SHATTER

FAMILY
LAW
IN THE REPUBLIC OF IRELAND

To Carol, Dylan and Kelly

SHATTER's

FAMILY LAW

IN THE REPUBLIC OF IRELAND

THIRD EDITION

Alan Joseph Shatter

T.D., B.A.Mod., Dip.E.I., Solr.

WOLFHOUND PRESS

British Library Cataloguing in Publication Data
Shatter, Alan Joseph
    Shatter's Family law in the Republic of
Ireland. — 3rd ed.
1. Domestic relations — Ireland
I. Title II. Shatter, Alan Joseph. Family
law in the Republic of Ireland
344.17061'5 KDK200

ISBN 0-86327-080-8

© 1986 Alan Shatter
First edition 1977, Second Edition 1981,
published by Wolfhound Press

WOLFHOUND PRESS
68 Mountjoy Square, Dublin 1.

Cover design: Jan de Fouw
Typesetting: Print Prep
Printed by Richard Clay (The Chaucer Press) Ltd., Bungay.

PREFACE

It is almost 6 years since the second edition of *Family Law in the Republic of Ireland* was published. Case law developments, the enactment of new statutory provisions, the publication of many reports proposing changes in family law and express government commitments to introduce reforms have all contributed to making this third edition essentially a new book. In it I attempt not only to state the current law but also to describe some of its deficiencies and discuss reforms proposed to resolve them. So that the current law can be easily ascertained when necessary without being lost in a maze of critical comment, in accordance with previous practice I have generally confined comment on the need for law reform to the end of the chapter to which it is relevant. However, where Bills are already before the Oireachtas which contain provisions which, if enacted, will substantially change existing law, I have made reference to such Bills in the sections discussing the current law to which they are relevant so that changes that might shortly come about are clearly signposted. New statistical material of relevance to family law is also included which illustrates changes that are occurring in Irish family life and developing demographic trends relating to marriage, births, illegitimacy, adoption, children in care and marital breakdown.

The book is written not only for the legal practitioner and law student but also as a reference book for all of those, who in professional or voluntary work, look to this area of the law for assistance. In it I have tried to cover those areas of family law that are of particular importance and that arise most often in practice whilst also including some areas that, to date, have received little attention but which, it is anticipated, will increase in importance in the coming years.

A continued difficulty in the area of family law is the number of unreported judgements. Whilst the publication of the *Irish Law Reports Monthly* has resulted in far more family cases being reported than in the past, a majority of the new cases discussed in this edition are unreported and most of the unreported cases first discussed in earlier editions remain unreported. Where a case is referred to in a footnote as unreported, unless otherwise indicated, a written judgement is obtainable. The record number of each such judgement can be found in the table of cases. There are no written judgements available, however, in certain cases of interest and where this is the position it is stated. Where a citation makes reference to a newspaper report only it can also be assumed that no written judgement is available other than that recorded in the newspaper report.

The emphasis in the book is on Irish case law and over 200 new Irish cases determined since publication of the second edition are referred to and discussed in this edition. There is, of course, also reference to pre-1922 English authorities and to cases determined after that date by both the English and Northern Ireland courts where relevant. Some reference by way of comparative material is also made to developments in the law of other countries. It should be noted that in the discussion of Irish case law the titles given to members of the judiciary correspond with the juridicial positions held by them at the date of delivery of the judgement discussed. For example, Mr. Justice Thomas Finlay is in some instances referred to as President of the High Court and in others as Chief Justice.

New legislation discussed includes the Health (Family Planning) (Amendment) Act, 1985, the Age of Majority Act, 1985, the Courts Acts, 1981 and 1986, the Irish Nationality & Citizenship Act, 1986, the Domicile & Recognition of Foreign Divorces Act, 1986 and various relevant Social Welfare Acts. Reference is also made to Bills of relevance currently before the Oireachtas such as the Status of Children Bill, 1986, and the Children (Care & Protection) Bill, 1985, as initiated. In critically examining the current law and proposed reforms, reference is made to various reports published by the Law Reform Commission relating to family law and to the Final Report of the Task Force on Child Care Services, the Report of the Review Committee on Adoption Services, the Report of the Joint Oireachtas Committee on Marriage Breakdown and to various governmental statements promising new statutory measures.

I am, of course, solely responsible for the law as stated in this book. I must, however, extend my thanks to my legal partner, Brian Gallagher, Solicitor, for his tolerance in never complaining at my taking time off from our practice for research and writing purposes and for his reading portions of the book and commenting on them prior to its going to print. I also have to thank Catherine McGuinness B.L., for reading the chapter on adoption and for her helpful comments thereon. Thanks are also due to those working in the Central Office of the High Court and the Supreme Court Offices, to Betty McGuigan, High Court Registrar, to Margaret Byrne in the Library of the Incorporated Law Society of Ireland and to the staff of the Oireachtas Library for their assistance in tracing unreported judgements and various other essential source material. Thanks are also due to those working in the Central Statistics Office, the Department of Justice and the Department of Health, without whose assistance much of the statistical information contained in the book would not have been so readily available to me. My special thanks also go to my secretary, Caroline Davies, who has typed and photocopied various drafts of this manuscript and whose help has been invaluable.

My greatest debt is owed to my wife, Carol, for her support, encouragement and assistance and for her patience in putting up with me regularly working late into the night and at weekends and holiday periods, to complete this new edition. Mention must also be made of my son Dylan (6½) and my daughter, Kelly (3½) both of whom on weekends regularly in exasparation enquired "why daddy had not yet finished the book". The main reason for celebrating the publication of this edition is that its completion affords to this family lawyer some real free time to spend with his own family.

In conclusion, I have stated the law as accurately as possible on the sources available to me on the 1st of November, 1986. Although the original manuscript went to my publishers early in July it has been possible to incorporate developments up to the 1st of November, 1986 at the proof stage.

A.J. SHATTER   *4th November, 1986.*

CONTENTS

Chapter 6

MARRIAGE AND THE LAW

Chapter 7

SEPARATION AGREEMENTS

Chapter 14

FAMILY RIGHTS TO MAINTENANCE

Chapter 15

MATRIMONIAL PROPERTY

Chapter 18

THE FAMILY OUTSIDE MARRIAGE

TABLE OF STATUTES

TABLE OF CASES

A

B

C

D

E

F

H

xxxiii

Kish & Ivaskovics v. Director of Vital Statistics (1973), 35 D.L.R. (3 rd.), 530 (Can.)   262
Knott v. Knott, [1955] P. 249; [1955] 2 All E.R. 305; [1955] 3 W.L.R. 162 (Assize)   223
Kowalczuk v. Kowalczuk, [1973] 2 All E.R. 1042; [1973] 1 W.L.R. 930; 117 S.J.
    373; (C.A.) 489, 494, 502
Kyne v. Tiernan & Anor. (July 1980) unreported (H.C.) Rec. No. 1978/6857P   546, 547,
                                                                               548

L

L. v. K. [1985] 3 W.L.R. 202 (Fam. D.)   416
L. v. L. [1949] 1 All E.R. 141; 65 T.L.R. 88; 93 Sol. Jo. 42; sub. nom. R.E.L. v.
    E.L., [1949] P. 211   281
L. v. L. [1978] I.R. 288 (H.C.) 521, 555, 623, 625
L. v. L. (December 1979) unreported (H.C.) Rec. No. 1979/378 Sp.   . 445, 446, 492,
                                                                 497, 498, 502, 504, 621
L. v. L. (falsely called W.) (1882), 7 P.D. 16; sub nom. L. v. W. (falsely called L.),
    51 L.J. (P.) 23; 47 L.T. 132; 30 W.N. 444 (H.C.)   124
L. v. L. [1984] 4 I.L.R.M. 607 (H.C.)   522
La Carte v. La Carte (1975) 60 D.L.R. (3d.) 507 (Can.)   262
Landers v. A.-G. (1973), 109 I.L.T.R. 1 (H.C.)   45
Lang v. Lang; [1955] A.C. 402; [1954] 3 All E.R. 571; [1954] 3 W.L.R. 762; (P.C.)   444
Lawrence v. Biddle, [1966] 2 Q.B. 504; [1966] 1 All E.R. 575; [1966] 2 W.L.R.
    930; (Q.B.D.) 162, 163
L.B. v. H.B. (July 1980) unreported (H.C.) Rec. No. 1979/449 Sp.   191, 268, 270, 271,
                                                                          433, 539
L.C. v. B.C. (otherwise known as B.L.) (November 1985) unreported (H.C.) Rec. No.
    1984/5M 106, 124, 129, 140
Leake v. Douglas (1952), 88 I.L.T.R. 4 (Cir. Ct.) 460, 462
Leake (formerly Bruzzi) v. Bruzzi, [1974] 2 All E.R. 1196; [1974] 1 W.L.R.
    1528 (C.A.)   487
Le Brocq v. Le Brocq. [1964] 1 W.L.R. 1085; [1964] 3 All E.R. 464 (C.A.)   ..   222
Legeyt v. O'Brien (1834), Milw. Rep. 325 (Cons. Ct.)   109
Lehr v. Robertson U.S.   — — —   597
Le Mesurier v. Le Mesurier, [1895] A.C. 517; [1895–9] All E.R. Rep. 836; 64
    L.J.P.C. 97; 72 L.T. 873; 11 T.L.R. 481 (P.C.) 257, 273
Lepre v. Lepre, [1965] P. 52; [1963] 2 W.L.R. 735; [1963] 2 All E.R. 49 (P.D.A.)   270
Lett v. Lett, [1906] 1 I.R. 618, 630 (M.R., C.A.) 200, 206, 214
Lewis v. Lewis, [1940] I.R. 42; (1939), 74 I.L.T.R. 170 (H.C.)   ..   18, 206, 208, 209
Lindo v. Belisario (1795), 1 Hag. Con. 216; appeal at (1796), 1 Hag. Con. at p. 7   196
L. (Minors) (Wardship: Jurisdiction), Re [1974] 1 W.L.R. 250; [1974] 1 All E.R.
    913; 118 Sol. Jo. 22 (C.A.); (Pet. Dis.) [1974] 1 W.L.R. 266 G (H.L.)   372
Lloyd v. Lloyd (1859) 1 Sw. & Tr. 567; 164 E.R. 862   227
Lloyd v. Sullivan (March 1981) unreported (H.C.) Rec. No. 1981/39 Sp.   545
Long v. Long and Johnson (1890), 15 P.D. 218; 60 L.J. (P.) 27; (P.D.A.)   218
Lonergan v. Morrissey (1947) 81 I.L.T.R. 130 (Cir. Ct.)   613
Long v. Keightley (1877) I.R. 11 C.L. 221 (Com. Pleas)   164
Looney, Michael Dec'd., In Re. O'Connor v. O'Keeffe (November 1970) unreported
    (H.C.) Rec. No. 1969/126 Sp. ..   ..
Lough v. Ward & Anor. [1945] 2 All E.R. 338; 173 L.T. 181; 89 Sol. Jo. 283
    (K.B.D.) 163, 165
Loveden v. Loveden (1810) 2 Hag. Con. 1; 161 E.R. 648 (Cons. Ct.)..   218
Lowe In Re, Stewart v. Lowe, [1929] 2 Ch. 210 (Ch. D.)   283
Lurie v. Lurie, [1938] 3 All E.R. 156; 159 L.T. 249; 54 T.L.R. 889 (Ch.D.)   ..   214
Lynch v. Lynch, [1966] N.I. 41 (Q.B.D.)   445
Lyons, In re, (1937) 72 I.L.T.R. 87 (N.I., C.A.)..   ..   ..   261, 263
Lyons v. Lyons [1950] N.I. 181 (K.B.D.)   218

M

M. (an Infant), In Re, [1946] I.R. 334; (1946), 80 I.L.T.R. 130 (H.C.)   ..   6, 594, 595
M. v. An Bord Uchtála, [1975] I.R. 86 (H.C.) also sub nom. J. McG. & W. McG. v.
    An Bord Uchtála & A.-G. (1975) 109 I.L.T.R. 62 (H.C.) 42, 297
M. v. J. (1977) 121 S.J. 759 (D.C.)   368
M. v. M. (Child: Access), [1973] 2 All E.R. 81 (Fam. D.) 367, 368
M. v. M. (orse B.), [1957] P. 139; [1959] 3 All E.R. 769 (P.D.A.)   124
M. v. M. (May 1978) unreported (H.C.); (October 1979) unreported (S.C.) Rec.
    No. 1977/26M; 1978/109   ..   ..   106, 143
M. v. M. (1978) 114 I.L.T.R. 46 (H.C.) 492, 494, 495, 502, 507

S

Y

Z

INTRODUCTION

Family life in Ireland, as in other countries, is changing. The family as a social institution is in a state of continuous evolution, its internal dynamic affected by the social relationships of its individual members and buffeted by outside forces frequently beyond its control.

Family Law in the Republic of Ireland, having remained unchanged for decades is gradually being reformed and developed by both legislators and the judiciary to accommodate the changing patterns of family life and the problems created by them that require resolution. The need to accommodate change and confront social reality has created tensions which have resulted in the laws relating to marriage and marital breakdown, divorce and family planning, abortion, illegitimacy, adoption and children at risk all, on occasion, becoming embroiled in national controversy. Irish family law, the existence of which was barely acknowledged prior to the 1970s, has frequently been centre stage in social and political debate during the past decade.

The sociological changes taking place in Irish society and in Irish family life can be gleaned from some of the statistical and demographic information contained in the appendices to this book. They show that the marriage rate climbed steadily throughout the 1960s and early 1970s to peak in 1974 at 22,833 marriages. It then levelled off in the second half of the 70s, declined to 18,355 marriages in 1984 to climb again slightly in 1985 to 18,552 marriages. The number of births having climbed from 59,825 in 1961 to 74,046 in 1980 declined to 62,250 in 1985, 8.5% of the latter births, i.e. 5,268 being recorded as illegitimate, the highest number of recorded illegitimate births in the history of the State. The continuous climb in the number of illegitimate births has been matched by a dramatic fall in the number of illegitimate children available for adoption. In 1985 only 882 adoption orders were made, being 16.74% of the total illegitimate births[1] and only 670 of the children adopted in that year were adopted by married couples unrelated to the natural mother or natural father of the child adopted. This can be compared with the peak figure for adoptions of 96.94% of all illegitimate births in 1967. This fall in the number of illegitimate children made available for adoption has coincided with an annual growth in the number of recipients of unmarried mother's allowance. By the 31st December, 1985, 11,530 mothers and 14,325 children were beneficiaries of this social welfare scheme.

The climb and then decline in the marriage rate has been matched by a continuous climb in the number of those whose marriages have irretrievably broken down. No comprehensive statistics exist as to the full extent of marital breakdown in Ireland or as to cohabitation outside marriage of partners to previously valid marriages. Such data as does exist records a continued growth in the number of matrimonial court proceedings instituted during the 1970s and 80s and an

---

1. Using a crude measure, see Appendix A:2.

1

annual increase in the recipients of Deserted Wives Allowance and Deserted Wives Benefit. It also records an increasing number of people whose marriages have collapsed, resorting to alternative forms and mechanisms outside the civil legal system to obtain some recognition of the factual end to their marriage. Thus, in the period 1976 to 1985, 7,128 people, 991 of whom were successful, sought decrees of annulment from the Marriage Tribunals of the Roman Catholic Church in Ireland although such decrees have no legal validity. Few of those who sought them have any prospect of obtaining a civil divorce of annulment and the possibility of a civil decree of divorce is denied to them all by the constitutional prohibition on the enactment of laws to permit the dissolution of marriage.

In developing legal and social policies for the family, all of the above trends must be taken into account as must outside influences and developments that directly impinge on family life. For example, increasingly sophisticated medical techniques, such as artificial insemination, test tube fertilisation and embryo implantation now provide alternatives to adoption for childless married couples. To date, however, Irish legislators have failed to even consider, let alone enact, legislation to determine the status of children conceived and born as a result of the use of such techniques. In the area of marital breakdown the issue of whether divorce should or should not be permitted has recently been the subject of an emotive and at times irrational referendum debate. However, in the aftermath of the referendum poll which resulted in a majority favouring the retention of the constitutional ban on divorce no one has yet confronted the sociological impact on Irish society of an increasing number of people who are parties to broken marriages cohabiting outside legal marriage and in many instances contracting bigamous second marriages, sometimes in collusion with the church of which they are members.

In this book I attempt, not only to describe the main legal rules applicable to various aspects of family life but also to examine the social impact of their application and discuss some of the many reforms that have been recently proposed and that are required to provide a modern and humane family law that responds to and reflects the changes that are occurring in Irish society and meets the needs of the family. Although the pages that follow deal with the family both inside and outside marriage, the emphasis is, of course, on the "marital family" with which the majority of legal rules that come within the subject matter of family law are concerned.

Marriage can be said to have two dimensions. On the one hand it is viewed by the law as a lifelong contract between a man and woman which creates a status giving rise to mutual rights and obligations. On the other, it is a personal relationship between two people subject to all the stresses and strains that fluctuations of physical and mental health as well as a variety of social pressures bring to it. In discussing the need to reform matrimonial law it is assumed that a functioning and viable marriage relationship is of fundamental importance to all married couples and that it is the relationship concept of marriage with which family law should be primarily concerned. Upon marital breakdown occurring, it is assumed that the object of social and legal policy should be to mitigate the harmful consequences of breakdown, to ensure that the welfare of any dependent children of the parties to the marriage is properly protected and to help the estranged spouses to re-organise their lives with the minimum of distress, bitterness and recrimination. It is an objective which is central to many of the suggestions made for reforming family law which are proposed and supported in the chapters that follow.

CHAPTER 1

THE FAMILY, MARRIAGE AND THE CONSTITUTION

INTRODUCTION

Under Articles 41 and 42 of Bunreacht na hÉireann (The Constitution of Ireland) the family is recognised as the most important social unit within the State. As such, the State guarantees its protection and pledges itself to defend the institution of marriage on which it states the family to be founded. Whereas the State can require that children receive a certain minimum education, its role is secondary to that of the family which is said to be the primary and natural educator of the child. Only if parents fail in their duty to their children may the State intervene.

Since 1937 the family has been placed on a constitutional pedestal. The earlier Constitution of the Irish Free State (in force from 1922-1937) contained no corresponding provisions concerning the family. As the provisions of Articles 41 and 42 are the principal subject matter of this chapter and are referred to in a number of subsequent chapters it is necessary to quote them in full. They read as follows:

Article 41 – *The Family:*

1.1. The State recognises the Family as the natural primary and fundamental unit group of Society, and as a moral institution possessing inalienable and imprescriptible rights, antecedent and superior to all positive law.

1.2. The State, therefore, guarantees to protect the Family in its constitution and authority, as the necessary basis of social order and as indispensable to the welfare of the Nation and the State.

2.1. In particular, the State recognises that by her life within the home, woman gives to the State a support without which the common good cannot be achieved.

2.2. The State shall, therefore, endeavour to ensure that mothers shall not be obliged by economic necessity to engage in labour to the neglect of their duties in the home.

3.1. The State pledges itself to guard with special care the institution of Marriage, on which the Family is founded, and to protect it against attack.

3.2. No law shall be enacted providing for the grant of a dissolution of marriage.

3.3. No person whose marriage has been dissolved under the civil law of any other State but is a subsisting valid marriage under the law for the time being in force within the jurisdiction of the Government and Parliament established by this Constitution shall be capable of contracting a valid marriage within that jurisdiction during the lifetime of the other party to the marriage so dissolved.

Article 42 – Education:

1. The State acknowledges that the primary and natural educator of the child is the Family and guarantees to respect the inalienable right and duty of parents to provide, according to their means, for the religious and moral, intellectual, physical and social education of their children.

2. Parents shall be free to provide this education in their homes or in private schools or in schools recognised or established by the State.

3.1. The State shall not oblige parents in violation of their conscience and lawful preference to send their children to schools established by the State, or to any particular type of schools designated by the State.

3.2. The State shall, however, as guardian of the common good, require in view of actual conditions that the children receive a certain minimum education, moral, intellectual and social.

4. The State shall provide for free primary education and shall endeavour to supplement and give reasonable aid to private and corporate educational initiative, and, when the public good requires it, provide other educational facilities or institutions with due regard, however, for the rights of parents, especially in the matter of religious and moral formation.

5. In exceptional cases, where the parents for physical or moral reasons fail in their duty towards their children, the State as guardian of the common good, by appropriate means shall endeavour to supply the place of the parents, but always with due regard for the natural and imprescriptible rights of the child.

THE FAMILY AND THE CONSTITUTION

The "family" and "parents" referred to in these Articles, although not defined within the Constitution itself, have been held by the courts to be confined to the family and parenthood that is based on marriage, that is a marriage which was a valid subsisting marriage under the law of the State.[1] A couple whose marriage is not valid according to the civil law of the State cannot form a family unit in the constitutional sense[2] but may do so if they subsequently enter into a valid and recognisable marriage[3] or if an initially invalid marriage is retrospectively validated.[4]

A married couple either with or without children may comprise a "family" within the meaning of the Constitution.[4a] Moreover, in the context of a married couple with children, the absence of one spouse does not necessarily impair the authority of the family or diminish parental rights. Thus, a separated,[5] deserted[6] or widowed spouse[7] and the child or children of his or her marriage have all been held to be a family in the constitutional sense. Moreover, orphaned children who were members of a marital family, it has been said, will continue to constitute a family for the purposes of the Constitution even though their parents have died.[8]

To date, no judicial pronouncement has been made as to the effect on the constitutional status of a married couple of their marriage ceasing to subsist as a result of the grant of a foreign decree of dissolution or divorce recognised by the civil law of the State.[8a] In this context, it should be noted that the courts have acknowledged that where spouses are estranged and separated the collapse of their marriage, of itself, may change the constitutional nature of their relationship, as a family divided ceases to function as a single unit.[8b] As a consequence, it has been held that an individual separated spouse may not be able to avail of all the rights guaranteed to the family under Article 41, as upon such a spouse being involved in legal conflict, a court may be called upon not simply to protect the rights of the family as a unit against the outside world but to reconcile the rights of the individual members of the family.[8c] As already stated, however, the courts have also held in a number of cases that a separated spouse with children may be regarded as a family in the constitutional sense when engaged in

1. *The State (Nicolaou) v. An Bord Uchtála & The Attorney General* [1966] I.R. 567 (S.C.); *G. v. An Bord Uchtála* [1980] I.R. 32; (1978) 113 I.L.T.R. 25 (S.C.); *O'B. v. S.* [1984] I.R. 316; *Sub Nom In the Goods of William Walker Dcsd.* [1985] 5 I.L.R.M. 86 (S.C.). See also *K.C. & A.C. v. An Bord Uchtála* [1985] 5 I.L.R.M. 302 (S.C.).
2. For example, a couple may marry in a Registry Office in England after one of them has had a first marriage dissolved by an English decree of divorce that is not recognised in Ireland. For the law as to recognition of foreign divorces see Chapter 10.
3. In the circumstances of footnote 2 above the parties to the second marriage could of course enter into a valid marriage at a later date if the spouse of the party who remarried died prior to any such "second" marriage ceremony taking place.
4. See, for example, *F.M.L. & A.L. v. The Registrar General of Marriages* [1984] 4 I.L.R.M. 667 (H.C.) in which the marriage between the plaintiffs that took place in a Roman Catholic Church subsequent to the first marriage of F.M.L. being annulled by that church was retrospectively validated upon the High Court later annulling F.M.L.'s first marriage due to his first "wife's" impotence. See also *A.M.N. v. J.P.C.* (December, 1985) unreported (H.C.). See further p. 105 *post*. See also the Marriages Act, 1972, section 2 which retrospectively validated certain Lourdes marriages. See further p. 94 *post*.
4a. See *Murray & Murray v. The Attorney General & Ireland* [1985] 5 I.L.R.M. 542 (H.C.) (This case is under appeal at the time of writing.)
5. See *Northampton County Council v. A.B.F. & M.B.F.* [1982] 2 I.L.R.M. 164 (H.C.); *Kent County Council v. C.S.* [1984] 4 I.L.R.M. 292 (H.C.). See, however, *The State (Bouzagou) v. Fitzgibbon St. Garda Station* [1986] 6 I.L.R.M. 98 (H.C.).
6. *In re Doyle, an Infant* [1956] I.R. 217 (H.C.) and (December, 1955) unreported (S.C.). See, however, *Dennehy v. The Minister for Social Welfare & A.G.* (July, 1984) unreported (H.C.). See further p. 41 *post*.
7. See *In re O'Brien, an Infant* [1954] I.R. 1; (1953) 87 I.L.T.R. 156 (S.C.).
8. See *G. v. An Bord Uchtála, supra*, judgement of Walsh J. [1980] I.R. at p. 70.
8a. See chap. 10. See also p. 19 *post*.
8b. See *Kent County Council v. C.S., supra; Dennehy v. Minister for Social Welfare, supra; The State (Bouzagou) v. Fitzgibbon St. Garda Station, supra.*
8c. See, in particular, *The State (Bouzagou) v. Fitzgibbon St. Garda Station, supra*, at p. 103.

a conflict with third parties. Whatever constitutional impact the granting of a
foreign divorce decree recognised under Irish law is held to have on the couple
whose marriage is dissolved, such decree does not affect the constitutional
status of any children of such couple. They remain the children of a family
based on marriage.

The rights and duties recognised and acknowledged[9] by the State as being
vested in the family and parents and the State's guarantees in relation to them
do not extend to the natural family or the family outside wedlock. In 1966
Walsh, J., delivering the judgement of the Supreme Court in *The State (Nicolaou)
v. An Bord Uchtála*,[10] stated:

> "While it is quite true that unmarried persons co-habiting together and the
> childrͻn of their union may often be referred to as a family and have many,
> if not all, of the outward appearances of a family, and may indeed for the
> purposes of a particular law be regarded as such, nevertheless so far as
> Article 41 is concerned the guarantees therein contained are confined to
> families based upon marriage."[11]

This view was re-affirmed by the Supreme Court in *G. v. An Bord Uchtála*[12] and
more recently in *O'B. v. S.*[13]

Although parents who have not married do not benefit from the rights enunciated in Articles 41 and 42 of the Constitution, it has been said that a child born
outside wedlock has the same "natural and imprescriptible rights" under Article
42 as a child born in wedlock. These rights include the right to religious and
moral, intellectual, physical and social education and the right to free primary
education.[14] Nevertheless, we shall see that despite the judicial articulation of
the existence of an equality of rights between children both born inside and
outside wedlock, the courts have held that in a number of instances it is con-

---

9. The rights and duties are "recognised" by the Constitution rather than "created" or
"conferred" by it. They have been said to exist as part of the natural law and the Constitution
merely "confirms their existence and gives them protection", *per* Walsh J., *McGee v. A.G.*
[1974] I.R. 284, p. 310. See also *Norris v. The Attorney General* [1984] I.R. 36 (S.C.) in
particular the judgement of McCarthy J.; *Finn v. A.G.* [1983] I.R. 154 (H.C., S.C.) particularly High Court judgement of Barrington J.; *Northampton County Council v. A.B.F. &
M.B.F. supra*; *Murray & Murray v. The Attorney General & Ireland, supra*. See further
J.M. Kelly, *The Irish Constitution* (Jurist Publishing Company Ltd., Dublin 1984), pp.
427–445.
10. *Supra*.
11. *Supra* at pp. 643–644.
12. *Supra*.
13. *Supra*. See also *McNally v. Lee* (January, 1970) unreported (H.C.); *E.M. v. M.M.*
(December 1982) unreported (H.C.).
14. *In re M., an infant* [1946] I.R. 334 (H.C.) at p. 344 "Under Irish law, while I do
not think that the constitutional guarantee for the family ... avails the mother of an
illegitimate child, I regard the innocent little girl as having the same 'natural and imprescriptible rights' (under Article 42) as a child born in wedlock" per Gavan Duffy P. confirmed
by the Supreme Court in *The State (Nicolaou) v. An Bord Uchtála and the Attorney General,
supra*, at p. 642 where Walsh J. stated: Article 42.5 "speaks of 'the natural and imprescriptible rights of the child'. Those 'natural and imprescriptible rights' cannot be said to be
acknowledged by the Constitution as residing only in legitimate children any more than it
can be said that the guarantee ... as to the provision of free primary education excludes
illegitimate children. While it is not necessary to explore the full extent of 'the natural and
imprescriptible rights of the child' they include the right to "religious and moral, intellectual,
physical and social education. An illegitimate child has the same natural rights as a legitimate
child." See also judgement of Walsh J. in *G. v. An Bord Uchtála* at [1980] I.R. at pp. 67–
69. In the latter case Henchy J. whilst acknowledging that "all children, whether legitimate
or illegitimate, share the common characteristic that they enter life without any responsibility for their status and with an equal claim to what the Constitution expressly or
impliedly postulates as the fundamental rights of children" stated that the natural and
imprescriptible rights referred to in Article 42.5 "are those of a child whose parents have

stitutionally permissible to treat children born outside wedlock differently to those born to a married couple.[15]

Unmarried persons co-habiting together with their children may have the guarantees and protections afforded by Articles 41 and 42 extended to them and become a family recognised by the Constitution if they validly marry. Moreover, if such marriage legitimates any children born to them outside marriage, the children will also form part of the constitutional family unit.[16] In *In re J.*,[17] dealing with this issue in the High Court, Henchy J. stated:

> "It is true that the child was born illegitimate and therefore outside a family, but by its parents' marriage it has clearly become a legitimate child of the marriage . . . I am of the opinion that . . . the father, mother and child constitute a family . . . I am satisfied that section 1 of the Legitimacy Act, 1931,[18] operated to endow the child, in this case with membership of a family founded on the institution of marriage. It is an example of the way in which certain constitutional rights . . . may be conferred by the operation of an Act of Parliament."[19]

In *K.C. & A.C. v. An Bord Uchtála & Ors.*[20] both the High Court and Supreme Court upheld this view.[21] As we shall see later, however, under current statute law a child or children born to parents who are not married to each other prior to or at the time of the child's birth may, in certain circumstances, remain illegitimate, even after the parents have validly married. It appears that such a situation can give rise to a constitutional anomaly whereby the parents themselves upon becoming a married couple are regarded as a "constitutional family" while children born to them prior to marriage and not legitimated by virtue of the marriage, do not form part of that constitutional family, the constitutional relationship between the parents and any such children continuing to operate as if the parents had not married each other.[22]

Just as a legitimated child and its parents may constitute a family under the provisions of Articles 41 and 42 so, similarly, it is submitted should an adopted

---

married (thereby creating a family in the constitutional sense . . .)". He held that an illegitimate child's right to the provision of religious and moral, intellectual, physical and social education was a personal right implicitly arising under Article 40.3. See further [1980] I.R. at pp. 85–87. See also the judgement of O'Higgins C.J. [1980] I.R. at p. 56. See further *E.M. v. M.M., supra.*

As for the constitutional right to free primary education and the State's duty to make provision for such education see *Crowley & Ors. v. Ireland, The Minister for Education & Ors.* [1980] I.R. 102 (S.C.) and p. 21 *post.*

15. See p. 26 *post et seq.* and p. 594 *post et seq.*

16. See Legitimacy Act, 1931, section 1. For detailed consideration of the law as to legitimacy and legitimation see Chapter 11. A couple who have already had a child could marry without their marriage legitimating their child. For example, if a man was already married at the time of his child's conception and only became free to marry the child's mother some time after the child's birth upon his wife's death, the marriage of the couple would not legitimate their child.

17. [1966] I.R. 295 (H.C.).

18. See footnote 16 *ante.*

19. *Supra* at pp. 306, 307.

20. [1985] 5 I.L.R.M. 302 (H.C., S.C.). Judgements were delivered in the High Court in this case by Lynch J. in August and October, 1984 and there was an appeal decision delivered by the Supreme Court in March of 1985. These three judgements are reported in [1985] I.L.R.M. A further judgement was delivered by Lynch J. in May, 1985 and this judgement is reported in [1986] 6 I.L.R.M. 65.

21. "There can be no doubt but that the child has been legitimated by the marriage of the parents and that these three persons now constitute a family within the meaning of that term as used in Articles 41 and 42 of the Constitution" *per* Lynch J. at [1985] 5 I.L.R.M. at p. 308. This statement of the law was upheld by the Supreme Court.

22. See further p. 282 *post et seq.*

child together with its adopters, if they are a married couple. It would seem, however, that if a child is adopted by an unmarried person or by a widowed person, the adopted child and its adoptive parent would not be recognised as a "constitutional family" as the relationship between the adopted child and the parent could not be regarded as being based upon the institution of marriage.[23] The courts have not, as yet, been asked to pronounce on the constitutional position of the adopted child and its parents or parent.

The constitutional family is the nuclear family, i.e. a husband, wife and their children, if any.[24] It is expressly recognised in the Constitution as the most important social group in the State and as possessing inalienable and imprescriptible rights antecedent and superior to all positive law.[25] Unlike other rights

23. See *T. O'G. v. The Attorney General* [1985] 5 I.L.R.M. 61 (H.C.) in which it was held that section 5(1) of the Adoption Act, 1974, was unconstitutional so making it possible for a widower with no previous children to adopt. Both widows and widowers as well as other categories of single people may now adopt (see p. 294 *post*). There can be little doubt but that a widowed person and his or her adopted child would be regarded as a family for the purposes of Article 41 and 42 if the adoption process had been completed during the lifetime of both spouses. In *T. O'G. v. The Attorney General* it had not been so completed, and if an adoption order was made subsequent to the decision in that case, the family formed by the making of the adoption order could not be regarded as a family "based on marriage".

24. In *McCombe and Another v. Sheehan and Another*, [1954] I.R. 183 (H.C.) a case on the Rent Restrictions Act, 1946, Murnaghan J. in the High Court referring to Article 41 said at p. 190 "... there can be no doubt, in my opinion, about the meaning to be attributed to the word 'family', namely, parents and children". In the later case of *Jordan and Another v. O'Brien* [1960] I.R. 363; (1959) 95 I.L.T.R. 115 (S.C.) the Supreme Court gave the word "family" a broader meaning for the purposes of the Rent Restrictions Acts but Lavery J. said, "I will accept, without deciding that the word, [family] as used in the Constitution does mean parents and children and does not include other relationships" – [1960] I.R. at p. 370 In *McGee v. A.-G.* [1974] I.R. 284 at p. 334 Griffin J. stated, "The word Family is not defined in the Constitution but, without attempting a definition it seems to me that in this case it must necessarily include the plaintiff, her husband and their children".

In *Murray & Murray v. The Attorney General & Ireland, supra* at pp. 546–547 Costello J. rejected the contention that a married couple without children was not a "family" within the meaning of Article 41. He stated:

"The Constitution does not attempt to define (the family) but instead describes it as the 'natural primary and fundamental group of society', as a 'moral institution', as 'the basis of the social order' and as being 'indispensable to the welfare of the Nation and the State'. Whilst it is true that the Article contains a pledge that the 'institution of marriage' will be guarded with special care and the Family is referred to as being based on marriage, I do not think that the reference to two distinct institutions necessarily concludes the matter ... A married couple without children can properly be described as a 'unit group' of Society just as is referred to in this Article and the lifelong relationship to which each married person is committed is certainly a 'moral institution'. The words used in the Article to describe the 'Family' are therefore apt to describe both a married couple with children and a married couple without children. It is true that the rights and duties of a married couple with children are more varied than a married couple without children but each 'unit group' has the same nucleus and it is reasonable to assume that both were given the same constitutional protection."

25. In *Ryan v. A.G.* [1965] I.R. 294 Kenny J. stated at p. 308 " 'inalienable' means that which cannot be transferred or given away whilst 'imprescriptible' means that which cannot be lost by the passage of time or abandoned by non-exercise." See, however, *G. v. An Bord Uchtála, supra*, where Walsh J. stated [1980] I.R. at p. 79 that "Some inalienable rights are absolutely inalienable while others are relatively inalienable." See further *Murray & Murray v. The Attorney General & Ireland, supra* at p. 548 where Costello J. states with reference to both Articles 41 and 42 and also Article 40.3.1 that:

"It is abundantly clear that too literal a construction of the Constitution could lead to absurdities ... the power of the State to de-limit the exercise of constitutionally protected rights is expressly given in some Articles and not referred to at all in others, but this cannot mean that where absent the power does not exist. For example, no reference is made in Article 41 to any restrictive power but it is clear that the exercise by the family of its imprescriptible and inalienable right to integrity as a unit group can be severely and validly restricted by the State when, for example, its laws permit a father to be banned from a family home (see Chapter 16 *post*) or allow the imprisonment of both parents of young children."

See also *Pok Sun Shum & Ors. v. Ireland* (June, 1985) unreported (H.C.) and *Sunday Osheku & Ors. v. Ireland & Ors.* (June 1986) unreported (H.C.).

enumerated in the Constitution, family rights are not expressly said to be confined to citizens of the State. In *Northampton County Council v. A.B.F. & M.B.F.*[26] Hamilton J. in the High Court rejected the contention that only citizens of the State are entitled to the protection afforded by Article 41 stating:

"that non-citizenship can have no effect on the interpretation of Article 41 or the entitlement to the protection afforded by it."[27]

This issue remains to be finally determined by the Supreme Court.

Rights recognised by Articles 41 and 42 vest in the family as a unit of society and attach to each individual member of the family, both parents and children.[28] The Constitution does not, however, specify or define all the rights possessed by the family and each of its members.[29] It has been left to the courts, Walsh J. has stated:

"to examine and to search for the rights which may be discoverable in the particular case before the court in which these rights are invoked[30] . . . According to the preamble, the people gave themselves the Constitution to promote the common good with due observance of prudence, justice and charity so that the dignity and freedom of the individual might be assured. The judges must, therefore, as best they can from their training and their experience interpret these rights in accordance with their ideas"[31]

of these virtues. Thus, the rights possessed by the family may vary from time to time, dictated by the ideas, concepts and prevailing notions of these virtues

---

26. *Supra.*
27. *Supra* at p. 166. See also *Abdelkefi v. The Minister for Justice* [1984] 4 I.L.R.M. 138 (H.C.) in which the court appears to have accepted that a Tunisian husband and his Irish wife and their child were a "family" protected by Article 41 although rejecting the plaintiffs' argument that the wife had a constitutional right to the company of her husband whenever she visited the State. The parties' permanent home was at the date of the proceedings outside Ireland. In *The State (Bouzagou) v. Fitzgibbon St. Garda Station, supra*, the court accepted "that the rights recognised by Articles 41 and 42 of the Constitution are not confined to citizens" [1986] 6 I.L.R.M. at p. 103 *per* Barrington J.
28. In *McGee v. The Attorney General, supra*, at p. 310 Walsh J. stated "the individual has natural and human rights over which the State has no authority; and the family as the natural, primary and fundamental group of society has rights as such which the State cannot control. However, as the Constitution acknowledges and claims . . . the State as the guardian of the common good and . . . the individual, as a member of society, and the family, as a unit of society have duties and obligations to consider and respect the common good of that society". Further on at p. 311 the learned judge continued stating that in Articles 41 and 42 "The State recognises the parents as the natural guardians of the children of the Family and as those in whom the authority of the family is vested and those who shall have the right to determine how the family life shall be conducted, having due regard to the rights of the children, not merely as members of that family but as individuals."
In *K.C. & A.C. v. An Bord Uchtála, supra*, Finlay C.J. in the Supreme Court (*supra*, at p. 316) referred to a legitimated child's rights "under the Constitution as a member of a family" as including the right "to belong to a unit group possessing inalienable and imprescriptible rights antecedent and superior to all positive law." See further *P.W. & A.W. & Othrs. supra*, discussed on p. 389 *post*. See however, *Murray & Murray v. The Attorney General & Ireland, supra*, at p. 547 where Costello J. expresses the view that "The rights in Article 41.1.1 are those which can properly be said to belong to the institution (of the family) itself, as distinct from the personal rights which each individual member might enjoy by virtue of membership of the family. No doubt if the rights of the unit group were threatened or infringed any member of the family could move the court to uphold them but the cause of action would then be the threat to the rights granted to the unit and not to those of its individual member." In the view of the learned judge individual rights of family members fell to be protected under the provisions of Article 40.3.1.
29. See p. 12 *et seq.*
30. *McGee v. A.G., supra*, at p. 318.
31. *Ibid* at p. 319. See also *The State (Healy) v. Donoghue* [1976] I.R. 325 where O'Higgins C.J. reiterated this view at p. 347.

possessed by the judges called upon to determine or discover their existence and ambit.[32]

THE INFLUENCE OF THE CONSTITUTION

The influence of the Constitution on Irish Family Law has not been confined to Articles 41 and 42, although it is these Articles that have arisen for consideration in the majority of constitutional and judicial pronouncements affecting this area of the law. In many of the decided cases, however, the courts have had to consider the inter-action between these two Articles and other Articles of the Constitution and in some instances have had to adjudicate upon, or strike a balance between, other fundamental rights protected by the Constitution *vis-à-vis* those rights recognised and enunciated in Articles 41 and 42 so as to resolve an apparent constitutional conflict between them. It is intended first to examine the effect on the legislature of the family articles and the court decisions, judicial pronouncements and juridical developments solely deriving from them and then to examine the inter-action between the family articles and other provisions contained in the Constitution. Finally, we shall examine other constitutional decisions directly relating to family law unconnected with Articles 41 and 42.

Protection of the Marital Family — The Legislative Response

Despite the constitutional emphasis on the importance of the marital family, it is now recognised, even by the Oireachtas itself, that it has, as a legislature, failed to adequately respond to the constitutional duty imposed on it to "protect the family" and to "guard with special care the institution of marriage".[33] Although new legislation has been enacted over the years to reform individual areas of Irish family law, many of the reforms introduced have been forced either by judicial constitutional pronouncements or by particular social problems or legal anomalies being highlighted by pressure groups and the news media.[34] Few

---

32. In *McGee v. A.G., supra*, p. 319 Walsh J. stated: "It is but natural that from time to time the prevailing ideas of these virtues may be conditioned by the passage of time; no interpretation of the Constitution is intended to be final for all time. It is given in the light of prevailing ideas and concepts."

In *The State (Healy) v. Donoghue, supra*, at p. 347, O'Higgins C.J. stated that "The Constitution was to be considered in accordance with concepts of prudence, justice and charity which may gradually change or develop as society changes and develops and which fall to be interpreted from time to time in accordance with prevailing ideas. The preamble envisages a Constitution which can absorb or be adopted to such changes. In other words, the Constitution did not seek to impose for all time the ideas prevalent or accepted with regard to these virtues at the time of its enactment." See, however, the judgement of O'Higgins C.J. in *Norris v. A.G.*, [1984] I.R. in particular at p. 54 and at pp. 64–65 in which the Chief Justice delivering the majority judgement of the court, appears to test the constitutionality of a pre-1937 statute by reference to the beliefs and convictions of the Irish people in 1937 when the current Constitution was enacted by way of a referendum. See further the powerful dissenting judgement of McCarthy J. where he rejected such an approach stating ([1984] I.R. at p. 96) that he found it "philosophically impossible to carry out the necessary exercise of applying what I might believe to be the thinking of 1937 to the demands of 1983", asserting that "the Constitution is a living document", he stated further on ([1984] I.R. at p. 99) that he could "not accept the approach based upon applying the test of the then contemporary mores to the issue of constitutionality. It must be the mores contemporaneous with the raising of the issue itself."

33. See *Report of the Joint Committee on Marriage Breakdown* (A select Committee of the Oireachtas consisting of 11 members of Dáil Éireann and 4 members of Seanad Éireann) published by the Stationery Office in April 1985, chapters 3–6 and in particular para. 5.9 on p. 30.

34. Reforming legislation within this category would include the Adoption Acts, 1974–76; the Family Law (Maintenance of Spouses & Children) Act, 1976; the Family Home Protection Act, 1976, and the Health (Family Planning) Act, 1979.

statutory reforms have resulted from any coherent social policy or organised research. Nevertheless, some of the family law legislation enacted by the Oireachtas since 1937 has been regarded by the courts as a legislative response to the constitutional duty imposed on the State to protect the marital family.[35] Two examples of this can be seen in recent judgements delivered by members of the Supreme Court.

In *Hamilton v. Hamilton*[36] referring to the Family Home Protection Act, 1976, and its statutory requirement that a spouse who wishes to sell a family home held by him in his sole name must first obtain the prior written consent of the other spouse, Henchy J. remarked that:

> "The Act of 1976 provides for the protection of the family home, presumably as an implementation of the constitutional duty that falls on the State to protect the family and to guard with special care the institution of marriage. To this end, the Act ... created a new right whereby (save in excepted cases) the non-disposing spouse is given the right to veto the disposition to a third party of any legal or equitable interest in the family home."[37]

In *O'B. v. S.*[38] referring to the rights conferred on a surviving spouse and children of a marriage by the Succession Act, 1965, Walsh J. stated that it could:

> "scarcely be doubted that the Act of 1965 was designed to strengthen the protection of the family as required by the Constitution and, for that purpose, to place members of a family based upon marriage in a more favourable position than other persons in relation to succession to property, whether by testamentary disposition or intestate succession."[39]

Despite such judicial statements, it is clear from the chapters that follow that very few of the legislative measures enacted by the Oireachtas in the family law area can be accurately described as resulting from a conscious recognition by the legislature of the duties imposed on it by Article 41. In this context, the Joint Oireachtas Committee *Report on Marriage Breakdown* published in April 1985 contains the first attempt by the Oireachtas, through a special committee appointed by it, to produce a detailed social policy and legislative analysis of the measures required to protect marriage and family life and to provide for the consequences of marital breakdown since the enactment of the present Constitution in 1937. Whether this report will produce the necessary governmental and legislative action in response to the constitutional duty imposed on the State to afford protection to the family and each of its individual members remains to be seen. The document *Statement on Government's Intentions with*

---

35. "The provisions of Article 41 of the Constitution of Ireland create not merely a State interest but a State obligation to safeguard the family" *per* Walsh J., in *O'B. v. S.* [1984] I.R. at p. 338.
36. [1982] I.R. 466 (S.C.).
37. *Ibid* at p. 485. See also *Weir v. Somers* [1983] I.R. 112 at p. 126 and [1983] 3 I.L.R.M. 343 at p. 347 where McCarthy J. delivering the judgement of the Supreme Court, stated with reference to the Family Home Protection Act, 1976, "I draw attention to the wide range of powers granted to the courts in section 5 as indicative of the concern of the Legislature in enacting the Act of 1976 to fulfil the function of the legislative branch of the State as set out in Article 41., s.1. of the Constitution. . . In my view, the Act of 1976 must be used, primarily, to secure the protection of the family in the family home, and all other claims to the premises that constitute such home must remain secondary to it. The judicial branch of Government of the State must also recognise its duty under Article 41 and seek to achieve the objectives as set out in that Article."
38. [1984] I.R. 316 (S.C.).
39. *Ibid* at p. 335.

Regard to Marriage, Separation and Divorce first published in April 1986, undertaking to implement many of the reforms proposed by the Oireachtas Committee
does, however, give rise to some optimism that the proposals of the Committee
will be implemented.[39a]

Protection of the Marital Family – The Judicial Response

There have been a number of important court cases in which either the constitutional validity of legislative enactments has been challenged as violating the
constitutional protection afforded to the marital family or in which the constitutional validity of impugned statutory provisions has been upheld by reliance
on the constitutional duty imposed on the State to protect the marital family.
The impact on the judiciary and the Irish legal system of Article 41 and the
interpretation and application of this Article by the courts is now examined.
Fluoridation: In the important case of *Ryan v. The Attorney General*[40] both the
High Court and, on appeal, the Supreme Court rejected the plaintiff's contention
that sections of the Health (Fluoridation of Water Supplies) Act, 1960, which provided for the addition of fluoride to public water supplies were unconstitutional.
Denying that the Act violated the State's guarantee in Article 41 to protect the
authority of the family in its constitution and authority, O'Dalaigh C.J. delivering
the judgement of the Supreme Court stated that :

> "The aspect of that authority which is in question is the authority of the
> family or the parents to provide for the health of its members in the way it
> thinks best. It is sought to establish, as a corollary, that parents are entitled
> to omit to provide for the health of their children if they so think fit. One
> of the duties of parents is certainly to ward off dangers to the health of their
> children and in the court's view there is nothing in the constitution which
> recognises the right of a parent to refuse to allow the provision of measures
> designed to secure the health of its child when the method of avoiding
> injury is one which is not fraught with danger to the child and is within the
> procurement of the parent . . ."[41]

Taxation: In *Murphy v. The Attorney General*,[42] a constitutional challenge based
on Article 41 was successful, the Supreme Court holding sections 192-198 of the
Income Tax Act, 1967, to be repugnant to the Constitution in so far as they
provided for the aggregation of the earned income of married couples. Upon
marriage, in the vast majority of cases, the effect of these provisions, if both a
husband and a wife had an independent income, was to impose on the husband
an income tax liability greater than the total sum of income tax which a husband
and a wife would have had individually to pay if they were assessed separately as
single people on what each earned. In essence, the income tax code provided an
incentive to many couples to live together outside marriage by requiring them to
pay less tax than they would have to pay if married and residing together. The
State contended that this extra income tax liability had to be viewed in the con-

---

39a. This document was published in conjunction with the publication of the Tenth
Amendment of the Constitution Bill, 1986, which provided the legislative vehicle together
with the Electoral (Amendment) Act, 1986, for the holding of a referendum on the 26th
June 1986 to amend Art. 41.2.3. by replacing it with a new provision to permit divorce
subject to certain constitutional restrictions. The amendment was rejected by the electorate.
See further p. 18 and chapt. 9. See also the revised version of the April document published
in June 1986, prior to the referendum.
40. [1965] I.R. 294 (S.C.).
41. *Ibid* at p. 350.
42. [1982] I.R. 241 (H.C., S.C.).

text of the other legislative advantages given by the State to married couples and their children. Delivering the judgement of the court, Kenny J. stated:

"The pledge given in (Article 41.3.1) to guard with special care the institution of marriage is a guarantee that this institution in all its constitutional connotations, including the pledge given in Article 41.2.2 as to the position of the mother in the home, will be given special protection so that it will continue to fulfil its function on the basis of the family and as a permanent indissoluble union of man and woman."[43]

As for the State's contention, the learned judge continued:

"The court accepts the proposition that the State has conferred many revenue, social and other advantages and privileges on married couples and their children. Nevertheless, the nature and potentially progressive extent of the burden created by section 192 of the Act of 1967 is such that, in the opinion of the court, it is a breach of the pledge by the State to guard with special care the institution of marriage and to protect it against attack. Such a breach is, in the view of the court, not compensated for or justified by such advantages and privileges."[44]

Following upon the above decision the State sought clarification from the Supreme Court as to whether it was obliged to repay any of the monies collected by way of taxation under the impugned provisions. The Supreme Court held by a majority that the plaintiffs were entitled to be repaid the sums collected from them by way of tax invalidly imposed from the first day of the financial year immediately following upon the issuing of their proceedings and limited the right to recover taxes already paid by other tax payers to any of those who had also issued proceedings challenging the constitutionality of the impugned legislation.[45] As a result, taxes which had been paid by married couples pursuant to

---

43. *Ibid* at p. 286.
44. *Ibid* at p. 287.
45. Henchy J., Griffin J., and Parke J. formed the majority. O'Higgins C.J. and Kenny J. dissenting. Dealing with entitlement to recover tax already paid, Henchy J. stated:

"The plaintiffs' right to recover the sums by which they claim the State was unjustly enriched, by the collection of the taxes that have now been held to have been unconstitutionally imposed, begins for the year 1978–9, that is, the first year for which they effectively objected to the flow of the taxes into the central fund. Up to that year the State was entitled, in the absence of any claim of unconstitutionality, to act on the assumption that the taxes in question were validly imposed, that they were properly transmissible to the central fund, and that from there they were liable to be expended according to the will of Parliament, for the multiplicity of purposes for which drawings are made on the central fund of the State. Equally, every taxpayer whose income was deducted from his earnings throughout a particular tax year, no matter how grudgingly or unwillingly he allowed the deductions to be made from his weekly or monthly income, could not avoid having imputed to him the knowledge that the tax he was paying was liable to be immediately spent by the State." (1982 I.R. at p. 318).

Further on he stated:

"The State was led to believe, by the protracted absence of a claim to the contrary, that it was legally and constitutionally proper to spend the money thus collected, the position had become so altered the logistics of reparation so weighted and distorted by factors such as inflation and interest, the *prima facie* right of the taxpayers to be recouped so devalued by the fact that, as members of the community, and particularly as married couples, they had benefited from the taxes thus collected, that it would be inequitable, unjust and unreal to expect the State to make full restitution." (see [1982] I.R. at p. 320).

Griffin J. dealing with the same issue and agreeing with the judgement of Henchy J. stated:

"Notwithstanding the invalidity of the statute under which such act was done, the

the impugned legislation could not generally be recovered. The court further ruled that its original decision had constituted a finding that the invalid sections in the income tax code were void *ab initio*. This clearly had the consequence that the State could no longer compute and levy taxes in reliance on them.[46]

Section 21 of the Finance Act, 1980, subsequently enacted, sought to impose on all married couples who had not paid the full amount of income tax for which they would have been liable prior to the decision in the *Murphy* case, the same liability for tax as they would have had under the invalid provisions of the Act of 1967 for all preceding tax years. In *Muckley v. The Attorney General*[47] the constitutional validity of section 21 of the Finance Act, 1980, was successfully challenged. It was stated that the purpose of this section was to achieve an equality between married tax payers who had not paid the tax derived from the invalid sections and married tax payers who had paid that tax and who were debarred from recovering it. Finlay C.J., affirming the decision of the High Court and delivering the judgement of the Supreme Court stated that section 21 of the Act of 1980 could not "be given validity by having been enacted for the purpose of achieving the equality sought."[48] Stating that the decision in the *Murphy* case was "essentially . . . that the invalid sections penalised the married state" he continued:

> "Section 21 of the Act of 1980 has the same effect and does not escape invalidity merely on the basis that though imposing an identical tax burden the effect is retrospective and not continuing or prospective. It still contains the fatal flaw in common with the invalidated sections of imposing on the married couples to whom it applies a greater burden of taxation than that imposed on a man and woman living together outside marriage."[49]

Although both the *Murphy* and the *Muckley* cases directly related to tax payable on earned income through the P.A.Y.E. collection system, it is submitted that as a result of these decisions it is no longer within the competence of the State to require married persons to pay additional tax of any nature simply because of the fact of marriage.

Homosexuality: In *Norris v. The Attorney General*,[50] the plaintiff, a male homosexual, unsuccessfully challenged the constitutional validity of sections 61 and 62 of the Offences against the Person Act, 1861 and section 11 of the Criminal Law (Amendment) Act, 1885. The provisions of the 1861 Act that were challenged render it a criminal offence to commit buggery with mankind and also deal with associated offences such as attempts and assaults for the purpose of committing buggery and specifically include indecent assaults on a male person. The impugned provision of the 1885 Act renders it an offence for a male person to commit "in public or in private" any "act of gross indecency with another male person". Delivering the majority judgement of the Supreme Court rejecting the plaintiff's claim, O'Higgins C.J. stated:

> "While the impugned legislation does not expressly deal with homosexual practices and conduct, it is accepted that the effect of the three sections,

---

courts recognise the reality of the situation which arises in such cases, and that it may not be possible to undo what was done under the invalid statute – as it was put so succinctly during the argument, 'the egg cannot be unscrambled'."
46. This was not, however, explicitly stated in the judgements delivered.
47. (July, 1984) unreported (H.C.); (November, 1985) unreported (S.C.).
48. See p. 4 of judgement.
49. See p. 6 of judgement.
50. *Supra*.

taken together, is to prohibit and criminalise such conduct between male persons"[51]

Having referred to the evidence and the text books produced as part of the evidence, the Chief Justice went on to consider "the effect of homosexual activity on marriage" and concluded that:

> "an open and general increase in homosexual activity in any society must have serious consequences of a harmful nature in so far as marriage is concerned"[52] (and that such) "conduct can be inimical to marriage and is *per se* harmful to it as an institution."[53]

Further on he continued:

> "Article 41, s.3, sub-s.1, of the Constitution provides:— 'The State pledges itself to guard with special care the institution of Marriage, on which the Family is founded, and to protect it against attack.' Surely, a law which prohibits acts and conduct by male citizens of a kind known to be particularly harmful to the institution of marriage cannot be regarded as inconsistent with a Constitution containing such a provision."[54]

Succession: In *O'B. v. S.*[55] the plaintiff challenged the constitutional validity of sections 67 and 69 of the Succession Act, 1965, in so far as they deprived an illegitimate child of the same rights to intestate succession as that of a legitimate child. The State contended that these provisions were consistent with the Constitution and relied heavily on Article 41, arguing that "the State's special duty of protecting the institution of marriage can be justification for ensuring that, on intestate succession, children born to either one of the married couple outside the marriage will not succeed on intestacy and that children born of the marriage will so succeed". It claimed that such provision ensured that "the family patrimony will be kept within the family on intestacy" and "is a reasonable and valid means open to the Oireachtas to adopt within the Constitution, if it considers it necessary to do so." By so doing it was contended the State ensures that the family based on marriage "is maintained in a position superior to that of an unmarried union, and thereby honours its guarantee under Article 41, s.1, sub-s.2, of the Constitution."[56] The Supreme Court, without there having been any evidence presented at the original High Court hearing as to the substance of the argument that the impugned sections of the Succession Act afforded protection to the marital family, accepted that they constituted "a law designed to protect the family" which was "aimed at maintaining the primacy of the family as a fundamental group of society"[57] and upheld the constitutionality of the impugned legislation.

Extending succession and other rights to a child adopted by a married couple has been held not to infringe the family's constitutional protection under Article 41. In *The State (Nicolaou) v. An Bord Uchtála*,[58] the applicant challenged the constitutionality of the Adoption Act, 1952, on a number of grounds and in

---

51. *Ibid* at pp. 51–52.
52. *Ibid* at p. 63.
53. *Ibid*. See further on, however, where the Chief Justice expresses a more qualified view stating that homosexuality "is potentially harmful to the institution of marriage." (*supra* at p. 65).
54. *Supra* at p. 65. See, however, the dissenting views expressd by McCarthy J. and Henchy J. See further p. 31 *post*.
55. [1984] I.R. 316 (S.C.).
56. *Ibid* at pp. 333, 334.
57. *Ibid* at p. 334.
58. *Supra*.

doing so argued that the Act, by permitting the adoption of a child by the
parents of an existing family and by providing that the child shall be considered
as one born in lawful wedlock, infringed the guaranteed rights of the family and
its members. Walsh J. on behalf of the Supreme Court rejected this contention
stating:

> "The adoption of a child by the parents of a family in no way diminishes
> for the other members of that family the rights guaranteed by the Con-
> stitution. Rights of succession, rights to compensation for the death of a
> parent and such matters may properly be the subject of legislation and the
> extension of such legal rights by legislation to benefit an adopted child does
> not encroach upon any of the inalienable and imprescriptible rights guaran-
> teed by the Constitution to the family or its members or upon the natural
> and imprescriptible rights of children referred to in section 5 of Article 42."[59]

Spousal Residence in the State: In *Mohammed Abdelkefi and Susanne Abdelkefi v. The Minister for Justice*,[60] the husband, a Tunisian citizen married to an
Irish citizen, had been refused permission to reside in Ireland prior to marriage
and at the date of the hearing of the proceedings both the plaintiffs and their
child had their home outside the State and had no present intention of establishing a home in Ireland. It was argued that the wife, as an Irish citizen had "a
constitutional right to the company of her husband whenever she comes to
and remains within the State"[61] and that as a consequence the authorities
had no discretion under the Aliens Act, 1935, and the relevant regulations made
under that Act, to refuse to permit her Tunisian husband into the State and
accompany her when she travelled to Ireland to visit her family.

Barron J. dismissing the wife's claim based on Article 41.1 stated that he
could:

> "see nothing in the refusal by the Aliens Registration Office to weaken the
> family as an institution or to weaken its position in our society nor is there
> anything in such refusal which can be said to undermine the status of
> marriage."[62]

In the *State (Bouzagou) v. Fitzgibbon Street Garda Station*[62a] a Moroccan
citizen (the husband) married to an Irish citizen was denied leave to land in the
State under the Aliens Act, 1935, on the grounds that he did not hold a valid
Irish visa and was not in a position to support himself. It was established that
domestic problems existed between the husband and the wife: that the husband
had been convicted of assaulting his wife and that two and a half years earlier
the wife had obtained an order barring the husband from the family home. At
the date of the proceedings the wife and the parties' two children resided in the
home which was local authority rented accommodation. The husband contended
that his exclusion from the State violated Articles 41 and 42 of the Constitution.
Dismissing the husband's proceedings and holding that the reasons given by the

---

59. *Ibid* at p. 645.
60. [1984] 4 I.L.R.M. 138 (H.C.).
61. *Ibid* at p. 143.
62. *Ibid* at p. 145. As for the wife's allegation that the refusal by the Aliens Registration Office was a denial of her personal rights under Article 40(3) of the Constitution
(see p. 25 *post*) Barron J. stated that he did "not regard the fulfilment of a desire to visit
her immediate family in the company of her husband as being of such a fundamental nature
as to be guaranteed by such constitutional provision." (*supra* at p. 145).
62a.[1986] 6 I.L.R.M. 98 (H.C.).

immigration officer for his exclusion were bona fide, Barrington J. stated:

> "The prosecutor's problem . . . is that he cannot automatically claim the rights guaranteed to the family under Article 41, because in this case, unfortunately, the family is divided. It is not a question of asserting the rights of a family, or even of parents, as against the outside world but of reconciling rights of individual members of the family when the family itself is divided. The wife and children now live as a separate unit and, when the prosecutor was last in the country had the protection of a barring order against him. In these circumstances . . . in the absence of agreement between husband and wife, the task of reconciling the rights of the prosecutor and those of other members of his family is one for the courts."[62b]

Barrington J. emphasised that he had not been required to state "what the position would be" if the spouses were not estranged and that "even in the case of an estranged husband, there might be circumstances in which he would be entitled to a visa or to enter Ireland for the purpose of sorting out his family difficulties by litigation or other lawful means."[62c] The husband had not made his case on this basis, however, having untruthfully told immigration officials he was returning to reside permanently in Ireland with his family.

Neither the *Abdelkefi* nor the *Bouzagou* case was concerned with determining the constitutional rights of a happily married Irish citizen to permanently reside in the State with a non-Irish spouse or with the rights of such a couple and their children to reside together as a family within the State. In *Pok Sun Shum & Ors. v. Ireland & Ors.*[62d] the husband who was a Chinese national and the wife who was an Irish citizen and their children challenged the constitutional validity of an order made by the Minister for Justice pursuant to the Aliens Act, 1935, requiring the husband to leave the State following his application for naturalisation having been refused. The couple had married in Ireland in 1979, the husband having originally been permitted to enter the State in 1978. Upon the ministerial order requiring him to leave being made in 1983 these proceedings were instituted.

Costello J. noted that

> "The plaintiffs seek a declaration that the second named plaintiff (the wife) who is married to the first named plaintiff is normally entitled to the society of the first named plaintiff within the State. That is so and I don't think it needs any declaration of the court for that to be made clear."[62e]

Further on, in his judgement he stated that it was submitted on behalf of the plaintiffs

> "that because of the very entrenched provisions of the family rights in the Constitution . . . these could not be trenched upon, in any way, by the State and, in particular by the Aliens order. (Counsel for the plaintiff) went so far as . . . to say that if an alien landed in the State on one day and married the next day to an Irish citizen in the State, the State was required by the Constitution, to safeguard the rights which were given to the family and these could not be taken away by the Aliens Act."[62f]

Rejecting the plaintiffs' submission, he continued:

62b. *Ibid* at p. 103; see also *Dennehy v. The Minister for Social Welfare, supra*.
62c. *Ibid*.
62d. (June, 1985) unreported (H.C.).
62e. See p. 4 of judgement.
62f. See p. 5 of judgement.

"I do not think that the rights given to the family are absolute, in the sense that they are not subject to some restrictions by the State and . . . restrictions are in fact permitted by law, when husbands are imprisoned and parents of families are imprisoned and, undoubtedly, whilst protected under the Constitution there are restrictions permitted for the common good on the exercise of its (the family's) rights."[62g]

The learned judge held that the Minister's powers under the Aliens Act and the regulations made under it, to be such "permissible restrictions". He further declined to grant a declaration sought by the wife that "she has a right under Article 41 . . . to have her family unit protected in its Constitution and in particular to be allowed to cohabit with her husband . . . and to reside within the State" rul:ng that "if the Minister has the power, as I believe he has, to order aliens deportation from the State, then even if he is married to an Irish citizen, no entitlement to (such) a declaration . . . can exist."[62h]

Dissolution of Marriage: In *Murray & Murray v. The Attorney General & Ireland*[63] Costello J. stated that:

"The Constitution makes clear that the concept and nature of marriage which it enshrines are derived from the Christian notion of a partnership based on an irrevocable personal consent given by both spouses which establishes a unique and very special life-long relationship."[64]

The irrevocability of the marriage vow is constitutionally copperfastened by Article 41.3.2 which prohibits the Oireachtas from enacting any law providing for the grant of a dissolution of marriage and by so doing denies to the Oireachtas the power to enact divorce legislation.[65] On the 26 June 1986 a Government proposal, contained in the Tenth Amendment of the Constitution Bill, 1986, to replace the prohibition on divorce by a new constitutional provision permitting divorce subject to prescribed constitutional restrictions was rejected in a referendum by 935,843 (63%) votes to 538,279 (37%).[65a]

The elevation of marriage to a constitutionally enshrined lifelong relationship does not and, of course, cannot guarantee the success of all marriages. Conscious of the social reality of marital breakdown within Irish society and of the constitutional indissolubility of the marriage bond, the Irish judiciary have in the past decade by reliance on modern developments in psychiatric and psychological learning, developed the civil law of nullity and considerably widened its scope. As a result of a liberal and humane development and application of the law of nullity, a number of marriages which at no stage were viable have been declared

62g.*Ibid.* See however, *McGee v. A.G., supra* - Griffin J. states p. 333 "the right of married persons to establish a home and bring up children is inherent in the right to marry."
62h. See p. 6 of judgement. See also *Sunday Osheku & Ors. v. Ireland & Ors.* (June 1986) unreported (H.C.).
63. [1985] 5 I.L.R.M. 542 (H.C.).   64. *Ibid* at p. 545.
65. See *Lewis v. Lewis* [1940] I.R. 42 (H.C.) p. 41 where Hanna J., referring to Article 41.3.2 stated that its effect "is that notwithstanding any kind of matrimonial offence the marriage tie still continues . . .".
65a. The Bill proposed that Art. 41.3.2 be replaced by: "Where, and only where, such court established under this Constitution as may be prescribed by law is satisfied that — i. a marriage has failed, ii. the failure has continued for a period of, or periods amounting to, at least five years, iii. there is no reasonable possibility of reconciliation between the parties to the marriage, and iv. any other condition prescribed by law has been complied with, the court may in accordance with law grant a dissolution of the marriage provided that the court is satisfied that adequate and proper provision having regard to the circumstances will be made for any dependent spouse and for any child of or any child who is dependent on either spouse." The total electorate eligible to vote was 2,440,907. See further Chapter 8.

null and void by the Irish courts in circumstances in which in other jurisdictions decrees of dissolution or divorce would have been sought and granted.[66]

Marriage Counselling: Article 41.3 pledges the State "to guard with special care the institution of marriage" and "to protect it against attack". In *E.R. v. J.R.*[67] Carroll J. held that communications made to a minister of religion who was acting as a marriage counsellor are privileged and cannot be revealed in family law proceedings, unless the privilege is waived by the spouses who participated in such counselling. Delivering judgement, Carroll J. stated that:

> "The provision of confidential marriage counselling which may help a married couple over a difficulty in their marriage is protection of the most practical kind for the family and should be fostered."[68]

Separation. The constitutional duty to protect marriage and safeguard it from attack has not resulted in any constitutional challenge being mounted to the court's statutory powers to grant decrees of judicial separation (divorce *a mensa et thoro*)[69] or to grant barring orders to exclude a spouse from the family home in order to protect the safety or welfare of the other spouse and/or the spouse's infant children.[70] Deeds of separation in which spouses agree to live apart from each other have also been held to be binding legal contracts unaffected by Article 41 and enforceable by the courts.[71] In *Dalton v. Dalton*,[72] however, considering a separation deed in which the parties, whilst domiciled in Ireland, had covenanted to obtain a foreign decree of divorce, O'Hanlon J. stated that:

> "considerations of public policy require that the court shall not lend its support to an agreement providing for the obtaining of a divorce *a vinculo* by a husband and wife and this may well be the position even if the parties are domiciled elsewhere than in Ireland when the application is made or propose to take up such foreign domicile in the future."[73]

It is clear from this decision that the Irish courts will not enforce a provision in a deed of separation whereby spouses domiciled in Ireland agree to obtain a foreign divorce and that if such a provision is contained in any such deed it may taint the entire deed, rendering all its provisions unenforceable, unless severable from them.

Foreign Divorce Decrees: Although the Irish courts will do nothing to "facilitate" or "assist" in the obtaining of a foreign decree of divorce, such a decree has been held recognisable under common law if the parties to the divorce were domiciled within the foreign jurisdiction from which it was obtained at the date of the initiation of the divorce proceedings. At one time it was judicially suggested that Article 41.3.3 prohibited in any circumstances the recognition in this country of a decree of divorce granted in any other State. It is now established that it has no such effect[74] and the Domicile and Recognition of Foreign Divorces Act,

---

66. See the dissenting judgement of Henchy J. in *N. (otherwise K.) v. K.* [1986] 6 I.L.R.M. 75 (S.C.). See further Ch. 5.
67. [1981] 1 I.L.R.M. 125 (H.C.).
68. *Ibid* at p. 126.
69. See Chapter 8.
70. See *Murray & Murray v. The Attorney General & Ireland, supra,* and the extract therefrom in footnote 25 above where Costello J. expressly accepts the constitutional validity of the State in its laws permitting a father to be barred from the family home. See further Chapter 17.
71. See Chapter 7.
72. [1982] 2 I.L.R.M. 418 (H.C.).
73. *Ibid* at p. 419. See also *Cohane v. Cohane* [1968] I.R. 176 (S.C.). See further p. 210 *post*.
74. See Chapter 10. See, in particular, *Mayo-Perrott v. Mayo-Perrott* [1958] I.R. 336 (S.C.); *Gaffney v. Gaffney* [1975] I.R. 133 (S.C.); *T. v. T.* [1983] I.R. 29; [1982] 2 I.L.R.M. 217 (S.C.); *K.E.D. (otherwise known as K.C.) v. M.C.* (September, 1984) unreported (H.C.), (December, 1985) unreported (S.C.).

1986, discussed in chapter 10 extends by statute the circumstances in which a foreign decree of divorce may be recognised. It has also been held that it is not contrary to the provisions of Article 41 or to Irish public policy for the Irish courts to enforce maintenance or other financial orders for the support of a spouse made by a foreign court in divorce proceedings, as such support orders cannot be regarded as "facilitating" or "assisting" in the obtaining of a divorce decree.[75]

The Marital Family and Parental Rights

The courts in considering the influence of Articles 41 and 42 in this area have been concerned with examining the nature of parental rights, the limitations on the State's and third parties' capacity to interfere with those rights and with elucidating the principles applicable in the resolution of disputes relating to the custody and upbringing of children upon the possibility arising of a clash between parental rights and the rights of the child.

In *In re Art. 26 and the School Attendance Bill*, 1942[76] the Supreme Court held invalid a section in a bill aimed at giving the Minister for Education ultimate control over the manner in which children between the ages of 6 and 14 years of age should be educated. Sullivan C.J., delivering the judgement of the court referring to Article 42.3.2, said that:

> "The State is entitled to require that children shall receive a certain minimum education. So long as parents supply this general standard of education we are of opinion that the manner in which it is being given and received is entirely a matter for the parents and is not a matter in respect of which the State under the Constitution is entitled to interfere."[77]

Any such interference in the court's view was not "warranted by the Constitution".[78]

Similarly it has been held that testators cannot by will "override the sacred parental authority and defy the parental right and duty of education under Article 42 of the Constitution" so as to require a child to be brought up in a religion favoured by the testator and that any such provision contained in a will is invalid and contrary to public policy.[79]

In *Ryan v. The Attorney General*[80] it was unsuccessfully contended that the fluoridation of the public water supplies violated the "inalienable right of parents to provide for the physical education of their children". In dealing with this issue the Supreme Court for the first time considered the meaning of the term "education" in Article 42. O'Dalaigh C.J. referred to the contention that "the provision of suitable food and drink for children is physical education" and continued:

> "In the court's view this is nurture not education. Education essentially is the teaching and training of a child to make the best possible use of his

75. See *D.M. v. E.F.M.* (July, 1978) unreported (H.C.); *G. v. G.* [1984] I.R. 368 (H.C.); *Sachs v. Standard Chartered Bank (Ireland) Ltd. & Sachs* (July, 1985) unreported (H.C.), (July, 1986) unreported (S.C.). See further p. 462 *post*.
76. [1943] I.R. 334 (S.C.). See also *Report of the Committee on the Constitution* (Dublin, Stationery Office, December 1967) p. 46 and the comments on this case.
77. *Supra* at p. 346.
78. *Ibid.*
79. See *Burke & O'Reilly v. Burke & Quail* [1951] I.R. 216; (1950) 84 I.L.T.R. 70 (H.C.). See further p. 524 *post*.
80. *Supra.*

inherent and potential capacities, physical, mental and moral. To teach a child to minimise the dangers of dental caries by adequately brushing of his teeth is physical education for it induces him to use his own resources. To give him water of a nature calculated to minimise the danger of dental caries is in no way to educate him physically or otherwise for it does not develop his resources."[81]

Children's rights to education and the role of government and public authorities have been discussed in two relatively recent Supreme Court decisions.

In *Crowley & Ors. v. The Minister for Education & Ors.*,[82] the Supreme Court held by a majority decision that the State had not failed in its duty under Article 42.4 "to provide for" free primary school education when a strike by teachers who were members of the Irish National Teachers Organisation (I.N.T.O.) prevented children in Drimoleague, West Cork from attending at three schools in their parish. It was, however, held that a circular sent by the I.N.T.O. to all its members teaching in schools in the areas adjoining Drimoleague directing them not to enrol pupils from Drimoleague was an unlawful interference with the constitutional rights of the infant plaintiffs' free primary education.

In *McDonald v. Dublin County Council & Ors.*[83] the mother of an itinerant family claimed that a resolution passed by the elected members of Dublin County Council requiring the Dublin City & County Manager to remove her and her family from a site owned by the council on which they lived in their caravan was an invalid interference with her constitutional rights and those of her family. The Supreme Court held that it was not proper for the council as a housing authority to simply remove the family from the site without the council giving "attention" and "consideration" to the "provision of adequate and suitable" accommodation for the "plaintiff and her family". The injunction granted by the High Court against the council was discontinued by the Supreme Court prior to the hearing of the Supreme Court appeal as by that time appropriate accommodation had been offered by the council to the plaintiffs. In delivering the court's judgement, O'Higgins C.J. remarked that:

"this case highlights the continuing problem of itinerant families in and around this city and county. It appears that there are at present 210 such families occupying unauthorised sites. Nothing is solved merely by moving such families from place to place. By doing so, not only is the problem per- petuated but the claims and rights of the children to any possibility of education and a settled life and future are ignored."[84]

As between married parents, Articles 41 and 42 have been interpreted by the courts so as to terminate the paternal supremacy of the common law and replace it with joint parental authority, both the mother and father of a legitimate child being held under the Constitution to have equal rights and duties in matters relating to the guardianship, custody and upbringing of their children.[85] It is in seeking to reconcile the inalienable and imprescriptible rights of parents as a unit within the family (Article 41.1.1) and the inalienable right and duty of parents (Article 42.1) to bring up and provide for the education of their children with the inalienable and imprescriptible rights of children as members of the family

---

81. *Ibid* at p. 350.
82. *Supra.*
83. (July, 1980) unreported (S.C.).
84. *Per* O'Higgins C.J. at pp. 12–13 of his judgement, which was the judgement of the court.
85. See *In re Tilson, infants* [1951] I.R. 1 (S.C.). See further p. 350 *post et seq.*

(Article 41.1.1) and the natural and imprescriptible rights of children to care
and education (Article 42.5) that has caused both the legislature and the courts
the greatest degree of difficulty. It is in the area of disputes as to custody
between parents and third parties that this difficulty has been particularly
apparent.

In *In re Doyle, an Infant*,[86] a part of section 10 of the Children Act, 1941,
was held to be repugnant to the Constitution by the Supreme Court because it
empowered the authorities to retain custody of a child placed in an industrial
school with parental consent even after a parent had reacquired his ability and
expressed a desire to support his child. Maguire C.J. stated that while:

> "the provisions of section 10 in so far as they permit the State to supply
> the place of the parents because of lack of means are protected by (Article
> 42.5.), it cannot be that the mere fact that parents are at a given time
> unable to support their child would entitle the parents to surrender and the
> State to accept a surrender of the parents' rights, or would enable the
> parents by agreement with the State to rid themselves of the duty so plainly
> stated in Article 42.1. It seems clear that where such a surrender is sanctioned
> it can (only) be for a period limited by the parents' inability to provide for
> the education of a child ... In the view of this court, however, (Article
> 42.5.) does not enable the legislature to take away the right of a parent who
> is in a position to do so to control the education of his child where there is
> nothing culpable on the part of either parent or child."[87]

There is a suggestion arising from a number of court judgements that section 3
of the Guardianship of Infants Act, 1964, may be unconstitutional in so far as
it requires the child's welfare to be regarded "as the first and paramount consideration" in the determination of disputes relating to the custody and upbringing of legitimate children between a child's parents and third parties.[88] The
difficulties associated with this issue have resulted in two apparently conflicting
decisions being delivered by the Supreme Court in recent years in cases in which
the provisions of Articles 41 and 42 were discussed but in which the constitutional
validity of section 3 of the Act of 1964 was not formally challenged.

In *J. v. D. & Ors.*[89] determined in 1977, the court had no difficulty in
applying the welfare principle as required under the Act of 1964 in refusing to
give custody of four legitimate children to their father who was their sole surviving parent. In *K.C. & A.C. v. An Bord Uchtála*[90] determined in 1984, the
court held that parents could only be deprived of custody of their legitimate child
for "compelling reasons" or in "an exceptional case" where the parents have
failed and "continue to fail to provide education for the child for moral or physical
reasons".[91] Delivering the principal judgement of the court, Finlay C.J. stated
that in so far as the decision in *J. v. D.* could be construed

86. *Supra.*
87. See pp. 4–5 of judgement of court delivered by Maguire C.J. (December, 1955)
unreported (S.C.). Earlier at p. 4 of judgement the Chief Justice had stated: "Article 42.2.3
appears to us expressly to secure to parents the right to choose the nature of the education
to be given to their children and the schools at which such education shall be provided and
this right must be a continuing right. Parents must be entitled to change and substitute
schools as in their judgement they think proper and to hold that a choice once made is
binding for the period of a child's education would be to deny such right."
88. See Chapter 13, p. 383 *et seq*.
89. (June, 1977) unreported (S.C.).
90. [1985] 5 I.L.R.M. 302 (S.C.).
91. *Ibid* at p. 317.

"as clearly indicating that in the case of legitimate children (the) paramount consideration of their welfare ... can be applied as the sole test without regard to the provisions of Articles 41 and 42 of the Constitution, I must respectfully refuse to follow it."[92]

In dealing with the constitutional rights of the legitimate child, the court held that "in addition to the rights of every child which are provided for in the Constitution",[93] such child has rights under the Constitution as a member of a family

"(a) To belong to a unit group possessing inalienable and imprescriptible rights antecedent and superior to all positive law (Article 41.1.);

(b) To protection by the State of the family to which it belongs (41.2.) (and)

(c) To be educated by the family and to be provided by its parents with religious, moral, intellectual, physical and social education (Article 42.1.)."[94]

In effect, the court held that the duty of the parents of a legitimate child to provide for the upbringing and education of their child conferred a corresponding right on such child to be brought up and educated by its parents. This constitutional right of the child, in the Supreme Court's view as expressed in *K.C. & A.C.*, renders it constitutionally impermissible to regard the welfare of the child as the first and paramount consideration in any dispute as to its upbringing or custody between parents and third parties. This perception of a parental right and duty as conferring a corresponding right on the legitimate child which supercedes in importance other personal rights possessed by the child as an individual and as a member of the family, can be interpreted as placing such other rights of the legitimate child in a constitutionally inferior or subservient position to the rights of the legitimate child's parents. As we shall see, however, the Supreme Court has not as yet fully worked out or explained the constitutional and legal implications of its decision in *K.C. & A.C.* or how it is to be applied in practice to finally adjudicating on disputes relating to the custody and upbringing of legitimate children between parents and third parties. It has also not yet given any detailed consideration as to how the familial constitutional rights are to be applied and interact with the other constitutional rights which have been declared by the courts to vest in every child and which are discussed in the section that follows.

It has been recognised that there are practical limitations, in specific circumstances, to the application of the familial constitutional rights to all legitimate children. Thus, in *Kent County Council v. C.S.*[95] the High Court ordered that a legitimate child be returned to the applicants' care in England after his Irish father had brought him to Ireland to prevent the applicants obtaining custody

92. *Ibid* at p. 318.
93. *Ibid* at p. 316. See further p. 26 *post*.
94. *Ibid* at p. 317. The Supreme Court ordered that the proceedings be remitted to the High Court so that the original trial Judge could apply the principles enunciated by the Supreme Court, "namely ... the test of compelling reasons why the welfare of the child cannot be secured to it in the family unit and by the parents" (*per* Finlay C.J., *supra* at p. 318), to the evidence heard in the case or to such further evidence as the trial Judge considered material. In doing so, Lynch J., in his judgement of May 1985 ordered that the child, who was the subject of the proceedings, be returned to the natural parents — see [1986] 6 I.L.R.M. 65. See further p. 392 *et seq*.
95. [1984] 4 I.L.R.M. 292 (H.C.).

of the child pursuant to an order of the English Courts. The father relied on Articles 41 and 42 and contended that if his son was returned to England he would be placed for adoption by the plaintiffs. Rejecting the father's contention and ordering the child's return to the care of the applicants, Finlay P. stated that the only "reasonable interpretation" of the orders made by the English court was that the court was "hoping or expecting that it might be possible to place the child in the long term care of its mother with appropriate access to its father".[96] As for the father's contention that he and the child formed a family in the constitutional sense and that he should not be deprived of his right to take responsibility for the upbringing and education of his child Finlay P. stated:

> "Taken in its broadest and most usual sense the family of which the infant is a member has broken up and it is not possible any longer for the courts of this country or ... the courts of England to provide a unified right to the family to educate and bring up the child as (a) close united family unit."[97]

The fact that parents have separated and disagree as to a child's future upbringing does not mean, however, that one parent cannot rely on the family articles of the Constitution in a dispute with the other parent and a third party. In *Northampton County Council v. A.B.F. & M.B.F.*[98] the High Court refused to order the return of a child to the plaintiff's care without a full plenary hearing as it was clearly their intention, with the mother's consent, to place the child for adoption against the wishes of the father. Hamilton J. held that the court had to consider the constitutional rights of the father who was separated from the child's mother and also had to ascertain "whether the child's rights are being protected"[99] before making any order. Finlay P. distinguished this case from that of *Kent County Council v. C.S.*[100] on the basis that in the latter he was "satisfied there (was) no question of a deprivation of any of the constitutional rights" of the father[101] and that the possibility of the child being placed for adoption did not arise.

Irish adoption law does not currently permit the adoption of legitimate children unless they are orphans. It has been suggested by some commentators that if the law were changed and the possibility of adoption extended to such children, any such legislative measure would be unconstitutional in that parents cannot permanently deprive themselves of their "inalienable" and "imprescriptible" rights in relation to their legitimate children or deprive such children of their "right" to be educated by their parents. Accordingly, a change in the law extending adoption to legitimate children may require an amendment to be made to the Constitution by way of a referendum. This issue is discussed in Chapter 12.

THE FAMILY, FAMILY LAW AND PERSONAL RIGHTS

In the pages that follow the importance and relevance of other fundamental rights provisions contained in the Constitution to family law becomes readily apparent. Articles 40.1. and 40.3. are in this context the constitutional Articles

---

96. *Ibid* at p. 296.
97. *Ibid.*
98. *Supra.*
99. *Ibid* at p. 166.
100. *Supra.*
101. *Ibid* at p. 297.

that have received most judicial attention in the elucidation of the personal rights of the family and its individual members in conjunction with Articles 41 and 42. They state:

Article 40

1. All citizens shall, as human persons, be held equal before the law. This shall not be held to mean that the State shall not in its enactments have due regard to differences of capacity, physical and moral, and of social function.

3.1. The State guarantees in its laws to respect, and as far as practicable, by its laws to defend and vindicate the personal rights of the citizen.

3.2. The State shall, in particular, by its laws protect as best it may from unjust attack and, in the case of injustice done, vindicate the life, person, good name, and property rights of every citizen.

3.3 The State acknowledges the right to life of the unborn and, with due regard to the equal right to life of the mother, guarantees in its laws, to respect, and, as far as practicable, by its laws to defend and vindicate that right.[102]

In *Ryan v. The Attorney General*,[103] although rejecting the plaintiff's submission that the addition of fluoride to the public water supply violated her personal rights guaranteed by Article 40.3., which rights she alleged included a right to bodily integrity, Kenny J. agreed with the contention that:

"the personal rights which may be invoked to invalidate legislation are not confined to those specified in Article 40 but include all those rights which result from the Christian and democratic nature of the State."[104]

Included in these unspecified personal rights, he held, were the right to bodily integrity, the right to marry and the right to freedom of movement within the State.[105] The Supreme Court upheld Kenny J.'s view that there existed unspecified personal rights arising out of the Constitution which "the High Court and the Supreme Court have the difficult and responsible duty of ascertaining and declaring" and thereby laid the foundation for the judicial expansion and development of family, parental and children's rights.[106]

---

102. Sub-section 3 was added to this Article by the Eighth Amendment of the Constitution Act following upon its approval by the people in a referendum held on the 7th of September, 1983. From a total electorate of 2,358,651 the total poll was 1,265,994 (53.7%). In favour totalled 841,233, against totalled 416,136. There were 8,625 spoilt votes.

103. [1965] I.R. 294 (H.C., S.C.).

104. *Ibid* at p. 312.

105. *Ibid* at p. 313. Building on the right to freedom of movement, Finlay P. in *The State (K.M. & R.D.) v. The Minister for Foreign Affairs & Ors., supra*, enunciated the right to travel and the right of a citizen to a passport. In the context of a child the right, he stated, is one to be exercised "by the choice of its parent, parents or legally recognised guardian subject always to the right of the Courts by appropriate proceedings to deny that choice in the dominant interest of the welfare of the child." (See [1979] I.R. at p. 81). See also *Abdelkefi v. The Minister for Justice, supra*, in which the High Court rejected the contention that the plaintiff wife had a personal right under Article 40.3 to the company of her husband whenever she visited the State. See further p. 16 *et seq ante*.

106. In *The State (Nicolaou) v. An Bord Uchtála, supra*, Walsh J. at p. 642 stated: "The Constitution does not set out in whole what are the rights of the citizen which are encompassed in this guarantee and while some of them are indicated in sub-section 2 of section 3 ... the personal rights guaranteed are not exhausted by those enumerated in sub-section 2." In *G. v. An Bord Uchtála, supra*, at p. 66 Walsh J. noted that: "it is now well accepted that the view first enunciated by my learned colleague, Mr. Justice Kenny (in *Ryan v. The*

Children's Rights: In *The State (Nicolaou) v. An Bord Uchtála,*[107] the
Supreme Court, while rejecting the contention that Articles 41 and 42 applied
to the family outside marriage, held that a mother's right to the care and custody
of her illegitimate child was a personal right which fell to be protected by
Article 40.3 and this was re-affirmed in *G. v. An Bord Uchtála.*[108] In the latter
case, the Supreme Court for the first time, in detail, enumerated some of the
personal rights of the child.

O'Higgins C.J. stated:

> "The child also has natural rights . . . Having been born, the child has the
> right to be fed and to live, to be reared and educated, to have the oppor-
> tunity of working and of realising his or her full personality and dignity
> as a human being. These rights of the child (and others which I have not
> enumerated) must equally be protected and vindicated by the State."[109]

The duty of the State as guardian of the common good to afford protection to
the rights of the child, he asserted, arises under Article 42.5 in the case of a
legitimate child and under Article 40.3 in the case of an illegitimate child.[110]

Parke J. also stated that:

> "The child has personal rights (which are recognised by Article 40 of the
> Constitution) to life, to be fed, to be protected, reared and educated in a
> proper way."[111]

The child in question in this case was in fact illegitimate, but it is clear that
it was the court's view that these rights also vest in legitimate children. In the
same case, Henchy J. stated:

Attorney General) that there are rights guaranteed by the Constitution other than those
which are enumerated in the Constitution itself is the correct view."

In *McGee v. The Attorney General, supra,* Henchy J. stated at p. 325: "The infinite
variety in the relationships between the citizen and his fellows and between the citizen and
the State make an exhaustive enumeration of the guaranteed rights difficult, if not impossible." See also *Norris v. The Attorney General, supra,* in which the majority judgement of
O'Higgins C.J. and the dissenting judgement of McCarthy J. starkly illustrate the different
judicial approaches that can be adopted in the application of the Kenny J. principles in the
court's elucidation of unspecified constitutional rights.

For a detailed consideration of the unspecified personal rights found by the courts to
emerge out of and derive from Article 40.3, see J.M. Kelly, *The Irish Constitution, supra,*
p. 468 *et seq.* See also *Murray & Murray v. The Attorney General & Ireland, supra.*

107. *Supra.*

108. [1980] I.R. 32 (S.C.). See judgements of O'Higgins C.J., Walsh J. and Parke J.
Two members of the court dissented on this issue, Henchy J., and Kenny J. See also *E.M. v.
M.M.* (December, 1982) unreported (H.C.).

109. *Supra* at p. 56. See also *Northampton County Council v. A.B.F. and M.B.F.* [1982]
2 I.L.R.M. 164 (H.C.).

110. In the case of a legitimate child, the Chief Justice was of the view that the State
could intervene "where the parents fail in their duty towards (the) child for physical or
moral reasons" while in the case of an illegitimate child it could do so if the mother's rights
were "used in such a way as to endanger the health or life of the child or to deprive him of
his rights." [1980] I.R. at p. 56. On the basis of this analysis the State can afford greater
protection to the illegitimate child than to the legitimate child under the 1937 Constitution.
See also *K.C. & A.C. v. An Bord Uchtála, supra,* and the discussion of this case on p. 22
ante et seq. and p. 392 *post et seq.*

111. *Supra* at p. 100. Although Henchy J., in the minority, was of the view that the
mother did not possess a personal constitutional right to the custody of her child, he expressed
the view that "the constitutional rights of an illegitimate child will require that the mother
be given custody, particularly in the case of a very young child. In such a case the custody
has a constitutional footing in so far as it satisfies a constitutional right of the child" subject
to the proviso that "if (because of factors such as physical incapacity, mental illness, personality defect, chronic alcoholism, drug addition, moral depravity or dereliction of parental
duty) the mother's custody could be incompatible with the child's constitutional rights,"
the child's rights would take precedence. See [1980] I.R. at pp. 87–88.

"all children, whether legitimate or illegitimate, share the common characteristic that they enter life without any responsibility for their status and
with an equal claim to what the Constitution expressly or impliedly postulates as the fundamental rights of children."[112]

Moreover, Walsh J. stated that in his view there is

"no difference between the obligations of the unmarried parent to the
child and those of the married parent. These obligations of the parent
or parents amount to natural rights of the child and they exist for the
benefit of the child[113] ... Not only has a child born out of wedlock the
natural right to have its welfare and health guarded no less well than that of
a child born in lawful wedlock, but *a fortiori* it has the right to life itself
and the right to be guarded against all threats directed to its existence
whether before or after birth. The child's natural rights spring primarily
from the natural right of every individual to life, to be reared and educated,
to liberty, to work, to rest and recreation, to the practice of religion and to
follow his or her conscience. The right to life necessarily implies the right
to be born, the right to preserve and defend (and to have preserved and
defended) that life and the right to maintain that life at a proper human
standard in matters of food, clothing and habitation. It lies not in the
power of the parent who has the primary natural rights and duties in respect
of the child to exercise them in such a way as to intentionally or by neglect
to endanger the health or life of the child or to terminate its existence. The
child's natural right to life and all that flows from that right are independent
of any right of the parent as such ... In these respects the child born out
of lawful wedlock is in precisely the same position as the child born in lawful wedlock."[114]

It is, thus, clear that both legitimate and illegitimate children possess rights
guaranteed by the Constitution other than those enumerated in the Constitution
itself and that there are personal and individual rights vested in children independent of parental rights. It is these personal and individual rights of legitimate
children to which the Supreme Court failed to give sufficiently detailed consideration in *K.C. & A.C. v. An Bord Uchtála*.[115]

The equality of rights as between children, it has been held, does not require
identical legislative treatment of all children in all circumstances. Henchy J. in
G. v. An Bord Uchtála[116] pointed out that due to

"the central and fundamental position accorded by the Constitution to the
family in the social and moral order, there is a necessary and inescapable

---

112. *Supra* at pp. 86–87.
113. *Ibid* at p. 68.
114. *Ibid* at p. 69. See also the High Court judgement of Finlay P. in *G. v. An Bord
Uchtála* [1980] I.R. at p. 44 where the learned judge referring to the rights of the child
stated she has "an unenumerated right to an opportunity to be reared with due regard to
her religious, moral, intellectual, physical and social welfare."
115. See p. 23 *ante*. It should, however, be noted that in *G. v. An Bord Uchtála, supra*,
Walsh J. did raise the issue of the constitutional difficulties that could arise in the context
of the application of section 3 of the Guardianship of Infants Act, 1964, to disputes between
parents and third parties in relation to legitimate children. He stated *supra* at p. 76 with
reference to section 3 that "the word 'paramount' by itself is not by any means an indication of exclusivity; no doubt if the Oireachtas had intended the welfare of the child to be
the sole consideration it would have said so. The use of the word 'paramount' certainly
indicates that the welfare of the child was to be the superior or the most important consideration, *in so far as it can be, having regard to the law or the provisions of the Constitution applicable to any given case.* (Author's italics)
116. *Supra*.

difference of moral capacity and social function between parents or a parent within a family and the parents or parent of an illegitimate child" (and) "thus one will find throughout the laws of the State many instances where parents within a family are treated differently from the parent of an illegitimate child. Likewise, with the same constitutional justification, instances may be adduced (e.g. in the law of succession) where illegitimate children are treated differently from legitimate children."[117]

It was on the basis of similar reasoning that in *O'B. v. S.*[118] the Supreme Court held that the Succession Act, 1965, did not unconstitutionally discriminate against an illegitimate child by denying to the child the same rights of intestate succession as it conferred on legitimate children. Walsh J., delivering the judgement of the court, acknowledged that:

"It cannot be contested that a person born outside marriage is, as a human person, equal to one born within marriage"[119]

and that no difference of physical or moral capacity, or social function arose from the mere fact of illegitimacy that could justify the different legislative treatment of an illegitimate child on the basis of the proviso to Article 40.1. However, he stated that:

"Legislation which differentiates citizens or which discriminates between them does not need to be justified under the proviso (to Article 40.1.) if justification for it can be found in other provisions of the Constitution"[120]

and held, as we have already seen, that the 1965 Act in so far as it discriminated between legitimate and illegitimate children was justified by the State's constitutional duty to protect the marital family, noting that

"The provisions of Article 41 of the Consitution ... create not merely a State interest but a State obligation to safeguard the family."[121]

As the Constitution does not require identical treatment of all children it has been held that the State may, by legislation, redress some of the inequalities imposed by circumstances on illegitimate children. It has been held that the State may by legislation treat an illegitimate child differently to the treatment afforded to a legitimate child if such differences in treatment are to afford protection to the welfare of the illegitimate child.[122] Thus, it may by the enactment of adoption legislation provide an opportunity for illegitimate children to receive the advantages of family life.[123] However, it is clear, having regard to the judgement delivered in *O'B. v. S.* that the courts could strike down as unconstitutional any legislation extending rights to the family outside marriage or to any of its members, including the illegitimate child, if in the view of the Supreme Court the extension of any such rights violated the duty imposed on the State to protect the marital family.

Parental Rights Outside Marriage: As we have already seen, a mother's constitutional right to the care and custody of her illegitimate child or children is

---

117. *Ibid* at p. 86.
118. [1984] I.R. 316 (S.C.).
119. *Ibid* at p. 332.
120. *Ibid* at p. 335.
121. *Ibid* at p. 338.
122 See *The State (K.M. & R.D.) v. The Minister for Foreign Affairs & Ors., supra.*
123. *The State (Nicolaou) v. An Bord Uchtála* [1966] I.R. at p. 642.

protected by Article 40.3.[124] As the natural mother's rights do not arise under Articles 41 and 42 they are not inalienable or imprescriptible. Thus, whilst there may be a doubt as to whether the State can by way of adoption legislation permit parents of a legitimate child to entirely divest themselves of their rights and duties in relation to such child by agreeing to transfer such rights and duties to adopters,[125] there is no constitutional impediment to the mother of an illegitimate child waiving or abandoning her constitutional rights so as to permit her child to be adopted.[126] Neither can there be any doubt about the constitutionality of section 3 of the Guardianship of Infants Act in so far as it requires that the welfare of the child is to be regarded "as the first and paramount consideration" in the determination of custody disputes between the natural parent or parents of an illegitimate child and a third party.[127] As for the father of a child born outside marriage, it has been held that he has no constitutional rights in relation to his child at all.[128]

Right to Privacy: In *McGee v. The Attorney General*[129] the Supreme Court by a 4–1 majority recognised the existence of a "right to marital privacy". The plaintiff, a married woman, decided with her husband's agreement that she would have no more children as she had been medically advised that another pregnancy would have serious physical repercussions and could put her life at risk. She sought to import by post a contraceptive jelly which was unavailable in Ireland but the package was seized by the Customs Authorities. In subsequent proceedings, the Supreme Court held section 17(3) of the Criminal Law Amendment Act, 1935, the effect of which[130] was to prohibit the importation of contraceptives for any purpose to be inconsistent with the Constitution and no longer in force.[131]

Three members of the court relied on Article 40.3. in their judgement. Henchy J. stated:

> "In my opinion, s.17 of the Act of 1935 violates the guarantee in subs-s.1 of s.3 of Article 40 by the State to protect the plaintiff's personal rights by its laws; it does so not only by violating her personal right to privacy in regard to her marital relations but, in a wider way, by frustrating and making criminal any efforts by her to effectuate the decision of her husband and herself, made responsibly, conscientiously and on medical advice to avail themselves of a particular contraceptive method so as to ensure her life and health as well as the integrity, security and wellbeing of her marriage and her family."[132]

124. *The State (Nicolaou) v. An Bord Uchtála, supra; G. v. An Bord Uchtála, supra; McNally v. Lee, supra; S. v. The Eastern Health Board* (February, 1979) unreported (H.C.); *E.M. v. M.M., supra.*
125. If there is a doubt as to the likely constitutional validity of any such legislation, current legislation which permits the adoption of a legitimated child must also be constitutionally suspect. For a detailed discussion of this issue see p. 329 *post.*
126. See in particular *G. v. An Bord Uchtála, supra; S. v. E.H.B., supra.* For a detailed consideration of this area see p. 329 *post.* See also P.A. O'Connor, "Constitutional Conflict in Adoption Proceedings" (1985) 3 (n.s.) I.L.T. 58, 89, 107 and 161.
127. See further p. 597 *post et seq.*
128. *The State (Nicolaou) v. An Bord Uchtála, supra.* See further p. 595 *post.*
129. [1974] I.R. 284 (S.C.).
130. Together with sections 42 and 186 of the Customs Consolidation Act, 1876.
131. The prohibition on the importation of contraceptives together with the prohibition on their sale, had the effect of making them unavailable within the law. There was no prohibition either on their manufacture or use within the State. In practice "the pill" was imported and sold in chemist's shops throughout the country and taken by many thousands of women for purely contraceptive purposes. The law was evaded by the legal fiction that it was used for health reasons only.
132. [1974] I.R. at p. 328.

Griffin J. stating the right of marital privacy to be one of the personal rights guaranteed by Article 40.3.1 continued:

> "In my opinion, a statute which makes it a criminal offence for the plaintiff or her husband to import or to acquire possession of contraceptives for use within their marriage is an unjustifiable invasion of privacy in the conduct of the most intimate of all their personal relationships."[133]

Budd J. said:

> "Whilst the 'personal rights' are not described specifically, it is scarcely to be doubted in our society that the right to privacy is universally recognised and accepted with possibly the rarest of exceptions and that the matter of marital relationship must rank as one of the most important of matters in the realm of privacy ... This Act does not defend or vindicate the personal rights of the citizen or his or her privacy relative to matters of the procreation of children and the privacy of married life and marital relations."[134]

Walsh J. relying primarily on Article 41 stated that:

> "The sexual life of a husband and wife is of necessity and by its nature an area of particular privacy[135] ... the rights of a married couple to decide how many children, if any, they will have are matters outside the reach of positive law where the means employed to implement such decisions do not impinge upon the common good or destroy or endanger human life ... it is outside the authority of the State to endeavour to intrude into the privacy of the husband and wife relationship for the sake of imposing a code of private morality upon that husband and wife which they do not desire.
>
> In my view, Article 41 of the Constitution guarantees the husband and wife against any such invasion of their privacy by the State. It follows that the use of contraceptives by them within that marital privacy is equally guaranteed against such invasion and, as such, assumes the status of a right so guaranteed by the Constitution. If this right cannot be directly invaded by the State, it follows that it cannot be frustrated by the State taking measures to ensure that the exercise of that right is rendered impossible."[136]

As a consequence of this judgement it was no longer contrary to the law to import contraceptives. However, the other provisions contained in section 17 of the Criminal Law Amendment Act, 1935, remained in force prohibiting the importation for sale, or the sale of contraceptives in the State. The Health (Family Planning) Act, 1979 which came into operation on the 1st of November 1980 repealed the whole of section 17 of the 1935 Act and made statutory provision for the operation of family planning services and the supply of contraceptives. This legislation was recently amended by the Health (Family Planning) (Amendment) Act, 1985.[137]

---

133. *Ibid* at p. 335.
134. *Ibid* at p. 322.
135. *Ibid* at p. 312.
136. *Ibid* at p. 313. Section 17(1) of the Act of 1935 rendered it unlawful "for any person to sell or expose, offer, advertise or keep for sale or to import or to attempt to import ... for sale any contraceptive." The section was not here challenged. However, Walsh J. stated in *McGee v. The Attorney General, supra,* at p. 315: "if, in the result, notwithstanding the deletion of sub-s.3, the prohibition on sale had the effect of leaving a position where contraceptives were not reasonably available for use within marriage, then that particular prohibition must also fall. However, at the moment I do not think it necessary to make any declaration in respect of that."
137. See further p. 171 *post.*

In *Murphy v. The Attorney General*[138] the right to privacy was again considered, Hamilton J. in the High Court rejecting the argument that each spouse has a right to privacy in respect of his or her income and that legislation obliging a spouse to disclose his or her income to the other spouse violated that right. In the learned judge's opinion

> "the Constitution does not guarantee any such privacy to either the husband or the wife ... it is clear that the right of privacy (referred to in *McGee v. The Attorney General*) was the right to the privacy of their relationships which did not impinge upon the common good or destroy or endanger human life ... The common good of ... society requires that revenue be raised for the purposes of that society by taxation and that information be made available for the purposes of determining the amount payable by any individual. The Constitution does not guarantee the right to either spouse not to disclose to his or her spouse the source or amount of his or her income for the purpose of making (income tax) returns."[139]

No reference was made to this issue by the Supreme Court.

In *Norris v. The Attorney General*[140] the Supreme Court for only the second time gave detailed consideration to the right to privacy. O'Higgins C.J. denying that the impugned legislation violated the plaintiff's right to privacy said:

> "I regard the State as having an interest in the general moral wellbeing of the community and being entitled, where it is practicable to do so, to discourage conduct which is morally wrong and harmful to a way of life and to values which the State wishes to protect. A right of privacy or ... a right 'to be let alone', can never be absolute. There are many acts done in private which the State is entitled to condemn, whether such be done by an individual on his own or with another. The court has always condemned abortion, incest, suicide attempts, suicide pacts, euthanasia, or mercy killing. These are prohibited simply because they are morally wrong and regardless of the fact, which may exist in some instances, that no harm or injury to others is involved."[141]

The Chief Justice delivering the majority judgement concluded stating that:

> "On the ground of the Christian nature of our State and on the grounds that the deliberate practice of homosexuality is morally wrong, that it is damaging to the health, both of individuals and the public and, finally, that it is potentially harmful to the institution of marriage, I can find no inconsistency with the Constitution in the laws which make (homosexual) conduct criminal."[142]

Both Henchy J. and McCarthy J. vigorously dissented from this view. Henchy J. stated that the right to privacy which "inheres in each citizen"[143] compendiously described "a complex of rights which vary in nature, purpose and range, (each necessarily a facet of the citizen's core of individuality within the constitutional order)."[144] Saying that it was unnecessary to explore all aspects of the right of privacy, he continued:

---

138. [1982] I.R. 241 (H.C., S.C.).
139. *Ibid* at p. 266.
140. *Supra.*
141. *Ibid* at p. 64.
142. *Ibid* at p. 65.
143. *Ibid* at p. 71.
144. *Ibid.*

"It is sufficient to say that they would all appear to fall within a secluded area of activity or non-activity which may be claimed as necessary for the expression of an individual personality, for purposes not always necessarily moral or commendable but meriting recognition in circumstances which do not engender considerations such as State security, public order or morality or other essential components of the common good."[145]

In the learned judge's view the Attorney General had signally failed to discharge the onus of proof necessary to establish that to allow the plaintiff consensually in private to engage in homosexual acts "would be inconsistent with the maintenance of public order and morality." Stating that "the sanctions of the criminal law may be attached to immoral acts only when the common good requires their proscription as crimes,"[146] he asserted that the "consensus of the evidence was that the sweep of the criminal prohibition . . . goes beyond the requirements of the common good; indeed, in the opinion of most of the witnesses it is inimical to the common good. Consequently, a finding of unconstitutionality was inescapable on the evidence."[147]

McCarthy J. in his judgement in directly contradicting the approach adopted by the majority in the judgement of the Chief Justice, expressly identified the "nature of the personal right of privacy" as "the right to be let alone"[148] and stated that the right could only be delimited by "a compelling State interest" which would, by example be "overwhelming in the protection of minors, persons under incapacity of one kind or another, public decency, discipline in the armed forces or the security forces and so on".[149] In the absence of a compelling State

---

145. *Ibid* at p. 72.
146. *Ibid* at p. 78.
147. *Ibid*. See also [1984] I.R. at p. 77 where Henchy J. stated that: "whether the constitutional provisions he relied on gave the necessary justification depended on a complex of expert evidential considerations — social, moral, medical and others — and, since the unrebutted consensus of the evidence was against the existence of such justification, the (trial) judge was debarred from holding otherwise." Henchy J. also asserted, however, that in his view not all homosexual acts could be decriminalised. Referring to possible future legal developments he stated:

"One way or the other, the impugned provisions seem doomed to extinction. Whether they be struck down by this court for being unconstitutional or whether they be deemed invalid elsewhere in accordance with *Dudgeon v. United Kingdom** (for being in contravention of the European Convention for the Protection of Human Rights and Fundamental Freedoms) they will require to be replaced with appropriate statutory provisions. It would not be constitutional to decriminalise all homosexual acts, any more than it would be constitutional to decriminalise all heterosexual acts. Public order and morality; the protection of the young, of the weak-willed, of those who may readily be subject to undue influence, and of others who should be deemed to be in need of protection; the maintenance inviolate of the family as the natural primary and fundamental unit of society; the upholding of the institution of marriage; the requirements of public health; these and other aspects of the common good require that homosexual acts be made criminal in many circumstances. The true and justifiable gravamen of the complaint against the sections under review is that they are in constitutional error for over-reach or overbreadth. They lack necessary discrimination and precision as to when and how they are to apply."

**Dudgeon v. United Kingdom* (1981) 4 E.H.R.R. 149 is a decision of the European Court of Human Rights which held sections 61 and 62 of the Offences Against the Person Act, 1861, and section 11 of the Criminal Law (Amendment) Act, 1885, as they applied in Northern Ireland to violate Article 8 of the European Convention for the Protection of Human Rights and Fundamental Freedoms. See further, A.M.C. Connelly, "Irish Law and the Judgement of the European Court of Human Rights in the Dudgeon Case" (1982) 4 D.U.L.J. 25. Subsequent to the Supreme Court decision *Norris* brought proceedings pursuant to the European Convention against Ireland and his application was declared admissible by the European Commission of Human Rights on 16 May 1985. The matter has not been determined by the European Court of Human Rights at the date of writing — see further (1986) 4 I.L.T. (n.s.) 118.

148. *Supra* at p. 101.
149. *Ibid*.

interest he was of the opinion that:

> "A very great burden lies upon those who would question personal rights
> in order to justify State interference of a most grievous kind (the policeman
> in the bedroom) in a claim to the right to perform sexual acts or to give
> expression to sexual desires or needs, in private, between consenting adults,
> male or female."[150]

Agreeing with Henchy J., he held that the State had not satisfied that burden.

Right to Beget Children: In *Murray & Murray v. The Attorney General &
Ireland*,[151] the constitutional right of a married couple to beget children was
asserted by the plaintiffs, a married couple serving sentences of life imprisonment. They had no children and it was alleged by them and judicially assumed
that by the date of their likely release from prison, the age of the wife would be
such that the chances of her conceiving a child would be small. They sought a
declaration either that they were entitled to bail so as to enable them to exercise
this constitutional right outside prison or alternatively, that the prison authorities
were obliged to provide facilities to enable them to exercise this right within the
confines of the prison.

Costello J., delivering judgement in the High Court, stated that according to
the concept of marriage enshrined by the Constitution "the procreation and
education of children by . . . spouses is especially ordained" and that by explicitly
recognising and protecting this concept of the institution of marriage, it would
follow that the right of each spouse to beget children is implicitly recognised and
protected.[152] This right was said by the trial judge to be "distinct from the
constitutional right to privacy"[153] but, like the right to privacy, he held it was
a personal right within the meaning of Article 40.3.1 and not derived from
Article 41 as in his view:

> "the rights in Article 41.1.1. are those which can properly be said to belong
> to the institution (of the family) itself as distinct from the personal rights
> which each individual member might enjoy by virtue of membership of the
> family"[154] (which he stated) "find recognition and protection as personal
> rights under Article 40.3.1."

As to whether the restrictions on the plaintiffs' right to beget children caused
by the State exercising its legal power to imprison them were permissible, following upon their being convicted and sentenced in a criminal trial, Costello J.
stated:

> "When the State lawfully exercises its power to deprive a citizen of his
> constitutional right to liberty many consequences result, including depri-

---

150. *Ibid* at p. 102. McCarthy J. also noted that the legislation impugned rendered it
unlawful for a married couple to commit buggery. He disagreed with the majority view that
the plaintiff could not in his constitutional challenge rely on the right to marital privacy and
assert that the challenged legislation violated that right. In dealing with this contention, he
stated that if a statute containing similar prohibitions were now enacted by the Oireachtas,
"it would, on its face, be clearly in conflict with that right of privacy in marriage and,
therefore repugnant to the Constitution" (*Supra* at p. 91) . . . "there is no statable argument
that can support the intrusion of the criminal law in the sphere of life that is described as
the privacy of marriage, unless, as is nowhere shown to be the case here, there is a pressing
social need or compelling State necessity to permit it." (*Supra* at p. 92).
151. [1985] 5 I.L.R.M. 542 (H.C.).
152. *Ibid* at p. 545.
153. *Ibid* at p. 546.
154. *Ibid* at p. 547.

vation of the liberty to exercise many other constitutionally protected rights, which prisoners must accept. Those rights which may be exercised by a prisoner are those:
(a) which do not depend on the continuance of his personal liberty (so a prisoner cannot exercise his constitutional right to earn a livelihood), or
(b) which are compatible with the reasonable requirements of the place in which he is imprisoned or, to put it another way, do not impose unreasonable demands on it."[155]

He continued further on:

"As the plaintiffs' claim — that they be permitted to leave prison from time to time to exercise their rights to beget children — is clearly incompatible with the restriction on their liberty which is constitutionally permitted by their imprisonment, I do not think that it is a valid one."[156]

As for the plaintiffs' claim that facilities be provided to enable them to exercise their right within the prison, he stated that:

"The reasonable requirements of the prison service would not . . . permit the exercise by all married prisoners of their right to beget children."[157]

Moreover, if exercise of this right was confined to all married couples who could establish that at the end of the imprisonment of one or other spouse the chances of their begetting a child or an additional child, would be small or non-existent,

it would also, he continued:

"place unreasonable demands on the prison service to require prison authorities to make facilities available within the confines of the prison to enable all prisoners who fall within this category to exercise their right to beget children."[158]

Costello J. concluded, holding that the plaintiffs had not established that the exercise of their constitutional rights had been invalidly infringed by their imprisonment and dismissed their claim. At the date of writing this case is under appeal to the Supreme Court.

---

155. *Ibid* at p. 551.
156. *Ibid*.
157. *Ibid* at p. 552.
158. *Ibid*. It was argued that the special features of the plaintiffs' case required the State to make special provision for them. Referring to this argument, Costello J. stated:

"It is accepted that the State has the power to deprive wrong doers of their liberty but it is urged that in doing so the right to beget children which inheres in married persons cannot be 'totally extinguished', and it is said that in 'extreme cases' the State has a duty to intervene to protect the right where otherwise it would be abolished. This will happen, it is said, in this case; if the plaintiffs cannot exercise their rights now, they will be unable to beget children when they are jointly released from custody. I think that it is more correct to refer to the effect of sentences of imprisonment as restricting the exercise of the plaintiffs' constitutional rights rather than as extinguishing them, but for the purposes of the argument I will accept that there may be cases, and this is one, in which the effect of a prison sentence is to deprive married couples of an opportunity ever to conceive a child . . . the effect of a long term of imprisonment on the enjoyment of other rights, for example, the right of a father to educate his child, may be such that the prisoner may in practice never be able to exercise it. But if its exercise is not compatible with the reasonable requirements of the prison or would impose unreasonable demands on it, then the State in my view commits no constitutional breach as these are the consequences of the lawful deprivation of the plaintiffs' liberty. That is the situation in this case."

Right to Life of Unborn Child: In *McGee v. The Attorney General*[159] members of the Supreme Court, in December 1973, for the first time considered the constitutional right to life with reference to the unborn child. Referring to the constitutional limitations on the right to marital privacy, Walsh J. asserted that:

> "Any action on the part of either the husband and wife or of the State to limit family sizes by endangering or destroying human life must necessarily not only be an offence against the common good but also against the guaranteed personal rights of the human life in question."[160]

In the same case, Griffin J. emphasised that:

> "this judgement is confined to contraceptives as such: it is not intended to apply ᵗo abortifacients, though called contraceptives, as in the case of abortifacients entirely different considerations apply."[161]

As we have already seen, Walsh J. returned to the same subject in *G. v. An Bord Uchtala*[162] in 1978, again asserting the constitutional right to life of the unborn child. In *Norris v. The Attorney General*,[163] McCarthy J. also referred to this issue, stating:

> "It is not an issue that arises in the instant case, but it may be claimed that the right of privacy of a pregnant woman would extend to a right in her to terminate a pregnancy, an act which would involve depriving the unborn child of the most fundamental right of all — the right to life itself . . . nothing in this judgement, express or in any way implied, is to be taken as supporting a view that the provisions of section 58 of the (Offences Against the Person) Act of 1861, making it a criminal offence to procure an abortion, are in any way inconsistent with the Constitution[164] . . . the provisions of the preamble (to the Constitution) . . . would appear to lean heavily against any view other than that the right to life of the unborn child is a sacred trust to which all the organs of government must lend their support."[165]

At the time when the above judicial statements were made Article 40.3.3 had not been added to the Constitution. Amid considerable controversy it became part of the Constitution by virtue of the Eighth Amendment of the Constitution Act following its approval by the people in a constitutional referendum held on the 7th of September 1983. The proponents of the amendment argued that the amendment was necessary so as to ensure that existing legislation prohibiting abortion could not at a future date be found to be unconstitutional and argued, despite the judicial statements cited above, that the Constitution did not afford protection to the right to life of the unborn child.[166] In *Finn v. The Attorney General*,[167] the plaintiff sought to prevent the referendum relating to the Eighth Amendment being held on the grounds that it was superfluous, contending that the right to life of the unborn child was already protected by the Constitution.

159. [1974] I.R. 284 (S.C.).
160. *Ibid* at p. 312.
161. *Ibid* at p. 335.
162. *Supra.* See p. 27 *ante.*
163. *Supra.*
164. See pp. 57, 58 of judgement.
165. See p. 60 of judgement.
166. See in particular J. O'Reilly, "Marital Privacy and Family Law" (1977) 65 Studies 8; W. Binchey, "Marital Privacy and Family Law: A Reply to Mr. O'Reilly" (1977) 65 Studies 330.
167. [1983] I.R. 154 (H.C., S.C.). See also *Roche v. Ireland & Ors.* (June, 1983) unreported (H.C.).

Both the High Court and Supreme Court dismissed the plaintiff's action, the Supreme Court holding that the courts possess "no jurisdiction to construe or review the constitutionality of a Bill" other than one referred to the Supreme Court by the President under Article 26 of the Constitution, the court's power of constitutional review being confined to Acts that have completed the legislative process.[168] Although Barrington J. in dismissing the plaintiff's proceedings on the same ground in the High Court had stated that he

> "would have no hesitation in holding that the unborn child has a right to life and that it is protected by the Constitution",[169]

the Supreme Court held that as the proceedings could "not be maintained" it was unnecessary for it to consider the matter in the context of the particular proceedings and did not comment on the substantive issue. Article 40.3.3 has not been the subject of any judicial interpretation since its insertion in the Constitution.

Right to Equality: Although Article 40.1 asserts that "all citizens shall as human persons be held equal before the law" the proviso contained in the article permits the State, in its enactments, to have due regard to differences of physical and moral capacity and social function.[170] Thus, it has been held that legislative discrimination may be constitutionally inviolate if it results "from some special abilities or some deficiency or from some special need"[171] or from "differences in relevant circumstances"[172] but it cannot be "invidious", that is "unjust, unreasonable or arbitrary and constitutionally offensive".[173]

Legislation that does not come within the proviso to Article 40 will not be regarded as invidious if justification can be found for it in other provisions of the Constitution. Thus, as we have already seen, in *O'B. v. S.*[174] legislation which discriminated against illegitimate children was held to be constitutionally justified by the provisions of Article 41.

It is intended first to examine a series of different cases affecting the family and family law legislation in which Article 40.1 has arisen for consideration and then to examine its interaction with Articles 41 and 42 in a number of cases not yet discussed in which the courts have sought to balance the guarantee of equality with the rights afforded to the family.

In *The State (Nicolaou) v. An Bord Uchtála*[175] it was held that it was not constitutionally offensive and contrary to Article 40.1 to confer a statutory right to be heard by the Adoption Board before it determined an adoption application on the mother of an illegitimate child, while denying such right to the child's father, the Supreme Court being of the view that the different treatment afforded to the father was justified under the proviso to the Article, there

---

168. For an account of the judicial powers of constitutional review see J.M. Kelly, *The Irish Constitution, supra,* p. 269 *et seq.*

169. *Supra* at p. 160.

170. For a comprehensive discussion of Article 40.1 and its judicial interpretation, see J.M. Kelly, *The Irish Constitution, supra* at p. 446 *et seq.* See also F.X. Beytagh, "Equality under the Irish and American Constitutions: A Comparative Analysis" (1983) 18 I.J. (n.s.) 56, 219.

171. *The State (Nicolaou) v. An Bord Uchtála, supra,* at p. 639 *per* Walsh J.

172. *O'Brien, an Infant v. Keogh* [1972] I.R. 144 (S.C.) *per* O'Dalaigh J. at p. 156.

173. *O'B. v. S., supra, per* Walsh J. at p. 332. See also *Murphy v. The Attorney General, supra,* at p. 286; *De Burca & Anderson v. The Attorney General, supra,* in particular Walsh J. at p. 68 and O'Higgins C.J. at p. 59. See further *King v. The Attorney General* [1981] I.R. 233 (S.C.).

174. *Supra.*

175. *Supra.*

being a difference in "moral capacity and social function" between the natural father and mother of the child.

In *The State (K.M. & R.D.) v. The Minister for Foreign Affairs*,[176] Finlay P. rejected the contention that section 40 of the Adoption Act, 1952, offended Article 40.1. in so far as it permitted the removal of a legitimate child from the State with its parents' consent but only permitted the removal of an illegitimate child from the State, if it was going to reside abroad with its mother. The learned judge stated he was satisfied

> "that for an illegitimate child and a legitimate child there is a difference of moral capacity and social function, at least in the context of the removal of the child out of the State. A legitimate child is part of a family unit; the rights and, in a sense, the duties of the family being specially provided for in the Constitution. In the generality of cases the legitimate child has the protection of a joint decision by its parents ... on the other hand an illegitimate child has not the benefit of being a member of a family unit ... further, in my view, there is much weight in the submission made on behalf of the Repondents to the effect that in the generality of cases the mother of an illegitimate child may be subjected to strains, stresses and pressures arising from economic and social conditions which fully justify the legislature in making special provisions with regard to the welfare of that child, which provisions are not considered necessary for the welfare of a legitimate child."[177]

A challenge to the constitutionality of the section did, however, succeed under Article 40.3., the court holding the child to have a constitutional right to travel outside the State.[178]

In *Somjee & Anor. v. The Minister for Justice & Anor.*[179] it was alleged that section 8 of the Irish Nationality & Citizenship Act, 1956, was unconstitutional in that it permitted an Irish man who married an alien to confer Irish citizenship on his wife but did not permit an Irish woman who married an alien to confer Irish citizenship on her husband, although the husband could under other provisions contained in the legislation apply for naturalisation. It was also contended that as a result, a woman's right to marry the person of her choice was restricted. Dismissing the plaintiff's claim, Keane J. noted that the 1956 Act provided "a diversity of arrangements"[180] for the obtaining of citizenship and continued stating:

> "the Act does not provide for any discrimination between male and female applicants for citizenship as such. Persons of each sex are equally entitled to apply for and become Irish citizens by naturalisation. It is only in the case of aliens becoming married to Irish citizens ... that a distinction is drawn and in my view, the distinction is more properly regarded as conferring a form of privilege on female aliens rather than as being invidiously discriminatory against male aliens."[181]

---

176. [1979] I.R. 73 (H.C.).
177. *Ibid* at pp. 78, 79.
178. See p. 188 *post*.
179. [1981] 1 I.L.R.M. 324 (H.C.).
180. *Ibid* at p. 325.
181. *Ibid*. The learned judge expressed no view as to whether the first named plaintiff, who was not an Irish National, was precluded from asserting rights afforded to "citizens" by Article 40.1. Keane J. also held that the section did not violate Article 9.1.3 of the Constitution. The decision in this case was not appealed to the Supreme Court. See also *Pok Sun Shum & Ors. v. Ireland & Ors.* (June, 1985) unreported (H.C.) and *Sunday Osheku & Ors. v. Ireland & Ors.* (June 1986) unreported (H.C.).

The Irish Nationality and Citizenship Act, 1986, has repealed and replaced the original provisions contained in section 8 of the Act of 1956 and both husbands and wives are now placed in a position of legal equality with reference to the acquisition of Irish citizenship arising from marriage.[181a]

The presumption of law that if certain criminal offences were committed by a wife in the presence of her husband, they were done under his coercion was held no longer to be extant in *The State (D.P.P.) v. Walsh.*[182] Delivering the judgement of the Supreme Court on this issue Henchy J. stated:

> "The idea that, where a wife performs a criminal act, there should be a *prima facie* presumption that the mere physical presence of her husband when she did it overbore her will, stultified her volitional powers, and drove her into criminal conduct which she would have avoided but for his presence, presupposes a disparity in status and capacity between husband and wife which runs counter to the normal relations between a married couple in modern times. The conditions of legal inferiority which attach at common law to the status of a married woman and which gave rise to this presumption have been swept away by legislation and by judicial decisions. ... A legal rule that presumes ... that a wife has been coerced by the physical presence of her husband into committing an act prohibited by the criminal law, particularly when a similar presumption does not operate in favour of a husband for acts committed in the presence of his wife, is repugnant to the concept of equality before the law guaranteed by the first sentence of Article 40.s.1., and could not, under the second sentence of that Article, be justified as a discrimination based on any difference of capacity or of social function as between husband and wife. Therefore, the presumption contended for must be rejected as a form of unconstitutional discrimination."[183]

In *Murphy v. The Attorney General*[184] the Supreme Court, while holding in favour of the plaintiffs on the grounds already discussed, rejected the argument that the taxation provisions challenged were contrary to Article 40.1. The court said that this Article "is not a guarantee of equality before the law in all matters or in all circumstances. It is a qualified guarantee to all citizens as human beings that they will be held equal before the law. It therefore relates to those attributes which make us human; it is concerned with the essentials of human personality."[185] Noting that the Article recognised that inequality may arise from differences of capacity or social function, Kenny J., delivering the judgement of the court, stated that the inequality in treatment for income tax purposes "as between on the one hand, married couples living together and, on the other hand unmarried couples living together" was justified by the different "social function" of married couples. He continued:

> "numerous examples could be given from the income tax code of types of income tax payers who are treated differently, either favourably or unfavourably, because of their social function. This particular unfavourable tax treatment of married couples living together, set against the many

181a. See further p. 185 *post.*
182. [1981] I.R. 412 (S.C.).
183. *Ibid* at pp. 449, 450.
184. *Supra.*
185. *Ibid* at p. 283.

favourable discriminations made by the law in favour of married couples does not ... constitute an unequal treatment forbidden by Article 40.1. particularly having regard to the vital roles under the constitution of married couples as parents or potential parents and as heads of a family."[186]

In *Norris v. The Attorney General*[187] a majority of the Supreme Court rejected the contention that the impugned legislation, contrary to Article 40.1, sexually discriminated against men in that it rendered criminal homosexual conduct between males but did not criminalise homosexual conduct between females, O'Higgins C.J. stating:

"The legislature would be perfectly entitled to have regard to the difference between the sexes and to treat sexual conduct or gross indecency between males as requiring prohibition because of the social problem which it creates, while at the same time looking at sexual conduct between females as being not only different but as posing no such social problem."[188]

In three different cases the courts have sought to balance the provisions of Article 40.1 with those of Article 41.2. *DeBurca & Anderson v. The Attorney General*[189] was the first case in which the interaction between these two articles was judicially considered. A majority in the Supreme Court granted a declaration that the Juries Act, 1927, discriminated against women and was inconsistent with the Constitution in so far as it provided that women were to be exempt from jury service but entitled to serve on a jury if they applied to do so. O'Higgins C.J. dissented from this finding, being of the view that the proviso to Article 40.1 taken together with Article 41.2 justified the making of a "special provision" for women. During the course of his judgement he stated that:

"When one considers the special recognition of women and mothers in Article 41 of our Constitution, it does not appear inappropriate that the State in its laws should give preference to woman; particularly when the exercise of her right in relation to jury service also involves the acceptance of a burden ... this is a discrimination which is not invidious because it

186. *Ibid* at p. 284. In the High Court, Hamilton J. had found that the provisions of the Income Tax Act, 1967, relating to the aggregation of the earnings of a married couple were in violation of both Articles 40.1 and 41. The Supreme Court relied solely on the latter Article in making its finding. In the High Court it had also been contended that income tax provisions which provided for a lower personal allowance to be allowed as a deduction against the taxable income of a married couple living together and working than that afforded to single people living together and working were unconstitutional. Hamilton J. rejected this argument on the ground that "the legislature was entitled to take into consideration the fact that when a husband and wife are living together certain expenditure is common to both." Rejecting the argument that this is also true of single people living together, he continued: "there is a difference of social function between a husband and wife living together and single people living together to which the legislature was entitled to have regard. The husband and wife living together do so as a family recognised by the Constitution. The law or the Constitution does not recognise or have regard to any other union or liaison between single persons." (1980 I.R. at p. 268). The Supreme Court, in its judgement, did not refer to the issue of income tax allowances. It is submitted with respect that the learned High Court judge was incorrect. It is submitted that the difference in social function permits the State to treat a married couple differently to the manner in which it treats a single couple but that it does not permit the State by legislation to treat the married couple more oppressively. If it does so, the State is in breach of the duty imposed upon it by Article 41 as enunciated by the Supreme Court in its appellate decision in the same case.
187. *Supra*.
188. *Ibid* at p. 59. Henchy J. supported the majority view – see pp. 70–71. See, however, the vigorous dissenting views expressed by McCarthy J., and in particular at p. 102 where the learned judge refers to the "gross hypocrisy that frequently prevailed ... amongst the ranks of the legislators" during the reign of Queen Victoria when the impugned legislation was enacted.
189. [1976] I.R. 38 (S.C.).

does not amount to an exclusion and because some preferential treatment of women citizens seems to be contemplated by the Constitution."[190]

Walsh J., in the majority viewed the matter differently. He stated that Article 41.2:

"draws attention to and stresses the importance of woman's life within the home and makes special provision for the economic protection of mothers who have home duties" but that women also "fulfil many functions in society in addition to or instead of those mentioned in Sect. 2 of Article 41 ... there can be little doubt that the Oireachtas could validly enact statutory provisions which could have due regard within the provisions of Article 40, to differences of capacity both physical and moral and of social function in so far as jury service is concerned ... However, the provision made in the Juries Act, 1927, is undisguisedly discriminatory on the ground of sex only ..." It "does not seek to make distinction between the different functions that women may fulfil and it does not seek to justify the discrimination on the basis of any social function. It simply lumps together half of the members of the adult population, most of whom have only one thing in common, namely, their sex. In my view, it is not open to the State to discriminate in its enactments between the persons who are subject to its laws solely upon the ground of sex of those persons. If a reference is to be made to the sex of a person then the purpose of the law that makes such a discrimination should be to deal with some physical or moral capacity or social function that is related exclusively or very largely to that sex only."[191]

In *T. O'G. v. The Attorney General & Ors.*[192] a proviso contained in Section 5(1) of the Adoption Act, 1974, which imposed far greater restrictions on adoption by widowers than applied to widows was held by the High Court to be unconstitutional, McMahon J. holding that the different treatment of men as compared to women in the legislation violated the guarantee to human equality contained in Article 40.1. He stated:

"Widowers as a class are not less competent than widows to provide for the material needs of children and their exclusion as a class must be based on a belief that a woman, by virtue of her sex has an innate capacity for parenthood which is denied to a man and the lack of which renders a man unsuitable as an adopter. This view is not supported by any medical evidence adduced before me ... the culture of our society has assigned distinct roles to father and mother in two parent families in the past just as families on the land recognise a distinction between men's work and women's work but this is a feature of our culture which appears to be changing as the younger generation of married people tend to exchange roles freely. No medical or psychological evidence has been adduced to explain the difference between these roles and its significance for the welfare of the child or to establish that the roles are mutually exclusive or that both are essential for the proper upbringing of children or to establish that there is any difference in capacity for parenthood between a widow and a widower."[193]

As for Article 41.2.1 and the State's contention that it conferred "on a widow

---

190. *Ibid* at p. 67.
191. *Ibid* at pp. 70–71. As a consequence of this case the Juries Act, 1976, was enacted by the Oireachtas. See J. Connolly, "The New Irish Jury", 110 I.L.T. and S.J. 119 *et seq.*
192. [1985] 5 I.L.R.M. 61 (H.C.).
193. *Ibid* at p. 64.

an advantage over a widower as an adopter" the learned judge continued:

> "The Article recognises the social value of a mother's services in the home but that does not involve a denial of the capacity of widowers as a class to be considered on their merits as suitable adopters."[194]

In *Dennehy v. The Minister for Social Welfare*,[195] Article 41.2 was held to constitutionally justify a discrimination against fathers embodied in the social welfare code. The plaintiff husband had been deserted three years earlier by his wife and left by her with their two children in his care. The High Court rejected his contention that a portion of the Social Welfare (Consolidation) Act, 1981, which provides for the making of social welfare payments to deserted wives was unconstitutional in that it does not make similar provision for deserted husbands. In dealing with the plaintiff's submission that the legislation contravened Articles 41 and 42, Barron J. expressed the view that:

> "The failure to provide benefit to a deserted husband is not *per se* an attack on the family since the family has already been broken up by the desertion of the wife. It cannot be suggested that to make provision for the husband in such circumstances would in any way cause the parties to come together again."[196]

As for the contention that the legislation was contrary to Article 40.1 he stated:

> "The evidence adduced on behalf of the defendants indicates that the sections which are impugned were originally enacted to meet what was then an increasing problem of wives being deserted by their husbands and being left without proper provision. Similar provision was not made for husbands because the desertion of husbands by their wives was not causing any problem which required to be resolved."[197]

He concluded stating:

> "Having regard to the provisions of Article 41(2) it does not seem to me that as a matter of policy it would be unreasonable, unjust or arbitrary for the Oireachtas to protect financially deserted wives who are mothers who have dependant children residing with them or to recognise that mothers who have had to care for children will have lost out in the labour market and so are likely to need similar protection when similarly deserted."[198]

In the judge's view the discrimination embodied in the legislation could reasonably have been arrived at as a matter of policy by the Oireachtas.

The decision in this case was not appealed to the Supreme Court as the plaintiff husband died between the date when the action was heard and the judgement delivered. Accordingly, in the absence of a decision by the Supreme Court on this issue some doubt must still remain as to the constitutionality of this legislation.

THE FAMILY, FAMILY LAW AND RELIGIOUS RIGHTS

In the areas of guardianship and custody of children, adoption, family plan-

---

194. *Ibid.* at p. 65. See further p. 294.
195. (July, 1984) unreported (H.C.).
196. See p. 6 of judgement. See also *The State (Bouzagou) v. Fitzgibbon Street Garda Station, supra*, extract from judgement of Barrington J. cited on p. 17 *ante.*
197. See p. 17 of judgement.
198. See pp. 18–19 of judgement.

ning, abortion, nullity and divorce some of the religious tensions and conflicts which arise in Irish society have been reflected in the area of family law and family litigation. Nevertheless, only once since 1937 has a family law enactment been invalidated for being contrary to the guarantee contained in Article 44 of the Constitution.[199] Under this article freedom of conscience and the free profession and practise of religion are, subject to public order and morality, guaranteed to every citizen and the State pledges itself not to impose any disabilities or make any discrimination on the ground of religious profession, belief or status. Relying on this pledge, the High Court, in *J.McG. & W.McG. v. An Bord Uchtála and the Attorney General*[200] found unconstitutional section 12(2) of the Adoption Act, 1952, the effect of which was to prevent married couples from adopting if the husband and wife who wished to adopt were of a different religion to each other, or of a religion different to that of the child they wished to adopt.[201]

In *McGee v. The Attorney General*[202] the plaintiff also invoked Article 44 arguing that her decision and that of her husband to use contraceptives was a matter of conscience which fell to be protected under this Article. This argument was rejected in both the High Court and the Supreme Court, members of both courts clearly being of the view that the freedom of conscience protected under this Article relates to a freedom to practise or not to practise a religion, Walsh J. in the Supreme Court stating that:

> "because a person feels free, or even obliged in conscience to pursue some particular activity which is not in itself a religious practice it does not

---

199. Article 44:

1.1.   The State acknowledges that the homage of public worship is due to Almighty God. It shall hold His Name in reverence, and shall respect and honour religion.
1.2.   The State recognises the special position of the Holy Catholic Apostolic and Roman Church as the guardian of the Faith professed by the great majority of the citizens.
1.3.   The State also recognises the Church of Ireland, the Presbyterian Church in Ireland, the Methodist Church in Ireland, the Religious Society of Friends in Ireland, as well as the Jewish Congregations and the other religious denominations existing in Ireland at the date of the coming into operation of this Constitution.
2.1.   Freedom of conscience and the free profession and practice of religion are, subject to public order and morality, guaranteed to every citizen.
2.2.   The State guarantees not to endow any religion.
2.3.   The State shall not impose any disabilities or make any discrimination on the ground of religious profession, belief or status.
2.4.   Legislation providing State aid for schools shall not discriminate between schools under the management of different religious denominations, nor be such as to affect prejudicially the right of any child to attend a school receiving public money without attending religious instruction at that school.
2.5.   Every religious denomination shall have the right to manage its own affairs, own, acquire and administer property, movable and immovable, and maintain institutions for religious or charitable purposes.
2.6.   The property of any religious denomination or any educational institution shall not be diverted save for necessary works of public utility and on payment of compensation.

The Report of the Committee on the Constitution (Stationery Office, Dublin, 1967) recommended the deletion of Articles 44.1.2 and 44.1.3, see pp. 47–48 of their Report.

In 1972, following a Referendum, the Fifth Amendment of the Constitution Act deleting these Articles came into force. See judgement of Walsh J. in *McGee v. Attorney General, supra*, where the effect of the deletion of these Articles is discussed.

For a detailed account of Article 44, see J.M. Kelly, *The Irish Constitution, supra*, p. 662 *et seq.* See also Kelly, *Fundamental Rights*, Chapter 10; L. Beth, *Development of Judicial Review*, pp. 139–143; A. O'Rahilly, *Thoughts on the Constitution*, pp. 65–68; J.H. Whyte, *Church and State in Modern Ireland*, pp. 53–61, 158–171, 349–350.

200. [1975] I.R. 81; (1974) 109 I.L.T.R. 62 (H.C.).
201. See further p. 296 *post*.
202. *Supra*.

follow that such activity is guaranteed protection by Article 44."[203]

THE FAMILY, THE RIGHT OF ACCESS TO THE COURTS AND TO FAIR PROCEDURES

The constitutional rights of a litigant in the area of family law have been considered in three recent cases. In *R. v. R.*[204] the High Court held that having regard to the provisions of Article 34.3[205] of the Constitution the Oireachtas cannot deprive the High Court of its jurisdiction in family law matters and "cannot create validly, in accordance with the Constitution, a new juridical jurisdiction and withhold it from the High Court"[206] but that where courts of limited local jurisdiction are conferred with a family law jurisdiction, the High Court is not "compellable to provide any person, as a matter of constitutional right, with access" to it as "it is competent for the High Court to decline to entertain applications for orders obtainable in such other courts, or to remit to such other courts for hearing applications brought in the High Court which are within the jurisdiction of such other courts."[207] Accordingly, the High Court was held to possess an original jurisdiction to determine family law disputes arising under three different statutes,[207a] although the statutory provisions themselves only expressly confer such jurisdiction on the District and Circuit Courts and make no express reference to the High Court as either retaining or being conferred with the necessary jurisdiction.[208] The decision in this case was not appealed to the Supreme Court and in the light of the recent judgement of that court in *Tormey v. Ireland & the Attorney General*[209] the authority of the decision in *R. v. R.* is open to serious question. Dealing with the constitutional capacity of the legislature to require a defendant to undergo a criminal trial in the Circuit Court and to deprive him of a right to a trial in the Central Criminal Court (which is the name given by statute to the High Court when exercising criminal jurisdiction), Henchy J., delivering the judgement of the Supreme Court stated:

"The full original jurisdiction of the High Court referred to in Article 34.3.1 must be deemed to be full in the sense that all justiciable matters and questions (save those removed by the Constitution itself from the original jurisdiction of the High Court) shall be within the original jurisdiction of the High Court in one form or another. If, in exercise of its powers under Article 34.3.4 Parliament commits certain matters or questions to the jurisdiction of the District Court or of the Circuit Court, the functions of hearing and determining those matters and questions may, expressly or by necessary implication be given exclusively to those courts."[210]

---

203. [1974] I.R. at p. 316. See also O'Keeffe P., who heard the case at first instance in the High Court, *supra*, at p. 291 and Fitzgerald C.J. who delivered a dissenting judgement in the Supreme Court but who agreed with the majority on this issue, *supra* at p. 302.
204. [1984] I.R. 296 (H.C.).
205. Article 34.3.1 reads: "The courts of First Instance shall include a High Court invested with full original jurisdiction in and power to determine all matters and questions whether of law or fact, civil or criminal."
206. *Supra* at p. 308.
207. *Ibid* at p. 310.
207a. The Guardianship of Infants Act, 1964, the Family Law (Maintenance of Spouses & Children) Act, 1976, and the Family Law (Protection of Spouses & Children) Act, 1981.
208. See p. 47 *post*.
209. [1985] 5 I.L.R.M. 375 (S.C.).
210. *Ibid* at p. 380. Article 34.3.4 states "The courts of First Instance shall also include courts of local and limited jurisdiction with a right of appeal as determined by law."

The approach of the Supreme Court in the *Tormey* case cannot be reconciled with the approach of the High Court in the earlier case of *R. v. R.*[211] The extent of the High Court's current jurisdiction in family law matters will remain unclear until this issue is finally determined by the Supreme Court.

In *E. v. E.*[212] the husband contended that he could not afford to pay for legal representation for High Court maintenance and custody proceedings brought against him by his wife. He claimed that the State should be prepared to indemnify him "against any legal costs and expenses incurred in order to ensure that his personal and family rights" were defended and vindicated under the Constitution. He alleged that the failure of the State to provide him with free legal aid was in breach of his guaranteed right of access to the High Court to defend and vindicate his personal rights and those of his children. The husband had sought legal aid through the State's Scheme of Civil Legal Aid & Advice[213] and at the date of the court hearing was awaiting a decision under the Scheme on an appeal lodged by him against the rejection of his original application for legal aid. O'Hanlon J. dismissed the husband's application as he had not yet "exhausted the procedure which was open to him under the Legal Aid Scheme for obtaining legal aid before coming to court to assert his rights under the Constitution"[214] and stated that he was satisfied that the husband "cannot establish that any existing right he enjoys under Irish law has been infringed."[215]

In *S. v. S.*[216] the High Court held that a rule of evidence and procedure which prior to the enactment of the Constitution in 1937 had prohibited the admission of evidence of either a husband or wife to prove that a child born to the wife was not that of the husband was no longer part of Irish law. O'Hanlon J. held the rule to be inconsistent with the Constitution[217] describing it as contrary to the "constitutional guarantee of fairness in procedures"[218] and no longer applicable.

CONCLUSION

In the pages that follow reference is again made to some of the constitutional matters discussed in this chapter. It was merely intended here to give an overview of the impact of the Constitution on Irish family law and to illustrate how its tentacles have reached out to affect its development in a number of important areas. Whilst its influence has not been confined to Articles 41 and 42, there can be little doubt that it is these Articles that have had the most profound impact on the majority of judicial constitutional pronouncements affecting this area of the law.

Articles 41 and 42 have been described both as "very long winded, unnces-

211. *Supra*. See further G.W. Hogan, "Constitutional Aspects of the Distribution and Organisation of Court Business" (1984) 6 D.U.L.J. 40 where the author discusses the constitutional implications of the decisions of the High Court in *R. v. R.* and in *Tormey v. Ireland* prior to the determination of the Supreme Court appeal in the latter case.
212. [1982] 2 I.L.R.M. 497 (H.C.).
213. See p. 56 *post*.
214. *Supra* at p. 50.
215. *Ibid*. Considerable reliance was placed by the husband on the judgement of the European Court in *Airey v. Ireland* (1979) 2 E.H.R.R. 305. This matter is further discussed on p. 57. See also G.F. Whyte, The Application of the Euorpean Convention on Human Rights Before the Irish Courts (1982) 31 I.C.L. Q. 856.
216. [1983] I.R. 68 (H.C.).
217. And not carried forward as part of Irish Law after the enactment of the 1937 Constitution. See Article 50 of the Constitution.
218. *Supra* at p. 80. The learned judge made reference in this context to the provisions of Articles 34, 38.1 and 40.3 and described their "combined effect" as guaranteeing "something equivalent to the concept of 'due process' under the American Constitution in relation to causes and controversies litigated before the courts." (*supra* at p. 79).

sarily detailed and rather rhetorical"[219] and as formulating "first principles with conspicuous clarity of power".[220] On the one hand they can be criticised for rigidifying the law, for example by prohibiting divorce legislation, while on the other they can be praised for encouraging and contributing to its development.[221] They have in a number of areas acted as a catalyst to judicial creativity, yet they have failed as a general stimulant against legislative inertia. As shall be seen further on, the challenge they throw out to the Oireachtas to develop, within the limits they prescribe, a modern and humane law based on the needs of the family has not yet been acted upon.[222]

219. A. O'Rahilly, "Thoughts on the Constitution", p. 6.
220. *In re Tilson, Infants* [1951] I.R. 1 at p. 14 *per* Gavan Duffy P.
221. For a critic of the assumptions upon which Articles 41 and 42 are based see article by W. Duncan, "Supporting the Institution of Marriage in the Republic of Ireland" in *Marriage and Co-habitation in Contemporary Societies* edited by J.M. Eekelaar & S.N. Katz at p. 82 *et seq* (1980, Butterworth & Co., Canada Ltd.) [also published in (1978) 13 I.J. (n.s.) 215].
222. See also Art. 45 of the Constitution which contains "Directive Principles of Social Policy", which are intended for the general guidance of the Oireachtas. This Article provides
"1. The State shall strive to promote the welfare of the whole people by securing and protecting as effectively as it may a social order in which justice and charity shall inform all the institutions of the national life.
2. The State shall, in particular, direct its policy towards securing
    i. That the citizens (all of whom, men and women equally, have the right to an adequate means of livelihood) may through their occupations find the means of making reasonable provision for their domestic needs.
4. 1° The State pledges itself to safeguard with especial care the economic interests of the weaker sections of the community, and, where necessary, to contribute to the support of the infirm, the widow, the orphan, and the aged.
    2° The State shall endeavour to ensure that the strength and health of workers, men and women, and the tender age of children shall not be abused and that citizens shall not be forced by economic necessity to enter avocations unsuited to their sex, age or strength."
The Article states that the application of the above principles "in the making of laws shall be the care of the Oireachtas exclusively, and shall not be cognisable by any Court under any provisions of this Constitution." Despite this Kenny J. interpreted subsection 2(i) above as indicating the existence of a right to an adequate means of livelihood which came under the protection of Art. 40.3 as one of the personal rights of the citizen – *Murtagh Properties v. Clery* [1972] I.R. 330 (H.C.). The provisions of Art. 45 were also relied on by the plaintiff in *McGee v. A.-G. supra*. In that case Fitzgerald C.J. stated at p. 303 that:
"Article 45 refers to principles of social policy which are intended for the general guidance of the Oireachtas in its making of laws and which are declared to be exclusively its province and not cognisable by any Court. In my opinion, the intervention by this or any other Court, with the function of the Oireachtas is expressly prohibited under this article. To hold otherwise would be an invalid usurpation of legislative authority."
No other members of the Supreme Court commented on the effect of this Article. However, see comments of O'Keefe P. in the High Court at p. 291 where he suggested that the Article could be considered by the courts in certain circumstances. See also *Landers v. The Attorney General* (1973) 109 I.L.T.R. 1 (H.C.) in which Finlay P. stated that he was entitled "to look at Article 45.4.2 in determining a constitutional challenge to a statutory provision which had the effect of prohibiting the plaintiff, a child aged eight and a half years from giving singing performances on licensed premises at night.
Article 45 has had little influence in the area of family law. For a detailed discussion of the Article, see J.M. Kelly, *The Irish Constitution*, 2nd Ed., *supra*, p. 679 *et seq*.

CHAPTER 2

THE FAMILY LAW JURISDICTION OF THE COURTS
AND RELATED MATTERS

In looking at the court system this chapter is only concerned with proceedings that can solely be classified within the category of Family Law, e.g. questions relating to marital breakdown, family maintenance, custody of children, decrees of nullity, etc. The jurisdiction of the courts over family law matters and the manner in which that jurisdiction is exercised is briefly examined. Questions relating to family law may, of course, arise in a variety of different categories of legal proceedings. For example, it may be necessary to determine whether a defendant's spouse is a competent or compellable witness in criminal proceedings or whether a husband is generally liable for a wife's debts. The jurisdiction of the courts in relation to such matters is not within the scope of this chapter.

THE JURISDICTION OF THE COURTS

The Jurisdiction of the Ecclesiastical Courts

In Ireland, as in England, the law relating to matrimonial causes and matters was formerly administered exclusively by the Ecclesiastical Courts of the Established Church. These courts had exclusive jurisdiction to hear suits for nullity of marriage, divorce *a mensa et thoro*, restitution of conjugal rights, and jactitation of marriage. They possessed no jurisdiction to dissolve a marriage (i.e. to grant a decree of divorce *a vinculo matrimonii*), as the Church upheld the doctrine of indissolubility. This latter jurisdiction was exercised by Parliament.[1]

Up until the reign of Henry VIII the law administered by the Ecclesiastical Courts was based on the canon law of the Roman Catholic Church.[2] After the Reformation, the administration of the Ecclesiastical Courts passed from the Roman Catholic Hierarchy to that of the Established Church of England and Ireland, and canon law rules prevailed only insofar as they were unaffected by Acts of Parliament and the common law and custom of England.[3] The Ecclesiastical law administered by the Ecclesiastical Courts after the Reformation ceased to be affected by progress within the canon law of the Roman Catholic Church, and became known as the King's Ecclesiastical law.[4]

---

1. See *McM. v. McM.* and *McK. v. McK.* [1936] I.R. at pp. 187–190, (H.C.); see also *Mason v. Mason (otherwise Pennington)* [1944] N.I. 134 (K.B.D.).
2. *Ussher v. Ussher* [1912] 2 I.R. 445 at p. 458 (K.B.D.); *R. v. Millis* (1844) 10 Cl. & Fin. 534 at p. 678; 8 E.R. 844; (H.L.).
3. Lord Hale, *History of the Common Law*, Chapter 2; *McM. v. McM., supra*; *S. v. S.* (July 1976) unreported (S.C.). See judgement of Kenny J.
4. *McM. v. McM., supra*; *R. (Kelly) v. Maguire and others* [1923] I.R. 58; (1923) 57 I.L.T.R. 57 (K.B.D.); *Hunt v. Hunt* [1861] 4 De G.F. & J. 221 at p. 227; 45 E.R. 1168 (Chancery) *MacMahon v. MacMahon* [1913] I.R. 428 (C.A.); *Courtney v. Courtney* [1923] 2 I.R. 31; (1923) 57 I.L.T.R. 42 (C.A.).

The Irish Church Act of 1869 dissolved, as from the 1st January 1871, the union of the Established Churches of England and Ireland and declared that the Church of Ireland should cease to be established by law. Section 21 of that Act provided that on or after the 1st January 1871, the jurisdiction of the Ecclesiastical Courts would cease. The latter's jursidiction over matrimonial causes and matters were vested in the Court of Matrimonial Causes and Matters set up by the Matrimonial Causes and Marriage Law (Ireland) Amendment Act, 1870. Section 13 of this Act provides that:

> "In all suits and proceedings the said Court for Matrimonial Causes and Matters shall proceed and act and give relief on principles and rules which in the opinion of the said court shall be as nearly as may be comfortable to the principles and rules on which the ecclesiastical courts of Ireland have heretofore acted and given relief."

Under the Judicature (Ireland) Act, 1877, this jurisdiction became vested in the permanent division of the Supreme Court of Judicature in Ireland described as Her Majesty's High Court of Justice in Ireland and was exercised by the Judge of the Probate and Matrimonial Division. On the establishment of Saorstat Eireann the jurisdiction passed to a new High Court of Justice created by the Courts of Justice Act, 1924.[5] Finally, in 1961 with the enactment of the Courts (Establishment and Constitution) Act it vested in the High Court established under the present Constitution.[6]

The Present Jurisdiction of the High Court

The High Court still administers the law relating to matrimonial causes and matters inherited by it from the Ecclesiastical Courts over one hundred years ago. In addition, the High Court exercises an original jurisdiction over family law matters pursuant to the Married Women's Status Act, 1957, the Family Home Protection Act, 1976, the Family Law Act, 1981, the Adoption Acts, 1952–76, the Marriages Act, 1972, the Legitimacy Declaration Act (Ireland), 1868, the Succession Act, 1965,[7] and the President of the High Court has inherited the old jurisdiction of the Court of Chancery over Wards of Court.[8] Until the coming into force of the Courts Act, 1981, on the 12th of May, 1982,[9] the High Court also exercised an original jurisdiction under the Guardianship of Infants Act, 1964, and the Family Law (Maintenance of Spouses & Children) Act, 1976. In *R. v. R.*[10] Gannon J. held that although the Courts Act, 1981, had deleted from the latter two Acts the provision contained in each whereby an originating jurisdiction was conferred on the High Court,[11] such jurisdiction was still exercisable by that court under Article 34.3.1 of the Constitution which vests the High Court with "full original jurisdiction in and power to determine all matters and questions whether of law or fact, civil or criminal." He also held

---

5. Sect. 17.
6. Sect. 2 of the Act of 1961.
7. To commence proceedings for a decree of divorce *a mensa et thoro*, nullity, restitution of conjugal rights, jactitation of marriage or for a declaration under the Legitimacy Declaration Act (Ireland), 1868 as amended, a petition must be filed in the Central Office of the High Court. See R.S.C. (S.I. No. 15 of 1986); the whole of Order 70 and Order 36, Rules 4 and 13 which relate to the above matrimonial causes; and Order 71 which concerns proceedings under the Act of 1868. Other family law matters coming before the High Court are commenced by special summons; see Order 3 and Order 38, *supra*.
8. Courts (Supplemental Provisions) Act, 1961, Sect. 9.
9. Courts Act, 1981, Sect. 33(3).
10. [1984] I.R. 296 (H.C.). See also *O'R. v. O'R.* (December, 1984) unreported (H.C.) discussed in footnote 14 below.
11. See the Courts Act, 1981, Sect. 12 & 15.

that by virtue of this provision the High Court could also exercise an original jurisdiction under the Family Law (Protection of Spouses & Children) Act, 1981.[12] The authority of this decision is now in doubt having regard to the decision of the Supreme Court in *Tormey v. Ireland & the Attorney General*[13] and although no written judgement has been delivered on the issue to date, it appears that the High Court may no longer possess any jurisdiction to make original orders in any proceedings issued in the High Court on or after the 12th of May 1982, under either the Guardianship of Infants Act, 1964, or the Family Law (Maintenance of Spouses & Children) Act, 1976, or in any proceedings issued since its enactment under the Family Law (Protection of Spouses & Children) Act, 1981.[14] As a result of the coming into force of the Courts Act,

---

12. See in particular [1984] I.R. at pp. 307–310. Gannon J. stated at p. 309 that he rejected "as wrong in law, the contentions (advanced on behalf of the Attorney General) that under Article 36 of the Constitution* the Oireachtas may confer upon and withdraw from the High Court, or confer upon other courts to the exclusion of the High Court, jurisdiction in the matters of family law, custody of children and maintenance which are under consideration in these proceedings." Further on (1984 I.R. at p. 310) he stated, however, that "in so far as other courts of first instance established by law have jurisdiction in matters of family law, custody of children and maintenance of the nature under consideration in these proceedings, it is competent for the High Court to decline to entertain applications for orders obtainable in such other courts, or to remit to such other courts for hearing such applications brought in the High Court as are within the jurisdiction of such other courts." The proceedings in *R. v. R.* itself were eventually heard and determined in the High Court following this judgement. Subsequent to *R. v. R.* the following practice direction was issued by the President of the High Court:—

"Having regard to the decision of Mr Justice Gannon in *R. v. R. and the Attorney General*, delivered on 16 February 1984 the notice of practitioners is drawn to the following practice direction.

In any case where relief is sought in The High Court, under any of the above-named Acts, the summons shall be returnable before the Master in the ordinary way and thereafter shall be put in the list before the judge sitting for Family Law on a Friday Motion day.

The parties must on that occasion attend and submit such evidence or arguments as they see fit as to whether the case is one appropriate for The High Court to exercise its jurisdiction under one or other of the above Acts or whether it is a case which should be remitted to the Circuit Court or District Court. A decision will then be made on that issue and depending upon the nature of that decision the case will be listed for hearing, but such listing will not determine the appropriate scale of costs, if any, to be awarded which will be subject to the provisions of section 17(4) of Courts Act, 1981."

The Acts referred to in the Direction are – the Guardianship of Infants Act, 1964, the Family Law (Maintenance of Spouses and Children) Act, 1976, and the Family Law (Protection of Spouses and Children) Act, 1981.

*Article 36 of the Constitution states "Subject to the foregoing provisions of this Constitution relating to the Courts, the following matters shall be regulated in accordance with law, that is to say: . . .

"iii The Constitution and organisation of the said Courts, the distribution of jurisdiction and business among the said courts and judges and all matters of procedure."

13. [1985] 5 I.L.R.M. 375 (S.C.) discussed on p. 43 *ante*. See also G.W. Hogan, "Constitutional Aspects of the Distribution and Organisation of Court Business" (1984) 6 D.U.L.J. 41; D.G. Morgan, *Constitutional Law of Ireland* (The Round Hall Press, Dublin 1985) at pp. 192–194.

14. See also *O'B. v. O'B.* [1984] I.R. 182 (S.C.) in particular O'Higgins C.J. at pp. 187–188. The Courts Act, 1981, whilst extending the jurisdiction of the Circuit Court in proceedings issued under the Married Women's Status Act, 1957, the Succession Act, 1965, and the Family Home Protection Act, 1976, did not delete the provisions contained in those Acts which expressly confer an originating jurisdiction on the High Court. In *T. v. T.* proceedings issued in the High Court on the 9th day of December, 1983 in which the plaintiff sought orders pursuant to the Married Women's Status Act, 1957, and the Family Home Protection Act, 1976, were remitted by McMahon J. to the Circuit Court in reliance on the President's practice direction (see footnote 12) on the 16th of March, 1984, stating that in his opinion the case was "an appropriate one" to be so remitted. The plaintiff successfully appealed to the Supreme Court which held (on the 3rd day of May, 1984) that unless the party seeking to remit an action to the Circuit Court could establish that the action was "not fit to be prosecuted in the High Court" under Order 49 Rule 7 of the Rules of the

1981, and the decision in the *Tormey* case it also appears that the High Court may no longer possess an original jurisdiction to make orders under the Illegitimate Children (Affiliation Orders) Act, 1930, in any proceedings initiated on or after the 12th of May 1982.[15]

The High Court jurisdiction to make *Habeas Corpus* orders may also be invoked in the family law context, in particular in child custody proceedings. Prior to the coming into force of the Guardianship of Infants Act, 1964, it was usual to initiate custody proceedings by using the *Habeas Corpus* procedure and if it is established that such proceedings can no longer be issued in the High Court under the Act of 1964, the remedy of *Habeas Corpus* may be increasingly relied

Superior Courts (S.I. No. 72 of 1962) then a High Court judge should not remit the matter to the Circuit Court.

*Order 49 Rule 7 of the current rules states:

"(i) Where any action or proceeding is pending in the High Court which might have been commenced in the Circuit Court or the District Court, any party to such action or proceeding may apply to the High Court that the action be remitted or transferred to the Circuit Court or the District Court (as the case may be) and if the High Court should not consider the action or proceeding fit to be prosecuted in the High Court it may remit or transfer such action or proceeding to the Circuit Court or the District Court (as the case may be) to be prosecuted before the Judge to such Circuit or (as the case may require) the Justice assigned to such District as may appear to the Court suitable and convenient, upon such terms and subject to such conditions as to costs or otherwise as may appear just.

(ii) An application under this rule to remit to transfer an action may be made at any time after an appearance is entered and before service of notice of trial."

*S.I. No. 15 of 1986.

In the later case of *O'R. v. O'R.* (December, 1984) unreported (H.C.) proceedings were initiated by the plaintiff pursuant to the Family Home Protection Act, 1976, and pursuant to the three Acts in which proceedings had been issued in *R. v. R.* Murphy J. stated that the absence of any express provision conferring an original jurisdiction on the High Court in the Family Law (Maintenance of Spouses and Children) Act, 1976, and in the Family Law (Protection of Spouses and Children) Act, 1981, was "a clear indication on the part of the Oireachtas that such applications (i.e. applications under the two Acts) should be made in the first instance to the court of limited local jurisdiction." Stating that the court should "give effect to the intention of the Oireachtas," he asserted that "it must be recognised that in accordance with Article 36 of the Constitution the Oireachtas is bound to enact legislation regulating in accordance with the law (among other things) the constitution and organisation of the courts and the distribution, jurisdiction and business among the courts." (See p. 10 of judgement.) Further on he stated that "It seems to me that the only circumstances in which the court would be justified in departing from the procedure envisaged by the legislature would be where the High Court was satisfied that in the circumstances of a particular case there was a serious danger that justice would not be done if that court declined to exercise the jurisdiction vested in it by the Constitution in relation to that case." As no such circumstances existed, he held it to be "appropriate . . . to decline to exercise the inherent or constitutional jurisdiction of the court to determine the issues in this case and to leave the parties to pursue their remedies in those courts on which the Oireachtas has expressly conferred jurisdiction." Murphy J. did not in his judgement advert to the fact that the High Court still retained an original jurisdiction under the Family Home Protection Act, 1976, expressly conferred on it by section 10 of that Act. An appeal was filed in the Supreme Court in this case but was subsequently withdrawn by consent, the spouses having entered into a settlement.

O'R. v. O'R. was determined before the decision of the Supreme Court in *Tormey v. Ireland & The Attorney General, supra*. Murphy J.'s reference to jurisdiction vested in the High Court by the Constitution derives from the view of Gannon J. in *R. v. R., supra*, that the High Court still retained an original jurisdiction to make orders in proceedings initiated after the 12th of May, 1982, under the Guardianship of Infants Act, 1964 and the Family Law (Maintenance of Spouses & Children) Act, 1976, and that it possessed an original jurisdiction to make orders under the Family Law (Protection of Spouses & Children) Act, 1981. See also *M. McD. v. P. McD.* (April, 1986) unreported (H.C.) in which orders were made under both the Guardianship of Infants Act, 1964, and the Family Law (Maintenance of Spouses and Children) Act, 1976 by MacKenzie J. in proceedings instituted in the High Court in 1985. Although no reference is made to the Courts Act, 1981, in the judgement, the trial judge had earlier ruled the case to be an appropriate case to be determined in the High Court in accordance with the direction of the President of the High Court, (see footnote 12, *supra*).

15. See the Courts Act, 1971, Sect. 19 as amended by the Courts Act, 1981, Sect. 14.

upon in appropriate cases to invoke the original jurisdiction of the High Court to determine such cases.[16]

Jurisdiction of the Circuit Court

The Circuit Court has an original jurisdiction in family law matters to hear suits for divorce *a mensa et thoro*,[17] proceedings initiated under the Married Women's Status Act, 1957, the Guardianship of Infants Act, 1964, the Family Law (Maintenance of Spouses & Children) Act, 1976,[18] the Family Home Protection Act, 1976,[19] the Family Law (Protection of Spouses & Children) Act, 1981,[20] the Family Law Act, 1981, the Succession Act, 1965,[21] the Illegitimate Children (Affiliation Orders) Act, 1930,[22] and the Legitimacy Declaration Act (Ireland), 1868. The Circuit Court may also hear wardship proceedings.[23]

Jurisdiction of the District Court

The District Court has a limited family law jurisdiction. It may hear proceedings under the Guardianship of Infants Act, 1964,[24] the Family Law (Maintenance of Spouses & Children) Act, 1976,[25] the Family Home Protection Act, 1976, Sect. 9,[26] the Family Law (Protection of Spouses & Children) Act, 1981,[27] the Family Law Act, 1981, the Illegitimate Children (Affiliation Orders) Act, 1930, as amended,[28] the Children Acts, 1908–57 and the School Attendance Acts, 1926–67. The Children Act, 1908,[29] as amended, requires the District Court when dealing with children under 17, to sit either in a different place or at different times or on different days from those on which the ordinary sittings of the court are held. When such a special sitting of the court is taking place, the Act describes it as a juvenile court. The Courts of Justice Act, 1924, Sect. 80, provides for special court sittings in Dublin, Cork, Limerick and Waterford and such sittings are referred to as "Children's Courts". The only full time Children's Court is the Dublin Metropolitan Children's Court.

Appellate Jurisdiction

The Circuit Court hears and determines appeals in family law matters from the District Court. The High Court hears and determines appeals in family law matters from the Circuit Court and the Supreme Court hears and determines

---

16. In relation to Habeas Corpus see Article 40.4 of the Constitution. See also Order 84 of the Rules of the Superior Court, (1986) *supra*. See further Chapter 13.

17. See the Courts Act, 1981, Sect. 5. See also the Circuit Court Rules (No. 6) 1982 (S.I. No. 158 of 1982) Order 69.

18. See the Courts Act, 1981, Sects. 3, 12 & 15. See also the Circuit Court Rules (No. 6) 1982, *supra*, Order 68.

19. See the Courts Act, 1981, Sect. 13. See also the Circuit Court Rules (No.7) 1982 (S.I. No. 244 of 1982).

20. See the Circuit Court Rules (No. 3) 1982 (S.I. No. 152 of 1982).

21. See the Courts Act, 1981, Sect. 4.

22. *Ibid*, Sect. 14. See also the Circuit Court Rules (No. 6) 1982, *supra*, Order 68.

23. Courts (Supplemental Provisions) Act, 1961, Sect. 22(1); See Third Schedule, Ref. No. 24 as amended by the Courts Act, 1981, Sect. 2(1).

24. See the Courts Act, 1981, Sect. 15. See also the District Court (Guardianship of Infants Act, 1964) Rules, 1982. (S.I. No. 141 of 1982).

25. See also the District Court (Family Law . . . Act, 1976) Rules 1976 (S.I. No. 96 of 1976).

26. See the Family Home Protection Act, 1976, Sect. 10.

27. See also District Court [Family Law (Protection of Spouses & Children) Act, 1981] Rules, 1981 (S.I. No. 246 of 1981.

28. See also District Court Rules (No. 2) 1962 (S.I. No. 8 of 1962).

29. Sect. 111 as amended by the Children's Act, 1941, Sect. 26.

appeals in family law matters from the High Court. Both Circuit Court and High Court appellate hearings are by way of an oral rehearing of the relevant evidence in the case appealed. A Supreme Court appeal is based on the evidence presented at the original hearing in the High Court and although an original decision made by the High Court may be reversed on a point of law or fact, the Court is slow to reverse a finding of fact by a judge who has had an opportunity of listening to and assessing the credibility of witnesses in an oral hearing.

PRIVACY

Article 34(1) of the Constitution states that "Justice shall be administered in courts established by law . . . and save in such special and limited cases as may be prescribed by law, shall be administered in public." Almost all family law court proceedings result in a disclosure by parties of various confidential details of their family life and personal relationships. In order to prevent unnecessary distress, it is particularly important for the protection of the parties and their families that such proceedings are heard in private. As a consequence, the great majority of such proceedings come within the "special and limited" category of cases envisaged in the above article from which the public may be excluded.

Section 45(1) of the Courts (Supplemental Provisions) Act, 1961, provides that

"Justice may be administered otherwise than in public in . . . matrimonial causes and matters . . . and minor matters."

The Act does not define the meaning of "matrimonial causes and matters" and it is uncertain as to whether its meaning is confined to those matters traditionally so called, over which the Ecclesiastical Courts had jurisdiction, or whether it has a wider application.

Proceedings that may be heard in private in reliance on this section are all proceedings formerly within the jurisdiction of the Ecclesiastical Courts,[30] proceedings under the Guardianship of Infants Act, 1964,[31] the Adoption Acts, 1952–76 and wardship proceedings. Other family law matters may be heard in private in accordance with express legislative enactment. These include proceedings under the Married Women's Status Act, 1957 and the Family Home Protection Act, 1976 to determine proprietary disputes between spouses.[32] Proceedings under the Family Law . . . Act, 1976,[33] proceedings under the Family Law

---

30. See also the Matrimonial Causes & Marriage Law (Ireland) Amendment Act, 1970, Sect. 14 and the Circuit Court Rules (No. 6) 1982, *supra*, Order 69 Rule 4. The latter provides that all divorce *a mensa et thoro* proceedings that come before the Circuit Court "shall be heard in camera".

31. See also Circuit Court Rules (No. 6) 1982, *supra*, Order 68 Rule 17.

32. Sect. 12(4) of the 1957 Act: "If either party so requests, the court may hear the application in private". Sect. 10(6) of the Act of 1976: "Proceedings under or referred to in this Act in which each spouse is a party (whether by joinder or otherwise) . . . shall be heard otherwise than in public". Sect. 10(7) provides that "Proceedings in the High Court and in the Circuit Court under or referred to in this Act in which each spouse is a party (whether by joinder or otherwise) shall be heard in chambers".

33. Sect. 25(1) Proceedings under this Act shall be conducted in a summary manner and shall be heard otherwise than in public. (2) Proceedings in the High Court and the Circuit Court under this Act shall be heard in chambers. See also District Court (Family Law . . . Act, 1976), Rules 1976; S.I. No. 96 of 1976, Rule 6 – "Proceedings shall not be heard in public and only the parties, their legal representatives and witnesses shall be per-

(Protection of Spouses & Children) Act, 1981,[34] proceedings dealing with children in the District Court when acting as a Juvenile or Children's Court under the Children Act, 1908,[35] proceedings under the Illegitimate Children (Affiliation Orders) Act, 1930,[36] the Succession Act, 1965,[37] the Legitimacy Declarations Act (Ireland), 1868,[38] as amended, and applications under the Marriages Act, 1972,[39] to be exempt from the prohibition to marry imposed on persons under 16 years of age or from the need to obtain a guardian's consent to marry.

The law as to hearing matters in private is not, under the above provisions, identical in all respects. In some proceedings the court merely has a discretion to hear matters in private, in others it must do so.[40] Further, the language of the legislative provisions permitting privacy varies. Thus proceedings may be heard "in private" or "otherwise than in public" or "in chambers" or "in camera".

THE PRESS

If the press is admitted to family proceedings, a limited amount of protection is afforded to parties by the Censorship of Publications Act, 1929, and by the Illegitimate Children (Affiliation Orders) Act, 1930, as amended.

Section 14 of the 1929 Act reads as follows:

(1) It shall not be lawful to print or publish or cause or procure to be printed or published in relation to any judicial proceedings —

(a) any indecent matter the publication of which would be calculated to injure public morals, or

(b) any indecent medical, surgical or physiological details the publication of which would be calculated to injure public morals.

---

mitted to be present." and the Circuit Court Rules (No. 6) 1982 *supra*, Order 68 Rule 17 – "Every application shall be heard otherwise than in open court." See Nineteenth Interim Report of the Committee on Court Practice and Procedure, para. 48 which stated that "in maintenance proceedings the court should be given power to exclude witnesses until it is ready to hear their evidence". Witnesses may be excluded under existing rules of court. See The District Court Rules, 1948 (S.I. No. 431 of 1947) Rule 6(2); Rules of the Circuit Court, 1950 (S.I. No. 179 of 1950) Order 30, Rule 9.

34. Sect. 14(1) Proceedings under this Act shall be heard otherwise than in public. (2) Proceedings under this Act in the Circuit Court, and in the High Court on appeal from Circuit Court, may be heard in chambers. See also District Court [Family Law (Protection of Spouses & Children) Act, 1981] Rules, 1981 (S.I. No. 246 of 1981), Rule 5 – "Proceedings under the Act shall be heard otherwise than in public and only the parties, their legal representatives and witnesses shall be permitted to be present." As for the entitlement of witnesses to be present, see footnote 33 above.

35. Sect. 111(4) of the Children Act, 1908, provides that "In a juvenile court no person other than the members and officers of the court and the parties to the case, their solicitors and counsel, and other persons directly concerned in the case, shall, except by leave of the court, be allowed to attend;

Provided that bona fide representatives of a newspaper or news agency shall not be excluded."

36. Sect. 3(5) as amended by Sect. 28(1)(d) of the 1976 Act *supra*. "Proceedings under this Act shall be conducted otherwise than in public".

37. See Sects. 56 (11), 119 and 122 of the 1965 Act, "All proceedings in relation to this part shall be heard in chambers".

38. See The Courts Act, 1971, Sect. 20 which provides that proceedings under the above Act "shall be heard in chambers".

39. Sect. 1(3)(c) and Sect. 7 by which such application "may be heard in private".

40. If a court does not comply with a statutory requirement to exclude the public, the validity of the order made by the court will not necessarily be at risk. See *The State (Lee) v. Circuit Court Judge for Cork* (1947) 82 I.L.T.R. 22 (H.C.) – non-compliance with statutory provision that the judge "shall" exclude certain persons from the court held not to invlidate affiliation proceedings. The word "shall" held to be directory, not imperative.

(2) It shall not be lawful to print or publish or cause or procure to be printed or published any report, statement, commentary or other matter of or in relation to any judicial proceedings for divorce, nullity of marriage, judicial separation, or restitution of conjugal rights save and except all or any of the following particulars of such proceedings, so far as the same can be printed and published without contravening any other subsection of this section, that is to say:

(a) the names, addresses and occupations of the parties and witnesses,

(b) the court in which and the Judge before whom the proceedings were tried and the names of the solicitors and counsel professionally engaged in the proceedings,

(c) a concise statement of the charges, defences, and counter-charges in support of which evidence was given,

(d) particulars of any point of law raised and discussed in the proceedings and the decision of the court thereon,

(e) the summing-up of the Judge and the findings of the jury or the decision of the court and the observations of the Judge when pronouncing his decision.

(3) Nothing in this section shall apply:

(a) to the printing of any pleading, transcript of evidence, or other document for use in connection with any judicial proceedings or the communication thereof to persons concerned in the proceedings, or

(b) to the printing and publishing of any order, notice, or report in pursuance of the directions of the court, or

(c) to the printing or publishing of any matter in any separate volume or part of any *bona fide* series of law reports which does not form part of any other publication and consists solely of reports of proceedings in courts of law, or in any publication of a technical character *bona fide* intended for circulation among members of the legal or medical profession.

The Act of 1930 as well as providing that all proceedings under it "shall be conducted otherwise than in public" further provides in section 3(6)[41] that:

"It shall not be lawful to print or publish or cause to be printed or published any material relating to proceedings under this Act which would tend to identify the parties to the proceedings".

Both Acts then provide that:[42]

"If any person being the proprietor, editor or publisher of any book or periodical publication or being a master printer engaged in the printing of such book or publication prints or publishes or causes, procures or permits to be printed or published therein in contravention of any of the (above) provisions ... any matter, details, or particulars in relation to any judicial proceedings such person shall be guilty of an offence under this section and shall be liable on summary conviction thereof to a fine not exceeding five

41. As amended by the Family Law ... Act, 1976, Sect. 28(1)(e).
42. Sect. 15 of the 1929 Act, Sect. 3(8) of the 1930 Act.

hundred pounds or at the discretion of the court to imprisonment with or without hard labour for any term not exceeding six months or to both such fine and such imprisonment."

In 1971, the six leading Irish national newspapers were fined in total over £23,000 in the only prosecutions ever brought for breach of the above sections of the 1929 Act.[43] The prosecution arose following their publication a year earlier of evidence given in a suit of divorce *a mensa et thoro*. The divorce proceedings reported by the papers had been held in open court.

In 1976, the editor of the Sunday World newspaper and a reporter of that paper were fined £600 and £300 respectively for contempt of court. The contempt arose out of the publication by that paper of an article concerning a case under the Guardianship of Infants Act which had been heard in private in the High Court and was under appeal to the Supreme Court. The newspaper in its report had revealed the names of the parties to the proceedings, published pictures of the mother and the children, and had given a grossly inaccurate account of the High Court hearing.[44]

JURY ACTIONS

In the High Court, if a question of fact has to be determined in any of those matrimonial proceedings that were formerly within the jurisdiction of the Ecclesiastical Courts it may be determined by a jury. Either party can request a jury.[45] Even if such request is made the court is not bound to comply with it. It may decide, without the consent of the parties, that a matter of fact should be tried by a judge alone. In matrimonial matters the parties are not entitled as of right to a jury if they desire one. However, upon the court refusing an application for a jury, such refusal may be appealed to the Supreme Court.[46]

COSTS

It has been said in a number of cases that "one of the privileges of a husband is to provide his wife with the sinews of war".[47] Put simply, a married woman is entitled to have the means required to employ a lawyer so as to obtain legal protection against violence or misconduct on the part of her husband.[48]

The Rules of the Superior Courts, Order 70, Rules 74–80 set down special rules as to costs which are applicable to those matrimonial causes and matters that come before the High Court.[49] Order 70 Rule 75 states

"After directions have been given as to the mode of hearing or trial of a

---

43. See *Irish Times*, 30 June, 1971 and 7 July, 1971.

44. *Re McCann and Kennedy* [1976] I.R. 382 (S.C.).

45. If the petitioner does not within 14 days from the filing of the last pleading, by motion on notice to the Master of the High Court apply to fix time and mode of trial, the respondent may do so. The Master, or the Court if the Master places the motion on the court list, fixes time and mode of trial.

46. See Sects. 15 and 27 of the Matrimonial Causes and Marriage Law (Ireland) Amend. Act, 1870 and R.S.C. (S.I. No. 15 of 1986), Order 36 Rules 4–7, Order 70, Rule 33; See also *B. (falsely called B.) v. B.* (1875) I.R. 9 Eq. 551 (Ct. for Mat. Causes). See further *Bradley v. Bradley* (Jan. 1971) unreported (H.C.) where Murnaghan J. stated that having regard to the above statutory provisions and rules of court there was some doubt as to whether in matrimonial matters the Master had power to order a trial by jury.

47. See *Bradley v. Bradley, supra*.

48. *Robson v. Robson* (1891) 29 L.R.Ir. 152 (Matr. Ct.); *Mecredy v. Taylor* (1873) I.R.7 C.L. 256 (Exch. Cham.). (It is submitted that in this case the dissenting judgements are more convincing than the judgements for the majority), *Sullivan v. Sullivan* [1912] 2 I.R. 116, 125; (1911), 45 I.L.T.R. 198 (K.B.D.), (C.A.).

49. See also the Matrimonial Causes and Marriage Law (Ireland) Amendment Act, 1870, Sect. 27 provides that the Court may make such order as to costs as "may seem just".

cause, or in an earlier stage of a cause, where special circumstances are shown, the Court may, on the application by motion of a wife who is a petitioner or who has entered an appearance (unless the husband shall prove that the wife has sufficient separate estate or show other good reason) make an order directing him to pay her costs of the cause up to the date of such application, and her further costs *de die in diem* up to the trial or hearing, and directing the Taxing Master to tax such costs and at the time of such taxation (if directions as to the mode of hearing or trial have been given before such taxation) to ascertain and certify what is a sufficient sum of money to be paid into court or what is a sufficient security to be given by the husband to cover the costs of the wife of and incidental to the hearing or trial of the cause".

Order 60 Rule 78 states:

"When on the hearing or trial of a cause the decision of the Court or the verdict of the jury is against the wife, no costs of the wife of and incidental to such hearing or trial shall be allowed as against the husband, except such as shall be applied for, and ordered to be allowed by the Court at the time of such hearing or trial".

A husband will be held liable for all costs reasonably and properly incurred by his wife, whether she is petitioner or respondent, if she has no separate property of her own. This is so even if he succeeds against her[50] or if the trial is abortive,[51] or if the parties settle their differences and resume cohabitation after commencing proceedings.[52] If, however, she has some property of her own she may be held liable for all or part of her costs. If she possesses no property the court may only refuse an order for costs[53] if her action was vexatious, frivolous or without reasonable grounds and "where the attorney had the means of seeing before instituting the suit that it was one that ought not to be instituted".[54]

The duty imposed on a husband to pay a wife's costs arises both out of the former practice of the Ecclesiastical Courts to hold him so bound and from the common law duty of a husband to supply his wife with necessaries. Necessaries are said to include the necessary costs of obtaining legal protection against a husband's misconduct. Thus, as well as High Court matrimonial matters, a wife's right to obtain costs extends to costs arising from other necessary legal work done or proceedings brought to seek protection or obtain support from her husband.[55] However, if costs are recoverable from the husband but the wife's solicitors sue and recover costs from her, only to subsequently discover that she is unable to pay them, they are barred from proceeding against the husband.[56]

The law as to costs is based on the principle that if a husband was not obliged to discharge his wife's legal costs as many wives are financially dependent on

50. *Courtney v. Courtney, supra; McM. v. McM., supra.*
51. *Bradley v. Bradley, supra;* see also *Kemp-Welch v. Kemp-Welch* [1910] P. 233 (C.A.), *Sanders v. Sanders* [1911] P.D. 101, (C.A.).
52. *Ballance v. Ballance* [1899] 2 I.R. 128 (Matr.); *O'Neill v. O'Neill* (1908) 42 I.L.T.R. 281 (K.B.D.).
53. *Robson v. Robson, supra; Cooney v. Cooney* (1947) 81 I.L.T.R. 131 (S.C.).
54. *Bradley v. Bradley, supra; Carnegie v. Carnegie* (1885) 15 L.R. Ir. 513 (Mat. Ct.); *Flower v. Flower* (1873) L.R. 3 P. & D. 132 (Ct. of P. & D.), *Sullivan v. Sullivan, supra.*
55. *Ottaway v. Hamilton* (1876) 3 C.P.D. 393 (C.P.D.); *Sullivan v. Sullivan, supra; Wilson v. Ford* (1876) L.R. 3 Ex. 63; 37 L.J.Ex. 60 (Ct. of Exch.); *Mecredy v. Taylor, supra; Turner v. Rookes* (1839) 10 Ad. & E. 47; 2 P. & D. 240; 113 E.R. 18 (Ct. of K.B.), *J.N. Nabarro v. Kennedy* [1954] 2 All E.R. 605; [1955] Q.B. 575 (Q.B.D.). See, however, the Family Law . . . Act, 1976, Sect. 26 — "The costs of any proceedings under this Act shall be in the discretion of the court."
56. *Sullivan v. Sullivan, supra.*

their husbands they would be unable to obtain legal assistance when such assistance is required to resolve a family difficulty.[57] In reality, the help afforded to wives by this area of the law is not great. Many solicitors in private practice are unwilling to act for wives who are not in a position to discharge the legal fees incurred by them as even if a court order for costs is obtained against a husband it is often not possible to make the husband comply with the order made against him. However, where an award for costs is made in maintenance proceedings brought under the Family Law ... Act, 1976, or the Guardianship of Infants Act, 1964, or in proceedings for alimony or proceedings under the Illegitimate Children (Affiliation Orders) Act, 1930, and the party against whom the award is made subsequently defaults in his maintenance, alimony or affiliation payments, it is possible to secure payment of the costs by an attachment of earnings order, if such an order is made to enforce the maintenance, alimony or affiliation order.[58]

LEGAL AID

The most fundamental defect in the Irish legal system is the absence of a comprehensive statutory scheme of free legal aid and advice.[59] Whilst the State has by legislation provided free legal aid in limited circumstances for persons charged with criminal offences since 1962,[60] no legislation has been enacted to provide free legal aid and advice in civil matters, including family law, for those who cannot afford to pay for legal assistance. However, in December, 1979, the Minister for Justice laid before both Houses of the Oireachtas a booklet containing details of a non-statutory scheme the Government intended to set up to provide civil legal aid and advice. On the 8th of September, 1980, the scheme formally came into operation.

The need for the State to provide free legal assistance in family law matters was clearly demonstrated by the work of the Free Legal Advice Centres (F.L.A.C.) in Dublin during the 1970s. This voluntary organisation in the period from the 1st of April, 1969 to the 1st of November, 1979, assisted 33,254 clients, 13,418 of whom sought help with a problem classified as coming within the category of family law.[61] Despite the number of persons that sought its help, FLAC believed that it was only dealing with "a small proportion of the problems that arise within the particular areas of Dublin City where the centres operate."[62]

In December, 1977, the Pringle Report on Civil Legal Aid and Advice was published.[63] This report contained detailed recommendations for the establishment of a comprehensive State financed scheme of civil legal aid and advice. In relation to family law the Report stated:

"While in no way detracting from our view that a comprehensive scheme of

---

57. *Bradley v. Bradley, supra; Flower v. Flower, supra.*
58. See the Family Law ... Act, 1976, Sect. 10(4)(a). See also the Defence Act, 1954, Sect. 98 as amended by the Family Law ... Act, 1976, Sect. 30 which provides a procedure for enforcing orders for costs made against a man of the Permanent Defence Force.
59. See F.L.A.C. Reports 1972, 1974, 1976, 1977, 1978.
60. Thus, children charged with a criminal offence may get free representation under the provisions of the Criminal Justice (Legal Aid) Act, 1962. See the case of *The State (Healey) v. Donoghue and Ors.* [1976] I.R. 325; (1976) 112 I.L.T.R. 37 (S.C.) in which the constitutional right of a person to be informed of his entitlement to legal aid was enunciated by the Supreme Court.
61. From figures supplied by F.L.A.C.
62. F.L.A.C. Report 1976. See also F.L.A.C. Report 1978 where the organisation stated that its statistics represented "only the tip of the iceberg".
63. *The Report of the Committee on Civil Legal Aid & Advice* (The Pringle Report) (December 1977, Dublin Stationery Office) (Prl. 6862).

legal aid and advice should be introduced at the earliest possible opportunity, we consider that family law cases merit immediate consideration because of the particular social problems which they present, the peculiar sensitivity of their nature and the consideration which must be given to the welfare of the children."[64]

In November, 1979, the European Court of Human Rights in the case of *Airey v. Ireland*[65] held the State to be in breach of Article 6(1)[66] and Article 8[67] of the European Convention for the Protection of Human Rights and Fundamental Freedoms, due to its failure to provide free legal aid in a family law matter. The applicant, Mrs. Airey, was unable to find a solicitor willing to represent her in proceedings for divorce *a mensa et thoro* (judicial separation) as she did not have the means to pay for legal representation. The Court held that the failure of the State to provide her with the necessary legal assistance constituted a denial to her by the State of an effective right of access to the High Court and a failure on the part of the State to respect her private family life.

The Court in its judgement stated:

"In Ireland, many aspects of private or family life are regulated by law. As regards marriage, husband and wife are in principle under a duty to cohabit but are entitled, in certain cases, to petitition for a decree of judicial separation; this amounts to recognition of the fact that the protection of their private or family life may sometimes necessitate their being relieved from the duty to live together.

Effective respect for private or family life obliges Ireland to make this means of protection effectively accessible, when appropriate, to anyone who may wish to have recourse thereto. However, it was not effectively accessible to the applicant: not having been put in a position in which she could apply to the High Court . . . she was unable to seek recognition in law of her de facto separation from her husband."[68]

The Government had argued that Mrs. Airey was not deprived of access to the court as she was free to bring proceedings herself without legal assistance. In reply to this contention the Court stated that:

"it is not realistic . . . to suppose that in litigation of this nature, the applicant could effectively conduct her own case . . . Litigation of this kind, in addition to involving complicated points of law, necessitates proof of adultery, unnatural practices or, as in the present case, cruelty; to establish the facts,

---

64. *Ibid*. at p. 47 para. 2.7.2.

65. See the judgements delivered by the court on the 9th October 1979 and on the 6th February 1981. In the latter judgement Mrs Airey was awarded £3,140 compensation. See also the Report on the European Commission on Human Rights adopted on the 9 March, 1978 (Application No. 6289/73).

66. Article 6(1) provides "In the determination of his civil rights and obligations or of any criminal charge against him, everyone is entitled to a fair and public hearing within a reasonable time by an independent and impartial tribunal established by law. Judgement shall be pronounced publicly but the press and public may be excluded from all or part of the trial in the interests of morals, public order or national security in a democratic society, where the interests of juveniles or the protection of the private life of the parties so require, or to the extent strictly necessary in the opinion of the court in special circumstances where publicity would prejudice the interests of justice."

67. Article 8 provides "1. Everyone has the right to respect of his private and family life, his home and his correspondence. 2. There shall be no interference by a public authority with the exercise of this right except such as is in accordance with the law and is necessary in a democratic society in the interests of national security, public safety or the economic wellbeing of the country, for the prevention of disorder or crime, for the protection of health or morals or for the protection of the rights and freedom of others."

68. See Section 33 of judgement.

expert evidence may have to be tendered and witnesses may have to be found, called and examined. What is more, marital disputes often entail an emotional involvement that is scarcely compatible with the degree of objectivity required by advocacy in court."[69]

Following the judgement of the European Court in the *Airey* case, the Government published details of the Scheme of Civil Legal Aid & Advice which came into operation in 1980. This scheme is considerably different to that proposed in the Pringle Report. Under the scheme, free legal assistance is provided through law centres only on a means tested basis. The scheme is administered by a Legal Aid Board whose duties include determining an applicant's eligibility for legal assistance and the establishment and provision of law centres with the Minister's consent.[70] The addresses of all the law centres operating under the scheme as at the 30th of September 1986 can be found in Appendix B.

Legal advice under the scheme can only be given on "the application of Irish law to any particular circumstances which have arisen in relation to the person seeking the advice" and "as to any steps which that person might appropriately take ... having regard to the application of Irish law to those circumstances." It may also include any assistance given by a law centre solicitor to any person "by taking any such steps on his behalf or by assisting him in taking them on his own behalf."[71] Legal aid under the scheme is confined to proceedings conducted in the District, Circuit, High or Supreme Court.[72] The scheme, which provides advice and aid in the area of civil and not criminal law, applies to most areas of family law. However, proceedings before social welfare appeal tribunals are not included in the scheme and as a consequence, a deserted wife or unmarried mother cannot be represented by a legal aid solicitor under the scheme before a tribunal determining an application for deserted wife's allowance or benefit[73] or unmarried mother's allowance.[74]

Legal assistance also cannot be extended under the scheme to provide for representation before a foreign court in a family law matter. For example, a wife living in Ireland whose husband issues divorce proceedings against her in a foreign court, cannot through the scheme employ a lawyer in the country in which the divorce proceedings are brought to represent her before the courts of that country. Similarly, if there is a custody dispute between parents and one parent kidnaps a child and removes it from Ireland to a foreign country, whilst legal aid may be obtained under the scheme to obtain an Irish court order that the child be returned to the jurisdiction of the Irish Courts, no provision is made in the scheme for the payment of legal fees to lawyers in a foreign jurisdiction to bring court proceed-

---

69. See Section 24 of judgement. See further S. Maidment, The Airey Case (1980) 10 Fam. Law 69. See also *E. v. E.* [1982] 2 I.L.R.M. 497 (H.C.) discussed on p. 44 *ante*.
70. See Scheme of Civil Legal Aid and Advice (Dublin Stationery Office) (Prl. 8543) laid by the Minister for Justice before each House of the Oireachtas, December, 1979. For a critique of the Minister's scheme see, *It's Rough Justice With Legal Aid* published by the Free Legal Advice Centre (Dublin, May, 1980). The scheme has been amended on five occasions since December, 1979. See Ministerial Policy Directives Nos. 1 and 2 of 1980 (22nd July, 1980), No. 3 of 1981 (1st February, 1981), No. 4 of 1983 (3rd May, 1983) and No. 5 of 1986 (29th May, 1986). It is the scheme of Civil Legal Aid and Advice (Dublin Stationery Office, Prl. 1532) laid by the Minister for Justice before each House of the Oireachtas in May, 1983, as amended in May, 1986, which incorporates all the amendments made to the original scheme published in December, 1979. It is this scheme to which reference is made in the rest of this section. It should be noted that the amendments of May, 1986 were solely concerned with financial eligibility and the financial provisions relating to the assessment of means and contributions.
71. See Scheme of Civil Legal Aid and Advice, supra (May, 1983), p. 12, section 3.1.
72. *Ibid.*, p. 13, section 3.2.
73. For a discussion of Deserted Wife's Allowance/Benefit see p. 470 *post*.
74. For a discussion of Unmarried Mother's Allowance see p. 617 *post*.

ings within that jurisdiction to seek to have such child returned to Ireland pursuant to an order made by an Irish Court.

A legal aid certificate cannot be granted for legal representation before the courts unless the Legal Aid Board is of the opinion that the applicant

(a) has as a matter of law reasonable grounds for taking, defending or being a party to proceedings and

(b) satisfies the specified financial eligibility criteria;

(c) is reasonably likely to be successful in the proceedings, assuming that the facts put forward by him in relation to the proceedings are proved before the court, and

(d) there is no available method other than court proceedings, which is satisfactory (having regard to all the circumstances, including the cost to the applicant) by which the result which the applicant hopes to derive or a more satisfactory one, could be achieved.[75]

The Board must also be of the opinion, having regard to all the circumstances of the case, including the probable cost of taking or defending the proceedings, measured against the likely benefit to the applicant, that it is reasonable to grant a legal aid certificate[76] and that the granting of such certificate "would be in conformity with the purpose and terms of the scheme."[77] Provision is also made for the granting of emergency legal aid certificates in cases of urgency.[78] Many such certificates have been granted in practice in the family law area, for example, in cases in which wives have required immediate legal protection against violent husbands and also cases in which immediate orders have been required to prevent children from being removed from the jurisdiction of the Irish Courts.

A legal aid certificate may not be granted under the scheme "where the Board is of the opinion that the application is not being made in the sole interests of the applicant or of a member of his family or other person for whom he has special responsibility but is of a kind commonly described as a test case."[79] Therefore, a person who wishes to bring a constitutional action in the family law area may be excluded from assistance under the scheme. Moreover, the

---

75. See Scheme of Civil Legal Aid and Advice, *supra*, pp. 13–14, section 3.2.3.

76. *Ibid.*, at p. 14, section 3.2.3. The application of this provision has, in practice, given rise to particular difficulties in the family law area where fathers have sought legal aid certificates to obtain representation in custody proceedings. Determining that the mother is more likely to succeed in such proceedings the Legal Aid Board have refused to make legal aid available to impecunious fathers in a number of cases, in which on the principles enunciated in the *Airey* case, it is arguable legal aid should have been available.

77. *Ibid.*, at p. 13, section 3.2.3. The purpose of the scheme is stated (p. 6, section 1.2.1.) to be "to enable any person whose means are within the limits specified in the Scheme to obtain legal services in a situation where –

1. A reasonably prudent person whose means were outside those limits would be likely to seek such services at his own expense, if his means were such that the cost involved, while representing a financial obstacle to him, would not be such as to impose undue financial hardship, and

2. A competent Lawyer would be likely to advise him to obtain such services."

78. Part 4 of the Scheme provides the procedure for the granting and refusal of legal aid certificates. Section 4.6. is concerned with the granting of emergency certificates.

79. Scheme of Civil Legal Aid and Advice, *supra*, at p. 14, section 3.2.4(3). See also section 3.2.4(2). Section 3.2.6. provides – "Notwithstanding the other provisions of the Scheme the Board may grant a certificate where it is satisfied that the application is concerned with a matter in respect of which the State has a duty to provide civil legal aid under an International Instrument which specifically states that the State is obliged to provide such aid and the requirements, if any, to be satisfied by such an applicant in connection with the grant of a certificate will be determined on the basis of the requirements of the International Instrument."

Legal Aid Board cannot grant a legal aid certificate in relation to any proceedings taken in the court other than the lowest court having jurisdiction in relation
to those proceedings, unless an applicant is obliged by virtue of a decision taken
by an unaided litigant to take or defend proceedings in a higher court.[80] This
provision, if strictly applied, can result in the Legal Aid Board requiring that
maintenance proceedings brought on behalf of a dependent wife in need of
support be initiated in the District Court, even where there is a possibility that
if such proceedings were initiated in the Circuit Court, the wife could obtain a
maintenance order for her own support in excess of the sum of £100 per week
which is the maximum the District Court can presently order.

A person who is "aggrieved" by a decision of the Legal Aid Board may submit
further information to it and request that the decision made be reviewed. An
"aggrieved" person may also appeal against any decision made to an appeals
committee of the Board.[81]

However, the scheme is non-statutory and does not confer a right to free legal
assistance. Thus, if an application for legal assistance is unsuccessful, the applicant
has no right of appeal to the courts.[81a]

CRITICISMS AND SUGGESTED REFORMS

1. The establishment of a State funded scheme of civil legal aid and advice
through law centres has provided many people with access to legal assistance
who would not otherwise have been able to afford such assistance. The need for
the scheme in the area of family law has been clearly established. In the period
September, 1980 to December, 1984, a total of 12,113 people were assisted by
law centres in family law matters.[82] Approximately 75% of the cases handled
by the law centres in the years 1981 to 1984 inclusive fell into the family law
category. The scheme, however, has to date failed to provide the comprehensive
service necessary to make legal assistance available to all of those who require it
and who do not have the financial means to obtain it to resolve a family law
problem. It is not possible within these pages to detail all the defects in the
scheme. Some of these have already been referred to briefly. Many others have
been documented by one of the scheme's most frequent critics, the Legal Aid
Board that administers it.[83] The Board have stated the need

(i) To put the scheme on a proper statutory basis.[84]

(ii) To provide extra funding both for additional staff and to permit
expansion, noting that the suspension from time to time of legal services
to new clients has become an unavoidable feature of the service as demand
for services still outstrips supply and that the scheme is still "some distance"
from the goal of providing a nationwide Legal Aid Scheme.[85]

---

80. *Ibid.*, p. 19, section 4.3.6.
81. *Ibid.*, p. 22, section 4.7.
81a. If the Legal Aid Board acts contrary to natural or constitutional justice or in excess
of or without jurisdiction there may be a right to apply to the High Court to review a
decision made by the Board. See *The State (Hayes) v. The Criminal Injuries Compensation
Tribunal* [1982] 2 I.L.R.M. 210 (H.C.) in which orders made by the Criminal Injuries
Compensation Tribunal were held to be open to review by the High Court. This tribunal,
like the Legal Aid Board, was set up by direct executive act and not as a result of any
statutory provision or in pursuance of any direct statutory power. The Tribunal, in these
proceedings, however, accepted that its orders were open to such review. See also *E. v. E.*
[1982] 2 I.L.R.M. 497 (H.C.) discussed at p. 44 *ante*.
82. See the Annual Reports of the Legal Aid Board for the years 1980, 1981, 1982 and
1983/84.
83. For a comprehensive examination and critique of the Civil Legal Aid and Advice
Scheme see G. Whyte, "And Justice for Some" (1984) 6 D.U.L.J. 88.
84. See in particular the Legal Aid Board Report 1983/84 at pp. 2 and 8.
85. *Ibid.*, at pp. 2 and 6.

(iii) For a regular revision of the means test applied to determine eligibility for legal assistance, noting that there is a "recurring problem" of having to turn away applicants for whom the legal aid scheme was clearly intended, on the ground that they fail to satisfy the financial eligibility criteria.[86] This problem was temporarily resolved by changes made by the Minister for Justice in the means test provisions which came into effect on the 29th of May, 1986. This was, however, the first such revision since 1983 and the problem described by the Legal Aid Board will again occur unless the means test applicable is more regularly revised.

The Joint Oireachtas Committee on Marriage Breakdown in its Report published in April, 1985, called for a "fundamental reassessment of the Legal Aid Scheme and its means of operation" and were of the view that "the present structure is grossly inadequate . . . does not ensure equality of treatment for all (and) is quite inadequate to meet existing needs".[87] It has also been suggested that the scheme as currently constituted may not properly fulfil the obligations imposed on the State by the European Convention for the Protection of Human Rights and Fundamental Freedoms as articulated by the European Court in the *Airey* case.[88]

2. The law applicable to costs in family cases has developed piecemeal. Many of those who do not qualify for State legal aid and advice also cannot afford the legal fees that can be incurred if Circuit or High Court proceedings are required to resolve a family law problem. In the area of marital breakdown, wives are particularly vulnerable as husbands are still in the overwhelming majority of cases either the sole or principal income earner in the family. If an order for costs is obtained against a husband who refuses to comply with it, frequently in the family law area no practical action can be taken to enforce compliance. The provision whereby the husband of a wife who has no substantial means or assets of her own may be required to lodge costs in court or provide security for costs in High Court matrimonial proceedings[89] should be extended to apply to all family proceedings initiated in either the Circuit or High Court. Moreover, this provision should be amended so as to extend a discretionary power to both the Circuit and High Court to make such orders upon the application of either spouse, rendering it possible for a dependent husband to obtain such order against a wife in appropriate cases. The remedy of attachment of earnings should also be extended so as to provide a general enforcement mechanism in respect of costs ordered in all family matters.

3. The statutory provisions which permit jury actions in High Court matrimonial causes such as petitions for a decree of divorce *a mensa et thoro* (judicial separation) should be repealed. Juries serve no useful purpose in such proceedings and their presence can cause much unnecessary distress.

4. All family law proceedings should be automatically heard in private. The right to privacy should extend to domestic disputes that result in the invocation of a court's criminal jurisdiction, for example, proceedings in which a husband is prosecuted for assaulting his wife. Privacy, however, must not result in family

---

86. *Ibid.*, at pp. 2 and 13.
87. See Report of Joint Oireachtas Committee at p. 111.
88. See G. Whyte, "And Justice for Some", *supra*. See further *E. v. E.* [1982] 2 I.L.R.M. 497 (H.C.) discussed on p. 44 *ante*.
89. See p. 54 *ante*.

law matters being shrouded in secrecy and mystique. Both the legal profession and the general public are entitled to information as to the manner in which family law is administered, interpreted and applied by the courts. It is submitted that a central registry of family law judgements accessible to all persons wishing to obtain information about a family law matter should be established and that written court judgements delivered in family law cases should be made available for publication by the press. In order to protect the right of privacy of parties to proceedings, there should be deleted from all family judgements, the names and addresses of the parties and witnesses involved in a family law case and any other details which might result in the parties being identified.

Whether the press and other members of the media should be permitted to be present and report evidence given in family proceedings, provided the anonymity of the parties is preserved, is a matter that needs to be examined. Whereas their presence in certain types of proceedings may be harmful, their exclusion from all family proceedings may be equally detrimental in so far as it inhibits or prevents informed public discussion of the manner in which the law is administered and of the effect it has on the lives of those who look to it for assistance. Referring to this issue, the Joint Oireachtas Committee in its Report on Marriage Breakdown was of the opinion that in camera hearings "do have a detrimental effect" in that "public scrutiny is the natural enemy of arbitrariness and injustice in a legal system" and that "our courts, while hearing family cases, have operated without this salutary check."[90]

5. In the area of family law the type of forum within which and the way that substantive rules are administered can have as far reaching an effect on the lives of people as the content of the rules themselves. The existing institutions and structures by which family legislation is administered can be criticised on a number of grounds. These include:

(a) Upon a family dispute occurring which cannot be solved by the parties by themselves or with legal assistance, no independent nationwide structure exists to help those in dispute to resolve their differences by agreement as an alternative to court proceedings. The absence of an accessible alternative mechanism results in many spouses, upon marital breakdown occurring, commencing court proceedings against each other who would not have to do so if some alternative procedure was available to afford assistance to them.[90a]

(b) The District Court, the Circuit Court and the High Court exercise both an overlapping and fragmented jurisdiction to hear and determine family cases while the Circuit Court, the High Court and the Supreme Court also exercise an appellate jurisdiction. This multiplicity of court jurisdiction results in a large number of judges and justices hearing and determining family matters and, in practice, has resulted in a lack of uniformity in approach and decision making. The disparity in the manner in which similar cases are heard and determined in both original and appellate proceedings can result in considerable injustice, the outcome of many cases being too dependent on the subjective approach of the member or members of the judiciary before whom the cases are heard.[91]

---

90. See the Report of the Joint Oireachtas Committee at p. 110.
90a. A pilot mediation scheme set up under the auspices of the Department of Justice opened in Dublin in July 1986. It can be found on the 5th Floor, Block 6, Irish Life Centre, Dublin 1. (Phone Nos. 728697 and 728708.)
91. *Ibid.*, at p. 106.

(c) The manner in which jurisdiction to hear different types of family proceedings is distributed throughout the juridicial hierarchy is unsatisfactory and lacking in logic. For example, if maintenance proceedings are initiated by a wife in either the District or Circuit Court under the Family Law . . . Act, 1976, and the husband alleges that he is not liable to maintain the wife because their marriage is a nullity, neither of the lower courts possess jurisdiction to hear nullity proceedings and the husband must initiate a separate nullity action in the High Court. Further, if barring proceedings are initiated by a wife in the District Court under the Family Law (Protection of Spouses & Children) Act, 1981, and if the husband defending such application wishes to obtain a court order that the home be sold, he cannot seek such an order in the District Court and must issue separate proceedings in either the Circuit or High Court.

Family conflicts, particularly those that arise as a consequence of marital breakdown, frequently require legal solution to a variety of issues. For example, disputes concerning maintenance, the family home and other property, the right to live apart, guardianship and custody of children, may all need to be determined. At present each spouse may seek legal remedies to deal with some of these issues in different courts and as a result each matter may be judicially examined and determined in isolation rather than as part of one family controversy. This not only adds to the stress of family proceedings but can result in an unnecessary duplication of legal costs.

(d) In exercising jurisdiction over family actions, the courts do not always have to give a simple legalistic determination between opposing rights and duties but also, in many cases, have to decide what order should be made so as to ensure that the welfare of a particular individual is properly protected. This is particularly the case when a court is exercising its jurisdiction over children. At present, the judiciary receive no specialist training in the skills required to deal with family cases and there is no legal obligation imposed on any court to obtain an independent welfare report before finally resolving a dispute concerning the guardianship, custody or upbringing of children. Whilst limited use is made mainly by the District Court of the Probation and Welfare Service for this purpose,[92] the Report of the Joint Oireachtas Committee on Marriage Breakdown states that "one of the most disturbing aspects of the present court structure for

---

92. There is no legislative provision relating to the use of the Probation & Welfare Service in family cases. However, limited use has been made of it by the courts as can be seen from the following table derived from the annual reports of the Probation & Welfare Service:

Reports prepared for the Courts in relation to Family Law Matters

Year	In proceedings initiated for maintenance and barring orders.	In proceedings initiated under Guardianship of Infants Act, 1964.
1980	191	–
1981	186	12
1982	116	11
1983	85	8

Use of the service in maintenance and barring proceedings is, in practice, largely confined to the District Court. The Report for 1980 notes that during that year the service offered support and advice in some cases of access, custody of children and other related matters that came before the High Court. It is assumed that the 1981 statistic relating to proceedings initiated under the 1964 Act also applies to High Court proceedings as the District Court did not acquire jurisdiction to make orders under the Act of 1964 until the 12th of May, 1982, following the coming into force of the Courts Act, 1981.

The above information is derived from the Reports on Probation and Welfare Service for the years 1980, 1981, 1982 and 1983. No later reports had been published as at the 1st of September, 1986.

dealing with family cases is the total lack of any proper in-court welfare service."
Noting that "the majority of family cases are heard without the benefit of any
professional evidence and without any investigation of family circumstances by
an independent agency" the committee states "decisions made in such a vacuum
are much more likely to be unsatisfactory; the subjective evidence of both
spouses is a very unreliable basis on which to decide the future of a family."[93]

(e)   The majority of court buildings in which family cases are heard lack
proper basic facilities. Referring to this, the Joint Oireachtas Committee state
"at the moment many family cases are heard in inadequate and unsuitable
accommodation. Hearings take place in the same building as ordinary cases, the
difference being that the court is cleared of members of the general public. Some
judges and justices hear family cases in their chambers, an indication in itself of
the unsuitable nature of the accommodation available. Often there are no suitable
consultation facilities and parties end up seeing their solicitor in the street or in
the foyer of the court."[94]

(f)   The type of documentation necessary to initiate family proceedings
varies from court to court and can also vary within a single court structure
depending on the remedy sought. For example, to initiate Circuit Court proceedings on behalf of a wife seeking maintenance for her support and for the
support of dependent children and also seeking a decree of divorce *a mensa et
thoro*, two separate sets of initiating documentation must be used in relation to
which different procedural steps have to be taken.[95]

The need for a radical restructuring of the institutions and procedures by
which family legislation is administered has been asserted by the Joint Oireachtas
Committee. Dealing with the area of marital breakdown, the Committee states
that the "primary emphasis in dealing with marriage problems should be to
assist the parties to reach a resolution of their difficulties by agreement."[96] It
proposes the establishment of a nationwide "independent mediation service" to

---

The relevant statistics are to be found on page 19 of each of the first three reports
and on page 51 of the 1983 Report. See also p. 13 of the 1980 Report, p. 12 of the Reports
of 1981 and 1982 and p. 42 of the 1983 Report.

The limited use made of the Probation & Welfare Service by the District Court in family
cases can be seen from the following statistics of the number of relevant cases initiated in
the District Court in the years to which reference is made above.

Number of District Court Family Proceedings Initiated

Year ending 31 July	Maintenance proceedings	Barring proceedings	Guardianship of Infants Act proceedings
1980	1,842	1,917	
1981	2,095	2,225	
1982*	1,812	2,428	Not available
1983*	872	1,697	110
1984	2,160	3,478	605

*1982-83 figures are reduced due to District Court Clerks going on strike following on
the coming into force of the Courts Act, 1981, on the 12th of May, 1982. It should be
noted also that the District Court did not obtain a jurisdiction under the Guardianship of
Infants Act, 1964, until the 12th of May, 1982 when the aforesaid Act came into operation.
See further Appendix C.

93. See Report of Joint Oireachtas Committee at p. 107.

94. *Ibid.*, at p. 108. See also the *Task Force on Child Care Services: Final Report*
(Stationery Office, Dublin, September 1980) at p. 248.

95. *Ibid.*, at p. 109.

96. *Ibid.*, at p. 105.

which people would have direct access and the cost of which would be borne by the State.[97] Such service would "interact with other organisations, both statutory and voluntary" so that "persons attending marriage counselling who came to the conclusion that they wished to separate could be ... referred to the mediation service before relations between them deteriorate further" and "if during mediation meetings a prospect of reconciliation emerges" the parties could be referred to a marriage counselling service.[98] So as to ensure that following its establishment all of those who could be assisted by such a service are made aware of it, the Committee also propose that the service should be widely publicised and that there should be a statutory obligation imposed on solicitors to inform a client of the existence and advantages of using the mediation service, rather than going to court, upon a solicitor being first instructed to represent a person with a marital difficulty. It also states that originating documents in all family proceedings should inform the parties involved in such proceedings about the availability of a mediation service.[99]

Use of the mediation service would be voluntary[100] and open to spouses not involved in legal proceedings.[101] The purpose of such a service, the Committee emphasise, is not to force a reconciliation between estranged spouses but is "to minimise the stress and bitterness resulting from a broken marriage and to assist couples to deal with the consequences of breakdown."[102] It would also provide the basis for "continued interaction and co-operation"[103] where necessary after separation, for example, where there are minor children of a marriage and a couple, as parents of their children, will continue to be in regular contact with each other for many years after separating so as to make arrangements for and to implement joint decisions made relating to their children.

It is envisaged that the proposed mediation service would assist estranged spouses to reach agreement on all matters arising from the breakdown of their marriage that need to be resolved, including all disputes concerning children, family finances and property.[104]

The Oireachtas Committee acknowledge that "no matter how successful and attractive ... a mediation service may be, it is unfortunately inevitable that a certain proportion of cases will still require an adjudication."[105] Stating the need for the introduction of structures and procedures which keep bitterness and dispute to a minimum, the Committee proposes the establishment of a

---

97. *Ibid.*, at pp. 97, 98 and 101.
98. *Ibid.*, at p. 98.
99. *Ibid.*, at pp. 101 and 102.
100. *Ibid.*, at p. 101. See also the Law Reform Commission Report on Divorce *a Mensa et Thoro* and Related Matters (L.R.C. No. 8–1983) at p. 63 where the Commission states that "if proper counselling services are available whether provided by private agencies or the State, it could be made a necessary preliminary to the institution of court (matrimonial) proceedings that recourse be had by the spouses to those services. We appreciate that there is a substantial body of opinion opposed to any degree of compulsion in relation to counselling and conciliation on the basis that it is ineffective but we consider that there is some merit in investigating the approach we have tentatively recommended possibly on a pilot and experimental basis." Referring to this issue, the Oireachtas Committee states (p. 101 of their report) that "coercion would appear to be contrary to the concept of mediation. As one commentator has noted: 'the first requirement for effective conciliation is the voluntary participation of bóth parties'.* To force persons to go through a meaningless charade would be likely to undermine the whole basis and effectiveness of a mediation service."

*Lisa Parkinson, 'Bristol Court's Conciliation Service' (1982) 12 Fam. Law 13.
101. *Ibid.*, at p. 97.
102. *Ibid.*, at p. 94.
103. *Ibid.*
104. *Ibid.*, at pp. 98–99. A pilot mediation scheme along the lines recommended by the Oireachtas Committee was opened in Dublin in July, 1986. See footnote 90a *ante*.
105. *Ibid.*, at p. 105.

unified family court or family tribunal "with full and exclusive power to deal with all types of family cases."[106] It states that the main objective of a family court should be

"— To provide a sympathetic means for the taking of decisions in regard to family disputes, which causes the minimum disruption and upset for the members of a family.

— To safeguard the welfare of children affected by marriage breakdown or family difficulties.

— To reduce the adversarial element inherent in the resolution of family disputes.

— To provide a uniform approach in the adjudication of family disputes.

— To minimise the costs involved in family proceedings."[107]

The Committee proposes that the family court "should be staffed with a sufficient number of judges to ensure that family cases are heard fully and speedily at locations which are reasonably convenient to the parties" and which have "proper accommodation".[108] The need to modify the manner in which such cases are heard and to reduce "the formal adversarial nature of such proceedings" in so far as that is possible is also acknowledged, the Committee expressing the opinion there should be "a greater degree of informality and flexibility" and that judges should play "a more inquisitorial role" in the hearing

---

106. *Ibid.*, at p. 106. See also p. 105. See also the *Report of the Review Committee on Adoption Services* (Stationery Office, Dublin, May, 1984), p. 69 where the Committee recommend the establishment of an Adoption Court which could "be expanded to deal with other family matters if and when a system of family courts is devised." See also the *Task Force on Child Care Services: Final Report, supra*, Supplementary Report at p. 348 *et seq* where the authors recommend the provision of a new system of children's courts. The recommendations made by the majority of the Task Force are less radical, see the main report at p. 247 *et seq*.
  In referring to the establishment of a family court, the Oireachtas Committee states that "under the present constitutional structure, the Committee has been advised that to set up such a body with full and exclusive powers, it is necessary that it should form part of the High Court." On this issue see also the *Report of the Review Committee on Adoption Services, supra*, at p. 69; J.P. Casey, "The Judicial Power Under Irish Constitutional Law" (1975) 24 I.C.L.Q. 305; G.W. Hogan, "Constitutional Aspects of the Distribution and Organisation of Court Business" (1984) 6 D.U.L.J. 40; D.G. Morgan, *Constitutional Law of Ireland* (Round Hall Press, Dublin, 1985) at pp. 192–194. The necessity for a family court to form part of the High Court is now open to question having regard to the judgement of the Supreme Court in *Tormey v. Ireland* [1985] 5 I.L.R.M. 375 (S.C.) which was delivered after the Oireachtas Committee concluded its deliberations. See p. 43 *ante*. See further the Report of a Working Party on Women's Affairs and Family Law Reform, *Irish Women: Agenda for Practical Action* (Stationery Office, Dublin, 1985) which stated (at p. 291) that "the question of family courts is of very great significance and deserves special consideration" and "is an issue involving constitutional, social and economic questions which do not lend themselves to easy answers." This section of the report, which is a product of the Department of Justice, suggested that the establishment of such a court should be examined by the Law Reform Commission or by a separate Department of Justice Committee. The Law Reform Commission itself in its published "First Programme for Examination of Certain Branches of the Law with a View to their Reform (Dublin, January, 1977) stated at p. 9 that "in examining the various aspects of family law the Commission will consider the question of the best type of judicial or court structure or structures appropriate to deal with the different matters which fall under the general heading of family law." No working paper or report has to date been published by the Law Reform Commission on this issue. See further "Statement on Government's Intentions with regard to Marriage, Separation and Divorce" first published by the Department of Justice (Dublin, April, 1987) discussed at the end of this chapter.
107. See the Report of the Joint Oireachtas Committee at pp. 105–106.
108. *Ibid.*, at pp. 107, 108.

of family cases.[109] The Committee also states that there is a need to provide simplified standard documentation for the initiation of family proceedings.[110]

The need to ensure that judges appointed to a family court or tribunal have the required expertise and temperament is emphasised. The Committee states that "judges should be appointed solely to hear family cases and different criteria should be applied in selecting judges for the purpose. Consideration should be given to the capacity of a potential judge to carry out the objectives of a new tribunal, to have a real understanding of the types of difficulties with which he or she is dealing and in particular to hear such cases in a compassionate and sympathetic way". The need to "broaden" the "present statutory requirement to become a judge" and the need to provide "suitable training . . . to give both judges and lawyers who regularly deal with family law matters a proper insight into the social and psychological aspects of the type of cases that occur" is also stated.[111]

The Committee also proposes that there should be a "comprehensive welfare service" staffed by social workers attached to the new court or tribunal and that a member of the service should be present in court during the hearing of all family cases.[112] The tasks of such a service should be to

(a) carry out investigations into family circumstances on behalf of the court,

(b) report to the court on family circumstances,

(c) arrange for the provision of further professional advice, such as the assessment of children by a child psychiatrist or psychologist,

(d) help the parties with the practical difficulties resulting from their marital problems such as child care and finance,

---

109. *Ibid.*, at p. 110. See the Australian Family Law Act, 1975, Sect. 97 under which the traditional court trappings and ceremonial are reduced to a minimum in the family court established by the Act. Neither judge nor counsel are to wear wigs or robes in court and there is a general requirement that the court shall proceed without undue formality and that proceedings are not to be protracted. See H.A. Finlay, *Family Law in Australia*, 3rd ed. (Butterworths 1983), p. 24 *et seq*. See also Law Reform Commission Report No. 8, *supra*, at p. 62.

110. *Ibid.*, at p. 110.

111. *Ibid.*, at p. 107. See Australian Family Law Act, 1975, Sect. 22, which specifically provides for a person to be appointed as a judge of the family court; in addition to having legal training, he must "by reason of training, experience and personality" be "a suitable person to deal with matters of family law". See also the Report of the Committee on Non-Accidental Injury to Children (Stationery Office, Dublin, 1976) which recommended that judges dealing with children "should have some special training in the field of child care" (p. 21 of the report). The Task Force Supplementary Report, *supra*, at p. 349 recommended that "the children's courts should be headed by a specially qualified professional children's judge" stating that the children's judges should be recruited "from among qualified barristers and solicitors with at least 5 years practical experience" and that "their appointment should be conditional on their successfully completing an appropriate course of studies and practical experience designed to equip them for the specialised work" in which a children's court would be engaged. The main report in also recommending the establishment of a Children's Court stated that "In selecting a justice . . . regard should be had to . . . training and experience" and that justices of the District Court appointed to the Children's Court "should be encouraged and facilitated to acquire knowledge and training necessary for dealing with problems involving children" (*supra* at p. 247).

The Report of the Review Committee on Adoption Services, *supra*, at p. 70 in proposing the establishment of an adoption court stated the judge of such "new court should be specifically appointed for the purpose" and suggested that the requirements of Sect. 22 of the Australian Family Law Act provided a guideline that "might be used here" in the appointment of a judge to such court. See further *Irish Women: Agenda for Practical Action, supra*, at pp. 293–294.

112. Report of Joint Oireachtas Committee at p. 107.

(e) provide referrals to other agencies, such as mediation and suitable counselling, and

(f) provide support and assistance for the members of the family, especially children, during and after the determination of the proceedings.[113]

The court welfare service as proposed would be entirely separate from and independent of the mediation service. Whereas the primary function of the welfare service would be to assist the family tribunal in the adjudication process and to provide social supports for those who come before the tribunal, the primary function of the mediation service would be to obviate the necessity for any court hearing or adjudication and to assist estranged spouses in resolving their own difficulties. All communications between spouses in the context of mediation, the Committee state "must be privileged" and a "mediator should not be a competent or compellable witness in any family proceedings."[114] Communications to a court welfare officer would not be so privileged. It is envisaged, however, that there would be some interaction between the family court and the mediation service in that it is proposed that the court itself should be empowered to refer a couple to the mediation service[115] and that "a simple and inexpensive procedure should exist" to allow parties who have reached agreement through mediation to have such agreement "noted and accepted by the family tribunal."[116]

Government Intentions: In April, 1986, when publishing the Tenth Amendment of the Constitution Bill, 1986, for the holding of a referendum on the divorce issue the Government, in a Statement of its Intentions "with regard to Marriage, Separation and Divorce" stated that judicial separations "in future" will be "dealt with by a family court presided over by one of a number of judges of the Circuit Court specially assigned for the purpose" and that "its procedures will be less formal and less confrontational than the procedures that exist at present."[117] It also stated that "appeals from the Family Court will be heard in the High Court."[118]

In the first instance it was stated that the Family Court will "enquire into whether counselling services have been or should be availed of by the spouses to assist them in attempting a reconcilliaton and will have power to adjourn the proceedings so that recourse may be had to these services where it considers it necessary or appropriate to do so."[119] The Statement further referred to the provision of a "mediation process"[120] designed to secure agreement between

113. *Ibid.*, at pp. 107–108.
114. *Ibid.*, at p. 103.
115. *Ibid.*, at p. 102.
116. *Ibid.*, at p. 103. The provisions contained in Sect. 8 of the Family Law . . . Act, 1976, could be adapted for this purpose. See p. 211 *post*.
117. "Statement" at p. 2. See also revised "Statement" (Department of Justice, June, 1986) at p. 7.
118. *Ibid.* The "Statement" did not clarify whether any member or members of the High Court would be newly appointed or "specially assigned" to determine such appeals.
119. See revised "Statement" (June, 1986) at p. 7. It states that "it is proposed that the counselling process be undertaken by recognised counselling agencies" and stated that "three such bodies exist at present which will be invited to undertake this work" – The Catholic Marriage Advisory Council of Ireland, The Marriage Counselling Service and the Marriage & Family Institute" – see further footnote 121. See also original "Statement" (April, 1986) at p. 2.
120. There was a terminological confusion in the original "Statement" published in April, 1986, in that the Marriage Guidance Counselling Services were wrongly referred to as "Mediation Services". This reference is changed to "Counselling Services" in the revised "Statement". The original "Statement" referred to a "conciliation process" and it was

estranged spouses "in a non-confrontational manner" on terms of separation, such a process to be undertaken by "the existing voluntary bodies[121] or should these bodies prefer not to undertake this mediation work on behalf of the court, through a mediation service attached to the court itself."[122] The Statement also envisaged that the proposed family court would exercise a jurisdiction to make separation agreements a rule of court,[123] to hear divorce applications and to determine applications to marry of under age persons or from persons seeking to abridge a newly proposed minimum notice period for marriage.[124]

As the Government's Statement of Intent proposed that in determining applications for a judicial separation or a divorce "questions relating to maintenance, custody of children and property owned by the spouses, including the family home" will all come under the scrutiny of the court,[125] it is assumed that a comprehensive jurisdiction in matrimonial matters will be conferred on the proposed family court.[126] At the time of writing, however, no statement has been made clarifying whether all of the High Court's current matrimonial jurisdiction is to be transferred to such court or as to whether the District Court is to continue to exercise its current limited jurisdiction. The arrangements that will be made so as to enable the newly proposed family court to exercise its jurisdiction separate and apart from the current Circuit Court structure have also not been fully clarified. It is also not certain whether the Government intends to fully implement the proposals for the establishment of a family court contained in the Joint Oireachtas Committee's Report (e.g., is the welfare service proposed

---

clear that the conciliation process referred to in the "Statement" was based on the Joint Oireachtas Committee's concept of a mediation service. "Mediation Services" instead of "Conciliation Services" are referred to in the revised "Statement". See "Statement" (April, 1986) at p. 2 and revised "Statement" (June, 1986) at p. 7.

121. The existing bodies that the Government identified in this context were the same as those referred to in the context of marriage counselling services, that is, the Catholic Marriage Advisory Council of Ireland set up by the Roman Catholic Church in Ireland in the 1960s which has its principal office in Harcourt Street in Dublin, the Marriage Counselling Service which is a non-denominational service with its headquarters at 24 Grafton Street, Dublin 2 and the Marriage & Family Institute which is also a non-denominational service based at 5 Clare Street, Dublin 2. Only the latter body currently works in the area of mediation, the two former bodies being concerned with marriage counselling. The Advisory Council currently provides a network of services throughout the country whilst the Marriage Counselling Service provides services only in Dublin and Cork. The Marriage & Family Institute operates in Dublin only.

122. "Statement" (June, 1986) at p. 7. See also "Statement" (April, 1986) at p. 2.

123. See p. 211 *post*.

124. See "Statement" (April, 1986) at p. 5 and revised "Statement" (June, 1986) at p. 6.

125. See "Statement" (April, 1986) at p. 4 and revised "Statement" June, 1986 at p. 10.

126. For a selection of additional reading material on family courts and mediation/concilliation services see H.A. Finlay, *Family Law in Australia, supra*, chap. 1; P.E. Nygh, *Guide to the Family Law Act, 1975* (Butterworths - Sydney, 1975) chap. 3; K. Enderby, "The Family Law Act, 1975" (1975) 49 A.L.J. 477; J. Wade, "The Family Court of Australia and Informality in Court Procedure" (1978) 27 I.C.L.Q. 820; The Law Reform Commission of Canada, *The Family Court* (Working Paper No. 1, January, 1974); *The Report of the Committee on One Parent Families (The Finer Report)* 1974 H.M.S.O. Cmnd. 5629, Sects. 13 & 14; J. Eekelaar & S.N. Katz, *The Resolution of Family Conflict — Comparative Legal Perspectives* (Butterworths, Toronto, 1984); L. Parkinson, *Conciliation in Separation and Divorce* (Croom Helm Ltd., Kent, 1986); J. Eekelaar, *Family Law & Social Policy*, 2nd ed. (Weidenfeld & Nicolson, London, 1984) pp. 53–63. See also A. Samuels, "Family Courts – the Future" (1972) 122 N.L.J. 133 E.J. Griew, "Marital Reconciliation – Contexts and Meanings" (1972) 30 C.L.J. 294; A.H. Manchester, "Reform and the Family Court" (1975) 125 N.L.J. 984; A.H. Manchester & J.M. Whetton, "Marital Conciliation in England and Wales" (1974) 23 I.C.L.Q. 339; M.M. Mayo, "Responsibility of the Law in Relation to Family Stability" (1976) 25 I.C.L.Q. 409; P.T. Horgan, "Family Court – The Need and the Obstacles" (1976) 27 N.I.L.Q. 120; The Council for Social Welfare (a Committee of the Catholic Bishops Conference) – Statement on Family Law Reform, chaps. 3 & 8; C.R. Cripps, "A Family Court for England" (1984) 14 Fam. Law 71; Irish Bishops' Pastoral, *Love is for Life* (Veritas Publications, 1985) Part IV.

by the Committee to be established) or whether the court will exercise jurisdiction to determine other types of family law litigation, such as child care,
adoption or affiliation proceedings.

CHAPTER 3

THE ENGAGEMENT

INTRODUCTION

The majority of couples become engaged to marry before they go through a marriage ceremony. An exchange of promises to marry at common law constituted a legally binding contract breach of which rendered the party responsible liable to be sued for damages in an action for breach of promise to marry.[1] The desirability of preserving such an action as an instrument of social policy was questionable in that it could be used to pressurise people into marriages they would not otherwise enter into and which, as a consequence, were potentially unstable. The engagement period is seen by many as affording to a couple some time not only to prepare for marriage but also to give final consideration to the full implications and consequences of their agreement to marry and to the viability of their interpersonal relationship. The opportunity the engagement period afforded for a change of mind prior to the exchange of marriage vows was offset by the pressure to marry that could be imposed by the threat of an action for breach of promise. Recognising that the continued existence of the action for breach of promise undermined the usefulness of the engagement period, the Law Reform Commission in 1978 recommended its abolition.[2] This recommendation was implemented by the Oireachtas upon the enactment of the Family Law Act, 1981, section 2(1) of which states that:

> "An agreement between two persons to marry one another, whether entered into before or after the passing of this Act, shall not under the law of the State have effect as a contract and no action shall be brought in the State for breach of such an agreement, whatever the law applicable to the agreement."

Consequently, no action for breach of promise can be brought before the Irish courts upon the termination of an agreement to marry even if the couple entered into such an agreement outside the jurisdiction of the Irish courts. Moreover, even if an agreement to marry was entered into prior to the coming into force of the Act on the 23rd of June, 1981, no proceedings could be initiated after that date for breach of such agreement upon it being terminated by either party.[3]

In abolishing the action for breach of promise, the Act of 1981 recognised that various property and financial disputes may arise following upon the termination of an engagement, not only between the formerly engaged couple but

---

1. See A.J. Shatter, *Family Law in the Republic of Ireland*, 2nd ed. 1981, Chapter 3.
2. See The Law Reform Commission: The Law relating to Breach of Promise of Marriage (Working Paper no. 4, November 1978) and First Report on Family Law (March 1981), in particular pp. 21–24. See also The Episcopal Council for Social Welfare (a committee of the Catholic Bishops Conference): Statement on Family Law (1974), p. 7.
3. Section 2(2) provided that subsection (1) was not to have effect in relation to any action commenced before the passing of the Act.

also involving third parties. Accordingly, it prescribes the substantive law applicable to the resolution of such disputes and also extends to the parties of a broken engagement the right to use the same legal procedures for the resolution of proprietary disputes between themselves as may be availed of by a married couple. It is these provisions of the Family Law Act, 1981, which are discussed in the following pages. It should be noted, however, prior to embarking on this discussion that proceedings to enforce a right conferred by the Act of 1981 arising out of the termination of an engagement to marry must be commenced within 3 years of such termination by either party to the agreement or, where the Act extends a right of action to a third party, by such third party. No such proceedings can be commenced after the expiration of the three year period.[4]

THE RESOLUTION OF PROPRIETARY AND FINANCIAL DISPUTES

A couple who become engaged and plan to marry will normally make arrangements for their future accommodation. This may involve the acquisition of rented accommodation or the purchase of a home or the expenditure of money on the renovation, repair and re-decoration of a home which prior to the engagement was already owned by or in the possession of one of the parties to the engagement. Upon the termination of their engagement a dispute may arise as to the parties' respective proprietary rights in any such home and section 5 of the Act of 1981 permits a party to "an agreement to marry which is terminated" to institute proceedings against the other party under section 12 of the Married Women's Status Act, 1957, for the determination of

> "Any dispute between them or claim by one of them, in relation to property in which either or both had a beneficial interest while the agreement (to marry) was in force."[5]

Until 1981, section 12 of the Act of 1957 could only be utilised to resolve proprietary disputes between married couples.

Under this provision proprietary disputes relating not only to a home but also to any other property, real or personal, in which either party had a beneficial interest during the engagement period can be determined. Moreover, the section expressly provides that in the determination of any such disputes

> "The rules of law relating to the rights of spouses in relation to property in which either or both of them has or have a beneficial interest shall apply"

as if the parties to the terminated agreement were married.[6]

In order for section 5 to apply there must be an agreement to marry which has been "terminated" and at least one of the parties must have had a beneficial interest in the disputed property while the agreement was in force. Thus, the section may apply to the resolution of a proprietary dispute between a couple who were engaged but cannot apply to the resolution of a proprietary dispute between a couple who co-habited but were never engaged.[7] It also cannot be

---

4. Section 9.
5. Section 5(2).
6. Section 5(1). For a full discussion of section 12 of the Married Women's Status Act, 1957, and the law applicable to the resolution of proprietary disputes between spouses, see Chapter 15.
7. Proprietary disputes between co-habitees can be litigated by the bringing of declaratory or other proceedings. See p. 619 *post*.

used to resolve a dispute as to the ownership of property acquired by a party subsequent to the termination of an agreement to marry or disposed of by a party prior to a couple agreeing to marry.

The main advantage of section 5 is that it affords to formerly engaged couples the benefit of the speedier summary procedure provided by section 12 of the Married Women's Status Act, 1957, for the resolution of proprietary disputes. Moreover, by applying to the resolution of such disputes the legal principles applicable to the resolution of proprietary disputes between husband and wife, it confirms that the doctrine of advancement as it applies to spouses may apply to property purchased by a man with his own money and conveyed by him to his fiancée, so as to give rise to the legal presumption that he intended that such property be owned by her.[8] No such presumption arises in respect of property purchased by a male co-habitee and conveyed by him to a woman to whom he is not engaged and with whom he is co-habiting.[9]

A difficulty relating to section 5 which also arises in the context of other provisions of the Act is that it prescribes no rules or specific evidential requirements as to how it may be established in court proceedings that an "agreement to marry" existed for cases in which the existence of such an agreement is disputed. As the section only applies to a claim to a beneficial interest which either party had in property during the currency of an agreement to marry, it may be important to ascertain when an arrangement to marry became an agreement for the purposes of the Act. For example, the status of a secret, informal or unofficial engagement is unclear.

In order to recover damages in an action for breach of promise to marry, the testimony of the plaintiff that the defendant had agreed to marry, had to be corroborated by some other material evidence supporting the making of such promise. While it is clear that if a dispute arises under the Act of 1981, as to whether a couple ever agreed to marry, a court faced with two conflicting accounts of the couple's relationship will require some corroborative evidence to establish the existence of an agreement to marry, such evidence is not an essential pre-requisite to establish the existence of the necessary agreement. In the event of the existence of an agreement to marry being in dispute, such evidence will merely form part of the normal proofs such as are required in contested court proceedings in which a fundamental factual allegation is in dispute and has to be determined.[10]

---

8. See *Moate v. Moate* [1948] 2 All E.R. 486 from which it appears that the presumption of advancement applies to property purchased by a man and placed in his fiancée's name even prior to the enactment of the Act of 1981. See also the Law Reform Commission: First Report on Family Law, *supra*, at p. 20 where the commission notes that as between spouses "the presumption appears to have applied only where a husband made the purchase and it may well involve discrimination proscribed by the Constitution." Since the publication of the report the courts have continued to apply the presumption and no judgement has been delivered suggesting that its continued application is incompatible with the Constitution.

9. See p. 619 *post*. It has been suggested that section 5(1) could have wider implications and have the effect of applying the provisions of the Family Home Protection Act, 1976, and the Succession Act, 1965, to property owned by parties during the period of their engagement. See A. Power, "The Family Law Act, 1981 – Yet Another Pandora's Box" (1985) 79 *Gazette of the Incorporated Law Society of Ireland* 169. It is submitted that such an interpretation of this section is not warranted. See R. O'Donnell, "Conveyancing and the Family Home" (April 1983) S.Y.S. Lecture no. 146 in particular appendix F. See also pp. 29–46 where the author queries whether section 5(1) has any substantive effect of any nature whatsoever and considers in detail the conveyancing implications of the section.

10. In relation to the action for breach of promise, see the Evidence (Further Amendment) Act, 1869, section 2. See further *Bessela v. Stern* (1877) 2 C.P.D. 265 (C.A.); *O'Shea*

ENGAGEMENT RINGS AND GIFTS

It is not unusual that a couple who contemplate marriage give gifts to each other and that either one or both of them receive gifts from relations and other third parties relating to their intended marriage. The traditional gift given by a man to his future wife during such period is the engagement ring. At common law if a man unjustifiably terminated an engagement he could not require his fiancée to return the engagement ring, while he could do so if she terminated the engagement or if it was terminated by mutual consent.[11] Whether or not a party to a broken engagement could reclaim other gifts given during the engagement period depended on whether such gifts were conditional on the marriage taking place. Moreover, it was uncertain as to whether a party who was regarded as at fault for the breakup of an engagement could recover gifts given by him/her even if they were so conditional.

The Law Reform Commission recommended that "the law should remove any consideration of fault from the determination of whether gifts between parties to an intended marriage were returnable" and that the rules applicable to gifts generally should apply to engagement rings.[12] Section 4 of the Act of 1981 implemented this recommendation and has rendered the question of fault irrelevant. It provides that where a party to an agreement to marry makes a gift of property (including an engagement ring) to the other party, it shall be presumed, in the absence of evidence to the contrary, that the gift

(a) was given subject to the condition that it should be returned at the request of the donor or his personal representative if the marriage does not take place for any reason other than the death of the donor, or

(b) was given unconditionally, if the marriage does not take place on account of the death of the donor.

Thus, if a party terminates an engagement it is presumed that it was intended that the donor of the gift, or his personal representative, if the donor subsequently dies, is entitled to recover the gift from the party who received it. If, however, the engagement is terminated due to the death of the donor, it is presumed that it was intended that upon such an event occurring the person who received the gift would retain it. If there is evidence available of an intention contrary to that presumed such evidence may be given so as to rebut the presumption that arises under this section.

It should be noted that the presumption under (a) only applies to gifts given after parties have become engaged and does not apply to gifts given by one to the other prior to an engagement or after an engagement has been terminated. Thus, if a gift is given by one person to another to create an impression or by way of an introduction in the hope that the recipient of the gift will ultimately agree to marry the donor at some future date, if the donor does not succeed in his ambitions neither the common law nor section 4 of the Act of 1981 provides him with any help to recover any gift so given. Similarly, if a party to a

---

v. Roche [1952] 18 Ir. Jur. Rep. 11 (Circ. Ct.) in which the judge remarked on the similarity of the corroboration required in a breach of promise action to that required by the Illegitimate Children (Affiliation Orders) Act, 1931. See also *Cleeland v. M'Cune* (1908) 42 I.L.T.R. 201 (C.A.); *Wiedmann v. Walpole* [1891] 2 Q.B. 534 (C.A.); *Hickey v. Campion* (1872) I.R. 6 C.L. 557 (Exch); *Wilcox v. Gotfrey* (1872) 26 L.T. 48 (Ct. of Exch.).

11. *Jacobs v. Davis* [1917] 2 K.B. 532 (K.B.D.); *Cohen v. Sellar* [1926] 1 K.B. 536 (K.B.D.).

12. Law Reform Commission: The Law Relating to Breach of Promise to Marry, *supra* at p. 42.

broken engagement gives a present to his ex-fiancée in the hope of persuading her to resume their relationship and to marry him, he has no right to reclaim any gift so given upon failing to achieve his aspiration.

Section 3 of the Act of 1981 is concerned with wedding gifts given to engaged couples by third parties. It provides that any property given by a third party "as a wedding gift" to an engaged couple or to one of them, "in the absence of evidence to the contrary", is presumed to have been given to them as joint owners and to be subject to the condition that it will be returned at the request of the donor if the marriage does not take place "for whatever reason". Consequently, a wedding gift can be recovered by a third party not only if a couple agree not to marry but also if their marriage does not take place due to the death of either party prior to the marriage ceremony.

Proceedings to recover property by an ex-fiancé(e) pursuant to section 4 or by a third party pursuant to section 3 can be commenced at any time within three years of the termination of an engagement. During such three year period the ownership rights of the recipient or recipients of any gift recoverable under either section are qualified to the extent that the property to which they are applicable cannot be fully transferred to another without the original donor being a party to such transfer. For example, if a parent of one party to an engagement gives a house as a wedding gift to an engaged couple, in the event of the death of one of the parties to the engagement preventing the wedding taking place, the parent is entitled to request that the house be returned to his ownership and can institute proceedings to recover it at any time during such three year period. If within the three year period the surviving fiancé(e) transfers the house to a purchaser without the parent joining in such transfer or expressly waiving his right to recover the property pursuant to section 4 of the Act, proceedings instituted under this section within the three year period could effectively render any such transfer null and void.[13] If no such proceedings are instituted, however, the parent's right to recover the property expires and the validity of the transfer and the purchaser's title in the house is immune from challenge.

If a party to an agreement to marry that has been terminated "has received a benefit of a substantial nature" from a third party "in consequence of the agreement to marry" other than a wedding gift, the court may under section 6 of the Act make "such order (including an order for compensation) as appears to it just and equitable in the circumstances" upon application being made to the court by such third party. Thus, if a relative of one of the parties to an engagement carries out or pays for substantial works to be done on the improvement of a home owned by either party to an engagement, so that the property might be used by the engaged couple as their family home, the court can make an order enabling the relative to recover the money spent by him on such home or requiring that he be paid for any improvement works directly undertaken by him on it. For an order to be made under this section against a party to a broken engagement, it must be established that he has received a "benefit of a substantial nature". The Act of 1981 nowhere defines the exact meaning of this term and it is left for the court to decide what benefits are to be regarded as of a sufficiently "substantial nature" as to warrant the making of an order under section 6. It should be noted, however, that in order for such order to be made, it is not necessary to prove that the third party who makes application under the

---

13. See A. Power, *supra* at p. 169; R. O'Donnell, *supra*, at pp. 35—38 in which he discusses the additional requisitons on title required as a result of the enactment of these sections. See further *The Incorporated Law Society of Ireland Standard Requisitons on Title* (1985 Edition) Requisition 31.

section incurred "substantial expenditure", the principle matter of relevance for the court to ascertain being whether the party to the engagement received a substantial benefit from the third party as a consequence of entering into an engagement.

The extent to which this section can be used remains uncertain. For example, following upon the termination of an engagement could a father whose daughter's engagement was terminated, successfully obtain an order under this section against her ex-fiancé, if the father was instrumental in obtaining employment for the ex-fiancé and would not have done so if he had not become engaged to his daughter?

THE RECOVERY OF SUBSTANTIAL EXPENDITURE

The action for breach of promise did have merit to the extent that it enabled a party to a broken engagement to recover expenditure incurred in contemplation of marriage. In abolishing the action, the Act of 1981 sought to protect the right of each party to recover such expenditure and, in so doing, also extended a right of action to third parties to recover expenditure incurred on behalf of a party to a broken engagement. Section 7 provides that if a party to an agreement to marry or another "on behalf of a party to such agreement" incurs expenditure of a substantial nature "by reason of the agreement" from which the engaged party did not benefit, the court may, following upon the termination of the engagement, make such order against the other party "as appears just and equitable in the circumstances," including an order for the recovery of the expenditure incurred. Thus, if a woman, having become engaged, flies from Australia to Ireland for a wedding, only to discover that the man she was to marry has changed his mind, proceedings can be brought by her to recover the expenditure incurred in travelling to and residing in Ireland during the engagement period. Moreover, her father, if he contributed all or part of such expenditure, could also institute court proceedings to recoup the monies spent. An interesting question arises as to whether this section could be utilized by an unmarried mother to seek extra financial provision over and above that available to her pursuant to the Illegitimate Children (Affiliation Orders) Act, 1930.[14] For example, if a woman after becoming engaged agrees to have sexual intercourse with her fiancé and, as a result, becomes pregnant, if the engagement is terminated and she subsequently gives birth to the child, can she obtain such financial order as is "just and equitable" against her ex-fiancé in reliance on this provision by proving that she had only agreed to engage in intercourse with him because of their agreement to marry and consequently, contend that she had become pregnant "by reason of the agreement"? Whilst an arguable case could be made as to her entitlement to recoup substantial expenditure incurred by her as a result of her pregnancy, it is submitted that the courts are unlikely to regard the provisions of section 7 as applicable to such circumstances.

COURT JURISDICTION

The District Court is conferred with jurisdiction to hear and determine proceedings instituted under section 6 or section 7 of the Act where the amount claimed does not exceed £2,500.[15] The Circuit Court and High Court are conferred with concurrent jurisdiction to hear and determine proceedings under the

14. See p. 604 *post et seq*.
15. Section 8(2).

latter sections save that if proceedings are instituted for a sum in excess of £15,000 such proceedings cannot be dealt with in the Circuit Court save by the consent of both parties.[16] The Circuit and High Courts' jurisdiction to determine proprietary disputes under section 12 of the Married Women's Status Act, 1957, between parties to a terminated engagement is the same as the jurisdiction applicable to determine such a dispute between spouses.[17]

16. See section 8(1) and the Courts (Supplemental Provisions) Act, 1961, section 22.
17. See p. 485 *post*.

CHAPTER 4

MARRIAGE

INTRODUCTION

Marriage Defined: The classic legal definition of marriage is that given by Lord Penzance in the case of *Hyde v. Hyde*[1]: "I conceive that marriage, as understood in Christendom may . . . be defined as the voluntary union for life of one man and one woman to the exclusion of all others."[2] This definition involves four conditions: a marriage must be voluntary; the parties must intend it to be for life;[3] it must be monogamous; it must be between parties of a different sex.

The Contract of Marriage: Marriage is both a contract and a relationship. For persons to become husband and wife in the eyes of Irish law they must comply with the conditions the law sets down for the entering into of a valid marriage contract. Firstly, they must both possess the capacity to marry each other and secondly, they must observe the necessary formalities. Generally speaking, capacity to marry is determined by the law of each party's pre-nuptial domicile, whilst the formalities to be observed are those required by the *lex loci celebrationis*, i.e. the law of the place where the marriage is celebrated.[4] However, if a marriage is celebrated outside Ireland in accordance with the required formalities of the common law in a country in which use of the local formalities is impossible, such marriage will be recognised in Ireland even though the formalities of the *lex loci celebrationis* have not been complied with, provided the marriage so celebrated is not by its nature potentially polygamous.[4a] Moreover, it appears from the only modern Irish authority on this issue,[4b] that whereas the

---

1. (1866) L.R. 1. P. & D. 130; [1861-73] All E.R. Rep. 176, (Ct. of P. & D.) cited with approval in *Griffith v. Griffith* [1944] I.R. 35 (H.C.).
2. (1866) L.R. 1. P. & D. 130, at p. 133.
3. *Nachimson v. Nachimson* [1930] P. 217 (C.A.).
4. See the Law Reform Commission: *Report on Private International Law Aspects of Capacity to Marry and Choice of Law in Proceedings for Nullity of Marriage* (L.R.C. Report No. 19, October 1985) Chap. 2; Dicey & Morris, *Conflict of Law*, 10th Ed. (Sweet & Maxwell, London, 1980) Chap. 13. For Irish authorities as to private international law rules as to formalities of marriage see *Du Moulin v. Druitt* (1860) 13 I.C.L.R. 212 (Q.B.); *In the estate of M'Loughlin* (1878) 1 L.R. Ir. 421 (H.C.); *Swifte v. A.G. for Ireland* [1912] A.C. 276 (H.L., Ir.); *Ussher v. Ussher* [1912] 2 I.R. 445 (K.B.D.). For Irish authorities as to private international law rules as to capacity to marry see *Davis v. Adair* [1895] 1 I.R. 379 (H.C.) and *K.E.D. (otherwise K.C.) v. M.C.* (September, 1984) unreported (H.C.) in particular judgement of Carroll J. at p. 9–10. The respondent's appeal to the Supreme Court was dismissed in December 1985. This issue is not referred to in the judgements delivered by members of the Supreme Court in the appeal which was concerned solely with the basis upon which Irish law will recognise foreign decrees of divorce. See further p. 261 *post*. See also *C.S. (otherwise L.) v. J.L.* (July, 1985) unreported (H.C.)., Murphy J.
4a. *Conlan v. Mohamed* (July, 1986) unreported (H.C.).
4b. *Ibid.*

presence of an episcopally ordained priest is essential to the formal validity under common law of a marriage celebrated in Ireland, this does not apply to a marriage celebrated in a foreign country in the circumstances here described.[4c]

CAPACITY TO MARRY

For a person domiciled in Ireland to have capacity to contract a valid marriage he must comply with the following conditions:

Age: Section 1(1) of the Marriages Act, 1972, states that

> "A marriage solemnised between persons either of whom is under 16 shall . . . not be valid in law."

This section did not come into force until 1st January, 1975.[5] Prior to 1975, a valid marriage could be contracted in the case of a boy, when he reached the age of 14, and in the case of a girl when she reached the age of 12. Since the beginning of 1975 a person under 16 years of age who wishes to marry may apply to the President of the High Court (or a judge of that court nominated by the President) for exemption from the application of section 1(1). Such an application may be made informally through the Registrar of Wards of Court and is heard and determined in private. An exemption order can only be granted if "the applicant shows that its grant is justified by serious reasons and is in the interests of the parties to the intended marriage".[6] No fee is charged by the court for hearing the application.

In practice an application may be made to the Registrar either by letter or personally. The Registrar then sends the applicant a simple form which is designed to ascertain relevant information such as the age of the applicant and the name and address of the intended spouse and of both parties' parents or guardians. Copies of the parties' birth certificates are also sought. After this information has been received by the Registrar an appointment is made for the parties and their parents to meet the President of the High Court and separate interviews with the parties and their parents or guardians take place. If the parties are willing, a report may be sought from other interested third persons such as a social worker. After the interviews have been completed and all information sought has been obtained an order granting or refusing exemption is made.[7]

From the 1st January 1975 until the 31st December, 1982, 42 applications for exemption orders were made, 21 were granted, 14 were refused and 9 were withdrawn. As there are no reported cases on the exercise of this jurisdiction it is not known in what circumstances exemptions have been granted.[8]

If a person knowingly solemnises or permits the solemnisation of a marriage which, as a consequence of the provisions of section 1 is not valid or is a party

---

4c. The mere exchange of marital vows *per verba de presenti* may be sufficient. See further p. 82 *post*.

5. See S.I. No. 324 of 1974.

6. Marriages Act, 1972, Sect. 1(3).

7. See The Law Relating to the Age of Majority, The Age for Marriage and Some Connected Subjects, The Law Reform Commission Working Paper No. 2, 1977, at p. 39.

8. There are also no unreported written judgements setting out the facts of a case in which exemption was granted. In Australia the courts in exercising a similar jurisdiction have granted permission for under age marriages where the girl was pregnant, the parents' consent and the maturity and compatibility of the parties make it probable that their marriage will succeed: *Re K.* (1963), 5 F.L.R. 38; *Re W.* [1968] Q.W.N. 45; *Re Z* (1970), 15 F.L.R. 420. The permission has been refused, however, where parties simply belong to a class of persons or ethnic group that customarily expects young girls to marry: *Re S.G.* (1968), 11 F.L.R. 326. See further, H.A. Finlay, *Family Law in Australia* (Butterworths 1983) at p. 107 *et seq*.

to such marriage, he is guilty of a criminal offence and liable on summary conviction to a penalty not exceeding £50.[9]

Prohibited Degrees: Parties within the prohibited degrees of relationship cannot marry. Prohibitions are based either on consanguinity (blood relationship) or affinity (relationship by marriage).[10] Until 1835 a marriage within the prohibited degrees was merely voidable, but the Marriage Act (known as Lord Lyndhurst's Act) of that year made all such marriages void.

The prohibited degrees apply to a wide range of family relationships and do not distinguish between relationships of the half blood and those of the whole blood. The extent of their application to both consanguinity and affinity can be seen from the table of prohibited degrees that follows.

Table of Prohibited Degrees

(The relationship of the half blood is of the same effect as of the whole blood).

A Man may not Marry his

1. Grandmother.
2. Grandfather's Wife.
3. Wife's Grandmother.
4. Father's Sister.
5. Mother's Sister.
6. Father's Brother's Wife.
7. Mother's Brother's Wife.
8. Wife's Father's Sister.
9. Wife's Mother's Sister.
10. Mother.
11. Stepmother.
12. Wife's Mother.
13. Daughter.
14. Wife's Daughter.
15. Son's Wife.
16. Sister.
17. Son's Daughter.
18. Daughter's Daughter.
19. Son's Son's Wife.
20. Daughter's Son's Wife.
21. Wife's Son's Daughter.
22. Wife's Daughter's Daughter.
23. Brother's Daughter.
24. Sister's Daughter.
25. Brother's Son's Wife.
26. Sister's Son's Wife.
27. Wife's Brother's Daughter.
28. Wife's Sister's Daughter.

A Woman may not Marry her

1. Grandfather.
2. Grandmother's Husband.
3. Husband's Grandfather.
4. Father's Brother.
5. Mother's Brother.
6. Father's Sister's Husband.
7. Mother's Sister's Husband.
8. Husband's Father's Brother.
9. Husband's Mother's Brother.
10. Father.
11. Stepfather.
12. Husband's Father.
13. Son.
14. Husband's Son.
15. Daughter's Husband.
16. Brother.
17. Son's Son.
18. Daughter's Son.
19. Son's Daughter's Husband.
20. Daughter's Daughter's Husband.
21. Husband's Son's Son.
22. Husband's Daughter's Son.
23. Brother's Son.
24. Sister's Son.
25. Brother's Daughter's Husband.
26. Sister's Daughter's Husband.
27. Husband's Brother's Son.
28. Husband's Sister's Son.

---

9. Marriages Act, 1972, Sect. 1(6). See also Sects 1(4), (5) & (7).

10. See 28 Hen. 8. c.2. (1537); 33 Hen. 8. c.6. (1542); 3 & 4 P. & M. c.8. (1556); 2 Eliz. 1 c.1. (1560); Statute Law Revision (Ireland) Act, 1878 and the Statute Law Revision (Pre-Union Irish Statutes) Act, 1962. See also *Wing v. Taylor (falsely calling herself Wing)* 2 Sw. & Tr. 276; 164 E.R. 1002 (Ct. for Div. & Matr. Causes) — Affinity can only be created by marriage.

The prohibition on marriage by persons related within the prohibited degrees was amended in 1907, after much controversy, by the Deceased Wife's Sister's Marriage Act which permitted a man to marry his deceased wife's sister and in 1921 by the Deceased Brother's Widow's Marriage Act which permitted a woman to marry her deceased husband's brother. However, if a marriage is terminated as a result of a divorce as opposed to a spouse's death, the prohibition on a woman marrying her husband's brother or on a man marrying his wife's sister still remains. For example, Joe O'Neill marries Mary O'Brien in Ireland and they go to live in England where they establish domicile. While domiciled there they obtain a divorce which is recognised in Ireland as terminating their marriage. Subsequently, Joe returns to live in Ireland and marries Pat O'Brien who has lived in Ireland all her life and has an Irish domicile. Pat being Mary's sister, her marriage to Joe is invalid.

No specific reference is made in existing legislation to the application of the prohibited degrees to persons related by or through adoption. Section 24 of the Adoption Act, 1952 provides that upon an adoption order being made, the adopted child "shall be considered with regard to the rights and duties of parents and children in relation to each other as the child of the adopter or adopters, born to him, her or them in lawful wedlock" and it has been suggested that this section could be interpreted so as to apply the prohibition that applies to a marriage between a natural child and one of his parents to one between an adopted child and one of his adoptive parents. Whether it could also be interpreted so as to prohibit a marriage between an adopted child and such child's adoptive brother or sister must be doubtful. It appears, however, that the prohibited degrees continue to apply to prevent a marriage between an adoptive child and his natural relations. The practical difficulty that arises in the latter case is that an adopted child may unknowingly marry contrary to the prohibited degrees due to not knowing the identity of his natural parents.[11]

Monogamy: Marriage being a union between "one man and one woman", if at the time of the marriage ceremony either party is already validly married to a third party, the marriage is void.[12] In such a case it does not matter whether one or both of the parties knew of the continued subsistence of the first marriage at the time of the ceremony.[13] Further, the fact that either or both of them may have a valid defence to a charge of bigamy, such as a mistaken but honest belief on reasonable grounds that the former spouse is dead, is immaterial. A person who has already contracted one marriage cannot validly contract another until the first spouse dies or the earlier marriage is terminated by a valid and recognisable foreign decree of divorce.[14]

If a person is a party to a marriage which is void, he may contract a new marriage without obtaining a decree of nullity. Although such a decree is not

---

11. See the Law Reform Commission: *Report on Nullity of Marriage* (L.R.C. Report No. 9, July 1984) 48. In their report the Commission recommends that all prohibitions based on affinity should be abolished and that legislation should expressly prohibit and render void marriages between a parent and his or her adoptive child and between adoptive brothers and sisters (see pp. 130–144 of report). See also the *Report of the Review Committee on Adoption Services* (May 1984, Dublin, Stationery Office) at p. 93, para. 13.11.

12. See *Johnson (falsely called Cooke) v. Cooke* [1898] 2 I.R. 130 (Q.B.D.); *K.E.D. (Otherwise K.C.) v. M.C.* (September, 1984) unreported (H.C.); (December, 1985) unreported (S.C.); *C.S. (Otherwise L.) v. J.L.* (July, 1985) unreported (H.C.).

13. *Miles v. Chilton (falsely calling herself Miles)* (1849) 1 Robb. Ecc. 684; 27 Digest (Repl) 448; 163 E.R. 1178; *Hayward v. Hayward (orse Prestwood)* [1961] P. 152; [1961] 1 All E.R. 236 (P.D.A.).

14. See Chapter 10.

essential, it is, however, desirable that it first be obtained so as to ensure that a party does not enter into a "second marriage" under the mistaken belief that a previous marriage is void. Where a previous marriage is voidable, the parties to it are not free to marry another person until a decree of nullity is obtained; if, however, either party does enter into a "second marriage" upon such a decree being granted, the second marriage is regarded as having always been valid, the first marriage as a result of such decree being regarded as never having existed.[14a]

Sex: One party must be male and the other female. While this may seem almost a truism, this requirement did give rise to some difficulty in the English case of *Corbett v. Corbett*.[15] A marriage ceremony had been performed between a man and a person who had been born with male characteristics, but had undergone surgery to give him all the external characteristics of a female. The latter had been issued with a national health card and passport appropriate to females and dressed as a woman. The court held, however, that this did not make him a female for the purpose of marriage. In doing so it stated that while a person may be of the female gender, the same person may be biologically male. It held that, in determining a person's capacity to marry, it is the biological sex that is important.

FORMALITIES OF MARRIAGE

Certain formalities are laid down by statute that parties wishing to enter into marriage in Ireland must observe. The general purpose of these formalities can be said to achieve the following: to ensure that the marriage ceremony is easily identifiable from the normal interaction of everyday life so that persons do not marry by accident; to facilitate the maintaining of public records of married persons; to enable persons easily prove that they themselves or others are married; and to prevent persons not free to marry from marrying.

The law as to formalities is complex and obscure, being contained in a labyrinth of statutes stretching from 1844 to 1972. There now follows a brief historical introduction and then a detailed examination of the formalities required under the present law for the celebration of a marriage to be lawful.

Historical Introduction

Prior to the Reformation both Ireland and England were Roman Catholic countries and the formalities to be observed for a valid marriage ceremony were left by the common law to be determined by the canon law as decreed from Rome.[16] There were, according to its rules, three methods of contracting a valid marriage:

(a) *Sponsalia per verba de praesenti*; this was a simple declaration by the parties, in the present tense, agreeing to take each other as husband or wife.

(b) *Sponsillia per verba de futuro et copula*; this was a promise to marry in the future, the parties becoming husband and wife upon a subsequent consummation.

14a. *F.M.L. & A.L. v. The Registrar General of Marriages* [1984] 4 I.L.R.M. 667 (H.C.). See also *A.M.N. v. J.P.C.* (December, 1985) unreported (H.C.).
15. [1970] 2 All E.R. 33; [1971] P. 83 (P.D.A.).
16. See G.H. Joyce, *Christian Marriage*, Ch. 2.

(c) *In facie ecclesiae*; this was a marriage contracted at the church door *per verba de praesenti* in the presence of a priest. Such a ceremony took place after the publication of banns, unless they were dispensed with by papal or episcopal licence.

By a decree of the Council of Trent in 1563, no marriage of a Roman Catholic was to be regarded as valid by the Church unless celebrated in the presence of a priest and at least two witnesses, but by this time the Reformation having taken place, the common law and the canon law had gone their separate ways. Thus, whilst this decree governs the question of the Roman Catholic Church's recognition of a marriage as valid, it is not relevant to the formalities required by the common law.[17]

The three above methods were accepted as valid means of contracting a marriage in Ireland until 1844. In that year, in the much criticised case of *R. v. Millis*,[18] it was decided by the House of Lords that at common law the presence of a clergyman in holy orders, either of the Roman Catholic or Protestant Episcopal Church, at the time of the solemnisation of the marriage was essential for the valid constitution of a marriage contract. This view was later confirmed by the House of Lords in 1861 in *Beamish v. Beamish*.[19]

As a consequence of the decision of *R. v. Millis*, the Marriages (Ireland) Act, 1844, which is at the foundation of our present law as to formalities of marriage, was passed.

Roman Catholic Marriages

The great majority of marriages that take place in the State are celebrated in accordance with the rites and ceremonies of the Roman Catholic Church — 17,692 out of a total of 18,552 marriages were so celebrated in 1985.[20] These marriages are generally unaffected by legislative enactments, the 1844 Act and subsequent amending legislation being largely inapplicable to them. In the main the formalities to be observed for a Roman Catholic marriage are left by the State to be determined according to the rites of the Church, whilst the question of the civil validity of such marriages is determined by the common law, i.e. the common law will regard them as valid if celebrated by an episcopally ordained clergyman.[21] There is, however, a limited amount of legislative interference in this area. The law lays down certain formalities that must be observed for the valid celebration of a mixed marriage. The main purpose of this legislation

---

17. See *Ussher v. Ussher* [1912] 2 I.R. 445; (1912) 46 I.L.T.R. 109 (K.B.D.).
18. 10 Cl. & Fin. 534; 8 Jur. 717; 8 E.R. 844 (H.L.).
19. 9 H.L.Cas. 274; 11 E.R. 735. See also *Ussher v. Ussher, supra*; See also W.J. Walshe "Two Famous Irish Marriage Cases" (1912), 31 *Irish Ecclesiastical Record*, 4th Series, 449–75, 579–605 and (1912) Vol. 32, 10–30; 118–136.
20. From yearly summary of Births, Deaths and Marriages (1985) compiled by the Central Statistics Office. See further Appendix A.
21. See W.H. Faloon, *Marriage Law of Ireland*, p. 9. There the author writes "They (Roman Catholic marriages) might be celebrated privately or publicly, at any time or place, and in any form or manner the celebrating priest thought proper, without banns, licence, notice, residence or consent; and so far as the state is concerned this seems still the law;" This is no longer the case in respect of third party consents, see p. 98. See also J. Blanchard, *The Church in Contemporary Ireland*, p. 61. See also *Report of the Committee on the Constitution* (Dublin, Stationery Office, December 1967), pp. 45–46. The Committee suggests · that the law in prescribing requirements that have to be complied with by parties to non-Roman Catholic marriage, while not prescribing such requirements for a Roman Catholic marriage, may be unconstitutional, being contrary to Article 44.2.3 in that such provisions constitute discrimination on the grounds of religious profession of belief.
In *I.E. v. W.E.* [1985] 5 I.L.R.M. 691 (H.C.) the possibility of such a constitutional challenge was raised but the issue was never pursued.

which was enacted in the second half of the last century, was to repeal the penal laws which prevented the valid celebration of such marriages by Roman Catholic clergymen. To facilitate the registration of Roman Catholic marriages, an Act of 1863 imposes a duty on the husband in the case of all marriages celebrated by a Roman Catholic clergyman, to furnish the registrar of the district in which the marriage is solemnised with certain information after the marriage has taken place. Finally, the statutory provisions as to parental consent required for the lawful celebration of a marriage by a minor apply to all marriages celebrated in the State.

A Roman Catholic marriage may be celebrated by I. Episcopal dispensation; II. After publication of the banns; III. By ordinary licence; IV. On production of a Registrar's Certificate.

I & II. The proceedings in these cases are regulated by the law of the Church. Both parties must be Roman Catholics.[22]

III: An ordinary licence can be granted by a person nominated by the bishop if either both or one of the parties are Roman Catholic. If only one of the parties is a Roman Catholic notice must be given to the licence issuer 7 days before the licence can be used, and he must send by post a copy of the notice to the clergyman who officiates at the places of worship where the parties have been in the habit of attending.[23] In this latter case the marriage must be solemnised in a Roman Catholic church or chapel with open doors in the presence of two or more witnesses.[24]

IV: For a Roman Catholic marriage to take place on production of a registrar's certificate one of the parties must be of a different persuasion than Roman Catholic.[25] The certificate, (or certificates, where the parties reside in different districts) must be given to the officiating clergyman at the time of the solemnisation of the marriage and the marriage must be solemnised in a Roman Catholic church or chapel in the district of the registrar who issued the certificate, with open doors and in the presence of two or more witnesses.[26] For the procedure to be followed to obtain a certificate see "Marriage in the Office of the Registrar."

Registration of Marriage celebrated by a Roman Catholic Clergyman: By the Registration of Marriages (Ireland) Act, 1863, Sect. 11, the parties to a Roman Catholic marriage are required to obtain from the registrar of the district in which the marriage is to take place, a certificate which they must produce to and

---

22. See the Code of Canon Law (Collins Liturgical Publications, London 1984) Canons 1108–1133.
23. Matrimonial Causes and Marriage Law (Ireland) Amendment Act, 1871, Sect. 26. Under 19 Geo. II, c. 13 all marriages celebrated by a Roman Catholic priest, between a Protestant and a Roman Catholic were void. See *Thelwall v. Yelverton* (1862), 14 I.C.L.R. 188, (Ct. of C.P.). The Matrimonial Causes and Marriage Law (Ireland) Amendment Act, 1870, Sect. 39, repealed this Act in so far as it rendered all such marriages void, and Sect. 38 laid down the procedure to be followed whereby such a mixed marriage celebrated by a Roman Catholic priest would be valid. Under this section it is necessary for the certificate of the district registrar to be obtained for such a marriage to be valid. However, Sect. 27 of the Act of 1871 lays down that whenever a licence is issued for marriage pursuant to Sect. 25 of the same Act it is not necessary to obtain the registrar's certificate.
24. Under Sect. 27 of the Act of 1871 the licence is to have the same effect under the provisions of the Act of 1870 (i.e. Sect. 38 of that Act) as a certificate of the registrar would have had. See Sir Robert Edwin Matheson, *Digest of the Irish Marriage Law* (Dublin 1908).
25. Sect. 38 of the 1870 Act.
26. *Ibid.*, Sect. 38 as amended by Sect. 17(1)(*e*) of the Marriages Act, 1972.

which must be filled in by the clergyman celebrating the marriage. The certificate must contain the following particulars:[27]

    I. The date when married.

    II. The name and surname of each party.

    III. Their date of birth.

    IV. Their status at time of marriage, i.e. whether bachelor, spinster, widow or widower.

    V. Their occupation.

    VI. The normal residence of each party before marriage.

    VII. The name and surname of the father, and the name and maiden name of the mothers of both parties.

    VIII. The place in which the marriage was solemnised.

    IX. The intended future permanent residence of the parties.

The certificate must be signed by the parties married, the officiating clergyman and by two witnesses. It must be delivered or sent by post to the registrar of the district in which the marriage was solemnised, within three days of the ceremony. Non-compliance with the above provision in no way affects the validity of the marriage. It merely renders the husband liable to a penalty not exceeding £10.

In practice, the above described procedure is not followed. Normally it is the officiating clergyman that acquires the necessary certificate. He writes in the necessary information, has it signed as required, and returns it himself to the registrar.

Church of Ireland Marriages

Prior to the disestablishment of the United Church of England and Ireland, the rules prescribed by the Rubric in the book of Common Prayer and the canons of the Church, except in so far as they were modified by the Act of 1844, determined the formalities to be observed in a marriage solemnised in that church. The Irish Church Act, 1869, brought about the dissolution of the union between the two churches and the disestablishment of the Church of Ireland. As a consequence of that Act, the Matrimonial Causes and Marriage Law (Ireland) Amendment Acts, 1870 and 1871, were passed. These acts, slightly amended, now regulate the formalities to be observed in a Church of Ireland marriage.

A Church of Ireland marriage may be celebrated by: I. Special Licence; II. Ordinary Licence; III. After publication of the banns; IV. On Production of a Registrar's Certificate.[28]

I. A special licence may be granted by any Bishop of the Church of Ireland to marry at any convenient time in any place within his episcopal superintendence. Formerly both parties had to be Protestant Episcopalians but now only one of them need be.[29] "Protestant Episcopalian" is defined to mean a member of the

---

27. See Vital Statistics and Births, Deaths and Marriages Registration Act, 1952, Sect. 7 and S.I. No. 47 of 1956.
28. Sect. 33 of the 1870 Act.
29. Sect. 36 of the 1870 Act as amended by Sect. 13 of the 1972 Act. The latter section makes provision for the granting of the above licence by a deputy, in the absence of the bishop.

Church of Ireland, the Church of England, the Episcopal Church of Scotland and any other Protestant Episcopal Church.[30] Parties to a marriage by special licence must give to the clergyman celebrating the marriage a certificate identical to that required for the registration of Roman Catholic marriages. The certificate must be filled in by the clergyman and the husband is under a duty to deliver or send it to the Registrar-General of Marriages (an tÁrd Chláraitheoir)[31] within three days of the ceremony. Failure on his part to do so renders him liable to a penalty not exceeding £10.[32]

II. An ordinary licence can be granted by a person nominated by the Bishop if either both or one of the parties to be married are Protestant Episcopalians. The marriage may be celebrated in any church or chapel in the licensor's district (a) in which Divine Service is performed according to the rites of the Church of Ireland and in which marriages could have been solemnised on 10th August, 1870, or (b) in any church or chapel of the Church of Ireland licensed since that date for the celebration of marriage by the bishop.

Before a licence can be issued, notice of the intended marriage must be given to the licensor (in person or in writing) by one of the parties who must have either (a) resided for not less than 7 days then next preceding in such licensor's district or (b) been for not less than three months then next preceding a member of the congregation of the church or chapel.[33] The notice to the licensor must state the church or chapel in which it is intended to solemnise the marriage. If the church or chapel is in a parish in which neither party resides at the time of the service of the notice, before a licence can be granted they must obtain the consent of the incumbent of the parish in which they reside to the celebration of the marriage in the place stipulated.[34] Before the licence can be given one of the parties must appear in person before the licensor and swear or affirm that there is no lawful impediment to the marriage; that one of the parties has had his or her usual place of abode for 14 days immediately before the day of the grant of such licence within the district attached to the church or chapel in which the marriage is to be solemnised, or for more than 3 months immediately preceding the day of the grant been a member of the congregation of such church or chapel; that they have both reached 21 years of age or if either is under 21, that the consent of the person or persons whose consent is required by law has been obtained, or that there is no person with authority to give such consent, or that the person under 21 is a widow or widower.[35]

The licensor is required to enter a copy of the notice in his "Marriage Notice Book", which must be open at all reasonable times for inspection by the public. A copy must also be sent to the officiating minister of the places of worship attended by the parties. On the expiration of 7 days from the service of the notice, the licence may be granted. If the licensor refuses to grant a licence the applicant can appeal to the bishop who appointed him or his successor.[36] If

---

30. Sect. 4 of the 1870 Act.
31. Vital Statistics Act, 1952, Sect. 3.
32. Sect. 22 of the 1871 Act as amended by the 1952 Act, Sect. 7 and S.I. No. 47 of 1956.
33. Sect. 35 of the 1870 Act, as amended by the 1972 Act, Sect. 12(1)(b).
34. Sect. 35 of the 1870 Act, as amended by the 1972 Act, Sect. 12(1)(c). If the parties reside in different parishes the consent of the incumbents of both parishes must be obtained. Under this section every reference to an incumbent is said to include a curate in charge, and if there is no incumbent or curate in charge, it is to be construed as a reference to the bishop of the diocese.
35. Sect. 35 of the 1870 Act as amended by the 1972 Act, Sect. 12(1).
36. Sect. 35 of the 1870 Act.

the marriage does not take place within three months from the date of the notice, the notice and licence become void.[37]

III. The publication of banns is regulated in accordance with the rules of the Church of Ireland in force at the time when the parties seek to marry.[38] For marriage after publication of banns both parties must be Protestant Episcopalians.

IV. A certificate of a registrar can be used instead of banns, for the solemnisation of a marriage in a Church of Ireland church or chapel within the registrar's district.[39] For the procedure to be followed to obtain a certificate see "Marriage in the Office of the Registrar."

Solemnisation of Church of Ireland Marriages: Every marriage by ordinary licence, after publication of banns, or upon production of a registrar's certificate must be publicly solemnised in the presence of two or more witnesses and the officiating clergyman must immediately after solemnisation register the marriage in each of the Duplicate Marriage Register Books supplied to him by the Registrar-General.[40]

Presbyterian Marriages

Presbyterian marriages may be celebrated **I.** By Special Licence; **II.** By Ordinary Licence; **III.** After publication of banns.

I. By Section 37 of the Act of 1870 special licences to marry at any convenient time at any place in Ireland may be granted by any of the following persons:

(a) The Moderator of the General Assembly of the Presbyterian Church in Ireland;

(b) The Moderator of the Remonstrant Synod of Ulster;

(c) The Moderator of the Presbytery of Antrim;

(d) The Moderator of the Synod of Munster.[41]

Formerly both parties had to be of the same religion as the Moderator who granted the special licence. Now only one of them need be.[42] Marriage by special licence is subject to the same rules concerning registration as apply to special licences issued by the Bishops of the Church of Ireland.

II. Marriage by ordinary licence takes place in a certified place of worship or church, pursuant to a licence granted by one of the authorised ministers of the church, specially appointed by the presbytery to issue such.[43] Such a licence can be granted if either both or one of the parties are Presbyterians. To obtain such a

37. *Ibid.*
38. Sect. 33 of tne 1870 Act as amended by Sect. 11 of the 1972 Act.
39. Sect. 33(1) of the 1870 Act; Sects. 13–16 of the 1844 Act; and Sects. 26–27 of the 1871 Act.
40. See Sects. 63 and 64 of the 1844 Act; Marriage Law (Ireland) Amendment Act, 1863, Sect. 6 Matrimonial Causes and Marriage Law (Ireland) Amendment Act, 1870, Sect. 33.
41. The 1972 Act, Sect. 14(*e*) authorises a deputy appointed by one of the above persons to issue special licences in his absence.
42. Sect. 14(*b*) and (*c*) of the 1972 Act.
43. Sects. 7 and 8 of the 1844 Act.

licence one of the parties must, 7 days prior to its issue, give to the licensing minister a certificate from the minister of the congregation of which he or she has been a member, stating that he has been a member for at least one preceding calendar month and that notice of the intended marriage has been entered in the congregation book kept for that purpose. The certificate also states the church or chapel in which it is intended to solemnise the marriage.[44]

Before the licence can be granted one of the parties must appear personally before the licensor and swear or affirm as to the same matters required to be sworn or affirmed before the grant of an ordinary licence for a Church of Ireland ceremony. The only matter of difference is that one of the parties must have had, for 15 days immediately preceding the grant, his or her usual place of abode in the Presbytery within which the marriage is to be solemnised.

The licensor is required to enter a copy of the certificate into his marriage notice book, which must be kept open at all reaonable times for inspection by the public. Any person may enter a caveat against the issuing of a licence. If upon examination of the matter stated in the caveat the licensing minister is satisfied that it ought not to obstruct his granting a licence, or if the caveat is withdrawn by the person who entered it, the licence may issue. But if the minister has any doubt he can refer the matter to the Presbytery for decision.[45]

If a licensing minister for any reason refuses to grant a licence the applicant may appeal against the refusal to the Presbytery by which he was appointed.[46] On the expiration of 7 days from the delivery of the certificate the licence may be granted. If the marriage does not take place within a month from the date of the licence and within 3 months of the entry of the notice in the Marriage Notice Book, the notice and licence are void.[47]

III. For a marriage by publication of banns both of the parties to the marriage must be Presbyterians. Banns must be read on three consecutive Sundays preceding the solemnisation of the marriage by or in the presence of one Presbyterian Minister in the church of each congregation to which the parties belong. The marriage must be solemnised in a church in which the banns have been read. At least six days prior to the first reading of the banns the persons to be married must deliver or cause to be delivered to the minister or ministers by whom or in whose presence banns are to be read, a notice in writing stating their christian name, surname, the congregation of which they are members, their respective abodes and the time during which they have resided in them.[48]

Solemnisation of Presbyterian Marriages: Every marriage by ordinary licence, or after publication of banns, must be publicly solemnised in the presence of two or more witnesses and the officiating minister must immediately after solemnisation register the marriage in each of the Duplicate Marriage Register Books supplied to him by the Registrar-General.

---

44. *Ibid.*, Sect. 10.
45. *Ibid.*, Sect. 11.
46. *Ibid.*, Sect. 8.
47. *Ibid.*, Sect. 45.
48. *Ibid.*, Sects. 5 and 6.

Protestant Marriages other than Church of Ireland or Presbyterian; and Marriages of any other Community of Christians not Roman Catholics who do not describe themselves as Protestants

Other Protestant marriages may be celebrated by I. Special Licence; II. Registrar's Licence; III. Registrar's Certificate.

I. Special Licences to marry at any convenient time at any place in Ireland may be granted by:[49]

(a) The Moderator of the Eastern Reform Presbyterian Synod;

(b) The Moderator of the United Presbyterian Presbytery of Ireland;

(c) The Moderator of the Secession Church in Ireland;

(d) The Moderator of the Reformed Presbyterian Synod of Ireland;

(e) The Chairman of the Congregational Union of Ireland;

(f) The Secretary of the Conference of the Methodist or Wesleyan Church in Ireland;

(g) The President or Head of the Methodist New Connexion Church;

(h) The President or Head of the Association of the Baptist Churches in Ireland.[50]

Formerly both parties had to be of the same religion as the person who granted the special licence. Now only one of them need be.[51] Marriage by special licences is subject to the same rules concerning registration as apply to special licences issued by the Bishops of the Church of Ireland.

II. & III. For the obtaining of a Registrar's licence or certificate see "Marriage in the Office of the Registrar".

Marriages by any other community of Christians other than Roman Catholics, and who do not describe themselves as Protestants may be solemnised by methods II. & III.[52]

Solemnisation: Every marriage by a registrar's licence or certificate must be solemnised by a minister of the Church or denomination to which the parties to the marriage or either of them belong, in the place of worship named in the notice with open doors and in the presence of two or more witnesses other than the person solemnising the marriage.[53] As in the case of marriages in accordance with the rites of religious denominations previously discussed all such marriages must be registered in the Duplicate Marriage Register Books.

Marriages in accordance with (a) the usages of The Society of Friends and (b) The Jewish religion

Such marriages may be solemnised by I. Special Licence; II. Upon production of a Registrar's Certificate.

---

49. Sect. 37 of the 1870 Act as amended by the 1871 Act, Sect. 21.
50. Sect. 14(e) of the 1972 Act authorises a deputy appointed by one of the above persons to issue special licences in his absence.
51. Sect. 14(b) and 14(c) of the 1972 Act.
52. See Marriage Law (Ireland) Amendment Act, 1873.
53. Marriage Law (Ireland) Amendment Act, 1863, Sect. 7.

I. Special licences to marry at any convenient time or place in Ireland may be granted by the Clerk to the Yearly Meeting of the Society of Friends or by the Chief Rabbi of the Jewish Communities in Ireland.[54] One of the parties to whom such a licence is granted must be of the same religion as the person granting it.[55] Marriages by special licence are subject to the same rules concerning registration as apply to special licences issued by the Bishops of the Church of Ireland

II. For the obtaining of a registrar's certificate see "Marriage in the Office of the Registrar". The certificate must be given to the registering officer of the place where the marriage is to be solemnised.

Solemnisation: Every marriage by a registrar's certificate must be solemnised according to the practice of the respective bodies, in the place named in the notice, with open doors in the presence of two or more witnesses.[56] All such marriages must be registered in the Duplicate Marriage Register Books by the registering officer. In the case of a Jewish marriage it must be registered by the Secretary of the Synagogue to which the husband belongs.[57]

Marriage in the Office of the Registrar

The 1844 Act provided for the appointment of registrars with powers to solemnise marriages by civil contract after compliance with various conditions. A marriage may be solemnised in this way after parties have obtained a district registrar's certificate or licence. As we have already seen such a certificate or licence may be required not only for marriage in the office of the registrar, but also for marriage in accordance with the rites of the religious denominations previously discussed.

For a licence or a certificate to be issued, notice of the intended marriage must be given by one of the parties to the district registrar. If they reside in different districts the notice must be served on the registrar of each district.[58] The notice must state:[59]

    (a) The name and surname of the parties;

    (b) Their status, i.e. whether bachelor, spinster, widow or widower.

    (c) Their rank or profession;

    (d) Whether or not they are of full age to marry, i.e., over 21 years of age.[59a]

    (e) The church, chapel or place of worship the parties or either of them usually attends;

---

54. Sect. 37 of the 1870 Act as amended by the 1972 Act, Sect. 14(a). Sect. 14(e) authorises a deputy to issue special licences in the absence of the clerk or the Chief Rabbi.
55. Sect. 37 of the 1870 Act as amended by the 1972 Act, Sect. 14(b) and Sect. 14(c).
56. Marriage Law (Ireland) Amendment Act, 1863, Sect. 7.
57. Sect. 63 of the 1844 Act as amended by the 1972 Act, Sect. 4. This amendment provides for registration by a secretary's deputy. See also Sect. 5 of the 1972 Act, which concerns the Dublin Jewish Progressive Congregation.
58. Sect. 13 of the 1844 Act.
59. Marriage Law (Ireland) Amendment Act, 1863, Sect. 2.
59a. Although the age of majority was reduced to 18 years by the Age of Majority Act, 1985, the Marriages Acts of 1844, 1863, 1870 and 1972 are unaffected by the Act of 1985. See, in particular, Sect. 2(4) of the 1985 Act.

(f) The parties' usual dwelling place, each having resided there for not less than 7 days;[60]

(g) The church, chapel or other place in which the marriage is to be solemnised. Except in the case of members of the Jewish faith, it must be within the district of the registrar, or one of the registrars to whom notice is given;[61]

(h) Whether the marriage is intended to be celebrated by virtue of the registrar's certificate or licence.

When the registrar is served with the notice he must[62]

1. File the notice and keep it in his Office Records;

2. Enter a true copy of the notice in the Marriage Notice Book which he must keep open for the inspection of all persons at all reasonable times without payment of fees;

3. On the day on which he receives notice or on the next day, send by post in a registered letter, a copy of the notice —

   (a) to the Minister of the church, chapel or registered place of public worship in which the marriage is intended to be solemnised;

   (b) to the Minister of the church, chapel or place of public worship which the parties to the marriage or either of them usually attend;

   or

   (c) to the Registering Officer of the Society of Friends, or to the Clerk of a branch of the Church of Christian Scientists[63] or to the Secretary of a Synagogue by whom the marriage is to be registered;

4. If the marriage is to be contracted in the registrar's office, then in addition to (b) he has to suspend a copy of the notice in some conspicuous place in his office, and keep it there (i) for 21 days if the marriage is to be celebrated by virtue of a certificate, or (ii) for 7 days, if it is to be celebrated by licence.

In the case of a marriage in the registrar's office, if the parties have no minister of a place of worship to which they ordinarily go, and are not Quakers or Christian Scientists or Jewish, the registrar must publish at the expense of the parties, once at least in 2 consecutive weeks after the receipt of the notice, a copy of the notice in a newspaper circulating in the district in which the marriage is to be solemnised. If there is no such newspaper, then in one circulating in the county in which such district is situated.[64]

Marriage by Licence: The party giving notice is required to declare in writing — that there is no lawful impediment to the intended marriage; that the parties have for one month preceding usually attended Divine Worship in the building

---

60. By Sect. 6 of the 1972 Act, however, if there is not a church or building used by the religious denomination according to the rites of which the marriage is to be solemnised within the district where the parties have for the previous 7 days resided, the marriage may be celebrated in a church or building situate in another district.

61. Sect. 13 of the 1844 Act as amended by the 1871 Act, Sect. 28.

62. Marriage Law (Ireland) Amendment Act, 1863, Sect. 3.

63. Sect. 10(1) of the 1972 Act.

64. Sect. 41 of the 1870 Act, as amended by the 1972 Act, Sect. 10(2).

named in the notice (if one is so named); that one of them has resided for 15 days in the district of the registrar on whom notice is served; and, in cases of persons under 21 years of age, that the necessary consents have been obtained.[65] In cases where both parties reside in the same district a residence of 15 days is necessary for one party and not less than 7 days for the other. But if they reside in different districts a residence of 15 days in each is necessary at the time of the service of the notice.[66] The registrar may grant a licence after the expiration of 7 days from the date of entry of the notice.[67] The ceremony may then take place.

Marriage by Certificate: At the time of giving notice for marriage by certificate a declaration similar to that required for marriage by licence must be made. The requirement of 15 days residence by one party is here replaced by a requirement that each party must reside within the registrar's district 7 days immediately preceding the giving of notice. Thus here the declaration is to 7 days residence.[68] After the expiration of 21 days from the entry of the notice, the registrar may issue his certificate and the ceremony can take place.

Caveats: Any person may enter a caveat with a registrar against the issuing of a certificate or licence to an applicant. Such a caveat must be signed by or on behalf of the person entering it and must state his address and the grounds for objection. No licence or certificate can issue until the registrar has examined the matter of the caveat and is satisfied that it ought not to obstruct his issuing a certificate or licence or until it is withdrawn by the party who entered it. The registrar, if in doubt, can refer the matter to the Registrar-General to decide. If the registrar refuses to grant a certificate or licence the applicant may appeal to the Registrar-General.[69]

Registrar's Special Marriage Licence:[70] The Registrar-General may grant a special licence to marry on being satisfied that one of the persons to be married is, for health reasons certified by a doctor, unable to go to a registry office for a marriage ceremony. A marriage authorised by such a licence may be solemnised, in the presence of two witnesses, at any time and place by the registrar of marriages for the registration district in which that place is situated.

Solemnisation of Marriage: The following declaration must be made by both parties, in the presence of the registrar and witnesses, in the case of a marriage in a registry office or following the granting of a special licence by the Registrar-General.[71]

"I do solemnly declare that I know not of any lawful impediment why I, A.B. may not be joined in matrimony to C.D."

Each of the parties must say to each other

"I call upon these persons here present to witness that I, A.B. do take thee C.D. to be my lawful wedded wife (husband)."

---

65. Marriage Law (Ireland) Amendment Act, 1863, Sect. 4.
66. *Ibid.*
67. *Ibid.*, Sect. 5.
68. *Ibid.*, Sects. 2 and 4.
69. Sect. 23 of the 1844 Act. See also Sect. 18.
70. Sect. 16 of the 1972 Act.
71. *Ibid.*, and Sect. 29 of the 1844 Act.

Marriages in the registrar's office may take place between eight in the morning and five in the afternoon on any day except Sunday, with open doors in the presence of the registrar and two witnesses.[72]

NON-OBSERVANCE OF FORMALITIES

The general principle is that the non-observance of, or a defect in the formalities does not invalidate a marriage unless both parties were aware of it at the time of the ceremony. Only if both parties "knowingly and wilfully" disregard certain requirements will their marriage be void.[72a] Thus, a marriage is void if parties knowingly and wilfully marry (except in the case of a marriage celebrated by a Roman Catholic priest)[73]

(a) in any place other than the church or chapel in which the banns of matrimony between the parties were duly and lawfully published;[74] or

(b) in any place other than the church or chapel specified in the licence , where the marriage is by licence; or

(c) in any place other than the church or chapel, registered building or office specified in the Notice and Registrar's Certificate; or

(d) without due notice to the registrar or without certificate of notice duly issued or without licence from the registrar where a notice or licence is necessary;[74a] or

(e) in the absence of a registrar where the presence of a registrar is necessary; or

(f) in any certified Presbyterian Church without publication of banns or any licence.

A marriage celebrated by a Protestant Episcopalian clergyman between a person who is a Protestant Episcopalian and a person who is not, or by a Roman Catholic clergyman between a person who is a Roman Catholic and a person who is not is void if the parties to such marriage knowingly and wilfully marry without[75]

(a) due notice to the registrar; or

(b) without certificate of notice duly issued; or

(c) without the presence of two or more witnesses; or

(d) in a building not set apart for the celebration of divine service according to the rights and ceremonies of the religion of the clergyman solemnising such marriage.

A marriage may also be void if not celebrated within three calendar months after notice has been given to the registrar. After the passage of such time the

---

72. Sect. 30 of the 1844 Act as amended by the 1972 Act, Sect. 17(2).

72a. See *I.E. v. W.E., supra.* Although the formalities required for the celebration of a marriage in a Lutheran Church were not complied with, Murphy J. declined to hold the marriage to be invalid.

73. Sect. 49 of the 1844 Act.

74. See *Courtenay v. Miles* [1876] I.R. 11 Eq. 284 (Ct. for Matr. Causes) – The use of a false name in the publication of banns with the knowledge of both parties prior to the marriage for the purpose of deception or concealment was held to render the marriage void.

74a. See *I.E. v. W.E., supra.*

75. Sect. 39 of the 1870 Act.

notice, certificate and any licence issued and all "other proceedings thereupon" are void.[76]

There are also certain specified defects, evidence of the existence of which can never be given so as to render a marriage void. Evidence may not be given[77]

    (a) that any of the statutory requirements as to the residence of the parties prior to the marriage were not fulfilled; or

    (b) that the consent of any third person required to be given was not so given;[78] or

    (c) that either of the parties was not a Presbyterian in the case of a marriage solemnised in a Presbyterian church; or

    (d) if the marriage was by licence, that the certificate required to be delivered to the Minister granting such licence had not been delivered, or that a certificate of the publication of banns had not been produced to the Minister by whom the marriage was solemnised where such production was required.

The Acts are silent as to the effect on the validity of a marriage of non-observance of a number of other requirements, e.g. would a marriage be valid if celebrated by a registrar in his office without any witnesses present, or behind closed doors or after 5 p.m.? As a general rule it is submitted that unless a defect is said expressly to invalidate a marriage, the marriage is completely valid. Whilst the non-observance of certain formalities may not invalidate a marriage, as usually one of the parties has to make an oath or declaration, he or she may be rendered liable to prosecution for perjury or for the commission of an offence under the Statutory Declarations Act, 1938, Sect. 6. A person convicted under the latter provision is rendered liable to a fine not exceeding £50 and/or to a term of imprisonment not exceeding three months.

LOURDES MARRIAGES

The Marriages Act, 1972, Sect. 2, provides that a marriage to which it applies "shall be, and shall be deemed always to have been valid as to form if it would have been so valid had it been solemnised in the State". The section is said to apply to marriages which were solemnised, before the passing of the Act, solely by a religious ceremony in the department of Hautes Pyrenees, France, and were between "persons both or either of whom were or was citizens or a citizen of Ireland on the day of the marriage". The section further provides that the Registrar-General upon "production of such evidence as appears to him to be satisfactory" may cause such a marriage to be registered in a register to be maintained in his office. The need for section 2 arose out of the fact that a number of Irish Roman Catholic couples in previous years had gone to Lourdes to marry, and probably believing French law to be the same as Irish law had only gone through a religious ceremony while there. According to French law, however, a marriage ceremony must take place before an official of the State for it to be valid. The parties may then have their marriage celebrated according to the rites of their own religion. We have already seen that generally speaking the formal validity of a marriage is determined by the *lex loci celebrationis* i.e. the law of the place where the marriage is celebrated. Thus under both French and

76. See Sect. 25 of the 1844 Act.
77. Sect. 32 of the 1844 Act.
78. See "Consents of Third Parties" at p. 98 *post.*

Irish law such Lourdes marriages, not being preceded by a civil ceremony, were invalid and of no effect. Section 2 was enacted so as to retrospectively validate all such marriages that took place prior to 20th December 1972, i.e. the date of the passing of the Act. Any marriages that have taken place in Lourdes since that date and that have not complied with French formalities are unaffected by the section, and are thus invalid.

There are a number of matters about this section worth noting:

I. Whereas the marriages to which the section applies are retrospectively validated in this country, the section cannot, and of course does not, affect the law of any other country. Generally speaking under private international law a marriage is only regarded as valid as to form if it complies with the formalities required by the country in which the marriage is celebrated. Thus, if the parties to a marriage validated by Section 2 go to live in England, English law will test the validity of the marriage by looking to see whether the parties complied with the formalities required by French law. Upon making a finding that they did not, an English court would hold the marriage to be invalid under English law.

II. The section applies to marriages celebrated by a couple either or both of whom were Irish citizens at the time of the marriage. It is submitted that for a provision retrospectively validating in this State a marriage celebrated in another State, Irish domicile or at least residence at the time of the ceremony would have been a more appropriate connecting factor with this country. As the law stands at present Irish law regards as valid the marriages of Irish citizens to which the section applies irrespective of whether they were domiciled or resident in this country at the time of the celebration of the marriage, or at any other time.

III. In retrospectively validating such marriages the Act makes no provision for a person who having discovered the invalidity of his or her Lourdes ceremony, married another prior to section 2 coming into operation. In such circumstances having regard to the wording of the section it seems that the first marriage would be regarded as valid. Such a result could have particularly unjust consequences for a party's 'second' spouse.

IV. The section applies to marriages solemnised prior to the passing of the Act, i.e. prior to 20th December 1972. The provisions of the Act could not come into force until a ministerial order rendered them operative. Section 2 was not brought into force by such an order until 1st February 1973.[79] It is submitted that it would have been more appropriate for the section to have recognised marriages solemnised prior to the coming into operation of the section rather than prior to the passing of the Act.[79a]

CONFLICT AS TO FORMALITIES OF MARRIAGE BETWEEN ROMAN CATHOLIC CHURCH AND STATE

There are a number of situations in which a marriage will be regarded as formally valid by the State but as invalid by the Roman Catholic Church. The most noteworthy are the following:

(a) A marriage of Roman Catholic parties celebrated by a Roman Catholic

79. S.I. No. 12 of 1973.
79a. See further The Law Reform Commission: Report No. 19, *supra*, at p. 22 *et seq.*

priest with no witnesses present is a valid civil marriage *per verba de praesenti* but is not valid in the eyes of the Church, such ceremony not being in compliance with the decree of the Council of Trent.[80]

(b) A marriage celebrated in a registry office between two Roman Catholics or between a Roman Catholic and a Protestant if the required formalities are properly observed is a valid marriage by the law of the State but is invalid according to the Church. Further it has not been unknown in the past for a Roman Catholic previously married in a registry office, to be married by a Roman Catholic priest to another person, and as a consequence convicted of committing bigamy.[81] In one such case, tried in Limerick in 1962, in the course of passing sentence the President of the Circuit Court, Judge Barra O'Briain, discussed the relationship between the canon law and the law of the State:

> "The position of a Judge who is called upon to administer the civil law that for historical reasons conflicts with the canon law which is binding upon the majority of the people of this State is ... unenviable. I do not intend to let that affect my interpretation of the criminal law or in any way to derogate from its effect. I might add, however, that after 40 years of independence, it should be possible to amend the law here which for historical reasons now raises a grave problem of conscience among the majority of Irish citizens. It should be possible to amend the law without in any way creating a new problem of conscience for the majority, Protestants or otherwise."[82]

Where a person does marry bigamously any person who with knowledge of the circumstances persuades him to so marry may be convicted of bigamy as an accessory before the fact. Moreover any clergyman who with knowledge of the circumstances officiates at such a marriage may be convicted as a principal in the second degree. The bigamist, persuader and clergyman could all receive, if convicted, a maximum sentence of 7 years penal servitude.[83]

CRITICISMS AND SUGGESTED REFORMS

In 1868 a Royal Commission, looking at Irish Marriage law stated that "a good general marriage law ... ought to embrace the maximum of simplicity and the maximum of certainty". To say that the present law does not go near to doing so is to state the obvious. It is the product not of a systematic and coherent development but of piecemeal legislative action stretching across over 140 years. In all that time no effort has been made by the legislature to clarify and simplify the general procedures that have to be followed by persons wishing to marry, or to codify or rationalise the extremely complex statutory position.

---

80. *Ussher v. Ussher, supra.*
81. See *People (A.-G.) v. Ballins* [1964] Ir. Jur. Rep. 14, (Cir. Ct.); *People (A.-G.) v. Hunt* [1945] 80 I.L.T. & S.J. 19 (C.C.C.).
82. *People (A.-G.) v. Ballins, supra* at p. 15.
83. See p. 180 *post.* See also W. Conway, "Marriage in Ireland: Church and State" (1946) 68 *Irish Ecclesiastical Record* 361–6; D. Fennell, *The Changing Face of Catholic Ireland,* chap. 1; G.A. Lee, *Canon and Civil Marriage Law in Ireland* (1946) 67 *Irish Ec. Record,* pp. 154–158; "Family Law" by D. Barrington (Society of Young Solicitors Lecture No. 33); C. Davitt, "Some aspects of the Constitution and the Law in Relation to Marriage", *Studies,* 1968, p. 6 (see also the comments by V. Grogan on p. 20 of the same issue of *Studies*).

The confusing legal situation is exacerbated by the fact that there are a number of circumstances in which the State regards as formerly valid, a marriage between Roman Catholics that the Roman Catholic Church does not accept as valid, and *vice versa*. There are also circumstances in which a marriage between Roman Catholics solemnised in accordance with the formalities required by the Council of Trent, and thus valid in accordance with both the Civil law and Canon law, may be declared a nullity by the Matrimonial Tribunals of the Church. The civil law as to nullity is discussed in a later chapter. Suffice it here to say that a declaration of nullity by a Church Tribunal does not affect the validity of a marriage in the civil law.

The fact that marriages celebrated in accordance with the rites of the Roman Catholic Church, but subsequently annulled by the Marriage Tribunals of that church, may be regarded still as valid subsisting marriages under the civil law, has created confusion in the minds of the general public. Looked at simply, it seems that at one stage the State leaves the matter to the religious sphere and recognises its actions, while at another stage it refuses to do so.

The most obvious reform and solution to the present diverse statutory provisions would be to adopt the formula followed in many foreign countries and stipulate that a civil ceremony is the only legally effective way of contracting a marriage. The parties could then go through any religious ceremony they wish. Such a division of ceremonies would help to maintain in the public mind a distinction between the civil contract of marriage, and its effects under civil law, and the religious ceremony and its religious consequences. It would help to instil in people the fact that the religious and civil spheres do not coincide and thus help to prevent confusion arising as to the effects in the civil law of a church decree of nullity, or of the church not regarding a marriage as validly celebrated. Moreover such a system by making the law both more simple and more certain would greatly facilitate the solution of any disputes that arise as to the formal validity of a marriage.[84] Such a reform of the law, however, could arouse very strong opposition from the various churches and religious bodies in the State.

The Report of the Joint Oireachtas Committee on Marriage Breakdown acknowledging the need for reform in this area states that "the formalities for validly marrying . . . should be simplified, uniformly applicable and given clear legislative force" and that "wilful non-observance of the simplified formalities should render a marriage null and void."[85] The report agrees that the dual-purpose ceremony of marriage, i.e. a single ceremony having both religious and civil consequences, "can give rise to difficulties in understanding"[86] and makes reference to the fact that there are situations in which a marriage between two Roman Catholics will be considered valid by the civil courts under common law but invalid under Canon law and that it is equally possible to have marriages valid under the Canon law but invalid under the civil law.[87] However, the report falls short of proposing that a separate civil ceremony should be the only effective way of contracting a valid marriage according to the civil law. With reference to such a proposal it states that "the committee feels that to require parties to undergo a separate civil ceremony in addition to the religious ceremony of their

---

84. See S. Ryan, "Irish Marriage Law: The Need for Change", *Irish Times* 16th and 17th May 1973; A. Samuels, "Capacity and Formalities of Marriage" (1971), Fam. Law 118 — Although the author is here writing about the English situation nearly all the comments made are equally applicable to the law of this country.

85. *Report of the Joint Oireachtas Committee on Marriage Breakdown* (Stationery Office, Dublin, March 1985) at p. 42.

86. *Ibid.*

87. *Supra* at p. 35.

choice would create considerable administrative and financial difficulties for all concerned." Acknowledging, however, that "it would be desirable that the nature of the contract (of marriage) and its legal consequences should be made clear to the parties at the time of the ceremony" it proposes that the law should require that a specific reference to the civil contract of marriage be made in a separate part of the marriage ceremony prior to the exchange of the marriage vows in a religious service.[88]

REQUIRED CONSENTS OF THIRD PARTIES TO MARRIAGE

The basic policy of the law is that parental consent is required before a person under 21 is permitted to marry. This requirement, however, is by no means absolute and a marriage solemnised without such consent is regarded as valid. Consequently, the obtaining of consent is classified as part of the formalities, and not as a question concerning capacity.

Whose Consent is Required

The requirements as to consents are set down in section 7 of the Marriages Act, 1972. They are applicable to all marriages including those celebrated according to the rites of the Catholic Church. Section 7 taken in conjunction with the provisions of the Guardianship of Infants Act, 1964, sets down the following rules:

I. Where the minor is legitimate:

Circumstances:	*Person or persons whose consent required:*
(a) If both parents are living.	(a) Consent of both parents.
(b) If one parent dead and there is no other guardian.	(b) The surviving parent.
(c) If one parent dead and if a guardian has been appointed by deceased parent.	(c) Consent of both if acting jointly. If parent still sole guardian, consent of parent only.
(d) Where both parents dead and guardians or guardian appointed by deceased parents or by the court under the Guardianship of Infants Act, 1964.	(d) The guardian or guardians so appointed.
(e) Where both parents dead and no guardian has been appointed.	(e) The President of the High Court (or a Judge of that court nominated by the President).

---

88. *Supra* at p. 42 and p. 115.

II. Where the minor is illegitimate:

Circumstances:	*Person whose consent is required:*
(a) If the mother is alive.	(a) The mother.
(b) If the mother of the infant is dead and a guardian has been appointed by her or by the court.	(b) The guardian so appointed.
(c) If mother dead and no guardian has been so appointed.	(c) The President of the High Court (or a Judge of that court nominated by the President).

If the minor is a widow or widower, the above consents are not required. In the case of a ward of court, the consent of the court must be obtained.

Dispensing with Consent

The requirement of the consent of a guardian can be dispensed with if a guardian:

(a) refuses or withholds consent; or

(b) is unknown; or

(c) is of unsound mind; or

(d) is of whereabouts which would be unreasonably difficult to ascertain,

and the President of the High Court (or a judge of that court nominated by him) consents to the intended marriage.

An application to the President under section 7 of the 1972 Act can be made informally through the Registrar of Wards of Court and is heard and determined in private. No fee is charged by the court in respect of such an application and the procedure is substantially the same as that used for determining applications for exemption orders under section 1 of the 1972 Act. As there are no reported cases on the exercise by the President of the High Court of the above jurisdiction, it is impossible to say what reasoning is applied upon an application for dispensation of consent coming before him.[89] In making a determination under the section, however, the court must regard the child's welfare as the paramount consideration by virtue of section 3 of the Guardianship of Infants Act, 1964.

THE AGE FOR MARRIAGE – SUGGESTED REFORM

The law as to the minimum age for marriage and the necessity for parental consent was examined by the Law Reform Commission in its Second Working Paper published in 1977.[90] The Commission having proposed that the age of majority be reduced from 21 years to 18 years[91] stated:

"In most European States the age of majority is the same as the free age for marriage (i.e. the age at which persons are free to marry without parental

---

89. There are also no unreported written judgements available setting out the facts of a case and the decision reached.

90. The Law relating to the Age of Majority, the Age for Marriage and Some Connected Subjects: The Law Reform Commission, Working Paper No. 2 (Dublin 1977). See also A. Shatter, "What is the Age of Consent?", *Irish Times*, 2nd May 1978.

91. A proposal now implemented by the Age of Majority Act, 1985.

consent). . . when no question of principle is involved uniformity with other legal systems, particularly those of the E.E.C., is desirable. If it is correct to reduce the age of majority there seems to the Commission to be no reason why a similar reduction should not be made in the free age for marriage. A person who is fit to manage his own affairs, who is fit to serve on a jury, to make a will, to vote, should, in the Commission's view, be responsible enough to enter into a marriage contract without requiring the consent of any person or tribunal."[92]

The Commission recommended that the free age for marriage be reduced to 18 years and reiterated this recommendation in its Report on the Age of Majority published in 1983.[93] Following upon the enactment of the Age of Majority Act, 1985 which reduced the age of majority to 18 years the Commission's recommendation that the free age for marriage also be 18 years was endorsed by the *Report of the Joint Oireachtas Committee on Marriage Breakdown*.[94]

In its working paper the Law Reform Commission proposed two possible approaches in relation to persons under 18 years of age. It suggested either (a) that the minimum age for marriage should be the same as the "free age for marriage", i.e. 18 years and that no person below that age be permitted to marry in any circumstances or (b) that the minimum age for marriage should remain 16 years and that persons between 16 and 18 years should be permitted to marry with either the prior written consent of their parents or guardians or with the consent of some other appropriate authority, such as the President of the High Court, where there are no parents or guardians or where one or both of the parents or guardians refuse or withhold consent.[95] In addition, it proposed with reference to (b) that no person under 16 should be permitted to marry and that the current jurisdiction to grant exemptions to persons under 16 years should be abolished.

Proposal (a) had much to commend it as if, as a society, we believe that persons under 18 years of age do not have sufficient experience and understanding of life to be able to enter into marriage on the basis of their own judgement, it is logical that 18 years should be the minimum age for marriage. In this context, it is to be noted that research has shown that teenage marriages are more at risk than older marriages and there is no evidence that the giving of a parental consent or of any other consent to marriages of persons under 18 years reduces the risk.[95a]

Despite the above argument, in its *Report on the Age of Majority*, the Commission favoured the adoption of proposal (b) subject to the provision that if both guardians or parents opposed the marriage of a person over 16 but under 18 years of age it expressed the view that such person should not be able to appeal against combined parental opposition to the President of the High Court as originally suggested, on the basis that "it would not be oppressive to require a minor in such circumstances to wait for what in many cases will be a period of months rather than years before being able to marry." Where guardians or parents disagreed, however, the Commission was of the view that the possibility of such an appeal should remain an available option. It also recommended that

---

92. *Ibid* at p. 48.
93. Report on the Law relating to the Age of Majority, the Age for Marriage and Some Connected Subjects: L.R.C. Report No. 5 (April 1983).
94. *Report of the Joint Oireachtas Committee on Marriage Breakdown, supra*, p. 19.
95. Working Paper No. 2, pp. 50–51. See also pp. 79, 87.
95a. See *Report of the Joint Oireachtas Committee on Marriage Breakdown, supra*, at pp. 17–18. See also Working Paper No. 2 at p. 122 *et seq*.

marriages of persons between 16 and 18 years without a required parental or judicial consent should be null and void.[96]

In a study entitled "Age of Marriage and Marital Breakdown" published as an appendix to the Law Reform Commissions's Working Paper,[97] Dr. Helen Bourke suggests that if the marriage of persons between 16 and 18 years is to be permitted both parental consent and judicial permission should be required before such a marriage could be validly celebrated. She states:

> "Judicial permission to marry is regarded as necessary in these cases as well as parental consent (a) to protect a couple from being pressurised into marriage by parents who might persuade them to marry to avoid the stigma of illegitimacy; (b) judicial consent, if it is tied in with a system of pre-marital counselling could provide a very positive service for underage couples."[98]

The purpose of such pre-marital counselling is, she emphasises, "not to talk the couple out of marriage but rather to explore with them why they need to marry now and help them to face more realistically what marriage involves."[99] Moreover, a report from a marriage counsellor would assist the court in its assessment of the couple's readiness for marriage.[100]

The approach of Dr. Bourke has now been supported by the Joint Oireachtas Committee on Marriage Breakdown which stated that marriages of persons between 16 and 18 years should only be permitted if such persons obtain both the prior consent of their guardian(s) and the prior consent of a court. The committee also states that marriages of persons under 18 years of age without the necessary consents should be null and void.[101] It is submitted that the approach of the Oireachtas Committee is preferable to that of the Law Reform Commission. If the free age for marriage is reduced to 18 years, parental consent should not, by itself, be sufficient to enable persons between 16 and 18 years to enter into marriage. The concern of the law in establishing a minimum age for marriage should be to prevent minors from entering into precipitate and ill-advised marriages. It should provide them with protection not only from their own actions but also from those of their parents. The need for such protection is clear from information contained in the Law Reform Commission's Working Paper. In it it states that in 1975 there were 9 applications to the President of the High Court for an exemption order to marry by persons under 16 years of age. Eight of the applicants were girls, 7 of whom were pregnant.[102] A law as to the age for marriage must protect minors from being forced into marriage by parents anxious to cover up the embarrassment of a daughter's pre-marital pregnancy.

If persons between the ages of 16 and 18 years are to be permitted to marry, the Joint Oireachtas Committee's proposal should, it is submitted, be modified

96. Report No. 5 at pp. 24–25. See also the Law Reform Commission: *Report on Nullity of Marriage* (L.R.C. Report No. 9, October 1984), pp. 8–10 and 92.
97. Appendix D, at p. 117.
98. Working Paper No. 2, at p. 139.
99. *Ibid*, p. 136.
100. *Ibid*, pp. 139–140.
101. *Report of the Joint Committee, supra*, p. 19. See further p. 18 of the report where the committee states that consideration should be given to the introduction of a 3 month "waiting period" in civil law between the time a couple decide to marry and the date of marriage. Such a waiting period is suggested for all marriages and not just those of persons between 16 and 18 years of age.
102. *Ibid*, pp. 40, 128. Three of the applications to marry were granted, 3 were refused and 3 were withdrawn.

to permit such a person to marry without parental consent if the parent or guardian whose consent is required

(a) is incapable of consenting by reason of mental disability; or

(b) cannot after reasonable enquiries be found; or

(c) is dead,

and the court is satisfied that it is in the interests of the applicant's welfare that the marriage take place.

Finally, the proposal that marriages of persons under 18 years of age without the required consents should be null and void if implemented, will give substance to the content of any new law which prohibits marriages of persons under 18 years without such consents. If a person is regarded as too immature to make a proper judgement as to whether to enter into marriage or not and if the law only regards it correct to give effect to his decision upon his obtaining the consent of his parents or guardians and some other appropriate judicial authority, a marriage without such consents should be null and void. As we have already seen, however, at present if persons under 21 years of age marry without first obtaining the necessary consents, the validity of their marriage is unaffected.[103]

Government Intent: In the government's "Statement of Intent" first published in April 1986 it announced that it proposed to change the law in this area and that the minimum age for marriage "will in future be 18" with provision that the proposed "Family Court may authorise in exceptional circumstances the marriage of people between the ages of 16 and 18, having heard the parents." The Statement did not clarify whether the court will be empowered to authorise the marriage of a person or persons between 16 and 18 years without parental approval. The government also stated that it intended to introduce a new requirement of a minimum three month period of notice for marriage, which period could only be abridged with the consent of the Family Court. Such consent it stated will only be obtainable "where the Court is satisfied that there are substantial grounds justifying such an abridgement".[104] The three month notice period was originally suggested by the Joint Oireachtas Committee and is to apply to all intended marriages. To implement its proposals the government will have to publish and the Oireachtas will have to enact the necessary legislation.

---

103. Marriages (Ireland) Act, 1884, Sect. 32. See p. 98 *ante*. See further, the Law Reform Commission: Report No. 19, *supra*, p. 136 *et seq*.

104. See "Statement on Government's Intentions with regard to Marriage, Separation and Divorce" (Dept. of Justice, April 1986) at p. 5 and Revised "Statement" (June 1986) at p. 6. See also Footnote 101 *ante*.

CHAPTER 5

NULLITY OF MARRIAGE

JURISDICTION

The former jurisdiction of the Ecclesiastical Courts of the Church of Ireland over suits for nullity of marriage has been vested in the High Court since 1871. By the Matrimonial Causes and Marriage Law (Ireland) Amendment Act, 1870, Section 13, in exercising this jurisdiction, the High Court is to "proceed and act and give relief on principles and rules which in the opinion of the said court, shall be as nearly as may be conformable to the principles and rules which the Ecclesiastical Courts of Ireland have heretofore acted on and given relief."[1] This statutory provision and the failure of the legislature to enact any reforming legislation resulted in a total stagnation of nullity law for over a century. In the last decade, however, many members of the judiciary have abandoned the conservative and cautious approach of their predecessors and have, despite the jurisdictional constraints imposed by section 13 of the Act of 1870, radically developed this area of law.[2] As a consequence, nullity law, more than any other area of law, is rapidly becoming a juridical monument to the powerful impact of a dynamic judicial creativity.

Nullity and Dissolution: Whilst the constitutional prohibition on the dissolution of marriage contained in Article 41.3.2 does not prevent the High Court from granting decrees of nullity, it has in recent years clearly influenced both the High Court and the Supreme Court in expanding and liberalising the nullity jurisdiction. The courts have, nevertheless, always been careful to distinguish clearly as between the effect of a decree of dissolution and the effect of a decree of nullity. It has been emphasised that a decree of dissolution terminates a valid subsisting marriage and that a decree of nullity determines that a marriage never came into being. Referring to this distinction in *Griffith v. Griffith*[3] Haugh J. stated that:

"The question of nullity of marriage is best understood as part of the law of contract. A particular country may or may not permit of divorce; but in

---

1. See Chapter 2.
2. See *N. (otherwise K.) v. K.* [1986] 6 I.L.R.M. 75 (S.C.); *S. v. S.* (July, 1976) unreported (S.C.) judgement of Kenny J. See also *R.S.J. v. J.S.J.* [1982] 2 I.L.R.M. 263 (H.C.) Barrington J.; *D. v. C.* [1984] 4 I.L.R.M. 173 (H.C.) Costello J. (Supreme Court Appeal but withdrawn); *M.F. McD. v. W. O'R.* (January, 1984) unreported (H.C.) Hamilton J.; *W. v. P.* (June, 1984) unreported (H.C.) Barrington J.; *R. v. R.* (December, 1984) unreported (H.C.), Costello J.; *D.C. v. D.W.* (February, 1986) unreported (H.C.) Blayney J. See further *B. v. D.* (June, 1973) unreported (H.C.) Murnaghan J.; *S. v. O'S.* (November, 1978) unreported (H.C.) Finlay P., *M.K. (otherwise M. McC.) v. F. McC.* [1982] 2 I.L.R.M. 277 (H.C.) O'Hanlon J., *C. O'K. (otherwise C.P.) v. W.P.* (April, 1984) unreported (H.C.) McMahon J.
3. [1944] I.R. 35; (1943), 78 I.L.T.R. 95 (H.C.).

every country that treats of marriage . . . there must be a law of nullity, i.e. a law laying down the conditions under which the marriage contract is valid and binding."[4]

Thus, in this chapter, we are concerned with discovering the conditions under which, what on the surface appears to be a valid marriage contract, may in fact be a nullity.

VOID OR VOIDABLE

A marriage may either be void or voidable. As Bromley has pointed out,

"A void marriage is strictly speaking a contradiction in terms; to speak of a void marriage is merely a compendious way of saying that, although the parties have been through a ceremony of marriage, they have never acquired the status of husband and wife owing to the presence of some impediment."[5]

Such a marriage will be regarded as never having taken place. Being void *ab initio* it does not need a decree to annul it. Any such decree can only be declaratory and cannot effect any change in status. A decree, however, may be sought if desired not only by the parties to the purported marriage, but also by any other interested person, even after the death of the parties. Whereas a party to a void marriage may remarry without first obtaining a decree, such a decree is desirable in order to remove any doubt that may exist as to the validity of the former ceremony. In Irish law a marriage may be void because of:

   I. Lack of Capacity;

   II. Non-observance of Formalities;

   III. Absence of Consent.

A voidable marriage is for all purposes a valid subsisting marriage until a decree of annulment is pronounced and such a decree can only be made upon one of the parties to the marriage bringing nullity proceedings. Such proceedings cannot be initiated after the death of one party to the marriage or by a third party.[6]

The rationale behind the distinction between void and voidable marriages has been said to express a real difference in the substance upon which an allegation of nullity is made. In *A. v. B.*[7] explaining the difference, Wilde J. said:

"In all cases in which the incapacity to marriage is one in which society has an interest and which rests on grounds of public policy, it would be wrong and illogical that the validity or invalidity should depend upon the option of the parties and in all such cases the marriage is absolutely void"

---

4. [1944] I.R. at p. 41.
5. Bromley's *Family Law* 6th Ed. (Butterworths, London 1981), p. 75.
6. See *D. v. C.* [1984] 4 I.L.R.M. at p. 190. See also *A. v. B.* (1868) L.R. 1 P & D. 559 (Ct. of P & D.). See further *De Renville v. De Renville* [1948] 1 All E.R. 56, (C.A.) at p. 60 where Lord Greene M.R. stated:

"A void marriage is one that will be regarded by every court in any case in which the existence of the marriage is in issue as never having taken place and can be so treated by both parties to it without the necessity of any decree annulling it; a voidable marriage is one that will be regarded by every court as valid subsisting marriage until a decree annulling it has been pronounced by a court of competent jurisdiction."

See further, Law Reform Commission: *Report on Nullity of Marriage* (L.R.C. Report No. 9, October 1984) at pp. 88–89.
7. *Supra.*

but where the incapacity is "a matter of personal complaint only" and the parties

> "prefer to maintain the bond of matrimony intact, would it not be almost intolerable that a third party should have the right to insist upon an inquiry into the nature of their co-habitation and the revelation of their physical defects?"[8]

Until 1983 impotence was the only ground upon which a marriage was voidable in Irish law. In *D. v. C.*,[9] decided in May 1983, Costello J. held that a marriage is also voidable if at the time of the marriage ceremony a party suffers from a psychiatric illness which renders him or her unable to enter into and sustain a normal marital relationship.[10] This concept was further developed in the subsequent cases of *W. v. P.*,[11] where it was held to apply to a personality disorder, and *M.F. McD. v. W. O'R.*[12] in which it is suggested that such an inability may arise in other circumstances, for example, if it is proved that at the time of marriage a party was by reason of being homosexual incapable of entering into and sustaining the relationship which should exist between a married couple.

A decree annulling a voidable marriage retrospectively invalidates the marriage, the parties to it being regarded in law as never having been married to each other. Thus, in *F.M.L. & A.L. v. An tArd Chláraitheoir Na mPósadh*[13] (The Registrar General for Marriages), the first named plaintiff's second marriage was held to have been valid as and from the date of the marriage ceremony as a result of his first marriage being annulled on the grounds of his first wife's impotence, although the decree of annulment was not granted until a year after the second marriage ceremony had taken place. The granting of the nullity decree retrospectively invalidating the first marriage was held to retrospectively validate the second marriage.[13a]

ONUS OF PROOF

There is a general presumption that once parties have gone through a marriage ceremony they have contracted a valid marriage. Thus, the onus is on the petitioner (i.e. the party alleging invalidity) to rebut the presumption.[14] This onus was said by the court in *Griffith v. Griffith* to be "severe and heavy".[15] In *S. v. S.*[16] Kenny J. in the Supreme Court stated that "a petitioner must establish his or her case with a high degree of probability" or "must remove all reasonable doubt".

---

8. *Supra* at pp. 561-562, approved of by Costello J. in *D. v. C.* [1984] 4 I.L.R.M. at p. 190. See, however, *N. (otherwise K.) v. K., supra,* judgement of McCarthy J. at p. 94 where he states that he reserves "for further consideration, in an appropriate case, the question as to whether or not the issue of the contract being void or voidable is a true distinction."

9. *Supra.*

10. This ground for the granting of a nullity decree was first articulated by Barrington J. in *R.S.J. v. J.S.J., supra,* but no decree of nullity was granted in that case and it was not finally determined whether proof of such illness rendered a marriage void or voidable. See further p. 130 *post.*

11. (June 1984) unreported (H.C.).

12. (January, 1984) unreported (H.C.). See further p. 133 *et seq.*

13. [1984] 4 I.L.R.M. 667 (H.C.); See also *Mason v. Mason (otherwise Pennington)* [1944] N.I. 134 (K.B.D.).

13a. See also *A.M.N. v. J.P.C.* (December, 1985) unreported (H.C.).

14. *Griffith v. Griffith, supra; B. v. D.* (June, 1973) unreported (H.C.); *S. v. S.* (November, 1974) unreported (H.C.); (July, 1976) unreported (S.C.); *I.E. v. W.E.* [1985] 5 I.L.R.M. 691 (H.C.); *N. (otherwise K.) v. N. supra.*

15. *Supra* at p. 39. In *I.E. v. W.E., supra* at p. 693 Murphy J. stated that there was "a heavy burden imposed on the husband" in seeking to dispute the validity of his marriage.

16. *Supra.*

In the later case of *N. (otherwise K.) v. K.*,[17] McCarthy J. in the Supreme Court asserted that a petitioner must establish his case "upon the balance of probabilities standard."[18] While there is some judicial disagreement as to the standard of proof applicable, it has been generally emphasized that "the court must proceed with great caution before giving relief."[19] In this context it has been said that "it is not the function of the court by the exercise of this important jurisdiction to relieve parties from hasty and ill advised marriages."[20]

The courts have been anxious to ensure that spouses have not colluded to present a false case.[21] Whereas many decrees of annulment have, in practice, been granted in cases which have not been defended or in which only the applicant spouse has appeared before the court,[22] in some instances the failure of the other spouse to defend a case or appear in court has given rise to judicial suspicion. Thus, in *E.P. v. M.C.*[23] Barron J. refused to grant a decree because of "a suspicion that if the respondent (spouse) had given evidence the case might well have appeared differently".[24] The mere fact that both spouses are anxious that a decree be granted will, however, not of itself prevent a petitioning spouse from being successful, if the evidence given is accepted as truthful.[25] Consequently, the availability of convincing corroborative evidence can be crucial.[26]

GROUNDS FOR RENDERING A MARRIAGE VOID

I. Lack of Capacity

A: If parties go through a ceremony of marriage and

   (i) either party is at the time of the ceremony validly married to another person; or

   (ii) the parties are within the prohibited degrees of relationship; or

   (iii) are of the same biological sex

the ceremony is of no effect, and the marriage is void. See further chapter 4.

---

17. *Supra.*

18. See p. 6 of judgement. See also *M.F. McD. v. W. O'R.* (January, 1984) unreported (H.C.) at pp. 5–6 of judgement where Hamilton J. states that the onus is on the petitioner to prove what is alleged "to a high degree of probability".

19. *B. v. D., supra.* See also *R.S.J. v. J.S.J., supra*, "a judge should be cautious before accepting the evidence put forward for a petition in a nullity suit". [1982] 2 I.L.R.M. at p. 265.

20. *R.M. v. M.M.* (1941) 76 I.L.T.R. 165, (H.C.) per O'Byrne J. at p. 169. In *N. (otherwise K.) v. N., supra*, Finlay C.J. emphasized that parties to a marriage cannot, in nullity proceedings "successfully impugn the marriage merely because it could be considered to have been an unwise one." [1986] 6 I.L.R.M. at p. 82.

21. See further p. 142 *post.*

22. See, for example, the recent cases of *L.C. v. B.C. (Otherwise known as B.L.)* (November, 1985) unreported (H.C.); *A.M.N. v. J.P.C., supra*. See also *Griffith v. Griffith, supra*.

23. [1985] 5 I.L.R.M. 34 (H.C.).

24. *Supra*, see p. 38. The approach of the learned judge is open to question having regard to the approach of the Supreme Court in *M. v. M.* (October, 1979) unreported (H.C.). See footnote 26. See further p. 143.

25. See *N. (otherwise K.) v. N. supra*; *M. v. M.* (October, 1979) unreported (S.C.). See also *A.M.N. v. J.P.C., supra*, in which Barron J. granted a decree of annulment on the ground of impotence although the respondent did not appear as he was "satisfied" on the evidence that the marriage was never consummated.

26. See, for example, *N. (otherwise K.) v. N., supra*; *M.K. (otherwise M. McC.) v. F. McC.* [1982] 2 I.L.R.M. 277 (H.C.); *W. v. P.* (June, 1984) unreported (H.C.). In *M. v. M., supra*, although evidence given by the parties of their inability to consummate their marriage was corroborated by two medical witnesses, Murnaghan J. declined to grant a decree of annulment. On appeal, the Supreme Court granting the nullity decree stated that having regard to the evidence given it was not open to the trial judge to refuse a decree of nullity.

B: As we have already seen,[27] section 1(1) of the Marriages Act, 1972 which
came into force on 1st January 1975,[28] states that a marriage between persons
either of whom is under the age of 16 "shall not be valid in law" unless exemption
from this subsection is obtained. Prior to the coming into force of this section,
under the common law, a marriage by a boy under 14 or a girl under 12 although
not valid, could be ratified by the continued cohabitation of the parties after
both of them had attained the requisite age. Thus a marriage by parties under
age prior to 1975 was in essence voidable and not void.[29] Ratification made the
marriage irrevocably binding.

Having regard to the wording of section 1(1) and the power to obtain exemption from it prior to marriage, but not after marriage, a marriage between persons
either of whom is under 16, it is submitted, is now void and cannot be subsequently
validated. There is, however, no express statement to this effect to be found
anywhere in the Act.[30]

II. Non-observance of Formalities

That the parties have married in disregard of certain formal requirements
relating to the marriage ceremony. See Chapter 4, page 93 *et seq.*

III. Absence of Consent

In *N. (otherwise K.) v. K.*[31] the Supreme Court emphasized that the voluntary consent of the parties to a marriage is essential for a marriage to be valid.
Finlay C.J. stated:

> "The entry into of a valid marriage is not only the making of a contract but
> is also, in law, the acquisition of a status. The status thus acquired and the
> related concept of a family receives special protection from the provisions
> of the Constitution. Furthermore, the provision of the Constitution pro-
> hibiting the enactment of legislation permitting the dissolution of a valid
> marriage makes the contract of marriage absolutely irrevocable. Consent
> to the taking of such a step must therefore, if the marriage is to be valid, be
> a fully free exercise of the independent will of the parties."[32]

McCarthy J. in the same case stated:

> "Marriage is a civil contract which creates reciprocating rights and duties
> between the parties but, further, establishes a status which affects both the
> parties to the contract and the community as a whole. The contract is

---

27. See "Capacity to Marry", p. 79 *ante.*
28. S.I. No. 324 of 1974.
29. See *McM. v. McM.* and *McK. v. McK.* [1936] I.R. 177 at p. 215.
30. It is arguable that in the light of the fact that marriages celebrated by parties under
age prior to the coming into operation of this section could be validated, that marriages of
persons under 16 are under Sect. 1(1) voidable, such marriages not being valid at the date of
the ceremony but being capable of validation by the continued cohabitation of the parties
after both have passed the age of 16. See the English Age of Marriage Act, 1929, Sect. 1(1)
where marriages of persons under 16 were expressly declared void.
Moreover, in the Act of 1929, it was thought necessary to state that the validity of a
marriage selebrated prior to the passing of the Act would not be affected by the Act,
see Sect. 1(2). Thus, if the intention of Sect. 1(1) of the 1972 Act is to render marriages
of persons under 16 void, unless exempt, it is also arguable that marriages by persons under
16 that took place prior to the Act may now also be regarded as void, the section containing
no provision excluding marriages already solemnised prior to it coming into force from
its operation. Such a result would be preposterous and such an interpretation of the section
highly unlikely.
31. [1986] 6 I.L.R.M. 75.
32. *Ibid.*, at p. 82.

unique in that it enjoys, as an institution, a pledge by the State to guard it with special care and to protect it against attack, with a prohibition against the enactment of any law providing for the grant of a dissolution of marriage. ... This constitutional prohibition emphasizes the durability that is peculiar to the contract of marriage and the consequent need for a full appreciation of what that contract entails and that one is wholly free to enter into it or not."[33]

Thus "the essence of a valid marriage is the full and free consent of the contracting parties."[34] What on the surface appears to be a valid consent can be shown by proof of the presence of insanity or unsoundness of mind, intoxication, mistake, misrepresentation, fear, duress, intimidation or undue influence to have been no consent at all. It has also been suggested that proof of an intention not to fulfil a fundamental term of the marriage contract by a party to a marriage at the date of the ceremony may vitiate consent.

Whilst all of these factors are of assistance in describing the legal concepts the courts should have regard to in determining a challenge to the validity of a marriage based on absence of consent, it has to be remembered that they are "subservient to the ultimate objective" of ascertaining whether the consent of each party to a marriage "was real or apparent".[35] This warning should be kept in mind as we embark on a discussion of the various legal concepts that currently fall under the umbrella of absence of consent.

A. *Insanity:*[36] A person who has been certified as a lunatic or "a lunatic or person under a phrenzy" whose person and estate have been committed to the care and custody of trustees under any statute is incapable of marrying until declared sane, by virtue of the Marriage of Lunatics Act, 1811. The marriage of such a person is absolutely void even if it takes place during a lucid interval.[37]

If a person suffers from mental illness at the time of the marriage ceremony, a decree of annulment can be granted on the ground of insanity upon proof that at the date of marriage he or she was incapable of understanding the nature of the duties and responsibilities which marriage created[38] "free from the influence of morbid delusions upon the subject."[39] To succeed in proving this ground, it is not sufficient to establish that a party has before or after the marriage suffered from mental illness. It must be proved that at the time of the ceremony his state of mind was such that he was incapable of understanding the nature of the contract into which he was entering. Thus, unlike insanity under the Act of 1811, it is necessary to prove that the marriage did not take place during a lucid interval.[40]

---

33. *Ibid.*, at p. 93. See also Hederman J. *supra* at p. 91 where he states "a personal and full internal and informed consent is essential to a valid marriage." See also Murray & Murray Ireland [1985] 5 I.L.R.M. at p. 545 where Costello J. states that "The Constitution makes clear that the concept and nature of marriage which it enshrines are derived from the Christian notion of a partnership based on an irrevocable personal consent given by both spouses which establishes a unique and very special life-long relationship."

34. *Per* Griffin J., in *N. (otherwise K.) v. N., supra* at p. 89.

35. *Per* Finlay C.J. in *N. (otherwise K.) v. N., supra* at p. 82.

36. "Mental Capacity and Marriage" – see (1964), 98 I.L.T. & S.J. p. 159–161.

37. This had already been the position in Britain: see 15 Geo. 2, C. 30. See judgement in *Turner v. Meyers (Falsely called Turner)* (1808) 1 Hag. Con 414; 161 E.R. 600.

38. *Durham v. Durham* (1865), 10 P.D. 80; 1 T.L.R. 338, (P.D.A.).

39. *Hunter v. Edney (Otherwise Hunter)* (1885), 10 P.D. 93, *per* Sir J. Hannen P. at p. 95 (P.D.A.).

40. *B. (otherwise A.) v. B.* (1891) 27, L.R. Ir. 587 (Matr. Ct.).

It has been said that the contract of marriage is a very simple one which does not require a high degree of intelligence to comprehend it.[41] As a consequence, there are no recent written judgements delivered by the courts granting a decree of annulment based on a successful allegation of insanity as defined in this section. Although it was established in two recent cases determined by the High Court in which this ground was alleged that one of the parties in each case suffered from mental illness or a serious personality disorder, the court in both instances declined to hold that the illness rendered the party unable to fully understand the nature, purpose and consequences of the marriage contract.[42] Nevertheless, in both cases, the court indicated a willingness to develop the law and held that it if was proved that a party at the time of the marriage was, due to mental illness, unable to enter into and sustain a normal marital relationship, even though he was able to understand the nature of the marriage contract, a decree of nullity could be granted.[43] However, the High Court has held that proof of such an allegation renders a marriage voidable and not void,[44] whereas proof of insanity as defined in the preceding paragraph renders a marriage void. Until such time as there is a written judgement delivered by the Supreme Court confirming the existence within our law of this new concept as a ground of nullity, the law in this area will remain uncertain. A detailed discussion of this ground for nullity commences on page 130.

B. *Intoxication:* A marriage contracted by a party so drunk as to be incapable of giving proper consent is invalid. Sir William Scott in the old case of *Sullivan v. Sullivan* stated[45] that:

> "Suppose three or four persons were to combine to effect such a purpose by intoxicating another, and marrying him in that perverted state of mind, this Court would not hesitate to annul a marriage on clear proof of such a cause connected with such an effect."

Similarly it is submitted that a marriage contracted by a party under the influence of drugs or otherwise deprived of his capacity to consent is invalid. In all cases it is a question of whether a person is in "a state of disability, natural or artificial, which created a want of reason or volition amounting to incapacity to consent".[46]

C. *Mistake and Misrepresentation:* Both mistake and misrepresentation are given a very restrictive role in the annulment of marriages. In *Swift v. Kelly*[47] it was said that:

---

41. *Durham v. Durham, supra.* See also *In the Estate of Park Decsd.* [1945] P. 112, where it was held that although the deceased was "not of sound mind, memory and understanding" so as to execute a valid will, a different standard of capacity is required for entering into marriage, and that the consent given by him in a ceremony of marriage a few hours earlier was a valid consent, creating a valid marriage.
42. See *R.S.J. v. J.S.J., supra; D. v. C., supra.* See also *R. v. R.* (December, 1984) unreported (H.C.) and *D.C. v. D.W.* (February, 1986) unreported (H.C.) in which such an allegation was also made but upon which no determination had to be made.
43. *Ibid.* See also *W. v. P., supra; R. v. R., supra; D.C. v. D.W., supra.*
44. See *D. v. C., supra; W. v. P., supra* and *D.C. v. D.W., supra.*
45. 2 Hag. Con. 238; 161 E.R. 728 at p. 731 (Consistory Court).
46. See *Legeyt v. O'Brien* (1834) Milw. Rep. 325 at p. 333 *et seq.* (Consistory Court). In this case it was alleged that the husband was of unsound mind at the date of the ceremony and incapable of consenting. The unsoundness of mind it was alleged was caused by his grossly drunken habits which caused delirium tremens. The court rejected the contention that the marriage was invalid on this ground, holding that the evidence did not prove incapacity at the time of the ceremony.
47. (1835) 3 Knapp 257; 12 E.R. 648 (P.C.) cited with approval in *Griffith v. Griffith, supra.*

"... No marriage shall be held void merely upon proof that it had been
contracted upon false representations and that but for such contrivances,
consent never would have been obtained. Unless the party imposed upon
has been deceived as to the person and thus has given no consent at all,
there is no degree of deception which can avail to set aside a contract of
marriage knowingly made".[48]

Thus if X marries Y believing him to be Z there is no valid marriage. On the other
hand if X marries Y believing him to be rich and he turns out to have no money
the validity of the marriage is not affected. When fraud is spoken of as a ground
for avoiding a marriage it "does not include such fraud as induces a consent, but
is limited to such fraud as procures the appearance without the reality of consent."[49] It is not the presence of fraud by itself, but the absence of consent that
is a ground for a decree of annulment. Thus the fact that a woman concealed
from her husband at the time of their marriage that she was then pregnant by
another man did not invalidate their marriage.[50] Similarly, concealment by a
man, from the woman he was marrying, of the fact that on the night immediately
preceding their wedding he had slept with another woman was held not to render
their marriage void.[51] If each party knows that he is going through a ceremony
of marriage with the other, there is no evidence of mistake by which the marriage
may be invalidated. However, if one party did not know what the ceremony was
that took place, then there is no marriage. Thus, in *Ford (falsely called Stier) v.
Stier*[52] a decree of nullity was pronounced upon the judge being satisfied that
the petitioner believed she was going through a ceremony of betrothal and that
she did not consent to marry the respondent.

D. *Intention not to fulfil fundamental term of marriage contract:* In *S. v. S.*[53]
which is discussed in detail in the section entitled "Impotence" further on in this
chapter, Kenny J. delivering a minority judgement in the Supreme Court, held
that the intention of a spouse at the time of marriage not to have sexual intercourse with his or her spouse, without prior agreement between them, has the
result that "the consent necessary for the existence of a valid marriage does not
exist" as an "intention to have sexual intercourse is a fundamental feature of the
marriage contract". This judgement created the possibility that proof of the
existence of an intention of one party to a marriage not to fulfil a fundamental
term of the marriage contract, without the knowledge of the other, at the time
of the marriage ceremony, could vitiate a consent to marry and render a marriage
void. It remains to be seen whether this approach will be approved by a majority
of the Supreme Court, as in *S. v. S.* the other members of the court who delivered
written judgements gave different reasons for their decision and did not refer to
the judgement of Kenny J. If the Supreme Court does at some subsequent date
accept this as a ground for nullity, it would also have to be determined what other
obligations of marriage are to be regarded as so fundamental by the courts as to
give rise to the possibility of a marriage being a nullity if one or other party to
the marriage at the date of the ceremony does not intend to fulfil such obligation.

48. *Ibid.*, 12 E.R. 648, *per* Lord Brougham at p. 661.
49. *Moss v. Moss (otherwise Archer)* [1897] P. 263 approved in *Griffith v. Griffith*; see
also *Wakefield v. Mackay* (1807) 1 Hag. Con. 394; 161 E.R. 593; *Ussher v. Ussher* [1912]
2 I.R. 445; (1912), 46 I.L.T.R. 109, (K.B.D.).
50. *Moss v. Moss (otherwise Archer), supra.*
51. *S. v. S., supra.*
52. [1896] P. 1; see also *Valier v. Valier (otherwise Davis)* (1925), 133 L.T. 830;
Kelly (otherwise Hyams) v. Kelly (1932), 49 T.L.R. 99, (P.D.A.); *Mehta v. Mehta* [1945]
2 All E.R. 690, (P.D.A.).
53. *Supra.*

In *E.P. v. M.C.*[54] relying on the judgement of Kenny J., the petitioner, in addition to seeking a decree of nullity on the ground of duress,[55] also relied upon the ground that the respondent never intended to enter into a proper and lasting marriage. The petitioner had married the respondent because she was pregnant. Five months after the marriage their baby was born. Four months later the parties acquired their own home and six weeks after its acquisition the respondent left home, never to return. Evidence was given that she had only married to avoid the shame of pregnancy and to provide a name for her child and that "she said that having got what she wanted the marriage was over."[56]

Barron J. declined to grant a nullity decree on this ground as he was not satisfied that the petitioner had discharged the onus of proof. Nevertheless, he made it clear that even if he had done so, no decree would have been granted by him on this ground as there was "no evidence whatsoever" that the respondent had suffered from any illness. In rejecting this ground, the learned judge, however, stated: "undoubtedly the evidence shows that she (the respondent) was spoilt, that she preferred life as a single person and that she was totally unprepared to accept the obligations of marriage."[57]

It is respectfully submitted that if the proofs had been held to be satisfactory and the approach of Kenny J. followed, a nullity decree could have been granted. Proof of mental illness is not an essential ingredient to establish that at the date of the marriage ceremony a spouse intended not to fulfil a fundamental feature of the marriage contract and there is no suggestion in the judgement of Kenny J. in *S. v. S.*[58] that such proof is required. Indeed, the existence of a mental illness may in fact prevent a party to a marriage from forming any coherent long-term intentions. It is submitted that an intention at the time of marriage to continue life as a single person and not to reside permanently with the person you are marrying can be nothing other than an intention not to fulfil a fundamental term of the marriage contract. Barron J., in his judgement, appears to have failed to take into account the different components of this ground of nullity as compared to an allegation alleging that at the date of marriage a party was, due to mental illness, unable to enter into and sustain a normal marriage relationship.[59]

E. *Duress, Intimidation and Undue Influence:* If a person is induced or forced to go through a ceremony of marriage by fear, threats, intimidation, duress or the undue influence of another person, such a marriage is invalid. Although it has been stated in some High Court cases that fear or pressure which is not improper or which is justly imposed cannot ground a decree of nullity[60] such an approach has now been rejected by the Supreme Court.[61]

The amount of duress required to vitiate consent has been said to be "a question of degree" dependent on the facts of the particular case.[62] It is clear from the decided cases that the courts use a subjective test to determine whether duress has vitiated consent. The question the court must decide is not whether a

---

54. [1985] 5 I.L.R.M. 34 (H.C.).
55. See p. 118 *post*.
56. *Supra* at p. 36.
57. *Supra* at pp. 38–39.
58. *Supra*.
59. See also *M.F. McD. v. W. O'R., supra*.
60. See *Griffith v. Griffith* [1944] I.R. 35 (H.C.); *A.C.L. v. R.L.* (October, 1982) unreported (H.C.).
61. See *N. (otherwise K.) v. N., supra*.
62. In *Griffith v. Griffith* [1944] I.R. at p. 52 Haugh J. said "duress must be a question of degree and may begin from a gentle form of pressure to physical violence accompanied by threats of death . . .".

reasonable person would have succumbed to the pressure imposed but whether the alleged pressure was such that it overbore the free will of the particular petitioner in the particular case before the court.[63] Thus, pressure sufficient to amount to duress in the case of one person may not be sufficient to do so in the case of another person of stronger character.[64]

Griffith v. Griffith[65] was the first Irish case in this century in which the High Court declared a marriage null and void on the ground of duress. The petitioner had married at the age of nineteen. Prior to the marriage he had been accused by the respondent and her mother of having unlawful carnal knowledge of the respondent (then under 17 years of age) and so causing her to become pregnant. They threatened him with criminal prosecution. This threat, with the consequent scandal and publicity to him and his family, along with a fear of conviction and imprisonment, induced him to go through with the marriage. The petitioner had not in fact engaged in sexual intercourse with the respondent and the statement as to the paternity of the respondent's child was false. Haugh J. when granting a decree of annulment stated:

> "that the consent to marry . . . given by the petitioner was in fact given not because of the usual inspirations caused by love and affection, but because of a real and grave fear inspired by an unjust and fraudulent misrepresentation of a very grave and vital matter, going to the root of his consent; and that it was this fear, so unjustly imposed, that led to the marriage now impugned . . . I feel bound to hold that a consent so obtained by this combination of fraud and fear, the first producing the second, is not a consent that binds the petitioner – and there being no real consent in law, there was accordingly no valid marriage."[66]

If in this case the allegation of paternity had been true and the petitioner had been induced by fear of prosecution to marry the respondent, Haugh J. made it clear that he would have held the marriage to be valid:

> "Assuming that marriages have resulted from a fear so imposed, they are clearly valid and binding on both parties. The man is free to elect between

63. *N. (otherwise K.) v. N., supra*, see judgement of Griffin J. at pp. 90 and 91. See also judgement of McCarthy J. at pp. 93 and 94 and the dissenting judgement of Henchy J. at p. 85. See further *B. v. D., supra; S. v. O'S., supra.*
64. See *Scott (falsely called Sebright) v. Sebright* (1886) 12 P.D. 21 at p. 24 where Butt J. stated:

> "It has sometimes been said that in order to avoid a contract entered into through fear, the fear must be such as would impel a person of ordinary courage and resolution to yield to it. I do not think that is an accurate statement of the law. Whenever, from natural weakness of intellect or from fear – whether reasonably entertained or not – either party is actually in a state of mental incompetence to resist pressure improperly brought to bear, there is no more consent than in the case of a person of stronger intellect and more robust courage yielding to a more serious danger."

See *N. (otherwise K.) v. N., supra*. See further *B. v. D.* (June, 1973) unreported (H.C.); *S. v. O'S.* (November, 1978) unreported (H.C.); *M.K. (otherwise M. McC.) v. F. McC.* [1982] 2 I.L.R.M. 277 (H.C.); *C. O'K. v. W.P.* (April, 1984) unreported (H.C.).
In the English cases of *Szechter (Orse. Karsov) v. Szechter* [1971] P. 286; [1970] 3 All E.R. 905 (P.D.A.); *Buckland v. Buckland* [1968] P. 296; [1967] 2 All E.R. 300 (P.D.A.) and *H. v. H.* [1953] 2 All E.R. 1229 the court was of the opinion the fear must be reasonable. It is submitted that this approach by the English Courts was wrong and contrary to precedent (see in addition to *Scott v. Seabright, supra, Cooper v. Crane* [1891] P. 369 and *Parojcic v. Parojcic* [1959] 2 All E.R. 1 (P.D.A.)) and appears to have been finally over-ruled in the recent decision of the Court of Appeal in *Hirani v. Hirani* [1983] 4 F.L.R. 232 (C.A.). See further T. Ingman & B. Grant, "Duress and the Law of Nullity" (1984) 14 Fam. Law 92.
65. *Supra.*
66. *Supra* at p. 52.

the scandal and possible punishment on the one hand or the marriage to the girl he has wronged on the other."[67]

In the similar case of *Kelly v. Kelly*[68] there was held to be no true marriage where a woman fraudulently induced a man to go through a marriage ceremony by falsely (unknown to him at the time) alleging she was pregnant by him and threatening that if he did not marry her she would inform his parents, his sister who was a nun and that she would bring legal proceedings against him that would result in adverse publicity. The marriage was said to be "induced by fraud and fear to the point that his (the petitioner's) consent to the marriage was no true consent." The fact that the marriage was never consummated was regarded as an important indication of the petitioner's mental attitude to the marriage at the time of the ceremony.

In *B. v. D.*[69] the pressure brought to bear on the petitioner was of a different nature to that which occurred in the two preceding cases. The petitioner and respondent were both national school teachers and having known each other for five years, married in Dublin in August, 1970. Throughout their relationship there was no evidence of any real affection between them. From the time they first met the respondent used the petitioner's car as if it was his own, spent most of his time gambling and borrowed (in the later stages demanded) money from her which he did not repay. Notwithstanding the petitioner telling her family two days prior to the ceremony that she did not wish to marry the respondent, she kept an arrangement to meet him and travel to Dublin with him by car for the ceremony. On the way to Dublin the petitioner rang her sister and told her that the respondent was very aggressive and that she thought the best thing to do would be to drop him in Dublin and return home. However, she did not have the opportunity to carry out this intention and the ceremony took place. Murnaghan J. stated that *prima facie* having regard to the petitioner's age,[70] her social and educational standing, it was very difficult to take any view other than that she had consented to all that had occurred. However, he continued:

"The picture of the respondent which I get . . . is that, towards the petitioner, he was generally arrogant and domineering and that he cut her off from her family and friends . . . I consider that he is very forceful, mentally arrogant and disinclined to take no for an answer."[71]

Acknowledging that the petitioner "certainly had nothing resembling a strong personality", Murnaghan J. continued:

"I have very little doubt but that gradually from the first time they met, the petitioner found herself in her relationship with the respondent in a groove, which as time went on got deeper and deeper and out of which she was constitutionally unable to extract herself, and in which perhaps she was prepared in the circumstances, if not content, to remain . . . I have . . . come to the conclusion after long consideration that the reasonable probabilities

---

67. *Supra* at p. 43. See also *Buckland v. Buckland, supra,* which followed Haugh J.'s judgement in *Griffith v. Griffith.* See also "Marriage or Prison: The Case of the Reluctant Bridegroom", by A.H. Manchester in (1966), 29 M.L.R. 622. Griffith and Buckland are here discussed and criticised. Pre 1966 Irish and English authorities on duress are here discussed at length.
68. (February, 1971) unreported (H.C.).
69. *Supra.*
70. She was over 27 at the date of the marriage.
71. See pp. 6 and 7 of judgement.

are that the degree of duress was such as to render the contract of marriage in this case one that the law should consider to be a nullity."[72]

In *B. v. D.* the parties' marriage had been consummated but it was held that "such intercourse that did take place, took place under the same duress as compelled the petitioner to marry the respondent."[73]

In *S. v. O'S.*[74] the petitioner and respondent having known each other for almost one and a half years married in June, 1974. At the time of the marriage the petitioner was twenty two and the respondent was twenty five. Initially the parties had a normal courtship and planned to marry when the respondent, who was a medical student, completed his studies and finished his year's internship. One night during their courtship the petitioner went to a dance without the respondent This act by the petitioner had a traumatic emotional effect on the respondent. He reacted by developing a condition known as Munchausen Periodic Syndrome. This condition consisted of projecting with elaborate detail bizarre sicknesses. The only cure for these alleged sicknesses, according to the respondent, was in the first instance the almost exclusive attention and physical presence of his fiancée, the petitioner, and secondly an early marriage. By May of 1974 the petitioner was persuaded by the respondent that if their marriage did not take place within six weeks she would be responsible for his rapid decline and death or his suicide. The petitioner in evidence admitted that she was totally taken in by the respondent and that she believed she would be responsible for his death if she refused to marry him. The psychiatric evidence established that at the time of the marriage she was "in the emotional bondage of the respondent". Holding the marriage to be void, Finlay P. stated:

> "Essentially, it seems to me that the freedom of will necessary to enter into a valid contract of marriage is one particularly associated with emotion and that a person in the emotional bondage of another person couldn't consciously have the freedom of will."[75]

In all of the above cases the duress was imposed by the respondent. However, duress can be imposed, not only by one of the parties to the marriage but also by a third person[76] or persons[77] or external circumstances.[78]

In *M.K. v. F. McC.*[79] the petitioner was aged 19 at the date of the marriage and the respondent 21. They had known each other for about two years, going out regularly with a group of friends but they had never contemplated the possibility of marriage. In the summer of 1972 they engaged in sexual intercourse for the first time and as a result the petitioner became pregnant. Upon their mutual parents learning of the petitioner's pregnancy each of them was told that they would either have to marry or leave home. The petitioner described the situation in her home at that time as "tense and disastrous" with her mother in bed "crying and broken up".[80] The respondent's father refused to talk to him and the situation in his home became so bad he had to leave and stay temporarily with a friend. Both sets of parents met and decided in the absence of

---

72. See p. 8 of judgement.
73. See p. 9 of judgement.
74. (November, 1978) unreported (H.C.).
75. See p. 2 of judgement.
76. See for example *Parojcic v. Parojcic, supra*. (Fear imposed by petitioner's father).
77. See, for example, *Hirani v. Hirani, supra*. (Threats and pressure imposed by both parents); See also *McLaron v. McLaron* (1968) 112 *Solicitors Journal* 419.
78. See *H. v. H.* [1954] P. 258; [1953] 2 All E.R. 1129; *Buckland v. Buckland, supra*; *Szechter (orse. Karsov) v. Szechter* [1971] P. 286; [1970] 3 All E.R. 905 (P.D.A.).
79. [1982] 2 I.L.R.M. 277 (H.C.).
80. *Ibid.* at p. 278.

both parties that the petitioner and the respondent would have to marry as quickly as possible before the petitioner's pregnancy became noticeable. The petitioner was ordered by her mother to see a priest to arrange the wedding and she did so without any prior communication with the respondent. Six weeks after the petitioner's pregnancy became known to her parents, the wedding took place. Two weeks after the ceremony she suffered a miscarriage. The parties separated early in 1975. Although they had marital relations on a number of occasions there were no children of the marriage.

O'Hanlon J. comprehensively reviewed all the relevant Irish and English authorities. He noted that many of the English nullity cases in which decrees of annulment had been sought on the ground of duress required proof of danger to the life or liberty or physical well-being of the petitioner.[81] Moreover, referring to *Griffith v. Griffith*,[82] he noted that:

> "It may be inferred from Haugh J.'s summary of the principles applicable ... that he took the view that if the allegations made against the petitioner were well founded, it could be permissible to apply pressure of such kind against him to induce him to enter into marriage and that he would not be allowed to allege lack of true consent at a later stage."[83]

He acknowledged, however, that less stringent requirements were accepted as being sufficient to ground an application for nullity in *B. v. D.*[84] and *S. v. O'S.*[85] and concluded that he would take "the broader view of the concept of duress"[86] illustrated by these two cases which is "more consonant with the related topic of undue influence than with legal duress in the stricter sense of the term."[87] In this case he found that:

> "An unwilling bride and a resentful husband were dragged to the altar and went through a ceremony of marriage which neither of them wanted and without any genuine feelings of attraction or affection which might have led on to a happy union in the course of time."[88]

Holding the marriage to be null and void he was satisfied:

> "that the will, not merely of one partner but of both husband and wife, was overborne by the compulsion of their respective parents and that they were driven unwillingly into a union which neither of them desired or gave real consent to ... and which was doomed to failure from the outset[89] ...

81. See in particular *Szechter (orse. Karsov) v. Szechter, supra; Buckland v. Buckland, supra; Singh v. Singh* [1971] P. 226, (C.A.); *Singh v. Kaur* (1981) 11 Fam. Law 151 (C.A.). See, however, the later judgement of the Court of Appeal in *Hirani v. Hirani, supra*, in which the court denied that proof of a threat to "life, limb or liberty" was essential in order to make a finding of duress and in a remarkable volte face the court held at (p. 234) that "the crucial question ... is whether the threats, pressure or whatever it is, is such as to destroy the reality of the consent and overbear the will of the individual ... thus invalidating or vitiating her consent." See further D. Bradley, "Duress & Arranged Marriages", (1983) 46 M.L.R. 499.
82. *Supra.*
83. *Supra* at pp. 280–281.
84. *Supra.*
85. *Supra.*
86. *Supra* at p. 282.
87. *Supra* at p. 281.
88. *Supra* at p. 279. See also p. 283.
89. *Supra* at pp. 282–283.

and that the duress exercised was of a character that they were constitutionally unable to withstand."[90]

Following upon the above decision of O'Hanlon J. a series of cases came
before the High Court in which it was alleged that the petitioning spouse had
been forced to marry by reason of a pre-marital pregnancy. In *A.C.L. v. R.L.* [91]
the parties had met in 1975 when the petitioner was 28 years of age and the
respondent 32. Within a short time of their meeting the respondent proposed
marriage. Early in 1976 the parties commenced living together and again the
respondent proposed. In May, 1976, the petitioner learnt that she was pregnant.
She concealed the pregnancy from her family and in September, 1976, went to
live with the respondent in London. The parties returned to Ireland shortly
after Christmas following the birth of their child. Upon their return, the petitioner's parents and other members of her family were told of the baby's birth
and that they were going to get married eventually. The general reaction from
the petitioner's parents and brother was that she had to get married as soon as
possible. In March, 1977, the ceremony took place. For the following nine
months the parties had a normal marital relationship. The petitioner again
became pregnant and this time miscarried and from that date their relationship
deteriorated and they eventually separated.

The petitioner contended that she did not want to get married, that she had
reservations about doing so and that she only agreed to marry because she was
forced to do so by her parents. The respondent stated that the petitioner had
been perfectly willing to get married and that she was above reacting to the
pressures caused by their unconventional relationship. Barron J. expressed the
view that the petitioner's evidence was "coloured by the breakdown" of their
relationship and, expressing a preference for that of the respondent, he stated:

> "on only one point do I not accept the respondent's evidence. It is when
> he says that he thought the petitioner was above all that. I feel that he was
> fully aware that the petitioner was allowing herself to be persuaded to get
> married almost immediately when he knew that she had wanted her decision
> to be reached gradually."[92]

As for the allegation of duress, he continued:

> "I am satisfied that the parties came home intending to live together as a
> family and to get married sometime in the future. On her return home the
> petitioner realised that this scheme of things could not be adhered to. It
> was causing conflict with her family. She accordingly agreed to get married
> as soon as possible to please them. Without their persuasion the parties
> would have got married but not as soon . . . she had a free choice and . . .
> she expressed it to please her parents."[93]

Referring to the concept of duress as enunciated by O'Hanlon J. in *M.K. v.*

---

90. *Ibid.* at p. 283. The fact that the parties' marriage had been annulled by the Roman
Catholic Church clearly had some influence on the approach adopted by O'Hanlon J. (See
[1982] 2 I.L.R.M. at p. 282). See, however, *N. (otherwise K.) v. K., supra,* in particular
judgement of Finlay C.J. where he states that:

> "the fact of such an ecclesiastical decree of nullity cannot, of itself, be a contributing
> factor to our decisions" [but] "the seeking of such a decree soon after a purported
> marriage and some time before the petition for nullity in the civil courts could, in
> certain cases, be accepted as evidence corroborating the allegation of an absence of real
> consent." (See [1986] 6 I.L.R.M. at p. 82).

91. (October, 1982) unreported (H.C.).
92. See p. 8 of judgement.
93. See pp. 8–9 of judgement.

F.McC., Barron J. stated that for such an allegation to succeed:

> "the compelling facts must be pressure improperly brought to bear ... and also the fear must arise from some external circumstance for which the petitioner is not herself responsible[94] ... there is no evidence that the petitioner's parents, brothers or sisters acted ... improperly. They were doing what they believed was for her best. Undue influence at least is fastening on to another's weakness and seeking to obtain a benefit from such behaviour. No such suggestion can be made here. The position in which the petitioner found herself was brought about by her own conduct. She had the choice between marriage on the one hand and the possible alienation of her parents on the other."[95]

While it is arguable that on the evidence given the pressure imposed on the petitioner in the circumstances of this case was not such as to warrant the granting of a nullity decree, it is clear that Barron J. in his judgement took the more restrictive view of duress articulated in *Griffith v. Griffith* as opposed to the broader view taken in *B. v. D.*, *S. v. O'S.* and *M.K. v. F. McC.* Moreover, there is no basis in precedent for the learned judge's suggestion that duress imposed by a third party can only ground a decree of nullity if the third party was "seeking to obtain a benefit from such behaviour".

In two subsequent cases, *J.R. v. McG.*[96] and *E.P. v. M.C.*,[97] Barron J. again declined to grant decrees of annulment. In neither of these cases did the respondent appear before the court to give evidence.

In *J.R. v. McG.* twenty years after her marriage the petitioner sought a decree of annulment on the ground of duress. The petitioner had discovered in December 1963, that she was pregnant and nine days later had become engaged to the respondent, the parties marrying in February 1964. Their child was born in August 1964 and a second child was born in February 1966. There were many difficulties during the course of their marriage but the parties did not separate finally until 1980. The petitioner alleged that she had been forced into marriage by virtue of her pregnancy, that her mother had initially told her to pack her

---

94. See p. 10 of judgement.
95. See p. 11 of judgement. Barron J. also stated:

> "It seems to me that, even if the evidence supported a compelling pressure which would otherwise have justified the granting of the relief sought, such relief should be denied because the respondent would not have been aware that the will of the petitioner had in fact been overborne."

If this statement of law is correct it would be impossible for any petitioner, no matter how great the coercion imposed that resulted in marriage, to successfully seek a declaration of nullity if the respondent could prove that he or she was unaware that the petitioner was acting under duress. This principal has never formed part of the law of nullity, in relation to the ground of duress and no authority was given by the learned judge for this statement which is *obiter*. Moreover, see *Hirani v. Hirani, supra*, in which an arranged marriage of a young Hindu girl, forced upon her by her parents who had threatened to turn her out of her home if she did not go through with it, was declared null and void. The respondent did not meet the petitioner until the wedding ceremony and there is nothing in the judgement to indicate that he was aware that the petitioner was being coerced by her parents prior to the marriage. Ormrod, L.J. stated that the "crucial question in these cases ... is whether the threats, pressure or whatever it is, is such as to destroy the reality of consent and overbear the will of the individual." See [1983] 4 F.L.R. at p. 234. What is relevant is the petitioner's state of mind at the time of the ceremony, not the respondent's level of awareness of the petitioner's state of mind. Although Barron J. refers to many of the English precedents in this area, neither in this case or in his later judgement in *J.R. v. McG., supra*, is *Hirani v. Hirani* cited or discussed. The above passage in *Hirani* was subsequently cited with approval by Griffin J. giving judgement in the later Supreme Court case of *N. (otherwise K.) v. K., supra*.

96. (February, 1984) unreported (H.C.).
97. (March, 1984) unreported (H.C.).

bags and leave the family home and that when she had not done so had ostracised her; that she was told she could not remain in the house after her baby was born and had nowhere else to go; that the respondent had been assaulted by her mother when he called to her home; that no help was available to the petitioner from any of her relations; and that the respondent had only agreed to marry when he realised the petitioner's situation in her family home.

Referring to the difficulty of assessing the position in which the petitioner found herself 20 years after the marriage took place, Barron J. stated that he did not totally accept her evidence. He stated:

> "there were undoubtedly pressures on her which resulted in her agreeing to get married . . . these were resolved in an amazingly short time if she herself was against the idea of marriage."[98]

Referring to the judgement of O'Hanlon J. in *M.K. v. F. McC.* he stated:

> "That was a case where the evidence showed that the decision that the parties should marry was made not by the parties themselves but by their respective families and that the two parties to the ceremony were in fact given no choice in the matter and accordingly there was no true consent on either of their parts.[99]
>
> It (duress) can operate so that the party under the duress fails to apply his or her mind to the question of giving consent. In such cases, the duress creates a form of bondage. The party concerned may not even be aware that such bondage exists. *M.K. v. McC.*[100] and *S. v. S.*[101] . . . are examples of this form of duress. Duress can also operate to compel the party under the duress to make a decision to give his or her consent to escape the consequences which will otherwise follow. Such a party knows that his or her consent is not a true consent and is in effect consenting not to being married but to escaping from the threat. Such a marriage is a sham or a device to procure a particular result, i.e. freedom from the particular threat to which he or she is subjected."[102]

Stating that it was the latter type of duress which was alleged in this case, he continued that:

> "to test whether or not duress has affected the mind of a party to a marriage so that the marriage is a mere device to escape the pressure imposed it is necessary to look to how that party acted, not only before the marriage ceremony but also afterwards."[103]

In this case the parties had resided together after the marriage for many years and the marriage had been consummated. The marriage, Baron J. held "was not brought about through duress."[104]

In *E.P. v. M.C.*[105] the parties started going out together in February 1979. In August 1979 the respondent told the petitioner that she was pregnant and that he was the father. They became engaged and attended a pre-marriage counselling course for five weeks and got married early in November 1979. The court

---

98. See pp. 4–5 of judgement.
99. See p. 7 of judgement.
100. *Supra.* This decision is an illustration of the second type of duress referred to in this passage by Barron J. and not of the first type as the learned judge suggests.
101. The reference should be to *S. v. O'S., supra.*
102. See p. 7 of judgement.
103. See p. 8 of judgement.
104. See p. 9 of judgement.
105. *Supra.*

accepted that the respondent had told the petitioner that if he did not marry her she would have an abortion as she believed if she did not marry her parents would put her out of their home. The petitioner in these circumstances felt he had no option but to agree to marry. It was further accepted by Barron J. that the evidence established that "the parties would not have married when they did but for the respondent's pregnancy". Subsequent to the marriage the parties lived with the respondent's parents until they acquired their own home in August 1980. Six weeks later the respondent left the petitioner, having told him that she had only married to avoid the shame of pregnancy outside marriage and to provide a name for her child.

The respondent did not appear before the court and Barron J. declined to grant a nullity decree as two letters from the respondent's solicitor produced in evidence had indicated that the respondent was also anxious that a decree be granted and led him to suspect "that if the respondent had given evidence the case might well have appeared differently". He held that the petitioner had not discharged the required onus of proof.[106] Even if this onus had been established however, it is clear that Barron J. would have refused to grant a decree. Referring to the allegation of duress he stated:

> "Duress must be of such a nature that there is the appearance without the reality of consent. Where consent is procured through fear for the life of another, the party consenting is fully aware that he is giving his consent to a ceremony of marriage but at the same time is in reality consenting to save that life ... If the petitioner had given his consent in this case solely for the purpose of saving the life of his unborn child, this would have constituted a ground for a decree of nullity. But the petitioner would have had to establish that the marriage was such a device to procure this end. If, as in this case, the parties had a normal engagement followed by a normal marriage and held themselves out as being a married couple, it cannot be said that the marriage ceremony was a sham."[107]

It is respectfully submitted that it is impossible to reconcile the learned trial judge's conclusion with the evidence given in this case, which was accepted by him as truthful. The fact that the parties would not have married but for the respondent's pregnancy, that they did marry just two months after she first discovered she was pregnant because the petitioner believed that if they did not do so she would have an abortion and that they co-habited as a married couple for only ten months should, on the basis of the earlier authorities, such as *B. v. D.*, *S. v. O'S.*, and *M.K. v. F. McC.* have been held to be a sufficient basis upon which to grant the nullity decree sought. The case of *C. O'K. v. W.P.*[108] decided a month later starkly illustrated the differing approaches being taken by judges of the High Court in determining nullity proceedings grounded on duress.

In *C. O'K. v. W.P.* the parties had met when the petitioner was under 16 years of age, the respondent being 18 years old. The respondent showed himself from an early stage to be "extremely jealous, possessive and domineering" and got "angry if he saw (the petitioner) speaking to another man". Within a year "at his insistence the petitioner acquiesced in sexual intercourse with him" and McMahon J. noted that "in all matters of making a choice she had to yield to what he wanted".[109] The parties first became engaged in 1972 and on a number

---

106. *Ibid.*, at p. 38.
107. *Ibid.* As for the concept of a "normal engagement period" see also the dissenting judgement of Henchy J. in *N. (otherwise K.) v. K., supra.*
108. (April, 1984) unreported (H.C.).
109. See p. 2 of judgement.

of occasions the petitioner tried to extricate herself from the relationship. When she did so, the respondent, McMahon J. stated:

> "went to extraordinary lengths to get her back. He carried on a process of watching and besetting her home and place of work, following her to and from work in his car, ringing up . . . her place of work with messages . . . and threatening to tell her parents and her work mates that she had sexual relations with him . . . He treated her with occasional acts of violence, not of a serious kind but his conduct conveyed to her that he was a person capable of great violence and she regarded him with a certain amount of fear."[110]

The petitioner's mother was unwell and she never told her parents of her difficulties. Following the final occasion when she returned the engagement ring, the respondent made a scene at her home "threatening to do away with himself and crying".[111] Believing the respondent might commit suicide in February 1974, the petitioner gave in and reinstated the engagement. Thereafter she made no further effort to terminate the engagement and the parties married 9 months later, in November 1974. The couple co-habited until March 1981, when the petitioner returned to her parents' home. During the period they lived together there were frequent rows and no real communication. Although they did engage in sexual intercourse the petitioner never became pregnant. In June 1983, the petitioner issued nullity proceedings.

McMahon J. stated that he was satisfied that from the time when the petitioner reinstated the engagement up to the date of marriage

> "She had not the freedom of will necessary to enter into a valid contract of marriage" and that "the means used by the respondent to procure her agreement to marry went far beyond persuasion and were oppressive and improper."[112]

He concluded, granting a decree of annulment, stating:

> "Duress need not be physical violence or the threat of it . . . any pressure improperly brought to bear may amount to duress . . . any degree of duress which in fact causes a person to agree to a marriage to which he or she would not otherwise have agreed invalidates the marriage. I am satisfied that the methods employed by the respondent to obtain the petitioner's consent to this marriage amounted to duress and undue influence and caused the petitioner to agree to a marriage she did not wish to contract."[113]

Having regard to the length of the parties' engagement prior to marriage and the number of years they co-habited after marriage, it is submitted that if the above case had fallen to be determined by Barron J. instead of McMahon J., on the basis of the principles enunciated in the trilogy of cases discussed prior to *C. O'K. v. W.P.*, and, in particular, the law as applied in *E.P. v. M.C.*, it is highly unlikely that a decree of nullity would have been granted.

In *N. (otherwise K.) v. K.*[114] in November 1985, it finally fell to the Supreme Court to determine whether a narrow or broad view of the concept of duress should be applied in nullity proceedings.

The petitioner was 19 and the respondent 20 years of age when they married

---

110. See pp. 3–4 of judgement.
111. See p. 5 of judgement.
112. See pp. 5–6 of judgement.
113. See p. 6 of judgement.
114. [1986] 6 I.L.R.M. 75 (H.C., S.C.).

in February 1979. The couple had met in August 1978, and in November 1978, the petitioner was persuaded by the respondent to have sexual intercourse with him. Shortly afterwards the parties ceased meeting each other. By Christmas 1978 the petitioner realised she was pregnant, informed her parents who were both very upset and shortly afterwards was brought by her father to the respondent's parents' home. On arrival, the petitioner was left in a room on her own whilst her father informed the respondent's parents of her pregnancy and presented them with two alternatives: an abortion or marriage. He dismissed the suggestion that the petitioner could keep the baby but remain unmarried. The respondent upon his arrival home, learnt of the situation, spoke to the petitioner who was crying and upset and agreed that they would marry. Six weeks later the wedding took place, all the arrangements having been made by both sets of parents without the intervention of the parties or any interest displayed by them in the necessary arrangements. The couple lived together for three months after the wedding in the respondent's parents' home and then the petitioner returned to live in her parents' home. They again co-habited for a short time before the birth of their baby and for a further period of three months approximately 12 months after its birth. In November 1983, the petitioner issued nullity proceedings.

In the High Court, Carroll J. concluded that the parties would not have married but for the pregnancy; that the respondent was completely immature and unsuited for marriage; that the petitioner was little more than a school girl and did not see any alternative to getting married; that she would not consider an abortion and that if she did not get married she believed she would get no support from her parents and would have to leave home. The trial judge also concluded that the shock of discovering that she was pregnant had put the petitioner into a state in which she could not think clearly, that she thought her parents knew best in their view that she should marry and that she had not been counselled or advised on any alternative approach she could have taken, such as bringing up her child as a single mother or placing it for adoption. Despite the above findings, Carroll J., at first instance declined to grant a nullity decree stating that it was not a case in which the petitioner "definitely did not want to marry and was coerced, forced or even persuaded to marry. She had no clear idea what to do and her father made up her mind for her. I do not think that amounts to duress at law."[115]

The Supreme Court by a 4 − 1 majority[116] decided in favour of the petitioner and declared the marriage to be null and void. In so doing, the court rejected the more restrictive approach illustrated by the judgements of Haugh J. and Barron J. and adopted and approved of the "broader view of duress"[117] articulated by O'Hanlon J. in *M.K. v. F. McC.* Referring to the latter case, Finaly C.J. stated:

> "The fundamental *ratio decidendi* of (that) decision . . . appears to me . . . to be a rejection of the earlier decisions which restricted the concept of duress in nullity to threats of physical harm or threats falsely based, of other harmful consequences."[118]

Rejecting the contention that a decree of nullity can only be granted if the pressure imposed was improper, the Chief Justice stated:

---

115. *Ibid.*, at p. 79.
116. Finlay C.J., McCarthy J., Griffin J., Hederman J. A dissenting judgement was delivered by Henchy J.
117. See judgement of Griffin J., *supra*, at p. 90.
118. *Supra* at p. 82.

"If . . . the apparent decision to marry has been caused to such an extent by external pressure or influence, whether falsely or honestly applied, as to lose the character of a fully free act of that person's will, no valid marriage has occurred."[119]

Taking up a similar theme, McCarthy J. referred to the need for:

"A true voluntary consent based upon adequate knowledge and freed from vitiating factors commonly described as undue influence or duress, particularly those emanating from third parties"[120]

and further on he continued, stating that:

"If a fear leading to marriage is produced by duress or intimidation or, indeed, ignorance itself, I can find no logic in excusing such fear because it is 'justly imposed'. It may well be that options are presented to the prospective spouse but if it is an option without any real choice, it is no option at all. If a partner to the alleged contract has entered into it as a result of pressure offering little option, however *bona fide* that pressure may be, however well meaning . . . the sources of that pressure, how can it be said that the prospective partner is exercising a true free will?"[121]

Griffin J., also finding in favour of the petitioner, emphasized that it was:

"of the utmost importance that the contract of marriage should be entered into with the full and free consent of the contracting parties and (that) if . . . the apparent decision to marry on the part of one of the parties has been caused to such an extent by external pressure as to lose the character of a fully free act of that party's will, no valid marriage has taken place."[122]

The decision of the Supreme Court in *N. (otherwise K.) v. K.* has now firmly established that a broad view is to be taken of the concept of duress in nullity petitions brought before the High Court and that the more restrictive approach articulated in some of the earlier cases discussed is no longer part of Irish law.[123]

---

119. *Ibid.*
120. *Supra* at p. 93.
121. *Ibid.*
122. *Supra* at p. 90. See further *P.C. (otherwise O'B.) v. D. O'B.* (October, 1985) unreported (H.C.) in which Carroll J. declined to grant a decree of nullity on the ground of duress stating that pre-marital pregnancy *per se* is not a ground for annulment and that she was satisfied that there was no evidence to establish that the "petitioner's will was overborne so as to destroy the reality of her consent to marry". There was no evidence in this case of any pressure being imposed on the petitioner by any other person, although there was medical evidence that she was "an immature personality" and Carroll J. accepted that she may have married when she did "because she could not see any other solution to her problems." The parties had become engaged 6 months before the petitioner's pregnancy.
123. Although Henchy J. delivered a dissenting judgement, it was largely based on his view of the facts of the particular case. In referring to the concept of duress applicable to determine a nullity petition the learned judge stated that he was:

"prepared to assume that the test for duress is entirely subjective and that the source or nature of the duress is not of consequence provided the coercive matters relied on by the wife are such either to have affected her mind to the point of making her incapable of understanding what she was doing, or, even if she did so understand, overbearing her power of volition to the extent that it could not be said that she really consented to the marriage." (*Supra* at p. 85).

In the learned judge's view the furthest the wife's case could be put was:

"to say that she entered into the marriage because she was unduly influenced by the wishes of her parents" [but he concluded that] "no influence short of duress can produce nullity" (*Supra* at p. 88).

It is this latter part of Henchy J.'s dissenting judgement that is at variance with that of other members of the court, as it is clear from the majority decision that if undue influence is exercised to the extent of vitiating the consent of a party to marriage, it may, in the majority view, of itself, ground a decree of nullity. See further P. O'Connor, "Duress and the Supreme Court" (1986) 4 I.L.T. (n.s.) 4 and 22.

GROUNDS RENDERING A MARRIAGE VOIDABLE

Impotence

If at the time of the solemnisation of a marriage either of the parties to it is impotent, the court may upon the petition of one of them pronounce a decree declaring it null and void. A marriage is only voidable and not void on this ground. A third person cannot sue for a decree of nullity on the ground of impotence, nor can the validity of the marriage be challenged on such a ground after the death of one of the parties.[1] Such a marriage is valid for all legal purposes during the lifetime of the parties, unless a decree of nullity is pronounced. If such a decree is pronounced, however, it is then regarded as void *ab initio*.[2]

The Meaning of Impotence: A decree for impotence is granted on the basis of a party's inability to consummate the marriage. A marriage is regarded as consummated once the parties have engaged in "ordinary and complete"[3] sexual intercourse after the solemnisation. A party's inability to engage in such intercourse is the basis for a decree. Thus, it is essential to understand what is meant by "ordinary and complete" sexual intercourse.

The question to be considered is whether a party is capable of *vera copula* i.e. capable of the natural sort of coitus without the power of conception.[4] Inability to procreate or a party's sterility affords no ground for obtaining a decree of nullity. What has been said to be important in determining whether one or other party is impotent is the question of the "practical possibility" of full penetration by the male into the female.[5] It is not necessary to show that such penetration is physically impossible; it is sufficient to show that it is only possible under conditions to which a spouse would not be justified in resorting.[6] As the fertility of the spouse is irrelevant, so is the question of a spouse's ability to ejaculate.[7] Once "full and complete" penetration is achieved, a marriage is regarded in law as consummated and a petition on the ground of impotence cannot succeed.[8]

Impotence can arise from a number of causes. There may be some physical defect such as a total lack of sexual organs or a malformation of sexual organs rendering intercourse impossible. Alternatively, there may be some psychological or neurotic cause rendering it impossible for a perfectly formed individual to engage in the sexual act, i.e. a person may have an invincible repugnance to the

---

1. *A. v. B.* [1868] L.R. 1 P. & D. 559 (Ct. of P. & D.).
2. See *F.M.L. & A.L. v. tArd Chlaraitheoir na mPosadh* [1984] 4 I.L.R.M. 667 (H.C.); *A.M.N. v. J.P.C.* (December, 1985) unreported (H.C.). See also *Mason v. Mason* [1944] (N.I.) 134 (K.B.D.).
3. *D-e v. A-g (falsely calling herself D-e)* [1845] 1 Robb. Eccs. 279; 173 E.R. 1039.
4. *Ibid.*
5. If the parties have not had intercourse, the birth of a child as a result of fecundation ab extra or artificial insemination will not amount to consummation – *Clarke (otherwise Talbott) v. Clarke* [1943] 2 All E.R. 540; *R.E.L. (otherwise R.) v. E.L.* [1949] P. 211 [1949] 1 All E.R. 141; (P.D.A.). As only full penetration by the male into the female is required, the fact that the husband used a contraceptive sheath does not prevent consummation from taking place, *Baxter v. Baxter* [1948] A.C. 274; [1947] 2 All E.R. 886 (H.L.). Similarly if the husband practises coitus interruptus consummation is not prevented – *White v. White* [1948] 2 All E.R. 151; [1948] P. 330, (P.D.A.). *Cackett (otherwise Trice) v. Cackett* [1950] 1 All E.R. 677; [1950] P. 253, (P.D.A.).
6. *G. v. G.* (1871) L.R. 2 P. & D. 287 (Ct. of P. & D.).
7. *R. v. R. (otherwise F.)* [1952] 1 All E.R. 1194, (P.D.A.); *M. M. (otherwise G.) v. P.M.* (December, 1985) unreported (H.C.).
8. See *W. (otherwise K.) v. W.* [1967] 3 All E.R. 178, (P.D.A.). Husband able to enter wife but following entry his erection collapsed. Penetration held not to be "full and complete" and decree granted.

sexual act resulting in a paralysis of the will,[9] or may suffer nervousness or hysteria.[10] A person's incapacity does not necessarily have to be general and may be *quoad hanc* or *quoad hunc* a particular spouse, i.e. a person may be unable to have sexual intercourse with the person he marries, but be able to with other persons.[11] Thus, in both *S. v. S.*[12] and *R. (otherwise W.) v. W.*[13] there was evidence that the impotent spouse was engaging in sexual intercourse with a third party although psychologically impotent *vis-à-vis* the other spouse.

Curability: The disability alleged must be incurable. Impotence will be regarded as incurable if the condition can be remedied only by an operation attended by danger, or if the spouse at fault refuses to submit to an operation. A spouse cannot compel the other spouse to have an operation and is only expected to use reasonable means of persuasion.[14] Moreover, even if a physiological disability can be or is resolved by medical intervention, the court may still regard a party to a marriage as impotent if satisfied that the latter still suffers from a psychological difficulty that will continue to prevent sexual intercourse taking place.[15]

Proof of Impotence: The onus of proof of impotence is on the party alleging it, and the impotence or "practical impossibility" of consummation must still exist at the date of the hearing.[16] This onus, as in all nullity petitions, is a heavy one. It has been said that to succeed, "the petitioner must remove all reasonable doubt" as to the respondent's incapacity[17] or must establish his or her case "with a high degree of probability".[18]

Wilful Refusal to Consummate: Until the decision of the Supreme Court in 1976 in *S. v. S.*[19] wilful refusal of sexual intercourse had always been held to be insufficient to justify the court annulling a marriage.[20] In *McK. v. McK.*[21] the repeated attempts by a potent husband to consummate his marriage were repelled by his wife. It was contended for the wife that she was neurotic and had an invincible repugnance to the husband amounting to a paralysis of her will, so that she was unable to consummate the marriage. On medical inspection she was found to be perfectly formed and *apta viro*; there was no suggestion of neurosis or hysteria or of any physical defect suggesting any kind of incapacity. It was

9. *S. v. S.* (July, 1976) unreported (S.C.); *R. (otherwise W.) v. W.* (February, 1980) unreported (H.C.); *A.M.N. v. J.P.C., supra; R.M. v. M.M.* (1941) 76 I.L.T.R. 165 (H.C., S.C.); *McM. v. McM.* and *McK. v. McK.* [1936] I.R. 177 (H.C.); *G. v. G.* [1924] A.C. 349 (H.L. (Sc.)).
10. *G. v. G.* (1871) *supra; S. v. A. (otherwise S.)* (1878) 3 P.D. 72 (P.D.).
11. *S. v. S., supra; R. (otherwise W.) v. W., supra; McM. v. McM., supra; R.M. v. M.M., supra; G. v. G., supra; C. (otherwise H.) v. C.* [1921] P. 399; [1921] All E.R. 268.
12. *Supra.*
13. *Supra;* see also *L.C. v. B.C. (otherwise known as B.L.)* (November, 1985) unreported (H.C.); *A. O'H. (otherwise F.) v. F.* (December, 1985) unreported (H.C.).
14. See *D-e v. A-g (falsely called D-e), supra; G. v. G.* (1871), *supra; L. v. L. (falsely called W.)* (1882) 7 P.D. 16, (P.D.A.); *G. v. G. (falsely called K.)*, (1908) 25 T.L.R. 328; *S. v. S. (otherwise C.)* [1956] P. 1; (1954) 3 All E.R. 736, (Assize); *M. v. M. (otherwise B.)* [1957] P. 139; [1956] 3 All E.R. 769.
15. See *N.F. v. M.T. (otherwise known as F.)* [1982] 2 I.L.R.M. 545 (H.C.) at p. 547. See also *L.C. v. B.C. (otherwise known as B.L.), supra.*
16. *S. v. S. (otherwise C.), supra.*
17. *Per* Lord Birkenhead in *C. (otherwise H.) v. C. supra;* approved by Kenny J. in *S. v. S.* (1976) *supra,* and Hanna J. in *McM. v. McM.* and *McK. v. McK. supra;* see also *U. (falsely called J.) v. J.* (1867) L.R. 1 P. & D. 460 (Ct. of P. & D.).
18. See *S. v. S., supra,* judgement of Kenny J.
19. Discussed further on p. 125 *et seq.*
20. *Napier v. Napier (Goodban)* [1915] P. 184 (C.A.); *McM. v. McM.* and *McK. v. McK., supra; R.M. v. M.M., supra.*
21. *Supra.*

stated to be a "difficult and delicate task to distinguish between impotence and wilful obstinacy" but such a difficulty "had to be faced and a determination come to". Hanna J. concluded that in his opinion the cause of the trouble was that the wife "had resolved from the first not to have any children" and that if the husband "had been a man of more determined and inconsiderate personality he would have succeeded in overcoming . . . the wilful and continued refusal on the part of the wife." Consequently the petition for nullity was refused.

In the later case of *R.M. v. M.M.*[22] the court also refused to grant a nullity decree. O'Byrne J. was satisfied that the wife was "genuinely shocked and disgusted" by attempts at consummation and that she had "a strong and real aversion to the sexual act". However, he was not satisfied that this aversion was of such an "invincible character as to produce a paralysis and distortion of the will". The marriage had not been consummated due to the wife's wilful refusal and he believed that he was fortified in his view by her statement that "she would never allow her husband or any other man to have sexual intercourse with her". On appeal, the Supreme Court affirmed this decision.

Since 1941 when the case of *R.M. v. M.M.* was decided, there have been considerable psychiatric advances in the understanding of psycho-sexual problems. It is questionable as to whether in the light of these developments *R.M. v. M.M.* would necessarily be decided today as it was in 1941.[23] It is certainly arguable that today the facts of the case would be regarded as involving a real impotence.[24]

The distinction between "real" incapacity to consummate and wilful refusal to consummate enunciated by the civil courts can be examined against the more enlightened approach adopted by the canon law of the Roman Catholic Church. By Canon 1142 an unconsummated marriage may be dissolved by the Roman Pontiff.[25] Mr. Justice Davitt, a former President of the High Court, in 1968 pointed out[26] that since 1941 the High Court has had to decide cases where the facts were almost identical to those in *R.M. v. M.M.* In some of these cases the parties involved were Roman Catholics and their marriages had been dissolved by Papal Dispensation. Thus they remained married according to civil law but were unmarried in the view of the Church.[27] Mr. Justice Davitt argued that a marriage in which one of the parties wilfully "refuses to accept and perform one of its fundamental obligations can hardly be regarded as in every sense a real marriage. The offending party has in one sense repudiated it. It would seem in the interests of justice, as well perhaps as in the interests of morality, that the unoffending spouse should be able to obtain relief".[28]

In *S. v. S.*[29] Kenny J. in the Supreme Court appears to have adopted the above reasoning. In this case the husband and wife had known each other for two years prior to their marriage. During this two years they engaged in sexual

---

22. *Supra.*

23. See Article by Gerald Clarke in *Studies* 1968, p. 24 — A response to an article in the same issue by the ex-President of the High Court, Mr. Justice Davitt.

24. See, in particular, the judgements in *S. v. S., supra* and *R. (otherwise W.) v. W., supra.*

25. See *The Code on Canon Law* (Collins 1983) prepared by The Canon Law Society of Great Britain and Ireland at p. 201.

26. See 1968 *Studies*, p. 6 — "Some Aspects of the Constitution and the Law in Relation to Marriage".

27. See Jean Blanchard, *The Church in Contemporary Ireland* p. 70, where the unreported case of *Begley v. Begley* is cited as an example of a case involving parties who were refused a civil annulment but were granted a canonical dissolution for impotence.

28. In England since the passing of the Matrimonial Causes Act, 1937, a marriage has been voidable on the ground of wilful refusal to consummate. The present English law is contained in the Matrimonial Causes Act, 1973, Sect. 12. See K. Hayes — *The Matrimonial Jurisdiction of the High Court.* (1973) 8 I.J. (n.s.) 55 at p. 69.

29. (July, 1976) unreported (S.C.).

intercourse on many occasions. After their marriage they went on honeymoon for eight days and then made their home in Dublin. Although the parties slept together both during their honeymoon and when living in the matrimonial home, they did not at any time after their marriage have sexual intercourse. When the wife discussed this matter with her husband he said that he did not like her, that she made him sick, that the marriage was a mistake and that he did not want any children. Six months after the wedding the husband left the wife and went to live with another woman. There was also evidence of the husband having sexual relations with this other woman immediately prior to the marriage.

Subsequent to his departure the wife, (the petitioner in the proceedings) obtained an annulment in the marriage tribunal of the Roman Catholic Church for the diocese of Dublin. Despite the fact that the church decree had no effect on the civil validity of her marriage, three days after obtaining it, she married another man in a Roman Catholic church. At the date of these proceedings she had had a child by her second husband. The Supreme Court, on appeal from the High Court,[30] granted the wife's petition for a decree of nullity on the ground of her husband's impotence. Two members of the court, while agreeing that the husband was obviously potent, concurred in holding that this was a case of relative impotence, "i.e. *impotence quoad hanc*" and issued a decree of nullity on that ground. They both rejected the contention that the marriage was also invalid on the ground that the petitioner had been induced by fraud to marry her husband. Henchy J. in rejecting this ground stated that:

> "There is no doubt that the wife entered into the marriage on the inducement of a concealed falsity, but that falsity (by which I mean falsity as to emotional and sexual capacity on the part of the husband) may or may not have been known to the husband at the time of the marriage. For all we know, he may have genuinely believed or hoped that he would be able to make the marriage a success. Because of that, fraud must be discounted."[31]

The above judgement leaves open the possibility of the marriage being annulled, due to absence of proper consent, upon proof that a party had an intention not to consummate at the date of the marriage ceremony. Henchy J. merely held that on the facts of the case non-consummation was due to the husband's real sexual incapacity in relation to his wife and not to a conscious decision by him prior to or at the time of the ceremony, not to consummate the marriage.

Kenny J. however, in annulling the marriage, did not agree that the husband had become impotent *vis-à-vis* his wife, but was of the opinion that at the date of the ceremony he had formed the intention not to have intercourse with her. He stated that:

> "Section 13 of the Act of 1870 did not have the effect of fossilising the law in its state in that year. That law is, to some extent at least, judge made and Courts must recognise that the great advances made in psychological medicine since 1870 make it necessary to frame new rules which reflect these[32] . . . It seems to me that the intention to have sexual intercourse is such a *fundamental feature of the marriage contract*[33] that if at the time of the marriage

---

30. (November, 1974) unreported (H.C.).
31. See p. 4 of judgement.
32. This passage has been cited with approval and relied upon to develop the law in the following High Court cases: *R.S.J. v. J.S.J., supra; D. v. C., supra; W. v. P., supra; M.F. McD. v. W. O'R., supra.* See, however, the comments of Henchy J. at p. 17 of his dissenting judgement in *N. (otherwise K.) v. K., supra.*
33. Author's italics.

either party has determined that there will not be any during the marriage and none takes place, and if the parties have not agreed on this before the marriage . . . a spouse who was not aware of the determination of the other is entitled to a declaration that the marriage was null. The intention not to have or permit intercourse has the result that the consent which is necessary to the existence of a valid marriage does not exist."[34]

As a consequence of this case, despite earlier judicial pronouncements to the contrary, it seems that a marriage may now be annulled on the ground of a spouse's wilful refusal to consummate, provided the latter intended not to consummate at the time when the marriage took place. However, it is only the judgement of Kenny J. that unequivocally supports wilful refusal as a ground. It remains to be seen whether this judgement will be followed in future cases.

Curiously, despite judicial assertions in cases prior to *S. v. S.* that wilful refusal to consummate will not afford a sufficient ground for the granting of a nullity decree, the Rules of the Superior Court seem to contemplate the granting of a decree on such a ground. Order 70, Rule 32(4) makes explicit provision for the medical inspection of parties "in proceedings for nullity on the ground that the marriage has not been consummated owing to the wilful refusal of the respondent to do so."

In practice there are great difficulties distinguishing between wilful refusal and psychological inability to consummate. The approach of Kenny J. lessens the importance of this distinction. However, one essential difference does seem to exist. Impotence renders a marriage voidable. Proof of an intention not to consummate on the part of one spouse at the time of the wedding causes the consent necessary to constitute a valid marriage to be absent. As we have already seen, absence of consent renders a marriage void.

Medical Inspection:[35] It is the practice of the court, borrowed from the Ecclesiastical Courts, in a nullity suit for impotence to require a medical inspection of the parties. This is done by two medical practitioners experienced in gynaecology appointed from a rota of medical inspectors by the Master of the High Court. Either side can obtain a copy of the medical reports and the inspectors may be called as witnesses and cross-examined. Such an inspection is not obligatory and where a party refuses to submit to inspection, the court may nevertheless still grant a decree.[36] The fact that the marriage has not been consummated despite the co-habitation of the parties for a reasonable time, and the willingness of the petitioner to consummate, together with a refusal on the part of the respondent to undergo a medical examination can raise an inference of impotence on the part of the respondent.[37]

Petition of impotent spouse: As a result of the High Court decision in *McM. v. McM.*[38] it seems that a spouse cannot be granted a decree as petitioner on the ground of his own impotence unless he can satisfy the court that there has been

34. See p. 5 of judgement.
35. R.S.C. Order 70, Rule 32 (S.I. No. 15 of 1986).
36. *E.M. v. S.M.* (1942) 77 I.L.T.R. 128; See also *S. (otherwise B.) v. S.* [1943] N.I. 87 (K.B.D.); *S. v. S.* (July, 1976) unreported (S.C.); *N.F. v. M.T. (otherwise known as F.)*, *supra.*
37. *S. (otherwise B.) v. S., supra; B. (otherwise H.) v. B.* [1901] P. 39 (P.D.A.); *W. v. S. (orse W.)* [1905] P. 231 (P.D.A.). See also *F. v. P. (falsely called F.)* (1869) 75 L.T. 192, where it was held that after a reasonable period of co-habitation during which one party was always willing to consummate, the court can draw an inference that something more than mere wilful refusal must have animated the other.
38. *Supra.*

conduct on the part of the other spouse which would prevent the latter from denying the "just cause" of the petition. An example of such conduct would be the latter's repudiation of the marriage contract and its obligations.

Hanna J. stated:

> "The decree for nullity of marriage cannot . . . be granted to a petitioner on the ground merely of a petitioner's own impotence, but it is clearly established that if a petitioner can, in addition to proof of his own impotency, satisfy the Court that there had been, and is, conduct on the part of the respondent which has destroyed the *verum matrimonium* e.g., by a genuine and deliberate repudiation of the marriage contract and its obligations, the Court may *ex justa causa* grant the relief."[39]

In this case both parties were Roman Catholics. The petitioner, the husband in 1934 sought a decree on the ground of his own impotence. Three years earlier the respondent had left him and the court found that she would not return to him on account of his violence and neurasthenic condition over sexual matters. She refused to defend the proceedings and was content that he should obtain any redress to which he was entitled. However, her attitude was that she recognised the marriage until the Church dissolved it.

Hanna J. refusing to grant a decree of annulment stated that:

> "it would be contrary to reason and justice to hold that, where the respondent is a Roman Catholic, it is a repudiation of the status of wife and of her marriage contract for her to say to the Court: 'Though I have left him on account of his violence, and will not return for fear of violence, I shall take no part in the proceedings in the civil Court and shall adhere to my marriage until it is terminated by my Church'."[40]

At the time of the court hearing the respondent had taken no steps to obtain a church dissolution or annulment. Rather than repudiating the marriage, as a matter of conscience and religious belief, she regarded it as still subsisting.

In both the earlier case of *A. v. A.* (sued as *B.*)[41] and the more recent case of *R. (otherwise W.) v. W.*[42] decrees of annulment were granted on the application of an impotent petitioner, the respondent in each case being held to have repudiated the marriage by seeking a decree of annulment in the Ecclesiastical Courts of the Roman Catholic Church. Finlay P. giving judgement in the latter case stated:

> "The parties were both Catholics at the time of the purported marriage and the marriage took place according to the rites of the Catholic Church. I have no doubt on the evidence that the respondent's immediate concern after the separation between the parties had become final and complete was to try and free himself of this marriage according to the law of the Church of which he was a member. There can be no other explanation of his very rapid institution of proceedings seeking a decree of nullity in the Ecclesiastical Courts. It is irrelevant to the issue at present before me that those proceedings have not been yet terminated since they are being persisted in by the respondent. That must, in my view, be a clear and unequivocal repudiation

---

39. *Ibid.* at pp. 219, 220.
40. *Ibid.* at p. 206.
41. (1887) 19 L.R. (Ir.) 403. (Matr. Ct.).
42. (February, 1980) unreported (H.C.).

by him of the marriage and, therefore, in my view entitles the petitioner to a decree of nullity based on her own impotency."[43]

In *R. (otherwise W.) v. R.* it was argued that a repudiation of the marriage is not required in all cases for the petition of an impotent spouse to succeed. The respondent's behaviour provided conclusive evidence of repudiation, however, and the learned judge reserved this question to be decided in a future case upon it arising.

It is difficult to understand why a spouse who, upon marrying, discovers his own impotence should not be able to rely on it alone to obtain a decree of nullity, when such impotence can be relied upon by the other spouse to obtain a decree. The premise running through the decision in *McM. v. McM.* seems to be that an impotent spouse has committed some sort of wrong by marrying and that he should not be permitted to rely simply on his own wrong in order to terminate the marriage.

It is submitted that the court in *McM. v. McM.* fails to distinguish between two quite different situations. The first is the case of the person who marries fully aware of the fact that he is impotent, and knowingly deceives the other spouse. The second is the person who does not discover his own impotence until after the marriage has taken place.

Hanna J. admitted that the majority of commentators on the Canon Law were in favour of the proposition that a spouse can secure annulment on the grounds of his own impotence if he was unaware of it at the time of the marriage. In reaching the conclusion that a petitioner's impotence by itself is insufficient to ground a decree of nullity, he relied to a great extent on the case of *Norton v. Seton.*[44] He stated:

"In my opinion a fair reading of that judgement is that the learned Judge was of opinion that the petitioner could not maintain the claim solely on the ground of his own impotence."[45]

This, however, is not the basis of the decision in that case. In that case, Sir John Nicholl quoted the maxim that "No man shall take advantage of his own wrong" and it is evident that his judgement is founded on the belief that the husband entered marriage well knowing his physical defects and deceived the wife into marrying him. Whereas the decision of the Irish Court of Appeal in *A. v. A.* (sued as *B*).[46] does support Hanna J.'s conclusion, two other cases he cites certainly do not. In *G. v. G. (falsely called K.)*[47] the Court of Appeal purporting to follow the previously mentioned case, decided that a decree of nullity can be granted at the suit of an impotent spouse and the Master of the Rolls did not deem it necessary for the other spouse to repudiate the marriage. Finally in *Davies (orse Mason) v. Davies*[48] Langton J. expressly refrained from deciding whether the court possesses jurisdiction to annul a marriage on the petition of an impotent spouse if there has been no repudiation by the other spouse.

McM. v. McM. itself was a case in which the spouse did not discover his impotence until after the marriage ceremony. It is submitted that the balance of

43. See p. 13 of judgement. See also *L.C. v. B.C. (otherwise known as B.L.), supra*, in which Lynch J. held that a wife who had left her husband and was residing with another man by whom she had a child had repudiated her marriage.
44. (1819) 3 Phill. Ecc. 147; 27 Digest 266; 161 E.R. 1283.
45. *Supra* at p. 211.
46. *Supra.*
47. (1908) 25 T.L.R. 328 (C.A.).
48. [1935] P. 58 (P.D.A.).

authority is against the decision reached by Hanna J. and that the ratio of that case should be overruled upon a similar case arising.[49]

It is further submitted, however, that if a spouse enters marriage knowing himself to be impotent, the other spouse being unaware of his condition, it is only just that he should be denied relief. If he knew of his impotence at the time of the ceremony, he entered the marriage with a full realisation of the fact that it would not be consummated. His own impotence in such circumstances could make no difference to a situation which he had voluntarily accepted. In such a situation only the potent spouse should be permitted to petition the court. The present law, however, seems to be that if the potent spouse does some act repudiating the marriage, the impotent spouse can succeed on the grounds of his own impotence. It is difficult to understand why a spouse who enters a marriage fully knowing that it cannot be consummated due to his own incapacity, should be permitted to plead such incapacity to obtain an annulment in one situation − i.e. where the other spouse also repudiates the marriage − and be prevented from relying on it in another situation, i.e. where there is an absence of such repudiation. In both situations the impotent spouse enters marriage knowing that it cannot be consummated and the principal cause of action is his own impotence. In such a situation only the other spouse should be permitted to petition.

Inability to Enter into and Sustain a Normal Marriage Relationship

Prior to 1982 there was no precedent in Irish law for the granting of a decree of annulment on this ground. In *R.S.J. v. J.S.J.*,[50] determined in that year, the petitioner alleged that at the date of marriage he suffered from schizophrenia or some similar illness and contended that as a result he was "incapable of contracting a valid marriage because he was so ill that he was unable to maintain and sustain a normal relationship with his wife"[51] and sought a decree of annulment. In considering whether it was open to the court to grant a nullity decree in such circumstances Barrington J. stated:

> "The law has always accepted impotence as a ground for avoiding a marriage . . . what is contended for here is a much more serious impediment to marriage. No doubt there have been happy marriages where one of the parties was impotent. But it is impossible to imagine any form of meaningful marriage where one of the parties lacks the capacity of entering into a caring or even a considerate relationship with the other."

Referring approvingly to the dictum of Kenny J. in *S. v. S.*[52] he held:

---

49. See *Harthan v. Harthan* [1949] P. 115; [1948] 2 All E.R. 639 (C.A.), in which *McM. v. McM.* is discussed on this point and disagreed with. It was held that the husband, who had been unable to consummate his marriage was entitled to succeed. In this case the husband petitioner clearly did not know of his impotence until after the celebration of the marriage; see also *J. (orse. S.) v. J.* [1947] P. 159; [1947] 2 All E.R. 43 (C.A.) and *Pettit v. Pettit* [1963] P. 177; [1962] 3 All E.R. 37 (C.A.); see also Webb and Bevan, *Source Book of Family Law* (Butterworths, London 1964), pp. 92–93; H.K. Bevan (1960), 76 L. Q.R. 267 "Limitations on the Right of an Impotent Spouse to Petition for Nullity".
50. [1982] 2 I.L.R.M. 263 (H.C.).
51. *Supra* at p. 264. The petitioner also sought to have the marriage annulled on the grounds of insanity and duress. Rejecting these allegations on the evidence, Barrington J. held "that the petitioner was at all material times able to understand and did understand the nature, purpose and consequences of the marriage contract" and that "there was no pressure, fear, duress or undue influence exercised by the respondent on the petitioner." See *R.S.J. v. J.S.J.* unreported judgement (January, 1982) at p. 14. Only a part of this judgement is reported in [1982] 2 I.L.R.M.
52. *Supra*, see p. 126 *ante*.

"If . . . it could be shown that at the date of the marriage, the petitioner, through illness lacked the capacity to form a caring or considerate relationship with his wife I would be prepared to entertain this as a ground upon which a decree of nullity might be granted".[53]

However, he held that a "heavy onus of proof"[54] rested on the petitioner and that whereas from the evidence he accepted "that the petitioner, both before and after his marriage suffered from some form of personality defect or illness similar to schizophrenia" and that "this made it difficult for him to have a successful marriage" and "that the marriage in fact broke down", the petitioner's own evidence was unsatisfactory.[55] Refusing to grant a decree of annulment the learned judge stated that he was "not satisfied that . . . on the date of his marriage he (the petitioner) was so incapacitated as to make the marriage void or voidable."[56]

In *D. v. C.*[57] Costello J. approved of and expanded upon the law as developed by Barrington J. He stated:

"Marriage is by our common law (strengthened and reinforced by our consitutional law) a life long union, and it seems to me to be perfectly reasonable that the law should recognise (a) the obvious fact that there is more to marriage than its physical consummation and (b) that the life long union which the law enjoins requires for its maintenance the creation of an emotional and psychological relationship between the spouses. The law should have regard to this relationship just as it does to the physical one. It should recognise that there have been important and significant advances in the field of psychiatric medicine since 1870 and that it is now possible to identify psychiatric illnesses, such as for example manic-depressive illness, which in some cases may be so severe as to make it impossible for one of the partners to the marriage to enter into and sustain the relationship which should exist between married couples if a life long union is to be possible. Extending the law by reasoning by analogy is as old as the common law itself . . . and so it seems to me . . . that if the law declares to be null a marriage on the grounds that one spouse is through physical disability incapable of the physical relationship required by marriage it should do likewise where one spouse is through a psychiatric disability unable to enter into and sustain the whole inter-personal relationship which marriage also requires."[58]

In *D. v. C.* the petitioner succeeded in her application for a decree of annulment successfully establishing that the respondent "suffered from a manic depressive illness which was present thoughout the duration of his relationship with the petitioner both before, at the time of, and after their marriage."[59] Referring to the respondent's illness Costello J. stated:

---

53. [1982] 2 I.L.R.M. at p. 265.
54. *Ibid.*
55. [1982] 2 I.L.R.M. at pp. 267, 268.
56. *Ibid.* See further *R. v. R.* (December, 1984) unreported (H.C.) and *D.C. v. D.W.* (February, 1986) unreported (H.C.), in which it was established that the respondent suffered from paranoid schitzophrenia at the date of the marriage and a nullity decree was granted. See p. 133 *post*.
57. [1984] 4 I.L.R.M. 173 (H.C.).
58. *Ibid.* at p. 189.
59. *Ibid.* at p. 184. The court declined to grant a decree of annulment on the ground of insanity which was also alleged in the petition, Costello J. stating that whereas the petitioner had established that the respondent was suffering at the time of the marriage from the incapacitating illness alleged in the petition, he was not "satisfied that she has shown that the respondent was unable fully to understand the nature, purpose and con-

"It was a cyclical manic-depressive disorder which resulted in disturbance in mood states which affected his personality and behaviour. The empathy which ought to develop between spouses did not occur because of these changes in mood and his erratic behaviour, and they explain why the petitioner felt that at no time during her marriage did she have a sharing relationship with her husband. I am satisfied that the respondent's illness at the time of his marriage was sufficiently severe to impair significantly his capacity to form and sustain a normal, viable marriage relationship with the petitioner."[60]

Costello J. also went on to hold that "the illness alleged and established in the case is one which renders the marriage voidable and not void"[61] stating that "there is no public interest in seeing that a marriage subject to this illness is void."[62]

In *W. v. P.*[63] the parties met in 1977, became engaged in September 1978, married in May 1979 and parted in August 1981. Seeking a decree of annulment the petitioner alleged that the respondent's mental instability and emotional immaturity was such that he lacked the capacity to form a normal marriage conceived of as a caring or considerate relationship between two adults of the opposite sex.[64] The evidence established that subsequent to marriage the respondent had regular temper tantrums during which he had boxed his head with his own clenched fists and broken up furniture in the home. On various occasions he locked himself in his bedroom, stamped on the floor and cried, having to be coaxed out of the room like a sulky child. Other incidents included the respondent hitting himself with a poker, putting his head over a gas ring and inhaling gas and an attempt to hang himself in a cattle shed. Prior to marriage the respondent had threatened that he would shoot himself if the petitioner refused to marry him and after the marriage the petitioner discovered that love letters she had received from the respondent had in fact been written by his mother, as the respondent could not write properly himself. The parties' local doctor in evidence stated that the respondent had the emotional maturity of a five year old child and that his relationship "with the petitioner was immature and possessive like the relationship of a small child with its mother."[65] Psychiatric evidence established that the respondent's "degree of under-development and immaturity of personality was such as markedly to impair his capacity to sustain a normal and viable marriage relationship" and that "he could never have a marriage consisting of a normal relationship between two adults."[66]

Delivering judgement, Barrington J. acknowledged that:

"modern medicine gives us new insights into the institution of marriage and

sequences of the marriage contract." In this context the learned judge remarked that although the petitioner was "in a manic state on the day of his marriage" he had prior to that "taken part in the arrangements for the wedding and the decision to marry was a longstanding one". (See [1984] 4 I.L.R.M. at p. 187.)

60. *Supra* at p. 186.

61. *Ibid.* at p. 190. In the earlier case of *R.S.J. v. J.S.J., supra*, Barrington J. did not finally determine whether a marriage was void or voidable on this ground. In the later case of *W. v. P., supra*, he expressly approved of and followed the finding of Costello J. that such marriages are voidable.

62. *Supra* at p. 190. See further Law Reform Commission: *Report on Law of Nullity* (L.R.C. Report No. 9, October 1984) at pp. 14–28 where the law as stated in *R.S.J. v. J.S.J.* and *D. v. C.* is comprehensively examined.

63. (June, 1984) unreported (H.C.).

64. See pp. 2 and 20 of judgement. The petitioner also alleged duress but Barrington J. did not make a final determination on this allegation. (See pp. 2, 3, & 20 of judgement.)

65. See p. 18 of judgement.

66. See p. 19 of judgement.

the principles of law which govern it"[67] [and that the law by regarding marriage] "as a life long association between one man and one woman ... seems to contemplate that each partner should have the capacity to live in society with the other."[68]

Having regard to the evidence presented and adopting the legal analysis contained in *D. v. C.*[69] he held that:

"the petitioner is entitled to a declaration that her marriage to the respondent is and was null and void because the respondent at the time of this marriage was suffering from such psychological or emotional disability or incapacity as made it impossible for him to enter into and sustain a normal marriage relationship."[70]

In two subsequent cases *R. v. R.*[71] and *D.C. v. D.W.*[72] decrees of annulment were granted, the court in each case being satisfied that at the date of marriage, one of the parties was suffering from paranoid schizophrenia rendering such party incapable of entering into and sustaining a normal marriage relationship. In both cases, psychiatric evidence was given as to pre-marital psychiatric treatment received by the parties and this evidence was said to be "very persuasive" (*R. v. R.*) and to carry "great weight" (*D.C. v. D.W.*). In granting a decree in *R. v. R.*, Costello J. emphasised that "it did not follow" from his decision "that every unfortunate sufferer from paranoid schizophrenia is as a matter of law incapable of entering into a valid ceremony of marriage".[72a]

In *M.F. McD. v. W. O'R.*[73] the petitioner alleged that the respondent was prior to and at the time of the marriage a homosexual and also alleged that he had engaged in homosexual relationships prior to and after marriage. Hamilton J. accepted that prior to marriage the respondent had engaged in one homosexual relationship but rejected the other allegations made by the petitioner. He held that the mere fact of a person having a pre-marital homosexual relationship did not "of itself"[74] provide a ground for a decree of nullity. If the petitioner had established that "at the time of the marriage to him and by reason of his homosexuality" the respondent "was incapable of entering into and sustaining the relationship which should exist between married couples if a life long union is to be possible"[75] the learned judge stated he would have granted a nullity decree. The evidence established that the parties had married in 1972 and that for a number of years they had a satisfactory and normal sexual relationship. Hamilton J., declining to grant a decree, held the petitioner had not established that the respondent suffered from the inability or incapacity alleged.[76]

The judgements of Hamilton J. in *M.F. McD. v. W. O'R.* and of Barrington J. in *W. v. P.* have developed further this ground of nullity so as to extend the courts' jurisdiction to granting decrees of annulment to cases in which there is no allegation of mental illness, as such, but where it can be proved that for

---

67. See p. 21 of judgement.
68. *Ibid.*
69. *Supra.*
70. See p. 23 of judgement. See further P. O'Connor, "Inability to Enter into a Normal Marital Relationship – Further Developments" (1984) I.L.T. (n.s.) 218.
71. *Supra.*
72. *Supra.*
72a. See p. 5 of judgement.
73. (January, 1984) unreported (H.C.).
74. *Supra.*, see p. 8 of judgement.
75. *Supra.*, see p. 5 of judgement.
76. For a further discussion of this case see "Homosexuality as a Ground for Nullity" (1984) 2 I.L.T. (n.s.) 163.

reasons other than mental illness a person lacked the ability or capacity to enter into and sustain a normal marital relationship. The outer limits of the judicial development of this ground are difficult to predict. It is clear, however, that whether a mental illness or a personality disorder is relied upon to seek a decree, it must be of a very serious nature. In this context, it should be noted that in *R.S.J. v. J.S.J.* Barrington J. stated that this ground could not be relied upon to obtain a decree merely based on an allegation that "one party did not love or had not the capacity to love the other".[76a] Moreover, in *P.C. (otherwise O'B.) v. D. O'B.*,[76b] Carroll J. declined to grant a nullity decree, although accepting that at the time of marriage, the petitioner had an "inadequate or immature personality". She stated this to be a "mental condition rather than a mental illness" which "cannot be a ground for nullity unless it exists to an abnormal degree".[76c]

Onus of Proof and Medical Evidence: The onus of proof is on the party seeking the decree of nullity. In *R.S.J. v. J.S.J.*[77] Barrington J. remarked that "a judge should be cautious before accepting the evidence put forward for a petition"[78] in a nullity suit. In *M.F.McD. v. W. O'R.*[79] Hamilton J. stated that the allegation made must be established "to a high degree of probability".[80] Evidence arising from a psychiatric examination before marriage of the person who it is alleged was unable to marry due to mental illness can be of considerable assistance in the obtaining of a decree, although it is not essential. No such psychiatric evidence may be available in many cases.[81]

To obtain a decree, it is not sufficient to simply establish the existence of a psychiatric illness or personality disorder or some other factor causing marital difficulties at the date of the court hearing. It must be established that it existed at the time of the marriage. It has been said that evidence of the pre-marital history and the post-marital relationship is necessary, the latter being of relevance "in so far as it may help in throwing light on . . . pre-marital psychiatric health."[82] However, if it can be established that at the date of marriage a person suffered from a psychiatric illness rendering such person incapable "of entering into and forming a normal marriage relationship" a decree may be granted even if such person by the date of the nullity proceedings has recovered from such illness.[82a]

None of the decided cases have yet determined whether the courts may order one or both parties to undergo psychiatric examination when a petition brought on this ground is based on an allegation of mental illness. In *D. v. C.*[83] the respondent refused the petitioner's solicitor's request that he be examined by the petitioner's psychiatrist but, nevertheless, the court accepted the latter's diagnosis of the respondent's illness from the description the petitioner gave of the respondent's behaviour. In *W. v. P.*[84] the hearing was adjourned and both parties voluntarily agreed to an examination by a psychiatrist at the request of the trial judge who indicated he was anxious to hear psychiatric evidence, as the only medical evidence given had been that of two general practitioners. In his judgement, Barrington J. expressly stated that he did not "direct the examina-

---

76a. [1982] 2 I.L.R.M. at p. 264.
76b. (October, 1985) unreported (H.C.).
76c. See p. 8 of judgement.
77. *Supra.*
78. *Supra* at p. 265.
79. *Supra.*
80. See p. 6 of judgement.
81. See *D. v. C., supra.* Such evidence was available and given in *R. v. R., supra,* and *D.C. v. D.W., supra.*
82. *D. v. C., supra,* at p. 176.
82a. See *D.C. v. D.W., supra.*
83. *Supra.*
84. *Supra.*

tion".[85] It will clearly be impossible in many future cases brought on this ground for a court to properly adjudicate upon whether particular behaviour is proof of a condition upon which a decree of annulment can be granted without the assistance of psychiatric evidence. As this ground of nullity has been developed by way of a judicial analogy to the concept of impotence, it is possible that the courts may be willing to develop the analogy further, by developing the jurisdiction inherited from the ecclesiastical courts to order a medical inspection in cases in which a physical incapacity, i.e. impotence, is alleged, to a jurisdiction to order a psychiatric examination where a mental incapacity or some other disability is alleged[86] to affect a person's capacity to enter into a normal marital relationship.[87]

Petition of Spouse Suffering Disability: In *R.S.J. v. J.S.J.*[88] the petitioner sought a decree of annulment on the basis of his own inability to maintain and sustain a normal relationship with his wife. The respondent wife denied the marriage was a nullity although she accepted that it had broken down. The court held that she had left the family home "for good and sufficient reason"[89] and that in view of the marital history she had been justified in rejecting the respondent's request that she return home. Barrington J. rejected the petition for nullity being "not satisfied" that the petitioner had proved incapacity at the date of the wedding.[90] However, drawing a further analogy with the law of nullity and the ground of impotence, he stated:

> "Under the law of Ireland impotence makes a marriage voidable but an impotent spouse can rely upon his own impotence to avoid the marriage only if the other party has previously repudiated the marriage[91] . . . even if the marriage in this case were a voidable marriage[92] . . . *prima facie*, it would be a marriage voidable at the instance of the wife and not the husband. In the circumstances of this case it would be necessary for the husband to show that the wife had repudiated the marriage."[93]

On the facts as stated he held that she had not done so.

In *D.C. v. D.W.*,[94] Blayney J. adopted the above approach. As the wife was seeking a decree of nullity on the basis of her own psychiatric illness, he held a decree could not be granted unless the husband had repudiated the marriage. As he had sought and obtained a canonical decree of nullity from the Marriage Tribunals of the Roman Catholic Church, he was held to have "clearly repudiated the marriage".[94a]

---

85. See p. 19 of judgement.

86. See p. 127 *ante* in which the court's power to order a medical examination where impotence is alleged is discussed. In *D.C. v. D.W., supra*, there is a reference to the petitioner complying with an order of the Master of the High Court providing for a psychiatric examination. As she was the moving party in the proceedings and as her evidence was not disputed by the respondent, she presumably sought the Master's order and was a voluntary participant in the psychiatric examination.

87. See *M.F. McD. v. W. O'R., supra*. As no independent medical practitioner or psychiatrist had examined the respondent, Hamilton J. held he could not consequently hold "that at the date of the marriage the respondent was not capable of maintaining and sustaining a lasting marital relationship". See p. 9 of judgement.

88. *Supra.*

89. *Ibid.* at p. 268.

90. *Ibid.*

91. *Supra* at p. 265.

92. *Supra* at p. 268.

93. *Ibid.*

94. *Supra.*

94a. See p. 8 of judgement.

For a further discussion of the doctrine of repudiation and its relevance to impotence as a ground for nullity see page 127 *et seq ante.*

BARS TO RELIEF[95]

Approbation of Voidable Marriage

Impotence: It is well established that a person seeking a decree of annulment on the ground of impotence may be prevented by his own conduct from denying the validity of the marriage. It has been said that a person cannot both approbate and reprobate a marriage. In *G. v. M.*[96] Lord Selborne L.C., stated:

> "I think I can perceive that the real basis of reasoning which underlies that phraseology is this . . . that there may be conduct on the part of the person seeking this remedy which ought to stop that person from having it; as, for instance, any act from which the inference ought to be drawn, that during the antecedent time the party has, with a knowledge of the facts and of the law, approbated the marriage which he or she afterwards seeks to get rid of, or has taken advantages and derived benefits from the matrimonial relation which it would be unfair and inequitable to permit him or her, after having received them to treat as if no such relation had ever existed . . . that explanation can be referred to known principles of equitable and . . . general jurisprudence".[97]

Thus, a judge will consider the conduct of the person seeking a decree and may on general equitable principles refuse to permit him to obtain it.

Sir Ignatius J. O'Brien L.C. in the Court of Appeal pointed out in *P. v. P.*[98]:

> "It is not an uncommon case that two very old people go through a form of marriage, knowing well that a true marriage cannot take place. Again, a woman may take large benefits under this supposed marriage, and may have allowed ten, twenty, or thirty years to have elapsed without making any complaint, in which case, having . . . approbated the marriage, to allow her to reprobate it in proceedings for a decree of nullity would not be in accordance with the public interest, nor in most cases with common justice".

Similarly, if a spouse with knowledge of the other's impotence agrees to adopt a child, he may be regarded as approbating the marriage and barred from successfully challenging its validity.[99]

---

95. For a more detailed exposition of the law as to Bars to Relief see J. Jackson, *The Formation and Annulment of Marriage*, 2nd ed. (London, Butterworths 1969), chapter 8. See further D. Lasok – Approbation of Marriage in English Law and the Doctrine of Validation (1963) 26 M.L.R. 249.

96. (1885) 10 App. Cas. 171 (H.L. (Sc.)); see also *P. v. P.* (by amendment *McD. v. P.)* [1916] 2 I.R. 400, 414; (K.B.D.) (C.A.); 50 I.L.T.R. 149.

97. *Supra*, p. 186. See also *A.M.N. v. J.P.C., supra.*

98. *Supra* at p. 421–2; see also *G. v. G.* [1924] *supra; McM. v. McM., supra; R.M. v. S.M., supra.*

99. *W. v. W.* [1952] P. 152; [1952] 1 All E.R. 858 (C.A.). (Decree refused. Husband taken to know that the remedy of nullity was available to him before adoption order made); *Slater v. Slater* [1953] P. 235; [1953] 1 All E.R. 246 (C.A.). (Decree granted. Wife unaware that remedy of nullity available to her at time of adoption); See also *D. v. D.* [1979] Fam. 70 (Fam. D.); See further *Tindall v. Tindall* [1953] P. 63; [1953] 1 All E.R. 139 (C.A.), in which a spouse with full knowledge of her husband's impotence and the possibility of her obtaining a decree of nullity, having first brought proceedings in the Magistrates Court against him on which she relied on the validity of their marriage, sub-

The court in all cases in which non-consummation is alleged is said to have power to consider the general justice of the case. It may examine the surrounding facts of the parties' married life and marital relationship so that the conduct, as well as the position of the parties can be properly considered.[100] Thus, for example, if parties live together for 20 years and then upon the impotent spouse becoming confined to bed, the other petitions for a decree of nullity, the court may hold it to be unjust and inequitable to grant a decree. This, however, can be seen as simply another branch of the doctrine of approbation. In the case, however, of the impotent spouse who only discovers his impotence after the marriage, if it is accepted that the repudiation of the other spouse is not required to permit him to petition, this doctrine can be important. Rather than a spouse being granted a decree as of right on the ground of his own impotence, it becomes necessary for the court to look at the whole of the circumstances including the other spouse's attitude and reaction to the situation created by the petitioner's impotence, in order to see whether it is just and equitable to grant a decree against a spouse in no way responsible for the non-consummation. In such a situation it should be recognised that both parties are aggrieved. Thus, in the case of an impotent husband who lives with his wife for many years and then when she is crippled and old brings proceedings for nullity on the ground of his own impotence, the court, on the above principles, could hold that to grant a decree would be unjust having regard to the length of time the parties have lived together and the incapacitated spouse's present vulnerable condition.

If the law was to develop in this way, an impotent spouse would be entitled to obtain a decree of annulment on the basis of his own impotence unless in the circumstances of the case it was unjust that he should do so.[101] The onus would fall on the respondent who wished to defend the marriage to allege and prove consequent injustice and there would no longer be an onus on the petitioner to establish that the respondent had repudiated the marriage before a decree of nullity could be granted.

Inability to enter into and sustain a normal marital relationship: In *R.S.J. v. J.S.J.*[102] Barrington J. envisaged extending the doctrine of approbation to apply to marriages alleged to be a nullity on this ground stating that "the illness of one of the parties . . . could not under any circumstances make a marriage void[103] provided both parties knew of the illness and wished to get married."[104]

In *D. v. C.*[105] Costello J. examined the application of the doctrine of approbation in detail. The parties had been married for 8 years prior to the institution of nullity proceedings and there were two children born subsequent to their marriage. Moreover, a year earlier the petitioner had instituted High Court

---

sequently alleged her husband's impotence as a ground for annulling their marriage. She was held to have approbated the marriage and it was said to be inequitable and contrary to public policy to allow her the decree sought. In *A.M.N. v. J.P.C.*, *supra*, Barron J. held that by denying the validity of her marriage to her second husband (C.S.) in proceedings in which he sought access to the parties' children, the petitioner had not approbated her marriage to her first husband (the respondent) so as to bar her from having her first marriage annulled due to the respondent's impotence. He held that he was "satisfied that there was no intention to indicate that she intended to return to the respondent or to give up her right to apply . . . for the relief which she now seeks." (See p. 4 of judgement.)

100. *McM. v. McM.* and *McK. v. McK.*, *supra*. See also *N.F. v. M.T.* [1982] 2 I.L.R.M. 545 at p. 549.
101. See *Pettit v. Pettit* [1963] P. 177; [1962] 3 All E.R. 37 (C.A.).
102. *Supra.*
103. "Voidable" would be the correct terminology in view of the judgements delivered in *D. v. C.*, *supra*, and *W. v. P.*, *supra*.
104. *Supra* at p. 264.
105. *Supra.*

proceedings against the respondent and obtained an order barring him from the family home and an order granting custody of their children to her. In the latter proceedings she had filed an affidavit in which she had sworn that she was married to the respondent and there had been no dispute as to the validity of their marriage. Rejecting the respondent's allegation that the petitioner had approbated the marriage, Costello J. stated:

> "The defence now relied on can only succeed where it has shown that the petitioner acted not only with knowledge of the facts which entitled her to a nullity decree but also with knowledge that those facts would, as a matter of law, have entitled her to the right she now seeks to enforce. It is perfectly clear that in the present case the petitioner (a) did not know that her husband had suffered from a psychiatric illness at the time of her marriage until several years after the ceremony had taken place and (b) until she obtained legal advice shortly before the institution of these proceedings she was unaware that her husband's illness entitled her to a nullity decree."[106]

Moreover, although the High Court orders made in the earlier proceedings had been on the basis that the parties were "spouses" as no dispute had arisen in those proceedings as to the validity of the marriage, he held, the court had "made no pronouncement on the status of the petitioner or the respondent"[107] so as to estop the petitioner from challenging the validity of their marriage. The court had not been called upon to previously determine this issue and the respondent's plea of *res judicata* could not be upheld.[108]

Although he rejected the allegation of approbation in *D. v. C.*,[109] it is clear that Costello J. regarded it as applicable to petitions for annulment on this ground. It will require further judicial development of the law to clarify the exact type of behaviour that in practice the courts will hold to be approbation. Consummation of the marriage and the parties having regular sexual intercourse subsequent to marriage will clearly not, in itself, be regarded as approbation as in both *D. v. C.*[110] and *W. v. P.*[111] in which the petitioners were successful, the parties' post-marital sexual intercourse was not held to be a bar to the granting of a decree.[112] Neither was the fact that two children had been born following the "marriage" in *D. v. C.*[113] regarded as an impediment to a declaration of nullity.[114]

Delay

Impotence: Delay in presenting a petition on the ground of impotence is not an absolute bar to the remedy.[115] The reason for the delay is of the utmost importance, as a long delay may be proof of approbation of the marriage, or

---

106. *Supra* at p. 191. Costello J. expressly referred to and approved of the passage from *G. v. M., supra,* quoted on p. 136 *ante*.
107. *Supra* at p. 192.
108. *Supra,* see pp. 191–195.
109. *Supra*.
110. *Ibid*.
111. *Supra*.
112. In *R.S.J. v. J.S.J., supra,* and *M.F. McD. v. W. O'R., supra,* although nullity decrees were refused, there is no suggestion in the judgements delivered that the parties' post-marital sexual intercourse would have been held to be a bar to the granting of a decree. See further *R. v. R.* (December, 1984) unreported (H.C.) in which the nullity petition was successful although the marriage was consummated.
113. *Supra*.
114. See, however, footnote 79 *ante*. See further the dissenting judgement of Henchy J. delivered in *N. (otherwise K.) v. K.* [1986] 6 I.L.R.M. 75 (S.C.) at p. 88.
115. *G. v. M., supra; B. (otherwise A.) v. B., supra.*

may render it inequitable that a decree be granted. Everything depends on the circumstances of the particular case.

By the very nature of the ground of impotence long delay will render it more difficult to establish the necessary proof and it has been said that following such a delay evidence to support the suit must be of the clearest and most satisfactory.[116] The objection of delay cannot be surmounted by the uncorroborated testimony of the petitioner.[117]

Long delay may throw so heavy a burden on a petitioner of proving the fact of incapacity that it may deprive him of his remedy. Thus in *B. (otherwise A.) v. B.*[118] despite the petitioner discovering her husband's impotence in 1873 she did not present a petition until 1891. The petitioner had lived apart from her husband since 1873 and had married another in 1874. There could be no medical evidence as to the condition of the wife and the husband refused to submit to medical examination. He denied being impotent at the time of the marriage, but the medical officer appointed by the court was satisfied as a result of his interviw with him that he was impotent at the date of the interview. There was no excuse given by the petitioner for her delay in bringing proceedings. The court held that considering the length of time which had elapsed since the marriage and since the petitioner became aware of her husband's imperfection, in view of the lack of medical testimony (in that even if he was impotent in 1891 this did not necessarily mean he was in 1873) and the want of corroborative evidence, there was no sufficient or satisfactory proof that the respondent was impotent at the date of the marriage. A decree was refused.

When, however, there are valid reasons for a petitioner's delay and the impotence of the respondent can be adequately proved a decree will be granted.[119] In *Pettit v. Pettit*[120] Donovan L.J. stated:

"In a case where a potent spouse discovers after a marriage that his partner is incapable, he may or may not know that the law grants him a remedy. If he does not know, and he goes on living with the incapable partner, he will almost invariably do things which afterwards can be used as evidence that he approbated the marriage. Outwardly he may be just an ordinary husband taking his wife about as his wife, and no doubt asserting in writing year after year that he is a married man living with his wife and, therefore, entitled to the appropriate tax relief. But as from the moment that he knows that he has a remedy, the situation alters. If he decides to seek it, it seems to me it would be quite unfair to deny it to him simply because, when ignorant of the law, he behaved like any ordinary decent husband. If, after knowing of his remedy, he acts in such a way as to show that he does not wish to avail himself of it, but on the contrary acquiesces in the situation, then it may well and fairly be said that he has approbated the marriage. I think, therefore, that knowledge of the facts and the law should be regarded as prerequisites of approbation."[121]

Accepting and adopting this statement of principle in *N.F. v. M.T.*,[122] O'Han-

---

116. *Castleden v. Castleden* (1861) 9 H.L. Cas. 186; *B. (otherwise A.) v. A., supra.*

117. *B. (otherwise A.) v. B., supra; V. (falsely called J.) v. J.* (1867) L.R. 1 P. & D. 460 (Ct. of P. & D.).

118. *Supra.*

119. *G. v. M., supra; Castleden v. Castleden, supra; Mansfield (falsely called Cuno) v. Cuno* (1873) 42 L.J. (P. & M.) 65; *T. v. T. (otherwise J.)* (1963) 47 T.L.R. 629; *H. (falsely called C.) v. C.* (1860) 1 Sw. & Tr. 605; 164 E.R. 880 (Ct. for Div. & Matr. Causes).

120. [1963] P. 177.

121. *Ibid.,* at p. 191.

122. *Supra,* see p. 458.

lon J. granted a decree of annulment on the basis of the respondent's impotence holding that the petitioner by his delaying instituting nullity proceedings until almost six years after the marriage ceremony had not approbated the marriage. The parties had lived together for three and a half years and the petitioner gave evidence, which was accepted as truthful, that he had not instituted nullity proceedings earlier as he had been originally advised he had no real prospect of success. It was only when he changed solicitors that he learned that he had good grounds for instituting such proceedings. In the earlier case of *G. v. R. (otherwise known as G.)*[123] a decree of annulment was granted on the grounds of the respondent wife's impotence seventeen years after the marriage had taken place. The parties had lived together continuously for the first fifteen years of the marriage. The petitioner in evidence stated that he only became aware of the possibility of instituting nullity proceedings when watching a programme on television a year prior to the court hearing.[123a]

Inability to enter into and sustain normal marital relationships: The longer a petitioner delays instituting proceedings the more difficult it may become to prove that the illness alleged to invalidate the marriage existed at the date of the marriage ceremony. The degree of difficulty experienced will in many instances depend on the nature of the alleged illness or personality defect and the type of evidence available to the court. Evidence of the results of a psychiatric examination conducted prior to or very soon after a marriage will be of particular importance.[124] The absence of such evidence may render it impossible to obtain a decree in some cases.

In *D. v. C.*[125] the psychiatrist called to give evidence on behalf of the petitioner gave evidence not only as to the mental health of the respondent at the time of the proceedings but also speculated as to the exact state of the respondent's health at the date of the marriage ceremony over eight years earlier, although he had not examined the respondent and his diagnosis was based on what the petitioner had told him of the respondent's behaviour. Evidence was also given by a psychiatrist who had treated the respondent subsequent to marriage who declined to comment on his state of health at the time of marriage as he considered it was not possible to make a retrospective diagnosis. In *W. v. P.*,[126] however, no difficulty was experienced in giving a retrospective diagnosis by the psychiatrist who gave evidence following the court's request that both parties participate in a psychiatric examination almost five years after the ceremony of marriage. In *R.S.J. v. J.S.J.*[127] there was a conflict between the psychiatrists as to whether the nature of the illness suffered by the petitioner merely impaired his ability to form a normal marital relationship at the date of the ceremony or rendered it impossible for him to do so. Although the petitioner

---

123. Decision of Barrington J. February 1980. Record No. 1979/11M. There was no written judgement in this case.

123a. See further *L.C. v. B.C. (otherwise known as B.L.), supra*, in which a decree of nullity on the ground of impotence was granted 11 years after the parties' marriage; *A. O'H. (otherwise F.) v. F., supra* in which a decree on the ground of impotence was granted 15 years after the parties' marriage and *A.M.N. v. J.P.C., supra* in which a decree on the ground of impotence was granted 17 years after the parties' marriage.

124. See *R. v. R., supra* in which evidence was given that the respondent had been diagnosed as suffering from paranoid schizophrenia 5 years prior to his marriage which the High Court anulled. See also *D.C. v. D.W., supra*.

125. *Supra.*

126. *Supra.*

127. *Supra.*

had been under the care, prior to marriage, of two of the three psychiatrists who gave evidence, the court declined to grant a decree of nullity. This was partially due to the conflict in the psychiatric conclusions and partly because some of the evidence of the petitioning husband who was seeking the decree on the basis of his own illness was not believed. Nevertheless, the case establishes that even if a person is under psychiatric care prior to marriage, it will not automatically afford a ground for the granting of a decree.

In some instances, delay will be essential to provide sufficient proof to successfully establish this ground of nullity as detailed evidence of post marital behaviour will be required to enable the court to ascertain whether at the date of marriage there existed "a lack of capacity to enter into and sustain a normal marital relationship". As in *D. v. C.*, it may be necessary for some time to pass before a spouse may become aware of an illness suffered by the other spouse. Consequently, whether delay, of itself, will lead a court to conclude that a marriage has been approbated or that it is unjust or inequitable to grant a decree, will largely depend on the reasons for the delay and the judicial conclusions reached on the facts of the individual case that arises for determination before the court.

Ratification of Void Marriages

At first sight the notion of validating or ratifying that which is void is strange. There is, however, some authority for the proposition that a marriage, void for lack of consent, may be ratified by the subsequent behaviour of the parties.[128] This doctrine of ratification is purely canonical in origin and cannot be explained on logical grounds. In the words of Lord O'Brien in *Ussher v. Ussher*[129]

"how could the marriage be validated if it was altogether void? Such a proposition, it was contended, finds no support from 'reason'. I am afraid there are many things lying at the root, at the foundation, of the christian religion, mysteries of faith, for an elucidation of which we should appeal to 'reason' in vain."

The case law in support of this doctrine is sparse and it mainly rests on commentators' statements as to the principles applied by the Ecclesiastical Courts.[130] In effect, it renders the status of marriages void for lack of consent, similar to that of marriages voidable on the grounds of impotence. In both cases a party can by his or her own conduct prevent such a marriage from being annulled.[131]

---

128. See *Valier v. Valier* (1925) 133 L.T. 830 at p. 832; *Ash's Case* (1702) *Freem. Ch.* 259; Prec. Ch. 203; 22 E.R. 1196 (Chan.).

129. [1912] 2 I.R. 455 at p. 480. In this case no validation of the marriage was attempted. Validation was not however necessary. The parties to the marriage were both Roman Catholics. The marriage was celebrated by a Roman Catholic priest and was valid at common law, although invalid by the law of the Roman Catholic Church, only one witness being present at the ceremony.

130. See Tolstoy, Void and Voidable Marriages (1964) 27 M.L.R. 385, and The Validation of Void Marriages (1968) 31 M.L.R. 656, and the authorities therein cited. See also J. Jackson *supra*, p. 357; Law Commission (Law Com. No. 33), *Family Law – Report on Nullity of Marriage* (London – H.M.S.O. 1970), p. 4; Law Reform Commission: *Report on Nullity of Marriage* (L.R.C. No. 9, Dublin 1984), pp. 66–67.

131. See further judgement of McCarthy J. in *N. (otherwise K.) v. K., supra*, where he states (*supra* at p. 94) that he reserves for further consideration, in an appropriate case, "whether or not there can be a valid and enforceable approbation* of what was initially an invalid contract of marriage."

*As this case concerned an allegation of duress the reference should have been to "ratification" and not "approbation".

A "void" marriage may also be rendered valid by statutory enactment. Thus, as we have already seen, the Marriages Act, 1972 rendered valid certain marriages celebrated in Lourdes, that prior to its enactment were void.

Collusion: Order 70 Rule 4 of the Rules of the Superior Courts requires a petitioner seeking a decree of nullity to state in an affidavit filed with the petition that no collusion or connivance exists between the petitioner and the respondent.

As has been seen the High Court has constantly reiterated the need to ensure that "discontented spouses" will not use the nullity jurisdiction to obtain release from the bonds of matrimony, and the courts have in a number of cases looked at the evidence presented to them to ensure that there is no suggestion of collusion between the parties.[132]

The exact effect of collusion in proceedings seeking a declaration of nullity is, however, uncertain. Collusion between the parties may affect the veracity of their evidence and thus prevent the court granting a decree on the ground of impotence. But if a marriage is void due, for example, to under age, prohibited degrees or prior marriage, collusion should not act as a bar to a decree. If it does so act, the doctrine is anomalous in that a void marriage will remain void even if a decree is refused on such a ground. The concept of collusion has been discussed in detail in two recent cases.

In *E.P. v. M.C.*[133] Barron J. considered whether there had been collusion in determining a petition for annulment based principally on the ground of duress. The respondent did not give evidence in the proceedings but two letters sent by her solicitors to the petitioner's solicitors were tendered in evidence. In the first letter they stated that "provided proper arrangements are entered into" to provide for the maintenance of the child born to the parties the respondent would not defend the proceedings. The second letter stated that the respondent was prepared to co-operate with the petitioner "and agrees that it was not her intention at the time of the alleged marriage . . . to co-habit with (the petitioner)," and proposed that a consultation be arranged for the respondent with the petitioner's counsel.[134]

Barron J. stated that he was satisfied that "no efforts were made" by either the petitioner or his lawyers to act on the proposals contained in either letter. Referring to the doctrine of collusion he stated:

"Collusion means essentially an agreement between the parties so that the true case is not presented to the court."[135]

He stated, however, that the letters led him "to have a suspicion that if the respondent had given evidence the case might well have appeared differently" and he declined to grant a decree because the petitioner had not discharged the onus of proof "to establish that there are no reasonable grounds for thinking that the true case has not been presented to the court".[136]

---

132. See, for example, *Griffith v. Griffith, supra*, at pp. 46, 50; *R.M. v. M.M., supra* at p. 169; *Kelly v. Kelly* (February, 1971) unreported (H.C.) at p. 3 of judgement; *S. v. S.* (July, 1976) unreported (S.C.), see judgement of Henchy J., p. 4; *N. (otherwise K.) v. K., supra*, see judgement of Finlay C.J. *supra* at p. 80. See also the old case of *Pollard, falsely called Wybourn v. Wybourn* (1828) 1 Hag. Ecc. 725; 162 E.R. 732 (Consistory Court).
133. [1985] 5 I.L.R.M. 34.
134. *Ibid.*, at p. 36.
135. *Ibid.*, at p. 37.
136. *Ibid*, at p. 38. It is difficult to reconcile the approach of Barron J. in this case with that adopted in *A.M.N. v. J.P.C., supra*, in which he granted a nullity decree.

As the learned judge stated that the failure of the respondent to appear did "not establish collusion"[137] and as he acknowledged that there was "no specific agreement nor . . . any specific fact . . . concealed"[138] from the court, the reasoning behind the finding made is unclear. It cannot be part of nullity law that a letter proposing possible collusion from a respondent, who does not appear to give evidence, sent to a petitioner or his legal advisors and ignored by them, throws a heavier onus of proof on to the petitioner than would exist if no such letter had been received. Such an approach would afford a facility to every respondent in every nullity case to severely jeopardise a petitioner's chance of succeeding in obtaining a decree by the sending of such correspondence. It is submitted that on the basis of the evidence given and conclusions reached in this case as disclosed in the written judgement there was no basis upon which the trial judge could have properly concluded "that the true case" had not been presented to the court.[139]

The authority of *E.P. v. M.C.* on this issue is seriously in doubt having regard to the earlier judgement of the Supreme Court in *M. v. M.*,[140] which is not cited or referred to in the former case.

In *M. v. M.* in the High Court[141] Murnaghan J. refused to grant a decree of nullity on the ground of impotence, principally because he suspected collusion between the parties. In the proceedings, the petitioner's evidence as to the respondent's inability to consummate the marriage was admitted in evidence as truthful by the respondent, and was corroborated by two medical witnesses from whom the parties had sought help with their difficulties some time prior to the initiation of nullity proceedings. Each of the four witnesses "left court without any suggestion having been made that their evidence was not truthful or credible".[142] A fortnight later, however, Murnaghan J. rejected the petitioner's application stating he was not satisfied that consummation had not taken place, nor was he satisfied as to the "bona fides of the parties". He was of the belief that they had mutually agreed to have their marriage annulled and, in effect, held that he was not satisfied that the husband and the wife had not acted collusively.

The Supreme Court, on appeal, granted the decree of nullity. Delivering the judgement of the court[143] Henchy J. stated:

"Having regard to the unanimity of the evidence given and the conduct of the case generally, it was not open to the judge to refuse a decree of nullity for the reasons given. It is not in accordance with the proper administration of justice to cast aside the corroborated and unquestioned evidence of witnesses, still less to impute collusion or perjury to them, when they were not given any opportunity of rebutting such an accusation. To do so in this case was in effect to condemn them unheard, which is contrary to natural justice. Having due regard to the degree of proof required to be established by the petitioner in a case such as this, I consider that a decree of nullity was the only verdict that was open on the evidence given."[144]

It is submitted that it follows from the above judgement that it is not open to

---

137. *Ibid.*, at p. 37.
138. *Ibid.*
139. For further discussion of *E.P. v. M.C.* see p. 118 *ante*.
140. (October, 1979) unreported (S.C.).
141. (May, 1978) unreported (H.C.).
142. See Supreme Court judgement of Henchy J. at p. 3.
143. With which Kenny J. and Parke J. agreed.
144. See pp. 3–4 of judgement.

a trial judge to withhold the grant of a decree of nullity if he suspects collusion or suspects that the full story has not been told, if there is no specific evidence given during the course of a nullity hearing upon which such a suspicion could be validly based.

THE CONSEQUENCES OF A DECREE OF NULLITY

If a marriage is void no legal consequences can flow from the relationship which in law did not exist. The parties have no succession rights or obligations of support *vis-à-vis* each other and any accommodation in which they have resided together will not be a "family home" under the Family Home Protection Act, 1976, as the parties are not "spouses" and none of the protections extended by that act to "family homes" can apply to such accommodation. Neither can either party to a void marriage obtain a protection or barring order under the Family Law (Protection of Spouses and Children) Act, 1981. Moreover, any children born to the parties are regarded as illegitimate,[145] their mother being their sole guardian. The father may, however, seek a court order of custody or access under the Guardianship of Infants Act, 1964, section 11.

If a voidable marriage is annulled, the decree acts so as to retrospectively invalidate the marriage. It is then said to be void *ab initio* and the legal position of the parties is identical to that of parties to a void marriage. A decree annulling a voidable marriage retrospectively bastardises any children born to the parties.[146]

Whilst a "wife" can obtain alimony *pendente lite* (pending the hearing of the case) from her husband, upon declaring a marriage to be a nullity, the court has no power to order the "husband" to contribute anything towards her future maintenance or the maintenance of their children. The only manner in which he can be compelled to give some financial support is if affiliation proceedings are subsequently brought to force him to contribute towards his children's maintenance.

---

145. See *N. (otherwise K.) v. N., supra,* and *K.E.D. (otherwise K.C.) v. M.C.* (December, 1985) unreported (S.C.).

146. See *Newbold v. A.G.* [1931] P. 75 approved of by Lynch J. in *F.M.L. & A.L. v. an tArd Chlaraitheoir na mPosadh* [1984] 5 I.L.R.M. 667 (H.C.). See further *D. v. C., supra,* in which the decree of annulment granted resulted in the two children born to the parties being rendered illegitimate. In *D.C. v. D.W.* (February 1986) unreported (H.C.) the decree of annulment granted resulted in the one child born to the parties being rendered illegitimate.

CRITICISMS AND SUGGESTED REFORMS[1]

A Discussion Paper entitled "The Law of Nullity in Ireland" prepared in the Office of the Attorney General and published in August, 1976, concluded that there "is a real and pressing need for reform" of the law of nullity.[2] This need, it stated, arose because many aspects of the law "are uncertain" and the law "has not developed in a significant way and has not kept pace with developments in other countries . . . or with the law administered in the Ecclesiastical Courts in Ireland."[3] Recommending that a "comprehensive codifying and reforming measure be enacted" it stated that such a measure "would greatly assist the public in understanding rights in relation to nullity matters and make the law more easily accessible."[4]

In the ten years that have elapsed since publication of the Discussion Paper significant judicial development has radically changed and expanded the law of nullity.[5] Nevertheless the need for reform remains. Judicial development whilst clarifying some aspects of nullity law and extending its scope has added to the uncertainty by rendering it impossible to define the exact parameters of its application.[6] As a consequence it is currently not possible for some "spouses" to obtain definitive legal advice as to whether they are parties to a valid marriage or as to whether their marriage could be set aside by either party at some future date seeking and obtaining a nullity decree.

In the first half of the 1970s much of the pressure to reform the law of nullity derived from the considerable divergence between the civil law and the canon law administered by the Marriage Tribunals of the Roman Catholic Church. By virtue of its jurisdiction over the marriages of Roman Catholics, the church has always exercised a power to declare a marriage of a Roman Catholic to be a nullity according to Church or canonical law. Developments in the canon law in the decade immediately preceding publication of the Discussion Paper rendered it possible to obtain relief on grounds far wider than those entertained by the civil courts.[7] As canonical annulments are not recognised by the State those

1. See Office of the Attorney General: The Law of Nullity in Ireland (Stationery Office, Dublin, August, 1976); The Law Reform Commission Report on Nullity of Marriage (L.R.C. Report No. 9, October 1984); Report of the Joint Oireachtas Committee on Marriage Breakdown (Stationery Office, Dublin, March 1985), pp. 33–44.
   With reference to the Age for Marriage and Nullity see also, The Law Relating to the Age of Majority, the Age for Marriage and Some Connected Subjects (Working Paper No. 2 – November 1977 and Report No. 5 – April 1983). See further p. 99 *et seq*. For a discussion of nullity law and the need for reform in the area of private international law see Report on Private International Law Aspects of Capacity to Marry and Choice of Law in Proceedings for Nullity of Marriage (L.R.C. Report No. 19 – October 1985).
2. The Law of Nullity in Ireland, *supra*, p. vii.
3. *Ibid*. The "Ecclesiastical Courts" to which reference is made are the Marriage Tribunals of the Roman Catholic Church.
4. *Ibid*.
5. See L.R.C. Report No. 9, *supra*, at p. ix.
6. See Report of Joint Oireachtas Committee at p. 39 and L.R.C. Report No. 9 at pp. 19 and 27. See also P.A. O'Connor, "Recent Developments in the Irish Law of Nullity" (1983) 5 D.U.L.J. 168, "Inability to Enter into a Normal Marital Relationship – Further Developments" (1984) 2 I.L.T. (n.s.) 218 and "Duress and the Supreme Court" (1986) 4 I.L.T. (n.s.) 4 & 22, W. Duncan, "Sex and the Fundamentals of Marriage" (1979–80) D.U.L.J. 29.
7. For the grounds upon which a marriage may be annulled pursuant to the canon law of the Roman Catholic Church see The Code of Canon Law prepared by the Canon Law Society of Great Britain and Ireland (Collins Liturgical Publications, London 1983) Title VII. See also Irish Bishops' Pastoral, Love is for Life (Veritas Publications, Dublin 1985), p. 81 *et seq*. For a detailed discussion of the canon law of nullity see R. Brown, *Marriage Annulment* (Chapman, London 1971) and R. Brown, *Marriage Annulment in the Catholic Church – A Practical Guide* (Kevin Mayhew Ltd., Essex, England, 1977); *The Church's Matrimonial Jurisprudence, A Statement of Current Position*, The Canon Law Society Trust

who obtain them remain married to each other according to civil law[8] although in accordance with their religious convictions many regard themselves as free to remarry.[9] If they do so, however, any such "second" marriage is invalid and participation in a "second" marriage ceremony may render a person liable to criminal prosecution for bigamy.[10] Whilst the judicial innovation and reform of recent years has narrowed the gap between the civil law of nullity and the canon law of the Roman Catholic Church, considerable differences still remain in that the jurisdiction exercised by the Church Tribunals is still wider and more liberal than that exercised by the High Court.[11] This is evidenced by the fact that in the period 1976–85 inclusive there were 991 decrees of annulment granted by the church whilst there were only 91 decrees of annulment granted by the courts.[12] There is consequently a growing number of Irish people regarded by the civil law as having validly married whose marriages have been canonically annulled and which their church holds never to have existed.

In his dissenting judgement in *N. (otherwise K.) v. K.*,[13] Henchy J. in the Supreme Court in November 1985, emphasised "the need for a modern statute providing for the grant of decrees of nullity of marriage on fair, reasonable and clearly stated grounds."[14] In the twelve month period immediately preceding the Supreme Court hearing of that case, the Law Reform Commission[15] and the Joint Oireachtas Committee on Marriage Breakdown[16] both published reports containing proposals for the enactment of such a statute. As the report of the Law Reform Commission contains a more detailed discussion of this area than that of the Oireachtas Committee it is the recommendations contained in the

---

(Westminster 1975); L.G. Wrenn, *Annulments* 4th ed. (Canon Law Society of America, Connecticut 1983); L. Orsey, *Marriage in Canon Law* (M. Glazier Inc., Delaware, USA, 1986); B.A. Siegle, *Marriage According to the New Code of Canon Law* (Alba House, USA, 1986). Interesting case studies illustrating the circumstances in which the church will annul a marriage are contained in *Matrimonial Jurisprudence, United States 1968–1971*, published by the Canon Law Society of America (1973) and L.G. Wrenn, *Decisions* (Canon Law Society of America, 1983). See further J.A. Coulter, "The Pastoral Problem of Annulments", Vol. 29 (November 1978) The Furrow, p. 680; "Marriage Annulments in the Catholic Church" (1978), 72 *Gazette of the Incorporated Law Society of Ireland* 135.

8. See further p. 180 *post*.

9. See L.R.C. Report No. 9, p. 93. See for example *S. v. S.* (July, 1976) unreported (S.C.) where the wife after obtaining a church decree of nullity remarried prior to the Supreme Court annulling her first marriage. See also *N.A.D. v. T.D.* [1985] 5 I.L.R.M. 153 (H.C.) in which the husband sued for maintenance by his first wife had, prior to the maintenance proceedings, remarried in church subsequent to his obtaining a church decree of annulment. There is no suggestion in the court judgement that there was any ground in civil law upon which he could obtain a civil decree of annulment in respect of his first marriage.

10. If, however, a party obtains a civil decree of nullity subsequent to a second marriage, as the first marriage is then retrospectively invalidated the second marriage is then rendered valid – see *F.M.L. & A.L. v. The Registrar General of Marriages* [1984] 4 I.L.R.M. 667 (H.C.).

11. See L.R.C. Report No. 9, *supra*, at p. 89.

12. See Appendix C.

13. [1986] 6 I.L.R.M. 75 (S.C.).

14. *Ibid.*, at p. 89.

15. L.R.C. Report No. 9, *supra*.

16. *Supra*.

former report to which primary reference is made in the discussion that follows. Prior to entering upon our discussion it should be noted that in April 1986 the government promised that "the law relating to nullity of marriage will be reviewed" taking into account the recommendations contained in both reports but did not state when a Nullity Bill might be published and gave no indication as to its likely content.[16a]

Reform of the Grounds for a Decree of Nullity

The Law Reform Commission discuss in detail recent developments in the law of nullity and propose four new grounds for rendering a marriage voidable, three of which incorporate many of the legal principles enunciated by the courts in recent years in the judicial development and expansion of the law of nullity.

1. Noting that "the law relating to want of mental capacity is in a state of development"[17] the Commission recommends that "a marriage should be invalid on the ground of want of mental capacity where, at the time of the marriage, either spouse is unable to understand the nature of marriage and its obligations or where a spouse enters a marriage when, at the time of the marriage, on account of his or her want of mental capacity, he or she is unable to discharge the essential obligations of marriage".[18]

This recommendation incorporates within it the traditional ground of insanity and partially incorporates the newly developed ground of "inability to enter into and sustain a normal marriage relationship".[19] Although the Commission, itself, points out the ambiguity of the present law and the difficulty of making "any confident prediction as to where the courts will draw the line in deciding whether to annul" marriages,[20] it does not define what is meant by "want of mental capacity" or "the essential obligations of marriage"[21] or prescribe what will constitute an inability to discharge such obligations so as to warrant the granting of a nullity decree. The Commission merely states that this "broadly defined ground will afford the courts the appropriate degree of flexibility in deciding cases where want of mental capacity is alleged to have invalidated a marriage".[22]

The Discussion Paper produced by the Attorney General's Office in 1976 proposed that "mental disorder" existing at the date of marriage rendering a person unfit for marriage should be a ground for nullity and that the term "mental disorder" should be defined so as to mean "mental illness, arrested or incomplete development of mind or personality, psychopathic disorder and any other disorder or disability of mind or personality".[23] Although the Com-

---

16a. See "Statement on Government's Intentions with Regard to Marriage, Separation and Divorce published by the Department of Justice (April 1986) at p. 5 and revised "Statement" (June 1986) at p. 13.

17. See L.R.C. Report No. 9, *supra*, at p. 95.

18. *Ibid.*, at p. 104.

19. See p. 130 *ante*. It does not fully incorporate this ground of nullity in that a person may be able to discharge the essential obligations of marriage but may not be able to enter into and maintain a normal marriage relationship.

20. See L.R.C. Report No. 9, *supra* at pp. 27–28. See also pp. 18–19.

21. See, however, the four grounds upon which the Commission recommends the law should permit the grant of a decree of nullity for a fraudulent non-disclosure, discussed on p. 150 *post*.

22. L.R.C. Report No. 9, *supra*, at p. 104.

23. The Law of Nullity in Ireland, *supra* at p. 34 defined in Draft Nullity of Marriages Bill included in the Discussion Paper. See also pp. 7–8. "Psychiatric disorder" within this definition in the draft bill was said to mean "a persistent disorder (whether or not including sub-normality of intelligence) which results in abnormally aggressive or seriously irrespon-

mission in its report discusses this proposal in detail, by failing to define the meaning of "want of mental capacity" it effectively leaves it to the courts to determine the extent to which this concept should incorporate within it the concept of "mental disorder" as defined in the Discussion Paper.[24]

Referring to both the Law Reform Commission's Report and the Discussion Paper, the Joint Oireachtas Committee states that there is a "need for greater certainty in this area of the law" and that neither approach "would remove or sufficiently reduce, the present uncertainty".[25] Accepting that "there is a need for the court to have regard to the fact that in certain cases a person is suffering from a mental disorder *so serious in nature*[26] as to render him or her incapable of discharging the essential obligations of marriage" the Committee state that "mental disorder" as a ground for rendering a marriage voidable should only apply to "those unfortunate people who suffer from a really serious mental disorder who can positively be stated in human terms to be incapable of marriage".[27]

Recommending that "mental disorder of such a nature as to render a person incapable of discharging the essential obligations of marriage" should be a ground for nullity, the Committee states that the definition of mental disorder should not include the concept of "arrested or incomplete development of personality".[28] Moreover, whilst the Law Reform Commission states that "want of mental capacity" should in all cases render a marriage voidable and not void, the Oireachtas Committee favour "mental illness at the time of the marriage which causes an

---

sible conduct on the part of the person." Costello J. was Attorney General at the date of the publication of the Discussion Paper and is generally acknowledged to have been its principal author. It is interesting to note that although the draft bill did not become statute law, as a member of the High Court judiciary he has been one of the principal judicial innovators in the development of the new ground of nullity based on a person's "inability to enter into and sustain a normal marriage relationship" due to the existence of a psychiatric illness at the date of marriage. See *D. v. C.* [1984] 4 I.L.R.M. 173 (H.C.) and *R. v. R.* (December, 1984) unreported (H.C.).

24. The cases of *R.S.J. v. J.S.J., supra; D. v. C., supra; R. v. R., supra* and *D.C. v. D.W., supra,* were concerned primarily with an alleged mental illness whilst *W. v. P.* (June, 1984) unreported (H.C.) and *P.C. (otherwise O'B.) v. D. O'B.* (October, 1985) unreported (H.C.) were concerned with an alleged personality disorder or defect.

25. See Report of Joint Oireachtas Committee, *supra*, at p. 41.

26. Author's italics.

27. Report of Joint Oireachtas Committee, *supra*, p. 41. This view is an endorsement by the Committee of the approach of Ormrod J. in the English case of *Bennet v. Bennet* [1969] 1 W.L.R. 430 at 434. The English Matrimonial Causes Act, 1973, Section 12 provides that a marriage celebrated after the 31st of July, 1971 is voidable on the ground "that at the time of the marriage either party, though capable of giving a valid consent, was suffering (whether continuously or intermittently) from mental disorder within the meaning of the Mental Health Act, 1959, of such a kind and to such extent as to be unfitted for marriage." The definition of mental disorder contained in the 1959 Act is the same as that proposed in the Discussion Paper published by the Attorney General's Office except it does not include the concept of a personality disorder. See L.R.C. Report No. 9, pp. 97–104. In the context of recent Irish case law developments Ormrod J.'s emphasis on the need for a "really serious mental disorder" is mirrored by the approach of Carroll J. in *P.C. (otherwise O'B.) v. D. O'B, supra,* where the learned judge stated that for a decree of nullity to be granted on the ground of "inability to enter into and sustain a normal marriage relationship" it had to be established that at the date of marriage a person suffered from a mental condition "to an abnormal degree" (see p. 8 of judgement).

28. Report of Joint Oireachtas Committee at p. 41. In reaching this conclusion the Committee cites an extract from a submission made to it by Dr. D. Walsh of the Medical-Social Research Board in which he states that "the insights which advances in psychiatry and psychology have given into aspects of the human personality are not yet of a kind to enable the expert witness to establish 'beyond doubt' or even 'on the balance of probability' that a particular individual's personality on his marriage day many years ago was 'immature' or 'irresponsible'." See p. 40 of report. However, where evidence is available as to a party's behaviour before or immediately after marriage it may be possible to establish that at the date of marriage a person suffered from such a serious personality disorder as to render it impossible for such person to discharge the essential obligations of marriage. In this context, see *W. v. P., supra*.

inability to understand the nature of marriage" continuing to be a ground of nullity which renders a marriage void but states that it should fall under the category of "lack of capacity" and cease to fall under the category of "defective consent".[29]

2. Referring to the judgement of Hamilton J. in *M.F.McD. v. W.O'R.*,[30] the Law Reform Commission states that "it seems to us proper that a marriage should be capable of being annulled where one of the parties has so strong a homosexual orientation as to make it impossible for the couple to live a normal married life."[31] Recommending that proof of such an orientation so "as to make it impossible for the couple to form a genuine life-long marriage relationship" should be a separate ground for nullity rendering a marriage voidable, the Commission states that:

> "In many cases the true orientation of a homosexual person may take some years to reveal itself fully to that person and his or her partner. This does not mean, of course, that the person 'just becomes' homosexual — rather is it the case that the innate characteristic present at the time the marriage was celebrated is manifested later. In this respect there are legal parallels between a homosexual orientation and a condition of impotence which may reveal itself fully only after the marriage has been celebrated. Although the time scale may be far longer in the case of a homosexual orientation, we do not consider that this factor, in itself, would involve undue difficulties for the court."[32]

The Commission states that this ground should not be placed within the category of "want of mental capacity" as it may "encourage litigants to raise the issue of whether a homosexual orientation is an illness" and that "it does not seem . . . necessary or appropriate to require petitioners to make the case that such orientation is an illness."[33]

3. Referring to the limited role currently played by fraud and mistake in the law of nullity, the Commission states that a marriage should not be regarded as valid where a party consented to it "on account of mistake or of fraud practised on him".[34] The Commission recommends a new ground for nullity, namely "that a party was induced to enter into a marriage as a result of fraudulent mis-representation made by or on behalf of the other party to the marriage."[35] Acknowledging that "the range of facts capable of falling within the scope of the new ground is broad" it states that it is "satisfied that the courts will be able to ensure that a decree will be granted only in cases where, but for the misrepre-sentation (a) party would not have entered the marriage."[36] In addition the Commission recommends that "certain cases of fraudulent non-disclosure" should also afford grounds for nullity of marriage.[37] These are

---

29. Report of Joint Oireachtas Committee, *supra*, at p. 43.
30. (January, 1984) unreported (H.C.).
31. L.R.C. Report No. 9, *supra*, at p. 106.
32. *Ibid.*, at p. 107.
33. *Ibid.*, at p. 106. The Commission refers to homosexuals. It is presumed that it intended the term to include both men and women and that this proposal is intended equally to apply to a woman with a lesbian orientation.
34. *Ibid.*, at p. 110.
35. *Ibid.*, at p. 112.
36. *Ibid.*, at p. 113.
37. *Ibid.*, at p. 118.

a)   fraudulent non-disclosure of an intention at the time of entering the marriage not to consummate the marriage.[38]

b)   fraudulent non-disclosure of an intention permanently to desert one's partner immediately after the marriage.[39]

c)   fraudulent non-disclosure of an unqualified intention never to have children.[40]

d)   fraudulent non-disclosure of sterility, the sterile party being aware of his/her condition at the date of marriage.[41]

The ground of fraudulent misrepresentation as proposed by the Commission would considerably broaden the law. A fraudulent misrepresentation prior to marriage as to a person's character, wealth, religion, education, employment, family or personal background or medical history could each afford a basis for obtaining a decree of annulment subsequent to a marriage ceremony, provided a court was satisfied that "but for the fraudulent misrepresentation" a person would not have married. The Law Reform Commission acknowledge that such a ground for nullity could result in the law being "seen to support social policies of dubious merit in certain cases". For example, it states "where a woman married a man earning £5,000 per annum believing his representation that he is worth £20,000 per annum" or "believing his representation that he has obtained a professional qualification", it could be considered "improper" for the law to permit her to obtain a nullity decree. While acknowledging "the force of this objection" it concludes that "if it can be shown that they entered a marriage by reason of a fraudulent misrepresentation relating to such a matter made by or on behalf of the other party and that they would not otherwise have entered the marriage, then we consider the balance of the argument is in favour of permitting the general ground of fraudulent misrepresentation to apply."[42]

The ground of fraudulent non-disclosure brings within its compass the additional factor suggested by Kenny J. in *S. v. S.*[43] as providing proof of absence of consent and extends its scope. Thus, while the Commission does not favour extending the ground of nullity to wilful refusal to consummate,[44] a spouse who enters a marriage not intending to consummate may be held to have fraudulently induced the other party's consent and the marriage may be declared a nullity on this ground. Similarly, if a spouse, unknown to the other party, is at the time of the marriage ceremony sterile or has decided not to have children or to desert the other party, the latter's consent to marry may be held to have been

---

38. *Ibid.*
39. *Ibid.*, at p. 119. The Commission states that "the desertion must in fact have taken place immediately and (so far as may be discerned by the court) permanently." It is of the view, however, that "it would be imprudent for the legislation to specify an exact time limit (24 hours or 7 days, for example) within which desertion must have taken place" but stresses "that the legislation should make it clear that 'immediate' should be understood narrowly and that this requirement should not in any circumstances be construed broadly". This recommendation if implemented in the manner proposed by the Commission would not extend the possibility of obtaining a nullity decree to the husband in *E.P. v. M.C.* [1985] 5 I.L.R.M. 34 (H.C.) whose wife deserted him eleven months after marriage, five months after the birth of their child.
40. *Ibid.*, at pp. 119–121.
41. *Ibid.*, at pp. 121–123.
42. *Ibid.*, at p. 117.
43. (July, 1976) unreported (S.C.). See pp. 110 and 125 *ante*.
44. See L.R.C. Report No. 9 at p. 146. The Discussion Paper produced by the Attorney General's Office also rejected this as a separate ground for nullity – see pp. 15–16 of Discussion Paper. The Report of the Joint Oireachtas Committee, however, expressed the opposite view – see p. 43 of Report.

induced by the former's fraudulent non-disclosure and may be declared null and void.[45]

The Commission recommends that the proposed new grounds of fraudulent misrepresentation and fraudulent non-disclosure should render a marriage voidable and not void.[46] It also recommends that these two grounds for nullity should not be retrospective and should only apply to marriages celebrated after the enactment of nullity legislation, save for fraudulent non-disclosure of an intention not to consummate the marriage, which it states, appears already to be part of Irish law.[47]

4. Other recommendations made by the Law Reform Commission which, if enacted, would affect the grounds upon which a decree of nullity may currently be granted include

(a) all prohibitions that apply to persons related by affinity to marry should be abolished.[48]

(b) marriages between a parent and his or her adoptive child and between adoptive brothers and sisters should be void.[49]

(c) a spouse should be permitted to petition for a decree of nullity on the grounds of his own impotence and not only after the other spouse has repudiated the marriage.[50]

(d) the distinction between void and voidable marriages should remain but that lack of consent to marry should render a marriage voidable and not void, as should the four new proposed grounds for nullity.[51]

(e) as a general principle void marriages should not be capable of ratification.[52]

---

45. The draft Nullity Bill contained in the Discussion Paper published by the Attorney General's Office proposed that in deciding whether the "apparent consent" of a party to a marriage was a true consent, the court should have regard to "deceit practiced on the party by any person as regards a feature of the marriage which in the particular circumstances of the case the court considers the party reasonably regarded as fundamental and which induced, to a material extent, the marriage" – see p. 34 of Discussion Paper.
The Joint Oireachtas Committee proposed no changes in existing nullity law in relation to mistake, fraud or misrepresentation – see p. 43 of Report.
46. See L.R.C. Report No. 9, *supra*, at p. 166.
47. *Ibid.*, at pp. 181–182. Whether this ground is already part of Irish law is dependant on whether the courts in the future follow the minority judgement of Kenny J. in *S. v. S.*, *supra*.
48. See L.R.C. Report No. 9, *supra*, at pp. 135–141.
49. *Ibid.*, at p. 143.
50. *Ibid.*, at p. 145. See also Report of Joint Oireachtas Committee at p. 43.
51. *Ibid.*, see p. 160 *et seq.* The Commission recommends that all marriages vitiated by mental incapacity should be voidable but that in order to give protection to an incapacitated person against being victimised, it should be possible for nullity proceedings on this ground to be brought on behalf of the spouse alleged to be incapacitated by any person "who appears to the court to be a proper person to take such proceedings in the interest of such spouse" (see p. 165 of Report). The Joint Oireachtas Committee recommends that nullity based on the traditional ground of insanity continue to render a marriage void but that the new ground based on mental disorder rendering a person incapable of fulfilling the essential obligations of marriage, render a marriage voidable. On the latter ground as proposed by the Committee a third party could not initiate nullity proceedings. The Discussion Paper published by the Attorney General's Office recommended that the distinction between void and voidable marriages be abolished altogether, proposing a new distinction – that between "void" marriages subject to such an impediment that no subsequent conduct can act as a bar to relief and "void" marriages that can be validated by subsequent conduct (see p. 12 *et seq* of Discussion Paper). See also A.J. Shatter, *Family Law in the Republic of Ireland*, 2nd ed., pp. 82–83.
52. L.R.C. Report No. 9, *supra*, at p. 153.

(f) nullity legislation should confer a general discretion on the court to refuse to grant a nullity decree in respect of a voidable marriage "where in all the circumstances it would not be proper to grant one" and the concepts of approbation and collusion should cease to apply. In applying such discretion the Commission states that the conduct of the parties before and after the marriage "would clearly appear to be a matter worthy of consideration as well as the time that had elapsed since the ceremony and the position of the parties and their children at the time of the proceedings."[53]

Commentary

A Nullity of Marriages Act containing all the grounds upon which a nullity decree may be granted in Irish law has never been enacted and it is clear that such a legislative measure is long overdue. Whilst many of the reforms proposed by the Law Reform Commission are welcome, the four new proposed grounds for nullity call for further comment.

Prior to making any recommendations for reform, the Law Reform Commission stresses that

"The law of nullity of marriage is concerned with circumstances in which a marriage is from its commencement invalid: this is in contrast to divorce and legal separation which are not concerned with the circumstances prevailing at the commencement of the marriage, but rather with circumstances arising after the commencement of the marriage."[54]

Moreover, the Commission stresses that as nullity law focuses on the state of affairs prevailing at the time a couple enter into marriage it "cannot be an answer to all problems which bring about marital breakdown."[55]

Judicial development of the law of nullity has, however, already blurred the conceptual distinction between nullity as compared with divorce or legal separation. Prior to 1982[56] the jurisdiction of the High Court to annul a marriage was based entirely on the contractual concept of marriage. It involved the court examining the circumstances existing prior to and at the time of the marriage in order to discover whether as a result of the presence of a particular impediment, the parties did not or could not contract a valid marriage. Thus, the parties' post-marital relationship was largely irrelevant to nullity proceedings, whilst the existence or not of the marriage "contract" was all-important.[57] The new judicially developed ground of "inability to enter into and sustain a normal marriage relationship" has brought about a radical change in the nullity jurisdiction in so far as it emphasises the relationship as opposed to the contractual concept of marriage. If the four new grounds for nullity proposed by the Law Reform Commission become part of Irish law, this change will be statutorily copperfastened. Like the present nullity jurisdiction exercised by the Marriage Tribunals of the Roman Catholic Church, the civil courts if conferred with the new proposed jurisdiction will be much concerned to discover whether at the

---

53. *Ibid.*, at p. 154.
54. *Ibid.*, at p. 88.
55. *Ibid.*, at p. vii. This quotation is adopted by the Joint Oireachtas Committee — see p. 33 of its Report.
56. When judgement was delivered by Barrington J. in *R.S.J. v. J.S.J.*, *supra*.
57. In the case of impotence, however, evidence of failure to consummate after the ceremony is used to prove the existence of impotence at the time of the ceremony. Post-marital conduct is also relevant in determining whether a party is barred from obtaining a decree.

date of marriage both parties had the capacity to discharge the essential obligations of a marital relationship and the intention to carry out the responsibilities of such a relationship. Whilst a movement away from the formal contractual approach is to be welcomed, arguments can be made both in favour of and against the new judicially developed grounds of nullity and the new statutory grounds proposed by the Commission.

The following arguments can be made in favour of the new grounds:

(a)   The new grounds take into account modern psychiatric and psychological learning as to the ability of parties to enter into a true marriage. They enable a court to look behind the exchange of marital vows so as to ascertain whether parties to a marriage possess the personal commitment and personal attributes essential for the creation of a viable marital relationship at the date of the marriage ceremony.

(b)   The new proposed grounds will bring the law more into line with the law administered by the Marriage Tribunals of the Roman Catholic Church. By doing so, it will greatly reduce the number of limping marriages, i.e. marriages held to be null and void by the church but valid by the State. A great majority of those who in the future have their marriages annulled by the Church Tribunals will be able to obtain a civil decree of nullity from the State, similar principles being applicable under both civil and canon law to determine the validity of marriages.

(c)   In determining a person's suitability for marriage the new proposed grounds will allow the court to decide each case on its individual circumstances by examining both the pre-marital and post-marital behaviour of the parties. Thus, where a marriage breaks down, proof of breakdown and the reasons for it, may disclose an initial incapacity on the part of one or both parties to enter marriage or establish that one party was induced to marry by fraudulent misrepresentation or a fraudulent non-disclosure. As a consequence legal release will be possible from a failed marriage out of which the parties would otherwise be prevented from extricating themselves by the constitutional prohibition on divorce.

The following arguments can be made against the new grounds:

(a)   It should be possible to ascertain with certainty at the time a marriage is celebrated whether it is valid or not. If many years after a marriage has taken place a party suffers from a mental illness, it may be alleged that such illness although not apparent, also existed at the date of marriage so as to constitute "a want of mental capacity to fulfil the essential obligations of marriage." Unless the concept of want of mental capacity is defined so as to relate solely to a very serious mental illness or personality disorder that becomes apparent within a short period of time after marriage, this ground as proposed will introduce greater uncertainty into the law of nullity than exists at present and will render it impossible to determine whether any marriage is valid or potentially voidable.

(b)   The proposed new ground of nullity based on fraudulent misrepresentation is so broad as to extend the possibility of obtaining a nullity decree to all couples whose marriage breaks down. For example, in reliance on this ground it appears that upon marital breakdown occurring, a "wife" could allege that she was induced to marry by a representation made to her by her "husband" at the date of marriage that he loved her and always would love her but that his behaviour since marriage clearly established that his profession of love was "fraudulent" and that, accordingly, her consent to marry should be held to be a nullity. Such a broad concept of nullity would be nothing but a legal fiction for divorce enabling a spouse whose marriage has failed to use the nullity jurisdiction to circumvent the constitutional prohibition on divorce. Divorce, not nullity, should provide for the legal termination of such marriages.

Even if the courts declined to regard proof of a fraudulent profession of love inducing marriage as justifying the grant of a decree of nullity on this ground,[58] as a broad range of facts could be held to fall within this concept of nullity considerable doubt would be created as to the validity of many marriages. For example, proof of any of the following facts could provide the basis for the grant of a nullity decree:

(i) Prior to marriage a wife promises she will not use contraceptives after marriage and agrees that she and her husband will have a child as soon as possible after marriage. During the first three years of marriage the wife without her husband's prior consent, avoids pregnancy by use of the contraceptive pill.

(ii) Prior to marriage a couple agree that after marriage they will live in the wife's parents' home in Cork. Unknown to the wife, the husband purchases a home in Cork, insists after marriage that they reside in the newly purchased home and refuses to live with his wife's parents in their home.

(iii) Prior to marriage a husband and wife each agree that after marriage they will not have a sexual relationship with any third party. Two years after marriage the husband commences a liaison with another woman.

(iv) A Church of Ireland woman marries a Roman Catholic man agreeing that any children born to them will be brought up in the Roman Catholic faith. After marriage the wife refuses to implement the couple's pre-marital agreement as to their children's education.

(v) Prior to marriage a husband promises that after marriage he will take his wife to Barbados for an annual holiday and will buy her a new sports car every third year. After marriage the husband does not keep his promises.

In each of the above cases, upon the petitioner proving that he/she would not have married but for the promise of the other spouse, the court could grant a nullity decree on the basis that the fraudulent misrepresentation of the respondent spouse induced the petitioner to enter into marriage.

In addition to increasing uncertainty as to the validity of many marriages, this ground could be easily invoked by spouses anxious to extricate themselves speedily from failed marriages, in that an inventive couple wishing to obtain an annulment would have little difficulty in fabricating a story to rely upon to seek a decree of annulment. As a consequence, such a ground of nullity would not only be seen as a legal fiction for divorce but would also bring nullity law generally into public disrepute.[59]

---

58. A court would have great difficulty in declining to accept such a ground as falling within this concept of nullity.

59. The L.R.C. Report No. 9, at p. 111, states that an extension of the existing ground of nullity based on mistake and fraud would be desirable, provided the new ground would meet the following tests:
"(1) its scope is clear,
 (2) it is not capable of undue extension,

(c) The four grounds subsumed within the ground based on fraudulent non-disclosure are arbitrary and lacking in logic. For example, if it is accepted that one of the fundamental obligations of marriage is that spouses should cohabit and if marriage is held to be an indissoluble union for life, why should "non-disclosure of an intention to desert immediately and permanently" only be a ground for nullity? Why should an intention to desert one year, two years or five years after marriage not also afford such a ground? In support of "fraudulent non-disclosure of an unqualified intention never to have children" as a ground for nullity, the Law Reform Commission states that "most people would agree that the desire to have children is a justifiable expectation on the part of a spouse when entering marriage".[60] However, it can also be argued that most people would agree that it is a justifiable expectation on the part of a spouse when entering marriage that a marital partner will be faithful and not subject the other to marital misconduct. On this basis it could be argued that fraudulent non-disclosure of an intention to commit adultery or cruelty should also be a ground of nullity.

(d) Upon marital breakdown occurring, in the majority of cases, it is possible to discover something in a person's background and mental makeup which can be regarded as a factor contributing to the breakdown. The Roman Catholic Church by developing its nullity jurisdiction may annul many marriages which under the civil law of most States can only be terminated by divorce. It is to a certain extent using nullity as a legal fiction for divorce. The changes proposed by the Law Reform Commission if they become law will result in parties to broken marriages, many years after the celebration of their marriage, seeking decrees of annulment by alleging that one of them suffered a "want of mental capacity" at the date of the marriage or that the marriage was induced by a "fraudulent misrepresentation" or would not have taken place but for a "fraudulent non-disclosure". Contrary to the Law Reform Commission's own perception of the role of the law of nullity, circumstances arising after the marriage will be relied upon to seek to establish that a marriage was invalid from the date of its commencement. Such use of the law of nullity will exacerbate the distress and bitterness that can arise upon marital breakdown occurring rather than contribute towards ameliorating the consequences of breakdown. Instead of encouraging estranged spouses to settle their differences in a dignified and humane manner, it will encourage the assignment of blame and require a finding of "fault" by the court, thus lessening the possibility of co-operation between parties to a broken marriage in the future. The consequences of this approach will be particularly damaging where such co-operation is essential if the welfare of any children born to the parties is to be secured. Moreover, if such nullity proceedings are successful, the granting of a decree of nullity will extinguish any familial constitutional rights vested in any children of the parties, as such children will be regarded as never having been part of a constitutional family unit, their parents' marriage being held to be invalid *ab initio*.

(e) The proposed ground of nullity based on homosexual orientation requires

---

(3) it cannot easily be invoked by spouses who are merely anxious to seek a way out of marriage."
The new ground as proposed by the Commission does not appear to satisfy any of these tests. See further, W. Duncan, "Sex and the Fundamentals of Marriage", *supra*, in which the author discusses the more restrictive proposal based on the concept of deceit contained in the Discussion Paper produced by the Attorney General's Office and raises similar objections to it.
60. L.R.C. Report No. 9, *supra*, at p. 119.

that such orientation would render it impossible for a couple to form a genuine life-long marriage relationship. However, sexual incompatibility which poses a threat to the permanence of a marital relationship can arise from many other causes. For example, a husband and wife may both be heterosexually orientated but the wife may permit intercourse only for the purpose of conception or permit intercourse only once a year, or upon the marriage being consummated, one party may discover he/she is sexually repulsed by the other and refuse to again have intercourse. To permit arbitrarily a decree of nullity to be granted on the ground of sexual incompatibility proposed by the Commission and refuse to extend it to other forms of sexual incompatibility will give rise to considerable injustice. Moreover, this ground as proposed is insufficiently defined and lacking in clarity. For example, if one party to a marriage is hetero-sexual and the other is bisexual will the latter be held to have "so strong an homosexual orientation" as to enable the court grant a nullity decree or will a bisexual's homosexual orientation not be sufficiently "strong" so as to qualify? The collapse of a marital relationship due to sexual incompatibility, whether it arises from one spouse having a homosexual orientation or from other causes, should not be a matter for the law of nullity.

(f) Marital breakdown should be the concern of the law of judicial separation and dissolution or divorce and not the concern of the law of nullity. Upon a marriage collapsing the fundamental question a court should ask is whether the relationship of the parties is still viable at the time when its jurisdiction is called upon. Its sole concern should not be to try to discover whether a person suffered from a psychiatric illness at the date of marriage or whether a person was fraudently induced to marry or married as a result of a fraudulent non-disclosure so as to render a marriage invalid.

Reform of the Consequences of a Decree of Nullity

The effects of a decree of nullity are unnecessarily harsh. The Discussion Paper produced by the Attorney General's Office stated that "It is clearly desirable that the hardships which may result from a decree of nullity should be minimised as far as possible and, accordingly, it is recommended that powers be given to ' the Court to enable the Court to give financial relief to the parties of the marriage and to the children of the marriage so as to do justice between the parties and their children. The Court should be empowered to order that either party to the marriage should make to the other periodical payments or a lump sum; that a party to the marriage should make a payment for the benefit of a child of the marriage; that a party to the marriage should transfer to the other party, or to any child of the marriage, such property as may be specified in the order. Power to vary any ante-nuptial or post-nuptial settlement should also be given. The legislation should set out guidelines on which the discretion of the Court should be exercised, making it clear that the Court should take into consideration the income of the parties to the marriage, their financial needs, the standard of living enjoyed by the family, the age of each party to the marriage and any benefit accruing to the party which might result from the annulment of the marriage".[61]

The Law Reform Commission in its Report on Nullity of Marriage adopts a similar approach, recommending that "wide ranging powers" be conferred on

---

61. Discussion Paper at p. 16.

the court to make orders "regarding property and maintenance rights of parties to an invalid marriage."[62]

Neither in the Discussion Paper nor the Report of the Law Reform Commission is it suggested that any succession rights should be conferred on a party to a void marriage. Referring to this issue, the Commission states that "on the question of succession rights of the parties to a void marriage or a voidable marriage that has been annulled we consider that the best approach would be for legislation not to create any succession rights; the court, in making financial orders at the time it makes a decree of nullity will . . . do so on the basis that no succession rights will accrue to either party."[63] In many cases, however, a party may not discover that his or her marriage is void until after the death of the other party to such "marriage". In such circumstances on the basis of the above proposals as no nullity decree will have been granted during the lifetime of both parties, no jurisdiction will vest in the court to make any financial or property transfer orders. If it is deemed just to minimise the hardship that may arise from a decree of nullity during the lifetime of the parties, it is submitted that the hardship which may occur upon a person who married in good faith discovering his or her marriage to be void after the death of the other party, should also be minimised. Such a person should be empowered to apply to the court for reasonable provision out of the deceased's estate. This proposal should not, however, extend any such legal right to a person who celebrated a marriage ceremony knowing at the date of the ceremony that the marriage was invalid, for example, because it was bigamous.

The Discussion Paper also recommends that a child born of an annulled marriage should:

(a) be treated as a legitimate child of its parents,[64]

(b) have a right to share in the estate of both of his deceased parents.[65]

On the basis of this proposal, a child would be treated as legitimate or be able to obtain a share in his father's estate if his parents have gone through a ceremony of marriage that is declared void by a court, but if the parents merely live together and are not parties to an invalid (i.e. non-existent) marriage, he would not be so treated or acquire any such succession rights. A more logical solution would be to enact legislation abolishing the concept of illegitimacy altogether and equalising the rights of children so that the legal relationship between parents and children is based on the fact of parenthood and is not affected by whether or not parents are validly married to each other. The Law Reform Commission recommends the enactment of such legislation.[66]

The Status of Children Bill, 1986, proposes to remove many of the provisions in the current law which discriminate against children born outside marriage but as published does not fully adopt the approach proposed by the Law Reform Commission, in that it preserves a distinction in law between marital and non-marital children. In the context of nullity proceedings it pro-

---

62. L.R.C. Report No. 9, *supra*. at p. 173. See further Chapter 15 at p. 535 *et seq*.
63. L.R.C. Report No. 9, at p. 175.
64. Discussion Paper at p. 15.
65. *Ibid*., at p. 16.
66. See generally Report on Illegitimacy (L.R.C. Report No. 4 – September 1982) and L.R.C. Report No. 9 at p. 167. The Joint Oireachtas Committee in its Report (at p. 43) "urges the speedy introduction of legislation to remove the status of illegitimacy" and also proposes that the court should be empowered to make ancillary orders relating to children of an annulled marriage as to guardianship, custody and maintenance. See further the Status of Children Bill, 1986, discussed in chaps. 11 and 18.

vides that a child of a void marriage shall be deemed to be the legitimate child of its parents "if either or both of his parents reasonably believed (whether or not such belief was due to a mistake of fact or of law) that their ceremony of marriage resulted in a valid marriage." and that "where a nullity decree is or has been granted in respect of a voidable marriage" any child of such marriage shall be deemed to be legitimate. A child deemed legitimate under the Bill is said to be a "marital child". Consequently, under the terms of the Bill as drafted some children born to a couple whose marriage is void or has been annulled will be regarded as "marital children" whilst others will be regarded as "non-marital" children. As all marriages in respect of which a decree of nullity is granted are in law void *ab initio*, statutory classification of children in such circumstances as "marital children" will not result in the relationship between such children and their parents being governed by Articles 41 and 42 of the Constitution as these provisions only apply to a family based on a valid marriage. The statutory distinctions under the new proposed law between marital and non-marital children are briefly discussed in chapters 11 and 18. It need merely be noted here that if the Bill, as initiated, is enacted by the Oireachtas, both "marital" and "non-marital" children will possess similar rights to share in the estate of each of their parents, although some differences in the legal position of non-marital children when compared to that of marital children will still exist in the laws of succession.

CHAPTER 6

MARRIAGE AND THE LAW

Marriage creates a status to which the law attaches various rights and duties, which affect both the legal relationship of the parties between themselves, and with other people. The most fundamental right that marriage creates is the right that each party has to the other's company (consortium). The corollary of this right is the legal duty imposed on spouses to cohabit. In this chapter we discuss the legal means of enforcing the duty to cohabit and the remedies the law provides for loss of consortium. We then look to see how marriage historically affected the position of parties under various other categories of the law and the present day position. In conclusion we look at the procedure available whereby a person can obtain a declaration as to his marital status and the remedy available to prevent a person falsely asserting that he is another's spouse.

REMEDY TO ENFORCE DUTY TO COHABIT

Restitution of Conjugal Rights

The primary duty of a husband and wife under Ecclesiastical Law was the duty to cohabit. This duty was enforced by the Ecclesiastical Courts upon petition by a deserted spouse for a decree of Restitution of Conjugal Rights. This decree called upon the spouse in desertion, to resume cohabitation with the petitioner. If it was disobeyed, the respondent could be excommunicated. The power to excommunicate was abolished in England by the Ecclesiastical Courts Act, 1813, and replaced by a power to impose a six-month sentence of imprisonment. This Act did not apply to Ireland and until the abolition of the Ecclesiastical Courts in 1870 the power to excommunicate remained.[1]

Today the jurisdiction to hear proceedings for restitution of conjugal rights is vested in the High Court[2] and failure to comply with such an order of that Court renders a person liable to committal for contempt.[3] In order to obtain

---

1. *Contra* K. Hayes, "Matrimonial Jurisdiction of the High Court", (1973) 8 I.J. (n.s.) 55.
2. See *Hood v. Hood* [1959] I.R. 225 (H.C.).
3. See *Bell v. Bell* [1922] 2 I.R. 103, 152 at p. 158; 56 I.L.T.R. 46; (K.B.D.); In England in 1884 the Matrimonial Causes Act (which did not apply in Ireland) abolished the courts' power of attachment. From then on in England refusal to comply with a decree of restitution gave the other spouse a right to petition for a judicial separation, or until 1923, in the case of a wife, for divorce, if the husband had also committed adultery. See A.W. Samuels K.C., "Divorce Jurisdiction in Ireland" (1911) 45 I.L.T. & S.J. 6; also Westropp's Divorce Bill (1868) 11 A.C., p. 294n, (H.L.). Sect. 20 of the Matrimonial Proceedings and Property Act, 1970, abolished the action totally in England. By Sect. 120(2) of Succession Act, 1965, a spouse who fails to comply with a decree for restitution of conjugal rights obtained by the deceased is precluded from taking any share in the estate of the deceased as a legal right or on an intestacy. A spouse who fails to comply with an order for restitution of conjugal rights may also be held to be in desertion and thereby deprived of his or her right to obtain a maintenance order pursuant to the provisions of the Family Law (Maintenance of Spouses and Children) Act, 1976 (see p. 439 *post*). Moreover, an order could also be made

such a decree a petitioner must give evidence of the respondent having refused to comply with a written demand to resume cohabitation and restore conjugal rights.[4] If at any time after the commencement of proceedings the respondent becomes willing to resume cohabitation, the petitioner may apply for an order to stay the proceedings.[5]

A defence to a petition for restitution is afforded by proof by the respondent that the petitioner has committed a matrimonial offence sufficient to ground an action for a divorce *a mensa et thoro*.[6] If a respondent succeeds in substantiating such a charge he or she is in turn able to obtain such a divorce decree.[7]

Moreover, it has been stated that evidence of matters of a less aggravated character than are sufficient to ground an allegation of cruelty or adultery for the purpose of *a mensa et thoro* decree may be held sufficient to justify a refusal to cohabit.[8] However, the fact that the petitioner has previously deserted the respondent without just cause, affords no answer to a suit for restitution, desertion not being a ground for *a mensa et thoro* decree.[9]

A decree for restitution of conjugal rights is the only lawful means whereby one spouse can force another to cohabit against the latter's will. In the case of *R. v. Jackson*[10] it was decided that a husband cannot resort to extra-judicial methods to enforce his right to his wife's consortium. In this case a wife who had gone to live with relations while her husband was away, refused to return to him and failed to comply with a decree for restitution of conjugal rights. One Sunday when she was leaving church the husband with two other men seized her, took her to his home and refused to permit her to leave. An application was made on her behalf for a writ of *habeas corpus*. The application was successful, the Court of Appeal holding that it was no defence that the husband was merely attempting to enforce his right to consortium.

Commentary: Mr. A.W. Samuels, K.C. in giving evidence on Irish Marriage Laws before the Royal Commission on Divorce in 1910[11] referring to the power to make an order of restitution, stated:

"This is a peculiar jurisdiction exercised by the divorce tribunal, by which it purports to compel two people who detest one another to live together. It would be a very difficult thing to discover a case in which the husband or wife was by the promptings of affection urged to bring a suit for the restitution of conjugal rights. To quote the words of Lord Hannen in *Marshall v. Marshall*[12] 'I must observe that so far as suits for restitution

dispensing with the necessity to obtain the prior written consent of such a spouse to a conveyance of an interest in a family home pursuant to the provisions of the Family Home Protection Act, 1976 (see p. 560 *post*).

4. See Order 70, Rule 4 of the Rules of the Superior Courts. See also *Molloy v. Molloy* (1871) I.R. 5 Eq. 367 (Ct. for Mat. Causes).
5. *Ibid.*, Order 70, Rule 58.
6. *Ruxton v. Ruxton* (1880) 5 L.R. Ir. 19, 455 (P. & M.), (C.A.); *D'Arcy v. D'Arcy* (1887) 19 L.R. Ir. 369 (P. & M.).
7. *Seaver v. Seaver* (1846) 2 Sw. & Tr. 665; 164 E.R. 1156 (Consistory Ct.).
8. *Carnegie v. Carnegie* (1886) 17 L.R. Ir. 430 (P. & M.); *Sopwith v. Sopwith* (1860) 2 Sw. & Tr. 168; 164 E.R. 954; *Russell v. Russell* [1895] P. 315, (C.A.); [1897] A.C. 395 (H.L.) affirming C.A. See, however, *D. v. D.* (December, 1966) unreported (H.C.); *Manning v. Manning* (1873) I.R. 7 Eq. 520; (1872) I.R. 6 Eq. 417; (1873) I.R. 7 Eq. 365 (Ct. of App. in Ch.).
9. *Dunne v. Dunne* [1947] I.R. 277; (1947) 81 I.L.T.R. 80 (H.C.); *Manning v. Manning, supra.*
10. [1891] 1 Q.B. 671 (C.A.); see also *R. v. Reid* [1972] 2 All E.R. 1350 (C.A.) — in this case a husband was convicted of kidnapping his wife; see further (1972) 2 Fam. Law 135.
11. See (1911) 45 I.L.T. & S.J. 6.
12. (1879) 5 P.D. 19 (P.D.A.), at p. 23.

of conjugal rights from being in truth and in fact what theoretically they purport to be, proceedings for the purpose of insisting on the fulfilment of the obligation of married persons to live together, I have never known an instance in which it has appeared that the suit was instituted for any other purpose than to enforce a money demand'."

Today such proceedings are not even necessary for this latter purpose as a dependent spouse who is not supported can bring maintenance proceedings so as to compel the other spouse to provide proper maintenance and support.

The Law Reform Commission in its 6th report dealing with the action for restitution of conjugal rights, notes that "international experience strongly suggests that reconciliation and conciliation are more successfully encouraged where the procedures are voluntary rather than compulsory."[13] It is submitted that if a spouse genuinely desires to bring about a reconciliation, a court order directing the other spouse to co-habit is hardly an appropriate method of effecting one and is more likely to exacerbate than ameliorate matrimonial disharmony. The action for restitution of conjugal rights is rarely used today, the last written judgement in proceedings seeking such an order having been delivered by the High Court over 20 years ago. It is a valueless anachronism and, as is recommended by the Law Reform Commission, it should be abolished.[14]

---

13. The Law Reform Commission: *Report on Restitution of Conjugal Rights* (L.R.C. Report No. 6, November 1983) at p. 12.

14. *Ibid*. See also K. Hayes, *supra*, at pp. 74–77.

REMEDIES FOR INTERFERING WITH THE RIGHT TO WIFE'S SOCIETY AND SERVICES

Action for loss of Society and Services (per quod servitum et consortium amisit)

In the eyes of the common law a husband has a proprietary or at the very least a quasi proprietary interest in the society and services of his wife. As a consequence, if he is deprived of her society or services as a result of a wrong[1] committed against her by a third person, he has a right of action against that person. The husband's action is quite distinct from any claim which the wife may have, and his claim is not affected by any contributory negligence on her part.[2] There is no analogous right in the wife to sue for the loss of her husband's society or companionship.[3]

Damages may be recovered for loss of her services or society or both. The usual damages recovered for loss of services are for the cost of providing an alternative housekeeper to look after the husband and children while the wife was in hospital, together with medical expenses. Damages are also recoverable for the cost of domestic assistance that the husband may have to obtain in the future by reason of his wife's incapacity to carry out her domestic duties.[4] Where a husband has suffered any loss of earnings in order to be with his wife during her illness, he is able to recover these earnings to the extent that they were incurred in order to mitigate the damage flowing from the loss of consortium.[5]

Damages can be recovered for the total loss of a wife's society or consortium but they cannot be recovered for an impairment of consortium. Thus in *Spaight v. Dundon*[6] whereas a husband could recover damages for the total loss of his wife's companionship during the period of one year which she had to spend in hospital, he was not entitled to be compensated because she was disfigured or because her temperament or mental outlook might be affected. In *O'Haran v. Divine*[7] it was said that consortium is "the sum total of the benefits which a wife may be expected to confer on her husband by their living together – help, comfort, companionship, services and all the amenities of family and marriage. If by the negligent action of the defendant a husband was deprived of all these, even for a limited period he was entitled to recover damages; but if the deprivation was merely of one or more elements of consortium while other elements continued to be engaged no action lay".[8] The fact that a husband may visit his incapacitated

---

1. The wrong is usually a tort, but such a claim may arise from a breach of contract. In *Jackson v. Watson & Sons* (1909) 2 K.B. 193 (C.A.) – A husband was held entitled to sue for compensation the vendor of bad salmon which his wife ate and which caused her death by food poisoning.
2. See the Civil Liability Act, 1961, Sect. 35(2) as amended by the Civil Liability Act 1964, Sect. 4. See also *Mallet v. Dunne* [1949] 2 K.B. 180 (K.B.D.).
3. *Best v. Samuel Fox* [1952] A.C. 716 (H.L.).
4. *Spaight v. Dundon* [1961] I.R. 201; 96 I.L.T.R. 69 (S.C.).
5. *McNeill v. Johnstone* [1958] 3 All E.R. 16 (Q.B.D.). Moreover, if in his employment, a husband is particularly dependent on his wife's presence or assistance, and it is reasonable for him to refuse employment while she is incapacitated, he may be able to recover damages for his loss of earnings – *Behrens v. Bertram Mills Circus Ltd.* [1957] 2 Q.B. 1 (Q.B.D.); see, however, *Kirkham v. Boughey* [1958] 2 Q.B. 388 (Q.B.D.) in which the authority of the previous case was doubted.
6. *Supra.*
7. (1966) 100 I.L.T.R. 53 (S.C.).
8. *Per* Kingsmill Moore J. at p. 55. See also *Cutts v. Chumley* [1967] 2 All E.R. 89 (C.A.), where damages were given for impairment of consortium, but what was regarded as an impairment of consortium on the facts of that case – the total incapacitation and institutionalisation of the wife – would be regarded on the basis of the decision in *O'Haran v. Divine* as a total loss of consortium. There "a healthy companion and helper was reduced to a condition where she had to be separated from her husband" and "all the innumerable advantages, pleasures and consolations of married life were brought to an end – save a limited measure of communication –" (1966) 100 I.L.T.R. at p. 56; see also *Lawrence*

wife in hospital is not regarded as preventing him from recovering for loss of consortium.

This action has been condemned by both the English and Irish judiciary as an anachronistic survival of a medieval outlook. When it was argued in the English case of *Best v. Samuel Fox Ltd.*[9] that it was anomalous to permit a husband to bring such an action while denying the wife a similar right, the House of Lords replied that the real anomaly was the husband's right of action in the first place, and that the action should not be extended. The Supreme Court in *Spaight v. Dundon* agreed with this opinion of the House of Lords, stating that the action would not be extended and that damages for loss of consortium should not be too generous.[10]

Harbouring, Enticement and Criminal Conversation

At common law a husband could bring proceedings seeking damages from any person who provided accommodation for and harboured his wife or who engaged in criminal conversation, i.e. had sexual intercourse, with her. Moreover, any person who procured, enticed or persuaded a spouse to leave the other could be sued for damages by the deserted spouse.[11] All of these actions are now abolished by section 1 of the Family Law Act, 1981.[12]

REMEDIES FOR INTERFERING WITH RIGHT TO CHILDREN'S SERVICES[13]

Just as a husband at common law has a right to his wife's services, a parent is regarded as having a legal right to the services of his unmarried minor children who ordinarily live at home.[14] If a third party wrongfully deprives a parent of such services, for example by enticing, harbouring,[15] or seducing a child,[16] the parent acquires a right of action against the former, in which, if he is successful, he can obtain damages.[17] In practice, the great majority of such actions are brought by a parent for the seduction of his daughter. Although in theory such

---

v. Biddle [1966] 2 Q.B. 504 (Q.B.D.). See further The Law Relating to Loss of Consortium and Loss of Services of a Child, The Law Reform Commission Working Paper No. 7 (Dublin 1979) at p. 2 *et seq*. See also B.M.E. McMahon & W. Binchy, *Irish Law of Torts* (Professional Books, 1981) at p. 414 where the authors state that the decision in *O'Haran v. Divine* may be interpreted as a relaxation of the previous requirement that the loss of consortium be total, in favour of a more flexible standard.

9. *Supra.*

10. See, however, the Law Reform Commission, Working Paper No. 7, *supra*, at p. 4 *et seq*. where it is suggested that the courts may extend the action so as to enable a wife sue for loss of consortium. See also McMahon & Binchy, *supra* at p. 414.

11. See A.J. Shatter, *Family Law in the Republic of Ireland*, 2nd ed., pp. 91–93; McMahon & Binchy, *supra*, pp. 406–412.

12. See the Law Reform Commission's Working Paper No. 5 (Dublin 1978) and *First Report on Family Law* (Dublin 1981) where the Commission recommend that these actions be replaced by a new family action enabling members of the family unit (i.e. spouses and their children) to seek damages from any person who committed adultery with a spouse of the family. This recommendation was rejected by the government and the actions for criminal conversation, harbouring and enticement were simply abolished. For a critique of the Commission's Working Paper see A.J. Shatter, *supra*, at pp. 95–98.

13. See McMahon & Binchy, *supra*, pp. 415–424.

14. *Lough v. Ward* [1945] 2 All E.R. 338 (K.B.D.). A parent's entitlement to his child's services has been held to continue until a child attains 21 years of age. The Age of Majority Act, 1985, reduced the age of majority to 18 years and it is submitted so reduces a parent's right to his child's services.

15. *Lough v. Ward, supra.*

16. All reported cases of seduction relate to the seduction of a girl. See cases cited in the following footnotes.

17. See the interesting case of the *People (A.-G) v. Edge* [1943] I.R. 115 (S.C.), in which the Supreme Court held that the defendant could not be convicted of the criminal offence of kidnapping, following his taking a boy of fourteen and a half years of age away from his parents, with the boy's, but without the parents', consent.

an action is brought for loss of services, this is little more than a legal fiction. In reality, the action is for a wrong done to the honour and feelings of the parent.[18]

Loss of services: The legal basis of the action is loss of services and not the familial relationship between a parent and child.[19] Thus, if a child is too young to give any services,[20] or is in the service of another and not living with his parents,[21] a parent cannot obtain damages for a wrong committed against his child. However, it is possible for a child to remain in the service of a parent, although also employed by another,[22] whilst if a child quits another's service a parent's right may revive.[23] A parent may obtain damages without proving that a child in fact renders any services. If the child lives with the parent and is old enough to provide services the law will conclusively presume that service is given.[24] Such an action can be brought by any parent living with his child whether the parent is married or unmarried,[25] or whether the child is the natural or adopted child of the parent.[26]

In the old case of *Hamilton v. Long*[27] it was held that if both parents are alive and living together with their child, the latter's services are owed exclusively to the father as master of the household. The court held that the mother could not sue for loss of services arising out of her daughter's seduction during the father's lifetime. Now that it is accepted that a mother has the same constitutional rights with respect to a legitimate child as the father,[28] it is submitted that she must have the same right as the father to recover damages for loss of her child's services.

Damages: The court in such proceedings has no power to order a child to return to a parent. It may, however, as well as awarding damages, restrain the defendants by way of injunction from harbouring a child or otherwise depriving

---

18. A parent may of course have a right to the service of a child who has attained his majority. However, such a right is presumed in relation to a minor child but will not be presumed in relation to an older child – see *O'Reilly v. Glavey* (1893) 32 L.R. (Ir.) 316 (Ex. Div.); *Farrelly v. Donegan* (1931) 65 I.L.T.R. 102 (Cir. Ct.); *Beetham v. James* [1937] 1 K.B. 527 (K.B.D.). See also *Murray v. Fitzgerald* [1906] 2 I.R. 254 (C.A.) where a brother successfully claimed damages for the seduction of his older sister. Both were over twenty one years. The brother managed the family farm while the sister performed the domestic chores around the house. In *Clements v. Boyd* (1894) 28 I.L.T.R. 44 (C. Ct.) and *Brennan v. Kearns* (1943) 77 I.L.T.R. 194 (Cir. Ct.) similar actions were unsuccessful. See further W. Binchy, "Seduction and the Irish Law" (November 1977) Vol. 71, Gazette of the Incorporated Law Society of Ireland 187.
19. *Grinnel v. Wells* (1844), 7 Man & G. 1033; 135 E.R. 419 (Ct. of C.P.); *Beetham v. James, supra.*
20. *Hall v. Hollander* (1825) 4 B. & C. 660; 107 E.R. 1206 (K.B.). (Accident-son).
21. *Hedges v. Tagg* (1872) L.R. 7 Ex. 283 (Ct. of Ex.); *Gladney v. Murphy* (1890) 26 L.R. Ir. 651 (Q.B.D.); *Kearney v. M'Murray* (1894) 28 I.L.T.R. 148 (C. Ct.); *Barnes v. Fox* [1914] 2 I.R. 276 (C.A.). All these cases are concerned with the seduction of a girl and establish that for a parent to obtain damages for loss of services he must show a right to his daughter's services both at the time of the seduction and during her confinement. See, however, *Long v. Keightley* (1877) I.R. 11 C.L. 221 (Com. Pleas); *Connell v. Noonan* (1883) 17 I.L.T.R. 103 (C. Ct.) in which it is held that it is not necessary for a daughter to remain in the plaintiff's service during the confinement. See further (1877) I.L.T. & S.J. at pp. 402 and 428 where the case of *Long v. Keighley* is disucssed.
22. *Dent v. Maguire* [1917] 2 I.R. 59 (Appeal).
23. *Terry v. Hutchinson* (1868) L.R. 3, Q.B. 599 (Q.B.).
24. *Ibid.*
25. *Beethan v. James, supra.*
26. *Peters v. Jones* [1914] 2 K.B. 781 (K.B.D.).
27. [1903] 2 I.R. 407 (K.B.D.) affirmed [1905] 2 I.R. 552 (Appeal), *Thompson v. Fitzpatrick* (1920) 54 I.L.T.R. 184 (K.B.D.); *O'Donnell v. Neely* (1940) 70 I.L.T.R. 120 (Cir. Ct.); see also *Peters v. Jones, supra; Beetham v. James, supra.*
28. See p. 350 *et seq.*

a parent of the child's services.[29] Damages are not limited to the financial worth of the services lost, which in the majority of cases is not very great, but may also be awarded as compensation for the damage done to the pride and honour of the parents. They may further include all reasonable and necessary expenses incurred as a consequence of the defendant's actions. Thus, if a baby is born as a result of the dependant's seduction, it has been held that the costs of maintaining such a child may be taken into account.[30] However, the behaviour of the parents[31] or the child[32] may be such as to mitigate damages, whilst the behaviour of the defendant may be such as to justify the award of exemplary damages as an indication of the court's disapproval of his conduct.[33]

PROPOSALS FOR REFORM

The Law Reform Commission has extensively examined this area of the law and made a number of recommendations for reform.[34]

(i)   The Commission has recommended that the existing actions for loss of the services and society of a wife and for the loss of the services of a child should be replaced by a single family action that could be brought for the benefit of all members of the family unit residing together. For the purposes of such action, the family unit is to be defined as being parents and their children, including adopted children and children to whom either parent is *in loco parentis*.[35] Damages, which would be without monetary limitation in the new legislation, would cover:

(a)   All reasonable expenses and other financial losses incurred by the members of the family of the victim;

(b)   Mental distress resulting to the members of the family;

(c)   Damage to the continuity, stability and quality of the relationships between members of the family.

The Commission further recommends that only one action should be capable of being brought and the court should be empowered to award such damages to each member of the family unit as it considers fit. It also states that the defence of contributory negligence should be available to the defendant in such proceedings.[36]

These recommendations by the Commission are to be welcomed. The new proposed action would remove the medieval foundations on which the present law is based by extending the action to all members of the family unit and no longer requiring proof of a service relationship. It would end artificial distinctions between total and partial loss of consortium and concentrate on the consequences

29. *Lough v. Ward, supra.* (Young girl entered religious society without parental consent.)
30. *Flynn v. Connell* [1919] 2 I.R. 427 (K.B.D.).
31. *Beetham v. James, supra,* (unmarried parents cohabiting); see also *Reddie v. Scoolt* (1795), Peake 316; 170 E.R. 169 (Nisi Prius) — where it was held that a father who permitted a married man to make visits to his daughter, could not maintain an action against him for seduction.
32. *Verry v. Watkins* (1836), 7 Car. & P. 308; 173 E.R. 137 (Nisi Prius), (child sexually promiscuous).
33. *Lough v. Ward, supra.*
34. See the Law Reform Commission: The Law Relating to Loss of Consortium and Loss of Services of a Child (Working Paper No. 7, Dublin 1979); The Law Relating to Seduction and the Enticement and Harbouring of a Child (Working Paper No. 6, Dublin 1979); and *First Report on Family Law* (Report No. 1, Dublin 1981).
35. See Report No. 1, *supra*, p. 9; Working Paper No. 7, *supra*, p. 58.
36. See Report No. 1, *supra*, p. 10; Working Paper No. 7, *supra*, p. 44.

to the family unit of an injury to one of its members. It would also remove the existing legal anomaly whereby damages for mental distress can be obtained for the death of a spouse, child, or parent as a result of a deliberate or negligent act by a third party but cannot be obtained for their permanent incapacitation.

The expenses incurred by a family as a result of one of its members being wrongfully injured can give rise to considerable hardship. The proposed action would enable members of the family to recover reasonable expenses properly incurred in consequence of the injury. Such expenses could include loss of earnings, costs of visits to hospital and costs of any domestic help required as a result of such injury.

(ii) The Commission has recommended that the existing action of seduction of a child be abolished and replaced by a single family action for seduction and that the actions for enticing and harbouring a child be retained, subject to certain amendments.[37] All of these actions would have the following characteristics in common:

(a) The actions would be in the nature of a single family action for the benefit of all members of the family unit to be defined as comprising the parents and their children[38] and the requirement of a service relationship would be abolished.

(b) The child's right of action would be merged in the family action, allowing the child to be awarded damages where the circumstances so warrant.

(c) The actions would be limited to cases of unmarried children under 18 years of age and in the case of an action for seduction, the seduction must have resulted in pregnancy and such action would not lie if the seduced child was married at any time prior to the seduction. In all cases the evidence of the child would require corroboration.

(d) The present law as to damages would be retained and in the case of actions for enticement and harbouring, in assessing damages or granting discretionary relief, the court would be required to have regard to the extent, if any, to which the welfare of the child had been affected by the enticement or harbouring. The Commission gives no explanation as to why this requirement should not apply in an action for seduction.

It is submitted that the Commission's recommendations are misconceived and that the actions for seduction, harbouring and enticement of children should simply be abolished. If a parent does not wish a child to associate with a third party, it is submitted that the welfare of the child can be better protected by bringing proceedings under section 11 of the Guardianship of Infants Act, 1964, or by bringing wardship proceedings. In the context of the action for seduction, any suggestion that the continued availability of such action could deter would-be seducers is dismissed by the Commission itself, which acknowledges that in countries where such action is available "it has no significant deterrent effect on

---

37. See Report No. 1, *supra*, pp. 11–15 and Working Paper No. 6, *supra*, pp. 73–75.
38. Children would include legally adopted children and children to whom either parent is *in loco parentis.*

behaviour."[39] Moreover, if the Commission intended that the continued availability of such action should act as a deterrent it is difficult to understand why it should be confined to cases in which a seduction results in a pregnancy and not apply to all alleged seductions, including seduction of boys under 18, as well as girls under 18. There is no evidence that the existing actions that are available in this country have had any deterrent effect whatsoever and the rarity of such proceedings is indicative of their irrelevance to modern social relationships.

The Law Reform Commission's work in this area exhibits a total lack of understanding of intra-family relationships. The seduction of a young girl or the departure from home of a young child is in the great majority of instances a symptom or consequence of a deep family malaise. The Commission's proposals merely deal with some of the symptoms and fail to suggest a method to help parents come to terms with or understand the causes. In practice, the proceedings proposed could aggravate rather than ameliorate family difficulties by further alienating from the family the child in respect of whom such proceedings are instituted. The Commission's proposals have been stated to be currently "under consideration in the Department of Justice"[40] and it is hoped that in this area they will be rejected.

---

39. Working Paper No. 6, *supra*, p. 58.
40. See "Irish Women — Agenda for Practical Action — Report of Inter-departmental Working Party" (Stationery Office, Dublin, February 1985), p. 284.

DEATH OF A RELATION[1]

The case of *Baker v. Bolton*[2] in 1808 laid down that at common law "in a civil court the death of a human being could not be complained of as an injury".

Thus, whereas a husband could recover damages for the loss of his wife's consortium and services if she suffered an injury at the hands of another, if the injury caused her death he could not recover for the permanent deprivation suffered as a result of her death. The legislature intervened to ameliorate the position by the passing of the Fatal Accidents Acts. The present law is set down in Part IV of the Civil Liability Act, 1961.[3] By its provision dependants of a deceased may recover damages where his death is caused by the wrongful act of another, if the act was such as would have entitled the deceased, but for his death, to maintain an action and recover damages against the other.[4] If during the deceased's lifetime he has accepted full compensation from the defendant in respect of the injury, no action can be brought as a result of his death.[5]

The relatives whose interests are protected are the wife, father, mother, grandfather, grandmother, stepfather, stepmother, son, daughter, grandson, granddaughter, stepson, stepdaughter, brother, sister, half-brother and half-sister. An adopted child is to be considered as the legitimate child of the adopter or adopters, an illegitimate person, if not adopted by another, is to be considered as the legitimate child of his mother and reputed father,[6] and a person *in loco parentis* to another is considered as the parent of that other.[7]

In order for any of the above persons to recover damages it must be shown that they suffered injury or mental distress as a result of the deceased's death. Only one action may be brought against the same person and such action is to be for the benefit of all the dependants.[8]

The action is to be brought by the deceased's personal representative but if at the expiration of 6 months from the death there is no personal representative, or no action has been brought by a personal representative, all or any of the dependants may sue. The plaintiff must provide the defendant with particulars of the person or persons for whom and on whose behalf the action is brought, and of the nature of the claim in respect of which damages are sought.[9] The action must commence within 3 years of the death.[10]

Assessment of Damages[11]

Damages are recoverable for injury, mental distress and for funeral and other expenses.

---

1. For a more detailed account of this area of the law see B.M.E. McMahon & W. Binchy, *Irish Law of Torts*, Chap. 10.
2. (1808) 1 Camp 493 (Assize); 170 E.R. 1033.
3. See "Some Aspects of Damages Under the Civil Liability Acts of 1961 and 1964", Michael Knight (1966) 1 I.J. (n.s.) 35; see also Article in (1962–63) Vol. XXVIII-XXIX, I.J. 30, "Assessment of damages in Fatal Injury cases" by V.T.H. Delany.
4. Sect. 48(1); also see *Malone v. C.I.E.* (1953) 94 I.L.T.R. 179 (S.C.).
5. See *Swords v. St. Patrick's Copper Mines Ltd.* [1965] Ir. Jur. Rep., 63 (S.C.). (The Workmens Compensation Acts, 1934–55 therein referred to, were repealed by the Social Welfare (Occupational Injuries) Act, 1966).
6. See *O'Mahoney v. E.S.B.* (1959) 93 I.L.T.R. 4 (S.C.).
7. Sect. 47(1) and (2); see also *Waters v. Cruikshank* [1967] I.R. 378, (1963) 103 I.L.T.R. 129 (S.C.).
8. See *Swords v. St. Patrick's Copper Mines Ltd., supra.*
9. Sect. 48(5).
10. Sect. 48(6).
11. See Sect. 49 of Act.

I. Injury: Injury is measured solely by reference to the financial loss suffered by a claimant as a result of a person's death. The loss is estimated by reference to the actual pecuniary loss incurred, together with any reasonable expectation of benefit (either money or money's worth) the claimant would have had, whether as of right or otherwise, if the life had continued,[12] set off against any pecuniary benefit and any reasonable expectation of such benefit the claimant has as a result of the death.[13] The court requires information showing as accurately as possible the net pecuniary loss sustained by each dependant in consequence of the death. The courts have constantly stated that there must be affirmative evidence of the extent of the loss. Damages will not be awarded merely on a basis of guesswork.[14] Any damages given are purely by way of compensation and are not of a punitive nature. If the deceased was guilty of contributory negligence, the damages awarded may be reduced proportionately.[15]

II. Mental Distress: Since the enactment of the 1961 Act[16] "reasonable compensation"[17] has been recoverable for mental distress caused to a dependant as a result of a death. Prior to the coming into force of the Act no such damages were recoverable.[18] Whereas the amount of damages for "injury" suffered by a dependant may be assessed by a jury, damages for purely mental distress are to be assessed solely by a judge. The total amount of damages that could be awarded for such distress under the 1961 Act originally could not exceed £1,000 but this limit was increased to £7,500 by the Courts Act, 1981.[19]

In determining the amount of damages to be awarded Walsh J. stated in *Dowling v. Jedos Ltd.*[20]

"The correct approach is for the judge to make a notional award in the sum which he would on the evidence be justified in giving to each of the persons who suffered mental distress without taking into account at that stage that the maximum possible total is £1,000. When the notional figures have been arrived at and if their total exceeds £1,000 then as the ratio between them is already known they should be scaled down proportionately so that the total is reduced to £1,000."[21]

As for the meaning of mental distress, Lavery J. in *Cubbard v. Rederij Viribus Unitis & Another*[22] stated:

"Mental distress is something very different from being moved or affected by the death of a relative. Everyone is moved or affected by the death of a

---

12. *Gallagher v. E.S.B.* [1933] I.R. 558 (S.C.); *Horgan v. Buckley* (No. 1) [1938] I.R. 115 (S.C.); *Byrne v. Houlihan and Ano.* [1966] I.R. 274 (S.C.); *Murphy v. Cronin* [1966] I.R. 699 (S.C.); *O'Sullivan v. C.I.E.* [1978] I.R. 409 (H.C., S.C.).
13. *Byrne v. Houlihan and Ano., supra; Murphy v. Cronin, supra; O'Sullivan v. C.I.E., supra.*
14. *Hull v. Great Northern Railway Co. of Ireland* (1890) 26 L.R. Ir. 289 (Ex. Div.); *Appelbe v. West Cork Board of Health* [1929] 1 I.R. 107 (S.C.); *Horgan v. Buckley, supra; Gallagher v. E.S.B., supra; Byrne v. Houlihan, supra.*
15. *McCarthy v. Walsh* [1965] I.R. 246 (S.C.); *Murphy v. Cronin, supra.*
16. See also Civil Liability (Amendment) Act, 1964.
17. See *McCarthy v. Walsh, supra*, where the meaning of reasonable compensation is discussed.
18. *Gallagher v. E.S.B., supra.*
19. Courts Act, 1981, Sect. 28(1). In *McCarthy v. Walsh, supra*, Lavery J. criticised the original limit of £1,000 put on such damages. This criticism could equally be applied to the current limit of £7,500.
20. (March, 1977) unreported (S.C.).
21. The Courts Act, 1981, Sect. 28(1) increases the limit of such award to £7,500 but does not affect the reasoning of Walsh, J.
22. (1965) 100 I.L.T.R. 40 (H.C.).

relative or a friend . . . The view I take of the section is that it is not intended to provide monetary compensation for every member of the family. If it were there would be no end to it. It would mean that there would be damages recovered by a group of people that ordinarily would be very large. I think the section must be considered in the light of some real intense feeling or being grievously affected by the death."[23]

In *McCarthy v. Walsh*[24] it was decided that the fact that a relative could not show a financial loss arising from the death entitling him to damages for "injury", was not a bar to his obtaining damages for mental distress.

III. Funeral & Other Expenses: Damages may also be recovered for funeral and other expenses incurred by the deceased, the dependants or personal representative by reason of the wrongful act. "Other expenses" could include medical expenses incurred before death and wages or salaries lost by a dependant as a result of the deceased's injury and subsequent death.[25]

Finally, section 50 of the Act provides that in assessing damages no account is to be taken of any sum payable on the death of the deceased under any insurance contract, or any pension, gratuity or other like benefit payable under statute or otherwise in consequence of the death of the deceased.[26] However, in assessing damages for funeral expenses account is to be taken of any death benefit granted under Part II Chapter 5 of the Social Welfare (Consolidation) Act, 1981, in respect of such expenses.[27] The rights conferred by Part IV of the 1961 Act are in addition to the rights conferred by Part II of the Act, under which certain causes of action vested in the deceased at the time of his death survive for the benefit of his estate.[28] There cannot, however, be a duplication of damages.

---

23. *Ibid.* at p. 40.
24. *Supra.*
25. See *Byrne v. Houlihan, supra.* The cost of an ordinary tombstone but not of an extravagant monument may also be recovered, *O'Brien v. Higgins* (March, 1967) unreported (S.C.).
26. See, for example, *Murphy v. Cronin supra* – sum payable to widow from deceased husband's superannuation fund a "gratuity" and not to be taken into account in assessing damages.
27. See Sect. 68 of 1981 Act. See also article entitled "The Occupational Injuries Act: Some Reflections" by J. Casey, (1969), 4 I.J. (n.s.) 234 (particularly pp. 242–246). See article by M. Knight, *supra*; see also "Ten years of the Civil Liability Act", by Earnán P. de Blaghd (1972) 106 I.L.T. & S.J. 206, 211, 219.
28. See Part II of the 1961 Act, Sects. 6–10. Under Sect. 8 certain causes of action subsisting against the deceased at the time of his death also survive against his estate. See further, McMahon & Binchy, *supra*, at Chap. 9.

MARRIAGE AND THE LAW AS TO FAMILY PLANNING

The decision of the Supreme Court in *McGee v. Attorney General*[1] recognised the existence of a constitutional right to marital privacy which conferred on married couples a right to obtain contraceptives for their own use. The Health (Family Planning) Act, 1979, which came into operation on the 1st November 1980 makes provision for family planning services and for the availability, importation, manufacture, sale, and advertisement of contraceptives.[2] It also amends the grounds upon which the Censorship Board may ban a publication.

The Health (Family Planning) (Amendment) Act, 1985, which came into operation on the 1st of October, 1985, amends the provisions of the Act of 1979 in relation to the sale of contraceptives.[3] In the discussion that follows, reference to "the Act" is a reference to the Act of 1979 as amended by the Act of 1985.

Family Planning Service: A family planning service is defined in the Act as a service for the provision of information, instruction, advice, or consultation in relation to one or more of the following: (a) family planning; (b) contraception; (c) contraceptives[4]. A family planning service as defined does not include within its functions the provision or supply of contraceptives.

The Act imposes a duty on the Minister for Health to secure the orderly organisation of family planning services, and to provide a comprehensive natural family planning service, that is, one that is concerned with methods of family planning that do not involve the use of contraceptives.[5]

A Health Board is bound by the regulations made under the Act to make available "a family planning service",[6] but it appears that if a Health Board makes available a natural family planning service alone, this will be sufficient for the purpose of the duty imposed on it by the Act. A Health Board itself does not have to provide the service. It may make such a service available by way of an arrangement with another person or body.[7] A family planning service established by a person other than a Health Board and which gives advice or instruction about contraceptives can only operate with the consent of the Minister for Health and any such service must operate under "the general direction, and supervision" of a doctor.[8] However, a natural family planning service can operate without the necessity of obtaining any such consent.[9] Moreover, there is a statutory obligation imposed on a Health Board or any other person providing a service that gives advice as to the use of contraceptives also to give advice about methods of family planning that do not involve the use of contraceptives. The Act does not, however, prevent a doctor "in his clinical relations with a patient" or a chemist selling contraceptives from giving advice as to their use.[10]

The Sale of Contraceptives: The Act defines a contraceptive as "any appli-

1. [1974] I.R. 284; (1973) 109 I.L.T.R. 29 (S.C.). See p. 29 *ante*.
2. See the Health (Family Planning) Act, 1979 (Commencement Order) 1980 (S.I. No. 247 of 1980).
3. See the Health (Family Planning (Amendment) Act, 1985 (Commencement Order) 1985 (S.I. No. 316 of 1985).
4. Health (Family Planning) Act, 1979, Sect. 1.
5. *Ibid.*, Section 2.
6. Health (Family Planning) Regulations, 1980 (S.I. No. 248 of 1980), para 3(1).
7. *Ibid.*, para 3(2).
8. Health (Family Planning) Act, 1979, Sect. 3(3) and 3(4); see also Health (Family Planning) Regulations, 1980, *supra*, para 4.
9. Health (Family Planning) Act, 1979, Sect. 3(2).
10. *Ibid.*, Sect. 3(6).

ance, instrument, drug, preparation or thing, designed, prepared, or intended to prevent pregnancy resulting from sexual intercourse between human beings".[11] Under section 4 of the Act contraceptives can only be supplied by way of sale, and the only persons authorised to sell contraceptives[12] to the general public are:

(a)   A chemist[13] who may sell contraceptives in a place where he "keeps open shop" for the compounding and dispensing of medical prescriptions in accordance with the provisions of the Pharmacy Acts, 1875–1977;

(b)   A doctor who may sell contraceptives "at a place where he ordinarily carries out his professional duties";

(c)   An employee of a Health Board acting as such who may sell contraceptives in a "health institution";

(d)   A person[14] making available a family planning service as defined by the Act, who may sell contraceptives "at the place where that service is being made available";

(e)   An employee acting as such of a hospital providing maternity services or services for the treatment of sexually transmitted diseases "who may sell contraceptives in such hospital".

Contraceptive sheaths or spermicides can be sold to any person over 18 years of age[15] without prescription. The sale of any type of contraceptive, including contraceptive sheaths or spermicides to persons under 18 years of age and of all other types of contraceptives, to persons either under or over 18 years of age, is restricted to a person named in a doctor's written prescription or authorisation, and prior to issuing any such prescription or authorisation a doctor must be satisfied that the person seeking it requires contraceptives "for the purpose bona fide, of family planning, or for adequate medical reasons and in appropriate circumstances."[16] Where a prescription indicates that contraceptives are to be given for such purposes, section 4 states "it shall be conclusively presumed" that the person named in it is a person who in the opinion of the doctor requires contraceptives for the purpose or reasons stated in the Act.[17] A prescription or authorisation can be issued for any period up to one year, but its validity cannot extend beyond one year.[18] Section 4 also permits a licensed importer or manufacturer to sell contraceptives to any of those persons who are authorised to sell them to the general public under the Act.[19]

Paragraph 6 of the regulations provides that a sale of contraceptives under section 4 "shall not be made unless the quantity sought to be purchased is not such as to indicate they are not solely for the purchaser's own use". This provision applies to the sale of all types of contraceptives, including the sale of contraceptive sheaths to persons under 18 years of age by prescription or persons over 18 years of age without prescription.[20] Neither the Act, nor the regulations

---

11. *Ibid.*, Sect. 1.
12. *Ibid.*, Sect. 4(1)(b)(i) as amended by the Health (Family Planning) (Amendment) Act, 1985, Sect. 2.
13. Or his servant or agent.
14. Or his servant or agent.
15. Health (Family Planning) Act, 1979, Sect. 4(1)(b)(i) as amended by Health (Family Planning) (Amendment) Act, 1985, Sect. 2.
16. See Health (Family Planning) Act, 1979, Sect. 4(1)(b)(i) and (ii) and Sect. 4(2).
17. *Ibid.*, Sect. 4(2).
18. Health (Family Planning) Regulations, 1980, para 5(1)(e).
19. Health (Family Planning) Act, 1979, Sect. 4(1)(c).
20. Prior to the coming into operation of the Act of 1985 the lawful sale of all such contraceptives had to be by prescription. This regulation has not been amended since the passage of that Act.

made under it, provide any criteria by which a person authorised to sell contraceptives can determine whether "the quantity sought" is for a purchaser's own use. Curiously, this regulation also appears to apply to all sales of contraceptives under section 4 of the Act and it seems that an importer or manufacturer selling contraceptives to any of those persons authorised to sell them to the general public is bound by it!

Importation and manufacture of contraceptives: Under section 5 of the Act, a person may import contraceptives if "they are part of his personal luggage accompanying him when he is entering the State and if their quantity is not such as to indicate they are not solely for his own use."[21] As in the case of paragraph 6 of the regulations, the Act lays down no test for determining whether contraceptives imported are solely for a person's own use. Moreover, a person who so imports contraceptives does not require a prescription irrespective of the type of contraceptives imported and regardless of age. Thus, a 17 year old could import contraceptive sheaths under this provision without the necessity of first obtaining a prescription.

Section 5 also provides for the granting of licences for the importation of contraceptives by persons authorised to sell them to the general public or by persons (wholesalers) who wish to sell contraceptives to those authorised to sell them to the general public. The Act does not permit a person to import contraceptives by post for his own use.

Section 6 of the Act provides for the granting of licences for the manufacture of contraceptives within the State.

Advertisements and publications: Advertisements concerning contraception or contraceptives may only be published or displayed in relation to family planning services authorised under the Act, and in the case of a family planning service provided by a person other than a Health Board, the publication or display must accord with any consent given by the Minister to operate a family planning service that provides information about the use of contraceptives.

An advertisement relating to contraception or contraceptives can also be published for the purpose of providing information for

(i) Persons providing family planning services in accordance with the Act;

(ii) Registered medical practitioners;

(iii) Registered pharmaceutical chemists and registered dispensing chemists and druggists;

(iv) Persons registered in the Register of Nurses;

(v) Persons who are in training with a view to becoming a member of any of the classes of persons specified in (ii) to (iv).

Publication of advertisements may also be arranged by or on behalf of the Minister for Health.[22]

Section 12(3) of the Act removes the powers conferred on the Censorship Board by the Censorship of Publications Act, 1946, to ban a book or a periodical publication on the ground that it advocates or advocated the unnatural prevention of conception. A book may now only be banned if the Board is of the opinion that

21. Health (Family Planning) Act, 1979, Sect. 5(1)(a).
22. See Health (Family Planning) Act, 1979, Sections 7, 12(1) and 12(2) and the Health (Family Planning) Regulations, 1980, para 8.

(a) it is indecent or obscene, or

(b) it advocates the procurement of abortion or miscarriage or the use of any kind of method, treatment or appliance for the purpose of such procurement.

Periodical publications may be banned on similar grounds.[23]

Abortion: Section 10 provides that nothing in the Act shall be construed as authorising the procuring of abortion or the doing of any other thing which is prohibited under Sections 58 or 59 of the Offences Against the Persons Act, 1861 (which sections prohibit the administering of drugs or the use of instruments to procure abortion or the supplying of drugs or instruments to procure abortion) or sale, importation to the State, manufacture, advertising or display of abortifacients.

Consciencious objectors: Section 11 provides that nothing in the Act shall be construed as obliging any person to take part in the provision of a family planning service, the giving of prescriptions or authorisations for the purpose of the Act or the sale, importation into the State, manufacture, advertising or display of contraceptives.

Offences: Contravention of the provisions contained in the Act or the regulations made under it constitutes a criminal offence, punishable in the first instance, by a fine not exceeding £500 and/or imprisonment for a term not exceeding six months. A second or subsequent offence renders a person liable to a fine not exceeding £5,000 together with, in the case of a continuing offence, a fine not exceeding £250 each day or part of a day for which the offence is continued and/or to a term of imprisonment not exceeding 12 months.[24]

Commentary: Prior to the coming into force of the Act of 1985 it was suggested by some commentators that the Act of 1979 confined the availability of contraceptives to married couples. This was never the case as any person, single or married, could and still can import any quantity of contraceptives he wished for his own use in his personal luggage when entering the State. Moreover, under the Act of 1979 a doctor was at liberty to give a prescription for contraceptives to a single person, if satisfied that the contraceptives were required for the purpose, bona fide, of family planning or for adequate medical reasons and in

23. See further *Irish Family Planning Association Ltd. and Anor. v. Ryan and Ors.* [1979] I.R. 295 (S.C.) in which an order made by the Censorship Board banning a book entitled *Family Planning* which contained information about different methods of contraception, on the ground that it was "indecent or obscene" was declared null and void. Section 6 of the Censorship of Publications Act, 1946, conferred power on the Board when examining a book to communicate with its author, editor or publisher and to take into account any representations made in relation to the book. The Board did not communicate with the plaintiffs prior to making its order and from evidence given by the secretary in the High Court it was clear that prior to the date of these proceedings it had never so communicated prior to banning a book or periodical publication. The Supreme Court held that the Board had acted "unjustly" and that prior to banning the book it should have communicated with the plaintiffs who were responsible for its publication. Its failure to do so was a violation of the right to natural justice and, in particular, the obligation imposed on the Board to observe the rule of *Audi Alteram Partem*. The Court also expressed considerable doubt as to whether the book could have been lawfully banned as being "indecent and obscene" had the Board correctly observed the duty imposed on it. O'Higgins C.J. in his judgement (at p. 315) stated that "Far from being pornographic or lewdly commercial or pandering to prurient curiosity, it simply aimed at giving basic factual information on a delicate topic as to which there is genuine concern."
24. Health (Family Planning) Act, 1979, Sect. 14.

appropriate circumstances. The chemist to whom such prescription was tendered could not challenge the doctor's conclusions, although he could require proof of identity from the person tendering the prescription. The Act of 1985, passed through the Oireachtas amidst considerable controversy, has merely abolished the necessity for persons over 18 years of age to obtain a prescription or authorisation for a lawful sale of contraceptive sheaths or spermicides to be made to them. A lawful sale within the State of such contraceptives to persons under 18 years of age can still only be made by way of prescription or authorisation, whether or not the person under such age who wishes to acquire contraceptives is married or single.[25] Such person may still, however, import any type of contraceptive in his personal luggage that he wishes for his own use without prescription under the provisions of section 5 of the Act.

In conclusion, it should be noted that the Act of 1979 again renders it unlawful not only for a single person but also for a spouse to import contraceptives by post for his or her own use. In *McGee v. The Attorney General*[26] it was the constitutional right of Mrs. McGee to import contraceptives by post for her own use that was asserted by the Supreme Court and, as a consequence, some doubt must exist as to the constitutional validity of the provisions of the Act, in so far as they prevent married couples importing contraceptives by post for their own use. However, the decision in the *McGee* case was delivered at a time when it was also unlawful to sell contraceptives in the State and the prohibition on sale taken together with the prohibition on importation was held to frustrate the right of the McGees to have access to contraceptives and to be in violation of their right to marital privacy. As contraceptives may now be lawfully sold to married couples within the State and can be acquired by post from persons authorised to sell them within the State, the ban on their direct importation from other countries by post by a married couple, if ever challenged, may not be held to be in violation of the right to marital privacy.

25. The Act does not impose any duty on a doctor to consult with or obtain the consent of the parents of a person under 18 years of age prior to prescribing contraceptives for such a person. The question as to whether a doctor can lawfully prescribe contraceptives for a girl under 16 years of age without the consent of her parents gave rise to considerable controversy recently in England. See *Gillick v. West Norfolk & Wisbech Area Health Authorities* [1985] 3 All E.R. 402 (H.L.); [1985] 1 All E.R. 533 (C.A.) and [1984] 1 All E.R. 365 (Q.B.D.). The Family Articles contained in the Constitution and parental rights as therein articulated and interpreted by the Supreme Court could, it is submitted, result in the Irish Courts holding that there is such a duty under Irish law in the context of the prescribing of contraceptives to unmarried persons under the age of 18 years. In the *Gillick* case, the House of Lords concluded by a majority that a doctor had a discretion to give contraceptive advice or treatment to a girl under 16 without her parents' knowledge or consent, provided the girl had reached an age where she had a sufficient understanding and intelligence to enable her to understand fully what was proposed.

26. *Supra.*

MARRIAGE AND THE LAWS OF EVIDENCE[1]

At common law a party's spouse was generally incompetent as a witness for, or against him, in both civil and criminal proceedings. The only important exception to this rule arose in the case of a criminal charge involving personal violence by one spouse against the other. The incompetence of a spouse resulted from fear as to the trustworthiness of the evidence of a spouse and also out of recognition that undesirable consequences might follow if one spouse was compelled to give evidence against the other and perhaps forced to break matrimonial confidences.

The rule as to the incompetency of spouses in civil cases was abolished by the Evidence Amendment Act, 1853, which rendered spouses competent and compellable witnesses for any party to an action. A spouse, however, remained an incompetent witness to give evidence for or against her husband/his wife in any proceedings instituted in consequence of adultery. The Evidence Further Amendment Act, 1869, renders a spouse competent to give evidence in such proceedings but is silent as to compellability. Moreover, it restricts the nature of the evidence that a married witness can be required to give in family proceedings. Section 3 of the Act of 1869 states:

> "The parties to any proceedings instituted in consequence of adultery, and the husbands and wives of such parties, shall be competent to give evidence in such proceedings: provided that no witness in any proceeding, whether a party to a suit or not, shall be liable to be asked or be bound to answer any question tending to show that he or she has been guilty of adultery, unless such witness shall have given evidence in the same proceeding in disproof of his or her alleged adultery."

There has been no written judgement delivered by the Irish Courts in which the implications of the above section have been fully considered. In the event of the issue arising it is possible that it may be held at some future date, in accordance with the principles enunciated in the decision of the High Court in *S. v. S.*,[2] that this provision did not continue in force as part of Irish law after the enactment of the present Constitution as its application in court proceedings would be contrary to "fair procedures and the due administration of justice in the courts".[2a] Such a judicial determination may not, however, prove necessary as the Status of Children Bill, 1986, as initiated, if enacted, will repeal the proviso contained in the section.

The rule as to the incompetency of spouses in criminal cases was changed by the Criminal Justice (Evidence) Act, 1924. By section 1(e) the spouse of a person charged may be called as a witness upon the application of the person charged. Whereas such a spouse is now competent to give evidence he/she is not generally compellable.

A spouse is generally an incompetent witness for the prosecution. Thus, if a husband is charged with murder or bigamy his wife cannot be a prosecution witness. There are, however, a number of exceptions to this rule. The principle exception arises under section 4(1) of the Criminal Justice (Evidence) Act, 1924, by which a spouse of a person charged with an offence under any of the enactments listed in the schedule of that Act may be called as a witness, either for the

---

1. See generally, the Law Reform Commission: *Report on Competence and Compellability of Spouses as Witnesses* (Report No. 13, July 1985).
2. [1983] I.R. 68 (H.C.) − see p. 44 *ante*.
2a. *Ibid.*, at p. 79.

prosecution or defence, without the consent of the person charged.[3] It appears, however, that a spouse while competent is not compellable in such proceedings.[4] Moreover, a number of statutes enacted both prior and subsequent to the Act of 1924 make a spouse a competent prosecution witness against a spouse accused of specific offences committed under such statutes.[5] Thus, the Married Women's Status Act, 1957, expressly states that a spouse is a competent witness for the prosecution in any criminal proceedings brought against the other spouse for the protection and security of the former's property.[6]

Neither the Act of 1924 nor any other statutory provision has affected the circumstances under the common law in which the spouse of a person charged with an offence can be called as a witness for the prosecution without the consent of the spouse charged.[7] In practice, the principle example of this arises in charges involving personal violence by one spouse against the other. Until relatively recently, the balance of authority favoured the view that under common law a person who suffered violence at the hands of their spouse was not only a competent but also a compellable witness for the prosecution. However, in *Hoskyn v. The Metropolitan Police Commissioner*[8] the House of Lords in England held that a wife is not a compellable witness against her husband in such proceedings. Whether this decision will be followed by the Irish courts is uncertain.[9]

By virtue of section 1(d) of the 1924 Act and section 3 of the Act of 1853, neither a husband nor a wife are compellable to disclose in either criminal or civil proceedings any communication made by one to the other during the marriage. This privilege as to revealing the content of a communication between spouses is the property of the spouse being questioned in the witness box. Thus,

---

3. Since the coming into force of the 1924 Act the enactments referred to in the Schedule have been added to and some have been repealed and replaced. The offences now included in the Schedule under which a wife can give evidence for the prosecution include offences under the Prevention of Cruelty to Children Act, 1904; offences under Sects. 48, 52, 53, 54, so far as unrepealed, and 55 of the Offences Against the Person Act, 1861, (see Criminal Law Amendment Act, 1935, Sects. 6 & 20); see also Sect. 9 of Married Women's Status Act, 1957, repealing and replacing Sects. 12 & 16 of Married Women's Property Act, 1882.

Also see *McGonagle v. McGonagle* [1951] I.R. 123 (S.C.); [1952] Ir. Jur. Rep. 13 (S.C.). The appellant was convicted for that having the custody of a child aged six years he did "wilfully neglect said child in a manner likely to cause said child unnecessary suffering and injury to its health" contrary to Sect. 12 of the 1908 Children Act. By Sect. 133(28) it is provided that in any proceedings against any person for an offence under Part II of the Act (including Sect. 12) or for any offences mentioned in the First Schedule of the Act, a spouse of the accused shall be competent but not compellable to give evidence. It was contended that as the 1908 Act was not listed in the Schedule to the 1924 Act that Sect. 133(28) was repealed and the spouse of the accused was not a competent witness. The Supreme Court noted that *per incuriam* the legislature overlooked the fact that a great deal of the Act of 1904 had been repealed and re-enacted in the Act of 1908; that one of the sections repealed in the 1904 Act was Sect. 1 whereby a spouse of an accused may be called as a prosecution witness without the consent of the party charged; that provisions substantially the same as those in Sect. 1 were re-enacted in Sect. 12 of the 1908 Act, and that as a consequence there was a clear intention expressed by the legislature that a spouse of the accused should be a competent witness and this provision of the 1908 Act was unaffected by the Act of 1924. See also p. 404 *et seq*.

For a further discussion as to the statutory provisions included in the schedule, see the Law Reform Commission: Report No. 13, *supra*, pp. 7–10.

4. *R. v. Leach* [1912] A.C. 305 (H.L.).

5. See Law Reform Commission: Report No. 13, pp. 10–27.

6. See Married Women's Status Act, 1957, Sect. 9.

7. The Criminal Justice (Evidence) Act, 1924, Sect. 4(2) states that "nothing in this Act shall affect a case where the wife or husband of a person charged with an offence may at common law be called as a witness without the consent of that person."

8. [1979] A.C. 474 (H.L.).

9. See Law Reform Commission: Report No. 13, *supra*, at p. 29. See also (1978) 94 L.Q.R. 321.

if the spouse being questioned wishes to reveal what the other spouse has previously communicated, there is nothing the other spouse can do to prevent disclosure. The communication itself is not privileged and if a spouse refuses to reveal its contents, there is nothing to prevent a third party giving evidence as to what information it contained.[10] This of course is subject to the rules as to inadmissibility of hearsay evidence.

In two recent cases the courts have developed the rules of evidence with particular reference to the family law area. In criminal cases it has for long been determined by the Supreme Court that evidence obtained as a result of a deliberate and conscious violation of the constitutional rights of an accused, such as the inviolability of a private house, may not be admissible.[11] In *O.C. v. T.C.*[12] a deed of separation had been concluded and the husband and wife were living apart. Approximately 13 years after the conclusion of the deed, while the husband was abroad, the wife forced her way into his house, accompanied by two body guards, and removed amongst other things, letters and photographs from her husband's bedroom. She sought to tender these as evidence in maintenance proceedings subsequently instituted by her but McMahon J. ruled they were inadmissible having been obtained "in flagrant violation of the husband's constitutional right to the inviolability of his home."[13] In *E.R. v. J.R.*[14] Carroll J. extended the principle that a communication made to a priest acting in his pastoral capacity is privileged, to apply to communications made by spouses consulting with a priest as marriage counsellor. Moreover, it was stated "that the privilege is that of the people consulting" and that if both spouses have participated "the privilege must be waived clearly and unequivocally by both" before evidence can be given in matrimonial proceedings revealing the content of the communication. The court expressly reserved the question as to whether the privilege can arise where the counsellor is not a minister of religion.[15]

Proposals for Reform

(i)   The law as to the competence of a spouse of an accused to give evidence for the prosecution in criminal proceedings has developed in a haphazard and piecemeal way and is badly in need of reform. An extract from the comprehensive report on this area published in July 1985 by the Law Reform Commission[16] highlights the anomalous nature of the current statutory position. It states:

> "The present list of exceptions to the general rule that spouses are incompetent to testify is difficult to justify on any rational basis. Why should the wife of an accused be a competent witness on any charge involving bodily injury to a child and not on a charge of incest against the same child? Why should the wife of a person accused of a breach of a 'barring order' under the Family Law (Protection of Spouses and Children) Act, 1981, where no

---

10. See *Rumping v. D.P.P.* [1964] A.C. 814, 822 (H.L.) where Sect. 1(d) of the English Criminal (Evidence) Act, 1898, was discussed. This section corresponds to Section 1(d) of the Irish Act of 1924.

11. See *The State (Attorney General) v. O'Brien* [1964] I.R. 142 (S.C.). See further J.M. Kelly, *The Irish Constitution* (2nd ed.), pp. 283 *et seq.*

12. (December, 1981) unreported (H.C.).

13. See p. 6 of judgement. If the parties had not concluded a deed of separation and the wife had not lost her right to reside with the husband in his home, the evidence could have been successfully tendered by her as she would still have been entitled to enter the home.

14. [1981] 1 I.L.R.M. 125 (H.C.).

15. *Ibid*, at p. 127.

16. Report No. 13, *supra*. See also P.A. O'Connor, "Competence and Compellability of Spouses as Witnesses for the Prosecution" (1985) 3 I.L.T. (n.s.) 208.

violence to that spouse is involved not be a competent witness when she would be competent on a charge of an offence against her property under the Married Women's Status Act, 1957?"[17]

The Commission recommends that any rule of law making the spouse of an accused person incompetent, as such, to testify in criminal proceedings brought against his or her spouse should be abolished. It is submitted that this recommendation of the Commission should be implemented.

(ii)   The privilege conferred on a priest acting as marriage counsellor should be extended by statute to apply to other qualified persons so acting. If it is accepted that spouses with marital difficulties should be encouraged to take steps to resolve their problems, without fear that facts disclosed by them in a genuine attempt to bring about a reconciliation with an estranged spouse could ultimately be used in evidence against them, such a reform is necessary. If a spouse seeking help feels inhibited in fully disclosing to a counsellor all matters relevant to the breakdown of a marriage, the possibility of the counsellor being of real assistance is considerably reduced. This reform should be provided by statute and not have to await judicial development of the law.[18]

---

17. *Ibid.* at p. 35. See also p. 38 of report. The Family Law (Protection of Spouses & Children) Act, 1981, is discussed in detail in Chapter 17.
18. For a summary of the full recommendations of the Law Reform Commission see pp. 76–78 of Report No. 13.

MARRIAGE AND THE CRIMINAL LAW

1. Bigamy[1]

Bigamy is the only crime that cannot be committed by an unmarried person.[2] Originally it was only an ecclesiastical offence but it was declared to be a capital felony by statute in 1603.[3] The present law is contained in section 57 of the Offences Against the Person Act, 1861. Bigamy is committed when a person who is a party to a valid subsisting marriage goes through a ceremony of marriage with another. It is a defence to a charge of bigamy that the first marriage was void or voidable and has been validly annulled by the civil courts,[4] or that it has been validly dissolved.[5]

It is no defence to a charge of bigamy to show that the first marriage was not recognised by or has been annulled by the Roman Catholic Church.[6]

Thus, in the *People (A.-G.) v. Ballins*[7] where a Roman Catholic woman having been told that her marriage in a Registry Office was regarded as having no effect according to church law, went through a ceremony of marriage with another man in a Roman Catholic church she was convicted of bigamy. Moreover, in *F.M.L. & A.L. v. The Registrar General for Marriages*,[8] referring to the second marriage of the husband in a Roman Catholic church subsequent to the granting of a Papal decree of dissolution of his first marriage but prior to the determination of civil nullity proceedings, Lynch J. stated that:

> "A marriage which is voidable for impotence is not known to be voidable nor consequently void *ab initio* unless and until the High Court shall have pronounced it to be so. In the meantime, the spouse remains apparently validly married and open to prosecution for bigamy . . . if a trial for bigamy should pre-date the decree of nullity, the accused spouse would be liable to conviction and penalty."[9]

The learned judge said that he would express no view as to what would be the legal position if a decree of nullity were subsequently granted, stating that he merely wished to "emphasize the difficulties and dangers of the course and order of events adopted" by the husband.

A defence to the charge is afforded by an accused proving that the first spouse has been continuously absent for seven years and has not been known by the accused to be living within that time. Such absence for seven years merely provides a defence to a charge of bigamy and does not dissolve the first marriage. Thus, if the first spouse is alive, even though an accused may be held to be innocent of bigamy, his "second marriage" is still a complete nullity. It is also

---

1. For a more detailed discussion of the criminal law as to bigamy see Smith & Hogan, *Criminal Law*, 5th ed. (London, Butterworths 1983), Ch. 18. See also P.A. O'Siochain, *The Criminal Law of Ireland* (Dublin 1981), pp. 135–140.

2. An unmarried person can of course be convicted as an accessory or for aiding and abetting.

3. 1 Jac. 1, c. 11.

4. See Chapter 5.

5. See Chapter 10.

6. *People (A.-G.) v. Hunt* [1945] 80 I.L.T.R. & S.J. 19, *per* Haugh J. (C.C.C.); *People (A.-G.) v. Ballins* [1964] Ir. Jur. Rep. 14 (Cir. Ct.).

7. *People (A.-G.) v. Ballins, supra.*

8. [1984] 4 I.L.R.M. 667 (H.C.).

9. *Ibid.* at p. 670. See also *A.M.N. v. J.P.C.* (December, 1985) unreported (H.C.) in which the petitioner's first marriage was annulled on the ground of impotence whilst bigamy proceedings relating to her second marriage were pending before the courts.

a defence that the accused believed on reasonable grounds that his or her spouse was dead, although he or she has not been absent for seven years;[10] or that his first marriage was void[11] or that his first marriage was dissolved.[12]

2. Coercion

There was a rebuttable presumption of law that a misdemeanour or a felony other than treason or murder committed by a wife in the presence of her husband was committed under his coercion or duress. The presumption could be rebutted by proof that the wife was the instigator of the act or was the more active party in the committal of an alleged offence. In *The State (D.P.P.) v. Walsh*[13] the Supreme Court held the presumption to be no longer applicable, Henchy J. stating that:

> "Nowadays, to exculpate a wife for an *actus reus* because it was done when her husband was present is no more justifiable than if she were granted immunity from guilt because the act was done in the presence of her father, her brother or any other relative or friend."[14]

3. Conspiracy

Arising out of the notion of the unity of husband and wife, it has been held that spouses cannot be convicted of conspiring together to commit an offence. Both can, however, be charged with conspiring with other people.[15] In the light of the view taken in *The State (D.P.P.)v. Walsh*, referred to above, there must be a real possibility that the Supreme Court may take a different approach to this issue at a future date.

4. Rape

A man commits rape if he has unlawful sexual intercourse with a woman, knowing at the time of such intercourse that she does not consent to it or if he is reckless as to whether she does or does not consent.[16] A husband cannot be convicted of raping his wife during the subsistence of their marriage, even if he forces her to have sexual relations with him against her will, as by marriage a woman implicitly consents to having sexual intercourse with her husband. If, however, a decree of divorce *a mensa et thoro* has been granted or a separation agreement concluded, her implied consent is withdrawn and he may be liable to a charge of rape.[17] Moreover, if a husband undertakes to a court not to "assault,

10. *R. v. Tolson* (1889), 23 Q.B.D. 68 (C.C.R.).
11. *R. v. King* [1964] 1 Q.B. 285 (C.C.A.).
12. *R. v. Gould* [1968] 2 Q.B. 65; [1968] 1 All E.R. 849 (C.A.). This case overruled *R. v. Wheat and Stocks* [1921] 2 K.B. 119 (C.C.A.), in England which regarded bigamy as an offence of strict liability. Despite a *dicta* of Kenny J. in *Counihan v. Counihan* (July, 1973), (H.C.), unreported, citing *Wheat & Stocks* as being the law, it is submitted that *Gould* will be followed in Ireland.
13. [1981] I.R. 412 (S.C.).
14. *Ibid.* at p. 449. See also p. 38 *ante*.
15. *Mawji v. R.* [1957] A.C. 126; [1957] 1 All E.R. 385 (P.C.). See Smith & Hogan, *Criminal Law*, 3rd edition, p. 180 (Butterworths, London 1973). See also *Midland Bank Trust Co. Ltd. v. Green* [1979] 2 W.L.R. 594 (Ch. D); F. Graham Glover, "Conspiracy as between husband and wife" (1979) 9 Fam. Law 181.
16. See the Criminal Law (Rape) Act, 1981, Sect. 2.
17. *R. v. Clarence* (1888) 22 Q.B.D. (C.C.R.); *R. v. Clarke* [1949] 2 All E.R. 448, (Assize); *R. v. Miller* [1954] 2 Q.B. 282 (K.B.D.); [1954] 2 All E.R. 529. A husband may be prosecuted for aiding and abetting the rape of his wife – see *D.P.P. v. Morgan* [1975] 2 All E.R. 347 (H.L.). See also *R. v. O'Brien* [1974] 3 All E.R. 684 – grant of decree nisi of divorce revokes wife's implied consent. For criticism of the present law see P. English, "The Husband Who Rapes His Wife" (1976) 126 N.L.J. 1223, M.D.A. Freeman; "Rape by A Husband?" (1979) 129 N.L.J. 332; P. Matthews, "Marital Rape" (1980) 10 Fam. Law 221; A. Wallace, "Marital Rape – The Silent Crime" (1986) 4 I.L.T. (n.s.) 140.

molest or interfere" with his wife he may lose his immunity to a charge of
raping her.[18] It is to be assumed that the courts will hold that a husband can be
convicted of raping his wife if he has been barred by court order from entering
the family home or any other place in which his wife is residing under section 22
of the Family Law (Maintenance of Spouses & Children) Act, 1976 or its successor, the Family Law (Protection of Spouses & Children) Act, 1981. Even though
a husband has a right to marital intercourse, he is not entitled to use force or
violence for the purpose of exercising that right. If he does so, he may render
himself liable to other criminal charges such as assault.[19] Further, the use of
undue force may enable a wife to petition for a decree of divorce *a mensa et
thoro* on the grounds of cruelty or to obtain a barring order under the Family
Law (Protection of Spouses & Children) Act, 1981.[20]

5. Larceny

At common law neither spouse could steal from the other. This rule was
modified by the Married Women's Property Act, 1882, Sect. 12 and by the
Larceny Act, 1916, Sect. 36. The present law is to be found in the Married
Women's Status Act, 1957, Sect. 9. It provides that criminal proceedings may be
brought against either spouse for the protection and security of a spouse's
property, but forbids such proceedings being brought while they are living
together, or while they are living apart concerning any act done by a spouse
while living with the other, unless property was wrongfully taken by one of the
parties when leaving or deserting or about to leave or desert the other. If criminal
proceedings, to which this section relates, are brought against a spouse, the
other spouse may be called as a witness for the prosecution or the defence without the consent of the spouse charged.[21]

6. Assaults

Until 1976 the only District Court remedy available to a battered wife wishing to obtain protection from the assaults of her husband was a summons for
assault and breach of the peace. Since jurisdiction was conferred on the District
Court in that year to make barring orders, fewer wives have resorted to the
criminal law to seek protection from violent husbands than was the case in the
past. Nevertheless, on occasion the criminal law is used in this context.

Upon being assaulted a wife herself may issue a summons against her husband
or it may be issued by a Garda. Ironically, a wife who issued a summons for
assault against her husband could not before February 1981 obtain State free
legal aid, being the prosecutor, whilst her husband, being the accused, was able
to do so, provided he was eligible in accordance with the provisions of the
Criminal Justice (Legal Aid) Act, 1962. A husband may still obtain legal aid
under the 1962 Act whilst a wife may now obtain legal aid under the civil Legal
Aid Scheme.[22] If a Garda issues the summons he is then the prosecutor and

18. See *R. v. Steele* [1977] Crim. L.R. 290 (C.A.).
19. *R. v. Jackson* [1891] 1 Q.B. 671 (C.A.); *R. v. Miller, supra*.
20. See Chap. 17.
21. Sect. 9(5).
22. See original Scheme of Civil Legal Aid and Advice (Stationery Office, Dublin 1979)
laid before each House of the Oireachtas by the Minister for Justice in December, 1979. A wife
bringing criminal proceedings against her husband was not originally entitled to legal aid or
advice under the scheme but following an amendment made to Section 3.1 of the Scheme
on 1st February 1981 she may be granted legal aid for such proceedings. See now the
revised scheme laid before each House of the Oireachtas in May 1986. See further p. 56 *et
seq., ante.*

the wife merely a witness in the proceedings, and she does not require legal representation.

When such cases arise in the District Court most district justices adjourn the proceedings to obtain a report from a probation officer or court welfare officer before deciding on what course of action to take. However, if the assault charged is a particularly vicious one, or if a husband has been convicted of assaulting his wife previously, he may be imprisoned without further inquiries being made by the court. A remedy frequently employed by justices in such cases is to discharge the husband without proceeding to conviction upon his entering into a recognisance to be of good behaviour and to comply with such conditions as the court stipulates for a period of time not exceeding three years.[23] The court may also place the husband under the supervision of a probation officer.[24] If a husband fails to observe any of the conditions of his recognisance and for example again assaults his wife, she may so inform the court, which is empowered to issue a warrant for his arrest. By such behaviour the husband renders himself liable to conviction and sentence.[25] An alternative means used by the courts to protect a wife from further violence is an order binding a husband to keep the peace and be of good behaviour for a specified period of time.[26]

23. Probation of Offenders Act, 1907, Sect. 1.
24. *Ibid.*, Sect. 2.
25. *Ibid.*, Sect. 6(1).
26. On the power of the District Courts to make such orders, see J.F. Crotty, *Practice and Procedure in the District Court* (Cork University Press, Cork 1960), p. 171 *et seq.*

CHAPTER 6

MARRIAGE AND THE LAW OF TORT

At common law a husband had to be joined as a party to an action either brought by a wife in respect of a tort committed against her or brought by a third party in respect of a tort committed by the wife before, or during the marriage. If the wife was a plaintiff the husband could recover the damages; whilst if she was the defendant he was liable for them.

The necessity of joining the husband as a co-plaintiff was abolished by the Married Women's Property Act, 1882, which permitted a wife to retain damages and the Acts of 1874 and 1882 while not affecting his liability for torts committed during coverture, limited his liability for ante-nuptial torts to the amount of the property that he became entitled to on marriage. Now under section 2(1)(c) of the Married Women's Status Act, 1957, a married woman is liable in tort, and a husband by reason of only being her husband, cannot be sued or made a party to any legal proceedings brought, nor be made liable for any tort committed by her, by reason of the fact that she is his wife.[1]

Until 1865 no action in tort could be brought by one spouse against the other. The Married Women's Property (Ireland) Act of that year enabled a wife, deserted by her husband or separated from him by a decree of divorce *a mensa et thoro*, to sue him in tort. Her rights were further extended by the Act of 1870 by which she could bring an action to recover her separate property against anyone including her husband.[2] This remained the position until the Act of 1957, which permits a spouse to bring any action in tort against the other spouse.[3] Thus, if a husband uses force or violence against his wife she may, if she wishes, bring a civil action for assault to recover compensation for the damages inflicted. At present, many civil actions are brought by wives against husbands and *vice versa*, for damages for injuries due to the negligent driving of a motor vehicle. The named defendant is the spouse; the real defendant is that spouse's insurance company.

---

1. Sect. 2(1)(c).
2. See Sect. 11. He may of course under the general law of tort be vicariously liable on other grounds.
3. Sect. 2(2).

MARRIAGE AND THE LAW OF NATIONALITY AND CITIZENSHIP[1]

Section 6 of the Irish Nationality and Citizenship Act, 1956, provides that every person born in Ireland is an Irish citizen from birth. Moreover, a person is an Irish citizen if either his father or mother is an Irish citizen at the time of his birth. However, section 7 of the Act provides that if a person is born outside Ireland and if the father or mother from whom citizenship derives was also born outside Ireland, that person does not acquire Irish citizenship unless (a) his birth is registered in a foreign births entry book kept in an Irish diplomatic mission or consular office; or (b) the father or mother from whom citizenship derives is at the time of the birth resident abroad in the public service.

A foundling, unless the contrary is proved, is deemed to be an Irish citizen and a child, whose father died before his birth, will acquire Irish citizenship from his father, if he would have acquired such citizenship from the father if the latter had been alive at the time of the child's birth.[2] An adopted child, if it is not an Irish citizen, automatically acquires Irish citizenship when adopted, if the adopter or where the adoption is by a married couple, either spouse, is an Irish citizen.[3] In addition, a person born in Northern Ireland, who is not otherwise an Irish citizen, may acquire Irish citizenship by declaring himself to be an Irish citizen upon attaining full age or upon his being so declared by his parent or guardian.[4]

Under the nationality laws of some countries, a woman upon marrying automatically acquires her husband's nationality. By section 8 of the Act of 1956, as originally enacted, a woman who was an alien at the date of her marriage to an Irish citizen did not become an Irish citizen by virtue of her marriage unless she lodged a prescribed declaration with the Minister for Justice, or with any Irish diplomatic mission or consular office, either before or at any time after the marriage, accepting Irish citizenship as her post-nuptial citizenship. If such a declaration was lodged prior to marriage, she became an Irish citizen from the date of her marriage. If it was lodged after the marriage, it took effect from the day of lodgement. If a man who was not an Irish national married an Irish citizen, he could not avail of a similar procedure to acquire Irish nationality, but he could ultimately apply for a certificate of naturalisation.[5] He was not,

---

1. Article 9 of the Constitution provides:-
   - 1.1. On the coming into operation of this Constitution any person who is a citizen of the Saorstat Eireann immediately before the coming into operation of this Constitution shall become and be a citizen of Ireland.
   - 1.2. The future acquisition and loss of Irish nationality and citizenship shall be determined in accordance with law.
   - 1.3. No person may be excluded from Irish Nationality and citizenship by reason of the sex of such person.
   - 2. Fidelity to the nation and loyalty to the state are fundamental political duties of all citizens.

For a detailed discussion of these provisions see J.M. Kelly, *The Irish Constitution*, 2nd ed. at p. 39 *et seq*.

2. See Sects. 9 and 10 of the Act of 1956.
3. See Sect. 11 of the Act of 1956.
4. See Sects. 2 and 7(1) of the Act of 1956.
5. See Part III of the Act. This Part is now amended by the Irish Nationality and Citizenship Act, 1986. In *Somjee v. The Minister for Justice* [1981] 1 I.L.R.M. 324 an unsuccessful challenge was made to the constitutional validity of Sect. 8 of the Act of 1956, Keane J. holding that the section did not violate Article 9.1.3 or Article 40.1 of the Constitution. In the learned judge's view the distinction made "conferred a form of privilege on female aliens" but did not invidiously discriminate or sexually discriminate against male aliens. The legislation merely provided "a diversity of arrangements" for the obtaining of citizenship. (see further p. 37 *ante*). This decision was not appealed to the Supreme Court. See also *Pok Sun Shum & Ors. v. Ireland & Ors.* (June, 1985) unreported (H.C.) and *Sunday Osheku & Ors. v. Ireland & Ors.* (June, 1986) unreported (H.C.). Section 8 has now been replaced by a new provision contained in Sect. 3 of the Act of 1986.

however, entitled to obtain Irish citizenship simply by virtue of the fact that his wife was an Irish citizen.

The Irish Nationality Citizenship Act, 1986, enacted on the 1st July, 1986, places both men and women in a position of equality in relation to the acquisition of citizenship upon marriage. Section 3 of the Act replaces the provisions contained in section 8 of the Act of 1956 with a provision whereby any person who is an alien at the date of his or her marriage to a person who is an Irish citizen "shall not become an Irish citizen merely by virtue of the marriage" but may do so by lodging, not earlier than three years from the date of the marriage, a declaration with the Minister for Justice or with any Irish diplomatic mission or consular office, accepting Irish citizenship as post-nuptual citizenship, provided that

"(a) the marriage is subsisting at the date of lodgement of the declaration, and

(b) the couple are living together as husband and wife and the spouse who is an Irish citizen submits an affidavit to that effect when the declaration is being lodged."[6]

Thus, Irish citizenship can now be acquired by either a man or a woman following upon their marrying an Irish citizen but such citizenship can only be acquired by virtue of marriage, three years after the date of marriage and the marriage must still be "subsisting" at the date when the necessary declaration is lodged and the couple must be living together as husband and wife. The new provisions contained in the Act of 1986 do not affect the position of a woman who before its enactment married an Irish citizen and who by virtue of doing so can acquire Irish citizenship.[7] The Act also contains a transitional provision whereby for a period of six months from the date of its enactment any person who but for its enactment would have become an Irish citizen may still do so.[8]

---

6. If a person is married to another who subsequent to marriage becomes an Irish citizen, the former may under this section acquire Irish citizenship three years after it has been acquired by his or her spouse, if the couple are residing together as husband and wife.
7. However, see also Sect. 5 which confers a general discretion on the Minister to grant an application for naturalisation within the 3 year period.
8. See Sect. 8.

MARRIAGE AND THE LAW AS TO PASSPORTS

The Ministers and Secretaries Act, 1924, section 1(xi) provides that the Department of External Affairs (now called the Department of Foreign Affairs) shall "comprise the administration and business generally of public services in connection with . . . the granting of passports and of visés to passports and all powers, duties and functions connected with same." Apart from the provisions of the now defunct Spanish Civil War (Non-intervention) Act, 1937, this provision is the only statutory reference made to the issuing of passports in any legislation enacted since the foundation of the State.

No legislative provisions define or identify those persons who are entitled to Irish passports or lay down any conditions or criteria that must be complied with by an applicant for a passport. Moreover, no statute states the circumstances in which a parent or non parent is entitled to have a minor included in his or her passport or when a minor is entitled to obtain his own separate passport.

It is clear from the questions asked on passport application forms that the Department of Foreign Affairs has developed its own rules in connection with the issue of passports but the content of these are unknown and have no statutory force. Having regard to the practices followed by that Department, it appears that an individual Irish citizen, single or married, who is no longer a minor may be granted a passport provided the applicant's identity and signature is certified on the passport application form by a member of the Garda Siochána. In practice Irish citizens over 18 years experience little real difficulty in obtaining passports for themselves. An area of difficulty and confusion relates to passports for minors.

As a general rule, if a parent wishes his legitimate child to be included on his passport, the written consent of the other parent is sought. If an application is made for a legitimate child to have his own separate passport, the written consent of both parents is sought. There is no statutory provision which stipulates that the Department of Foreign Affairs must ensure that both parents agree to their legitimate child being granted passport facilities prior to their provision by the Department but the Department appears in this area to have regard to the fact that in law parents are joint guardians of their legitimate children and has taken it upon itself to enforce this provision in this way.

If one of the parents is deceased this can be certified by the person witnessing the passport application, if the latter is in a position to confirm this fact. Alternatively, the death certificate of the deceased parent may be submitted. An illegitimate child will be included on its mother's passport, on the mother's application and only the mother's consent is required for such a child to obtain its own separate passport. A passport when granted remains in force for a period of ten years. If a minor is included in a parent's passport, the minor's inclusion remains valid until either the parent's passport loses its validity or until the minor obtains his own passport or attains his majority.

In practice, difficulties are frequently experienced by spouses whose marriages have broken down when they seek passports for children in their custody. If in a deed of separation one spouse has consented to the other spouse obtaining passports for the parties' children or if a court order has specifically stated that a spouse may obtain such passports or have the children included on his or her own passport, little difficulty arises. If, however, one spouse has merely departed and his whereabouts are unknown and if no such court order has been obtained or no agreement containing such a consent concluded, the approach of the Department is unclear. In practice, it has not been unknown for the Department to refuse to grant any passport facilities for a minor in such circumstances without the applicant parent first obtaining a court order authorising the issuing of the requested passport. On other occasions, the Department has refused to grant a passport valid for a ten year period but has merely granted a temporary passport, while on some occasions the Department has granted a passport valid for ten years on foot of a court order or agreement granting the applicant parent custody but silent as to the question of passports.

There is one statutory provision indirectly of relevance to the issue of passports for minors. Section 40 of the Adoption Act, 1952, prohibits the removal from the State of a legitimate child under seven years of age who is an Irish citizen unless such removal is by or with the approval of a parent, guardian or relative of the child. A person who contravenes this section or causes or permits its contravention is guilty of an offence and liable to imprisonment for up to twelve months and/or to a fine not exceeding one hundred pounds. It is thus clear that a civil servant in the service of the Department of Foreign Affairs cannot issue a passport to enable a legitimate child under seven years of age to be removed from the State if he knows such removal will contravene this section. If, however, a parent wishes to take his or her legitimate child outside the State, whether the child is under or over seven years of age, this section does not provide any statutory authority for the Department's practice of seeking the other parent's consent before it will issue a passport for the child as it only requires the approval of one parent. It also does not provide the statutory justification for the different approaches adopted by the Department when a separated parent seeks a passport for one of his children.

Section 40 of the 1952 Act also prohibits the removal from the State of an illegitimate child under seven years unless such removal is by or with the approval of the child's mother, guardian or a maternal relation.[1] In *The State (K.M. & R.D.) v. The Minister for Foreign Affairs and Ors,*[2] a further provision in this section relating to illegitimate children was held to be unconstitutional. The provision in question prohibited the removal from the State of an illegitimate child less than a year old except for the purpose of residing with its mother or a maternal relative. The judgement delivered by the High Court, contains the first detailed examination by the Irish Courts of the law as to passports and, in particular, of the question as to whether an Irish citizen has a constitutional right to a passport.

In this case, the Department of Foreign Affairs refused to grant a passport for a two and a half month old illegitimate child upon the mother's application. The child's mother was an Irish national and the natural father a Nigerian national. Both of the child's parents wished to send the child to Nigeria to be brought up by the natural father's parents, pending the natural father's return to that country upon the completion of his studies. Finlay P. formed the view that the proposals of the natural parents were consistent with the child's welfare. He then considered whether the child had a constitutional right to travel. He held that a citizen has the right to travel as one of the unenumerated personal rights of Article 40.3 of the Constitution and stated that "subject to the obvious conditions which may be required by public order and the common good of the State the right to a passport," which latter right is "inextricably intertwined" with the right to travel. In the case of a child, this right is exercisable

"by the choice of its parent, parents or legal guardian subject always to the right of the courts by appropriate proceedings to deny that choice in

---

1. See Sect. 3 and Sects. 40(1) and 40(3) of the 1952 Act.
2. [1979] I.R. 73 (H.C.).

the dominant interest of the welfare of the child."[3]

He stated that the above provision failed to defend and vindicate the child's personal right to travel and held it to be unconstitutional. He concluded stating that unless the Department of Foreign Affairs are in a position to bring wardship proceedings as a result of which the court decides that "it is contrary to the child's welfare for it to travel out of Ireland . . . the child has a constitutional right to a passport."

In the later case of *Cosgrove v. Ireland & Ors.*[4] the father of two legitimate children brought proceedings against the State claiming damages. Passports had been issued by the Department of Foreign Affairs to the plaintiff's wife for the parties' two children, contrary to the plaintiff's express objections communicated to the Department. The wife took the children to Holland and did not return to Ireland, so depriving the plaintiff of regular contact with them.

McWilliam J. stated that as parents are joint guardians of their legitimate children "neither parent may deprive the other of his or her children without an order of the court".[5] In this case, he continued, the mother was aware of the father's opposition to her obtaining passports for their children and she ought to have made an application to the court for permission to take them out of the country. Referring to the Department of Foreign Affairs' practice of normally seeking written consent of both parents for the issue of passports to legitimate minors, he stated:

> "This is a very prudent practice to adopt, but there is no statutory provision requiring it and I am not satisfied that there is any duty imposed on the State or the Department by the Constitution or otherwise to take any particular steps to protect rights which they have no reason to suppose are being infringed.
>
> Here, the passport office was notified by the plaintiff that he was objecing to the issue of the passports after forms had been issued which the plaintiff had failed to sign. Under these circumstances the Department was put on notice that the plaintiff was exercising his rights as joint guardian under the Guardianship of Infants Act, and I am of opinion that the passports should not have been issued without an application to the court being made by the wife and that this should have been told to the wife."[6]

McWilliam J. held against the State and following a subsequent hearing determined that the plaintiff was entitled to damages for the "infringement of a statutory right".[7] However, only nominal damages of £1,250 were awarded to the plaintiff, having regard to all the circumstances and, in particular, the behaviour of the plaintiff during the course of his marriage which rendered it "inconceivable that he would have been given custody of the children when the parties separated" and which probably would have resulted in his access to them being "very greatly restricted had his wife and children remained in Ireland."[8]

As a result of the above two judgements it appears that if a parent applies to have a minor placed on his or her passport or consents to a minor obtaining a separate passport, the minor has a constitutional right to have the passport facilities sought afforded to him. If the minor is legitimate and one parent objects

---

3. *Ibid.*, at p. 81.
4. [1982] 2 I.L.R.M. 48 (H.C.).
5. *Ibid.*, at p. 52.
6. *Ibid.*
7. [1982] 2 I.L.R.M. 53 (H.C.) at p. 55.
8. *Ibid.*

to the issue of passports, the Department may not issue a passport and has a duty to advise the spouse seeking it that before a passport can be issued the spouse must apply to the appropriate court under the Guardianship of Infants Act, 1964, and obtain an order permitting the spouse to apply for a passport and to take the children out of the country. If, however, the Department is unaware of any objection to the issue of a minor's passport, it must issue the passport and can only deny the minor passport facilities by bringing wardship proceedings and establishing to the satisfaction of the court in those proceedings that it is contrary to the welfare of the particular minor to permit it to travel outside Ireland. It is, of course, open to a spouse who fears that the other spouse may remove children from the jurisdiction without the former's consent to apply to an appropriate court under the 1964 Act for an injunction to prevent the other spouse doing so. In practice, many such injunctions have been granted.[9]

In relation to married couples, both of whom are Irish citizens, it is clear from the judgement delivered in *The State (K.M. & R.D.) v. The Minister for Foreign Affairs & Ors.* that each spouse has an independent right to a passport. However, in relation to this right, Finlay P. stated:

> "There are obvious and justified restrictions, the most common being the existence of some undischarged obligation to the State by the person seeking a passport or seeking to use his passport – such as the fact that he has entered into a recognisance to appear before a Criminal Court for the trial of an offence."[10]

The question arises as to whether the restrictions referred to by the learned judge will be extended by the courts to prevent a spouse leaving the jurisdiction in order to renege on his obligation to maintain his spouse and children. Having regard to the constitutional protection afforded to the family, the courts may be willing to restrict the right to travel and the right to use or obtain a passport in such circumstances.

It is submitted that legislation should be enacted to clarify this whole area of the law. It should clearly set out the duties imposed on the Department of Foreign Affairs in relation to the issue of passports and the manner in which these duties are to be exercised. In particular, such legislation should clearly specify the circumstances in which parental consents are required for the issuing of a passport for a minor and should provide a simple and inexpensive court procedure for dispensing with the consent of a parent, where to do so is in the interests of a minor's welfare. In addition, the legislation should state the circumstances in which the Department may refuse to issue a passport and the circumstances in which the courts may place restrictions on the issuing or use of passports in the interests of "public order" and the "common good".

---

9. See further p. 588 *post et seq.*
10. [1979] I.R. at p. 81.

DOMICILE[1]

Many problems in family law are intimately bound up with the concept of domicile. Domicile is a connecting factor or link between an individual and the legal system that governs specific issues affecting his personal life. These include questions relating to a person's capacity to marry, the validity of his marriage, the recognition of any foreign decree of divorce obtained, issues concerning status, for example, whether a person is legitimate or illegitimate or can be legitimated, issues relating to succession and to a person's liability to taxation.

The law relating to domicile is relatively complex. Put simply, a person's domicile is said to be that of the country in which he has his permanent home.[2] However, as will be seen, the rules for determining domicile often require a far more complicated inquiry than one simply to discover the location of an individual's home. Moreover, it is not strictly accurate to equate the concept of domicile with that of a country. Domicile strictly signifies a separate law district, i.e. a territory subject to a single system of law. Thus, whilst the equation is accurate for example in the case of the Republic of Ireland or England, in the case of the U.S.A. it is not. There, each State is a separate law district, and persons are not domiciled in the U.S.A. as such, but in one of its states.[3]

The two basic rules as to domicile are that nobody can be without one and that no person can have more than one domicile, at the same time, for the same purpose.[4]

Domicile of Origin

Every person is deemed at birth to have a domicile of origin. The domicile of a legitimate child born during his father's lifetime, is that of the domicile of the father at the time of his birth. The domicile of a legitimate child born after his father's death or of an illegitimate child is that of his mother. The domicile of a foundling is in the country where he is found. Thus domicile of origin, as can be seen, in no way depends on the intention or actions of the person who acquires it.

Domicile of Choice

Every person who is not a minor, apart from a person of unsound mind, can acquire a domicile of choice. To do so a person must leave the country of his domicile of origin and take up residence in another country, with the intention of continuing to reside there permanently or at least indefinitely.[5] A person may

---

1. See generally, the Law Reform Commission: Domicile and Habitual Residence as Connecting Factors in the Conflict of Laws (Working Paper No. 10, 1981 & Report No. 7, 1983).
2. *Whicker v. Hime* (1858) 7 H.L. Cas. 124 at p. 160 (H.L.); see comments of Budd J. in *In re Adams* [1967] I.R. 424 (H.C.). Nationality and domicile may often coincide but they are not necessarily the same. Thus, a person of Irish nationality, may have an English or French domicile under Irish law, providing he acquires it in accordance with one of the rules under Irish Law for the acquisition of domicile. Similarly, a person may acquire a foreign nationality and still retain an Irish domicile, see *K.E.D. (otherwise K.C.) v. M.C.* (September, 1984) unreported (H.C.); (December, 1985) unreported (S.C.).
3. Dicey and Morris, *Conflict of Law*, 10th edition, ch. 7.
4. See Cheshire & North, *supra*, pp. 162–165.
5. Rule 10, Dicey and Morris, *supra*; see *In re Joyce, Corbet v. Fagan* [1946] I.R. 277 (S.C.); *In re Sillar, Hurley v. Wimbush* [1956] I.R. 344 (H.C.); *In re Adams, supra*; *Revenue Commissioners v. Shaw and Talbot Crosbie* (April 1977) unreported (H.C.); *Gaffney v. Gaffney* [1975] I.R. 133 (S.C.); *T. v. T.* [1983] I.R. 29 (S.C.); *K.E.D. (otherwise K.C.) v. M.C., supra*. See also *Sproule v. Hopkins* [1903] 2 I.R. 386 (K.B.D.); *Revenue Commissioners v. Iveagh* [1930] I.R. 386 (S.C.); *Revenue Commissioners v. Z.* (1967) 101 I.L.T. & S.J. 492 (Sp. Com.); *J.W. v. M.W.* (July, 1978) unreported (H.C.); *L.B. v. H.B.* (July, 1980) unreported (H.C.).

lose his domicile of choice by ceasing to reside there and abandoning his intention to reside there.[6] Upon abandoning a domicile of choice a person may
acquire a new domicile of choice. Alternatively, he may abandon his domicile
of choice without having any definite intention as to where to set up a home. In
such circumstances his domicile of origin revives.[7]

Domicile of Dependency

Neither minors (unmarried persons under 18 years of age) nor persons of
unsound mind can acquire a domicile of choice. They have what is known as a
domicile of dependence. Until the 2nd of October, 1986, married women also
had a domicile of dependency. Though a married woman may now acquire a
separate and independent domicile her legal position may still be affected by
the old rule as to dependency. Accordingly the domicile of married women must
be treated separately.

Married Women

Prior to the 2nd of October, 1986, the domicile of a husband was communicated to a wife immediately upon marriage and during the subsistence of
the marriage she was unable to acquire an independent domicile of her own.
This applied even if spouses were living apart, whether or not they were doing
so in pursuance of a separation agreement or a decree of divorce *a mensa et
thoro*.[8] Thus, if a husband deserted his wife and went to live permanently in
England, acquiring an English domicile of choice, even though the wife never
set foot in England, under Irish law she also acquired an English domicile. In
1975 it was suggested by Walsh J. in *Gaffney v. Gaffney*[9] that the rule as to
a wife's dependent domicile might be unconstitutional. This suggestion was
again repeated by McCarthy J. in 1985, at the conclusion of his judgement in
K.E.D. (otherwise K.C.) v. M.C.[10] This issue has, however, never been definitively
determined by the Irish Courts.

Upon the valid dissolution of her marriage, or the death of her husband, a wife
was free to acquire a domicile of choice of her own.[11] Until she did so, however,
she continued to retain her husband's domicile.[12] Upon the pronouncement of a
decree annulling a voidable marriage a wife was also free to acquire her own
domicile of choice. If she was party to a void marriage she never became a depen-

---

See further the interesting case of *Egan v. Egan* [1928] N.I. 159 (K.B.D.) where it was
held that a person who possessed an Irish domicile prior to 1922 could, upon the establishment of the Irish Free State, elect for domicile either in Northern Ireland or in the Irish
Free State.

6. Rule 13, Dicey and Morris, *supra*; see *Sproule v. Hopkins, supra, Revenue Commissioners v. Matthews* (1958) 92 I.L.T.R. 44 (S.C.); *In re Adams, supra*.

7. *Udny v. Udny* (1869) L.R. 1 Sc. & Div. 441 at p. 450, (H.L.); see Cheshire and
North, *supra*, pp. 177–178 where he criticises the doctrine of revival – The doctrine of
revival can result in a person being domiciled in a country with which he has little or no
connection and even upon which he has never set foot.

8. *A.-G. for Alberta v. Cook* [1926] A.C. 444 (P.C.); *Gaffney v. Gaffney* [1975] I.R.
133 (H.C., S.C.).

9. *Gaffney v. Gaffney, supra*.

10. (December, 1985) unreported (S.C.).

11. *In re Scullard deceased* [1957] Ch. 107 (Ch. Div.); see P.B. Carter – Domicile of
a Widow, (1957) 33 B.Y.I.L. 329–332. See also *Gaffney v. Gaffney, supra*.

12. *In re Wallach deceased* [1950] 1 All E.R. 199 (P.D.A.).

dent person, and so retained her independent domicile.[13]

Section 1 of the Domicile & Recognition of Foreign Divorces Act, 1986, makes provision for a married woman to acquire her own independent domicile and abolishes a wife's domicile of dependency from the date of the commencement of the Act. Pursuant to its provisions, the domicile of a married woman as at any time on or after the 2nd of October, 1986, "shall be an independent domicile and shall be determined by reference to the same factors as in the case of any other person capable of having an independent domicile."[13a] Thus, a married woman no longer acquires her husband's domicile upon marriage and is capable of acquiring a separate domicile of her own, though in relation to the majority of married couples a husband and wife will, in most instances, inevitably each independently acquire the same domicile. For the purpose of determining the domicile of a wife prior to the commencement of the Act, i.e. prior to the 2nd of October, 1986, section 2 provides that the wife's "domicile shall be determined as if the Act had not been passed." In effect the old domicile of dependency rule is preserved by the Act up to and including the 1st of October, 1986. On the 2nd of October, 1986, a wife's domicile of dependency ceases and under section 3 of the Act her domicile must be determined as if the Act "had always been in force."

The effect of these provisions is that a wife residing permanently in Ireland, who had at birth an Irish domicile of origin and who acquired an English domicile of choice dependent on the domicile of a deserting husband, continues to retain her dependent English domicile up to and including the 1st of October, 1986. The automatic acquisition by her on the 2nd of October, 1986, of a capacity to acquire an independent domicile results in her reverting to her Irish domicile of origin. If, however, an issue arises as to the wife's pre-2nd of October, 1986, domicile, under the statute, it remains a domicile dependent on that of her husband. Upon the issue arising in future litigation, it is of course still open to the Irish courts to further consider whether the rule as to a wife's domicile of dependency is consistent or inconsistent with the Constitution.

Minors

A person is a minor until he reaches the age of 18 years or until he marries.[14] As we have seen a legitimate infant acquires the domicile of his father, if born during the latter's lifetime, and of his mother if not. An illegitimate child acquires his mother's domicile, and if legitimated his father's. However, in the latter circumstances the mother's domicile is the domicile of origin and his father's, the domicile of choice. An adopted child acquires the domicile of his adopters. The generally accepted rule is that a minor is incapable of acquiring a domicile of choice of his own, the only exception being that a female minor acquires the domicile of her husband. A domicile of choice, however, may be acquired for him by the act of one of his parents.

The domicile of an infant follows any change which occurs in the domicile of his father. In the Northern Ireland case of *Hope v. Hope*,[15] it was said that

---

13. *In Gray v. Formosa* [1963] P. 259 (C.A.) – The rule of dependent domicile of a married woman was said to be "the last barbarous relic of a wife's servitude", – *per* Lord Denning M.R. at p. 267. The rule was abolished in England by the Domicile and Matrimonial Proceedings Act, 1973, Sect. 1.

13a. The legislation was enacted by the Oireachtas on the 2nd July, 1986. Sect. 6 provides that the Act is to come into operation "on the day that is three months after the date of the passing of this Act."

14. See the Age of Majority Act, 1985, Sect. 2.

15. [1968] N.I. 1 (Q.B.D.). See further (1969) 20 N.I.L.Q. 304.

this rule is based "on the authority and responsibility that a father has to act for his child."[16] The domicile of a minor at any time when his father or mother are living apart is that of his mother, if

(a) the minor then has his home with her and has no home with his father, or

(b) the minor has at any time had the mother's domicile by virtue of paragraph (a) and has not since had a home with his father.[17]

Upon the death of a father, an infant's domicile becomes dependent on and will, *prima facie*, change with that of his mother. This power to change her infant's domicile is said to be vested in a mother, to be exercised for the welfare of the infant. It was decided in *In re Beaumont* that if a mother changes her own domicile, she may abstain from changing that of her child provided she does so without fraudulent intention and with the child's welfare in mind.[18]

All the classical writers affirm that a father is incapable of conferring on his infant a domicile different to his own. The Irish case of *Spurway v. Spurway*[19] is frequently relied on to support this principle. However, anything said in that case about the respondent's domicile as an infant, was purely *obiter*.[20] There is no logical reason why a mother should be able to confer a domicile on her infant different to her own and a father prevented from doing so. Moreover *In re Beaumont*, although decided a year prior to *Spurway* was not mentioned in the latter case.[21] In conclusion, the domicile of a minor whose mother dies, is that of the mother at the date of death, even if she is survived by the father, if the minor had her domicile as a result of his parents living apart and if he "has not since had a home with his father."[21a]

Proposals for Reform

The desirability of radically reforming the law as to domicile so as to replace the concept of domicile with that of habitual residence was given detailed consideration by the Law Reform Commission[22] which concluded that "on balance the better course is to replace domicile by habitual residence".[23] The Domicile & Recognition of Foreign Divorces Act, 1986, although it does not implement the major recommendation of the Commission that the concept of habitual residence be adopted to replace domicile as a connecting factor[24] has introduced

16. *Supra* at p. 10, *per* Lord MacDermot, L.C.J.

17. See the Domicile & Recognition of Foreign Divorces Act, 1986, Sect. 4(1). The Act does not define what is meant by home. If a minor is in the legal custody of a mother pursuant to a court order or under the terms of a separation agreement but spends every weekend residing with the father in his home pursuant to a court access order or agreed access it is arguable that the minor has a home with both the father and the mother and has a domicile dependant on that of the father. It is submitted it would have been more appropriate to make a minor's domicile dependant on that of the principal custodial parent.

18. [1893] 3 Ch. 490 (Ch. Div.).

19. [1894] 1 I.R. 385, 401; (1893) 28 I.L.T.R. 2 (C.A.).

20. See W.R. Duncan, "The Domicile of Infants", (1969) 4 I.J. (n.s.) 36.

21. See *Stephens v. M'Farland* (1845) 8 Ir. Eq. Rep. 444 (Rolls Ct.) and the comments thereon by Duncan *supra* – However, note that the parent in M'Farland was the mother, although the Master of the Rolls does not mention that fact in his judgement.

21a. See the Domicile & Recognition of Foreign Divorces Act, 1986, Sect. 4(2).

22. Law Reform Commission Working Paper No. 10, *supra* and Law Reform Commission Report No. 7, *supra*.

23. Report No. 7 at p. 13.

24. See the Conflict of Laws Reform Bill, 1985, tabled in the Dáil by Mr. C.J. Haughey T.D., the leader of the Fianna Fáil party in opposition, which was defeated and did not obtain a second reading. This bill was similar in many respects to the draft bill published by the Law Reform Commission in its report.

a welcome reform by placing both husbands and wives in a position of legal equality by allowing each to acquire their own independent domicile. The Act does not unfortunately reform some of the other anachronistic rules as to domicile and it is suggested that until such time as the concept of domicile is replaced by that of habitual residence further reforming legislation should be enacted providing measures

(a) to abolish the rule as to the revival of the domicile of origin. It is submitted that there is no valid reason for retaining this rule and that upon a person leaving a domicile of choice, such domicile should be retained until a new one is acquired.[25]

(b) to provide that the same rules shall apply to determine whether a domicile of origin has been abandoned and a new domicile acquired as apply to determine whether a domicile of choice has been abandoned and a new domicile acquired. The great difficulty in shaking off a domicile of origin under current law can result in an artificial legal view as to with which country a person has his primary connection and it is submitted that there is no logic or purpose in retaining the current approach.[26]

---

25. See Law Reform Commission Working Paper No. 10 at pp. 79–81. An amendment to the 1986 Act which would have implemented this proposal was tabled by the author in the Dáil but ruled out of order as "outside the scope of the Bill" by the Cheann Comhairle.
26. *Ibid.*, at pp. 78–79.

JACTITATION OF MARRIAGE[1]

In 1871 the High Court inherited the old jurisdiction of the Ecclesiastical Courts to hear proceedings in which application is made for a decree of Jactitation of Marriage.[2] A petition in a suit for jactitation of marriage is designed to prevent a person (the respondent) from making false assertions that he or she is married to the petitioner.[3] Upon the court being satisfied that the parties to the proceedings are not married it makes a declaration to that effect together with an order forbidding the respondent from repeating the assertion. The declaration that the parties are not married does not bind third parties and is not therefore in any way equivalent to a decree of nullity.[4] There are three defences to the suit:

(a) A denial that the assertion was made;[5]

(b) An admission that it was made together with a statement as to its truth;[6]

(c) Proof that the assertion was authorised or acquiesced in by the petititioner.[7]

If the court upholds the respondent's claim that he or she is validly married to the petitioner, the court can make a declaration that the parties are validly married.[8]

There are no cases of suits for jactitation of marriage to be found in any of the modern Irish law reports. The remedy seems to have fallen into general disuse. It does, however, provide a useful procedure to enable a person stop another from causing him embarrassment by pretending in public to be married to him. A defect in the remedy is that it does not enable the court to make an order to silence or prevent third parties from making false statements as to a person's marital status, nor does it enable a husband or wife to obtain a court order to prevent a third party from claiming to be married to his or her spouse or to prevent such third party from assuming their spouse's name.[9]

The Law Reform Commission has recommended that this action be replaced by a new remedy which would enable a plaintiff to obtain orders to prevent a person falsely claiming to be married to him and also to prevent third parties from falsely stating (with knowledge of the falsity of such statement or reckless indifferences as to its truth), that another person is married to him. The remedy

---

1. See the Law Reform Commission: *Report on Restitution of Conjugal Rights, Jactitation of Marriage and Related Matters* (L.R.C. Report No. 6 – November 1983).
2. The word "jacitation" is derived from the Latin "jacitare" meaning to boast.
3. *Goldstone v. Smith* (1922) 38 T.L.R. 403 (P.D.A.).
4. *Duchess of Kingston's Case* (1776) 20 State Tr. 355; 168 E.R. 175 (H.L.). In this case, the Duchess, in a prosecution for bigamously marrying the Duke of Kingston, relied by way of defence on a decree of jacitation in respect of her first marriage to another man, but it was held the decree could only bind the parties to the suit and therefore was not binding on the Crown.
  Further, it seems that it is not even conclusive as between the parties, but that the case can be reopened upon the respondent showing on new evidence that the parties were married.
5. *Hawke (Lord) v. Corri* (1820) 2 Hag. Con. 280; 161 E.R. 743 (Consistory Ct.).
6. *Lindo v. Belisario* (1794) 1 Hag. Con. 216; appeal at (1796) 1 Hag. Con. 7; 161 E.R. 530, 636 (Consistory, Arches Cts.); *Hawke v. Corri, supra*; *Bodkin v. Case* (1835) Milw. Rep. 355 (Consistory Ct.); *Thompson v. Rourke* [1893] P. 70 (C.A.); *Goldstone v. Smith, supra*; *Schuck v. Schuck* (1950) 66 T.L.R. 1179 (P.D.A.); *Igra v. Igra* [1951] P. 404 (P.D.A.).
7. *Thompson v. Rourke* [1893] P. 11 (P.D.A.).
8. *Goldstone v. Smith, supra.*
9. See Working Paper No. 34 of the English Law Commission; see also Working Paper No. 48 of the same body.

would also, in appropriate places, entitle a plaintiff to obtain damages. However, the Commission does not appear to have considered whether such new remedy should also entitle the spouse of another to institute proceedings to prevent a third party claiming to be married to his or her spouse.[10]

MARRIAGE AND DECLARATORY JUDGEMENTS

A spouse may petition the High Court for a declaration that his marriage is valid under the provisions of the Legitimacy Declaration (Ireland) Act, 1868. The Attorney General must be joined as a respondent to any petition. A declaration made under the Act is binding on all persons given notice of, or made parties to the proceedings (including the State) and anyone claiming through them. However, a decree proved to have been obtained by fraud or collusion has no binding effect on anyone.[11] A second way in which a declaration may be obtained was discussed in the Court of Appeal in England in *Har-Shefi v. Har-Shefi.*[12] Here it was held that the court had jurisdiction to make an order declaratory of the parties' status under Order 25, Rule 5 of the English Rules of the Supreme Court. The English Order corresponds exactly with Order 19, Rule 29 of the Irish Rules of the Superior Courts which states that:

> "No action or pleading shall be open to objection on the ground that a merely declaratory judgement or order is sought thereby, and the court may if it thinks fit, make binding declarations of right whether any consequential relief is or could be claimed or not."

The jurisdiction of the High Court to give a declaratory judgement on the general question of a person's marital status could be a particularly useful method of testing the validity of foreign decrees of divorce under Irish law before a question as to the validity of such a decree arises in other proceedings. The jurisdiction of the court has not as yet, been used for such a purpose.

The Law Reform Commission in 1983 referring to the present law regarding declarations as to status, stated that it would benefit from restatement in clear terms in modern legislation. In the Commission's view such legislation should enable a person to apply to the High Court for a decree declaring that his or her marriage was or is a valid marriage and should be concerned specifically with the validity of marriages and would not relate directly to questions of legitimacy as does the Act of 1868.[13]

---

10. Law Reform Commission Report No. 6, *supra*, pp. 23–24.
11. See Order 71 of the R.S.C. (S.I. No. 15 of 1986).
12. [1953] P. 161; [1953] 1 All E.R. 783 (C.A.).
13. Law Reform Commission Report No. 6, 1983, see pp. 24–25.

CHAPTER 7

SEPARATION AGREEMENTS

"Whereas unhappy differences have arisen between the husband and the wife."

So traditionally commences the most depressing of all legal contracts, the Separation Agreement. When parties to a marriage no longer wish to cohabit a separation agreement affords the means whereby they can regularise their affairs without recourse to a court.

Prior to the Reformation marriage was regarded both by the Church and the law as a sacrament. The duty of cohabitation was the fundamental matrimonial duty and a contract made for giving effect to voluntary separation was regarded as *contra bonos mores* and of no effect. After the Reformation although such contracts were not regarded as contrary to common law, the Ecclesiastical Courts still refused to recognise them. It was not until the middle of the last century that the validity and enforceability of separation agreements was finally established.[1] In upholding the validity of separation agreements the courts recognised the desirability of estranged spouses settling their differences in private, rather than in open court.

It is now settled law that a contract between a husband and wife to live separate and apart and to regulate their respective legal rights is valid and enforceable. However, a contract by spouses living together, providing for a future separation, is void and inoperative as contrary to public policy.[2] The one exception to this arises if an agreement is made by spouses not cohabiting, providing for their resuming cohabitation and containing provisions to regulate their position if they should again separate.[3]

Form

A separation agreement need not be in any particular form, provided each spouse gives valuable consideration it will be valid and enforceable. Mutual oral promises simply not to cohabit, if intended to have legal effect, are enforceable.[4]

---

1. *Wilson v. Wilson* (1848) 1 H.L. Cas. 538 (H.L.).
2. *Westmeath (Marquis of) v. Westmeath (Marchioness of)* (1830) 1 Dow & Cl. 519; 6 E.R. 619 (H.L.); *Cohane v. Cohane* [1968] I.R. 176 (S.C.). See also *Brodie v. Brodie* [1917] P. 271 (P.D.A.), ante-nuptial agreement of non-cohabitation, void.
3. *MacMahon v. MacMahon* [1913] 1 I.R. 154, 428 (M.R., App.); *Purser v. Purser* [1913] 1 I.R. 422, 428 (Ch.D., App.).
4. *Courtney v. Courtney* [1923] 2 I.R. 31; (1922), 57 I.L.T.R. 42 (C.A.). See judgement of Dodd J. at p. 37 where he suggests mutual oral promises to live apart are not sufficient to create a binding agreement. See, however, judgement of Ronan C.J. at p. 42 where he states that such an agreement would be enforceable provided that the parties intended it to have legal consequences. As for the need for intention to create legal relations, see *Balfour v. Balfour* [1919] 2 K.B. 571 (C.A.); *Gould v. Gould* [1970] 1 Q.B. 275 (C.A.); *Merritt v. Merritt* [1970] 1 W.L.R. 1211 (C.A.).

Generally, however, an agreement is much more complex containing agreed provisions to resolve all the personal and financial consequences of a broken marriage for the separating spouses and their children. Thus, it will usually make provision for custody and access to children, maintenance of the dependant spouse (most often the wife) and children, division of matrimonial property and use of the family home, non-molestation by one spouse of the other and other appropriate matters arising out of the relationship of the spouses that if not resolved by agreement could subsequently become a matter of dispute. Such an agreement is normally written and is generally embodied in a deed signed by both spouses.

Formerly, owing to a married woman's inability to contract, it was necessary to join trustees to such an agreement to contract on behalf of the wife. Since the coming into force of the Married Women's Property Act, 1882 (now replaced by the Married Women's Status Act, 1957) this has not been necessary. A separation agreement is subject to the ordinary law of contract. If obtained by fraud or duress such an agreement will be voidable.[5] Whereas if it is entered into by unmarried parties, thinking themselves to be married, it is void.[6]

Terms That May Be Included in an Agreement

The following are the terms more usually found in separation agreements.

Agreement to Live Apart: This is the fundamental provision in every separation agreement. By it, each spouse is released from the duty of cohabiting with the other. However, this provision should be regarded with caution. If a deserted spouse consents to living apart, the desertion automatically comes to an end. Under the Family Law ... Act, 1976, a deserting spouse is barred from claiming maintenance for his or her own support.[7] Under the Family Home Protection Act, 1976, the courts may automatically dispense with the consent of a deserting spouse so as to permit the deserted spouse to validly sell or convey to another any interest in a family home owned by the deserted spouse without having to first obtain the prior consent of the spouse in desertion.[8] Under the Succession Act, 1965, a spouse in continuous desertion of a deceased spouse for two years or more prior to the latter's death automatically loses his or her statutory entitlement to a specific portion of the deceased spouse's estate.[9] Thus, by signing a separation agreement, a deserted spouse may render himself liable to contribute to the maintenance of the spouse in desertion or may revive the deserting spouse's Succession Act[10] or Family Home Protection Act[11] rights. Similarly, a deserted wife by agreeing to separate may render herself ineligible for deserted wife's benefit or allowance, a social welfare payment she might otherwise receive in the event of her husband failing to maintain her. Where the parties are not agreed on a separation but are agreed on financial and other arrangements subsequent to desertion by one, of the other, a "maintenance" or other type of agreement may be more appropriate than a "separation" agreement. Whereas a separation agreement normally recites that the parties "have agreed to live apart from each other" a maintenance or other agreement would

---

5. See *V.W. v. J.W.* (April, 1978) unreported (H.C.) in which the plaintiff failed to have an agreement declared void.
6. *Galloway v. Galloway* (1914) 30 T.L.R. 531 (K.B.D.), (D.C.).
7. See further p. 439 *et seq.*
8. See pp. 560 *et seq.*
9. See pp. 527 *et seq.*
10. One or both spouses may in the deed expressly waive succession rights. See p. 520.
11. The deed itself may contain a provision granting a general consent under the 1976 Act. See p. 211 *post.*

contain merely the factual statement that they "are living apart from each other" or that a named spouse has deserted the other spouse.

Non-Molestation Clause: There is generally a term that neither spouse will "molest, annoy, disturb or interfere with the other". Molestation must be some act done by the wife or husband, or on his or her authority, with the intent to annoy the other and in fact be an annoyance to him or her. A covenant not to molest is not broken by the subsequent bringing of a *bona fide* matrimonial action.[12] Neither adultery by a wife, nor adultery followed by the birth of an illegitimate child, is a breach of such a covenant, though if a wife held out such a child to be the legitimate child of her husband it would amount to molestation.[13] Behaviour in breach of such a clause may be restrained by an injunction.

Custody of Children: At common law any agreement whereby a father divested himself of the custody of his children was regarded as contrary to public policy and void. Now by the Guardianship of Infants Act, 1964, section 18(2)

> "A provision contained in any separation agreement made between the father and mother of an infant shall not be invalid by reason only of its providing that one of them shall give up the custody or control of the infant to the other."[14]

However, if provision is made in a separation agreement for the custody of, or for access to a child and subsequently proceedings are brought, the court will not enforce the provision if enforcement is contrary to the child's welfare.[15]

The spouse who does not obtain custody of a child is usually given reasonable rights of access to it. Such rights normally include as a minimum the right to visit and take out the child on one day each week and in addition, to have the child either reside with or go on holidays with such parent for part of the school holidays. It is also usual to state the circumstances in which a child may be taken outside the jurisdiction by either parent e.g. whether the other parent's consent is required, how much notice must be given, etc. The exact agreement reached as to access varies and is dependent upon the individual circumstances and the ages of the parties' children. To avoid dispute at a later date a separation agreement should also state whether it is agreed or not that a passport be obtained for a child or that a child's name be placed on the passport of either parent.

Maintenance Clause: If a wife is the dependant spouse or in a financially inferior position to that of the husband, provision is usually made for the husband to pay maintenance to the wife for her support, and if she has custody of the parties' children, a portion of the sum payable is normally allocated as being for the children's support. If the wife's financial circumstances are superior to those of the husband there may be provision for the husband to receive maintenance from the wife. The vast majority of agreements concluded, however, require husbands to pay maintenance to wives.

The amount of maintenance payable is the sum agreed as a result of whatever negotiations or discussions take place between the parties, their legal advisors or any other persons who assist them to reach agreement. Agreement must also be

---

12. *Courtney v. Courtney* [1923] 2 I.R. 31; (1923) 27 I.L.T.R. 42 (C.A.).
13. *Fearon v. Earl of Aylesford* (1884) 14 Q.B. 792 (C.A.).
14. This section in effect re-enacts Sect. 2 of the Custody of Infants Act, 1873; see also the article in (1883) 17 I.L.T. & S.J. 473-4 entitled, "The Right to the Custody of Children".
15. See Sect. 3 of the 1964 Act. See further Chapter 13, particularly p. 373.

reached as to when an obligation to pay maintenance for the support of any child or children will cease, and in the case of a family containing more than one child, an agreement will normally state the manner in which the maintenance is to be divided between each child. The agreement may provide for the payment of one lump sum[16] or for yearly payments. The more usual arrangement is for the husband to make weekly, fortnightly, or monthly payments, the exact arrangement agreed usually being dependent on the manner in which the husband receives his wage or salary from his business or place of employment. The maintenance may be secured or unsecured and it can be payable directly to a wife, to her agent or, if the agreement is made a rule of court under section 8 of the Family Law . . . Act, 1976, to a District Court Clerk.[17]

It is usual to make provision for the variation of the amount payable by way of maintenance if the financial circumstances of the parties change and also to provide a mechanism to take into account the effects of inflation on the sum it is originally agreed is to be paid. An agreement that does not do so, does not prevent a spouse in receipt of inadequate maintenance under a separation agreement from seeking a maintenance order under the Family Law . . . Act, 1976, but the spouse bound to pay maintenance, in the absence of a variation clause, may find himself legally contracted to pay a sum that is beyond his means and from which he cannot legally extricate himself.[18]

There are numerous types of variation clauses that may be inserted in an agreement to ensure that it keeps in step with the requirements and resources of the parties to the agreement. For example, at the end of each year an agreement may provide for:

(a) A fixed annual percentage increase in the maintenance payments; for example 10%.

(b) A fixed sum increase; for example £10 for a wife and £5 for each child. child.

(c) An annual percentage increase based on any increase in the cost of living as certified by the Central Statistics Office.[19]

(d) An increase proportionate to the annual increase in the husband's income or a specific proportion of any increase in income received by the husband.

(e) A renegotiation of the maintenance payable in the context of changes in either or both spouses' financial circumstances.

Each of the above methods has advantages and disadvantages. Methods (a), (b) and (c) are preferable to (d) and (e) in so far as they avoid annual arguments between the parties as to their true earnings. Further, they lessen the pressure on

---

16. See *Lett v. Lett* [1906] 1 I.R. 618, 630 (M.R., App.).

17. See p. 211. For a discussion of the application of income tax law to maintenance payments provided for under the terms of an agreement concluded prior to the 8th June 1983 see M.V. O'Mahoney, The Drafting of Separation Agreements, S.Y.S. Lecture No. 3 and F. Gannon, "The Tax Implications of Marital Breakdown" (1983) 77 *Gazette of the Incorporated Law Society of Ireland* 15. For a discussion of the application of income tax law to maintenance payments provided for under the terms of an agreement concluded on or after 8th June 1983 see p. 455 *post*. For a detailed analysis of the whole area of the law see N.E. Judge, *Irish Income Tax* (Butterworths, London 1986) p. 565 *et seq*.

18. See *O'S. v. O'S.* (November, 1983) unreported (H.C.); *J.D. v. B.D.* [1985] 5 I.L.R.M. 688 (H.C.).

19. The Central Statistics Office publishes quarterly and annual statistics as to increases in the cost of living in accordance with the Consumer Price Index.

the parties to "spy" on each other and thus prevent any further unpleasantness that such behaviour can cause. The main disadvantage of methods (a) and (b) is that in times of extreme inflation, despite such a provision, a wife's income in real terms could decline. Alternatively, in a more stable monetary situation her income could as a result increase in real terms, but such an increase could be beyond the means of her husband. Method (c) avoids many of the above difficulties. It is disadvantageous, however, in so far as it may give rise to uncertainty, in that the parties may not know until a short time before payment is due, the exact amount of the annual increase. Further, it does not make any allowance for a change in the financial circumstances of each party unconnected with cost of living increases. It is submitted that the best compromise clause is one that provides for an annual increase based on the cost of living together with provision for either party to serve notice on the other proposing an alternative sum payable "upon the occurrence of a fundamental change" in the financial circumstances of either. In the event of the parties being unable to resolve a dispute as to the exact sum to be paid, within a specified period of time after the service of such notice, the agreement may permit the paying spouse, if he is seeking to pay a reduced sum to unilaterally reduce the maintenance he is paying or, the spouse receiving maintenance, if she is seeking an increased sum, to apply to the appropriate court for a maintenance order under section 5 of the Family Law . . . Act, 1976.[20] The agreement may also provide for the maintenance recipient to make such application upon the paying spouse unilaterally reducing his maintenance payments following the expiration of the specified period of time, without the amount of future maintenance to be paid having been agreed. As a spouse is always entitled to make such application under the current law, however, it is not essential that the agreement so provide. While proceedings can always be issued by a maintenance recipient seeking increased maintenance, it should be noted that if an agreement does not contain an express provision permitting a reduction in maintenance payments in changed financial circumstances, the courts at present possess no statutory jurisdiction to reduce the sum payable under it by the maintenance paying spouse.[21]

Covenant not to sue for maintenance and courts' jurisdiction to vary maintenance clause: Prior to the coming into force of the Family Law . . . Act, 1976, it was not unusual for a separation agreement to contain a clause whereby a wife, in receipt of a weekly sum of maintenance or in receipt of a lump sum by way of final settlement, covenanted not to apply to the courts at any future time for a maintenance order. It is now clear that even if a wife does so covenant, she is not excluded from obtaining a maintenance order under the provisions of the Family Law . . . Act, 1976.

In *H.D. v. P.D.*[22] proceedings brought by the applicant wife against her

---

20. For detailed discussion of sections 5 and 6 of the Family . . . Act, 1976, see chapter 14 and in particular pp. 433 *et seq*.

21. See footnote 18 *ante*. See also *R.H. v. N.H.* (October, 1985) unreported (S.C.) in which the court declined to enforce a provision in a deed as to increased payments to be made by the husband on the ground that the parties had not been *ad idem* as to the meaning of the provision when the deed was concluded. The court held that instead a maintenance order should be made under Sect. 5 of the Act of 1976 to determine what sum should be paid by the husband to the wife. See also judgement of Costello J. in the High Court (June, 1983) unreported. Proceedings originally involving the parties had previously been settled on the basis of the terms contained in the agreement which the court declined to enforce.

22. (May, 1978) unreported (S.C.). See further G. McGann, "Maintenance Agreements and the Family Law (Maintenance of Spouses & Children) Act, 1976" (1979) 72 *Gazette of the Incorporated Law Society of Ireland* 115.

husband seeking a divorce *a mensa et thoro* had been settled in 1973. A written consent signed by the parties had been received and filed in court. In accordance with its terms the respondent husband had paid to the wife a sum of £10,000 which was stated in the consent to be "in full satisfaction of all claims in the petitition". In 1977, the wife issued further proceedings against her husband seeking a maintenance order under section 5 of the Family Law . . . Act, 1976, for the support of herself and two of her children.

It was contended on behalf of the husband that the wife was estopped from seeking maintenance by reason of the consent. The court, however, held that despite the covenant contained in the consent the claim fell within the provisions of section 5 of the Family Law . . . Act, 1976, under which a maintenance order may be made if it appears to the court that a spouse has failed to provide "such maintenance as is proper in the circumstances."

Walsh J. delivering the judgement of the court, held that the consent "was in effect a separation agreement" and went on to state:

> "The operation of the (Family Law) Act cannot be affected by a separation agreement or other document in the nature of the consent in this case entered into before the passing of the Act unless there is an express provision to the contrary in the Act. It is clear from the whole structure of the Act that its purpose is to deal with the situation of the parties at the time the proceedings were brought under the Act and that the primary function of the Act is to ensure that proper and adequate maintenance will be available in accordance with the provisions of the Act to spouses and children. The basic question to be decided is whether at any given time there is a failure by one spouse to provide reasonable maintenance for the support of the other spouse and for any dependent children of the family of the spouses. In my view it is not possible to contract out of the Act by an agreement made after the Act came into force or by an agreement entered into before the legislation was enacted."[23]

As for agreements entered into after the Act came into force and made rules of court under section 8 of the Act he continued:

> "a provision in any such agreement for periodical maintenance payments is not final and there is nothing to prevent the spouse receiving the payments from subsequently applying for a maintenance order if the circumstances have changed."[24]

Curiously, Walsh J. did not refer in his judgement to section 27 of the Act which provides that a provision in an agreement, in so far as it would have the effect of excluding or limiting the operation of any provision of the Act, is void. His judgement is, however, wholly consistent with the intent of this provision.

Although provisions contained in a separation agreement cannot exclude a court from hearing and determining an application for maintenance under the 1976 Act, a covenant whereby a spouse agrees not to seek future maintenance, taken together with the circumstances that gave rise to the conclusion of the agreement and the subsequent behaviour of the spouses and their current financial standing, it has been held, may lead a court to the conclusion that it "is proper in the circumstances" for a husband to pay no maintenance to his wife. In *O.C. v. T.C.*[25] a separation agreement was concluded whereby a wife waived

23. See p. 7 of judgement. See also *R.H. v. N.H., supra.*
24. See pp. 7–8 of judgement.
25. (December, 1981) unreported (H.C.).

all rights to be maintained by her husband and undertook to take no steps to compel him to pay maintenance to her. The agreement formed part of a settlement whereby the husband discontinued criminal conversation proceedings he had instituted against P., the man with whom the wife was living. Subsequent to the conclusion of the agreement, the Supreme Court granted the wife sole custody of two of her four children on the basis of the wife's evidence that she had terminated her adulterous relationship and ordered that neither party should take three of the children outside the jurisdiction without the other's consent. Shortly after the conclusion of these proceedings the wife left Ireland taking three of the children with her, one of whom had been placed in the husband's custody, and went to live with P. in London. Some years later two of the children returned to Ireland to reside with the father and one child, a son, continued to reside with his mother. Around the time of her departure the wife had received a sum of £50,000 under a family trust and while living in England had bought and sold property and engaged in different business ventures. She subsequently went to live in Texas in the United States of America, taking with her the one child that had continued to reside with her. Under the deed of separation the husband was bound to pay for his son's education up to the age of 22 years if he attended a university and the wife agreed to support him. Eleven years after the Supreme Court proceedings the wife instituted proceedings seeking maintenance for herself and her son.

McMahon J. stated:

> "The wife's adultery with P., the terms of the deed of separation and her conduct since the separation amount to an unequivocal repudiation by her of any relationship with the husband. Her flagrant breaches of the terms of the separation deed[26] and of the terms on which the Supreme Court awarded her custody . . . damaged the husband in his relationship with these (two of the) children. At the time the parties separated the wife became entitled to a large sum of money sufficient to make her financially independent for the remainder of her life. In these circumstances it would . . . clearly be unfair to the husband to revive the obligation to support his wife which was extinguished by her adultery."[27]

Although it is clear from the judgement that the husband was considerably wealthier than the wife, refusing the wife's application for maintenance for her own support the learned judge stated that:

> "In view of her nett asset position it does not appear to me that she is in need of support."

As for the husband's contractual obligation to pay his son's educational fees or his legal obligation to contribute to his maintenance, McMahon J. stated that whereas

> "The husband's liability to support (his son) is not affected by the wife's adultery . . . it was never contemplated that the husband should be liable for fees and maintenance at an American University . . . while he (the son) lives in the United States. I do not consider that . . . a contribution towards such expenses or to his maintenance is support which it is proper the husband should be liable for."[28]

26. Following her return to Ireland and while her husband was abroad, the wife removed a considerable quantity of furniture in two furniture removal vans from the husband's home. The police were alerted and prevented the wife from taking the furniture to England.

27. See pp. 7–8 of judgement. See further Family Law . . . Act, 1976, Sect. 5(3) and see p. 445 *post*. Contrary to what is implied by the learned judge in his judgement, adultery is not an absolute bar to the obtaining of maintenance.

28. See pp. 8–9 of judgement.

In essence, the wife's behaviour in this case can be regarded as having been such a fundamental breach of her contractual obligations as to extinguish her contractual rights. Moreover, as married parents remain the joint guardians of their children even when one parent has sole custody, the wife could not unilaterally determine the university and country in which the son should undertake third level education while a minor. As the wife excluded the husband from the decision-making process, it is submitted McMahon J. was correct in refusing to require the husband to contribute to his son's maintenance or discharge university fees.[28a]

A maintenance order made by a court pursuant to section 5 of the 1976 Act cannot by itself extinguish or vary an already existing contractual obligation to make maintenance payments. Thus, if a court orders a lesser sum to be paid by way of maintenance than that required by the agreement, the sum paid pursuant to the statutory order made will be in partial satisfaction of the contractual obligation. The fact that an agreement requires a husband to pay a larger sum than a court deems to be "proper" maintenance under the criteria laid down in the 1976 Act, does not affect a wife's contractual right to continue to receive the larger sum in the absence of a specific variation clause in the agreement expressly stating that any such court maintenance order made will automatically reduce the husband's contractual liability. If the court orders a greater sum to be paid than that stipulated in the agreement, the contractual payment, it has been held, will be regarded as being supplemented by payments made in pursuance of a maintenance order.

In *O'S. v. O'S.*[29] a separation agreement concluded in 1973 provided for the payment by the husband to the wife of £1,400 per year subject to an annual adjustment by reference to the cost of living index. It was an express term of the agreement that the payments should be reviewed only when the last of the children attained the age of 21 years. In 1980 the husband discontinued making the payments required by the agreement. The wife instituted maintenance proceedings under section 5 of the 1976 Act and Murphy J. rejected the husband's contention that the maintenance provisions of the agreement were invalidated by section 27 of the Family Law . . . Act, 1976.[30] He held that although the agreement could not exclude or limit the court's powers to make maintenance orders, the court had no power to set the agreement aside and the husband remained bound by it. The learned judge stated that in his view

---

28a. As the husband was held to have a complete defence to the wife's action, it appears that if the son had himself sought to require his father to pay his university fees under the separation deed in proceedings brought under Sect. 8 of the Married Women's Act, 1957, he would not have succeeded in doing so. Sect. 8 of the Married Women's Status Act, 1957, states:

> (1) "Where a contract (other than a contract to which Sect. 7 applies)* is expressed to be for the benefit of, or by its express terms purports to confer a benefit upon, a third person being the wife, husband or child of one of the contracting parties, it shall be enforceable by the third person in his or her own name as if he or she were a party to it."
> (2) "The right conferred on a third person by this section shall be subject to any defence that would have been valid between the parties to the contract."
> (3) "Unless the contract otherwise provides it may be rescinded by agreement of the contracting parties at any time before the third person has adopted it expressly or by conduct."
> (4) "This section applies whether the contract was made before or after the commencement of this Act.
> (5) "In this section, 'child' includes stepchild, illegitimate child, adopted person . . . and a person to whom the contracting party is *in loco parentis*."

*Sect. 7 applies to life assurance and endowment policies.
29. *Supra.*
30. Section 27 states: "An agreement shall be void in so far as it would have the effect of excluding or limiting the operation of any provision of the Act (other than section 21)."

"It would be unthinkable that the legislature was prepared to avoid a contractual obligation entered into for the benefit of a number of people who might have no corresponding or comparable right under the 1976 Act."[31]

In the context of the particular agreement the husband was required to continue to contribute towards the support of his children until the last child attained 21 years. As there were seven children of the marriage the obligation to pay maintenance for them clearly continued beyond the age of dependency as defined in the 1976 Act in relation to 6 of the children. Murphy J. also rejected the argument that the wife had, by invoking the 1976 Act, waived her contractual maintenance rights.[32]

The above case was concerned with an agreement concluded prior to 1976, but it is submitted that a similar approach would be adopted by the courts to maintenance provisions contained in a separation agreement concluded after the coming into force of the Family Law . . . Act, 1976.

The overall effect of the above decisions is that a spouse cannot be prevented by the terms of a separation agreement from seeking a court maintenance order for his or her own support or the support of dependent children or from seeking a larger sum or an additional sum of maintenance in excess of that provided for in an agreement. Moreover, a specific covenant not to bring maintenance proceedings will, of itself, act as no bar to a maintenance order being granted but is one of the matters that may be taken into account by the court, including other matters relating to the parties' personal and financial circumstances when deciding whether or not to make a maintenance order. Where a spouse is bound by an agreement to pay a specific sum of maintenance, the courts cannot vary the sum payable so as to reduce his contractual liability in the absence of a specific variation clause in the agreement stating that any future court maintenance order made is to have such effect, even if the sum he or she is bound to pay is in excess of the amount a court would regard as "proper" under the criteria laid down in the 1976 Act.[33]

Covenant not to sue for alimony and courts' jurisdiction to vary alimony clauses: The Family Law . . . Act, 1976, does not affect the jurisdiction of the High Court or the Circuit Court[33a] to make alimony orders. The question now arises as to whether a wife can bar herself in an agreement from applying for alimony if, at some later date she brings proceedings for a decree of divorce *a mensa et thoro*. Judicial pronouncements in the first half of this century held that a wife could be contractually bound by such a clause unless a state of things arose not contemplated by her when signing the agreement, i.e. unless she subsequently discovers her husband to be guilty of gross misconduct of a nature completely different from that known to her when entering into the agreement (e.g. incestuous adultery).[34]

---

31. See p. 8 of judgement.
32. See p. 9 of judgement.
33. If it is proved that the parties to an agreement were not at the time they entered into it *ad idem* as to the meaning or effect of a maintenance review or increase clause, the court will not enforce it — see *R.H. v. N.H., supra.*

33a. The Courts Act, 1981, Sect. 5 conferred jurisdiction on the Circuit Court to grant decrees of divorce *a mensa et thoro* and to make ancillary orders for alimony — see chaps. 8 and 14.

34. See *Morrall v. Morrall* (1881) 6 P.D. 98 (P.D.A.); *Gandy v. Gandy* (1882) 7 P.D., 77 (P.D.A.); on appeal, (1882) 7 P.D. 168 (C.A.); *Lett v. Lett, supra*; *Rose v. Rose* [1908] 2 I.R. 339 (K.B.D.); *Lewis v. Lewis* [1940] I.R. 42 at p. 50, also reported in (1939) 74 I.L.T.R. 170 (H.C.).

However, in 1929 in the English case of *Hyman v. Hyman*[35] Lord Atkin stated that

> "In my view no agreement between the spouses can prevent the court from considering the question whether in the circumstances of the particular case it shall think fit to order some reasonable payment to the wife . . . the wife's right to future maintenance is a matter of public concern which she cannot barter away."

It was pointed out that if a wife was prevented from seeking alimony the State might have to become responsible for her support.

In *Courtney v. Courtney,*[36] the facts of which are discussed further on, it was emphasised that there is nothing to prevent a spouse challenging a clause in an agreement on grounds of public policy. The question of whether a covenant by a wife not to seek alimony is contrary to public policy has never been determined by an Irish Court. It is submitted that the reasoning in *Hyman v. Hyman*, which was a case of divorce *a vinculo* is equally applicable to an award of alimony subsequent to a decree of divorce *a mensa et thoro.*[37] If, however, the courts hold a wife to be bound by a clause in an agreement not to sue for alimony, there is nothing to prevent her from seeking maintenance under the Family Law . . . Act, 1976.

If a separation agreement contains a provision whereby a support payment to be made by a husband to a wife is described as "alimony" instead of "maintenance" under the principles enunciated in *H.D. v. P.D.,*[38] the wife may always apply to the courts for a larger sum of money than that which she is receiving as "alimony" under the agreement by instituting maintenance proceedings under the Family Law . . . Act, 1976. It is submitted, however, that in the absence of a specific contractual provision empowering the courts to vary the husband's alimony liability, the courts have no power to reduce the sum payable by him and the law applicable is the same as that already discussed in the preceding section.

In the recent case of *M.C. v. J.C.*[39] Costello J. expressly reserved this point for determination at a later date when holding that in one specific instance an alimony agreement between spouses could, even in the absence of an express clause permitting review or variation, be varied so as to reduce the husband's financial liability.[40] In this case, an alimony agreement between a husband and a wife was recorded in the schedule to a court order granting the wife a decree of divorce *a mensa et thoro* on the ground of cruelty. Although the agreement contained no provision enabling the court to vary the payment, the husband applied to the court to reduce the sum he was obliged to pay under it. Rejecting the argument that the court had no power to vary the husband's contractual

---

35. [1929] A.C. 601 (H.L.). The law in England has since been affected by statute. See S.M. Cretney, *Principles of Family Law*, 4th ed. (Sweet & Maxwell, London 1984), pp. 896–904.

36. *Supra.* See p. 209 *post.*

37. See *Dempsey v. Dempsey* [1943] Ir. Jur. Rep. 47 (H.C.), in which Haugh J. did not disagree with a statement by counsel that "Permanent alimony for a judicially separated wife is and always has been inalienable". This case was, however, concerned with the question of whether a court having awarded alimony after granting a divorce *a mensa et thoro* could be prevented from making or varying the order for alimony at some future time by an agreement, assignment or release entered into by the spouses concerned, by which the wife deprived herself of the right to it. It was accepted that such an agreement only had binding force if made a rule of court. See further *M.C. v. J.C.* [1982] 2 I.L.R.M. 562 (H.C.).

38. *Supra.*

39. *Supra.*

40. See, *supra*, at p. 565.

obligation, Costello J. referred to the fact that if no agreement had been made, the court, pursuant to Order 70 of the Rules of the Superior Courts, would have been empowered to "allot" a sum payable by way of alimony and such allotment would have been subject to variation in the event of a change in either party's financial circumstances under the Rules of the Superior Courts.[41] He held that the agreement reached should be regarded as "an allotment of alimony" within the meaning of the Rules as not to so regard it "would place a very restrictive meaning on the Rule and impose an unjustified and unnecessary restriction on the court's power to review alimony payments."[42]

In the above case, the agreement reached was not made a rule of court under section 8 of the Family Law ... Act, 1976, but Costello J. was of the view that if it had been, there could have been no doubt as to the court's power to review.[43] As we shall see further on, this assumption by the learned judge is incorrect[44] and the authority of this decision must be open to question until such time as a similar issue arises for determination before the Supreme Court. No Supreme Court appeal arose in this case on this issue as in the subsequent variation hearing the court dismissed the husband's application to reduce his alimony payments having heard the financial evidence.[45]

Maintenance, Adultery, Remarriage and Dum Casta clauses: A clause may be included in an agreement terminating a spouse's obligation to maintain the other upon the latter committing adultery or ceasing to lead a "chaste" life. In the absence of such a clause, the courts have long held that no such term can be implied in an agreement so as to bring to an end a spouse's contractual right to receive maintenance.[46] The position was not changed by the family provisions in the 1937 Constitution and this was clearly stated in two cases in the 1940s.

In *Lewis v. Lewis*[47] a husband had covenanted under a separation deed to pay his wife a monthly sum for her maintenance. There was no clause making the continuance of its operation dependent on the wife's living single and chaste. The payment fell into arrears, but before the claim for arrears was heard the husband obtained a decree of divorce *a mensa et thoro* on the ground of his wife's adultery. On the hearing of the wife's claim, it was held by Hanna J. that, in the absence of a *dum casta* clause in the deed, she was entitled to recover arrears. As to whether it is contrary to public policy in this country to permit a wife, living an adulterous life, to recover under a deed, he went on:

41. See Rules of the Superior Courts (S.I. No. 15 of 1986) Order 70 r. 54:
"A wife who has obtained a final decree *a mensa et thoro* may apply to the court by motion for an allotment of permanent alimony provided that she shall 8 days at least before making such application give notice thereof to the husband or his solicitor."
Order 70 r. 55:
"A wife may at any time after alimony has been allotted to her, whether alimony pending suit or permanent alimony, apply by motion for an increase of the alimony allotted by reason of the increased faculties of the husband or by the reduction of her own faculties or a husband may apply by motion for a diminution of the alimony allotted by reason of reduced faculties or of the wife's increased faculties and the course of proceeding in such cases shall be the same as required by this order in respect of the original application for alimony and the allotment thereof so far as the same are applicable."
The case was determined under the preceding Rules (S.I. No. 72 of 1962). These provisions of Order 70 are the same in both.
42. *Supra* at p. 565.
43. *Ibid.*
44. See *J.D. v. B.D., supra*, discussed at p. 212 *post*. See also *Dempsey v. Dempsey, supra*, discussed in footnote 37 *ante*.
45. No written judgement was delivered following the subsequent hearing.
46. *Fearon v. Earl of Aylesford, supra.*
47. [1940] I.R. 42 (H.C.).

"To distinguish the public policy in Eire from that in England, reliance has been placed upon the provisions of Art. 41 of our present Constitution ... In my judgement the provisions of our Constitution do not help on the question of public policy in Ireland, which I have to decide, as regards a separation deed without a *dum casta* clause. I can find no public policy that I could legally rely upon as a guide upon this matter."[48]

In the similar case of *Ormsby v. Ormsby*[49] it was argued that a *dum castus* clause must be implied in every separation deed since it would be against Irish public policy as expressed in Art. 41 that a wife should have to support her husband while he maintained an adulterous household. This argument was rejected by the Supreme Court, Sullivan C.J. saying:

"Art. 41 of the Constitution has satisfied me as being the law of this country as it existed prior to the Constitution."[50]

If maintenance payments for the support of a spouse are to cease upon that spouse engaging in a sexual relationship with another person this must be clearly stated in the agreement. Modern agreements more usually state that maintenance will cease to be payable for the support of a spouse if that spouse and another "co-habit as husband and wife" for a continuous specified period or upon the spouse entitled to receive maintenance going through a ceremony of marriage with another "whether or not such ceremony creates a valid and recognisable marriage under Irish law." This latter provision is designed to deal with the position of the spouse who "remarries" after obtaining a decree of annulment from the Marriage Tribunals of the Roman Catholic Church or after obtaining a foreign decree of divorce that is not recognisable under Irish law.

If maintenance ceases to be payable to a spouse under the terms of a separation agreement, a spouse may still seek a maintenance order in proceedings issued under the Family Law ... Act, 1976. Moreover, a clause in an agreement terminating a spouse's maintenance in the above circumstances is usually expressly stated in the agreement not to affect the contractual obligation imposed on the paying spouse to continue to pay maintenance to the adulterous spouse for the support of dependent children that continue to remain in the custody of the adulterous spouse.

Covenant not to bring "Mensa et Thoro" proceedings for matrimonial misbehaviour prior to Deed: A covenant in a separation agreement not to bring *Mensa et thoro* proceedings against a spouse for behaviour prior to the execution of the agreement will be upheld by the court. In *Courtney v. Courtney*[51] a wife petitioned for a divorce *a mensa et thoro* from her husband on the ground of cruelty. Some time prior to the petition an agreement had been made by the parties whereby the wife returned her ring and a watch to the husband and he in turn gave her £150. Upon receiving the money she signed the following receipt: "Received from Mr. Michael Courtney the sum of one hundred and fifty pounds (£150), being in full discharge of all claims of every nature and kind by me against the said Michael Courtney".

The court held that the consideration from the wife was that if the husband agreed to the terms she would abstain from bringing proceedings for separation or for alimony. It was contended that if there was no express covenant not to

---

48. *Ibid.*, at pp. 51, 52.
49. (1945) 79 I.L.T.R. 97 (S.C.).
50. *Ibid.*, at p. 102.
51. *Supra.*

sue, no agreement not to sue was to be implied. To this Dodd J. stated:

> "If parties who are free to contract do in fact contract for the settlement of
> an action or for the abandonment of claims which might terminate in legal
> proceedings, can it be contended that the settlement having been entered
> into and completed by one party complying with it, the other party can
> keep the money and go on with the action?"

Parties to a binding contract

> "who agree so to settle a matrimonial controversy must be taken to contract
> that they will not go behind the settlement, and cannot be listened to saying
> that they did not make an express stipulation not to sue. The decision here
> must be kept within its legitimate limits, and is not to be taken to extend to
> contracts that are against the public policy."[52]

Covenant to obtain a decree of divorce a vinculo: A provision in an agreement whereby a husband and a wife agree to obtain a divorce *a vinculo* i.e. a
decree of dissolution of marriage, will not be enforced by the Irish courts as
being contrary to public policy. Moreover, such a provision contained in an
agreement may render the entire agreement unenforceable as the Irish courts will
not "give active assistance to facilitate in any way the effecting of a dissolution
of marriage."[53] In *Dalton v. Dalton*[54] O'Hanlon J. stated that:

> "Considerations of public policy require that the court shall not lend its
> support to an agreement providing for the obtaining of a divorce *a vinculo*
> by a husband and wife, and this may well be the position even if the parties
> are domiciled elsewhere than in Ireland ... or propose to take up such
> foreign domicile in the future."[55]

In this particular case the learned judge declined to make an agreement a rule
of court under section 8 of the Family Law ... Act, 1976, because of a provision
contained in it whereby the parties agreed to obtain a decree *a vinculo* and the
husband agreed not to contest any such proceedings issued by the wife. The
parties to the agreement were domiciled in Ireland. In a subsequent court
application, however, the agreement was made a rule of court after it had been
amended by the parties, by agreement, by the deletion of the offending clause.
Thus, if a clause in an agreement under which spouses agree to obtain a divorce
a vinculo is severable from the rest of the agreement, it may not affect the enforceability of the other provisions contained in it.

Clauses relating to property: The property provisions in a separation agreement vary according to the circumstances and wishes of the parties concerned.
Their content totally depends on the amount of property owned by the spouses
and the terms upon which agreement is reached. Thus, it may be agreed between
spouses that the family home be sold and the proceeds divided in agreed pro-
portions between them. Alternatively, it may be agreed that the home be transferred from one spouse to the other, or that a spouse be granted sole right of
residence in the home, the other spouse agreeing not to enter or approach the

---

52. See also *Rose v. Rose* (1883) 8 P.D. 98 (C.A.).
53. *Mayo-Perrott v. Mayo-Perrott* [1958] I.R. 336 (S.C.) at p. 360. See also *Cohane v. Cohane, supra.* See further *D.M. v. E.F.M.* (July, 1978) unreported (H.C.), *G. v. G.* [1984] I.R. 368 (H.C.), and *Sachs v. Standard Chartered Bank (Ireland) Ltd. & Sachs* (July, 1986) unreported (S.C.) − see p. 462 *post.*
54. *Supra.*
55. *Ibid.* at p. 419. For the law as to the Recognition of Foreign Decrees of Divorce A Vinculo, see Chap. 10.

home without the former's consent. If the family home is held in or transferred into the sole name of one spouse, the other spouse may give a general consent to the sale of the home at any future date for the purposes of the Family Home Protection Act, 1976, so as to obviate the necessity of the former spouse having to seek such a consent many years after the parties have separated prior to a sale taking place.

Agreement may also be reached as to which spouse is to discharge the mortgage repayments on the family home and to repay bank loans or other moneys owed by the parties. Provision may also be made for the manner in which the contents of the family home and other property is to be dealt with. If spouses jointly own a business, the agreement may specify the terms upon which it is to be wound up or the manner in which their interests are to be divided. Spouses may also renounce their succession rights under Part 9 of the Succession Act, 1965.[56] Finally, the parties to the agreement may exclude section 21 of the Family Law ... Act, 1976, from applying to any property purchased or money saved by one spouse out of any allowance payable to that spouse by the other under the provisions of any clause in the separation agreement.[57]

Medical Clause: Many separation agreements require the spouse who is obliged to pay maintenance to also discharge medical and dental expenses incurred by the dependent spouse and children of the family. For example, a husband may covenant to insure his wife and children with the Voluntary Health Insurance Board for in-patient private or semi private hospital treatment. Liability to insure the children would normally end when the obligation to pay maintenance for their support ceases under the agreement.

Indemnification Clause: It is usual for both the husband and the wife to indemnify each other from liability for all future debts incurred by either of them. Additionally, a deed may specifically provide that the sole financial obligations owed by each spouse to the other are those set down in the agreement. Such a clause will not prevent either seeking maintenance under the Family Law ... Act, 1976, at a future date.

Family Law ... Act, 1976, Section 8: Pursuant to the provisions of this section a spouse who has entered into a written agreement, including a separation agreement, after the commencement of the 1976 Act (the 6th of May 1976) may apply to either the Circuit or High Court to have the agreement made a rule of court provided the agreement includes either or both of the following provisions:

"(i) A provision whereby one spouse undertakes to make periodical maintenance payments for the benefit of the other spouse and/or any dependent children of the family;

(ii) A provision governing the rights and liabilities of the spouses towards one another in respect of the making or securing of payments (other than payments specified in (i) above) or the disposition or use of any property."

If the court is satisfied that the agreement is a fair and reasonable one which in all the circumstances adequately protects the interests of both spouses and

---

56. See p. 520.
57. See p. 516.

any dependent children of the family, it may by order make the agreement a rule of court.

The benefit of having an agreement made a rule of court is that it affords to the spouse receiving maintenance the right to have his or her maintenance payments paid through the District Court and the sum payable enforceable by way of an attachment of earnings order as if the payment was being made pursuant to a maintenance order made under the 1976 Act. By the ordinary Rules of the Circuit and High Courts the ruling of an agreement in this way also extends the remedy of contempt of court to either spouse who wishes to prevent the other spouse, who is a party to such agreement, from refusing or failing to comply with a provision contained in it. An agreement can be made a rule of court under this section even if no contentious matrimonial proceedings have been initiated between the parties prior to the signing of the agreement.

The maintenance clause in an agreement that is ruled under this provision is only deemed to be a maintenance order for the purpose of payment and enforcement and is not deemed to be a maintenance order for any other purpose.[58] Thus, if at a future date, the person receiving maintenance requires a sum larger than that provided in the agreement, maintenance proceedings have to be instituted. In the absence of an express provision in the agreement permitting the court to do so, it cannot vary the maintenance clause as if it were a maintenance order. Similarly, if a spouse is bound to pay a higher sum of maintenance than he can afford under the terms of a ruled agreement, in the absence of an express provision in the agreement the court cannot reduce the maintenance he is contractually bound to pay, although it may refuse to grant an attachment of earnings order for all or part of the sum, if the paying spouse satisfies the court that he has a reasonable excuse for failing to comply with his obligations.[59] It may, in similar circumstances, refuse to make a committal order for contempt of court.[59a] Even if no such orders are made, however, the paying spouse's liability for maintenance arrears continues to subsist and for as long as he fails to comply with the maintenance provisions contained in the agreement his financial debt will continue to accumulate and be enforceable under the ordinary laws of contract.

In *J.D. v. B.D.*[60] it was held that the High Court could not vary the terms of a maintenance agreement made a rule of court, under which a husband was bound to pay a specific weekly sum of maintenance which was to be annually increased in accordance with the cost of living, although the husband's evidence was accepted that he was financially incapable of complying with his contractual obligation. Carroll J. stated:

"This raises the question of whether a maintenance agreement which does

---

58. "An order making the separation agreement a rule of court (under Section 8 of the 1976 Act) is not a maintenance order except for the purpose of payments through the District Court Clerk and attachment of earnings." *per* Walsh J. in *H.D. v. P.D.*, *supra* at p. 8 of judgement. See also *J.D. v. B.D.*, *supra*, in which Carroll J. stated that as the 1976 Act precluded the maintenance provision in the separation agreement, made a rule of court under section 8, from being deemed a maintenance order for the purpose of section 6 of that Act "the court does not have power to vary it", see [1985] 5 I.L.R.M. at p. 690. See, however, *J.H. v. C.H.* (July, 1979) unreported (H.C.) in which Keane J. suggested that upon an agreement being made a rule of court under section 8 the defendant husband could apply to the court for a variation order if he considered the maintenance provisions in the agreement excessive. The judgement does not, however, fully reveal the contents of the settlement and it is possible that it contained a term permitting the husband to make such an application in such circumstances. If it did not do so, it is respectfully submitted that the learned judge was incorrect.

59. See Family Law . . . Act, 1976, Sect. 10(3). See *J.D. v. B.D.*, *supra*.

59a. See *J.D. v. B.D.*, *supra*.

60. *Supra*.

not contain a provision enabling application to be made to the court to vary it in the same way as if it were a maintenance order, is an order which is a fair and reasonable one . . . It is my opinion that unless there is such a provision for variation, the agreement is neither fair nor reasonable."[61]

It was clearly the learned judge's view that in future no agreement providing for periodical maintenance payments should be made a rule of court unless it contains a provision enabling the courts to vary the maintenance sum payable in circumstances similar to which court maintenance orders may be varied. Prior to the 6th of September 1984, when judgement in this case was delivered, many agreements had been made a rule of court under section 8 of the 1976 Act although not containing specific provisions to permit a variation of the sum of maintenance payable pursuant to such agreements. Whether the courts will continue to rule agreements in the future in the absence of such a clause remains to be seen. Nevertheless, on the basis of the judgement delivered in *O'S. v. O'S.*[62] it is clear that, whether or not a separation or maintenance agreement is made a rule of court, a spouse may under existing law continue to be contractually bound to pay maintenance at a rate higher than he can genuinely afford and be unable to legally extricate himself from such obligation, unless the agreement concluded expressly provides a mechanism whereby the maintenance clause can be varied.

The District Court has no power to make an agreement a rule of court under section 8 and, as we have already seen in *Dalton v. Dalton*,[63] the High Court has held that in order for an agreement to be ruled under this section, it must not only comply with the criteria laid down in the section but must also contain nothing that is contrary to public policy.

DISCHARGE OF SEPARATION AGREEMENT

An agreement may be discharged by the subsequent agreement of the parties, or in accordance with a term in the original agreement.[64] Alternatively there may be a repudiation of the agreement by one party, giving the other the right to treat it as discharged if he so wishes. Whether there is such a repudiation is purely a question of fact. Continued failure on the part of a husband to pay maintenance might be regarded as such.[65] A fundamental breach of the contract may also entitle the other party to regard himself as discharged from its obligations.[66] Non-observance of one particular covenant, however, is unlikely to be sufficient to entitle the other party to regard himself as so discharged. The fact that one party does not observe one covenant in a contract will not entitle the other party to renege from obligations arising under another covenant, unless they are so phrased as to be interdependent.[67]

---

61. *Ibid.* at p. 690. The learned judge also stated "the question of whether the order making the agreement a rule of court should or can be now set aside has not been argued and must be left for another day." Having regard to the judgement of Murphy J. in *O'S. v. O'S., supra*, it appears that a court may not set aside such a provision in a separation agreement so as to extinguish the husband's contractual liability.

62. *Supra.*

63. *Supra.*

64. *Newsome v. Newsome* (1871) L.R. 2, P. & D. 306 (Ct. of D. & M. Causes). Here the wife promised to be bound only if her husband "remained true to her". It was held that his subsequently committing adultery terminated the agreement.

65. The innocent spouse is not bound to inform the spouse in breach that he has accepted the repudiation. It is sufficient if there is evidence that upon repudiation he treated the contract as a dead letter. See *Pardy v. Pardy* [1939] 3 All E.R. 779; [1939] P. 288 (C.A.).

66. *Besant v. Wood* (1879) 12 Ch.D. 605, (M.R.); *Morrall v. Morrall, supra, O.C. v. T.C., supra.*

67. *Fearon v. Aylesford, supra.*

A separation agreement entered into in order to determine the rights of the parties while living apart is put to an end by reconcilement and renewed cohabitation. However, covenants in an agreement may be phrased so as not to be dependent on the parties living apart and may still remain binding after cohabitation has resumed, unless the parties agree to discharge them. Thus, financial provisions or a settlement made in a deed for the benefit of a wife and children may still be effective. Everything, however, depends on the construction of the particular deed.[68]

Finally, covenants in a separation agreement can still be held binding after a decree of divorce *a mensa et thoro*[69] or *a vinculo*[70] or it seems after a decree of nullity[71] for a voidable but not a void marriage.[72] In the case of the latter the agreement is regarded as having no effect, being made as a consequence of mistake, the parties at no time being married.

REMEDIES FOR BREACH OF AN AGREEMENT

Ordinary damages are always obtainable for breach of an agreement, specific performance is available to force a spouse to carry out a covenant, for example, to pay maintenance or to transfer property to trustees to be used for the benefit of his wife,[73] and the remedy of injunction is available to restrain a party from breaching a non-molestation[74] or non-interference clause or a promise not to bring proceedings for past misconduct[75] or not to remove children from the jurisdiction. Further, if an agreement is made a rule of court, a contempt of court application can be made for breach of a provision in an agreement with the remedies of attachment and committal to prison available, and in the case of an agreement ruled under section 8 of the Family Law . . . Act, 1976, as we have already seen, periodical payments of maintenance are also enforceable by an order for attachment of earnings.

THE NEED FOR REFORM

It is submitted that when marital breakdown occurs and spouses agree to resolve their differences by the conclusion of a separation agreement, the law should seek to achieve four objectives. It should ensure that the welfare of any children of the spouses is properly protected, that proper provision in relation to support and housing is made for the dependent spouse and children, that in so far as is possible the necessity for future litigation between the spouses is obviated and seek to encourage spouses to reorganise their lives and plan for the future with a degree of security and certainty. In order to achieve the latter three objectives some spouses wish to conclude 'once and for all' financial settlements, by which, more usually, the husband is to pay a lump sum to the wife and/or transfer property owned by him into the wife's sole name, in consideration for

68. *Negus v. Forster* (1882) 46 L.T. 675 (C.A.); *Ruffles v. Alston* (1875) L.R. 19, Eq. 539 (V.-C.M.); *Nicol v. Nicol* (1886) 31 Ch. D. 524 (C.A.). See Article entitled "Agreements for Separation followed by Re-cohabitation", (1886) 20 I.L.T. & S.J. 295–6.

69. *Gandy v. Gandy, supra.*

70. *May v. May* [1929] 2 K.B. 386 (C.A.); *Charlesworth v. Holt* (1873) L.R. 9 Exch. 38. See Article "Dissolution of Marriage – Effect on Separation Agreements", (1941) 75 I.L.T. & S.J. 289–90; 295–97.

71. *Adams v. Adams* [1941] 1 K.B. 536 (C.A.); *Fowke v. Fowke* [1938] 2 All E.R. 638; [1938] Ch. 774 (Ch. Div.).

72. *Galloway v. Galloway, supra.*

73. *Lurie v. Lurie* [1938] 3 All E.R. 156; 159 L.T. 249; (Ch. Div.).

74. *Sanders v. Rodway* (1852) 16 Beav. 207; 20 L.T.O.S. 122; 51 E.R. 757 (Rolls Ct.).

75. *Lett v. Lett, supra.*

the wife waiving her rights to future maintenance. However, as a result of the Supreme Court's decision in *H.D. v. P.D.* estranged spouses are no longer able to conclude permanent and binding settlements of this nature as there is no existing legal mechanism to protect the husband from future claims for maintenance by the wife.

To a husband this type of settlement is advantageous only if it terminates what is otherwise an open-ended legal obligation to support his wife and if it enables him to plan his future with a degree of financial certainty. To a wife such a settlement is advantageous if she is to receive a sum of money sufficiently large or property sufficiently valuable as to enable her to become financially independent of her husband and free of the problems that can be experienced by a wife in receipt of weekly maintenance payments, such as the fear that if the husband leaves the jurisdiction she may be left with no means of support other than social welfare payments.

It is submitted that amending legislation should provide that if a permanent financial settlement is concluded between spouses, under the terms of which a lump sum payment is to be made and/or property is to be transferred to the dependent spouse and (a) both spouses extinguish their rights to future maintenance, and (b) such settlement is approved by either the Circuit or the High Court[76] as properly protecting the interests of all the parties to it and their dependent children, and (c) is made a rule of court, such settlement is binding on the parties to it and is an absolute bar on either party applying for maintenance for his or her support at any future date. It is further submitted, however, that in order to properly fulfil the first objective, this provision should only apply to spouses' maintenance and should not extend to children's maintenance. The overriding public interest in protecting the welfare of children requires that the courts be in a position to vary all orders and agreements made in relation to children when circumstances change and financial orders and agreements relating to children should be open to such variation.

As we have seen, a dependent spouse in receipt of maintenance pursuant to provisions contained in a separation agreement may successfully apply to the courts for a maintenance order requiring that a larger sum of maintenance be paid than that provided for in the agreement, even if the agreement expressly prohibits the making of such application or contains no provision permitting such an application to be made. By contrast, the spouse obliged to pay maintenance pursuant to provisions contained in a separation agreement cannot reduce the amount of maintenance payable under such agreement or have his maintenance liability reduced by the making of a court maintenance order, unless the agreement expressly contains provision permitting such reduction. In practice, this has led to the result that many wives in receipt of inadequate sums of maintenance under deeds of separation have been able to obtain court maintenance orders to require husbands who can afford to do so to increase the maintenance payable to them, whereas husbands obliged to pay sums of maintenance in excess of amounts they can truly afford have been unable to extricate themselves from maintenance commitments beyond their financial resources.

The need to ensure, in so far as is possible, that both spouses of a broken marriage are left in a position whereby each can maintain a reasonable standard of living was recently stated by the Supreme Court.[77] It is submitted that any

---

76. Or a family court, upon such court being established.
77. See *R.H. v. N.H.* (October, 1985) unreported (S.C.) in particular, judgement of Finlay C.J. at pp. 7–8.

amending legislation enacted should expressly extend power to either party to
a separation or maintenance agreement to apply to the courts to review and vary
any financial arrangements contained in such agreement in so far as such arrangements make provision for annual, monthly, weekly or other forms of periodical
payment for the support of a dependent spouse and/or children. The jurisdiction
to review should extend to all agreements whether made a rule of court or not,
the only exception being in respect of agreements providing for a lump sum payment by way of a "once and for all" financial settlement approved by and made
a rule of the High Court as proposed above. Upon a review application being
made, in determining whether to vary financial arrangements contained in an
agreement, the courts should be bound to apply essentially the same financial criteria as are applicable by the courts in determining whether to vary a court maintenance order made under the Family Law . . . Act, 1976, and for this purpose such
financial provision should be treated as if made pursuant to a maintenance order.
This would have the effect of requiring the party seeking a variation order to
establish that (a) a change in circumstances had occurred since the conclusion of
the agreement and/or (b) that new relevant information had become available
to such party which was not available at the date when the agreement was
entered into, before the financial provisions contained in any agreement could
be altered.[78] Such a requirement would effectively preserve the integrity of the
original agreement and protect both spouses from the bringing of precipitate
court proceedings so as to upset financial arrangements entered into in good
faith as part of an overall family settlement.

---

78. See the Family Law . . . Act, 1976, Sect. 6(1)(b) by which the court may "vary a
maintenance order at any time, on the application of either party, if it thinks it proper to
do so having regard to any circumstances not existing when the order was made or . . . to
any evidence not available to that party when the maintenance order was made". See further
p. 447 *post*.

CHAPTER 8

DIVORCE A MENSA ET THORO[1]
(Judicial Separation)

Under section 13 of the Matrimonial Causes ... Act, 1870, the High Court inherited the jurisdiction of the Ecclesiastical Courts to grant decrees of divorce *a mensa et thoro*.[2] The Courts Act, 1981, conferred a concurrent jurisdiction on the Circuit Court to hear and determine such proceedings.[3]

The remedy is in a sense misleadingly named in that it does not amount to a divorce in the popular meaning of the term but only to a judicial separation of the spouses. In order to distinguish it from a divorce *a vinculo matrimonii* which the Irish courts have no power to grant, and for convenience sake, this remedy will, in the pages that follow, be occasionally referred to as a decree of judicial separation. As in the case of other jurisdiction inherited from the Ecclesiastical Courts, the court has to exercise its jurisdiction to grant such a decree on principles and rules "which shall be as nearly as may be conformable to the principles and rules on which the Ecclesiastical Courts acted". Thus, its powers to give relief are as limited as the powers possessed and exercised by the Ecclesiastical Courts in the first half of the 19th century.

The only grounds for which relief can be granted are cruelty, adultery or unnatural practices.[4] The latter ground arises so rarely that it is not discussed further in the text. The authorities for its existence are in footnote 4 below.

Effect of Decree

A decree of divorce *a mensa et thoro* does not dissolve a marriage so as to permit the parties to remarry. It merely relieves a spouse from the duty of cohabiting with the other. It can be said that it suspends the cohabitation obligation of marriage. The obligation is not terminated for all time as, if at some future date a reconciliation takes place and the parties again wish to cohabit, the decree may be discharged and the obligation thus revived.

---

1. For the procuedure to be followed to bring such proceedings, see R.S.C. Order 70 (S.I. No. 15 of 1986).
2. *A mensa et thoro* – latin for "from bed and board".
3. The Courts Act, 1981, Sect. 5.
4. See the Law Reform Commission: *Report on Divorce a Mensa et Thoro and Related Matters* (Report No. 8, December 1983), pp. 12–14.; Shelford's *Law of Marriage* (1841), p. 364. See also Kisby, *The Law and Practice of the Court on Matrimonial Causes and Matters* (Dublin 1871), p.5. This ground has been relied on in very few cases. See *Bromley v. Bromley,* (2) Burns Ecc. Law 499 n; 2 Add 158 n. In this case a woman founded her claim and was granted a divorce *a mensa et thoro* on the ground that her husband had been found guilty of assaulting another with intent to commit an unnatural act with him for which he was sentenced to two years imprisonment.
See also *Mogg v. Mogg* (1824), 2 Add 292; 162 E.R. 301 (Arches Ct.). The wife sought a decree on the grounds of cruelty and unnatural practices. The evidence for the latter ground was that her husband had been convicted of assaulting another with the intent of engaging in homosexual conduct.

It is intended first to examine the grounds upon which a decree can be obtained, the various bars to the granting of a decree and the ancillary relief available. We shall then discuss the need to reform this area of the law.

ADULTERY

Adultery may be defined as voluntary sexual intercourse between two persons of whom one or both are married but not to each other. In a suit for divorce *a mensa et thoro* on this ground, the only parties to the proceedings are the two spouses. The person with whom a spouse is alleged to have committed adultery is never a party but will usually be called as a witness.

Nature of the Act

For the commission of adultery it is not necessary for the complete act of sexual intercourse to have taken place, but there must have been at least some penetration of the female by the male organ.[5] Sexual play falling short of penetration does not constitute adultery.

In order to be guilty of adultery a person must have consented to sexual intercourse. Thus, the rape of a wife does not constitute adultery on her part.[6] Moreover, a spouse who is mentally ill may be regarded as incapable of giving the requisite consent.[7] Rarely will there be direct evidence of the fact of adultery.[8] The fact that adultery has occurred may be inferred from the behaviour of the alleged adulterous spouse and the surrounding circumstances.[9]

A confession by the adulterous spouse has been held not to be sufficient evidence by itself. It must be corroborated by other testimony or by the evidence of the surrounding circumstances in order to prevent a decree being granted as the result of collusion.[10]

Standard of Proof

In *J.M.H. v. J.P.H.*[11] when granting a decree of divorce *a mensa et thoro* upon proof of the husband's adultery, Ellis J. stated:

> "On a charge of adultery for a petitioner to succeed it is not necessary for her to prove actual sexual intercourse or adultery by the alleged offender. This fact is inferred from circumstances which lead to it by fair inference as a necessary conclusion, when adultery will be presumed, or taking all the evidence into account, the circumstances are sufficient to lead the guarded discretion of a reasonable man (to the conclusion) that adultery took place."[12]

---

5. *Dennis v. Dennis (Spillet cited)* [1955] P. 153; [1955] 2 All E.R. 51 (C.A.); *Sapsford v. Sapsford and Furtado* [1954] P. 394; [1954] 2 All E.R. 373 (Assize).

6. *Redpath v. Redpath and Milligan* [1950] 1 All E.R. 600 (C.A.), where it was said that once the act of intercourse is established, the burden is on the wife to show that the act was forced against her will.

7. *Long v. Long and Johnson* (1890) 15 P.D. 218 (P.D.A.); *Yarrow v. Yarrow* [1892] P. 92 (P.D.A.); *Hanbury v. Hanbury* [1892] 8 T.L.R. 559 (C.A.).

8. *Loveden v. Loveden* (1810) 2 Hag. Con. 1; 161 E.R. 648 (Consistory Ct.); *Allen v. Allen and Bell* [1894] P. 248 (C.A.); *Grant v. Grant* (1839) 2 Curt. 16; 163 E.R. 322 (Arches Ct.).

9. *J.M.H. v. J.P.H.* (January 1983) unreported (H.C.); *Loveden v. Loveden, supra*; *Chambers v. Chambers* (1876) 1 Hag. Con. 440; 161 E.R. 610 (Consistory Ct.).

10. *Burgess v. Burgess* (1817) 2 Hag. Con. 222; 161 E.R. 723 (Consistory Ct.); *Noverre v. Noverre* (1846) 1 Rob. Ecc. 428; 161 E.R. 1090 (Eccles. Ct.); *Owen v. Owen* (1831) 4 Hagg. Ecc. 259; 162 E.R. 1441 (Consistory Ct.). See also *Robinson v. Robinson & Lane* (1859) 1 Sw. & Tr. 362; 164 E.R. 767 (Consistory Ct.), and the comments thereon in Kisby, *Matrimonial Causes and Matters*, pp. 10—11.

11. *Supra.*

12. *Supra*, see p. 73 of judgement. See also p. 91 of judgement. See also *Loveden v. Loveden*, 161 E.R. at p. 648.

In this case the learned judge held that "adultery is presumed" if it is proved that a married man "goes to and spends the night with a woman in a brothel" or "if he spends the night with a woman other than his wife in a hotel bedroom, particularly if booked in advance or in such a way as to make it appear as if they are husband and wife."[13] Upon such presumption of adultery arising it was held that "the onus of proving no adultery then shifts to the respondent".[14] In the same case, Ellis J. held that when adultery is alleged to have taken place in a private residence "the onus of proving adultery to have occurred lies on the petitioner unaided by such presumption."[15]

In a number of cases determined before *J.M.H. v. J.P.H.* it was said that the standard of proof required to establish the fact of adultery is more stringent than that required of a plaintiff in other civil actions which may be determined on a mere balance of probability, but less stringent than the standard of proof "beyond reasonable doubt" which is required in criminal cases.[16]

It is submitted that the standard of proof should be the same as that required in all civil cases, i.e. simply the balance of probability. This is the standard required for proof of cruelty, when alleged as a ground for a decree.

The matter is, however, complicated by the common law rule that the presumption of legitimacy can only be rebutted by evidence putting the matter beyond reasonable doubt.[17] Thus, if the standard of proof for adultery is less, a court could find itself in a position whereby, arising from identical evidence, it would regard adultery as proved, but a child conceived around the time when the adultery was committed to be legitimate. This is not, however, as incongruous as it may at first appear. Proof of a wife's adultery does not imply that a child conceived by her, close to the time when the adulterous act was committed, is of necessity illegitimate. It is perfectly possible for a woman to have sexual relations with her husband while also having an affair with another man. In such circumstances although she may be guilty of adultery, it is also possible for her child to be the legitimate offspring of her marriage.[18] Finally, it should be noted in this context that the recently published Status of Children Bill, 1986, Sect. 48 specifies that the standard of proof required to rebut the presumption of legitimacy in civil proceedings shall be "the balance of probabilities". Before this becomes law the Bill must be enacted by the Oireachtas.

CRUELTY

Cruelty on the part of either spouse is a ground for a decree *a mensa et thoro*. What constitutes cruelty depends on the facts of each individual case. Conduct which may plainly amount to cruelty in one case may not do so in another. Much depends on the nature of the conduct, the attitude of the spouses and their physical and mental weaknesses.[19] Cruelty cannot be measured by a fixed

13. See p. 73 of judgement.
14. *Ibid.*
15. See p. 93 of judgement.
16. *Lyons v. Lyons* [1950] N.I. 181 (K.B.D.); see also *Ginesi v. Ginesi* [1948] P. 179, [1948] 1 All E.R. 373 (C.A.); *Blyth v. Blyth and Pugh* [1966] A.C. 643, [1966] 1 All E.R. 524 (H.L.); *Bastable v. Bastable and Sanders* [1968] 3 All E.R. 701 (C.A.).
17. See Chapter 11; see also *Morris v. Davies* (1837) 5 Cl. & Fin. 163; 7 E.R. 365 (H.L.); *Bosvile v. A.-G.* (1887) 12 P.D. 177 (D.C.); *Preston-Jones v. Preston-Jones* [1951] A.C. 391; [1951] 1 All E.R. 124 (H.L.); *Bastable v. Bastable, supra*; *F. v. F.* [1968] 1 All E.R. 242; [1968] P. 506 (P.D.A.).
18. See (1949) 65 L.Q.R. 220, "Standard of Proof of Adultery", by J.A. Coutts.
19. *Gollins v. Gollins* [1964] A.C. 644; [1963] 2 All E.R. 966 (H.L.).

invariable standard. It is relative to age, to strength, to health and to capacity of endurance upon the part of the sufferer.[20]

Nature of the Conduct

The courts have consistently refused to lay down a comprehensive definition of cruelty. However, it is established that no conduct amounts to legal cruelty unless it causes injury to life, limb or health, bodily or mental, or a reasonable apprehension of such.[21]

It has been frequently stated that it is not necessary to wait until a person's health is impaired for a decree to be granted.[22] It is sufficient if the conduct is such as to give rise to a reasonable apprehension of personal injury.[23] Whilst the main question to be determined is whether X's conduct in fact gave rise to Y fearing such injury (the test thus being subjective) it has been said that "it must not be an apprehension arising merely from an exquisite and diseased sensibility of mind".[24] Thus, if Y's fear of X has arisen as a result of abnormal hyper-sensitivity a decree may be refused.[25]

The character of the conduct must be "grave and weighty"[26] before a decree will be granted. In the face of such conduct the court grants a decree on the basis of it being impossible for the unoffending spouse to carry out her (his) marital duties in "a state of dread".[27]

In 1966, in *D. v. D.*[28] Butler J. emphasised the serious nature of the conduct required to constitute cruelty. He stated that:

> "The courts have never allowed a divorce on the grounds that a party has repented of his bargain and found life with his partner unpleasant or even intolerable. The conduct complained of in its effect on the petitioning spouse must have been such as to render the continued performance of the obligations of marriage impossible. In so far as the grounds relied on are cruelty this must be of such a nature as to have caused actual bodily harm

20. *Russell v. Russell* [1897] A.C. 395 (H.L.,); *D'Aguilar v. D'Aguilar* (1794) 1 Hagg. Ecc. 733, 162 E.R. 748; *Evans v. Evans* (1790) 1 Hag. Con. 35; 161 E.R. 466 (Consistory Ct.); *Westmeath (Earl of) v. Westmeath (Countess of)* (1827), 2 Hagg. Ecc. Supp. 1, 148; 162 E.R. 992, 1043 (Consistory Ct.); *Milford v. Milford* (1866) L.R. 1 P. & D. 295 (P. & D.).

21. *Evans v. Evans, supra*; *M'Keever v. M'Keever* (1876) I.R. 11 Eq. (Ct. for Matr. Causes); *Russell v. Russell, supra*; *Gollins v. Gollins, supra*; *Jamieson v. Jamieson* [1952] A.C. 525; [1952] 1 All E.R. 875 (H.L.), (Sc.); see also *Ward v. Ward* [1948] N.I. 60 (K.B.D.); *Bradley v. Bradley* (11th December 1970), *Irish Times*, in which the address of Murnaghan J. to the jury is reported.

22. See for example the old Irish case of *Carpenter v. Carpenter* (1827), Milw. Rep. 159, heard in the Consistory Court of Dublin.

23. See e.g. *Evans v. Evans, supra*; *Kirkman v. Kirkman* (1807) 1 Hag. Con. 409; 161 E.R. 598 (Consistory Ct.).

24. *Evans v. Evans, supra*, 161 E.R. 466 at p. 468, *per* William Scott.

25. *Jamieson v. Jamieson, supra*. See further *McA. v. McA.* [1981] 1 I.L.R.M. 361 (H.C.) at pp. 363–364 where Costello J. in holding the husband guilty of mental cruelty stated "It is true that before marriage the plaintiff (wife) whilst attending university had to seek psychiatric help due to the strain of her final year's examination, but I am satisfied that although she is a person who perhaps suffers anxiety more easily than others and although she may be more prone to depression than others she is by no means a neurotic person."

26. *Evans v. Evans, supra per* Sir William Scott at p. 467; *Russell v. Russell, supra*.

27. *Milford v. Milford, supra per* Lord Penzance at p. 299. See also *Evans v. Evans, supra*, where Sir William Scott (later Lord Stowell) stated at p. 467, "The causes must be grave and weighty, and such as to shew an absolute impossibility that the duties of the married life can be discharged. In a state of personal danger no duties can be discharged; for the duty of self-preservation must take place before the duties of marriage which are secondary both in commencement and obligation . . .".

28. (December, 1966) unreported (H.C.).

or its reasonable and probable apprehension or, if short of that, must have excited such 'feelings of horror and even loathing' as is said by the court of appeal in *Russell v. Russell*[29] ... to show the absolute impossibility that the duties of married life could be discharged."[30]

Physical Violence: Where physical violence is involved there is generally little difficulty in proving injury or a reasonable apprehension of injury to a person's health so as to be entitled to obtain a decree of judicial separation. There does not have to be proof of one individual act of cruelty. Proof of an aggregate of acts, each of which individually may be insufficient to obtain relief, may when taken together be sufficient.[31] Thus, in *Murphy v. Murphy*[32] a wife obtained a decree against her husband alleging misconduct by him towards her which included physical assault, threatening and abusive language, speaking offensively to her in the presence of their children, locking her out of the home at night, ordering her out of the house, throwing water over her, refusing to allow her to handle money, objecting to her friends and being mainly responsible for quarrels that occurred.

If the violence alleged is trivial or was perpetrated in self defence as the result of provocation, it may be excusable.[33] However, provocation will only afford a defence if it bears a direct relation to the subsequent violence.[34] The violence of a wife will only justify such force by the husband as is necessary to restrain her. In *Holden v. Holden*, Sir W. Scott said:[35]

"It is not necessary that the conduct of the wife should be entirely without blame. For the reason which would justify the imputation of blame to the wife will not justify the ferocity of the husband ... If the passions of the husband are so much out of his own control, as that it is inconsistent with the personal safety of the wife to continue in his society, it is immaterial from what provocation such violence originated."

Mental Cruelty: Where there is no allegation of physical violence or of a reasonable apprehension of such violence, the courts, historically, were reluctant to grant decrees of judicial separation and formerly adopted a very restrictive approach. Thus, in the 19th century case of *Evans v. Evans*[36] it was said that

"What merely wounds the mental feelings is in few cases to be admitted,

---

29. [1895] P. 315.
30. See pp. 6–7 of judgement. See also *Murphy v. Murphy* [1962–63] Ir. Jur. Rep. 77 (H.C.) at p. 81 where Davitt P. states that "Eventually a stage was reached when common life became impossible." In *McA. v. McA., supra* at p. 364 Costello J. referred to the husband's behaviour as having "adverse effects on the wife's health" which "have been serious and could very easily become more serious"; *G.L. v. M.L.* (December, 1982) unreported (H.C.) Murphy J. stated that the husband's behaviour had a "deleterious effect" on the wife and "if continued, must necessarily have an even more serious consequence" (see p. 29 of judgement).
31. See *G.L. v. M.L., supra*; *Murphy v. Murphy, supra*; *M'Keever v. M'Keever* (1876) I.R. 11 Eq. 26 (Ct. for Matr. Causes); *D'Arcy v. D'Arcy* (1887) 19 L.R. Ir. 369 (Ct. for Matr. Causes); *Cochrane v. Cochrane* (1910) 27 T.L.R. 107 (P.D.A.).
32. *Supra.*
33. *Waring v. Waring* (1813) 2 Hag. Con. 153; 161 E.R. 699; 2 Phill. Ecc. 132; 161 E.R. 1098 (Consistory Ct.).
34. In *O'Reardon v. O'Reardon* (February, 1975) unreported (H.C.), in his direction to the jury Finlay P. stated "In order for cruelty to be justified there must be a reasonable relationship between the cruelty and the provocation ... you have to relate the provocation to the extent of the cruelty".
35. (1810) 1 Hag. Con. 453; 161 E.R. 614 at p. 616 (Consistory Ct.); see also *Stick v. Stick* [1967] 1 All E.R. 323 (Assize).
36. *Supra.*

while unaccompanied with bodily injury either actual or menaced. Mere austerity of temper, petulance of manners, rudeness of language, a want of civil attention and accommodation, even occasional sallies of passion if they do not threaten bodily harm do not amount to legal cruelty."[37]

However, acts which one hundred years ago would not have been regarded as causing injury or reasonable apprehension of injury would today, with greater medical understanding of mental ill health and its causes, be more readily accepted as having such an effect.

In *McA. v. McA.*[38] Costello J., asserting that "it is clear that in the Ecclesiastical Courts a decree could be granted on the ground of the cruelty of the respondent even in the absence of proof of physical violence," stated that the test to be applied in determining whether conduct constituted cruelty was whether the conduct alleged "renders the co-habitation unsafe or . . . makes it likely that co-habitation will be attended by injury to the person or health of the party."[39]

In this case it was alleged that the husband had been guilty of mental cruelty which had injured the wife's health. The evidence established that for a considerable period of time the husband had refused to communicate with his wife except through their three year old daughter or by means of notes; that he had "deliberately withdrawn himself emotionally from her"[40] seeking "protection from the strain in the family home in the practise of transcendental meditation";[41] that there had been no sexual intercourse between the couple for over three years, the husband no longer sleeping with his wife and that the husband had refused to co-operate with her in trying to find a solution to their marital difficulties. In addition there was medical evidence that the wife had been on antidepressant medication for over two and a half years and suffered from anxiety and depression as a result of the husband's behaviour. Costello J. stated that he was satisfied that if the couple continued to reside together, the wife could develop "a chronic neurotic depression"[42] and holding that "the major blame for what happened to this marriage must lie on the conduct of the defendant"[43] (husband) granted the wife's application for a decree of judicial separation.[44]

Standard of Proof: Cruelty must be proved on the balance of probabilities by the person alleging it. It is a question of whose version of the facts is "the more probable".[45] Thus, the standard required is less than that required for

37. 161 E.R. 466 at p. 467, *per* Sir William Scott. See also *Harris v. Harris* (1813) 2 Hag. Con. 148; 161 E.R. 697 (Consistory Ct.); 2 Phill. Ecc. 111; 161 E.R. 1093 (Consistory Ct.); *Le Brocq v. Le Brocq* [1964] 3 All E.R. 464 (C.A.).
38. [1981] 1 I.L.R.M. 361 (H.C.).
39. *Ibid.*, at p. 362.
40. *Ibid.*, at p. 363.
41. *Ibid.*
42. *Ibid.*, at p. 364.
43. *Ibid.*, at p. 363.
44. In the earlier case of *D. v. D.* (December, 1966) unreported (H.C.) Butler J. declined to grant a decree where it was alleged that the husband behaved in a way similar to the behaviour of the husband in *McA. v. McA., supra*. In *D. v. D.*, however, there was no evidence that the husband's behaviour posed a threat to the wife's health in the same manner as in *McA. v. McA*. The evidence was in fact to the contrary, the trial judge referring to the wife as "cool and self possessed and able to look after her own interests . . .". In the later case of *G.L. v. M.L., supra*, in which there were also some allegations of physical assault (but which were said by Murphy J. to be insufficient of themselves to ground the granting of a decree) (see p. 9 of judgement) behaviour similar to that of the husband in *McA. v. McA*. was held to warrant the granting of a decree as the trial judge was satisfied that the husband's conduct would have serious consequences for the wife if continued. See p. 29 of judgement.
45. *O'Reardon v. O'Reardon, supra*.

adultery. It is not essential to show that the respondent intended to injure the petitioner or that his conduct "has been deliberate in the sense that it was consciously adopted by him."[46] It is sufficient if having regard to all the circumstances a person's conduct can fairly be called cruel. Proof of intention, however, may be an important element in a particular case, especially where mental cruelty is alleged.[47]

Conduct Constituting Cruelty

A wide variety of different types of conduct apart from the application of physical violence by one spouse against the other has been held to constitute cruelty. These include nagging,[48] threats,[49] abuse,[50] spitting on a spouse,[51] wilful communication of venereal disease,[52] uncontrollable fits of drunkenness,[53] refusal of sexual intercourse[54] and the use of contraceptives or the practice of coitus interruptus against the other's wishes.[55] Desertion by itself, however, is not cruelty[56] and does not afford a ground for granting a decree. Moreover, cruelty to children may be regarded as cruelty to the other spouse. Thus, cruelty by a husband to his children in the presence of his wife (the children's mother) has been held sufficient ground for a decree.[57]

No conduct or act carries with it an inherent quality of cruelty. The essential question is "whether this conduct by this man to this woman or *vice versa* is cruelty". The answer to this question depends on the particular facts of the case and the temperament and character of the spouses concerned.

BARS TO RELIEF

Condonation

It is a complete defence to a charge of cruelty or adultery that the petitioner

---

46. *McA. v. McA., supra* at p. 363; see also *G.L. v. M.L., supra*, at p. 26 of judgement.

47. *McA. v. McA., supra*; *G.L. v. M.L., supra*. See also *Gollins v. Gollins, supra*; *Williams v. Williams* [1964] A.C. 698 (H.L.); *Jamieson v. Jamieson, supra*; in *Holden v. Holden* (1810) 1 Hag. Con. 453; 161 E.R. 614 (Consistory Ct.), *per* Sir W. Scott at p. 616, "It is not necessary . . . to inquire from what motive such treatment proceeds, it may be from turbulent passion, or sometimes from causes which are not inconsistent with affection . . .".

48. *Atkins v. Atkins* [1942] 2 All E.R. 637 (P.D.A.).

49. *Carpenter v. Carpenter, supra*; *Bostock v. Bostock* (1858) 1 Sw. & Tr. 221; 164 E.R. 701 (Ct. for Div. & Matr. Causes).

50. *Harris v. Harris, supra*; *Kelly v. Kelly* (1869) L.R. 2 P. & D. 31 and, on appeal, (1870) L.R. 2 P. & D. 59 (Ct. for Div. & Matr. Causes).

51. *Saunders v. Saunders* (1847) 1 Rob. Ecc. 549; 163 E.R. 1131 (Consistory Ct.); *O'Reardon v. O'Reardon, supra*.

52. *Brown v. Brown* (1865) L.R. 1 P. & D. 46 (Ct. for Div. & Matr. Causes); *Durant v. Durant* (1825), *supra*; *Browning v. Browning* [1911] P. 161; 104 L.T. 750 (P.D.A.).

53. *Power v. Power* (1865) 4 Sw. & Tr. 45 and 173; 164 E.R. 1483 (Ct. for Div. & Matr. Causes); *Baker v. Baker* [1955] 1 W.L.R. 1011 (Assize).

54. *Sheldon v. Sheldon* [1966] P. 62; [1966] 2 All E.R. 257 (C.A.); *Slon v. Slon* [1969] P. 122; [1969] 1 All E.R. 759 (C.A.).

55. *Knott v. Knott* [1955] P. 249; [1955] 2 All E.R. 305 (Assize), *Forbes v. Forbes* [1956] P. 16; [1955] 2 All E.R. 311 (P.D.A.).

56. *Evans v. Evans, supra*, at p. 496.

57. *Suggate v. Suggate* [1859] 1 Sw. & Tr. 489, 492, 497; 164 E.R. 827, 828, 830 (Ct. for Div. & Matr. Causes); *Wright v. Wright* [1960] P. 85; [1960] All E.R. 678 (C.A.).

It has been suggested that cruelty by a mother to her child cannot ground a petition by the father. "It may well be that violence practised on a child in its mother's presence, would be injurious to the health of a woman, gifted as most women are, with tender sensibility when their offspring suffers, but men are supposed to be made of sterner stuff;". *Manning v. Manning* (1873) I.R. 7 Eq. 520 (Matr. Causes). It is submitted that the question of the effect of such behaviour on the father and whether it is such as to amount to legal cruelty must depend on the facts of the particular case. It is unlikely that a court would today refuse to regard violence practised on a child by its mother, in the father's presence as cruelty to the father.

has condoned the matrimonial offence of the respondent. Condonation is effected by the voluntary forgiveness and reinstatement of the erring party to the marriage by the wronged spouse with knowledge of the offence of the former.[58] In the case of cruelty the question of the petitioner's knowledge of the acts of cruelty will hardly arise. In the case of adultery it is necessary to show that the act or acts of alleged condonation were done with knowledge of the other's adultery.

Condonation may be express or implied. The best evidence of the latter is the continuance or resumption of sexual intercourse, or the fact that the parties continued to live or have resumed living in the same house. But such evidence is not conclusive.[59] For example, a wife who remains in the home with the adulterous spouse may do so simply because she has nowhere else to go and no means of her own. Mere delay in bringing a petition after a spouse's misconduct does not necessarily amount to condonation, but if the delay is very long and there is no good excuse it may bar a remedy. Much depends upon the validity of the reason for the delay. If it is due to a hope of reconciliation, or a lack of means to bring a suit, or a desire to avoid upsetting a close relation it should not be an obstacle to obtaining relief.[60] As a wife was regarded by the Ecclesiastical Courts as being under the power of her husband, condonation has been said not to be presumed as a bar so readily against her as it is against the husband.[61]

The forgiveness and reinstatement of the guilty spouse is subject to an implied condition that the injury shall not be repeated, and that the unoffending spouse shall in every respect be "treated with conjugal kindness".[62] Subsequent matrimonial misconduct revives condoned cruelty or adultery.[63] The principle being that "much less is sufficient to destroy condonation than to found an original suit".[64] Thus, intimacy falling short of adultery, or misbehaviour insufficient in itself to found a suit for cruelty, is sufficient to revive condoned adultery and

---

58. *D'Aguilar v. D'Aguilar* (1794) *supra*; *Turton v. Turton* (1830) 3 Hagg. Ecc. 338; 162 E.R. 1178 (Consistory Ct.); *Burch v. Burch* [1958] 1 All E.R. 848; [1958] 1 W.L.R. 480 (P.D.A.); *Swan v. Swan* [1953] P. 258, [1953] 2 All E.R. 865 (P.D.); *O'Reardon v. O'Reardon* (February, 1975) unreported (H.C.). in his direction to the jury, Finlay P. stated "If one of the parties to a marriage commits an offence against the marriage, and if with knowledge of that offence, the other party resumes or continues ordinary marital relations then the act condones the marital offence". If P. condones D.'s adultery with X. not knowing that D. has also committed adultery with Y. the former condonation in relation to X. is not avoided. *Bernstein v. Bernstein* [1893] P. 292 (C.A.); see also *Inglis v. Inglis and Baxter* [1968] P. 639 (P.D.A.); *Wells v. Wells* [1954] 1 W.L.R. 1390 (C.A.).

59. If a husband has sexual intercourse with his wife knowing that she has committed adultery, the husband's act in consenting to intercourse amounts to condonation. On the other hand a wife's sexual intercourse with a husband after he has committed a matrimonial offence does not automatically establish that she condones his conduct. *Henderson v. Henderson* [1944] A.C. 49 (H.L.); see also *Mackrell v. Mackrell* [1948] 2 All E.R. 858 (C.A.); *Blyth v. Blyth* [1966] A.C. 643 (C.A.).

60. *Coode v. Coode* (1838) 1 Curt. 755; 163 E.R. 262 (Consistory Ct.); *Newman v. Newman* (1870) L.R. 2 P. & D. 57 (P.D.); *Durant v. Durant* (1825) 1 Hagg. Ecc. 733; 162 E.R. 734 (Arches Ct.); *Turton v. Turton* (1830) 3 Hagg. Ecc. 338; 162 E.R. 1178 (Consistory Ct.); *Beeby v. Beeby* (1799) 1 Hagg. Ecc. 789; 162 E.R. 755 (Consistory Ct.); *Kirkwall (Lady) v. Kirkwall (Lord)* (1818) 2 Hag. Con. 277; 161 E.R. 742 (Consistory Ct.).

61. *Durant v. Durant, supra, per* Sir John Nicholl at p. 744; *Beeby v. Beeby, supra.*

62. *Durant v. Durant, supra, per* Sir John Nicholl at p. 744; see also *Dent v. Dent* (1865) 4 Sw. & Tr. 105; 164 E.R. 1455 (Ct. for Div. & Matr. Causes).

63. *Durant v. Durant, supra; Dent v. Dent, supra;* see also *Murphy v. Murphy, supra; O'Reardon v. O'Reardon, supra.*

64. *Cooke v. Cooke* (1863) 3 Sw. & Tr. 126; 164 E.R. 1221 at p. 1226 (Ct. for Div. & Matr. Causes); *M'Keever v. M'Keever, supra; Westmeath v. Westmeath, supra; Bostock v. Bostock, supra.*

cruelty.[65] After condonation an offence can be revived by an act not *eiusdem generis*. Thus cruelty can revive adultery and *vice versa.*[66]

A spouse who condones another spouse's offence and subsequently commits an offence of his own, may have a *mensa et thoro* decree made against him in the absence of a revival of the condoned offence.[67] Finally, in the case of *Rose v. Rose*[68] it was held that an agreement between spouses not to take proceedings against each other in respect of any offence already committed, precluded either spouse from obtaining relief on the ground of such offence, and, further, that any matrimonial wrong committed after the date of the agreement would not, if the parties had so agreed, revive the offence 'condoned' by the agreement.[69]

Recrimination

A plea of recrimination provides a complete answer to a suit whether brought by the husband or wife. Thus, if the petitioner alleges and proves adultery on the part of the respondent, the respondent may answer that the petitioner has also committed adultery. Proof of the latter's allegations may be established by evidence less than that necessary to prove an original suit.[70]

In order for a plea of recrimination to succeed it is not necessary that the misconduct of the petitioner should have occurred prior to that of the respondent.[71] Moreover, it is possible upon proof of the charge of recrimination, and failure on the part of the petitioner to prove his original charge, for the Court to pronounce a decree *a mensa et thoro* in favour of the respondent.[72]

Connivance

Connivance on the part of the petitioner to the respondent's adultery constitutes a complete bar to his alleging such adultery as a ground for a decree of divorce *a mensa et thoro.*[73] Mere negligence or inattention on the part of the unoffending spouse is not sufficient, there must be proof that it was his inten-

---

65. *M'Keever v. M'Keever, supra; Westmeath v. Westmeath, supra; Winscom v. Winscom* (1864) 3 Sw. & Tr. 380; 164 E.R. 1322 (Ct. for Div. & Matr. Causes); *Bramwell v. Bramwell* (1831) 3 Hagg. Ecc. 618; 162 E.R. 1285 (Consistory Ct.); *Worsley v. Worsley* (1730) 1 Hagg. Ecc. 734; 162 E.R. 735 (Consistory Ct.); *Gardiner v. Gardiner* [1949] N.I. 126 (K.B.D., N.I.); *Cooke v. Cooke* [1948] N.I. 46 (K.B.D., N.I.).

66. From Finlay P.'s direction to jury in *O'Reardon v. O'Reardon, supra. Bramwell v. Bramwell supra; Durant v. Durant, supra.*

67. *Anichini v. Anichini* (1839) 2 Curt. 210; 163 E.R. 387 (Consistory Ct.); *Beeby v. Beeby, supra; Seller v. Seller* (1859) 1 Sw. & Tr. 482; 164 E.R. 823; see also *Everett v. Everett and McCullum* [1919] P.D. 298 (C.A.) – If a petitioner is still committing the condoned or connived at offence, he or she cannot get a decree on the basis of the misconduct of the other spouse.

68. (1883) 8 P.D. 98; [1881–85] All E.R. Rep. 141 (C.A.).

69. See also *Courtney v. Courtney* [1923] 2 I.R. 31; (1923) 57 I.L.T.R. 42 (C.A.), discussed at p. 111. In this case there was no evidence of the commission of a matrimonial offence after the date of the agreement.

70. *Forster v. Forster* (1790) 1 Hag. Con. 144; 161 E.R. 504 (Consistory Ct.); see, however, *Chettle v. Chettle* (1821) 3 Phill. Ecc. 507, 161 E.R. 1399 (Arches Ct.). It seems from this case that for a plea of recrimination to succeed in reply to a petition on the ground of adultery, the respondent must allege and prove adultery on the part of the petitioner. On the other hand adultery on the part of the petitioner may afford a good defence to the petitioner's allegation of cruelty.

71. *Proctor v. Proctor* (1819) 2 Hag. Con. 292; 161 E.R. 747 (Consistory Ct.); *Beeby v. Beeby, supra.*

72. *Harris v. Harris* (1829) 2 Hagg. Ecc. 376; 162 E.R. 894 (Consistory Ct.); *Kenrick v. Kenrick* (1831), 4 Hagg. Ecc. 114; 162 E.R. 1389 (Consistory Ct.).

73. *Harris v. Harris., supra; Forster v. Forster, supra.*

tion that adultery should take place or continue.[74] Once evidence of the presence of such "corrupt intention" has been given it is not necessary to prove "express" or "active" consent, mere passing acquiescence being sufficient to raise the implication of consent.[75] Such consent must be freely given; the principle on which connivance is based being *volenti non fit injuria*.[76] Connivance by its very nature must be precedent to the occurrence of the adultery alleged.[77] Moreover, there must be a distinct connection between the connivance and subsequent acts of adultery. Even if such connection did exist at one stage, it seems that it may be held to have "spent". This may occur where subsequent to the act of connivance there has been a complete reconciliation between the parties, or where considerable time has elapsed before the commission of a further matrimonial offence.[78] A spouse who keeps watch or hires a private detective to keep watch on the other spouse whom he suspects of adultery is not guilty of connivance. It has been said that

> "A man who suspects his wife of adultery is allowed to keep watch on her with suitable witnesses, so that he may give proof of her adultery; for that is not conniving at her sin, but discovering her guilt so that he can get his remedy. It is one thing to request, counsel, or commend evil to be done; that is not allowed, but it is quite another thing to permit, or not to interfere with the doing of evil. That is sometimes allowed as being the greater good."[79]

The evidence to establish connivance is generally, as in the case of condonation, circumstantial, and if the facts are equivocal there is a presumption against the presence of the requisite corrupt intention.[80] The petitioner in all *mensa et thoro* cases must swear in an affidavit, filed with his or her petition, that there is no connivance or collusion between the petitioner and the other spouse.

Wilful Neglect Conducing to Adultery

It is suggested in a case determined in 1895 that wilful neglect by a husband which conduces to his wife's adultery is a discretionary bar to the granting of a decree of divorce *a mensa et thoro*.[81] The authority of this decision is open to question, however, as it was largely based on a development in English statute law relating to the granting of decrees of divorce *a vinculo* that did not apply to Ireland.[82]

Collusion

Collusion can be looked on as another aspect of connivance. It is an absolute

---

74. *Rix v. Rix* (1777) 3 Hagg. Ecc. 74; 162 E.R. 1085 (Arches Ct.); *Hoar v. Hoar* (1801) 3 Hagg. Ecc. 137; 162 E.R. 1108 (Consistory Ct.); *Gipps v. Gipps and Hume* (1864) 11 H.L. Cas. (H.L.); *Rogers v. Rogers* (1830) 3 Hagg. Ecc. 57; 162 E.R. 1079 (Arches Ct.); see also *Harris v. Harris, supra*; *Phillips v. Phillips* (1844) 1 Rob. Ecc. 144; 163 E.R. 993 (Consistory Ct.).
75. *Moorsom v. Moorsom* (1792) 3 Hagg. Ecc. 87; 162 E.R. 1090 (Consistory Ct.).
76. i.e. a person cannot complain of an act to which he has freely consented. *Rogers v. Rogers, supra*; *Moorsom v. Moorsom, supra*; *Harris v. Harris, supra*; *Reeves v. Reeves* (1813) 2 Phill. Ecc. 125; 161 E.R. 1097 (Arches Ct.); *Douglas v. Douglas* [1951] P. 85; [1950] 2 All E.R. 748 (C.A.).
77. *Churchman v. Churchman* [1945] P. 44; [1945] 1 All E.R. 190 (C.A.).
78. See *Godfrey v. Godfrey* [1965] A.C. 444; [1964] 3 All E.R. 154 (H.L.).
79. *Timmings v. Timmings* (1792) 3 Hagg. Ecc. 76 at p. 82; 162 E.R. 1086; *Phillips v. Phillips, supra*; *Douglas v. Douglas, supra*.
80. *Rogers v. Rogers, supra*; *Kirkwall v. Kirkwall, supra*; *Turton v. Turton* (1830) 3 Hagg. Ecc. 338; 162 E.R. 1178 (Consistory Ct.).
81. *Scovell v. Scovell* [1897] I.R. 162 (Ct. for Matr. Causes).
82. See further Law Reform Commission Report No. 8, *supra*, at pp. 23–24.

bar to the obtaining of a decree. In order for there to be collusion it is not necessary for there to be an agreement between the parties for one to commit a matrimonial offence so as to enable the other to bring separation proceedings. In *Churchward v. Churchward*[83] it was stated that:

> "If the initiation of a suit be procured, and its conduct (especially if abstention from defence be a term) provided for by agreement that constitutes collusion, although no one can put his finger on any fact falsely dealt with, or withheld".

Collusion today has no practical importance, as, if spouses agree to separate, there is no sense in their colluding to bring proceedings for a divorce *a mensa et thoro*. They can simply enter into a separation agreement.

Ancillary Relief

In proceedings for a judicial separation, the court has ancillary power to determine a husband's liability to pay alimony to his wife[84] and to make a declaration that the spouse, by reason of whose misconduct the decree is made, is unfit to have custody of any children of the marriage.[85] Both the High Court and the Circuit Court have in practice in appropriate cases granted orders excluding a violent spouse from the matrimonial home following upon the granting of a decree of divorce *a mensa et thoro* on the grounds of cruelty.[86] The Ecclesiastical Courts possessed no such jurisdiction and until the jurisdictional basis upon which such orders are granted is fully clarified by way of a detailed written judgement delivered by the Supreme Court, the courts' powers to grant such exclusion orders by way of ancillary relief in separation proceedings remains questionable.[87]

A decree of divorce *a mensa et thoro* also automatically deprives the guilty spouse of his or her right to a share in the estate of the other spouse, either as a legal right or on intestacy under the Succession Act, 1965.[88]

The court does not possess jurisdiction to determine any other disputes between the spouses and may not make any other orders in relation to the family home or other family property, nor can it grant custody of a child to a particular

---

83. [1895] P. 7 and P. 30 (P.D.). See further *Crewe v. Crewe* (1800) 3 Hag. Ecc. 123; 162 E.R. 1102; *Lloyd v. Lloyd* (1859) 1 Sw. & Tr. 567; 164 E.R. 862; *Barnes v. Barnes* (1867) L.R. 1 P. & D. 505.

84. See p. 450 *post*.

85. See p. 373 *post*.

86. In *F.W. v. K.W.* (26 January, 1984) Finlay P. determining a Circuit Court appeal to the High Court, affirmed orders made by the President of the Circuit Court, Judge Neylon, granting a decree of divorce *a mensa et thoro* on the grounds of physical and mental cruelty and excluding the husband from the family home, stating that the husband "must leave the matrimonial home and must not seek to enter it again." The learned President stated that he was upholding the exclusion order made by the President of the Circuit Court as "The wife was fully entitled to live separately from her husband . . . particularly in a case where molestation was likely to arise." No written judgement was delivered in this case but a note of the President's judgement was taken by Catherine McGuinness B.L. and this note was signed and approved by Finlay P. on the 21st of March 1984.

87. If separate proceedings are instituted in either the Circuit or High Court seeking an injunction or a barring order (see, however, p. 586 *post* as to the extent of the High Court's current jurisdiction to grant barring orders), such proceedings may be heard together with the separation proceedings and at the end of the hearing a barring order or an injunction may be granted. What is questioned here is merely the court's jurisdiction to grant such orders by way of ancillary relief without the institution of separate proceedings seeking either a barring order or an injunction.

88. See p. 527 *post*.

parent[89] or resolve other disagreements between the parties over a child's up-bringing.[90] It cannot order the payment of maintenance for the support of children or of a husband and orders for alimony are limited to ordering periodical payments, the court being unable to make lump sum orders in favour of a spouse.

So as to circumvent the limited jurisdiction of the court and to avoid dupli-cation of litigation, the practice has grown up in recent years of simultaneously instituting and attempting to have tried together, proceedings claiming whatever other relief is required to finalise all matters in dispute between spouses. The latter proceedings may contain claims under all or any of the following enact-ments – the Married Women's Status Act, 1957, the Guardianship of Infants Act, 1964, the Family Law (Maintenance of Spouses & Children) Act, 1976, the Family Home Protection Act, 1976, and the Family Law (Protection of Spouses and Children) Act, 1981. Although this manoeuvre saves spouses the expense of a second and completely new court hearing, the necessity to use two totally separate sets of proceedings results in much unnecessary paperwork, expense and duplication.

---

89. Pursuant to the Guardianship of Infant Act, 1964, Sect. 18(1) the court may declare the parent by whose misconduct the decree is made unfit to have custody of children (see p. 373 *post*). In practice there is no written judgement delivered in which any such order has been made since the enactment of the 1964 Act.

90. A.W. Samuels K.C. as long ago as 1910 criticised this limitation on the jurisdiction of the court in the context of High Court proceedings. See, "Divorce Jurisdiction in Ireland" (1911) I.L.T. & S.J. 6.

CRITICISMS AND SUGGESTED REFORMS

Until 1982, divorce *a mensa et thoro* proceedings were becoming increasingly irrelevant due to the anachronistic nature of the proceedings themselves and the courts' limited powers to make ancillary orders.[1] The fact that *a mensa et thoro* actions could only be brought in the High Court and that a multiplicity of paper-work was required and a series of preliminary court applications necessary, prior to a full court hearing taking place, made such proceedings unnecessarily expensive and caused estranged spouses to use other family law actions as a substitute for an action for separation.

In practice, *mensa et thoro* proceedings were mainly instituted when one or both estranged spouses were relatively wealthy and such proceedings were used as a means to force a respondent spouse to conclude a separation agreement and an appropriate financial settlement. The fact that a court decree could terminate the "guilty" spouse's succession rights, whilst the petitioning spouse's were retained, conferred a negotiating advantage on the latter. Moreover, the threat of a jury trial with attendant publicity together with the fear of being required to discharge the large legal costs that could result from a fully contested court case, put pressure on a respondent to settle and not to proceed to a full court hearing. The action was rightly described as a "privilege" of the richer members of society.[2] Its inadequacies were highlighted by Mr. Justice Kenny in a speech to the Society of Young Solicitors in 1970, where he said:

"One of the most serious failings of our legal system is the absence of an expeditious, cheap method of hearing separation proceedings. The cases involve petitions, answers, applications for alimony, settlement of issues before the Master, motions to fix the amount of security to be given by the husband and finally a jury trial lasting 3 or 4 days. It is a risk which a hus-

---

1. In the period 1970 to 1981 (being the last year in which the jurisdiction to grant decrees of divorce *a mensa et thoro* was vested solely in the High Court) there were only an average of 5 decrees a year granted by the High Court. The following are the statistics for the total number of petitions issued in each year and the number of decrees granted:

Year	Number of Petitions issued	Number of Decrees granted
1970	40	11
1971	27	5
1972	30	9
1973	26	2
1974	51	10
1975	43	4
1976	37	3
1977	29	5
1978	39	1
1979	34	2
1980	27	2
1981	25	2

(See the Law Reform Commission: *Report on Divorce a Mensa et Thoro and Related Matters*, Report No. 8, December 1983 at p. 90).

By comparison in the High Court in the years 1976 to 1981 inclusive, 1,621 special summonses were issued initiating proceedings under the Guardianship of Infants Act, 1964, and 1,455 special summonses were issued under the Family Law (Maintenance of Spouses and Children) Act, 1976. In the years 1978 to 1981 in the High Court 772 special summonses were issued initiating proceedings between spouses under the Married Women's Status Act, 1957, and 787 special summonses were issued initiating proceedings under the Family Home Protection Act, 1976. In the three year period the 1st of August 1978 to the 31st of July 1981 inclusive in the District Court 5,635 applications were made by spouses seeking barring orders and 5,643 were made by spouses seeking maintenance orders. See Appendix C.

2. See the *Report of the Free Legal Advice Centres*, 1972 (Dublin), p. 23.

band cannot insure against and if he has to pay the costs of both sides, the result is usually financial ruin. So never bring a separation action if any other method is available of procuring a reasonable financial settlement.[3]

The acquisition by the Circuit Court of a jurisdiction to grant decrees of divorce *a mensa et thoro* in May 1982[4] and the speedier and simpler procedures used in that court, taken together with the provision of a limited form of civil legal aid in family law matters, has resulted in the action becoming more accessible to estranged spouses. The practice of the former President of the Circuit Court Judge Neylon (approved by Finaly C.J. when President of the High Court) of making ancillary orders excluding a spouse from living in the family home in appropriate cases, has also made the action for judicial separation a more practical and useful remedy.[5] As a result, there has been an increase in its use during the last four years.[6] Nevertheless, the need for reform remains. The substantive law applicable to the granting of separation decrees continues to be based on the legal principles articulated and applied by the Ecclesiastical Courts prior to their abolition in 1871 and provides no legal remedy for many spouses whose marriages have totally collapsed and who require legal intervention to resolve the consequences of such collapse. It is the need to reform the substantive law applicable to the granting of separation decrees and the court's powers to make ancillary orders that is the concern of the remaining part of this chapter.

The Grounds for Obtaining a Separation Decree

The *Report of the Joint Oireachtas Committee on Marriage Breakdown* published in April 1985 acknowledges that:

"The problems caused by marriage breakdown have not been adequately

---

3. Kenny J., "Some Aspects of Family Law", Society of Young Solicitors Lecture No. 48 (Cork 1970), p. 5.
4. Following upon the commencement of the Courts Act, 1981, which extended jurisdiction to grant decrees of divorce *a mensa et thoro* to the Circuit Court in accordance with the recommendations contained in the *20th Interim Report of the Committee on Court Practice & Procedure* (Dublin 1978, Stationery Office, Prl. 7459).
5. See p. 227 *ante.* See also the *Report of the Joint Oireachtas Committee on Marriage Breakdown* (April 1985), p. 47.
6. The Circuit Court acquired jurisdiction to grant decrees of divorce *a mensa et thoro* on the 1st of May 1982. The following are the available statistics of the number of cases initiated in the Circuit Court in each of the last three years commencing on the 1st of August 1982 and ending on the 31st of July 1985 and the number of decrees granted.

Year	Number of app. made	Number of decrees granted
1 Aug 1982/31 July 1983	53	14
1 Aug 1983/31 July 1984	115	51
1 Aug 1984/31 July 1985	197	71

In the period 1983 to 1985 inclusive, 3 decrees of divorce *a mensa et thoro* granted by the Circuit Court were set aside on appeal by the High Court.
In the period 1982 to 1985 the statistics as to divorce *a mensa et thoro* proceedings before the High Court were:

Year	Number of app. made	Number of decrees granted
1982	20	6
1983	8	6
1984	5	0
1985	15	0

The above statistics derive from replies received to Dáil questions. See Vol. 364 Dáil Reports Cols. 691 and 771–772 (4 March 1986), and from L.R.C. Report No. 8 at p. 90. In relation to both Circuit Court and High Court applications many of the cases initiated would have been settled without the necessity of an ultimate court hearing. See further Appendix C.

dealt with by the Oireachtas in the past. The present laws which purport to deal with marriage breakdown are not comprehensive nor are they reactive to the current changes in society and in personal attitudes to the family and to marriage."[7]

The report states that the "essence of marriage" is the making of a formal commitment between two people "to create and maintain a lasting and stable relationship"[8] but accepts that the stability of the marital relationship can be undermined both by spouses themselves and by social, economic and environmental pressures which can result in marital breakdown.[9] Stating that "the scale and extent of (the) problems which are caused by marriage breakdown are considerable"[10] the report continues:

> "The Committee recognises that an increasing number of couples are separating and that the separation of spouses is essentially a public demonstration of the end of a marital relationship. The Committee also recognises, however, that many couples (whose) marital relationship has irretrievably broken down are still residing under the one roof and that although residing together are, effectively leading separate lives. Many such couples wish to separate but are unable to do so as they cannot reach agreement between themselves as to the basis upon which they should separate. Under the existing legal system there are no legal remedies available whereby the courts can resolve disputes as to the basis upon which a separation should take place without proof of fault such as adultery, cruelty, or unnatural practices."[11]

The Committee in its report favours greater emphasis on the concept of marital breakdown than on the notion of the matrimonial offence which requires the courts to assign blame for the collapse of a marriage by determining which spouse is primarily at fault for such collapse. The report states that "the court should grant a decree of judicial separation if it is satisfied that the marriage of the person to his or her spouse has irretrievably broken down" and that "irretrievable breakdown should be the one overall ground" for the granting of a decree.[12] It goes on to state that "the court should be satisfied that such a breakdown has occurred if an applicant spouse proves one of the following:

(a) that his or her spouse has behaved in such a way that the applicant cannot reasonably be expected to co-habit with that other spouse;

(b) that his or her spouse has been guilty of adultery;

(c) that his or her spouse is in desertion or in constructive desertion of the applicant;

(d) that the applicant has been living separate and apart from the other spouse for a continuous period of not less than one year where the other spouse consents to the making of the decree;

(e) that the applicant has been living separate and apart from the other spouse for a continuous period of three years;

---

7. See *Report of Joint Oireachtas Committee, supra*, at p. 30.
8. *Ibid.*, at p. 21.
9. *Ibid*, see Chapter 4.
10. *Ibid.*, at p. 28.
11. *Ibid.*
12. *Ibid.*, at p. 49.

(f)   that such other facts and/or reasons exist or existed which in all circum-
      stances make it reasonable for the applicant to live separate from, and
      not co-habit with, the other spouse."[13]

The above proposal, if implemented, would result in irretrievable breakdown
becoming the sole ground upon which a decree of separation could be granted
and proof of any of the facts listed in (a) to (f) would oblige the court to grant a
decree upon an application being made to it.

     The approach of the Oireachtas Committee differs from that taken by the
Law Reform Commission in its *Report on Divorce A Mensa Et Thoro and Related
Matters* published in December 1983[14] to the extent that the Commission recommended an extension of the existing grounds upon which a separation decree
might be granted but did not propose that irretrievable breakdown of marriage
should be the one overall ground for the granting of a decree.[15] The Commission
did, however, recommend that in addition to cruelty and adultery, the grounds
upon which a decree could be granted should be extended to include as separate
grounds (a), (c) and (d) above, proof of which the Oireachtas Committee propose
would require a separation decree to be granted on the basis of irretrievable
breakdown.[16] The Commission differed from (e) only to the extent that it proposed that proof of 5 years separation as opposed to 3 years should entitle an
applicant to obtain a separation decree.[17] In the context of (a) the Commission
was of the view that it should form an additional ground upon which a decree
could be granted and stated that cruelty should remain as a separate and distinct
ground.[18] Under the Oireachtas Committee's proposal the current concept of
cruelty would be subsumed within (a) and would not form a separate fact, proof
of which could result in the granting of a decree. Cruelty as such would be fully
incorporated under the umbrella of (a).

     While the Law Reform Commission did not propose that irretrievable break-
down should be the one overall ground upon which a decree could be granted, it
did recommend that proof of "breakdown of marriage" should be an additional
distinct and separate ground by itself.[19] In doing so, however, it failed to describe
how the ground of "breakdown of marriage" should interact as a distinct and
separate ground with the existing grounds of cruelty and adultery and the new
additional grounds proposed by the Commission, proof of any of which can also
be regarded as indicative of marital breakdown. The Commission in support of
"breakdown of marriage" as an extra ground for judicial separation acknowledged
that:

     "Some people may prefer not to involve themselves in making allegations
     that their spouses have been guilty of matrimonial mis-conduct" and "they
     wish to seek a legal separation on the basis that the marriage has broken

13. *Ibid.*, at p. 50.
14. L.R.C. Report No. 8.
15. See L.R.C. Report No. 8, Chapter 3.
16. The Commission also recommended that unnatural practices should be abolished as
a specific ground and the Oireachtas Committee did not specifically list proof of the committal of unnatural practices as one of the specific facts upon which a court could conclude
that a marriage had irretrievably broken down. It is clear, however, that proof of such
behaviour by a spouse could establish facts (a) or (f) in the Oireachtas Committee's proposal
and the Law Reform Commission expressly stated that proof of such behaviour could warrant
a finding that a spouse could not reasonably be expected to live with a spouse who so
behaved (see L.R.C. Report No. 8, at pp. 35—37).
17. See L.R.C. Report No. 8, at pp. 45—46.
18. *Ibid.*, at pp. 36—37.
19. *Ibid.*, at pp. 42—46. See also the dissenting view expressed by Mr. Roger Hayes in
Chapter 4 of the Commission's Report.

down – a ground that involves no name-calling or criticism of the other spouse's behaviour."[20]

It did not, however, consider whether as a matter of social policy the State should permit estranged spouses to use the court system to obtain, by way of court decree, a judicial condemnation of the other spouse's marital behaviour or whether upon proof of the collapse of a marriage, the courts should be confined, in so far as is just and equitable, to extending judicial recognition to the factual breakdown of the marital relationship without having to irrevocably identify and criticise one spouse as being more responsible than the other for such breakdown.

It is submitted that, by proposing that irretrievable breakdown should be the sole ground upon which a decree of separation should be granted, the Oireachtas Committee recognised that the commital of adultery or cruelty or the desertion by one spouse of the other, is most often simply an external manifestation or symptom of marital failure but is rarely the sole cause of marital breakdown. In the vast majority of cases both spouses by their behaviour, either intentionally or unintentionally, to varying degrees contribute to the permanent sundering of a marital realtionship.[21] A law founded on the doctrine of breakdown would accord with social reality by recognising this fact and effectively accepting that the purpose of separation proceedings is not to provide a procedure designed to assign blame or determine the guilt for marital failure but is to provide a juridical recognition of the factual inability of both parties to a marriage to maintain a stable and lasting relationship with each other, despite their original commitment to do so. By emphasizing the importance of the relationship as opposed to the contractual concept of marriage, such an approach also implicitly acknowledges that there is nothing to be gained by ultimately labelling spouses as either guilty or innocent, particularly where there are infant children of a marriage in whose interests separated spouses as guardians and parents of their children may have to co-operate and interact with each other for many years after the granting of a separation decree.[21a] Where the necessity for such future co-operation exists society in general has an interest to ensure that the law as to separation, in so far as is possible, minimises family division and promotes future harmony and does not unnecessarily perpetuate and exacerbate family conflict. It is submitted that this should be a major social policy consideration in determining the nature of any new law as to the granting of separation decrees.[22] Any law based on the concept of breakdown is more likely to be successful in this, than is one based on the concept of the matrimonial offence.

20. *Ibid.*, at p. 43.
21. The Free Legal Advice Centres' Report of 1972 stated that "The idea that marriages break up because only one party has committed an offence against the other is unreal. In the vast majority of cases both parties are at fault in varying degrees." See p. 24 of Report.
The *Report of the Joint Oireachtas Committee* includes a number of extracts from submissions received by it in support of its approach. An extract from the submission received from a group of solicitors working in the State Law Centres stated:

"A matrimonial breakdown is the failure of a relationship between spouses. Both spouses are responsible to various degrees. The law should reflect this and not try to assign fault and make orders as rewards for good behaviour. It should be possible for spouses to obtain judicial separation in the courts when a marriage has irretrievably broken down." (See p. 49 of the Report).

21a. See the *Report of the Joint Oireachtas Committee* at p. 60 where the Committee states that "A considerable body of evidence has been produced to this committee as to how important it is for both spouses to continue to play a full and proper role as parents of (their) children despite the breakdown of their relationship as husband and wife."
22. See further W. Duncan, "Desertion and Cruelty in Irish Matrimonial Law" (1972 7 I.J. (n.s.) 213, particularly pp. 237–239, "Statement on Family Law" by the Council for Social Welfare, a Committee of the Catholic Bishops Conference (Dublin 1974).

Government Intentions: In the government's "Statement of Intent" published in April, 1986, it announced that it proposed to extend the grounds upon which decrees of judicial separation can be granted to include "desertion, including constructive desertion (viz. conduct on the part of one spouse that results in the other spouse leaving and living apart); and separation for three years, or separation for one year with the consent of the respondent." It did not adopt (f) above as a ground, proof of which the Oireachtas Committee proposed should satisfy a court that irretrievable breakdown had occurred, stating that the government believes the new grounds proposed by it "cover all appropriate cases, and that the wording proposed by the (Joint Oireachtas) Committee . . . is unduly vague."[22a]

The government did not adopt the Joint Committee's proposal that irretrievable breakdown constitute the one overall ground for the granting of a separation decree or that proof of simple "breakdown of marriage" as proposed by the Law Reform Commission permit the granting of such decree. Whilst legislation implementing the government's proposals will, for the first time, permit the Irish courts to grant judicial separations where mere separation has taken place without either party having to prove fault, the government's rejection of (f) and failure to accept "breakdown of marriage" as the basis upon which a decree may be granted, denies to a totally incompatible couple who cannot agree on a basis for separation, the possibility of using this jurisdiction to ask a court to determine the basis upon which they should separate, unless one can prove the other guilty of a matrimonial offence.[22b]

Bars to the Granting of a Decree

The report of the Oireachtas Committee recommends that all of the bars to the granting of a separation decree should be abolished.[23] The Law Reform Commission recommends abolition of the bar of recrimination stating "we do not believe that it is a sound policy to require spouses to live with each other as a penalty for previous misconduct on the part of both of them."[24] It also recommends abolition of the bar of collusion on the basis that in this area of the law it has "no practical importance".[25] The Commission proposed that connivance as a bar be retained[26] and also that "conduct conducing to adultery" should be incorporated in any new legislation, as an additional bar.[27] It is submitted that if legislation was enacted in accordance with the proposal of the Oireachtas Committee there would be no purpose in retaining either of the latter "bars"

22a. See "Statement of Intent" (April, 1986, Dept. of Justice) at p. 3. See also Revised "Statement" (June, 1986, Dept. of Justice) at p. 8. The latter document omits to make any reference to (f).

22b. Such couple may, however, be able to reach agreement through use of the proposed mediation service. As already discussed in chapter 2 the "Statement of Intent" envisages that in future judicial separation proceedings will come before a family court, that such court will have power to enquire into whether marriage counselling services have been or should be availed of by estranged spouses and will be able to adjourn separation proceedings so that recourse may be had to such service. Where no reconciliation is possible the "Statement" appears to envisage a couple then participating in a compulsory mediation process "designed to secure agreement . . . in a non-confrontational manner on the terms of separation." It continues stating that "the decision as to a judicial separation and the terms of such a separation will be determined by the court having heard the parties and any other appropriate evidence, including *a report on the results of this mediation process*" (Author's italics). The "Statement" does not clarify the relevance of the "mediation report" to the granting of a decree where cruelty, adultery or desertion is established.

23. See p. 51 of Report.
24. L.R.C. Report No. 8 at p. 50.
25. *Ibid.*, at p. 52.
26. *Ibid.*, at p. 51.
27. *Ibid.*, at p. 54.

as such behaviour by a spouse would, of itself be indicative of marital break-down. Moreover, there would be no reason for a spouse to connive at another's adultery and then allege adultery so as to obtain a separation decree, as proof of either cruelty, or adultery to which connivance is essentially relevant, would no longer be essential to obtain a decree of separation. There would, consequently, be little if anything to be gained by a spouse so behaving.

Unlike the Oireachtas Committee which favours its abolition, the Law Reform Commission recommend that condonation be retained as a discretionary, as opposed to an absolute, bar to the obtaining of a separation decree.[28] It is sub-mitted that any law on separation should operate in a way that encourages voluntary reconciliation between spouses and should not place legal obstacles in the path of spouses who wish to try and resolve their difficulties. The bar of condonation effectively discourages reconciliation by encouraging a spouse to stand his ground upon the other spouse stepping outside the matrimonial bond and, for example committing adultery, since if an attempted reconciliation fails, the latter may find himself barred from relying on the former's matrimonial misconduct to obtain a separation decree. For this reason alone, it is submitted the bar of condonation should simply be abolished.

Finally, it is submitted that the retention of any of the bars the Law Reform Commission propose be retained cannot be reconciled with the Commission's own proposal that proof of "breakdown of marriage" be a separate and distinct ground for the obtaining of a separation decree. One of the arguments made by the Commission in favour of this ground is

> "that where a marriage has broken down, either spouse should be per-mitted to obtain a decree relieving him or her from the obligation of living with the other spouse since it would be futile for the law to require spouses to live together where their relationship has ceased to be viable."[29]

Thus, where a marital relationship has completely collapsed, proof that it had done so would, on the basis of this proposal, afford a ground for the obtain-ing of a separation decree. If it is acknowledged that the law cannot require spouses who do not wish to do so to continue to reside together, it is difficult to see any basis for retaining the above three bars to the granting of a separation decree.

Government Intentions: The "Statement of Intent" makes no reference to the current bars to the granting of a decree and it is unknown what future role, if any, they will play.

Reform of Court Jurisdiction to Grant Ancillary Relief

Upon the granting of a decree of separation, the court should be empowered to make all ancillary orders necessary to properly and efficiently regulate the consequences of marital breakdown without the parties having to institute any additional proceedings. Both the Law Reform Commission and the Joint Oireachtas Committee express the opinion that the court should be empowered to make ancillary orders as to guardianship and custody of children[30] and financial provision for dependent spouses and children.[31] They also agree that

28. *Ibid.*, at pp. 52, 53.
29. *Ibid.*, at p. 43.
30. See *Report of the Joint Oireachtas Committee* at p. 51; see L.R.C. Report No. 8 at pp. 57, 58, 63.
31. See *Report of the Joint Oireachtas Committee* at p. 51; see L.R.C. Report No. 8 at pp. 54–57.

the court should be empowered to make orders in relation to the division and transfer of property and as to succession rights, although they differ about the powers the court should exercise in this area.[32]

The Law Reform Commission expressly declined to make any recommendation as to the nature of the jurisdiction that should be exercised by way of ancillary relief regarding property orders, noting the government's intention to introduce new legislation relating to ownership of the family home and stating that any new jurisdiction "should not be treated in isolation" and "must depend on the structure of matrimonial property regimes that will become the basis of the law in the future."[33] The Oireachtas Committee, however, did not display such reticence expressing the opinion that:

> "The court should have an ancillary power to decide who shall have the right to live in the family home as and from the date of the making of a decree of judicial separation (and) an ancillary power to divide the various property or properties of the spouses, between the spouses, . . . and the court should have the power to transfer the title of any relevant property as it deems just and equitable."

In exercising these powers the Committee stated:

> "The court should be obliged to base its decision on what is in the best interests of the family as a whole and, in the event of a conflict as to the best of interests of the various members of a family, the interest of the children should be paramount during their minority."[34]

Referring to succession rights, the Law Reform Commission proposed that the granting of a decree of separation should automatically preclude both spouses from taking any share in the other's estate, stating that the loss of succession rights was a factor the court could take into consideration when making ancillary financial and proprietary orders.[35] This proposal, if implemented, could result in many dependent spouses being left destitute upon the death of the maintenance-paying spouse in circumstances where at the date of the granting of a separation decree there is no family property in existence that can be transferred to the maintenance recipient or dependent spouse to provide some security for the future. This proposal of the Law Reform Commission was not adopted by the Joint Oireachtas Committee. The latter recommended that the court should merely be empowered to vary or discharge a spouse's rights of succession following the granting of a decree of separation "having regard to the circumstances of the parties, in the context of determining what orders, if any, should be made for the division or transfer of property between spouses."[36]

Government Intentions: The "Statement of Intent" undertakes that new legislation relating to the granting of separation decrees will include provision for the making of ancillary orders for maintenance, for the payment of lump sums and for property transfer orders.[37] It is silent as to whether any change will be introduced affecting succession rights.[38]

---

32. See *Report of the Joint Oireachtas Committee* at pp. 50–51; L.R.C. Report No. 8 at pp. 57, 59–62.

33. L.R.C. Report No. 8 at p. 57.

34. *Report of the Joint Oireachtas Committee* at p. 50.

35. L.R.C. Report No. 8 at pp. 61–62.

36. *Report of the Joint Oireachtas Committee* at p. 51.

37. "Statement of Intent" (April 1986) at p. 3 and Revised Statement (June 1986) at pp. 8, 10–12.

38. Succession is only referred to in the context of the effect of divorce *a vinculo* legislation in the event of the divorce referendum being successful.

CHAPTER 9

DIVORCE A VINCULO MATRIMONII

INTRODUCTION

Article 41.3.2.° of the Constitution states that:

"No law shall be enacted providing for the grant of a dissolution of marriage".

The Irish courts have never possessed jurisdiction to pronounce a decree of divorce *a vinculo matrimonii* (for brevity referred to simply as divorce in the following pages) so as to dissolve a valid marriage and permit the parties to remarry. In England prior to the Reformation marriage was regarded as a sacrament and indissoluble. Whilst after the Reformation a marriage could be dissolved by an Act of Parliament, the Ecclesiastical Courts still adhered to the doctrine of indissolubility and the jurisdiction that they passed on to the High Court in 1870 has never been extended so as to enable it to pronounce a decree of divorce.

In Ireland before the Act of Union divorce proceedings could take place in the Irish Parliament. Prior to the dissolution of the Irish Parliament there were nine divorce Bills passed and one rejected. Thereafter, the jurisdiction was transferred to the Imperial Parliament.

In 1857, the Matrimonial Causes Act set up the Court of Divorce and Matrimonial Causes in England and jurisdiction was conferred upon it to grant decrees of divorce. This Act, however, did not apply to Ireland and until 1922 a marriage of spouses domiciled in Ireland could only be validly dissolved, according to Irish Law, by a Bill of Divorce passed by the British Parliament.[1]

A husband could obtain a Bill on the ground of his wife's adultery. Adultery alone would not suffice in the case of a Bill submitted on behalf of the wife. She had to show that the adultery was accompanied by some other matrimonial offence, such as bigamy, incest or an unnatural offence. Although the Act of 1857 and the subsequent Matrimonial Causes Act, 1884, did not apply to Ireland, it was decided that in so far as they set down grounds for divorce,[2] the Acts were to apply to Parliamentary divorces sought by persons domiciled in Ireland.[3] As a consequence, following their enactment, a husband could present a petition for divorce on the ground of his wife's adultery; whilst a wife could petition on the grounds that her husband had committed incestuous adultery, adultery with

---

1. See generally J. Roberts, "Divorce Bills in the Imperial Parliament" (Dublin, 1906). See also W. Duncan, "Desertion and Cruelty in Irish Matrimonial Law" (1972) 7 I.J. (n.s.) 213–216. *Mayo-Perrott v. Mayo-Perrott* [1958] I.R. 336 (S.C.); *Bank of Ireland v. Caffin* [1971] I.R. 123 (H.C.).

2. See Sect. 27 of the Act of 1857, and Sect. 5 of the Act of 1884.

3. *Westropp's Divorce Bill* (1886) 11 App. Cas. 294 (H.L.); *Parker's Divorce* [1922], 2 I.R. 154n (H.L.); see also *Bell v. Bell* [1922] 2 I.R. 103, 152; (1922) 56 I.L.T.R. 46 (K.B.D.).

bigamy,[4] adultery with cruelty, adultery coupled with a failure on the husband's part to comply with a decree of restitution of conjugal rights,[5] rape, sodomy, or bestiality.

Before a petitioner could successfully bring parliamentary divorce proceedings he or she had to bring proceedings for divorce *a mensa et thoro* in the Irish High Court.[6] Moreover a husband alleging his wife's adultery was required to bring an action of criminal conversation against the adulterer or to provide a satisfactory reason for not having done so. As a consequence of the enormous costs involved in bringing such divorce proceedings they were completely outside the reach of the great majority of people.[7]

1922 and After

The Constitution of the Irish Free State contained no prohibition against divorce legislation. By the beginning of 1925 three bills for divorce *a vinculo* had been deposited in the Private Bill Office of the Oireachtas. In February, 1925, the Dáil without a division passed the following resolution:

> "That the Joint Committee on Standing Orders relative to Private Business be requested to submit additional Standing Orders regulating the procedure to be adopted in connection with Private Bills relating to matrimonial matters other than Bills of divorce *a vinculo matrimonii*, and to propose such alterations in the Standing Orders as will prevent the introduction of Bills of Divorce *a vinculo matrimonii*; and that a message be sent to the Seanad requesting its concurrence in this resolution".[8]

In his speech introducing this motion, Mr. W.T. Cosgrave[9] said:

> "I have no doubt but I am right in saying that the majority of people of this country regard the bond of marriage as a sacramental bond which is incapable of being dissolved. I personally hold this view. I consider that the whole fabric of our social organisation is based upon the sanctity of the marriage bond and that anything that tends to weaken the binding efficacy of that bond to that extent strikes at the root of our social life".[10]

On the resolution coming before the Senate, the Cathaoirleach ruled that the proposal was *ultra vires* the Constitution, inasmuch as if divorce *a vinculo* was to

---

4. i.e. he had married another after marrying the petitioner. If the petitioner was a party to the second "marriage" such marriage would be void, and there would be no necessity to obtain a divorce.

5. *Parker's Divorce, supra.*

6. *Sinclair's Divorce Bill* [1897] A.C. 469 (H.L.); see also *Sinclair v. Sinclair* [1896] 1 I.R. 603 (Ch. Div.).

7. See A.W. Samuels, "Evidence to the Royal Commission on Divorce" in 1910 reported in (1911) 45 I.L.T. & S.J. 6, or see "Reports of the Royal Commission on Divorce and Matrimonial Causes" Vol. III 1912—13 Cmnd. 6481, xx 455. Samuels, although referring to the exorbitant costs involved in obtaining a Divorce Bill, was adamant that public opinion in Ireland would be totally against the introduction of a court to deal with full dissolution of marriage in this country; see also M.J. Roberts' evidence to the same commission in Reports Commissioners, Vol. III, 1912—13 XX.

8. Dáil Debates, Vol. X cols. 156 and 182; see also D. O'Sullivan, *The Irish Free State and its Senate*, 161—5; J.H. Whyte, *Church and State in Modern Ireland 1923—1970*, (Gill and Macmillan, Dublin 1971), pp. 36—37; C. Davitt, "Some Aspects of the Constitution and the Law in Relation to Marriage", (1968), *Studies*, at p. 16; M. Nolan, "The Influence of Catholic Nationalism on the Legislation of the Irish Free State" (1975) 10 I.J. (n.s.) 128 at pp. 133—137.

9. W.T. Cosgrave led the Government of the Irish Free State from 1922—1932. Eamon de Valera led the Free State Government from 1932—1937.

10. Dáil Debates, Vol. X, col. 158.

be prohibited it could be done only by legislation and not by standing orders.[11] In June 1925 the Senate proposed an alternative method by resolution that such bills should be read a first time in each House before being proceeded with in the Senate. However, the Dáil rejected this proposal, the Senate rescinded its previous resolution, and there the matter ended.[12] Thereafter until the enactment of the present Constitution there were no Standing Orders providing for private bills of divorce and no legislation on the subject.[13]

The 1937 Constitution

Mr. de Valera in his introductory speech on the second stage of the Draft Constitution in the Dáil said in relation to Article 41:

"We pledge the State to protect the family in its constitution and its rights generally. This is not merely a question of religious teaching; even from the purely social side, apart altogether from that, we would propose here that we should not sanction divorce. Therefore no law can be passed providing for divorce".[14]

Later on he said:

"With regard to the question of divorce in general there is no doubt that sometimes there are unhappy marriages, but from the social point of view, without considering any other point of view, the obvious evil would be so great, and it has been proved to be so great in other countries that I do not think any person would have any difficulty — at least I would not — in making a choice in this matter".[15]

Article 41.3.2. has, since its enactment, been criticised as being an imposition of Roman Catholic teaching on the non-Roman Catholic minority in the State[16] and as being based on an unsustainable sociological premise, i.e. that the prohibition on divorce, of itself, either prevents or considerably reduces the extent of marital breakdown and provides a protection for marriage. It is now intended to examine the degree to which Article 41.3.2. reflects Roman Catholic canon law. We shall then consider the approach taken to this Article by two different Oireachtas Committees and the governmental action taken to implement their

11. Seanad Debates, Vol. IV, cols. 929 to 945.

12. Seanad Debates, Vol. V, cols 426 to 482 (434 to 443 reports a famous speech by W.B. Yeats in defence of the right to divorce) and cols. 820 to 824 and 933 to 938; Dáil Debates, Vol. XII, cols. 1563 to 1572; see also *McM. v. McM* and *McK. v. McK* [1936] I.R. 177 at pp. 187–189; see also J. White, *Minority Report* (Gill and Macmillan, Dublin 1975) pp. 116–118.

13. See J.H. Whyte, *supra*, pp. 57–60 where he discusses the Protestant opposition to the Dáil's attitude to divorce and other legislation. For an invaluable insight into attitudes to divorce in the 1920s, see, *correspondence regarding divorce in the Irish Free State (24 Jan 1923–1 Aug 1929)* File No. S.4127 – Cabinet Papers, State Records Office, Dublin Castle.

14. Dáil Debates, Vol. 67, col. 63.

15. Dáil Debates, Vol. 67, col. 1886.

16. See J. White, *Minority Report, supra*, at pp. 114–120; J.H. White, *Church & State ... supra*, at pp. 51–53; *Report of the Committee on the Constitution* (December, 1967) at pp. 43–44; "The Constitution" a Report of a Working Party of the Irish Theological Association (1972) 23 *The Furrow* 374; *New Ireland Forum, The Legal Systems North & South* (A study prepared for the New Ireland Forum by Profs. C.K. Boyle and D.S. Greer) (Dublin Stationery Office, 1984) in particular p. 17; see also *New Ireland Forum, Proceedings* (A Publication of the Public Sessions of the New Ireland Forum, 30th May, 1983 –2nd May, 1984); Minutes of Evidence taken by the Joint Oireachtas Committee on Marriage Breakdown (21st March, 1984–21st June, 1984) – in both see, in particular, the submissions of the Church of Ireland and the other minority Churches.

recommendations. We shall conclude by examining the impact of the divorce prohibition on marital breakdown in Ireland today.

THE CANON LAW OF THE ROMAN CATHOLIC CHURCH

Under the Canon Law of the Roman Catholic Church a valid sacramental and consummated marriage between two christians is indissoluble and remains in force throughout the lifetime of the parties.[17] Thus, if a civil decree of dissolution could be granted by the State, it would not be recognised by the Church. The Church can, however, in specific limited circumstances itself dissolve a marriage.[18] These are described below.

Non-consummation

According to Roman Catholic doctrine the rite of marriage is a sacrament. The union between husband and wife is representative of the union between Christ and the Church. It is symbolic of the inseparable alliance between the Son of God and mankind. This symbolism, however, is only found fully in the consummated marriage. A validly celebrated marriage[18a] of a Roman Catholic only becomes indissoluble when the husband and wife have in fact become "one flesh". For centuries the Roman Pontiffs have exercised power to dissolve an unconsummated marriage so permitting the parties to remarry. Such a dissolution can be granted upon request of either both parties or of one party to the marriage and a decree of dissolution will be granted provided there is "a just cause" or "a just reason" to terminate the marriage.[19] A justifying cause or reason can be an intention to enter religious life, or to receive sacred orders or a desire to remarry another within the church and to lead a normal family life.[20]

Dissolution in Favour of the Faith

(a) *Pauline Privilege:* A marriage between two unbaptised persons is regarded by the Roman Catholic Church as a true marriage but as lacking the sacramental

---

17. *The Code of Canon Law*, English translation by the Canon Law Society Trust (Collins Liturgical Publications, London, 1983) Canon 1141.
18. For an interesting discussion from the point of view of Roman Catholic theology of the basis for the continuous assertion by Catholic theologians and philosophers of the indissolubility of marriage see "The Indissolubility of Marriage in Natural Law", by Liam Ryan (1963) 30 *Irish Theological Quarterly*, 293–310 and I.T.Q. 62–71; W.J. Harrington, "Jesus' Attitude Towards Divorce" (1970) 37 I.T.Q. 199, and "The New Testament and Divorce" (1972), 39 I.T.Q. 199. For an interesting critique of the Church's attitude to civil divorce see P.J. McGrath, "Marriage Annulments: A Second Look" (Nov. 1975) Vol. 1, *Maynooth Review* 45. See also W. Cosgrove, "Rethinking the Indissolubility of Marriage", (1980) 31 *The Furrow* 8 in which the author argues that the Church could, under canon law, extend its power to grant decrees of dissolution of marriage. See further the responses to this article by M.C. McGuickian and Monsignor G. Sheehy in (1980) 31 *The Furrow* p. 194 *et seq* and at p. 269.
18a. A "validly celebrated marriage" here means validly celebrated according to Roman Catholic doctrine. See further F. O'Callaghan, "Faith and the Sacrament of Marriage" (1986) 52 I.T.Q. 163.
19. *The Code of Canon Law, supra*, Canon 1142.
20. See further B.A. Siegle T.O.R., *Marriage According to the New Code of Canon Law* (Alba House, New York, U.S.A., 1986) pp. 169–173 L. Orsy S.J., *Marriage in Canon Law* (Michael Glazier, Wilmington, Delaware, U.S.A., 1986) pp. 211–215. See also R. Browne, *Marriage Annulment* (London, 1971) chap. 6 and *Marriage Annulment in the Catholic Church* (Kevin Mayhew, England, 1977) chap. 7 (both of these books predate the publication of the *New Translation of the Code of Canon Law*). See further Irish Bishops Pastoral, *Love is for Life* (Veritas Publications, Dublin, 1985), at pp. 82–83.

character attached to a christian marriage.[21] By virtue of the Pauline Privilege[22] the Church is able to dissolve such a marriage if one of the parties becomes a baptised Roman Catholic[23] and the other does not wish to convert and refuses to live peacefully with the convert, or departs after baptism has taken place and such departure is not the fault of the convert.[24] Provided these three conditions can be properly established the convert is permitted by the local Bishop to proceed to a new marriage. The former valid marriage subsists until the moment when the second marriage, valid by reason of the Pauline Privilege, takes place, i.e. the first marriage is dissolved by the exercise of the Pauline Privilege.[25]

(b) *Petrine Privilege:*[26] A marriage between a baptised and a non-baptised person may be a valid marriage in the eyes of the Church[27] but also lacks the sacramental character of the marriage of two baptised persons. Such a marriage can be dissolved by the Pope upon the baptised party[28] wishing to marry a Roman Catholic.

In the case of both the Pauline and Petrine Privileges a dissolution is said to be granted in *favorem fidei*, i.e. in favour of the faith. The Roman Catholic Church in Ireland has not published detailed statistics as to the numbers of persons who annually have either sought a church dissolution or succeeded in obtaining one. However, in the Irish Bishops Pastoral, *Love is for Life*, published in 1985, it was stated that in the year 1982, 15 decrees of dissolution were granted on the grounds of non-consummation and 7 marriages were dissolved in *favorem fidei.*[29]

Just as the State does not recognise a church decree of nullity, it also does not recognise a church dissolution, the parties to a marriage so dissolved remaining in the eyes of the civil law validly married to each other. Some of those who obtain a church decree of dissolution on the ground of non-consummation may, as we have already seen, regularise their position under civil law by seeking and obtaining a civil decree of annulment on the ground of impotence. However,

---

21. The Roman Catholic Church regards the marriages of all baptised christians as sacramental unions. Thus, the marriage of two members of the Church of Ireland would be so recognised by the Roman Catholic Church and could not be dissolved by means of the Pauline Privilege. Alternatively, a marriage of two members of the Jewish faith is not regarded as possessing this sacramental character and could be dissolved.
22. See the *Code of Canon Law, supra,* Canons 1144–1149.
23. Valid baptism outside the Roman Catholic Church is sufficient foundation for the use of the privilege but there would be practical difficulties in the procedure unless the person became a Roman Catholic – see B.A. Siegle, T.O.R., *supra,* at pp. 173–174.
24. See B.A. Siegle T.O.R., *supra,* at pp. 173–177; L. Orsy, *supra,* pp. 215–227 and 231–234; Irish Bishops Pastoral, *supra,* at p. 83.
25. Intervention by the Pope or any other Ecclesiastical authority is not required. It is the local Bishop who is empowered to verify that the necessary conditions have been complied with.
26. See the *Code of Canon Law, supra,* Canon 1150. See also B.A. Siegle T.O.R., *supra,* at pp. 173, 177–180; L. Orsy, *supra,* at pp. 227–228; R. Browne, *Marriage Annulment, supra,* chap. 7 and *Marriage Annulments in the Catholic Church, supra,* chap. 8; Irish Bishops Pastoral, *supra,* at p. 83.
27. By the impediment of disparity of cult a marriage between a person baptised as a Roman Catholic and a non-baptised person is invalid unless the necessary dispensation is obtained. This only applies to Roman Catholics and does not affect the status (in the eyes of the Roman Catholic Church) of a baptised non-catholic who marries an unbaptised person. See, the *Code of Canon Law, supra,* Canons 1086, 1125 and 1126. See also B.A. Siegle T.O.R., at pp. 77–84 and 153–160.
28. If the non-baptised party becomes baptised subsequent to the marriage, for a dissolution to be granted, it must be established that the couple did not live together as man and wife after the baptism.
29. See Irish Bishops Pastoral, *supra,* at p. 83.

the canonical concept of "non-consummation" is broader than the legalistic civil concept of "impotence". Thus, some persons who can have their marriages dissolved by the church on the former ground are unable to obtain civil release from their bond, the State holding it to be indissoluble.[29a]. There is, of course, no civil law equivalent of the Pauline or Petrine Privileges.

Whereas the civil prohibition on dissolution is an accurate reflection of the Church's general attitude to marriage, in specific instances it is stricter, in that it holds marriages indissoluble that the Church, itself, exempts from such categorisation. Moreover, the State not only refuses to dissolve marriages that the Church regards as dissoluble but also regards as indissoluble marriages that the Church has annulled and marriages that it does not recognise as having taken place, for example, those celebrated by Roman Catholic parties in Registry Offices.

1967 DÁIL COMMITTEE ON THE CONSTITUTION

Thirty years after the adoption of the present Constitution, Article 41.3. was examined by an All Party Dáil Committee on the Constitution whose report was published at the end of 1967.[30] The Committee pointed out that the prohibition on divorce had been criticised for ignoring "the wishes of a certain minority of the population who would wish to have divorce facilities and who are not prevented from securing divorce by the tenets of the religious denominations to which they belong". It drew attention to

"the more liberal attitude now prevailing in Catholic circles in regard to the rites and practices of other religious denominations, particularly since the Second Vatican Council"

and noted, as shown above, that the present law

"deprives Catholics also of certain rights to which they would be entitled under their religious tenets. There are several circumstances in which the Catholic Church will grant dissolutions of valid marriages or will issue declarations of nullity ... The absolute prohibition in our Constitution has therefore the effect of imposing on Catholics regulations more rigid than those required by the law of the Church".[31]

The Committee suggested the replacement of the present article by one such as the following: —

"In the case of a person who was married in accordance with the rite of a religion no law shall be enacted providing for the grant of a dissolution of that marriage on grounds other than those acceptable to that religion."

It went on to state that:

29a. See, for example, the recent case of *M.M. (otherwise G.) v. P.M.* (December, 1985) unreported (H.C.) in which McMahon J. refused the petitioner's application for a decree of annulment. Seeking a decree on the ground of impotence the petitioner gave evidence that the husband was able to achieve an erection and penetration but not the emission of seed. It was held that erection and penetration are sufficient to consummate the marriage in the civil law and that inability to inseminate was not a "necessary element in the consummation of a marriage" and to regard it as such "would amount to adding a new ground of nullity." The judge records that during the course of the court hearing evidence was given that for the purpose of Roman Catholic canon law consummation required "erection, penetration and insemination" and that "under it ejaculation is essential to consummation".

30. See Report of the Committee on the Constitution, *supra*, at pp. 43–45.

31. See also "Church & State in the Constitution of Ireland", Rev. E. McDonagh (1961) 28 I.T.Q. 131.

"This wording would . . . meet the wishes of Catholics and non-Catholics alike. It would permit the enactment of marriage laws acceptable to all religions. It would not provide any scope for changing from one religion to another with a view to availing of a more liberal divorce regime. While it would not deal specifically with marriages not carried out in accordance with the rights of a religion, it would not preclude the making of rules relating to such cases".

According to J.H. Whyte[32] no religious leaders of any denomination were consulted as to the content of this recommendation. Upon its publication, it met instant opposition from Cardinal Conway, the Roman Catholic Archbishop of Armagh and from both Archbishops of the Church of Ireland. Leaders of other Protestant denominations gave the Committee's recommendation a reserved welcome.[33]

Leaving aside the question of whether the laws of the State should seek to enforce the various religious teachings on marriage in the manner suggested by the Committee,[34] the recommendations of the Dáil Committee if implemented would have created more problems than they would have resolved. If implemented, the Irish Courts would have found themselves embroiled in complex assessments of the matrimonial doctrines of the various religious denominations, and couples who changed their religion subsequent to their marriage would have found themselves bound by the doctrines of a religion they no longer adhered

32. See *Church and State in Modern Ireland, 1923–1970* by J.H. Whyte, pp. 347–349; see also *The Changing Face of Catholic Ireland*, D. Fennell, p. 187. The Catholic Bishops particularly condemned it as being the first step on the way to permitting civil divorce for the whole population. Cardinal Conway stated "The proposal would involve the setting up of divorce courts in the Republic. In the beginning they would be limited in scope but, inevitably, this would only be the first step. Everyone knows how these things spread once the gates are opened. Already, within 24 hours, one national newspaper has suggested that there should be divorce for all.

One must have the greatest possible respect for the tenets of our fellow-Christians. Yet, in fact, comparatively few of them believe in divorce, and still fewer of them want it. Even these few have little difficulty in securing a divorce elsewhere, and many of them have done so. One may ask whether what inconvenience there is, affecting very few, would justify such a radical and far-reaching break with our national traditions.

One thing is certain. Once the first divorce law has been introduced it will only be a matter of time till it is extended to apply to everybody. I am sure that Irish husbands and wives will ponder very carefully on what the committee's proposal to open the gates to divorce will almost inevitably lead to in terms of family life". *Irish Times*, 15th December 1967, p. 1.

The then Bishop of Dublin, Dr. McQuaid, two months later said "Civil divorce, as a measure which purports to dissolve a valid marriage, is contrary to the law of God. The experience of other countries has proved that civil divorce produces the gravest evils in society. The effort, even if well-intentioned, to solve hardships within marriage by civil divorce has invariably resulted for society in a series of greater sufferings and deeper evils". *Irish Times* (26th February 1968), p. 9.

See also comments of Dr. Daly, the Roman Catholic Bishop of Ardagh and Clonmacnois, *Irish Times* (December 21st, 1967); and see "Socio-Political Aspects of Divorce" by Rev. (now Bishop) Jeremiah Newman (1969), 23 Christus Rex p. 5.

The Church of Ireland Archbishop of Dublin, Dr. Simms, and the Church of Ireland Archbishop of Armagh both stated that their church upheld the indissolubility of the marriage bond. The latter, however, stated that he also wished to respect the rights of others who do not accept the principle of indissolubility. See *Irish Times* (16th December, 1967), p. 1.

See also Editorial of Church of Ireland Gazette reprinted in *Irish Times* (27th December, 1967), p. 9, "If there is to be freedom to divorce it is a freedom that ought to be open to all so far as the state is concerned. What the churches may lay down as a discipline to be accepted by their members is a different matter altogether. If it is right that divorce should be available to those whose consciences allow them to avail of it, then it should be left to their consciences to decide".

33. See *Irish Times* (16th December, 1967), pp. 1 and 6.
34. See "Revision of the Constitution; Religion and Marriage", by J.M. Kelly, *Irish Times* (5th January, 1968).

to. Moreover the recommendation gave no guidance as to the circumstances in which State legislation ought to permit the grant of a divorce in accordance with the tenets of a person's religion, e.g. it is certainly arguable that it would not be good public policy for the State to permit Roman Catholics to obtain a divorce under the civil law in accordance with the Petrine Privilege or Pauline Privilege. Nor did it give guidance as to the grounds upon which a divorce should be permitted in the case of parties married other than in accordance with the rites of a religion, i.e. in a registry office. The Dáil Committee reached a unanimous decision to permit a limited measure of divorce, a measure that is both undesirable and impossible to implement, without considering the one question that is fundamental in reaching a decision as to whether divorce legislation should be permitted and enacted, i.e. whether such legislation is socially desirable.[35]

REPORT OF THE JOINT OIREACHTAS COMMITTEE ON MARRIAGE BREAKDOWN[36]

Sixteen years after the Report of the Dáil Committee on the Constitution was published, in 1983, the Joint Oireachtas Committee on Marriage Breakdown was established "to consider the protection of marriage and of family life and to examine the problems which followed the breakdown of marriage and to report to the Houses of the Oireachtas thereon."[37] This All Party Committee composed of members of both the Dáil and the Seanad published its report in April of 1985 and in it gave detailed consideration to Article 41.3.2. The Committee received in excess of 700 written submissions and took oral evidence from 24 different groups, the overwhelming majority of which made reference to the constitutional prohibition on divorce.[38]

In summary the arguments the Joint Committee records as being made to it against divorce and in favour of the constitutional prohibition include the following:

(a) The introduction of divorce "would be contrary to the religious views of the vast majority of the people" residing in the State and contrary to the teachings of the church of which the overwhelming majority are members, i.e. the Roman Catholic Church.[39]

(b) The introduction of divorce would "open the flood gates" and would "cause persons who were having difficulties in their marriage to work less hard at achieving a solution to those difficulties" and as a result the incidents of marital breakdown would be greatly increased.[40]

(c) "The introduction of divorce would fundamentally change the nature and perception of marriage by making it into a temporary as opposed to a permanent union between a husband and wife" and into a temporary as opposed to a permanent contract. Divorce would "undermine the institution of marriage

---

35. See P. Hannon, "Catholics and Divorce", Vol. 27, *The Furrow*, p. 470 (Aug. 1976). In discussing whether divorce legislation should be introduced the author writes that the question should be regarded "not as a religious but as a socio-legal one . . . To consider it in terms of the respective rights of religious majorities and minorities is confusing and likely to obscure the real question. That question is how best is the state through legislation to cope with the fact that some marriages break down irretrievably?"
36. (Stationery Office, Dublin, 1985).
37. See *Joint Oireachtas Committee Report on Marriage Breakdown*, at p. vii.
38. The oral hearings are published as Minutes of Evidence taken by the Joint Committee.
39. See *Joint Oireachtas Committee Report, supra*, at p. 82.
40. *Ibid.* at pp. 80–81.

and the family and since the family is the fundamental unit of society", society itself, would be "undermined and destabilised."[41]

(d) The introduction of divorce would "reduce the protection at present given to the institution of marriage and the family under Article 41 of the Constitution" and would "have a detrimental effect on child development and would increase the number of children whose upbringing is damaged by the fact that they come from a broken home.[42]

(e) Divorce would result in women and children suffering "financial hardship" as "it costs more to look after two homes and two families" and "an inevitable reduction of the standards of living of the parties involved must take place." As the wife usually obtains custody of the children, divorce places her financially in a "particularly vulnerable position being unable to take up full time employment". Moreover, divorce would result in a loss of valuable rights currently guaranteed by law to spouses and children, such as inheritance or succession rights.[43]

In summary, the arguments the Joint Committee records as being made to it in favour of divorce and against the constitutional prohibition include the following:

(a) All the minority churches and religions in the State (with the exception of the Church of the Latter Day Saints) favour constitutional change and favour the provision of civil divorce arguing that the "civil law in this area should not reflect only the views expressed by the church of which the majority of the population are members, and that by doing so at present it discriminates against members of other churches and religions and those who profess no religious faith."[44] Moreover, the "absolute prohibition on divorce has the effect of imposing on Catholics regulations more rigid than those required by the law of the church."[45]

(b) The constitutional ban on divorce and the absence of divorce legislation "has not prevented marital breakdown from occurring and that in the past decade the level of marital breakdown has increased.[46] (Appendix C of this book contains some statistics as to the current level of marital breakdown — Author.)

(c) The breakdown of a marriage "is due to the collapse of the relationship between the parties" to the marriage and "divorce does not cause that collapse, but merely affords a facility to give legal recognition to the fact that a marriage has ended while leaving the parties thereto free to remarry."[47]

(d) "To deny the right to remarry to a battered wife or husband has no social advantage to the State and is in fact detrimental to society in general and lacking in compassion."[48]

(e) "It is the factual breakdown of a marriage and not the availability of divorce which has an adverse effect on children. The integration of a child into

41. *Ibid* at p. 80.
42. *Ibid*. at p. 81.
43. *Ibid*. at p. 82.
44. *Ibid*. at pp. 76–77.
45. *Ibid*. at p. 79.
46. *Ibid*. at p. 78.
47. *Ibid*. at p. 78.
48. *Ibid*. at pp. 78–79.

a new loving family unit can, in some circumstances, reduce the trauma resulting from the breakdown of a parents' marriage."[49]

(f) "Divorce is not the source of financial hardship to parties whose marriage has broken down. Such financial hardship results from the need to finance two separate homes, which in turn results from the need to live separate and apart. The forming of a relationship with a third party can either ease or exacerbate such financial difficulties."[50]

(g) "The prohibition on divorce is unjust to those persons whose marriages have irretrievably broken down and who have become involved in other relationships" because

(i) they cannot obtain any "recognition for their new relationship" or "any adequate legal definition of their status"

(ii) there is no legislation in force to protect the "parties to and the children of such relationships"

(iii) "the children of such a relationship are illegitimate"

(iv) "the parties suffer substantial disadvantages in areas such as taxation and the right to social welfare benefits."[51]

(h) The absence of divorce is resulting in spouses whose marriages have broken down trying to use other mechanisms and legal forms as a substitute for divorce. These include:

(i) marrying another person either in Ireland or outside Ireland after first obtaining a foreign decree of divorce not recognised in Ireland, having the result that the State does not recognise the second marriage and still regards the divorced couple as married to each other.

(ii) marrying another person in a Roman Catholic church after first obtaining a church decree of annulment or dissolution, the State not recognising the Church annulment or dissolution having the result that it does not recognise the second marriage and still regards the parties to the annulled or dissolved marriage as married to each other.

(iii) completion of a deed poll whereby a woman or man changes his or her name to correspond with that of the person with whom they are residing, where one or both parties are already married to someone else, so that they both have the same surname and appear to be married.[52]

Having considered the above arguments the Committee noted that "it is almost 48 years since the present Constitution came into force" and acknowledged that "many people in this country are affected by the problem of marital breakdown". Stating that "strong argument can be made both for and against the introduction of divorce" and accepting that "the holding of a referendum . . . is likely to be socially divisive" a majority of the Committee expressed the view that a referendum should be held. Moreover, "so as to ensure that no constitutional ambiguity results from any such referendum", the Committee stated "that any amendment to be voted upon should be in a positive format" and should "be drafted in such way as to ensure that the basic emphasis of Article 41

---

49. *Ibid.* at p. 79.
50. *Ibid.* at p. 80.
51. *Ibid.* at p. 75.
52. *Ibid.* at pp. 29 and 84.

is not altered, in that the Article should continue to place a duty on the State to protect the family and the institution of marriage and to recognise the family as the natural, primary and fundamental unit group of society."[53]

The Committee did "not express any views on the wider question of whether divorce legislation is either necessary or desirable" and took the view that "it would not be appropriate or feasible for it to recommend the details of any divorce legislation which might be provided in the event of a change in the Constitution."[54] It did, however, indicate "its views as to what should be the main feature of any such legislation" stating that:

> "Adequate safeguards must be built into any legislation to take account of the State interest in fostering and protecting marriage and the family. Also the Committee feels that there is an obvious need to ensure in any such legislation that proper provision is made for the protection of dependent spouses and the welfare of dependent children who might be affected by the grant of a decree of divorce."[55]

Recording that the constant theme in its "opinions and observations" has "been the need as far as possible to reduce the adversorial element in marriage breakdown" it concluded that "any divorce law should be based on the concept of marital breakdown", as such an approach, the Committee believed, "would reduce acrimony and bitterness and would assist separated parents in the continuing relationship between themselves and their children."[56]

Having already proposed that irretrievable breakdown should be the basis for granting decrees of judicial separation it was of the belief "that the grant of a decree of judicial separation should be a first step, whereby a person could apply after a fixed period of time, after the granting of a judicial separation for a decree of divorce."[57]

THE 1986 DIVORCE REFERENDUM

Following the Committee's Report being debated in both the Dáil[58] and the Senate[59] the Taoiseach consulted with the leaders of the main churches and religious denominations and on the 23rd of April, 1986, the government announced its intention to hold a referendum.[60] The Tenth Amendment of the Constitution

53. *Ibid.* at p. 89.
54. *Ibid.* at p. 90.
55. *Ibid.* at p. 90.
56. *Ibid.* at p. 90.
57. *Ibid.* at p. 91.
58. See (14th November, 1985) 361 Dáil Debates Cols. 2260–2337 & Cols. 2396–2415; (29th November, 1985) 362 Dáil Debates Cols. 713–806; (6th December, 1985) 362 Dáil Debates Cols. 1467–1564; (13th December, 1985) 362 Dáil Debates Cols. 2364–2386 and the (24th January, 1986) 363 Dáil Debates, Cols. 527–572.
59. See (27th June, 1985) 108 Seanad Debates Cols. 1142–1192; (18th July, 1985) 108 Seanad Debates Cols. 2066–2086; (26th September, 1985) 109 Seanad Debates Cols. 163–221; (2nd October, 1985) 109 Seanad Debates Cols. 273–293; (13th October, 1985) 109 Seanad Debates Cols. 467–478; (24th October, 1985) 109 Seanad Debates Cols. 632–727; (6th November, 1985) 109 Seanad Debates Cols. 943–1022 & 1057–1082.
60. On two occasions after the publication of the Committee's Report and prior to the publication of the government's Bill attempts were made to start the legislative process for the holding of a referendum. A Private Members Bill, the 10th Amendment to the Constitution Bill, 1985, sponsored by M. O'Leary, T.D., was denied a first reading in the Dáil on the 5th day of November, 1985, prior to the completion of the Dáil and Seanad debates on the Joint Committee's Report – see 361 Dáil Debates Cols. 1253–1261. A further Private Members Bill entitled the 10th Amendment to the Constitution (No. 2) Bill, 1985, sponsored by the Labour Party was given an unopposed first reading on the 17th of December, 1985 (see 362 Dáil Debates Col.2513) but was denied a second reading on the 26th of February, 1986 (see (18th of February, 1986) 363 Dáil Debates Cols. 3001–3034); (19th February, 1986) 363 Dáil Debates Cols. 3222–3252; (25th February, 1986) 364 Dáil Debates Cols. 214–244 and (26th February, 1986) 364 Dáil Debates Cols. 450–483.

Bill, 1986, proposed that the prohibition on divorce be deleted from the Constitution and be replaced by the following provision:

> "Where, and only where, such court established under this Constitution as may be prescribed by law is satisfied that —
>
>   i.   a marriage has failed,
>
>   ii. the failure has continued for a period of, or periods amounting to, at least five years,
>
>   iii. that there is no reasonable possibility of reconciliation between the parties to the marriage, and
>
>   iv. any other condition prescribed by law has been complied with,
>
> the court may in accordance with law grant a dissolution of the marriage provided that the court is satisfied that adequate and proper provision having regard to the circumstances will be made for any dependent spouse and for any child who is dependent on either spouse."

The other provisions contained in Articles 41 and 42 were to remain unchanged.

A document published at the same time as the Bill entitled "Statement of Government's Intentions With Regard to Marriage, Separation and Divorce" to which reference has already been made in earlier chapters, contained proposals setting out the form of divorce legislation that the government intended to introduce if the referendum were successful, the substance of which substantially accorded with the views expressed by the Joint Oireachtas Committee. It envisaged that obtaining a decree of judicial separation or a court order approving the contents of a deed of separation and making it a rule of court would be an essential prerequisite to the institution of divorce proceedings. It emphasised that "a period or periods of not less than 5 years separation will be required before an application for divorce will be entertained" and that "no decree of divorce will be granted within 2 years from the date of judicial separation or the order making a separation agreement a rule of court".[61] The "Statement" promised that new legislation would also contain comprehensive provisions to enable a family court[62] determining applications for either divorce or judicial separations, "to make various financial orders with a view to ensuring that the interests of a dependent spouse and children are adequately protected and appropriately provided for."[63] Such orders, it stated would "relate to maintenance, lump sum payments and property owned by the spouses, including the family home".[64] Moreover in any divorce proceedings instituted, the effectiveness of any arrangements made by the court in separation proceedings or in a separation agreement made a rule of court, relating to a dependent spouse or children was to be reviewed.[65]

In a later revised statement, the government affirmed that "in the case of a widow's or widower's pension under an occupation pension scheme, (including, of course public service pension schemes) where in the absence of special provision the pension would be lost on divorce, the court will have power to order

---

61. "Statement" (April, 1986) at p. 3.
62. Which it is promised would be established – see Statement, *supra*, at p. 2 – see also p. 68 *ante*.
63. "Statement", *supra* at p. 3.
64. *Ibid.*
65. "Statement", *supra* at p. 5.

that the whole or part of the pension be paid to a spouse who is divorced".[66]
It also undertook to make any necessary changes that were required in Social
Welfare legislation "to ensure that no spouse will be disadvantaged in terms of
his or her social welfare entitlements" as a result of a change in legal status
"from 'married', 'separated' or 'deserted' to 'divorced' ".[67] It was also stated
that any divorce legislation would be framed so as "to enable the court to take
account of loss of succession rights arising from divorce" and that "the court
will be empowered to order that compensation be given where it is appropriate
to do so." As an alternative to a court ordering that a spouse retain a pension
entitlement, the court was also to be empowered "to order compensation to be
made" to a spouse in some other form where appropriate, for example, by lump
sum or property transfer orders.[68]

The Tenth Amendment of the Constitution Bill completed its passage through
the Dáil[69] and the Senate[70] on the 24th day of May, 1986. The arguments both
in favour and against divorce synopsised above from the Report of the Joint
Oireachtas Committee were relied upon by the proponents and opponents of
divorce in the debate that took place in the two Houses of the Oireachtas and in
the public debate and campaign that ensued.[71] The Roman Catholic Church and
the many religious organisations and bodies associated with it vigorously opposed

---

66. "Statement" (June, 1986) at p. 11.
67. *Ibid.*
68. *Ibid.*
69. See (14th May, 1986) 366 Dáil Debates Cols. 790–857, Cols. 919–990 & 1033–
1067; (15th May, 1986) 366 Dáil Debates Cols. 1077–1134 & 1218–1354; (16th May,
1986) 366 Dáil Debates Cols. 1356–1466; (20th May, 1986) 366 Dáil Debates Cols. 1609–
1750; (21st May, 1986) 366 Dáil Debates Cols. 1752–1802 & 1881–1977.
70. See (22nd May, 1986) 112 Seanad Debates Cols. 1447–1700; (23rd May, 1986)
112 Seanad Debates Cols. 1704–1806 and (24th May, 1986) 112 Seanad Debates Cols.
1898–2040.
71. In addition to the arguments synopsised from the *Joint Oireachtas Committee
Report* two books published prior to the holding of the referendum comprehensively
reflect the substantive arguments made on both sides of the debate. See W. Duncan, "The
Case for Divorce in the Irish Republic", revised edition (I.C.C.L. Report No. 5, 1982) and
W. Binchy, *Is Divorce the Answer* (Irish Academic Press, Dublin, 1984). See also Review of
the original edition of Duncan's *The Case for Divorce* by W. Binchy at (1980) 15 I.J. (n.s.)
361 and the reply of W. Duncan (1981) 16 I.J. (n.s.) 186. In the campaign that preceded
the holding of the referendum a majority of the Oireachtas members of both the Fine Gael
and Labour parties who formed the coalition government favoured change while a minority
of the members of each party opposed change. The principal opposition party, Fianna Fáil,
officially maintained a neutral stance but the overwhelming majority of its members of the
Oireachtas made it known that they opposed the removal of the prohibition on divorce
from the Constitution. Outside the formal political party structure much of the argument
in favour of divorce was made by the Divorce Action Group and that made against divorce
was spearheaded by the Anti-Divorce Campaign Group of which Mr Binchy was a leading
protagonist.
The following articles clearly illustrate the various arguments made during the course
of the referendum campaign by those who supported the government's proposal and by
those who opposed it. See articles in support by – Sen. M. Robinson, *Irish Times*, 2nd
June, 1986, p. 8 & 3rd of June, 1986, p. 18; D. Spring, T.D., An Tanaiste, *Irish Independent*, 23rd June, 1986, p. 8; K. Boyle, *Irish Times*, 24th June, 1986, p. 9. See also inter-
views with Alan Dukes, T.D., Minister for Justice, 25th of May, 1986, *Sunday Press*, p. 10;
An Taoiseach, Dr Garrett Fitzgerald, T.D., 8th June, 1986, *Sunday Tribune*, p. 9 and 22nd
June, 1986, *Sunday Independent*, p. 8.
See articles in opposition by – Paul Bowe, O.P., *Irish Independent*, 27th May, 1986, p.
6; Anti-Divorce Campaign Group, *Irish Independent*, 28th May, 1986, p. 10; W. Binchy,
Irish Independent, 15th June, 1986, p. 9.
See also interview with P. Cooney, T.D., Minister for Education, 5th June, 1986, *Sunday
Independent*, p. 8. For an article summarising the arguments on both sides see K.D. O'Con-
nor, 6th June, 1986, *Irish Independent*, p. 8.

constitutional change[72] whilst the minority churches and religions made known their support for change.[73] Finally, on the 26th of June, 1986, the people went to the polls and the proposal to amend the Constitution was rejected by 935,843 votes to 538,279 votes. The total electorate eligible to vote was 2,440,907.

---

72. The Irish Bishops Pastoral, *Love is for Life, supra*, published in 1985, a year prior to the calling of a referendum comprehensively sets out the opposition of the Irish Hierarchy to the introduction of divorce. Three weeks prior to the referendum vote a documentary extract from the pastoral entitled "Marriage, The Family and Divorce — A Statement by the Irish Bishops" was distributed at all churches throughout the country. There are two appendices attached to this statement. Appendix 1 contains an extract from the written submission made by the Irish Bishops to the Taoiseach in talks that took place prior to the calling of the referendum and Appendix 2 contains a statement issued by the Irish Hierarchy on the 26th of April, 1986, after the announcement was made that a referendum was to be held. The contents of both of these appendices can be found in Appendix D of this book.

Much public comment was made and a considerable number of addresses were delivered and sermons preached by members of the Roman Catholic Hierarchy in the period following the announcement of the holding of a referendum up until polling day. Much of the comment made is reported in the *Irish Times, Irish Independent, Irish Press* and *Cork Examiner* in the period from the 24th of April, 1986, to the 26th of June, 1986. The following are references to some of the comment reported:

Interview with Dr Newman, Bishop of Limerick, 5th of May, 1986, *Irish Times*, p. 9 in which he states that divorce will be "disastrous" for Ireland and that "the government has no right either under christian law or natural law to introduce this (divorce)". See also address of Dr Newman reported in the 23rd of May, 1986 *Irish Times*, at p. 8.

Address of the Archbishop of Dublin, Dr K. McNamara, 7th of May, 1986, *Irish Times* at p. 8 in which he states "civil divorce holds out the offer of what God does not allow. It may meet the desires of some, but it cannot bring happiness or secure God's blessings for society as a whole. On the contrary, it makes stable and permanent marriages more difficult for everyone. May the spirit of God guide and support the Irish people in their defence of marriage and the stability of family life."

See also addresses of Archbishop McNamara reported on the 31st of May, 1986, *Irish Times* at p. 10, 6th June, 1986, *Irish Times* at p. 8, the 14th of June, 1986, *Irish Times* at p. 8 and the 23rd of June, 1986, *Irish Times* at p. 8. See also the interview given by Dr McNamara to *Magill Magazine* (June, 1986) p. 17 in which he states that "if divorce legislation were to be introduced, it would seem to conflict with the whole tenor of what the Constitution has to say in regard to marriage and the family, and not just with the existing prohibition on divorce. The introduction of divorce and remarriage could well lead to increasing pressure that the very notion of marriage and the family as understood by the Constitution should be changed. . . . Law has an impact on people's values. It creates a climate of opinion which influences and either helps them or hinders them in maintaining their personal ideals and convictions and acting according to them. . . . The Chernobyl disaster of recent weeks can be a useful reminder of how negative radiation can filter across and permeate society. Divorce legislation has had a somewhat similar effect in the way it has permeated western societies and undermined the stability of married life."

Statement issued by the Irish Bishops Conference on the 12th of June, 1986, *Irish Times* at p. 7, *Irish Independent* at p. 8 and *Irish Press* at p. 1 in which the Bishops stated "Once divorce is introduced marriage in civil law is no longer binding unless and until 'death do us part'. It becomes binding unless and until 'divorce do us part' . . . we are convinced that the proposed amendment would weaken rather than strengthen marriage and the family. It would damage rather than protect the genuine rights and wellbeing of both spouses and children. While it would alleviate the pain of some it would, we believe, release in society a force which would bring pain to a much greater number."

Address of Cardinal O'Fiaich, 18th June, 1986, *Irish Times*, p. 10 where he states that "despite the Church's best endeavours only a few states remain unharmed by what the Second Vatican Councils calls 'the plague of divorce'. The people of the Republic have, therefore, a grave responsibility . . . they will decide whether to open or bar the door." See also comments by Cardinal O'Fiaich, 24th June, 1986, *Irish Press*, p. 1.

See also the address of the Bishop of Ferns, Dr Comiskey, 19th June, 1986, *Irish Times* at p. 8 and addresses of the Archbishop of Cashel, Dr T. Morris, the Bishop of Clare & Ross, Dr M. Murphy, the Bishop of Killala, Dr T. McDonnell, the Bishop of Clonfert, Dr Cassidy, the Bishop of Kerry, Dr O'Suilleabhain, all reported in the 23rd of June, 1986, *Irish Times* at p. 8. See further Pastoral letter of the Archbishop of Tuam, Dr J. Cunnane, 5th of June, 1986, *Irish Independent* at p. 9.

73. Dr Eames, the Church of Ireland Archbishop of Armagh, addressing the Churches General Synod in Dublin stated that civil divorce provided an "opportunity for couples to end the human misery they may encounter through a complete failure to maintain their (marriage) vows" and that the uncomfortable fact had to be recognised that "the numbers of those marriages which are ending in hardship and disillusionment is increasing" (21st of

THE PROHIBITION ON DIVORCE AND THE PROBLEM OF
MARITAL BREAKDOWN

The result of the divorce referendum makes it unlikely that there will be another referendum on the divorce issue in Ireland for at least a decade. Marriages will, of course, continue to break down and husbands and wives whose marriages have collapsed will continue to separate. Some will separate by agreement, some will separate as a result of the granting of a decree of judicial separation or the making of a court barring order. Some will live apart following one spouse simply walking out on or deserting the other. The fact that in law such couples will continue to be regarded as married to each other will not, in social reality, camouflage the fact that many Irish marriages will remain, and an increasing number of Irish marriages will become, marriages in name only.[74] The funding of two separate households by the same income that previously funded one after husbands and wives have separated will continue to result in many spouses whose marriages have collapsed suffering financial hardship and a reduced standard of living.[75] Moreover, the absence of divorce will not prevent the courts from recognising that the factual separation of spouses can change the constitutional complexion of the family under Articles 41 and 42 in circumstances where the family ceases to function as a single unit.[76]

The Joint Oireachtas Committee acknowledged that if the Constitution remained unchanged and the prohibition on divorce was retained it was "inevitable" that "many" of those who are parties to a broken marriage will "form stable permanent relationships with other men and women" and that a "significant number" will continue to "resort to alternative forms and mechanisms in second relationships, in order to extend the appearance of 'marriage' to their relationship".[77] In this context, the alternative forms and mechanisms referred to by the Committee include those already mentioned above, i.e. spouses celebrating second ceremonies of marriage with other persons, having first obtained either a church annulment or dissolution that has no effect on the civil validity of their first marriage or a foreign decree of divorce not recognised by Irish law. There is little doubt that if divorce was available in Ireland the great majority of those who have so behaved in the past and who will do so in the future would obtain a divorce and remarry under Irish law. As one writer remarked some years prior to the 1986 divorce referendum, it is ironic that the very absence of divorce facilities is contributing to the growing phenomena of cohabitation out-

---

May, 1986, *Irish Times* at p. 1). Dr Empey, the Church of Ireland Bishop of Meath & Kildare also addressing the General Synod, referring to the need for divorce stated "we wish dearly that there would be no necessity for such legislation, but we feel that it is the only rational response to an escalating problem" (22nd May, 1986, *Irish Times* p. 6). See also the comments of the Dean of St Patricks Cathedral, the Rev. Victor Griffin, in the same report. See further, comments reported from the Presbyterian General Assembly, 6th June, 1986, *Irish Times* at p. 8 and the statement by the Irish Council of Churches, 11th June, 1986, *Irish Press*, p. 4 and by the Dublin Council of Churches, 29th June, 1986, *Irish Times* at p. 8.

74. The statistical information contained in Appendix C clearly shows an escalating number of marital cases being brought before the courts annually as a result of marriages breaking down. As more marriages break down, the number of those who are parties to a broken marriage must steadily increase. The best statistical illustration of this can be seen from the annual increase in the number of wives who are recipients of deserted wives allowance and benefit.

75. See *R.H. v. N.H.* (October, 1985) unreported (S.C.) and the comments therein of Finlay C.J. cited on p. 435 *post*.

76. See p. 5 *ante*.

77. *Joint Oireachtas Committee Report, supra*, at p. 84.

side legal marriage when divorce is prohibited by Article 41 on the basis of a philosophy of providing support for family life based on marriage.[78]

It is important to note that couples who set up home having celebrated a ceremony of marriage, either civil or religious, after one or both of them have had a first marriage annulled or dissolved by the Roman Catholic Church or have obtained an unrecognisable foreign decree of divorce are, in Irish law, merely cohabitees. Consequently, the law applicable to their relationship and any children born to them is no different to that applicable to a man and woman who simply set up home together having neither validly married each other nor ever having been married to any other person. The fact that a party's first marriage still subsists and that any second marriage ceremony in which he or she has participated has no legal validity means that under Irish law:

1. Any second marriage ceremony celebrated is not only void but may render the person attempting to acquire a second spouse liable to a criminal charge of bigamy.[79]

2. The parties to the second marriage acquire no rights of succession or to maintenance as between each other and none of the protections afforded by the Family Home Protection Act, 1976, or the Family Law (Protection of Spouses & Children) Act, 1981, extend to their relationship.

3. Any children born to the parties to the second marriage are illegitimate and if they are unable to have children of their own, they cannot

---

78. W. Duncan, "Second Marriages After Church Annulments – A Problem of Legal Policy" (1978) 72 *Gazette of the Incorporated Law Society of Ireland* 203. See also W. Duncan, "Supporting the Institution of Marriage in Ireland" (1978) 13 I.J. (n.s.) 215 where he states that "there are . . . signs that the absence of divorce is giving rise to practices of evasion and avoidance which characterise pre-divorce Italy" (p. 227). The same article can be found in *Marriage & Cohabitation in Contemporary Societies*, edited by J.M. Eekelaar & S.N. Katz (Butterworths, Toronto, Canada, 1980) p. 82 *et seq*.

79. For examples of cases determined by the courts in which a second Church marriage has been celebrated after a Church decree of annulment or dissolution has been granted without the party to the annulled or dissolved marriage first obtaining a civil decree of annulment see *N.A.D. v. T.D.* [1985] 5 I.L.R.M. 153 (H.C.); *F.M.L. & A.L. v. The Registrar General of Marriages* [1984] 4 I.L.R.M. 667 (H.C.); *A.M.N. v. J.P.C.* (December, 1985) unreported (H.C.). In the latter two cases previously married parties subsequently obtained a civil decree of annulment. The granting of such a decree retrospectively validated the parties' second marriage. In *F.M.L. & A.L. v. The Registrar General of Marriages, supra*, Lynch J. emphasised the "difficulties and dangers" of adopting such a course of action stating that "if a trial for bigamy should pre-date the decree of nullity the accused spouse would be liable to conviction and penalty" (*supra* at p. 670). In *A.M.N. v. J.P.C.* a criminal prosecution for bigamy was instituted by a wife's second husband subsequent to her marrying him in Church after her first marriage had been annulled by the Roman Catholic Marriage Tribunals. The bigamy proceedings were still pending at the time when the High Court was asked to grant a decree of annulment of the wife's first marriage on the ground of her first husband's impotence. Such a decree was granted and as a result it is presumed that the proceedings for bigamy were terminated.

For examples of cases determined by the courts where a second marriage was celebrated after the granting of an unrecognisable foreign decree of divorce see *Gaffney v. Gaffney* [1975] I.R. 133 (S.C.); *K.E.D. (otherwise K.C.) v. M.C.* (September, 1984) unreported (H.C.), (December, 1985) unreported (S.C.) and *C.S. (otherwise L.) v. J.L.* (July, 1985) unreported (H.C.).

See also *The People (Attorney General) v. Ballins* (1964) Irish Jur. Rep. 14 (Cir. Ct.) and *People (A.G.) v. Hunt* (1945) 80 I.L.T. & S.J. 19 where bigamy prosecutions resulted from a spouse celebrating a second ceremony of marriage to a third party in a Roman Catholic Church after a previous registry office marriage to another. The Church was willing to celebrate such marriage as it did not recognise the validity of the registry office marriage. See further C. Davitt, "Some Aspects of the Constitution and the Law in Relation to Matrimony" (1968) *Studies* 6.

together adopt a child as they are not in law a married couple.[80]

4. The family formed by the parties to the second marriage is not recognised as a family within the meaning of the Constitution and none of the constitutional protections afforded to the family as a constitutional unit extends to it.

During the recent referendum debate those opposed to constitutional change, including the Roman Catholic Church, failed to adequately address the growing problem being created for Irish society by the increasing number of couples cohabiting outside legal marriage. Moreover, the Irish Catholic Bishops in their pre-referendum submission to the Taoiseach, referring to the remarriage of persons in Church after the granting of a church decree of annulment, confirmed the Church's intention to continue to celebrate such marriages. In the context of a discussion headed "The Enforcement of the Law Proscribing Bigamy" they stated that

"If a particular country's laws differ from those of the Catholic Church on the question of what constitutes a valid marriage, it is not possible for the Church to change the conditions of validity in order to adjust in every respect to the provisions contained in the civil law. Where the Catholic Church recognises as invalid a marriage which initially had the appearance of validity, it is obliged to take account of the status of the partners concerned as persons who were not in Church law united as husband and wife in virtue of that ceremony."[81]

It is noteworthy that in their written published submission under the above heading the Catholic Bishops avoided making explicit reference to the remarriage of persons in church after the granting of church decrees of dissolution or after the celebration of a marriage in a civil registry office. Whilst it is assumed that it is the Church's intention to continue celebrating second marriages after church dissolutions, it cannot necessarily be assumed that the Church intends to so act after the celebration of registry office marriages, as criminal prosecutions instituted by the State for bigamy following such second marriages have in the past secured criminal convictions.[82]

The number of civilly invalid and bigamous second marriages that have been celebrated by the Roman Catholic Church and the number of couples who are parties to such marriages is unknown, as is the number of those spouses who have celebrated a second marriage ceremony after first obtaining an unrecognisable foreign decree of divorce. Indeed, as the Joint Oireachtas Committee noted, no comprehensive and detailed statistics exist as to the full extent of marital breakdown in Ireland today.[83] At the time of writing, figures are being collated by the Central Statistics Office derived from the 1986 census which may for the first time comprehensively indicate the extent of the problem. The results of this census, taken together with the continuing growth in the numbers

---

80. Such child will be categorised as a "non-marital child" if the Status of Children Bill, 1986, as initiated, becomes law. However, if a decree of nullity is granted in respect of the second marriage and either party to such marriage "reasonably believed that the ceremony of marriage resulted in a valid marriage" such child may be "deemed" to be a legitimate child and a "marital child" within the meaning of the proposed statute (see Sects. 2 & 6 of the Bill as initiated). See further p. 289 *post*.

81. See *A statement of the Irish Bishops, Marriage, the Family and Divorce, supra.* Appendix 1 para 1.

82. See *The People (A.G.) v. Ballins, supra* and *The People (A.G.) v. Hunt, supra*.

83. See *Report of the Joint Oireachtas Committee, supra*, at pp. 31–32.

of people who find themselves not only legally tied to broken marriages but also parties to invalid and bigamous marriages, many of which are sanctioned and approved of by the Roman Catholic Church, will inevitably force both Irish legislators and the Irish people to again consider the need for constitutional change and the provision of divorce legislation.[84] The question is not whether there will ever again be a referendum on this issue but when will such referendum next be held.

---

84. As an alternative to divorce it has been suggested that the State should permit "bigamy under licence" and allow a person to enter into a second marriage when all the outstanding obligations of a first marriage have been "arranged under the terms of a judicial separation". Such an approach, it is suggested, could resolve the difficulties that arise in civil law and extend civil legal protections to the parties to a marriage celebrated in a Roman Catholic church where a party to such marriage has previously obtained a church decree of annulment or dissolution. See M.C. McGuckian S.J., "Civil Remarriage without Divorce — A Creative Alternative" (1985) 51 I.T.Q. 193.

CHAPTER 10

RECOGNITION OF FOREIGN DECREES OF DIVORCE A VINCULO[1]

INTRODUCTION

Prior to 1937 the Irish courts generally recognised foreign decrees of divorce *a vinculo matrimonii* if at the date of the institution of the divorce proceedings both spouses were domiciled within the jurisdiction of the foreign court which granted the decree of divorce.[2] As a wife's domicile was dependent on that of her husband, this meant in effect that a foreign decree of divorce was recognised if the husband was domiciled in the jurisdiction of the foreign court at the date of the institution of the divorce proceedings. Upon the enactment of the 1937 Constitution, there was a degree of judicial uncertainty as to its impact on this common law rule. However, in a number of cases determined by both the High Court and the Supreme Court it was held to be still part of Irish law.[3] The law relating to the recognition of foreign decrees of divorce *a vinculo* remained unchanged until the Domicile & Recognition of Foreign Divorces Act, 1986, came into force on the 2nd of October, 1986.[4] This Act makes provision for a wife to acquire an independent domicile of her own[5] and provides for the recognition of a foreign decree of divorce *a vinculo* if either spouse is domiciled within the jurisdiction of the foreign court which grants the divorce decree, at the date of the institution of the divorce proceedings.[6] The Act also makes special

---

1. See generally, P.M. North, *The Private International Law of Matrimonial Causes in the British Isles and the Republic of Ireland* (North Holland Publishing Co., 1977) pp. 372–386; The Law Reform Commission, *Recognition of Foreign Divorces & Legal Separations* – Working Paper No. 11 (Dublin, September 1984) and Report No. 10 (Dublin, April 1985); J.M. Kelly, *The Irish Constitution* (Jurist Publishing Co. Ltd., Dublin 1984) pp. 617–623 and the earlier work of the same author, *Fundamental Rights in the Irish Law & Constitution*, 2nd Ed. (Dublin, 1967) pp. 199–204; C. Jones, "The Non-Recognition of Foreign Divorces in Ireland" (1968) 3 I.J. (n.s.) 299; G. Lee, "Irish Matrimonial Law & The Married Status", 16 N.I.L.Q. 385; J. O'Reilly, "Recognition of Foreign Divorce Decrees" (1971), 6 I.J. (n.s.) 293; A.W. Kerr, "The Need for a Recognition of Divorces Act" (1976) 1 D.U.L.J. 11; P.A. O'Connor, "The Recognition of Foreign Divorce Decrees" (1986) 4 I.L.T. (n.s.) 45; W. Duncan, "The Future for Divorce Recognition in Ireland" (1970) 2 D.U.L.R., and by the same author, "Desertion & Cruelty in Irish Matrimonial Law" (1972) 7 I.J. (n.s.) 213, "Foreign Divorces Obtained on the Basis of Residence & the Doctrine of Estoppel" (1974) 9 I.J. (n.s.) 59 and "Collusive Foreign Divorces – How to Have your Cake and Eat it" (1981) D.U.L.J. 17.
2. See *Maghee v. M'Allister* (1853) 3 Ir. Ch. Rep. 604 (Ct. of Ch.); *Sinclair v. Sinclair* [1896] 1 I.R. 603 (Ch. D.). See also *Mayo-Perrott v. Mayo-Perrott* [1958] I.R. 336 (S.C.).
3. See *Mayo-Perrott v. Mayo-Perrott, supra*; *Bank of Ireland v. Caffin* [1971] I.R. 123 (H.C.); *Counihan v. Counihan* (July, 1973) unreported (H.C.); *Gaffney v. Gaffney* [1975] I.R. 133 (S.C.); *T. v. T.* [1983] I.R. 29 (S.C.); *K.E.D. (otherwise K.C.) v. M.C.* (September, 1984) unreported (H.C.), (December, 1985) unreported (S.C.); *C.S. (otherwise L.) v. J.L.* (July, 1985) unreported (H.C.).
4. The Statute was enacted by the Oireachtas on the 2nd of July, 1986. Sect. 6(2) provides that "it shall come into operation on the day that is three months after the date of the passing of this Act."
5. See sects. 1–3. See further p. 192 *ante*.
6. See sect. 5.

provision for decrees of divorce granted by courts within the British Isles and Northern Ireland.[7] The new rules as to the recognition of foreign decrees of divorce only apply under the Act to decrees granted after its commencement.[8] As the Act came into force on the 2nd of October, 1986, it does not extend recognition to decrees of divorce granted prior to that date that were not recognisable under Irish common law. Accordingly, different rules now apply to the recognition of foreign decrees of divorce granted prior to the 2nd of October, 1986, than apply to those granted on or after that date. It is intended first to examine the impact of the Irish Constitution on this area of the law. We shall then discuss the law as to recognition of foreign divorces as it relates to decrees granted prior to the 2nd of October, 1986 and thereafter examine the law applicable to decrees granted on or after that date. Finally, we shall examine the relevance of estoppel to this area of the law and the public policy grounds upon which the courts may refuse to extend recognition to foreign divorce decrees, even though the basic recognition requirement in relation to domicile has been complied with.

ARTICLE 41.3.3. AND ITS INTERPRETATION

Constitutional reference to the dissolution of marriage by a foreign decree of divorce is to be found in Article 41.3.3. This Article states that:

> "No person whose marriage has been dissolved under the civil law of any other State but is a subsisting valid marriage under the law for the time being in force within the jurisdiction of the Government and Parliament established by this Constitution shall be capable of contracting a valid marriage within that jurisdiction during the lifetime of the other party to the marriage so dissolved".

The 1922 Constitution contained no article corresponding to Art. 41.3.3.° Its meaning was first judicially considered in *Mayo-Perrott v. Mayo-Perrott.*[9] The plaintiff had obtained a divorce *a vinculo matrimonii* in England, where she and her husband had been domiciled. Having been awarded the costs of the petition by the English court she sought to recover the sum remaining unpaid in the Irish courts, her former husband having come to reside within the jurisdiction of the Irish courts. The Supreme Court on appeal, however, refused to enforce the order for costs partly on the ground that the cause of action was of such a character that it could not have supported an action in this country and partly that to enforce an order which assisted the obtaining of a divorce decree was contrary to public policy.[10]

Referring to whether Irish law should "give active assistance to facilitate in any way the effecting of a dissolution of marriage in another country where the parties are domiciled" Kingsmill Moore J. stated:

> "It cannot be doubted that the public policy of this country as reflected in the Constitution does not favour divorce a vinculo ... (the law) would fail to carry out public policy if, by a decree of its own courts, it gave assistance

---

7. See, in particular, sect. 5(3).
8. See, in particular, sect. 5(5).
9. [1958] I.R. 336 (S.C.).
10. See judgement of Kingsmill Moore J. and O'Daly J., especially.

to the process of divorce by entertaining a suit for the costs of such proceedings."[11]

However, while the Irish courts would do nothing to facilitate or assist the bringing of divorce proceedings, this did not of necessity mean that they would not recognise the change of status brought about by the grant of a decree of divorce. The meaning of Article 41.3.3. and the question as to whether the Irish courts would recognise a divorce granted by the courts of a foreign country was discussed by Maguire C.J. and Kingsmill Moore J.[12]

Maguire C.J. regarded the Article as

"clearly . . . designed to double bar the door closed in sub-s.2. Far from recognising the validity of a divorce obtained outside the country it seems to me expressly to deny to such a divorce any recognition for it prohibits the contracting of a valid marriage by a party who has obtained a divorce elsewhere. The sub-section says as plainly as it could be said that a valid marriage which is dissolved under the law of another State remains in the eyes of our law a subsisting valid marriage. It may be that the Constitution recognises that a decree of dissolution of marriage elsewhere may be valid in the country where it has been obtained, but to my mind as I have said, it denies it any validity here".[13]

Kingsmill Moore J. disagreed with the above interpretation. He reviewed a number of pre-1922 English and Irish decisions,[14] and on the basis of these, concluded that prior to that date the Irish courts would have recognised a divorce decree granted by a foreign court within the jurisdiction of the common domicile of the parties. The law was not affected by the enactment of the 1922 Constitution, nor by the coming into force of the 1937 Constitution. Article 41.3.3.°, he stated, only denied recognition to divorces

---

11. *Supra* at p. 350. In *D.M.* v. *E.F.M.* (July 1978) unreported (H.C.) Hamilton J. held that the enforcement by the Irish courts of a maintenance order made in and consequent to English divorce proceedings could not be said to assist or facilitate the process of divorce, the maintenance order having been made approximately 6 years after the divorce decree was granted. However, in *G.* v. *G.* [1984] I.R. 368 (H.C.) Finlay P. appeared to raise a doubt as to whether there were public policy objections to the enforcement of a maintenance order which commenced only upon the granting of a divorce decree. This doubt has now been dispelled by the judgement of the Supreme Court delivered by Finlay C.J. in *Sachs* v. *Standard Chartered Bank (Ireland) Ltd.* (July, 1986) unreported (S.C.) in which the Supreme Court upheld the unreported judgement delivered in the High Court by Barrington J. (July, 1985). See further p. 462 *post*.

On the issue of the Irish courts not assisting in the obtaining of a divorce decree see also J.M. Kelly, "The Irish Constitution", *supra*, at p. 619 where the author refers to two further cases. These are Ex.p. Minister for External Affairs: *Hovells* v. *Hovells* (1962) unreported (S.C.) in which the Supreme Court on the application of the Minister for External Affairs, on appeal from the High Court, ordered the examination within the jurisdiction of the Courts of the Republic of Ireland of a witness in divorce proceedings then pending before a foreign court and *Heffernan* v. *Heffernan* (1955) unreported (H.C.) in which the High Court refused to make a similar order. The latter decision was not appealed. There are no detailed written judgements available in either case.

With reference to the enforceability of Deeds of Separation concluded in contemplation of divorce proceedings see *Cohane* v. *Cohane* [1968] I.R. 176 (S.C.) and *Dalton* v. *Dalton* [1982] 2 I.L.R.M. 418 (H.C.). See further p. 210 *ante*.

12. The Chief Justice found it "not easy to construe" whilst Kingsmill Moore J. stated the words to be "not without difficulty".

13. *Supra* at 344.

14. *Shaw* v. *Gould* (1868) L.R. 3, H.L. 55; *Le Mesurier* v. *Le Mesurier* [1895] A.C. 517; (P.C.); *Bater* v. *Bater* (1906) P. 209 (P.D.A.); *Sinclair* v. *Sinclair* [1896] 1 I.R. 603, 613 (Ch.D.). See also *Maghee* v. *M'Allister* (1853) 3 Ir. Ch. Rep. 604 (Ct. of Ch.) which was not referred to by the learned judge.

"where, under the law for the time being in force within our jurisdiction
(i.e. the jurisdiction of the Irish courts), the original marriage is regarded as
valid and subsisting or in other words, where, by that law the divorce is
regarded as not being effectual to put an end to the original valid marriage.[14a]
No doubt the Oireachtas could pass a law that no dissolution of marriage
wherever effected, even where parties were domiciled in the country of the
court pronouncing the decree, was to be effective to annul[15] the pre-
existing valid marriage. If it did so, then by the law for the time being in
force, the first marriage would still be valid and subsisting within our jurisdiction. But the Oireachtas has not done so and the law as existing when
the Constitution was passed was that a divorce effected by a foreign court
of persons domiciled within its jurisdiction was regarded as valid in our
jurisdiction . . . I cannot find anything in Article 41.3, to suggest that the
courts (in the absence of further legislation) are entitled to do otherwise
than regard as valid and effectual a divorce *a vinculo* granted by the courts
of a foreign country, where the parties at the time of the suit were domiciled
in that country.[16]

Further there was nothing contained in the Constitution to invalidate the remarriage of such persons.

The sub-section next came up for judicial pronouncement in the English case
of *Breen (orse Smith) v. Breen.*[17] Karminski J. considering whether the Irish
courts would recognise a divorce decree granted by the English courts, to a couple
of English domicile, favoured the construction given by Kingsmill Moore J. He
stated:

"I am bound to say that I do not understand the section to say either plainly
or at all that a valid marriage dissolved by the court of another State remains
in the eyes of the Irish law a subsisting valid marriage".[18] Later he added,
"The principle of recognising the validity of a decree pronounced by the
court of the domicile has been long established, and indeed forms an essential
part of the comity of nations . . . If the article intended to depart from this
established principle it could no doubt have done so; but it would have
expressed the intention in clear and unequivocal terms".[19]

In 1971 in the High Court, in *Bank of Ireland v. K. Caffin and Y. Caffin,*[20]
Kenny J. followed the reasoning of Kingsmill Moore J. and expressly disagreed
with Maguire C.J. Stating the purpose of Art. 41.3.2.° was to deprive the National
Parliament of its power to pass legislation dissolving a marriage, or the courts of
jurisdiction to grant a divorce, he went on:

14a. Further on as an example of a divorce decree that would not be recognised in Ireland he suggested the case of one granted to persons not domiciled in the place where the
divorce is granted. He went on to state however that whereas such persons "shall not be
capable of contracting a valid marriage within that jurisdiction" (within Ireland) there is
nothing to stop them remarrying elsewhere. "The words do not declare that such a person
cannot *anywhere* contract 'a marriage valid within our jurisdiction' but merely prohibit the
contracting *within our jurisdiction* of a valid marriage", (at p. 349). Kingsmill Moore J. went
on to say that there is nothing to make such a marriage invalid if contracted elsewhere. Undoubtedly such a second marriage contracted in a foreign country which recognised the
divorce would be valid in that country, but if the parties to such a marriage entered Ireland,
as the divorce would not be recognised, it is difficult to see how the second marriage would
not be regarded as invalid and perhaps even bigamous here.
15. "Dissolve" would have been more appropriate.
16. *Supra.*
17. [1964] P. 144.
18. *Supra* at p. 149.
19. *Supra* at p. 152.
20. [1971] I.R. 123 (H.C.).

"The recognition of orders of divorce made by the courts of another country where the husband and wife had their domicile has no logical connection with the power of the Oireachtas to dissolve a marriage; and the restrictions imposed on it by the Constitution do not involve a general principle that the Courts should not, or cannot, recognise orders for the dissolution of a marriage made by the courts of another country when the parties to the marriage were domiciled in that country at the time of the court proceedings. This gets support from the words 'under the law for the time being in force within the jurisdiction of the Government and Parliament established by this constitution' for they give the National Parliament jurisdiction to decide by legislation that some decrees of dissolution made by the courts of other states are to be recognised by our courts".[21]

The Oireachtas had not so legislated, and so he held that the pre-1937 law prevailed.

Kenny J. also rejected the argument that the court should refuse to recognise the English divorce because it was given on the ground of desertion which was not a ground on which divorce *a vinculo* could have been granted to those domiciled in Ireland by the Imperial Parliament before 1921. As Mr. C. and Y. were domiciled in England he held that the grounds upon which a divorce *a vinculo* could be granted were to be determined by English law. In deciding whether a foreign divorce is to be recognised or not, the grounds on which such a divorce are granted are generally irrelevant.[22] The sole question to be determined is whether in the eyes of Irish law the foreign court could exercise jurisdiction over the parties.[23]

The court consequently recognised the English divorce of H., the testator, and Y. his first wife which was granted when they were domiciled in England. It further held that K., his wife by a second marriage was thus entitled to one half of the deceased's estate under the provisions of the Succession Act, 1965.[24]

In two decisions in 1973 (*Gaffney v. Gaffney*[25] and *Counihan v. Counihan*[26]), Kenny J. reiterated the principle that a divorce *a vinculo*, if granted by a court of the parties' common domicile, is recognised as validly dissolving their marriage.[27] In *Counihan v. Counihan* the wife had been resident in England for

---

21. *Supra* at p. 129.

22. See, however, *L.B. v. H.B.* (July, 1980) unreported (H.C.) discussed on p. 270 *post*.

23. See *In re Adams, Bank of Ireland Trustee Co. Ltd. v. Adams* [1967] I.R. 424 (H.C.) – It is the court of the forum which must determine whether the foreign court had jurisdiction.

24. Sect. 111 of the Act states that "If the testator leaves a spouse and no children the spouse shall have a right to one half of the estate." See further p. 518 *post*. Also see J. O'Reilly, "Recognition of Foreign Divorce Decrees" (1971) 6 I.J. (n.s.) 293 where the author suggests that Kenny J. in *Caffin* by recognising K. as the wife of Caffin for the purpose of the Succession Act was not only recognising the divorce but enforcing it. Thus, he suggests that Kenny's judgement was inconsistent with the judgement of the Supreme Court in *Mayo-Perrott* in which the court could not enforce the decree for costs made in favour of the plaintiff. It is submitted that the author confuses the concepts of "enforcement" and "recognition" of a decree – see, Dicey & Morris, *Conflict of Law*, 10th Ed., (Stevens & Sons, London, 1980) at pp. 1035–1037. Kenny J. was not enforcing the divorce decree between Caffin and Y. (his first wife), he was merely recognising the change of status brought about by the decree, which resulted in Caffin being able to enter into a valid marriage with K. (his second wife). On this, see also W. Duncan, "Desertion & Cruelty in Irish Matrimonial Law" (1972) 7 I.J. (n.s.) 213 especially pp. 231-235.

25. [1975] I.R. 133 (H.C., S.C.).

26. (July, 1973) unreported (H.C.).

27. See also *In re McComisky; Gibson v. Patterson* [1939] I.R. 573 (H.C.), where Gavan Duffy J. held on the construction of a will that Mrs. Cottu did not die "unmarried" but she did die without a surviving husband. Dr. Cottu the person to whom she was married was alive at her death but he said "I must take Dr. Cottu to have been domiciled in England at . . . the dissolution of the marriage, and in the absence of an Irish law invalidating that decree, the law of his domicile must determine whether he is married or not, when that question arises on a claim of which a marriage is the foundation".

three years at the date when the divorce proceedings were instituted and the husband was domiciled in Ireland. Refusing to recognise the divorce decree, Kenny J. stated:

> "The domicile of a wife is that of her husband unless their marriage is validly terminated by a divorce *a vinculo*, and as the husband was at all times domiciled in the Republic of Ireland, the courts in this country do not recognise the divorce in England as having the effect of dissolving the marriage. While a divorce given by the courts of the country in which the husband and wife are domiciled will be recognised . . . a divorce granted to a wife who was resident in England against a husband who was domiciled in the Republic of Ireland does not have the effect, in so far as the courts in Ireland are concerned, of dissolving the marriage. I know that the courts in England now have jurisdiction under legislation to grant divorces to wives who have been resident for three years in England but this jurisdiction did not exist in 1921 and the doctrine of comity of courts does not require that the courts in the Republic of Ireland should recognise this divorce. No legislation has been passed by the National Parliament giving recognition to divorces granted to a wife resident in England who was domiciled in the Republic of Ireland, and in my opinion, the husband and wife are, under our law, married."[28]

Two years later, in 1975, determining an appeal from the decision of Kenny J. in *Gaffney v. Gaffney*[29] a majority in the Supreme Court[30] accepted that a foreign decree of divorce was recognised, if granted by a court of the parties' common domicile. Walsh J. stated that:

> "In the course of his judgement in *Mayo-Perrott v. Mayo-Perrott*, Kingsmill Moore J. stated the Irish law to have been that the recognition of foreign divorces in Irish courts depended upon establishing that the domicile of the parties was within the jurisdiction of the court pronouncing the decree. Recognition and application of this principle of private international law

---

28. See pp. 5–6 of judgement. At the date when the English divorce was obtained by the wife divorce proceedings could be instituted in England by a wife who had "been ordinarily resident in England for 3 years immediately preceding the presentation of the petition". Such period of residence by a wife in English law at that time was sufficient to confer on the English Court jurisdiction to hear a wife's petition for divorce – see the English Matrimonial Causes Act, 1965, sect. 40(1)(b) now repealed and replaced by the Domicile & Matrimonial Proceedings Act, 1973, Sect. 5(2) which confers jurisdiction on the English courts to entertain divorce proceedings if either of the parties to the marriage (1) is domiciled in England at the date when the proceedings are begun* or (2) was habitually resident in England throughout the period of 1 year ending with that date.

*The 1973 Act brought to an end a wife's domicile of dependency in England and extended to a wife the opportunity of acquiring her own independent domicile.

In the context of Kenny J.'s reference to the common law divorce recognition jurisdiction which existed in 1921, see further the remarks of Walsh J. in *Gaffney v. Gaffney, supra*, where he emphasised that the law as to recognition was part of the common law and that "neither Article 73 of the Constitution of Saorstat Eireann nor Article 50 of the present Constitution could be construed as freezing our common law, or other non-statutory law in the condition in which it was found at the coming into force of the Constitution in 1922 so that it could never be departed from save by enactment of the Oireachtas." (*supra* at p. 151).

29. *Supra.*

30. See judgements of Walsh J., O'Higgins C.J. and Parke J. In his judgement, Griffin J. also seems to accept that a decree will be recognised if granted in the place of the parties' common domicile. However, he concludes (*supra* at p. 159) stating "for the purpose of the present case, it is not necessary to decide whether and to what extent, if at all, the recognition of a decree of divorce *a vinculo* made by a foreign court is inconsistent with or repugnant to any of the Articles of the Constitution, and I express no view on this question." Henchy J. expressed no opinion on the matter.

was part of the common law in Ireland and, like Kingsmill Moore J. in the *Mayo-Perrott* case and Mr. Justice Kenny in this case, I am satisfied that it is still part of our law. It follows, therefore, that the courts here do not recognise decrees of dissolution of marriage pronounced by foreign courts unless the parties were domiciled within the jurisdiction of the foreign court in question."[31]

In two subsequent cases determined by the Supreme Court, *T. v. T.*[32] and *K.E.D. (otherwise K.C.) v. M.C.*,[33] the law as stated in *Gaffney* was expressly followed.

In *T. v. T.* an English decree of divorce was recognised, the Supreme Court [34] holding that the husband and wife had their common domicile in England. The couple had moved from England to Ireland in 1974 and the divorce proceedings had not been filed by the husband in the English courts until 1977. The decree absolute of divorce was granted in 1978. The husband had come to reside in Ireland for the purpose of taking up employment and he was held not to have abandoned his English domicile of origin. Henchy J. during the course of his judgement stated:

> "The net point is still the same. At the time of the divorce, was the husband's domicile Irish or British?[35] If it was British, the divorce qualifies for recognition in our courts; if it was Irish, the divorce was given without jurisdiction and cannot be acted on here: see the decision of this court in *Gaffney v. Gaffney*. Before the husband's domicile could be held to be Irish, it would have to be established that he had abandoned his British domicile of origin and had opted for an Irish domicile of choice instead. This is a mixed question of law and fact, an affirmative answer to which depends on whether it appears from the husband's conduct and the general course of events that he had cast off his British domicile of origin and had chosen to acquire in its place an Irish domicile. The rebuttable presumption is that a person retains his domicile of origin."[36]

As a consequence of this decision, a maintenance order made against the husband under the Family Law (Maintenance of Spouses & Children) Act, 1976, could no longer remain in force, the wife ceasing to be a "spouse" within the meaning of that Act.[36a]

In *K.E.D. (otherwise K.C.) v. M.C.* divorce proceedings had been filed in England against the husband by his first wife in 1959 after she had been resident there for over 3 years. A decree absolute of divorce was granted in 1962 and later that year the husband married the petitioner. Over 20 years later, the petitioner sought a decree of annulment and her contention, that the English decree of divorce granted dissolving the husband's first marriage was not recognised under Irish law, was upheld and her marriage declared null and void. In

---

31. *Supra* at p. 150. See also *Re E.E.L. (an infant)* [1938] N.I. 56 sub nom *In re Lyons* (1937) 72 I.L.T.R. 87 a decision of the Northern Ireland Court of Appeal referred to by Walsh J. in which a divorce decree granted in Florida was not recognised as at the date of the commencement of the proceedings the parties were not domiciled in Florida. It was clearly the view of the court that the decree would have been recognised if the rule as to domicile had been complied with.
32. [1983] I.R. 29.
33. (December, 1985) unreported (S.C.).
34. O'Higgins C.J., Henchy J. and Griffin J.
35. The reference should have been to whether the husband's domicile was English.
36. *Supra* at p. 33.
36a. For a detailed discussion of the provisions of the Family Law (Maintenance of Spouses & Children) Act, 1976, see chapter 14.

the High Court[37] Carroll J. held that the husband had not at any relevant time acquired an English domicile and ruled that

> "The divorce granted by the English courts is not valid in this jurisdiction as it was not based on domicile."[38]

On appeal to the Supreme Court, it was contended that domicile was not the only appropriate test for recognition. It was argued on behalf of the husband that the principle enunciated in the House of Lords case of *Indyka v. Indyka*[39] should be adopted in Irish law and that a foreign decree of divorce should be recognised where there is a real and substantial connection between the parties and the country granting the decree of divorce. This argument was rejected[40] on the following grounds:

(a) It had not been raised in the High Court and no evidence had been given or finding made at first instance as to any real and substantial connection between the wife of the first marriage,[41] or the husband,[42] with England. Moreover, at the time of the commencement of the proceedings there was "no question" of the husband being resident in England and he had not disputed the statement made in the divorce petition when it was issued that "he was not resident or domiciled in England" and which designated his residence as in Ireland.[43]

(b) The test of real and substantial connection enunciated by the English courts in *Indyka* partially derived from the existence of statutory provisions in English law which conferred jurisdiction on the English courts to determine divorce proceedings on a jurisdictional basis other than domicile and as a con-

---

37. (September, 1984) unreported (H.C.).
38. See p. 9 of judgement. See also *C.S. (otherwise L.) v. J.L* (July, 1985) unreported (H.C.) where Murphy J. followed the judgement of Carroll J. In this case the court declined also to recognise a divorce granted by the English courts dissolving the respondent husband's first marriage. The proceedings had been instituted by the husband's first wife and he was stated in the proceedings to be domiciled in Ireland. As a consequence, the husband was held under Irish law to be still married to his first wife at the date of marriage to the petitioner and their marriage was declared null and void.
39. [1969] A.C. 33 (H.L.). See further Cheshire & North, *Private International Law*, 8th Edition, 362–368 and cases there discussed; Dicey & Morris, *Conflicts of Law*, 9th Edition, pp. 316–319 and cases cited therein; *Indyka* was subsequently followed in Australia – *Nicholson v. Nicholson* (1971), 17 F.L.R. 47; and in Canada – *Kish v. Director of Vital Statistics* (1973), 35 D.L.R. (3d.) 530, *Mac Neill v. Mac Neill* (1974) 53 D.L.R. (3d.) 486; *La Carte v. La Carte* (1975) 60 D.L.R. (3d.) 507; *Holub v. Holub* (1976) 71 D.L.R. (3d.) 698; *Keresztessy v. Keresztessy* (1976) 73 D.L.R. (3d.) 347; *Siebert v. Siebert* (1978) 82 D.L.R. (3d.) 70; *Clarkson v. Clarkson* (1978) 86 D.L.R. (3d.) 694; *El-Sohemy v. El-Sohemy* (1979) 89 D.L.R. (3d.) 145. See, however, *Powell v. Cockburn* [1977] 2 S.C.R. 218. See further, C. Davies, *Family Law in Canada* (Carswell Legal Publications, Canada, 1984) at p. 575 *et seq.*
English law on recognition has now changed. See the Recognition of Divorces and Legal Separations Act, 1971 and the Domicile & Matrimonial Act, 1973. See also Dicey & Morris, 10th Ed., *supra*, at p. 338 *et seq* and the supplement to that edition. For the present Australian law as to recognition, see the Australian Family Law Act, 1975, Sects. 104–106.
40. (December, 1985) unreported (S.C.). The decision was unanimous. The members of the court were Finlay C.J., Henchy J., Griffin J., McCarthy J., and McMahon J.
41. The evidence established that the first wife had resided in England between 1955 and 1962, the proceedings being issued in 1959 on the jurisdictional basis of her having been 3 years resident in England. See also *Counihan v. Counihan* discussed earlier.
42. The husband had an Irish domicile of origin and had lived in Ireland for most of his life. He had been educated for a period in a boarding school in England, served in the British Army during the second world war and had in 1952 accepted British citizenship. From 1946 until 1961 he had lived permanently in Ireland, going to reside in England in the Autumn of 1961. He returned to reside permanently in Ireland in 1965. See judgements of Carroll J. and Finlay C.J.
43. See judgement of Finlay C.J. at pp. 8 and 10.

sequence the courts developed reciprocal rules of recognition. In Ireland, where there is no provision for divorce, such a principle could not apply.[44]

(c) Although anomalies might exist in the law of domicile when applied to the recognition of foreign divorces, these should be resolved by legislation. It is not a reason for considering a "test other than the well-established test of domicile."[45] Actions of Irish citizens and the "affairs of the community as a whole over the last decade (since *Gaffney*) or over 28 years (since *Mayo-Perrott*) had been based upon that law.[46]

Although in theory it still remains open to a future litigant to again argue the issue by raising it at first instance in the High Court, it is submitted that there is virtually no possibility that the Supreme Court will so radically develop the rules as to recognition, particularly following the enactment of the Domicile & Recognition of Foreign Divorces Act, 1986.[47] The Act does not, however, entirely preclude the Supreme Court from developing the law, as it merely amends the domicile rules applicable to the recognition of foreign divorces granted on or after 2nd October 1986, without expressly stating that either the common law or the statutory law as to domicile is to remain the sole basis for recognition.[48]

RECOGNITION OF FOREIGN DECREES OF DIVORCE GRANTED PRIOR TO THE 2ND OF OCTOBER, 1986

The Domicile & Recognition of Foreign Divorces Act, 1986, does not affect the rules applicable to the recognition of foreign decrees of divorce granted prior to the 2nd of October, 1986. Accordingly such decrees of divorce are generally recognised by Irish law if at the date of the institution of the divorce proceedings, both spouses were domiciled within the jurisdiction of the foreign court that granted the decree.[49] For the purpose of determining whether a divorce

44. *Ibid.*, at pp. 9–11.
45. *Ibid.*, at p. 10.
46. See judgement of McCarthy J. at pp. 4–5.
47. Even if the Act of 1986 had not been enacted, this statement, it is submitted, accurately reflects the approach to this issue by the current members of the Supreme Court. In stating that there were no grounds for entertaining a consideration of the real and substantial connection test in *K.E.D. (otherwise K.C.) v. M.C.*, Finlay C.J. expressed the view "that to do so would be much more likely to lead to substantial injustice in the application of any decision of this court to other parties in different cases than it could possibly contribute to any requirement of justice in the instant case before us" (p. 11 of judgement). McCarthy J. remarked that it would be "utterly wrong to embark upon such an enquiry" (see p. 5 of judgement).
48. The court may hold at a future date that the concept of a wife's dependent domicile did not remain part of Irish law after the coming into force of the present constitution and so have to modify the law as to recognition of foreign divorce decrees granted prior to 2nd October 1986. See p. 192 *ante*.
49. See *Mayo-Perrott v. Mayo-Perrott, supra*; *Gaffney v. Gaffney, supra*; *T. v. T., supra*; *K.E.D. (otherwise K.C.) v. M.C., supra*; see also *Bank of Ireland v. Caffin, supra*; *Counihan v. Counihan, supra*; *C.S. (otherwise L.) v. J.L., supra*. See further *D.M. v. E.F.M., supra*; *G. v. G., supra*; *Sachs v. Standard Chartered Bank (Ireland) Ltd., supra*. Sect. 5 of the Act of 1986 defines domicile as meaning domiciled at the date of the institution of the proceedings. For case law authority as to the crucial date in relation to domicile see, in particular, *In re E.E.L. (an infant) supra*, sub nom *In re Lyons supra*, cited with approval by Walsh J. in *Gaffney v. Gaffney* [1975] I.R. at p. 150) where in [1938] N.I. at p. 77 Andrews L.J. stated that "the law is clear that our courts will not recognise a decree of divorce as possessing any extra-territorial validity unless at the commencement of the proceedings the parties were domiciled within the jurisdiction of the court pronouncing the decree." In *Mayo-Perrott v. Mayo-Perrott, supra*, in [1958] I.R. at p. 349 Kingsmill Moore J. states that "I cannot find anything in Article 41.3. to suggest that the courts (in the absence of future legislation) are entitled to do otherwise than regard as valid and effectual a divorce *a vinculo* granted by the courts of a foreign country, where the parties at the time of suit were domiciled in that country." In *K.E.D. (otherwise K.C.) v. M.C.* the husband went to reside in England after his first wife had issued divorce proceedings before the decree absolute was granted. As he was held at no time to have acquired an English domicile, Carroll J. held that "the

decree granted prior to the 2nd of October, 1986, is recognised under Irish law, a wife's domicile remains dependent on that of her husband.[50] It should be noted, however, that Walsh J. in *Gaffney v. Gaffney*[51] commented that:

> "The law has been that during the subsistence of a marriage a wife's domicile remains the same as and changes with that of her husband. For the purpose of this case it is proper to adopt this view, although it is possible that some day it may be challenged on constitutional grounds in a case where the wife has never physically left her domicile of origin while her deserting husband may have established a domicile in another jurisdiction."[52]

In *K.E.D. (otherwise K.C.) v. M.C.*,[53] McCarthy J. also raised the issue of the constitutionality of a wife's dependent domicile.[54] To date, there has been no case in which the Supreme Court has been expressly asked to determine whether the common law rule that a wife's domicile is dependent on that of her husband survived the enactment of the 1937 Constitution.[55] In the event of the court being requested to do so and finding that this rule ceased to be part of Irish law after the adoption of the present Constitution, a determination will also have to be made as to whether foreign decrees of divorce *a vinculo*, granted prior to the 2nd of October, 1986, are only recognisable if both spouses were independently domiciled in the foreign jurisdiction at the date of the institution of the divorce proceedings, or whether there should be incorporated into the common law the provision contained in the 1986 Act, which extends recognition to a decree granted by a foreign court if either spouse was domiciled within the jurisdiction of the foreign court at the date of the institution of the proceedings.

In *Bank of Ireland v. Caffin*,[56] Kenny J. expressly reserved to be determined at a future time the "difficult" question of whether a divorce decree granted by the courts in Northern Ireland to persons domiciled there would be recognised and an issue as to the recognition of such a decree has not as yet arisen for determination by the High Court or the Supreme Court. As we have already seen, domicile merely signifies a territory which is a separate law district.[57] Northern Ireland is such a law district with an established legal system different to that of the Republic of Ireland. It is recognised as such in Article 3 of the

---

question of whether a change of domicile after the presentation of the petition and before the granting of the decree absolute affects the validity of the divorce, does not arise" (see p. 9 of judgement). In the Supreme Court, Finlay C.J. remarked that "it seems probable on the authorities, though I do not decide the point, that the time at which the test of jurisdiction should arise is the commencement of the proceedings and not their conclusion" (see p. 10 of judgement). See further *Mansell v. Mansell* [1967] P. 306 (P.D.A.).

50. See *Counihan v. Counihan, supra*. It should be noted that in *T. v. T., supra, K.E.D. (otherwise K.C.) v. M.C., supra* and in *C.S. (otherwise L.) v. J.L., supra* it was assumed that the wife's domicile was dependent on that of the husband.

51. *Supra.*

52. *Supra* at p. 152.

53. *Supra.*

54. See p. 5 of judgement.

55. In *T. v. T., supra*, the wife was an Irish citizen when she married the husband. The husband was British and they lived in England from the date of their marriage in 1966 until 1974 when they moved to Ireland. In determining whether the divorce obtained by the husband in England was recognised in Ireland, the Supreme Court at no stage considered whether the wife could have acquired an Irish domicile independent of her husband. In *K.E.D. (otherwise K.C.) v. M.C., supra*, it was uncontroverted that the husband's first wife had moved to England in 1955 and continued to reside there up to the date when the decree absolute was granted in 1962. At no stage was evidence presented or was it argued that the wife had acquired a domicile independent to that of her husband.

56. *Supra.*

57. See p. 191 *ante.*

Constitution;[58] in various statutes enacted by the Oireachtas, such as the Maintenance Orders Act, 1974, and in a number of cases determined by the Supreme Court.[59] There is no reason why divorce decrees granted in Northern Ireland prior to the 2nd of October, 1986, should be treated any differently for recognition purposes to divorce decrees granted elsewhere.[60]

Finally, in the old English case of *Armitage v. A.G.*[61] it was held that a foreign decree of divorce would be recognised if it is recognised by the courts of the country of the couple's common domicile. In this case, a divorce decree granted to the wife in South Dakota after 90 days residence there was recognised as validly dissolving the marriage by the English courts, as the law of New York, the place of the parties' common domicile, recognised the validity of the decree. To date, no case has arisen before the Irish courts so as to require a determination to be made, as to whether the extension of the domicile principle embodied in *Armitage* is applicable under Irish law.

RECOGNITION OF FOREIGN DIVORCE DECREES GRANTED ON OR AFTER THE 2ND OF OCTOBER, 1986

In *Gaffney v. Gaffney*,[62] Walsh J. acknowledged that Article 41.3.3. empowered the Oireachtas "by legislation to define what foreign judicial decrees of dissolution of marriage shall or shall not be recognised in our courts as legally changing the status of the parties."[63] The Domicile & Recognition of Foreign Divorces Act, 1986, is the first such legislative enactment since the foundation of the State. Section 5 provides that

> "For the rule of law that a divorce *a vinculo* is recognised if granted in a country where both spouses are domiciled at the date of the institution of the proceedings for divorce there is hereby substituted a rule that a divorce *a vinculo* shall be recognised if granted in the country where either spouse is domiciled at the date of the institution of the proceedings for divorce."[64]

In relation to a country which is split into two or more territorial units within which different legal systems operate in matters of divorce, section 5 has "effect as if each territorial unit were a separate country."[65] Thus, as each State in the United States of America has its own divorce jurisdiction, for the purposes of section 5, each State is treated as if it were a separate country for the purposes of domicile. For example, a divorce obtained in a State within the U.S.A. will be recognised if either spouse was domiciled in that State at the date when the divorce proceedings were instituted.

---

58. Article 3 states "Pending the re-integration of the national territory and without prejudice to the right of the Parliament and the Government established by this Constitution to exercise jurisdiction over the whole of that territory, the laws enacted by that Parliament shall have the like area and extent of application to the laws of Saorstat Éireann and the like extra territorial effect."

59. See, for example, *The State (Gilsenan) v. McMorrow* [1978] I.R. 360 (S.C.) *McGlinchey v. Wren* [1982] I.R. 154 (S.C.); *Shannon v. A.G. & Ireland* [1985] 5 I.L.R.M. 449 (S.C.).

60. Sect. 5 in the 1986 Act expressly contains special provisions to extend the jurisdictional basis for recognising decrees of divorce granted in the British Isles and Northern Ireland.

61. [1906] P. 135 (P.D.A.).

62. *Supra.*

63. *Ibid.*, at pp. 150–151. See also judgement of O'Daly J. in *Mayo-Perrott v. Mayo-Perrott, supra,* at p. 351.

64. See Sect. 5(1) and Sect. 5(7).

65. Sect. 5(2).

Where a country is split into territorial units but a divorce law applies throughout the country, the country is treated as a single unit for the purpose of domicile. For example, a divorce obtained in Australia will be recognised if a spouse is domiciled in any part of Australia at the date when the divorce proceedings are instituted, as a federal divorce law is uniformly applicable throughout that country.

Special provision is made for the recognition of decrees of divorce granted by a court in the British Isles or Northern Ireland. Such a decree will, of course, be recognised if either spouse is domiciled within the jurisdiction of the court which grants the decree at the date of the institution of divorce proceedings. In addition, section 5(3) provides for the recognition of a divorce granted in

(a) England and Wales

(b) Scotland

(c) Northern Ireland

(d) The Isle of Man

(e) The Channel Islands

if either spouse is domiciled in any of those jurisdictions at the date of the institution of divorce proceedings.[66] Thus, if a wife with a Northern Ireland domicile, resident in England, institutes English divorce proceedings against her husband domiciled in the Republic of Ireland, the English divorce decree subsequently granted is recognised pursuant to this provision. If an English divorce decree was so obtained prior to the 2nd of October, 1986, no recognition could be given to it under the common law rules applicable prior to the commencement of the 1986 Act, as the husband and the wife would be held to have had their common domicile in the Republic of Ireland at the date of the institution of the proceedings, the wife's domicile being dependent on that of her husband.

The Act of 1986 also gives statutory expression to the common law rule of recognition derived from *Armitage v. The A.G.*[67] Section 5(4) provides for the recognition of a foreign decree of divorce where neither spouse is domiciled in the Republic of Ireland and a divorce decree is granted within a jurisdiction in which neither spouse was domiciled at the date of the institution of proceedings but which is recognised by the law of the State where both spouses were domiciled when the proceedings were brought, or if they were domiciled in different States, if it is recognised by the law of each of those States. Thus, under this provision Irish law will recognise a German decree of divorce obtained by a couple resident in Germany, both of whom are domiciled in England at the date of the institution of the divorce proceedings, if the decree is recognised as validly terminating their marriage under English law. Recognition will not, however, be granted to such a decree if one party is domiciled in England and the other is domiciled in the Republic of Ireland at the date of the institution of the proceedings.

In concluding this part it is essential to note that the Act of 1986 is not retrospective and that its provisions as to both domicile and recognition of foreign divorce decrees only apply on and after the 2nd of October, 1986.[68] As a consequence, where foreign divorce proceedings are instituted prior to that date but the decree of divorce is granted some time later, such decree will

---

66. See Sect. 5(3) and Sect. 5(7).
67. *Supra.* See p. 265 *ante.*
68. The Act completed its legislative passage on the 2nd of July 1986. Sect. 6(2) provides that it is to commence three months after that date.

only be recognised if the spouses had their common domicile within the foreign jurisdiction at the date of the institution of the divorce proceedings. This is due to the fact that until the 2nd of October, 1986, under common law a wife retains a domicile dependent on that of her husband. This proposition is illustrated by the following example: A wife living in Northern Ireland issues divorce proceedings against her husband domiciled in the Republic of Ireland on the 1st of June, 1986, and the decree absolute of divorce is granted on the 1st of November, 1986. Although the divorce decree is granted after the commencement of the Act, it is not recognised in the Republic of Ireland. The crucial question for determining whether the decree is recognised relates to whether either spouse was domiciled in Northern Ireland or in the British Isles[69] on the 1st of June, 1986, the date when the proceedings were instituted. As the husband was at all relevant times domiciled in the Republic of Ireland, the wife under Irish law retains a domicile dependent on him until the 2nd of October, 1986, even if for many years prior to that date she has had her permanent home in Northern Ireland. Whilst she may acquire an independent domicile of her own on the 2nd of October, 1986, as she possessed no such domicile at the date of the institution of the proceedings, the divorce granted by the courts in Northern Ireland is not recognised in the Republic of Ireland. If, however, she discontinues the original proceedings before a final decree of divorce is granted (a decree absolute), upon her acquiring an independent domicile of her own in Northern Ireland on or after the 2nd of October, 1986, she may then issue new divorce proceedings and obtain a decree of divorce from the courts in Northern Ireland that will be recognised in the Republic of Ireland as validly dissolving her marriage.

DOCTRINE OF ESTOPPEL AND FOREIGN DECREES OF DIVORCE

In *Gaffney v. Gaffney*,[70] the question arose as to whether "a spouse domiciled in one State who obtains an invalid divorce in another State is estopped in the State of the domicile from establishing that the divorce was invalid."[71] The facts of *Gaffney v. Gaffney* were as follows: The plaintiff and her husband were both resident and domiciled in the Republic of Ireland until the husband's death in 1972. Despite the plaintiff not wanting a divorce, her husband instructed a firm of solicitors in Manchester in 1957 to prepare a petition by her seeking a divorce *a vinculo* from him. By threatening her with physical violence he forced the plaintiff to swear an affidavit stating that he resided in Blackburn and that they were both domiciled in England. Believing that he would assault her if she did not do what he demanded, she flew to Manchester with him on the morning of the divorce proceedings. Upon arriving at the court they were coached by the husband's solicitors as to what they were to say, and the case was concluded in the court in a few minutes. On the same day she returned to Dublin. In January 1959 the English court granted a decree absolute of divorce. In April 1959 the husband married the defendant, his second wife, in a Registry Office in Blackburn. They then came to live in Dublin.

The husband died intestate in 1972. Upon his death, the plaintiff successfully brought proceedings claiming that she was his widow for the purpose of succession, and that she was entitled to obtain a grant of letters of administration to his estate. Kenny J. held that the divorce proceedings had not validly dissolved the marriage in the eyes of Irish law because:

---

69. See Sect. 5(1), 5(3) and 5(7).
70. *Supra*.
71. *Supra* at p. 141 *per* Kenny J.

1.   The parties were at all times domiciled and resident in Ireland and the courts in this country will only recognise decrees of dissolution pronounced by a court of the parties' common domicile.

2.   The decree was procured by the fraudulent invocation of the English court's jurisdiction, neither party being domiciled or resident in England when the court's jurisdiction was invoked. If the English court had itself known of the true position it would not have pronounced a decree, and further if today the true facts were made known there, the decree could be set aside.

3.   The plaintiff had obtained the decree under duress.

The Supreme Court confirmed that the decree was invalid on grounds 1 and 2.

In this case, however, the respondent further contended that the wife being the petitioner in the divorce proceedings could not now give evidence that the divorce was improperly obtained, i.e. she could not deny the validity of such proceedings having instituted them herself. Kenny J. pointed out the extraordinary consequences that would result if she was estopped from establishing the invalidity of the divorce; e.g. whereas the spouse who obtained the divorce would be prevented from proving its invalidity, if the other spouse remarried he or she might be successfully prosecuted for bigamy.[72] If there were children of such second marriage, upon the husband dying intestate, the first wife could not dispute their legitimacy, but her children could do so. On grounds of public policy such estoppel was undesirable. It was held and confirmed by the Supreme Court that estoppel did not apply either to the question of the existence of a valid marriage, or in relation to determining property rights between the spouses. Walsh J. giving judgement in the Supreme Court stated:

> "Apart from other legal incidents in this country, certain constitutional rights may accrue to a woman by virtue of her being a wife which would not be available to her if she were not. The matter cannot, therefore, by any rules of evidence be left in a position of doubt nor could the Courts countenance a doctrine of estoppel, if such existed, which had the effect that a person would be estopped from saying that he or she is the husband or wife, as the case may be, of another party when in law the person making the claim has that status".[73]

In the above case the plaintiff was not a free agent, but even if she had been, her application to the courts in England would not have estopped her contesting the validity of the divorce. In *Counihan v. Counihan*[74] the fact that the plaintiff had voluntarily invoked the jurisdiction of the English courts and there obtained a divorce was not held to estop her from asserting in the Irish courts that the English divorce decree lacked validity in this country.[75] Moreover, in *K.E.D. (otherwise K.C.) v. M.C.*[76] the High Court held that the petitioner could not be

---

72. Even more extraordinary would be the result that whilst the spouse who petitioned for the divorce would be prevented from asserting its invalidity, if she remarried she would be liable to a charge of bigamy.

73. *Supra* at p. 152. See further Duncan (1974) 9 I.J. (n.s.) 59, *supra*. See also E.M. Clare Canton, "Duress and Estoppel in Matrimonial Causes" (1978) 94 L.Q.R. 15.

74. *Supra*.

75. See also *L.B. v. H.B.* (July, 1980) unreported (H.C.). in which Barrington J. held a wife who had colluded with her husband in the obtaining of a French divorce decree was not estopped from challenging its validity (see p. 270 *post*). See further, the old case of *Maghee v. M'Allister, supra*, in which the court held that a husband who had applied for and obtained a divorce from a Scottish Court was not estopped from impugning the validity of the divorce decree.

76. *Supra*.

refused a decree of nullity either because she had "acquiesced for many years in the marriage" or "because she knew she was marrying a person who, having been married in Ireland, was divorced in England." Carroll J. stated that there "is no estoppel of record where there was no jurisdictional competence to make the order."[77]

Thus, neither party involved in foreign divorce proceedings which resulted in a decree of divorce *a vinculo* being granted, nor any person with whom either party subsequently celebrates a ceremony of marriage, is estopped from challenging the validity of such a divorce under Irish law. The fact that the parties to the divorce proceedings co-operated with each other or consented to using the foreign jurisdiction to obtain a divorce is irrelevant. Spouses by consent cannot confer a jurisdiction on a foreign court that, according to Irish law, it does not possess.[78]

GROUNDS UPON WHICH RECOGNITION MAY BE WITHHELD

Even where the requirements as to domicile have been complied with, there are a number of grounds upon which recognition can be withheld from a foreign decree of divorce granted either before or after the 2nd of October, 1986, and these are unaffected by the Act of 1986. Section 5(6) of the Act states

"Nothing in this section shall affect a ground on which a court may refuse to recognise a divorce, other than such a ground related to the question whether a spouse is domiciled in a particular country, or whether the divorce is recognised in a country where a spouse is domiciled."

Below we discuss the various grounds upon which recognition may be withheld.

(a) *Fraud*: As we have already seen, one of the grounds on which validity was denied to the English decree in *Gaffney* was that it was procured by the fraudulent invocation of the jurisdiction of the English court, i.e. the parties had fraudulently misrepresented facts (domicile) in order to lead the court to believe it had jurisdiction. But whereas fraudulent invocation of jurisdiction will overthrow a foreign decree, fraud as to the merits of the petition will be ignored[79] unless such fraud constitutes a "substantial defeat of justice".[80]

(b) *Duress*: Kenny J. further denied recognition to the divorce decree in *Gaffney* because the plaintiff had acted under duress. She had only gone to Manchester because of "genuine and reasonable fear of immediate physical danger if she refused"[81] to go. He stated that:

"It is established law that a marriage may be declared null if it is entered

---

77. See judgement of Carroll J. at pp. 10–11.
78. In *Gaffney v. Gaffney*, Walsh J. stated "consent cannot confer jurisdiction to dissolve a marriage where that jurisdiction does not already exist" (*supra* at p. 152). See also the nullity case of *Addison (otherwise McAllister) v. Addison* [1955] N.I. 1 (Q.B.D.) "in cases involving status jurisdiction cannot be conferred by the submission of a party to the jurisdiction of the court." See also *Papadopoulos v. Papadopoulos* [1930] P. 55 (P.D.A.).
79. *Bonaparte v. Bonaparte* [1892] P. 402 (P.D.A.); *Bater v. Bater* [1906] P. 209 (C.A.); *Crowe v. Crowe* [1937] 2 All E.R. 723, (1937) 157 L.T. 557 (P.D.A.); *Middleton v. Middleton* [1967] P. 62 (P.D.A.), where a divorce granted in Illinois was denied recognition by the English courts on the ground that the husband petitioner had fraudulently invoked the jurisdiction of the Illinois court. It was denied recognition despite the fact that it would have been recognised in Indiana where the petitioner was domiciled. Thus fraud as to jurisdiction intervened so as to prevent recognition on the *Armitage v. A.-G.* rule. See J. Unger (1966) 29 M.L.R. 327; P.B. Carter (1966) 41 B.Y.I.L. 445.
80. See p. 270 *post*.
81. *Supra* at p. 139.

into because of duress and, in my view, a similar principle applies to an application for a decree of divorce. There is no reason in logic or in principle why, if the doctrine of duress applies to contracting a marriage, it should not apply to its termination by divorce".[82]

Walsh J. in the Supreme Court, however, suggested that if the divorce court had possessed jurisdiction and the facts as to coercion still existed, in order to successfully assert her status as wife the petitioner may have had to apply to the court that granted the decree to set it aside.[83]

(c) *Denial of Justice*: Finally, it has been said that a divorce decree will be refused recognition if granted in circumstances which amount to a denial of substantial or natural justice. This ground for refusing recognition has had very limited application in England[84] and has on only one occasion been relied upon by an Irish Court.

In *L.B. v. H.B.*[85] the parties in 1958 when domiciled in France obtained a divorce decree from the French courts. For the purpose of obtaining the decree they had employed French lawyers to manufacture evidence to present to the court and at the date of the proceedings, the parties' circumstances were such that no real grounds existed upon which either party could obtain a divorce. Both during the divorce proceedings and after the granting of the divorce decree the parties continued to reside together. They subsequently came to live in Ireland and in 1979 the wife issued proceedings in the Irish High Court seeking a maintenance order and certain other orders against the husband. In these proceedings the wife submitted that the divorce should not be recognised in Ireland as it had been obtained by collusion and constituted a substantial denial of justice. Evidence was given that had the French court been aware of the collusive nature of the proceedings in 1958, it would have dismissed them but that the French court would not now set aside the divorce decree.

Barrington J. finding in favour of the wife's submission stated:

"I have no doubt whatsoever that the divorce was a collusive divorce ... it represented the worst form of collusion as the evidence on which the court decided the case was manufactured to achieve that precise result".[86]

He stated that under the principles of private international law as stated in *Re Caffin, decsd.* and *Gaffney v. Gaffney* the divorce decree was entitled to recog-

---

82. *Ibid.* Agreeing with the views expressed by Bagnall J. in *In re Meyer* [1971] P. 298 (P.D.A.). See also *Hughes v. Hughes* (1932) 147 L.T. 20 (P.D.A.).

83. See *In re Meyer, supra.* There was no doubt that the German Court had, in the eyes of English law, jurisdiction to grant a decree. The decree was denied recognition in England as the petitioner had been overborne by extreme duress into seeking the divorce. The duress was said to be such that when seeking the divorce decree the petitioner "was overborne by a genuine and reasonably held fear caused by present and continuing danger to life, limb or liberty arising from external circumstances for which [she] was not responsible" – *per* Bagnall J. at p. 307. See further, Clare Canton, *supra.*

84. See *Pemberton v. Hughes* [1899] 1 Ch. 781 (C.A.); *Middleton v. Middleton* [1967] P. 62 (P.D.A.); *Qureshi v. Qureshi* [1972] Fam. 173 at p. 201 (P.D.A.). See also the nullity cases of *Gray (orse Formosa) v. Formosa* [1963] P. 259 (C.A.); *Lepre v. Lepre* [1965] P. 52 (P.D.A.); *Macalpine v. Macalpine* [1958] P. 35; [1957] 3 All E.R. 134 (P.D.A.); *Rudd v. Rudd* [1924] P. 72 (P.D.A.); *Igra v. Igra* [1951] P. 404 (P.D.A.); *Wood v. Wood* [1957] P. 254, [1957] 2 All E.R. 14 (C.A.); *Viswalingham v. Viswalingham* (1980) 1 F.L.R. 24 (C.A.). Cheshire 8th Edition pp. 655–658. Dicey 9th Edition p. 1033, *supra.* In England the law is now governed by the Recognition of Divorces and Legal Separations Act, 1971, Sect. 8.

85. (July, 1980) unreported (H.C.).

86. See p. 22 of judgement.

nition as it was granted by a court of competent jurisdiction to people domiciled within its jurisdiction. However, he continued:

"in the present case . . . I am satisfied that there was such a measure of collusion between the parties in the proceedings before the French Court as to amount to a fraud upon that court. I am also satisfied that if the French Court had known of the collusion it would have rejected the (divorce) petition . . ."[87]

This was not one of those cases, he stated, in which

"one of the parties has committed a fraud, or suppressed the truth, or where there has been collusion between the parties about peripheral matters. Clearly matters which have been fully heard and determined before a competent tribunal should not lightly be reopened . . . (Here) the entire suit was manufactured and conducted in such a way that it amounted to a fraud upon the French court . . ."[88]

Whilst there was no fraud or substantial denial of justice as between the parties

"The collusion . . . between the parties was such that the entire proceedings became a charade and the French court was unwittingly led to a conclusion which had been pre-determined by the parties. There was a substantial defeat of justice for which the parties and not the court bear the responsibility . . . it is accordingly no disrespect to the French court if (this court) refuses to recognise a divorce obtained in such circumstances. Indeed, once this court has been fixed with knowledge of what happened in the French divorce proceedings it is hard to see how it could recognise the validity of the divorce and at the same time observe the constitutional duty of the State to uphold the institution of marriage."[89]

Having refused to recognise the French divorce decree, Barrington J. concluded making a maintenance order against the husband under the Family Law . . . Act, 1976, and holding the home in which the parties resided to be a "family home" within the meaning of the Family Home Protection Act, 1976.[90]

The denial of recognition to the French divorce decree on the ground that recognition of it would have constituted "a substantial denial of justice" introduced considerable uncertainty into the law, as at no stage did Barrington J. fully define or determine the exact parameters of application of this concept. In the 6 years that have elapsed since this case was determined no other case has arisen before the Irish courts in which recognition has been withheld from a foreign decree of divorce on this ground.[91]

---

87. See p. 25 of judgement.
88. See p. 26 of judgement.
89. See p. 34 of judgement.
90. An appeal to the Supreme Court was lodged in this case but the appeal was withdrawn.
91. See further, W. Duncan, "Collusive Foreign Divorces — How to Have Your Cake and Eat it" (1981) D.U.L.J. 17.

CRITICISMS AND SUGGESTED REFORMS

Although the Domicile & Recognition of Foreign Divorces Act, 1986, has both clarified and reformed some aspects of the law relating to the recognition of foreign divorces a number of difficulties remain.

1. Foreign courts assume jurisdiction to grant decrees of divorce in accordance with their own laws not only on the jurisdictional basis of domicile but also on the basis of residence and nationality. Moreover, some countries that use domicile have a less exacting definition of domicile than that applied by the Irish courts. The absence of a domestic divorce jurisdiction has resulted in spouses domiciled in Ireland seeking and obtaining divorces outside the State, following marital breakdown occurring in circumstances in which a foreign court is, according to its own laws, jurisdictionally competent to grant decrees of divorce, but where any decree, if granted, is not recognised under Irish law.[1] For example, the divorce jurisdiction of the courts of Northern Ireland, Scotland, England and Wales can be invoked to obtain a decree of divorce on a substantive ground prescribed by the statutory provisions applicable in each of those jurisdictions,[2] by a spouse who has been habitually resident in either jurisdiction throughout the period of one year up to the date proceedings are instituted.[3] A divorce obtained on the jurisdictional basis of simply one year's habitual residence dissolving the marriage of spouses domiciled in Ireland will, as has been seen, not be recognised under Irish law.

There are in Ireland a growing number of limping marriages, i.e. marriages regarded as valid and subsisting in Ireland but held to be dissolved and terminated elsewhere[4] as a result of spouses domiciled in Ireland resorting to the divorce jurisdiction of the United Kingdom and Northern Ireland and elsewhere. A continued adherence to domicile as the only jurisdictional basis for divorce recognition taken together with the continued absence of a domestic divorce jurisdiction guarantees that the growth in the number of limping marriages created in this way will continue.

---

1. See for example, *Counihan v. Counihan* (July, 1973) unreported (H.C.); *N.A.D. v. T.D.* [1985] 5 I.L.R.M. 153 (H.C.); *K.E.D. (otherwise K.C.) v. M.C.* (September, 1984) unreported (H.C.), (December, 1985) unreported (S.C.).

2. Under the substantive law of each of these jurisdictions the sole ground upon which a petition for divorce may be presented to the court by either party to a marriage is that the marriage has irretrievably broken down. To prove that such breakdown has occurred a petitioner must satisfy the court of one or more of the following facts:

(a)   that the respondent has committed adultery and the petitioner finds it intolerable to live with the respondent;

(b)   that the respondent has behaved in such a way that the petitioner cannot reasonably be expected to live with the respondent;

(c)   that the respondent has deserted the petitioner for a continuous period of at least two years immediately preceding the presentation of the petition;

(d)   that the parties to the marriage have lived apart for a continuous period of at least two years immediately preceding the presentation of the petition and the respondent consents to a decree being granted;

(e)   that the parties to the marriage have lived apart for a continuous period of at least 5 years immediately preceding the presentation of the petition.

See the Matrimonial Causes Act, 1973, Sect. 1(2) (England); the Divorce (Scotland) Act, 1976, Sect. 1(2) and the Matrimonial Causes (Northern Ireland) Order, 1978, Sect. 3(2).

3. See the Domicile & Matrimonial Proceedings Act, 1973, Sects. 5(2), 7(2) and 13(2).

4. This term is also used for marriages annulled or dissolved by the marriage tribunals of the Roman Catholic Church that are still held to be valid and subsisting marriages under civil law. See chap. 6 at p. 153.

2. The limitation of the law of recognition of foreign divorces to the narrow ground of domicile can be attributed to a desire to prevent or discourage forum shopping, i.e. to prevent or discourage spouses living in Ireland from seeking a divorce in a more accommodating jurisdiction so as to evade the constitutional prohibition on dissolution of marriage. In an era of greater mobility, however, this policy of the law can produce absurd results that have a devastating impact on the lives of those it affects. This proposition can be illustrated by the following example: A husband, whose family home is in Dublin, unable to obtain employment in the Republic of Ireland is offered a job in Derry in Northern Ireland and sets up home there with his wife and family. Both spouses intend ultimately to return to reside in Dublin upon a suitable employment opportunity arising and both retain Irish domicile. Five years later while still residing in Derry their marriage breaks down. The wife and her two children return to reside in Dublin and the husband issues divorce proceedings in Northern Ireland seeking a decree of divorce in accordance with the statutory provisions applicable. A divorce decree is granted and two years later the husband, who is still residing in Derry, remarries in Northern Ireland.[5] According to the laws of the Republic of Ireland the husband is still validly married to his first wife. According to the laws of Northern Ireland their marriage has been validly terminated. Examining the social reality of the situation, the wife in the Republic of Ireland is held in the bonds of a marriage to which there is no other party. There is something very wrong with a law that fosters such a situation. Rather than simply preventing spouses from evading the constitutional prohibition on divorce, it is perpetuating a legal fiction that marriages that have long since ceased to exist and which have been dissolved under the laws of neighbouring jurisdictions, still remain in being.

3. The current law can be supported on the grounds that upon marital breakdown occurring "the differences of married people should be adjusted in accordance with the laws of the community to which they belong"[6] or with which they have the closest connection. However, the artificiality and peculiarities of some of the rules relating to domicile can have the result that a couple's personal life is governed by the laws of a country with which they have had little or no connection for most of their married life. For example, within a few weeks of marriage an Irish couple take up residence in England, the husband obtaining employment there. They reside in England for 20 years always intending to return to Ireland, thus retaining their Irish domicile. Their marriage breaks down and a divorce is obtained. It is not recognised in the Republic of Ireland as at the date of the institution of the divorce proceedings neither party has an English domicile, although for virtually their entire married life the couple have resided in England, reared their children in England and England is in real terms the country with which they have together had the closest connection. If the husband or the wife in the foregoing example returns to Ireland after the granting of the English divorce decree, as their divorce is not recognised, neither party can validly marry under Irish law. Moreover, if either of them having remarried in England set up home in Ireland with their new spouse, Irish law does not recognise the validity of the second marriage.

---

5. See footnote 3 above.
6. *Le Mesurier v. Le Mesurier* [1895] A.C. 517 at p. 540 (H.L.) approved by Griffin J. in *Gaffney v. Gaffney* [1975] I.R. at p. 158.

4. In its Tenth Report[7] published in 1985, prior to the publication and enactment of the Domicile & Recognition of Foreign Divorces Act, 1986, the Law Reform Commission, having recommended that habitual residence replace domicile as a jurisdictional connecting factor in Irish private international law,[8] proposed the introduction of a dual system of divorce recognition which would have enabled the State to ratify and incorporate into Irish law the Hague Convention on the Recognition of Divorces and Legal Separations subject to certain reservations permitted by the Convention.[9] The Commission effectively proposed that one set of rules apply to the recognition of foreign divorces obtained by those it deemed to have "close connections with Ireland" and that a different set of rules apply to those it deemed not to have such connection.[10]

The Commission recognised "the desirability of avoiding limping marriages"[11] in respect of persons "who do not have close connections with Ireland."[12] but stated that "the policy of preventing evasion of the constitutional prohibition on divorce must take precedence over that of avoiding limping marriages,"[13] in respect of persons who do have such connections. It emphasised that "whatever recognition rules we adopt should not subvert the policy of existing internal law",[14] stating, however, that such rules should also not "operate unfairly and unjustly in so far as they effect different individuals in our society."[15] In essence, the Commission took the view that the avoidance of "limping marriages" should not be the major or primary aim of any new rules as to the recognition of foreign divorces adopted in so far as they would affect persons who "have close connections with Ireland".

The Commission proposed

(a) A foreign decree of divorce should not be recognised where both spouses are habitually resident in the State (the Republic of Ireland) at the date of the institution of the foreign divorce proceedings.[16]

(b) Where

(i)   one of the spouses is an Irish citizen and

(ii) only one spouse is habitually resident in the State and

(iii) the spouses last habitually resided together in the State

a foreign decree of divorce should only be recognised if the spouse habitually resident in the State submitted to the jurisdiction of the foreign court (by entering an appearance as respondent which was not solely to protest the court's jurisdiction) and if the divorce was obtained in a country where

---

7. *Report on Recognition of Foreign Divorces and Legal Separations* (L.R.C. Report No. 10 – April, 1985). See also on the same subject Working Paper No. 11 (W.P. No. 11, September, 1984). See further, *Report on Domicile & Habitual Residence as Connecting Factors in the Conflict of Laws* (L.R.C. Report No. 7, December, 1983) and on the same subject Working Paper No. 10 (W.P. No. 10, September, 1984).
8. See L.R.C. Report No. 7, *supra*.
9. The full text of the Hague Convention is published at the end of both the Report and the Working Paper published by the Law Reform Commission relating to the recognition of foreign divorces. The reservations that the Commission proposed be adopted would provide for the most restrictive recognition rules permissible under the Convention.
10. See W.P. No. 11 at p. 20 *et seq* and L.R.C. Report No. 10 at pp. 24–27.
11. W.P. No. 11 at p. 39.
12. *Ibid.*
13. *Ibid.*, at p. 62.
14. *Ibid.*, at p. 21.
15. *Ibid.*
16. *Ibid.*, at p. 27. See also L.R.C. Report No. 10 at p. 24.

the other spouse who instituted the proceedings was habitually resident at the date of their being instituted.[17]

(c) Save for the circumstances outlined in (a) and (b) the Commission proposed that generally speaking a foreign decree of divorce should be recognised if proceedings were instituted in a country in which either the petitioner or respondent was habitually resident or of which both spouses were nationals or of which the petitioning spouse was a national. In the latter instance, if the petitioning spouse did not also have his habitual residence in the State of which he was a national, in order for a divorce obtained in proceedings instituted by him in such State to be recognised the petitioner had to

(i)   be in such State at the date of the institution of the proceedings, and

(ii)   the spouses had to have last resided together in a State whose law, at the date of the institution of the proceedings, did not provide for divorce.[18]

So as to ensure that Irish domestic law would not be undermined by the above proposals, the Commission also stated that "where the residence abroad is only a temporary residence acquired with evasive intent in order to obtain a foreign divorce for which recognition might be sought here, it should not be treated by our courts as a genuine habitual residence for divorce recognition purposes. Accordingly, the legislation should specify that a person should be deemed to be habitually resident in the State who, having been habitually resident here, has temporarily ceased to reside here and has acquired a temporary residence abroad for the primary purpose of acquiring a foreign divorce." [19]

There is no doubt that the use of habitual residence as a jurisdictional basis for the recognition of foreign divorces either instead of or in addition to the concept of domicile as it currently applies would resolve some of the difficulties already discussed.[20] It offers both "a more practical and appropriate basis for recognition"[21] and is more readily understandable. However, the above proposals of the Law Reform Commission, if implemented, would introduce unnecessary complexity to what is an already difficult area of law and create as many anomalies as they would resolve. This is illustrated by the following example: A husband and wife are both Irish nationals, they last habitually resided together in Ireland where one spouse continues to reside and the other spouse institutes divorce proceedings in the foreign State in which he has established a habitual residence following the parties separating. Any divorce granted in such proceedings will be recognised.[22] If, however, the same circumstances pertain save that one spouse is an Irish national and one is not, such a divorce will not be recognised unless the spouse habitually resident in Ireland submitted to the foreign jurisdiction. Moreover, where both spouses are Irish nationals a recog-

---

17. L.R.C. Report No. 10 at p. 24 and W.P. No. 11 at pp. 27–30.
18. See W.P. No. 11 at p. 31 *et seq* where the commission proposes that the Hague Convention on Recognition of Divorces and Legal Separations should be the basis for the new rules of recognition of foreign divorces. See also L.R.C. Report No. 10 at pp. 24–25.
19. W.P. No. 11 at pp. 25–26. See also L.R.C. Report No. 10 at p. 24.
20. It should be noted that the Commission envisaged replacing the concept of domicile with that of habitual residence, not using habitual residence as an additional connecting factor.
21. See W.P. No. 11 at p. 23.
22. For the purpose of this example it is assumed that such spouse is properly habitually resident, not having established a "temporary residence" with "evasive intent".

nisable foreign divorce can be obtained by either spouse instituting proceedings in the courts of the foreign country in which one of them is habitually resident, whereas if one spouse only is an Irish national a recognisable foreign decree of divorce can only be obtained if the spouse habitually resident in the foreign jurisdiction institutes divorce proceedings. Under the current law if one spouse has a foreign domicile either spouse can institute divorce proceedings and obtain a recognisable decree of divorce in the courts of the foreign domicile.

It is possible that although it did not so state, the Law Reform Commission intend that (b) above would apply not only where one spouse is an Irish national but also to where both spouses are Irish nationals. If that is so, the position of a couple where both spouses are Irish nationals as compared to that where one spouse is an Irish national and one is not would be no different under its proposals. The proposals of the Commission as so stated, however, would introduce a discrimination on the basis of nationality between couples who could be regarded as having an equally close connection with Ireland and which does not presently exist under Irish law. This can be illustrated by the following example: A couple of English nationality who made their permanent home in Ireland and have resided in Ireland for 20 years live next door to a couple of Irish nationality who have never resided outside Ireland. Each of their marriages break down and in each case one spouse subsequently establishes both domicile and habitual residence in England. In the case of the couple of English nationality, the spouse remaining in Ireland can petition the English courts and obtain a divorce that will be recognised in Ireland. No recognisable divorce can, however, be obtained by the spouse remaining in Ireland instituting such divorce proceedings in the case of the Irish couple. Under current law either spouse could institute proceedings which would result in the obtaining of a recognisable foreign divorce decree. Moreover, in the case of a deserted Irish wife whose Irish husband sets up a permanent home in a foreign country and acquires foreign domicile, the implementation of the Law Reform Commission's proposals would deprive such wife of the possibility of instituting divorce proceedings and obtaining a decree recognised by Irish law, in circumstances where a wife has been able for decades to institute foreign divorce proceedings and obtain a decree of divorce that is recognised due to the old common law rule as to a wife's domicile of dependancy.

Not only would the Law Reform Commission's proposals, if implemented, "operate unfairly and unjustly",[23] they also lack clarity and logic in the manner in which they seek to distinguish between those designated as having close connections with Ireland and those designated not to have such connections. This can be illustrated as follows: A Scottish national and an Irish national marry and reside for the first year of their marriage in Ireland, for 20 years in Scotland and then return to reside in Ireland for 2 years. The marriage breaks down and one of the spouses returns to Scotland to reside, the other remaining in Ireland. The spouse resident in Ireland cannot, by instituting divorce proceedings in Scotland, obtain a decree that will be recognised in Ireland, although such a decree can be obtained if the spouse residing in Scotland institutes the proceedings and the spouse in Ireland submits to the jurisdiction of the Scottish court. By contrast, a Scottish national and Irish national marry and reside for the first year of their marriage in Scotland, for 20 years in Ireland then return to Scotland for 2 years. The marriage breaks down and one of the spouses returns to Ireland to reside, the other remaining in Scotland. Either spouse can institute divorce proceedings in the Scottish courts and obtain a divorce decree that will

---

23. To use the Commission's own test – see W.P. No. 11 at p. 21.

On appeal, a majority in the Supreme Court rejected this approach[95a] and held that once the mother had validly agreed to an adoption placement, any constitutional rights she possessed as a mother ceased to be a determining factor that should influence the court's decision.[95b] O'Higgins C.J. stated:

> "Once her agreement is such as to permit the operation of the section . . . the decision to grant or refuse the order sought must be taken on the sole test as to what, in relation to the grant or refusal of the order sought is in the 'best interests of the child'[96] . . . I interpret s.3 as giving to the child the statutory right to have her interests considered without regard to the clashing claims and competing rights of others . . . I conceive it to be the clear duty of this court to ensure that this right is both recognised and protected."[97]

A majority of the court[98] held that the "best interests of the child" were consistent with her being returned to the mother and upheld the decision of the High Court. Kenny J. stated:

> "The blood link between the (mother) and her child means that an instinctive understanding will exist between them which will not be there if the child remains with the (prospective adopters). A child's parent is the best person to bring it up as the affinity between them leads to a love which cannot exist between adoptive parents and the child. The child is now 12 months old and children of that age are infinitely adaptable."[99]

O'Higgins C.J. and Parke J., however, dissented from this finding. Referring to the judgement delivered by Finlay P. in the High Court, O'Higgins C.J. stated:

> "While he dealt with the welfare of the infant, having regard to the circumstances of each of the parties, he does not appear ever to have considered the one question which arises under s.3 of the Act of 1974 namely, what was 'in the best interests of the child.' "[100]

95a. Although Henchy J., in the minority, denied that the mother had a constitutional right to the custody of her child, the test applied by the learned judge in determining whether it was in the best interests of the child to dispense with the mother's consent, was in similar terms to that applied by Finlay P. It did not accord with the approach to this issue applied by the other members of the court.

95b. See, however, *R.C. & P.C. v. An Bord Uchtála & Anor.* (February, 1985) unreported (H.C.) where O'Hanlon J. remarked (at p. 13 of his judgement) that "The impact of the Constitution on the statutory provisions (of section 3 of the 1974 Act) has never been fully clarified."

96. [1980] I.R. at p. 58.

97. *Ibid.*, at p. 60.

98. Walsh J., Kenny J., and Henchy J.

99. [1980] I.R. at p. 98. Kenny J. gave no explanation as to how he formed the view that there is "an instinctive understanding between a natural parent and child as a result of the 'blood link' ". Neither did he explain the reasoning behind his conclusion that there is an affinity between a child and its natural parent that leads to a love which cannot exist between a child and its adoptive parents. Recent studies in this area emphasise that psychological rather than biological parenthood is what is important. See J. Goldstein, A. Freud, A.J. Solnit, *Beyond the Best Interests of the Child* (The Free Press, New York 1973) particularly Ch. 2) and *Before the Best Interests of the Child* (Burett Books Ltd., London 1980) particularly Ch. 4; M. Rutter, *Maternal Deprivation Reassessed* (Penguin Books Ltd., England 1972); J. Triseliotis, *New Developments in Foster Care & Adoption* (Routledge & Kegan Paul, London 1980) in particular Ch. 9; see also J. Rowe, "Parents and Substitute Parents" (Spring 1977) Children First Newsletter No. 7, p. 27; F. Bates, "Beyond the Best Interests . . . in the American Courts" (1978) 8 Fam. Law 46; W. Binchy, "The American Revolution in Family Law" (1976) 27 N.I.L.Q. 371 at p. 410 *et seq.*; G. McGann, "G. v. An Bord Uchtála — the best interests of the child and constitutional rights in adoption" (1979), vol. 73 *The Gazette of the Incorporated Law Society of Ireland* 203.

100. [1980] I.R. at p. 60.

The Chief Justice and Parke J., in the minority, both held that the case should be remitted to the High Court for that question to be determined.[101]

The High Court decision in *G. v. An Bord Uchtála* was given eight months after the child had been placed with adopters when the child was ten months old. When delivering judgement in the High Court, Finlay P. had stated that he accepted:

> "that the immediate removal of the child from its present whereabouts[101a] to the custody of its mother must represent to it some harmful dislocation, though I am not satisfied that it is a major one or that it is one which is likely to last."[102]

It is clear that the majority in the Supreme Court three months later were of a similar view when confirming the High Court order that the child be returned to the mother and, in this context, it should be noted that neither Walsh J. nor Henchy J., who, together with Kenny J. formed the majority, commented on the latter's statement as to the importance of the "blood link".[103]

During the course of the 1970's important studies into parenting and child development emphasised the pre-eminent importance of psychological as opposed to simple biological parenthood and documented how the newly born baby forms attachments and bonds with parenting adults and their extended family.[104] It is now accepted in the area of child development that a child can bond or form attachments equally as well with persons who are not blood relations as it can with its biological parent or parents. It is also accepted that to remove a child from an entire family with whom it has bonded and to place it in the care of a person or persons with whom it has never formed a relationship can have serious adverse short term and long term repercussions on the child's development and personality. There is, however, no unanimity between experts working in this area as to the exact period of time a baby or young child must be in the care of a family[105] before bonds or attachments are formed to the extent that the total removal of the child from all of those with whom the child has bonded

---

101. Finlay P. in the High Court had stated (1980 I.R. at pp. 48–49) "If the issue in this case was analogous to that which arises where separated parents are each seeking the custody of a child of the marriage, then I would be forced to the conclusion that the welfare of the child would be marginally better if the child remained with her present custodians (in the event of their obtaining an adoption order concerning her) than it would be if she returned to the custody of her mother and into the family home consisting of her grandmother, her grandfather and her aunt."

101a. Residing with the adopters in their home.

102. [1980] I.R. at p. 49. Walsh J. referring to the judgement delivered by Finlay P. in the High Court stated (1980 I.R. at pp. 81–82): "but even on the question of 'best interest', if that point had been reached, I am satisfied that on the evidence, the learned President of the High Court would be justified in holding that those interests would not have required him to authorise the board to dispense with the plaintiff's consent. His findings of fact are to the effect that the constitutional rights of the child are not in any way exposed to danger and are much less likely to be damaged by being brought up in the manner contemplated and planned by the mother, and that the mother has not in any way surrendered or abandoned her own constitutional rights to both the guardianship and the custody of her child."

103. See p. 309 *ante*.

104. See footnote 99 *supra*.

105. "Family" here is used in its broadest sense and refers to the extended family with whom a child forms close relationships. It can include not only the adoptive parents and their children but persons within an entire network of family relationships and friendships, i.e. aunts, uncles, neighbours, friends, etc., who have had close and regular contact with the particular child.

and formed attachments can be predicted to cause such serious repercussions.[105a] In the judicial consideration of the issue of the "child's best interests" in *G. v. An Bord Uchtála* no reference is made in any of the judgements delivered to the importance of psychological parenting and bonding and it appears from them that no witnesses who were called to give evidence in the High Court dealt with this issue. It arose for consideration by the High Court for the first time in an application brought under section 3 of the 1974 Act in *S. v. The Eastern Health Board*[106] and the decision in that case has been regarded as an issue of crucial importance in considering the "best interests of the child" in all subsequent cases decided under this section.

In *S. v. E.H.B. & Ors.*[107] the plaintiff having given birth to an illegitimate child on the 3rd June 1977 in St. Patrick's Home in Dublin, remained in the home for ten days and then resumed employment. She regularly visited the child until August 1977 and was encouraged to make a decision as to what future arrangements should be made for the child's upbringing. Her visits ceased from August until December 1977, when she agreed to the child being placed for adoption. The child was so placed on the 19th December 1977. In April of 1978, upon the child being returned to her by the adopters at her request, she retained the child in her custody for only three days and then placed it in another children's home as she was unable to cope.

On the 2nd May 1978, the mother signed a consent to the making of an adoption order and the child was returned at her request to the original adopters. Sixteen days later she withdrew her consent. The child was still residing with the adopters[108] early in 1979 when the case was heard and was nineteen months old.

The court held that it was in the best interests of the child that it remain with the adopters and that the mother's consent be dispensed with. Finlay P. stated that he accepted, on the evidence, that the child had integrated into the adopters' family, that the separation in April of 1978 had had an injurious effect on the child's development which had taken some months to repair and that it was presently developing normally and well. Referring to the psychiatric evidence,[109] he stated that he was satisfied:

"that this child is essentially a child who has significantly suffered in its emotional and psychiatric development by the first period of six months

---

105a. This is evident not only from the literature on this issue but also from the judicial references made to evidence given by various child psychiatrists in many of the judgements delivered in cases determined under section 3 of the Act of 1974 which are discussed in this chapter. Compare, for example, the psychiatric evidence given in *S. v. The Eastern Health Board, supra, Mc.C. v. An Bord Uchtála, supra*, and *R.C. & P.C. v. An Bord Uchtála, supra*, as referred to in the judgements delivered in these cases. This issue is discussed in detail by the authors of *Before the Best Interests of the Child, supra*, who state that although the process of forming "psychological parent-child relationships" can be described, "its time-table cannot be set precisely" (see p. 42) and that "there is no litmus paper for testing when a substitute parent has become a particular child's psychological parent" (p. 45). While acknowledging that the timespan required for the formation of such a relationship can vary having regard to the circumstances and history of the individual child, the authors nevertheless propose the provision of specific statutory periods during which if a child is in the direct and continuous care of the same adult(s) it should be presumed that a child's residual ties, if any, with absent parents are less significant for the child than those that have developed between the child and his longtime caretakers (see p. 46 *et seq*.) and which if disrupted could have serious repercussions for the child.

106. (February, 1979) unreported (H.C.).

107. *Ibid*.

108. The adopters also had two children of their own. At the date of the court hearing their daughter was 7 years of age and their son 4 years of age.

109. Given by Professor Brendan McCarthy, of the Tavistock Child Guidance Clinic, London, England.

in which it remained in St. Patrick's Home.[110] (The child psychiatrist's) account of his interview with and observations of the child in the environment of its present family indicates clearly to me that it has the badges of an institutional child and that there are very real dangers to its ultimate intellectual and emotional development unless a continuity of an existing caring custody is maintained. My view is not that the child would particularly suffer from now being transferred to the custody of its mother but rather that the child would be most likely seriously to suffer now from being transferred from the custody of the applicants for adoption."[111]

In the later case of *The State (P.M.) v. G.M.*[111a] dispensing with the consent of a natural mother so as to enable the Adoption Board make an adoption order in respect of a child who was at the date of the court judgement sixteen months old, and who hadbeen placed with adopters when ten days old, Finlay P. stated that he had

"very carefully considered the importance or potential importance of a blood link between the child and her parents"

and that on the evidence he had heard in the case, he could find

"no strong or serious support for the importance of that as a feature in the future welfare of the child.[111b]

In *Mc.C. v. An Bord Uchtála*[112] a four week old baby was placed with adopters in February 1979. The mother signed the final consent on the 23rd of April 1979 but changed her mind and withdrew her consent two months later, before the Adoption Board had made an adoption order. The adopters refused to return the child to the mother and, in March 1981, she instituted court proceedings seeking custody and the adopters sought to dispense with her consent to adoption. Delivering judgement in the High Court at the end of July 1981, when the child was eighteen months old, finding in favour of the adopters and dispensing with the mother's consent, McWilliam J. stated:

"I have had the benefit of the evidence of two psychiatrists in the case and, by a coincidence, of a third in a case I heard immediately after it.[113] They all agree that a child becomes assimilated into its family or 'bonded' from the age of six months and that a change after a year is usually difficult and may even be dangerous unless accomplished carefully. Apart from this, the evidence is that the child is living in a stable, caring household in which the mother[114] is always available and that the child has become a member of the family in the fullest sense, whereas the plaintiff appears to have a certain lack of appreciation of what would be required for the proper care of her child and has an unsatisfactory 'on and off' relationship with the father of the child which could be very disturbing for the child, quite apart from the

110. Professor McCarthy in evidence stated that in his view the child had formed no significant bonds or attachments during its time in St. Patrick's as a variety of different people had cared for it and that no bonds had been formed with the mother (the plaintiff) due to the lack of contact between her and the child and that it had for the first time in its young life started to formulate bonds or attachments after being placed with the adopters.
111. See p. 25 of judgement.
111a.(November, 1984) unreported (H.C.).
111b.See p. 20 of judgement.
112. [1982] 2 I.L.R.M. 159 (H.C.).
113. The reference is to *McF. v. G. & G. & Ors.* [1983] 3 I.L.R.M. 228 (H.C.). See p. 304 *ante* and p. 313 *post*.
114. The reference should be to the adopting mother.

emotional disturbance caused by the separation from his present family."[115]

Referring to submissions made on behalf of the plaintiff mother as to "the importance for the child of the blood link with his mother", he continued:

"I have had no evidence that there is any importance to be attached to this and one of the doctors denied that it has any importance at all."[116]

Three days later, delivering judgement in *McF. v. G. & Ors.*[117] McWilliam J. expressing similar views[118] held it to be in the best interests of a child aged two years and two months that he dispense with the consent of the child's mother, so as to enable adopters with whom the child had been placed when three months old obtain an adoption order.

In *The State (M.G.) v. A.H. & M.H.*[119] a child had been in the adopters' care for nineteen months, being only seven days old when first placed with them. Dealing again with the question of bonding, McWilliam J. noted that the opinion of the only child psychiatrist called as a witness in the proceedings was that:

"Moving the child now out of the family with which it has become so well assimilated would have disastrous effects on her (the child) and (that the psychiatrist) enumerated a number of short term and long term adverse developments, some of which she considered probable and others possible."[120]

He concluded dealing with this issue noting that the psychiatrist

"particularly emphasised that there is no such thing as a re-bonding in a new family when bonding has already taken place to the extent in which it has done here."[121]

An order was made dispensing with the mother's consent.

In the later case of *R.C. & P.C. v. An Bord Uchtála*[122] an entirely different approach to the issue of re-bonding was accepted by the trial judge. The child was just one year old at the date of the court judgement, having been in the care of prospective adopters for ten months. Until placed for adoption the child had spent seven weeks in foster care and had been visited regularly when in fosterage by the natural mother. Four months after placement, the natural mother withdrew her consent to adopt.

O'Hanlon J. accepted that the child had "thrived" in the care of the adopters and stated that there was a "conflict of opinion" between the psychiatrists called to give evidence as to the likely effect on the child if it were transferred from the adopters' to the mother's custody. He noted that the child psychiatrist called on behalf of the adopters had said that the baby was very definitely bonded to the adoptive parents; that bonding takes place in the first six months of the baby's life and "if broken the child may be marked for life, both physically and psychologically, with a tendency to become a superficial adult, unhappy and unable to relate on a deep level to another human being" and that the prognosis given

115. [1982] 2 I.L.R.M. at pp. 162–163.
116. *Ibid.*, at p. 163. A notice of appeal lodged by the mother in the Supreme Court against the High Court decision was subsequently withdrawn and no Supreme Court appeal hearing took place.
117. *Supra.*
118. See [1983] 3 I.L.R.M. at p. 233.
119. [1984] 4 I.L.R.M. 237 (H.C.).
120. *Ibid.*, at p. 245.
121. *Ibid.*
122. (February, 1985) unreported (H.C.).

for the child's future, if taken from the adopters, was "a very gloomy one".[122a] The child psychiatrist called on behalf of the mother, while accepting that a transfer of custody to the mother would cause "an initial period of stress and upset for the baby" was of the view that there would be no long term ill-effects if the mother and her family provided "the loving and caring environment which the child needed for its proper development" stating that "there was no reason to suppose that the child would not form a new bond with its natural mother."[122b]

O'Hanlon J., stating it was very hard to resist the claims of the natural mother, continued:

> "The adoptive parents appear to be as good a choice as one could make when placing this child for adoption but I cannot help feeling that a baby and growing child would always be better off with its natural mother if she is a devoted and concerned parent and can provide in a reasonable manner for the physical as well as the emotional needs of the child. If too long a period is allowed to elapse before the return of the child from the adoptive parents is sought, I accept that the bonds of attachment between the child and its psychological parents may have been so strongly formed as to be incapable of being broken without lasting damage to the child's personality but I do not think, after carefully reviewing the conflicting medical testimony in this case, that that point of no return has yet been reached."[122c]

He declined to dispense with the mother's consent and ordered that the child be returned to her custody.

In *N.B. & T.B. v. An Bord Uchtála & Ors.*[123] Barron J. declined to return a child aged three years and three months to the mother's custody and granted an order dispensing with the mother's consent. During the first seven months of his life, the child had resided with his mother, then spent five months in care, then lived a further fifteen months with his mother and then remained a further year in care before being placed with adopters. According to the mother, on her own evidence, she had placed her son for adoption as she had been violent towards him, had rejected him and had been unable to cope with him. Finding that if the child was returned to the mother there was "nothing to suggest that she will be able to cope with him any better than she did in the past"[124] Barron J. went on to consider the evidence of three child psychiatrists, from which he accepted

> "that the infant is now in the first secure home which he has ever known, that he is an integrated member, not only of the applicants' (adopters') home but also of their family in an extended sense. He is happy and well adjusted and regards this family as his family. He has had too many placements and upsets in his routine in the past. If he is moved now, he will have a grief reaction. This will manifest itself with tears, nightmares, bedwetting, loss of appetite and general misbehaviour. The longer term reaction could involve delinquency and general behavioural problems and he will run a

---

122a. See p. 9 of judgement.
122b. See pp. 9 and 10 of judgement.
122c. See p. 14 of judgement. During the course of his judgement O'Hanlon J. stated that the onus lay on the prospective adopters "to satisfy the court, as a matter of probability" that the best interests of the child required that the mother's consent be dispensed with for such order to be made. The judge's statement that the child "would always be better off with its natural mother" appears to again raise the issue of the importance of the "blood link". See P. O'Connor, "Constitutional Conflict in Adoption Proceedings — A Postscript" [1985] 3 I.L.T. 161.
123. (February, 1983) unreported (H.C.).
124. See p. 10 of judgement.

serious risk of being unable to form lasting personal relationships."[125]

The Supreme Court, without delivering a written judgement, upheld the High Court decision and rejected the mother's appeal at the conclusion of a full appeal hearing.[126]

In all of the above discussed cases no doubt arose as to the capacity of the prospective adopters to properly care for the child placed with them and in all of them the validity of the mother's agreement to place was challenged. *S.M. & M.M. v. An Bord Uchtála & Ors.*[127] was unusual in that no challenge was made to the validity of the agreement to place, the mother withdrawing her consent to adopt as information had been given to her suggesting that it was not appropriate that an adoption order be made in favour of the adopters with whom her child had been placed.

The child (a boy) having been born in March 1982, had been in Temple Hill Nursery for over seven months prior to being placed with the adopters in November 1982. He had only been visited once by his mother when in the nursery and had been in the care of the adopters for almost eighteen months at the date of the court hearing. The adopters had failed to disclose to the Adoption Board or Adoption Society that the adoptive father had suffered from depression and mood swings and had required medical treatment. It was also suggested during the course of the court hearing that the adopters had marital difficulties. The trial judge held on the evidence that the adoptive parents enjoyed a stable, happy marriage and that the adoptive father's illness had been stabilised by medication. Accepting evidence that

> "if the child were now removed from this environment[128] and placed into another environment either by being given back to the mother and her family or placed for adoption with other persons, this would probably result in grave psychological injury to the child, possibly resulting in delinquency at a later age."

Lynch J. found in favour of the adopters and dispensed with the mother's consent.[129]

Form and Effect of Order Made Under Section 3 of Adoption Act, 1974

Upon adopters succeeding in proceedings initiated under this section the court, in practice, makes a two-part order, granting custody to the adopters for a specific period of time under section 3(2)(a) of the Act and authorising the Adoption Board to dispense with a necessary consent or consents under section 3(2)(b) of the Act during the period of time for which the custody order remains in force. The order of the court does not require the Adoption Board to make an adoption order, it merely enables it to do so.[130] If the Board declines to make an adoption order, then the question of the future custody of the child arises for determination. In the majority of cases determined under this section, the court has not indicated its views as to the arrangements that should be made for the future custody of a child, if the Adoption Board subsequently declines

---

125. See pp. 9–10 of judgement. The learned judge also stated that even if the mother was able to cope, such difficulties would arise. See p. 11 of judgement.
126. In January 1984.
127. (May, 1984) unreported (H.C.). Lynch J.
128. The adopters' home.
129. On the issue of bonding see also *T. O'G. v. A.G. & Ors.* [1985] 5 I.L.R.M. 61 (H.C.). In particular McMahon J. at p. 65.
130. See *S. v. E.H.B., supra*, at p. 14 of judgement.

to make an adoption order after the court has authorised it to dispense with a consent. In *S. v. E.H.B.*[131] and *The State (P.M.) v. G.M.*, Finlay P. held that if the Board did not make an adoption order the child who was the subject of the court proceedings should be returned to the custody of its natural mother.[132] In *S.M. & M.M. v. An Bord Uchtála & Ors.*[133] Lynch J. held that in such circumstances the courts should, subsequent to the Adoption Board's decision, hear further evidence as to what order it should make having regard to the provisions of section 3 of the Guardianship of Infants Act, 1964, under which "the first and paramount consideration must be the welfare of the child".[134] It is submitted that the approach adopted by Lynch J. is preferable, as if the Adoption Board does decline to make an adoption order after a court decision that it is "in the best interests" of a child that a consent be dispensed with, prior to any further decision being made as to the arrangements to be implemented for the future upbringing of the child, it is essential that the court is informed of the circumstances which gave rise to the Adoption Board's decision. In the absence of such information being given to the court, it would be unable to fulfil its statutory duty by ensuring that all matters relating to the child's welfare were fully considered by it prior to making a decision as to the child's future custody.

Section 3 Proceedings – Outstanding Problems

Section 3 of the Act of 1974 has resolved some of the problems that arose from the limited power to dispense with a necessary consent as originally conferred by the Act of 1952 and has enabled the adoption process to be completed and adoption orders made in respect of a number of children whose adoptions could not have been finalised prior to its enactment. By the end of February 1986, 48 applications had been made to the courts to dispense with the consent of a natural mother under the section, 35 of which were granted, 3 of which were refused and 3 of which were not finally determined. Of the remaining 7 applications, 3 were adjourned generally by the High Court and 4 were struck out.[134a]

A number of difficulties still remain to be resolved in this area. These include:

(a) It appears from the judgement of Finlay P. in *S. v. Eastern Health Board & Ors.* that where a mother concludes a valid agreement to place but later changes her mind and requests that her child be returned to her, if the prospective adopters comply with her request and the mother subsequently proves incapable of caring for her child, if she refuses to again agree to the placing of her child for adoption or, in the absence of such agreement, to consent to the making of an adoption order, the court has no power to make an

---

131. *Supra*.
132. *Supra*.
133. *Supra*.
134. See p. 14 of judgement. Finlay P. in *S. v. E.H.B.*, *supra*, and *The State (P.M.) v. G.M.*, *supra*. He appears to have held the view that if no adoption order was made and if the mother's conduct was not such as to warrant her forfeiting custody under the provisions of sections 14 or 16 of the Guardianship of Infants Act, 1964 (see pp. 377–78 *post*), the mother would have a right to have her child returned to her custody. Lynch J. in *S.M. & M.M. v. An Bord Uchtála, supra*, adopted the approach that even if the mother's behaviour would not result in her forfeiting the right to custody under either of those two sections, that the issue of custody would have to be determined on the basis of the welfare principle as stated in section 3 of the Act of 1964. See further, *J.M. & G.M. v. An Bord Uchtála* (April, 1986) unreported (H.C.) in which Barron J. did not dispense with the mother's consent but held the child should remain with the adopters. See reference also to this case in footnote 58 *ante*.
134a. See Vol. 364 Dáil Reports, Cols. 95 and 96 (25th February 1986).

order permitting the Adoption Board to dispense with her consent so as to enable the adoption process to be completed.

(b) If an illegitimate child is placed in institutional or foster care for all or most of its infancy and the mother, whose whereabouts are known, refuses to agree to the child being placed for adoption, no order can be made permitting the Adoption Board to dispense with the necessity for her agreement to an adoption placement and with her consent to an adoption order being made.

(c) In *K.C. & A.C. v. An Bord Uchtála*[135] in the context of a custody dispute determined under the Guardianship of Infants Act, 1964, between the natural parents of a legitimated child and a couple with whom the child had originally been placed for adoption, Lynch J. referred to evidence given as to the likely psychological consequences to a child of the breaking of bonds or attachments as "predictive" and "not certain evidence"[136] and stated that "such adverse effects as may result" from the transfer of the child to its natural parents from the couple with whom it had originally been placed for adoption and with whom it had lived for the first three years of its life had "not ... been sufficiently established" as to warrant a finding that the child's welfare required that it remain in the latter's custody.[137] This case was considerably complicated by the constitutional issues already referred to in chapter 1 and discussed in chapter 13.[138] It was also not a case which ultimately fell to be determined on the basis of the best interest test prescribed by section 3 of the Act of 1974. It, nevertheless, casts a shadow over this area of the law and creates the possibility that the courts may start to question the degree to which reliance should be placed on evidence given by child psychiatrists as to the nature and importance of bonding in future cases that arise under section 3.

Procedure for the Making of an Adoption Order

As has been seen, before accepting a child for adoption, the placement agency is obliged to furnish the mother or guardian, who proposes to place the child at its disposal, with a statement explaining the effect of an adoption order upon the rights of the mother or guardian, and the provisions of the Act relating to consents. The agency must ensure that the person understands the statement and signs a document to that effect.[139] This document has a dual function. It is both a receipt for the explanatory statement and a written agreement to the placing for adoption of the child. The child is then placed with prospective adopters. Prior to the Adoption Board making an adoption order the final consent to the making of such an order must be obtained by the Society. If no such consent is forthcoming, an adoption order cannot be made unless the consent is dispensed with in accordance with the provisions described earlier.

Section 9 of the 1974 Act empowers the Adoption Board to prescribe a period during which a child must be in the care of the applicants before an order can be made. The Board, however, has not at the time of writing yet made an order under the powers conferred by this section. In practice, however, in the absence

---

135. See the judgement of Lynch J. of May 1985 reported in [1986] 6 I.L.R.M. 65. See also [1985] 5 I.L.R.M. 302 (S.C.).
136. See [1986] 6 I.L.R.M. at p. 66.
137. *Ibid.*, at p. 67.
138. See p. 22 *ante* and p. 392 *post*.
139. Adoption Act, 1952, Sect. 39.

of very special circumstances it requires a child to be in the care of the applicants for a minimum of six months before it will make an order.

Upon an adoption application being made the Board is empowered to hold an oral hearing, can summon witnesses, examine on oath, and require any witness to produce to the Board any document in his power or control. The Board may make whatever enquiries it thinks necessary to fulfil its function. A member or officer of the Board may visit the homes of the child, the guardian of the child, the applicants and the person to whom custody of the child has been given under an interim order.[140] Unless a person whose consent is required informs the Board that he does not wish to be heard, the Board must inform that person of a date on which he will be heard by it.[141] It must also ensure that such person properly understands the nature and effect of giving consent and of an adoption order.[142]

The following persons are entitled to be heard on an application for an adoption order:[143]

(a) the applicants;

(b) the mother of the child;

(c) the guardian of the child;

(d) a person having charge of or control over the child;

(e) a relative of the child;

(f) a representative of a registered adoption society which is or has been at any time concerned with the child;

(g) a priest or minister of religion (or, in the case of any such religion which has no ministry, an authorised representative of the religion) where the child or a parent (whether alive or dead) is claimed to be or to have been of that religion;

(h) an officer of the Board;

(i) any other person whom the Board, in its discretion, decides to hear.

If the application is in respect of a legitimated child whose birth has not been re-registered under the Legitimacy Act, 1931, the natural father of the child is also entitled to be heard.[144]

Any of these persons may be legally represented.

As has been seen the Board may state a case for the determination of the High Court on any question of law arising out of an application for an adoption order and such a case may be heard in camera.[145] If the Board has been notified that custody proceedings are pending in regard to the custody of a child in respect of whom an application is before the Board, it can make no order until the proceedings have been disposed of.[146]

---

140. See First Schedule to the Adoption Act, 1952. For interim orders see further p. 320.
141. See Adoption Act, 1976, Sect. 3.
142. See p. 297 *ante*.
143. Adoption Act, 1952, Sect. 16(1).
144. Adoption Act, 1964, Sect. 2(2).
145. Adoption Act, 1952, Sect. 20.
146. *Ibid.*, Sect. 16(4).

Administrative Duties of the Adoption Board and of Adoption Societies

The staff of the Adoption Board consists of a full-time registrar, administrative staff and welfare officers who are responsible for reporting to the Board on the suitability of adoption applicants.

The Board must produce a yearly report stating the number of applications for adoption and the decisions thereon, the names of the registered societies concerned in the applications, the number of applications for registration of societies and the decisions of the Board thereon, and the name and address of each registered society or of the societies whose registration has been cancelled.[147]

An Adoption Societies Register is kept by the Board and nobody can be entered into the register unless it exists only for the purpose of promoting charitable, benevolent or philanthropic objects and the Board is satisfied that it is competent to discharge the obligations imposed on adoption societies.[148] A registered adoption society must furnish the Board with whatever information it requires in regard to its constitution, membership, employees, organisation and activities. It must also permit the Board to inspect all books and documents relating to adoption in the possession of the society.[149] The Board may cancel the registration of a society on any ground which would entitle them not to register the society or if it appears to the Board that the requirements of the Act are not being complied with by the society or its members.[150] The Board does not, however, have a statutory power to set down a minimum code of practice for adoption societies. Although it did in 1970 produce some guidelines for the societies, these are not mandatory.

In *McL. v. An Bord Uchtála & A.-G.*[151] the applicants sought a declaration that the making of an adoption order was not the exercise of a limited judicial power or function and that accordingly section 9 of the 1952 Act which confers such power on the Board was repugnant to the Constitution.[152] Butler J. in the High Court dismissed this contention, holding that the Board exercises an administrative and not a judicial function. On appeal, the Supreme Court left the matter undecided, holding that the adoption order was invalid for reasons already discussed.

In *G. v. An Bord Uchtála,*[153] Walsh J. also stated that the Board was exercising an administrative and not a judicial function. The other members of the Supreme Court, however, expressly reserved their opinion on the issue as it did not arise for consideration and had not been argued before them.

On the 5th of July 1979 following the holding of a Constitutional Referendum, the Sixth Amendment of the Constitution (Adoption) Act, 1979, became law and the following provision was inserted into Article 37 of the Constitution as Article 37.2:

"No adoption of a person taking effect or expressed to take effect at any time after the coming into operation of this Constitution under laws enacted

---

147. See *Ibid.*, First Schedule.
148. *Ibid.*, Sect. 36.
149. *Ibid.*, Sect. 38.
150. *Ibid.*, Sect. 37.
151. (October, 1974) unreported (H.C.); [1977] I.R. 287 (S.C.).
152. Article 37.1 of the Constitution provides "Nothing in this Constitution shall operate to invalidate the exercise of limited functions and powers of a judicial nature, in matters other than criminal matters, by any person or body of persons duly authorised by law to exercise such functions and powers, notwithstanding that such person or such body of persons is not a judge or a court appointed or established as such under this Constitution." For a detailed discussion of this article see J.M. Kelly, *Irish Constitutional Law*, 2nd ed. (1984) p. 363 *et seq.*
153. *Supra.*

by the Oireachtas and being an adoption pursuant to an order made or an authorisation given by any person or body of persons designated by those laws to exercise such functions and powers was or shall be invalid by reason only of the fact that such person or body of persons was not a judge or a court appointed or established as such under this Constitution."

As a result of the addition of this provision to the Constitution, adoption orders made by the Board are no longer open to challenge on the ground that the Board is exercising a judicial function.[153a]

Interim Orders[154]

On an application for an adoption order the Board is empowered to adjourn the application and make an interim order giving the custody of the child to the applicant for a probationary period of not more than two years. Conditions as to the maintenance, education and supervision of the welfare of the child can be attached to such an order, and the order can be revoked by the Board under its own initiative or at the request of the person to whom custody of the child has been given or of the mother or guardian of the child.

The Position of the Natural Father of an Illegitimate Child

For the purpose of the Adoption Acts the role of the father of an illegitimate child is only given limited recognition. Whereas he is one of those who are eligible to apply to adopt the child, he is not regarded as a parent or as a relation of the child. Relatives under the Act are traced through the mother only. The only instance in which the consent of a natural father is required before the making of an adoption order is when a child has been legitimated by the subsequent marriage of his parents.[155] In all other cases, the feelings and views of the natural father are irrelevant.

The natural father as such is not one of those entitled to be heard by the Board in an oral hearing prior to determining whether an order to adopt should be made. He may of course acquire a right to be heard as an applicant for adoption, as a person having charge or control over the child, or as the guardian of the child.[156] The Board may also hear him in exercise of their discretion to hear "any other person".[157]

In the *State (Nicolaou) v. An Bord Uchtála*[158] the constitutional validity of the Adoption Act, 1952, was challenged on the ground that it violated the constitutional rights of the natural father of an illegitimate child by enabling the Board to make an adoption order without hearing his views.

Nicolaou, a Greek Cypriot of Greek Orthodox faith and English domicile,

---

153a. See further, *J.M. & G.M. v. An Bord Uchtála* (April, 1986) unreported (H.C.) and the reference therein by Barron J. to Art. 37.2 at pp. 16–17 of judgement. See reference also to this case in footnote 58 *ante*.

154. Adoption Act, 1952, Sect. 17.

155. See *K.C. & A.C. v. An Bord Uchtála, supra*.

156. The Guardianship of Infants Act, 1964, Sect. 11(4) conferred on the natural father of an illegitimate child the right to apply to the Circuit or High Court for the custody of such child. Thus, if the father of an illegitimate child does not wish it to be adopted he may strengthen his hand by making such an application. Even if he does not succeed in getting custody he will at least delay the making of an order by bringing such proceedings. This Act was not in force at the time when Nicolaou commenced the proceedings discussed further on. The Courts Act, 1981, Sect. 15 conferred jurisdiction on the District Court to make orders under section 11(4) and may have deprived the High Court of such jurisdiction. See further Chapter 2.

157. Adoption Act, 1952, Sect. 16(1)(i).

158. [1966] I.R. 567 (S.C.).

was the father of the illegitimate child of a Catholic Irishwoman with whom he had lived in London. The child was born on 23rd February 1960 and on 16th June 1960, the mother returned to Dublin with the child and on the 23rd September 1960, she left it in the custody of the Catholic Protection and Rescue Society for adoption. Towards the end of September, Nicolaou learnt that the child was being put forward for adoption, and on 7th October 1960 his solicitors wrote to the Adoption Board stating that they had been instructed to institute proceedings in the High Court to prevent the adoption of the child and that they were putting the Board on notice in accordance with section 16 of the Act. Nothing more was done by Nicolaou or his solicitors and in September 1961 the mother signed the papers necessary for the adoption to take place and an order was made for the child's adoption by a married couple.

At all times Nicolaou had been willing to marry the mother but she would not agree to a marriage unless he became a member of the Catholic Church. In mid 1963 Nicolaou learnt that the child had definitely been adopted and having been refused a conditional order of Habeas Corpus directed to the registrar of the Board and the secretary of the adoption society, he sought to have the adoption order quashed by an order of *certiorari*. One of the arguments on his behalf was the contention that the Adoption Act discriminated against him by according a status to the mother which was not accorded to the father contrary to Article 40.1. In reply to this, Walsh J. delivering the judgement of the court, said:

> "In the opinion of the court each of the persons described as having rights under S.14, sub-s.1, and S.16, sub-s. 1, can be regarded as having, or capable of having, in relation to the adoption of a child a moral capacity or social function which differentiates him from persons who are not given such rights. When it is considered that an illegitimate child may be begotten by an act of rape, by a callous seduction or by an act of casual commerce by a man with a woman, as well as by the association of a man with a woman in making a common home without marriage in circumstances approximating to those of married life" (*the latter was the situation here* – Author.) "and that, except in the latter instance, it is rare for a natural father to take any interest in his offspring, it is not difficult to appreciate the difference in moral capacity and social function between the natural father and the several persons described in the sub-sections in question."[159]

The court also held in *Nicolaou* that the Act was not contrary to Article 40.3 as, on the evidence presented, the father had no "personal rights" in relation to the child, nor was it contrary to Articles 41 and 42 as these articles related solely to a family and parenthood based on marriage.[160]

---

159. *Supra* at p. 641.
160. See also *O'B. v. S.* [1984] I.R. (S.C.); *G. v. An Bord Uchtála, supra*. See further p. 6 *ante* and p. 594 *post*.

Invalid Orders

The Supreme Court decision in *McL. v. An Bord Uchtála & A.-G.*[161] caused considerable public controversy. At the date when the judgements were delivered the 'adopted' child was six years old and had been in the custody of its adoptive parents since the age of three months, its mother having placed the child with an adoption society within five weeks of its birth. A year after the making of the order the natural parents married and went to live in West Africa. It was not until the child was four years old that the parents commenced the proceedings that resulted in the court holding the adoption order to be invalid and the natural parents entitled to custody of the child.[162]

Section 5 of the Adoption Act, 1976, enacted as a result of the above case, provides that an adoption order shall not be declared invalid if the court is satisfied

> "(a) that it would not be in the best interests of the child concerned to make such a declaration, and
>
> (b) that it would be proper, having regard to those interests and to the rights under the Constitution of all persons concerned, not to make such a declaration."

In the *McL.* case, the court granted custody to the natural parents although the adoptive parents were not parties to the proceedings and had no opportunity to present their case.[163] Section 6 of the Act of 1976 provides that if an adoption order is declared invalid at the request of a person who does not have custody of the child subject to the order, the court cannot make an order of custody unless

> (a) such an order is sought and
>
> (b) any person having custody of the child is joined in the proceedings, and
>
> (c) it is in the interests of justice that the question of custody be determined without the necessity of bringing separate proceedings.

If the court decides to determine the question of custody the section states that "it shall do so subject to the provisions of section 3 of the Guardianship of

---

161. *Supra.*

162. See dissenting judgement of Henchy J. The child was never actually returned to the custody of the natural parents.

163. Subsequent to the Supreme Court decision, the adopters commenced proceedings seeking a declaration that they were not bound by the Supreme Court order as they were not afforded any opportunity to be heard, and sought an order that the child remain in their custody. The natural parents sought an order of Habeas Corpus requiring the adopters to return their child to them. On 6th Oct. 1976, it was announced to the President of the High Court that the actions had been settled. A consent was executed by the parties in which they agreed that the child be made a ward of court and remain in the custody and care of the adopters. See the *Irish Times* 24th July and 7th Oct. 1976.

Infants Act, 1964" which requires the court to regard the welfare of the child as the first and paramount consideration in the determination of any dispute as to custody.[164] Whilst there should be no difficulty in the courts applying the "best interests" test or the welfare test under section 3 of the Act of 1964 as required by sections 5 and 6 of the Act of 1976 in determining proceedings initiated by a mother seeking to have an adoption order declared invalid and to obtain custody of her child, the application of either test in the determination of such proceedings initiated by a married couple in respect of a child that would be legitimated upon an adoption order being declared invalid or which is legitimated as a result of such declaration is considerably complicated by the judgement of the Supreme Court in *K.C. & A.C. v. An Bord Uchtála*[165] discussed in detail in chapter 13.

The persons in whose favour an adoption order is made can only be heard in proceedings in which the validity of an adoption order is challenged with the consent of the court. In deciding whether to give consent, the court may hear submissions from the Adoption Board or any other interested person relating to the identification of the person or persons concerned or to any other relevant matter.[166]

Prohibition on Advertisements and Payments

The Adoption Act, 1952, prohibits the publication of any advertisements indicating

(a) that a parent or guardian of a child desires to have the child adopted, or

(b) that a person desires to adopt a child, or

(c) that a person (other than a registered Adoption Society or Health Board) is willing to arrange for the adoption of children.[166a]

The Act also prohibits an adopter, parent or guardian of a child from receiving or agreeing to receive "any payment or other reward in consideration of the adoption of the child" and prohibits any person from giving or agreeing to give any such payment or reward.[167] Moreover, a person "who makes arrangements for the adoption of a child" is prohibited from receiving, making or giving any payment or other reward for making any such arrangements or for agreeing to do so.[168] Adoption arrangements for which payment is prohibited include

(a) the making of any agreement or arrangement for, or facilitating the adoption or maintenance of the child by any person, and

(b) the initiation of or taking part in negotiations of which the purpose or effect is the making of any such agreement or arrangement, and

(c) the causing of another to initiate or take part in any such negotiations.[169]

---

164. See further Chapter 13.
165. [1985] 5 I.L.R.M. 302 (S.C.). See p. 392 *et seq*.
166. Adoption Act, 1976, Sect. 6(2).
166a. Adoption Act, 1952, Sect. 41(1) as amended by the Adoption Act, 1974, Sect. 13.
167. Adoption Act, 1952, Sect. 42(1).
168. *Ibid.*, Sect. 42(3)(a).
169. *Ibid.*, Sect. 4.

The section does not, however, prohibit adopters, parents or guardians of a child from making or receiving payments for the maintenance of a child being adopted or prohibit remuneration being paid to or received by a solicitor for professional services arising out of or relating to the making of arrangements for an adoption.[170]

Contravention of any of the above prohibitions is an offence. A person who contravenes the prohibition on advertising is liable on summary conviction to a fine not exceeding £100.[171] A person who contravenes the prohibition on payments or other rewards is liable on summary conviction to a fine not exceeding £100 and/or to a sentence of imprisonment for a term not exceeding twelve months.[172]

SECRECY, ANONYMITY AND ORIGIN TRACING

There is no specific statutory provision contained in the Adoption Acts which requires complete secrecy in the adoption process. If the mother of an illegitimate child places her child directly with a married couple for adoption, she will of course be aware of the identity of the adopters and usually of where they live. The vast majority of adoptions are, however, arranged through Adoption Societies and Health Boards and in the case of most adoption placements, as a matter of practice, both the placement agency and the Adoption Board seek to ensure that the anonymity of the parties involved in the adoption process is preserved. Consequently, natural mothers and adopters are usually unaware of each other's identity.

The Act of 1952 expressly confers power on the Adoption Board to hear adoption applications "wholly or partly in private" and in practice all proceedings before the Board are held in private.[173] Where it is necessary for a case to be stated to the High Court, the Act enables the court to hear the proceedings "in camera".[174] Moreover, in practice proceedings under section 3 of the Adoption Act, 1974, are also heard in camera, although that section confers no express power on the High Court to hear such applications in camera.[175]

A practice direction of the President of the High Court relating to proceedings brought under section 3 of the Act of 1974 seeks to ensure that the contending parties involved do not either meet or discover the other's identity. Proceedings initiated under section 3 are issued and served on the Adoption Board, which is named as a nominal defendant, and which is responsible for arranging that both the natural mother and the adopters receive court papers and affidavits filed by each other, having first deleted their names and addresses and any other identifying information from the court papers. The court hearing is split into two parts: the mother is only permitted to be present in court on the day or days when her side of the case is being presented and the adopters are only permitted to be present in court on the day or days when their case is being presented. If the court reserves judgement and delivers it some weeks after the case has been heard, neither mother nor prospective adopters are allowed to be present. Explaining the reason for this procedure in *G. v. An Bord Uchtála*, Finlay P. stated "it is vital for the welfare of the infant that her mother and the

---

170. *Ibid.*, Sect. 42(3)(b).
171. *Ibid.*, Sect. 41(2).
172. *Ibid.*, Sect. 42(4).
173. Adoption Act, 1952, Sect. 16(3).
174. *Ibid.*, Sect. 20(2).
175. The court may rely on the Courts (Supplemental Provisions) Act, 1961, Sect. 45(1) to hear such proceedings "otherwise than in public".

person seeking to adopt her should not now become aware of each other's identity."[176]

Section 22 of the Act of 1952[177] provides for the establishment of an Adopted Children Register by an tArd-Chlaraitheoir (The Registrar General of Births) and the Adoption Board is obliged to send the Registrar particulars of each child in respect of whom an adoption order is made. Such particulars must include the date and country of birth of the child, the child's first name and sex, and the name, address and occupation of the adopter or adopters and the date of the adoption order. The Registrar is also obliged to keep an index "to make traceable the connection between each entry in the Adopted Children Register and the corresponding entry in the Register of Births."[178] To enable him to do so, the Adoption Board also supplies the Registrar with the name and address of the child's natural mother. The legal obligation imposed on the Registrar General to maintain such an index guarantees the existence of a statutory record as to the original identity of the adopted child, through which a child born in Ireland and subsequently adopted in Ireland can discover or trace the name of his natural mother. The information contained in the index could also enable the natural parents of an adopted child to trace the identity of the child's adopters and enable adopters to trace the identity of the child's natural mother.[179]

At the time of the passing of the Act of 1952, the legislature was anxious to ensure that the index was maintained as a private record of a child's origins and section 22(5) of that Act provides that the index "shall not be open to public inspection" and that "no information from it shall be given to any person" except by order of a court or the Adoption Board. Section 8 of the Act of 1976 prohibits a court from requiring that any such information be given to any person unless the court is satisfied that it is "in the best interests" of the child concerned to do so. The best interests test also has to be applied by the courts under this provision in determining whether to make an order against the Adoption Board in court proceedings "for the discovery, inspection or production or copying of any book, document or record (or any extracts therefrom) of the Board." To date, only two written judgements have been delivered by the courts demonstrating the effect of these provisions.

In *P.C. v. An Bord Uchtála*[180] the plaintiff alleged that he was the natural father of a child that had been adopted some years earlier. In a preliminary application brought in the proceedings in which he was seeking a declaration that the adoption order made was invalid, McWilliam J. declined to require the Adoption Board make available to the plaintiff documents in their possession from which he would have been able to trace the adoptive parents. The learned judge held that he was "satisfied that it is not in the best interests of the child to disclose to the plaintiff the information sought."[181]

In *S.M. & M.M. v. G.M. & Ors.*,[182] making an order for discovery in pro-

---

176. [1980] I.R. at p. 36.
177. As amended by the Adoption Act, 1964, Sect. 7.
178. Adoption Act, 1952, Sect. 22(5).
179. See also Sect. 14(1) of the First Schedule to the Adoption Act, 1952, which requires the Adoption Board to publish in *Iris Oifigiuil* a notice of every adoption order made. The notice, which is inserted in the form prescribed by the Adoption Rules, 1976, Form 11, includes the first name(s) of the adopted child and the name and address of the adopters. A natural parent aware of the date upon which her child was adopted would have little difficulty in tracing the adopters from this publication. The Review Committee on Adoption Services, *supra*, recommend the abolition of this requirement (see p. 91 of the Report).
180. (April, 1980) unreported (H.C.). McWilliam J.
181. See p. 7 of judgement.
182. [1985] 5 I.L.R.M. 186 (H.C.).

ceedings instituted under section 3 of the 1974 Act, Finlay P. stated that he
had

> "no doubt that the best interests of the child in regard to the determina-
> tion of (these) proceedings . . . depends upon discovery of such documents
> being made as would enable all the parties . . . to present their case to the
> full . . . This means that the plaintiffs as prospective adoptive parents should
> be in a position to adduce the maximum amount of evidence establishing
> their suitability as custodians of the child and to defend themselves against
> any challenges or criticisms of that suitability and that the mother should
> have a like advantage and opportunity."[183]

Among the documents that the court ordered be discovered were a number of
welfare officers' reports including a report of an interview by an officer of the
Adoption Board with the mother in relation to the section 3 application and a
medical report on the mother. Before the discovered documents were to be
made available to the parties, the court required that "any name or address
which could reveal the identity of either the prospective adoptive parents or of
the mother . . . be excluded from each document."[184]

The courts have yet to fully come to terms with those provisions in the
Adoption Acts which seek to ensure the privacy of records and the practices
which have been developed by the Adoption Board, Adoption Societies and
Health Boards that seek to prevent natural parents and adopters learning of
each other's identities. As yet, no written judgement has been delivered in any
case in which the court has been asked to determine proceedings instituted by
an adopted person seeking to trace his origins and, in particular, trying to discover
the identity of his natural mother. In the event of such proceedings being
instituted and an adopted person seeking to obtain documents held by the
Adoption Board which would reveal the natural mother's identity or seeking to
obtain from the Registrar General of Births information contained in the index
maintained by him, the only statutory guidance available to the court is that
contained in section 8 of the Act of 1974 which requires that such applications
be determined on the basis of what is in the best interests of the child concerned.[185] Accordingly, contrary to popular belief, the Adoption Acts provide
a natural mother with only limited protection against her identity being revealed
to her child many years after its birth and adoption. If an adopted child is sufficiently determined to go to court to obtain information contained in the
Adoption Board's records and the Registrar General's index, the Court, in
deciding whether the information sought should be made available to him,
appears at present to be statutorily required to order that the information
sought be disclosed if to do so is in the best interests of the child, regardless of
the possible consequences for or the possible impact on the mother of her identity being revealed.[186]

---

183. *Ibid.*, at p. 187.
184. *Ibid.*, at p. 188.
185. In *S.M. & M.M. v. G.M. & Ors., supra*, it can be noted that Finlay P. stated that
once it had been established that it is in the best interests of a child that discovery be made
or papers produced "there cannot arise, in my view, any question of balancing the interests
of an individual child concerned in a particular case against the general proceedings and
efficiency of the activities of the Adoption Board." (see p. 2 of judgement.)
186. In the event of such an application being brought, the courts could hold that
section 8 of the Act of 1976 has no application and is only of relevance while the adopted
person is a "child". See Adoption Act, 1952, Sect. 2., which provides that under theAdop-
tion Acts "child" means (save where the context otherwise requires) any person under 21
years of age. This provision is unaffected by the Age of Majority Act, 1985 – see Sect. 2
of that Act.

In conclusion, it should be noted that in its Reports for the years 1983 and 1984, the Adoption Board states that upon receiving enquiries from adopted persons seeking information on their background it is "willing to make available to adoptees such non-identifying information as it has on file and to give any other assistance possible" but notes that "regretfully, in many of the earlier cases, the amount of information is scant." Thus, in practice, while the Board is willing to release some background information to adopted persons upon their seeking it, in so far as it is available, it will not, when responding to enquiries made to it, reveal to an adopted person the identity of his or her natural mother or natural parents.

THE LEGAL CONSEQUENCES OF THE MAKING OF AN ADOPTION ORDER

The effect of an adoption order is to establish the legal relationship of parent and legitimate child between the adopter and the adopted child. Section 24 of the 1952 Act states:

"Upon an adoption order being made —

(a) the child shall be considered with regard to the rights and duties of parents and children in relation to each other as the child of the adopter or adopters born to him, her, or them in lawful wedlock;

(b) the mother or guardian shall lose all parental rights and be freed from all parental duties with respect to the child."

The child thus attains the same status as if born in lawful wedlock to the adopters and the legal rights and duties arising from the relationship between the child and his natural mother or guardian automatically cease. Any affiliation order or any agreement by the father of an illegitimate child to make payments for its benefit is discharged unless the mother is an adopter.[187] Similarly a court order under the Children Act, 1908, committing a child to the care of a fit person, ceases to have effect.[188] The child obtains the same property and succession rights as a child born in lawful wedlock.[189] Further, he is placed in the same position as the latter in respect of his right to claim damages under Part IV of the Civil Liability Act, 1961.[190] If the adopter is an Irish citizen and the child is not, it becomes an Irish citizen.[191] The adoption of a child is not affected by the subsequent marriage of its natural parents and the Legitimacy Act of 1931 will not apply to the child unless the adoption order is set aside.[192] Where the child has been adopted by one of his natural parents who subsequently marries the other parent, the 1931 Act is applicable, and the child can be legitimated and his name removed from the Adopted Children Register.[193]

As already noted in Chapter 1 in *The State (Nicolaou) v. An Bord Uchtála* the submission made that the Adoption Act, 1952, by permitting the adoption of a child by the parents of an existing family and by enacting that the child shall be considered as one born in lawful wedlock, in some way infringed the

---

187. Adoption Act, 1952, Sect. 31(1).
188. Adoption Act, 1952, Sect. 31(2) and Sect. 33.
189. Adoption Act, 1952, Sect. 26 and see also Sect. 110 of the Succession Act, 1965.
190. Adoption Act, 1952, Sect. 28; see also Part IV of the Civil Liability Act, 1961.
191. Adoption Act, 1952, Sect. 25 and the Irish Nationality and Citizenship Act, 1956, Sect. 11.
192. Adoption Act, 1952, Sect. 29(1). See also *In re J. supra; McL. v. An Bord Uchtála and the A.-G., supra*.
193. Adoption Act, 1952, Sect. 29(2).

guaranteed rights of the family and its members under Article 41, was rejected. Finally, where an Act of the Oireachtas passed after July, 1976, refers to a child of a person, unless there is a contrary intention, the reference is to be construed as including a child adopted by that person.[194]

RECOGNITION OF FOREIGN ADOPTION ORDERS

An adoption order can be made by the Adoption Board in respect of a child who resides in the State in favour of applicants who are ordinarily resident in the State and have been so resident during the year ending on the date of the order. Consequently, the Adoption Board's jurisdiction to make adoption orders is based on a residential period of one year and, in relation to the child, on simple residence without any statutory specification as to its minimum length.

The Adoption Acts are silent as to the circumstances in which recognition is to be afforded to adoption orders made in foreign jurisdictions and there have been no decisions delivered by the Irish courts since the provision of adoption legislation in this State laying down the legal principles applicable to determine the validity in Ireland of adoptions completed in a foreign State. At the very least, it is submitted that the Irish courts will afford recognition to adoption orders made in a foreign jurisdiction if the Irish Adoption Board would have had jurisdiction to make an adoption order in relation to a particular child, if the particular circumstances in which the foreign adoption order was made had arisen in respect of the child and its adopter or adopters in this State. Whether the application of this principle would also lead the Irish courts to confine recognition to the adoption of those categories of children who can currently be adopted under Irish law is a matter of conjecture. For example, would an Irish court refuse to recognise the validity of a foreign adoption order made in respect of a legitimate child, one or both of whose parents was alive at the making of the order, as Irish law does not currently permit the adoption of such a child unless it is an orphan.

In 1964, the Hague Conference on Private International Law produced a Convention On Adoption which seeks to provide international regulations for the reciprocal recognition of foreign adoption orders. The provisions of this convention provide for mutual recognition of adoption orders between countries who are signatories to the convention. An increasing number of Irish couples have in recent years adopted children outside Ireland and there is considerable uncertainty as to the status of such children. Our law in this area should be clear and should not be a matter of speculation.

---

194. Adoption Act, 1976, Sect. 8.

CRITICISMS AND PROPOSALS FOR REFORM[1]

In April 1983 a Review Committee on Adoption Services was established to examine the standards, practices and laws in regard to adoption and was asked to make such recommendations as it considered necessary for their improvement or amendment. It reported in May 1984 and it is the principle proposals for reform made by the Review Committee that are primarily considered in this section.

1. Under existing legislation, there are no circumstances in which a legitimate child, who is not an orphan, can be adopted. A number of different circumstances arise in which it would clearly be in the interests of such a child if it could be adopted. For example, there are children in the care of health boards and voluntary organisations who have been permanently abandoned by parents or who are destined to remain in such care for all or most of their childhood as a result of a total disintegration of their family unit or due to parental inadequacy, neglect or cruelty. While an increasing number of legitimate children taken into care are placed with foster parents, many still remain in residential institutions. As they are all unadoptable they are denied the opportunity of becoming fully integrated members of a stable family unit with a permanent home.[2]

The Review Committee states that "adoption should be one of the options available to provide care for all children, whether they are born in or out of wedlock, who cannot grow up in their natural families"[3] and recommend that legitimate children should be eligible for adoption.[4] This recommendation, the Review Committee notes, may have constitutional implications as it has been suggested that a law permitting the adoption of legitimate children who are not orphans may be unconstititional.[5] The need to clarify the constitutional position is emphasised and the committee suggests that either a Bill permitting the adoption of legitimate children be referred by the President to the Supreme Court for a determination under Article 26 of the Constitution as to its constitutionality or that, in the alternative, the Constitution be amended by way of referendum.[5a] The question thus arises as to whether a constitutional amendment is required prior to the enactment of legislation to permit the adoption of legitimate children so as to ensure its constitutional validity. Moreover, if such an amendment is required, as there is no difference between the constitutional position of a legitimate and a legitimated child, a question mark must also hang over the constitutional validity of section 2 of the Adoption Act, 1964, which permits the adoption of legitimated children.[6]

1. See generally *Report of the Review Committee on Adoption Services* (Dublin Stationery Office, May 1984); Harold J. Abramson, *Issues in Adoption in Ireland*, E.S.R.I. Broadsheet No. 23 (Dublin, July 1984); *Task Force on Child Care Services: Final Report* (Dublin Stationery Office, September 1980) in particular supplementary report by O'Daly and O'Cinneide; V. Darling, *Adoption in Ireland* (CARE Discussion Paper No. 1, Dublin 1974). See also V. Richardson, *Whose Children?* (Family Studies Unit, University College Dublin, March 1985); C. Mollan & L. LeFroy, *New Families* (Turoe Press, Dublin 1985); Children First, Second submission to the TASK Force on Child Care Services (Dublin, February 1976) and Children First Newsletter, No. 7, "Proceedings of the Children First Conference on Substitute Parenting" (Dublin, Spring 1977).
2. See, in particular, V. Richardson, *Whose Children?, supra,* Chapter 8. See also Rev. J. O'Mahony, "Key Issues Facing Adoption Today", Children First Newsletter, No. 7, *supra,* p. 35. See also Children First, "Second Submission ..." at pp. 3 and 9; and footnote 44 *post.*
3. See *Report of Review Committee, supra,* at p. 12.
4. See also TASK Force, Supplementary Report, *supra,* at p. 329; V. Richardson, *Whose Children? supra,* Chap. 9.
5. See *Report of the Review Committee, supra,* at p. 13.
5a.*Ibid.,* at p. 14.
6. *Ibid.* See also Fr. James Good, "Are the Adoption Acts Constitutional?", *Irish Times,* 25th August 1973.

The constitutional problem that could arise upon the enactment of legislation to permit the adoption of legitimate children derives from Articles 41 and
42 in which both the family and parents are stated to possess inalienable and
imprescriptible rights. It is argued that if parental rights are inalienable they
cannot be totally extinguished by an adoption order.[7] As these articles do not
apply to the relationship existing between an illegitimate child and its parents,
they present no obstacle to the adoption of illegitimate children. Moreover, no
constitutional problem arises upon the natural parents of an illegitimate child
marrying subsequent to the making of an adoption order, as upon such a marriage
taking place the Legitimacy Act, 1931, has no application and the adopted child
is not legitimated, unless the adoption order made is invalid and set aside.[8]

The judgement delivered by Walsh J. in *G. v. An Bord Uchtála*[9] contains the
only detailed reference to this issue made to date by a member of the Supreme
Court. Having regard to its importance, it is quoted *in extenso*. Walsh J., during
the course of his judgement, stated:

> "In my view, there is nothing whatever in the Constitution, to prevent a
> member of a family passing out of that family ... I do not see any impedi-
> ment in principle to a child's passing out of one family and becoming a
> member of another family in particular circumstances[10] ... parents are the
> natural guardians of the children of the family. Guardianship may be sur-
> rendered or abandoned provided that doing so does not infringe any con-
> stitutional rights of the child and is not inimical to the welfare of the
> child."[11]

Further on, he continued:

> "There is nothing in the Constitution to indicate that in cases of conflict
> the rights of parents are always to be given primacy[12] ... Article 42 s.5 of
> the Constitution speaks of the case where parents fail in their duty towards
> their children for physical or moral reasons; it provides that the State as
> *guardian* of the common good, by appropriate means shall endeavour to
> supply the place of the parents, but *always with due regard for the natural
> and imprescriptible rights of the child*. Under that section the State may very
> well by legislation provide for the failure of the parents, and in appropriate
> cases it may very well extend the law beyond simple provisions for a change
> of custody. A parent may for physical or moral reasons decide to abandon
> his position as a parent or he or she may be deemed to have abandoned that
> position; a failure in parental duty may itself be evidence of such an aban-

---

7. See W. Duncan, "Substitute Parenting and the Law", Children First Newsletter, No.
7, *supra*, p. 9 and see also speech delivered in March 1977 by the then Minister for Justice,
Mr. P. Cooney at the Children First Conference on Substitute Parenting reported in the
same newsletter at p. 5; M. Staines, "The Concept of the Family under the Irish Constitution"
(1976) 11 I.J. (n.s.) 223. See further The Irish Council for Civil Liberties, Report No. 2,
Children's Rights under the Constitution (Dublin 1977).
8. See the Adoption Act, 1952, Sect. 29(1). See *In re J., supra*, in which an adoption
order was set aside as the mother had given her consent too soon and *McL. v. An Bord
Uchtála, supra*, in which an adoption order was set aside upon the mother's consent being
held to be invalid. In both cases the natural parents had married after the adoption order
had been made. Upon the adoption order being set aside the child in each case was legitimated. See also *K.C. & A.C. v. An Bord Uchtála* [1985] 5 I.L.R.M. 302 (S.C.) in which a
child was legitimated following its being placed for adoption but prior to the making of an
adoption order. With reference to the issue of a court declaration of invalidity in respect of
an adoption order already made see p. 322 *ante*.
9. [1980] I.R. 32 (S.C.).
10. *Ibid.*, at p. 71.
11. *Ibid.*, at p. 75.
12. *Ibid.*, at p. 78.

donment . . . Where there is a complete abandonment of the parental right and duty, the State may be justified in taking measures by statute or otherwise to protect the rights of the child; these measures may include the enactment of adoption legislation."[13]

As for the inalienability of parental rights, Walsh J. stated:

"It is also to be borne in mind that some inalienable rights are absolutely inalienable while others are relatively inalienable."[14]

In the above judgement Walsh J. clearly states that he is referring to both legitimate and illegitimate children. Whilst the above cited extracts are clearly *obiter dicta* with reference to the position of legitimate children, they are a clear indication that the adoption of such children is constitutionally permissible in certain specified circumstances.[15] Moreover, it should be noted that while it is difficult in some respects to reconcile the recent Supreme Court judgements delivered by Finlay C.J. and McCarthy J. in *K.C. & A.C. v. An Bord Uchtála*[16] with the above judgement of Walsh J. in *G. v. An Bord Uchtála*, it was accepted by the Supreme Court in the former case that the State can "supplant the role of parents" in exceptional cases which come within the provisions of Article 42.5 where parents have failed to fulfil their role as parents[17] or where there are compelling reasons which establish that a child's welfare "cannot be achieved within the family" and that the child should be in a custody other than that of the natural parents.[18] However, the court did not in *K.C. & A.C.* consider whether parental rights could be entirely extinguished in such circumstances by the making of an adoption order as is suggested by Walsh J. in his judgement.

It is clear that the constitutional validity of legislation permitting the adoption of legitimate children will remain open to doubt until such time as the constitutionality of a Bill providing for their adoption is tested under Article 26 of the Constitution or until a specific amendment is made to the Constitution by way of a referendum.[19]

2. The Review Committee states that "the principal objective of adoption is to secure a permanent caring environment for the child and this . . . can normally best be provided for by a married couple in a family setting."[20] However, it also recognises the need to ensure a degree of flexibility which would allow a single person to adopt when to do so is in the best interests of the child although stating that it would "expect that it would be unusual for a single person to be considered as an adoptive parent if an equally suitable married couple were willing and available to adopt."[21] While not opposing adoption by a

---

13. *Ibid.*, at p. 79.
14. *Ibid.* See also *Murray & Murray v. The Attorney General & Ireland* [1985] 5 I.L.R.M. 542 (H.C.); *Pok Sun Shum & Ors. v. Ireland & Ors.* (June 1985) unreported (H.C.) and *Sunday Osheku & Ors. v. Ireland & Ors.* (June 1986) unreported (H.C.).
15. See also The Law Reform Commission: *Report on Illegitimacy* (Report No. 4 — September 1982), p. 165.
16. [1985] 5 I.L.R.M. 302 (S.C.).
17. *Ibid.*, see judgement of Finlay C.J. at p. 317.
18. *Ibid.*, see judgement of McCarthy J. at p. 319.
19. The constitutional difficulty that could arise in relation to legislation permitting the adoption of legitimate children would not be eliminated by the enactment of legislation abolishing the concept of illegitimacy and equalising the statutory rights of children born outside marriage with those of children born within marriage. See further, The Law Reform Commission Report No. 4, *supra*, pp. 163–170 and the brief reference to adoption at p. 9 of the Memorandum laid by the Minister for Justice before the Oireachtas in May 1985 entitled "The Status of Children". See p. 383 *et seq. post.*
20. *Report of Review Committee*, at p. 18.
21. *Ibid.*, at p. 20.

child's relatives, the Committee emphasises that a child adopted "within the family circle may create its own special difficulties" and that adoption by a relative "changes significantly the natural relationship between a natural parent and the child"[22] and that "artificial and distorted relationships are created in place of natural ones."[23] The Committee proposes that prior to any such adoption being finalised, the applicants to adopt should be referred to an adoption agency for advice on the implications of the proposed adoption, if they have not already sought such advice.[24] It also recommends that upon such an adoption application being made, an order appointing the applicants' guardians and awarding them custody of the child to which they are related should be an alternative available option in circumstances in which such an order would be appropriate.[25] The welfare of the child should be the first and paramount consideration, the Committee states in deciding whether a guardianship order, instead of an adoption order, should be made in favour of adoption applicants.[26] Research has established that adoptions by relatives are mainly adoptions by grandparents[27] and it is clear that the Committee envisaged guardianship orders being made primarily upon grandparents seeking to adopt a child in circumstances in which the child would continue to have contact with the natural parent(s).

Curiously, the Committee makes no express reference to the need to reform the Adoption Acts so as to place both widows and widowers in a position of statutory equality in relation to eligibility to adopt.[29] As already stated, it is arguable that the present law in this area is unconstitutional. It is submitted that there is no valid reason for rendering it more difficult for a widower than a widow to adopt and appropriate amending legislation should be incorporated in any new adoption bill that comes before the Oireachtas to place each in an equal position as adoption applicants.

3. The minimum age requirements for eligibility to adopt specified in the Adoption Acts are based on no coherently articulated social policy. The Review Committee states that a uniform age should apply in the case of all prospective adopters, recommending 21 years as the minimum age both for single people and married couples. In relation to applications to adopt by married couples, the Committee recommends there should be a general rule of adoption practised whereby a child should only be placed for adoption with a married couple who have been married and living together for at least three years and that this practice should be waived only in cases where the adoption agency judges that the circumstances merit its waiver.[30] The Committee does not, however, propose that this be a statutory requirement.

4. Adoption laws should seek to minimise the risk of uprooting a young

---

22. *Ibid.*, at p. 61.
23. *Ibid.*, at p. 83.
24. *Ibid.*, at p. 61.
25. *Ibid.*, at p. 83.
26. *Ibid.*
27. See V. Darling, *Adoption in Ireland, supra*, at p. 45. See also Appendix F.
28. See *Report of Review Committee* at pp. 82–83. The committee also envisage such orders being made where it may be in the interests of a child's welfare that the child remain with adoption applicants who have been deemed ineligible to adopt or where a mother seeks to jointly adopt with her husband and a reasonable relationship exists between the child and its natural father. In the latter instance, the committee states "the best solution in such cases may be to give the husband of the natural mother guardianship rights over the child with access by the natural father."
29. See p. 294 *ante*.
30. See the *Report of Review Committee* at p. 30. See also TASK Force, Supplementary Report, *supra* at p. 336.

child from a family with which the child has been placed for adoption and with whom it has lived for a number of months. At least six months normally pass from the time when a mother agrees to the placing of her child for adoption[31] until the Adoption Board makes an adoption order. Following the placement of a child with adopters, a mother (or father, in the case of a legitimated child) may refuse to consent to the making of an adoption order, or may revoke a consent already given before the order is made. The imposition of a continuing obligation on the mother to confirm her initial decision and several opportunities to change her mind, the Review Committee acknowledges "adds to the pain and heart searching, encourages indecisiveness and may interfere with or cause her to postpone other important decisions bearing on her own future".[32] Moreover, the fear of a change of mind on the part of the mother adds unnecessary uncertainty to the adoption process and can cause considerable anxiety to prospective adopters. Such anxiety may, in turn, harm or interrupt the development of a secure and stable relationship between a child and the adopters with whom it is placed.[33] The need to resolve these difficulties is recognised by the Review Committee but is not adequately dealt with in the recommendations made by it.

The Committee proposes that the existing two stage process whereby a mother concludes both an agreement to place and a subsequent consent to adoption should remain unchanged, save that it recommends that a consent having been given should be irrevocable.[34] If a mother seeks the return of her child after its placement with adopters but before giving her final consent the Review Committee recommends:

(a)   She should be statutorily entitled to have her request complied with, if made within three months of placement, except where a court[35] otherwise determines upon the application of an adoption agency[36]

(b)   She should be required to do so by way of court application if her request is made after three months of placement and a court determination should be required in relation to such request.[37]

The above recommendation of the Review Committee, if implemented, would eliminate the possibility of a consent being revoked but would only partially eliminate the difficulties created for all parties involved in the adoption process by the two stage procedure currently in use. Many months can elapse between

31. As the vast majority of adoptions are of illegitimate children placed for adoption with a mother's agreement, it is such adoptions that are primarily referred to in this discussion.

32. See *Report of the Review Committee* at p. 28.

33. *Ibid*. See also TASK Force, Supplementary Report, *supra* at p. 330.

34. At p. 31 of their report the committee states "While a natural parent's consent to adoption would be irrevocable, she would retain her other rights and responsibilities in relation to the child until he was legally adopted. Similarly, the child's succession and other rights would not be affected. In the event of a placement breaking down after consent to adoption has been given, the natural parent should be entitled to seek the return of her child without the prior approval of the Adoption Court (see p. 337 *post*) unless the agency concerned contests the return on specified grounds."

35. The committee recommends the establishment of an Adoption Court and it is this court which it envisages determining any disputes relating to adoption, including any of those that could arise under the proposals made by the committee discussed in this section. For a discussion of the proposed Adoption Court see p. 337 *post*.

36. See *Report of Review Committee* at p. 29. The committee also states that it considers that the grounds upon which the court would refuse to order the return of a child to its natural parent under this proposal should be the same as those which a court may, under general child care legislation, order that a child be taken out of the custody of a parent and placed in care. (See p. 30 of Report).

37. See *Report of Review Committee* at p. 30. Although the committee does not fully tease out this proposal, it is assumed that after the passage of three months, no statutory entitlement to have her request complied with would arise.

the completion of an agreement to place and the signing of a consent to adopt during which time both mother and adopters may be under severe stress and suffer considerable anxiety.[38] Implementation of the proposal that three months after placement a child should only be returned to the mother upon a court ordering the child's return would not, of itself, resolve the problem. The Review Committee nowhere states what criteria the court should apply in determining whether it should order the return of a child after more than three months have elapsed from the date of placement. If the approach taken was to be the same as that applied by the courts in determining proceedings under section 3 of the Adoption Act, 1974, on the basis of the cases determined to date, the court would generally order the return of a child to its natural mother if it had been in the care of adopters for less than one year whilst it would generally permit the child to remain with adopters if it had been in their care for more than one year.[39] Thus, the uncertainty that is caused by the current two stage procedure and by the absence of any specific statutory time limit within which a mother must make a final decision as to whether or not she wishes her child to be adopted, would remain.

As an alternative to the two stage procedure, the Review Committee states that it should be possible for a natural parent to conclude a comprehensive consent, embodying both an agreement to place and a consent to the making of an adoption order, at the start of the adoption process. Such a consent, it states, should only be used "in exceptional circumstances" where there is likely to "be considerable delay in finding an adoptive family, for say, an older or handicapped child."[40] Such a comprehensive consent, it is envisaged, should only be given with court approval and would have the effect of vesting responsibility for the care and maintenance of a child in an adoption agency.[41] The Committee do not envisage the comprehensive consent procedure being used where there are prospective adopters available at the time when a mother indicates that she wishes her child to be placed for adoption.

It is submitted that the Committee's recommendation concerning the provision of a comprehensive consent procedure is also inadequate. Even with comprehensive counselling and a court hearing being required before such consent could take effect, cases could arise in which a mother could be wrongly deprived of her child. For example, the mother of an illegitimate child might only realise the enormity of what she had agreed to a few days after or a week after the conclusion of a comprehensive consent and even if she changed her mind within such a short period of time, her consent would be irrevocable.

It is submitted that there is a need to provide a procedure which fully and properly protects the welfare of the child and which strikes a balance between the need to provide certainty in the adoption process and eliminate unnecessary stress and anxiety, while also affording to a mother placing her child for adoption

---

38. The committee recommends (at p. 76 of its report) that new regulations should prescribe three months as the *minimum* period between the placement of a child for adoption and the making of an adoption order. Although it is of the view that it should be possible in the generality of cases to establish whether a placement has been successful within such a period of time, it makes no recommendation for regulations to provide a maximum period within which a decision should be taken as to whether an adoption order should be made.

39. See p. 299 *ante*. This is accurate as a general overview of the decided cases but it must be remembered that the specific facts of an individual case may vary the court's approach. For example, a child in the care of adopters for only 5-6 months may be permitted to remain in their care if it has previously spent a lengthy period of time in a residential institution or if the mother seeking to regain custody is unfit as a parent or has been guilty of neglect or is incapable of properly caring for her child.

40. See *Report of Review Committee* at p. 32.

41. *Ibid.*, at pp. 32 and 33.

a reasonable time to reflect on and fully consider her position after the placement of the child. The difficulties inherent in the Review Committee's recommendations could be avoided if the current two stage procedure was entirely
replaced by a single form of authorisation for adoption, such as the comprehensive consent proposed by the Committee, which would comprise both a
placement agreement and a consent to the making of an adoption order and
which would upon completion vest in an adoption agency responsibility for the
care and maintenance of a child. Prior to the completion of such authorisation,
a mother should be fully counselled as to its effect and it should only become
irrevocable an exact number of days, weeks or months after being concluded.
In Australia, for example, a consent to the making of an adoption order is
irrevocable after 30 days have elapsed.[42] Such a period can be criticised as being
too short and it is submitted that a period of three months would be more
appropriate. The procedure for the completion of such an authorisation should
not require a court hearing but should require the conclusion by a mother of a
statutory declaration stating that she had freely made her decision and signed
such authorisation after fully considering the alternative courses of action open
to her and after a full explanation being given to her as to its legal effect. As is
recommended by the Review Committee in the context of its proposal for the
provision of a comprehensive consent procedure, in the event of a child not
being placed for adoption within twelve months of the completion of such
authorisation, the adoption agency should be required to so inform the mother
and a similar obligation should apply after every subsequent twelve month
period during which the child remains unplaced. On being so informed, the
mother should be entitled to apply to the court for the return of her child
but the right to make such application should automatically terminate upon a
placement being made.

It is submitted that the provision of a single authorisation procedure such as
that proposed would fully and properly protect the welfare of children, eliminate
much of the stress and anxiety caused to both adopters and natural parents by
the present adoption process, simplify what is an unnecessarily complex and
duplicatory procedure and considerably reduce the necessity for litigation under
section 3 of the Adoption Act, 1974.[43]

5. We have already seen that circumstances can arise in which a mother may
be incapable of caring for her illegitimate child and in which such a child may be
destined to spend all or most of its life in a residential institution or in fosterage
and be denied the possibility of adoption due to the mother's refusal to permit
her child to be placed for adoption. Reference has already been made also to the
existence of many legitimate children in the care of health boards and voluntary

---

42. See H.A. Finlay, *Family Law in Australia*, 3rd ed. (Butterworths, 1983), p. 402
- *et seq.*
43. In the implementation of this proposal regard may have to be had to the Council
of Europe Convention on Adoption of Children to which Ireland is a signatory. Article
5.4 of the Convention provides that "A mother's consent to the adoption of her child
shall not be accepted unless it is given at such time after the birth of the child, not
being less than six weeks, as may be prescribed by law, or, if no such time has been prescribed, at such time as, in the opinion of the competent authority, will have enabled her
to recover sufficiently from the effects of giving birth to the child." In order to comply
with this provision it may be necessary to provide that an authorisation to adopt cannot be
given until the child has attained 6 weeks of age or if concluded earlier shall not take effect
as a consent to adopt and shall not be accepted as such until the child has attained 6 weeks.
See further S.M. Cretney, *Principles of Family Law*, 4th ed. (London, Sweet & Maxwell, 1984), pp. 459–461 in which the author discusses the procedure available since May
1984 in England whereby an order can be made "freeing a child for adoption" pursuant to
the provisions of the English Children Act, 1975, as amended.

organisations who have no prospect of being brought up and cared for by their parents.[44] The Review Committee recommends that jurisdiction should be conferred on the court to dispense both with the necessity for parental agreement and consent to the placement of a child for adoption and to the making of an adoption order in relation to such children.[45] The Committee states that the first consideration in determining such applications should be the best interests of the child and that such jurisdiction should only be exercisable, if the person whose consent is required

"(i)   cannot be found; or

(ii) has ceased without reasonable excuse to maintain regular and responsible contact with the child for a period of at least 12 months and has not proposed realistic alternative arrangements for the child's long-term care which adequately safeguard the child's physical and emotional welfare; or

(iii) has persistently ill-treated or neglected the child and where the rehabilitation of the child without hazard in his household is unlikely."[46]

The Committee also emphasises the need to resolve any constitutional difficulties that could arise upon the enactment of any reforming legislation.

In recommending that the "best interests" test be used by the court in ultimately determining whether to dispense with the necessity for an agreement to place in accordance with the above discussed recommendation of the Committee or to dispense with an adoption consent in proceedings brought under section 3 of the Act of 1974, the Committee gave no consideration to the difficulties that currently arise in practice in section 3 proceedings. Although the court is asked in such proceedings to determine what course of action is in the best interests of a child, any evidence given by child psychiatrists on this issue usually derives solely from the contesting parties and it is not unusual for contradictory evidence to be given by child psychiatrists called to give evidence by each side. Upon this occurring a trial judge, with no specialist expertise or training, is ill-equipped to determine which psychiatrist's evidence is correct and what approach should be taken in the best interests of the child. It is submitted that amending legislation should confer power on the court in appropriate cases to appoint a children's advocate to represent the child's legal needs by gathering for and providing the court with all the information it requires and by calling

---

44. On the 19th of May 1983, in reply to a Dáil question the Minister for Health stated that there were approximately 650 legitimate children in residential care who had been in such care for more than 5 years – see Vol. 342 Dáil Reports, Col. 1800. The same Minister in response to a question as to the number of children in long-term foster care stated that as at the 17th day of May 1983 there were 589 legitimate children in long-term foster care, 248 of which had been in foster care for 5 years or more. See Vol. 342 Dáil Reports, Col. 1251.
On the 25th of February 1986, the Minister for Health stated that as at the 30th of June 1985, there were 965 children in residential care and 1,645 in foster care but stated that he did not have available to him information on the length of stay and the status of children currently in care. See Vol. 364 Dáil Reports, Cols. 13 & 14.
45. See *Report of Review Committee* at pp. 38–41.
46. *Ibid.*, at p. 40. See also TASK Force, Supplementary Report, *supra*, pp. 331–336. See further H.A. Finlay, *Family Law in Australia, supra*, at p. 405. Under Australian law the grounds upon which parental agreement and consent may be dispensed with include where the parent or parents (a) cannot, after reasonable enquiry, be found or identified, (b) is in such physical or mental condition as not to be capable of properly considering whether to give consent, (c) has abandoned, deserted or persistently neglected or ill-treated the child, (d) has failed for not less than one year and without reasonable cause to discharge the obligations of parent or guardian. Under English law parental consent can be dispensed with in similar circumstances – see S.M. Cretney, *Principles of Family Law, supra*, at pp. 446–459.

evidence from any independent witnesses that are necessary to assist the court in making a determination. It is clearly unsatisfactory that adjudications as to what is in a child's best interests be allowed to continue to be made in section 3 proceedings in which a child psychiatrist called by a mother recommends the child be returned to her, whilst the child psychiatrist called by prospective adopters recommends that a child remain with them without the court having available to it, if necessary, the evidence of an independent child psychiatrist uninvolved with either side. Moreover, having regard to the final judgement delivered by Lynch J. in the *K.C. & A.C.* case,[47] it is submitted that there is also an urgent need for legislative clarification as to what weight should attach to psychiatric evidence given in future adoption and custody cases concerning the likely consequences for a child of the breaking of bonds or attachments already formed. In particular, there is a need to clarify whether the fact that such evidence is "predictive" means it cannot be the determining factor in an adjudication as to what course of action is in the best interests of a child.[48]

6. The Review Committee recommends that the Adoption Board should be replaced by a specialist Adoption Court which would be presided over by a single judge specially appointed to it and which would sit with two assessors in all contested cases.[49] It proposes that the court should not only make adoption orders but also determine all contested court proceedings in the adoption area such as custody disputes arising at any stage during the adoption process and applications for dispensation orders. It also suggests that the court's jurisdiction could be expanded to deal with other family matters at a later date.[50]

The Review Committee recommends the provision of a new system of registration for adoption societies and states that the Minister for Health should be vested with powers to make statutory regulations in regard to the requirements for registration. It proposes adoption societies should have to apply to renew their registration every three years and that the Minister should be empowered to cancel a registration at any time if "proper standards are not being maintained". The establishment of a statutory committee to monitor the performance of adoption societies and to advise the Minister on registration applications is also recommended.[51]

Considerable criticism has been voiced in recent years of the total lack of uniformity in the practices of adoption societies and of the failure by some societies to employ an adequate number of properly qualified personnel.[52] The Committee recommends that all societies should be in a position to provide a minimum range of facilities before they are granted authority to function as adoption agencies, which should include:

"(i) the provision of assistance and counselling to the mother during her pregnancy as well as guidance about the alternative options open to the natural parents in regard to the future of their child;

(ii) pre-placement casework with natural parents, including the capacity to

47. See [1986] 6 I.L.R.M. 65 (H.C.).
48. See p. 394 *post et seq.*
49. See *Report of Review Committee, supra*, pp. 67–72.
50. *Ibid.*, p. 69. What the committee envisage is somewhat uncertain as the report refers to the Adoption Court's jurisdiction expanding "when a system of family courts is devised." The committee appear to contemplate the Adoption Court either becoming a separate division within a family court or expanding into becoming a family court.
51. *Ibid.*, see pp. 51–53.
52. See, for example, V. Darling, *Adoption in Ireland, supra*, p. 19 *et seq*; TASK Force, Supplementary Report, *supra*, p. 317 *et seq*; C. Mollan, *New Families, supra*, p. 113 *et seq*.

assist and advise them for a time where they choose an alternative to adoption;

(iii) the capacity to recruit, interview, assess and select suitable adoptive parents;

(iv) the professional skills to counsel natural parents after they have given up their child and to provide continuing support and advice for adoptive parents and adoptees; and

(v) the capacity to arrange temporary care for children pending placement for adoption.[52a]

In the case of a small society, the Committee states some of the above services could be made available through a close working arrangement with a health board or another voluntary organisation.

The Committee also states that the following requirements should be essential for registration:

"(i) each adoption agency should be required to employ at least one social worker with a Certificate of Qualification in Social Work or an equivalent qualification either on a full-time or part-time basis, depending on the workload involved;

(ii) where a society has long-serving existing staff who do not meet the foregoing requirements, it should suffice to show that their experience is adequate and relevant. All future appointments should, however, be confined to professionally qualified social workers;

(iii) it should not be sufficient to acquire the services of a social worker on a voluntary basis. The person should be engaged by the society in a professional capacity; and

(iv) every society should have a legal and a medical adviser.[53]

The failure of adoption societies to keep adequate records has also been the subject of criticism. The Committee recommends that all agencies be required to preserve records in properly secured facilities for an indefinite period of time which should include the following minimum information:

name, address and date of birth of father, mother and child;

medical records of father,[53a], mother and child;

physical description of parents;

full background and social history of parents, including reasons for adoption;

personality and talents of parents;

degree and nature of contact between natural parents and the child; and

contact subsequent to placing of child for adoption.[54]

52a. *Report of the Review Committee* at p. 54.
53. *Ibid.*, at p. 55.
53a. The Review Committee note that "A natural father may not have acknowledged paternity, that a mother might not be certain of who the father was and that an alleged father may not, in fact, have been the father." It nevertheless recommends that "the natural father's name should be retained in the records whether paternity has been acknowledged or not" stating that "where there are doubts about paternity, this should be clearly stated in the records (see p. 58 of report). The desirability of an alleged father's name being included in adoption records without an acknowledgement of paternity having been made or a court order as to paternity having been first granted must be open to serious question.
54. *Ibid.*, at p. 57.

Currently five adoption societies are operated by or in association with health boards.[55] Where there is no local adoption agency, the area health board may itself provide an adoption service. There is, however, no specific legal obligation requiring a health board to do so and a number of health boards have had very little involvement in adoption over the years.[56] In the context of extending the possibility of adoption to many of those children who are currently destined to spend most of their childhood in care, there is clearly a need to ensure that there is an adoption service avialable in all health board areas. The Committee recommends that all health boards be statutorily required to ensure the availability of an adoption service within their areas.[57] While stating that it would be anomalous to require a health board, statutorily required to provide an adoption service, to be subject to the registration procedure proposed for voluntary adoption agencies, the Review Committee states that health boards should apply the same minimum standards and that their performance should also be subject to a three yearly review.[58]

While the majority of the recommendations made by the Review Committee for the re-organisation and re-structuring of the adoption service are welcome, the desirability of implementing its proposal to abolish the Adoption Board is open to serious question. In 1952 the decision to establish the Adoption Board was made on the basis that it would create a flexible system for processing adoption applications, that would be less costly, more accessible and more speedy than the courts. The fact that it is the sole body responsible for the making of adoption orders has enabled it to develop a specialised knowledge of the subject and has ensured a uniformity of approach and decision making. As the Board is

---

55. See Appendix E.
56. The lack of involvement by health boards in the adoption process and the failure of some health boards to maintain adequate records as to the adoption service provided can be seen from the following reply by the Minister for Health to a Dáil question tabled relating to the adoption services provided by all health boards in the State in the last 5 years.

Health Board	No. of children placed for adoption in the years:					No. of adoption orders made in each of the last 5 years pursuant to an adoption placement made by a Health Board					No. of applicants for adoption on the books of each H.B. awaiting the placement of a child for adoption at 25 February 1986	No. of children in the care of each of the H.B.s available for adoption but not placed for adoption, and their ages at 25 February 1986
	1981	1982	1983	1984	1985	1981	1982	1983	1984	1985		
Eastern	5	9	10	14	13	5	6	11	12	11	10 couples	2 yrs, 6 months, 6 − 2 months, 7 months, 4 months, 4 weeks
Midland	16	14	20	11	3	16	14	20	8	6	6 "	1 − 8½ years
Mid-Western	0	0	0	1	0	0	0	0	0	1	0 "	0
North Eastern	na	na	na	na	na	na	na	na	9	6	0 "	7 − all under 3 months
North Western	1	1	1	2	1	1	1	1	3	0	1 "	3 − 18 mths; 16 yrs; 17 yrs.
South Eastern	na	na	na	na	na	na	na	na	4	1	36 "	0
Southern	52	43	28	32	19	40	47	34	41	24	21 "	6− 5, 3, 3, 2, 1, months.
Western	na	na	na	na	na	5	8	10	8	5	23 "	4 − 5, 5, 1, 1, months

Source: (1986) 364 Dáil Reports Cols. 93 & 94 and Report of Adoption Board for 1985. (An error in the 1984 statistics contained in the Dáil Report is corrected by the Adoption Board Report.)

*The above statistics do not include adoption orders made following an adoption placement by a registered adoption society operated by a health board or run in conjunction with a health board. For these see Appendix E.

In the period 1976−1985 inclusive a total of 715 adoption orders were made pursuant to health board placements − see Appendix F.
57. See *Report of Review Committee* at p. 49.
58. *Ibid.*, at p. 53.

in the centre of the workings of the adoption system it also is in a unique position to assess the strengths and weaknesses of the various adoption agencies.

The Review Committee acknowledges that whereas valid criticism was voiced in submissions made to it as to the Board's methods of operation, little criticism was made of the concept of the Board itself.[59] Much of the criticism made of the Board relates to the fact that unnecessary delays occasionally occur in the processing of adoption applications; the administrative staff of the Board are ill-equipped to respond adequately to general queries about adoption; not all of the Board's adoption personnel have adequate specialist knowledge of adoption work or a sufficient understanding of the adoption laws they are administering; and the annual reports until recently contained the minimum information statutorily required to be published, rendering it impossible for those involved in the adoption service, for legislators and for the general public to evaluate the efficiency of the service and to learn of any weaknesses that require correction.[60]

Procedural changes in the Board's method of operation and the statutory prescription of specific qualifications or experience in adoption work for membership of the Board or for recruitment as a Board social worker together with the provision of specialist training for the Board's administrative staff would resolve many of the above difficulties. A statutory regulation prescribing the maximum time within which the Board must determine an application to adopt in the absence of court proceedings would ensure delays were kept to a minimum and a statutory obligation requiring the Board to publish annually a more detailed report than is required at present, would render it easier to evaluate the workings of the adoption service and pinpoint inadequacies. The obligations the report proposes be imposed on a statutory committee to monitor the performance of adoption societies and health boards could, it is submitted, be more efficiently and effectively exercised by the Board, whose regular interaction with the societies and the health boards place it in a unique position to monitor how each society or health board performs and to ensure that minimum standards are maintained. The Board should also be given a statutory role in advising the Minister as to the contents of any statutory regulations to be enacted to ensure that minimum standards are observed.

The abolition of the Adoption Board and its replacement by an adoption court as proposed by the Committee, while having certain superficial attraction would result in an unnecessary division of functions between the proposed adoption court, the specialist monitoring committee and officials of the Department of Health which could be more efficiently and effectively carried out by a reformed Adoption Board. Moreover, unless the adoption court was established as part of a unified family court dealing with all family litigation, its establishment would also further fragment existing court structures in the area of family law, in that not only the District, Circuit and High Court could exercise jurisdiction to determine custody disputes, but those disputes with an adoption ingredient would be hived off to be dealt with by a specialist judge sitting in an adoption court. It is submitted that the recommendation of the Review Committee to abolish the Adoption Board in the manner in which it is framed should not be implemented.

---

59. *Ibid.*, at p. 65.

60. For an evaluation of the existing service from the limited information published in the annual reports of the Adoption Board, see Harold J. Abramson: *Issues in Adoption in Ireland, supra*, Part 3. Since ministerial responsibility for adoption was transferred from the Department of Justice to the Department of Health this is no longer the case. See, in particular, the Reports of the Adoption Board for the years 1984 and 1985.

7. We have seen that adoption laws and practices have evolved on the basis of preserving anomimity and confidentiality, although the relevant statutory provisions are haphazard and flawed. The importance to an adoptee of knowing his origins and the desirability of making detailed information available to an adoptee as to the identity of natural parents has been well documented.[61] A change in the law in this area, conferring a statutory right on all adopted children to have access to such information is complicated by the fact that since the introduction of legal adoption in Ireland both natural and adoptive parents have been assured by adoption agencies that their anonimity will be protected and, in particular, the identity of a natural parent will not be revealed to an adopted child. We have seen, however, that the substantive legal provisions in this area may afford no such guarantee.

In Scotland since the introduction of adoption in 1930, adopted persons, upon attaining 17 years of age, have had the right to obtain a copy of their original birth records. In England and Wales, adopted persons upon attaining 18 years have had a similar right since November 1976, but those adopted before the enactment of the Children Act, 1975, are first required to undergo counselling. In Northern Ireland, the Black Committee in their report published in 1982 recommended that birth records should be made available to adoptees who attain the age of 18 years who are adopted after the enactment of legislation providing for the disclosure of records but the Committee failed to reach agreement on the issue of retrospection.[62] The Review Committee on Adoption Services was also divided on this issue. A majority were of the view that all future adoptees should have a right of access to their original birth certificates upon attaining the age of 18 years and should receive counselling before exercising this right, stating that at the time of placement for adoption natural parents should be informed that their child would have such a right. A majority of the Committee, however, opposed giving all adoptees such access to their original birth certificates, because it was considered that such a measure would be a breach of faith with those parents who had placed children for adoption in the past on the assumption that there would be no change in the law. A minority of members disagreed with both approaches.[63] There is little doubt that this issue will give rise to considerable debate and public discussion in the context of any reforming measure introduced into the Oireachtas.

8. Finally, other recommendations made by the Review Committee not yet mentioned include:

(a) The natural father of a child, where paternity has been established, should have a statutory right to be heard on an adoption application.[64]

(b) The Minister for Health should be empowered by statute to designate countries whose adoption orders are recognisable in Ireland.[65]

---

61. See, for example, J. Triseliotis, *In Search of Origins — The Experience of Adopted Persons* (Routledge & Kegan Paul, London 1973) and *New Developments in Foster Care and Adoption* (Routledge & Kegan Paul, London 1980), in particular, Chap. 14; TASK Force: Supplementary Report, *supra*, p. 336 *et seq*; *Report of Review Committee, supra*, Chap. 12; C. Mollan, *New Families, supra*, p. 114 *et seq*. See also Children First Newsletter, No. 11 (Dublin, Spring 1978).
62. See *Adoption of Children in Northern Ireland*: Report of the Children and Young Persons Review Group (June 1982, H.M.S.O. Belfast) at pp. 73–74.
63. *Report of the Review Committee* at pp. 88–90.
64. *Ibid.*, at p. 79.
65. *Ibid.*, at p. 95.

(c) The Department of Health should instigate and fund a programme of research into the adoption service.[66]

---

66. *Ibid.*, at p. 97. The lack of research has been the subject of considerable criticism. See Harold J. Abramson, *Issues and Adoption in Ireland, supra*, Part VI; C. Mollan, *New Families, supra*, at p. 21.

CHAPTER 13

GUARDIANSHIP AND CUSTODY OF CHILDREN

INTRODUCTION

There are two concepts central to any discussion of the law as to parent and child. These are "guardianship" and "custody".

Guardianship: Parents have both rights and duties in respect of the upbringing of their children, e.g. a duty to maintain and rights to make decisions as to education. This whole relationship, both rights and duties, is one of "guardianship". Persons other than parents can be a child's guardian. Thus, as we shall see in the pages that follow, a person may be appointed guardian either by a parent under a deed or will, or by a court of competent jurisdiction.

Custody: Custody essentially means the right to physical care and control. Thus, a parent deprived of custody is not prevented from having any further say in the upbringing of his child. The right to custody is merely one of the rights that arise under the guardianship relationship. It is the enforcement of this right that has given rise to the greatest amount of litigation and with which the courts in recent years have been mainly concerned. Consequently, the pages that follow concentrate on the law as to determination of disputes concerning the custody of children.

The law as to guardianship and custody of children is governed by the Guardianship of Infants Act, 1964. The Act gives statutory expression to the equitable rule that all matters concerning guardianship and custody of children should be decided on the basis of the welfare of the child being regarded as the first and paramount consideration and to the constitutional principle[1] that parents have equal rights to and are the joint guardians of their children.[2]

Part II of the Act asserts the equality of rights as between parents as joint guardians of their children and, as amended by the Courts Act, 1981, expressly confers jurisdiction on the District Court and Circuit Court to determine disputes between parents or guardians on matters affecting a child's welfare.[3] Prior to the coming into force of the Courts Act, 1981, on the 12th of May 1982, the District Court possessed no such jurisdiction and although this jurisdiction was vested in both the Circuit and High Courts, in practice the vast majority of pro-

---

1. See *B. v. B.* [1975] I.R. 54 (S.C.) particularly the judgements of O'Dalaigh C.J. & Walsh J.
2. An infant or child under the Act of 1964 for the purpose of court orders relating to guardianship or custody is a person under 18 years of age. (See sect. 2 of the Act of 1964 as amended by the Age of Majority Act, 1985, sect. 2.)
3. See Guardianship of Infants Act, 1964, s.5 as amended by the Courts Act, 1981, s.15.

ceedings initiated under Part II of the Act of 1964 were initiated and determined
in the High Court.

Part III of the Act is concerned with the enforcement of a right to custody of
a child and is usually invoked in custody disputes between parents and third
parties. Until the 12th of May 1982 only the High Court could exercise jurisdiction under this part of the Act and apply the provisions contained in it to the
determination of custody disputes but the Courts Act, 1981, has now transferred
the jurisdiction contained in Part III of the Act to the District and Circuit
Courts.[4]

The Guardianship of Infants Act, 1964, is now silent as to the jurisdictional
competence of the High Court to determine guardianship and custody disputes
under either Part II or Part III of the Act. In *R. v. R.*[5] it was held that the High
Court still retained an original jurisdiction in this area, but as has been previously
stated, the authority of this decision is now in question.[6] Even if the High Court
can no longer apply the provisions of Parts II or III of the Act of 1964 to the
resolution of disputes concerning children, its jurisdiction to determine Habeas
Corpus applications is unaffected by the Courts Act, 1981. Consequently a
parent or third party entitled to the custody of a child being wrongfully withheld by another may use the latter jurisdiction to seek the child's return. Both
the High Court and the Circuit Court may also determine issues relating to children
through their Wards of Court jurisdiction, which provides a juridicial mechanism
separate to that originating under the Act of 1964.

It is intended to first deal with the development of the law up to the present
day in the area of rights and the determination of disputes between parents as
to the custody and upbringing of their legitimate children and then similarly to
deal with the position between parents and third parties.

DISPUTES BETWEEN PARENTS

Methods of Resolving Disputes: Formerly such disputes were resolved upon
an application for a writ of Habeas Corpus by which one parent sought to
obtain custody from the other. Today such disputes are usually determined
upon an application to the appropriate court under section 11 of the 1964 Act.
It is also possible for a parent to have a child made a ward of court so as to
enable the court resolve a parental dispute over a child, but this is rarely done in
practice.

History of Parental Right

At common law a father was the sole guardian of his legitimate child and his
right to the custody[7] of such child until the age of 21 was almost absolute,
forfeited only in those exceptional cases where he had been guilty of such grave
misconduct as was likely to cause physical or moral harm to the child. This paternal
right to custody was a corollary to the paternal duty to protect and maintain
one's legitimate minors, but whereas the former right was enforceable by the
father, the machinery for enforcing the duties was almost wholly ineffectual.

Equity, on the other hand, derived from the prerogative of the Crown a jurisdiction to act as supreme parent to all children and took a far broader view of

---

4. *Ibid.*
5. [1984] I.R. 296 (H.C.).
6. See *Tormey v. Ireland* [1985] 5 I.L.R.M. 375 (S.C.). See further p. 43 *ante.*
7. See "The Right to the Custody of Children" (1883) 17 I.L.T. & S.J. 417–8, 431–2,
445–6, 459–60, 473–4, 483–4.

the jurisdiction it exercised over children and parents. Stressing the welfare of the child as the paramount consideration, it showed greater willingness to deprive the father of his right to custody, even exceptionally where he had been guilty of no misconduct.

Whilst *prima facie* the father's rights were to be enforced, upon their exercise being shown to be clearly contrary to the child's welfare, they were pushed aside. After the passing of the Judicature Act, 1877, the equitable rule stressing the importance of the child's welfare prevailed in all courts.[8]

During the father's lifetime the mother possessed no real power, but on the death of the father without having appointed a testamentary guardian,[9] she was entitled to the custody of her infant children and acquired all the father's rights and responsibilities. But where a testamentary guardian had been appointed, a mother as such had no right to interfere with him. Even if in a deed of legal separation, the father voluntarily gave up his rights to his children, the courts held that such a provision was void in so far as it deprived the father of his powers over his children or provided that the mother should have possession of them to his exclusion.

In the first half of the 19th century a number of factors combined to bring about a gradual reform of the law by limiting the exclusive powers of the father by statute. The development of the Chancery jurisdiction on the basis of the welfare of the child resulted in a gradual judicial realisation of the anomalous and unequal position of the mother, and a growing judicial concern about the restrictive nature of the common law courts' jurisdiction over children. Much publicity was also given to extreme cases where mothers were deprived of their children's custody in situations where such a decision seemed contrary to the child's benefit and this helped to bring about pressure for reform.[10]

Talfourds Act of 1839 which conferred on the mother the right to seek custody of her children until they reached the age of seven, was the first of a number of 19th century Acts which gradually whittled down the paternal authority and power. This Act specifically provided that no custody order was to be made in favour of the mother if she had been guilty of adultery. The Custody of Infants Act, 1873, empowered the court to give the mother custody until the child reached the age of 16 and omitted the provision relating to adultery. The Act also rendered enforceable a provision in a deed of separation whereby a father surrendered custody of his children to their mother "except where the court might deem it contrary to the benefit of the child to enforce it". The Guardianship of Infants Act, 1886, enabled the mother to obtain custody of her children until they reached 21 and for the first time in a statute stated that such an application was to be decided having regard to the welfare of the infant, as well as the conduct and wishes of both parents. A father could no longer defeat a mother's rights after his death by appointing a testamentary guardian, for if one was appointed she was to act jointly with him. The mother was also empowered in the Act to appoint a guardian to act after both her and her husband's death and one to act after her death jointly with the father "if it be shown to the

---

8. *R. v. Gyngall* [1893] 2 Q.B. 232 (C.A.); *In re O'Hara, an Infant* [1900] 2 I.R. 232; (1899) 34 I.L.T.R. 17 (C.A.); *In re Kindersley an Infant* [1944] I.R. 111; (1943) 78 I.L.T.R. 159 (S.C.).

9. A testamentary guardian could be appointed by the father under the Tenures Abolition Act, 1662.

10. See *Children in English Society*, Vol. II by I. Pinchbeck & M. Hewitt (Routledge & Kegan Paul, London 1973), Ch. XIII.

satisfaction of the court that the father is for any reason unfitted to be the sole guardian of his children".[11]

Disputes as to Custody between Parents from 1886 to the Present Day

Effect of Act of 1886: Despite the fact that the 1886 Act was described as "essentially a mother's Act"[12] it did not result in the stage being reached whereby it could be said "that the respective rights of the parents of a child are equal". Thus, in *In The Matter of N.P. An infant*[13] it was said that whilst the primary question is the welfare of the child

> "The father is the head of the household and is liable to contribute to the cost of maintenance of his wife and family. If the circumstances show that he has not disentitled himself I rather lean in favour of conceding to him a greater claim than to the mother.[14] This, however, is subject to an important exception, namely, that where the child is of very tender years her claim is substantially increased".[15]

But if she was regarded by the court as being primarily responsible for the breaking up of the family she was denied custody irrespective of the age of the child.[16]

A considerable number of parental disputes as to custody involved a dispute as to the education and particularly the religious education[17] of the children of the marriage. At common law not only was the father's right to custody fundamental, but he also had an absolute right to determine a child's education and in particular its religious upbringing. These rights could of course be overridden by equity and by all the courts after 1877 upon their exercise being proved contrary to the child's welfare.[18]

In disputes as to the religious upbringing of a child the courts constantly stated that they would never attempt to adjudicate between the merits of different faiths.[19] They did, however, regard it as a matter of great importance

---

11. Now under the Guardianship of Infants Act, 1964, both parents have identical powers of appointment of testamentary guardians (see p. 375).

12. *Per* Lord Justice Lindley, *In re A. & B., (Infants)* [1897] 1 Ch. 786 (C.A.).

13. *In the matter of N.P. an Infant* (1943) 78 I.L.T.R. 32 (H.C.).

14. *In re McNally, an Infant* (1949) 84 I.L.T.R. 7 (H.C.). "If the conditions are equal *prima facie* the father is entitled to the custody of the child". *Per* Haugh J. at p. 8. See also *In re Kindersley an Infant, supra*.

15. *Supra per* Maguire J. at p. 34.

16. *In re Mitchell* [1937] I.R. 767, 776 (S.C.). In which a mother was denied custody of her three year old child because she returned to her home in Dublin leaving her husband in Glasgow, because of homesickness. See also *In re McNamara, Infants* (1948) 86 I.L.T.R. 75 (H.C.) – In which a father was denied custody on the grounds of his responsibility for breaking up the family; see also *In re Kevin Isherwood, An Infant* (1948) 82 I.L.T.R. 85 (H.C.)

17. For a dispute as to a child's educational upbringing but not his religious education see *In re Kindersley, an Infant, supra*.

18. *In re Kindersley, an Infant, supra* – however, in this case it was emphasised that in the case of a dispute as to a child's education in determining what course is best for the child's welfare "greater weight should be attached to the view of the father".

19. *In re Grimes* (1877) I.R. 11 Eq. 465 (Chancery) Ball L.C. stated "of religious systems how far true, how far in error it (the court) pronounces nothing; it neither favours nor condemns any; and views the claims and rights of all with perfect impartiality." In *In re Connor* [1919] 1 I.R. 361, 367 (M.R.) (C.A.), Ronan L.J. stated "We are bound to treat the Catholic and Protestant religions as equally beneficial to the minor. We are prohibited from considering the respective merits of the two religions, and therefore from saying that as between the two religions, as such, it is more for the welfare of the minor that he should be brought up in one of them than in the other". See also *In re Story, Infants* [1916] 2 I.R. 328; (1916) 50 I.L.T.R. 123 (K.B.D.).

that a child should be brought up in some religion.[20] The courts, moreover, regarded it as essential that such belief as a child was taught should not be disturbed by controversy "the result [of which] may be to unsettle the foundations of belief in the mind, and substitute a scepticism fatal to the existence of any religious faith whatever".[21] "The child must be taught dogmatically that the religion in question is true. The child must soon learn that there are other religions, but must be taught that its own is the true one. The religious belief of a child is not the result of a consideration of arguments as to which is the true religion."[22] The father's authority over a child's religion was such that his wishes were still to be adhered to after his death, despite the fact that the mother who had custody of the child, did not agree with them. Ante-nuptial agreements that children should be brought up in a religion different from that of the father were held not to be binding.[23]

Although wishing to ensure that children should be educated in the religion of their father, the courts constantly reiterated that the law was not so rigid as to compel them to order children to be so educated regardless of the consequences to themselves.[24] Thus, if it was clearly contrary to the child's welfare the parental right was not enforced.[25]

The Influence of the 1937 Constitution

The court's right to deprive a mother of the custody of her children in order to ensure that they should be educated in their deceased father's religion was challenged in *In re Frost, Infants*.[26] It had been agreed in an ante-nuptial agreement that the children should be brought up as Catholics; after the marriage and before the father's death, the mother under pressure of economic circumstances agreed to their being placed in one of Mrs. Smyly's homes, "the Bird's Nest" in Dún Laoghaire, a Protestant institution. The decision of the High Court resulted in the mother getting custody of the two youngest children, but not of the others. The mother contended that the court must regard the family as a unit by virtue of Article 41.1 of the Constitution, the control and management of which is vested in both parents while they are both living and, on the death of either of them, in the parent who survives. This, the court stated, as a general proposition was unquestionable. It was contended, however, that "So long as either parent is alive, the court has no power to interfere with the education, religious or otherwise of the children, contrary to the parents' wishes, except for the special reasons set out in Article 42 of the Constitution; nor should a surviving mother's right be displaced merely because the court is of opinion that the welfare of the

---

20. See *In re Greys* [1902] 2 I.R. 684; (1902) 36 I.L.T.R. 170 (K.B.D.); see also *Shelley v. Westbrooke* (1817), Jacob 266n.; 37 E.R. 850 (Chancery). In this case the poet Shelley was denied custody of his children on the grounds of his declared atheism.
21. *In re Grimes, supra per* Ball L.C. at p. 471.
22. Ronan L.J., *In re Connor, an Infant, supra* at p. 389.
23. *In re Browne* (1852) 2 Ir. Ch. Rep. 511 (Rolls); *In re Meades, Minors* (1871) 2 I.R. 5 Eq. 98 (Chancery); *Andrews v. Salt* (1873) 8 Ch. App. 622 (C.A. in Ch.); *Agar-Ellis v. Lascelles* (1878) 10 C. Div. 49 (C.A.); *In re Kevin Isherwood, an infant, supra*; *In re Story, Infants, supra* — see however statement by Dodd J. at p. 352 that "A promise by a father to bring up his children in his wife's religion though it is not a promise that can be enforced in law or equity, . . . still is a circumstance to which weight, and perhaps even great weight, should be attached".
24. *In re Meades, Minors, supra*; *In re M'Grath (Infants)* (1893) 1 Ch.143 (C.A.); *In re Story, Infants, supra*; *The State (Kavanagh) v. O'Sullivan* [1933] I.R. 618; (1931) 68 I.L.T.R. 110 (S.C.).
25. *Ward v. Laverty* [1925] A.C. 101 (H.L.); see also [1924] 2 I.R. 19 (C.A.).
26. *In re Frost, Infants* [1947] I.R. 3; (1945) 82 I.L.T.R. 24 (S.C.). See also *In re Keenan, Infants* (1949) 84 I.L.T.R. 169 (H.C.). (This case also involves children being brought up in the Bird's Nest in Dún Laoghaire).

children requires a religious education other than that which the mother proposes to provide".

Sullivan C.J. in answer to this stated:

"I cannot, however, accept ... that the rights of the parents, or of the surviving parent, are absolute rights, the exercise of which cannot in any circumstances be controlled by the Court. That a child has natural and imprescriptible rights is recognised by the Constitution (Article 42.5), and if ... (this) proposition were accepted, it would follow that the Court would be powerless to protect those rights should they be ignored by the parents. I am satisfied that the Court has jurisdiction to control the exercise of parental rights, but in exercising that jurisdiction it must not act upon any principle which is repugnant to the Constitution. The Constitution does not define the respective rights of the parents during their lifetime. Where as in the present case, the parents could not agree on the particular religion in which their children should be brought up and educated, the children should not be deprived of all religious education. If that be so then the only alter- native is that one or other of the parents should have the legal right to determine the religion in which the children shall be educated. The rule which the courts both in this country and in England have consistently followed, is that the father has that legal right, and that when that right has been exercised by him, the children must be educated in the religion which he has chosen, by his wife should she survive him. In my opinion that rule is not inconsistent with any Article of the Constitution, and the Courts are entitled to act upon it."[27]

A case which illustrates the extreme lengths to which the courts would go to ensure that a child would be brought up in his father's religion is that of *In re Corcoran, Infants.*[28] In this case, the applicant, the mother, after a short and unhappy marriage finally left her husband on 11th November 1943, being unable when leaving to bring her child of two and a half years with her. On 24th December upon visiting her husband's residence to see the child, she discovered that the child had been brought by her husband to her mother-in-law's residence in Bishopswood, Dundrum, Co. Tipperary. The child remained in the custody of the mother-in-law, the respondent, until the date of an application for Habeas Corpus by the mother on 18th November 1949.

Prior to this application, the mother stated that she had frequently tried to persuade her husband to bring the child back to England where the parties lived before separating. This he denied. In 1947 the applicant's husband instituted proceedings against her in England for divorce, grounded on alleged desertion on her part. The applicant cross-petitioned for divorce on the grounds of cruelty, and a decree of dissolution was granted on the ground alleged by her. The English High Court granted her custody of the child but the husband refused to comply with the order and was eventually lodged in Winchester Gaol because of his refusal. The mother applied for an order of Habeas Corpus to obtain custody of the child from the grandparents. The court accepted that the grand- parents were merely an instrument in the case and that in reality it was a dispute

---

27. *Supra* at pp. 28–9; Sullivan J. also said at p. 29 that "it is not necessary in this case to consider the question whether the provisions of the Constitution affect what had been the established law as to the validity and effect of ante-nuptial agreements, in respect of the religion of children, in view of the fact that subsequent to their marriage the parents agreed that their children should be educated in a different religion from that stated in the ante-nuptial agreement". See also *In re Keenan, Infants, supra.*

28. (1950) 86 I.L.T.R. 6 (S.C.).

between parents. The mother in this case was a Protestant and the father a Catholic. Prior to the marriage the mother had signed an undertaking to bring up any children of the marriage in the Catholic religion and did not contend in this application that the child should be brought up in any other religion. The High Court decided that the child should remain in its grandparents' home on the grounds that it would be contrary to the child's welfare and happiness to be removed from her paternal grandmother's home and sent to live in England with her mother in strange surroundings, since she had from the earliest age lived apart from her, and also that if the child went to England the court could not guarantee that the child would be brought up a Roman Catholic as the mother had promised.

On Appeal, the majority judgement of the Supreme Court, given by Murnaghan J., affirmed the High Court decision. He stated that the father "apart from his temper and violence"[29] was "hardworking and industrious". He went on "I do not, however, overlook the consideration that the character of the father is always an important element in any case involving the custody of a child", but there is no rule that "cruelty to a wife should deprive the father of the custody of his child". Murnaghan J. suggested that the notion that the welfare of the child was the paramount consideration was unconstitutional and concluded that the child should not go outside the jurisdiction, as if it did the court could not be certain that it would be educated as a Catholic.

Black J. in a remarkable dissenting judgement criticising the decision and reasoning of those who found in the father's favour, stated:

> "the learned judges who held against the mother in the High Court left the important factors of living space, hygiene and income, out of consideration altogether in forming their view of the child's welfare ... I should have thought that without giving due and great weight to all of them it would be impossible to arrive at a wise and balanced opinion as to the child's welfare. A weightier matter is the supreme asset of a loving mother's intimacy and care – in sickness and in health, in happiness and in trouble – a blessing which I had thought was recognised by all mankind as unique, irreplacable and priceless".[30]

As to the father's rights in relation to religious upbringing

> "This religious (or as I think it would be more accurate to call it, sectarian) dictatorship of the father is often referred to as his absolute right ... The extremity, fanatical as it seems to me, to which the 'right' of the father has been carried is shown by the rule that it must be upheld even if the father has induced the mother to marry him on the faith of a solemn undertaking that he will renounce the right in question and let the children be brought up in the mother's religion. The law is that even that solemn undertaking is unenforceable."

> "The father has the right to have the child brought up in his religion ... When I speak of his religion I mean the religion for which he professes zeal ... Such zeal may, for all I know, co-exist with intolerable cruelty, but I wonder whether it can exist in the soul of an individual who, like this man, does his best to get a divorce *a vinculo* which would set him free to re-marry and might lead his wife to do so, knowing well that such a divorce is contrary to the most solemn inhibitions of his professed religion."[31]

---

29. *Ibid.*, at p. 17.
30. *Ibid.*, at p. 19.
31. *Ibid.*, at p. 21.

He concluded by holding that in his opinion custody should be awarded to the mother and that she should be trusted to keep her undertaking to continue the child's education in the Roman Catholic faith.

In 1950 shortly after *In re Corcoran, Infants*, the whole question of the paternal supremacy to determine a child's religious upbringing and the validity of ante-nuptial agreements was re-examined in the light of Irish public policy and the 1937 Constitution. The case of *In re Tilson, Infants*,[32] came before the High Court and on an appeal, the Supreme Court, and gave rise to considerable public interest and controversy.

Tilson, a Protestant, having signed an ante-nuptial undertaking that any children of the marriage would be brought up as Catholics, had married a Catholic woman in a Catholic Church in Dublin in 1941. They had four children, all boys, who were baptised as Catholics. Differences having arisen between the spouses, Tilson removed the three elder children from the home of his wife's parents (where the whole family was then living) and took them to live with his parents; he subsequently removed them to Mrs. Smyly's home "The Bird's Nest" in Dún Laoghaire. The eldest child was eight at the time. The mother obtained a conditional order of Habeas Corpus against the trustees of the institution and on her motion to have the order made absolute, Gavan Duffy J. held that it was for both the spiritual and temporal welfare of the children to be returned to their mother's custody. He considered at length the basis of the rule against enforcing ante-nuptial agreements, noting that the marriage could not have been celebrated in a Catholic Church without the parties having reached such an agreement. In reply to the argument that to enforce such an agreement against the father's wishes was contrary to public policy he stated:

> "The plea implies that the paternal trust is more sacred in the eyes of the law than a man's sacred ante-nuptial agreement; . . . I have the temerity to prefer a principle of public policy that would imperatively require a man to keep faith with the mother whom he has induced to wed him by his categorical engagement to respect her convictions in the supernatural domain of her children's creed, at least when that promise is shown to have been of grave importance to her, as it must be to a Catholic . . .[33] The doctrine of Articles 41, 42 and 44 of the Constitution appears to me to present the ante-nuptial agreement of the parties upon the creed to be imparted to their future children in a new setting and, subject to the welfare of the particular infants concerned, to invite recognition of the agreement in our Courts as a compact that serves the social order in Ireland, because the agreement, far from conflicting in any way with those Articles, is consonant with their spirit and purpose and tends directly (a) to safeguard a marriage which cannot be dissolved; (b) to safeguard the harmony of the projected family; and (c) to safeguard the innate and imprescriptible right of the child to religious education, its most precious inheritance in the eyes of a Christian state."[34]

He remarked that he thought it possible that a man might estop himself in law by signing an ante-nuptial agreement subsequently acted upon, but that he proposed to decide the issue on other grounds.

> "In my opinion, an order of the Court designed to secure the fulfilment of an agreement peremptorily required before a mixed marriage by the Church

---

32. [1951] I.R. 1; (1950) 86 I.L.T.R. 49 (S.C.).
33. [1951] I.R. at p. 12.
34. *Ibid.*, at p. 17.

whose special position in Ireland is officially recognised as the guardian of the faith of the Catholic spouse, cannot be withheld on any ground of public policy by the very State which pays that homage to that Church."[35]

Pointing out that the Tilson children had not been long enough in the "Bird's Nest" to have acquired fixed Protestant views he concluded that:

"There is no question here of any attempt (such as no Court would entertain) to coerce into the Church of Rome any young person who by a Protestant education, in disregard of an ante-nuptial agreement, has in fact acquired Protestant convictions; the Church itself would condemn any such attempt."[36]

He held that for the boys' spiritual and temporal welfare they should remain with their mother.

The decision of Gavan Duffy J. was upheld in the Supreme Court by a majority of 4 to 1. The judgement of the majority was delivered by Murnaghan J. and was based primarily upon the court's interpretation of Article 42.1.

"This article includes among 'Fundamental Rights' the inalienable right and duty of parents to provide according to their means for the religious and moral, intellectual, physical and social education of their children. Where the father and mother of children are alive this article recognises a joint right and duty in them to provide for the religious education of their children. The word 'parents' is in the plural and naturally should include both father and mother. Common sense and reason lead to the view that the mother is under the duty of educating the children as well as the father and both must do so according to their means."[37]

Later on in the judgement, Murnaghan, J. stated:

"The parents — father and mother — have a joint power and duty in respect of the religious education of their children. If they together make a decision and put it into practice it is not in the power of the father — nor is it in the power of the mother — to revoke such decision against the will of the other party. Such an exercise of their power may be made after marriage when the occasion arises; but an agreement made before marriage dealing with matters which will arise during the marriage and put into force after the marriage is equally effective and of binding force in law."[38]

Having regard to the views expressed by him in *In re Corcoran Infants*, Black J. surprisingly dissented from the majority judgement. While regarding it as desirable to construe Article 42.1 as altering the common law, which was in this area described by him as

---

35. *Ibid.*, at p. 19; Gavan Duffy J. is here referring to Article 44.1.2.° which stated "The State recognises the special position of the Holy Catholic Apostolic and Roman Church as the guardian of the faith professed by the great majority of the citizens". This Article together with the one following it, was deleted from the Constitution following a Referendum held in 1972.

Murnaghan J. delivering the majority judgement in the Supreme Court stated (at p. 35) that "It is right . . . to say that the Court in arriving at its decision, is not now holding that the last mentioned Articles (44 & 41) confer any privileged position before the law on the Roman Catholic Church . . ." and Black J. stated (at p. 44) "Unequivocally" that the "constitution does not confer any such privileged position before the law upon members of any religious denomination whatsoever".

36. [1951] I.R. at p. 21.

37. *Ibid.*, at p. 32.

38. *Ibid.*, at p. 34.

"an archaic law and a relic of barbarism — a law derived from another law, that of the serfdom of women, which . . . emanated from the cave-men, long ages before the art of writing was discovered",[39]

he thought it did no more than reflect an already existing paternal right and duty.[40]

Seven years later in *In re May, Minors*[41] the law as established in *In re Tilson* was applied where no express agreement had been made between parents as to their children's religious upbringing. Mr. and Mrs. May were both Roman Catholics and had been married in a Roman Catholic Church. There were five children of the marriage who, for over 10 years had been brought up as Roman Catholics and no differences of any kind had previously arisen as to their religious up-bringing. In 1954 Mr. May became a follower of the beliefs of the Jehovah's Witnesses and a year later attempted to interfere with his children's religious upbringing. Davitt J. held that as both parents had for many years followed the Catholic faith there was an implied agreement between the parties as to the children's religious upbringing and as the children had been educated in that faith, that agreement had been exercised and could not be abrogated by the unilateral act of one of the parties. Mr. May could not change the children's religion without Mrs. May's consent.

1964 AND AFTER

The Tilson case in 1951 firmly established that the rights and duties of parents in relation to their children under the Constitution are equal. This equality was finally given statutory expression in the Guardianship of Infants Act, 1964. Section 6(1) of the Act provides that "the father and mother of an infant shall be guardians of the infant jointly". This section has since been said to be "no more than a reiteration of the principles enunciated in Article 42 of the Constitution".[42] Each parent now has the same rights in relation to the person of their child, i.e. to custody, to determine the child's upbringing and education, both secular and religious, and the same powers to appoint a testamentary guardian.

Section 11 of the 1964 Act provides that

---

39. *Ibid.*, at p. 37.
40. The judgement in the Tilson case caused considerable controversy at the time — see J. White, — *Minority Report*, pp. 125–128. J.H. Whyte, — *Church and State in Modern Ireland 1923–1970*, pp. 169–71; V.T.H. Delaney, "The Custody and Education of Children" 18 I.J. 17; J.M. Kelly, — *Fundamental Rights*, pp. 229–230; P.C. Moore, — *Support and Custody of Children*" (the International Bar Association of Ireland 1968), pp. 11–14.
41. 92 I.L.T.R. 1 (H.C.).
42. O'Dalaigh C.J., *B. v. B.* [1975] I.R. 54 (S.C.) at p. 58. Although not reported until 1975 judgement was in fact delivered by the Supreme Court in this case in April 1970. Walsh J. in the same case stated: "The main purpose of the Guardianship of Infants Act, 1964 was to give both parents of an infant equal rights in guardianship matters. In doing so it provided a statutory expression of the rights already guaranteed by the Constitution". See J.M. Kelly, — *Fundamental Rights*, p. 229 where the author remarks that "it is very difficult to read in Article 42.1 the intention that paternal supremacy is to be replaced by joint parental authority". See also "Private Law Aspects of the Irish Constitution", by J. Temple Lang (1971) 6 I.J. (n.s.) 237, where the author points out in a section on Family Law that "if parents have equal rights over their children's upbringing, they presumably have equal duties, and responsibilities in relation to it. This suggests that a father having custody of children would have the same right to be financially supported by a wealthy wife, as a wife would have if the situation were reversed". On this point see The Report of the Committee on Court Practice & Procedure entitled "Desertion & Maintenance". See now Family Law (Maintenance of Spouses and Children) Act, 1976, Sect. 5, discussed in Chap. 14.

(1) "Any person being a guardian of an infant may apply to the court for its direction on any question affecting the welfare of the infant and the court may make such order as it thinks proper".[43]

(2) "The court may by an order under this section —

(a) give such direction as it thinks proper regarding the custody of the infant and the right of access to the infant of his father or mother.

(b) order the father or mother to pay towards the maintenance[44] of the infant such weekly or other periodical sum as having regard to the means of the father or mother, the court considers reasonable."

An order can be made under section 11 on the application of either parent, even if they are still living together.[45] However, an order made pursuant to section 11(2)(a) is not enforceable while they continue to do so and ceases to have effect if the parties continue to reside together for three months after it is made.[46] Until the 1st of March 1985, a person remained an infant for the purposes of the 1964 Act until he attained the age of 21 years and orders could be made by the court pursuant to section 11(1) and (2) in respect of any person until he attained the age of 21 years. The Age of Majority Act, 1985, which came into force on that date has reduced the age of persons in relation to whom the court may make an order pursuant to section 11(1) and (2)(a) to that of 18 years, although maintenance orders may still be made by the court pursuant to section 11(2)(b) for the support of a person up to the age of 21 years.[47]

Whilst prior to 1964 the courts stressed that the most important factor in parental disputes concerning children was the welfare of the child, it was not until that date that statutory force was given to the equitable principle that the child's interests are paramount. Section 3 states

"Where in any proceedings before any court the custody, guardianship or upbringing of an infant, or the administration of any property belonging to or held on trust for an infant, or the application of the income thereof, is in question, the court in deciding that question, shall regard the welfare of the infant as the first and paramount consideration."

In *J. v. C.*[48] in the House of Lords it was stated that this requirement means: "More than that the child's welfare is to be treated as the top item in a list of

---

43. An application can be made to the court under section 11(1) for directions with regard to the administration of the assets or estate of an infant on the application of the guardian or guardians. See *In re Meade, Applicant* [1971] I.R. 327 (H.C.). See, however, *In the Matter of J.S. an infant* (1977) 111 I.L.T.R. 146 (H.C.) where Finlay P., expressing a preference for such applications being made under the Wards of Court procedure, stated "Whilst it is not possible nor desirable to attempt an exclusive or comprehensive classification of the cases which might be appropriate for directions concerning the estates or assets of minors under Section 11(1) rather than by the Wardship of Court procedure, in general it would appear that they are appropriate only where one or at most two or three applications would be necessary and where a fixed and final straightforward scheme not requiring variations and not requiring the continued supervision of the Court is appropriate in the interests of the children".

44. Maintenance is said to include education — Sect. 2 of the 1964 Act.

45. See *J. O'C. v. M. O'C.* (August, 1975) unreported (H.C.); *O'D. v. O'D.* (June, 1976) unreported (H.C.).

46. Sect. 11(3) of the Act of 1964 as amended by the Age of Majority Act, 1985, sect. 6(a).

47. See the Age of Majority Act, 1985, sect. 2.

48. [1970] A.C. 666 (H.L.).

items relevant to the matter in question". It connotes "a process whereby, when all the relevant facts, relationships, claims and wishes of parents, risks, choices and other circumstances are taken into account and weighed, the course to be followed will be that which is most in the interests of the child's welfare as that term has now to be understood. That is the first consideration because it is of first importance and the paramount consideration because it rules on or determines the course to be followed".[49]

Welfare in relation to an infant is said to comprise its religious and moral, intellectual, physical and social welfare.[50]

The great majority of disputes heard under the Act are disputes as to the custody of children. In reaching a decision the court must take into account all the factors comprised in the concept of welfare. The matter, Walsh J. has stated, is

> "not ... to be decided by the simple method of totting up the marks which may be awarded under each of the five headings ... all the ingredients which the Act stipulates ... are to be considered globally ... It is the totality of the picture presented"[51]

that the court must consider and on which it must make its decision. Often the court has an almost impossible task in determining which parent should be awarded custody.

The Conduct of the Parents

Whilst prior to 1964 it was extremely unlikely that the spouse responsible in the eyes of the court for a marriage breaking down would obtain custody of the children of the marriage,[52] the courts have since that date constantly reiterated that

> "An award of custody is not a prize for good matrimonial behaviour".[53]

> "So far as the custody of the children is concerned ... evidence (as to which of the parties contributed to or caused the breakdown of the marriage) was relevant only to the character of the respective parents with a view to deciding whether the welfare of a particular child would best be served by its being left in the custody of one parent rather than the other."[54]

Thus, the fact that a husband (or by analogy a wife) must bear the bigger share

---

49. Per Lord MacDermott, ibid., at p.p. 710–711 adopted by the Supreme Court in the judgement of Henchy J. (with whose judgement Kenny J. expressed agreement) in MacD. v. MacD. (1979) 114 I.L.T.R. 60 (S.C.); see also E.K. v. M.K. (July, 1974) unreported (S.C.) judgement of Henchy J.; O. v. O. (May, 1979) unreported (H.C.).
50. Guardianship of Infants Act, 1964, sect. 2.
51. M.B. O'S. v. P.O. O'S. (1974) 110 I.L.T.R. 57 (S.C.) per Walsh J. at p. 61. See also judgements of Walsh J. and Budd J. in E.K. v. M.K., supra, and judgement of Griffin J. in MacD. v. MacD., supra.
52. See In re Mitchell, supra; In re McNamara, supra; In re Kevin Isherwood, an Infant (1948) 82 I.L.T.R. 85 (H.C.). Unless the child was being educated in the religion of the spouse so responsible, the parties being of different faith – see In re Corcoran, Infants (1950) 86 I.L.T.R. 6 (S.C.); on the other hand see In re Story, supra.
53. Kenny J. in J.J.W. v. B.M.W. (1971) 110 I.L.T.R. 45 (H.C.) at p. 47. See also M. O'B. v. P.M. O'B. (January, 1971) unreported (H.C.); J.C. v. O.C. (July, 1980) unreported (H.C.); P.G. v. C.G. (March, 1982) unreported (H.C.); P.G. v. C.G. (No. 2) (July, 1983) unreported (H.C.).
54. Fitzgerald J. in B. v. B., supra. See also Hamilton J. – "The Guardianship of Infants Act 1964 and Recent Decision in Relation Thereto", S.Y.S. Lecture No. 91 (Nov. 1975), p. 10. See further section on moral welfare below.

of the blame does not mean that he "has by his conduct forfeited the right to have the custody of the children if it be found that it is in the best interests of any one or more of the children to be placed in his custody".[55] "The conduct, wishes and needs of the parents are irrelevant except in so far as such considerations bear on the welfare of the children."[56] However,

> "Where a marriage has broken down, whether temporarily or permanently, it may be possible to show that the welfare of the children requires that one or other parent should by reason of character or conduct be excluded from consideration, as being a person unfit to have custody . . . The courts should always be reluctant to reach such a conclusion, because the welfare of the children will rarely be advanced by a verdict of condemnation of one or other of the parents".[57]

Such a condemnation will only be made in the most extreme cases, for example where a parent is likely to be an extreme danger to the physical or moral welfare of his children.

It is now intended to examine in detail the matters that the courts have regard to in reaching a determination on the basis of the child's welfare. However, it is to be remembered that the importance of any given factor depends on the circumstances of each individual case. Thus a decision in any one case cannot be completely relied upon to give an accurate prediction of the outcome of any other case.

Physical Welfare of the Child

Physical welfare primarily appears to be concerned with the health, bodily comfort, nourishment and hygiene of children with the qualification that their health may be affected by emotional or psychiatric disturbances which are also of relevance to their intellectual welfare.[58] Mothers are regarded by the courts as *prima facie* the best persons to minister to the physical and emotional needs of young children[59] and all things being equal a mother will normally be given

---

55. Budd J. in *B. v. B., supra*, at p. 66. Similarly Kenny J. in *B. v. B.* (January, 1969) unreported (H.C.) stated "A hot tempered, emotional difficult incompetent wife may be a much more suitable person to have custody of young children than a cold, unsympathetic self-righteous and very able husband". See also *M.B. O'S. v. P.O. O'S., supra* (S.C.) at p. 65, judgement of Griffin J. "If this was a contest simpliciter between the wife and the husband . . . and if only the right and interests of the parents were to be considered . . . the wife would be entitled to custody". He went on to hold, however, that the welfare of the children being paramount, they should remain in the custody of the father. In *MacD. v. MacD., supra*, Henchy J. stated "If custody of children could be granted as a badge of moral approval, the father, who has been steadfast as a husband and a father would come first. But the right to custody may not be determined in that way". He went on to grant custody in this case to the wife.

56. Henchy J. in *MacD. v. MacD., supra*. See, however, dissenting judgement of Griffin J. where he states "the conduct of the parents is relevant in so far as inferences can be drawn from it to show where the priorities of the parents lie in relation to the children, as this is an important factor to consider in relation to their welfare".

57. O'Dalaigh C.J. in *B. v. B.* [1975] I.R. 54 (S.C.) at p. 59.

58. See judgement of Finlay P. in *MacD. v. MacD.* (February, 1979) unreported (H.C.). Although the decision of the High Court in this case was reversed on appeal, the Supreme Court did not disagree with the learned trial judge's definitions of the different factors comprised in the concept of welfare.

59. See *MacD. v. MacD.* (April, 1979) unreported (S.C.), judgements of Henchy J. and Kenny J. See also *J.C. v. O.C.* (July, 1980) unreported (H.C.).

custody of children under twelve years of age.[60] The availability of the mother in the home during the day has been one of the factors that has influenced the courts to favour mothers on the ground that a father working outside the home cannot give to young children the time and attention which their welfare requires.[61] As children get older, the courts take the view, especially in the case of boys, that they have more need of the father. There are, however, no hard and fast rules and everything depends on the circumstances of the particular case. Thus, in *J.J.W. v. B.M.W.*[62] three young girls (aged nine, seven and three years) were placed in their father's custody, in *H. v. H.*[63] a boy aged two and a half was placed in his father's custody, and in the recent case of *A.H. v. B.H.*[64] three children, aged seven and a half, six and a half, and five, were placed in their father's custody.

As all orders as to custody are interlocutory and not final, the court can vary its orders and it is possible for a child to be given into its mother's custody until it reaches a certain age and then given into its father's custody. Thus, in *M. O'S. v. M. O'S.* a boy was given into his mother's custody until he reached 12½ years of age and then given into the custody of his father.[65]

The court has, however, stated that it is essential that children of a broken marriage should establish roots and not be constantly moved from place to place, from parent to parent and from school to school.

> "The main psychological need for children if they are to become happy citizens is a feeling of security, a conviction that people care for them and about them and a feeling of continuity. They should have a chance of

---

60. In *J.J.W. v. B.M.W.*, Fitzgerald J. said "children of tender age and particularly girls would . . . other things being equal, be better in the custody of their mother". (1971) 110 I.L.T.R. 45, 49, at p. 52 (S.C.). See also judgement of Walsh J. in *E.K. v. M.K.* (July, 1974) unreported (S.C.) and judgement of Griffin J. in *MacD. v. MacD., supra* (S.C.). See further *O'D. v. O'D.* (June, 1976) unreported (H.C.); *J.W. v. M.W.* (July, 1978) unreported (H.C.). Moreover, when faced with the choice of placing a 19 month old child in the custody of an inadequate father residing with paternal grandparents or an inadequate mother residing with maternal grandparents in *P.G. v. C.G., supra*, Finlay P., placing the child in the mother's custody held that "in the overall welfare of the child he must at least be given a chance of being brought up by his own mother" although he stated that he had "no real doubt that the child is at present happy, contented and well cared for in her general and continuous custody" and "that it is probable . . . that the child will suffer significantly and immediately from being separated from his paternal grandmother."

61. See particularly judgement of Henchy J. in *MacD. v. MacD., supra* (S.C.). See also *E. v. E.* (February, 1977) unreported (H.C.) in which the plaintiff wife was granted custody although she suffered from depression. See further *J.C. v. O.C., supra*.

62. See judgement of Fitzgerald J. where he states "the circumstances in the present case are by no means equal as regards either the character of the respective parents or the benefits which they are in a position to provide for any of the children". See also *W. v. W.* (December, 1974) unreported (S.C.).

63. (February, 1976) unreported (H.C.).

64. (January, 1982) unreported (H.C.). See also *J. O'C. v. M. O'C.* (August, 1975) unreported (H.C.); *McC. v. McC.* (January, 1976) unreported (H.C.); *O. v. O.* (May, 1979) unreported (H.C.) and (June, 1979) unreported (H.C.); *M.K. v. P.K.* (November, 1982) unreported (H.C.); *F.M. v. J.M.* (November, 1983) unreported (H.C.); see further *B. v. B.* [1975] I.R. 54 (S.C.) in which a boy almost ten years old and a girl aged eight and a half years old were placed in their father's custody and the children's brother who was six and a half years old was placed in the mother's custody. For an interesting discussion on the judicial stereotyping of parental roles see W. Binchy, "The Sex of a Parent as a Factor in Custody Disputes" (1983) 77 *Gazette of the Incorporated Law Society of Ireland* 269.

65. (April, 1970) unreported (H.C.). See also *M. O'S. v. M. O'S.* (April, 1972) unreported (H.C.).

putting down roots and should not have the fear that they will be moved around."[66]

The fact that one parent is financially better off does not necessarily mean that that parent will get custody. In the majority of cases the husband will be better off financially than the wife, and where this is the case, the making of a maintenance order by the court can ensure that the children, if given into the wife's custody, will not suffer any great material disadvantages. Moreover, it has been persistently reiterated that it is the happiness of the child and not its material prospects with which the court is concerned.

A parent who frequently employs corporal punishment to discipline his children may find it particularly difficult to obtain an award of custody. In *J. O'C. v. M. O'C.*[67] four children (two boys aged 12 and 6½ and two girls aged 9½ and 8½) were placed in their father's custody. Kenny J., in the course of his judgement stated

> "I am satisfied that the wife has consistently inflicted severe corporal punishment on the children, has humiliated them before each other and that the position now is that all the children are very frightened of her. Each husband and wife have their own standards and their own theories about bringing up children and it may be necessary on some rare occasions to punish them but severe corporal punishment administered consistently to young children and particularly to girls is certain to cause emotional trouble. The parents who use corporal punishment on young children may think that it is for their good but civilized human beings have long since abandoned this barbaric practice."[68]

When a marriage has broken down the courts regard anything which may tend towards preserving the unity of the family as being for the welfare of the children. It was suggested in *B. v. B.* that where the custody of a number of children was in question one parent should not be totally deprived of custody as this might lead to further ill-feeling and be "a major stumbling block to any worthwhile type of reconciliation between the parents".[69]

Whereas it is always desirable to bring about a reconciliation between estranged spouses, there is a danger in such an approach that children will be regarded merely as tools or instruments to re-unite their parents. It is submitted that a child's welfare is more likely to be protected if it is living with a single parent in a stable, peaceful and loving home environment than with both parents in a warring, embittered and tension-filled situation. An important factor in maintaining some sort of family unity is to preserve the unity of the children. Children should not be separated unnecessarily. Any spirit of comradeship that exists between them, should be fostered, not extinguished.[70]

---

66. Kenny J. in *M. O'S. v. M. O'S.* (April, 1970) unreported (H.C.); in *W. v. W.* (April 1972) unreported (H.C.), Kenny J. stated "They (the children) should be given an opportunity to put down roots somewhere, because a sense of security is essential for children's happiness". See also *J.J.W. v. B.M.W.* (1971) 110 I.L.T.R. 49 (S.C.). In his judgement, Walsh J. also spoke of the need for stability in the lives of children.

67. *Supra.*

68. See p. 7 of judgement.

69. [1975] I.R. 54, *per* Budd J. at p. 69.

70. See *B. v. B.* [1975] I.R. at p. 59 where O'Dalaigh C.J. states: "After the separation of the parents, there remains two lesser points of unity around which one would wish, if possible to build: the first of these is the unity or comradeship of the three children and the second is the family home where these children have grown up together." See also *E. v. E., supra.*

The importance of this was fully recognised by Finlay P. in *J.C. v. O.C.* [71] when he declined to make an order transferring two children to the custody of their father with one child remaining in the custody of the mother. He referred to the desirability of keeping the three children together and the considerable importance "of their social development as a family unit", stating that "unless there were very good reasons to split them up it is better they should remain one unit." [72]

If a child is particularly attached to one parent such very good reason may be held to exist. In *P.G. v. C.G.* (No. 2) [73] the parties' three children (a girl aged 16 and two boys aged thirteen and a half and two years) were in the mother's custody. The thirteen and a half year old boy had an "exceptionally good" relationship with the father and on two occasions had run away from the mother's home going to stay with the father. Ellis J. was satisfied that the boy did not wish to return to live with his mother and that "to require him to do so would cause him great distress" and would be "fraught with . . . dangers and risks to (his) safety and physical and mental well being" and accordingly declined to order that the child return to his mother's custody. [74]

Intellectual and Religious Welfare

Intellectual welfare is concerned with the emotional security, settled affections and psychiatric stability of children, with plans for their education and intellectual development, the manner in which their environment and their parents contribute to this aspect of their development and with ensuring that children can take the maximum advantage of the educational opportunities available to them. If a child has a particular gift or aptitude the courts will often seek to ensure that the child has an opportunity of developing it. [75]

The religious welfare of children is concerned with their education in and practice of the religion in which they are being brought up. [76] It also involves ensuring, in so far as is possible, that the arrangements made for the custody of a child will not jeopardise the child's religious education.

As has already been seen, a great number of pre-1964 disputes as to custody between parents involved the question as to which parent should determine the children's education and in particular the religious education. Until *Tilson*'s case the courts permitted the father alone to dictate his children's religious upbringing and secular education. The 1964 Act expressly replaced paternal supremacy with joint parental authority. Now a mother and father have an equal say in the upbringing and education of their children and where agreement has been reached between parents as to a child's education, religious or secular, one parent cannot deviate from that agreement, [77] without the assent of the other. [78] If in a custody

---

71. *Supra.*
72. The importance of keeping children together was also the deciding factor in granting custody to the father in *M.K. v. P.K.* (November, 1982) unreported (H.C.).
73. (July, 1983) unreported (H.C.).
74. See pp. 18 & 20 of judgement. Ultimately a custody order was made in favour of the father.
75. See particularly judgement of Finlay P. in *MacD. v. MacD., supra* (H.C.).
76. *Ibid.*
77. As we have seen such an agreement can be either express, (*In re Tilson, supra*) or implied (*In re May, Minors, supra*). See *H. v. H.* (February, 1976) unreported (H.C.) where Parke J. expressly followed *In re May*.
78. That third parties cannot coerce parents into educating their children in the religion that the third party favours has been laid down in a number of cases. See *Burke and O'Reilly v. Burke and Quail* [1951] I.R. 216 (H.C.); (1950) 84 I.L.T.R. 70; *In re Blake, decd.* [1955] I.R. 89 (H.C.).

case today there is a dispute as to a child's religious upbringing the court would hold any agreement previously reached by the parties as binding, unless contrary to the child's welfare.[79]

It is arguable, however, that a remnant of paternal supremacy still survives. Whereas both parents have the "right and duty" to determine their children's education and religion, it was stated in *In re May, Minors*,[80] that in the absence of agreement the father's wishes are still to prevail. Thus, in a dispute between a couple of a mixed marriage, who have never come to any agreement[81] as to their children's religious education, it seems that it is the father's wishes that will prevail. Certainly the court could not decide that the practice of one religion was better for the welfare of a child rather than another.[82] On the other hand the court may not regard itself as bound by *In re May* and simply decide that it is for the child's welfare to be educated in the religion of that parent in whose custody it is for its welfare to be placed. The latter seems the more likely and desirable solution.[83]

If there is still a remnant of paternal religious dictatorship it could arise in another situation. Both the *Tilson* and *May* cases were concerned with express and implied agreements that were acted upon by the parties. There was no clear statement as to what the position would be if having made an agreement one of the parties renounced it before there was an opportunity to act upon it, i.e. before any children of the marriage were born. Would this be a case of "disagreement", and as a consequence the old common law rule of paternal supremacy could prevail or would the parties be held bound by the unexercised agreement? Upon a dispute arising following the birth of a child to the parties, Gavan Duffy J. undoubtedly would have enforced such an agreement upon grounds of public policy[84] and whereas Murnaghan J. and Davitt J. spoke primarily of an agreement acted upon, Murnaghan J. stated

> "I cannot accept the contention . . . that where a joint agreement has been made by a father and mother entitled under the Constitution to make it, the father at his mere wish can substitute an arrangement of his own".[85]

In the light of this statement and section 6(1) of the present Act such an unexercised agreement would more than likely be held to bind the parties and to be enforceable.

Prior to the 1964 Act the courts were very unwilling to grant custody to a parent of a religion different from that in which the child was being brought up.[86] Since that date there have been few written judgements delivered in cases involving disputes between parents of different religions. Certainly, the fact of a

---

79. *Cullen v. Cullen* (May, 1970) unreported (S.C.). See O'Dalaigh, C.J. part V of judgement.

80. *In re May, Minors*, (H.C.), *supra*.

81. Express or implied.

82. See comments of Parke J. in *H. v. H.* (February, 1976) unreported (H.C.).

83. This would not, however, solve the problem where parents intended to continue to cohabit but could not agree on their child's religious upbringing and made an application to the court for a direction under Sect. 11(1). Such a problem, however, is unlikely to arise, as if such a dispute between parents reached the stage where they applied to a court for its determination it is unlikely that they would continue to live together and thus the question of custody would also arise.

84. See *In re Tilson, Infants* [1951] I.R. 1 (H.C., S.C.).

85. *Ibid.*, at p. 35.

86. See *In re Keenan, Infants* (1949) 84 I.L.T.R. 169 (H.C.); *In re Corcoran, Infants* (1950) 86 I.L.T.R. 6 (S.C.); alternatively see *In re Begley, Infants* (1949) 82 I.L.T.R. 89 (H.C.).

parent being of a religion different to that of his or her children has not in practice been a major obstacle to a parent succeeding in an application for custody.[87] In such circumstances, however, it is a frequent condition of an award of custody, that a child will continue to receive proper instruction in a particular faith. In a number of cases discussed in the next section the interaction between the concepts of religious and moral welfare are examined. As shall be seen, in deciding disputes as to custody, the courts have been much influenced by the fact that the parent was living or intending to live in a manner condemned by the religion in which he proposed to bring up his children, that is, he was or was going to be, a party to an adulterous liaison.

Social and Moral Welfare

Social Welfare has been said to mean "the type of welfare which is to be judged by what is best calculated to make them (the children) better members of the society in which they live."[88] Social Welare is concerned with enabling the children to grow up to be "good citizens"[89] and well integrated members of society.[90] It is much concerned with ensuring that the child will be inculcated with "correct values" and imbued with a "proper" outlook on life. It is in fact a nebulous concept, difficult to pin down, its importance and influence in an individual case being much dependent on the subjective assessment of the facts by the individual judge.

Moral Welfare is concerned with the moral example given by a parent to his child, with the influence that the behaviour of the parent may have on the child's development and the manner in which the parent's conduct is likely to affect the child's religious, intellectual and social welfare.[91] The danger of the moral corruption of a child as a result of a parent's adulterous conduct has been a matter of particular concern to the courts and has given rise to a variety of conflicting judicial opinions and approaches in the application of the welfare principle.

In *J.J.W. v. B.M.W.*[92] the parties lived in England and were both Roman Catholics. The wife left the husband in 1969 and went to live with L. There were

87. *B. v. B.* [1975] I.R. 54 (S.C.) and *B. v. B.* (July, 1972) unreported (H.C.); *MacD. v. MacD., supra* (S.C.); *Healy v. Healy* (July, 1969) unreported (H.C.); *S. v. S.* (May, 1978) unreported (H.C.); In *Cullen v. Cullen, supra* the fact that the mother had ceased to practise her religion did not prevent her being awarded custody of her youngest son (5½) upon her giving assurances that he would receive proper religious instruction. In *H. v. H.* (February, 1976) unreported (H.C.) both parents were Catholics and married in accordance with the rites of the Church. The husband was found by the judge to drink heavily and to have previously assaulted his wife. Subsequent to the husband's assaults, the wife formed a liaison with an English man (Mr. G.) of the Jewish faith. She sought to have the marriage dissolved in England and intended to convert to Judaism and marry Mr. G. The court refused to grant custody of her 2½ year old son to the wife. Much weight was given to the wife's desire to change her son's religion and to the fact that she could not constitutionally do so without the father's consent. The question of her educating the boy in the Catholic religion was not considered.
88. *M.B. O'S. v. P.O. O'S., supra* (S.C.), *per* Walsh J. at p. 61. See also *H. v. H.* (February, 1976) unreported (H.C.).
89. *E.K. v. M.K.* (May, 1974) unreported (H.C.). Kenny J.
90. *M.B. O'S. v. P.O. O'S., supra* (S.C.) Henchy J. — Social welfare taken to mean "well-being as members of society". He went on to state that the children lead "an active, normal well-integrated existence". See also *J.C. v. O.C., supra*, in which Finlay P. referred to social welfare as being concerned with the children's "capacity to mix with and enter into and become part of the society in which they will be brought up."
91. See, in particular, judgements of Finlay P. in *MacD. v. MacD., supra*, and *J.C. v. O.C., supra*.
92. (1971) 110 I.L.T.R. 49 (S.C.). See also (1971) 110 I.L.T.R. 45, the High Court judgement of Kenny J. delivered in May 1971.

three children of the marriage, all girls, aged nine, seven and three. When the wife left home she took the two youngest girls with her but the husband regained custody of the children.

The husband came to live in his parents' house in Dublin with the children. His parents being elderly, three children were too much for them and as a result the two eldest were placed in a school run by nuns of the Poor Clare Order. They were visited at weekends by their father and spent their holidays with him and their grandparents.

In 1971 the wife, who was then living in England in a large flat with L.,[93] came to Dublin and with the help of her parents, brought the two eldest children back to England. She brought divorce proceedings in England and asked the English court to give her custody. The English court decided that the custody of the children was a matter to be decided by the Irish courts and directed her to return the children to her husband. Subsequently proceedings were brought in the High Court in Dublin.

Kenny J. decided that the religious, moral and intellectual welfare of the children would be better promoted by leaving them with the father. They would get a good secular and religious education in Ireland. They had been in school in Dublin for two years and it was not in their interests to be moved from school to school. Also, he stated,

"They will not have the corrupting example of their mother living with a man to whom she is not married".

However, these were not the only considerations.

"In my view the ages of the children, their sex, the certainty that they would be happier if they were living at home rather than in a school and the necessity that they should grow up together . . . make it so desirable that they should be with their mother that these elements should be held to outweigh the arguments based upon the moral, religious and intellectual aspects".[94]

Accordingly, the judge awarded custody of the three children to the mother.

However, the Supreme Court reversed Kenny J.'s decision and granted custody of all three to the father. His conclusions as to the religious, moral and intellectual welfare of the children were accepted. The fact that the father was compelled by circumstances to keep two of the children in boarding school for the greater part of the year and was therefore unable to let them all grow up together in one household, whereas the mother could do so, was not such a decisive factor as should give the mother custody. Walsh J. stated:

"As matters stand at the moment the children are leading a stable existence . . . the school in question specialises in catering for children from broken homes" and "the evidence does not disclose that the children are not happy . . . the present position of their mother offers no such stability and there is nothing to suggest that in the immediate future any such stability will be available".[95]

Fitzgerald C.J. stated:

"The fact is that the home which she has to offer to her children is one in which she continues an adulterous association with a man who has deserted

93. Who had by this time been divorced by his wife.
94. *Supra*, at p. 49.
95. *Ibid.*, at p. 50.

his own wife and his own two children. A more unhealthy abode for the three . . . children would be difficult to imagine".[96]

The fact that Mr. L. had divorced his wife and that Mrs. W. had obtained a decree nisi for divorce in the English Courts against her husband was regarded as irrelevant. The learned judge stated that even if Mrs. W. had entered into marriage with L. "her status in relation to her own children would not appear to me to be thereby in any way advanced".[97]

In *M.B. O'S. v. P.O. O'S.*[98] the moral welfare of the children was again considered. Here the husband P. left his wife B. and with her agreement kept their three young children in his custody. They lived for a year and a half with P.'s married sister, then for half a year with P.'s mother and finally came to Dublin to live in a large house with P. and a woman with whom he was living, and who had assumed his name by deed poll. A year later B. instituted proceedings to obtain custody of the children intending to live with them in her parents' house in Cobh.

Kenny J. in the High Court held that the intellectual, physical and social welfare of the children would best be served by the father retaining custody, but that

"having regard to my obligation to follow *J.J.W. v. B.M.W.* I have no doubt whatever that I should award the custody of the three children to the wife . . . The moral welfare of the children would not be promoted by the fact that their father is with a lady to whom he is not married and by whom he has had one child. As the children grow up they will be taught the virtues of chastity and the importance of marriage and they will be living in a household where each of them will be aware that the lady with whom their father is living is not his wife."[99]

On appeal the Supreme Court, by a majority decision, held that the father should retain custody. There was no principle in *J.J.W. v. B.M.W.* which Kenny J. was obliged to follow.

"[*J.J.W. v. B.M.W.*] was decided on the facts in that case, as indeed must all cases of this unhappy nature."[100]

The majority referred to the dangers of again uprooting the children[101] and to the fact that all aspects of their welfare including their religious welfare was being properly attended to. Griffin J. stated that:

"In my view, the moral danger to the children does not outweigh the other advantages to them in living with their father."[102]

The majority emphasised the fact that the father's relationship with the second Mrs. O'S. had all the appearances of being a permanent union and that, as such, the children would have to come to terms with it. Henchy J. stated that:

---

96. *Ibid.*, at p. 52.
97. See the contrasting approach of McWilliam J. in *MacC. v. MacC., supra* (H.C.).
98. (1974) 110 I.L.T.R. 57 (H.C., S.C.).
99. *Ibid.*, at pp. 58, 59.
100. *Ibid., per* Griffin J. at p. 65.
101. Henchy J. thought that their intellectual welfare "would be retarded by the emotional disturbance that the change would cause and by the rupture of the continuity of their schooling" *ibid.*, (at p. 62). The children when interviewed by the court gave evidence that they dreaded the prospect of being removed to Cobh where the mother lived.
102. *Ibid.*, at p. 66.

"Beyond the mere fact that the father and the stepmother are living together in an unmarried state there is nothing in the evidence to suggest that the children do not live in a healthy moral atmosphere."[103]

Walsh J. dissenting stated that:

"The Constitution recognises the family as the natural primary and fundamental unit group of society; that is the keystone of the social structure which the Constitution undertakes to maintain. The household in which these children now reside with their father is not a family in that sense . . . These three children would in my view, be far more of a family unit if they lived with their mother instead of residing with their father in the mixed menage in which they now find themselves . . . So far as the social, moral and religious aspects are concerned the present atmosphere in which they are found . . . is one which is a manifest repudiation of the social and religious values with which they should be inculcated at this stage of their lives . . . The welfare of the children requires that they should be returned to their mother to form the natural family unit from which, unfortunately, only the father is missing but in which there is no element alien or hostile to ordinary family life."[104]

In *E.K. v. M.K.*[105] the Supreme Court in a majority decision (3-2) granted custody of two children, a boy aged five and a half years and a girl aged three and a half years, to the father. In the High Court the mother had been granted custody.

In the High Court both parties agreed that their marriage had irretrievably broken down. Evidence was given that a year prior to the parties separating the wife had committed "an act of adultery" with one of her husband's employees but it was not alleged that this act by the wife had been a major factor in the breakdown of the marriage. The parties separated and agreed that the children would reside with the wife. However, a short time later, the wife became friendly with a Mr. M. and the evidence established that M. and Mrs. K. had engaged in sexual intercourse on many occasions in the latter's home after the children had gone to bed. It was also established that M. was well known to the children, was liked by them and was referred to by them as "uncle". There was no suggestion that the wife's association with M. commenced before the Ks. separated. Walsh J., awarding custody to the father, stated that:

"a removal of the children from the custody of their mother at such an age would be justified only when it has been found that the mother has been so greatly wanting in her duty to her children that the removal would be warranted."

Having regard to the mother's behaviour such removal was justified. The life she was leading, Walsh J. stated, was

"a manifest repudiation of the social and religious values with which the

---

103. *Ibid.*, at p. 64. He further stated that "Where the Supreme Court differed from the High Court in, [*J.J.W. v. B.M.W.*] was in holding that in spite of the fact that the father had to keep two of the children in a boarding school, it was to their intellectual and social welfare that he should retain custody . . . [*J.J.W. v. B.M.W.*] is a decision on its own facts". See also *M. O'B. v. P.M. O'B.* (January 1971) unreported (H.C.).

104. *Supra*, at p. 61. See also *H. v. H., supra.*

105. (July, 1974) unreported (S.C.). In this case both parents accepted that their marriage was "irretrievably broken down". The court regarded the mother responsible for the breakdown.

children should be inculcated and which she believes she can teach them while at the same time clearly repudiating them herself in the sight of her own children."[106]

In the later case of *W. v. W.*[107] the Supreme Court affirmed a High Court order to transfer the custody of two boys (14 and 11) from their father to their mother. Two years earlier the High Court had granted custody of the boys to their father. While they were in his custody, the father was found to have committed acts of adultery, one of which took place when the children were present in the house. It was stated that:

"such misconduct would have a devastating effect on the moral standards of the children at their present age."

Six months later, however, the High Court transferred custody back to the father. Mrs. W. had brought proceedings to commit her husband to prison for breach of the previous order of the court. Contrary to the court's order, the boys had returned to live with their father. Upon being interviewed by Kenny J., the boys were adamant that they wished to remain with their father and stated that if the court placed them in their mother's custody they would run away. Stating that

"when children of this age express . . . a strong preference for living with one of their parents, the court should give effect to it,"

Kenny J. granted custody to the father. A year later, the Supreme Court affirmed this latter order.[108]

The most recent case in which the Supreme Court has had to consider the concept of moral welfare is that of *MacD. v. MacD.*[109] The parties had married in 1969 in a Roman Catholic Church, the husband being Roman Catholic and the wife a member of the Church of Ireland. At the date of the proceedings they had two children, a girl aged six and a half years and a boy aged four and a half years. By the beginning of 1975 a relationship had developed between the wife and D. who was a divorcee. When the husband learned of the relationship, the marriage had broken up and in January 1977 a deed of separation was concluded which provided that the husband was to have custody of the children. In Decem-

106. The majority judgements were delivered by Walsh J., Budd J. and Fitzgerald C.J. Dissenting judgements were delivered by Henchy J. and Griffin J. It is interesting that in this case the dissenting judgements were given by the two judges in the majority in the earlier case of *M.B. O'S. v. P.O. O'S.* in which only a three man Supreme Court sat. See also *A.H.S. v. M.S.* (November, 1982) unreported (H.C.). The mother suffered from manic depressive psychosis and had been hospitalized on a number of occasions. The child (a seven and a half year old boy) had been residing for the preceding 18 months with his father and P.G., with whom the father had an adulterous relationship. Granting custody to the mother, Barron J. stated that:

"If he continued to reside with his father and P.G. he is going to be confused by a situation in which something he is taught to be totally wrong is being given the appearance of propriety . . . the Supreme Court has essentially regarded the moral danger to the child as being more important than its physical and social welfare unless it can be shown that it would be harmful to its latter welfare to remove it from a settled home."
107. (December, 1974) unreported (S.C.). The members of the Supreme Court in this case were Walsh J., Henchy J. and Griffin J. and the decision was unanimous.
108. Four unreported written judgements were delivered by Kenny J. in the High Court in *W. v.W.* (April 1972, July 1974, Oct. 1974, June 1975). No written judgement was delivered by the Supreme Court in July 1976 when affirming the June 1975 High Court decision. See also *P.G. v. C.G.* (No. 2) (July, 1983) unreported (H.C.) discussed on p. 358 in which a seven and a half year old boy was allowed to remain living with his father and E.W., with whom the father had an adulterous relationship. Ellis J. accepted that the child had "a good relationship" with E.W. "who looks after (him) well and although of a different religion sees to it that he attends to his religious duties as a Roman Catholic."
109. (1979) 114 I.L.T.R. 66 (S.C.).

ber 1977 the wife issued proceedings seeking custody of the children. In April 1978 these proceedings were settled and a further agreement concluded, under the terms of which the wife obtained custody and neither child was "to come into contact with D."

In December 1978 the wife took up residence in D.'s home with the two children. The husband re-entered the proceedings and sought custody. He proposed that the children should reside with him and stated that he would retain a housekeeper during the day to look after them when he was at work.

In the High Court, Finlay P., granting custody to the father, held that the children's physical and intellectual welfare would be equally safeguarded by both parents but that their moral, social and religious welfare would be better protected by the father. He stated:

> "It seems to me clear on the evidence that at present at least the household of the father of these children is one based upon the importance, sanctity and integrity of the family carrying no hint of approval of any permissive standards with regard to the sanctity of marriage."

As for the mother, her behaviour, he stated "is a firm and clear repudiation both of the fundamental integrity of the family as a unit and of these moral standards with regard to the sanctity of marriage and condemnation of adultery."[110]

The Supreme Court, on appeal, reversed the order of the High Court and in a majority decision granted custody to the mother.[111] The age of the children and the fact that the mother would be available during the day to look after them, whereas the father would be at work, greatly influenced the majority in holding that it was in the interests of the children's physical, social and intellectual welfare that the mother be granted custody. As for the children's religious and moral welfare Henchy J. stated:

> "The mother's relationship with D. is already an accomplished fact in the children's lives ... The mother has given evidence (which has not been doubted in cross examination and which is supported by her conduct when she already had custody), that she is prepared to bring up the children as Catholics ... In other words, she is prepared, so far as in her lies, to look after the religious and moral welfare of the children ... The unfortunate extra-marital situation in which she finds herself, which cannot be regularised so as to acquire constitutional propriety, detracts considerably from her willingness and ability to satisfy the religious and moral welfare of the children. But so long as she is ready as a loving and caring mother to do her best to see to that welfare, the obvious need of these young children for her as a mother should weigh heavily in the balance in favour of her claim to be given custody."[112]

In conclusion, he emphasised that:

> "custody is awarded not as a mark of approbation or disapprobation of parental conduct but solely as a judicial determination of where the welfare of the children lies."[113]

110. See also *S. v. S.* (May, 1978) unreported (H.C.) and *J.C. v. O.C.* (July, 1980) unreported (H.C.), judgements of Finlay P.; *N. O'D. v. M. O'D.* (November, 1977) unreported (H.C.), judgement of McMahon J.; *H. v. H.* (February, 1976) unreported (H.C.), judgement of Parke J.; *A.H.S. v. M.S.* (November, 1982) unreported (H.C.), judgement of Barron J., discussed in footnote 106 above.

111. Henchy J. and Kenny J. A dissenting judgement was delivered by Griffin J.

112. *Supra* at pp. 77, 78.

113. *Supra* at p. 78. Kenny J. stated that "an award of custody must not be used as a method of punishing the wife for her adultery." He also stated that he reserved "for future

The case law in this area lacks coherence and is difficult, if not impossible, to reconcile. The fact that a spouse is engaged in an adulterous relationship without doubt renders it more difficult for that spouse to succeed in any application for custody. It is, however, impossible to predict with accuracy the likely outcome of such proceedings having regard to the varying judicial opinions as to the likely damage to the welfare of a child if it is placed in the custody of an adulterous parent. Nevertheless, it is clear from existing authorities that a less serious view of the "moral danger" is taken in the case of the spouse who has formed an adulterous liaison some time after his or her marriage has broken down and separation has occurred, than in the case of the spouse who commits adultery while still living with the other spouse and who leaves the family home to set up home with a third party. In both circumstances, but particularly in the latter one, the adulterous parent's chances of success will improve if the children whose custody is sought are aware of the adulterous relationship and have resided with the adulterous parent and third party for a period prior to the matter arising for judicial decision. Moreover, a parent who can prove that an adulterous association has terminated will further increase his or her chances of success. Thus, in *Cullen v. Cullen*[114] a mother held to be the parent responsible for the breakdown of the marriage was granted custody of her youngest child on the condition and subject to the understanding that her association with her former lover was at an end.

In a society whose courts possess no jurisdiction to dissolve the matrimonial bond upon the breakdown of a marital relationship, the number of cases coming before the courts in which one or both parties to a broken marriage are engaged in an adulterous relationship is likely to increase. In such circumstances the application of the "welfare" principle is particularly difficult. This difficulty is exacerbated by the Supreme Court's failure to clearly enunciate the principles applicable in deciding such cases.[115]

Access

Where parents can agree between themselves about duration, frequency and circumstances of access, the court will not usually interfere. If they cannot agree and if custody is granted to one parent, the other will normally be given access by the court to the child if he wants it, and frequently access includes the right to have a child or children reside with and go on holidays with the non-custodial parent for a proportion of each school holiday period, and may include a right to have a child reside overnight with such parent on occasional weekends during school term.[116] Where a parent is living in an adulterous relationship with another, a condition of access may be that the other person must not be present when the parent has access to the children.[117] This, however, depends very much on the

---

consideration by a full court the questions of whether the decisions of this court in (*J.J.W. v. B.M.W.*) and (*E.K. v. M.K.*) were correct". *Supra* at pp. 81, 82. See also the decision of the English Court of Appeal in *S. (B.D.) v. S. (D.J.)* [1977] Fam. 109; [1977] 2 W.L.R. 44 referred to with approval by Henchy J. See further *K. (Minors) (Wardship)* [1977] 1 All E.R. 647 (C.A.).

114. (May, 1970) unreported (S.C.).

115. See J. O'Reilly, "Custody Disputes in the Irish Republic: the Uncertain Search for the Child's Welfare" (1977) 12 I.J. (n.s.) 37.

116. See for example *M.K. v. P.K.* (November, 1982) unreported (H.C.), Finlay P. See also *A. MacB. v. A.G. MacB.* (June, 1984) unreported (H.C.), Barron J.

117. Thus, in *Braun v. Braun* (December, 1973) unreported (H.C.) the mother was permitted to have access to her children in the house in which she was living on condition that R. the person with whom she was living would not be present at the time. See also the judgement of Fitzgerald J. in *J.J.W. v. B.M.W.*, *supra*.

circumstances of the case.[118]

In determining a dispute as to access the welfare of the child is the first and paramount consideration. The court is reluctant to refuse a parent access but it will do so if the child's welfare demands it. In *B. v. B.*[119] the behaviour of the father almost resulted in such a refusal. In this case the parents were living apart and the father having been given custody of two of his three children, used his children to spy on their mother, and place microphones in her bedroom. He turned both the children completely against their mother engaging in "violent verbal onslaughts" against her in their presence. Upon a new application by both parents to the High Court, the mother was granted custody of all three children and the father's access was curtailed to once a month.

In *N.A.D. v. T.D.*[120] the High Court declined to make the access order sought by a mother to her five children aged 20, 19, 18, 17, and 14 respectively. The mother deserted her husband in 1971 and her father remained in the family home, residing with the husband and assisting him in bringing up the children. She had no contact with her children until May 1980 when a meeting was arranged between the parties at which the children attended. Prior to the meeting, the five children of the marriage were totally unaware of the existence of another child born to the wife in England when she was residing with another man. Barron J. in his judgement noted that "A difficult reunion was made more difficult because the wife brought her six year old son to that meeting"[121] and that the mother had not since that time met the five children. Delivering judgement four years after the meeting had taken place, he stated that in "their present home circumstances" the children were "secure and well supported". He could see no benefit to any of the children "in any form of access" along the lines of that arranged in May 1980 when the parties had met in the grounds of a hotel half way between Dublin, where the mother resided and Galway, where the children resided. Declining to make an access order he stated:

> "The present relationship between the wife and her children could only be hampered by seeking to impose a solution, particularly one which would not appear to have any hope of producing a better relationship between them."[122]

As for the youngest child, a fourteen year old girl, she was "too old to be forced to see her mother with whom her older brothers and sisters may have no communication." He concluded dealing with this issue by stating that in the event of the wife going to live in Galway "then the position as to access should be reconsidered depending on the new circumstances."[123]

In *M. v. M.*[124] the English Court of Appeal stated that access to a child by a

---

118. See, for example, *J.C. v. O.C.* (July, 1980) unreported (H.C.), Finlay P., in which no order was made by the court preventing children coming into contact with and having a relationship with the woman with whom the father was living in adultery. Whilst stating that "the moral and religious welfare" of the children indicated that they should remain in their mother's custody, Finlay P. also observed that the children must understand "their father is living with someone to whom he is not married and has two children of that union. That is a situation they will have to live with and should treat with understanding and compassion . . .". See also, *A. MacB. v. A.G. MacB.*, *supra*, in which Barron J. held it was in the best interests of three children (eleven and a half, ten and seven) that they have regular access to their father in his home although he was residing there "with a woman to whom he is not married and by whom he has had a child."

119. See Kenny J.'s judgement of (July, 1974) unreported (H.C.).

120. [1985] 5 I.L.R.M. 153 (H.C.).

121. *Ibid.*, at p. 156.

122. *Ibid.*, at p. 157.

123. *Ibid.*

124. [1973] 2 All E.R. 81 (Fam. D.).

parent is a basic right of the child rather than of the parent. Wrangham J. stated that:

> "No court should deprive a child of access to either parent unless it is wholly satisfied that it is in the interests of that child that access should cease, and that is a conclusion at which a court should be extremely slow to arrive."[125]

In making access orders the courts essentially seek to ensure, in so far as that is possible, that a child continues to maintain a full and meaningful relationship with the non-custodial parent. In reality this is only effectively achieved if both parents fully co-operate with each other in implementing whatever access arrangement is provided for by way of court order. It is also necessary for each parent to apply a degree of common sense and flexibility to vary such arrangements by mutual agreement, if necessary, without having to regularly and continually apply to the courts to resolve access disputes between them. If one parent withholds his or her co-operation, refuses to be reasonable or flexible, or continuously fails to comply with access orders made, the child or children to whom access is a right all too often become the damaged victims of a matrimonial war of attrition fought by parents engaged in continuous and never-ending litigation.

The Child's Wishes

Formerly, chancery frequently consulted a young child not for the purpose of obtaining the child's agreement or consent to being put into a particular parent's custody but in order to help the court determine for itself what was for a child's welfare. At common law a boy was regarded as reaching the age of discretion at 14 and a girl at 16 and the court regarded itself as bound by the wishes of the children when they reached the above ages. After 1877 the court exercised both jurisdictions and where a boy of 14 or a girl of 16 wished to be in the custody of a particular parent the court regarded itself as being under an obligation to respect the child's wishes, even if it believed that the implementation of them would be contrary to the child's welfare.[126]

In applications brought under section 11 of the 1964 Act, interviews of children have been undertaken by both the High Court and Supreme Court where appropriate. Such interviews are of an extremely informal nature[127] and usually take place in the trial judge's room or chambers. Not only what is said by children at such interviews but also their general behaviour and appearance may influence the court and form part of the basis of any decision made.[128] A

---

125. *Ibid* at p. 85. At p. 88 in the same case Latey J. stated: "I do not accept that . . . a parent should have access to the child although such access is contrary to the child's interests". This case was cited by Kenny J. but not commented on in *Braun v. Braun* (December, 1973) unreported (H.C.). See also *M. v. J.* (1977) 121 S.J. 759 (D.C.).

126. *State (Meagan) v. Meagan* [1942] I.R. 180 (H.C.). See also *R. v. Gyngall, supra; In re Elliott, an Infant* (1893) 32 L.R. Ir. 504 (C.A.); *In re O'Hara, an Infant, supra; In re Kevin Isherwood, an Infant, supra; In re Frost, Infants, supra.* Statutory authority was given to the practice of the courts interviewing the child in Habeas Corpus proceedings in the Custody of Children Act, 1891. See now Sect. 17(2) of the 1964 Act.

127. See, for example, *N.A.D. v. T.D.* [1985] 5 I.L.R.M. 153 (H.C.) in which Barron J. in his judgement refers to having seen two of the children in chambers. On rare occasions some members of the judiciary have taken a less conventional approach. See *M. O'S. v. M. O'S.* (April, 1972) unreported (H.C.) where Kenny J. describes how he met the children for lunch and strolled around the Boat Show at the R.D.S. and then went into the jumping enclosure with them.

128. See *M.K. v. P.K.* (November, 1982) unreported (H.C.) in which Finlay P. stated that "having interviewed two of the children (a daughter aged fifteen and a son aged eleven) I am satisfied that they both have close and affectionate ties with each of their parents."

judge is under no obligation to accede to a request to interview a child or children prior to deciding a custody or access dispute[128a] and it has been acknowledged that when such interviews take place the court has to be on its guard as to what a child says, as it may have been coached by one of its parents.[129] Whether the court would uphold the wishes of a 14 year old boy or 16 year old girl today if it believed them totally contrary to the child's welfare and long-term interests is doubtful.[130] It is submitted that it would not do so. If it did, it is certainly arguable that any such decision would be contrary to section 3 of the Act. On the other hand, it has been recognised that it would be impractical to transfer the custody of a 17½ year old girl from her mother to her father against the girl's own wishes.[131] Upon a child reaching such an age, in the absence of grave danger to its welfare, it is very unlikely that its wishes will not be complied with.[132]

Effect of Award of Custody

The fact that a parent is deprived of his right to custody does not mean he has no further say in the upbringing of his child. Such a parent is still a guardian of the child, and is entitled to be consulted on all matters affecting the child's welfare. As seen earlier, this applies to all matters that comprise the religious, moral, intellectual, physical and social welfare of the child. "Section 6 of the Act stated the equality of the parents and recognised them as the guardians of the infant and there is nothing in any provision of the Act which purports to confer upon any court or other body the power to displace either one or both of the parents from the position of guardian or guardians."[133]

Custody and Parental Kidnapping

A problem that has become more frequent in recent years is that of the parent who seeks to resolve a dispute as to the custody of children by removing them unilaterally from one jurisdiction to another without the consent of the other parent. Such behaviour is commonly described as parental kidnapping although it is not usually kidnapping in the criminal sense. It is proposed first

---

128a. See *F.M. v. J.M.* (November, 1983) unreported (H.C.) where O'Hanlon J. declined to interview three children (aged eighteen, sixteen and eleven years) stating "on the view I have taken of the evidence . . . the wife has disqualified herself for the time being, at any rate, as a person to whom the custody of the children, or any of them, should be entrusted."

129. In *B. v. B.* (January, 1969) unreported (H.C.) Kenny J. said that he did not interview the children as he thought it would be of no assistance and might upset them. He also complained that in another case he had interviewed a child obviously coached by his father. On the other hand, the Supreme Court, on appeal, did interview the children. In *J.C. v. O.C.* (July, 1980) unreported (H.C.) the father expressed the view that if interviewed, the children would be persuaded by their mother to express a particular point of view and that the actual interview itself would pressurize them. Although Finlay P. asserted that he had "a right to interview the children and to see them either separately or jointly for the purpose of coming to a conclusion" he held he did not need to do so but would "see them after all the issues had been decided but with nothing hinging on it so that nobody need think their answers will affect me." The learned President stated he just wanted "to see what kind of children they are."

130. See *In re S. Infants* [1967] 1 All E.R. 202 (Ch. D.).

131. See *Cullen v. Cullen* (May, 1970) unreported (S.C.). See also *W. v. W.* (June, 1975) unreported (H.C.) discussed on p. 364 *ante*.

132. An example of a circumstance in which the court would not agree to comply with the wishes of such a child would be perhaps where a parent was engaging in incest with the child. Here, despite the child's desire to remain with the parent, it is highly unlikely that such a parent would be permitted to retain custody.

133. Walsh J. in *B. v. B.* [1975] I.R. 54 (S.C.). In *J.J.W. v. B.M.W., supra* (S.C.) Walsh J. stated: "The award of custody does not affect the rights which accrue to the parents as guardians of the children". See also *W. v. W.* (December, 1974) unreported (S.C.).

to deal with the parental kidnapping of children living in this jurisdiction and then to look at the problem of children brought to Ireland from other jurisdictions.

Kidnapping within the jurisdiction: a parent who fears that the other parent may seek to remove a child from this jurisdiction can in proceedings brought under Section 11 of the 1964 Act obtain an order prohibiting the latter from removing the child from the jurisdiction without either the consent of the parent seeking the order or, in the alternative, the consent of the court. The court in making such an order may also require the parent against whom it is made hand into court any passport issued in respect of the child, that is in his possession.

If a parent has already kidnapped a child, an ex parte application can be made to the Circuit or High Court by the other parent seeking an immediate order prohibiting the removal of the child from the jurisdiction. In such circumstances it is also usual for the court to make an order authorising the solicitor acting for the applicant to notify by 'phone and telegram the Commissioner of the Gardai and all points of departure from the State of the content of the order. The court would also usually order the kidnapping parent to produce the child before the court within one or two days. If the whereabouts of the kidnapping parent are unknown, the court may further authorise the publication of a notice in a national or local newspaper containing the court order to bring it to the attention of the kidnapping parent. In practice, in an emergency, the High Court has granted such orders upon hearing the evidence of a parent even before proceedings have been drafted and issued.

If a parent knowingly breaks an order prohibiting the removal of a child from the jurisdiction, or if a third party knowing that such an order has been made, assists a parent to break it, he is guilty of contempt of court.[134]

Kidnapping outside the jurisdiction: in cases in which a parent has unilaterally brought a child to Ireland from another jurisdiction in which it has had its home, without the consent of the other parent, the Irish courts have in practice been reluctant to engage in a comprehensive examination of all the issues involved in a dispute as to custody and have generally approached the matter on the basis that the proper courts to determine such disputes are those of the home jurisdiction. Thus, in *A. v. H.*[135] the High Court peremptorily ordered that an illegitimate child just over two years of age be returned to the custody of its mother stating that any dispute as to its custody should be determined by the courts of Northern Ireland. Five days earlier the child, which was residing with its mother in Belfast, had been kidnapped by the father and brought to Dublin. In *O.D. v. O'D.*[136] the High Court ruled that the proper forum to determine a dispute as to the custody of three legitimate children kidnapped by their father from Alberta in Canada was the Supreme Court of Alberta. Two months prior to these proceedings the plaintiff had been residing with her children in Alberta and prior to her instituting proceedings in Ireland she had successfully applied to the Supreme Court in Alberta for custody.

Northampton County Council v. A.B.F. & M.B.F.[137] and *Kent County Council v. C.S.*[138] are the only cases in this area in which there have been delivered

134. See *D. v. D.* (April, 1974) unreported (H.C.).
135. 1978 No. 484 Sp. Decision of D'Arcy J. 23rd August 1978. There was no written judgement in this case.
136. See (July-August, 1979) Vol. 73 *Gazette of the Incorporated Law Society of Ireland,* "Recent Irish Cases" in which there is a summary of this case. No written judgement was delivered.
137. [1982] 2 I.L.R.M. 164 (H.C.).
138. [1984] 4 I.L.R.M. 292 (H.C.).

detailed written judgements. Although the applicants in both cases were English local authorities, it is clear that the cases themselves also involved a dispute between parents as to the future upbringing of children.

In *Northampton County Council v. A.B.F. & M.B.F.*, the plaintiffs sought an order that a child just under four years of age be returned to England after it had been brought to Ireland by the father and placed by him in the temporary care of the defendants. The parents were English citizens who were married and domiciled in England. The child had always lived in England until brought to Ireland by the father shortly after an order had been made by the Kettering Juvenile court placing the child in the care of Northampton County Council. It was the council's intention to place the child for adoption. The child was legitimate and while the mother was agreeable to it being adopted, the father, who was a notice party in the proceedings, opposed the adoption of his child. It was submitted by the County Council that the High Court should not undertake a detailed examination of the issues involved and that it should simply order that the child be returned to the jurisdiction of the English courts. Delivering judgement, Hamilton J. stated that in the ordinary course, without considering the merits of the case, he would have granted such an application

> "having regard to the orders made by Kettering Juvenile court, placing the infant in the care of the applicants and the degree of comity which exists between the courts of (the) relevant jurisdictions ... both parents being English citizens who married in England, were domiciled in England and whose only child ... was born in England and having regard to the fact that the infant had been unlawfully removed from the jurisdiction of the English courts."[139]

However, he declined at this stage to make the orders sought as, if made, "the child would have been adopted without the consent and in spite of the opposition of his lawful father, a development which is not permissible under the Irish law of adoption."[140]

Referring to the rights conferred on the family by Article 41 of the Constitution, the learned judge continued:

> "The natural law is of universal application and applies to all human persons, be they citizens of this State or not, and in my opinion it would be inconceivable that the father of the infant child would not be entitled to rely on the recognition of the Family contained in Article 41 for the purpose of enforcing his rights as the lawful father ... or that he should lose such entitlement merely because he removed the child to this jurisdiction for the purpose of enforcing his said rights."[141]

Noting that the child also had natural rights which had to be protected and vindicated by the State,[142] Hamilton J. concluded ordering that there be a full plenary hearing on the merits "for the purpose of ascertaining whether the child's rights are being protected" before any final order was made.

---

139. [1982] 2 I.L.R.M. at p. 165.
140. *Ibid.*
141. *Ibid.*, at p. 166.
142. Citing with approval a passage from the judgement of O'Higgins C.J. in *G. v. An Bord Uchtála* [1974] I.R. at p. 56 quoted at p. 26 in Chapter 1.

In the later case of *Kent County Council v. C.S.*,[143] a child just under three years of age was brought to Ireland by the father after an order had been made by the English High Court placing the child in the care of Kent County Council, empowering the council to ultimately place the child in the "care and control" of the mother upon it deciding that the child could "be entrusted" to the mother. The English courts had also ordered that the child was not to be removed "from England and Wales without leave of the court" and following its removal, ordered that it be returned to England. Finlay P. declined to order a full hearing into the merits of the case, expressing himself satisfied that the County Council had no intention of placing the child for adoption and that there was no question of the father being deprived of his constitutional rights pursuant to Article 41 or 42 of the Constitution, and made an order that the child be returned to the care of Kent County Council. In doing so he noted that "The witnesses who are material to the long-term question of the welfare of the infant" were all resident in England and "not ordinarily amenable to be brought before the courts in this country"[144] and referred to

> "the fundamental importance of the appropriate forum for the determination of the future welfare of the child being the courts in the country in which it was born and intended to be brought up."[145]

Although to date there has been no Supreme Court judgement delivered in this area, it is clear from the above authorities that in dealing with such cases the Irish courts are bound by the welfare principle as stated in section 3 of the Act of 1964 and will normally regard it as being in the best interests of a child that any dispute as to its future upbringing be determined by the courts of that country in which the child is being ordinarily brought up. The courts must also, however, be conscious of the rights and duties created by or deriving from the Constitution and may refuse to order the return of a child to a foreign jurisdiction until there has been a full substantive hearing to determine whether the rights possessed by each of the parents and the child under the Irish Constitution will continue to be fully protected if the court orders that the child be returned.[146]

---

143. [1984] 4 I.L.R.M. 292 (H.C.).
144. *Ibid.*, at p. 296.
145. *Ibid.*, at p. 297.
146. See further "Kidnapping and the Irish Courts" [1984] 2 I.L.T. (n.s.) 4. For an excellent discussion of English law up to 1979, see Lowe & White, *Wards of Court* (London, Butterworths 1979), Chap. 12. See also G. Ritchie, "Wardship and Kidnapping" (1979) 129 N.L.J. 873; N.V. Lowe, "Wardship and Kidnapping — A Reply" (1980) 130 N.L.J. 584; D.W. Fox & A.N. Khan, "Kidnapping Ones Own Child" (1979) 9 Fam. Law 68. See in particular the following cases: *Re H. (Infants)* [1966] 1 W.L.R. 381 (C.A.); *Re E. (An Infant)* [1967] Ch. 287; [1967] 1 All E.R. 329 (Ch.D.); [1967] 2 All E.R. 881 (C.A.); *Re T. (Infants)* [1968] Ch. 704 (C.A.); *Re A. (Infants)* [1970] Ch. 665 (C.A.); *Re L. (Minors) (Wardship: Jurisdiction)* [1974] 1 W.L.R. 250 (C.A.); (Pet. Dis.) [1974] 1 W.L.R. 266, G. (H.L.); *Re M.-R. (A Minor)* (1975) 5 Fam. Law 55 (C.A.); *Re C. (Minors) (Wardship: Jurisdiction)* [1978] Fam. 105 (C.A.); *Re: O. (Minors) Wardship: Jurisdiction* [1982] 3 F.L.R. 146 (C.A.).
    See further *R. v. D.* [1984] 2 All E.R. 449 (H.L.) in which the House of Lords held that the common law or criminal law offence of kidnapping can be committed by a parent who takes and carries away by force or fraud his own unmarried child under the age of majority without the child's consent and without lawful excuse. See also *People, The (A.G.) v. Edge* [1943] I.R. 115 (S.C.). A specific statute has been enacted entitled The Child Abduction Act, 1984, making it a statutory criminal offence for a parent to abduct a child from the United Kingdom — see V. Lowe, "Child Abduction and Child Kidnapping — The New Laws Affecting Parents" (1984) 134 N.L.J. 960 & 995.
    There is a growing problem of parental child abduction. The Hague Convention on the Civil Aspects of International Child Abduction, 1980, contains measures designed to ensure that the signatories to the Convention will, subject to certain exceptions, return a child that has been abducted to the country in which it was habitually resident prior to the abduction

Agreements as to Custody

As has been seen, at common law, as in the case formerly of an agreement by a father to curtail his rights to determine a child's education, any agreement by which he purported to assign the custody of his minor to another, was contrary to public policy and void. As a consequence of this, section 2 of the Custody of Infants Act was enacted in 1873. This section was re-enacted in Section 18(2) of the 1964 Act and reads:

"A provision contained in any separation agreement made between the father and mother of an infant shall not be invalid by reason only of its providing that one of them shall give up the custody or control of the infant to the other."

If any agreement made is contrary to a child's welfare it will not be enforced by the courts[147] and irrespective of the contents of any such agreement, either parent may apply to the court to vary arrangements formerly agreed in respect of a child's custody. The court in determining such application is bound by section 3 of the Act of 1964 to regard the welfare of the child as the first and paramount consideration and is not in any way bound by the terms of the parties' agreement.

An agreement between parents and third parties is unaffected by section 18(2) and is still void, though it might be evidence of a parent having abandoned his parental rights.[148]

Effect of a Mensa Et Thoro Decree

Section 18(1) of the 1964 Act states:

"In any case where a decree for divorce *a mensa et thoro* is pronounced, the court may thereby declare the parent by reason of whose misconduct the decree is made to be a person unfit to have the custody of the children (if any) of the marriage or of any children adopted under the Adoption Act, 1952, by the parents jointly; and in such case, the parent so declared to be unfit shall not, on the death of the other parent, be entitled as of right to the custody of the children."

This sub-section is in essence a re-enactment of section 7 of the Act of 1886. The effect of such a declaration is not to award custody of a child to a particular parent. Upon a petition for a decree of divorce *a mensa et thoro* the court has no

---

and the Council of Europe Convention on the Recognition and Enforcement of Decisions Concerning Custody of Children and on the Restoration of Custody of Children, 1980, is concerned with the recognition and enforcement of custody decisions made in other jurisdictions. Domestic effect has now been given to these conventions in the United Kingdom with the enactment of the Child Abduction & Custody Act, 1985. The Irish Law Reform Commission in its report on the Hague Convention (Report No. 12, June 1985) recommends that Ireland should become a party to it and that domestic legislation should be enacted giving the force of law to the convention. The report also refers to the European Convention, which was signed by Ireland, subject to ratification, on the 20th of May 1980 and notes that the Department of Justice is currently considering the issue of its ratification. The full text of the Hague Convention can be found in the appendix to the Law Reform Commission's Report. See also, Anton, "The Hague Convention on International Child Abduction" (1981) 30 I.C.L.Q. 537. See further, J.P. McCutcheon, "Child Abduction: A New Offence" (1985) 3 I.L.T. (n.s.) 233.

147. See *Cullen v. Cullen, supra* where O'Dalaigh C.J. stated "the court's duty in considering the interests of the children transcends the agreement of the parents as to the custody of the children". Also see *In re Besant* (1879) 11 Ch. D. 508 (C.A.).

148. See p. 377 *et seq.*

jurisdiction to do so. Its effect is to put an onus on the parent against whom a declaration is made, to show, if and when the question of the custody of the child arises, that he has so altered his mode of conduct from what it was before the declaration was made, to have become a fit and proper person to be entrusted with the care of his child.[149] In exercising its discretion to declare such a parent unfit, the court must be guided by the paramount consideration of the welfare of the child. As the welfare of the child is the paramount consideration, the parents' conduct, as in the case where no *mensa et thoro* action has been brought, should only be relevant in assessing their character as parents, not as spouses. It has been constantly stated that an award of custody is not a prize for good matrimonial behaviour. It is submitted that in *mensa et thoro* proceedings the court is more concerned with the parents' character as spouses and that in the absence of jurisdiction to examine their character as parents, the court cannot properly decide whether such a declaration would be in the interest of a child's welfare or not. As yet no order has been made under this section. The section is anomalous and should be repealed.[150]

Appeals/Variations

If a case is first determined in the District Court, an appeal lies to the Circuit Court. If a case is first determined in the Circuit Court, an appeal lies to the High Court. Both Circuit and High Court appeals are determined on oral evidence after a complete rehearing of the case appealed. If a case is first determined by the High Court, an appeal lies to the Supreme Court. A Supreme Court appeal is normally determined on the basis of the original evidence presented in the High Court. However, the Supreme Court has stated that if it is necessary or desirable, in the interests of a child's welfare, evidence not presented to the High Court can be examined by it on appeal, although it has expressed a preference for such new evidence normally being presented before the High Court by way of a case being re-entered before that court.[151]

Any order made by a court under Part II of the Act is not final and may be varied upon the application of either party establishing that it is in the interests of a child's welfare that a variation order be made.[152] A variation application is usually made to the court that made the original order. Section 15 of the Courts Act, 1981, however, also provides that either the District Court or Circuit Court may vary or revoke an order made by the High Court prior to the 12th of May 1982, if the circumstances to which the order of the High Court related have changed. In the case of the variation or revocation of such an order by the District Court, it should also be established that the provisions of the order would have been within the jurisdiction of the District Court if the Courts Act, 1981, had been in force at the date when the order was made.

---

149. See *Carey v. Carey* [1935] N.I. 144 (C.A.).

150. The Law Reform Commission in its report on Divorce *a Mensa et Thoro* (Report No. 8 at p. 58).

151. *B. v. B.* [1975] I.R. 54 (S.C.). See, however, *E.K. v. M.K.* where the Supreme Court refused to hear medical evidence that had not been heard in the High Court. See in particularly judgement of Henchy J.

152. Guardianship of Infants Act, 1964, Sect. 12 – see particularly *B. v. B.* (December, 1974) unreported (H.C.) this case was the subject of continual application for variation over a period of six years. See also the recent case of *C.O.B. v. A.O.B.* (November, 1985) unreported (H.C.) in which Lynch J. varied a custody order previously made and transferred the custody of a 12 year old boy from the mother to the father. The mother suffered from alcoholism and did not appear at the two day court hearing. Evidence was given that she had said she "had no intention of coming to court".

Guardianship and Custody on Parents' Death

By section 6 of the 1964 Act, on the death of either parent, the surviving parent is guardian of any infants of the marriage. Both parents have the power to appoint a testamentary guardian to act after their death, and if one is appointed, he acts jointly with the surviving parent. If the surviving parent objects to the testamentary guardian or the testamentary guardian considers the surviving parent unfit to have the custody of the infant, the latter may institute proceedings. In such proceedings the court may decide that the parent is to be the sole guardian, that both parent and testamentary guardian are to act jointly or that the latter is to act as guardian to the exclusion, so far as the court thinks proper, of the surviving parent. If the last decision is made the court must make an order as to custody and access to the infant and may order the parent to pay a reasonable sum to the guardian for the maintenance of the infant.[153]

A parent may appoint a guardian by either deed or will.[154] The court has power to appoint a guardian also if a deceased parent has not done so or if the appointed guardian or guardians are dead or refuse to act.[155] Any person interested in a child's welfare can apply to the court to be appointed guardian.[156] The court has a general power to remove from office any guardian appointed by will or deed or by order of the court.[157] It may appoint another guardian in place of one so removed or in place of a guardian appointed by court order who dies.[158]

A guardian appointed to act jointly with a surviving parent continues to act upon the death of such parent.[159] Where guardians are appointed by both parents, after the death of the surviving parent they act jointly.[160] Finally, where two or more persons are appointed to be guardians, on the death of either of them, the survivor continues to act.[161]

Generally speaking a guardian has the same rights and duties *vis-à-vis* a child as a parent. However, in relation to a child's education, secular or religious, he must observe the wishes of the child's parents unless they are contrary to the child's welfare. In relation to any property belonging to the child over which he has control, he is regarded as a trustee.

The guardian or guardians, as we have already seen, can apply to the court for its direction on any question affecting the welfare of the infant.[162] The court in reaching a determination must give paramount consideration to the welfare of the infant.[163] The guardians' duties automatically terminate upon a child becoming 18 years of age, or upon the death of the child.

---

153. Guardianship of Infants Act, 1964, Sect. 7.
154. *Ibid.*, Sect. 7(1) and Sect. 7(3).
155. *Ibid.*, Sect. 8(2). See *J. v. D. and others* (January, 1977) unreported (H.C.); June, 1977) unreported (S.C.).
156. *Ibid.*, Sect. 8(1).
157. *Ibid.*, Sect. 8(4).
158. *Ibid.*, Sect. 8(5).
159. *Ibid.*, Sect. 8(3).
160. *Ibid.*, Sect. 9(2).
161. *Ibid.*, Sect. 9(1).
162. *Ibid.*, Sect. 11(1). See *In re Meade, Applicant* [1971] I.R. 327 (H.C.). For the limitation on such applications see *In the Matter of J.S. an Infant* (1977) 111 I.L.T.R. 146 (H.C.).
163. *Ibid.*, Sect. 3.

Part III of Act of 1964

Part III of the Act of 1964, sections 14 to 17, in effect re-enact the provisions of the Custody of Children's Act, 1891. These provisions historically applied to Habeas Corpus applications to the High Court.[1] The Courts Act, 1981, now provides for their application to proceedings brought in both the District and Circuit Courts. Part III of the Act of 1964 primarily relates to disputes between parents and third parties. It may also apply to a dispute between parents[2] if either parent brings proceedings against the other to enforce a right to custody,[3] but in practice such a dispute is normally resolved by the courts without any judicial reference to Part III of the Act. It is thus intended to discuss Part III in the following section.

DISPUTES BETWEEN PARENTS AND THIRD PARTIES[4]

Methods of Resolving Custody Disputes

If a parent wishes to regain custody over his child from a third party he can bring Habeas Corpus proceedings, proceedings under section 11 of the Act of 1964, or wardship proceedings. Alternatively, if a third party wishes to bring a custody action against a parent he will have to commence proceedings to have the child made a ward of court and himself awarded custody.[5] Wardship proceedings are dealt with in the next section. This section is concerned with the bringing of either of the first two above mentioned proceedings by a parent so as to enforce the parental right to custody.

History of Parental Right

At common law the general rule was that a parent had an absolute right, unless guilty of extreme misconduct, as against a third party to the guardianship and custody of his children. Any agreement between a parent and another whereby a parent deprived himself of custody of his children was absolutely ineffective and the parent could at any time resume control over them. However, if a parent did relinquish control after 1877, the courts were governed by the Chancery rule that if they were satisfied that to return the child to the

---

1. In practice, in recent years, both the High Court and the Supreme Court have referred to the provisions in Part III of the Act when determining custody disputes between parents and third parties in proceedings instituted by parents under section 11 of the Act which is contained in Part II. See for example, *J. v. D. & Ors.* (January, 1977) unreported (H.C.); (June, 1977) unreported (S.C.); *S. v. The Eastern Health Board & Ors.* (February, 1979) unreported (H.C.); *P.W. v. A.W. & Ors.* (April, 1980) unreported (H.C.).
2. See e.g. *In re Story, Infants, supra*. See, however, *Campbell v. Campbell* [1956] S.C. 285 (Ct. of Sess.) in which it was held that these provisions of the Act of 1891 only applied to disputes between a parent and a third party and not as between parents; see also Halsbury – "Law of England", 3rd Edition, Vol. 21 (Butterworths, London 1957), 196.
3. See, e.g. *Donnellan v. Donnellan, Irish Times* 22nd and 27th Oct. 1976. Mrs D. was granted custody of her five year old daughter by the High Court. Four months later, Mr D. disappeared with the child when exercising his right of access to it. Upon the wife's application, a conditional order of Habeas Corpus was granted, requiring Mr D. to produce the child in Court. Upon him failing to do so, a warrant was issued for his arrest.
4. A "third party" in the pages that follow refers to a person who is neither a parent nor a legally appointed guardian of the child in question.
5. It has been held, however, that upon an application for custody by a parent in proceedings brought against a third party, the court may make a custody order in favour of the third party. See *J. v. D. and Ors., supra*. See *P.W. v. A.W. and Ors., supra*. See also *Re J.L. (a · Minor)* (March, 1978) unreported (H.C., P.) in which Finlay P. stated: "I would be prepared to hold that the powers conferred by Sections 14 and 16 of the Act of 1964 to deprive a parent of the custody of its child must imply as a necessary corollary a power to place the child in the custody of another".

custody of its parent would be harmful to its welfare, then, even though the parent was guilty of no misconduct, they could refuse to do so. However, the attitude of the courts was that, *prima facie*, it was contrary to a child's welfare to remove it from the custody of its natural parents and to place it in the custody of persons with no natural relationship to it, that "generally speaking, the best place for a child is with its parents".[6]

The Act of 1964 and Disputes as to Custody

Today the principle laid down in section 3 of the Guardianship of Infants Act, 1964, that the welfare of the child is to be regarded as the first and paramount consideration applies to all disputes as to the custody of a child. Thus, the matters previously discussed as comprising the various elements in a child's welfare also apply in disputes between parents and strangers. There has emerged, however, over the past twenty years a considerable divergence in the judicial approach to the application of the welfare principle to custody disputes between parents and third parties as compared to its application to custody disputes simply between parents. This has now become one of the most difficult problems in family law. It is intended first to examine the specific statutory provisions contained in Part III of the Act of 1964 and then to consider the difficulties that have been encountered in the application of the welfare principle to the resolution of custody disputes between parents and third parties.

Sections 14 to 16 of the 1964 Act are of particular relevance in custody disputes between parents and third parties. They read as follows:

14.—Where a parent[7] of an infant applies to the court for an order for the production of the infant and the court is of opinion that that parent has abandoned or deserted the infant, or that he has otherwise so conducted himself that the court should refuse to enforce his right to the custody of the infant, the court may in its discretion decline to make the order.

15.—Where, upon application by a parent for the production of an infant, the court finds—

(a) that the infant is being brought up at the expense of another person,[8] or

(b) that at any time assistance has been provided for the infant by a health authority under section 55 of the Health Act, 1953,

the court may, in its discretion, if it orders the infant to be given up to the parent, further order that the parent shall pay to that person or health authority the whole of the costs properly incurred by the person or health authority in bringing up or providing assistance for the infant or such portion thereof as the court considers reasonable, having regard to all the circumstances of the case, including, in particular, the means of the parent.

---

6. Lord Esher in *R. v. Gyngall, supra*, at p. 243.
7. Under Part III, "Parent" includes a guardian of the person and any person at law liable to maintain an infant or entitled to his custody — Sect. 13 of the 1964 Act.
8. "Person" includes any school or institution; *ibid.*

16.–Where a parent has–

(a) abandoned or deserted an infant, or

(b) allowed an infant to be brought up by another person at that person's expense, or to be provided with assistance by a health authority under section 55 of the Health Act, 1953, for such a length of time and under such circumstances as to satisfy the court that the parent was unmindful of his parental duties,

the court shall not make an order for the delivery of the infant to the parent unless the parent has satisfied the court that he is a fit person to have the custody of the infant.

The provisions of section 14 and 16 are essentially inter-related. A parent found to have misbehaved in a manner described in section 16 must satisfy the court that he is "a fit person" to have custody before an order for custody can be made in his favour. However, even if he so satisfies the court, the court may by virtue of the discretion conferred upon it by section 14, refuse to grant custody to the parent, if the court when having regard to the child's welfare concludes that it is in the interests of the child's welfare that a different order as to custody be made.[9] If the court is of the opinion that a parent ought not to have custody of a child, it may make such order as it thinks fit to ensure that the child is brought up in the religion in which the parent or parents desire it to be brought up. The court is given statutory authority to consult the wishes of a child in considering what order ought to be made and any right which the child possesses to exercise his own free choice is said not to be diminished by the 1964 Act.[10]

Sections 14–16 of the 1964 Act basically re-enact the statutory provisions contained in the Custody of Children Act, 1891. It is thus intended to examine a number of leading pre-1964 cases in which the provisions of the 1891 Act were discussed and interpreted and then to look at more recent cases, and discuss the effects of the Constitution on the present Act. As will be seen in the pages that follow, a number of the cases that precede the coming into force of the Adoption Act, 1952, involve parents attempting to regain custody of a child some time after concluding an "adoption agreement" with a third party, whilst many of those after 1952 concern natural parents seeking to regain custody of a child in respect of whom an adoption placement or an invalid adoption order has been made. Where a section of the 1891 Act is referred to in the text that follows, the corresponding provision in the 1964 Act is set down in the footnotes.

The case which is at the foundation of the modern law in this area is *R. v. Gyngall*.[11] In this case a widowed Roman Catholic mother was refused custody of her 15 year old daughter, who had been brought up for a number of years in a Protestant institution. The Court of Appeal found that the mother had been "obliged to earn her living by moving from place to place, and from country to country", and had not been able herself to bring up the child, the child being

9. See *S. v. The Eastern Health Board & Ors.* (February, 1979) unreported (H.C.). This case involved a custody claim by an unmarried mother. Whether the abandonment or desertion of an infant would, of itself, be regarded as a "compelling reason" or a failure on the part of a parent under Article 42.5 of the Constitution so as to justify depriving a "fit" parent of custody of a legitimate child in accordance with the new test articulated by the Supreme Court in *K.C. & A.C. v. An Bord Uchtála* [1985] 5 I.L.R.M. 302 (S.C.) is now open to question. See further p. 392 *et seq.*

10. See Guardianship of Infants Act, 1964, Sect. 17 and see p. 368 *ante.*

11. *Supra.*

placed with other people for long periods. It was thought likely that if she was granted custody, within a short time the girl would be again institutionalised. The court was satisfied that the mother had been guilty of no misconduct or fault but as the overriding consideration was the child's welfare and happiness, taking into account her age, her wish to stay where she was, the fact that she now entertained Protestant views and that she would very shortly be in a position to earn her own living, it held that the mother's natural right must be superseded.

In the Irish Court of Appeal in *In re Elliott an Infant*[12] the court followed the principle laid down by the Divisional Court[13] in Gyngall's case. In 1884 Mary Elliott when only six years old with her mother's assistance or connivance was committed to nine years in an industrial school by the Thurles magistrates. Mary's mother was a Catholic and the industrial school was under the charge of Roman Catholic nuns. Upon the termination of the nine years her uncle, who was a Protestant, attempted to obtain custody of Mary. The mother, who had remarried and was living in England, permitted her name to be used in an application for a writ of Habeas Corpus. Holmes J.[14] noted that the mother was not seeking custody for herself:

> "I would not consider this, taken by itself, as a very important element in the case, for I think that a mother, if she is not possessed of means herself, may select a relative who has means, and who is willing to undertake to stand in her place as the custodian of her child, but it withdraws from our consideration such topics as the cultivation of filial affection and the personal association of the parent with a child, to which great weight ought to be given. Secondly, the education of this girl has been hitherto conducted in the industrial school upon a definite and distinct plan, leading to a definite and distinct end, namely, to placing her in a position in life where she would be able to earn a respectable livelihood by her own exertions; and if she be now removed from the nuns' care this plan will be broken in upon".[15]

Having interviewed the girl the court was satisfied "that as far as she herself is concerned she wishes to remain with the nuns, in the belief that her material prospects, and her hopes of becoming independent will be more advanced by this course". The court regarded her views as sound and reasonable and also bore "in mind the fact that this application comes before us within six weeks of the time when the child, having attained 16 years of age will be able to select her own place of residence".[16]

In re O'Hara, an Infant,[17] was the first Irish case in which the Custody of Children's Act, 1891 was discussed. On the 5th October 1897 an agreement in writing was entered into between the mother and one McMahon, whereby she agreed to give her nine year old daughter to McMahon and to have no more claim on her, and McMahon agreed to adopt the child. The child had resided in

---

12. (1893) 32 L.R. Ir. 504 (C.A.).
13. 9 Times Rep. 47.
14. Stating (at p. 508) the question to decide was "what order will be best for the moral, mental and material welfare of the infant?"
15. *In re Elliot, an Infant, supra*, at pp. 507, 508.
16. *Ibid.*, p. 508; Holmes J. also stated at p. 509 that "the question of religion . . . has not affected our decision. At her age and after nine years of conventual instruction Mary Elliot has now received fixed religious convictions if her mind is capable of them, and her uncle disclaims any inclination to interfere with them. On the one hand, it is much too late to have her instructed in her father's religion. On the other hand, we would not be justified in refusing this application on the grounds that the relatives, with whom her mother wishes her to live, are Protestants".
17. [1900] 2 I.R. 232; (1899) 34 I.L.T.R. 17 (C.A.).

an orphanage since she was two years of age due to her mother's poor circumstances following the death of her husband, the child's father. In May 1898 the mother married a small farmer. In the beginning of 1899 she demanded the return of her daughter from McMahon who refused to give her back unless he was paid £8.50 expenses for her support and maintenance. The High Court refused to return the child to the mother, one of the reasons being the child's express desire to remain with the McMahons. Fitzgibbon L.J. in the Court of Appeal, while approving of the practice of ascertaining the views of a young child, commented that

> "the parent's *prima facie* right must also be considered and the wishes of a child of tender years must not be permitted . . . to subvert the whole law of the family, or to prevail against the desire and authority of the parent, unless the welfare of the child cannot otherwise be secured".[18]

Referring to the agreement signed by the mother, he stated that the law did "not recognise the power of bindingly abdicating either parental right or parental duty".[19]

As for the general principles applicable in determining proceedings of this nature, he noted that since the Judicature Act the court was bound by the chancery jurisdiction under which "the main consideration was the welfare of the child" and continued,

> "In exercising the jurisdiction to control or to ignore the parental right (to custody) the court must act cautiously . . . and (act) in opposition to the parent only when judicially satisfied that the welfare of the child requires that the parental right should be suspended or superseded[20] . . . It appears to me that misconduct or unmindfulness of parental duty or inability to provide for the welfare of the child must be shown before the natural right can be displaced. Where a parent is of blameless life and is able and willing to provide for the child's material and moral necessities . . . the court is, in my opinion, judicially bound to act on what is equally a law of nature and of society and to hold . . . that 'the best place for a child is with its parent'. Of course I do not speak of exceptional cases . . . where special disturbing elements exist, which involve the risk of moral or material injury to the child, such as the disturbance of religious convictions or of settled affections, or the endurance of hardship or destitution with a parent, as contrasted with solid advantages offered elsewhere. The court, acting as a wise parent, is not bound to sacrifice the child's welfare to the fetish of parental authority, by forcing it from a happy and comfortable home to share the fortunes of a parent, however innocent, who cannot keep a roof over its head, or provide it with the necessaries of life."[21]

---

18. [1900] 2 I.R. 232 at p. 240.
19. *Ibid.*, at p. 241.
20. In *B. v. B.* [1975] I.R. 54 (S.C.) a custody dispute between parents, Walsh J. discussing the provisions of the Act of 1964 stated (pp. 61–62) that:
> "The Act does not purport to encourage any alteration of the established practice of the courts that they must act very cautiously in exercising the jurisdiction to interfere with parental rights, and the court will act in opposition to the parent or parents only when judicially satisfied that the welfare of the child requires that the wishes of the parent or parents should be over-ruled."
21. [1900] 2 I.R. 232 at pp. 239, 240, 241.

Referring to section 3[22] of the 1891 Act, he continued

"The phrase in the Act which most nearly fits the present case is that which speaks of a parent having 'allowed his child to be brought up by another person at that person's expense'; but that phrase occurs in connection with abandonment and desertion and is qualified by the words 'for such a length of time and under such circumstances as to satisfy the Court that the parent *was unmindful of his parental duties*'. On the construction of the Act I hold that the surrender of a child to an adopted parent as an act of prudence or of necessity, under the pressure of present inability to maintain it, being an act done in the interest of the child, cannot be regarded as abandonment or desertion or even as unmindfulness of parental duty within the meaning of the Act."[23]

Holmes J. felt that the provisions of the 1891 Act gave "little or no assistance" in determining the application for custody. The court, he stated, must decide

"(1)   whether the mother by her conduct has disabled herself from making the application; and, if she has not

(2)   whether it is more for the welfare of the child that she should remain in the house and under the care of the McMahons".[24]

Further on, he stated:

"A mother entitled *prima facie*, as guardian by nurture, to the custody of her child may fail to make good her right to such custody, by reason of her own conduct, or, where no valid objection can be taken thereto, for reasons connected with the welfare of the child."[25]

He went on to hold, as did the other members of the court, that the mother had not misconducted herself and that it was in the interests of the child's welfare that she be returned to her mother's custody.

That a parent forced by economic circumstances to give custody of his children to third parties was not guilty of abandonment or unmindful of his duties was further stated in the *State (Kavanagh) v. O'Sullivan.*[26] Kavanagh's wife after the birth of their three children became mentally ill and was confined to a mental home. Kavanagh was a Protestant and the children with their mother's agreement had been baptised and brought up as Protestants. The mother was a Catholic. Kavanagh lived in a tenement house and sometimes worked nights. With no one to mind the children in his absence, he got heavily in debt and, wishing to prevent their starvation, agreed to their being admitted to a Catholic institution whose main pre-condition was that the children be baptised Roman Catholic. A year and a half later he obtained a writ of Habeas Corpus to regain custody of the children. In the action it was alleged that he was not a fit person to have their custody by virtue of sub-s. (b) of section 3 of the 1891 Act.[27]

---

22. The equivalent of Sect. 16 of the 1964 Act.

23. *Ibid.*, at p. 244. See also *Re Hyndman, Infants* (1905) 39 I.L.T.R. 191 (K.B.D.); *In the matter of M.E. Bell, an Infant* (1909) 43 I.L.T.R. 35 (K.B.D.). On the other hand, see *In re Boyd* [1918] 2 I.R. 98 (K.B.D.) — In this case, a mother claimed the custody of her 13 year old son who had resided with her sister for six years. The Court being of the opinion that it was for the child's benefit to remain with the sister, refused the mother's application for a writ of Habeas Corpus. See also article "The Custody of Infants" in (1918) 52 I.L.T. & S.J. pp. 295—6.

24. [1900] 2 I.R. at p. 251.

25. *Ibid.*

26. [1933] I.R. 618; (1931) 68 I.L.T.R. 110 (S.C.).

27. The equivalent of Sect. 16(b) of the 1964 Act.

To this contention, Kennedy C.J. said:

> "So far from deserving censure for his action or being driven from a defence
> of his parental rights to the setting up under the Act of 1891 of his fitness
> as a parent to have custody of his children, he is rather to be commended
> for that, anxious for the well-being of his children, on the failure of his
> attempt to continue to carry on anything like a home . . . he took the most
> prudent action, the action best calculated in his unhappy situation to
> secure their welfare and to afford them protection against the danger
> surrounding them during the absence of their mother".[28]

If a parent has been unmindful of his duties or abandoned his child, the Act
gives him an opportunity of showing that notwithstanding the abandonment he
is a fit person and that it is in the interests of the child's welfare that he be
entrusted with its custody.

Thus, in the *State (Williams) v. Markey*[29] the Supreme Court gave parents
custody of their child, their having previously given it to another couple for
fear that the wife's mother would discover that its birth took place within five
months of the parents being married. It held that in the circumstances the
abandonment of the child was understandable and it did not indicate that the
parents were unfit to have custody. Having regard to the parents' better financial
circumstances, their desire to regain custody and to the fact that a "cloud of
suspicion always darkens the life of a child where the circumstances of its
adoption are obscure"[30] it was for the welfare of the child that it should return
to the custody of its parents.

Alternatively, in *In the Matter of M. Skeffington*[31] the court refused to grant
a writ of Habeas Corpus to a father so as to force his child's grandmother to
return the child to his custody. The child had been in the custody of the grandmother from the age of three and was 11 years old at the date of the application. The parents had had an unhappy marriage having been separated and
reconciled on numerous occasions. At the time of the application to the court
they were again living together. The court held that the father had allowed the
child to be brought up at another's expense and had been unmindful of his parental
duties. Further, having regard to the history of the marriage it felt that there was
"nothing in the nature of permanency in the home",[32] and that consequently
the father was not a fit person to be granted custody, having regard to the
interests of the child.[33]

In the recent case of *S. v. E.H.B. and Ors.*[34] the court held that the mother
of an illegitimate child had not abandoned her child by leaving it in a children's
home. The child had been born in June 1977 and the mother regularly visited it
in the home until August. From August until December 1977 she did not visit

---

28. [1933] I.R. 618 at p. 636.
29. [1940] I.R. 421; (1939) 74 I.L.T.R. 237 (S.C.).
30. [1940] I.R. 421 at p. 437 *per* Meredith J.
31. (1908) 43 I.L.T.R. 245 (K.B.D.). See also *In re Boyd, supra*.
32. *Supra* at p. 246 *per* Palles L.C.B.
33. See further, *O'N. v. O'B. and Ors.* (January, 1980) unreported (H.C.) in which
Finlay P. returned to the mother's custody a child that had been in the custody of the
mother's parents for six years.
   In *In re Cullinane, an Infant* [1954] I.R. 270 (H.C.), a case involving a dispute as to the
custody of an illegitimate child, the limitations of the 1891 Act were demonstrated. Here,
the court stated that the *wishes* of a mother as to who should have custody of her child
were not to be disregarded, even if she had let it be brought up at another's expense for so
long as to satisfy the court that she had been unmindful of her parental duties. As she was
not seeking custody, the section was said to have no application to the proceedings.
34. (February, 1979) unreported (H.C.). See also p. 311.

and made no contact with the home. Referring to section 14 and 16 of the 1964 Act, Finlay, P. stated

"Abandonment in these two sections must, in my view, be construed as total neglect, the leaving of an infant with the knowledge that there is nobody to care for it or look after it."

There was no abandonment in this case as there was no possibility that those in charge of the home would fail to care for the child. However, the mother was held to have deserted her child, as "she took no steps of any description to ascertain its welfare, to provide for its welfare or to engage the services of others who would provide for its welfare". In particular during that period she refused to communicate with the authorities of the children's home and that "must be viewed in the light of the fact that some urgent question of the welfare of the child might have required to be dealt with ... Her conduct was prompted to a large extent by an escapism and one which is understandable. Desertion however does not necessarily mean heartless or wanton desertion."

Finlay P. concluded on the evidence that the mother was, at the date of the proceedings, a fit person to have custody stating "that finding constitutes a finding only that there is nothing in her make-up arising from her personality or from any physical, emotional or psychiatric abnormality which would prevent her from being capable of caring for a young infant."

Nevertheless, having regard to the best interests of the child the court made an order dispensing with the mother's consent to the making of an adoption order, as sought by the prospective adopters with whom the child had been placed. The child at the date of the proceedings was 20 months old and had resided continuously with the adopters since the age of 6 months save for a two week break.[35]

THE 1937 CONSTITUTION AND THE WELFARE PRINCIPLE

Since the enactment of the 1937 Constitution there has been discernible in some judicial decisions a change of emphasis on the part of the courts. In making reference to the provisions of Articles 41 and 42 of the Constitution greater stress has been placed on parental rights and the parental position appears to

---

35. See also *The State (P.M.) v. G.M.* (November, 1984) unreported (H.C.) in which Finlay P. held that an unmarried mother who had placed her child for adoption and had made regular enquiries as to its well being had neither deserted nor abandoned her child nor so conducted herself that the court should refuse to enforce her right to custody under section 14 of the Act of 1964. It was also held that the mother had not been "unmindful of her parental duty" within the meaning of section 16 of the Act. Nevertheless, the court's view was that it was in the best interests of the child that the mother's consent be dispensed with so as to enable the Adoption Board make an adoption order in favour of adopters. At the date of the court judgement, the child was sixteen months old and had resided with the adopters since it was ten days old, never having resided with the mother. In *S.M. & M.M. v. An Bord Uchtála & Ors.* (May, 1984) unreported (H.C.) Lynch J. also made a finding that an unmarried mother who had placed her child for adoption had not "abandoned or deserted the child or was (not) unmindful of her parental duty so as to forfeit, pursuant to section 14 or section 16 of the 1964 Act her right to custody under that Act. See further p. 315 *ante.*

36. See *In re Art. 26 and the School Attendance Bill* 1942 (1943) I.R. 334; (1943) 771 I.L.T.R. 96 (S.C.); *In re Doyle, an Infant* [1956] I.R. 213 (H.C.); (21st December, 1955) unreported (S.C.); see also J.M. Kelly, *Fundamental Rights*, p. 211 and *The Irish Constitution*, Second Ed. p. 631 *et seq*; "Children's Rights Under the Irish Constitution", Irish Council for Civil Liberties Report No. 2 (Dublin, January 1977); M. Staines, "The Concept of 'The Family' under the Irish Constitution" (1976) 11 I.J. (n.s.) 223.

have been strengthened *vis-à-vis* other individuals and the State.[36] This strength-
ening of parental authority and emphasis on parental rights has given rise to the
suggestion that section 3 of the Act of 1964 may be unconstitutional in so far
as the section requires the courts to regard a legitimate child's welfare as the first
and paramount consideration in the determination of custody disputes between
parents and third parties.[37] A considerable divergence in judicial approach is evident in the decided cases in which written judgements have been delivered on this
issue and, as a result, the current law in this area is unclear and the exact principles applicable to the resolution of such disputes uncertain

It is now intended to examine those cases involving a dispute as to the custody
of a legitimate child between parents and third parties in which the effect of the
family provisions contained in the Constitution on section 3 of the Act of 1964
has been discussed and a number of other cases in which written judgements
have been delivered, to which this issue is of relevance.

In *In re J.*[38] an unmarried mother gave birth to a child in November 1964
and a month after its birth signed a written consent to its adoption. Less than a
week later, the child was placed with prospective adopters and in July 1965 an
adoption order was made. One and a half weeks after the making of the order
the mother married the child's father. In February 1966 the adoption order was
quashed as the mother's consent was invalid, being given in breach of a statutory
provision. The natural parents sought custody of the child and obtained a conditional order of Habeas Corpus. At the hearing it was submitted that the infant
had been legitimated[39] and that they were entitled to have custody of the infant
as its parents, because they, with the infant, constituted a family within the
meaning of Articles 41 and 42 of the Constitution. The adopters submitted that
they could provide a more secure financial background for the child, that the
child would be harmed by a change in custody and that the court should regard
the welfare of the infant as the first and paramount consideration. The High
Court ordered that the child be returned to the custody of its married parents.
Henchy J. having held that the father, mother and child constituted a family for
the purposes of Articles 41 and 42,[40] stated that the case was not one that
could be brought within Article 42.5, there being nothing culpabale on the part
of the parents, and that it would be impossible to give effect to the parents'
right and duty of education if they were deprived of custody. He continued:

> "If I am correct in my application of the Constitution to the facts of this
> case, the parents' right to the custody of the child is conclusively established
> without looking further than Articles 41 and 42. But counsel for the adopters
> say that S. 3 of the Guardianship of Infants Act, 1964 requires that in
> deciding the question of custody we must regard the welfare of the infant as
> the first and paramount consideration . . . Having regard to the inalienable
> right and duty of parents to provide for the education of their children and

37. *In re Corcoran, supra* — Murnaghan J. referring to the English Guardianship of
Infants Act, 1925 suggested that a law which did not allow the rights and claims of a parent
to the custody of his child to be considered except in their relation to "considerations
affecting the welfare of the child" would be inconsistent with the Constitution. *In re O'Brien*
[1954] I.R. 1; (1953) 87 I.L.T.R. 156 (S.C.), Byrne J. stated that the court assumed without deciding that Sect. 3 of the Custody of Children Act, 1891 was consistent with the
Constitution. See also *In re Blake*, deceased [1958] I.R. 89 (H.C.); *In re Doyle, an Infant,
supra*. See further (1956) 90 I.L.T. & S.J. pp. 53—55, "Some Observations of The Children's
Act 1941"; M.V. O'Mahony, "Legal Aspects of Residential Child Care" (1971) 6 I.J. (n.s.)
217; *Burke and O'Reilly v. Burke and Quail* [1951] I.R. 216; (1950) 84 I.L.T.R. 70 (H.C.).
38. [1966] I.R. 195 (H.C.); see also p. 7 and p. 283 *ante*.
39. By virtue of Legitimacy Act, 1931; see Chapter 11.
40. See p. 7 *ante*.

their right in appropriate cases to obtain custody of the children for that purpose, I consider that S. 3 must be interpreted in one or other of the following ways: first by regarding it as unconstitutional, or secondly, by reading it in conjunction with Articles 41 and 42 as stating, in effect, that the welfare of the infant in the present case coincides with the parents' right to custody ... I expressly reserve an opinion (counsel not having raised the matter) as to whether it was competent for the Legislature to provide that in a case such as this, where the parents are jointly seeking custody of their child for the purpose of giving effect to their inalienable right and duty to provide for its education, the Court should be bound to decide the question of custody by regarding the welfare of the infant as the first and paramount consideration."[41]

Teevan J. stated that it was well established that the child had an excellent home[42] and it would be "a sad parting and one that *must*[43] deeply affect the child, with the undoubted prospect of some permanent effect".[44] He stated however, that the parents' right to custody was absolute until forfeited in a way already well defined in many authoritive cases and in section 14 of the 1964 Act

"Nothing has been or can be urged to suggest their unfitness for their responsibilities and duties as parents ... In such circumstances the court must presume that restoration to her parents is the best thing for the child's welfare".[45]

As for section 3 and the argument that the child's welfare would be more secure in the adopters' home he went on

"To be valid it would have to be shown that S. 3 ... effects a change in the law as it stood prior to that enactment, and that the section purports to diminish or curtail the rights of parents to the absolute control over their children. If it does then ... a question of its constitutionality might arise. We are not however, confronted with any such question in this case."[46]

In *McL. v. An Bord Uchtála and the A.-G.*[47] no reference was made either to section 3 of the 1964 Act or its constitutionality. The Supreme Court granted declarations that an adoption order made five years earlier, in 1971, was null and void and that as a consequence the child in respect of whom the proceedings were brought was legitimated by its natural parents' marriage in 1972. The natural parents also sought an order directing that the child be placed in their custody. The child, who was by this time six years old, had never known its natural parents and had been in the care of its adoptive parents since the age of three months. The Supreme Court in granting custody to the natural parents made no mention of the provisions of the 1964 Act and in particular omitted to refer to the fact that the court was bound under section 3 of the Act in custody proceedings to regard the welfare of the infant "as the first and paramount consideration". The court seems to have presumed that once the adoption order was invalid, an order of custody had to be made. It failed to realise that the

41. *Supra* at p. 308.
42. With the adopters.
43. Author's italics.
44. *Supra* at p. 302.
45. *Ibid.*, at p. 304.
46. *Ibid.*, at p. 303.
47. [1977] I.R. 287 (S.C.). See also pp. 298 and 322 *ante*.

question as to whether the natural parents should be granted custody was a separate issue. Further, it determined the question of custody in the absence of the adopters.[48] As they were not parties to the proceedings, they had no opportunity to oppose the natural parents' application for custody.[49]

In *J. v. D. and Ors.*,[50] the plaintiff sought custody of his four children (three girls aged 14, 12 and 5 years and a boy aged 8½ years) following the death of his wife. The parties had married in 1961 and resided together in England. Twelve years after their marriage the parties separated and in July 1973 the plaintiff's wife, who was Irish, came to live in her father's home in Ireland with her children. Shortly afterwards, the plaintiff formed a relationship with another married woman, who subsequently was divorced. On the evidence, the court found that in the period that followed, the plaintiff showed no interest in his wife and children and made no contact with them. In October 1975 the wife died. The children remained in Ireland residing with their maternal aunts and their husbands.

In July 1976 the plaintiff issued proceedings under section 11 of the 1964 Act and in December 1976 he married the woman with whom he had been having a relationship. At the date of the hearing of the proceedings the two eldest girls were residing with one of the aunts and the youngest girl and the boy were each residing with a different aunt.

The plaintiff was unsuccessful in both the High Court and, on appeal, to the Supreme Court. It was held on the evidence that the plaintiff's failure to properly support his wife and children following their return to Ireland resulting in their being supported by his wife's sisters, his failure to defray even a portion of their expenses either before or after his wife's death and his failure to maintain contact with them amounted to an abandonment of his children. The maternal aunts were granted custody of each of the children in their care and were appointed guardians of them jointly with the plaintiff.

Referring to the Act of 1964, O'Higgins C.J. in his judgement noted that:

> "Neither in this court nor in the High Court has any question been raised as to the validity of the Guardianship of Infants Act or any part thereof having regard to the provisions of the Constitution. It falls therefore to this court to decide this appeal in accordance with the provisions of that Act and without regard to the difficult problems which could arise had its compatability with the provisions of Article 41 of the Constitution been raised."[51]

Further on, he said he was of the opinion that

> "in this case the welfare of each infant is best served by refusing the order sought by the plaintiff. For this reason alone in accordance with the provisions of Section 3 of the Act I would feel compelled to decide against the plaintiff ... I must add, however, that in my view the plaintiff's claim ought to fail both under Section 14 and under Section 16 of the Act. In my

48. The court order perfected in July 1976 does not contain a declaration as to custody although a majority of the Supreme Court made such a declaration when delivering judgement.
49. Subsequent to the Supreme Court decision, the adopters commenced proceedings seeking a declaration that they were not bound by the Supreme Court order as they were not afforded any opportunity to be heard and sought an order that the child remain in their custody. The natural parents sought an order of habeas corpus requiring the adopters to return their child to them. On the 6th of October 1976, it was announced to the President of the High Court that the actions had been settled. A consent was executed by the parties in which they agreed that the child be made a ward of court and remain in the custody and care of the adopters. See the *Irish Times*, 24th of July and 7th of October 1976.
50. (January, 1977) unreported (H.C.); (June, 1977) unreported (S.C.).
51. See p. 4 of judgement.

view, the plaintiff's conduct in relation to the infants would justify the court in declining to make an order under each of these sections."[52]

Kenny J. in his judgement agreed:

"that the welfare of all the children to whom this case relates requires that they should remain where they are now. It would be monstrous to hand them over to their father: they have roots, a settled way of life and a feeling of security where they are now . . . I have no doubt that giving them to their father would cause permanent psychological damage to them."[53]

As for the contention that "there is a *prima facie* parental right to custody" he stated:

"I deny that there is any natural or *prima facie* right of a parent to custody of his children: there is a rule of prudence that in most cases the best place for a child is with its parent".[54]

In disputes relating to custody the principles applicable, he continued, had not altered from those stated by Holmes L.J. in *Re O'Hara*, that is, a parent may be deprived of custody of a child "for reasons connected with the welfare of the child" even when a parent's conduct has been unobjectionable. In the learned judge's opinion

"The Constitution has not . . . altered this. Article 41 deals with the Family: the children are part of that unit and the authority of the family referred to in Article 41, Section 2, is that of the parents and children considered as a unit."[55]

However, in *G. v. An Bord Uchtála and Ors.*[56] Kenny J. again referring to the family provisions in the Constitution appeared to acknowledge that parents do have a constitutional right to the custody of their legitimate children. He stated:

"While the Constitution deals with the rights of parents of legitimate children and 'the natural and imprescriptible rights' of the child, it says nothing about the custody of legitimate or illegitimate children. As Article 42 acknowledges that the family is the primary and natural educator of the child and guarantees to respect the inalienable right and duty of parents to provide, according to their means for the religious and moral, intellectual, physical and social education of their children, it inferentially gives those who have married and are living together a constitutional right to the custody of their children."[57]

In the same case Henchy J. stated:

"The Constitution does not pronounce specifically on rights of custody, but it is necessarily inherent in the (constitutional) provisions I have cited that in the case of children whose parents were or have become married, the primary right to custody is vested in the parents."[58]

---

52. See p. 10 of judgement. The reference to Article 41 section 2 is mistaken. It is submitted that the learned judge in fact intended to refer to Art. 41.1.2.
53. See p. 1 of judgement.
54. See p. 2 of judgement.
55. See p. 4 of judgement.
56. [1980] I.R. 32 (S.C.).
57. *Ibid.*, at p. 97.
58. *Ibid.*, at p. 85.

In *G. v. An Bord Uchtála* the majority held that the natural mother of an illegitimate child has a constitutional right to the custody of her child which falls to be protected under Article 40.3. Both Henchy J. and Kenny J. dissented from this finding and denied that the mother of an illegitimate child has any such constitutional right. It is submitted, however, that it is clear that all members of the Supreme Court in this case were of the view that the parents of a legitimate child have such a constitutional right arising under Article 42 of the Constitution. This right is not, however, an absolute right. Walsh J., emphasising that the rights of both legitimate and illegitimate children are also protected by the Constitution, stated:

> "There is nothing in the Constitution to indicate that in cases of conflict the rights of the parent are always to be given primacy."[59]

Further on in his judgement he continued:

> "In Article 42.1 of the Constitution, the State recognises that the family itself is the primary and natural educator of the child, but it goes on to say that the State guarantees to respect the inalienable right and duty of parents to provide in accordance with their means for the religious and moral, intellectual, physical and social education of their children. Therefore such education is regarded both as a right and a duty of the parents; correlatively it is the right of the children to look to their parents and family for the fulfilment of their duty to supply, arrange for, or provide that education. If there is a failure to perform the duty, then the circumstances may be such that a transfer of custody is warranted."[60]

Referring to the Act of 1964, he stated:

> "Where the Guardianship of Infants Act, 1964 defines 'welfare' it is, as has been previously remarked in other cases, following the wording of the Constitution itself. It is also to be borne in mind that some inalienable rights are absolutely inalienable while others are relatively inalienable."[61]

In none of the above cases was the question of the constitutionality of section 3 an issue. The various judicial statements made merely confirmed that a question mark hangs over the constitutionality of the section and are illustrative of conflicting judicial approaches to the application of the welfare principle in the determination of disputes between parents and third parties. The statements are also clearly indicative of some judicial confusion as to the historical development of the law as to custody. In *In re J.* it is clear that the court held the view that prior to 1964, in the absence of fault on the part of parents, parental rights could not be curtailed and that a parent was automatically entitled to custody of his legitimate child unless he had done something culpable or committed some wrong in relation to the child. This, however, is not so. It is clear from the decided cases discussed earlier that since the Judicature Act, 1877, the courts have deprived parents of custody when to do so has been in the interests of the child's welfare, even when the parent has not been culpable or guilty of any misconduct. On the other hand, contrary to the view expressed by Kenny J. in

---

59. *Ibid.*, at p. 78. Walsh J. then cited with approval the first half of the passage from *In re Frost, Infants* [1947] I.R. 3 (S.C.) quoted on p. 348 *ante*.
60. *Ibid.*, at p. 79.
61. *Ibid.* See also *O'N. v. O'B. & Ors.*, *supra*, where Finlay P. stated that in deciding a dispute as to custody between a mother and grandparents "I can only do so looking at the problem from the dominant view of the welfare of the child" (see p. 18 of judgement).

J. v. D., it is also clear that in the absence of parental fault, the courts regarded it as *prima facie* in the interests of a child's welfare for it to be in its parents' custody.[62] In essence, the courts took the view that a child should be in its parents' custody unless judicially satisfied that the welfare of the child required that the wishes of the parents be overruled.[63]

In *P.W. v. A.W. and Ors.*[64] the constitutionality of section 3 finally arose for direct consideration. The facts of the case were found by the court to be as follows: The husband (P.W.) and wife (A.W.) had married in July 1963, and had four children. Since 1971, the wife had been in ill health, primarily due to a psychiatric illness and had required both in-patient and out-patient hospital treatment. Shortly after the fourth child's birth, in March 1974, due to A.W.'s inability to cope, the child went to live with the husband's sister (M.) and her husband. Originally, this was a temporary arrangement and the intention was that the child would return to reside with A.W. when she had sufficiently recovered her health. However, A.W. continued to be unwell and when the child was a few months old she "gave" the child to M. permanently. The child then continued to reside with M. In 1976 P.W. and A.W. separated. In November 1976 the High Court granted A.W. custody of the three eldest children and granted custody of the youngest child to M. In December 1977, the court provided for A.W.'s access to the child and the court was advised by her counsel that she wanted a further hearing relating to the child's custody. This hearing took place in April 1978, but no judgement was delivered, the court indicating that it wished to seek further assistance from a child psychiatrist who had given evidence at the hearing. The child continued to reside with M. and further access arrangements were made. The case came on for a final hearing in November 1979. By that date the child was 5½ years of age and the court found that she regarded M. and her husband as her parents.

Ellis J., holding that the child's welfare required that it remain in the custody of M., stated:

> "There is no natural or *prima facie* right of a parent to custody of his or her children but . . . there is a rule of prudence that in most cases the best place for a child is with its parents, but that there can be circumstances varying with each case, (not necessarily amounting to intentional misconduct or misbehaviour) to which valid objection can be taken in the interests of the welfare of a child, whereby the parent can lose custody of the child not only to another contending parent but to a stranger . . .[65] A removal now from the home and environment which Mr. and Mrs. M. have been providing for (the child) continuously since she was a few weeks old baby and the sundering of the relationships and the continuity which existed and had been built up between (the child) and M. over these most formative years in a mother and child existence would in my view be prejudicial to her welfare as would placing her in the changed custody of A.W. where no such mother and child relationship has existed in the true sense and where she would be exposed to and endangered by physical and emotional risks and potential

---

62. See *R. v. Gyngall, supra; In re O'Hara, an Infant, supra; State (Williams) v. Markey, supra; In re Kindersley, an Infant, supra;* See also *J. v. C,* [1970] A.C. 668; [1969] 2 W.L.R. 540 (H.L.) in particular the judgement of Lord MacDermott. The learned judge's summary of the law was subsequently approved of in *E.K. v. M.K.* (July, 1974) unreported (S.C.) and *MacD. v. MacD., supra,* (S.C.).
63. See *B. v. B.* [1975] I.R. 54 (S.C.) judgement of Walsh J. at p. 62.
64. (April, 1980) unreported (H.C.).
65. See p. 17 of judgement.

if not actual present domestic conflicts ... (this child) has now a sense of security and a feeling of protection with the Ms. which she would lose if given to A.W."[66]

The learned judge then went on to consider the submission made on behalf of the wife that under the Constitution she was entitled to be granted custody of her child even if the child's welfare under section 3 required that she should remain in the custody of M. He also dealt with the further submissions that

(i) in so far as section 3 impinged on A.W.'s constitutional rights it was incompatible with and repugnant to the Constitution;

(ii) a stranger can only take the place of parents in the exceptional cases referred to in Art. 42.5 of the Constitution where the parents for physical or moral reasons failed in their duty towards their children;

(iii) that A.W. and her child formed part of a family unit under the Constitution, that the natural and imprescriptible rights of the child can only be found within the inalienable rights of the family which rights emanate from the same source and cannot be in conflict and that therefore the rights of the family should prevail by the child being returned to it.

Due to the importance of the constitutional issues involved, it is intended to quote in extenso from the judgement of Ellis J. Dealing with the submissions made on behalf of A.W., he stated:

"In my opinion, I am not necessarily concerned with nor do I have to determine an issue of conflicting constitutional rights either as between (the child) and her mother A.W. or between (the child) in the custody of M. and the constitutional recognition of the family ... I am concerned to protect and uphold the infant's constitutional rights. In finding this can best be achieved in the custody of M. I do not think I am trespassing on the constitutional rights of A.W. or on the W. family. As already mentioned in the judgement of Walsh J. in *G. v. An Bord Uchtála*, there is nothing in the Constitution to indicate that in cases of apparent or alleged conflict the rights of a parent are always to be given primacy ... the natural (and constitutional) rights of A.W. in respect of (the child) are preserved by her retention of her natural and statutory rights as (the child's) guardian, even if custody is given to M. ...

If, however, there is a conflict between the constitutional rights of a legitimate child and the *prima facie* constitutional right of its mother to its custody I am of opinion that the infant's rights which are to be determined by regard to what is required for its welfare should prevail, even if its welfare is to be found in the custody of a "stranger" if for good and justifiable reason, to be ascertained on the facts and in the circumstances of any particular case, valid objection can be taken to the mother's inability to provide for her child's welfare, either emanating from the mother herself or for reasons connected with the child's welfare and not necessarily confined to failure by the parents (here A.W.) of their duty towards their children for physical or moral reasons, whereby the parents or as here the mother's

66. See p. 43 of judgement. There was evidence given in the proceedings of disagreements occurring on a number of occasions between the husband and the wife when the husband exercised his rights of access to the three children in the custody of the wife.

custody would or could not vindicate, protect or be compatible with the child's constitutional rights including its welfare.

Having regard to these conclusions I do not think it necessary for me to make a finding under Art. 42.5 of the Constitution. If, however, such a finding may be regarded as necessary or material to the issues involved I hold that this is an exceptional case. I also hold that in so far as it was or is the duty of the parents (and in the circumstances of this case, the duty of A.W.) to provide for the requirements of (the child) specified in Art. 42.1 or generally, that A.W. has failed in such for physical reasons. In my view the word physical as used in Art. 42.5 need not include intentional or purposeful reasons and would include reasons of health . . . which have combined to prevent and render her (A.W.) unfit or unable to carry out her required duty or duties towards (the child) . . ."

The learned judge then referred to the similarity in the wording of Art. 42.1 of the Constitution when compared to the definition of "welfare" in section 2 of the 1964 Act and continued:

"Such similarity accords with the view that the welfare of the child under the Act was intended to be of similar paramount consideration under the Constitution."

He concluded stating:

"Finally . . . it was held in *In Re Frost Infants*[67] . . . that the rights of parents are not absolute rights and that a child also had natural and imprescriptible rights of its own and further that to afford protection to the rights of the child the court regarded itself as having the jurisdiction to control the exercise of parental rights. In my opinion, the inalienable and imprescriptible rights of the family under Art. 41 of the Constitution attach to each member of a family including the children.[68] Therefore, in my view, the only way the "inalienable and imprescriptible" and "natural and imprescriptible" rights of the child can be protected is by the courts treating the welfare of the child as the paramount consideration in all disputes as to its custody, including disputes between a parent and a stranger. I take the view also that the child has the personal right to have its welfare regarded as the paramount consideration in any such dispute as to its custody under Art. 40.3 and that this right of the infant can additionally arise from 'the Christian and democratic nature of the State.' "[69]

He concluded directing that the child should remain in the custody of M. In essence, Ellis J. delivering judgement in the High Court held that to regard the welfare of the child as the first and paramount consideration in the determination of custody disputes between parents and strangers or third parties was not contrary to but in accordance with constitutional principles. Five years later, eight years after its decision in *J. v. D.*[70] the Supreme Court took a completely different view.

---

67. [1947] I.R. 3, see in particular, judgement of O'Sullivan C.J. at p. 28. See also *Landers v. A.G.* (1973) 109 I.L.T.R. 1 (H.C.).
68. See further the *State (Nicolaou) v. An Bord Uchtála* [1966] I.R. 567 (S.C.); *McGee v. The Attorney General* [1974] I.R. 284 (S.C.).
69. See pp. 69–74 of judgement.
70. *Supra.*

In *K.C. & A.C. v. An Bord Uchtála*,[71] an unmarried mother gave birth to a
child in September 1982. The child was placed with foster parents one week
after the birth and in November 1982 the mother agreed to its placement for
adoption. A month later it was placed with adopters. A year later, in December
1983, the mother withdrew her consent to adoption and in March 1984 she
married the father of her child, thereby legitimating the child. In proceedings
issued by the adopters, Lynch J. delivering judgement in the High Court in
August 1984 held that no order could be made by the court pursuant to section
3 of the Adoption Act, 1974, dispensing with the necessity to obtain the consent
of the natural parents to the making of an adoption order so as to enable the
Adoption Board to make such order, as the natural father had at no stage agreed
to the child being placed for adoption.[72]

There then remained for determination the issue as to whether the child
should be returned to the custody of its married parents or remain in the custody
of the adopters. In October 1984, Lynch J. found in favour of the adopters on
this issue. At the date of his decision the child had been in the care of the
"adopters" for almost two years. Delivering judgement the learned trial judge
expressed the view that:

> "The child is clearly bonded to the adopting parents and (their son) as
> though they were its own parents and brother respectively. Any sundering
> of these relationships will cause considerable immediate suffering to the
> child and a real possibility, if not a probability, which it is impossible to
> say one way or the other, of long term harm."[73]

In holding that he was bound by section 3 of the Act of 1964 to regard the welfare of the child as the first and paramount consideration, he stated:

> "In the context of this case and bearing in mind the secure and happy home
> which the child presently enjoys I think that I can best give effect to that
> section by asking and answering the question 'is there anything really worth-
> while to be gained for the child by transferring her from the adopting
> parents to the parents?' "[74]

He concluded that there was not.

On appeal, the Supreme Court unanimously held that the trial judge had not
applied the correct legal principles to determine the custody issue, having regard
to the constitutional protection afforded to the family by Articles 41 and 42
and the rights possessed by the child of married parents as a member of a family
under these Articles.[75] Finlay C.J., delivering the judgement of the court stated
that the Act of 1964 must, if possible, be given an interpretation consistent
with the Constitution and continued:

71. There were four sets of written judgements delivered in this case. Lynch J. delivered
written judgements in the High Court in August 1984, October 1984 and May 1985. There
was only one Supreme Court hearing and the principle judgement of the court was delivered
by Finlay C.J. There is also a brief judgement of McCarthy J. The Supreme Court delivered
its decision in March 1985. The members of the Supreme Court were Finlay C.J., McCarthy
J., Griffin J., Hederman J., and O'Hanlon, J. All the judgements except the May 1985 judgement of Lynch J. are now reported in [1985] 5 I.L.R.M. 302. The judgement of May
1985 can be found in [1986] 6 I.L.R.M. 65.
72. As the child had been legitimated not only the mother's but also the father's "agreement to place for adoption" was an essential pre-requisite before the court could consider
whether it would be in the best interests of the child to dispense with parental consent to
enable the Adoption Board make an adoption order pursuant to section 3 of the Adoption
Act, 1974. See further p. 300 *ante*.
73. [1985] 5 I.L.R.M. at p. 312.
74. *Ibid*.
75. See p. 22 *ante et seq*.

"In the case . . . of a (custody) contest between the parents of a legitimate child, who with the child constitute a family within the meaning of Articles 41 and 42 of the Constitution and persons other than the parents . . . it does not seem to me that section 3 of the Act of 1964 can be construed as meaning simply that the balance of welfare as defined in section 2 of the Act of 1964 must be the sole criterion for the determination by the court of the issue as to custody of the child or, to put the matter in another way, that it is a case as would be the situation in a contest between the parents of a legitimate child as to which of them should have general custody where the court could or should determine the matter upon the basis of the pre-ferred custody having regard to the welfare of the child . . .[76]

A child of over 2 years of age, as this infant is, in the dominant or general custody of persons other than its parents and continuing in such custody against the wishes of its parents, cannot be said to enjoy the right of educa-tion by its family and parents granted by Article 42.1 . . . I would therefore accept the contention that . . . Section 3 of the Act of 1964 must be con-strued as involving a constitutional presumption that the welfare of the child which is defined in Section 2 of the Act in terms identical to those contained in Article 42.1 is to be found within the family unless the court is satisfied on the evidence that there are compelling reasons why this cannot be achieved or unless the court is satisfied that the evidence estab-lishes an exceptional case where the parents have failed to provide education for the child and continue to fail to provide education for the child for moral or physical reasons."[77]

Referring to the judgement of O'Higgins C.J. in *J. v. D.*,[78] Finlay C.J. said that the specific findings made in that case, that the father was guilty of conduct which under the provisions of sections 14 and 16 of the Act of 1964 would have disentitled him to custody, "go close to equating with a finding . . . of an excep-tional case where for moral or physical reasons, the parent has failed in his or her duty to provide for the education of the child and in which the State can accordingly intervene to provide for that care and education by other means."[79] In so far, however, as O'Higgins C.J.'s judgement in *J. v. D.* could be construed as indicating that the paramount consideration of the child's welfare was to be applied as the sole test to determine a custody dispute over a legitimate child between parents and strangers "without regard to the provisions of Articles 41 and 42 of the Constitution", Finlay C.J. stated he must "respectfully refuse to follow it."[80]

The case was remitted back to the High Court for further determination by Lynch J. on the basis of the new principles applicable as articulated by the Supreme Court.[81] Delivering his third written judgement in the case in May of 1985, Lynch J. this time ordered that the child be returned to the custody of

---

76. [1985] 5 I.L.R.M. at p. 317.
77. *Ibid.*
78. *Supra.*
79. *Supra* at p. 318.
80. *Ibid.*
81. McCarthy J. in his judgement expressed the view that there could be "no suggestion" of this being an "exceptional case" within the terms of the test to be applied by the High Court in determining the issue as enunciated by the Chief Justice and continued "the key issue is whether or not the court is satisfied on the evidence that there are compelling reasons why the welfare of the child, as defined, cannot be achieved within the family, in other words that there are compelling reasons why the child should be in custody other than that of her parents". As for the burden of proof, he emphasized "that the compelling reason or reasons must in my view be clearly established." [1985]5 I.L.R.M. at p. 319.

its natural parents, having been in the care of the adopters for two and a half years. Referring to the judgement of the Supreme Court, he stated that the issue

> "Must be decided on the basis of section 2 and section 3 of Guardianship of Infants Act, 1964, read in the light of Articles 41 and 42 of the Constitution. In effect ... this means that the welfare of the child, meaning the religious and moral, intellectual, physical and social welfare of the child is the first and paramount consideration, but it must be assumed that such welfare is to be found within the family ... unless there are compelling reasons as to why this cannot be achieved."[82]

He continued:

> "The evidence on the previous occasions and even more strongly on this occasion is that there will be a very considerable short term upset for the child and I accept that evidence. The evidence of medium and longer term psychological consequences is also even stronger on this occasion than on the previous occasions, although it remains subject to the reservation that it is predictive evidence and not certain evidence, and to some extent at least it depends on the quality of the parenting which the parents will be able to provide for the child."[83]

Although he was "uncertain and apprehensive regarding the medium and long term effects of a transfer of custody" he was "satisfied that the parents can and will provide a good home for the child if it is transferred to them."[84] He concluded:

> "I do not think that such adverse effects as may result from such transfer have been sufficiently established to such a degree as to rebut the constitutional presumption that the welfare of the child is to be found within its constitutional family or amount to compelling reasons why this cannot be achieved."[85]

An appeal was lodged in the Supreme Court against this latter decision but was subsequently withdrawn.

It is arguable that the possible consequences for the child of a transfer of custody so graphically described by the trial judge in the extracts quoted from his judgements could have been held by him to be "compelling reasons" for permitting the child to remain with the adopters. Lynch J.'s ultimate decision appears to have been based on two factors. Firstly, in his view the "adverse effects" which might result from a transfer of custody to the parents had not been "sufficiently established" and, in this context, the psychiatric evidence given on this issue is described by him as "predictive evidence" and as such insufficiently persuasive. Secondly, he was satisfied that the natural parents "can and will provide a good home for the child".

As for the first factor, any evidence as to the likely impact of a court decision as to custody on the welfare of a child is by its nature "predictive" and any judicial decision made to determine a custody dispute, leaving aside the constitutional complication involved in this particular case, must be based on a judicial assessment of the evidence leading to the prediction that a child's welfare

---

82. [1986] 6 I.L.R.M. at p. 66.
83. *Ibid.*
84. *Ibid.*, at p. 67.
85. *Ibid.*

will be better promoted or protected if the child is placed in or remains in the custody of one person or couple as opposed to another. The evidence in this case presented two options — either that the child should remain in the custody of the adopters who it loved as parents, with whom it was developing normally, and to whom it had formed attachments and bonded, and be permitted to develop normally; or that it should be transferred to the custody of natural parents it did not know, terminate its relationship with the only parents it had known in the two and a half years since its birth, end its relationship with another child it had always regarded as a brother, suffer immediate distress and disruption in its development and be placed at risk of long term psychological harm.[86] Clearly, if the court had been in a position to determine the issue on the basis of the best interests of the child, having regard to the manner in which that test has been applied in the many adoption cases in which the courts have possessed jurisdiction to dispense with the necessity for a consent to adopt, a finding would have been made in favour of the adopters.[87] Equally, if the court had been in a position to choose the "course to be followed" that "is most in the interests of the child's welfare"[88] untrammelled by the constitutional assumptions that the Supreme Court held arise from Articles 41 and 42, a finding in favour of the adopters would appear inevitable. Looked at from the child's perspective it is respectfully submitted that the evidence was such as could be properly described as clearly establishing[89] compelling reasons to deny the natural parents custody.

In the context of the second factor, Lynch J. had no doubts as to the capacity of the natural father "to fulfil the role of father to the child"[90] and whereas he had some doubts as to the mother,[91] he did not regard these doubts as constituting "compelling reasons why the welfare of the child cannot be achieved in the parents' home". In other words, there was no evidence of serious inadequacies or misconduct on the part of the natural parents indicating unfitness to care for a child which could, in itself, provide compelling reasons for withholding custody from them. Application of the compelling interest test as enunciated by the Supreme Court, however, does not appear to require proof of parental unfitness or misconduct so as to empower the courts to deny custody to natural parents as the test is an alternative and additional test to that applicable under Article 42.5 of the Constitution. Whilst there was nothing done by or relating to the natural parents themselves which provided any compelling reason for denying them custody, having regard to the serious implications for the child of being transferred to them, it is submitted Lynch J., in applying the law as laid down by the Supreme Court, could have properly ordered that the child remain in the custody of the adopters.

The Supreme Court judgement in this case has left the law in a state of confusion and badly in need of clarification. In particular, there is a need to clarify the following matters:

(i) The strength and nature of the evidence required to rebut the constitutional presumption that a legitimate child's welfare "is to be found within

---

86. See, in particular, judgement of Lynch J. in October 1985, reported in [1985] 5 I.L.R.M. at p. 312 and judgement of Lynch J. (May 1985) reported in [1986] 6 I.L.R.M. at pp. 66–67.
87. See p. 308 *ante et seq.*
88. See *J. v. C.* [1970] A.C. 668 (H.L.) *per* Lord McDermott at p. 710 quoted on p. 353 *ante* and approved previously in the Supreme Court. See also footnote 49 on p. 354 *ante*.
89. In the words of McCarthy J. — see [1985] 5 I.L.R.M. at p.319.
90. See judgement of May 1985 [1986] 6 I.L.R.M. at p. 66.
91. *Ibid.*, at pp. 66–67.

the family". Must it be proved "beyond reasonable doubt" or "upon a balance of probability" that based on the particular facts of an individual case, a particular child's future welfare will not, cannot, or may not coincide with it being in the custody of its natural parents? McCarthy J. expressed the view in the Supreme Court that proof of compelling reasons had to be "clearly established" and Lynch J. was of the view that such reasons in the *K.C. & A.C.* case had not been "sufficiently established". The type of evidence that could have clearly established compelling reasons was not at any stage clarified either by members of the Supreme Court or by Lynch J. in his final judgement.

(ii) The type of behaviour which may constitute a "physical or moral" failure by parents "in their duty towards their children", so as to permit the courts deprive parents of the custody of a legitimate child in accordance with Article 42.5., was also at no stage clarified. Is such failure confined to education within the restrictive meaning of that word or does it apply to the totality of care a parent is obliged to provide in the upbringing of a child, described in Article 42.1 as religious, moral, intellectual, physical and social education?[91a] Is behaviour condemned by sections 14 or 16 of the 1964 Act, by itself, sufficient to deny custody to natural parents and what is the position if parents, despite such behaviour, prove that at the date of the hearing of court proceedings they are fit persons to have custody? What is the position of parents who do not physically abuse their legitimate child and are guilty of no moral failure, caring for it as best they can but who are totally inadequate as parents? If their behaviour is placing or could place the child at risk must the child remain in their custody so as to enable it "enjoy the right"[92] of being educated by its natural married parents or can it be placed in the custody of others? Does parental inadequacy constitute a sufficient physical reason under Article 42.5 on the basis of which the parent can be deprived of custody in the absence of deliberate fault or misconduct?

(iii) In what circumstances may the courts deprive parents of custody of a legitimate child for "compelling reasons"? No statutory provision or constitutional Article expressly prescribes judicial intervention permitting the courts to deprive parents of the custody of legitimate children for such reasons. Can "compelling reasons" be reasons relating to the child alone, deriving from its care and development up to the date of the court hearing and if so what weight is to be given to "predictive" evidence by child psychiatrists, psychologists or social workers as to the likely short term and long term impact on a child of a particular custody proposal? If the parents are fit and able parents, guilty of no moral or physical failure within the meaning of Article 42.5 and willing and able to provide a "good home" for their child, can they in any circumstances be deprived of custody of their legitimate child on this ground? Can there ever be compelling reasons in the case of such parents? Must such parents always be awarded custody irrespective of the consequences to the child?

(iv) What remaining relevance has section 3 of the Act of 1964 to custody

---

91a. See *Ryan v. The Attorney General* [1965] I.R. 294 (S.C.) in which O'Dalaigh C.J. states that "education essentially is the teaching and training of a child to make the best possible use of his inherent and potential capacities, physical, mental and moral." and the distinction made between "education" and "nurture". See [1965] I.R. p. 350. See further p. 20 *ante*.

92. See judgement of Finlay C.J. [1985] 5 I.L.R.M. at p. 317.

disputes between parents and third parties. As a result of the approach adopted by the Supreme Court in the *K.C. & A.C.* case, the child's welfare cannot any longer be regarded as "the first and paramount consideration". The Supreme Court's approach is clearly not compatible with the approach adopted by it in *J. v. D.*[93] or compatible with the approach of Ellis J. in *P.W. v. A.W.*[94] It is also at variance with the approach of the House of Lords in *J. v. C.*,[95] an approach previously approved and adopted by the Supreme Court in two earlier decisions concerned with custody disputes between parents.[96] It does, however, accord with the approach of the High Court in *In re J.*[97] Neither the *K.C. & A.C.* case nor *In re J.* involved any direct constitutional challenge to the validity of section 3 of the Act of 1964 such as was mounted in *P.W. v. A.W.*[98] but in *In re J.*, Henchy J. expressly reserved the issue as to whether the section could withstand a direct constitutional challenge[99] and there must be serious doubts now as to whether the section could survive any such challenge. Whether or not one is brought, however, is to a certain extent academic as the direct effect of the Supreme Court decision is to water down the welfare principle to such a degree as to render it impossible, without further clarification by the Supreme Court, to determine the extent to which it may be of relevance in deciding the outcome of future custody cases between parents and third parties over legitimate children.

The K.C. & A.C. Case – A Final Comment: The Supreme Court in the *K.C. & A.C.* case at no stage undertook a detailed examination and analysis of the inalienable and imprescriptible rights of the family as a unit and the relationship between family rights and the inalienable and imprescriptible rights possessed by the individual component parts which make up the family, i.e. parents and children. While it clearly recognised that parents possess inalienable and imprescriptible rights, it at all stages assumed that the constitutional rights of legitimate children were subsumed by and inferior to parental rights. In effect, parental rights were held to be superior to children's rights. The parental duty to provide education was turned into a right vested in the child to be educated by his/her parents, even if such "right" was at variance with the child's welfare. At no stage did the court acknowledge or give consideration to the proposition that inalienable and imprescriptible rights may vest in a legitimate child, independent of parental duty, which are of equal constitutional strength to parental rights and which require that the child's welfare be the paramount consideration in any adjudication between competing parental and children's rights. Finlay C.J. referred to the judgement in *P.W. v. A.W.*, as one of the cases the court had been referred to in legal argument and made a passing reference to it, but at no stage did the learned Chief Justice or any other member of the Supreme Court give any explanation as to why the court did not follow the approach adopted by Ellis J. in that case. It is respectfully submitted that it is an approach that deserves more detailed consideration.

93. *Supra.*
94. *Supra.*
95. *Supra.*
96. See *MacD. v. MacD.* (1979) 114 I.L.T.R. 66 (S.C.); *E.K. v. M.K.* (July, 1974) unreported (S.C.), in particular the judgement of Henchy J.
97. *Supra.*
98. *Supra.*
99. See p. 384 *ante et seq.*

GUARDIANSHIP AND CUSTODY: ENFORCEMENT OF ORDERS

If a person fails to comply with an order made by either the Circuit or High Court concerning the guardianship or custody of children, the person in default can be brought before the relevant court and may be committed to prison for contempt of court. If a person fails to comply with an order as to custody or access made by the District Court pursuant to the jurisdiction exercised by it under the Guardianship of Infants Act, 1964, as conferred on it by the Courts Act, 1981, there was until recently no penalty that the District Court could impose on the defaulter. Section 5 of the Courts Act, 1986, has now made it an offence rendering a person liable to a fine not exceeding £200 and/or to imprisonment for a term not exceeding 6 months for any person "having the actual custody of an infant" to "fail or refuse" to comply with a custody or access order made by the court.[100] To commit an offence under the section a person must have "been shown or given a copy of the order" made. A person present at the sitting of the District Court at which the order was made, is, however, deemed to have been given or shown a copy of it. It should be noted that this provision only applies to custody or access orders made by the District Court. Thus, it appears that, where the District Court makes other orders relating to children under the Act of 1964, such as an order relating to a child's education under section 11(1), there is no penalty that the District Court can impose against a person who fails to comply with such order.

In practice it should be noted that the courts are most reluctant to use the jurisdiction vested in them to imprison a parent who fails to comply with orders made under the Guardianship of Infants Act, 1964, relating to guardianship, custody or access.

---

100. The Act was enacted by the Oireachtas on the 12th July 1986.

WARDS OF COURT

The jurisdiction over wards of court is vested in the President of the High Court and in the Circuit Court.[1] This jurisdiction historically originates in the feudal obligation of the Sovereign, as *parens patriae*, to protect the person and property of his subjects particularly those unable to look after themselves, including infants or minors. The courts' jurisdiction to make a minor a ward of court is in the majority of instances invoked where it is necessary to protect the property interests of the minor.

Until recently if parties wished to make use of the wardship jurisdiction and a minor had no proprietary interests, it was common to settle a small sum, e.g. £50 on the minor in order to commence proceedings. In recent years, however, minors have been taken into wardship without the use of this expedient[2] and the President of the High Court has stated that he is satisfied that he has jurisdiction to take a minor into wardship when no property matter is involved, if to do so is in the interests of the minor's welfare.[3] This approach of the President was relied upon and approved by Keane J. in *The State (at the prosecution of C. Bruton) v. A. Judge of the Circuit Court & P. Bruton*[4] who stated that:

> "The wardship jurisdiction of the High Court and the Circuit Court in the case of infants does not depend for its existence on the possession of property by the infant sought to be made a ward of court."[5]

Wardship proceedings differ from proceedings under the Guardianship of Infants Act, 1964, in that they can be commenced by a third party even though the parents or guardians of a child are alive and even though such third party has no "right" to the custody of the child. Proceedings under the Act of 1964 can be initiated by a third party only if a child has no guardian or if a deceased parent or guardian has failed to appoint a testamentary guardian[6] and Habeas Corpus proceedings can only be brought by a third party already entitled to custody of a child, to regain such custody upon a parent or another wrongly depriving such third party of his "right" to custody.[7] It is by bringing wardship proceedings that a third party can initially seek custody of a child against a

---

1. Courts (Supplemental Provisions) Act, 1961, Sect. 9 (The President may assign another judge of the High Court to exercise the jurisdiction on his behalf). See also R.S.C. (S.I. No. 72 of 1962) Order 65. The Circuit Court has jurisdiction in proceedings for the wardship of infants and the care of infants' estates provided that any property in the estate of an infant taken into wardship in so far as it consists of land does not exceed the rateable valueation of £200 – Courts (Supplemental Provisions) Act, 1961, Sect. 22(1) as amended by Courts Act, 1981, Sect. 2(1). See Third Schedule, Ref. No. 24 of the 1961 Act. See also *The State (at the prosecution of C. Bruton) v. A Judge of the Circuit Court & P. Bruton* (July, 1984) unreported (H.C.).
2. See, for example, *Re J.L. (A Minor)* (March, 1978) unreported (Finlay P., H.C.). See also *In re Meades, Minors* (1871) I.R. 5 Eq. 98 (Ch. L.C.) at p. 114 where it is stated that exercise of the wardship jurisdiction is not dependent on the existence of property. See further T.W. Bell and R. Armstrong, *Minor Matters* (Dublin 1886) at p. 2.
3. Stated after delivering his written judgement in *Re J.L. (A Minor)*, *supra*. Unfortunately this statement is not contained in the judgement.
4. *Supra*.
5. See p. 3 of judgement.
6. See Sect. 8 of the 1964 Act. A third party or non-guardian cannot in any circumstances issue proceedings under Sect. 11 of the 1964 Act.
7. See *Northampton County Council v. A.B.F. & M.B.F.* [1982] 2 I.L.R.M. 164 (H.C.); *Kent County Council v. C.S.* [1984] 4 I.L.R.M. 192 (H.C.).

parent[8] or seek to obtain protection for a child against the actions of a parent.[9] A parent seeking to regain custody from a third party can commence proceedings under section 11 of the 1964 Act or bring Habeas Corpus proceedings. Parents and guardians of a minor may of course themselves commence wardship proceedings in various circumstances.

When a minor is made a ward of court all matters affecting the ward's upbringing become the responsibility of the court. The court may determine in whose care and custody the minor should be placed, the manner in which his property should be managed, and may make orders relating to the residence, education and holidays of the minor.[10] The court may also order maintenance to be paid for the benefit of the minor out of funds held on his behalf.[11] Further, the minor may not marry without the consent of the court.

The paramount consideration in all questions brought before the court is the ward's welfare[12] subject to any constitutional right that vests in parents to custody of their legitimate child.[13] The court exercises a continuing supervisory function and any person in whose custody the ward is placed must comply with the directions of the court. The power of the court to give directions on matters affecting a ward's welfare is unfettered by statute and has been held to be more extensive and flexible than that conferred by the Guardianship of Infants Act, 1964.[14]

Upon a minor attaining 18 years[15] of age the court will make an order of discharge from wardship. Failure to comply with an order of the court constitutes contempt of court and may result in the committal to prison of the person held in contempt.[16] In the case of such behaviour on the part of a person granted custody of the ward it can also result in the loss of such custody. The court may also enforce its orders by injunction.

---

8. See *Re J.L. (A Minor), supra.* See also *Re Farrell (Minors)*, Orders dated October 1977 and January 1978; (Gannon J., H.C.). *Re Williams (Minors)*, order dated August 1978 (D'Arcy J., H.C.). No written judgements were delivered in the last two mentioned cases. In the former, two children were made wards of court although the maternal grandmother and aunt who made the application failed to obtain custody of them. The court granted joint custody to their mother with another aunt who was not originally a party to the proceedings. In the latter case, on the application of Leeds City Council 3 children who had been kidnapped by their mother and brought over to Dublin were made wards of the Irish High Court and subsequently returned to England. Prior to the Irish proceedings, the English Courts had placed the children in the care of the City Council.

9. See the English case *Re D. (A Minor)* [1976] Fam. 185 (Fam. D.); in a novel application a mentally retarded child of 13 years was made a ward of court on the application of a third party so as to prevent her mother having a sterilisation operation carried out on her. For a discussion of this case see A.L. Polak – "Sterilisation of a minor", (1976) 6 Fam. Law 37.

10. See *In re Westby, Minors* (No. 2) [1934] I.R. 311 (S.C.); *Re J.L. (A Minor) supra.* See also *In re Gills' Minors* (1891) 27 L.R. Ir. 129 (Ch. L.C.) – a female infant ward of court should not become a novice in a convent without the consent of the court.

11. See for example in *In re Birch's Trusts* (1885) 15 L.R. Ir. 380 (Ch. M.R.); *In the Matter of R.J. Duddy & A.M. Duddy, Minors* [1925] 1 I.R. 196 (C.J.).

12. Guardianship of Infants Act, 1964, Sect. 3. See *J. v. C.* [1970] A.C. 668 (H.L.); *Re H. (A Minor) (Wardship Jurisdiction)* [1978] Fam. 65 (C.A.).

13. See *K.C. & A.C. v. An Bord Uchtála* [1985] 5 I.L.R.M. 302 (S.C.) discussed at p. 392 *ante.* The effect of this decision on the exercise of the wardship jurisdiction remains to be determined.

14. See *In the Matter of J.S., an Infant* (1977) 111 I.L.T.R. 146 (Finlay P., H.C.); *Re J.L. (A Minor), supra.*

15. See the Age of Majority Act, 1985, sects. 2, 3, 4 and the schedule thereto.

16. See *In re McLorinan, a Minor* [1935] I.R. 373 (S.C.) – The court may not punish a ward in contempt by placing restrictions on her rights of ownership of property to which she is entitled upon discharge from wardship.

Circumstances in which Wardship Jurisdiction May be Used

I Where parents seek to prevent a teenage son or daughter from marrying,[17] leaving home, or associating with undesirable persons, they may apply to have him/her made a ward of court.

II If a child is placed with or is living with relations, foster parents, potential adopters or any other persons who wish to retain custody of the child, contrary to the wishes of the natural parent or parents, the former may apply for a custody order under the wardship jurisdiction.[18]

III A Health Board, Local Authority or other such agency may apply to have a child whose welfare is threatened made a ward of court[19] and seek orders enabling it to have the child assessed or supervised in its place of residence or taken into care.

IV To restrict the removal of a minor from the jurisdiction[20] or to have a minor returned to the jurisdiction from where he was brought. Thus, the wardship jurisdiction may be invoked by an estranged spouse upon the "kidnapping" of a child by the other spouse.[21] If it is in the best interests of a ward of the Irish Court to leave this jurisdiction, permission will be granted by the court.[22]

V To determine a dispute between spouses as to their child's upbringing[23] or custody.[24] It is, however, more appropriate normally to use the provisions of section 11 of the Act of 1964 for this purpose.

---

17. A teenager of course requires parental consent to marry unless a court order is obtained dispensing with consent – Marriages Act, 1972, Sect. 7; where the marriage of a ward takes place without the court's consent the parties to the marriage and any person who helps to bring about the marriage commits contempt of court – see *In Re H.'s settlement H. v. H.* [1909] 2 Ch. 260 (Ch. Div.).

18. See *Re J.L. (A Minor), supra.* In this case the court took a child of eight and a half years into wardship and made the child's mother and a Miss M. joint guardians of the person of the child. The application had been made by F., a widower, whose household consisted of three sons and Miss M., who looked after the family and assisted F. in his business. The child had resided in F.'s household since the age of fifteen months. The mother originally resided in F.'s home but had not done so for almost four years prior to these proceedings. At the date of the proceedings, the child was under the belief that Miss M. was her mother and she had no relationship with the real mother. The court placed the child in the custody of Miss M. See further *J. v. C., supra.*

19. See *Williams (Minors) supra*, footnote 8. In this case, prior to the children being returned to Leeds, the court placed them under the care of the Eastern Health Board.

20. See *The State (K.M. and R.D.) v. The Minister for Foreign Affairs and Ors.* [1979] I.R. 73 (H.C.) where the constitutional "Right to Travel" was enunciated. It is clear from this judgement that if parents wish a child to travel outside the jurisdiction, the child has a constitutional right to a passport and if the Dept. of Foreign Affairs and the Passport Office believe that it is contrary to the interests of the child to issue a passport, it must bring wardship proceedings and prove its case. See further pp. 187 *ante et seq.*

21. For example, see the cases cited in footnote 146 on p. 372 *ante.*

22. *In re Westby, Minors, supra*, see also the English case of *Re R. A Minor* (1974) 4 Fam. Law 153; see also *In re Kindersley* [1944] I.R. 111; (1943) 78 I.L.T.R. 159 (S.C.). This case concerned a Habeas Corpus application on behalf of the father to have his son taken out of his mother's custody and sent to a school in England, i.e. sent outside the jurisdiction. The boy had previously been made a ward of court in England.

23. See *In re May, Minors* (1957) 92 I.L.T.R. 1 (H.C.).

24. See *The State (at the prosecution of C. Bruton) v. A. Circuit Court Judge & P. Bruton* in which a mother's challenge to the validity of a Circuit Court order making a child a ward of court and granting custody of the child to the father was dismissed.

VI The most common circumstance in which a minor is made a ward is where it is thought desirable to obtain independent protection for a minor's property interests.[25]

---

25. See *In the Matter of J.S., an Infant, supra*, in which Finlay P. held that if directions of the court are sought concerning the estates or assets of minors, as a general rule such directions should be sought by use of the wardship procedure. Such applications should only be made under section 11(1) of the Guardianship of Infants Act, 1964, when very few court applications are necessary and "where a fixed and final straightforward scheme not requiring variations and not requiring the continued supervision of the court is appropriate in the interests of the children". See further *In re Meade* [1971] I.R. 327 (H.C.).

THE CHILDREN ACT, 1908 AND RELATED LEGISLATION

It is not within the scope of this book to give a comprehensive account of the law relating to children. It is, however, intended to briefly examine circumstances other than those already discussed in which a parent may be deprived of the custody of his or her child. As will be seen in the pages that follow, this may happen either when a child is held to be in need of care and attention or is charged with or found guilty of a criminal offence. A parent may also voluntarily surrender custody of his or her child to third parties, such as foster parents or a health board, and reference is also made to the law and legislation applicable thereto in so far as it has not already been discussed in earlier sections of this chapter.

The Children Act, 1908, is at the foundation of the statutory provisions discussed in this section. Other relevant legislative enactments are the Children Acts, 1934 & 1941, the Children (Amendment) Acts, 1949 & 1957, the Health Act, 1953, and the School Attendance Acts, 1926–67.

For the purposes of the Children Acts, 1908 to 1957, a child is defined as a person under the age of 15 years and a young person as a person who is 15 years or upwards and under the age of 17 years.[1] Reference to a child or a young person in the following pages, thus refers to persons defined as such in the Children Acts unless otherwise indicated.

CHILDREN IN NEED OF CARE AND PROTECTION

Over 3,650 children each year spend some time in care, that is in either residential or foster care. Over one-third of these children are in long-term care and will remain in such care for most, if not all, of their childhood. The majority of children taken into care are received into care on a voluntary basis without the intervention of the courts. Others are taken into care following the making of court orders necessary to secure their safety and protection.[2]

The Children Act, 1908, states the main circumstances in which children may be taken into care by court order and contains provisions for the speedy obtaining of court orders to extend immediate protection to children and young persons seriously at risk where emergency intervention is required.

In practice, proceedings to extend care and protection to children and young persons are today usually brought by a health board, through one of its social workers. It should be noted, however, that the bringing of such proceedings is not restricted to health boards or health board personnel by the relevant legislation.

The discussion that follows examines the present law and also briefly refers to some of the proposed reforms that will be introduced if the Children (Care & Protection) Bill, 1985, as initiated, is enacted by the Oireachtas. At the date of writing, this Bill has been referred to a Select Committee of Dáil Éireann which is to process the Dáil Committee Stage of the Bill and substantial amendments to its original provisions are to be considered by the committee. It is clear that some considerable time will elapse before the Bill completes its passage through the legislative process and comes into force. It is also clear that many amendments may be made to the substance of the Bill before it is enacted. Accordingly, it should be remembered that some of the provisions discussed here contained in the Bill, as initiated, may be changed prior to it becoming law.

---

1. Children Act, 1908, Sect. 131 as amended by the Children Act, 1941, Sect. 29.
2. See Appendix G.

Place of Safety Orders[3]

The "Place of Safety" provisions contained in sections 20 and 24 of the Children Act, 1908, contain the main legislative mechanisms within the Children Acts for emergency intervention to obtain protection for children in immediate and serious risk.

Section 20 of the Act of 1908, empowers a member of the Garda Siochana, or any person authorised by a District Justice, to take to a place of safety, any child or young person in respect of whom an offence under Part II of the Act or any offence mentioned in the First Schedule to the Act "has been, or there is reason to believe has been, committed".[4]

A child or young person taken to a place of safety or seeking refuge in one may be kept there until he can be brought before the District Court. The court may make such order as the circumstances require until the charge against the person alleged to have committed the offence is determined. Where it appears to the court that such an offence has been committed and that it is in the interests of the child that an order be made, the court may make "such order as circumstances require for the care and detention of the child or young person" until a reasonable time has elapsed for a charge to be made, and if one is made within that time, until the charge is determined. In the case of a person being convicted on such charge, the child may be kept in care for a further 21 days.[5] These provisions are essentially of a 'holding' nature. They are designed to ensure that where there is a possibility that a person has committed an offence against a child, the child may be taken out of the offender's custody until the matter is determined.

---

3. See also the Summary Jurisdiction Rules, 1909 (S.R.O.) 1909 No. 952 Rules 6 & 12.

4. Children Act, 1908, Sect. 20(1). The offences under Part II of the Act are as follows: Sect. 12(1) of 1908 as amended by Sect. 4 of 1957 provides that it is a criminal offence "If any person over the age of seventeen years, who has the custody, charge, or care of any child or young person, wilfully assaults, ill-treats, neglects, abandons, or exposes such child or young person, or causes or procures such child or young person to be assaulted, ill-treated, neglected, abandoned, or exposed, in a manner likely to cause such child or young person unnecessary suffering or injury to his health (including injury to or loss of sight, or hearing, or limb, or organ of the body, and any mental derangement)". See *McGonagle v. McGonagle* [1951] I.R. (S.C.), see further p. 177 *ante*. See also *Re Arkins* [1966] 3 All E.R. 651 (Q.B.D.) in which the court refused to grant an order of Habeas Corpus and upheld a magistrate's order that the applicant be extradited from England to Ireland to answer a charge made against him under Section 12(1).

Sect. 13 provides that "Where it is proved that the death of an infant under three years of age was caused by suffocation (not being suffocation caused by disease or the presence of any foreign body in the throat or air-passages of the infant) whilst the infant was in bed with some other person over sixteen years of age, and that that other person was at the time of going to bed under the influence of drink, that other person shall be deemed to have neglected the infant in a manner likely to cause injury to its health within the meaning of this Part of this Act".

Sect. 14 makes it an offence for a person to cause or procure a child or young person in their custody or care to beg. Sect. 15 makes it an offence for a person not to properly protect a child under 7 years of age in their custody or care against the risk of being burnt so that the child is killed or suffers serious injury. *Sect. 16 makes it an offence for a person to allow a child or young person under 17 in their custody or care reside in or frequent a brothel. *Sect. 17 makes it an offence for a person to cause or encourage the seduction or prostitution of a girl under 17 in their custody or care.

*Both these sections were amended by the Criminal Law Amendment Act, 1935, Sect. 11.

The offences set down in the first Schedule to the Act consist of: Any offence under sections twenty-seven, fifty-five or fifty-six of the Offences Against the Person Act, 1861, and any offence against a child or young person under sections five, forty-two, or sixty-two of that Act, or under the Criminal Law Amendment Acts, 1885 to 1935.

Any offence under the Dangerous Performances Acts, 1879 and 1897.

Any other offence involving bodily injury to a child or young person.

5. Children Act, 1908, Sect. 20(2) and (3).

Section 24 of the Act of 1908, provides that if it appears to a District Justice, upon information on oath being laid by any person acting in the interests of a child or young person

"that there is reasonable cause to suspect —

(a) that the child or young person has been or is being assaulted, ill-treated, or neglected . . . in a manner likely to cause the child or young person unnecessary suffering, or to be injurious to his health; or

(b) that an offence under this Part of this Act or any offence mentioned in the First Schedule to this Act, has been or is being committed in respect of a child or young person,

the justice may issue a warrant authorising any constable named therein to search for such child or young person, and if it is found that he has been or is being assaulted, ill-treated, or neglected in manner aforesaid, or that any such offence as aforesaid has been or is being committed in respect of the child or young person, to take him to and detain him in a place of safety, until he can be brought before a court of summary jurisdiction, or authorising any constable to remove the child or young person with or without search to a place of safety and detain him there until he can be brought before a court of summary jurisdiction; and the court before whom the child or young person is brought may commit him to the care of a relative or other fit person[6] in like manner as if the person in whose care he was had been committed for trial for an offence under this Part of this Act."

A member of the Gardai authorised by warrant under section 24 to search for and/or remove a child or young person "may enter (if need be by force) any house, building or other place specified in the warrant, and may remove the child or young person therefrom."[7]

In practice, section 24 is used more frequently to protect children at risk than is section 20 as it permits the removal of a child to a place of safety and subsequently, a fit person order to be made, even if no offence has been committed against the child[8] — a "reasonable cause to suspect" that a child is being "ill treated or neglected" in a manner likely to cause "unnecessary suffering" being sufficient to permit intervention under the section. In an extreme emergency, however, intervention under section 20 can provide speedier protection, as it permits the removal of a child by a member of the Gardai, without a court order having to be first obtained.[9] A garda can only so act, however, if one of the specified offences "has been, or there is reason to believe has been committed". Section 27 of the Children (Care & Protection) Bill, 1985, as initiated, proposes to extend the grounds upon which place of safety orders can be obtained and to permit a child to be taken to a place of safety by a member of the gardai, without warrant, "where his immediate safety requires it" and "the circumstances are such that it would not be sufficient" to refer the case to a health board so

---

6. For the meaning of a fit person, see section entitled "Fit Person Orders", p. 409 *post*.
7. Sect. 24(3).
8. See D. Greene, "The Child and the Law" (1979) 73 *Gazette of the Incorporated Law Society of Ireland*, 143 and "Legal Aspects of Non-Accidental Injury to Children" (1980) 74 *Gazette of the Incorporated Law Society of Ireland* 152. See also Department of Health, *Guidelines on the Procedures for the Identification, Investigation and Management of Non-Accidental Injury to Children* (Revised Edition, February, 1983) pp. 16—17.
9. See Department of Health, *Guidelines, supra*, at p. 17.

that the board might determine whether to seek a place of safety order or to take care proceedings.[9a]

A place of safety under the Act of 1908 means a Garda Station, a hospital, a doctor's surgery, or "any other suitable place, the occupier of which is willing, temporarily, to receive an infant, child or young person."[10] It can, under this definition include an appropriate school or institution under the ownership or control of a health board, a local authority or a government department such as the Departments of Health, Justice or Education.

Care Proceedings

Section 58 of the Children Act, 1908[11] confers power on a District Court to send a child under 15 years in need of care and protection to an industrial school,[12] if the child

(a) is found begging or receiving alms (whether or not there is any pretence of singing, playing, performing, offering anything for sale, or otherwise), or being in any street premises or place for the purpose of so begging or receiving alms;[13] or

(b) is found not having any home or settled place of abode, or visible means of subsistence, or is found having a parent or guardian who does not exercise proper guardianship;[14] or

(c) is found destitute, and

   (i)   is an orphan

   (ii)   is not an orphan and either both parents, or where one is dead, the surviving parent is undergoing penal servitude or imprisonment

   (iii)   is an illegitimate child whose mother is undergoing penal servitude or imprisonment.[15]

(d) is under the care of a parent or guardian who, by reason of reputed criminal or drunken habits is unfit to have the care of the child;[16] or

(e) is the daughter, whether legitimate or illegitimate, of a father who has been convicted of an offence under Section 4 or 5 of the Criminal Law Amendment Acts, 1885 to 1935, in respect of any of his daughters, whether legitimate or illegitimate;[17] or

(f) frequents the company of any reputed thief, or any common or reputed prostitute[18], is lodging or residing in a house or part of a house used by

9a. See, generally, Sects. 26–32 of Bill.
10. See the Children Act, 1908, Sect. 131.
11. See also the Summary Jurisdiction Rules, 1909, *supra*, Rules 16–19.
12. The Children Act, 1908, Sect. 44(1) provides that an "industrial school means a school for the industrial training of children in which children are lodged, clothed and fed as well as taught." A child suffering from a "mental or physical defect" may also be sent to a special school (see Children Act, 1908, Sect. 62(2)).
For a discussion of the different types of residential homes or schools that cater for children in care see the *Task Force on Child Care Services: Final Report* (Stationery Office, Dublin, 1980) at p. 61 *et seq.*
13. Children Act, 1908, Sect. 58(1)(a).
14. *Ibid.*, Sect. 58(1)(b) as amended by the Children Act, 1941, Sect. 10(1)(b).
15. *Ibid.*, Sect. 58(1)(c) and Sect. 133(17).
16. *Ibid.*, Sect. 58(1)(d) as amended by Children Act, 1941, Sect. 10(1)(c).
17. *Ibid.*, Sect. 58(1)(e).
18. *Ibid.*, Sect. 58(1)(f).

any prostitute for the purpose of prostitution, or otherwise living in circumstances calculated to cause, encourage, or favour seduction or prostitution of the child;[19] or

(h) is under the care of a parent or guardian who has been convicted of an offence under Part II of this Act or mentioned in the First Schedule to this Act[20] in relation to any of his children, whether legitimate or illegitimate;[21] or

(i) is uncontrollable by his parent or guardian;[22] or

(j) if a public assistance authority satisfied the court that a child maintained in a county home is refractory or is the child of parents either of whom is convicted of an offence punishable with penal servitude or imprisonment and that it is desirable that the child be sent to an industrial school.[23]

A child may not be treated as coming within (f) above if the only prostitute whose company the child frequents is the child's mother, and she exercises proper guardianship and care over the child.[24] If an application is made under (i) above, the court may, instead of sending the child to an industrial school, place him under the supervision of a probation officer.[25]

A child found to come within one of the categories of neglect or ill-treatment listed in section 58(1) — i.e. within one of those listed in (a) to (h) above — may, as an alternative, be placed in the care of a fit person.[26]

"Any person" may bring a child before a district court to apply for a care order on any of the above grounds, other than (i) and (j).[27] Under (i) an application is brought by a parent or guardian. Moreover, there is a duty imposed on the Garda Siochana to take such proceedings in relation to any child who appears to come within one of the descriptions mentioned in section 58(1), unless — (i) the case is one in which the local school attendance committee are bringing proceedings; or (ii) proceedings are being taken by some other person; or (iii) the gardai are satisfied that the taking of proceedings is undesirable in the interests of the child.[28]

The requirement in section 58(1) to bring the child before the court has been interpreted by some district justices to mean that the child must be physically present in the court throughout the hearing of an application brought under that sub-section. The presence of a child in court during the hearing of such proceedings, particularly if the application is contested by the child's parents, must be extremely traumatic both for the child and parents and place at considerable risk the welfare of the child. It is submitted that it is sufficient for the purposes

---

19. *Ibid.*, Sect. 58(1)(g).
20. See footnote 4 *ante*.
21. Children Act, 1908, Sect. 58(1)(i) as amended by Children Act, 1941, Sect. 10(1)(d). See *In re Doyle, an Infant* (December, 1955) unreported (S.C.) in which the whole of Sect. 10(1)(d) and (e) was held to be repugnant to the Constitution and invalid, with the exception of only the introductory words and paragraph (i) in subs. 1(d).
22. Children Act, 1908, Sect. 58(4).
23. *Ibid.*, Sect. 58(5) as amended by the Public Assistance Act, 1939, Sect. 89(2). See, however, the Social Welfare (Supplementary Allowances) Act, 1975, Sect. 24. Under this provision section 89(2) of the 1939 Act is repealed but not replaced. In practice provision (j) in the text is obsolete.
24. Children Act, 1908, Sect. 58(1).
25. *Ibid.*, Sect. 58(4).
26. For the meaning of a fit person see section entitled "Fit Person Orders" at p. 409 *post*.
27. Children Act, 1908, Sect. 58(1).
28. *Ibid.*, Sect. 58(8).

of this provision if the child is identified to the court and that it is not necessary for a child to be kept in court throughout the hearing.[29]

Today, the majority of proceedings under section 58 are brought by social workers employed by the health boards and the principle ground upon which such applications are made is that of the failure of a guardian or parent to exercise "proper guardianship".[30] An application on this ground gives the court an opportunity to examine in detail all matters of relevance in determining what order, if any, should be made to protect a child's welfare. In determining such application the court should regard itself as bound by section 3 of the Guardianship of Infants Act, 1964, "to regard the welfare of the infant as the first and paramount consideration". However, no written judgement has ever been delivered by an Irish court stating the manner in which section 3 of the Act of 1964, is to interact with section 58 or any other section of the Act of 1908. It should also be noted that to date no written judgement has been delivered in which the effect of the constitutional provisions contained in Articles 41 and 42 on the provision which enables a care order to be made for parental failure "to exercise proper guardianship" has been judicially considered.

Section 33 of the Children (Care & Protection) Bill, 1985, as initiated, proposes to update and change the grounds upon which a child may be taken into care. In so doing it proposes that a child may be the subject of care proceedings if

(a) he has been or is being ill-treated, neglected or assaulted, or

(b) he is or has been under the care of a parent or guardian who does not exercise proper guardianship or has otherwise received or is receiving inadequate care such as to cause or to be likely to cause him physical or mental suffering or injury to his health or to impair substantially his proper development, or

(c) his parent or guardian is not capable of exercising proper guardianship, or

(d) he has been or is being sexually abused.

In addition, the section proposes that a child may also be taken into care if he has been the victim of a scheduled offence or is a member of a household in which a person has been convicted of such an offence, or in which another child has been the victim of such offence.

Health boards only, will be able to institute care proceedings under the Bill, as initiated, and upon a court holding a child to be in need of care and protection it will be empowered to make either a supervision order, empowering a health board to supervise the care of a child in its own home or an order placing the child in the care of the health board that instituted the proceedings.

Under existing legislation the courts have no statutory powers to make supervision orders although, as will be seen in the following section, on occasion health boards, having had a child placed in their care by way of the making of a fit person order, have allowed the child to remain residing in its own home under health board supervision. Under the provisions of the Bill of 1985, upon a care order being made it will be left to the health board in whose care a child is placed, to decide the manner in which the child should be looked after, i.e. whether in

---

29. The similar requirement in the Children Act, 1908, Sect. 24 has also been so interpreted. This submission also applies thereto.
30. See D. Greene, *supra*.

residential or foster care. The court will, however, be able to impose conditions regarding access by or consultation with a parent or guardian.[31] If these provisions are enacted, the District Court will no longer be empowered to commit a child directly to residential care in an industrial school as it may do currently under the provisions of the Children Act, 1908.

It has been suggested that some of the grounds upon which the Bill, as initiated, proposes to permit care orders to be made will be open to constitutional challenge, in particular in the light of the recent decision of the Supreme Court in *K.C. & A.C. v. An Bord Uchtála*.[32] Whether the President of the State will refer the Bill of 1985 to the Supreme Court pursuant to Article 26 of the Constitution following its passage through the Dáil and Senate for a determination to be made as to the constitutionality of section 33 remains to be seen.

The School Attendance Acts, 1926–67[33]

The School Attendance Act, 1926, section 17 provides for

(i) the issue of a warning notice to parents who fail to send a child to school,

(ii) the fining of parents who fail to comply with such a warning,

(iii) the commital of a child to an industrial school or to the care of a fit person.

The District Court may act under (iii) above if a parent, in proceedings brought against him satisfies the court that "he has used all reasonable efforts" to cause the child to whom the proceedings relate, to attend school or the parent is convicted for a second time or for a subsequent offence in respect of the same child.[34]

Fit Person Orders

Under the Children Act, 1908, section 58[35] the court may place a child under 15 in the care of a "fit person" if the child is refractory,[36] or beyond control[37] or convicted of his first offence[38] (or of any offence if under 12 years[39]) or if the child comes within any of the categories of neglect or ill-treatment listed in section 58(1). Under section 59 a person of 15 years may also be so placed if so circumstanced that if he were a child within the meaning of the Act (i.e. a person

---

31. See sections 34–36 of Bill, as initiated.
32. [1985] 5 I.L.R.M. 302 (S.C.) discussed on p. 392 *ante*. See speech of A. Shatter T.D. in the Dáil during second stage debate on Bill reported in (30 May 1985) 359 Dáil Reports Cols. 161–173 and (5 June 1985) 359 Dáil Reports Cols. 471–524.
33. See also the School Attendance Act, 1926 (Extension of Application) Order 1972, *supra* which provides that "the provisions of the School Attendance Act, 1926 ... shall extend to children who have attained the age of fourteen years and have not attained the age of fifteen years".
34. School Attendance Act, 1926, Sect. 17(4). This subsection provides that Part IV of the Children Act, 1908, so far as applicable, shall apply if the court thinks fit to send a child to an industrial school, whilst Part II of the same Act shall apply in so far as applicable to a fit person order.
35. Subs. 7.
36. See Sect. 58(5).
37. See Sect. 58(4).
38. See Sect. 58(3). See further p. 416 *post*.
39. See Sect. 58(2).

under 15) he would come within one of the categories of neglect listed in section 58(1).

Section 21 of the Act provides for the making of a fit person order in respect of a child or young person following the criminal conviction of such person's parent or guardian. It provides in sub-s. 1 that

> "Where a person having the custody, charge, or care of a child or young person has been —
>
> (a) convicted of committing in respect of such child or young person an offence under this Part of this Act or any of the offences mentioned in the First Schedule to this Act;[40] or
>
> (b) committed for trial for any such offence; or
>
> (c) bound over to keep the peace towards such child or young person,
>
> by any court, that court, either at the time when the person is so convicted, committed for trial, or bound over, . . . or at any other time, and . . . may, if satisfied on inquiry that it is expedient so to deal with the child or young person, order that the child or young person be taken out of the custody, charge, or care of the person so convicted, committed for trial, or bound over, and be committed to the care of a relative of the child or young person, or some other fit person, named by the court (such relative or other person being willing to undertake such care), until he attains the age of sixteen years, or for any shorter period, and that court or any court of like jurisdiction may of its own motion, or on the application of any person, from time to time by order renew, vary, and revoke any such order".

Sub-s. 2 provides that

> "If the child or young person has a parent or legal guardian, no order shall be made under this section unless the parent or legal guardian has been convicted of or committed for trial for the offence, or is under committal for trial for having been, or has been proved to the satisfaction of the court making the order to have been, party or privy to the offence, or has been bound over to keep the peace towards the child or young person, or cannot be found."

Sub-s. 4 provides that

> "Where an order is made under this section in respect of a person who has been committed for trial, then, if that person is acquitted of the charge, or if the charge is dismissed for want of prosecution, the order is rendered void, except with regard to anything that may have been lawfully done under it."

In practice, a fit person order is only made in relation to a child under section 21 after the parent or guardian has been convicted of one of the offences mentioned in the section. As we have already seen,[41] a fit person order may also be made

---

40. Sect. 21 is in Part II of the Act. For the offences under Part II and those listed in the schedule see footnote 4 *ante*.

41. See p. 405 *ante*.

under section 24 of the Act of 1908 subsequent to the court making a place of safety order.[42]

A fit person under the Act may be a friend or relation or any other appropriate person or "any society or body corporate established for the reception or protection of poor children or the prevention of cruelty to children."[43] Clearly the Irish Society for the Prevention of Cruelty to Children comes within this definition and until the 1970s many of the care proceedings brought pursuant to the Children Act, 1908, were instituted by the society. Nowadays, the overwhelming majority of such proceedings are brought by health boards and in practice, a health board is usually named as a fit person, although no express authority is conferred on health boards by the Health Acts to so act. Section 5(1) of the Health Act, 1970, does, however, provide that a health board is a "body corporate" and as, undoubtedly, part of a health board's function is to "provide for the reception or protection of poor children"[44] it appears that the health boards may properly come within the concept of a fit person as defined in the Act of 1908.[45]

Section 22 of the Act of 1908 provides that any person named as a fit person shall have "like control over the child or young person as if he were his parent" and a health board, upon being named as a fit person, may determine whether a child should be placed with foster parents or placed in a residential school or institution. Moreover, in appropriate cases, following the making of a fit person order in its favour, health boards have also permitted children to remain residing in their own home under the supervision of health board personnel, such supervision including regular visits to the child's home by a health board social worker.[46]

In making a fit person order, the Act requires the court to "endeavour to ascertain" the religious persuasion to which the child belongs and to "select a person of the same religious persuasion or a person who gives such undertakings as seems to the court sufficient that the child shall be brought up in accordance with his own religious persuasion."[47] Consequently, a court may make a fit person order in favour of a person of a different religion to the child, if the necessary undertakings are obtained.

It should be noted that it appears from the wording of the Act, that a fit person order can only be made in favour of one person. Thus, if a child is to be placed in the care of a married couple, only one of the spouses can be formally named by the court as a fit person. However, if a health board is named as a fit person, it can enter into a foster care arrangement with either an individual or a married couple, as the health board under the terms of such order acquires

---

42. A child or young offender may also be placed with a fit person temporarily (see p. 423 *post*). See also the Employment of Children Act, 1903, Sect. 5, which provides that a child under sixteen years of age convicted of contravening any bye-law as to "street trading made under the Act" is liable in the case of a second or subsequent offence to be sent to an industrial school or to be "committed to the charge and control of some fit person".

43. Children Act, 1908, Sects. 38(1), 58(7) and 59.

44. See the Health Act, 1953, Sect. 55.

45. It could, however, be argued that to come within the above definition, a body must be established *solely* for the above stated purposes. If such an argument was upheld, health boards would have no authority to act as fit persons. The power to perform certain functions under the Children Act, 1908, is expressly conferred on health boards by the Health Act, 1970. Sect. 6(2)(g) provides for the performance by health boards of functions which previously were performed by local authorities under "Part I of the Children Act, 1908 and Sections 2 and 3 of the Children (Amendment) Act, 1957". These provisions do not apply to the making of fit person orders. See, however, Department of Health, *Guidelines, supra*, at pp. 17–18.

46. See *Task Force . . . Final Report, supra*, at p. 54.

47. Children Act, 1908, Sect. 23(1).

parental control over the child. Whether or not such arrangement is entered into, third parties caring for a child following the making of a fit person order, essentially act as foster parents to such child, although they are not legally described as such under the relevant legislation.

Finally, if the Children (Care & Protection) Bill, 1985, as initiated, is enacted, the District Court will no longer be empowered to make fit person orders. The making of a care order will result in a child being placed in the care of a health board, which will be empowered to decide whether the child should be placed by it with foster parents or be looked after in residential care.[48]

THE HEALTH ACT, 1953, AND HEALTH BOARD FOSTER CARE PLACEMENTS[49]

Children may not only be taken into care through the making of court orders in the circumstances already described but may also be received into care pursuant to the provisions of the Health Act, 1953. Section 55 of this Act empowers health boards to have a child cared for in one of three ways: by boarding him out; by sending him to a school approved by the Minister for Health, or if the child is over 14 by placing him in employment or in a course for the learning of a trade, calling or business.[50] The health board may so act in relation to any child eligible for institutional assistance under section 54 of the same Act, and who is

(a) a legitimate child whose parents are dead or who is deserted by his parents or (where one of them is dead) by the surviving parent, or

(b) an illegitimate child whose mother is dead or who is deserted by his mother.[51]

Further, with the approval of the Minister for Health, a health board may assist any person eligible for general assistance within the meaning of the Public Assistance Act, 1939, by having any child such person is liable to support, cared for in one of the above stated ways with that person's consent.[52] The provisions for general assistance contained in the Act of 1939 were repealed and replaced by the Social Welfare (Supplementary Welfare Allowance) Act, 1975, which has now, in turn, been subsumed within the Social Welfare (Consolidation) Act, 1981.[53] In practice, parents who are now eligible to receive supplementary welfare allowance under the Act of 1981 may ask a health board to arrange for the care of their child under this provision.

The "Boarding Out" of children under the above provisions is the statutory terminology used for the placing of children in foster care where such care is arranged and paid for by a health board. Detailed provisions relating to the

---

48. Upon the enactment and coming into force of the Children (Care & Protection) Bill, 1985, as initiated, they will be so described — see Parts III and IV of Bill and in particular Sect. 43.

49. See generally the *Task Force . . . Final Report, supra*, chapter 13; The Irish Foster Care Association, *Open Door: An Introduction to Foster Care in the Republic of Ireland* (Dublin, 1984) in particular at p. 65 *et seq.*

50. See, however, School Attendance Act, 1926 (Extension of Application) Order, 1972 (S.I. No. 105 of 1972) which raised the school leaving age from 14 to 15 years.

51. Health Act, 1953, Sect. 55(2). Sect. 54(2) provides that "a person who is unable to provide shelter and maintenance for himself or his dependants shall, for the purposes of this section, be eligible for institutional assistance." Sect. 54(1) states "institutional assistance" to mean "shelter and maintenance in a county home or similar institution."

52. Health Act, 1953, Sect. 55(3).

53. See p. 467 *post et seq.*

placement of children in fosterage by health boards are contained in the Boarding Out of Children Regulations, 1983.[54] These regulations include the following provisions:

(i) No child shall be sent by a health board to an approved school[55] unless he cannot be suitably and adequately assisted by being boarded out.[56]

(ii) potential foster parents must be properly assessed by the health board and their suitability and the suitability of their home determined.[57]

(iii) the "available history" of a child and the reports relating to proposed foster parents must "indicate" that the boarding out of a child in a particular home "would be conducive to the welfare of the child."[58]

(iv) a child cannot be boarded out with a person who is of a different religion to the child unless

    (a)   each of the child's parents or

    (b)   where the child is illegitimate, the mother, or

    (c)   the child's guardians

know the religion of that person and consent. If a legitimate child is an orphan or has been deserted by his parents, or where one parent is dead, has been deserted by the survivor, or if an illegitimate child's mother is dead or if he has been deserted by his mother, such child may board out with a person who is not of the same religion as the child, if such a person undertakes in writing that "the child will be brought up in the religion to which the child belongs."[59]

(v) within one month after a child has been placed with foster parents, the child and the home in which he is living must be inspected by an officer of the health board and such an inspection must take place thereafter "at such intervals not exceeding 6 months" as the health board determines. The health board must also similarly review the health and wellbeing of every child boarded out by it, and maintain a register and a case record of every child boarded out.[60]

(vi) funds necessary for the maintenance, clothing and education of a child boarded out and for such other assistance as the health board considers "reasonable" must also be provided.[61]

Under the Health Act, 1953, a health board may only board out or take into an approved school, children who are under 16 years of age. However, with the consent of the Minister for Health a health board may continue to support such child upon his attaining 16 years of age until "the completion of the child's education".[62] If a child is adopted by a person or persons with whom it was

54. S.I. No. 67 of 1983.
55. See the *Task Force . . . Final Report, supra,* at p. 64 where the names of schools approved by the Minister for Health are listed.
56. Reg. 5.
57. Reg. 7.
58. *Ibid.*
59. Reg. 8.
60. Regs. 11 to 14.
61. Reg. 15.
62. Health Act, 1953, Sect. 55(5). See also "Boarding Out" Regulations, Reg. 6. See further Sect. 55(4) which makes similar provision for a child over 16 years engaged in "learning a trade, calling or business."

boarded out, the health board may continue to contribute to the maintenance of such child as if he continued to be boarded out.[63]

The regulations provide for a form of contract to be entered into between the health board and foster parents. This contract requires foster parents to return a child to a health board "at any time where the health board, with the consent of the Minister for Health, decides to remove the child from the foster parents" or where the Minister requires the health board to so act.[64] In this context it should be noted that section 56 of the Act empowers the Minister, who exercises a supervisory function, not only to require a health board to remove a child from foster parents but also to require the removal of a child from an approved school or from the custody of any person with whom the child has been placed in employment by a health board. A person who "wilfully refuses or neglects" to deliver up such custody is liable on summary conviction to a fine of £10. Upon so convicting a person the District Court that determined such case is required by the Act to make an order for the return of the child to the health board.[65]

Both the Kennedy Report[66] and the Task Force Final Report[67] noted that the main reason for distinguishing between children committed to care under the Children Acts and children received into care by health boards under the Health Act is the channels through which they arrive in care rather than their background.[68] However, an important difference in relation to the latter, is that upon parents or a parent being again able to care for a child, a child taken into care under the Health Acts may be returned to its parents without court proceedings having to be instituted to set aside a court order made by which such child was taken into care.

Where a parent seeks the return of a child taken into care under the Health Act, 1953, and a health board is of the belief that the child is in need of care and protection, it is, of course, open to the health board to bring proceedings under section 58 or any other appropriate section of the Children Act, 1908. Moreover, if foster parents with whom a child has been placed believe it is contrary to a child's welfare that he be removed from their custody, they may apply to the Circuit or High Court to have such child made a ward of court and may seek an order for custody in their favour.[69] Wardship proceedings can also be brought by a health board, if it deems such proceedings appropriate and if it is of the belief that necessary protection cannot be extended to a child pursuant to the provisions of the Children Acts, 1908–1957. Upon a health board or foster parents refusing to comply with a request made by a child's natural parents or parent that a child received into care under the Health Acts be returned to parental custody, a parent may issue Habeas Corpus proceedings to enforce the parental right to custody or issue proceedings under section 11 of

63. Health Act, 1953, Sect. 55(9)(c).
64. See Appendix I which contains the standard form of contract prescribed by the regulations.
65. Health Act, 1953, Sect. 56(5).
66. *The Reformatory & Industrial Schools Systems Report, 1970* (The Kennedy Report) (Stationery Office, Dublin, 1970).
67. *Supra.*
68. See The Kennedy Report at p. 112 and the Task Force Report at p. 62.
69. See "Wards of Court" p. 399 *ante.* See the Children (Care & Protection) Bill, 1985, as initiated, Part V of which is designed to provide a simpler procedure for foster parents to seek custody orders in relation to children who have resided with them for some time. This part of the Bill is badly drafted in that it fails to state how it is to interact with the provisions of the Guardianship of Infants Act, 1964 and will require extensive amendment during the passage of the Bill through the Oireachtas. See speech of Alan Shatter T.D. (5th June 1985) 356 Dáil Debates Cols. 520–522.

the Guardianship of Infants Act, 1964, to obtain court orders requiring the return of such child.[70]

Section 25 of the Children (Care & Protection) Bill, 1985, as initiated, proposes to extend the circumstances in which health boards are legally empowered to receive children into "voluntary care", i.e. without the institution of care proceedings. Under this provision a child "who has no parent or guardian able to provide for his proper care, maintenance and upbringing" may be received into care in appropriate circumstances even where his parents are not eligible for supplementary welfare allowance. Thus, under this provision, a health board will be able to receive into care a child whose parents are temporarily unable to care for it due to illness, or a child whose mother wants some time prior to deciding whether to place her child for adoption. In practice, despite the absence of the necessary legislation, health boards do currently make arrangements for the care of children in such circumstances. Moreover, upon a parent voluntarily placing a child in care, a health board will be permitted under the Bill, as initiated, to place such child with foster parents, if such placement accords with the child's needs.[71] Under the current law, if a child is received into care with parental agreement, the consent of the parent or parents is required in order to place the child in fosterage. As a result, if parental agreement to a fostercare placement is not forthcoming, the child who has been voluntarily placed by parents in care may have to be brought up in a residential institution by a health board even if the health board is of the belief that the child could benefit from the type of upbringing that foster parents could provide.[72]

THE CHILDREN ACT, 1908–1957 AND PRIVATE FOSTER CARE PLACEMENTS

A parent or parents may enter into a private arrangement for a legitimate child to live permanently with and be brought up by a married couple or any other persons or person and no statutory requirements of any nature have to be complied with in respect of such an arrangement. If a written agreement or contract is concluded between the parents of the child and foster parents, in which the natural parents agree that their child shall remain with the foster parents throughout its minority, as has already been seen, such agreement or contract is unenforceable at law[72a] and no legal relationship in such circumstances exists between the natural and foster parents. In the event of a dispute arising between them and the natural parents seeking the return of their child and the foster parents wishing the child to be left in their custody, the former may institute proceedings by way of making a Habeas Corpus application in respect of such child or pursuant to Guardianship of Infants Act, 1964, whilst the latter may invoke the wardship jurisdiction as discussed in the preceding section.[73]

Section 2 of the Children Act, 1957, requires parents of a legitimate child, who arrange that their child under 16 years be cared for by foster parents or

---

70. See "Custody Disputes Between Parents and Third Parties" starting at p. 376 *ante*.
71. See Part IV of Bill, as initiated.
72. The Task Force Final Report (*supra* at p. 178) notes that many of the children who need long term family placements do so because of the incapacity of their parent or parents to meet their needs and that such incapacity can "itself ... inhibit their ability to recognise the needs of their children." It goes on to recommend (*supra* at p. 218) that "consideration be given to making provision for dispensing with a parent's consent to the placement of a child in foster care where the withholding of such consent is not in the best interests of the child."
73. See footnotes 69 and 70 *ante*.

by any other person in return for payment or other reward by them, to notify their area health board 7 days in advance of their intention to implement any such arrangement. Moreover, if the mother of an illegitimate child makes such an arrangement for the care of her child, whether or not for payment or other reward by her, she is similarly obliged to so notify the health board. A person or body other than a child's parent who makes any such arrangement for the care of a child must also give a health board 7 days notice of the proposed arrangements.[74] In all instances, there is also an obligation imposed on foster parents or any other persons receiving children into their care in such circumstances to give 7 days advance notice to the area health board.[75] If a "body" as opposed to a person receives a child into its care, it appears that there is no obligation on the body to give advance notice to a health board of a child being so placed in its care.[76] Failure to give a necessary notice is a criminal offence, creating a liability to a sentence of 6 months imprisonment or to a fine not exceeding £25.

The Children Acts impose a duty on health boards to make regular enquiries as to whether legitimate children in fosterage for payment or reward, or illegitimate children in fosterage, are being properly cared for and where they are not, authorises the removal to a place of safety of a child in such circumstances and its return to its parents or any other relatives.[77]

Finally, it should be noted that the statutory provisions governing fosterage, including the notification requirements, do not apply where a child is placed by a registered adoption society with prospective adopters and where the adoption procedures are in the course of implementation.[78] They also do not apply to a child being placed in fosterage with "a relative" which for the purposes of section 2 of the 1957 Act is defined as meaning "grandparents, brothers, sisters, uncles, aunts" and in the case of illegitimate children "the person who would be so related if the infant were legitimate."[79]

Part II of the Children (Care & Protection) Bill, 1985, as initiated, contains provisions intended to eliminate the differences in the law in this area in so far as it distinguishes between legitimate and illegitimate children.

CHILDREN AND THE CRIMINAL LAW

Criminal Liability[80]

A child may be held criminally responsible for his acts from the age of seven. Under common law there is an irrebuttable presumption that a child below that age cannot commit a criminal offence, in that such a young child could not

---

74. See the Children Act, 1957, Sect. 2(2) and 2(7).
75. *Ibid.*, Sect. 2(1). See further Sect. 2(3) which relates to a person for reward, caring for a child already in his care without reward.
76. *Task Force . . . Final Report, supra* at p. 174.
77. Children Act, 1908, Sect. 5.
78. Adoption Act, 1964, Sect. 10.
79. Children Act, 1908, Sect. 11.
80. Under the Summary Jurisdiction over Children (Ireland) Act, 1884, as amended by the Children Act, 1941, Sect. 28, a child or young person charged with an indictable offence other than homicide may be dealt with by a court of summary jurisdiction, if the parent or guardian does not object. The court of summary jurisdiction that hears such cases is the District Court, sitting as a juvenile or children's court (see p. 50). In practice the great majority of criminal charges whether of a minor or serious nature, brought against children are dealt with by the District Courts. Although a child has a right to a jury trial for a nonminor offence – (see Articles 38.2 and 38.5 of the Constitution) in practice the number that opt for jury trial is small.

distinguish between right and wrong. From the age of seven to 14 years there is a rebuttable presumption of innocence,[81] i.e. a presumption that a child lacks criminal capacity or is *doli incapax*.[82] To override this presumption it must be established that at the time of committing the act charged, the child knew it was wrong.[83] Unfortunately, in practice the necessity to prove such knowledge is often ignored.

The decided cases are unclear as to the exact meaning of "knowledge of wrongfulness".[84] Does the requirement of knowledge of wrong refer to legal wrong or moral wrong; or may a child be convicted if he knew that his act belonged to either class of wrong? No definite answer has yet been given by the courts to this question.

It has been held that in order to prove the requisite knowledge, evidence that the child committed the act in question is not sufficient.[85] Evidence of a child's home background, however, may determine the matter. Thus, proof that a boy, nearly nine years of age, came from a respectable home and had been properly brought up was held sufficient to establish knowledge of wrongfulness in respect of a charge of breaking and entering.[86] Evidence that an eight year old upon being accused of "stealing" a cash box and money, admitted it, has also been held to rebut the presumption.[87] In this case, evidence as to a child's "home background and all his circumstances" was said to be "highly material to the question of whether a child knows what he is doing is wrong and should be admitted in spite of the risk that it will disclose information highly prejudicial to him.[88] Moreover, the English Court of Appeal has held that evidence of

---

81. See cases cited in footnote 83 below. See further *Monagle v. Donegal Co. Council* [1961] Ir. Jur. Rep. 37 (H.C.) – "The law does not presume children under the age of seven to be responsible for their acts and there is a rebuttable presumption that children under fourteen years are not so responsible" *per* Murnaghan J. at p. 39. See also *Goodbody v. The Mayor of Waterford* [1954] Ir. Jur. Rep. 39 (H.C.); J.F. Crotty, *Practice and Procedure in the District Court* (Cork University Press, Cork 1960), p. 44.

However, in recent years a number of District Justices have accepted the contention that it applies until a child's fifteenth birthday. See *Reformatory and Industrial Schools Systems Report* (The Kennedy Report) (Stationery Office, Dublin 1970), p. 68 where the presumption is said to apply to children "from the age of seven to fifteen". See also E. Stewart, "Young Offenders: Children and the Criminal Law" (1976) 110 I.L.T. & S.J. pp. 279, 286, 291, 297, 303, at p. 292 where it is also stated that the presumption applies from "the age of seven years to fifteen years". The Children Act, 1941, Sect. 28 is relied upon to support this contention. However, that provision merely amends the definition of child for the purposes of the Summary Jurisdiction Over Children (Ireland) Act, 1884. The latter Act says nothing about the age of criminal responsibility. The *Task Force . . . Final Report* affirms that the presumption applies to children between the ages of 7 and 14 years (see p. 230 of Report).

82. For criticism of the use of the phrase *doli incapax* see G.L. Williams, "The Criminal Responsibility of Children", (1954) Crim. L.R. 493. The author states that the use of this phrase suggests that proof of fraud or intention on the part of a child is sufficient to rebut the presumption. However, a child may intend to do the act in question, without knowing that it is wrong. It is knowledge by a child of the wrongfulness of his act that is required to rebut the presumption.

83. *R. v. Owen* (1830) 4 Car. & P. 236; 172 E.R. 685 (*Nisi Prius*); *R. v. Manley* (1844) 1 Cox C.C. 104 (Assizes); *R. v. Smith* [1845] 1 Cox C.C. 260, 393 (Assizes). See also *R. v. Vamplew* (1862) 3F & F. 520; 176 E.R. 234 (*Nisi Prius*); *R. v. Kershaw* (1902) 18 T.L.R. 357 (Assizes); *R. v. Gorrie* (1918), 183, J.P. 136, *W. (An Infant) v. Simpson* [1967] Crim. L.R. 360 (Q.B.D.); *B. v. R.* (1960) 44 Cr. App. Rep. I., sub nom. *X. v. X.* [1958] Crim. L.R. 805 (Q.B.D.); *F. v. Padwick* [1959] Crim. L.R. 439 (Q.B.D.). (The minimum age at which a child could be convicted of an offence was raised in England to 8 in 1933 and to 10 in 1963).

84. See G.L. Williams, *supra*. See also N. Osborough, "Rebutting The Presumption of Doli Incapax" (1975) 10 I.J. (n.s.) 48.

85. *R. v. Owen, supra; R. v. Smith, supra; R. v. Kershaw, supra.*

86. *B. v. R., supra.*

87. *F. v. Padwick, supra.*

88. *Ibid.*, at p. 440.

previous convictions may be given provided such evidence is relevant to the issue of the child's capacity to know good from evil.[89] However, such evidence may only be introduced if it has a bearing on the latter issue. If it does not, it will generally be excluded due to the prejudicial effect of such evidence. Finally, a boy under 14 years of age cannot be found guilty of rape or certain other sexual offences, there being an irrebuttable legal presumption that all boys under that age are physically incapable of having sexual intercourse.[90] This presumption has been described as absurd by one commentator[91] and in a recent English case was held not to extend to affiliation proceedings, the court holding that a boy aged thirteen and three-quarters at the date when a child was conceived, could properly be held to be the father of the child.[92] Whether the courts will at some future date review the application of this presumption to criminal proceedings remains to be seen.

Determination as to Age

There is an obligation imposed on a court to take some evidence on oath with regard to the question of the age of a person brought before it, if it appears that such person is a child or young person. Section 123(1) of the Children Act, 1908, as amended,[93] provides

"Where a person whether charged with an offence or not is brought before any Court otherwise than for the purpose of giving evidence and it appears to the Court that he is a child or young person the Court shall make due enquiry as to the age of that person and for that purpose shall take such evidence as may be forthcoming at the hearing of the case but an order or judgement of the Court shall not be invalidated by any subsequent proof that the age of that person has not been correctly stated to the Court and the age presumed or declared by the Court to be the age of the person so brought before it shall for the purposes of this Act be deemed to be the true age of that person and where it appears to the Court that the person so brought before it is of the age of 17 years or upwards the person shall for the purposes of this Act be deemed not to be a child or young person".

In the *State (Kenny) v. D.J. O'hUadhaigh*[94] Finlay P. made absolute a conditional order of Certiorari quashing three District Court convictions for which the applicant had been sentenced to six months imprisonment. The applicant should have been dealt with under the Children Acts as she was only fifteen at the date of the District Court hearing, but she had told the District Justice and the arresting guard that she was 18 years of age and had been treated as an adult. No inquiry as to her age had been made when she was giving evidence on oath.

89. *R. v. B.*] 1979] 3 All E.R. 460 (C.A.). See also J.S. Fisher, "Rebutting the Presumption of a Child's Criminal Incapacity" (1980) 130 N.L.J. 752.
90. See e.g. *R. v. Groombridge* (1836) 7 Car. and P. 582; 173 E.R. 256 (*Nisi Prius*); *R. v. Brimilow* (1840) 2 Mood. 122; 169 E.R. 49 (Crown Cases); *R. v. Eldershaw* (1828) 3 Car. & P. 396 172 E.R. 472 (Assizes); *R. v. Philips* (1839) 8 Car. & P. 736; 173 E.R. 695 (*Nisi Prius*); *R. v. Waite* [1892] 2 Q.B. 600 (C.C.R.). Although this rule rests on the principle that such a young child is physically incapable of committing a sexual offence, no evidence is admissible to prove that the particular child charged was capable – *R. v. Philips, supra*; *R. v. Jordan* (1838) 9 Car. & P. 118; 173 E.R. 765 (*Nisi Prius*); *R. v. Waite, supra*. However he may be convicted of indecent assault – *R. v. Williams* [1893] 1 Q.B. 32 (C.C.R.).
91. See Smith & Hogan, "Criminal Law", 5th Ed. (London, Butterworths, 1983) at p. 412.
92. *L. v. K.* [1985] 3 W.L.R. 202 (Fam. D.).
93. By the Children Act, 1941, Sect. 27.
94. [1979] I.R. 1 (H.C.).

Finlay P. stated that the proper construction of the above quoted section imposes "upon the Court an obligation to take some evidence on oath with regard to the question of the age of the person before it". As no such evidence as to age had been obtained the convictions could not stand.

Pre-trial Detention

A child or young person charged with an offence may be released on bail pending trial or held in custody.[95] The relevant legislation is contained in Part V of the Act of 1908. Section 94[96] provides that

"Where a person apparently under the age of seventeen years is apprehended with or without warrant, and cannot be brought forthwith before a court of summary jurisdiction, a superintendent or inspector of police, or other officer of police of equal or superior rank or the officer in charge of the police station to which such person is brought, shall inquire into the case and may in any case, and shall

(a) unless the charge is one of homicide or other grave crime; or

(b) unless it is necessary in the interest of such person to remove him from association with any reputed criminal or prostitute; or

(c) unless the officer has reason to believe that the release of such person would defeat the end of justice,

release such person on a recognizance, with or without sureties, for such an amount as will, in the opinion of the officer, secure the attendance of such person upon the hearing of the charge, being entered into by him or by his parent or guardian".

Where a person under 17 is not released under the above provision he must be held in a place of detention provided under Part V of the Act[97]

"until he can be brought before a court of summary jurisdiction, unless the officer certifies —

(a) that it is impracticable to do so; or

(b) that he is of so unruly a character that he cannot be safely so detained; or

(c) that by reason of his state of health or of his mental or bodily condition it is advisable so to detain him;

and the certificate shall be produced to the court before which the person is brought".[98]

Section 97 provides that

"(1) A court of summary jurisdiction, on remanding or committing for trial a child or young person who is not released on bail, shall instead of committing him to prison, commit him to custody in a place of detention provided under this Part of this Act and named in the commitment, to be

---

95. As for the general circumstances in which bail may be refused see *People (A.G.) v. O'Callaghan* [1966] I.R. 501 (S.C.).
96. As amended by the Children Act, 1941, Sect. 24.
97. See Children Act, 1908, Sect. 108. There is, at the date of writing, only one place of detention in Ireland, St. Laurence's School in Finglas, Dublin.
98. Children Act, 1908, Sect. 95, as amended by Children Act, 1941, Sect. 25.

there detained for the period for which he is remanded or until he is thence delivered in due course of law:

Provided that in the case of a young person it shall not be obligatory on the court so to commit him if the court certifies that he is of so unruly a character that he cannot be safely so committed, or that he is of so depraved a character that he is not a fit person to be so detained.

(2) A commitment under this section may be varied or, in the case of a young person who proves to be of so unruly a character that he cannot be safely detained in such custody, or to be of so depraved a character that he is not a fit person to be so detained, revoked by any court of summary jurisdiction acting in or for the place in or for which the court which made the order acted, and if it is so revoked the young person may be committed to prison".[99]

Consequences of Conviction[100]

A child cannot be sentenced to imprisonment and neither a child nor a young person can be sentenced to death or penal servitude.[101] If a child or young person is convicted of an offence punishable with penal servitude and if the court considers that the imposition of a period of detention is the only suitable punishment to impose, it may commit the child or young person to a place of detention for such term as may be specified in the order but in no case exceeding one month.[102] A young person can only be imprisoned for the commission of an offence if the court certifies that he is of so unruly a character that he cannot be detained in a place of detention, or that he is so depraved a character that he is not a fit person to be so detained.

If a young person is so certified, there is no maximum term of imprisonment beyond which he cannot be sentenced which derives from the fact that he is a

---

99. See the *State (Ward and others) v. Superintendent of the Bridewell Garda Station, Irish Times* 24th & 25th Jan. 1975. The High Court granted an order of Habeas Corpus in respect of six children between the ages of 9 and 13 who had been remanded in custody in the Bridewell Garda Station in Dublin. The Bridewell was not a scheduled place of detention as provided under Part V of the Act of 1908 and there was no evidence of the children being unruly. Consequently, their detention was unlawful. No order was made in relation to two other children in respect of whom the application was also made, as they had been detained in St. Laurence's School in Finglas, which was a place of detention provided under Sect. 108 for the purpose of detaining children and young persons on remand. See also *The State (fifteen year old girl) v. Deputy Governor of Mountjoy Prison, Irish Times* 27th Feb. 1975. An order of Habeas Corpus was granted in the High Court in respect of a fifteen year old girl held in Mountjoy Prison on remand.

100. It is intended here to briefly look at the consequences of the conviction of children under 16. A child over 17 may be sentenced in the same manner as an adult whilst a child of 16 years or over may also be detained in St. Patrick's Institution or Shanganagh Castle. For a full discussion of the history of, and the law applicable to these institutions see N. Osborough, *Borstal in Ireland* (I.P.A., Dublin, 1975).

A person under 16 cannot be sent to St. Patrick's, see *State (Two Limerick girls) v. Limerick Circuit Court Judge, (Irish Times* 23rd Jan. 1975). The High Court held an order sentencing a girl under 16 to St. Patrick's Institution to be invalid. See also D.C. Mitchell, A Report on the Law and Procedure Regarding the Prosecution and Disposal of Youthful Offenders (Commissioned by the Director of Public Prosecutions, Dublin, 1977). pp. 63–67. See further *The People v. Howard, Irish Times*, 1 April 1977, where the Court of Criminal Appeal in confirming a sentence of ten years penal servitude imposed on the defendant held that in relation to determining sentence, the relevant age was the defendant's age at the date of sentence and not at the date of the commission of the offence. The defendant was seventeen years old when sentenced.

101. Children Act, 1908, Sect. 103 and 102(1) and (2). See also the *State (O) v. O'Brien* [1973] I.R. 50 (S.C.).

102. Children Act, 1908, Sect. 106.

young person and which is less than the maximum sentence that can be imposed on an adult.[103]

In the *State (Hanley) v. Governor of Mountjoy Prison*[104] the court certified that the applicant was of so unruly a character that he could not be detained in a place of detention in safety, and he was sentenced to one month's imprisonment in Mountjoy Prison. No express evidence was adduced to show unruly character and at the time of conviction no place for detention after sentence[105] existed for the Dublin Metropolitan District in which the applicant had been tried.[106] On an application for Habeas Corpus, it was held by Finlay J. that since the crimes to which the applicant pleaded guilty involved, in part, crimes of violence, this in itself amounted to some evidence of unruly character. However, he granted the application on the ground that a District Justice could not certify a person as being unsuitable to detain in a place of detention when no such place existed.

In the later case of the *State (Holland) v. District Justice Kennedy and Another*,[107] Hamilton J., in the High Court, making absolute a conditional order of *Certiorari* stated that

> "It is the duty of the Courts to protect the rights of citizens and in particular the rights of 'young persons' within the meaning of the Children's Act, 1908 . . . very definite and specific evidence of the unruly nature of the general character of a convicted young person would be necessary before he was committed to prison rather than to a place of detention . . . the Court must conduct an enquiry as to the general character of the convicted young person and the convicted young person should have the right to challenge and rebut any evidence given".[108]

As no such inquiry had been made by the District Justice, an order made by her certifying the applicant to be of so unruly character that he could not be detained in a place of detention and sentencing him to one month's imprisonment in Mountjoy Prison, was quashed. The Supreme Court, on appeal, affirmed the decision of Hamilton J. The Court held that the word "character" means "nature or disposition". Henchy J. stated that the relevant provision of the 1908 Act requires that a District Justice must be satisfied that a young person

> "*is* of so unruly a character (not that he *has been* so unruly) that he *cannot be* (not that he ought *not to be*) detained in the provided place of detention".[109]

Thus, proof of the committal of a particular offence is not sufficient by itself. The court must fully examine the young person's antecedents and behavioural pattern in so far as that is possible. The mere conviction of Holland for assault without further enquiries being made as to his character was not sufficient to support the ruling of the District Justice.[110]

In *The State (Donohue) v. District Justice Kennedy*[111] the High Court again

---

103. See *The State (Laffrey) v. Esmonde* [1983] I.R. 229 (S.C.).
104. (1974) 108 I.L.T.R. 102 (H.C.).
105. As envisaged under the Children Act, 1908, Sect. 108.
106. St. Laurence's in Finglas was at that time only a place of detention for the purpose of detaining young persons on remand.
107. [1977] I.R. 193 (H.C., S.C.).
108. *Ibid.*, at pp. 197, 198.
109. *Ibid.*, at p. 200.
110. The ground on which the applicant was successful in Hanly's case could not be relied on by Holland as by the time the District Justice made her order St. Laurence's in Finglas had been designated as a place of detention for young persons after sentence. See further, *The State (Laffey) v. Esmonde, supra* where all appropriate enquiries were made.
111. (July, 1979) unreported (H.C.).

made absolute a conditional order of certiorari quashing an order of the District Justice certifying that the applicant, who was fifteen years of age, was a person of unruly character and remanding him in custody in Mountjoy Prison. At the date when the district court order was made there was no sworn evidence given to the court of unruly behaviour, the District Justice basing her decision on an assessment report received by her from the Child Assessment Centre in St. Laurence's School, Finglas. Neither the applicant nor his solicitor saw or read the report and the solicitor had not objected to the District Justice reading it at the District Court hearing.

Giving judgement in favour of the applicant, Finlay P. stated:

> "I have come to the conclusion that a decision to certify a young offender as of unruly character is of the same status as any other decision in a criminal proceeding and as such can only be reached by a court upon sworn evidence properly admissible before it, the accused having an opportunity through his solicitor to cross-examine the witnesses deposing to the facts concerned. I am therefore satisfied that the procedure which was operated . . . notwithstanding the willingness of the District Justice to let the report be read by the solicitor for the prosecutor was not in accordance with natural justice and that therefore the order of remand in custody must be quashed."

In the same case Finlay P. referred to the desirability of assessment reports being made available to the courts dealing with young offenders and stated:

> "A District Justice should be in a position having received an appropriate report from the social workers and other persons concerned at the Remand Centre to obtain as a matter of practicality the consent of the solicitor representing the young offender to the reading of those reports making them available to the solicitor and hearing any submissions or comments he should make upon them. For such a procedure it would be necessary presumably for the reports to be received but not read by the District Justice until he or she has obtained the consent of the solicitor for the young offender. This procedure would in my view not only be lawful but is most desirable so as to prevent the District Justice dealing with young offenders from being deprived of the valuable recommendations and observations of persons concerned with the Children's Centre."

It is clear that in the absence of the necessary consent being forthcoming the court may not read or take into consideration the contents of any such report.

A child under 12 years of age convicted of an offence punishable in the case of an adult by penal servitude or a lesser punishment, may be sent by the court to an industrial school[112] if the court is satisfied "that it is expedient so to deal with him".[113] A child of 12 years or upwards but less than 17 years of age convicted of a similarly punishable offence may be sent to a reformatory school.[114] A child who has reached 12 years of age and is under 15 years of age, however, with no previous conviction, may be sent to an industrial school, if having regard to the special circumstances of the case the court is satisfied he should not be sent to a reformatory. The court must be satisfied that "the character and ante-

---

112. An "industrial school means a school for the industrial training of children, in which children are lodged, clothed and fed, as well as taught" — Children Act, 1908, Sect. 44(1).
113. Children Act, 1908, Sect. 58(2).
114. *Ibid.*, Sect. 57(1) as amended by the Children Act, 1941, Sect. 9(1). A "reformatory school" means a school for the industrial training of youthful offenders in which youthful offenders are lodged, clothed and fed as well as taught. Children Act, 1908, Sect. 44(1).

cedents of the child are such that he will not exercise an evil influence over the other children" in the school and that the manager of the school is willing to accept the child.[115]

A number of alternative options are available to the court other than detaining a child or young person who commits an offence.[116]

(a) The court may (i) dismiss the information or charge; or (ii) may discharge the child or young person conditionally on his entering into a recognisance with or without sureties to be of good behaviour and to appear for conviction and sentence when called on at any time during a specified period not exceeding three years. In the case of (ii) the court may impose a further condition that he be placed on probation under the supervision of any person named in the order.[117]

(b) The court may fine the child or young person or order him to pay damages and the costs of the proceedings. The maximum amount a child can be required to pay in respect of each is two pounds.

(c) If a child or young person is charged with an offence for the commission of which a fine, damages, or costs may be imposed, and the court is of opinion that the case would be best met by the imposition of a fine, damages, or costs, whether with or without any other punishment, the court may in any case, and shall if the offender is a child, order that the fine, damages, or costs awarded be paid by the parent or guardian of the child or young person, unless the court is satisfied (a) that the parent or guardian cannot be found or (b) that he has not conduced to the commission of the offence by neglecting to exercise due care of the child or young person.[118]

(d) Where a court thinks that a charge against a child or young person is proved, it may make an order on the parent or guardian for the payment of damages or costs or requiring him to give security for good behaviour, without proceeding to the conviction of the child or young person.[119]

(e) The court also has a general power to order a parent or guardian to give security for the good behaviour of a child or young person.[120]

(f) The court may make a fit person order.[121]

Finally, a child who commits an offence of a minor nature may not be brought

115. *Ibid.*, Sect. 58(3) as amended by Children Act, 1941, Sect. 10(2).
116. See generally the Children Act, 1908, Sect. 107.
117. See the Probation of Offenders Act, 1907, Sects. 1 and 2, as amended by the Criminal Justice Administration Act, 1914. Under the provisions of Sect. 1 a justice may dismiss the charge or information or conditionally discharge the offender without proceeding to conviction if the court thinks the charge is proved; "but is of opinion that, having regard to the character, antecedents, age, health, or mental condition of the person charged, or to the trivial nature of the offence, or to the extenuating circumstances under which the offence was committed, it is inexpedient to inflict any punishment or any other than a nominal punishment, or that it is expedient to release the offender on probation". See also the Summary Jurisdiction Over Children (Ireland) Act, 1884, Sect. 7.
118. Children Act, 1908, Sect. 99(1).
119. *Ibid.*, Sect. 99(3).
120. *Ibid.*, Sect. 99(2).
121. See p. 409 *ante*.

into court at all, but may simply come under the supervision of a juvenile liaison officer.[122]

DETENTION AND RELEASE

Temporary Detention and Assessment

A detention order may take effect immediately, or at a later date. The court may make such order as it thinks fit having regard "to the age or health of the youthful offender or child".[123] If —

(a) a detention order is made, but is not to take effect immediately; or

(b) at the time specified for the order to take effect the youthful offender or child is unfit to be sent to a reformatory or industrial school; or

(c) the school to which the youthful offender or child is to be sent cannot be ascertained until inquiry has been made,

the court may make an order committing him either to custody in any place to which he might be committed on remand under Part V of the 1908 Act, or to the custody of a relative or other fit person, until he is sent to a reformatory or industrial school in pursuance of the detention order.[124]

(c) above is the provision which may be utilised by the court if it wishes to send a child to an assessment centre prior to determining where he should be detained.

Period of Detention

The period for which a child or young person may be detained in an industrial school or a reformatory, is called the period of detention and is determined by the court. Under section 65 of the 1908 Act, the period of detention in an industrial school is to be for such time as seems proper to the court, for the teaching and training of the child but may not extend beyond the child's 16th birthday.[125] The Minister for Education, however, may extend the period until the child reaches 17 years of age "for the purpose of the completion by the child of any course of education or training" provided the consent of the child's parents, surviving parent, mother (in the case of an illegitimate child) or guardian is obtained.[126] The above provision applies irrespective of the reason why a child was first sent to an industrial school, i.e. whether he was sent to the school for the commission of an offence or simply because he was in need of care and attention. A youthful offender may be detained in a reformatory for not less than two years and not more than four years, but not beyond the time when he attains 19 years of age.[127]

Finally, a child or young person convicted of murder, manslaughter, or

---

122. See P. Shanley, "The Formal Cautioning of Juvenile Offenders" (1970) 5 I.J. (n.s.) 262; *Children Deprived — The Care Memorandum on Deprived Children and Children's Services in Ireland* (Dublin, 1972) p. 21; *Task Force . . . Final Report, supra* at pp. 126 and 246.

123. Children Act, 1908, Sect. 61.

124. *Ibid.*, Sect. 63.

125. Children Act, 1908, Sect. 65(b).

126. Children Act, 1941, Sect. 12. In the case of a girl sent to St. Anne's school, Kilmacud, it seems that the Minister may make such an order without the consent of her parents — see the Children (Amend.) Act, 1949, Sect. 6.

127. Children Act, 1908, Sect. 65(a) as amended by Children Act, 1941, Sect. 11.

GUARDIANSHIP AND CUSTODY OF CHILDREN

attempted murder or wounding, may be detained for such period as is specified by the court.[128]

Release

A child or youthful offender may be released prior to completing the period of detention laid down by the court in the following ways.

(1) *By Order of discharge*: The Minister for Education may at any time order a child or youthful offender to be discharged from an industrial school or reformatory with or without conditions. If a discharge is conditional the Minister may revoke the discharge if a condition is breached.[129] If an application is made to the Minister for Education by a parent or guardian for the release of a child committed to an industrial school under section 58, if the Minister is satisfied

(a) that the circumstances which led to the making of the committal order have ceased and are not likely to recur upon the release of the child, and

(b) that the parent or guardian is able to support the child,

he may either discharge the child or refer the application to the court. If the court is satisfied as to (a) and (b) above it may order the discharge of the child.[130]

(2) *Release on licence*:[131] A youthful offender or child detained in an industrial school or reformatory may be released on licence by the manager of the place where he is detained,

(a) at any time with the consent of the Minister for Education, *or*

(b) after six months without any consent.[132]

A licence permits a child to live with any "trustworthy and respectable person" named in the licence willing to receive and take charge of him. Unless the licence is revoked, a child remains on licence until such time as his period of detention would have expired. The Kennedy Report noted that this system is rarely used.[133]

(3) *Leave of absence*: At any time during the period of detention the manager of an industrial school or reformatory may give a child or youthful offender leave to be absent. A child is granted leave to be placed in the charge "of such person and for such period" as the manager shall think fit, *or* "to attend a course of instruction at another school, either as a boarder or a day pupil". During leave of absence a child is deemed to be still in detention and under the manager's care. The latter may at any time require the child to return to the reformatory or industrial school.[134]

---

128. See Children Act, 1908, Sects. 103 and 104 and the *State (O) v. O'Brien, supra*. See also *R. v. Fitt* [1919] 2 I.R. 35; 53 I.L.T.R. 7 (Cr.C.R.) in which it was held that for the purpose of sentencing a youthful offender the relevant time for determining his age is when he is being sentenced by the court and not when he commits the offence.
129. Children Act, 1908, Sect. 69.
130. Children (Amendment) Act, 1957, Sect. 5.
131. Children Act, 1908, Sect. 67 as amended by Children Act, 1941, Sect. 15. Strictly speaking a person released under the circumstances described in this section is released under a supervision certificate. However the word "licence" has been preserved here so as to distinguish it from release on supervision discussed further on.
132. Children Act, 1908, Sect. 67 as amended by Children Act, 1941, Sect. 13(a).
133. *Supra*, at p. 76.
134. Children Act, 1957, Sect. 6(1).

(4) *On supervision*: A youthful offender sent to a reformatory school whose period of detention has expired remains under the supervision of the managers of the school up to the age of 19.[135] Further, if the Minister for Education directs that "it is necessary for the protection and welfare of the youthful offender" the supervision period can be extended until he reaches 21 years of age.[136] A child sent to an industrial school remains under the supervision of the managers of the school from the expiration of the period of detention until he reaches 18 years of age.[137] Further, as in the case of a reformatory school, the Minister can extend supervision until a child reaches 21 years of age. A child detained in an industrial school for the purpose of enforcing an attendance order however, upon release, is not subject to such supervision.[138] Where a supervision certificate has been granted, a person or child subject to it may be recalled if the managers are of the opinion that it is necessary for such person's protection. A person upon being recalled may be detained in the school for no longer than three months and may at any time again be placed out on a supervision certificate.[139] If the Minister discharges a child under (1) above the managers have no further responsibility for him.

CRITICISMS AND SUGGESTED REFORMS

In 1980 the Task Force on Child Care Services in its Final Report[140] to the Minister for Health noted that over the preceding 150 years "the services for deprived children and children at risk were initiated and developed piecemeal", that they were the result of "fragmented planning" and were "lacking in cohesion".[141] The need for a complete overhaul and reform of both children's law and children's services had been apparent and well documented long before the Task Force reported. The Task Force Report is merely the most recent detailed report relating to this area. Whilst it makes a vast number of worthwhile recommendations to provide a modern, coherent and efficient children's service responsive to the needs of children, it should be noted that in crucial areas, such as those relating to children at risk and in need of care, and those concerned with the reform of the criminal law as it applies to children, the members of the Task Force failed to fully agree as to what new measures were required.[142]

It is not possible in these pages to engage in a detailed discussion of the many recommendations for reforming this area of the law contained not only in the Task Force Report but also contained in a large number of other works

---

135. Children Act, 1908, Sect. 68(1).
136. *Ibid.*, as amended by Children Act, 1941, Sect. 14(a).
137. *Ibid.*, Sect. 68(2) as amended by the Children Act, 1941, Sect. 14(b).
138. *Ibid.*, Sect. 68(2).
139. *Ibid.*, Sect. 68(3).
140. *Task Force . . . Final Report, supra* (see also the very useful summary and index of the Task Force Report published by CARE in June, 1981).
141. *Ibid.*, at p. 81.
142. See the Supplementary Report by O'Daly and O'Cinneide, *ibid*, at p. 279 *et seq* and the reservations of O'Grady (*ibid* at p. 408) and O'Gilin at p. 419.

published both prior to and since the Task Force Report's publication. Footnote 143 below lists some of the relevant Irish literature published in the last 20 years in which the deficiencies of the present child care system and children's legislation are discussed. It is intended here to briefly mention only some of those reforms that the author believes are required in the law relating to children, to which reference has not as yet been made in the preceding pages. Those reforms that are contained in and proposed to be implemented by the Children (Care & Protection) Bill, 1985, as initiated, are omitted from this list, although reference is made to some reforms that could be accommodated within the format of that Bill and introduced into it by amendment during the course of its passage through the Oireachtas. Reference is also omitted to the many amendments that need to be made to the substantive detail of the 1985 Bill, as initiated, so as to remedy provisions in it that are defective. Many of these defects have already been fully documented elsewhere.[144]

---

143. See generally *Some of our Children: A report on the Residentail Care of the Deprived Child in Ireland*, Tuairim (London 1966); *Reformatory and Industrial Schools Systems Report* 1970 (The Kennedy Report), (Stationery Office, Dublin 1970); *Children Deprived – The CARE Memorandum on Deprived Children and Children's Services in Ireland*, (CARE Dublin, 1970); A.R. Byrne, *Report on Children's Hearing in Scotland* (N.Y.C. of Ireland, Jan. 1974); J.P. Grant, "The Children's Hearing System in Scotland: Its Strength and Weaknesses" (1975) 10 I.J. (n.s.) 24; First and Second Interim Reports of the Inter-Departmental Committee on Mentally and Maladjusted Persons (Stationery Office, Dublin 1974); North Dublin Social Workers, Suffer Little Children (Dublin 1976); Task Force on Child Care Services – *Interim Report* (Stationery Office, Dublin 1975); *Report of Joint Committee on Non-Accidental Injury to Children* (I.S.P.C.C. and North Dublin Social Workers, Dublin, Nov. 1975); *Report of the Committee on Non-Accidental Injury to Children* (Stationery Office, Dublin 1976); "Second Submission to the Task Force on Child Care Services", *Children First* (Dublin 1976); C. Delaney, "Child Battering in Ireland", Children First Newsletter No. 3, Spring 1976; P. Brennan, "The Role of Residential Care Services of Ireland", Children First Newsletter No. 6, Winter 1976; "Proceedings of The Children First Conference on Substitute Parenting", Children First Newsletter No. 7, Spring 1977; "Containment of Young Offenders", Children First Newsletter Nos. 12 and 13, Summer and Autumn 1978; *Care Newsletter* (Vol. 1 No. 2, Nov. 1974); *Care Newsletter* (Vol. 1 No. 3, July 1975); M.V. O'Mahony, "Legal Aspects of Residential Child Care" (1971) 6 I.J. (n.s.) 219; F.J. Elliott, "Residential Child Care Health Act Admissions (1972)", 7 I.J. (n.s.) 358; Dr. P.E. McQuaid, "Reform in the Law Relating to Children", S.Y.S. Lecture No. 67 (1972); Dr. P.E. McQuaid, "Problem Children and their Families", *Studies*, Vol. 60 (Summer 1971); *Planning for our Children: The Report of a Care Conference* (Dublin 1977); *Children's Rights Under the Constitution* (I.C.C.L. Report No. 2 (Dublin 1977); C. Mollan, *Children First* (Arlen House, Dublin 1979); D. Green, "The Child and the Law – The Practising Lawyer's Viewpoint" (1979) 73 *Gazette of the Incorporated Law Society of Ireland* 143 and "Legal Aspects of Non-Accidental Injury to Children" (1980) 74 *Gazette of the Incorporated Law Society of Ireland* 152; "The Child and the Law – The Child Psychiatrist's Viewpoint" (1979) 73 *Gazette of the Incorporated Law Society of Ireland* 189; F. Bates, "The Family Society and Myth" (1980) 15 I.J. (n.s.) 195; *Task Force . . . Final Report, supra*; C. Mollan, *Families & Children* (Care, Dublin 1983); C. Mollan & L. Lefroy, *New Families* (Turoe Press, Dublin 1984); W. Duncan, "Decision-Making Relating to Children in the Republic of Ireland – Restraints on Introducting New Models", contained in *The Resolution of Family Conflict* (Butterworths, Toronto 1984) edited by J.M. Eekelaar & S.N. Katz; *Report of the Working Party on Child Care Facilities for Working Parents* (Stationery Office, Dublin 1983); V. Richardson, *Whose Children?* (Family Studies Unit, U.C.D., Dublin 1985); Irish Fostercare Association, *Open Door* (Dublin 1984); *Report of the Review Committee on Adoption Services* (Stationery Office, Dublin 1984); *Report of the Joint Oireachtas Committee on Marriage Breakdown* (Stationery Office, Dublin 1985); Law Reform Commission, *Report on Hague Convention on the Civil Aspects of International Child Abduction* (Report No. 12, 1985).

144. See speech of A. Shatter T.D., on 2nd stage debate of Bill reported in (30th May, 1985) 359 Dáil Reports Cols. 161–173 and (5th June, 1985) 359 Dáil Reports Cols. 471–525. See further the papers delivered at the seminar on the Bill held in Dublin University (1st February, 1986) and the major submission published under the auspices of 14 voluntary and professional groups proposing detailed amendments to the Bill entitled "Response to Children (Care & Protection) Bill 1985" (Summer 1986). There have been many other submissions made relating to the contents of the Bill by various groups and organisations but it is not possible to list all of these here.

1. At present responsibility for children's services and legislation is divided among various government departments, particularly those of Health, Justice, and Education. There is a need to centralise administrative and legislative responsibility for all aspects of child care within one government department, and that department should be the Department of Health.

2. A National Children's Council independent of government should be established which would have advisory, monitoring and research functions in relation to children's services and legislation.

3. An entirely new court structure should be established to deal with children in need of care or children who have committed offences. Upon the establishment of a family court or a family tribunal, such a court should be taken into the family court structure. In addition to legal training, the personnel of such a court should have specialised training in child care.[145]

4. The law relating to children should be reformed to tackle a number of issues not referred to or adequately dealt with by the Children (Care & Protection) Act, 1985, as initiated. New legislation should

(a) recognise adoption as an important part of the child care system and integrate adoption law within children's law generally. In particular, there is a need for greater integration of adoption and fostering services. Because of their historical development, these services have been in general provided by different agencies. Thus, whilst some adoption placements are made by health boards, the great majority are still made by adoption agencies.[146] Similarly, while some adoption agencies place children in foster care, the majority of children are so placed by health boards. This division of responsibility is not conducive to ensuring the best service is made available to either children or their parents and can result in the agency approached taking an unnecessarily narrow view as to what alternative options should be considered in respect of a particular child.[147]

(b) empower the courts when adjudicating on a dispute as to the custody of a child between parents or between parents and third parties pursuant to section 11 of the Guardianship of Infants Act, 1964, or in Habeas Corpus proceedings, to make a supervision order[148] or a care order where it is of the opinion that circumstances exist which would justify the making of such order, if proceedings were instituted for the care and protection of the child, the custody of whom is in dispute. At present even if all the parties before the court in custody proceedings are

---

145. See further chapter 2 at p. 62 *et seq.*
146. See Appendix F.
147. See further chapter 12, in particular at p. 329 *et seq* where reference is made to the need to reform adoption laws so as to extend the possibility of adoption to children in long term residential or fostercare. It should be noted that failure to suggest fosterage as an alternative possibility to adoption could, in some instances result in the High Court holding that a mother who placed her child for adoption was not fully informed prior to doing so and could result in a challenge being made to the validity of "an agreement to place" signed by her. See p. 300 *ante et seq.*
148. The courts currently do not have power to make supervision orders under the Act of 1908. The Children (Care & Protection) Bill, as initiated, contains provisions for the making of such orders as an alternative to the making of care orders. See, in particular, Sect. 35 of the Bill, as initiated. See also p. 411 *ante.*

totally inadequate or if it could be positively harmful to a child to place the child in any of their custody, the court has no power to make any such order and has no statutory jurisdiction to make any order to ensure the child is properly protected against parental abuse.

(c) provide for the automatic assessment, by a professionally qualified social worker attached to the court, and where appropriate, a child psychiatrist, and/or psychologist of each child who comes before a court as in need of care and protection or for the commission of an offence. Upon a dispute arising between parents or parents and third parties in custody proceedings or upon a dispute arising in relation to the adoption of a child between its parent or parents and prospective adopters, the court determining such dispute should also be empowered to obtain independent reports from such persons to assist it in determining what course of action is in the interests of a child's welfare.

(d) empower a court that has to determine any proceedings relating to children, such as care, custody or adoption proceedings, to appoint a separate legal representative or children's advocate to ensure that the child's interests are properly represented before the court.

(e) raise the age at which a child becomes liable to criminal prosecution or at which a child can be held criminally responsible for his acts. In the Task Force, Supplementary Report of O'Cinneide & O'Daly it was proposed that the age of criminal responsibility should be raised to 15 years and that persons under that age should not be subject to the criminal law. It was proposed that children under that age who engaged in what is presently regarded as criminal conduct should be dealt with by the bringing of (a) welfare or care proceedings or (b) restraint proceedings, the latter proceedings being used where such children are "seen as a threat to the community" and if the taking of "measures for the purpose of promoting their welfare" will not afford adequate protection to the community.[149]

In concluding this chapter and the brief reference that has been made to some of the legislative reforms required in the law relating to children it should not be forgotten that the judgement delivered by the Supreme Court in the case of *K.C. & A.C. v. An Bord Uchtála*[150] has raised a major question mark as to the constitutional capacity of the Oireachtas, through legislation, and of the courts to protect the welfare of children, where a conflict arises between parental rights and children's welfare. On the basis of the judgement delivered in that case, it presently seems that upon a custody conflict arising between the parents of a legitimate child and third parties, such as a health board or foster parents, it is no longer constitutionally possible to ensure, by legislation, that the welfare of the child will be regarded as paramount in the juridicial determination of such conflict. In particular, it seems that the courts may be obliged to uphold the custodial rights of non-culpable parents even where the interests of the child may dictate otherwise.[151] Unless the Supreme Court modifies its current approach, for the paramountcy principle to be applicable in the future to such cases, a constitutional amendment to protect the rights and welfare of children will be required.

149. See Report, *supra* at p. 361 *et seq*. See also the specific reservation to this proposal raised by K. O'Grady at p. 408 *et seq*.
150. [1985] 5 I.L.R.M. 302 (S.C.). See p. 392 *ante et seq*.
151. See *Task Force . . . Final Report, supra* at p. 212, where this is also stated.

CHAPTER 14

FAMILY RIGHTS TO MAINTENANCE

MAINTENANCE FOR SPOUSES

Introduction

A husband at common law has always been under a legal duty to maintain his wife. The duty, however, only extends to the provision of the bare necessities of life. The wife on the other hand has never been under a corresponding common law duty to maintain her husband.

Prior to 1922, if a husband sought a Private Divorce Bill, an official of the House of Commons, who became known as "the lady's friend", was empowered to ensure that the husband made provision for his wife so as not to leave her destitute upon being divorced. While supervision of all other matrimonial matters was vested in the Ecclesiastical Courts, the common law courts provided no remedy whereby a wife could compel her husband to give her a sum of money specifically for her support. The Ecclesiastical Courts themselves would only order a husband to support his wife pending the hearing of a suit or upon making a decree of divorce *a mensa et thoro*.

The transfer of the Ecclesiastical Jurisdiction over marriage to the Court for Matrimonial Causes in 1870 effected no direct change in the substantive law relating to the maintenance of wives. It retained the principle that maintenance of the wife was only an ancillary matter to the main matrimonial reliefs of annulment, restitution of conjugal rights, or divorce *a mensa et thoro*, and this power to award alimony (as maintenance in such proceedings is called) was in any case available only to a small fraction of the population who could afford litigation in this court.

It was not until the passing of the Matrimonial Causes Act, 1878, that magistrates were given the power to order a husband to pay maintenance directly to support his wife. This Act provided that a husband convicted of an aggravated assault[1] upon his wife, could be ordered to pay her a weekly sum by way of maintenance. If the court in which the husband was convicted was satisfied that the future safety of the wife was in peril, it could order that she was no longer bound to cohabit with her husband. The order was to have the same force and effect as a decree for judicial separation on the ground of cruelty. No limit was placed on the amount of maintenance the court could order, and it was empowered to grant to the wife legal custody of any children of their marriage under ten. This Act was repealed in 1895 by the Summary Jurisdiction (Married Women) Act which extended the powers of magistrates in England and Wales but did not apply in Ireland. Thus, if the Act of 1878 applied to Ireland it continued to operate here after 1895. There is, however, some doubt as to whether

---

1. See Sect. 43 of Offences Against the Person Act, 1861.

it ever applied in this country.[2] Even if it did, it seems that it no longer has any effect, the offence of aggravated assault being abolished by the Criminal Justice Act, 1951.

The Married Women (Maintenance in Case of Desertion) Act, 1886, repealed in England by the Act of 1895, was until relatively recently the principal provision under which the courts could make a maintenance order. It conferred on magistrates (now District Justices) jurisdiction to make a maintenance order in favour of a deserted wife if her husband was able, wholly or in part, to maintain her and wilfully refused or neglected to do so. This jurisdiction was extended to the High Court by the Courts Act, 1971. The present law is contained in the Family Law (Maintenance of Spouses & Children) Act, 1976, as amended by the Courts Act, 1981, and under its provisions a court may now make a maintenance order if it appears, upon an application by either spouse, that the other spouse has failed to provide such maintenance as is proper in the circumstances.[3]

The Poor Relief (Ireland) Act, 1838, imposed upon a husband a statutory obligation to reimburse a Poor Law Union for relief paid by it to support his wife.[4] By section 59 of that Act and later section 2 of the Vagrancy (Ireland) Act, 1847, a husband was rendered liable to prosecution and imprisonment for wilfully neglecting to maintain her.[5] These provisions were repealed and replaced by the Public Assistance Act, 1939, by which spouses were under a mutual obligation of support,[6] each being liable to reimburse a local authority in respect of any money paid by it for the other's maintenance.[7] Section 83(1) of that Act provided that it was a criminal offence punishable by three months imprisonment for a husband to desert, or wilfully neglect to maintain his wife so as to render her eligible for assistance. The Act of 1939 was repealed by the Social Welfare (Supplementary Welfare Allowances) Act, 1975, which has now been superseded by the Social Welfare (Consolidation) Act, 1981. Under this Act spouses are still under a mutual obligation of support, each being liable to contribute towards repayment of any allowance granted to the other spouse. However, neither spouse is liable to criminal prosecution for failing to provide the required maintenance.

In 1970 the financial protection afforded a wife was extended when the State partially recognised that it had a specific responsibility to provide support for spouses of broken marriages. The Social Welfare Act, 1970, created deserted wife's allowance, by which a wife, deserted by her husband and unable to obtain maintenance from him, is guaranteed a specific income each week for herself and her children until the desertion terminates or until the husband meets his financial obligations to his family. The concept of the allowance, which is payable subject to a means test, was extended by the Social Welfare Act, 1973, which

---

2. Sect. 2 of the Act which refers to divorce proceedings did not apply in this country. See also (1896) 30 I.L.T. & S.J. 471; and W. Duncan, "Desertion and Cruelty in Irish Matrimonial Law" (1972) 7 I.J. (n.s.) 213 at 217.

3. See below.

4. See *M'Evoy v. The Guardians of Kilkenny Union* (1896) 30 I.L.T.R. 156 (Q.B.D.) under the Married Women's Property Act, 1870, a wife with separate property became liable to the Poor Law Authorities for the maintenance of her husband.

5. *Phillips v. The Guardians of South Dublin Union* [1902] 2 I.R. 112 (1900) 34 I.L.T.R. 171; 1 N.I.J.R. 3 (Q.B.D.); *The Guardians of the Poor of the Drogheda Union v. M'Cann* (1905) 39 I.L.T.R. 210, 5 N.I.J.R. 216 (K.B.D.).

6. See Sect. 27.

7. This duty was not absolute. Thus, if a wife left her husband without reasonable cause his duty was suspended until her desertion ended and the local authority could not recover money paid by it for her maintenance – *South Cork Board of Public Assistance v. O'Regan* [1949] I.R. 415 (S.C.). The duty of reimbursement was absolute under the 1838 Act – see *M'Evoy v. The Guardians of Kilkenny Union, supra.*

created deserted wife's benefit whereby a specific weekly sum of money is payable to a deserted wife unsupported by her husband if either spouse has satisfied the relevant contribution conditions. Today, the principal statutory provisions relating to deserted wife's allowance and benefit are to be found in the Social Welfare (Consolidation) Act, 1981.

It is now intended to engage in a more detailed discussion of the above law and the problems connected with it.

Necessaries

Necessaries can be defined as matters suitable to a person's station or condition in life and in accordance with his needs. They include food, clothes, lodgings and medical attention. One of the essential obligations imposed upon a husband at common law is to maintain his wife by providing her with necessaries. The rules as to the enforcement of this obligation were developed in a context where a wife had no legal power to contract on her own behalf, and lacking the capacity to hold property, usually had no resources of her own to meet any liabilities. The common law rule that neither spouse could sue the other, prevented a wife from enforcing her right to maintenance by a direct action against her husband. Thus, the presumption arose that a wife had power to pledge her husband's credit for the purchase of necessaries if he did not supply them to her himself. The husband's duty to pay the debts incurred by his wife stemmed from his express or implied authority to her to act as his agent. Her presumed authority to so act in the purchase of necessaries lasts while the spouses are living together.[8]

This presumption of agency can be rebutted. Proof that the husband has revoked his implied authority by express prohibition is sufficient. It is not necessary that such prohibition be communicated to a trader.[9] Thus a trader can be in a very weak position if he grants credit to a married woman. However, if a husband holds his wife out to a trader as having authority to pledge his credit, he is bound to give notice of the revocation of his authority to the particular trader in order to escape liability.[10]

The husband alone is the judge of the sufficiency of the allowance he gives to his wife and no finding of the court that the allowance is insufficient can render him liable for goods once the wife's authority is properly revoked.[11] Where a wife is in receipt of her husband's whole income which is ample to support both herself and her family, it has been held that she cannot pledge his credit.[12] Moreover, proof that the trader regarded the credit as being given to the wife alone, and not to the husband, frees the husband from any liability.[13]

If a wife is forced out of the matrimonial home or is deserted, her husband cannot forbid her to pledge his credit in order to support herself and her children.[14]

---

8. A mistress can also pledge the credit of the man she is living with. See *Munro v. De Chemant* (1815) 4 Camp. 215; 171 E.R. 69 (*Nisi Prius*) and *Ryan v. Sams* (1848) 12 Q.B. 460; 116 E.R. 940 (Ct. of Q.B.).

9. *Ryan v. Nolan* (1869) I.R. 3 C.L. 319 (Ct. of C.P.).

10. *Moylan v. Nolan* (1865) 16 I.C.L.R. 427 (Ct. of Q.B.).

11. *Ryan v. Nolan, supra*; *Jolly v. Rees* (1864) 15 C.B. (n.s.) 628, 143 E.R. 931 (Ct. of Q.B.); *Debenham v. Mellon* (1880) 6 App. Cas. 24 (H.L.), affirming (1880) 5 Q.B.D. 394.

12. *Chappell v. Nunn* (1879) 4 L.R. Ir. 316 (Q.B.D.); *Russell v. Mulcahy* (1897) 31 I.L.T. 215 (Cir. Cas.).

13. *Switzer and Co. Ltd. v. Kennan* (1930) 64 I.L.T.R. 222 (Cir. Ct.). See also *M'Grath v. Burke* (1897) 31 I.L.T. & S.J. 429 (Cir. Cas.), where it was held that a shopkeeper cannot recover from a husband the price of goods supplied to his drunken wife, whose habit of drink was so notorious that the trader must have been aware of it.

14. *Bazeley v. Forder* (1868) L.R. 3, Q.B. 559 (Ct. of Q.B.); *Mecredy v. Taylor* (1873) I.R. 7 C.L. 256 (Ct. of Exch. Cham.).

Thus where a wife was driven out of her home by the behaviour of her sister-in-law who also lived in the house, the wife's brother was held entitled to recover from her husband the rent due for her lodgings.[15] A husband who does not comply with a court order for the payment of alimony is also liable for debts incurred by his wife in the purchase of necessaries.[16]

As has already been seen, if legal proceedings are necessary for a wife's protection from her husband, she may pledge his credit for any costs she incurs in such proceedings.[17] Finally, at common law a husband is not liable to maintain an adulterous wife unless he has connived at[18] or condoned the adultery[19]. Thus in such circumstances a wife has no presumed authority to act as his agent. Similarly if a wife is in desertion he is not bound to maintain her. In such circumstances her right to maintenance is only suspended and upon the desertion coming to an end her agency may again arise.

Whilst the doctrine of the agency of necessity may have proved useful in the past its use today is very limited. The Married Women's Property Acts, now replaced by the Married Women's Status Act, 1957, removed a married woman's disabilities relating to contracts and the ownership of property. Under the Family Law ... Act, 1976, she may obtain a maintenance order if inadequately supported and if unable to do so, may be entitled to Deserted Wife's Allowance or Benefit or Supplementary Welfare Allowance. Its usefulness in obtaining solicitor's costs so as to enable her to bring court proceedings against her husband is not great. As for traders, few, understandably, will grant credit to a deserted wife on the basis that at some future time they may be able to secure payment from her husband, if and when he turns up.

Family Law (Maintenance of Spouses and Children) Act, 1976[20]

Grounds for Application: The Act seeks to make financial need rather than matrimonial misdeed the central issue in an application by a spouse for a maintenance order. Under it, the court may make an order if it appears "on application to it by a spouse, that the other spouse has failed to provide such maintenance for the applicant spouse as is proper in the circumstances".[21]

The application must be made by a spouse. Thus, if a foreign decree of divorce *a vinculo* has been made which is recognised under Irish law as dissolving a marriage, no maintenance order can be obtained by a former spouse.[22] Similarly, a maintenance order cannot be made in favour of a party to a marriage declared to be a nullity by the High Court. Prior to 1976 the courts were restricted to ordering that maintenance be paid to a wife. Now either spouse can be ordered

---

15. *Devine v. Monahan* (1932) 67 I.L.T.R. 44 (H.C.).
16. Married Women's Status Act, 1957, Sect. 11(2).
17. See p. 54 *ante.*
18. *Wilson v. Glossop* (1888) 20 Q.B.D. 354 (C.A.).
19. *Harris v. Morris* (1801) 4 Esp. 41; 170 E.R. 635 (*Nisi Prius*); see also Article entitled "Husband's liability for necessaries supplied to adulterous wife"; (1887) 21 I.L.T. & S.J. 427.
20. See generally P. Horgan, "The Irish Republic's New Maintenance Provisions" (1977) 127 N.L.J. 743; W. Binchy, "Family Law Reform in Ireland" (1976) 25 I.C.L.Q. 901.
21. Sect. 5(1)(a).
22. *T. v. T.* [1983] I.R. 29; [1982] 2 I.L.R.M. 217 (S.C.). See also *L.B. v. H.B.* (July, 1980) unreported (H.C.) in which the court refused to recognise a foreign decree of divorce and made a maintenance order against the husband and *N.A.D. v. T.D.* [1985] 5 I.L.R.M. 153 (H.C.) in which a husband domiciled in Ireland obtained an English divorce while his wife was residing in England. It was not suggested in the proceedings that the granting of the English divorce decree could in any way prevent the wife from pursuing her claim for maintenance.

to maintain the other and a maintenance order can be made, not only when spouses are living apart but also when spouses are still residing together, if it appears to the court that there is a failure to provide "proper maintenance".

Whether a spouse is providing "proper maintenance" for the other is a question of fact to be determined by the court, having regard to the circumstances of the particular case. The Supreme Court in *H.D. v. P.D.*[23] held that it is not possible for spouses to contract out of the maintenance provisions of the Act, in that spouses cannot by agreement prevent each other from applying for maintenance or oust the jurisdiction of the court so as to prevent it from making a maintenance order if it appears to the court, upon hearing a maintenance application, that there is a failure to provide proper maintenance.[24] If there is no evidence adduced of such failure, however, no maintenance order can be made under the Act.[25] Moreover, if a spouse is required to pay a larger sum by way of maintenance than a court could require him to pay under the criteria laid down in the Act, under the provisions of a separation or maintenance agreement, in the absence of an express clause in the agreement empowering a court to do so, it cannot by making a maintenance order vary the spouse's contractual rights and obligations.[26]

A person on whose application a maintenance order is made is called a maintenance creditor, whilst the spouse ordered to pay maintenance is the maintenance debtor. Despite the court's power to make a maintenance order in favour of husbands, the overwhelming majority of orders under the Act are made in favour of wives. Thus, normally the husband will be the maintenance debtor and the wife will be the maintenance creditor.

Criteria for making an order: The court in deciding whether to make a maintenance order and the amount to be awarded must have regard to all the circumstances of the case, and in particular:

(a) the income, earning capacity (if any), property and other financial resources of the spouses and of any dependent children of the family, including income or benefits to which either spouse or any such children are entitled by or under statute, and

(b) the financial and other responsibilities of the spouses towards each other and towards any dependent children of the family and the needs of any such dependent children, including the need for care and attention.[27]

The Act does not distinguish between those matters relevant in determining whether an order should be made in favour of a spouse, or a spouse and child, or a child alone. It is intended that all the financial circumstances of the parties

23. (May, 1978) unreported (S.C.).
24. See further p. 202 *ante*. See also the Family Law . . . Act, 1976, Sect. 27.
25. See *St. J. v. St. J.* (June, 1980) unreported (H.C.).
26. *O'S. v. O'S.* (November, 1983) unreported (H.C.); *J.D. v. B.D.* [1985] 5 I.L.R.M. 688 (H.C.). If the parties to a separation agreement were not at the date of its conclusion *ad idem* as to its financial terms the court may decline to enforce it – see *R.H. v. N.H.* (October, 1985) unreported (S.C.).
27. Sect. 5(4). Earnings are defined as "any sums payable to a person –
   (a) By way of wages or salary (including any fees, bonus, commission, overtime pay or other emoluments payable in addition to wages or salary or payable under a contract of service);
   (b) by way of pension or other like benefit in respect of employment (including an annuity in respect of past services, whether or not rendered to the person paying the annuity, and including periodical payments by way of compensation for the loss, abolition or relinquishment, or diminution in the emoluments, of any office or employment);" – Sect. 3(1).

be taken into account. However, the financial resources and needs of dependent children are essentially relevant to an application for maintenance for the support of such children. Children's maintenance is discussed in a separate section further on in this chapter.

In practice, judicial application of the above criteria has produced varied and inconsistent results, different members of the judiciary possessing different views as to what is a "proper" sum of maintenance to order in particular financial circumstances. Although the Supreme Court[28] has recently outlined some of the broad principles applicable to the fixing of maintenance payments, detailed judicial guidelines have still not emerged from decided cases describing the manner in which awards of maintenance are to be calculated or determining the weight that is to be attached to all the factors the court is to have regard to prior to making a maintenance order. For example, if an applicant spouse is unemployed but could obtain employment, it is unclear what significance is to be given to her earning capacity. Moreover, to date, no detailed judgement has been delivered as to the manner in which maintenance payments are to be calculated in circumstances in which the paying spouse has a relatively small income and is the owner of very valuable capital assets, such as large property holdings.

In the majority of maintenance cases, the courts are solely concerned with "need". In such cases, it is clear that the family finances are such that if spouses separate there will be an inevitable reduction in the living standards of both spouses. The court making a maintenance order in such circumstances seeks to provide for the support of a dependent spouse while also ensuring that the paying spouse will have sufficient money available for his own support.

In *R.H. v. N.H.*[29] the Supreme Court remitted a case to the High Court to be reconsidered by Costello J., holding that the amount of maintenance that the husband had originally been ordered to pay "was not properly related to the capacity of the defendant (husband) to pay and provide for his own living expenses."[30] Finlay C.J., delivering the judgement of the Supreme Court, outlined the general approach to be adopted by the courts when determining a wife's claim for maintenance. He stated:

> "Certain broad principles are . . . applicable to the fixing of maintenance pursuant to section 5 of the Act of 1976, arising from the terms of that section as well as from general principles of law. The court . . . in carrying out that task must first have regard to the somewhat pathetic fact that upon the separation of a husband and wife and, particularly a husband and wife with children, it is inevitable that all the parties will suffer a significant diminution in the overall standard of living. The necessity for two separate residences to be maintained and two separate households to be provided for makes this an inescapable consequence of the separation. Subject to that over-riding consideration a court must . . . ascertain the minimum reasonable requirements of . . . the wife and the children for whose upkeep she is responsible; it must then ascertain the income earned or capable of being earned by the wife, apart from the maintenance for which the husband is responsible; its next task is to ascertain the true net take home pay and income of the husband and lastly it must ascertain the reasonable living expenses of the husband, bearing in mind the general consideration of

---

28. See *R.H. v. N.H.* (October, 1985) unreported (S.C.).
29. *Ibid.*
30. See judgement of the court delivered by Finlay C.J. at p. 12. Henchy J. and Hederman J. also sat and each agreed with the judgement of the Chief Justice.

economy affecting all the parties concerned, but leaving him with a reasonable s'. dard of living."[31]

In *R.H. v. N.H.* the parties had separated by agreement. In the earlier case of *E.D. v. F.D.*[32] Costello J. in the High Court adopted a different approach to that articulated above, holding that the additional expense caused by separation need not affect both parties and that any loss in living standard should primarily affect the husband who had deserted the wife. He stated:

> "In fixing maintenance I do not accept the view which was urged on the defendant's behalf that because the overall family expenses rise when a husband deserts the family home, the extra burden should be borne equally by the husband and the wife and children who are living with her, and that she must be prepared to accept a reduction in their living standards. When a husband deserts his wife and children, the court should be concerned to ensure that their financial position is protected, even if this means causing a drop in the husband's living standards."[33]

On the evidence given in that case the husband's earnings were considerable and while the order made may have had the effect of reducing his standard of living, it is arguable that he would still have been able to maintain a reasonable standard of living on the monies he was allowed to retain from his income. If the husband's earnings had been less, a reduction in the living standards of the wife would have been inevitable. Nevertheless, it is arguable that the approach articulated by Costello J. in this case is no longer correct having regard to the judgement of the Supreme Court in *R.H. v. N.H.*

In determining the amount of maintenance, if any, a husband should pay, the court must have regard not only to the spouses' income but also to the value of property owned by the spouses.[34] Thus, in *C.P. v. D.P.*[35] Finlay P. made an order for maintenance which he stated:

> "is not capable of being met out of the husband's income, but which must represent a charge on his capital assets and in particular . . . notwithstanding his proper sentimental attachment to them conceivably involve a charge on the family furniture and *objets d'art* which he has been hoping to keep for his children when they grow up."[36]

Moreover, in *R.F. v. M.F.*[37] D'Arcy J. held that:

> "For the purpose of measuring a person's income for assessing maintenance a husband is not entitled to arrange his financial affairs so that he diminishes his income at the cost of a wife in order to increase his capital"[38]

and refused to deduct from the husband's income monthly loan repayments he was making to the Agricultural Credit Corporation prior to assessing what pay-

---

31. See pp. 7–8 of judgement. See further *M. McD. v. P. McD.* (April 1986) unreported (H.C.). MacKenzie J. at p. 6 stated "two households cannot be provided as cheaply as one, and it is necessary for both parties . . . to consider their position and try and economise, remembering that their circumstances can never be, where two dwellings have to be provided for, as comfortable and as easy were the marriage still in existence."
32. (October, 1980) unreported (H.C.).
33. See p. 4 of judgement.
34. See *R.F. v. M.F.* (December, 1982) unreported (H.C.) in which D'Arcy J. stated that in determining how much maintenance should be paid he had "to take into account the relevant capital possessions of both parties" – see p. 15 of judgement.
35. [1983] 3 I.L.R.M. 380 (H.C.).
36. *Ibid.*, at p. 387.
37. *Supra.*
38. See p. 2 of judgement.

ment he should make to his wife by way of maintenance.

The earnings or needs of a person with whom a husband is residing are not to be taken into account in determining the amount of maintenance a husband can be required to pay, except in so far as the earnings of the third party are factually reducing expenditure the husband would otherwise have to meet.

In *M. O'K. v. M. O'K.*[39] Barron J. expressed the view that both the earnings and needs of a third party with whom the husband was residing were irrelevant in determining the amount of maintenance the husband should pay to his wife for her support. He stated:

> "Neither the fact that the husband is living in an adulterous association nor the fact that the third party is earning or not earning is a consideration which should be taken into account. The wife should not be entitled to any greater maintenance from her husband because he has the benefit of earnings of a third party with whom he is living nor should the wife suffer because the third party with whom her husband is living is not earning and has to be supported by him.[40]

The above statement of the learned judge was open to serious question as it clearly had not been judicially applied in practice in many preceding maintenance cases in which no written judgements had been delivered. Whereas the courts had in many cases held that a husband cannot be regarded as having any legal obligation to support a third person with whom he is residing, they had been willing to take into account payments made by a third party to meet expenditure for which the husband would otherwise have been solely responsible in assessing what proportion of his income the husband need retain to meet his own needs and the amount that should be paid by him to his wife for her support. For example, payments made by a third party towards discharging the rent payable for accommodation in which she is residing with a husband may reduce the sum a court considers a husband needs to retain out of his income for his own rental payments. In the more recent case of *M. McG. v. D. McG.*[40a] Barron J. appears to have modified his position. Referring to the basis upon which he should assess how much maintenance should be paid to the wife in the context of the husband's necessary expenditure, he stated that:

> "In the course of the hearing, I asked Counsel to assist me as to the extent, if any, I should take into account that the husband had set up home on a permanent basis with another partner. I am satisfied . . . that it is proper that I should do so. I have done so, however, only upon the basis of what is factual. By virtue of the factual situation, the level of the husband's expenses after tax is less than it might otherwise be. I can see no reason why I should not act upon the basis of that state of affairs."[40b]

Finally, in this context, it should also be noted that whereas a husband is regarded as having no legal obligation to support any other woman with whom he is residing, if there is a child or children born as a result of their relationship, the courts when assessing the amount of maintenance to be paid by the husband to his wife will take into account the husband's legal obligation to contribute towards the support of any child of which he is the father, in determining how much maintenance he should be obliged to pay.

---

39. (November, 1982) unreported (H.C.).
40. See pp. 6–7 of judgement.
40a. (February, 1985) unreported (H.C.).
40b. See p. 5 of judgement.

There is a suggestion arising from some judicial comments that "financial need" must always be proved by an applicant spouse before a maintenance order can be made.[41] It is clear, however, that the criteria set down in the Act are concerned with the totality of the parties' financial circumstances. Thus, a spouse may fail to provide an applicant spouse with "such maintenance as is proper in the circumstances" if the former is very wealthy, even though the maintenance provided meets all of that spouse's basic needs. In the case of the very affluent, the maintenance ordered to be paid may bear no relation to basic needs. In *L.B. v. H.B.*[42] on the wife's application for a maintenance order, Barrington J. concluded that "Mr. B. is a man of enormous wealth" and stated:

> "I am also satisfied that he has not maintained his wife in the style to which the wife of so wealthy a man may reasonably aspire and which she formerly enjoyed . . . I am satisfied therefore that the defendant has not maintained the plaintiff in the manner which is proper in the circumstances. I accept the evidence of the plaintiff that she cannot live with any measure of comfort, in a house the size of the family home without, at least, the services of a housekeeper and a gardener. On the assumption that she pays the housekeeper and the gardener I will fix maintenance in the sum of £300 per week."[43]

While in the case of those of ordinary means the courts are concerned to provide maintenance to meet "need", in the case of the wealthy, the courts, in practice, are also concerned with determining what should be the style of life and relevant standard of living of an applicant spouse.

Court Jurisdiction and Financial Orders that can be made: Section 23 of the Family Law . . . Act, 1976, initially conferred an originating jurisdiction to make maintenance orders only on the District and High Court, the Circuit Court's jurisdiction being confined to a power to determine District Court appeals. Section 12 of the Courts Act, 1981, amended the Act of 1976 by substituting a new section 23, which expressly confers an originating jurisdiction to make maintenance orders on both the District and Circuit Courts but contains no express reference to the High Court retaining the original jurisdiction to make maintenance orders conferred on it by the Act of 1976 in any proceedings initiated as and from the 12th of May 1982, the date of commencement of the Act of 1981. In *R. v. R.*[44] it was held that the High Court still retained an original jurisdiction to make maintenance orders in proceedings initiated after that date but, as has been previously stated, the authority of this decision is now in question.[44a] There is no doubt, however, that the High Court may still make maintenance orders under section 5 of the Act of 1976 in proceedings initiated under that section prior to the 12th of May 1976 where no maintenance order was made before the coming into force of the Courts Act, 1981.[45]

---

41. See *H.D. v. P.D., supra,* at p. 9 of judgement where Walsh J. said:

"It appears to me that in a case such as the present one the function of the court under the Act of 1976 is to determine whether or not there is a financial need justifying the making of the order sought under the Act."

See also *O.C. v. T.C.* (December, 1981) unreported (H.C.) in which McMahon J. declined to award maintenance to the wife, one of the reasons being that "in view of her net asset position it does not appear . . . that she is in need of support." A number of other reasons were also given by the learned judge (see p. 203 *ante*). See further *St. J. v. St. J., supra.*

42. *Supra.*
43. See p. 38 of judgement.
44. [1984] I.R. 296 (H.C.).
44a. See p. 43 *ante.*
45. See *R.H. v. N.H., supra.*

A court determining a maintenance application is limited as to the type of financial order that can be made under the Act, in that it only has power to order periodical payments. Moreover, the District Court, and the Circuit Court on appeal from the District Court, may not order payment of a periodical sum greater than £100 per week for the support of a spouse.[46] However, the Circuit Court exercising its originating jurisdiction and the High Court, in so far as it may retain such jurisdiction, are not similarly restricted by statute as to the amount of maintenance they can order a spouse to pay by way of periodical payments, each possessing an unlimited financial jurisdiction. In practice, the majority of maintenance orders require a weekly payment to be made but the court is not confined to making such orders. It may, for example, order fortnightly, monthly or quarterly payments. A maintenance order for the support of a spouse made under the Act must be paid without deduction of income tax.[47]

There is no express power conferred on the court by the 1976 Act to order the making of a lump sum payment to an applicant. The Minister for Justice, however, stated in the Special Dáil Committee set up to examine the provisions of the Act, as presented to the Dáil, that the court was empowered by it to order a payment of a large sum for the first period and a lesser sum thereafter if it so wished.[48]

The court under the Act may order "periodical payments . . . for such period . . . of such amount and at such times as the court may consider proper". The more usual interpretation of the power conferred by this section would be that it enables the court to order periodical payment of a set sum until the variation or termination of the order. It is doubtful whether an order may lay down that different amounts are payable at different periods, the Act merely empowers the court to order payment of "such amount" and not "such amounts" as it considers proper.

Bars to Relief: Under the Act there are two bars to the making of an order. Desertion is an absolute bar and adultery is a discretionary bar.

DESERTION

The court may not make a maintenance order for the support of a spouse where the spouse has deserted and continues to desert the other spouse.[49] Further, the court having made a maintenance order in support of a spouse must discharge that order "where it appears to it that the spouse has deserted and continues to desert the spouse liable under the order to pay maintenance".[50]

The role played by desertion in maintenance legislation has thus been completely reversed. Under the Act of 1886 the onus was placed on the applicant to prove desertion by the defendant, such desertion being an essential prerequisite to the granting of an order by the court. Today, it may be used by the defendant as a bar to the granting of a maintenance order, or to discharge an order already made, and the onus is placed on the defendant to prove that the applicant or supported spouse is in desertion. As in most cases it is the husband that deserts, and not the wife, the former possessing greater financial indepen-

---

46. See Courts Act, 1981, Sect. 12.
47. Family Law . . . Act, 1976, Sect. 24. See further p. 455 *post.*
48. See Family Law . . . Bill, 1975, – Special Committee of Dáil Eireann (Official Report Unrevised), pp. 15–18.
49. Family Law . . . Act, 1976, Sect. 5(2).
50. *Ibid.*, Sect. 6(2).

dence, desertion is playing a far lesser role under the present Act than it played under the Act of 1886.

Desertion consists of the following four elements:

(a) A factual separation of the spouses;

(b) Absence of consent to live apart;

(c) Intention to desert;

(d) Absence of just cause for leaving.

(a) *Separation:*[51] Unless the parties have separated and no longer live together there can be no desertion. The more usual case of separation involves spouses living in separate abodes. However, it is possible for spouses to be regarded as living separate and apart although still residing under the same roof.[52] Desertion it has been said is "not the withdrawal from a place, but from a state of things".[53] Thus, if parties still reside under the same roof but "cease to be one household and become two households"[54] the factum of separation is present. Whether this has happened depends on the circumstances of the particular case. As a general rule it can be said to be a question of whether all the usual interaction of matrimonial cohabitation has come to an end. Thus, if spouses sleep in separate rooms, cease to communicate, refuse to carry out their marital duties and no longer engage in the normal interaction of man and wife, the court will hold the fact of separation to be present.[55]

Although normally, parties will live together before one deserts the other, the court may find that there is sufficient separation to constitute desertion without any previous cohabitation.[56]

(b) *Consent:* If parties agree to separate neither is in desertion. Undoubtedly there must be many a battered wife who has been more than relieved to see the departure of her husband. The test used to determine whether the latter is in desertion is whether the separation is due primarily to the conduct of the deserting spouse or to the other's voluntary consent to live apart.[57]

Consent may be by oral or written agreement, or inferred from the conduct

---

51. See F. Bates, "Cohabitation and Separation in the Law of Desertion" (1970) 21 N.I.L.Q. 111.

52. *Powell v. Powell* (1922) P. 278 (P.D.A.); *Naylor v. Naylor* [1962] P. 253; [1961] 2 All E.R. 129 (P.D.A.); *Hopes v. Hopes* [1949] P. 227; [1948] 2 All E.R. 920 (C.A.).

53. *Per* Lord Merrivale, *Pulford v. Pulford* [1923] P. 18; at p. 21 (P.D.A.).

54. *Per* Denning L.J., *Hopes v. Hopes, supra* at p. 326. See also *Bull v. Bull* [1953] P. 224; [1953] 2 All E.R. 601 (C.A.).

55. *Naylor v. Naylor, supra*; *Walker v. Walker* [1952] 2 All E.R. 138 (C.A.); *Bartram v. Bartram* [1950] P. 1; [1949] 2 All E.R. 270 (C.A.). These were all cases where spouses were living under the same roof but as "two households" the wife being in desertion of the husband. See also *Hopes v. Hopes, supra* where the husband unsuccessfully alleged that the wife was in desertion, the parties still living under the same roof. Mere refusal to carry out some of the obligations of matrimony does not constitute desertion. See *Weatherley v. Weatherley* [1947] A.C. 628 (H.L.) where refusal by a wife to have sexual intercourse was held not to be desertion. Sect. 2(6) of the English Matrimonial Causes Act, 1973, provides that for the purposes of the Act a "husband and wife should be treated as living apart unless they are living with each other in the same household". For the manner in which the courts have interpreted this see *Mouncer v. Mouncer* [1972] 1 All E.R. 289; *Santos v. Santos* [1972] Fam. 247; [1972] 2 All E.R. 246 (C.A.); *Fuller v. Fuller* [1973] 2 All E.R. 650 (C.A.); *Bradley v. Bradley* [1973] 3 All E.R. 750 (C.A.). See also R.L. Denyer, "Living Apart" (1974) 124 N.L.J. 735.

56. *De Laubenque v. De Laubenque* [1899] P. 42 (P.D.A.); *Timoney v. Timoney* [1926] N.I. 75 (K.B.D.); *Wells v. Wells* [1940] N.I. 88 (K.B.D.).

57. *Harriman v. Harriman* [1909] P. 123 (C.A.); *Pizey v. Pizey* [1961] P. 101 (C.A.); *Bacon v. Bacon* [1946] N.I. 110 (K.B.D.).

of the parties.[58] If the parties have signed a separation agreement which is still in force neither can rely on separation subsequent to the agreement as being desertion. Similarly, if a separation agreement is signed following desertion by one spouse, the agreement terminates the desertion.[59] Thus, if a husband concludes a separation agreement with his wife after she has deserted him, he will no longer be able to rely on her desertion as a defence against a claim by her for maintenance. Alternatively, if they sign an agreement which does not contain a clause by which they consent to live apart, any preceding desertion will continue to subsist.

It is a question of fact whether a consent to separate is real or not. Thus, if a spouse is forced into signing a separation agreement by threats of the other spouse and without legal advice, the consent to live apart may be ineffective.[60] Where there is genuine consent it is still possible for one spouse subsequently to be held in desertion of the other. Agreement to live apart may be purely temporary e.g. for a given period of time, or until the fulfilment of a condition or until the happening of a particular event. If the period comes to an end and one of the parties then refuses to cohabit he or she will be in desertion.[61] On the other hand, if an agreement is intended to run forever, it will only terminate with the consent of both parties or upon a breach of a fundamental term by one party treated by the other as terminating the agreement.[62]

(c) *Intention:* Intention to remain permanently separated from the other spouse is an essential ingredient of desertion. Normally, desertion will commence as soon as spouses separate. But if when the original separation took place the parties intended to return to each other, desertion begins only when the intention (*animus deserendi*) is formed.[63] Thus, if a spouse goes to Cork to mind a sick parent and subsequently decides not to return to the matrimonial home in Dublin, it is only when the latter decision is made that he or she is in desertion. Whether an insane spouse is capable of forming the requisite intention is a question of fact in each case. Thus, it has been held that a spouse who leaves under the influence of an insane delusion that the other spouse is going to kill her is not in desertion.[64]. Similarly, supervening insanity may terminate desertion.[65]

---

58. See *Joseph v. Joseph* [1953] 2 All E.R. 710; [1953] 1 W.L.R. 1182 (C.A.); the court inferred that a wife consented to live apart by her obtaining a "ghet" which by Jewish Law effects a divorce. In *Counihan v. Counihan* (July, 1973) unreported (H.C.), the wife alleged that the husband was in desertion but the court held the original separation of the parties to be by consent. The wife had subsequent to the separation obtained an English divorce which was not recognised in this country. Kenny J. did not hold that her obtaining the divorce decree also inferred consent by her to separation.

59. *Piper v. Piper* [1902] P. 198 (P.D.A.).

60. *Holroyd v. Holroyd* (1920) 36 T.L.R. 479 (P.D.A.).

61. *Timoney v. Timoney, supra; Shaw v. Shaw* [1939] P. 269; 2 All E.R. 381 (P.D.A.); *Bosley v. Bosley* [1958] 2 All E.R. 167 (C.A.); *Hall v. Hall* (1960) 1 All E.R. 91 (Assize); If a spouse decides before the end of the agreed period not to return, desertion begins to run as soon as the other spouse becomes aware of the decision – *Huxtable v. Huxtable* (1899), 68 L.J., P. 83 (P.D.A.); *Nutley v. Nutley* [1970] 1 All E.R. 410 (C.A.).

62. *Pardy v. Pardy* [1939] P. 288; [1939] 3 All E.R. 779 (C.A.).

63. *Henty v. Henty* (1875) 33 L.T. 263 (Ct. for Div. and Matr. Causes); *Strickland v. Strickland* (1876) 35 L.T. 767 (P.D.A.); *Chudley v. Chudley* (1893) 9 T.L.R. 491; (1893) 10 T.L.R. 63 (Q.B.D.), (C.A.); *Pulford v. Pulford, supra; Pardy v. Pardy, supra*; see also (1897) 31 I.L.T. & S.J. 15, 29 – "Husband and Wife – Desertion".

64. *Perry v. Perry* [1963] 3 All E.R. 766 (P.D.A.); *Brannan v. Brannan* [1973] Fam. 20; [1973] 1 All E.R. 38 (Fam. Div.).

65. *Crowther v. Crowther* [1951] A.C. 723 (H.L.).

(d) *Just Cause:* "Grave and weighty"[66] conduct by one spouse will justify the other spouse separating so as to afford the latter a defence against desertion. Thus, if a husband assaults his wife and as a result she leaves the matrimonial home, upon her suing for maintenance, if the husband alleges that she is in desertion, she can justify her departure on the grounds of his conduct. Indeed as we shall see in the next section, it is the husband rather than the wife that may be held in desertion in such circumstances. It is, of course, not sufficient for a wife alleged to be in desertion to merely make allegations of misbehaviour against her husband. She must prove her case by satisfying the court that she had "just cause" for leaving the family home.

In *P. v. P.*[67] the wife was held to be in desertion for leaving the family home as she failed to prove that her departure, as she alleged, had been forced by her husband's violence and cruelty. As a consequence, the court ruled that it was debarred from making a maintenance order for her separate support.[68] Delivering judgement in this case, Barrington J. stated:

> "When parties marry they marry for better or for worse. This, as I understand it, includes accepting quirks and difficulties in the character of the other marriage partner.
>
> To establish 'just cause' for leaving the matrimonial home the partner who has left must establish some form of serious misconduct on the part of the other partner. Such conduct must, as Lord Asquith said: . . . exceed in gravity such behaviour, vexatious and trying though it may be, as every spouse bargains to endure when accepting the other 'for better or worse'. The ordinary wear and tear of conjugal life does not in itself suffice."[69]

Proof by a wife of misconduct on the part of a husband will not, in itself, prevent a finding of desertion if the court forms the view that the husband's conduct was not the main cause for the wife's departure from the family home. Thus, in *S.D. v. B.D.*[70] although Murphy J. held that the wife's "departure from the family home was indicative of some failure on her husband's part to make for her a suitable home and a happy marriage", he was satisfied:

> "that the dominant fact motivating (her) when she left the family home . . . was not any fear of the husband or . . . any distaste for him or the circumstances in which she lived. Rather it was a positive ambition on her part to achieve a greater happiness, as she saw it, in other circumstances and with another man."[71]

At the date of the maintenance application this relationship had long since terminated but her application failed, the court holding the wife still to be in desertion of her husband.

In *C.G. v. P.G.*[72] the wife, following her departure from the family home, went to England where she and another man took up employment in a holiday camp and resided together passing themselves off as husband and wife. Finlay P.

---

66. *Yeatman v. Yeatman* (1868) L.R. 1 P. & D. 489; see also *Oldroyd v. Oldroyd* [1896] P. 175 (P.D.A.), conduct that renders it "practically impossible for the spouses to live properly together"; *Buchler v. Buchler* [1947] P. 25; [1947] 1 All E.R. 319 (C.A.).
67. (March, 1980) unreported (H.C.).
68. See also *N.A.D. v. T.D., supra.*
69. See p. 6 of judgement. The quote of Lord Asquith derives from *Buchler v. Buchler* [1947] P. at p. 45; [1947] 1 All E.R. at p. 326. *P. v. P.* was expressly followed by Lynch J. in *A.H. v. A.H.* (December, 1985) unreported (H.C.).
70. (March, 1982) unreported (H.C.).
71. See p. 17 of judgement.
72. (March, 1982) unreported (H.C.).

took the view that at the date of their marriage the husband and wife "were tragically immature" and that "probably in the development of their personalities quite unfit for marriage" and that this was the "fundamental and over-riding reason why the marriage had failed". The husband had admitted assaulting the wife on two or three occasions "though not in a serious manner" and Finlay P. expressed the belief that the husband was "probably uncaring and insensitive during the marriage" but rejected the wife's contention that she was forced to leave the home due to the husband's conduct. He concluded that she was in desertion of her husband as she had "left the house as part of a pre-arranged plan and had decided to go away with this other man before she did so."[73]

In *M.B. v. E.B.*[74] the court held that the wife had just cause for leaving the family home. The parties married in June 1977 and separated in July 1979. The wife established in evidence that her husband drank to excess and that since their child had been born he had gone out to a public house on his own almost every night of the week. He frequently returned home drunk and she was worried that he might, when drunk, knock over the baby. The night prior to the wife's departure the husband returned home drunk. An argument took place between them and the wife went to bed locking the bedroom door. The husband remained in the sitting-room drinking whiskey and playing a tape recorder "at full blast". The following morning, the wife found him asleep in the sitting-room with an empty bottle of whiskey beside him. She left the family home taking the baby with her. Delivering his judgement Barrington J. stated:

"I have no doubt that she (the wife) felt that she had just cause for doing what she did. A marriage counsellor might well have advised the wife not to take so extreme a step and might have assisted the husband to a fuller awareness of the ways in which he was distressing his wife. But objectively, I have reached the conclusion that the wife had just cause for leaving the matrimonial home in the light of the picture she has given of the marriage and which I accept to be a true one."[75]

Whether a spouse's conduct is such as to justify the departure of the other is a question of fact dependent on the circumstances of the case. Misconduct towards the parties' children may also justify a spouse's departure. Thus, in an English case it was held that where a husband developed a mental illness that led him to frighten his children, the wife was entitled to remain apart from him for as long as it was necessary for the children's sake.[76] A party may also not be in desertion if separation from his spouse is beyond his control, e.g. a spouse serving a prison term. Moreover, if a spouse has a reasonable belief that he has a good cause for leaving, such belief arising out of the other's conduct, then he will not be in desertion, even if the belief is mistaken.[77] If a spouse ceases to have a good cause or ceases to have a reasonable belief of a good cause for remaining apart, he will be in desertion if he fails to resume cohabitation.[78]

---

73. See pp. 4, 13 & 14 of judgement.
74. (February, 1980) unreported (H.C.).
75. See p. 11 of judgement.
76. *G. v. G.* [1964] P. 133; [1964] 1 All E.R. 129 (P.D.A.).
77. *Ousey v. Ousey and Atkinson* (No. 2) (1874) L.R. 3 P. & D. 223; [1874–80] All E.R. Rep. 635 (P.D.A.); *Glenister v. Glenister* [1945] 1 All E.R. 513; [1945] P. 30; But if the belief does not arise from the other's conduct or if the conduct was procured by the departing spouse, the latter has no "just cause" – *Elliott v. Elliott* [1956] 1 All E.R. 122; [1956] P. 160 (C.A.); *Hartley v. Hartley* [1955] 1 All E.R. 626 (P.D.A.).
78. *Forbes v. Forbes* [1954] 3 All E.R. 461 (P.D.A.); *Allen v. Allen* [1951] 1 All E.R. 724 (C.A.); *West v. West* [1954] 2 All E.R. 505; [1954] P. 444 (C.A.).

Constructive Desertion: It is not only the person who leaves the matrimonial home who may be in desertion. It has for long been accepted that if a spouse behaves in such a way as to force the other to leave, the former spouse is in constructive desertion.[79] Thus, desertion under the Act is said to include "conduct on the part of one spouse that results in the other spouse, with just cause, leaving and living separately and apart from him.[80] As in the case of ordinary desertion, the parties must separate and the deserted spouse (this time the one that departs) must have a just cause for doing so. Habitual drunkenness, violence, adultery and mental cruelty have, in practice, all been regarded as sufficient grounds for a spouse's departure.[81] When a husband physically throws his wife out of the matrimonial home or a spouse refuses without good cause to permit the other spouse to enter, there is an obvious case of constructive desertion. On the other hand, financial irresponsibility or inability to give a wife the amount of money which she requires to run the house according to her standards, or absence from the home during the week on account of work, have been held not to justify a wife leaving.[82]

Prior to the coming into force of the present Act, for a party to be held in constructive desertion, it was necessary to prove that he intended to end cohabitation. The Act makes no reference to intention but it is submitted that it is still required. The necessity to prove intention does not mean that a person can treat his spouse intolerably and then defend himself by saying that he never intended to make the other leave.

In *Counihan v. Counihan*[83] the High Court for the first time in a written judgement, discussed the meaning of constructive desertion. Kenny J. approved of the judgements of the Judicial Committee of the Privy Council in *Lang v. Lang*[84] and of Lord MacDermott in the Northern Ireland case of *McLaughlin v. McLaughlin*.[85] As a consequence of these cases, for the behaviour of a spouse to constitute constructive desertion, an intention to disrupt the marriage or to bring the cohabitation to an end must be proved against the spouse alleged to have deserted. The conduct of a spouse and its natural and probable consequences can give rise to a presumption in favour of the existence of such intention. This presumption though rebuttable, will not necessarily be rebutted by showing that the offending spouse did not want the other to depart, it being possible for a person to wish one thing and intend another. The more serious the conduct of

---

79. *Graves v. Graves* [1864] 3 Sw. & Tr. 350; 164 E.R. 1310 (Matr. Ct.).

80. Family Law . . . Act, 1976, Sect. 3. See *P.G. v. C.G., supra,* in which Finlay P. stated that if the wife "is to be entitled to maintenance . . . it could only be as a result of a finding by me on the facts that the conduct of the husband was such as in effect to constitute constructive desertion of his wife and that he had made it impossible for her to remain living with him." On the evidence, he was satisfied this was not the case and held the wife to be in desertion.

81. See, for example, *J.C. v. J.H.C.* (August, 1982) unreported (H.C.) in which the husband was held to be in constructive desertion, Keane J. holding that the wife was justified in leaving the family home due to the husband's "occasional outbursts of violence". In *R.K. v. M.K.* (October, 1978) unreported (H.C.) the wife seeking maintenance suffered from a motor neurone disease and consequent depression and anxiety. Finlay P. stated that "The obligations of a husband or a wife are not obviated but may be heightened by the sickness of the spouse. From the diagnosis of the plaintiff's illness and her progressive incapacity caused by it, the defendant showed a gross lack of attention and sympathy with her real needs which amounted to cruelty justifying her departure from the family home." See also *M.B. v. E.B., supra.*

82. In *Counihan v. Counihan, supra,* Kenny J. remarked that "the standards to be applied in judging the conduct of husband and wife are those of men and women, not angels."

83. *Supra.*

84. [1955] A.C. 402; [1954] 3 All E.R. 571 (P.C.).

85. [1956] N.I. 73 (Q.B.D.).

the spouse the more difficult it becomes to rebut the presumption.

The facts of *Counihan* were the following:—After ten years of marriage the wife told the husband to leave the matrimonial home in Dublin. She did this because of what she said was his irresponsibility in financial matters, his recklessness in contracting large debts and his taking a job which meant he could be at home only at weekends. Kenny J. held that the matters relied on did not constitute cruelty or conduct which "a reasonable man would know would have the consequences that marriage would be disrupted". He stated that the wives of many circuit going barristers and commercial travellers very often only see their husbands at weekends, and whilst the husband was financially irresponsible it would not have justified her leaving him. Consequently, it was held that the husband was not guilty of constructive desertion upon leaving the matrimonial home upon being told to do so by his wife, as she did not have sufficient cause to require him to go. As a result, their separation was held to be by consent.[86]

Termination of Desertion: For desertion to bar an application for maintenance it is not enough that the party seeking an order deserted the defendant some time in the past, he or she must still be in desertion when the matter comes to court. Desertion is a continuing offence and may come to an end. It terminates if the parties resume cohabitation[87] or if the deserting spouse makes a genuine offer to resume cohabitation. Such an offer must be genuine and not just a ploy to obtain a maintenance order. If a spouse refuses a genuine offer of reconciliation the court may hold that desertion has ended. However, the conduct of the deserter may be such that the other spouse could not be expected to accept him back.[88] In such a case the party will remain in desertion. Finally, desertion terminates following an agreement to live apart,[89] or the obtaining by a spouse of a divorce *a mensa et thoro*.

ADULTERY

The court has a discretion to refuse to make a maintenance order for the support of an applicant spouse if that spouse has committed adultery.[90] However, if the other spouse has condoned or connived at, or by wilful neglect or misconduct, conduced to the adultery, the court has no discretion and the act of adultery is not a ground upon which the court can refuse to make an order. Further, even if the defendant spouse has not behaved in this way, the court may make an order notwithstanding the applicant's adultery, if having regard to all the circumstances (including the conduct of the other spouse) it considers it proper to do so.[91]

In *L. v. L.*[92] the husband (D.) had left his wife and continued to engage in an

---

86. Kenny J. did not consider the point that as the wife was unjustified in telling the husband to leave the house she may have been the party in desertion. The issue as to whether she had forced the husband to leave was never considered. It was assumed that as he had left home upon being told to do so, he had agreed to live apart from his wife.

87. *Abercombe v. Abercombe* [1943] 2 All E.R. 465 (P.D.A.). "Just as you can have an act of desertion where the parties are not living under the roof of a matrimonial home, so equally you can have a resumption of cohabitation without necessarily going under the same roof". Thus, where parties go away on holiday together and resume sexual intercourse the court may adopt an inference of resumed cohabitation. Alternatively, see *Perry v. Perry* [1952] 1 All E.R. 1076; [1952] P. 203 (C.A.); *Lynch v. Lynch* [1966] N.I. 41 (Q.B.D.).

88. *Edwards v. Edwards* [1948] 1 All E.R. 157; [1948] P. 268 (P.D.A.).

89. See p. 199 *ante*.

90. For the meaning of adultery, see p. 218 *ante*.

91. Family Law . . . Act, 1976, Sect. 5(3).

92. (December, 1979) unreported (H.C.).

adulterious relationship with another woman. At the date of the court hearing, the wife had formed a relationship with another man. Although she lived alone, this man did from time to time stay over night in the wife's home. The court accepted, on the evidence, that he did not regularly maintain her in any way.

D. contended that the wife's adultery terminated his liability to provide her with maintenance. The court rejected this contention. It was clear that the wife's liaison was subsequent to that of D. and there was no suggestion of the wife having committed adultery prior to D.'s departure from the family home.

Delivering the judgement of the court, Finlay P. stated:

"If the court is satisfied that the spouse against whom maintenance is claimed has condoned or connived at or by wilful neglect or misconduct conduced to the adultery then it has no discretion and must order maintenance provided that the other conditions contained in the Act of 1976 with regard to maintenance are fulfilled, that is to say that the other spouse has failed to provide such maintenance for the applicant spouse as is proper in the circumstances . . .

If on the other hand, the Court is not satisfied that the respondent spouse has condoned or connived at or by wilful neglect or misconduct conduced to the adultery then it has a discretion and may exercise that discretion having regard to all the circumstances. All the circumstances must in my view include the financial circumstances of the applicant spouse. It seems to me that if an applicant spouse who has been guilty of adultery not condoned, connived at or conduced to by the other spouse were notwithstanding that in a position of extreme want or considerable penury that the court might have regard to that as a circumstance which would entitle it to exercise its discretion in favour of making an order for maintenance. Furthermore, it seems to me that if an applicant spouse had committed adultery but has ceased at the time of application that adulterous relationship that may well be a consideration which the court should take into account. Furthermore . . . a spouse against whom maintenance was claimed who had not condoned, connived at or conduced to the adultery of the applicant spouse might by his own conduct including presumably a subsequent adultery on his part make himself liable where he otherwise would not be to the payment of maintenance. I do not intend that these should be considered an exhaustive list of the circumstances which the court may take into consideration which must, of necessity, vary with every case but they are the sort of circumstances which it appears to me may be material to this situation."[93]

Rejecting D.'s denial of liability for his wife's maintenance, the learned President held that on the facts of the case D.'s wilful misconduct "as a matter of probability" had conduced to his wife's adultery. Her adultery was thus not a relevant factor in the court's determination of the wife's maintenance application.[94] The court

---

93. See pp. 11–13 of judgement.
94. On the facts of the case the court held that D. had not condoned or connived at his wife's adultery. Referring to the concept of condonation, Finlay P. stated: "I am . . . satisfied that it must be interpreted in so far as it refers to a condoning of the adultery as intended to carry the ordinary legal meaning of condonation namely a co-habiting subsequent to the discovery of the adultery."

As for the word connived, he continued: "I must interpret this as indicating conduct on the part of the other spouse consisting of a knowledge of the adultery and a failure to make any remonstrance concerning it or to take any steps to try and persuade his partner from continuing with it." See further p. 223 *ante et seq.*

was merely concerned with the financial circumstances and needs of both spouses.[95]

Where, subsequent to the making of a maintenance order, an applicant spouse commits adultery, the court cannot discharge or vary the order if the other spouse behaved in a manner that would prevent adultery being relied on to bar the making of an order. Similarly, even if the other spouse has not behaved in such a manner the court may, notwithstanding the adultery, refuse to discharge or vary the order, where having regard to all the circumstances (including the conduct of the other spouse) it considers it proper to refuse to do so.[96]

Interim Orders: Section 7 of the Act of 1976 confers jurisdiction on the court before which maintenance proceedings are initiated, prior to finally determining such proceedings, to make an interim order for such periodical sum as the court thinks proper "if it appears to the court proper to do so having regard to the needs of the persons for whose support the maintenance order is sought and the other circumstances of the case." Such an order may be in force for a specified period of time or until the maintenance application is adjudicated upon. An application for an interim order is usually made when a spouse is in immediate financial need and has insufficient means available to her for her support to enable her to await the making of a maintenance order following upon a full court hearing of her maintenance application.

Discharge and Variation: A maintenance order may be discharged or varied at any time on the application of either party, if new circumstances exist or upon the production of evidence not available to the party applying when the order was made or last varied.[97] An increase in a party's earnings or a decrease in the value of the original order as a result of inflation could be a sufficient change in circumstances to justify the variation of a previous order.

If an application for maintenance fails and the parties' circumstances subsequently change, the applicant may be justified in applying a second time for an order. However, where a summons for maintenance has been dismissed the matter is *res judicata* and the court has no jurisdiction to hear a second summons on exactly the same cause of complaint.[98]

An order may also be discharged on the application of the maintenance debtor one year after being made, if it appears to the court that, having regard to the former's record of payments and to other circumstances, the persons for whose support it provides will not be prejudiced by its being dishcarged.[99] As we have already seen, the court must revoke an order if the maintenance creditor subsequently deserts,[100] and has a discretion to discharge or vary an order upon his committing adulty.[101]

Section 5 provides that an order is to remain in force "for such period during the lifetime of the applicant . . . as the court may consider proper". Thus, it is

---

95. See, however, *O.C. v. T.C., supra,* in which the wife's adultery was one of the reasons for the court declining to award maintenance to her. McMahon J. stated that there was "no suggestion that the husband condoned or connived at the wife's adultery" and that "it would . . . clearly be unfair to the husband to revive the obligation to support his wife which was extinguished by her adultery."
96. Family Law . . . Act, 1976, Sect. 6(4).
97. *Ibid.,* Sect. 6(1)(b).
98. *Downey v. Downey* [1943] Ir. Jur. Rep. 72 (Cir. Ct.).
99. Family Law . . . Act, 1976, Sect. 6(1)(a).
100. *Ibid.,* Sect. 6(2).
101. *Ibid.,* Sect. 6(4).

also possible that the court when making the original order may limit the period for which it is to remain in force.

Section 12 of the Courts Act, 1981, confers jurisdiction on the District Court and Circuit Court to vary or revoke a maintenance order made by the High Court before the 12th of May 1982 (the date of commencement of the 1981 Act)[102] if the circumstances to which the order related have changed and, in the case of the District Court, provided that the High Court order was one which would have been within the jurisdiction of the District Court if the Act of 1981 had been in operation at the time when it was made. Thus, if a High Court maintenance order was made in 1980 for the support of a wife in a sum not greater than £100 per week, an application to vary the order can be made to an appropriate District Court.[103] If, however, a wife is seeking a sum in excess of £100 per week for her own support, as the District Court cannot order weekly maintenance in excess of that sum, it would be of no assistance to the wife to bring such application before the District Court. In such circumstances the application could be made under Section 12 of the 1981 Act to the appropriate Circuit Court,[104] or in reliance on the judgement in *R. v. R.*[105] to the High Court. Any maintenance or variation order made by the High Court on or after the 12th of May 1982 cannot be varied or revoked by the District or Circuit Court. Moreover, the District Court cannot vary or revoke any maintenance or variation order made by the Circuit Court exercising the originating jurisdiction conferred on it by the Courts Act, 1981. The District Court can, however, vary a maintenance order made by the Circuit Court in exercise of its appellate jurisdiction. Similarly, the Circuit Court can vary an order made by the High Court in exercise of its appellate jurisdiction.

The 1981 Act is silent as to the power of the Circuit Court to make an order, otherwise than on appeal, in relation to a matter in which the District Court has already made an order. It is submitted, however, that a spouse may institute maintenance proceedings in the Circuit Court and seek a maintenance order there, even if one has already been obtained by her in the District Court, as if a spouse could not do so, she could find herself locked into the jurisdictional financial limits imposed on the lower court, even in circumstances in which it would appear proper for a court to make a maintenance award in excess of £100 per week for her support. This contention is supported by the decision of the Supreme Court in *J.E.C. v. D.O.C.*[106] in which it was held that the existence of a District Court maintenance order did not prevent the High Court from making a maintenance order for the support of a wife under either section 5 or 7 of the 1976 Act "on the understanding that in the event of the court so making an order under either section the plaintiff (wife) will consent to abandoning the benefit of the maintenance order made in the District Court."

Deemed Maintenance Orders: Section 8 of the Act provides that if spouses enter into a written agreement (including a separation agreement) on or after the 6th of May 1976[107] that includes either or both of the following provisions:

---

102. See Courts Act, 1981, Sect. 33(3).
103. See *ibid.*, Sect. 16(2).
104. See *ibid.*, Sect. 16(1). There must be some doubts as to the constitutional validity of a statutory provision which entitles courts of limited and local jurisdiction to vary or discharge an order of the High Court.
105. *Supra.*
106. There was no written judgement in this case. See order dated the 1st of March 1982, Supreme Court Record No. 198/1981.
107. See also Family Law ... Act, 1976, Sect. 2.

(a) a provision whereby one spouse undertakes to make periodical maintenance payments for the benefit of the other spouse and/or any dependent children of the family;

(b) a provision governing the rights and liabilities of the spouses towards one another in respect of the making or securing of payments (other than payments specified in 'a'), or the disposition or use of any property;

upon application by one or both spouses, the High Court or Circuit Court may by order make the agreement a rule of court, if satisfied that it is fair and reasonable and that it adequately protects the interests of both spouses and the dependent children.[108] As a consequence of such an order, the procedure provided for payment and enforcement of maintenance orders made under the Act, may be used for the payment and enforcement of any maintenance clause in the agreement by which a spouse is obliged to make periodical payments for the benefit of the other spouse or dependent children. It is important to note that any such maintenance clause does not become a maintenance order proper, it is merely deemed to be a maintenance order for the purposes of payment and enforcement.[109] Any maintenance order made under the Act of 1886 is also deemed to be a maintenance order made under the Act of 1976 and continues in force and is payable and enforceable in the same manner as an order made under the latter Act.[110]

Procedure for Payment: The court when making a maintenance order under the Act must direct that payments under the order be made to a local District Court clerk rather than the maintenance creditor. The court is bound to make such a direction unless at the request of the maintenance creditor the court considers that it would be proper not to do so. If a direction of payment to the clerk is not made, the court may at any time in the future make such a direction on the *ex parte* application of the maintenance creditor.[111]

The clerk is under a duty to transmit payments made to him to the maintenance creditor.[112] Where payments to the clerk are in arrears, upon a request in writing by the maintenance creditor, the clerk may proceed in his own name for enforcement of the arrears.[113] This does not prevent a person from taking proceedings in his or her own name for the recovery of arrears if he or she so wishes.[114] Where the court has directed payment to the court clerk it may discharge the direction on the application of the maintenance debtor if satisfied that having regard to his record of payment and other circumstances it would be proper to do so. The court must give the maintenance creditor an opportunity to oppose such an application.[115]

108. See *Dalton v. Dalton* [1982] 2 I.L.R.M. 418 (H.C.) and *J.D. v. B.D.* [1985] 5 I.L.R.M. 688 (H.C.). See further pp. 210 & 211 *ante.*
109. For a detailed discussion on the ruling of separation and maintenance agreements, see p. 211 *ante.*
110. Family Law ... Act, 1976, Sect. 30(2).
111. *Ibid.*, Sect. 9(1).
112. *Ibid.*, Sect. 9(4).
113. *Ibid.*, Sect. 9(2).
114. *Ibid.*, Sect. 9(5).
115. *Ibid.*, Sect. 9(3).

Alimony[1]

The High Court by virtue of the 1870 Act now exercises the powers formerly vested in the Ecclesiastical Courts to order a husband to pay his wife alimony pending suit (*pendente lite*) and to pay her permanent alimony after the granting of a divorce *a mensa et thoro*.[2] The court has no jurisdiction to order a wife pay her husband such alimony.

Alimony Pendente Lite: Provided the *"factum"* of marriage between the parties is established, alimony pending suit will be allotted to a wife, regardless of whether the suit is commenced by or against the husband,[3] in nullity petitions,[4] in suits for restitution of conjugal rights and in suits for a divorce *a mensa et thoro*.

A statement as to the husband's income must be set down in the wife's affidavit and the veracity of such statement can be contested by the husband. The amount of alimony that will be awarded depends on the discretion of the court which is formed from an equitable view of all the circumstances of the case, e.g. husband's income, wife's independent income, property interests of the parties, etc.

Permanent Alimony: A wife who has obtained a final decree of divorce *a mensa et thoro* may apply to the court for allotment of permanent alimony. A larger allowance will be made by way of permanent alimony than for alimony pending suit.[5] If a decree has been granted by reason of a wife's adultery the court has no power to order the husband to make any financial provision for her. There is, however, precedent for awarding some provision for the maintenance of a wife against whom a decree is made on the ground of cruelty.[6] If a decree of nullity is made, the marriage is regarded as invalid *ab initio* and the 'husband' cannot be compelled to support his former 'wife'.

Alimony is allotted for the maintenance of the wife from year to year (the payment can of course be weekly,[7] monthly or yearly). The court has no power to order a husband to pay his wife a lump sum either instead of or as well as periodic payments. Neither has the court power to award her a separate sum for the support of any children in her custody.

Variation: A wife can apply to the court any time after an order for payment of alimony has been made, whether it be alimony pending suit[8] or permanent alimony, for an increase of the sum allotted by reason of the increased income of her husband or by the reduction of her own income. Similarly, a

1. See R.S.C. (S.I. No. 15 of 1986), Order 70, Rules 47–57.
2. *Keyes v. Keyes* [1919] 2 I.R. 160; (1918) 53 I.L.T.R. 190 (K.B.D.).
3. *Bain v. Bain* (1824) 2 Add. 253; 162 E.R. 286 (Consistory Ct.); *Smyth v. Smyth* (1824) 2 Add. 254; 162 E.R. 287 (Consistory Ct.); *Wilson v. Wilson* (1797), 2 Hag. Con. 203; 161 E.R. 176 (Consistory Ct.).
4. *Bird, alias Bell v. Bird* (1753) 1 Lee 209; 161 E.R. 78 (Arches Ct.).
5. *Kemp v. Kemp* (1828) 1 Hag. Ecc. 532; 162 E.R. 668.
6. *Pritchard v. Prichard* (1864); 3 Sw. & Tr. 523; 164 E.R. 1378; *Godden v. Godden* [1892] P. 1 (C.A.). See, however, *White v. White* (1859) 1 Sw. & Tr. 591; 164 E.R. 874 and *Dart v. Dart* (1863) 3 Sw. & Tr. 208; 164 E.R. 1254.
7. See *Brolly v. Brolly* [1939] I.R. 562 (H.C.) where it was held that the husband was not entitled to deduct income tax from payments ordered to be made weekly. See also *Nolan v. Nolan* [1941] I.R. 419 (H.C.). See further p. 455.
8. See *McArdle v. McArdle* (1940) 74 I.L.T.R. 59 (H.C.) where it was held that the court had jurisdiction to hear an application to vary an order of alimony *pendente lite* upon the application of the respondent who failed to appear at the original hearing.

husband may apply for a diminution of the sum allotted by reason of his reduced, or the wife's increased, income.[9]

FINANCIAL PROVISION FOR CHILDREN OF SPOUSES

Introduction

Common Law: At common law a father was under a duty to maintain his legitimate children and to provide them with food, clothes, lodgings and other necessaries. This duty was, however, only a moral one and was never enforceable. Children never had an agency of necessity and thus a trader could never force the father of a child supplied with necessaries to pay for them.[10] The wife's agency of necessity did extend to the purchase of necessaries for the children of the marriage, however, so a father could be compelled, through her, to pay for such goods.[11]

The Poor Law: Poor Law legislation expressly imposed upon a father an obligation to maintain his children and made him criminally liable for failing to do so.[12] Under the Public Assistance Act, 1939[13] both parents were obliged to maintain their children under 16 years, and were liable to criminal prosecution for deserting or wilfully neglecting to do so, so as to render such child eligible for assistance under the Act.[14] Under the Social Welfare (Supplementary Welfare Allowances) Act, 1975, which replaced the Act of 1939, both parents were still obliged to maintain their children under the age of 16, but it was no longer a criminal offence to fail to do so.[15] This remains the position under the provisions of the Social Welfare (Consolidation) Act, 1981.

Alimony: The law was extremely slow in making provision for the direct payment by one parent to another of sums of maintenance for the support of a child. Whilst a wife could be awarded alimony by the Ecclesiastical Courts no provision could be made for her children, and this is still the position in respect of awards of alimony made in those proceedings heard in the High Court or the Circuit Court that were formerly within the jurisdiction of the Ecclesiastical Court.

Guardianship of Infants Act, 1964: Finally, with the coming into force of the 1964 Act, a parent was able to apply to the Circuit Court or High Court for a maintenance order to be made in his favour requiring the other parent to provide support for a child in the applicant's custody.

Family Law (Maintenance of Spouses and Children) Act, 1976

It was not until the coming into force of the Courts Act, 1971,[16] that a spouse

---

9. See R.S.C. Order 70, Rule 55; see also *McGowan v. McGowan* [1921] 2 I.R. 314 (K.B.D.) where the amount being paid having been fixed by the consent of the parties, the consent having been made a rule of court, the court held it had jurisdiction to vary the amount. See further, *M.C. v. J.C.* [1982] 2 I.L.R.M. 562 (H.C.) discussed on p. 207 *ante*.
10. The father could expressly make his child his agent and so render himself liable for the child's purchases.
11. *Bazely v. Forder* (1868) L.R. 3 Q.B. 559 (Ct. of Q.B.).
12. See Sects. 53 and 59 of the Poor Relief (Ireland) Act, 1838 and Sect. 2 of Vagrancy Act, 1847.
13. See Sect. 27.
14. Sect. 83.
15. A parent who fails to maintain his children may be liable to prosecution under the Childrens Acts, 1908–1957, however.
16. See Sect. 18.

upon applying for maintenance for her own support could simultaneously seek an extra sum for the support of her dependent children. Now a spouse may seek maintenance for dependent children under the Family Law (Maintenance of Spouses and Children) Act, 1976. Except in so far as it is differentiated below, the law under this Act in relation to the maintenance of children, is the same as the law in respect of the maintenance of spouses.

Grounds: When it appears to the court that a spouse has failed to provide such maintenance for his dependent children as is proper in the circumstances, the court may order that spouse to make periodical maintenance payments for their support.[17] The District Court, and Circuit Court on appeal from the District Court, cannot award more than £30 per week for the support of a child, child, whilst the Circuit Court exercising its originating jurisdiction and the High Court in so far as it still retains such jurisdiction, are not restricted by statute as to the amount each may award.[18]

Dependent Child: A dependent child of a spouse or spouses means any child under 16 years of age —

(a) of both spouses, or adopted by both spouses under the Adoption Acts, 1952 to 1974, or in relation to whom both spouses are in *loco parentis*, or

(b) of either spouse, or adopted by either spouse under the Adoption Acts, 1952 to 1974, or in relation to whom either spouse is in *loco parentis*, where the other spouse being aware that he is not the parent of the child, has treated the child as a member of the family.

A person over 16 may still be a dependent child if he —

(i) is or will be or, if an order were made under this Act providing for periodical payments for his support, would be receiving full-time education or instruction at any unviersity, college, school or other educational establishment and is under the age of 21 years, or

(ii) is suffering from mental or physical disability to such extent that it is not reasonably possible for him to maintain himself fully.

The definition of a dependent child for the purposes of making maintenance orders is unaffected by the Age of Majority Act, 1985, which reduced the age of majority from 21 to 18 years of age.[19]

Who May Apply: The great majority of applications for maintenance for the support of dependent children are made by a spouse when seeking maintenance for her own support. However, the Act also permits a third party to seek a maintenance order for the benefit of dependent children in certain circumstances. Where a spouse

(a) is dead;

(b) has deserted, or has been deserted by the other spouse; or

(c) is living separately and apart from the other spouse

---

17. Family Law ... Act, 1976, Sect. 5(1)(a) and (b).
18. See the Courts Act, 1981, Sect. 12 and *R. v. R.* [1984] I.R. 296 (H.C.). See further, pp. 43 & 47 *et seq.*
19. See Age of Majority Act, 1985, Sect. 2 and in particular Sect. 2(4)(b).

and there are dependent children of the family who are not being fully maintained by either spouse, the court may order a spouse to make periodical payments of maintenance for the support of each dependent child to the person applying for the order.[20]

This provision could be used, for example, by a grandmother or an aunt to force a grandson or nephew to support a child of his in either of their care. A social worker could also bring proceedings under this section to force a parent to maintain his or her child. An interesting question that arises is whether a child himself could bring proceedings against a parent to obtain support, in the absence of a third party or other parent seeking maintenance on his behalf. It is arguable that he could do so, as the section empowers "any person" to bring such proceedings. No such proceedings, however, could be brought against parents still living together.

Effect of Parent's Desertion or Adultery: Desertion or adultery by a spouse does not affect the other spouse's liability to contribute towards the maintenance of any of his dependent children in the former's custody.[21] Indeed, in *P. v. P.*[22] where the court held the wife to be in desertion and consequently, barred from receiving maintenance for her own separate support, it went on to hold that as the parties were agreed that the wife retain custody of their child and it was also "agreed that this means she cannot work for some years to come . . . the maintenance for the child must include a sum sufficient to enable the mother to look after the child." Thus, a spouse barred from receiving maintenance for her own separate support may, if she retains custody of the children of her marriage, obtain a sum of maintenance for her support indirectly through the maintenance paid to her for the support of the children.[22a]

Other Matters: A maintenance order must specify each part of the payment that is for the support of a child and may specify the period, during the lifetime of the person applying for the order, for which payment for a child's support is to be made.[23] An order for the support of a child is discharged upon the child ceasing to be a dependent child within the meaning of the Act.[24]

The Courts Act, 1981, confers the same powers on the District and Circuit Courts to vary or discharge maintenance orders made for the support of children by the High Court prior to the 12th of May 1982 as it does in the case of a maintenance order made by that court to support a spouse.[25]

The Guardianship of Infants Act, 1964

When it was first enacted, the Guardianship of Infants Act, 1964, conferred jurisdiction on both the Circuit and High Court to order the father or mother

---

20. Family Law . . . Act, 1976, Sect. 5(1)(b).
21. See *ibid.*, Sect. 6(5) and see *P.G. v. G.G.* (March, 1982) unreported (H.C.). See, however, *O.C. v. T.C.* (December, 1981) unreported (H.C.) in which a husband was held not to be liable to contribute towards his son's support. McMahon J. stated that "the husband's liability to support (his son) is not affected by the wife's adultery" but he should not be required to contribute towards the son's support as the son was living in the United States with the wife in breach of the provisions of a separation deed under which the son was to reside in Ireland and the husband was to have joint custody with the wife. See further p. 203 *ante.*
22. (March, 1980) unreported (H.C.).
22a. See also *A.H. v. A.H.* (December, 1985) unreported (H.C.) in which Lynch J. followed the approach of Barrington J. in *P. v. P., supra.*
23. Family Law . . . Act, 1976, Sect. 5(1)(c).
24. *Ibid.*, Sect. 6(3).
25. See p. 447 *ante.*

of a legitimate infant to pay such weekly or other periodical sum for the maintenance of such infant as the court considered reasonable, having regard to the means of the father or mother, upon an application for maintenance being made to the court by either parent or by a person appointed as testamentary guardian of such infant.[26] Section 15 of the Courts Act, 1981, amended the Act of 1964 by the substitution of a new section[27] which expressly confers an originating jurisdiction to make such maintenance orders on the District and Circuit Courts but which contains no reference to the High Court retaining the original jurisdiction conferred on it by the Act of 1964 to make maintenance orders in any proceedings initiated on or after the 12th of May 1982, the date of commencement of the Act of 1981. In *R. v. R.*[28] it was held that the High Court still retained an original jurisdiction to make orders under the Act of 1964 after that date, but as has been previously stated, the authority of this decision is now in question.[29]

The District Court, and the Circuit Court on appeal from the District Court, cannot award more than £30 per week for the maintenance of an infant under the Act.[30] The Circuit Court exercising its originating jurisdiction and the High Court, in so far as it retains such jurisdiction, are not similarly restricted by statute as to the amount they can order a parent to pay, each having a jurisdiction unlimited as to amount.

Formerly, for liability to arise under a maintenance order made pursuant to the Act of 1964, the parents of the infant for whose support it was made had to have ceased cohabiting and if they continued to cohabit for three months after the making of such order, it ceased to have any effect.[31] This is no longer the case and a maintenance order now made under the Act may come into force notwithstanding that the parents are still residing together and no longer ceases to have effect if they continue to do so.[32]

An order for the maintenance of a child under the Act of 1964 may be applied for and may continue in force until the child attains the age of 21 years[33] or indefinitely in respect of a child over that age who "is suffering from mental or physical disability to such extent that it is not reasonably possible for him to maintain himself fully."[34]

---

26. See Guardianship of Infants Act, 1964, Sects. 5, 7, & 11(2)(b).
27. Replacing the original section 5 with a new section.
28. [1984] I.R. 296 (H.C.).
29. See p. 43 *ante*.
30. See the new section 5(2) as substituted by the Courts Act, 1981, Sect. 15.
31. See original section 11(3) in Guardianship of Infants Act, 1964.
32. See Age of Majority Act, 1985, Sect. 6.
33. An infant is defined as a person under 21 years of age by the Act of 1964. The Age of Majority Act, 1985, preserved 21 as the age up to which maintenance orders may be made and remain in force for the support of dependant children, although a child now ceases to be an infant for all other purposes of the Guardianship of Infants Act, 1964, upon attaining the age of 18 years. See Sect. 2 and in particular Sect. 2(4) of the Act of 1985.
34. See the Age of Majority Act, 1985, Sect. 6. The new Sect. 11(5) inserted by it in the Act of 1964 provides that any reference to an infant in respect of whom a maintenance order may be made "shall include a reference to a child who has attained the age of 18 years and is suffering from mental or physical disability to such extent that it is not reasonably possible for him to maintain himself fully."
Having regard to the provisions of Sect. 2(4) of the Act the reference should have been to 21 years and not 18 years as a maintenance order can remain in force in respect of any child until he attains the age of 21 years. However, the Act as originally presented to the Dáil would have had the effect of terminating maintenance payments for children at 18 years of age but an amendment to permit such payments continue until 21 years of age was introduced at the committee stage. The necessary consequential amendment in Sect. 6 to the new Sect. 11(5) to be inserted in the Guardianship of Infants Act, 1964, was never made during the Act's passage through the Oireachtas.

The court has no power under the Act of 1964 to award any sum for the maintenance of a spouse and any question as to whether either spouse is guilty of a matrimonial offence is irrelevant in reaching a determination as to whether an order for the maintenance of a child should be made. The matrimonial conduct of a parent may, however, be relevant if a dispute as to custody has to be determined prior to a decision being made upon a maintenance application for a child's support.[35]

In conclusion, section 15 of the Courts Act, 1981, confers jurisdiction on the District Court and the Circuit Court to vary or revoke any maintenance order made by the High Court before the 12th of May 1982 (the date of commencement of the 1981 Act) if a change of circumstances has taken place, provided the High Court order was one which would have been within the jurisdiction of the court to which such application is made, if the 1981 Act had been operative at the date when it was made. The jurisdiction conferred by this provision on the District Court and Circuit Court to vary or revoke maintenance orders for the support of children made by the High Court prior to the 12th of May 1982 is the same as that conferred on those courts to vary maintenance orders made for the support of a spouse pursuant to the provisions of the Family Law . . . Act, 1976 as already discussed.

MAINTENANCE, ALIMONY AND INCOME TAX

Maintenance ordered for the support of a spouse under the Act of 1976 or alimony ordered must be paid without deduction of income tax[35a] and all monies paid to a spouse for his or her own support pursuant to a maintenance or alimony order made on or after the 8th of June 1983 are deductible from the paying spouse's gross earnings prior to their being assessed for income tax by virtue of the provisions of section 3 of the Finance Act, 1983. As a consequence, any maintenance received by a spouse for his or her support pursuant to such order is taxable in the hands of the spouse receiving it, as is any maintenance or alimony payable by one spouse to another pursuant to the terms of a separation agreement or maintenance agreement concluded on or after that date. If, however, spouses agree to elect for joint assessment of income tax, as they may do pursuant to the provisions of section 4 of the Finance Act, 1983, and section 195 of the Income Tax Act, 1967, the monies received by way of maintenance by the spouse to whom it is being paid are not taxable in the hands of such spouse, such payments being nett of tax. In the context of such an arrangement being agreed the spouse paying maintenance cannot deduct the maintenance sum paid from his gross salary before it is assessed for income tax but may retain for his benefit the full married persons tax allowances and double tax bands. Following an election, if both spouses each have income in their own right other than maintenance payments, the income tax applicable to their respective incomes is calculated by the separate assessment procedure but the husband's gross income for tax purposes is not regarded as diminished by the amount of maintenance he is paying.

Maintenance ordered to be paid for the support of children under the Act of 1976 or under the Guardianship of Infants Act, 1964, or pursuant to the terms of a Deed of Separation must also be paid without deduction of income tax. Such maintenance, however, is treated as being the income of the payer and is

---

35. See p. 360 *ante et seq.*
35a. See the Family Law . . . Act, 1976, Sect. 24. See also *Brolly v. Brolly, supra* and *Nolan v. Nolan, supra.*

not taxable in the hands of the custodial spouse to whom it is paid for the support of a child or children.[36]

ENFORCEMENT MACHINERY

The following is the machinery available for enforcing financial orders of support made by the High Court, Circuit Court, and District Court. Unless it is necessary to distinguish between them, all such orders are referred to below as maintenance orders. Thus, the procedure for attachment of earnings not only applies to financial orders made under the Act of 1976 but is also available to enforce orders deemed to be maintenance orders under the Act,[37] affiliation orders, orders for maintenance under the Guardianship of Infants Act, 1964, enforceable maintenance orders under the Maintenance Orders Act, 1974,[38] and orders for payment of alimony pending suit or permanent alimony.

Attachment of Earnings

The Act of 1976 introduced a new method of enforcing a maintenance order – attachment of the earnings of a maintenance debtor.[39] An attachment of earnings order may be applied for by the person for whose benefit maintenance is paid or by a District Court clerk to whom payment is made. It can only be made without the consent of the maintenance debtor if the court is satisfied that he has, without reasonable excuse, defaulted in the making of any payment.[40] Only the earnings of the maintenance debtor as defined in section 3(1) of the Act can be attached.[41] Attachment cannot apply to monies payable to a maintenance debtor other than earnings payable to him periodically (e.g. weekly, fortnightly, monthly or quarterly) by an employer. In *Ellen Byrne v. Francis Byrne*[42] it was held that a lump sum payable to a husband as a redundancy payment upon the termination of his employment could not be attached as it was not "earnings for the purposes of the Act".

An attachment of earnings order must specify two rates:

---

36. Maintenance payable pursuant to a maintenance order made or a separation agreement entered into prior to the 8th of June 1983 is not affected by the Finance Act, 1983. The provisions of the Act of 1983 can only apply to the financial arrangements affecting parties subject to any such order or agreement if they jointly elect in writing for their application or enter into a new agreement or if a new maintenance order is made. It is not within the scope of this book to deal in detail with the area of taxation. For a discussion of the application of the income tax code to Deeds of Separation concluded prior to the 8th of June 1983 see, M.V. O'Mahony, "The Drafting of Separation Agreements", S.Y.S. Lecture No. 93; F. Gannon, "The Tax Implications of Marital Breakdown" (1983) *Gazette of the Incorporated Law Society of Ireland* 15. For a detailed analysis of this whole area see N.E. Judge, *Irish Income Tax* (Butterworths, London 1986), p. 565 *et seq.*
   37. See p. 448 *ante*.
   38. See p. 461 *ante*.
   39. Family Law . . . Act, 1976, Sect. 10.
   40. *Ibid.*, Sect. 10(3).
   41. See p. 434 *ante*, footnote 27.
   42. See (July/August, 1982) 76 *Gazette of the Inc. L.S. of Ireland*, "Recent Irish Cases" at p. 26. See further *B.H. v. W.H.* [1983] 3 I.L.R.M. 419 (H.C.) in which the wife succeeded in obtaining a *mareva* injunction against her husband on the ground that she feared he was about to leave the jurisdiction and otherwise dissipate a sum in excess of £9,000 which he was about to receive by way of a redundancy payment, the monies being the sole asset from which maintenance arrears and future maintenance payments to her could be met. There was evidence available as to the husband's intention to leave the jurisdiction and an interim order was granted for two and a half weeks freezing the cheque drawn in favour of the husband by his employers in respect of the redundancy payment. The employers were joined as co-defendants in the proceedings and no further order had subsequently to be made as the proceedings were settled. See also P. Charleton, "Family Law – Mareva Injunctions" (1982) 4 D.U.L.J. 114.

(a) The normal deduction rate — the amount of earnings which the court considers reasonable to apply towards meeting payments falling due under an order in the future, together with arrears already due and unpaid and costs owing.

(b) The protected earnings rate — the amount below which the court considers it proper that the earnings should not be reduced by payment made in pursuance of an order of attachment, having regard to the resources and needs of the maintenance debtor.[43]

An attachment order is directed to the maintenance debtor's employer who is bound to make such periodical deductions from the debtor's earnings as specified by the order and to pay them over to the District Court clerk.[44] Thus, on each pay-day an employer will normally deduct the "normal deduction rate" and hand over the rest of the pay to his employee. However, if deduction of the normal deduction rate would bring the amount handed to the employee below the protected earnings rate, the employer may only withhold the amount by which the earnings exceed the protected earnings rate. When a deduction is made the employer must give the maintenance debtor a written statement of the total amount deducted.[45] The District Court clerk may post any payment received by him under an attachment order, to the person entitled to the payment.[46]

Upon the making of an attachment of earnings order, any proceedings previously commenced under section 8(1) of the Enforcement of Court Orders Act, 1940, lapse.[47] Similarly, an order made or a warrant issued under that section ceases to have effect.[48] An attachment of earnings order ceases to have effect upon the subsequent making of an order under the above provision for the enforcement of an obligation to pay maintenance.[49]

Statement of Earnings: In relation to an order of attachment or an application for such an order, the court may require the maintenance debtor to give to it a statement in writing of the name and address of any person by whom earnings are paid to him and particulars of his earnings and expected earnings, resources and needs. Notice to the debtor of an application for an attachment of earnings order may include a requirement that such particulars be given to the court within a specified time. Further, the court may order an employer of a maintenance debtor to furnish particulars of the latter's earnings and expected earnings.[50] When an attachment order is in force an employer, maintenance creditor or maintenance debtor may apply to the court for a determination as to whether payments to the debtor are earnings for the purpose of the order.[51]

Variation and Discharge: If an attachment order is served on a person and the maintenance debtor is not or subsequently ceases to be in his employment, the person served must inform the court within ten days of either being served with the order, or from the date of the maintenance debtor's departure.[52] An order

---

43. Family Law . . . Act, 1976, Sect. 10(4).
44. *Ibid.*, Sect. 10(2).
45. *Ibid.*, Sect. 11(3).
46. District Court, Family Law (Maintenance of Spouses and Children) Act, 1976, Rules 1976; (S.I. No. 96 of 1976), Rule 22.
47. See p. 458 *post.*
48. Sect. 19(1) of the 1976 Act.
49. *Ibid.*, Sect. 19(2).
50. *Ibid.*, Sect. 13.
51. *Ibid.*, Sect. 14.
52. *Ibid.*, Sect. 11(2).

in respect of an employer lapses upon his ceasing to employ the maintenance debtor. However, it still applies in respect of deductions of earnings paid by the employer after termination of employment, so as to enable payment to the person in whose favour the order was made of any deductions made by the employer.[53]

The maintenance debtor is himself under an obligation to notify the court in writing within ten days of his leaving or changing employment and must also give particulars of earnings under the new employment.[54] Upon a person employing a maintenance debtor and discovering that an order of attachment of earnings is in force and the court by which it was made, he must notify the court in writing that he is the debtor's employer and include a statement of the debtor's earnings.[55] The court clerk, upon learning of any employer other than the one to whom the order is directed, may serve such employer with a copy of the order.[56]

A weakness in the above provisions is the inability of the court to impose an effective sanction on the maintenance defaulter who takes up new employment without informing the court, and without telling his new employer that an order of attachment of earnings is in force against him. The Act merely provides that if a person without reasonable excuse fails to give the above required notices and a maintenance creditor, as a result, fails to obtain a sum of money due under an attachment order, the person in default may be sued for that sum as a simple contract debt. Whereas this provision may compel an employer to comply with his obligations, it will have little effect on the maintenance debtor himself, as he is already liable for the sum due. Further, whereas a maintenance debtor is guilty of an offence if he gives "false or misleading" information to the court on any of the above matters and is rendered liable to a fine not exceeding £200 and/or a term of imprisonment up to six months, he is liable to no such penalty if he fails to inform the court at all.[57]

The court has a general power to discharge or vary an attachment of earnings order.[58] Finally, an attachment order ceases to have effect upon the discharge of the maintenance order it sought to enforce, except in relation to money payable prior to the date of discharge.[59]

Enforcement of Court Orders Act, 1940, Sect. 8.[60]

This provision applies to financial orders made in the District Court under the Act of 1976, orders deemed to be maintenance orders under that Act[61], maintenance orders made under the Guardianship of Infants Act, 1964,[61a] and District Court affiliation orders.[62] The section renders a person who defaults in his

53. *Ibid.*, Sect. 17(3).
54. *Ibid.*, Sect. 14(a) and (b).
55. *Ibid.*, Sect. 14(c).
56. *Ibid.*, Sect. 11(4).
57. Sect. 20 of the 1976 Act.
58. *Ibid.*, Sect. 17(1).
59. *Ibid.*, Sect. 18 (1).
60. See District Court Rules (No. 2) 1962 (S.I. No. 8 of 1962) Part iv; District Court, Family Law (Maintenance of Spouses and Children) Act, 1976, Rules 1976 (S.I. No. 96 of 1976) Rule 30; See further, J.V. Woods, *District Court Guide* Vol. II (1977), pp. 241–244. See, in addition, the Courts Act, 1986, Sect. 3(5) which extends power to the District Court to enforce orders for costs made by use of section 8 of the 1940 Act, in those proceedings in which financial orders made for spousal or child support can be enforced under the section.
61. Sect. 29 of the Act of 1976.
61a. See the Courts Act, 1986, Sect. 5(4).
62. In this section the term "maintenance creditor" is used to include a person to whom money is payable under an affiliation order and the term "Maintenance debtor" includes the person against whom an affiliation order has been made.

payments liable to distraint or imprisonment and an application under the section may be made by either the maintenance creditor or a District Court clerk where maintenance payments are being made through the District Court. Only arrears payable in respect of the six months immediately preceding the institution of enforcement proceedings can be recovered under section 8.

An application under section 8 is made by the swearing of an information before a justice of the District Court setting out the arrears payable. A justice to whom such application is made may either issue a warrant for the arrest of the maintenance debtor or if he thinks fit, issue a summons requiring the maintenance debtor to appear before the court. A justice when issuing a warrant may certify in the warrant his consent to the maintenance debtor being released on his entering into recognisance, with or without a surety or sureties, for his appearance before the court on a date specified in the warrant and he must specify the amount in respect of which the maintenance debtor and his surety or sureties (if any) are to be bound.

Distraint: A district justice may if he thinks proper upon an application being made, direct that the arrears owed by a maintenance debtor be levied by the distress and sale of the debtor's goods. In practice this provision is rarely used.

Imprisonment: A maintenance debtor may be imprisoned for up to three months unless he shows that his failure to pay was due neither to his wilful neglect nor culpable negligence. The release of a person imprisoned can be obtained upon payment by him, or by another person, of the sum owing. Serving a prison sentence does not operate so as to extinguish the debt.

Defence Act, 1954, Sect. 98[63]

This section applies to maintenance orders made under the Family Law ... Act, 1976, and deemed maintenance orders made under that Act, financial orders made under the Illegitimate Children (Affiliation Orders) Act, 1930, orders for alimony or for payment of any monies due as alimony under a deed of separation and any arrears accrued and any costs and expenses payable under any of the aforesaid orders.

Under the section if any of the above orders are made against a person who is or subsequently becomes a "man of the Permanent Defence Force" and a copy of such order is sent to the Minister for Defence, the prescribed authority "shall order to be deducted from the pay of such person as a man of the Permanent Defence Force and to be appropriated in satisfaction or part satisfaction of the amount ... payable under the order such portion (not exceeding, in case he holds the rank of sergeant or a higher non-commissioned army rank or the rank of petty officer or a higher non-commissioned naval rank, two thirds or, in any other case, three fourths) of his daily pay as the prescribed authority thinks fit. This section also applies to a reservist called out on permanent service.

In effect this provision permits earnings to be attached even if the payer has not defaulted in payments. It is to be noted, however, that the section does not apply to a maintenance order made under the Guardianship of Infants Act, 1964.[64] Furthermore, section 107 of the 1954 Act prohibits the making of

---

63. As amended by Sect. 30 of the 1976 Act.
64. See, however, section 99 of the 1954 Act. Sub-section one states:
    "Where it appears to the Minister that a person who is or subsequently becomes a man of the Permanent Defence Force has deserted or left in destitute circumstances, without reasonable cause, his wife or any of his legitimate children under the age of sixteen

an order of imprisonment under the Enforcement of Court Orders Act, 1940, sect. 8 against a man of the Permanent Defence Force or a reservist who has been called out on permanent service.

Other Methods of Enforcement

In practice these are not relevant to the enforcement of District Court maintenance orders. A maintenance order is not a final judgement. Thus, the successful applicant for maintenance does not have the same rights of enforcement as the successful plaintiff in a tort or contract action. The court may exercise its discretion in determining how much arrears need actually be paid and may remit them in whole or in part. It will not enforce payment of arrears that go back many years. There is no inflexible rule, however, and much depends on the circumstances of the case.[65] Due to the court's discretionary power maintenance payable under an order of the Circuit or High Court cannot be recovered by action,[66] though it may be enforced by any of the appropriate forms of execution or by attachment and committal proceedings.

The usual means of enforcement in the High Court prior to 1976 was by use of the Debtors (Ir.) Act, 1872, Sect. 6. By this section, the court may order the payment of arrears of maintenance by instalments or may commit a defaulter to prison upon being satisfied that he had, since the date of the order, the means to pay the sum in respect of which he is in default and has refused or neglected to pay it.[67] The court upon ordering imprisonment normally stays the order for a short time to enable the defaulter to pay his debt.[68] Imprisonment may be for a term of six weeks or until payment is made.[69] It does not operate so as to extinguish the arrears due.

RECIPROCAL ENFORCEMENT OF MAINTENANCE ORDERS

At common law a valid foreign judgement *in personam* is enforceable if it is for a debt or definite sum of money and is final and conclusive.[70] This is subject to the proviso that no action can be maintained on such a judgement if it is in respect of a cause of action contrary to the public policy of the country in which it is sought to be enforced. A foreign maintenance order requiring a spouse to make periodical payments to the other spouse is a foreign judgement *in personam*. If, as is usually the case, the foreign court has power to vary the amount of the payments, the foreign order cannot at common law be enforced in this country as it is not "final and conclusive".[71] However, if the foreign court has power to

---

years, the Minister may order to be deducted from the daily pay of such person as a man of the Permanent Defence Force and applied in such manner as the Minister thinks fit towards the maintenance of the wife or such legitimate children such portion (not exceeding, in case he holds the rank of sergeant or a higher non-commissioned army rank or the rank of petty officer or a higher non-commissioned naval rank, two-thirds or, in any other case, three-fourths) of his daily pay as the Minister thinks fit."

65. *Keys v. Keys, supra* (concerned enforcement of Alimony order).
66. *Keys v. Keys, supra*.
67. Sect. 6(2) of the 1872 Act; see *Tees v. Tees* [1930] N.I. 156 (K.B.D.), (order of committal made in respect of non payment of permanent alimony); *Daly v. Daly* (1886) 17 L.R. Ir. 372 (Matr. Ct.).
68. See *Brolly v. Brolly, supra*; *Tees v. Tees, supra*.
69. See, however, the Defence Act, 1954, Sect. 107 which prohibits the imprisonment of a member of the Defence Forces under Sect. 6 of the Act of 1872.
70. *Rainford and Others v. Newell-Roberts* [1962] I.R. 95 (S.C.); *Mayo-Perrott v. Mayo-Perrott* [1958] I.R. 336 (S.C.); *G. v. G.* [1984] I.R. 368 (H.C.).
71. *Leake v. Douglas* (1954) I.L.T.R. 4 (Cir. Ct.); See Dicey & Morris, *The Conflict of Law*, 10th edition, p. 1092 *et seq*.

vary the amount of future payments, but may not vary arrears, then the arrears may be recovered by an action on the foreign judgement.[72] Application of the above rules meant that, at common law, an Irish maintenance order could not be enforced in any of the courts in the United Kingdom and any of the latter's maintenance orders providing for periodical payments, could not be enforced in the Irish courts. Due to the high instance of husbands deserting their wives and going to England, there was a definite need to set up some procedure whereby maintenance orders made here could be enforced in England.

The Maintenance Orders Act, 1974,[73] which came into force on the 1st April 1975, now provides for the reciprocal enforcement of maintenance orders between Ireland and a "reciprocating jurisdiction", i.e. England, Wales, Scotland or Northern Ireland.[74] A "maintenance order" is defined in the Act so as to include alimony and affiliation orders.[75] It also includes "an order which is incidental to a decision as to the status of a natural person".[76] Thus, if upon granting a divorce *a vinculo*, an English court makes a maintenance order, the Act clearly provides that any such maintenance order is enforceable in this country. The Act applies to maintenance orders made before and after its commencement, but does not apply to arrears which accrued prior to its commencement.[77]

The Act confers jurisdiction on the Master of the High Court at first instance to make an enforcement order.[78] A maintenance debtor may appeal to the High Court against the making of an enforcement order, whilst a maintenance creditor may appeal against a refusal by the Master to make such an order.[79]

Upon the making of an enforcement order, the maintenance order becomes an "enforceable maintenance order" for the purposes of the Act and the District Court acquires jurisdiction to hear enforcement proceedings against a maintenance debtor for arrears of maintenance. The District Court's jurisdiction in such proceedings is identical to the jurisdiction it possesses to enforce maintenance orders made in the State.[80] Thus, if enforcement proceedings are brought under the Enforcement of Court Orders Act, 1940, an order can be made only in respect of six months arrears of maintenance. The Act does not confer jurisdiction on the High Court or Circuit Court to enforce "enforceable maintenance orders".

The Act lays down three circumstances in which a maintenance order made in a reciprocating jurisdiction will not be recognised or enforceable here.[81] They are —

    (a) if recognition or enforcement would be contrary to public policy, *or*

---

72. *G. v. G., supra*. See also *Beatty v. Beatty* [1924] 1 K.B. 807; [1924] All E.R. Rep. 314 (C.A.).

73. See also Family Law (Maintenance of Spouses and Children) Act, 1976, Sect. 9(7) and (8), S.I. No. 58 of 1975 — District Court (Maintenance Orders Act, 1974), Rules, 1975. See further, J.V. Woods, *District Court Guide* (1977), pp. 245 *et seq*.

74. The corresponding legislation in the United Kingdom is Part I of the Maintenance Orders (Reciprocal Enforcement) Act, 1972 as applied to the Republic of Ireland by "The Reciprocal Enforcement of Maintenance Orders (Republic of Ireland) Order, 1974, (S.I. 1974/2140). For forms required for use in proceedings for the enforcement of orders under the Provisions of Part I of 1972 Act see Magistrates Courts (Reciprocal Enforcement of Maintenance Orders (Republic of Ireland) Rules, 1975 (S.I. 1975/286). See also (1975) 125 N.L.J. 435; and (1977) 127 N.L.J. 612; C. Latham, "Reciprocal Enforcement of Maintenance Orders in the E.E.C." (1975) 5 Fam. Law 145.

75. Sect. 3(1) of the 1974 Act.

76. *Ibid.*, Sect. 3(2).

77. *Ibid.*, Sect. 4.

78. *Ibid.*, Sect. 6.

79. *Ibid.*, Sects. 7 and 8.

80. *Ibid.*, Sect. 14.

81. *Ibid.*, Sect. 9.

(b) where it was made in default of appearance, the person in default not being served with notice of the institution of the proceedings in sufficient time to enable him to arrange for his defence, *or*

(c) if it is irreconcilable with a judgement given in a dispute between the same parties in this State.

Public Policy and Article 41 in the Enforcement of Maintenance and Lump Sum Orders

Prior to the enactment of the Act of 1974, it was suggested that Irish public policy as enunciated in *Mayo-Perrott v. Mayo-Perrott*[82] presented an obstacle to the enforcement in this country of maintenance orders made consequent to a foreign decree of divorce *a vinculo*.[83] In that case, the Supreme Court refused to enforce an order for costs made in English divorce proceedings on the grounds that it was contrary to Irish public policy "to give active assistance to facilitate" or to "aid" the effecting of a dissolution of marriage. In *D.M. v. E.F.M.*[84] the Master of the High Court ruled that an English maintenance order made consequent to the granting of an English divorce to require a former husband to contribute towards the support of his former wife was an enforceable maintenance order for the purposes of the Act. The maintenance debtor appealed to the High Court and submitted that enforcement of the maintenance order was contrary to public policy. Hamilton J., finding in favour of the maintenance creditor and dismissing the appeal, stated:

> "I accept unreservedly that if recognition or enforcement of a maintenance order would have the effect of giving active assistance to facilitate in any way the effecting of a dissolution of marriage or give assistance to the process of divorce that such recognition or enforcement would be contrary to public policy. In the case of *Mayo-Perrott* the Supreme Court decided that the terms of the judgement which was subject to be enforced was not severable. In this particular case the maintenance order sought to be enforced was made (in) . . . July, 1973, and though made in and consequent to proceedings for a decree of dissolution of marriage, such decree had been granted and made absolute (in) . . . August, 1967. In enforcing and recognising this maintenance order . . . it cannot be said that such enforcement or recognition is giving active or any assistance to facilitate in any way the effecting of a dissolution of marriage or is giving assistance to the process of divorce. It is merely providing for the maintenance of spouses and as such cannot be regarded as contrary to public policy."[85]

---

82. [1958] I.R. 336 (S.C.). See p. 256 *ante et seq.*

83. See article entitled "Recognition of Foreign Divorce Decrees", by J. O'Reilly (1971) 6 I.J. (n.s.) 293; and by the same author, "Enforcement Abroad of Irish Maintenance Decrees" (1972) 7 I.J. (n.s.) 106; it is submitted that the author confuses the concepts of "enforcement" and "recognition" of a divorce decree, (see Dicey & Morris, *Conflicts of Law, supra* at p. 1035 *et seq.* See also W. Duncan, "Desertion and Cruelty in Irish Matrimonial Law" (1972) 7 I.J. (n.s.) 213, esp. 231–235. See also *Leake v. Douglas, supra; M'Donnell v. M'Donnell* [1921] 2 I.R. 148; (1920) 54 I.L.T.R. 104 (K.B.D.); *Cohane v. Cohane* [1968] I.R. 176 (S.C.). See further, *Dalton v. Dalton* [1982] 2 I.L.R.M. 418 (H.C.).

84. (July, 1978) unreported (H.C.). See also *Leake v. Douglas, supra* where it was held by the Circuit Court that an order for maintenance made consequent to divorce proceedings affected status only and that the obstacle to its enforcement was that it was not final and conclusive. This obstacle has now been removed in the case of orders made in the United Kingdom.

85. See p. 9 of judgement. The parties in this case appear to have accepted that the divorce decree was recognised by Irish law. The evidence was that the parties had emigrated from Ireland to England in 1946 and were both still living in England in August 1967 when the decree of divorce *a vinculo* was made absolute. The maintenance debtor, the husband, had remarried and returned to Ireland to reside in 1974.

In the above case the maintenance order sought to be enforced, although made in divorce proceedings, could not be regarded as having "assisted in" or "facilitated" or "aided" the effecting of a divorce decree, as it was made almost six years after the granting of the decree. In the subsequent High Court case of *G. v. G.*,[86] to which the Maintenance Orders Act, 1974, was of no direct relevance, Finlay P. held a maintenance order made by a Massachusetts Court requiring a husband (the defendant) to pay maintenance to his wife (the plaintiff) for the support of their child to be enforceable by the Irish Courts.[87] The plaintiff having filed a divorce petition against the defendant in 1978 had issued separate proceedings against him seeking custody of and maintenance for their child. Prior to the granting of a decree *nisi* of divorce, the custody and maintenance proceedings were settled and a court order made in 1979 requiring the parties to comply with the terms of the settlement, including the maintenance provision contained in it. The decree *nisi* of divorce granted in 1980 and made absolute six months later, contained orders reiterating the terms of the maintenance and custody settlement which required the defendant to pay $40 per week by way of child maintenance.

In proceedings brought by the plaintiff in the High Court she claimed $3,230 arrears of maintenance and sought to enforce the order made by the Massachusetts Court in 1979. The defendant contended that this order formed part of and was inseparable from[88] the order of divorce and was, accordingly, not enforceable by the Irish Courts. Finlay P. rejected this contention. He accepted that the maintenance order for the child's support was made in "quite separate proceedings", would have continued in force even if the plaintiff's divorce petition had been unsuccessful and that the incorporation of the maintenance provision in the decree *nisi* of divorce was merely "a matter of procedure in the Courts of Massachusetts."[89] Referring, however, to the High Court's general power to enforce maintenance orders made in foreign divorce proceedings, the learned President stated that he was bound by the decision of the Supreme Court in *Mayo-Perrott* that unless he is satisfied "that the order for maintenance can be and is clearly separable from the decree of divorce", he cannot "having regard to the provisions of the Constitution enforce it."[90] Further on he continued:

> "The law of this country does not recognise divorce[91] and will not aid it. However, it does recognise and in recent years has developed a strict and efficient code for the imposition of liability on a parent to maintain a child . . . a claim by a mother who has custody of a child against the child's father for a payment towards its maintenance is a form of action known to the courts in this country and regularly enforced by them. It may well be that different considerations might apply where an order for custody of a child has been granted to one parent for the first time and as an integral part of a decree for divorce in a foreign jurisdiction and where maintenance commenced only upon the making of that order. That is not the situation in this case and I would not like to express a view upon it. It does not seem to me that the principles laid down in the *Mayo-Perrott* case and the true

---

86. [1984] I.R. 368 (H.C.).
87. It was held to be a foreign judgement *in personam* which was final and conclusive in that the maintenance arrears due could not be varied by the Massachusetts courts.
88. *Supra* at p. 370.
89. *Ibid.*, at p. 372.
90. *Ibid.*
91. This is a curious statement as Irish law does recognise foreign decrees of divorce in specific circumstances – see Chapter 10.

interpretation of the relevant provisions of the Constitution would justify me in relieving the defendant from his obligation to pay maintenance for the support of his infant child merely by reason of what, on the evidence . . . was a procedural convenience which altered the forum or particular vehicle whereby that liability was imposed without apparently, altering the liability or reaching a separate conclusion about it."[92]

The above judgement clearly raised some doubts as to what future approach might be adopted by the Irish Courts in general as to the enforcement of maintenance orders made in foreign divorce proceedings and, in particular, with reference to the enforcement of such orders under the Maintenance Orders Act, 1974.

The most recent case in which this issue has arisen for consideration is *Sachs v. Standard Chartered Bank (Ireland) Ltd & Sachs.*[93] An English decree of divorce *a vinculo* having been made three months earlier, in January 1985, a lump sum financial order was made in favour of the wife requiring her divorced husband to pay to her £35,000 sterling. No order for periodical maintenance payments was made. The wife sought to obtain payment of the monies due to her in proceedings brought in the High Court in Dublin as the husband held considerable funds in an Irish bank account. Barrington J. accepted that the lump sum order was "an ancillary order made in divorce proceedings"[94] but rejected the husband's contention that to enforce such an order was contrary to Irish public policy as articulated in *Mayo-Perrott* and in violation of Article 41 of the Constitution. Accepting the wife's contention that orders making financial provision upon the dissolution of a marriage "do not necessarily arise from the divorce decree but from the breakdown of the marriage"[95] he stated:

> "If a marriage breaks down, whether the parties look for judicial separation or divorce, problems may arise concerning the custody and maintenance of children or the maintenance of one of the parties to the dissolved marriage . . . these are universal problems which arise not from the divorce proceedings as such, but from the problems attendant on the breakdown of marriage."[96]

Noting that both the husband and the wife were domiciled in England at the time of the granting of the divorce decree and that, as a consequence, the Irish courts would recognise the divorce, he continued:

> "A woman's right to have . . . financial provision made for her arises not because she was divorced but because she was married and the marriage has broken down. It would be strange if the public policy of Ireland allowed one to recognise the divorce but debarred one from upholding the vestigial right of the wife."[97]

Holding the wife to be entitled to receive the money due to her pursuant to the lump sum order made, he stated:

> "It is, of course, true that our statute law does not expressly confer upon the courts power to order one party to a broken marriage to make a capital payment to the other but there does not appear to be anything repugnant to

---

92. *Supra* at p. 374.
93. (July, 1985) unreported (H.C.). The decision in this case has been appealed to the Supreme Court.
94. See p. 2 of judgement.
95. *Ibid.*, at p. 7.
96. *Ibid.*, at pp. 8 & 9.
97. *Ibid.*, at p. 10.

our law or Constitution in the making of a capital payment as distinct from periodical payments of income on the occasion of the breakdown of a marriage."[98]

In *Sachs*, Barrington J. relied upon and adopted the approach of Hamilton J. in *D.M. v. E.F.M.* No reference is made to the judgement of Finlay P. in *G. v. G.* and it does not appear as if that judgement was cited in counsel's submissions to the court. Consequently, there is no reference to the suggestion made by Finlay P. that different considerations could apply to the enforcement of financial orders made after the granting of a divorce decree where such orders form "an integral part of a divorce" and are not "separable" from it. Barrington J. does, however, clearly differentiate between the making of financial orders for the support of a spouse and/or children upon marital breakdown occurring, whether in divorce or in other types of family law proceedings and the making of orders for the costs of divorce proceedings. Noting that "costs are the sinews of litigation" he stated that it was not surprising that in *Mayo-Perrott* the Supreme Court held the order for costs could not be severed from the order granting a divorce but that there was "no evidence" that the problems of a court dealing with financial matters "consequent upon the dissolution of marriage" were

> "in any significant way different from the problem which would face a court in Ireland attempting to make proper financial provision for a wife or children consequent upon the granting of a decree of judicial separation."[99]

Any doubts that existed as to the future enforcement by the Irish courts of either maintenance or lump-sum financial orders made consequent upon the granting of a foreign decree of divorce *a vinculo* were finally removed by the Supreme Court in July, 1986, when determining an appeal from the decision of Barrington J. in *Sachs*. Delivering the judgement of the court,[100] Finlay C.J. dispelled the doubts that he himself had raised in the judgement he had delivered two years earlier in *G. v. G.* when President of the High Court. Agreeing with the approach of Barrington J., he stated that the lump-sum award

> "arose from the obligations which according to the law of England were imposed upon the former husband by the fact of marriage and by his apparent desertion of his wife and his having ceased to support her."[101]

Further on he continued:

> "It would seem to me to be an extraordinary anomalous position if the legal situation were that public policy permitted the recognition of the dissolution of the marriage, something which cannot, having regard to the provisions of the Constitution, be permitted in this State, and yet, the court was, by reason of public policy, deemed incapable of executing a final judgement for maintenance."[102]

He concluded:

> "The provision of maintenance arising from the obligation of a spouse in a marriage to a dependent spouse is something recoverable within the law of this country and something for which ample provision has been made by

---

98. *Ibid.*, at pp. 11 & 12.
99. *Ibid.*, at p. 9.
100. In addition to Finlay C.J., the other judges who sat were Hederman J. and McCarthy J.
101. See p. 5 of judgement.
102. See pp. 5–6 of judgement.

relatively modern legislation. In these circumstances, it seems to me that not only should public policy not be deemed to prevent the enforcement of this judgement, but that the requirements of public policy seem clearly to favour it."[103]

Other Matters

In addition to providing for the reciprocal enforcement of maintenance orders, the Maintenance Orders Act, 1974, also provides a procedure whereby maintenance proceedings can be brought in this jurisdiction against a person residing in a reciprocating jurisdiction.[104] An essential prerequisite to the institution of proceedings in this country to obtain a maintenance order, or to seek enforcement of an order already made, against a person residing in the United Kingdom, is knowledge of the whereabouts of such person. In the absence of such knowledge, no such proceedings can be successful.

In conclusion, the Convention of the European Economic Community on Jurisdiction and the Enforcement of Civil and Commercial Judgements provides for the reciprocal recognition and enforcement throughout the European Community of maintenance orders. Ireland acceded to the convention on the 9th of October 1978, but appropriate legislation has to be enacted by the Oireachtas before the convention can become part of Irish domestic law.[105]

---

103. See p. 7 of judgement.
104. Sects. 17 & 18.
105. See Vol. 21 of the *Official Journal of the European Communities* No. L 304 (30th October, 1978) and Vol. 22 of the *Official Journal of the European Community* No. C 59, (5th March, 1979). See further Dáil Debates (21 October 1980) Vol. 323 col. 251 where the Minister for Justice stated that the necessary legislation to ratify the Convention would be enacted "when other urgent domestic legislation has been disposed of." The *Report of the Joint Oireachtas Committee on Marriage Breakdown* (April, 1985) states that the convention "should be implemented as soon as practicable" and notes that it was informed "that enabling legislation is presently being prepared in the Department of Justice" – see pp. 58, 59 of *Report*.

SOCIAL WELFARE LEGISLATION

Social welfare legislation is essentially part of family maintenance law. It is outside the scope of this book, however, to examine the great variety of social welfare benefits and allowances that are available. It is intended in this chapter merely to examine the two schemes of social welfare most relevant to the marital breakdown situation — Supplementary Welfare Allowance and Deserted Wife's Allowance and Benefit — and one social welfare benefit that is paid to the great majority of families residing in the State, who have children — Child Benefit.[1]

Supplementary Welfare Allowance

The Social Welfare (Supplementary Welfare Allowances) Act, 1975, which made provision for the payment of supplementary welfare allowance, came into force on the 1st of July 1977.[2] This is now repealed and replaced by the Social Welfare (Consolidation) Act, 1981. By section 200 of the 1981 Act every person in the State whose means are insufficient to meet his needs and the needs of any dependants is entitled to claim the allowance.[3] Under the Act a wife is regarded as a dependant of her husband if living with him or wholly or mainly maintained by him; whilst a husband is regarded as a dependant of his wife if he is incapable of self-support by reason of some physical or mental infirmity and is wholly or mainly maintained by her.[4]

The Supplementary Welfare Allowance Scheme is administered by the Health Boards who are responsible for its day to day operation under the general direction and control of the Minister for Social Welfare.[5] A claim for the allowance is made to an officer of the health board in the area where the claimant lives and an appeal lies from his decision.[6]

The amount of supplementary welfare allowance to which a person is entitled is the amount by which his means fall short of his needs.[7] The means and needs of a claimant are assessed on a basis laid down in the Act. Whether a person has a right to claim the allowance, is determined on the basis of this assessment. It is possible, however, that according to the calculations of the assessment a person's means may be regarded as adequate when in reality they are not. Thus, section 209 of the Act provides that if a person is not entitled as of right to any

---

1. On 28 Feb. 1981, the Social Welfare (Consolidation) Act, 1981 came into force (see S.I. No. 63, 1981). While replacing all previous social welfare legislation it continued in force all relevant statutory instruments in force at the date of its commencement (see s. 112, 1981 Act). The relevant statutory provisions in the 1981 Act for Supplementary Welfare Allowance are in Part III, Ch. 6; for Deserted Wife's Allowance in Part III, Ch. 5; for Deserted Wife's Benefit in Part II, Ch. 13 and for Child Benefit in Part IV, as amended by the Social Welfare Act, 1986, Sect. 17.

2. See S.I. No. 156 of 1977; see also Social Welfare (Supplementary Welfare Allowances) Regulations, 1977 (S.I. No. 168 of 1977).

Supplementary Welfare Allowance replaced Home Assistance provided under the Public Assistance Act, 1939. The latter was a discretionary scheme whilst the former confers an entitlement to receive payments as of right in certain instances. For further information on Home Assistance see S. Ó Cinnéide, *A Law for the Poor* (I.P.A., Dublin 1970); The National Economic and Social Council, *Universality and Selectivity: Social Services in Ireland* (N.E.S.C. No. 38) (Stationery Office, Dublin 1978), p. 150 *et seq.*

3. With certain exceptions, see 1981 Act, sections 201, 202, 203 which relate to persons receiving full time education, persons in full time employment and persons affected by trade disputes.

4. Social Welfare (Consolidation) Act, 1981, Sect. 208.

5. *Ibid.*, Sect. 204. See *The State (Kershaw) v. The Eastern Health Board* [1985] 5 I.L.R.M. 235 (H.C.).

6. *Ibid.*, Sect. 205.

7. *Ibid.*, Sect. 207.

allowance, or where a weekly allowance is paid but his income is still not sufficient to meet his needs, such a person may receive

(a) Payment of an allowance, where he is receiving no allowance as of right, or

(b) an additional allowance where already in receipt of allowance.[8]

Such payments are "discretionary" and not as "of right" in the sense that entitlement to receive an allowance pursuant to section 209 is not based on any standardised assessment of means and needs, such as applies to determine an application for payment of the allowance to a person pursuant to section 200, but is based on the individual assessment of a supplementary welfare allowance officer of an applicant's particular needs and those of any dependants, in the context of the applicant's personal circumstances.[8a] It is a discretionary decision that is made on the facts of the particular case. Upon a determination being made that the applicant's means are insufficient to meet his needs, however, the High Court has held that the applicant then has a right to payment of an allowance pursuant to section 209.[8b] The amount to be paid must also be determined having regard to any statutory constraints imposed or any regulations made by way of statutory instrument in relation to supplementary welfare allowance. The Act provides that the Minister may make regulations prescribing (i) the circumstances in which such a payment may be made and (ii) the amount to be paid either generally or in relation to a particular class of person.

The present regulations provide that an additional allowance may be paid if

(a) the rent or mortgage interest payable by a person in respect of his place of residence exceeds £1.50 per week,

(b) a person is living alone or only with persons who are dependent on him and such person or his dependants due to ill health or infirmity have to maintain a high standard of heating in their place of residence,

(c) a person or any dependant has special dietary needs,

(d) where in circumstances other than those specified in (a) to (c) the Health Board, by reason of the exceptional needs of such person, determines that the weekly payment is not sufficient to meet the person's needs.[9]

The amount of additional payment is left totally to the discretion of the Health Board save that an additional payment under (a) above is only payable in respect of the amount payable by the person in excess of £1.50 per week and the person is not entitled as of right to the total sum above £1.50. The Health Board is only bound to give such part of that amount as it considers reasonable in the circumstances.[10] Moreover, no additional payment in excess of £5 can be made with-

---

8. *Ibid.*, Sect. 209 (formerly Sect. 11 of the 1975 Act).

8a. See *The State (Kershaw) v. The Eastern Health Board, supra* in which it was held that a valid decision was not made on the prosecutrix application for a fuel allowance under the Supplementary Welfare Allowance Scheme as no consideration had been given as to whether her means were insufficient to meet her needs, her application having been refused because she was included in a category of persons (recipients of short term unemployment benefit) who were expressly said to be excluded from the scheme by a ministerial circular issued to health boards. This circular was held to be purely administrative and to have no legal effect and was not a "regulation" made under either the original Act of 1975 or the Act of 1981.

8b. See *The State (Kershaw) v. The Eastern Health Board, supra.*

9. See The Social Welfare (Supplementary Welfare Allowances) Regulations, 1977, *supra*, Article 6.

10. *Ibid.*, Article 6(2).

out the Minister's consent.[11]

The regulations in making provision for a person not in receipt of an allowance "as of right" merely state that "a weekly allowance may be paid to such person of such amount when taken with his other income is determined as appropriate to meet his needs."[12] However, as in the case of an additional payment, the amount cannot exceed £5 per week without the consent of the Minister.[13]

Regulations under section 209 may also provide for the granting of an allowance in kind to meet a person's specific needs. Thus, under the regulations, upon a determination under the section that an allowance is payable to a person in respect of heating needs the allowance may be granted "in the form of an allowance in kind" (i.e. free coal or turf) if the Health Board deems it appropriate.[14] Moreover, a Health Board may pay a fuel allowance of £5 per week for a period of 30 weeks commencing on the first Monday in October of each year to recipients of supplementary welfare allowance and to a number of other categories of social welfare recipients including those in receipt of deserted wife's allowance, deserted wife's benefit and unmarried mothers allowance.[15]

Health Boards may also arrange for the provision of footwear for a child dependant of a person who because of insufficient means is unable to provide such footwear.[16]

In determining entitlement the needs and means of a husband and wife living together are aggregated,[17] and the needs of a child under 18 are included in the needs of a person on whom he is dependent for support.[18] Thus, if an unsupported wife is living apart from her husband with dependant children, her means and needs will be calculated on the basis of the income of herself and the children. However, if she is living with a husband who does not support her, as their means are aggregated, it is possible that on the basis of the Act's assessment her means will be regarded as sufficient, although she may be in receipt of no money. In such cases she may claim Supplementary Welfare Allowance under section 209 of the Act. In the former case, the allowance is paid as of right. In the latter, at the discretion of the officer of the Health Board having regard to his individual determination as to whether her means are insufficient to meet her needs and those of any dependent children.

Instead of making a payment, the Health Board may determine in exceptional circumstances that the needs of a person can best be met by the provision of goods or services.[19] Further, the latter may also be supplied when it is necessary to meet a sudden and urgent need. If a person has an exceptional need the Board

11. *Ibid.*, Article 6(b). See, *The State (Kershaw) v. The Eastern Health Board, supra.* See further, S.I. No. 220 of 1982 which contains special provisions for assisting tenants of formerly rent controlled dwellings with rental payments following upon the rent payable by such tenants for their homes being determined in accordance with the provisions of the Housing (Private Rented Dwellings) Act, 1982. See also S.I. No. 236 of 1985.

12. *Ibid.*, Article 6(3).

13. *Ibid.*, Article 6(6).

14. *Ibid.*, Article 6(5).

15. See S.I. No. 49 of 1985 and S.I. No. 334 of 1985. The first statutory instrument referred to introduced new regulations as a result of the High Court decision in *The State (Kershaw) v. The Eastern Health Board, supra.* In *The State (McLoughlin) v. The Eastern Health Board and Anor.* (July, 1986) unreported (H.C.) provisions contained in these regulations by which the Minister for Social Welfare designated what class or classes of persons could qualify for a free fuel allowance and by which he excluded persons in receipt of unemployment assistance from receiving such allowance were held to be *ultra vires.* At the date of writing this decision is under appeal to the Supreme Court.

16. Social Welfare (Supplementary Welfare Allowance) Regulations, 1977, *supra*, Article 7.

17. Social Welfare (Consolidation) Act, 1981, Sect. 207(2)(a).

18. *Ibid.*, Sect. 207(2)(b).

19. *Ibid.*, Sect. 211.

may dispense with an inquiry into means and determine that a single payment be made to such a person to meet that need.[20] Similarly, the Board has a wide discretion to make a payment of supplementary welfare allowance in an urgent case without being bound by Ministerial regulations, or the provisions of the Act as to the assessment of means and needs.[21]

For the purpose of the Act, a man is liable to maintain his wife, his legitimate children under 16 and his wife's children born before her marriage to him. A woman is liable to maintain her husband and both any legitimate or illegitimate children of hers under 16. A child is not under the Act liable to maintain his parents.[22] Where a spouse or child who is liable to be maintained by another is granted an allowance, the person liable for maintenance is liable to contribute according to his ability to such allowance. The Health Board is empowered to apply for a District Court order where necessary for this purpose.[23]

Under the supplementary welfare allowance scheme in specified circumstances a person is entitled to receive payments as of right. However, as has been seen, an officer of the Health Board has considerable discretion in certain circumstances in determining a person's entitlement to an allowance and the amount of allowance to be paid. A major difficulty in practice has been the considerable divergence in approach between different supplementary welfare allowance officers when dealing with applicants seeking a discretionary allowance. A further difficulty arises due to the fact that applicants for supplementary welfare allowance are generally unaware of their right to appeal against a decision made by the supplementary welfare allowance officer. Whereas the Act empowered the Minister to provide regulations for the making and determination of appeals no detailed regulations in respect of appeals have yet been made and no formal appeals procedure has been provided. The Minister has, however, appointed a person in each Health Board area to determine appeals.[24]

The role of supplementary welfare allowance in the area of marital breakdown is to provide interim relief for a spouse without means until a maintenance order is obtained against the other spouse or until, in the case of a wife, she becomes entitled to Deserted Wife's Allowance or Benefit. It also provides relief where a spouse fails to comply with a maintenance order or where a spouse requires the sum paid to her, on foot of such an order, to be supplemented.

Deserted Wife's Allowance and Benefit

The Social Welfare Act of 1970 made provision for payment by the Dept. of Social Welfare of an allowance to a wife deserted by her husband. This Act was repealed and replaced by the Social Welfare (Consolidation) Act, 1981. Stringent conditions are laid down for eligibility for deserted wife's allowance. As well as being deserted, the wife must satisfy a means test, and if she is less than 40 years of age[25] in order to get an allowance she must have at least one qualified[26] child residing with her. Formerly, a wife had to be resident in the State at any

---

20. *Ibid.*, Sect. 212.
21. *Ibid.*, Sect. 213.
22. *Ibid.*, Sect. 214.
23. *Ibid.*, Sect. 215.
24. *Ibid.*, Sect. 205. For further discussion on the workings of the S.W.A. scheme see *The Report of the Commission on Social Welfare* (Stationery Office, Dublin, 1986) Chap. 19. See also N.E.S.C. No. 38, *supra*, pp. 154–55.
25. Social Welfare (Consolidation) Act, 1981, Sect. 195(1)(b).
26. *Ibid.*, Sect. 195(3).

time for a period of two years to qualify for the allowance but in 1978 this requirement was abolished.[27]

A qualified child is one who

(a) is under 18 years of age or, if over that age, is under 21 years and is receiving full time instruction by day at any university, college, school or other educational establishment,

(b) is ordinarily resident in the State, and

(c) is not detained in a reformatory or an industrial school.

A woman is regarded as deserted for the purpose of the Act if:

(a) her husband has of his own volition left her and has not at any time during the three months immediately preceding the date of her claim for an allowance lived or cohabited with her; and

(b) her husband wilfully refuses or neglects to contribute to the support and maintenance of her and her children; and

(c) she has made and continues to make reasonable efforts within the means available to her to trace her husband's whereabouts and to prevail on him to contribute to the support and maintenance of her and her children; and

(d) her husband has not resumed living or cohabiting with her.[28]

In determining whether or not a husband contributes to the support and maintenance of his wife, monetary payments and other contributions which are inconsiderable may be disregarded.[29] Thus, if a husband in desertion, regularly or irregularly pays his wife small sums of maintenance, such payments may not disqualify her from entitlement to the allowance.

If a husband is still in the country and his wife knows of his whereabouts she is expected to bring maintenance proceedings against him to force him to contribute towards her support. If she does not do so, her application for the allowance may be refused due to her failure to make "reasonable efforts" to prevail on him to provide maintenance.[30] The underlying assumption of the Act is that the State's responsibility is secondary to that of the deserting husband. Originally Deserted Wife's Allowance payments ceased upon the husband obtaining a divorce abroad, the "wife" in such circumstances being regarded as no longer married.[31] This is no longer the position and now if a wife having been deserted is divorced abroad, the decree is ignored by the Department of Social Welfare and the allowance is paid. Finally, a wife is disqualified from receiving an allowance if and so long as she is cohabiting with any other man as husband and wife.[32] Upon the termination of such cohabitation she can again become eligible for an allowance.

27, Social Welfare (Deserted Wife's Allowance) Regulations, 1970 (S.I. No. 227 of 1970) Article 6, revoked by the Social Welfare (Deserted Wife's Allowance) (Amendment) Regulations, 1978 (S.I. No. 92 of 1978) Article 3.

28. *Ibid.*, Article 4(1) as amended by the Social Welfare (Deserted Wife's Allowance) (Amendment) Regulations, 1974 (S.I. No. 178 of 1974) Article 3.

29. Social Welfare (Deserted Wife's Allowance) Regulations, 1970, *supra*, Article 4(2) as amended by the Social Welfare (Deserted Wife's Allowance) (Amendment) Regulations, 1972 (S.I. No. 74 of 1972) Article 2.

30. See N.E.S.C. No. 38, *supra*, at pp. 120–122.

31. See Report of the Commission on the Status of Women, December 1972, paragraphs 464 and 465.

32. See 1970 Regulations, *supra*, Article 7. See further footnote 35 *infra*.

Section 17 of the Social Welfare Act, 1973, made provision for Deserted Wife's Benefit,[33] obtainable under conditions similar to those required for Deserted Wife's Allowance except the Benefit has no means test. Thus, if a deserted wife works or has some other income, it will not affect her entitlement to benefit or the amount she receives. The Benefit is payable if either the wife or husband have satisfied the relevant contribution conditions under the Social Welfare Acts.[34] The amounts receivable under benefit are slightly more than those under the allowance. As in the case of the allowance, a wife is disqualified from receiving the benefit if and so long as she is cohabiting with any other man as husband and wife.[35]

Child Benefit

Child Benefit becomes payable from the first day of the month following that in which a child is born to the person with whom the child normally resides. Usually the mother is the person with whom the child is regarded as residing and it is she who is entitled to claim the benefit. A sum is paid for each "qualified child" and is not dependent on any means test or social insurance contributions.

A child is a qualified child for the purpose of claiming or receiving the benefit if

(a) he is under 16 years or

(b) having attained the age of 16, he is under 18 years and —

   (i) is receiving full-time instruction by day at any university, college, school, or other educational establishment *or*

   (ii) is, by reason of physical or mental infirmity, incapable of self-support and likely to remain so incapable for a prolonged period,

and

(c) he is ordinarily resident in the State

(d) he is not detained in a reformatory or an industrial school and is not undergoing imprisonment or detention in legal custody.

The benefit is paid in respect of each qualified child and the sum payable increases as the number of qualified children increases.[36]

---

33. Now see the Social Welfare (Consolidation) Act, 1981, Part II, Ch. 13.
34. See, *ibid.*, Sect. 101. See further, Social Welfare (Deserted Wife's Benefit) Regulations, 1973 (S.I. No. 202 of 1973). See also S.I. No. 202 of 1974, S.I. No. 232 of 1975, S.I. No. 84 of 1978 and S.I. No. 229 of 1985.
35. Social Welfare (Deserted Wife's Benefit) Regulations, 1973, Article 3(2). In *The State (Hoolahan) v. The Minister for Social Welfare & The A.G.* (July, 1986) unreported (H.C.) it was alleged that this provision in the regulations was *ultra vires* the 1981 Act. The court did not have to determine the issue, however, as it made absolute a conditional order of *certiorari* quashing a decision that a wife was disqualified from receiving benefit under this Article as the deciding officer who made the original decision had failed to act "judicially". He had not advised the wife of the "nature and extent of the case made against her" nor afforded her a proper opportunity to comment on it.
36. See generally the Social Welfare (Consolidation) Act, 1981, Part IV; Social Welfare Act, 1982, Sect. 3; Social Welfare Act, 1983, Sect. 12 and the Social Welfare Act, 1986, Sect. 17. See also Social Welfare (Children's Allowances) (General) Regulations, 1952 (S.I. No. 222 of 1952); Social Welfare (Children's Allowances) (General) (Amendment) Regulations, 1974 (S.I. No. 197 of 1974); Social Welfare (Children's Allowances) (Normal Residence) Rules, 1974 (S.I. No. 198 of 1974).

CRITICISMS AND SUGGESTED REFORMS

Although undoubtedly the Act of 1976 has afforded far greater protection to unsupported spouses and their children than any preceding legislation, the law in relation to maintenance is still defective in a number of respects. In criticising the law and suggesting various reforms, the term "maintenance" is taken in the following pages as including alimony, unless otherwise stated.

1. The most fundamental defect in the current law is the absence of a consistent philosophy as to the relevance in maintenance proceedings of the committal by the maintenance applicant of a matrimonial offence or matrimonial misconduct. Under the Married Women (Maintenance in Case of Desertion) Act, 1886, which was repealed and replaced by the Act of 1976, maintenance could only be awarded against a spouse in desertion. The Act of 1976 whilst making financial need rather than matrimonial misdeed the central issue in maintenance proceedings, still retains the concept of the matrimonial offence and gives varied degrees of importance to the committal of different types of matrimonial offences by an applicant spouse. Thus, adultery is a discretionary bar and desertion an absolute bar to the making of a maintenance order. Curiously, cruelty by an applicant spouse is not specifically referred to at all as a bar to the making of such order, although such behaviour may influence a court in determining what award to make on the basis of the court having an obligation to "have regard to all the circumstances" of the case.[1]

The law in this area, it is submitted, is not only illogical but may give rise to considerable injustice. The Act of 1976 by making desertion an absolute bar to the making of a maintenance order and adultery only a discretionary bar, clearly regards proof of desertion as a more reliable indicator by which to attribute "guilt" or responsibility for the breakdown of a marriage than proof of adultery. Yet desertion by one party may no more indicate sole responsibility for the destruction of the marital bond than any other type of behaviour. For example, spouses may continuously bicker and argue, each being equally responsible for the unhappiness that is created in the home. The wife may decide that she can no longer tolerate the strain and tension in the family home and move out taking her children with her. Nevertheless, the behaviour of the husband may not be such as to justify her departure, each spouse being equally responsible for the collapse of their marriage, and the wife may be held to be in desertion and disentitled to maintenance. Such a decision, it is submitted would clearly be unjust.

The anomalous nature of the current law is further highlighted by the fact that whilst adultery is only a discretionary bar to the making of a maintenance order pursuant to the Act of 1976, a wife against whom a decree of divorce *a mensa et thoro* is granted on the grounds of adultery will not be awarded alimony under the principles of law enunciated by the ecclesiastical courts inherited by the High Court pursuant to the provisions of section 13 of the Matrimonial Causes . . . Act, 1870.

Whereas misconduct may bar a spouse from obtaining maintenance for her own support, the maintenance provisions providing for the support of children contained in both the Act of 1976 and the Guardianship of Infants Act, 1964, clearly intend that spousal misconduct by a parent awarded custody should not affect the maintenance ordered for the support of children. It is clear, however,

---

1. See Family Law . . . Act, 1976, Sect. 5(1).

that if a spouse is deprived of maintenance for her own support, the living standards not only of that spouse but also of any children in her custody will be affected. Whereas the court may assess separate sums payable for the support of a spouse and each child, it is inevitable that whatever money is obtained will be used to meet the needs of the household. If no such maintenance is ordered to be paid to support a spouse, undoubtedly the standard of living of all, not just the spouse punished for misconduct but also any children in her custody, will fall.[2]

The Committee on Court Practice and Procedure in their Report on Desertion and Maintenance, which preceded the enactment of the Act of 1976, completely omitted to discuss what role misconduct should play in maintenance proceedings.[3] Clearly, if proof of the committal of a matrimonial offence is no longer to be an essential prequisite to obtaining a decree of judicial separation[3a] the role of the matrimonial offence in maintenance legislation will have to be revised. Such a revision has been undertaken in many other common law countries in recent years. Thus, in England following divorce or separation proceedings, the court when assessing the amount of maintenance payable to a spouse now takes misconduct into account only if it "would in the opinion of the court be inequitable to disregard it".[4] In New Zealand, misconduct by the party seeking maintenance can only be taken into account if it "is of such a nature and degree that it would be repugnant to justice to require the other party to pay maintenance."[5] It is submitted that the enactment of a similar provision into Irish law would reserve to the courts a discretionary power to withhold ordering maintenance in circumstances in which it was clearly unjust to order that it be paid, while enabling the courts to take into account the totality of the applicant spouse's circumstances and needs at the date of the maintenance application in the context of the overall family history. Such an approach would obviate the necessity for the courts to apportion responsibility for the breakdown of a marriage in the vast majority of cases, while allowing the courts to refuse to make a maintenance order where it would be grossly unfair to do so.[6]

2. The *Report of the Joint Oireachtas Committee on Marriage Breakdown* expresses "concern at evidence contained in submissions to the committee of judicial inconsistency in administering the law in the area of maintenance" and the committee "emphasizes the importance of uniform judicial interpretation as to the levels of maintenance awards, having regard to the incidents of hard-

2. This appears to have been recognised by the High Court in *P. v. P.* (March, 1980) unreported (H.C.).

3. See the *19th Interim Report of the Committee on Court Practice & Procedure* (Dublin, Stationery Office 1974). The report of this Committee laid the foundations for the enactment of the Act of 1976.

3a. The government's "Statement of Intent" proposes the granting of such decrees not only upon proof of desertion, adultery, cruelty or unnatural practices but where parties have lived apart for one year and consent to a decree being granted or, where no consent is forthcoming, upon proof of three years separation. See p. 234 *ante*.

4. See the English Matrimonial Causes Act, 1973, Sect. 25 as amended by the Matrimonial & Family Proceedings Act, 1984, Sect. 3.

5. See the New Zealand Family Proceedings Act, 1980, Sect. 66.

6. See further, *Report of the Joint Oireachtas Committee on Marriage Breakdown*, p. 56, where the Committee expresses the opinion that "Desertion or adultery should be a discretionary bar to maintenance for the applicant spouse, unless the conduct of the defendant is or was such as to make it inappropriate and unfair that he or she should be entitled to rely on the applicant's desertion or adultery." The Law Reform Commission in their *Report on Divorce a Mensa et Thoro* (L.R.C. Report No. 8, December 1983) simply recommends that the law as stated in the Family Law . . . Act, 1976, should apply to the making of periodical payment orders to be made after the granting of a decree of divorce *a mensa et thoro* and that the role of misconduct should remain unchanged.

ship imposed by awards of maintenance that are either too high, from the point of view of the spouse against whom the award is made, or too low, from the point of view of the spouse and/or dependant children in favour of whom the award is made."[7]

It is essential that the courts have a broad discretion to determine the amount of maintenance that should be awarded in any individual case having regard to the particular circumstances and needs of the dependant spouse and children and the spouse from whom maintenance is sought. Subjective judicial application of the factors laid down in the Act of 1976 to which the court must have regard prior to making a maintenance order, has in practice resulted in a wide divergence of approach on the part of the individual members of the judiciary who have presided over maintenance proceedings. While the general principles applicable to the fixing of maintenance awards articulated by the Supreme Court in October of 1985 in *R.H. v. N.H.*[8] will be helpful in bringing about a more uniform application of the law, they are, it is submitted, insufficiently comprehensive to resolve the current difficulty in this area. There is an urgent need for amending legislation to set out in greater detail, in so far as is practicable, the various factors that are to be taken into account by the courts in determining maintenance applications and in assessing and calculating maintenance awards. Moreover, there is a need for such legislation to give some indication as to the importance or weight to be attached to each of the factors specified. For example, a query has earlier been raised as to the importance the courts should currently attach to the "earning capacity" of an applicant spouse when assessing what sum of maintenance should be paid to such spouse.[9] The relevance or importance of other factors is equally unclear. For example, what importance should be attached to the duration of the marriage, the contribution an applicant spouse has made to the welfare of the family or to looking after the home, or to the acquisition of family assets. Until greater guidance is given to the courts by the Oireachtas as to the relevance of such factors and as to the method to be applied in quantifying or calculating how much maintenance it is "proper in the circumstances" that a spouse receive, a lack of uniformity of judicial approach will continue to create difficulties for those both paying and receiving maintenance pursuant to court maintenance orders.[10]

3. The courts should be empowered to order the payment of a lump sum in

---

7. See p. 57 of Report.
8. (October, 1985) unreported (S.C.).
9. See p. 435 *ante*.
10. The Law Reform Commission in its *Report on Nullity of Marriage* (Report No. 9, July 1984) dealing with the making of financial orders subsequent to the making of a nullity decree recommends that "The contribution made by each of the parties to the welfare of the family, including any contribution made by looking after the home or caring for the family" should be a specific factor to be taken into account in determining what financial order should be made (see p. 174 of report). The Report does not, however, clarify how taking this factor into account should influence the quantification of any sum ordered to be paid by way of maintenance. Such a factor is currently specified as relevant in the calculation of maintenance payments in a number of common law jurisdictions. Curiously, the Law Reform Commission did not make a similar recommendation in the context of maintenance orders to be made subsequent to the granting of decrees of divorce *a mensa et thoro*. See *Report on Divorce a Mensa et Thoro, supra*, at p. 56. See also the *Report of the Joint Oireachtas Committee on Marriage Breakdown* at pp. 56–57 where the Committee states the factors to be taken into account in determining a maintenance award should include the making of a court order "granting the sole right to reside in the family home to either the applicant or the defendant (spouse)" and "the need of the spouse who does not have the right to reside in the family home to provide adequate and suitable accommodation for himself or herself together with any persons with whom they may be living."

addition to or instead of periodical payments.[11] There are a number of circumstances in which such a power might be useful. For example, between the time when a husband ceases providing maintenance and when the wife obtains a court order, considerable debts may be incurred by her. As a maintenance order only applies to future payments a court cannot currently order a husband to make retrospective payments. Power to make a lump sum order would provide a mechanism whereby the courts could require that a payment be made to discharge debts incurred prior to the date of the court hearing. Similarly, a wife forced to leave the family home by her husband's misconduct may incur considerable debt in obtaining alternative temporary accommodation prior to a court hearing and the power to order a lump sum payment would provide a means whereby she could require her husband to discharge any debts so incurred. Power to make a lump sum order would also confer on the courts a means of providing some financial security for a dependant spouse and children upon proof of a husband's intention to leave the jurisdiction. For example, if a wife discovers her husband is about to receive a £20,000 redundancy payment and leave the jurisdiction with his money, even if both she and her children may be left destitute, the courts currently have no statutory powers to make an order requiring the husband to pay a portion of such monies to his wife for her support and the support of dependant children. The desirability of conferring jurisdiction on the courts to make such an order in such circumstances is self evident.[12]

In the recent "Statement of Intent" published by the government it is stated that an ancillary power to order the making of lump sum payments will be provided in legislation promised to reform the law relating to the granting of separation decrees.[12a]

4. The court when ordering periodical payments, or following upon a maintenance debtor defaulting in his payments, should be empowered to require that the maintenance order be secured where it thinks appropriate when there are assets available upon which it could be secured. Such an order would have the effect that the maintenance sum would be secured on property owned by the maintenance debtor and such property would provide a specific and readily identifiable asset for enforcement upon a spouse defaulting in payments. A jurisdiction vested in the courts to require security would be particularly advantageous to ensure payment by self employed maintenance debtors against whom no order for attachment of earnings can be made. It could also provide additional protection for a maintenance creditor whose spouse might permanently leave the jurisdiction so as to evade his maintenance obligations.[13]

5. As already stated in the chapter on Nullity, the court upon declaring a "marriage" void or upon annulling a "voidable" marriage should be empowered

---

11. The Law Reform Commission in its *Report on Nullity of Marriage, supra*, states that subsequent to the making of a nullity decree "it seems desirable" to confer jurisdiction on the court "to award a lump sum payment" (see p. 173 of Report). In its *Report on Divorce a Mensa et Thoro, supra*, at p. 57 it makes a similar recommendation as to the courts' jurisdiction to make financial orders subsequent to the granting of such decrees. The Joint Oireachtas Committee on Marriage Breakdown did not reach agreement on this issue and merely state that "there is a need to examine this matter in greater depth" (see p. 57 of Report).

12. The Circuit and High Courts may by way of injunction be able to prevent the removal of money from the jurisdiction in such circumstances. See p. 456 *ante* and in particular footnote 42. This, however, has not as yet been finally determined.

12a. See "Statement of Intent" (April, 1986) at p. 3 and revised "Statement" (June, 1986) at pp. 10–11.

13. See, for example, the English Matrimonial Causes Act, 1973, Sect. 23.

to make financial orders for the support of a dependant "spouse" in appropriate circumstances and for the support of any dependant children of the parties.[14] It is further submitted that legislation should be enacted conferring jurisdiction on the Irish Courts to make maintenance orders in appropriate circumstances for the support of a dependent former spouse and dependent children of the parties following upon the granting of a foreign decree of divorce *a vinculo* recognised in this country, if at the date of the initiation of the divorce proceedings either party to the proceedings was domiciled within this jurisdiction.[15]

6. The Act of 1976 contains elaborate provisions to ensure that the court obtains accurate information in relation to a maintenance debtor's earnings prior to the making of an attachment of earnings order. It is submitted that similar provisions should apply when a maintenance order is first sought so that the court is in a position to accurately assess the relative financial position of the spouses. In this regard, the Oireachtas Committee on Marital Breakdown expressed the opinion that "the parties should be under a statutory obligation to provide the court with a statement of their income and assets, to assist the court in determining the level of maintenance to be awarded, if any."[16] Prior to the hearing of maintenance proceedings both spouses should be obliged to furnish the court with full information as to both their earnings and resources.

7. Jurisdiction conferred on the courts by the Act of 1976 to make attachment of earnings orders has undoubtedly rendered maintenance orders more easily enforceable and made it more difficult for a maintenance debtor in regular employment to evade his maintenance obligations. However, a spouse determined not to comply with a maintenance order may, by moving from job to job, lessen the effectiveness of the attachment of earnings procedure. Although the Act imposes a duty on a maintenance debtor to inform the court of any change in his employment, as we have already seen, there is no effective penalty that the court can impose if it is not so informed. It is submitted that the sanction that may be imposed on a maintenance debtor who gives "false and misleading" information to the court in relation to a change in his employment, should be extended to apply to the maintenance debtor who fails to inform the court that any change at all has taken place.

Liability to a fine or imprisonment may not, however, be an effective deterrent to spouses changing jobs to avoid their maintenance obligations. In *Separated Spouses*,[17] the authors point out that "a system of attachment may work very efficiently in countries which have a complete system of national registration and of reporting changes of address and occupation to the police",[18] but in countries that lack such a system they doubted the efficiency of attachment procedures and were sceptical that they could produce any significant improvements.

It is the author's experience that attachment of earnings has proved effective in Ireland in forcing maintenance defaulters to comply with maintenance orders made against them. No detailed research has, however, been carried out to assess

---

14. See p. 156 *ante*.
15. See p. 278 *ante*.
16. See p. 56 of Report.
17. By McGregor, Blom-Cooper & Gibson (London 1970), p. 200.
18. A.I.M. suggested the introduction of such a system in Ireland. *The A.I.M. Group Report* (Dublin 1972), p. 13. In *Separated Spouses*, the authors stated that "this degree of control over the citizen is not compatible with British notions of liberty". It is submitted that this equally applies to Ireland.

the impact of attachment of earnings on the general rate of recovery on maintenance orders since the coming into force of the Act of 1976. As this Act has
been in force for over ten years, research on the efficacy of attachment of earnings as a means of maintenance collection is now long overdue. In the context of
improving the efficiency of the attachment order as a mechanism to ensure
compliance with a maintenance obligation, it is submitted amending legislation
should impose a statutory obligation on employers to state on an employees
P45 form, upon that employee leaving employment, that an attachment order
has been made and to insert all relevant information concerning the order so
that, upon a change of employment, the new employer would automatically
discover the existence of such an order and become bound by its terms.

   8. The Committee on Court Practice and Procedure has noted that in evidence submitted to it "the sanction of imprisonment where a husband defaults
in payment of maintenance was criticised for being one that did not really help
the situation but rather aggravated it."[19] Despite this comment, no further
mention of the problems associated with imprisoning maintenance defaulters
was made by it and its report contained no recommendations as to the future
role of imprisonment in the maintenance process. This matter has not been
since adverted to in any detail by any other government appointed body in any
report produced relating to the area of family law.
   There is little doubt that cases arise in practice in which maintenance debtors,
required to make maintenance payments by court order, deliberately refuse or
fail to make such payments despite being in a financial position to do so. If a
maintenance defaulter is in employment, it is submitted, there should be an
initial statutory duty imposed on the maintenance recipient to seek an attachment of earnings order so as to enforce payment prior to the threat of imprisonment being used as an enforcement remedy. If attachment proves unsuccessful
or if a maintenance defaulter is self employed, the maintenance recipient should
be permitted to use the sanction of imprisonment to enforce compliance with
the maintenance order. It is submitted, however, that prior to any court hearing
to determine whether or not a maintenance defaulter should be imprisoned,
the defaulter should be required to attend an interview with a Court Welfare
Officer whose function would be to explain to the maintenance defaulter his
duty to comply with a maintenance order, the consequence of a failure to
comply, and his entitlement to seek to have any maintenance order in force
varied, if there is a genuine financial inability to comply with it. Such a procedure, if implemented, would both maximize compliance with court maintenance orders whilst ensuring that the sanction of imprisonment is used only as
a last resort remedy to bring about such compliance where no alternative option
is available.[20]

------

   19. *Supra* at p. 12.
   20. See J. Eekelaar, *Family Law & Social Policy*, 2nd ed. (Weidenfeld & Nicolson,
London 1984), p. 131 where the author discusses the usefulness of the various enforcement
methods adopted to ensure a maintenance debtor complies with his obligations. See in
particular, p. 132 where the author states that research has established that inability to pay
"is by no means necessarily the major cause of non/or insufficient payment of child support."
In New Zealand a maintenance defaulter can only be imprisoned by a court if it is satisfied,
amongst other matters, "that other methods of enforcing payment . . . have been considered
or tried and it appears to the court that they are inappropriate or have been unsuccessful"
– see the New Zealand Family Proceedings Act, 1980, Part VII and in particular Sect. 30.
In Australia, imprisonment has been abolished for a failure to comply with maintenance
orders – see the Australian Family Law Act, 1975, Part XII. In England in 1974 the Finer
Committee's *Report on One Parent Families* (Cmnd. 5629, H.M.S.O. 1974) recommended
the abolition of imprisonment for maintenance defaulters (see pp. 128–132) but to date

9. The District Court is limited to ordering weekly payments of £100 for the support of a spouse and £30 for the support of each dependent child. The financial limits of the District Court's jurisdiction were last adjusted upon the coming into force of the Courts Act, 1981. They should be again increased to take into account the increase in inflation since the enactment of the afore-mentioned Act and should be reviewed and revised, if necessary, every three years.

10. The existing social welfare scheme for deserted wives can be criticised on the following grounds:

(a) Desertion as a criteria for eligibility for payments under the scheme is arbitrary and illogical. For example, a wife whose husband leaves home to live with another woman may be eligible for deserted wife's allowance or benefit but a wife who enters into a deed of separation with a husband who has previously violently assaulted her is not eligible as she is not deserted, having separated by agreement. Rather than determining eligibility on the basis of financial need, the scheme places undue emphasis on the final events immediately preceding the separation of spouses.[21]

(b) In many cases establishing the fact of desertion is particularly difficult. In practice, an official of the Department of Social Welfare normally interviews both the applicant and her husband, if the latter's whereabouts are known. Few husbands admit to deserting their wives and there is no prescribed procedure laying down the manner in which the competing claims of the spouses are to be determined. The matter is essentially left to the judgement of the departmental official who carries out the interviews and there is no information available as to the criteria used by the officials in making the necessary determination.

(c) As desertion is no longer a prerequisite for the bringing of maintenance proceedings, it should similarly not be a prerequisite to obtaining a special welfare payment upon the principal family breadwinner ceasing to provide maintenance. Matrimonial misconduct should be irrelevant in determining a spouse's entitlement to such payments. Whereas it may be unjust in certain circumstances to require a spouse to maintain the other spouse, if that other has committed a matrimonial offence, such considerations are not relevant to the State's duty to provide support. Even if a spouse can be held solely responsible for the breakdown of a marriage, which is very rarely the case, the needs of that spouse and his or her children still need to be met. Retributive measures on the part of the State can only lead to further bitterness and exacerbate the matrimonial dispute between the spouses.

(d) To obtain the allowance or benefit a wife must be deserted for three months. The Commission on the Status of Women in 1972 recommended that the Department of Social Welfare be enabled to grant the allowance during the qualifying period if undue hardship would be caused by withholding payments

this recommendation has not been implemented. See also *Separated Spouses, supra*, at p. 200 *et seq.*

21. See The National Economic and Social Council, *Universality and Selectivity: Social Services in Ireland* (N.E.S.C. Report No. 38) (Stationery Office, Dublin 1978) at p. 120, para. 8.81. See also Report of the Commission on Social Welfare (Stationery Office, Dublin 1986), at pp. 359–361.

until the end of the period.[22] It is submitted that the qualifying period serves no useful purpose and should be abolished.

(e) In determining eligibility, maintenance payments of an "inconsiderable sum" made by a husband may be disregarded but this is a discretionary provision and there is no statutory guidance as to what is to be regarded as an "inconsiderable sum".[23] In practice, if regular payments of any nature are being made by a husband to his wife, it is extremely unusual for the latter to be successful upon her claiming assistance under the scheme.

(f) The permanent absence of a spouse from the family home can in many instances give rise to additional family expenditure. The provision of Deserted Wife's Benefit recognises the extra financial burden imposed on deserted wives by providing a weekly social welfare payment to wives who qualify for benefit on their own or their husband's insurance record without a means test. The benefit is paid to an eligible wife whether or not she is in employment and the amount paid to her is not affected by any other income that she receives. The provisions as to Deserted Wife's Allowance do not afford similar recognition to the burden imposed on wives who are in receipt of the allowance. The means test renders it impossible for a wife to make any significant financial gain by combining part-time work with the allowance as most of the earnings received in such work are offset against the allowance. It also acts as a disincentive to a deserted wife obtaining full-time employment, in that a wife will normally lose her total allowance upon obtaining such employment even though she has to meet the additional expenses that arise from her work, such as the employment of a child minder. As a consequence, there will often be little net improvement in her financial circumstances if she obtains such employment. Moreover, a wife in receipt of the allowance receives less money than a wife in receipt of the benefit, despite the fact that the latter is often in employment and in receipt of a salary, whilst the former is usually solely dependent on the allowance to support herself and her children. In essence, the deserted wife dependent on Deserted Wife's Allowance is liable to be caught in a poverty trap.[24]

(g) To a great extent the problems of a separated husband bringing up children and those of a separated wife bringing up children are identical. Each has to provide a home for the family and has to fill both parental roles. In financial terms, the expense of running a house does not vary greatly if one parent or spouse is absent. The costs of items such as heating, lighting, cooking, mortgage or rent and family transport remain largely the same. Additional expense is usually incurred in the necessity to employ others to do work usually done by the departed spouse. This can include items such as cooking, washing, shopping, house maintenance and decoration and household repairs. Child minding is a further expense for either fatherless or motherless families. This expense not only applies solely to those parents who go out to work but to all parents, if

22. *Report of the Commission on the Status of Women* (Dublin 1972, Stationery Office) paras 384 and 385. When the Commission made this recommendation there was a six months qualifying period.

23. See N.E.S.C. Report No. 38, *supra* at p. 119, para 8.80. The Report of the Commission on Social Welfare states that "this rule is taken to mean that if the maintenance being paid is greater than the appropriate rate of (long-term) unemployment assistance which the wife would receive if she were signing on, then she is considered to be maintained by her husband and not deserted" (*supra* at p. 359).

24. See the National Economic and Social Council, *Alternative Strategies for Family Income Support* (N.E.S.C. Report No. 47 (Stationery Office, Dublin 1980) at pp. 114–115.

they are to continue to lead a normal social life. The absence of an allowance or benefit payable to deserted or separated fathers is a further anomaly in the existing scheme and indicative of its failure to come to terms with the financial needs of the single parent family.[25]

It is submitted that the present scheme of social welfare assistance for deserted wives should be replaced by a scheme for single parent families. Within this scheme provision should also be made for dependent unsupported spouses who have no children or whose children have attained the age of majority.

Any such scheme should fully take into account the interaction between Family Law and Social Welfare Law in the provision of income maintenance. At present, the State plays a secondary role in providing support for the broken family, only intervening when the spouse obliged to provide it fails to do so. Despite the fact that maintenance payable under a court order normally is in excess of that payable to a deserted wife under the Social Welfare Acts, many wives after experiencing the difficulties involved in securing regular payments under the former, express a preference for the latter. The granting of a maintenance order very often marks not the end but merely the beginning of a wife's problems. Many wives never know from one week to the next whether they will receive the sum ordered to be paid by the court or whether they will have to rely on Supplementary Welfare Allowance. Moreover, every few weeks they may find themselves returning to court to seek payment of arrears. Alternatively, a wife in receipt of Deserted Wife's Allowance or Benefit avoids much of the stress and anxiety associated with maintenance proceedings and she has a guaranteed regular weekly income.[26]

In England, the Finer Committee has suggested that the primary responsibility for providing support for single parent families should be borne by the State in the form of a Guaranteed Maintenance Allowance.[27] In the hands of the recipient such an allowance would be a substitute for maintenance payments under a court order. Maintenance payments would be assessed and collected by the Welfare Authority administering the allowance and they would be offset against the allowance paid and any excess paid to the recipient of the allowance. A spouse could still, under such a scheme, bring maintenance proceedings against the other spouse, if he or she so wished, but the primary responsibility to do so would rest with the State.

The provision of such a State allowance would relieve the unsupported spouse, to the maximum extent possible, of the pressures and anxieties attendant upon court proceedings for the assessment and enforcement of maintenance orders and would ensure the receipt of a regular and stable income, regardless of the extent to which the absent spouse or parent fulfills his or her obligation to provide support. As all single parents and dependent unsupported spouses would be entitled to receive such an allowance as of right the anomalies and inequities in the existing scheme for deserted wives would be avoided.

In New Zealand, the Social Security Amendment Act, 1980, introduced a social welfare scheme very similar to the form of single parent allowance suggested

---

25. See further, N.E.S.C. Report No. 47 *supra*, at p. 120. In *Dennehy v. The Minister for Social Welfare* (June, 1984) unreported (H.C.), the plaintiff, a deserted husband, failed in his challenge as to the constitutionality of the present law. See p. 41 *ante*.

26. See K. O'Higgins, *Marital Desertion in Dublin* (Dublin 1974), pp. 98–102. See also *Irish Women: Agenda for Practical Action*, Report of Inter-departmental Working Party (Stationery Office, Dublin, February 1985), p. 257.

27. *Supra*, pp. 276–334; see also O'Higgins, *supra*, pp. 125–126; D. Marsden, *Mothers Alone* (Pelican Books, 1973), in particular Chapter 15. See further, S.M. Cretney, *Principles of Family Law*, 4th edition, *supra*., at pp. 938–939.

here.[28] Our present social welfare law in so far as it provides social assistance for deserted wives, unmarried mothers, prisoners' wives and widows already contains the foundations for such a scheme. Its introduction would bring to an end the present fragmented and unco-ordinated approach to income maintenance. It would not only provide a regular income for those entitled to it but would also enable the State to recover payments made from spouses who fail to meet their obligations, while eliminating the necessity for a direct confrontation between spouses before the courts.[29]

---

28. See Sim & Inglis, *Family Court Code* (Butterworths, Wellington, New Zealand 1983) at pp. 89–92 and p. 181 *et seq*.

29. The Committee on Court Practice and Procedure in its 19th interim report recommended that as a long term reform "all maintenance orders should be met in the first instance by the local authority or Department of Social Welfare". However, the Committee failed to work out the manner in which such a system could operate. For example, under the Committee's recommendation, following the making of a maintenance order, the welfare authority would be required to pay such amount of maintenance as the court considered it reasonable for the defaulting spouse to pay, rather than such amount as is necessary to meet the needs of the recipients. Under such a system people with identical needs would receive different social welfare payments. Further, the Committee's recommendation assumes that responsibility for proceedings against the defaulting spouse will rest with the other spouse. For a brief discussion of the Committee's recommendations see W.R. Duncan, "Desertion and Maintenance" (1974) 9 I.J. (n.s.) 321. See also N.E.S.C. Report No. 47, *supra*, at p. 19 where the Council recommends "that a deserted wife who has children should be entitled to the Deserted Wife's Benefit or Allowance and that the State should collect any maintenance due from the deserting husband." Chapter 5 of the same report examines the Social Welfare Benefits payable to one parent families. It does not, however, elaborate further on the manner in which the Council's recommendation should be implemented.

See further the Joint Oireachtas Committee, *Report on Marital Breakdown, supra*, at p. 55 where the Committee expresses the opinion "that the State should be empowered to make payments of maintenance to victims of (maintenance) default and to recoup monies owed by defaulters, with an appropriate system of sanction in the case of continued default" stating it "is conscious of the considerable time and expense involved for litigants in pursuing maintenance defaulters and the need to balance this against the constitutional responsibility placed on the State to protect marriage and the family." The initial criticism raised to the proposal of the Committee on Court Practice and Procedure can also be applied to this proposal. It does, however, appear to envisage that responsibility for recouping maintenance arrears would fall on the State.

See further *Irish Women: Agenda for Practical Action*, Report of Inter-departmental Working Party, *supra*, Chap. 9, in particular pp. 259 to 262 in which the working party recommends that the Commission on Social Welfare, appointed by the Government in 1983 to examine the entire social welfare code, examine and make recommendations on the general difficulties relating to the enforcement of maintenance orders and the interaction between maintenance payments and social welfare payments. The Working Party also recommends that the Commission on Social Welfare "examine" the issue of the provision of "one parent family payments" for males and states that it "sees no . . . merit in the adoption of a one parent benefit for all single parents." This conclusion is difficult to understand in the context of the working party's referral to the Commission on Social Welare of the issues mentioned which are of direct relevance to determining the desirability or not of the introduction of a single parent family allowance and the manner in which such allowance should interact with maintenance legislation.

In its Report published in July, 1986, the Commission on Social Welfare fails to comprehensively deal with these issues. Whilst it asserts that it "supports the principle that the primary obligation to support one another rests with the marriage partners" it recommends that "where the maintenance payment is irregular or uncertain the State should have power to award a deserted wife's benefit or allowance and itself pursue outstanding maintenance claims." The Commission does not consider in any detail the issue of making one-parent family payments to males. It does, however, recommend that eligibility for all assistance payments be based in the future on "the needs of claimants rather than on the categorical basis which exists at present" and states this "should entitle all one-parent families – regardless of cause of lone parenthood or sex of the parent – to a social assistance payment, where they experience an income need." (*supra* at p. 360). The Commission makes no reference to the extension of deserted wive's benefit to deserted husbands. It merely raises a question as to whether a benefit deriving from social insurance contributions should in fact be payable to wives who have been deserted whilst acknowledging that those wives currently in receipt of benefit should not be deprived of it.

CHAPTER 15

MATRIMONIAL PROPERTY: OWNERSHIP AND SUCCESSION

INTRODUCTION

At common law a married woman had no contractual capacity and any contract entered into by her prior to her marriage automatically vested in her husband. Similarly any property, whether real or personal, owned by her at the time of the marriage or acquired thereafter became his.

A husband's interest in his wife's freehold property only lasted during his lifetime. Upon his death, it reverted to his wife, if she survived him or to her heir, if she did not. An absolute disposition of a wife's freehold property could be made, however, if both spouses joined in the disposition.

A husband had greater power over his wife's leasehold property and could make an absolute disposition of it, during his lifetime without her consent but if he did not do so, she could claim it upon his death.[1] A wife's personal property was absolutely owned by her husband. An exception to this rule related to a wife's "paraphernalia" i.e. those articles of apparel and personal ornament as were suitable to her rank and degree, e.g. brooches or a coat. While these were the property of the husband during his lifetime, they reverted to the wife upon his death.

Equity mitigated the harshness of the common law rules by the development of the concept of property for a wife's 'separate use'. If property was transferred to trustees or to a wife's husband to apply it for the wife's 'separate use', it remained her separate property and she could deal with it as if she were unmarried. This doctrine conferred on a married woman a limited contractual capacity, as any property so held by her could become bound by a contract, although she herself was not personally bound on any agreement.[2]

The Married Women's Property Acts[3] extended a wife's contractual capacity but her liability still remained proprietary and not personal. The Act of 1882 provided that any property acquired by a wife after 1882 and all property belonging to a woman who married after that date, should remain her separate property and conferred capacity on a wife to avail of the same civil remedies for the protection and security of her own property as a *femme sole*. By the Act of 1893 every contract entered into by her, otherwise than as agent of her husband, was held to bind her.

The above Acts did not abolish the equitable concept of restraint upon anticipation. This doctrine arose in order to protect a wife from making an improvident disposition of her separate property. Upon equity vesting in the wife

---

1. See J.C.W. Wylie, *Irish Land Law* (Professional Books Ltd., London 1975), p. 876.
2. See G.W. Keeton and L.A. Sheridan, *Equity* (N.I.L.Q. Inc., 1969), Chap. XV.
3. 1865, 1870, 1874, 1882, 1884, 1893, 1907.

the beneficial interest in property given to her separate use, there was nothing to prevent her from conveying her interest to a money-grabbing husband. Thus, equity held that if a clause restraining alienation or anticipation was inserted in a grant of property, any disposition by which she purported to alienate such property or deal with its income was rendered void. Whilst this rule protected a wife against her husband's influence, it simultaneously prevented a wife from selling property subject to such restraint when it was in her interests to do so.[4] The Conveyancing Act, 1881, conferred power on the courts to remove a restraint and authorise a disposition of property, if a wife consented and it was for her benefit.[5] A restraint ceased to have effect upon the death of a husband.

The present law is governed by the Married Women's Status Act, 1957, under which a husband and wife are treated as two separate persons for all purposes of acquisition of property.[6] The doctrine of restraint upon anticipation is abolished.[7] A married woman can now acquire, hold and dispose of any property and is capable of contracting and being rendered personally liable in respect of her contracts and debts.[8] Any property she owns no longer automatically vests in her husband upon marriage and her husband is no longer liable for any contract entered into, or debt incurred, by her. As has been seen, however, he may be liable for necessaries supplied to his wife in certain circumstances and in accordance with the general law of contract, he may be bound by any contract entered into or debt incurred by her acting as his agent.

PROPERTY RIGHTS DURING MARRIAGE

The general principle of separate property is that each spouse has independent and equal power to acquire and deal with his or her own property. Marriage as such no longer affects rights of ownership during the parties' lifetime. Whatever a party owns prior to marriage continues to belong to him after the ceremony. Each spouse owns his own income and any property that he or she acquires with it.[9] It has been recognised, however, that certain statutory restraints are necessary to curb the proprietary freedom of spouses so as to ensure that a property owning spouse or the spouse who is the principal wage earner in the family does not abuse his position and cause the dependent spouse, more usually the wife, to be at risk of being rendered homeless, left destitute or the victim of serious ill treatment in the home.

The Succession Act, 1965, confers a specific right on a surviving spouse to a share in a deceased spouse's estate upon a spouse dying testate, and an entitlement to a specific proportion of such estate, in the event of the deceased spouse dying intestate. The Family Home Protection Act, 1976, protects a spouse's right of residence in the family home by prohibiting its sale or the disposition of any interest in it, without the prior written consent of the non-owning spouse and confers wide discretionary powers on the courts to make orders against a spouse or any third party whose behaviour is such as could lead to a loss of the family home or render it uninhabitable. The Family Law (Protection of Spouses and Children) Act, 1981, confers power on the courts to bar a spouse from the

---

4. See Keeton and Sheridan, *supra*; Wylie, *supra*, p. 877.
5. Sect. 39, subsequently replaced by the Conveyancing Act, 1911, Sect. 7.
6. Sect. 5.
7. Sect. 6.
8. *Ibid.*, Sect. 2 and Sect. 11. Although the Married Woman's Property Acts rendered a wife suable on her contracts and debts, she could only be sued to the extent of her separate estate. See *The State (Kingston) v. Circuit Court Judge of Cork* [1943] I.R. 611 (S.C.).
9. Any property acquired out of housekeeping money given by one spouse to the other may be regarded as jointly owned. See p. 516 *post*.

home in which the other spouse and any children of the family are residing, if his behaviour poses a serious threat to the safety or welfare of the spouse seeking such barring order or to any children of the family. Moreover, the ownership rights of a spouse over real and personal property purchased with his or her own income have been curtailed to a limited degree by the Family Law ... Act, 1976, under which any property purchased by a spouse out of any allowance provided by the other spouse for household purposes is regarded as jointly owned, as are any savings accumulated from such allowance.

Neither the Family Home Protection Act, 1976, nor the Family Law (Protection of Spouses and Children) Act, 1981, as such, affect a spouse's ownership of or beneficial interest in property, although they can be said to curtail some of the freedoms or rights that normally vest in an owner of property.[9a] For example, a violent spouse who owns the family home may be deprived of his right to reside in it and may also be prevented from disposing of it. Disputes between spouses as to the ownership of property are determined by the courts in proceedings initiated under section 12 of the Married Women's Status Act, 1957, and are resolved by application of the doctrine of separate property. It is the resolution of disputes between spouses as to the ownership of property and the rules and statutory provisions applicable thereto that now form the subject matter of the first part of this chapter. In the second part we examine the extent to which our succession laws curtail a spouse's proprietary freedoms and afford protection to a surviving spouse and children of the family. In the following two chapters we examine the specific protection the law gives to the family home and the protection extended to spouses against ill treatment in the home.

THE RESOLUTION OF PROPRIETARY DISPUTES

The doctrine of separate property does not in practice provide easy solutions to disputes between a husband and wife over the ownership of property. Spouses tend to regard their earnings and property as part of the family assets rather than as belonging to either of them to the exclusion of the other. Arrangements as to domestic expenditure and ownership of property tend to be informal and undocumented. This is, of course, as it should be and will rarely give rise to any problems while spouses are living happily together. It is when a marriage breaks down and a dispute occurs that the domestic arrangements have to be unravelled and a determination as to the rights of the parties over the "family property" has to be made. The great majority of disputes relate to rights of ownership and possession of the family home and its contents. The respective rights of a husband and wife to a proprietary interest in the family home and other property and the means for ascertaining these rights are examined in the following pages.

THE MARRIED WOMEN'S STATUS ACT, 1957, SECTION 12

The Married Women's Status Act, 1957, Section 12, provides a procedure for determining disputes "between husband and wife as to the title to or possession of any property". Either party may make a summary application to the Circuit Court or High Court for such determination. If an application is made to the Circuit Court and the dispute concerns land the rateable valuation of which

---

9a. It should be noted, however, that in making orders under the Family Home Protection Act, 1976, the courts have in certain limited circumstances been willing to transfer ownership of a family home from one spouse to the other — see p. 561 *post et seq.*

exceeds £200, upon a request by the defendant, the proceedings must be transferred to the High Court. Any order made or act done in the course of such proceedings before such transfer remains valid unless discharged or varied by order of the High Court.

In exercising its jurisdiction under section 12, the court "may make such order with respect to the property in dispute . . . as the court thinks proper."[10] Section 17 of the Married Women's Property Act, 1882, which it replaced, permitted the court upon such an application to make such order as it thought "fit". Despite the difference in phraseology between them, both sections have been regarded by the courts as purely procedural provisions. While they have been held to confer jurisdiction on the courts to determine disputes between spouses as to their ownership rights in property, neither section has been regarded as conferring any discretionary power on the courts to vary or transfer all or part of the title of one spouse in property to the other.

Section 12 procedure may be used for the determination of all proprietary disputes between spouses, whether the subject matter of the dispute is real or personal property and, if the former, whether the dispute concerns the family home or any other real property. In practice, the vast majority of court proceedings in which this section has been invoked have been concerned with the resolution of disputes as to the title in and ownership of the family home.

DISPUTES AS TO OWNERSHIP OF THE FAMILY HOME AND OTHER PROPERTY

The Married Women's Property Act, 1882, Section 17, is still in force in England and Northern Ireland.[11] The case law developed in those jurisdictions under section 17 is at the foundation of many of the decisions delivered by the Irish courts under section 12 of the Act of 1957. Thus, it is intended first to examine briefly the manner in which the courts in England and Northern Ireland have exercised their jurisdiction under section 17 of the Act of 1882. We shall then discuss in detail the relevant Irish case law.

Section 17 of the Act of 1882[12]

There has been much judicial controversy as to the scope of the court's power under section 17. At one time it was said that the jurisdiction conferred by this section was purely discretionary, enabling the court to make such orders as appear to be fair and just in all the circumstances of the case. Building on the court's discretion, a doctrine of "family assets" was enunciated.[13]

By this doctrine it was stated that:

---

10. Sect. 12(1); The provisions of Sect. 12 are said to be without prejudice to the rights conferred by Sect. 2. Thus, a spouse may, if he or she so wishes protect an interest in property by suing the other in tort rather than by bringing Sect. 12 proceedings.

11. Its importance in both jurisdictions has been greatly diminished, however, by the wide discretionary powers conferred on the English and Northern Ireland courts to make property transfer orders.

12. For a more extensive coverage of the English decisions under Sect. 17 see generally, J. Jackson & D.T.A. Davies, *Matrimonial Finance & Taxation*, 4th ed. (Butterworths, 1986) Chap. 16; P.M. Bromley, *Family Law*, 6th ed. (Butterworths, 1981) Chap. 13; J.G. Miller, *Family Property & Financial Provision*, 2nd ed. (Sweet & Maxwell, 1984) Chaps. 5–8; S.M. Cretney, *Principles of Family Law*, 4th ed. (Sweet & Maxwell, 1984) Chap. 21; B. Passingham & C. Harmer, *Law and Practice in Matrimonial Causes*, 4th ed. (Butterworths, 1985) Chap. 8.

13. See *Hine v. Hine* [1962] 3 All E.R. 345 (C.A.); *Appleton v. Appleton* [1965] 1 W.L.R. 25 (C.A.); *Fribrance v. Fribrance* (No. 2) [1957] 1 All E.R. 357 (C.A.); *Ulrich v. Ulrich* [1968] 1 All E.R. 67 (C.A.); *Gissing v. Gissing* [1969] 2 Ch. 85 (C.A.).

"Where a couple by their joint efforts, get a house and furniture, intending it to be a continuing provision for them for their joint lives, it is the *prima facie* inference from their conduct that the house and furniture is a 'family asset' in which each is entitled to an equal share. It matters not in whose name it stands; or who pays for what; or who goes out to work and who stays at home. If they both contribute to it by their joint efforts, the *prima facie* inference is that it belongs to them both equally: at any rate, when each makes a financial contribution which is substantial."[14]

The House of Lords in *Pettitt v. Pettitt*[15] and *Gissing v. Gissing*[16] denied the existence in English law of a doctrine of family assets. Section 17 of the Act of 1882 was held to confer on the court no wider powers than it had in relation to the determination of proprietary disputes in other types of proceedings.[17] The section was held to be purely procedural, giving the court no power to confer or vary property rights.[18] Lord Morris stated that in a question as to title or ownership of property the job of the court is to ask "whose is this" and not "to whom shall this be given".[19] The fact that the contesting parties' marriage has broken down does not affect the answer to that question. Their proprietary rights are in no way altered by their changed matrimonial circumstances.

While these cases determined the question of whether the court possessed any discretionary power, the difficulty of ascertaining the interest of the parties still exists. The following principles can be gleaned from the relevant English authorities:

I. The beneficial ownership of disputed property depends on the agreement of the parties at the time of acquisition. Where the conveyance or lease declares not merely in whom the legal title is to vest but in whom the beneficial title is to vest, that concludes the question of title as between the spouses for all time and in the absence of fraud or mistake at the time of the transaction, the parties cannot go behind it at any future time.[20]

II. If the title documents are silent as to beneficial interest, in the absence of all other evidence, property conveyed into the name of one spouse *prima facie* confers on that spouse the whole beneficial interest, whilst property conveyed to the spouses jointly *prima facie* results in a joint acquisition of the beneficial interest.[21]

---

14. *Per* Lord Denning, *Gissing v. Gissing, supra*, at p. 93 (C.A.).
15. [1970] A.C. 777 (H.L.).
16. [1971] A.C. 886 (H.L.).
17. "... in my opinion the decision in *Pettitt v. Pettitt* has established that there is not one law of property applicable where a dispute as to property is between spouses and another law of property where the dispute is between others" (*per* Viscount Dilhorne in *Gissing v. Gissing, supra* at p. 899).
18. See also *Cobb v. Cobb* [1955] 2 All E.R. 696 (C.A.); *National Provincial Bank v. Ainsworth* [1965] A.C. 1175 (H.L.); *Cowcher v. Cowcher* [1972] 1 All E.R. 943 (Fam. D.); *McFarlane v. McFarlane* [1972] N.I. 59 (C.A.).
19. *Pettitt v. Pettitt, supra* at p. 798; See also *Bothe v. Amos* [1976] Fam. 46 at p. 54 (C.A.). The question to be determined is "What the title is: not what the title ought to be" *per* Megaw L.J.
20. *Per* Lord Upjohn in *Pettitt v. Pettitt* at p. 813. See also *Goodman v. Gallant* [1986] 1 All E.R. 311 (C.A.); *Leake v. Bruzzi* [1974] 2 All E.R. 1196 (C.A.); *Re Johns Assignment Trusts, Niven v. Niven* [1970] 2 All E.R. 210 (Ch.D.); *Bedson v. Bedson* [1965] 2 Q.B. 666 (C.A.); *Wilson v. Wilson* [1963] 2 All E.R. 447 (C.A.). (As for fraud see footnote 28.).
21. *Per* Lord Upjohn, *Pettitt v. Pettitt, supra*, at p. 814.

CHAPTER 15

III. Evidence is admissible that the spouse in whom legal title is vested holds all or part of that title in trust for the benefit of the other spouse and may be given so as to enable the court to ascertain what was the intention of the parties at the time the property was acquired.[22] In the absence of an agreement between the parties, in order to discover their common intention, the court may draw an inference from their conduct both at the time of and subsequent to acquisition [23] and the circumstances may result in the court holding all or part of the property to be held on an implied or resulting trust or by way of a constructive trust.[24] However, no such trust will arise in favour of a spouse who is a mere "volunteer" and who has neither made a contribution to the acquisition of property nor been induced to act to his detriment under the belief that he has a proprietary interest in property.[24a]

IV. In practice, the English courts have not always clearly distinguished between the implied or resulting trust which derives from the intention of the parties, and the constructive trust based on the concept of unjust enrichment. Moreover, in seeking to ascertain the spouses' common intention from their conduct, the courts in many instances have imputed an intention to spouses at the time of the acquisition of property as to in whom the beneficial interest is to vest which the spouses in reality never had, having given no thought to the issue.[25]

V. Two equitable presumptions may assist the court. By the presumption of resulting trust, if property is conveyed into the name of a person other than the one that provides the purchase price, the former is presumed to hold the property on trust for the purchaser. Thus, if a wife provides all or part of the purchase money for a house that is bought in her husband's name, he is regarded as holding all or part of the property on trust for her, i.e. she owns a beneficial interest in the property, proportionate to her contribution to its purchase, although the whole legal estate is vested in him. The presumption of advancement,[26] however, comes into play where a husband puts property into his wife's name. By this, it is presumed that he intends to make a gift to her.[27] Both these presumptions are rebuttable by evidence that the wife intended a gift or that a husband intended to retain the beneficial interest. In recent English cases these presumptions have been said to have little relevance today and to be easily rebuttable.[28]

---

22. *Pettitt v. Pettitt, supra*; *Gissing v. Gissing, supra*; *Re Rogers Question* [1948] 1 All E.R. 328 (C.A.); *Bernard v. Josephs* [1982] Ch. 391 (C.A.).
23. *Per* Lord Upjohn, *Petititt v. Pettitt, supra*, at p. 813. See also Lord Diplock and Lord Dilhorne in *Gissing v. Gissing, supra*, at p. 906. See further *Re Densham (A Bankrupt)* [1975] 1 W.L.R. 1519 (C.A.); *Knightly v. Knightly* (1981) 11 Fam. Law 122; *Bernard v. Josephs, supra*; *Allied Irish Banks v. McWilliams & Anor.* (1982) Northern Ireland Law Reports, Bulletin of Judgements (No. 7) 1.
24. *Per* Lord Reid and Lord Diplock, in *Gissing v. Gissing, supra*, pp. 897, 905.
24a. See *Midland Bank PLC v. Dobson* [1986] 1 F.L.R. 171 (C.A.); see also (1985) 135 N.L.J. 751.
25. See S.M. Cretney, *Principles of Family Law, supra*, pp. 639–652.
26. See *Re Rogers Question, supra*; *Bull v. Bull* [1955] 1 Q.B. 234; *Cowcher v. Cowcher, supra*.
27. See J.C. Wylie, *Irish Land Law, supra*, p. 450. See further, *Watters v. Watters* (April, 1979) Northern Ireland Law Reports, Bulletin of Judgements (No. 3 of 1979) (H.C., N.I.).
28. See particularly the comments made in *Pettitt v. Pettitt, supra*. Evidence rebutting the presumptions is not admissible, however, if it discloses an improper or fraudulent motive, see *Gascoigne v. Gascoigne* [1918] 1 K.B. 223 (K.B.D.); *Re Emery's Investment Trust* [1959] Ch. 410 (Ch.D.); *Tinker v. Tinker* [1970] P. 136 (C.A.); *Heseltine v. Heseltine* [1971] 1 All E.R. 952 (C.A.).

VI. In determining the parties' proprietary interests, the court will look to both direct and indirect contributions made by the parties to the purchase of the property.[29] Thus, if the property is held in the name of one spouse (for example, the husband) but the other spouse has made a direct payment out of her own money towards the purchase price, the deposit, legal charges or mortgage instalments, the former will hold the property subject to a beneficial interest vested in the latter.[30] More complex is the position where a spouse contributes indirectly to the purchase. The relevant authorities concur in holding that for an indirect contribution to give rise to a share in the family home, it must be of a substantial nature, and agree that a wife's work in the home, keeping house and caring for her husband and children, is not a relevant contribution for this purpose.[31] That, however, is the extent of their agreement.

In *Gissing* and *Pettitt*, the Law Lords expressed conflicting views and as a result two streams of opinion have emerged.

(a). In a number of cases determined in the first half of the 1970's, the English Court of Appeal followed the *dicta* of Lord Reid in *Gissing v. Gissing* that if a wife assists a husband to purchase the matrimonial home by relieving him of other expenses which he would otherwise have had to bear, she makes an indirect contribution which entitles her to a share. Thus, in *Falconer v. Falconer* Lord Denning stated that the contribution

"may be indirect as where both go out to work and one pays the housekeeping and the other the mortgage instalments. It does not matter which way round it is. It does not matter who pays what. So long as there is a substantial financial contribution to the family expenses, it raises an inference of trust."[32]

In *Hazell v. Hazell* he stated:

"it is sufficient if the contributions made by the wife are such as to relieve the husband from expenditure, which he would otherwise have had to bear. By so doing the wife helps him indirectly with the mortgage instalments because he has more money in his pocket with which to pay them. It may be that he does not strictly need her help — he may have enough money of his own without it — but if he accepts it (and thus is enabled to save more of his own money) she becomes entitled to a share."[33]

In *Hargrave v. Newton*[34] the Court of Appeal held that a wife had a beneficial interest in the matrimonial home which was solely in the husband's name. The

---

29. *Gissing v. Gissing, supra*, Lord Reid at p. 896, Lord Pearson at p. 903, Lord Diplock at p. 907.
30. *Gissing v. Gissing, supra*, Lord Diplock at p. 908. See also *Bernard v. Josephs, supra*; *Re Nicholson, Desc'd* [1974] 1 W.L.R. 479 (Ch.D.); *Muetzel v. Muetzel* [1970] 1 All E.R. 443 (C.A.); *Cowcher v. Cowcher, supra*; *Falconer v. Falconer* [1970] 3 All E.R. 349 (C.A.); *Watters v. Watters, supra*.
31. *Burns v. Burns* [1984] 1 All E.R. 244 (C.A.). A wife may, however, acquire a beneficial interest by labour (other than housekeeping) instead of cash — see for example *Smith v. Baker* [1970] 2 All E.R. 826 (C.A.). H. & W. built home themselves. W. gave up job in order to participate in building. See also *Cooke v. Head* [1972] 2 All E.R. 38 (C.A.).
32. [1970] 3 All E.R. 449 at p. 452 (C.A.).
33. [1972] 1 All E.R. 923 at p. 926 (C.A.). See also *Cooke v. Head, supra*; *Kowalczuk v. Kowalczuk* [1973] 2 All E.R. 1042 (C.A.) — held that a wife's indirect contributions gave her no interest in the matrimonial home which was purchased by husband before the parties met each other. In the more recent case of *Burns v. Burns, supra*, it was emphasised that the indirect contribution made must be referable to the acquisition of the house.
34. [1971] 3 All E.R. 866 (C.A.).

money for the house was raised by the husband. So as to help meet all the family expenses, the wife went out to work. Some time later she was fortunate enough to obtain a reward upon finding stolen money. The wife's earnings and the reward money were used to meet household expenses such as clothes, food, telephone bills, etc. The court held that the substantial indirect contributions by the wife were such as to permit the court impute that the husband held the matrimonial home on trust for them both jointly, beneficially in equal shares. A comparison between the decision in this case and that of the House of Lords in *Gissing v. Gissing*[35] is instructive.

In the latter, the home was purchased by the husband and was also held solely in his name. The wife made no direct contribution to the purchase price but paid for some household items and the cost of laying the lawn. She went out to work and paid for her own clothes and those of her son. The House of Lords unanimously held that she possessed no interest in the home. The decisions in these two cases are not easy to reconcile. In both, the wife "relieved the husband from expenditure which he would otherwise have had to bear", yet in the former, she was held to have an interest in the home, whilst in the latter, she was held to have none.

(b). Lord McDermott in the Northern Ireland Court of Appeal in *McFarlane v. McFarlane*, relying on statements made by the majority in *Gissing*, stated that:

> "the indirect contributions of a spouse must, if they are to earn or generate a beneficial interest ... in the property acquired, be the subject of some *agreement* or *arrangement* between the spouses sufficient to show a mutual intention that the indirect contributions will benefit the contributor in this way ... I do not refer to a contractual relationship solely, but would include any understanding between the spouses, which shows a mutual intention that the indirect contributions of one or the other will go to create a beneficial proprietary interest in the contributor."[36]

An initial direct payment to the purchase price may constitute sufficient evidence of such mutual intention.[37]

In *McFarlane* it was held that the wife had no beneficial interest in the matrimonial home, which was held in the husband's name, despite the considerable indirect contribution made by her towards its acquisition. The wife had done part-time clerical work in her husband's business for no pay. The salary she earned from other work was used to meet ordinary household expenses including food for all the family and clothes for herself and her children. The husband paid rates, gas, electricity etc. Later on, she gave up her other job and entered her husband's business full-time and was paid a salary. This she also used for the household expenses. Subsequently the husband purchased a house, the title of

---

35. *Supra.*
36. [1972] N.I. 59, at p. 71. In *Gissing v. Gissing* Lord Dilhorne stated that "Proof of expenditure for the benefit of the family by one spouse will not of itself suffice to show any such common intention as to the ownership of the matrimonial home" (at p. 901). Lord Pearson stated "Contributions are not limited to those made directly in part payment of the price of the property or to those made at the time when the property is conveyed into the name of one of the spouses. For instance there can be a contribution if by arrangement between the spouses one of them by payment of the household expenses enables the other to pay the mortgage instalments", (at p. 903). See also *Cowcher v. Cowcher, supra*; *In re Barnes, a Bankrupt* (May, 1979) Northern Ireland Law Reports, Bulletin of Judgements (No. 4 of 1979) (H.C., N.I.).
37. *Per* Lord Diplock, *Gissing v. Gissing, supra*, at p. 907. See also *Watters v. Watters, supra.*

which was in his sole name. The court agreed that the wife's efforts made a substantial if indirect contribution to the funds out of which the house was purchased. As, however, there was no agreement or arrangement between the spouses as to ownership, the court held she had no beneficial interest in the property. On the principles used and applied by the English Court of Appeal in *Hargrave v. Newton* she would undoubtedly have been held to have a share in the home.[38]

Circumstances in which an indirect contribution *may* result in the acquisition of a beneficial interest in the matrimonial home

(a) If a spouse contributes to the finance available to purchase the home, by working for the other spouse in his business for no pay.[39]

(b) Where a spouse makes substantial improvements to property held by the other spouse.[40] Where, however, "do-it-yourself" jobs are done by one spouse on the property of the other, the former acquires no beneficial interest in the property.[41]

(c) Where a spouse assists in the building of the matrimonial home.[42]

(d) Where the wife's own finance is used to pay for food and other general family expenses, thus enabling the husband to make mortgage payments.[43]

(e) Where all or part of the purchase money comes from "joint savings" or a "common pool".[44]

Section 12 of the 1957 Act

The vast majority of cases determined by the Irish courts in proceedings instituted pursuant to section 12 of the Married Women's Status Act, 1957, have been concerned with determining disputes between spouses as to the ownership of the family home and its contents. Other property disputes have also been determined under section 12, such as disputes as to the ownership of farmland

---

38. See further Lord Justice Gibson, "A Wife's Rights in the Matrimonial Home" (1976) 27 N.I.L.Q. 333.

39. *Nixon v. Nixon* [1969] 3 All E.R. 1133 (C.A.). (Disapproved of by Lord McDermott in *McFarlane v. McFarlane*, the judgement in this case was delivered after the decision of the House of Lords in *Pettitt v. Pettitt* but before their decision in *Gissing v. Gissing*); see also *Muetzel v. Muetzel, supra; Re Cummins* [1972] Ch. 62; [1971] 3 All E.R. 782 (C.A.)

40. *Jansen v. Jansen* [1965] P. 478 (C.A.) approved by Lord Reid and Lord Diplock in *Pettitt v. Pettitt*, disapproved of by Lords Hodson and Upjohn. See English Law Commission *Report on Financial Provision in Matrimonial Proceedings*, paras 56–58. Law Commission No. 25 and The Matrimonial Proceedings and Property Act, 1970, Sect. 37. See also *Davis v. Vale* [1971] 2 All E.R. 1021 (C.A.); *Harnett v. Harnett* [1974] 1 All E.R. 764 (C.A.); *Re Nicholson, Nicholson v. Perks* [1974] 2 All E.R. 386 (Ch.D.).

41. *Button v. Button* [1968] 1 All E.R. 1064 (C.A.); *Pettitt v. Pettitt, supra; Gissing v. Gissing, supra.*

42. *Smith v. Baker, supra; Cooke v. Head, supra* – Here an unmarried couple together built a bungalow, in which they intended to live when finished. L. did a great deal of heavy building work and was held to have a beneficial interest in the property. See also *Eves v. Eves* [1975] 3 All E.R. 768 (C.A.).

43. See e.g. *Falconer v. Falconer, supra; Hazell v. Hazell, supra; Hargrave v. Newton, supra*; alternatively see *Gissing v. Gissing, supra; Cowcher v. Cowcher, supra; McFarlane v. McFarlane, supra.*

44. See *Re Densham* [1975] 3 All E.R. 726 (Ch. D.); *Davis v. Vale, supra; Jones v. Maynard* [1951] Ch. 572 (C.A.); *Heseltine v. Heseltine* [1971] 1 All E.R. 952 (C.A.); *Re Bishop* [1965] 1 All E.R. 249; [1965] Ch. 450 (Ch. D.); *Watters v. Watters, supra.*

and farm stock,[45] business premises,[46] public houses,[47] blocks of flats[48] and other types of investment properties.[49] Partnership and company disputes over property between spouses have also been litigated under the section,[50] as have disputes relating to the ownership of wedding presents, motor cars and monies held in either bank or building society accounts. As most of the written judgements delivered by the Irish courts in proceedings brought under section 12 are concerned with disputes as to the ownership of the family home, it is the law applicable to the resolution of such disputes that is the principal subject matter of the pages that follow. In discussing this area, it is intended first to examine the law applied by the courts in determining disputes as to the ownership of the family home and other property when the legal title is held in the sole name of one spouse and then to examine the law applicable in determining such disputes when the legal title is held in the joint names of both spouses.

LEGAL TITLE HELD IN NAME OF ONE SPOUSE

It is now established that if the legal title to the family home is held in the sole name of one spouse and the other spouse directly or both directly and indirectly contributes to its acquisition, the latter may successfully claim a proprietary or beneficial interest in it.[51] It is also established that if a spouse indirectly contributes towards the acquisition of the family home, such indirect contribution may, by itself, also result in the acquisition of a beneficial interest[52] but there is some diversity of judicial opinion as to the exact legal principles applicable to determine when such contribution will result in a beneficial interest being acquired.[53] If it is held that a spouse is entitled to a beneficial interest in the home, the size of such interest will be in direct proportion to the value of the contribution made to its acquisition unless there is proof of a contrary agreement or arrangement between the parties or evidence of their having a contrary common intention.[53a]

Conway v. Conway[54] was the first High Court case in which a written judge-

---

45. See for example, *B. v. B.* (July, 1978) unreported (H.C.); *W. v. W.* [1981] 1 I.L.R.M. 202 (H.C.); *J.M.H. v. J.P.H.* (January, 1983) unreported (H.C.).
46. See, for example, *K. v. K.* (1978) 114 I.L.T.R. 50 (H.C.); *T. v. T.* (July, 1985) unreported (H.C.).
47. See, for example, *J.M.H. v. J.P.H., supra; N.D. v. A.D.* (December, 1982) unreported (H.C.); *H.D. v. J.D.* (July, 1981) unreported (H.C.).
48. See, for example, *Heavey v. Heavey* (1974) 111 I.L.T.R. 1 (H.C.); *M. v. M.* (1978) 114 I.L.T.R. 46 (H.C.); *C.C. v. S.C.* (July, 1982) unreported (H.C.).
49. See, for example, *C.C. v. S.C., supra.*
50. See, for example, *K. v. K., supra; C.C. v. S.C., supra; T. v. T., supra.*
51. *D. McC. v. M. McC.* [1986] 6 I.L.R.M. 1 (S.C.). See also *Conway v. Conway* [1976] I.R. 254 (H.C.); (1975) 111 I.L.T.R. 133 (H.C.); *K. v. K., supra; W. v. W., supra; H.D. v. J.D., supra; N.D. v. A.D., supra; E.R. v. M.R.* (January, 1981) unreported (H.C.); *G.N.R. v. K.A.R.* (March, 1981) unreported (H.C.); and *A.L. v. J.L.* (February, 1984) unreported (H.C.).
52. See *D. McC. v. M. McC., supra.* See also the following judgements of Finlay P. — *L. v. L.* (December, 1979) unreported (H.C.); *H.D. v. J.D., supra; F.G. v. P.G.* [1982] 2 I.L.R.M. 155. See further *R. v. R.* (January, 1979) unreported (H.C.), McMahon J.; *M.B. v. E.B.* (February, 1980) unreported (H.C.), Barrington J. See, however, *C.R. v. D.R.* (April, 1984) unreported (H.C.) in which Lynch J. states that for an indirect contribution to result in the acquisition of an interest in the family home it must be "significant". See further p. 512 *post.*
53. For a completely different approach to that adopted in the cases referred to in the preceding footnote see *M.G. v. R.D.* (April, 1981) unreported (H.C.), Keane J., and *S.D. v. B.D.* (March, 1982) unreported (H.C.), Murphy J; *B. v. B.* (April, 1986) unreported (H.C.) MacKenzie J. (Supreme Court appeal pending). See further, p. 502 *post.* See also *McGill v. S.* [1979] I.R. 283 (H.C.), Gannon J.
53a. See further p. 505 *post.*
54. [1976] I.R. 254 (H.C.), Kenny J.

ment was delivered in the determination of a dispute as to the ownership of a family home under section 12 of the Act of 1957 and has been expressly cited and followed in a number of subsequent cases. It is this case which we shall examine first.

Two years after the parties had married the family home was purchased by the husband in his sole name. The wife had inherited a sum of £242 and she gave it to the husband so that he could pay the deposit and the expenses of the purchase of the house. The rest of the money was obtained by the husband by way of a mortgage of £2,005. At various times the husband was unable to make the mortgage repayments and as a consequence the wife gave him money of her own so that he could pay the instalments due. The total amount contributed by her to the purchase price of the house and the mortgage repayments was £1,027. Upon the parties' marriage breaking down, the wife brought proceedings and succeeded in claiming a right to half of the beneficial interest in the house. Giving judgement Kenny J. stated:

> "When the matrimonial home is purchased in the name of the husband either before or after marriage, the wife does not as wife become entitled to any share in its ownership either because she occupies the status of wife or because she carries out household duties. In many cases however, the wife contributes to the purchase price or mortgage instalments. Her contributions may be either by payment to the husband of moneys which she has inherited or earned or by paying the expenses of the household so that he has the money which makes it possible for him to pay mortgage instalments".[55]

He then noted that domestic arrangements between spouses are usually informal and continued:

> "When there is an agreement between them as to the ownership of the house which is in the husband's name only, the Court will enforce it but the number of cases in which this happens is small".[56]

Where there is no agreement, however, he stated:

> "Trying to infer what was the implied agreement which arose when payments were made or expenses paid by a wife is a futile task because when the spouses are living happily together, they do not think of stipulating that payments by one of them are made to acquire a share in the matrimonial home or furniture. I think that the correct and most useful approach to these difficult cases is to apply the concept of a trust to the legal relationship which arises when a wife makes payments towards the purchase of a house or the repayment of the mortgage instalments when the house is in the sole name of the husband. When this is done, he becomes a trustee for her of a share in the house and the size of it depends upon the amount of the contributions which she has made towards the purchase or the repayment of the mortgage".[57]

55. *Ibid.*, at p. 257.
56. *Ibid.*
57. *Ibid.*, at p. 258. See also *Curran v. Bamlett (Ireland) Ltd.* (March, 1981) unreported (H.C.), judgement of McWilliam J. at p. 7 where he states:

> "The effect of *Conway v. Conway* is that payments made by a wife towards the purchase of a house or the repayment of mortgage instalments creates a trust by the husband for the wife of a share in the house proportionate to the amount of such payments."

He concluded this part of his judgement by stating that the decisions in *Pettitt, Gissing, McFarlane, Hazell, Kowolczuk* and his earlier judgement in *Heavey v. Heavey*[58] supported such an approach which

> "has the advantage that it gives that flexibility which is essential in dealing with domestic matters."[59]

The contributions made by the wife in *Conway* by virtue of which she was held to be entitled to one half of the beneficial interest in the family home were all direct contributions being in respect of the house deposit, mortgage repayments and expenses incurred in the purchase and, whereas, Kenny J. did not expressly state that the interest vested in the wife was acquired by way of a resulting trust, it is clear that it was the concept of the resulting trust that the learned judge applied.

In *M. v. M.*[60] and *K. v. K.*[61] both direct and indirect contributions were made by the spouses who claimed an interest in property, the ownership of which was in dispute.

In *M. v. M.*[62] a property was purchased by the defendant wife in her sole name in 1972 to provide a source of income. The purchase price was £8,500 and renovations were carried out at a cost of a further £4,000 to convert it into a number of bedsittingrooms. A loan for the deposit was obtained by the wife from her sister in the sum of £2,225. The balance of the purchase price, a sum just in excess of £6,000, was obtained on loan from a bank. The sum of £4,000 was provided out of the proceeds of sale of a public house in which the court held the plaintiff's husband had a 19% share, the wife owning the remainder, 81%. For a considerable time after the purchase of the premises, the rents were used solely to pay off the two loans and at the date of the court hearing they had both been discharged. From the date of the purchase, the husband who was working in the United States, sent a large portion of his earnings home for the maintenance of his wife and children. It was admitted by the wife in evidence that if she had not received these moneys she could not have fully discharged both loans. Throughout the period when the loans were being paid off, the wife and her children lived rent free with the wife's sister.

Finlay P., delivering judgement, first considered whether the contributions made by the husband "direct or indirect . . . must be presumed to have been a gift or advancement by him to his wife."[63] He held that they were not but were intended as a contribution towards the acquisition of a property that was to be "a source of income and revenue for the maintenance of the entire family."[64] Saying that he was satisfied "he should apply . . . the principles laid down" by Kenny J. in *Conway v. Conway*, he stated that he must on the evidence:

> "take the view that (the) loans were ultimately equally discharged by the contributions of the plaintiff and the defendant. It is quite clear to me . . .

---

58. See pp. 507 & 508 *post*.

59. *Ibid.*, at p. 258. Kenny J. did not during the course of his judgement refer to or analyse the conflicting principles enunciated by the members of the English and Northern Irish judiciary who delivered judgements in the cases cited by him.

60. (1978) 114 I.L.T.R. 46 (H.C.), Finlay P.

61. (1978) 114 I.L.T.R. 50 (H.C.), Finlay P.

62. *Supra*.

63. For a general discussion as to the application of the presumption of advancement when property is purchased in a wife's sole name with monies provided by her husband see p. 507 *post*. As for whether the presumption of advancement continued to remain part of Irish law after the coming into operation of the 1937 Constitution under the provisions of Article 50 of the Constitution, see further p. 516 *post*.

64. *Supra*, at p. 49.

that the plaintiff's contributions from his salary and working in New York
to the family made a clear indirect contribution towards the clearing of
these loans. At the same time the arrangement made by the defendant (wife)
with her own family . . . in particular with her sister, which provided free
board and lodging for herself and her children together with what I am
satisfied, on the evidence, was an active participation by her in the running
and letting of the premises constituted a contribution on her part towards
the reduction of the loans. It is not possible for me to make any precise
calculation as to the shares in which these contributions were made but I
take the view that, having regard to the relationships of the parties and the
financial arrangements between them, the equitable conclusion is that they
contributed equally to the clearing of these amounts of loans off the property
and to the consequential enlargement of the equity in it."[65]

Having regard to both the direct and indirect contributions made by the
husband to the acquisition of the property[66] the court held that 40% of the
beneficial interest in it was vested in him and 60% in the wife.[66a]

In *K. v. K.*[67] Finlay P. held that the plaintiff wife had a 28% share of the
beneficial interest in the family home and a 50% share of the beneficial interest
in the leases of two shops, the legal title in all three being held by the husband
in his sole name. The former share arose as a result of contributions made by
the wife from her earnings towards the household expenses, including the
mortgage repayments, by virtue of which Finlay P. stated she was:

"entitled to a beneficial share by way of a resulting trust in the house
in accordance with the principles laid down" (in *Conway v. Conway*).[68]

The latter share arose due to the fact that rents payable for both shops came
out of profits made in a limited liability company in which the wife held a 50%
share and in which she was an active participant. No monies were paid for the
leases and neither spouse received any specific monies by way of dividend or
salary for their work in the two leasehold shops and the court held that the real
cost of their acquisition consisted of the payment of rent and observance of the
other covenants in the lease.[69]

In *W. v. W.*[70] it was established that if a property has been fully purchased, a
wife will not acquire a beneficial interest in it by contributing to its improvement
as opposed to its acquisition. However, if she contributes towards discharging a
mortgage or other charge on the property, she may be entitled to an equitable
share in the property which has been mortgaged proportionate to her contribution to the mortgage repayments, even if the mortgage or charge is raised
subsequent to the original acquisition of the property. Finlay P. explained the
principle behind this latter proposition on the basis that:

"The redemption of any form of charge or mortgage on property . . . con-

---

65. *Ibid.*
66. In *M. v. M., supra*, Finlay P. held the total cost of acquisition and renovation of the
property to be the purchase price, i.e. the sum of £12,500. Thus, the plaintiff husband
contributed directly with his 19% share in the sum of £4,000 spent on renovations and
indirectly with the monies sent home from New York. No other authorities were referred
to by the learned President in his judgement in this case other than *Conway v. Conway,
supra*.
67. *Supra.* See also the sequel to this case in the unreported High Court judgement
delivered by Barrington J. in October 1980. See further p. 551 *post*, footnote 73.
68. *Supra*, at p. 52.
69. See also *N.D. v. A.D.* (December, 1982) unreported (H.C.).
70. [1981] 1 I.L.R.M. 202 (H.C.).

sists of the acquisition by the owner or mortgagor of an estate in the property with which he had parted at the time of the creating of the mortgage or charge and . . . there can be no distinction in principle between a contribution made to the acquisition of that interest and a contribution made to the acquisition of an interest in property by an original purchase."[71]

In *W. v. W.*, Finlay P. for the first time gave a detailed exposition of the general legal principles applicable to determine when a spouse has acquired a beneficial interest in property, the legal title of which is held in the sole name of the other spouse.[72] In this case a farm had been voluntarily[73] transferred into the sole name of the defendant husband, subject to encumbrances, by his brother and mother. Both the husband and the wife applied their savings and monies kept in a joint account on equipping and stocking the farm and improving the land. The wife worked on the farm for a number of years and also put monies she received as a result of a car accident and as a gift into the farm bank account. A mortgage was raised on the farm to finance the building of a modern milking parlour and both it and the original encumbrances were fully discharged. The court upheld the wife's claim that in so far as both her work on the farm and the financial contribution made by her to it had contributed to the general farm income out of which the encumbrances and the loan was discharged, she was entitled to a beneficial interest in it but dismissed her claim that the contribution to other improvements, as such, entitled her to a further additional equitable interest.[74] In the course of his judgement in dealing with the issue of the circumstances in which a wife's contribution can give rise to the acquisition by her of a beneficial interest in property Finlay P. stated:

> "Where a wife contributes by money to the purchase of a property by her husband in his sole name in the absence of evidence of some inconsistent agreement or arrangement the court will decide that the wife is entitled to an equitable interest in that property approximately proportionate to the extent of her contribution as against *the total value of the property*[75] at the time the contribution was made . . .
>
> Where a wife contributes either directly towards the repayment of mortgage instalments or contributes to a general family fund thus releasing her husband from an obligation which he otherwise would have (to) discharge liabilities out of that fund and permitting him to repay mortgage instalments, she will in the absence of proof of an inconsistent agreement or arrangement be entitled to an equitable share *in the property which had been mortgaged and in respect of which the mortgage was redeemed*[76] approximately proportionate to her contribution to the mortgage repay-

71. *Ibid.*, at p. 204.
72. Prior to doing so he stated that he had been referred to and had carefully considered *Conway v. Conway, supra; Heavey v. Heavey, supra; McGill v. S., supra.* No other decided cases are referred to in the learned President's judgement.
73. "Voluntary" in the sense that no purchase price had been paid for the farm.
74. As to the issue of financing improvements to property in the sole name of the other spouse, see p. 509 *post.*
75. Author's italics.
76. *Ibid.*

ments: to the value of the mortgage thus redeemed and to the total value of the property at the relevant time."[77]

As for a husband who contributes either directly or indirectly in a like manner to the purchase of property or to mortgage repayments on a property which is in the sole name of his wife, the learned President stated that subject to the presumption of advancement being rebutted, he would have a similar claim to an equitable share in the estate of the property.[78]

Neither in *W. v. W.*, nor in a number of judgements delivered by him in other cases has Finlay P., in practice, made any distinction between direct and indirect contributions to the acquisition of property and the law applicable in determining when any such contribution or contributions will result in the acquisition of a beneficial interest in it by the contributing spouse. Put in the context of the family home, the view of the learned President is that proof of the making of either type of contribution by a wife will entitle her to a proportionate beneficial interest in the home, in the absence of proof of the existence of an agreement or arrangement inconsistent with the acquisition by her of such interest. Thus, it is not necessary for there to be proof of an agreement or arrangement between spouses for an indirect contribution, by itself, to result in the acquisition of a beneficial interest. Such an interest will be acquired by way of the application of the concept of the resulting trust to the contribution made, unless it is established that there was an agreement or arrangement that the contribution made was not to have such result.[79]

In many of the cases decided by Finlay P. in which a wife has successfully

---

77. *Supra* at p. 204. The learned President distinguishes between the interest a spouse may acquire if a monetary payment to the acquisition of property is made at the date of purchase, i.e. the date when the property is transferred into the sole name of the other spouse, as opposed to when no such payment is made but there is a subsequent contribution which is regarded as directly or indirectly contributing to the discharge of a mortgage. For example, if a house is purchased for £30,000 in a husband's sole name and at the date of purchase £2,000 of the wife's own money and £8,000 of the husband's money together with a sum of £20,000 by way of a mortgage is used to pay for the property, the wife can claim a beneficial interest against the total value of the property in proportion to the contribution made by her. See, for example, *A.L. v. J.L., supra*, discussed on p. 505 *post*. If, however, the initial £10,000 is provided by the husband alone and the wife subsequently contributes either directly or indirectly towards discharging the mortgage, her proportionate interest does not apply to the total value of the property but to a proportionate share based on two thirds of the value of the property less the undischarged portion of the mortgage. See, for example, *M.B. v. E.B., supra*, discussed on p. 500 *post* in which the wife confined her claim to a beneficial interest as being a proportionate interest in a two third share of the family home.

Having determined the proportion of the wife's interest in that portion of the property that has been mortgaged, the proportion can then be related to a percentage interest in the property as a whole. Thus, in *K. v. K., supra*, the house costs £4,500. £2,000 was paid at the date of purchase by the husband out of his earnings. This represented 44% of the total cost. The other 56%, i.e. £2,500, was obtained by way of a mortgage and Finlay P. concluded that the wife contributed one half of the mortgage repayments, i.e. she had a 50% interest in the equity of redemption which was then calculated as being a 28% beneficial interest in the total value of the property. See further *H.D. v. J.D., supra*; *F.G. v. P.G., supra*. If the monies to acquire the family home fully derive from a mortgage or loans obtained, the proportionate interest acquired by each spouse will be determined simply on the basis of the proportionate contribution made by each spouse towards discharging the loans. See *L. v. L.* (December, 1979) unreported (H.C.). See further p. 498 *post* and also footnote 85.

78. *Supra* at p. 204, para 2 and p. 205, para 4.

79. In this context the learned President appears to have adopted the approach enunciated by Lord Reid in *Gissing v. Gissing, supra* (see p. 489 *ante*) and to have rejected the more rigid approach of the majority in that case and the approach adopted by the court of appeal in Northern Ireland in *McFarlane v. McFarlane, supra*. Although he refers to *McGill v. S., supra*, in *W. v. W.*, the applicable legal principles enunciated by Finlay P. cannot, in the context of indirect contribution, be reconciled with the approach adopted by Gannon J. in that case.

claimed a beneficial interest in a family home or other property on the basis of an alleged indirect contribution to its acquisition, such as the discharge of debts that would otherwise have had to be discharged by the husband, the wife has been regarded as contributing to "a general family fund"[80] or "a general family pool"[81] or to a "joint family fund"[82] or a "joint pool",[83] even when payments have been made directly by her out of monies of her own which were never actually joined with funds or monies provided by the husband in a joint bank or savings account. This is illustrated by the following two cases.

In *L. v. L.*[84] the husband purchased a house in his own name in December 1973. The wife worked as a secretary until July 1976 and contributed a high proportion of her earnings towards the purchase of food and the discharge of other household expenses. During the same period the husband worked as an accountant and discharged all the mortgage repayments. Finlay P. held that the wife, by virtue of her contribution to "the joint family fund" during the above period, was entitled to a 35% beneficial interest in the family home having regard to the proportionate contribution by her to it as compared to that of her husband.[85] In *H.D. v. J.D.*[86] the husband purchased a family home in his own name in which the spouses resided from 1971 until early 1975. The wife worked for a period of 18 months and earned a sum of £15 per week which Finlay P. stated "she brought into the general family pool out of which the mortgage repayments were made." The husband brought "into the family pool" £100 per week during the same period and the wife was held to have an interest in the house in proportion to the financial contribution made by her to the mortgage repayments during the relevant period. As a result, upon the sale of the house

---

80. See *W. v. W., supra.*
81. See *H.D. v. J.D., supra; F.G. v. P.G., supra.*
82. See *L. v. L., supra.*
83. See *A.L. v. J.L., supra.*
84. (December, 1979) unreported (H.C.).
85. In his judgement in this case, Finlay P. did not state the authorities he was relying on. He merely stated that he was "satisfied in accordance with the decisions to which I have been referred and which I must follow . . . that what I must ascertain is the contribution made by the plaintiff (wife) and the defendant (husband) during the period December, 1973 up to December, 1976, towards the mortgage repayments on this house and that they are entitled in law to the beneficial ownership of the premises or as it can be more precisely put, of the equity of redemption in the premises in the proportion of those contributions" (see p. 6 of judgement). The husband had used a greater proportion of his salary for his own purposes than had the wife and Finlay P., as a consequence, took the view that the proportionate contribution each made towards "the joint fund out of which mortgage repayments were made" when the wife was at work should not be equated with the proportionate difference between the parties' salary. Although the gross earnings of the husband for the relevant period were £14,000 and those of the wife £4,500, the wife was held to have contributed during that period 40% of the mortgage repayments. Her beneficial interest was then adjusted downwards to 35% due to the fact that she did not work and had no independent income of her own for a period during which the husband continued to work and to discharge the mortgage.
   See also *G.N.R. v. K.A.R., supra*, a case in which direct and indirect contributions were made by both spouses and in which Carroll J. held that the husband "expended a considerable proportion of his income on his own pursuits" and expressly followed the approach adopted by Finlay P. in *L. v. L.* See further, *E.R. v. M.R., supra*, in which Carroll J. held that a husband "who was not contributing adequately out of his earnings towards the maintenance of his family" was entitled to no beneficial interest at all in a site purchased by the wife with her own monies. Where spouses use a similar proportion of their salary towards family expenses the beneficial interest that each may acquire in the family home as a result of the contributions made by each will be in the same proportion as their respective gross earnings – see *R. v. R.* (January, 1979) unreported (H.C.) , McMahon J.
   86. (July, 1981) unreported (H.C.). See, however, the contrasting approach of Lynch J. in *A.H. v. A.H.* (December, 1985) unreported (H.C.).

out of the sum of £11,500, she was held entitled to a sum of £330.[87] Work undertaken by the wife for no pay in a public house subsequently acquired by the husband was also held to give the wife a larger beneficial interest in a home purchased by the husband following the sale of the public house.[87a]

In *F.G. v. P.G.*[88] Finlay P. took the concept of indirect contributions a step further and held that a wife had contributed to the acquisition of the family home as her contribution to the family expenses had avoided her husband having to sell the home "so as to service and finance the general expenses of the family." In 1964 the husband had purchased a home in Dublin in his sole name and had then gone to live in America from where he discharged the mortgage repayments out of his own earnings. The wife joined him in 1966. Thereafter, the home was rented to successive tenants and the rents obtained used to discharge the mortgage repayments and to maintain the property. Subsequently, the home was used to raise a loan, which the rents received were used to service. A year after she arrived in America, the wife obtained employment and contributed to "a joint family fund" until 1978 when the parties separated. Between 1967 and 1978 the parties used a portion of the joint family fund and the monies borrowed on the home in Ireland to engage in various property transactions and to discharge the household and family expenses. Finlay P. rejected the husband's contention that the wife was entitled to no beneficial interest in the Dublin home as at no stage had any of her monies been used directly or indirectly to acquire it. He agreed with the wife's contention that it was irrelevant that no monies were ever remitted from the family pool to which she contributed for the purpose of discharging the mortgage repayments. He stated:

"I have no doubt that had the plaintiff not earned in the years 1967 to 1978 and had she not contributed her earnings to the extent that she did to the general family pool that there was no way in which the defendant could during those years have avoided disposing of the Dublin house so as to service and finance the general expenses of the family and the property deals in which he was engaged in America. She has . . . in my view contributed to the acquisition of the equity of redemption in the Dublin home

---

87. Finlay P. cited his earlier judgement in *W. v. W., supra*, as authority for the decision made on this aspect of the case and calculated the extent of the wife's interest on the basis laid down in that judgement. See further, footnote 77 *ante*. In *H.D. v. J.D.* the monies realised from the sale of the family home together with the husband's savings and a bank loan of £11,000 were used to acquire a residential public house in the husband's sole name. The wife without receipt of any salary or pay played a major part in the running of the pub and the profits earned from the pub and monies contributed by the husband from other activities were used to meet the family expenses and discharge the mortgage. The pub was sold in 1977 two years after its acquisition and a portion of the monies obtained was used by the husband to build a new family home in which the wife claimed a beneficial interest. Finlay P. held that having regard to the wife's original contribution of £330 for the purchase of the pub and to her contribution by her work in it to the family pool out of which the mortgage repayments were made on the pub, she was entitled to a one fifth beneficial interest in the home, the purchase money for which derived from the proceeds of the sale of the pub.
87a. See 87, *ibid*.
88. [1982] 2 I.L.R.M. 155 (H.C.). These proceedings were brought by plenary summons and there is no mention of the Act of 1957 in the judgement. Following the breakdown in the parties' marriage, they obtained a civil divorce in the United States and as they had emigrated to the United States the divorce would have been recognised under Irish law if obtained in the State in which they were domiciled. It is presumed that it was so obtained and that as the parties were no longer "husband and wife" for the purpose of section 12 of the Act of 1957, it was necessary to resolve the dispute as to the ownership of their former family home by way of a declaratory action. The legal principles applicable, however, are no different to those applicable where parties are still married to each other at the date of the proceedings, and for simplicity, the parties are referred to as husband and wife in the account that follows.

just as clearly as if the monies earned by her had been remitted to discharge the mortgage repayments."[89]

Having regard to the contribution made by her, the wife was held to have a 30% beneficial interest in the home.

An approach similar to that taken by Finlay P. (in determining when an indirect contribution made by a spouse will result in the acquisition by that spouse of a beneficial interest in property held in the sole name of the other spouse) has been taken by other members of the High Court[90] and has recently been endorsed by the Supreme Court.[91]

In *R. v. R.*[92] the parties married in 1968 and a year later the family home was purchased in the husband's sole name and the deposit and mortgage repayments were all paid by the husband. Between 1968 and 1973, when the parties separated, the wife worked on average thirty-three weeks per year.

The court held that had the wife not been working, the husband would not have been able to keep up the mortgage repayments, maintain their standard of living and run a car, which he required for his job. The wife spent some of her earnings on providing food and other household requisites and she spent some on clothes for herself and visits to the hairdressers.

McMahon J., holding that the wife had an 18% beneficial interest in the home, stated that there was no distinction between monies used by the wife for necessaries for herself or for household purposes. He stated "so far as the money was spent on the wife's needs it seems to me that these were expenses which the husband would have been forced to meet if she was not able to pay for them herself". He continued:

> "both kinds of expenditure come within the principles enunciated by Kenny J. in *Conway v. Conway* . . . namely that the wife's contribution which will give her a claim to a beneficial interest in the matrimonial home may take the form of paying the expenses of the household so that her husband has the money which makes it possible for him to pay the mortgage instalments. In either case there is a saving to the husband and if that enables him pro tanto to meet the mortgage repayments the wife should be regarded as contributing towards these repayments".[93]

In *M.B. v. E.B.*[94] a wife's financial contributions to the purchase of furniture and other household goods and towards the general household expenses were held to confer on the wife a beneficial interest in the family home. The legal title in the home was held by the husband in his sole name and no direct pay-

---

89. *Supra*, at p. 157. Finlay P. stated that the principles laid down in *Nixon v. Nixon* [1969] 3 All E.R. 1133 (see footnote 39 *ante*) constituted "a persuasive precedent" which he should follow.

90. See *R. v. R.* (January, 1979) unreported (H.C.), McMahon J.; *M.B. v. E.B.* (February, 1980) unreported (H.C.), Barrington J. See also *C.R. v. D.R.* (April, 1984) unreported (H.C.) in which Lynch J. introduces the element that the indirect contribution must be "significant" (see further p. 512 *post*). See also *N.A.D. v. T.D.* [1985] 5 I.L.R.M. 153 (H.C.), Barron J. in which the legal principles enunciated by Finlay P. are approved but the manner in which the learned trial judge applies them to the facts of the particular case is open to question. See further p. 510 *post*.

91. See *D. McC. v. M. McC.* [1986] 6 I.L.R.M. 1 (S.C.).

92. *Supra*.

93. See p. 3 of judgement. The learned judge took the view on the evidence that "the fairest approach" was to assume that the "respective contributions to the family purse and therefore to the mortgage repayments were in the same proportion as their (the spouses) respective gross earnings before tax." Such an approach is not always taken. See footnote 85 *ante*.

94. (February, 1980) unreported (H.C.).

ments had been made by the wife towards its acquisition.[95] The wife in evidence had stated that there was "a kind of an agreement" between them under which the husband paid the mortgage and the electricity bills and she bought virtually everything else that was required for the house.

Barrington J. stated that:

> "Marriage partners seldom enter into formal agreements when the marriage is going well. But, the understanding between them may, at times, be seen in their actions or course of conduct. If they appear to be acting on the principle that all things are common between friends, then . . . a court can readily infer that that principle gives the basic understanding between them."[96]

The wife merely claimed an interest in a two fifths share of the house, as three fifths of the purchase price had been paid in cash by the husband at the time of the purchase and the wife had made no contribution to this sum. The wife also claimed, in the alternative, an interest in the household goods and furniture.

Barrington J. found that on the facts of the case, there clearly was an understanding between the parties that they were, by their joint efforts, to buy and furnish a home and held that the wife was entitled to a one fifth share in the beneficial interest in the home and to a one half share in the household goods and furniture. However, it appears from the judgement delivered, that even in the absence of such a finding, the court would have held that the indirect contributions made by the wife gave rise to the acquisition by her of a beneficial interest in both the home and household chattels.[97]

In March 1984, the Supreme Court in *D. McC. v. M. McC.*[98] for the first time considered the legal principles applicable to determine a claim by a wife to a beneficial interest in a family home deriving from an alleged indirect contribution by her to its acquisition. The home was purchased by the husband in his sole name for a sum of £9,000. The husband obtained a mortgage for the full sum from his employers who deducted the mortgage repayments from his salary. A sum of £600 to which the wife was entitled from the sale of the parties' previous home was used by the husband to purchase furniture and fittings. The wife claimed that this sum had gone into a family fund and had eased the financial liability incurred by the husband in the purchase of the home and that by virtue of her contribution she was entitled to a proportionate beneficial interest in it. The Supreme Court, confirming the decision of the High Court,[99] rejected the wife's claim. It held that her contribution only entitled her to a one third beneficial interest in the furniture and fittings, as the £600 was applied by the husband not in acquiring the house but as part of a sum of £1,800 he spent on furniture and fittings. The wife had not, the court held, "relieved the husband of any share of the financial burden he incurred in purchasing the house".[100]

---

95. Save for a sum of £150 towards discharging the legal costs incurred in the purchase. This sum does not seem to have been regarded by the court as a contribution by the wife towards the acquisition of the property.

96. See p. 21 of judgement.

97. Barrington J. referred to the judgement of Kenny J. in *Conway v. Conway* and cited with approval the judgement of McMahon J. in *R. v. R., supra,* and the passage from Lord Denning's judgement in *Hazell v. Hazell* [1972] 1 All E.R. 923 (C.A.) quoted on p. 489 *ante.*

98. *Supra.* A three man court sat. Griffin J., Hederman J. and Henchy J. who delivered the judgement of the court.

99. By Costello J.

100. [1986] 6 I.L.R.M. at p. 2.

Delivering the judgement of the court and referring to the legal principles applicable to such proceedings, Henchy J. stated that:

> "Where the matrimonial home has been purchased in the name of the husband, and the wife has, either directly or indirectly, made contributions towards the purchase price or towards the discharge of mortgage instalments the husband will be held to be a trustee for the wife of a share in the house roughly corresponding with the proportion of the purchase money represented by the wife's total contribution. Such a trust will be inferred when the wife's contribution is of such a size and kind as will justify the conclusion that the acquisition of the house was achieved by the joint efforts of the spouses.
>
> When the wife's contribution has been indirect (such as by contributing, by means of her earnings to a general family fund) the courts will, in the absence of any express or implied agreement to the contrary, infer a trust in favour of the wife, on the ground that she has to that extent relieved the husband of the financial burden he incurred in purchasing the house."[101]

The above passage from the judgement delivered by Henchy J. clearly endorses the approach taken by Finlay P. and by other members of the High Court in the series of cases discussed and referred to in this section, although the only authority that is referred to by the learned judge is that of Kenny J. in *Conway v. Conway*.[102]

However, an alternative approach to the issue of indirect contributions has been enunciated by other members of the High Court in proceedings brought under section 12 of the 1957 Act and it is this approach which we shall now examine.

Indirect Contributions: An Alternative Approach

In *M.G. v. R.D.*[103] a member of the High Court, for the first time in a detailed written judgement in proceedings brought under section 12 of the 1957 Act referred to and discussed the leading cases determined in both England and Northern Ireland under the Act of 1882, and acknowledged that conflicting approaches had been adopted in many of the judgements delivered, in relation to ascertaining when an indirect contribution to the purchase of property will result in the acquisition of a beneficial interest in it.[104] Delivering judgement in this case, Keane J. adopted an entirely different approach to that adopted by Finlay P., McMahon J. and Barrington J. in the cases previously discussed[105] and to

---

101. *Ibid*.
102. See further (1984) 3 I.L.T. (n.s.) 124.
103. (April, 1981) unreported (H.C.).
104. The cases referred to in the judgement delivered are *Gissing v. Gissing, supra*; *McFarlane v. McFarlane, supra*; *Falconer v. Falconer, supra*; *Hargrave v. Newton, supra*; *Hazell v. Hazell, supra*; and *Kowalczuk v. Kowalczuk, supra*. Although these cases are cited and referred to in many of the Irish cases already discussed, in no other case brought under the 1957 Act has any member of the High Court judiciary examined and commented on the conflicting approaches enunciated in the various proceedings brought under the Act of 1882 to determine claims to a beneficial interest based solely on the making of indirect contributions to the acquisition of disputed property.
105. The learned judge in his judgement referred to and discussed the following Irish cases determined under the Act of 1957 – *Conway v. Conway, supra*; *R. v. R., supra*; *M.B. v. E.B., supra*; *M. v. M., supra*; *K. v. K., supra* and *L. v. L., supra*. He also referred to and agreed with the judgement of Gannon J. in *McGill v. S., supra*, a case concerned with determining a proprietary dispute between cohabitees. See further p. 619 *post*.

that subsequently enunciated by Henchy J. delivering the Supreme Court judgement in *D.McC. v. M.McC.*[106]

In *M.G. v. R.D.* the family home was purchased in the husband's sole name in 1973 entirely by loans obtained by him and the mortgage and loan repayments were made solely by the husband. The husband was a bank official and the wife an air hostess and she used part of her salary on housekeeping items, principally food. She also purchased a car which both parties used and because of the wife's job, the cost of some overseas holidays they took together were substantially reduced. The wife claimed a beneficial interest in the home on the basis that she had contributed indirectly to its acquisition and Keane J. held that it was "probable that (her) contributions to the joint expenses of the household over the 4 years of the marriage amounted . . . to one fifth of those expenses".[107] He also stated that "there was no evidence to suggest that the payments made by the plaintiff were on foot of any agreement or arrangement" and noted that the husband had urged the wife on a number of occasions "to agree to operate a joint bank account" but that she had refused to do so.[108] The learned judge then went on to consider whether the wife was, by virtue of the money spent by her, entitled to a beneficial interest in the home. Having expressed doubts as to the "validity of the proposition that the making of indirect contributions, of itself, and without any other evidence, can constitute sufficient evidence to justify the inference of a resulting or constructive trust"[109] he continued:

"The strongest argument in favour of that proposition appears to be that to hold otherwise would be to create an unreal and arbitrary distinction between the direct payment by the contributing spouse of mortgage instalments and indirect contribution by way of payment of other household expenses. It seems to me, however, that the distinction is a real one and supported by principle. In the absence of special circumstances, the payment on a regular basis by one spouse of the mortgage instalments is clearly capable of supporting the inference that it was intended that the payor should be entitled to a beneficial interest in the property in respect of which the instalments were paid. Different considerations may well apply, however, to the discharge by one spouse of liabilities which are the responsibility of the other but which are not related in any way to the acquisition of the property in question: as Lord McDermott points out in *McFarlane v. McFarlane*[110] in most cases such payments are made without any thought of building up a beneficial interest in any form of property but as part of 'a joint and unselfish adventure'. It seems to me entirely reasonable in such circumstances that the court should require at least some evidence to indicate that they were in fact made in pursuance of a common intention that the contributing spouse should be entitled to some beneficial interest in the property."[111]

The test to be applied in determining whether such common intention existed, Keane J. stated, is an objective one:

"It depends on the inferences as to the intentions of the parties which a reasonable man would draw from their words or conduct. The fact remains

---

106. *Supra.*
107. See p. 3 of judgement.
108. See p. 2 of judgement.
109. See p. 14 of judgement.
110. *Supra.* See also p. 490 *ante.*
111. See pp. 14–15 of judgement.

that it is the existence or non-existence of such a common intention, whether actually expressed or reasonably to be inferred from words or conduct, which is critical in determining whether the resulting trust has come into operation."[112]

In the context of the indirect contribution made by the wife and her claim in this case to a beneficial interest in the family home, he concluded:

"There is nothing in the evidence to suggest that either she or the (husband) thought for a moment that the fact that she was regularly using her own income to defray expenses for which he was responsible meant that she was acquiring a part ownership of the house in which they were living."[113]

In dismissing the wife's claim Keane J. acknowledged that if the law in this country was that the wife was automatically entitled to a beneficial interest in property if she made "substantial contributions . . . to household expenses which were the responsibility of the husband and which left him with more money to repay the mortgage instalments"[114] on such property, the wife in this case would have succeeded.

In *S.D. v. B.D.*[115] Murphy J. expressly approved of and followed the approach adopted by Keane J., dismissing a wife's claim to a beneficial interest in the family home as it was "not based on any direct contribution by her towards the purchase of the house or repayments of mortgage instalments"[116] but based on the discharge of household expenses "which would otherwise have been borne by her husband."[117] These indirect contributions he noted "were not paid or made available as a result of any agreement or understanding between her husband and herself"[118] and so accordingly her claim to a beneficial interest did not succeed.

It is interesting to note that the judgement of Keane J. in *M.G. v. R.D.* was delivered approximately seven weeks after the judgement of Finlay P. in *W. v. W.* but that the latter judgement is not anywhere cited in the former case. Moreover, if the approach of Keane J. had been adopted, for example, in *L. v. L.* or in *R. v. R.* the wives who succeeded in their claims to a beneficial interest in their family homes would not have done so. The legal principles enunciated in *M.G. v. R.D.* as applicable to the determination of a claim to a proprietary interest in a family home on the basis of an alleged indirect financial contribution towards its acquisition are clearly irreconcilable with the principles stated in *W. v. W.* and those subsequently articulated by Henchy J. when delivering the judgement of the Supreme Court in *D.McC. v. M.McC.* The Supreme Court judgement in the *McC.* case, however, contains no reference to the judgements delivered in either *M.G. v. R.D.* or *S.D. v. B.D.* and makes no reference to any of the decided cases other than *Conway v. Conway.* It cannot, therefore, be regarded as a final determination as to which of the two conflicting judicial approaches to the issue of indirect contributions is correct.

In the Supreme Court case of *Northern Bank v. Henry*,[119] having acknowledged

112. See p. 16 of judgement.
113. See p. 17 of judgement.
114. See p. 18 of judgement.
115. (March, 1982) unreported (H.C.).
116. See p. 18 of judgement.
117. *Ibid.*
118. See p. 19 of judgement. See also *A.H. v. A.H.* (December, 1985) unreported (H.C.) Lynch J., in particular at p. 6 of judgement. See further *B. v. B.* (April, 1986) unreported (H.C.) MacKenzie J. in which an appeal lodged with the Supreme Court has not, at the date of writing, been heard or determined.
119. [1981] I.R. 1 (S.C.).

that both in this country and in England there was

> "judicial authority ... that although a matrimonial home might be legally vested in one spouse ... the other spouse could have a claim in equity to at least some share in the ownership of the house"

Parke J. noted that there had

> "not ... been complete judicial unanimity as to how the nature of such a claim should be designated or the exact equitable principle upon which it vested".[120]

It is unfortunate that four years later the Supreme Court did not use the opportunity provided by the *McC.* case to fully examine and analyse the differing and varied strains of judicial opinion evident in the many cases decided to date in this area and make a final determination between them by delivering a comprehensive statement of the law applicable to the resolution of proprietary disputes between spouses, with particular reference to the issue of indirect contributions. Until such a detailed written judgement is delivered, the law in this area will continue to remain uncertain.[121]

Beneficial Interest is not Always Proportionate to Contribution Made

The beneficial interest in the family home or other property which may vest in a spouse will not in all cases correspond to a share proportionate to the contribution made to its acquisition. The circumstances relating to its acquisition may properly lead to the conclusion that it was intended that a greater or lesser share be acquired or, that it was intended, that a beneficial interest be acquired without the making of any contribution at all. In the latter context, the entire or a portion of the beneficial interest in a property purchased and paid for by a husband may vest in the wife by application of the presumption of advancement and the wife's interest in the family home or other property may bear no relation to the contribution made by her to its purchase.

In *A.L. v. J.L.*[122] the wife was held to have a joint beneficial interest in the family home although the husband claimed that the financial contribution made by her to its acquisition was considerably less than that made by him. The home was purchased a month prior to the parties' marriage and was financed from their savings, by a building society mortgage and two additional loans. The home was held in the husband's sole name but it was agreed during the course of the proceedings that it was originally the intention of the parties that it be acquired in their joint names, each to be entitled to a one half share interest in it, but that at the date of purchase the deed of conveyance could not be taken in the wife's name as she was under 21 years of age. Finlay P. noted that throughout the period when the parties resided together "they both contributed to a joint pool out of which there was discharged not only household expenses but also repayments of the loans raised ... and the repayments of the mortgage instalments."[123] He held that "it was the clear intention of these parties that the house should be purchased jointly by them and ... the events which happened and the circumstances under which it was purchased in the sole name of the

---

120. *Ibid.*, at p. 21.
121. See further, J.C. Brady, "Trusts, Law Reform and the Emancipation of Women" (1984) 6 D.U.L.J. 1. See also, P. O'Connor, "Indirect Contributions and the Acquisition of a Beneficial Interest in Property" (1984) 3 I.L.T. (n.s.) 40.
122. (February, 1984) unreported (H.C.), Finlay P.
123. See p. 3 of judgement.

husband when viewed through equitable principles must be given the same force
and effect as if their intention had been carried out . . ."[124] On the facts of this
case, he was satisfied, that "even if the evidence were clearly to establish a greater
contribution . . . by the husband to the repayment of loans and the discharge
of mortgage than that made by the wife" it would not affect the wife's entitlement to one half of the beneficial interest in the home.[125]

Where property is acquired in a husband's sole name with monies paid out of
a joint bank account to which both spouses have contributed, by virtue of such
account being held in joint names, a wife may be held to have a joint beneficial
interest in any property acquired by use of or with monies originally derived
from such account, even if the husband's actual payments into the account
exceed those of the wife. In *C.C. v. S.C.*[126] the husband purchased a property
in his sole name, renovated and sold the original house purchased and built a
block of flats in the grounds of the property. He financed the entire venture
by borrowing money on a joint bank account held in the names of his wife and
himself and securing the borrowings by depositing with the bank the title deeds
of another property held jointly with his wife. He also paid the rents obtained
from the newly built flats into the joint account. The wife had no recollection
of signing any deposit document but the evidence established that she must have
done so. There was also no evidence of any explicit agreement on the wife's part
that the husband could use the money in their joint account for the purpose of
property ventures, although the court was satisfied that the wife both knew and
permitted that the money be used in this way, regarding the property developments as a provision for the family's future. The wife had originally contributed
a portion of the funds by which the joint account had been established with
earnings derived from the other property held by the parties in joint names which
had been paid into the account. McMahon J. held that there was no doubt that
the husband and wife were beneficially as well as legally joint tenants of the
monies in the joint account. As a consequence he decided that the wife was
entitled to one half of the beneficial interest in the property as she had "provided a moiety of the money" for its acquisition, stating:

> "it is immaterial whether the development arising from the use of her money
> in this manner is regarded as subject to a resulting trust based on an implicit

124. See p. 4 of judgement.
125. See p. 5 of judgement. The home had been purchased in 1975 and following upon
her leaving the husband in February 1980 the wife had ceased contributing to household
expenses. The proceedings were determined in February 1984 and counsel for the wife
conceded that the husband was entitled to a credit "for the extra amounts paid by way of
mortgage instalments by him since February, 1980." Finlay P. held the wife's half share to
relate to a half share equal to the nett value of the home as at February 1980, i.e. the gross
value less the amount outstanding by way of the building society's loan. It was contended
by the husband's counsel that the wife's interest which was held in trust by the husband
was "conditional upon each party honouring the obligations of the contract of marriage"
and that as she had deserted the husband and left the family home "the trust should in
equity be terminated or cancelled". Rejecting this contention, Finlay P. stated that "there
is not . . . in the general principles of equity room for a voidable or conditional trust depending on the maintenance of the marriage nor can the courts investigate the true reasons for
the unfortunate breakup of the marriage in order to ascertain the reality of the beneficial
ownership of two people who agree jointly to purchase a house and make each of their
contributions towards the redemption of a mortgage and insert a question mark upon it."
See p. 5 of judgement. Where a house is purchased by a husband alone, placed in the joint
names of his wife and himself and is so purchased after the marriage has broken down pursuant to a promise made by the wife to return to reside with the husband, the wife's beneficial
interest may be dependent on her fulfilling the promise made – see p. 515 *post.*
126. (July, 1982) unreported (H.C.), McMahon J.

consent on her part or to a constructive trust based on the fact of the husband's use of the wife's money."[127]

Where a property is acquired in a wife's sole name with monies paid out of a joint account the entire beneficial interest in the property will vest in the wife by application of the presumption of advancement unless the presumption is rebutted. In *Heavey v. Heavey*[128] the evidence given reinforced the presumption. The husband having purchased a house in the sole name of his wife with monies held in a joint bank account gave two reasons for vesting title in the wife:

(a) To help avoid death duties after his death and

(b) To invest money given to him by his wife over a number of years.

Kenny J. held the entire beneficial interest in the property to be vested in the wife.

The presumption of advancement may be rebutted by proof that it was not the husband's intention to make a gift to his wife.[129] However, even if this can be established, the wife will not be denied a beneficial interest in property placed by her husband in her sole name if it was so placed by him for illegal or fraudulent reasons. Thus in *Parkes v. Parkes*[130] 222 acres of land in Waterford was purchased by the husband, who was a British subject, in the sole name of his wife, who was an Irish citizen. Thirteen years later the husband claimed that his wife held the entire beneficial interest in the land in trust for him. It was accepted that at the time of its acquisition the husband did not intend to give the land as a gift to his wife but the court refused to make a declaration that he was entitled to a beneficial interest in it. The lands had been acquired in the wife's name and the transfer to her had contained a certificate certifying that the wife was "entitled to the entire beneficial interest in the property" and that she was "an Irish citizen" so as to avoid the necessity of the husband, as a British citizen, having to seek the Irish Land Commission's consent for the purchase.[131] It was illegal to make a false statement in such a certificate and Costello J. stating that "the whole transaction is tainted with illegality"[132] held that the court would "not allow (the husband) to take advantage of his own dishonesty."[133]

If a spouse contributes towards the improvement, as opposed to the acquisition, of property in the name of the other spouse, such contribution will not result in the acquisition of a beneficial interest in the property and the spouse making the contribution may not be entitled to be reimbursed for any monies spent on such improvement. Thus, in *W. v. W.*[134] it was decided that the con-

---

127. See p. 6 of judgement. See also the Circuit Court judgement of McWilliam J. in *Galligan v. Galligan* (1976) 70 *Gazette of the Incorporated Law Society of Ireland*, "Recent Irish Cases" p. 25. Here a farm purchased from a joint bank account was held to belong to the spouses jointly although purchased in the husband's sole name. Both spouses worked putting their money into a "joint pool". Cases referred to in the judgement but not mentioned in the *Gazette* report included *Jones v. Maynard, supra* and *Gissing v. Gissing, supra*.
128. (1974) 111 I.L.T.R. 1 (H.C.), Kenny J.
129. See, for example, *M. v. M., supra*, discussed on p. 494 *ante*.
130. (July, 1980) unreported (H.C.), Costello J. The proceedings were brought by way of a plenary summons as the parties had been divorced in England four years after their marriage. Although the divorce was probably recognised in Ireland they are referred to as husband and wife in the judgement delivered in the proceedings between them.
131. In order for the husband to have purchased the land in his sole name he would have had to obtain the consent of the Land Commission pursuant to section 45 of the Land Act, 1965.
132. See p. 20 of judgement.
133. See p. 21 of judgement. During the course of his judgement Costello J. cited with approval *Gascoigne v. Gascoigne, supra; Re Emery's Investment Trust, supra* and *Tinker v. Tinker, supra*. See further footnote 28 *ante*.
134. [1981] 1 I.L.R.M. 202 (H.C.).

tribution the wife made towards improving the farm held by the husband in his sole name did not entitle her to any additional beneficial interest in it. Dealing with this issue, Finlay P. stated:

"Where a wife expends monies or carries out work in the improvement of a property which has been originally acquired by and the legal ownership in which is solely vested in her husband she will have no claim in respect of such contribution unless she establishes by evidence that from the circumtances surrounding the making of it she was led to believe (or of course that it was specifically agreed) that she would be recompensed for it. Even where such a right to recompense is established either by an expressed agreement or by circumstances in which the wife making the contribution was led to such belief it is a right to recompense in monies only and cannot and does not constitute a right to claim (an) equitable share in the estate of the property concerned.

A husband making contributions in like manner to a property originally acquired by and solely owned as to the legal estate by his wife may . . . subject to a rebuttal of a presumption of advancement which would arise have a like claim to compensation in similar circumstances but would not have a claim to any equitable estate in the property."[135]

If the spouse in whose name a property is held is aware that the other spouse has raised a loan to pay for its purchase and/or carrying out of improvements on it, the property owning spouse may be required to contribute to the discharge of the loan, even if the spouse who raised it was not led to believe that such a contribution would be made.

In *Heavey v. Heavey*,[136] the property, which was purchased in 1967 and was held to be in the full beneficial ownership of the wife, was converted into luxury flats by the husband at a cost of £16,560 which was financed by an overdraft he obtained from the Bank of Ireland. Until May 1973 the husband collected and retained most of the rents obtained from the property and thereafter they were collected by the wife. The wife applied for an account of the rents and profits received by the husband and then claimed the sum of £23,041 being that part of the rent received by him that had not been paid over to her. At the date of the court proceedings, a sum of £7,385 was still payable by the husband to the bank, being money originally raised by him to purchase the premises in his wife's name. The court held the husband to be entitled to credit against the rents which he collected for the amount which he owed to the bank in connection with both the purchase and conversion of the premises, together with the probable amount of interest which he had to pay. Kenny J. giving judgement stated that:

"It is a presumption of law that when a husband makes a purchase of property or transfers money or securities into the name of his wife solely, it is intended as a gift to her absolutely at once and there is no resulting trust in his favour . . . the same principle applies when a husband expends his own money on the property of his wife even if that property has been transferred by him to her. It is, however, not an absolute rule of law that the wife gets the benefit of the expenditure, it is a presumption only which may be rebutted by evidence so that if the wife leads the husband to believe

---

135. *Ibid.*, at p. 205.
136. *Supra.*

that money which he spends on improving her property will be repaid to him out of the rents of the property when improved he has a valid claim to be reimbursed out of the rents."[137]

In the absence of a husband being so led he had no claim to reimbursement. Kenny J. continued:

"This principle, however, does not apply when the husband has borrowed the money to purchase the property or to carry out the improvements. If the wife is aware that the husband is borrowing the money for either of these purposes, it would, in my view, be inequitable for her, when a dispute arises between them, to retain the rents for herself and to refuse to have the outstanding debt incurred by the husband paid out of them. In this case the wife was keeping the husband's books and knew that part of the cost of purchasing the property and the entire cost of converting (it) was being financed by a bank loan given to the husband."[138]

The Supreme Court dismissed an appeal made by the husband against this decision.[139] There was, however, no written judgement delivered by it.

If a site is purchased in the name of one spouse and a family home is built on the site with monies contributed by the other spouse there is considerable judicial conflict as to the approach to be adopted and the principles applicable to determine whether the latter's contribution may give rise to the acquisition of a beneficial interest in the home or alternatively, to a right to reimbursement for monies spent. It is also unclear as to whether a contribution made to the building of a family home on a site owned by the other spouse is a contribution towards the acquisition of the home or merely towards the improvement of the site.

In *E.R. v. M.R.*[140] it was held that the entire beneficial interest in seven acres of land was vested in the wife as she had provided the entire purchase monies for its acquisition, although the husband had been registered as full owner in 1964.[141] In 1968 planning permission was obtained to build a house on the lands and the house was finally completed in December 1971. Carroll J. held, having regard to the contribution made by both spouses to the provision of the home that if the home were "sold tomorrow", the wife would be entitled to two-thirds of the nett proceeds of sale and the husband entitled to one-

---

137. *Ibid.*, at p. 3.
138. *Ibid.*, at p. 4.
139. In July 1976. The perfected order of the Supreme Court did not, however, become available until January 1977.
140. (January, 1981) unreported (H.C.), Carroll J.
141. It is arguable that some beneficial interest in the land should have been held to vest in the husband. Carroll J. dealing with this issue, noted that the wife's contributions towards its acquisition were direct and stated that "at the time the defendant (husband) was not contributing adequately out of his earnings towards the maintenance of his family." Although his contribution was inadequate, and it is clear from the judgement delivered that the wife was the more financially responsible spouse, the husband was, nevertheless, relieving the wife of some expenditure she would otherwise have had to meet. If he had not done so, the wife may not have been able to pay for the land. Consequently, having regard to the judgement of McMahon J. in *R. v. R., supra*, the only authority to which Carroll J. referred in her judgement, the husband it is submitted should have been held to have a beneficial interest in the land proportionate to the contribution made by him. Curiously, the learned judge subsequently adopted such an approach to the husband's claim to a beneficial interest in the family home built on the lands.

third, after first deducting the site value from the purchase money.[142] She did not at any stage consider whether the payments made by the husband could be regarded simply as being in respect of improvements and assumed that he was entitled to a share in any proceeds realised from the sale of the property proportionate to the contribution made by him.[142a]

A totally different approach was adopted by Barron J. in *N.A.D. v. T.D.*[143] In this case, the site on which the family home was built was purchased by the husband in his sole name and the wife was held to have no beneficial interest in it. The husband was held to have contributed £1,950 towards the building of the family home on the site and the wife a sum of £1,200. The trial judge then went on to consider whether the wife's contribution gave her any proportionate interest in the home or entitled her to reimbursement for the monies spent by her. He stated that her contribution related "to the improvement of property which had been acquired by and was solely owned beneficially by her husband"[144] and continued[145] "such contribution would entitle her to recompense in monies only in the event of it being established by her that either by virtue of an express agreement between her and her husband or by other circumstances of which her husband would have been aware she was led to believe that such would be the case."[146] Although she was held to have "contributed a substantial proportion towards the cost of the home",[147] Barron J. dismissed the wife's claim as there was "no evidence whatsoever of any conduct upon the part of the husband which would make it inequitable to allow him to deny his wife's claim."[148]

The approach adopted by Carroll J. in *E.R. v. M.R.* is preferable to that adopted by Barron J. in *N.A.D. v. T.D.* In the latter case the site had been acquired by the husband in 1964 for a sum of £690, which he had borrowed from a bank. He then in the same year obtained a building society loan of £1,500 which was used to both discharge the bank loan and to contribute to the cost of building the home. The total sum borrowed by him of £1,500 was included in the sum of £1,950 which the court held the husband had contributed to the provision of the home. It appears from the judgement delivered that the acquisition of the site, the building of the home and the making of the various payments all took place between December 1963 and December 1964, and it would have been logical to have regarded the various steps taken as a single transaction intended to provide a family home for both spouses. The learned judge cited in his judgement extracts from the judgement delivered by Finlay P. in *W. v. W.* and it is submitted that on the principles enunciated in that case, each spouse should have been held to have a beneficial interest in the

---

142. There was no immediate intention to sell the home. Having regard to the fact that there was a mortgage, Carroll J. stated that as the primary obligation to pay the mortgage rested with the husband, his proportionate interest would increase in accordance with the mortgage payments made by him and the wife's would correspondingly decrease (see p. 11 of judgement). For further reference to a spouse increasing his beneficial interest in a family home by making mortgage repayments (a) after the other spouse has ceased contributing see *A.L. v. J.L., supra,* Finlay P. or (b) after the other spouse's contribution to the household expenses has become "too small to be taken into account" see *Containercare (Ireland) Ltd. v. Wycherley* [1982] I.R. 143, in particular judgement of Carroll J., pp. 151–152. See further *M. O'K. v. M. O'K.* (December, 1982) unreported (H.C.) in which Barron J. followed the approach of Carroll J. in the *Containercare* case.
142a. See also *G.N.R. v. K.A.R., supra.*
143. [1985] 5 I.L.R.M. 153 (H.C.).
144. *Supra* at p. 161.
145. Having cited an extract from the judgement of Finlay P. in *W. v. W., supra.*
146. *Supra* at p. 161.
147. *Ibid.*
148. *Supra,* at p. 163.

property (i.e. both the site and the home) in proportion to the contributions made by each and that the contribution made by the wife should not have been regarded merely as monies expended on improving property owned by the husband.[149]

For a Contribution to be Relevant it must be in Money or Monies Worth

It is clearly established that in order for an indirect contribution to give rise to the acquisition by a wife of a beneficial interest in the family home, it must be a monetary contribution or a contribution in monies worth, such as the work undertaken on the farm in *W. v. W.*[150] or in the public house in *H.D. v. J.D.*[151] In *Conway v. Conway*[152] Kenny J. expressly stated that a wife does not by carrying out "household duties" acquire an interest in the family home and this was reiterated by Finlay P. in *R.K. v. M.K.*[153] in which the wife's claim to a beneficial interest in the home failed. In the latter case Finlay P. acknowledged that "the extent of (the wife's) work in the household and in the care of her children was very considerable" but he continued:

> "Our law does not recognise so far at least a right arising from that type of work to a part ownership of any family or marriage property."[154]

The fact that a husband might have to employ a housekeeper to keep home if his wife did not do such work and that a wife by so doing contributes to the family finances, thereby saving the husband from expenditure he might otherwise have to meet, is not regarded as a contribution to household expenses which can be related to the purchase of the family home or any other property.[155]

---

149. Barron J. sought to determine whether the wife had a beneficial interest in the property by way of a constructive trust. For further comment on the approach adopted see P. O'Connor (1984) 3 I.L.T. (n.s.) 179 and J.C. Brady, *supra* (1984) 6 D.U.L.J. at p. 21 *et seq.*

150. *Supra.*

151. *Supra.* Actual physical building of the house can be regarded as a contribution in monies worth — see, for example, *N.A.D. v. T.D., supra.*

152. *Supra,* see p. 492 *ante.*

153. (October, 1978) unreported (H.C.).

154. See p. 9 of judgement.

155. See further P. O'Connor, "Indirect Contributions and the Acquisition of a Beneficial Interest in Property" (1984) 3 I.L.T. (n.s.), 40.

The approach adopted by the Irish courts to the relevance of a wife's work in the home as a contribution to its acquisition is identical to that adopted by the English and Northern Ireland courts in determining cases under section 17 of the Act of 1882. It is, however, submitted that in this area it is open to the Irish courts without statutory intervention to interpret the law differently and that having regard to the provisions of Article 41 of the Constitution it is arguable that there is a duty imposed on the courts to do so. Article 41.2 expressly recognises "that by her life within the home, woman gives to the State a support without which the common good cannot be achieved" and requires the State "to ensure that mothers shall not be obliged by economic necessity to engage in labour to the neglect of their duties in the home." In *DeBurca & Anderson v. A.G.* [1976] I.R. 385 (S.C.) it was stated by O'Higgins C.J. that "some preferential treatment of women citizens seems to be contemplated by the Constitution" [1976] I.R. at p. 61 and by Walsh J. that Article 41.2 "makes special provision for the economic protection of mothers who have home duties" [1976] I.R. at p. 70 (see further pp. 39 *ante et seq*). Moreover, McCarthy J. in *Weir v. Somers* [1983] I.R. at p. 126 stated that "the judicial branch of Government of the State must . . . recognise its duty under Article 41 and seek to achieve the objectives as set out in that Article," and Finlay C.J. in *K.C. & A.C. v. An Bord Uchtála* [1985] 5 I.L.R.M. at p. 317 referred to the duty of the Supreme Court as "an organ of the State" to implement the provisions of Articles 41 and 42. The failure of the courts to date to regard a wife's work in the home as of sufficient value to be recognised as an indirect contribution to its acquisition, it could be argued amounts to a failure by the judiciary to recognise the duty imposed on them to achieve the objectives set out in Article 41. Whilst it is unlikely that the courts will at some future date change their approach by the adoption of reasoning based on such judicial self criticism, it is possible that they may, by reliance on Article 41.2

If the alleged contribution made by a wife derives from work undertaken in a husband's business for which she received no pay, in order to constitute a valid contribution which can result in the acquisition by her of a beneficial interest in property acquired by the husband with the proceeds or profits of the business, the work undertaken must be such "as could attract remuneration" or which constitutes "an identifiable taking part" in the business.[156] In *R.K. v. M.K.* the carrying out each week of the family banking by the wife was not regarded as such. This involved calculating, writing out and cashing at the bank a cheque signed by the husband to cover wages, household expenses, spending money for the wife and, on some occasions, cash to discharge bills connected with the business.

In *D.McC. v. M.McC.*[157] referring to the type of direct or indirect contribution to the purchase price or towards discharging mortgage instalments made by a wife which will result in the acquisition by her of a beneficial interest in the family home, Henchy J. stated that it must be "of such a size and kind as will justify the conclusion that the acquisition of the home was achieved by the joint efforts of the spouses."[158] In the subsequent case of *C.R. v. D.R.*,[159] Lynch J. stated that a wife's indirect contribution will result in her becoming entitled to a beneficial interest in property acquired by a husband if it "significantly assists in the acquisition of the property".[160] Referring to work undertaken by a wife in her husband's business, he stated:

> "If a wife by her work in the husband's enterprise such as a farm or a business significantly increases the family income from such enterprise, thus increasing the funds available to the husband to enable him to pay for the acquisition of the property, she will probably become entitled to a (beneficial) interest . . . in the property in the absence of any express or implied agreement to the contrary and will certainly become so entitled if there was any understanding, however informal, between the husband and the wife to that effect."[161]

In this case, the husband who was a vet, purchased a family home and four and a half acres of land attached to it in his sole name in 1960, raising a bank loan for the purchase monies which was fully discharged by him by 1966. The husband suffered from alcoholism and during the time when the loan was being discharged, the wife frequently accompanied him in his car when carrying out his work so as to ensure that he would not drink. The wife also "looked after such activities"[162] as related to the land, which included "milking one cow and at times two cows, sending about 2 gallons of milk daily to the local creamery which was exchanged for butter or other dairy products."[163] She also sometimes kept poultry and between 2–5 calves. Lynch J. stated that the contributions made by the wife were "not comparable to the contributions which the wife of

---

and the constitutional duty to "protect the family", hold that a wife by her work in the home, acquires some proprietary or beneficial interest in it. To date no written judgement has been delivered by the Irish courts in a case determined under section 12 in which such an approach has been judicially considered or discussed.

156. *R.K. v. M.K., supra.* See p. 9 of judgement.
157. [1986] 6 I.L.R.M. 1 (S.C.).
158. *Ibid.*, at p. 2.
159. (April, 1984) unreported (H.C.).
160. See p. 14 of judgement.
161. See p. 15 of judgement.
162. See p. 9 of judgement.
163. *Ibid.*

a farmer whose sole means of livelihood is farming would make from similar activities".[164] They were, he held, "so small relevant to the monies which . . . the husband was earning" that they could not be regarded as entitling her to any share "in the property, the acquisition of which was directly financed by the husband's earnings."[165] Moreover, although the wife was held to have been of great help to the husband in relation to his veterinary practice it was "not clear that the husband would not have been able to earn the necessary funds to acquire the property if his wife had devoted her energies solely to the home".[166] As a consequence, it was held that part of the monies earned by the husband as a vet could not be regarded as being earned by the wife.

It is obvious that if the indirect contribution made by a wife to the acquisition of a family home is of no significance, it cannot be relied upon by her to claim a beneficial interest in it. As, however, the contribution made by a wife only entitles her to a proportionate interest in the home, it is not clear from this decision as to when a small contribution becomes so small as to be insignificant.[167] A curious aspect of the decision in *C.R. v. D.R.* is that the husband during cross examination gave evidence that when he acquired the family home he regarded himself as acquiring it as the family home and regarded the wife "as a partner and the house as jointly owned."[168] Despite this uncontradicted statement of the husband, the wife was held to have no interest in the property, as her contribution to its acquisition was not significant, Lynch J. stating that he had to decide the case "on the basis of the true facts and the law applicable thereto."[169] In reality, the decision made did not accord with the true facts, imputing to the husband an intention as to the ownership of the home which was the exact opposite of what he actually intended and of what he expressly stated he intended in the court proceedings held to determine the extent of each spouse's proprietary interest in it.

LEGAL TITLE HELD IN NAME OF BOTH SPOUSES

If the legal title to the family home or other property is purchased by spouses in both their names[170] and if both make a financial contribution towards its

---

164. See p. 16 of judgement.
165. *Ibid.*
166. See p. 17 of judgement. See also *A.H. v. A.H., supra*, in which Lynch J. held the assistance given by the wife to the husband in his business to be "minimal and no more than one would expect any spouse to perform" (see p. 5 of judgement).
167. In this context it could be argued that the wife's contribution in *H.D. v. J.D., supra* (discussed on p. 498 *ante*) was too insignificant to have given rise to the acquisition by her of an interest in the original family home. The same argument could apply in *M.B. v. E.B., supra* (see p. 500 *ante*) in which Barrington J. expressly stated that the indirect contribution made by the wife must have had a "minimal effect" in reducing the capital sum outstanding on the mortgage. See, however, *E.R. v. M.R., supra*, in which it was held by Carroll J. that the husband had made no contribution to the acquisition of the site on which the family home was built as he had not contributed "adequately out of his earnings towards the maintenance of the family" (see p. 7 of judgement) and *Containercare (Ireland) Ltd. v. Wycherley, supra*, at p. 152 in which Carroll J. held that after the severance of the joint tenancy the husband's "contributions to the household expenses" were "too small to be taken into account" in determining the extent of his beneficial interest in the family home. See further, M. Cooney, "Wives, Mistresses and Beneficial Ownership" (1979) 14 I.J. (n.s.), 1, in which the author states that "the contribution must be significant" and that "this point is implicit" in *R.K. v. M.K., supra*.
168. See p. 12 of judgement.
169. *Ibid.*
170. Property may be acquired by way of a joint tenancy or a tenancy in common. See J.C.W. Wylie, *Irish Land Law, supra*, at p. 357 *et seq.*

acquisition, the purchase in joint names is regarded as evidence of the parties' intention that each acquire an equal beneficial interest in it.[171] Each will be held to have such an interest in the event of a dispute between them as to its ownership in the absence of proof of a contrary agreement or intention.[172] If the purchase money is provided by the wife alone, the law presumes a resulting trust in her favour and the courts may hold the entire beneficial interest to be vested in her. If the purchase money is provided by the husband alone, the law presumes by application of the doctrine of advancement that the husband intended to vest a beneficial interest in his wife and, in the event of a dispute, the parties may be held to own the family home or other property in equal shares. Both the presumption of resulting trust and the presumption of advancement are rebuttable by evidence of the spouses having a contrary intention at the time of the acquisition of the property.[173] Both presumptions have been judicially considered in a number of recent disputes determined under section 12 of the Act of 1957 as to the ownership of family homes held by spouses in their joint names.

In *B. v. B.*[174] the wife claimed to be entitled to the sole beneficial ownership of the family home and farm land attached to it, although the property was registered as being jointly owned by herself and her husband. The wife's mother had purchased a house for the parties in their joint names for a sum of £20,000 two years after their marriage. Six years later having sold the house the £20,000 realised from its sale was used to purchase the disputed property together with an additional £2,500 also provided by the wife's mother. The wife's mother stated in evidence that she intended the original house acquired by them to be the "joint property" of her daughter and the husband and that she did not want the daughter's husband "to be dependent on his wife".[175] Finlay P. held both the original family home and the disputed property to be in the joint beneficial ownership of the parties and rejected the contention that the wife's mother's intention to benefit the husband should be construed "as an intention to do so, so long as the marriage lasted."[176]

The decision in the preceding case can be contrasted with that given in *M.O'K. v. M.O'K.*[177] The first home acquired by the parties was placed in their joint names, the entire monies for the purchase of the home having been provided by the wife's father. He had given each of his children a home on their marriage and the father's evidence was that he told his daughter that the house was a present for her and had advised her not to put it into joint names. However,

---

171. In *Containercare (Ireland) Ltd. v. Wycherley, supra* at p. 151 Carroll J. stated "A decision was made by the (spouses) that the premises would be taken in their joint names and a joint tenancy created. This is evidence of an agreement or arrangement which is inconsistent with monies paid by the (husband) being appropriated to a proportionate share of the premises for his benefit and with monies paid directly or indirectly by the (wife) being appropriated to a proportionate share for her benefit." See also *P. v. P.* (March, 1980) unreported (H.C.), Barrington J.
    A severance of the joint tenancy can result in the contribution made after severance being apportioned. See footnote 167 *ante*.
172. See *Containercare (Ireland) Ltd. v. Wycherley, supra; P. v. P., supra.* See, however, *M. O'K. v. M. O'K., supra*, in which a home was purchased in joint names, the wife contributing a sum of £8,000 at the time of the purchase and the husband assuming responsibility for mortgage instalments. The husband was held only entitled to a beneficial interest in it proportionate to the contribution made by him.
173. See *Heavey v. Heavey, supra; Conway v. Conway, supra; W. v. W., supra; C.C. v. S.C., supra; J.C. v. J.H.C.* (August, 1982) unreported (H.C.); *R.F. v. M.F.* (December, 1982) unreported (H.C.); (October, 1985) unreported (S.C.).
174. (July, 1978) unreported (H.C.).
175. See p. 4 of judgement
176. See also *A.L. v. J.L., supra*, and footnote 125 *ante*.
177. *Supra.*

the husband was anxious that his name appear on the title deeds and the father acceded to the wife's request to so arrange matters. The husband alleged, and the wife denied, that there was an express agreement that the house would be owned beneficially between them. Barron J. held that as the father had intended the monies provided by him for the acquisition of the home to benefit his daughter only, the placing of the home in joint names had not resulted in the acquisition by the husband of a beneficial interest in it. The wife was, therefore, held to be entitled to the entire beneficial interest in the property.[178]

In *J.C. v. J.H.C.*[179] the family home was purchased in the joint names of the husband and wife, the monies being provided entirely by the husband. The wife said that she understood that at the time the home was purchased it was to belong to both of them in equal shares. The husband said that he merely intended to ensure that if he died first, the wife would be the sole person entitled to the property. Finding that the property was jointly owned by the parties, Keane J. stated that it was "quite plain" that the husband intended to benefit the wife and that the evidence of the parties had "overwhelmingly reinforce(d) the presumption of advancement which would arise if there were no other evidence pointing to the intention of the parties."[180]

In *R.F. v. M.F.*[181] the circumstances surrounding the acquisition of the property in dispute were held to rebut the presumption of advancement. In 1976 a property was purchased by the husband for use as a family home in the joint names of himself and his wife with monies provided by him alone. At the time of the purchase of the property the husband and wife had been living apart for over 10 years, although they had maintained regular contact with each other, the husband having dinner in his wife's home three to four nights per week. The wife's claim to one half of the beneficial interest in the property failed. The husband gave evidence that he purchased the property in joint names as the wife promised to return to reside with him if he did so. She did not implement her promise and the court ruled that as the conveyance had been made on this definite condition with which the wife had failed to comply, she held her share in the home as a trustee for the husband, in whom was vested the entire beneficial interest. The Supreme Court, on appeal, upheld this decision.[182]

In holding that the presumption of advancement had been rebutted, D'Arcy J., in the High Court, noted that in England the presumption is so easily rebutted "it had ceased to exist altogether, except in exceptional circumstances" and that the basis for this was "the changed nature of social conditions". He continued stating:

---

178. See also *J.M.H. v. J.P.H.* (January, 1983) unreported (H.C.). Ellis J. at pp. 29–30 of judgement held that the wife had a 50% beneficial interest in land, the legal title of which she held with her husband in their joint names. Most of the purchase money for the lands was provided by the wife's father.

179. *Supra*.

180. See p. 4 of judgement. See also *J.M.H. v. J.P.H., supra* at pp. 30–34 of judgement, in which it was decided that the wife possessed a 50% beneficial interest in land held to have been fully paid for by the husband, Ellis J. being of the opinion that by registering the land in their joint names, the husband intended to benefit the wife. The husband in his evidence had explained that he had registered the lands in their joint names as his solicitor had advised him to do so "for the benefit of his family".

181. (December, 1982) unreported (H.C.).

182. (October, 1985) unreported (H.C.). Henchy J. delivered the judgement of the court. The other members of the court were Finlay C.J. and Hederman J. The decision was unanimous and no other judgement was delivered.

"I don't think social conditions here have changed yet to justify the view of
the House of Lords ... the law of presumption of advancement still exists,
but it has been whittled down in this country."[183]

Whether or not the presumption has been whittled down remains to be determined in future cases. It was suggested by the Law Reform Commission in 1981
that, as the presumption of advancement applies only where a husband purchases
property in the name of his wife and does not apply where a wife purchases property in the name of her husband it "may well involve discrimination proscribed by the Constitution."[184] To date, however, no detailed consideration has
been given by the courts to this issue.[185]

Finally, in *J.M.H. v. J.P.H.*[186] Ellis J. took the view that if a wife alleges that
the entire purchase price to acquire a property was provided either by her or on
her behalf, if the court disbelieves the claim made by her and the legal title of
the disputed property is held by her jointly with her husband, she cannot rely
on the presumption of advancement to claim a joint beneficial interest in it, but
will only be entitled to a share in proportion to the actual contribution made by
her or on her behalf. In this case the wife claimed a 50% beneficial interest in a
public house/guest house and a field all acquired for a sum of £6,000, alleging
that her father had provided the entirety of the purchase money with the
intention of "investing it wisely to provide for the (wife), her husband and the
children." The court disbelieved the wife's evidence and accepted the husband's
evidence that he had contributed £4,000 towards the acquisition of the property
and that £2,000 had been contributed by the wife's father, as he knew the wife
wished to acquire the field that was purchased as part of the transaction. In
holding that a one-third beneficial interest in the properties was vested in the
wife, Ellis J. stated that the properties:

> "were conveyed to the plaintiff (wife) and defendant as joint purchasers and
> tenants in fee simple. Any apportionment would therefore *prima facie* entitle
> each to a moiety. If, however, the extent of the financial contributions of
> the purchasers to the purchase price is in issue to determine or ascertain the
> proper beneficial interest or share of each, then, in my opinion it follows
> that the share of each has to be determined by the extent (to) which it is
> found each have contributed to the purchase price."[187]

If the wife had simply stated that she was entitled to one half of the beneficial
interest in the property and had not raised an issue as to the financial contribution
made to acquire it, it appears she would have succeeded in her claim, as the
presumption of advancement would have been held to apply.

PROPERTY IN HOUSEHOLD ALLOWANCE

If a husband gave his wife housekeeping money out of his own income, any
money not spent by her or any property acquired by her with it, was, at common
law, regarded as belonging to the husband, unless it could be shown that it was
his intention to make a gift to her.[188] The Commission on the Status of Women

---

183. See p. 12 of judgement. See also *J.C. v. J.H.C., supra* at pp. 3–4 of judgement and
A.H. v. A.H., supra, at p. 7 of judgement.
   184. See the Law Reform Commission: *First Report on Family Law* (March, 1981) at
p. 20.
   185. The constitutional issue was not raised or referred to by the Supreme Court in its
judgement in *R.F. v. M.F., supra*.
   186. *Supra*.
   187. See pp. 150–151 of judgement.
   188. *Blackwell v. Blackwell* [1943] 2 All E.R. 579 (C.A.); *Hoddinott v. Hoddinott*
[1949] 2 K.B. 406 (C.A.).

in 1972 recommended that money saved or property bought out of a wife's housekeeping allowance should be treated as belonging to the spouses in equal shares. The Family Law (Maintenance of Spouses and Children) Act, 1976, Sect. 21, implements this recommendation. It provides that

> "Any allowance made by one spouse to the other spouse after the commencement of this Act for the purpose of meeting household expenses, and any property or interest in property acquired out of such allowance, shall, in the absence of any agreement, whether express or implied, between them to the contrary, belong to the spouses as joint owners."

The following points should be noted:

(a) The section applies to a household allowance provided by either spouse.

(b) It only relates to allowances made on or after 6th May 1976, the date when the Act came into force.

(c) Its application can be excluded by an express or implied agreement between the spouses, e.g. a clause in a separation agreement.

(d) If an allowance is made for household expenses, the allowance, any money saved out of it and also any property acquired with it belongs to the spouses as joint owners. Thus, if a wife purchases furniture or a television out of housekeeping money that she has saved, in the absence of a contrary agreement, it will belong to both spouses jointly.

(e) On the death of one spouse it seems that the whole beneficial interest in money and property jointly owned by virtue of this provision, will pass to the surviving spouse, unless the joint interest has been severed by either of the parties.

There are, however, certain ambiguities in the section. For example, what is the meaning of the phrase "an allowance . . . made for the purpose of meeting household expenses."? If a wife is given an allowance every week by her husband, part of which she has to use to pay off mortgage instalments on the matrimonial home, does she thereby acquire an interest in the home? Or is that part of the allowance intended to meet mortgage repayments not made for the purpose of meeting a 'household expense', but rather for meeting the expense of purchasing or acquiring a house?[189] If a wife is given money every week by her husband to meet hire purchase or credit sale instalments payable for carpets or a washing machine, is that an "allowance given to meet a household expense" and will the wife by reason of making such payments acquire an interest in the property, or is she merely acting as the agent of her husband when making the weekly payments? In what circumstances will the court hold an implied agreement excluding the application of the section to exist? Will such an agreement be implied where money from the household allowance is used by the wife to purchase goods or clothes for her own use, or will a husband be held to be the joint owner of such purchases? If a wife uses part of the household allowance to buy a lottery ticket or to play bingo, will a husband be the joint owner of her winnings? Many of these questions will, without doubt, give rise to litigation.

---

189. The English Courts have not, as yet finally determined this question under a similar legislative provision in force there. (See the Married Women's Property Act, 1964, Sect. 1.) In *Tymoszczuk v. Tymoszczuk* (1964) 108 Sol. Jo. 676 it was held that mortgage repayments made by a wife from an allowance given by her husband were not "expenses of the matrimonial home". In *Re Johns Assignment Trusts, Niven v. Niven, supra* this point was referred but not decided. However, Goff J. stated that he must "not be taken as accepting the view that where Sect. 1 (of 1964) does apply, moneys paid to discharge a mortgage in the marital home are not expenses of the matrimonial home . . .".

SUCCESSION ON DEATH

Succession by Will

The Succession Act, 1965, came into force on the 1st of January 1967. It repealed and replaced nearly all the pre-existing succession law[1] and has been described as "a most important part"[2] of family law. In radically changing the law as to succession, the Supreme Court has stated that the Act of 1965 "was designed to strengthen the protection of the family as required by the Constitution."[3] The family referred to in this context is of course the family based upon marriage.

By section 77 of the Act of 1965 any person of sound disposing mind,[4] who has attained the age of eighteen years, or is, or has been married, may dispose of all his property by will.[5] Further, a person under eighteen and unmarried may appoint a guardian of an infant by will if entitled to make such appointment.

Prior to the coming into force of the above Act, a testator had complete freedom of disposition, and thus could disinherit both his wife and children and leave them penniless if he so desired.[6] This freedom of testamentary disposition has now been curtailed by Part IX of the Act.

The Legal Right of a Spouse

Moving the Second Reading of the Succession Bill, 1965 in Dáil Éireann, Mr. B. Lenihan, T.D., the then Minister for Justice, stated that the family provisions of Article 41 of the Constitution "cannot be reconciled with a system of law which allows a man to ignore the mother of his family and to leave his property to strangers".[7] The Act provides that if a testator leaves a spouse[8] and no children, the spouse has a legal right to one-half of the estate;[9] if a testator leaves a spouse and children, the spouse has a legal right to one-third of the estate.[10]

---

1. Save for the Legitimacy Act, 1931, Sect. 9. See *O'B. v. S.* [1984] I.R. 316 (S.C.).
2. By the Supreme Court in *O'B. v. S., supra*, at p. 335.
3. *Ibid*.
4. *In the Goods of Farrell, Deceased* (1954) 88 I.L.T.R. 57 (H.C.); *In the Goods of Mitten, Deceased* (1934) 68 I.L.T.R. 38 (H.C.); *In Bonis Corboy, Leahy v. Corboy* [1969] I.R. 148 (S.C.).
5. For a comprehensive account of the law as to Succession, see R.A. Pearce, *The Succession Act, 1965: A Commentary* (Incorporated Law Society of Ireland, Dublin 1986). See also J.C. Wylie, *Irish Land Law*, Part VI.
6. Since the coming into force of the (Irish) Statute of Distribution, 1695, a testator could deal with his property as he thought fit. Prior to that date there was not complete freedom, the law being governed by the 'custom of Ireland' described in, and abolished by Sect. 10 of the above Statute. The present law of succession in relation to spouses and children is very similar to the 'custom of Ireland' set out in that section. See *In Re Urquhart* [1974] I.R. 197 (S.C.) judgement of Walsh J. at pp. 208–209.
7. Dáil Debates Vol. 215 Col. 2018.
8. The question as to who is a deceased's spouse has given rise to some litigation in circumstances in which a deceased and his first spouse have been divorced in another jurisdiction and the former has married another. See *Bank of Ireland v. Caffin* [1971] I.R. 123 (H.C.) – See footnote 15 below; *Gaffney v. Gaffney* [1975] I.R. 133 (S.C.); See also *In the Matter of N.S.M., deceased* (1973) 107 I.L.T.R. 1 (H.C.). Here the deceased and his first wife were divorced, although at all times domiciled in Ireland. The deceased married a second time and in his will, left nothing to his first wife. She commenced proceedings to obtain her share as a legal right, but the proceedings were compromised. The case in which these matters are recounted, concerned a claim by children of the first wife and the deceased to a share in his estate.
9. Sect. 111(1); See also Sect. 109(2) which states that references to the estate of the testator under Part IX of the Act "Are to all estate to which he was beneficially entitled for an estate or interest not ceasing on his death and remaining after payment of all expenses, debts and liabilities (other than estate duty*) properly payable thereout."
*(See now the Capital Acquisitions Act, 1975 as amended.)
10. Sect. 111(2).

This legal right of a spouse is given priority over devises, bequests and shares on intestacy.[11]

If a devise[12] or bequest[13] to a spouse is said in a will to be in addition to the legal right, the testator is deemed to have made a gift consisting of both the property devised or bequeathed and a sum equal to the value of the share the spouse is entitled to as a legal right.[14] In any other case, a devise or bequest to a spouse is deemed to have been intended by the testator to be in satisfaction of the legal right of the spouse.[15]

If there is a devise or bequest to a spouse in the will of a testator, the spouse may elect to take either that which is left to him by the will or the share to which he is entitled as a legal right.[16] If the spouse fails to elect, he must take under the will and cannot claim any share as a legal right.[17] Where a person dies partly testate and partly intestate, a spouse may elect to take either a share as a legal right or a share under the intestacy, together with any devise or bequest made in the will.[18] In default of election, a spouse is only entitled to take the latter.[19]

The personal representatives of the deceased's estate must notify a spouse in writing of his right of election. The right is not exercisable either after the expiration of six months from the receipt by the spouse of such notification, or one year from the taking out of representation of the deceased's estate, whichever is the later.[20] If a spouse elects to take his share as a legal right, he may further elect to take any devise or bequest made to him less in value than the share in partial satisfaction thereof.[21]

If a spouse having elected in favour of the share to which he is entitled as a legal right dies before receiving such share, the election constitutes a claim against

---

11. Sect. 112.

12. A devise is a gift of real property.

13. A bequest is a gift of personal property e.g. money, furniture or jewellery. A gift of a leasehold interest in property is usually also referred to as a bequest.

14. Sect. 114(1).

15. Sect. 114(2).

16. Sect. 115(1)(a). See *Bank of Ireland v. Caffin* [1971] I.R. 123 (H.C.).

Y was the first wife of the deceased. His marriage to her was dissolved by an English court when both the deceased and Y had an English domicile. Subsequently the deceased married K. The deceased's will contained a bequest of a pecuniary legacy to his second wife, but she, claiming to be the spouse of the deceased, elected to take her legal right to one half of his estate, instead of the legacy. The executors and trustees of the will applied to the court to determine whether Y or K was the spouse of the deceased for the purpose of Part IX of the Act of 1965. The court held that K, the second wife, was the deceased's spouse for the purpose of the Act. See further Chapter 10.

17. Sect. 115(1)(b); See *In Re Urquhart, supra*, in which the Supreme Court decided that the share by way of legal right may not vest in a spouse until he elects to take it. Walsh J. in his judgement at p. 211 stated:

"The right to take the legal share requires a 'taking' to vest the share in the spouse. It may be an actual taking, as by an express election to take it instead of the legacy, or it may be a constructive taking by dealing with the legal share in a manner which is inconsistent with any explanation other than that the spouse, in so dealing with it, has not elected to take the legacy.

See also *Reilly v. McEntee & Murphy* [1984] 4 I.L.R.M. 572 (H.C.).

18. Sect. 115(2)(a).

19. Sect. 115(2)(b).

20. Sect. 115(4). A spouse may exercise the right of election before receiving a notice from the personal representatives – see *J.H. v. W.J.H.* (December, 1979) unreported (H.C.).

21. Sect. 115(3); Sect. 115(5) provides that in the case of a spouse being

"a person of unsound mind, the right of election conferred by this section may, if there is a committee of the spouse's estate, be exercised on behalf of the spouse by the committee by leave of the court which has appointed the committee or, if there is no committee, be exercised by the High Court or, in a case within the jurisdiction of the Circuit Court, by that Court."

the estate which can be enforced by the personal representatives of the deceased elector's estate.[22] If, however, a spouse dies without making any election, the right of election does not survive the spouse's death and cannot be exercised by the spouse's personal representatives for the benefit of the deceased spouse's estate.[23]

The legal right of a spouse may be renounced in an ante-nuptial contract made in writing between the parties to an intended marriage or may be renounced in writing by a spouse after marriage and during the lifetime of the testator, e.g. in a separation agreement.[24] Further, where a testator during his lifetime and prior to the 1st January 1967, has made permanent provision for his spouse, whether under contract or otherwise, all property which is the subject of such provision (other than periodical payments made for her maintenance during his lifetime) must be taken as being given in or towards satisfaction of the share as a legal right of that spouse.[25] The value of property is reckoned as at the date of the making of the provision[26] and if the value is equal to or greater than the legal right, the spouse is not entitled to take any share as a legal right.[27] If the value of the property is less than the legal right, the spouse is only entitled to receive so much of the estate as, when added to the value of the property, is sufficient to make up the full amount of the legal right, as nearly as can be estimated.[28]

Provision for Children[29]

Section 117 of the Act empowers the court, upon an application by or on behalf of a child of a testator,[30] to order such provision to be made for the child out of the estate as the court thinks just, if it is of the opinion that "the testator has failed in his moral duty to make proper provision for the child in accordance with his means whether by will or otherwise."[31] The court must "consider the

---

22. *R.A.H. v. G.A. & J.McC.* (May, 1983) unreported (H.C.).
23. *Reilly v. McEntee & Murphy, supra.*
24. Sect. 113.
25. Sect. 116(1).
26. Sect. 116(2).
27. Sect. 116(3).
28. Sect. 116(4).
29. See generally Fitzpatrick, "The Succession Act, 1965, Section 117" (1976) I.L.T. & S.J. 77, 83, 89, 95, 101; Cooney, "Succession & Judicial Discretion in Ireland: The Section 117 Cases" (1980) 15 Ir. Jur. (n.s.) 62; A. Bacon, "The Rights of Children and the Discretion of the Courts under Section 117 of the Succession Act, 1965" (1983) 77 *Gazette of the Incorporated Law Society of Ireland* 223; R.A. Pearce, *The Succession Act, 1965: A Commentary, supra* at p. 260 *et seq.*
30. See *R.G. v. P.S.G. & J.R.G.* (November, 1980) unreported (H C.) in which Carroll J. held a person is a "testator" for the purposes of section 117 of the Act of 1965 if he makes a valid will in accordance with the statutory provisions even if the will is wholly inoperative due to the sole beneficiary under the will pre-deceasing the testator, resulting in his estate devolving as on intestacy. As a consequence a child of such "testator" may under this section seek a greater share out of a parent's estate than he would be entitled to if the deceased parent had died intestate.
31. Sect. 117(1). See also *F.M. v. T.A.M. and others* (1972) 106 I.L.T.R. 82 in which Kenny J. stated that the 'estate' for the purposes of Part IX of the Act of 1965 does not include immoveable property of which a testator was seized or to which he was entitled outside the State – (at p. 86). However, he stated further on (at p. 87) that in deciding whether a testator has made proper provision in accordance with his means, "the court may have regard to immoveable property outside the Republic of Ireland owned by the testator". The court, therefore, when deciding whether the moral duty has been fulfilled, must take all the testator's property (including immoveable property outside the Republic of Ireland) into account, but if it decides that the duty has not been discharged, the provision for the child is to be made out of the estate excluding that 'immoveable property'.

application from the point of view of a prudent and just parent." It has to take into account the position of each of the children of the testator and any other circumstances which it considers of assistance in arriving at a decision that is "as fair as possible to the child to whom the application relates and to the other children".[32] An order under this section may not, however, affect the legal right of a surviving spouse or, if the surviving spouse is the mother or father of the child, any devise or bequest to the spouse or any share to which the spouse is entitled on intestacy.[33] Thus, if a surviving spouse is a step-parent, an order may not affect his legal right, but may affect any devise or bequest to him or his share on intestacy.[34]

The court under section 117 must decide (i) whether a testator had a moral obligation to make provision for one or more of his children under his will; (ii) if the testator had such an obligation, whether he failed to make proper provision for such child or children in accordance with his means;[35] and (iii) if he so failed, what provision should be made out of the estate.[36]

In *F.M. v. T.A.M. & Ors.*,[37] Kenny J. stated that:

"An analysis of section 117 shows that the duty which it creates is not absolute because it does not apply if the testator leaves all his property to his spouse[37a] ... nor is it an obligation to each child to leave him something. The obligation to make proper provision may be fulfilled by will or otherwise and so gifts or settlements made during the lifetime of the testator in favour of a child or the provision of an expensive education for one child when the others have not received this may discharge the moral duty ... It follows that the relationship of parent and child does not of itself and without regard to other circumstances create a moral duty to leave anything by will to the child".[38]

He held that the question as to whether a parent has a moral duty to make proper provision for a child must be judged by the facts existing at the date of death and must depend upon

"(a) the amount left to the surviving spouse or the value of the legal right, if the survivor elects to take this, (b) the number of the testator's children, their ages and their positions in life at the date of the testator's death, (c) the

32. Sect. 117(2); See also Sect. 63 which provides that advancements made by a deceased to his children may be brought into account in determining a child's share in the estate.
33. Sect. 117(3).
34. See *Falvey v. Falvey* (July, 1983) unreported (H.C.).
35. Examples of cases in which it has been held that the testator did not fail to make proper provision include *In the matter of the Estate of Bessie Elkinson, Decsd. Elkinson v. Jacob & Ors.* (January, 1980) unreported (H.C.); *M.H. & N.McG. v. N.M. & C.M.* [1983] 3 I.L.R.M. 519 (H.C.).
36. See *In the matter of the Estate of Henry Dowse, Decsd, Walsh v. A.I.B. and Ors.* (March, 1977) unreported (H.C.); See also *Woods & Ors. v. Dowd & Ors.* (May, 1975) unreported (H.C.); *L. v. L.* [1978] I.R. 288 (H.C.); *M.P.D. & Ors. v. M.D.* [1981] 1 I.L.R.M. 179 (H.C.); *M.F.H. & Ors. v. W.B.H.* (March, 1983) unreported (H.C.); *D. McN. v. B.C. & P. McE.* (February, 1984) unreported (H.C.); *N. O'H. v. G.R.* (Nov. 1985) unreported (H.C.).
37. (1972) 106 I.L.T.R. 82.
37a.This is not strictly accurate, as if a surviving spouse is a step parent an order made under section 117 may not affect his legal right but may affect a specific devise or bequest, i.e. if a husband left his entire property to a second wife, children of his first marriage could claim a portion of that property in a section 117 claim. See *Falvey v. Falvey, supra*.
38. *Supra* at p. 86. See also *In the matter of N.S.M. Deceased* (1973) 107 I.L.T.R. 1 (H.C.); *McNally, Decd., Jennings v. Clancy* (1974) 108 I.L.T. & S.J. 227 (H.C.); *Bray v. Bray* (February, 1977) unreported (H.C.); *In the matter of the Estate of Henry Dowse, Walsh v. A.I.B. and Ors.* (March, 1977) unreported (H.C.); *M.F.H. & Ors. v. W.B.H.* (March, 1983) unreported (H.C.).

means of the testator, (d) the age of the child whose case is being considered and his or her financial position and prospects in life and (e) whether the testator has already in his lifetime made proper provision for the child."[39]

The fact that a child contributed financially to a parent, looked after her interests for many years and helped in the upkeep of the parents' home has also been held to give rise to a moral duty.[40] It has been emphasised that the duty is not to make "adequate provision" but to make "proper provision in accordance with the testator's means."[41] Further, its existence must be decided by objective considerations having regard to the value of the entire estate at the date of the testator's death and the overall circumstances of each of the children of the testator.[42] The court must decide whether the duty exists and the opinion of the testator that he was not under any duty is not decisive.[43] Nevertheless, the court may support a testator's view that he had no moral duty to provide for all or some of his children having regard to their particular circumstances and it has been emphasised that section 117 does not oblige a parent to leave something by will to each of his children.[44]

The fact that a court finds a parent in breach of his duty does not of necessity mean that a parent is blameworthy. It is possible, for a will made by a testator, to be completely overtaken by events, for example, by a sudden and dramatic increase in the testator's wealth prior to his death.[45]

If a court decides that a testator had a moral duty and has failed to fulfil it, it must decide what provision to make for the applicant child out of the estate from the point of view of a prudent and just parent. It has been held that a prudent and just parent when making his will would take into account all his moral obligations and not just those that arise under the Succession Act.[46] Such obligations may require the provision of support for a testator's dependent parents or for dependent brothers, sisters, nephews or nieces. They may also extend to making provision for a testator's illegitimate children or for a second spouse, in the latter instance, even if the testator's second marriage is invalid. Thus, the court must have regard to such obligations when deciding whether the provision that has been made is proper and upon holding that it is not, when determining what provision should be made.[47]

The section confers on the court a wide discretionary power to reconstruct a

---

39. *Supra* at p. 87.

40. *In the Estate of Matilda McGarry Decsd., McGarry v. Byrne* (November, 1978) unreported (H.C.).

41. See *In the matter of the Estate of Henry Dowse, Walsh v. A.I.B. & Ors., supra*, where Hamilton J. held that the provision made by the deceased for his daughter was "adequate" but not "proper provision according to his means". See also *R.G. v. P.S.G. and J.R.G., supra*, where Carroll J. emphasized that "adequacy is not the test. There must be proper provision in accordance with the testator's means".

42. See, in particular, *M.P.D. & Ors. v. M.D., supra*, at p. 188.

43. *F.M. v. T.A.M., supra; In the matter of N.S.M. Deceased, supra*. See also *In the matter of J.R.: J.R. v. J.R.* (November, 1979) unreported (H.C.); *Falvey v. Falvey, supra*.

44. See *M.H. & N.McG. v. C.M.* [1983] 3 I.L.R.M. 519 (H.C.) in which Barron J. held a father did not fail in his moral duty when making no provision out of his estate for his two daughters and effectively leaving his entire estate to his two sons. The two sons for their livelihood were dependent on their continued involvement in their late father's business, whereas the daughters' livelihood was not so dependent.

45. *Woods & Ors. v. Dowd & Ors., supra*.

46. *L. v. L.* [1978] I.R. 288 (H.C.); *M.P.D. & Ors. v. M.D., supra; L. v. L.* [1984] 4 I.L.R.M. 607 (H.C.).

47. *L. v. L.* [1978] *supra; J.H. & C.D.H. v. A.I.B. & Ors.* (November, 1978) unreported (H.C.); *M.P.D. & Ors. v. M.D., supra; L. v. L.* [1984], *supra; D.McN. v. B.C. & P.McE., supra*.

testator's will in order to make proper provision for his children.[48] In deciding what provision the court should make, regard must be had to the value of the entire estate not only at the date of death but also at the date of the court hearing.[49] The section does not require that equal provision be made for each of the testator's children. The court may order that one child receive a greater share of a parent's estate than the other due to the former's particular or special circumstances or needs[50] and may take into account the desire of a parent to favour one child over another.[51] Moreover, the court is not required when dividing an estate to confer on a child an absolute interest in part of it. It may, if it deems it prudent, just and fair, grant a right of residence in or a life estate in property, such as the family home, or place property in trust for the benefit of one or more children, even if such children are over 18 years of age[52] and financially independent.[53]

An application for provision out of a parent's estate may be made by or on behalf of a child.[54] Section 110 of the Act provides that "in determining any relationship for the purposes of this part[54a] the provisions of the Legitimacy Act, 1931, and of section 26 of the Adoption Act, 1952, shall apply as they apply in relation to succession on intestacy." Consequently, an application may be made under section 117 for the benefit of children adopted under the Adoption Acts, 1952–76,[55] and children legitimated under the Legitimacy Act, 1931. There is no express reference in the Act to the illegitimate child and to date no written judgement has been delivered by the courts determining whether an application can be made on behalf of such child under this provision. It is clear, however, that the Supreme Court in its recent decision in *O'B. v. S.*[56]

---

48. See, however, *Woods and Ors. v. Dowd and Ors., supra*, where Parke J. stated "(Counsel for the defendant) argued . . . that the court should disturb or interfere with the provisions of a will to the minimum extent necessary to make provision for a child or children claiming under the section. I accept at once that this is a sound principle, and one which can and ought to be applied to the majority of cases which have arisen and will arise under the section."
See also *M.F.H. & Ors. v. W.B.H., supra*, where Barron J. stated "Although the court has very wide powers both as to when to make provision for an applicant child and as to the nature of such provision, such powers must not be construed as giving the court power to make a new will for the testator" (at p. 18 of judgement). Nevertheless, it has proved necessary for the court in many cases to change the provisions of a will to such an extent as to render it unrecognisable when compared with the original. See further, *N.O'H. v. G.R.* (November, 1985) unreported (H.C.) where the deceased's son was awarded the entirety of his deceased mother's small estate having been left nothing by her in her will.
49. *M.P.D. & Ors. v. M.D., supra*.
50. See, for example, *In the matter of F.F. Decsd., H.L. v. The Governor and Company of the Bank of Ireland* (July, 1978) unreported (H.C.); *In the estate of Matilda McGarry, Decsd., McGarry v. Byrne, supra; J.H. & C.D.H. v. A.I.B. & Ors., supra; R.G. v. P.S.G. & J.R.G., supra; M.F.H. & Ors. v. W.B.H., supra*.
51. See *E.M. v. S.McG. & Anor.* (July, 1983) unreported (H.C.).
52. See cases cited in footnote 50, above.
53. All of the cases discussed in this section were heard and determined before the Age of Majority Act, 1985, came into force on the 1st of March 1985, reducing the age of majority to 18 years. This Act does not, however, affect the application of this section or the powers of the court to make provision for adult children.
54. See *In the matter of Michael Looney Decsd: O'Connor v. O'Keeffe* (November, 1970) unreported (H.C.); *D. McN. v. B.C. & P.McE., supra*.
54a.Part IX which contains section 117.
55. See *F.M. v. T.A.M., supra*. See also the Adoption Act, 1952, Sect. 26.
56. *Supra*.

did not envisage the possibility of children born outside marriage being entitled to make such application.[57]

The right to make an application is not limited to minor children but extends to all children of the testator, including children over 18 years of age and married.[58] An application may also be made on behalf of a child of the testator, conceived prior to his death but born thereafter.[59]

In *F.M. v. T.A.M. and others*,[60] a testator left all his property upon trust for his wife for life and after her death for two nephews. He had one child, an adopted son (the plaintiff) who was at the time of the testator's death thirty-two years of age and married with two children. The testator had made no provision for the plaintiff prior to his death and left him nothing in his will. The High Court held that the testator had failed in his moral duty to make proper provision by his will for the plaintiff and ordered that he be given one half of the testator's estate.[61]

In *In the matter of N.S.M. deceased*,[62] the court held that a testator, who had left a substantial estate, had failed in his moral duty to make proper provision for two married daughters (thirty and twenty-five years of age respectively) and for one son (twenty-nine years of age) and went on to make appropriate provision for them.

An application for an order under section 117 must be made within twelve months from the first taking out of representation of the deceased's estate. The personal representatives of the deceased are placed under no obligation to inform children of the deceased of their right to make such an application, or of the time within which such an application must be made.[63]

Restrictive Clauses in Legacies and Trusts

A testator when making a disposition in a will cannot interfere with the parental right to determine a child's religious education. In *Burke and O'Reilly v. Burke and Quail*[64] a testator by her will left the residue of her property upon trust for the purpose of maintaining and educating G[65] in Ireland and bringing him up as a Roman Catholic. A direction in her will that the selection of a Catholic school for G was to be at the absolute discretion of the trustees was held to be inoperative as it "would override the sacred parental authority and defy the parental right and duty of education under Article 42 of the Constitution".[66]

In *Re Blake, deceased*,[67] a trust was set up, the income of which was to be

---

57. See further p. 15 *ante* and pp. 596 & 624 *post*. See, however, the Law Reform Commission, *Report on Illegitimacy* (1982), pp. 45–46, where it is suggested that by virtue of the phraseology of Sect. 110 of the 1965 Act, an illegitimate child may be entitled to apply for proper provision out of his mother's estate under Sect. 117 if the mother leaves no legitimate children. See further the Status of Children Bill, 1986, as initiated, which proposes in Part V to extend the right to make a section 117 application to children who are illegitimate under existing law.
58. See footnote 53 above. See also *M. O'H. v. G.R., supra*.
59. Sect. 3(2).
60. *Supra*.
61. Excluding immoveable property in England which was included in the estate. See footnote 31 above.
62. *Supra*.
63. See *M.P.D. & Ors. v. M.D. and M.S.D. v. M.D.* [1981] 1 I.L.R.M. 179 (H.C).
64. [1951] I.R. 216 (H.C.).
65. G. was the son of a Protestant father and Catholic mother.
66. As this was a condition subsequent its invalidity did not prevent G. from benefiting under the will.
67. [1955] I.R. 89 (H.C.).

applied for the benefit of the testator's grandchildren, subject to the condition that they be brought up in the Roman Catholic faith. If they were not so brought up, the trust was to fall into residue. The condition was held to be void as an unlawful infringement of the parental right to determine a child's education. Dixon J. stated that:

> "any attempt to restrict or fetter that right would be contrary to the solemnly declared policy and conceptions of the community as a whole".

In conclusion, a condition in a legacy that totally restricts a party's right to marry will also be declared void, whilst a partial restraint on marriage may be permitted.[68]

Revocation of Wills and Subsequent Marriage

Under section 85(1) of the Act a will is revoked by the subsequent marriage of the testator, "except a will made in contemplation of that marriage, whether so expressed in the will or not".[69]

Intestate Succession[70]

If a person dies intestate after 1st January 1967, leaving a spouse and no issue, the spouse is entitled to the entire estate.[71] If the intestate leaves both a spouse and issue, the spouse takes two-thirds of the estate and the remainder is distributed among the issue.[72] "Issue" may include both legitimated and adopted children but has been held by the Supreme Court in *O'B. v. S.* to exclude illegitimate children.[73] If the intestate leaves issue only, the estate is distributed among the issue.[73a]

If distribution is to take place among the issue, if the issue are in equal degree of relationship to the deceased, the distribution is in equal shares among them, if they are not it is *'per stirpes'*.[74] If an intestate leaves neither spouse nor issue,

---

68. There is extensive case law on this — see Wylie, *supra*, pp. 168–169. See also *Ryan v. A.-G.* [1965] I.R. 294 (S.C.) in which "the right to marry" was said to be one of the personal rights arising out of Art. 40.3.

69. For a general account of the Law of Revocation see Wylie, *supra*, pp. 666-669. See also *In the Goods of John Baker Decd.* (March, 1985) unreported (H.C.).

70. For the history of intestate succession in Ireland see *ibid*, chap. 15.

71. Sect. 67(1). See *Gaffney v. Gaffney, supra*, where the intestate's first wife was declared the lawful spouse of her husband at the date of his death, the parties' divorce not being recognised in this country. As a consequence the 'wife' of his second marriage had no rights of succession to the Estate of the intestate. See further Chapter 10.

72. Sect. 67(2). By the Adoption Act, 1952, Sect. 26(1) if an adopter or an adopted person or any other person dies intestate in respect of any property after the making of an adoption order, the property devolves as if the adopted person were the child of the adopter born in lawful wedlock. This does not apply to property subject to an entailed interest under a disposition made before the order. See further the remaining sub-section of Sect. 26. Sect. 63 of the Act of 1965 provides that advancements made by a deceased to his children may be brought into account in determining a child's share in the estate.

See also *Application of Meade* [1971] I.R. 327 (H.C.). In this case the wife of an intestate was authorised to use part of her children's share in the estate for the provision of maintenance for the children.

73. See p. 624 *post* and also Part V of the Status of Children Bill, 1986, as initiated, which proposes to extend to children who are illegitimate under existing law rights to intestate succession under section 67 of the Act of 1965 similar to those which currently vest in legitimate children.

73a. Sect. 67(3).

74. Sect. 67(4); Sect. 3(3) provides that "Where a deceased person's estate or any share therein is to be distributed per stirpes among his issue, any issue more remote than a child of the deceased shall take through all degrees, according to their stocks, in equal shares if more than one, the share which the parent of such issue would have taken if living at the death of the deceased, and no issue of the deceased shall take if the parent of such issue is living at the death of the deceased and so capable of taking."

his estate is distributed between his parents in equal shares, but if one parent only survives the intestate, that parent takes the whole estate.[75] Next in line, if none of the above survive an intestate, are his brothers and sisters, among whom the estate must be distributed in equal shares. If a brother or sister does not survive the intestate, the surviving children of the former, where any other brother or sister survives, take in equal shares that part of the estate that their parent would have taken.[76] If no brother or sister survives, the estate is distributed in equal shares among the children of the intestate's brothers and sisters.[77] In the event of the deceased being survived by none of the above, the estate is distributed between his next of kin,[78] and in default of next-of-kin, the state may take it "as ultimate intestate successor".[79] Finally, the Act provides that descendants and relatives conceived before an intestate's death but born alive thereafter, are to be regarded as having been born in the lifetime of the deceased and as having survived him.[80]

Right to Home and Household Goods

If the estate of a deceased person includes a dwelling[81] in which at the time of a deceased's death the surviving spouse was ordinarily resident, the latter may require the personal representatives in writing, to appropriate the dwelling, in or towards satisfaction of his or her share in the deceased's estate.[82] A surviving

---

75. Sect. 68.

76. Sect. 69(1).

77. Sect. 69(2).

78. See Sects. 70–72. See *In the Matter of the Estate of Norman Robert Wilson, Deceased, Eric John Wilson v. The Attorney-General and John Coughlan* (May, 1979) unreported (H.C.). Sect. 71(1) provides that "the person or persons, who at the date of the death of the intestate, stand nearest in blood relationship to him shall be taken to be his next of kin". In this case it was stated that "the legislature intended to include only legitimate blood relations in the ascertainment of next of kin". As a consequence it was held that the maternal cousins of the deceased, who were the nearest surviving "blood" relations of the deceased who died intestate were not entitled to succeed to his estate. This case was appealed to the Supreme Court but the appeal was subsequently withdrawn.

79. Sect. 73(1); but the Minister for Finance may waive this right if he thinks it proper to do so – Sect. 73(2).

80. Sect. 3(2).

81. Dwelling means "an estate or interest in a building occupied as a separate dwelling or a part, so occupied, of any building and includes any garden or portion of ground attached to and usually occupied with the dwelling or otherwise required for the amenity or convenience of the dwelling" – Sect. 56(14).

See further *Hamilton v. Armstrong & Anor.* [1984] 4 I.L.R.M. 306 (H.C.).

82. Sect. 56(1); See also 56(5)(b) and (6) which provides that this right is not exercisable

    (a)   where the dwelling forms part of a building, and an estate or interest in the whole building forms part of the estate;

    (b)   where the dwelling is held with agricultural land an estate or interest in which forms part of the estate;

    (c)   where the whole or a part of the dwelling was, at the time of the death, used as an hotel, guest house or boarding house;

    (d)   where a part of the dwelling was, at the time of the death, used for purposes other than domestic purposes . . .

unless the court, on application made by the personal representatives or the surviving spouse, is satisfied that the exercise of that right is unlikely to diminish the value of the assets of the deceased, other than the dwelling, or to make it more difficult to dispose of them in due course of administration and authorises its exercise.

In *H. v. H.* [1978] I.R. 138 sub nom *In the Matter of J.H. Decsd* (1977) 144 I.L.T.R. 1 (S.C.), it was held that the onus lies upon an applicant to so satisfy the court, that the words "assets of the deceased" refer to *all* the assets of the deceased other than the dwelling house and that the court must be satisfied that *neither* of the specified eventualities is likely to happen (i.e. the word 'or' in the subsection is not disjunctive). For the sequel to this case see footnote 88 *infra*.

spouse may also require the appropriation of any household chattels in or towards satisfaction of such a share.[83] If a spouse's share is insufficient to enable either or both appropriations to be made, the right may also be exercised in relation to the share of an infant for whom that spouse is a trustee.[84] Further, a spouse may require appropriation partly in satisfaction of a share in the deceased's estate and partly in return for a payment of money by the spouse on the spouse's own behalf and that of any infant for whom the spouse is trustee.[85]

While a surviving spouse's right of appropriation still subsists, that spouse may apply to the court, and if the court "is of opinion that in the special circumstances of the case, hardship would otherwise be caused" to the spouse, or the spouse and any children, it may "order that appropriation to the spouse shall be made without the payment of money . . . or subject to the payment of such amount as the court considers reasonable".[86] The court may also make such "further order in relation to the administration of the deceased's estate as may appear to be just and equitable having regard to the provisions of the Act and to all the circumstances."[87]

The personal representatives must notify a spouse of his or her rights of appropriation and, as in the case of the legal right, they are not exercisable later than six months from receipt by a spouse of such notification or one year from the first taking out of representation of a deceased's estate.[88] The above rights arise whether a deceased dies testate or intestate.

Part X of the Act of 1965: Unworthiness to Succeed and Disinheritance

Section 120 of the Act of 1965 sets down various types of persons who are excluded from benefiting from a deceased's estate. A sane person guilty of the murder, attempted murder or manslaughter of the deceased cannot take a share in the deceased's estate, unless a share is left to him by the latter in a will made after the act constituting the offence, and is not entitled to make an application under section 117.[89] A spouse against whom a deceased has obtained a decree of

---

83. Sect. 56(2). Household chattels means "furniture, linen, china, glass, books and other chattels of ordinary household use or ornament and also consumable stores, garden effects and domestic animals, but does not include any chattels used at the death of the deceased for business or professional purposes or money or security for money, Sect. 56(14)."

84. Sect. 56(3).

85. Sect. 56(9).

86. Sect. 56(10)(a) and (b).

87. Sect. 56(10)(c). See further Sect. 56(10)(d). See also *Hamilton v. Armstrong & Anor*, *supra*, where a widow having elected in favour of her legal right to one half of her deceased husband's estate and having applied for an appropriation of the dwelling house under section 56, died shortly after court proceedings were instituted by her asking the court to declare her entitlement to the house and the field surrounding it. The court held that the deceased wife's claim could be maintained by her personal representatives on behalf of her estate as upon the wife applying for the appropriation of the dwelling an "equity arises immediately in her favour" which could be enforced by her personal representatives.

88. Sect. 56(5). See also section 55 which enables a personal representative to appropriate "any part of the estate of a deceased person . . . in or towards satisfaction of any share in the estate". See further *H. v. O.* [1978] I.R. 194 sub nom *C.H. v. D.G. O'D. and Ors.* (1978) 114 I.L.T.R. 9 (S.C.). Whereas the deceased's wife did not succeed under section 56 in having her family home appropriated towards satisfaction of her share in her husband's estate (see *H. v. H.* sub nom *In the Matter of J.H. Decsd., supra*) it was so appropriated as a result of her bringing proceedings to compel the personal representatives to make an appropriation under section 55. The Supreme Court, however, emphasised that a spouse or other beneficiary does not possess any right to compel a personal representative to exercise a power of appropriation under section 55 and stated that the proceedings were misconceived. Nevertheless, it dealt with the application on the basis of the personal representative having chosen to operate the section so as to avoid further litigation between the parties.

89. Sect. 120(1).

divorce *a mensa et thoro*, a spouse who has failed to comply with a decree of restitution of conjugal rights obtained by the deceased, and a spouse guilty of desertion (or constructive desertion)[90] which has continued up to the death, for two years or more, is precluded from taking any share in the estate of the deceased as a legal right or on intestacy.[91] Such a spouse is not prevented from taking a share left to him or her in the will of the deceased. A person who has been found guilty of an offence, against the deceased, or his spouse or child, punishable by imprisonment for a maximum period of at least two years, or by a more severe penalty, is precluded from taking any share as a legal right or from making an application under section 117.[92] If a person is precluded from taking a share in a deceased's estate on one of the above grounds the share is distributed as if that person had died before the deceased.[93]

Section 121 seeks to prevent a spouse, or parent disposing of his property so as to evade the obligations to his spouse and children, imposed upon him by the Act. The section applies to a disposition of property (other than a testamentary disposition or a disposition to a purchaser) under which the beneficial ownership of the property vests in possession in the donee within three years before the death of the person who made it, or on his death or later.[94] If the court is satisfied that such a disposition was made for the purpose of defeating or substantially diminishing the share of the disponer's spouse, whether as a legal right or on intestacy, or the intestate share of any of his children or of leaving them insufficiently provided for, the court may order that all or part of the disposition be deemed a devise or bequest made by will and forming part of the deceased's estate.[95] Such an order may be made regardless of whether the disponer died testate or intestate. To the extent that the court orders, the disposition is deemed never to have had effect and the donee[96] becomes a debtor to the estate for such amount as the court directs.[97] The court may also make any further order as may appear just and equitable, having regard to the provisions and the spirit of the Act and all other circumstances.[98]

An order may be made under this section for the benefit of a spouse, upon application by the spouse or the personal representatives, or for the benefit of a child, upon an application being made under section 117.[99] If, however, an application is made by or on behalf of a child of the disponer, who is also a child

---

90. Sect. 120(3) states that "a spouse who was guilty of conduct which justified the deceased in separating and living apart from him shall be deemed to be guilty of desertion." For a discussion of the meaning of desertion see p. 439 *ante*.

91. Sect. 120(2); This is a further example of the matrimonial offence approach to the problem of marital breakdown.

92. Sect. 120(4).

93. Sect. 120(5). See further, *O'B. v. S.,* (*supra*, at p. 331) where referring to Article 43.1.2 of the Constitution, Walsh J. delivering the judgement of the court stated "It appears to the court that the phrase 'and inherit property' must necessarily be related to the exercise of the power to transfer property by bequest and that what the State has guaranteed in that Article is to pass no law attempting to abolish the general right to inherit property so bequeathed. That does not mean that the State may not, in appropriate cases, prevent the succession to property. In this context, the court draws attention to the provisions of Part X of the Act of 1965 without offering any views whatsoever on its validity."

94. Sect. 121(1); disposition includes a *donatio mortis causa* – Sect. 121(10). See also Sect. 121(8) – if a donee disposes of the property to a purchaser the section then applies to the consideration given by the purchaser.

95. Sect. 121(2). See *M.P.D. and Ors. v. M.D.* and *M.S.D. v. M.D.* [1981] 1 I.L.R.M. 178 (H.C.).

96. Or any person representing or deriving title under him.

97. Sect. 121(3).

98. Sect. 121(4).

99. Sect. 121(5).

of the surviving spouse, no order can be made in respect of a disposition made to the spouse.[100] Further, no order can be made affecting a disposition made in favour of any children of the disponer, if

(a) the spouse of the disponer was dead when the disposition was made, or

(b) the spouse was alive when the disposition was made but was a person who, if the disponer had then died, would have been precluded under any of the provisions of section 120 from taking a share in the estate, or

(c) the spouse was alive when the disposition was made and consented in writing to it.[101]

An application under section 121 must be made within one year from the taking out of representation of a deceased's estate. In *M.P.D. & Ors. v. M.D. and M.S.D. v. M.D.*[102] such an application failed as the proceedings were not instituted within the time stipulated by the Act. In this case the deceased had concluded a separation agreement with his wife, making specific provision for her and the four children of their marriage. Subsequent to the conclusion of the agreement but within three years of his death the deceased had transferred a 50% share in his business to the defendant with whom he was residing and purchased a house in which she was named as a joint tenant. There were two children of the relationship between the deceased and the defendant. Carroll J. concluded that even if the application under section 121 had been brought in time on behalf of the children of the marriage, she would not have set aside the two transactions and included the property in the deceased's estate as "the purpose of the transactions . . . was to provide for the deceased's second family and not necessarily intended to result in diminishing the provision for his children of his wife." The learned judge held that there was "no proof either directly or by inference, that the dispositions were made by the deceased for the purpose of leaving his children by his wife insufficiently provided for."[103]

It is clear from this decision that mere proof that a deceased transferred property to another with whom he was residing or engaged in an extra-marital relationship three years prior to his death will not, of itself, automatically result in the courts setting aside such a transaction so as to incorporate all or part of the transferred property into a deceased's estate.[104]

---

100. Sect. 121(6).
101. Sect. 121(7).
102. [1981] 1 I.L.R.M. 179 (H.C.).
103. *Ibid.*, at p. 185.
104. For a further discussion of section 121 see Sherrin, "Dis-inheritance of a Spouse: A Comparative Study of the Law in the United Kingdom and the Republic of Ireland" (1980) 31 N.I.L.Q. 21.

CRITICISMS AND SUGGESTED REFORMS

There is a notable distinction between the approach of the law and the powers of the courts when questions arise as to the ownership of property during the lifetime of the parties to a marriage and when they arise upon death. During the lifetime of both spouses, subject to certain limited exceptions, the law as to ownership of property applies in the same manner to a married couple as to single people. Ownership is in the main determined by reference to the spouse who contributed the finance used to acquire property.

This emphasis on the origin of the financial contribution has meant that whilst a wife is legally as free as her husband to acquire property, in social reality, the great majority of wives have no real economic independence. Their dependence arises out of the attitude the law takes to the traditional roles that the respective spouses play in the marital relationship.[1] In determining questions as to the ownership of property, the contribution which the majority of wives make towards the acquisition of family assets by their work in the home is wholly ignored. The law fails to recognise, as pointed out in 1972 by the Commission on the Status of Women, that the "property rights of the husband would be less if his wife's services in the home were not available to him"[2] and fails to regard her services as conferring on her any beneficial interest in property acquired by him. Put simply, the present law fails to take into account that marriage is a form of partnership in which the parties play interdependent roles and to which the different contributions of each are of equal importance to the family welfare.[3]

Upon the death of a spouse the law adopts a totally different attitude. The partnership element is then recognised and the right of a spouse to obtain a fixed share in the other's estate is protected. It is arguable that if it is thought just that a spouse should be entitled to a fixed share in the assets of the other spouse upon the latter's death, spouses should as a general principle be similarly entitled to a share in each other's assets during the subsistence of or upon the breakdown of their marriage. Such legal provision, commonly referred to as a system of community of property, is in force in a variety of forms in a number of other countries. In 1972, the Commission on the Status of Women recommended that the desirability of legislation providing for a community of property regime be investigated[4] but no government has acted upon this recommendation.[5] It was again reiterated in 1985 in the *Report of the Joint Oireachtas Committee on Marriage Breakdown.*[6]

---

1. Although "the number of married women in the Irish labour force is increasing, a great majority of married women continue to make their contribution to the economic and social life of the community as housewives. In 1983 the estimated number of married women in the economically active age groups outside the labour force was 524,400 as compared with 127,600 in the labour force, a ratio of 4.1 to 1." — Extract from *Irish Women — Agenda for Practical Action*, Report of a government appointed inter-departmental working party on Women's Affairs and Family Law Reform (Government Publications, February 1985) p. 40.
2. *Report of the Commission on the Status of Women* (Government Publications, December 1972) at p. 177.
3. See also the Law Reform Commission: *First Report on Family Law* (March 1981) at p. 20; *Report of the Joint Oireachtas Committee on Marriage Breakdown* (March 1985) at p. 64.
4. *Report of the Commission on the Status of Women, supra*, p. 178.
5. The Law Reform Commission in the *First Report on Family Law, supra*, in 1981 indicated that it intended to publish a working paper on community of property "in due course" (see p. 21 of report). No such paper has yet been published.
6. See pp. 65–66 of report.

Falling short of the provision of a community of property regime, substantial reforms could be enacted so as to remove many of the anomalies and much of the complexity and uncertainty from the current law:

1. Section 12 of the Act of 1957, can only be utilised to determine property disputes between a "husband and wife" or between a couple who are parties to "an agreement to marry which is terminated".[6a] Thus, such proceedings cannot be commenced to determine a dispute between a couple whose marriage has been annulled by the High Court or terminated by a foreign decree of divorce recognised under Irish law. Section 12 procedure should be extended by statute to the determination of all such proprietary disputes. There is no logical reason for permitting formerly engaged couples to bring proceedings under section 12 whilst prohibiting couples who celebrated a marriage ceremony from doing so, upon their marriage being annulled or validly terminated. A recommendation to so extend the application of section 12 procedure was made by the Law Reform Commission in 1981.[7]

2. The type of order that the court may make in exercise of its jurisdiction under section 12 is uncertain. For example, can it, upon determining that spouses have a joint beneficial interest in the matrimonial home, order that the home be sold and the proceeds divided between the parties? Alternatively, upon holding a spouse to have a one third interest in the home, the value of which for example is assessed at £12,000, can it order the spouse who owns the other two thirds to pay the former £4,000 and upon such payment require the one third share to be transferred to the latter? Both these questions have not as yet been finally determined.[8]

3. The principles of law to be applied by the courts in determining when an indirect contribution by a spouse will be regarded as conferring on that spouse a beneficial interest in the family home or any other property to which such contribution relates should be clarified. Moreover, the artificial distinction made as to the different effect in law of a contribution to the acquisition of property as opposed to the improvement of property should be removed. The current law is unnecessarily complex and the lack of uniformity in judicial interpretation and application of the law can give rise to considerable injustice. In practice, a spouse's possibility of establishing whether he or she has a beneficial interest in a family home or other property often depends not on the application of clearly defined legal principles to a particular set of facts but on the personal approach

---

6a. See the Family Law Act, 1981, Sect. 5. See further p. 72 *et seq ante*.

7. See Law Reform Commission: *First Report on Family Law, supra*, at p. 19.

8. See the English case of *Tunstall v. Tunstall* [1953] 2 All E.R. 319 (C.A.). After this case in England the Matrimonial Causes (Property & Maintenance) Act, 1958, was enacted section 7 of which provides that "for the avoidance of doubt it is hereby declared that any power conferred by (section 17 of the Act of 1882) to make orders with respect to any property includes power to order a sale of the property". See further *Bothe v. Amos* [1976] Fam. 46 (C.A.).

In Ireland in practice a spouse who seeks an order pursuant to section 12 of the Act of 1957 as to the extent of his beneficial interest in property may in addition, seek an order for sale or partition of such property under the Partition Act, 1868/1876. See Wylie, *Irish Land Law, supra*, p. 369. However, in *O'D. v. O'D.* (November, 1983) unreported (H.C.) Murphy J. raised doubts as to whether the courts still possessed power to make any such orders – see p. 559 footnote 106. Moreover, if an order for the sale of the family home is sought, it is clear that such order will only be made when there are grounds for dispensing with the consent of a spouse pursuant to section 4 of the Family Home Protection Act, 1976. See p. 557 *post et seq*.

adopted by the individual judge before whom his case has to be determined. More than in any other area of law, many of those spouses who seek to have their property disputes determined by the courts are involved in a game of judicial roulette.[9] The lack of clarity and certainty in the law is, of itself, a cause of litigation, resulting in many spouses whose marriage have broken down and who cannot agree to an amicable division of the family property resorting to court proceedings to determine their respective ownership rights in circumstances in which the lawyers representing each spouse cannot definitively advise each as to their property entitlements. If the law was clear and uniformly applied by the judiciary there would be a considerable reduction in the level of matrimonial property litigation and much of the money that spouses currently spend on the costs of such litigation would be saved.

4. In the vast majority of families, the principal and only capital asset is the family home and it is disputes as to ownership of the family home that are the main subject matter of matrimonial property litigation. The criticism of the law that it fails to recognise the contribution to the family welfare made by the wife in the home is raised most frequently with reference to the law's failure to regard such contribution as a relevant factor in determining the mutual ownership rights of spouses in the home. Commenting on this in 1981, the Law Reform Commission recommended that legislation should be enacted requiring that a "contribution in money or monies worth" capable of conferring a beneficial interest in the family home on the spouse who so contributes should be stated to include "the contribution made by each spouse to the welfare of the family, including any contribution made by looking after the home or caring for the family."[10] The Commission did not, however, clarify how the courts should determine the monetary value of such contribution.[11] Whereas its proposal, if implemented, would have the effect of requiring the courts to regard the work of the wife in the home as an indirect contribution to its acquisition in "monies worth", it would not reduce the current level of matrimonial property litigation, as spouses in dispute would still have to go to court to establish the extent of their ownership rights in the family home, which would still depend on the proportionate value of the contribution made by each to its acquisition.

In 1972 the Commission on the Status of Women suggested that consideration should be given to the introduction of a system of co-ownership of the matri-

---

9. See the report of the Joint Oireachtas Committee, *supra*, at pp. 64, 66; The Law Reform Commission: *First Report on Family Law*, *supra*, at pp. 19–20, see in particular section 22 of the draft bill prepared by the Commission (pp. 33–35 of the report) which makes provision for reforming the law not only as to direct and indirect contributions to the acquisition of the family home but also as to the making of such contributions to the improvement or maintenance of the family home. In the context of improvements see also the English Matrimonial Proceedings & Property Act, 1970, section 37 which applies not only to the family home but to contributions made by one spouse in money or monies worth to the improvement of any real or personal property in which either spouse has a beneficial interest.

10. The Law Reform Commission: *First Report on Family Law, supra*, at p. 20.

11. In *Irish Women – Agenda for Practical Action, supra*, Chapter 8 reference is made to the difficulty in measuring the monetary value of housework and to the different possible methods of doing so – "one method is based on the potential solely of the individual who carries out the housework and assumes that the value of housework is equal to the salary which the individual who carried out the work would earn were she in the labour market. The second method uses the cost of employing a domestic help to carry out the housework and the third method is based on the replacement cost of each separate function of housework." If the Law Reform Commission's proposal was implemented it would be essential that legislation state which of these methods referred to should apply in calculating the value of the contribution made by each spouse in the home.

monial home under which the home would legally be regarded as being jointly owned by the husband and wife by virtue of the marriage bond, subject to the right of spouses to agree to opt out of such joint ownership.[12] The Commission when making this suggestion recognised that the automatic sharing of one family asset could create anomalies and injustice. For example, it can be argued that there is no valid basis for providing for automatic joint ownership of the family home but not for automatic joint ownership of other property acquired during marriage. If a husband uses his earnings to purchase an investment property whilst insisting that rented accommodation be used as the family home, why should the law not also provide for such investment property to be jointly owned? Despite this and other objections that can be raised, in the absence of legislative acceptance of a regime of community of property, the arguments in favour of joint ownership of the family home, it is submitted, are persuasive.

A law providing for automatic joint ownership of the family home would reflect the realities of family life to the extent that the overwhelming majority of spouses regard the family home as "their home" without ever giving detailed consideration to whether the legal title should be held in the sole name of one spouse or in joint names or as to whether either has a beneficial interest in it according to the laws of equity. It would recognise the "partnership element in marriage"[13] and make the financial value of each spouse's contribution to the purchase of the home or its improvement an irrelevance, rendering it also unnecessary to put a specific monetary value on housework such as would be required by the Law Reform Commission's recommendation. It would also reduce the necessity for spouses to resort to litigation to determine ownership rights in the home as all homes would be jointly owned, save for those purchased by spouses who opt out of such statutory ownership.

In April 1983, the government announced that it had "decided in principle that legislation will be introduced which, generally, will give to each spouse equal rights of ownership in the family home and contents". It envisaged "that the form the new legislation will take is that co-ownership will be legally *presumed* in all cases but, where exceptional circumstances exist so that it would be unjust to insist on co-ownership, it will be possible to have the presumption set aside by a court." It was also stated that consideration was being given to "the extent, if any, to which married couples would have a right by agreement to opt out of such provision and to make their own arrangements about ownership."[14] To date no legislation has been published to implement the government's decision.[14a]

Whilst the government's proposal would resolve some of the problems that arise under the current law, if implemented in the manner proposed, it would not automatically result in all family homes being jointly owned. It would merely introduce a presumption of joint ownership which would be rebuttable in "exceptional circumstances". What will amount to such exceptional circumstances as will render it unjust to apply the presumption of co-ownership remains to be clarified, as do many other questions relating to the proposed legislation. The policy questions that will have to be answered before the desirability of

12. *Report of the Commission on the Status of Women, supra*, at p. 176.
13. *Ibid*.
14. The government's proposals were announced by the Minister for Justice whose statement is published in *Irish Women – Agenda for Practical Action, supra*, at pp. 274–275.
14a. In the *Statement of Government's Intentions with regard to Marriage, Separation and Divorce* (June 1986, Dept. of Justice) at p. 8 it states that "the government has already announced proposals which are at present being finalised, to give equal rights of ownership in the family home to both spouses".

legislation implementing the government's proposals can be judged include the following:

(i) Will the legislation apply to all family homes? Will it have a retrospective effect and apply to homes purchased prior to the enactment of the promised legislation or will it merely be prospective, applying to all future homes purchased? Will it apply to a family home inherited by a spouse from a deceased parent or another or one given to a spouse by way of a gift? Will the donor of a family home by will or gift be able to exclude the spouse of the person to whom the gift is given from acquiring a joint interest in it? Will joint ownership apply to a property used as a family home but acquired by one spouse many years prior to marriage?

If a couple move out of one home into another and the original home is retained and let to tenants, will co-ownership be presumed in relation to only one or both properties? Will it extend to a property which is used for both business and residential purposes or will joint ownership only apply to that portion of the premises that is used as a family home?

(ii) Where a marriage is civilly annulled or terminated by a valid and recognisable foreign decree of divorce, will the presumption of co-ownership apply to property situated in this country which was used as a 'family home" by the parties at any time prior to such a nullity or divorce decree being granted? Will it apply to a property vested in the sole name of a party to an engagement which has been terminatea, and which was owned by such party during the subsistence of the engagement, if prior to or during the course of the engagement it had been agreed that such property was to be the couple's family home after marriage?

(iii) What will constitute "exceptional circumstances" sufficient to rebut the presumption of joint ownership? Can such circumstances arise following upon a comparison of the value of property owned by each spouse other than the family home? Can such circumstances relate to the value of the contribution made by a spouse to the acquisition of the home? To what extent will the length of time a couple resided together after marriage or the circumstances relating to a marriage breaking down be relevant? Will proof that a spouse is guilty of cruelty, adultery, desertion or other matrimonial misconduct be sufficient to make it "unjust to insist on co-ownership"? If the legislation applies to property used as a "family home" by a couple whose marriage is civilly annulled will the ground upon which such a decree of nullity is granted be a basis, by itself, for a finding of "exceptional circumstances"?

(iv) Should there be a provision permitting spouses to opt out? Whilst an opt out clause would leave spouses to make their own arrangements about ownership of the family home, it could also deprive a dependent spouse for whom such a law is necessary of essential protection. For example, a domineering husband might force a wife who did not wish to do so, to opt out of joint ownership. If a wife cannot opt out of her entitlement to maintenance pursuant to the provisions of the Family Law ... Act, 1976, should she be permitted to opt out of her entitlement to a share in the ownership of the family home? If spouses are permitted to opt out, will a spouse who does so and who has no legal title in the family home but who subsequently contributes to its acquisition, retain a right to claim a beneficial interest in it as can be claimed at present?

(v) How will the proposed legislation affect the rights of third parties such as mortgagees and creditors? Will a creditor have a right to enquire and be informed as to whether spouses have opted out of automatic co-ownership? Will spouses who have done so be able to "opt in" again upon a judgement being obtained against the home owning spouse so as to reduce the value of the debtor spouse's interest in the home, prior to a judgement mortgage being registered against it? Similarly, will spouses who have opted out be able to "opt in" immediately prior to the home owning spouse being declared bankrupt so as to reduce the value of the bankrupt spouse's assets? Will a third party, such as a creditor or the Offical Assignee in bankruptcy be able to rebut the presumption of co-ownership in such circumstances?

If the new proposed legislation does not adequately and comprehensively provide answers to all of the above questions it may create more problems than it will resolve and thereby add to, rather than reduce, the current level of matrimonial property litigation.[15] Moreover, it should be noted that as the proposed presumption of co-ownership is confined to the family home, any such legislation will not obviate the need to reform and clarify the existing law applicable to the resolution of disputes between spouses as to the ownership of property other than homes to which this presumption is to apply.

5. Two reports concerned with the law of nullity have recommended that the High Court subsequent to granting a nullity decree, should be conferred with jurisdiction, not only to order one party to pay maintenance to the other but also to order the transfer of property from one party to the other or to any children of the parties and to vary any ante-nuptial or post-nuptial settlement.[16]

To help the court decide on the type of order that it should make, both reports set down specific matters that the court should investigate. Essentially, they require the court to take into account all matters relating to the financial and personal circumstances of the parties and their children. Of particular importance to the "wife" is the stipulation that in deciding whether to exercise its powers, the courts should have regard to "the contributions made by each of the parties to the welfare of the family, including any contribution made by looking after the home or caring for the family".[17] On the basis of this proposal, such contribution would be a relevant factor to be taken into account by the court not only in the context of determining what order should be made in relation to the family home but also in determining what orders should be made in relation to any other property owned by either spouse.[18]

The Joint Oireachtas Committee on Marital Breakdown has also recommended that subsequent to the granting of a decree of divorce *a mensa et thoro*, the court granting such decree should be conferred with a similar ancillary juris-

---

15. In February of 1985 the inter-departmental working party stated in *Irish Women – Agenda for Practical Action* that it understood that "work on the preparation of this legislation is proceeding as a priority." (see p. 275).

16. *The Law of Nullity in Ireland* prepared by the Attorney General's Office (Stationery Office, Dublin, August 1976) pp. 15–16; The Law Reform Commission: *The Report on Nullity of Marriage* (July, 1984) pp. 173–174.

17. See Law Reform Commission: *Ibid.*, p. 174. See also proposed Nullity of Marriage Bill, section 12, published in the report prepared by the Attorney General's Office.

18. See, however, footnote 11 above.

diction[19] and the government's recent "Statement of Intent" has confirmed that new legislation will be enacted conferring a court jurisdiction to order transfers of property between spouses in separation proceedings, including a power to order the transfer of the family home from one spouse to the other.[20] This legislation, if enacted, will be additional and complimentary to any legislation providing for joint ownership or a presumption of co-ownership of the family home and will afford the courts an opportunity to provide an economically dependent spouse with ownership rights over property acquired by the principal wage earner during the subsistence of the parties' marriage.[21]

---

19. See also the Law Reform Commission: *Report on Divorce a Mensa et Thoro and Related Matters* (Report No. 8, December 1983), p. 57 in which the Commission briefly refers to such jurisdiction being conferred on the courts. In the *Report of the Joint Oireachtas Committee, supra*, the Committee recommends that subsequent to the granting of a judicial separation the court should have an ancillary power to divide the various property or properties owned by the spouses between them and "to transfer the title of any relevant property as it deems just and equitable". In the context of exercising such jurisdiction it also proposes that the court should "be empowered to vary or discharge a spouse's right of succession" (see pp. 50–51). The Law Reform Commission favoured changing the current law so as to provide that the granting of a decree of judicial separation would automatically extinguish each spouse's succession rights. It is submitted that the former proposal is preferable in that it would confer a flexible jurisdiction on the court to vary property rights taking into account the overall financial circumstances and capital assets of both parties whilst not erecting a legal barrier that might discourage a dependent spouse whose marriage had totally broken down from invoking the court's jurisdiction to seek a decree of separation. See further p. 236 *ante*.

20. See *Statement of Intent* (April 1986) at p. 3 and revised *Statement* (June 1986) at pp. 8, 10–12.

21. For some comparative material on matrimonial property law see: English Law Commission, *Working Paper on Family Property Law* (P.W.P. No. 42, 1971); *First Report on Family Property, A New Approach* (Law Com. No. 52, 1973) and *Third Report on Family Property: Matrimonial Home and Household Goods* (Law Com. No. 86, 1978); Scottish Law Commission: *Consultative Memorandum on Matrimonial Property* (No. 57, 1983); Law Reform Commission of Canada: *Family Property* (Working Paper No. 8, 1975); A. Kiralfy, *Comparative Law of Matrimonial Property* (A.W. Sijthoff International Publishing Co., Netherlands, 1972); K.J. Gray, *Re-Allocation of Property on Divorce* (Professional Books, 1977); M. Rheinstein & M.A. Glendon, Vol. 3 *International Encyclopedia of Comparative Law* (1980) Chapter 4; S.M. Cretney, *Principles of Family Law* (1984) Chapter 24; O'Kahn Freud, "Matrimonial Property: 'Where do we go from here?'" (Joseph Unger Memorial Lecture 1971); M.P.A. Freeman, "Towards a Rational Re-Construction of Family Property Law" [1972] Current Legal Problems 84; A.A.S. Zuckerman, "Ownership of the Matrimonial Home – Common Sense and Reformist Nonsense" (1978) 94 L.Q.R. 26.

CHAPTER 16

PROTECTION OF THE FAMILY HOME

The most fundamental right that marriage creates is the right that each spouse has to the other's company.[1] Irrespective of in whose name the family home is held, each spouse possesses at common law a right to reside in it with the other.[2] If each spouse has a proprietary or beneficial interest in the home, the right to reside in it arises, in addition, by virtue of the ownership rights of each. If the entire ownership rights in the home are vested in one spouse, the other spouse's right of residence arises by virtue of the marriage relationship alone. Moreover, at common law, the primary duty to provide a home rests with the husband, whose obligation to provide support for his wife includes an obligation to provide a roof over her head.[3] This duty could be regarded as having been reinforced by Article 41.2. of the Constitution,[4] although no reference has to date been made by the courts to this Article in this context.

The right of the wife at common law to reside in the matrimonial or family home owned by her husband has been held to be a purely personal right enforceable against the husband but unenforceable against third parties.[5] Thus, while it could be invoked to restrain a husband from selling the home until he provided his wife with suitable alternative accommodation,[6] it could not be invoked to prevent a purchaser from obtaining possession of the home upon it being sold by the husband without the wife's knowledge[7] or to have a purchaser evicted from it, upon such sale rendering a wife homeless. It also did not confer any right on a wife to be consulted by her husband prior to his mortgaging the home to a third party. In the event of the husband so doing and subsequently defaulting on the mortgage, the mortgagee could force a sale of the home and render the wife homeless without her ever having had an opportunity to intervene to prevent her husband using the home as security to obtain a loan.[8] Moreover, the

---

1. See p. 159 *ante*.
2. See *National Provincial Bank Ltd. v. Ainsworth* [1965] A.C. 1175 (H.L.). See also extra-judicial comments of Kenny J. in "Some Aspects of Family Law", S.Y.S. Lecture no. 46 (1970).
3. *National Provincial Bank Ltd. v. Ainsworth, supra.*
4. See p. 3 *ante*.
5. *National Provincial Bank Ltd. v. Ainsworth, supra.*
6. See *Heavey v. Heavey* (1974) 111 I.L.T.R. 1 (H.C.) in which Kenny J. made an order restraining the husband from selling the family home "until he provided such alternative suitable accommodation for the wife as might be sanctioned by the court". The title to the family home was held by the husband in his sole name and the wife was entitled to no beneficial interest in it.
7. If the transaction was purely a sham to enable a husband to obtain possession, the wife's rights were protected – see *Ferris v. Weaven* [1952] 2 All E.R. 233 (Q.B.D.) approved of in *National Provincial Bank Ltd. v. Ainsworth, supra.*
8. See *National Provincial Bank Ltd. v. Ainsworth, supra.*

right of residence possessed by a wife at common law did not extend to her any right to obtain compensation from her husband if his behaviour resulted in a loss of the home or in it being rendered uninhabitable. Upon either event occurring and no alternative home being acquired for her by the husband, the sole course of action available to a wife was, in the context of maintenance proceedings, to seek to require a husband to contribute towards the cost to her of her obtaining alternative accommodation.

The Commission on the Status of Women in a report published in 1972 noted that the vast majority of homes were held by husbands in their sole name and referred to the necessity to enact legislation to protect the family home and the wife's right to reside in it.[9] As a response to this report and to a number of voluntary organisations publicly highlighting the vulnerable position of wives in the home, particularly upon marital breakdown occurring, the need for reform was finally acknowledged by the Oireachtas with the passage of the Family Home Protection Act, 1976. It is the provisions of this Act that are now considered in detail.

THE FAMILY HOME PROTECTION ACT, 1976[10]

The Family Home Protection Act came into force on the 12th July 1976. Its primary object is to ensure that a spouse will not sell or otherwise dispose of the family home behind the back of his family and without the prior consent of the other spouse.[11] The Act does not create or vest in a spouse any proprietary or beneficial interest in the family home but confers on the non-owning spouse a statutory right to veto any unilateral disposition of it by the other spouse by rendering invalid any disposition that takes place without the former's prior written consent.[12] In essence, the Act confers a negative right on the non-owning spouse.

In addition, it provides a specific right of action to enable a spouse to obtain appropriate court orders to protect the family home so as to prevent its loss or it being rendered uninhabitable, and it provides an entitlement to seek compensation from a spouse or third party whose actions deprive a spouse of her right to reside in the family home. The Act also contains a number of other measures designed to protect a spouse's right to reside in the family home and also the right of children of the family to do so.

While the Act applies equally to a husband and to a wife, for the sake of convenience in the discussion that follows it will be presumed that ownership of the family home is vested in the husband alone unless otherwise stated.

---

9. *Report of the Commission on the Status of Women* (December 1972), see in particular pp. 174—176.

10. See generally J.C.W. Wylie, *Irish Conveyancing Law* (Professional Books Ltd. 1978) p. 198 *et seq.*; P. Ussher, "The Position of a Purchaser Under the Family Home Protection Act, 1976" (January 1977) Vol. 71 *The Gazette of the Incorporated Law Society of Ireland* 3; J. Macken, "The Family Home Protection Act, 1976" (March 1977) 111 I.L.T. & S.J. pp. 52, 59, 65, 71; F. Daly, "The Effect on Conveyancing Practice of the New Law Society Contract for Sale and the Family Home Protection Act, 1976" (S.Y.S. Lecture No. 79, November 1976); M. Carroll, "The Family Home Protection Act, 1976" (S.Y.S. Lecture No. 124, April 1980); R. O'Donnell, "Conveyancing and the Family Home" (S.Y.S. Lecture No. 146, April 1983).

11. *Somers v. Weir* [1979] I.R. 94; (1979) 113 I.L.T.R. 81 (S.C.); *Hamilton v. Hamilton* [1982] I.R. 466 (S.C.). See also Dáil Debates Vol. 291, Cols. 54 *et seq.*

12. See *Nestor v. Murphy* [1979] I.R. 326 (S.C.); *Hamilton v. Hamilton, supra*; *Guckian v. Brennan* [1981] I.R. 478 (H.C.); *Murray v. Diamond* [1982] 2 I.L.R.M. 113 (H.C.); *Containercare (Ireland) Ltd. v. Wycherley* [1982] I.R. 143 (H.C.); *O'D. v. O'D.* (November, 1983) unreported (H.C.).

Family home: The term "family home" means primarily a dwelling in which a married couple ordinarily reside. The expression is said also to comprise a dwelling in which a spouse whose protection is in issue ordinarily resides, or if that spouse has left the other spouse, ordinarily resided before so leaving.[13] Thus, two separate houses could under this definition be regarded at the same time as a "family home". For example, B. owns house X and house Y; B. and Mrs. B. live together in house X for a number of years after their marriage, then B. forces Mrs. B. to leave and go and live in house Y with their children. House Y is the family home in which Mrs. B. is now ordinarily residing, whilst house X is the home in which she ordinarily resided before leaving.

The term dwelling includes any building, or any structure vehicle or vessel (whether mobile or not), or part thereof, occupied as a separate dwelling and includes any garden or portion of ground attached to and usually occupied with the dwelling, or otherwise required for the amenity or convenience of the dwelling. The Act does not apply to any dwelling[14] in which the wife has never resided. Thus, if a husband leaves his wife and goes to live elsewhere, if the wife never resides in his new home, it is outside the scope of the Act.

Whilst in general the Act does not apply to the sale of business premises, in certain circumstances a wife's consent will be required for such a sale. For example, where a portion of the premises are used for residential purposes by the family and another portion for business purposes, it may not be possible or practical to dispose of the latter part of the premises without the former.

The requirement of consent: By section 3(1) of the Act, if a spouse without the prior consent in writing of the other spouse, purports to convey any interest[15] in the family home to any person except the other spouse ... the purported conveyance is void, subject to certain specified exceptions.[16]

13. Sect. 2. A dwelling may be a family home for the purposes of the Act if a husband and wife ordinarily resided in it, either before or after the coming into force of the Act. See *Somers v. Weir, supra* and *H. and L. v. S.* (July, 1979), unreported (H.C.). In both of these cases the spouses resided together in the home until 1973 when the wife in each case left the home taking the children with her. See also *Hegarty v. Morgan* (1979) 113 I.L.T. & S.J. 173 (H.C.) and *Reynolds v. Waters* [1982] 2 I.L.R.M. 335 (H.C.).

14. See footnote 47 *post*.

15. The term "interest" is defined as referring to "any estate, right, title or other interest, legal or equitable" – Sect. 1(1).

16. A property may be a family home as defined by the Act but may not be caught by Sect. 3(1) where no such "interest" is vested in either spouse. Thus, in *B.M.C. v. P.J.C.* (May, 1983) unreported (H.C.) it was held that a property in the name of a limited company of which the husband's brother and sister-in-law were the directors could be sold without the wife's prior consent although she and her husband had resided in it as a married couple. The husband was secretary of the company and claimed that he and his wife and children were allowed to have the use and occupation of the property by leave and licence of the limited company owned and controlled by his brother and sister-in-law. O'Hanlon J. in his judgement stated that on the evidence produced before him the defendant husband "has not been shown to have an interest in the property ... within the meaning of that expression as defined in Sect. 1 of the Family Home Protection Act, 1976." (See p. 8 of judgement.)

In *L.B. v. H.B.* (July, 1980) unreported (H.C.) Barrington J. granted a declaration that a property in which the husband and wife had resided together was a family home, although it was held in the name of a company. He stated that he was "aware that the house is not owned directly by Mr. B. It is owned by a company called Movie News Ltd., which in turn is controlled by a company incorporated in Panama in which Mr. B. owns what he describes as the 'vast majority' of the shares although some are owned by his son. I do not think that this affects the issue that the house is a family home within the meaning of the Act." (See p. 36 of judgement.) The learned judge did not expressly state whether there was vested in the husband any interest within the meaning of the Act.

In *Walpoles (Ireland) Ltd. v. Jay* (November, 1980) unreported (H.C.) a similar issue arose for consideration by way of a vendor and purchaser summons.* The plaintiff company was the vendor of the property in which R.W., one of the principal members of the company, had resided with his wife between 1967 and 1971. The property was held to be a

1. By section 3(2), sub-s.(1) does not apply to a conveyance made by a spouse in pursuance of an enforceable agreement made before the marriage of the parties. For example, A. contracts to sell his house to B. Subsequently, A. marries C. and they reside in the house for some time before the conveyance is completed. C.'s consent to the conveyance is not required under this provision.

2. Section 3(3) provides that no conveyance is void by reason only of sub-s. (1).

(a) If it is made to a *bona fide* purchaser for full value.[17]

(b) If it is made by a person other than the spouse referred to in section 3(1) to a *bona fide* purchaser for value.[18]

(c) If its validity depends on the validity of a conveyance in respect of which any of the conditions mentioned in sub-s. (2) or para. (a) or (b) are satisfied.

The Act attempts to strike a balance between protecting the interests of a wife and those of a *bona fide* purchaser. For example, having regard to para. (a) above, if a vendor conceals the fact of his marriage and does not obtain his wife's consent to a conveyance of what, unknown to the purchaser, is the family home, the appearance of the vendor's wife subsequent to the closing of the sale will not affect the interest in the property conveyed to the purchaser, if the latter has no notice of the marriage or the wife's existence, is *bona fide* and has given "full value".

To be *bona fide*, the purchaser must not have notice that at the time of the conveyance the property purchased was a family home. Absence of notice does not mean, however, that the validity of a conveyance cannot be impugned if a purchaser remains quiet and asks no questions. By virtue of the Conveyancing Act, 1882, Sect. 3, a purchaser will be held to have notice, if the fact that the property conveyed was a family home was within his own knowledge or

---

family home and whilst McWilliam J. held that "there was no provision in Sect. 3 of the Act which can avoid a conveyance of the property by the plaintiff (company) to the defendant" (see p. 5 of judgement) he stated that "if there was any interest legal or equitable vested in R.W." he was of the opinion "that he could not disclaim or release that interest or assent to its disposition without the consent of his spouse." (See p. 6 of judgement.) Whether any such interest was vested in R.W. was said to be a matter "for an investigation of title in the ordinary way" and no determination on this issue was made in the proceedings. See further "An Unmarried Company" (1983) 77 *The Gazette of the Incorporated Law Society of Ireland* 217.

*For the circumstances in which it is appropriate to issue a summons under the Vendor & Purchaser Act, 1874, to ask the court to resolve a dispute between a vendor and a purchaser in relation to requisitions on title see *Mulligan v. Dillon* (November, 1980) unreported (H.C.). See also "Practice Note" (1981) 75 *Gazette of the Incorporated Law Society of Ireland* p. 241.

17. See Sect. 3(6) which states that: "Purchaser means a grantee, lessee, assignee, mortgagee, chargeant or other person who in *good faith* acquires an estate or interest in the property". Thus, a person who does not acquire an estate or interest in good faith, is not a purchaser within the meaning of the Act.

"Full value" is said to mean "such value as amounts or approximates to the value of that for which it is given" – Sect. 3(5).

In the text 2(a) and (b) above should merely refer to a purchaser for full value (a) or for value (b) and the word purchaser implies that the person acquired the interest in good faith. However, for clarity the more usual term of *bona fide* purchaser is used in the text, as it is easy otherwise to lose sight of the fact that, for example in (a), to be exempt from the requirement of consent, a person must not only give full value but must also be *bona fide*.

18. See footnote 17 *supra*. In *Walpoles (Ireland) Ltd. v. Jay, supra*, McWilliam J. stated that "applying the normal principles of interpretation . . . I must assume that the expression 'purchaser for value' in paragraph (b) is intended to have a meaning different from the defined meaning of the expression 'purchaser for full value' in paragraph (a)."

"would have come to his knowledge if such inquiries and inspections had been made as ought reasonably to have been made by him".

Moreover, notice may be imputed to him if in the same transaction, such a fact

"has come to the knowledge of his counsel or of his solicitor or other agent or would have come to the knowledge of his solicitor or agent if such inquiries and inspections had been made as ought reasonably to have been made by the solicitor or agent".[19]

In *Somers v. Weir*[20] the purchaser's solicitor failed to make the enquiries he reasonably ought to have made to properly ascertain whether a wife's consent was required for the valid conveyance of a house. Her consent was not obtained and as a result the conveyance was held to be null and void.

The husband and wife resided together in the house from 1961 until 1973, when their marriage broke down and the wife left the house taking her children with her. In 1974 the parties entered into a separation agreement. The husband continued to reside in the house and on the 2nd August 1976 entered into a written agreement to sell it. The sale was completed on the 17th August 1976.

The Supreme Court held that the property in question was a family home and could not have been properly conveyed by the husband without the prior consent of his wife. If the necessary enquiries had been made by the purchaser's solicitor he would have been aware of this and, thus, the purchaser was held, by imputation, to have notice of the position at the time of the conveyance. The purchaser's solicitor had without further enquiry, wrongly accepted as sufficient for the purposes of the Act, the husband's statutory declaration stating that since he had executed a separation agreement with his wife, she had not relied on the property in question as her family home and that "by virtue of said separation agreement she has now no interest therein". The solicitor had never seen the separation agreement which in fact made no reference at all to the family home.[21]

The guiding principle in a conveyancing transaction is *caveat emptor* — let the buyer beware.[22] It is the responsibility of the purchaser to investigate the vendor's title, and if he does not observe the appropriate conveyancing procedures, he will be held to have notice of matters which would have been discovered if the proper procedure had been observed by him. In order to comply with the above requirement and properly protect a purchaser's interests, it is now essential when purchasing property which could have been used as a family home to raise

---

19. Conveyancing Act, 1882, Sect. 3(1) para. (ii) as amended by Sect. 3(7) of the Family Home Protection Act, 1976. See *Somers v. Weir, supra; M.D. v. L.D. and Ors.* (December, 1978) unreported (H.C.). See also *Hegarty v. Morgan, supra* and *Reynolds v. Waters, supra*.

20. *Supra*. See also *H. and L. v. S., supra*, in which a conveyance was declared null and void in similar circumstances. See further *Hegarty v. Morgan, supra*, in which a contract for sale was rescinded due to the inadequacy of the vendor's Family Home Protection Act Statutory Declaration and the vendor's refusal to take further steps to establish that the property was not a "family home" within the meaning of the Act. On the other hand, see *Guckian and Anor. v. Brennan and Anor, supra*, in which it was held that the vendors of registered land are not required for the purposes of the Family Home Protection Act to furnish a purchaser with evidence that the provisions of the Act were complied with when the property was originally assigned to them (the vendors). The court held that the duty of ensuring that the original transfer to the vendors was valid and effective fell upon the registrar at the time of registration and that the "register thereafter, in the absence of fraud, affords conclusive evidence of the validity of the title". See further p. 553.

21. For the sequel to this case see *Weir v. Somers* [1983] 3 I.L.R.M. 343, *sub nom W. v. Somers* [1983] I.R. 122 (S.C.).

22. See generally J.C.W. Wylie, *Irish Conveyancing Law, supra*, Chapter 5.

the appropriate requisitions on title, enquiring as to whether the property comes within the provisions of the Act.[23] In the event of such requisitions not being made, the appearance of a spouse after the purchase of what turns out to have

---

23. In a guide to the Family Home Protection Act prepared for students of the Incorporated Law Society of Ireland by Peter Polden & Rory O'Donnell and published as a supplement to the (April 1981) 75 *Gazette of the Incorporated Law Society of Ireland*, the authors state what enquiries in their view are required in conveyancing transactions and how the replies received should be verified so as to fully and properly comply with the requirements of Section 3(1). A supplement to the (October 1983) 77 *Gazette of the Incorporated Law Society of Ireland* recommended the following Requisitions on Title – which are now incorporated into the Society's *Standard Requisitions on Title* (1985 Edition), Requisition 30:

1 (a) Is the property or any part thereof the Vendor's "family home" as defined in the Act?

  (b) If the answer to (a) is in the affirmative furnish the prior written consent of the Vendor's spouse and verify the marriage by statutory declaration exhibiting therein civil marriage certificate.

  (c) If the answer to (a) is in the negative, please state the grounds relied upon and furnish new draft statutory declaration for approval verifying these grounds.*

2. In respect of all "conveyances" (as defined in the Act) of unregistered property made on or after the 12th day of July 1976 furnish spouses' prior written consents where appropriate together with verification of marriage by statutory declaration exhibiting therein civil marriage certificate or where consent is not necessary please furnish evidence verifying same by way of statutory declaration.

3 (a) Was the property or any part thereof at any time or does it presently comprise the "family home" as defined in the Act of any person other than the Vendor or previous registered owner?

  (b) If so, please state the name of each person who resided in the property or any part thereof as a "family home" within the meaning of the Act and state the nature of that person's interest (if any) in the property.

  (c) In relation to any such person having an "interest" (as defined in the Act) please furnish the prior written consent of that person's spouse to any "conveyance" (as defined in the Act) of that person's interest in the property or any part thereof since 12th July 1976 and verify such spouse's marriage by statutory declaration exhibiting therein civil marriage certificate.

  (d) If such person did not have an "interest" (as defined in the Act) in the property or any part of it please state the grounds relied upon and furnish new draft statutory declaration for approval verifying these grounds.

*In *Hegarty v. Morgan, supra*, McWilliam J. stated that in his opinion "a statutory declaration should set out the facts establishing that the premises are not a family home," a bald statement simply stating that it is not will not be sufficient. In *Reynolds v. Waters, supra*, Costello J. considered the issue as to whether a purchaser should accept a statutory declaration which verifies such facts or whether he is entitled to have the vendor's word corroborated by a second statutory declaration and to insist on the purchaser applying to the court for a declaration that a dwelling is not a family home in the absence of such corroborative evidence. He held that if the statutory declaration clearly contains the necessary information and if neither the purchaser or his solicitor has any reason to doubt the accuracy or veracity of the statements in it, it will normally be sufficient and "there is no general principle to the effect that a prudent purchaser should not accept the uncorroborated statutory declaration of a vendor merely because the vendor is gaining financially from the transaction." (See p. 7 of judgement.) In the same case, referring to *Somers v. Weir, supra*, the learned judge remarked that "in holding that the purchaser's solicitors ought to have made further enquiries before closing the sale on the faith of a statutory declaration which he himself drafted following totally inadequate enquiries, the court did not decide that a prudent purchaser can never rely on a vendor's uncorroborated statutory declaration (see p. 10 of judgement).

been the family home may render the transaction void.[24]

Section 3(1) only applies to a conveyance by a "spouse" of any interest in a family home. Thus, it does not apply to the conveyance by any other person of any such interest. Section 3(3)(b) also expressly excludes its application to a conveyance made by a person other than a spouse. Consequently, a mortgagee,[25] or, if a house owning spouse goes bankrupt, the Official Assignee in Bankruptcy, may convey a family home free from the requirement of obtaining a prior consent. A company in which is vested the full legal and beneficial interest in a family home may also validly sell or convey its interest in it without having to obtain a consent.[26] Since a limited company as such cannot have a spouse, the question of a company requiring a prior consent under the Act cannot arise. If, however, a company holds a family home in trust for a spouse in whom is vested the entire beneficial interest, a spouse's prior consent may be required to effect a valid transfer of the whole or any part of such beneficial interest to a third party.[27] It may also be required if there is any other estate or interest vested in a spouse such as a leasehold interest, in order to give vacant possession to a purchaser.[28]

In *Containercare (Ireland) Limited v. Wycherley*[29] and *Murray v. Diamond*,[30] it was held that section 3(1) has no application to the registering of a judgement mortgage pursuant to the provisions of the Judgement Mortgage (Ireland) Acts, 1850 and 1858 and that a spouse's prior consent is not required to render a judgement mortgage effective. In *Containercare (Ireland) Limited v. Wycherley* a judgement for £6,000 obtained against the husband was successfully registered against the family home. Carroll J. rejected the wife's contention that the judgement mortgage, having been registered without her prior consent, was void stating that:

---

24. For a general discussion of the Doctrine of Notice see J.C.W. Wylie, *Irish Land Law*, (Professional Books Ltd., London 1975), p. 102 *et seq*. See also *Northern Bank Ltd. v. Henry and Ors.* [1981] I.R. 1 (H.C., S.C.). See, in particular, the judgements of the Supreme Court in which section 3 of the Conveyancing Act, 1882 and the Doctrine of Constructive Notice are given detailed consideration. In his judgement Kenny J. referring to decided cases stated that "a purchaser or mortgagee who omits to make such enquiries and inspections as a prudent and reasonable purchaser or mortgagee acting on skilled advice would have made will be fixed with notice of what he would have discovered if he had made the enquiries and inspections which ought reasonably to have been made by him." *Supra* at p. 16. Further on he continued "the test then is the prudent purchaser acting on skilled advice. Such a purchaser would certainly not abstain from enquiry in an attempt to avoid having notice." *Supra* at p. 18.

The court held that the test to determine whether a conveyancer has fully complied with the duty imposed on him is an objective one. Henchy J. stated "the test of what enquiries and inspections ought reasonably to have been made is an objective test which depends not on what the particular purchaser thought proper to do in the particular circumstances, but on what a purchaser of the particular property ought reasonably to have done in order to acquire title to it . . . (a purchaser) must expect to be judged by what an ordinary purchaser, advised by a competent lawyer, would reasonably enquire about or inspect for the purpose of getting a good title . . . and a reasonable purchaser is one who not only consults his own needs or preferences but also has regard to whether the purchase may prejudicially and unfairly affect the rights of third parties in the property." (*Supra* at p. 9). See also Kenny J., *supra*, at p. 19.

25. See further p. 549 *infra*.

26. See *B.M.C. v. P.J.C., supra*.

27. In *B.M.C. v. P.J.C., supra*, in finding against the wife, O'Hanlon J. noted that there was not sufficient evidence "to support a finding that the property was . . . purchased in trust for the defendant although registered in the name of the limited company and assigned to it" (p. 7 of judgement).

28. See *Walpole (Ireland) Ltd. v. Jay, supra*, discussed in footnote 16 *ante*.

29. [1982] I.R. 143 (H.C.).

30. [1982] 2 I.L.R.M. 113 (H.C.). This judgement was delivered two weeks after the judgement delivered in the preceding case.

"A judgement mortgage, if registered against a family home, is not a disposition by a spouse purporting to convey an interest in the family home. It is a unilateral act by a judgement creditor . . ."[31]

In *Murray v. Diamond*, dealing with the same issue, Barrington J. stated that it is clear that a "judgement mortgage comes into existence by operation of the statute and not by virtue of any positive act by the judgement debtor".[32] He continued stating:

"I do not think that the mere fact that a man has irresponsibly allowed himself to get into debt, or allowed a judgement to be obtained against him and thereby allowed a situation to develop in which his creditor registers a judgement against his interest in the family home, would justify a court in saying that he has conveyed or purported to convey his interest in the family home to the judgement mortgagee."[33]

The learned judge emphasised, however, that he was not "dealing with a case of fraud or with a case of connivance between one spouse and his or her judgement creditor to defeat the rights of the other spouse."[34] If such case does arise, it is clear that the court may regard such judgement creditor as the *alter ego* of the spouse and regard any judgement mortgage lodged as invalid under section 3(1) of the Act of 1976. Moreover, a judgement mortgage cannot, of course, be registered against a family home, if the spouse against whom judgement was obtained has no proprietary or beneficial interest in the home.[34a]

Section 3(3)(b), as we have already seen, appears to be largely superfluous. Its purpose and that of section 3(3)(c) is not easy to construe.[35] It appears that one of their purposes may be to prevent a series of invalid transactions. For example, although a conveyance from X to Y may be void by reason of section 3(1), a subsequent conveyance by Y to Z may vest a valid title in the latter if he is a *bona fide* purchaser for value, as the conveyance is by a person (Y) other than the spouse making the purported conveyance (X) referred to in section 3(1).[36] In the event of a sale by (Z), paragraph (c) appears to guarantee the validity of Z's title. If a dispute arises as to the validity of a conveyance under the Act, the burden of proving that validity is placed on the person alleging it.[37] The language of section 3 is unnecessarily complicated. It has been and will continue to remain a source of much unnecessary and difficult litigation until such time as amending legislation is enacted clarifying some of its more obscure and mystifying provisions.

Spouse's prior written consent: The spouse whose prior consent is necessary to fulfil the requirements of the Act is the legally recognised spouse of the

---

31. *Supra* at p. 150.
32. [1982] 2 I.L.R.M. at p. 115.
33. *Ibid.*
34. *Ibid.*
34a. See *Allied Irish Banks v. McWilliams & Anor.* (1982) Northern Ireland Law Reports, Bulletin of Judgements (No. 7) 1. As for the protection of a family home jointly owned by a husband and wife upon a judgement mortgage being registered against it, following upon a judgement being obtained against one spouse, see *Tubman v. Johnston* (1980) Northern Ireland Law Reports, Bulletin of Judgements (No. 12).
35. In *Walpole (Ireland) Ltd. v. Jay, supra*, McWilliam J. stated that he did "not know what is the proper interpretation" to be put on paragraph (b) of sub-sect. 3(3).
36. The problem with this interpretation is that Y's conveyance vests an interest in Z which Y never had, the conveyance to Y being void; i.e., by Y conveying what to him is a "nothing" he turns it into a "something".
37. Sect. 3(4).

person conveying the family home. The Act of 1976 placed no age limit on a spouse's capacity to grant a consent but, following its enactment, it was suggested[38] that as a consequence of a minor's contractual incapacity and the provisions of the Infants Relief Act, 1874, a minor spouse lacked the capacity to give a consent under the Act or, in the alternative, that a minor's consent was voidable and could be repudiated by the minor upon attaining the age of 21 years. Thus, in conveyances for which the consent of a minor spouse was required, the practice grew of an application being made to the High Court by the minor spouse's guardian under section 11(1) of the Guardianship of Infants Act, 1964, for a court order approving of the minor spouse giving a required consent and asking the court to hold that the giving of such consent was in the interests of the minor.[39] Moreover, in *Lloyd v. Sullivan*[40] it was held that a vendor had failed to show good title upon his refusing a purchaser's request that an application be made to the High Court on behalf of the vendor's wife, a minor, to obtain the court's approval to her consenting to sell the family home. McWilliam J. stated that:

> "if the transaction were not shown to be to her advantage, she would be entitled to repudiate her consent on attaining her majority."

The Family Law Act, 1981, resolved this difficulty and the question mark that hung over the capacity of a minor to give a valid consent was removed by it. Section 10(1) of the Act of 1981 provides that:

> "No consent given by a spouse, whether before or after the passing of this Act[41] for the purposes of section 3(1) of the Family Home Protection Act, 1976 . . . shall be, or shall be taken to have been invalid by reason only that it is or was given by a spouse who has not or had not attained the age of majority."

This provision is also said to apply to any such consent given by a guardian or a court on behalf of a minor spouse prior to the passing of the Act of 1981.[42] The Age of Majority Act, 1985, by lowering the age of majority and providing that a person attains full age at 18 years or upon marriage, if he marries before attaining 18 years, has now reduced the importance of this provision.

The requirement of a spouse's "prior consent" to render a conveyance valid, raises the question of what is meant by "prior consent". Speaking on the Bill in the Seanad the then Minister for Justice, Mr. Cooney, expressed the opinion that for a wife's written consent to fulfil the requirement of the section it must be endorsed on the conveyance.[43] In the absence of such an endorsement, he stated, the title would be faulty. This interpretation of section 3(1) is questionable in that what the section requires is a written consent prior to the conveying of the family home. Use of the word "prior" indicates that it must be given in

---

38. See J.C.W. Wylie, *Irish Conveyancing Law, supra*, pp. 208–210; M. Carroll, *The Family Home Protection Act, 1976, supra*.

39. The court was bound by section 3 of the Guardianship of Infants Act, 1964, in determining any such application to regard the welfare of the minor "as the first and paramount consideration".

40. (March, 1981) unreported (H.C.).

41. The Act was passed on the 23rd of June 1981.

42. See Sect. 10(2) of Act of 1981.

43. Seanad Debates, Vol. 84, Cols. 1060–1062.

writing before the conveyance is executed. It does not require a wife to be a party to the execution of the conveyance itself. Moreover, in *Kyne v. Tiernan & Anor.*[44] the High Court held that a letter signed by a wife unequivocally consenting to the sale of a family home was sufficient to comply with the requirements of the section and that a further consent endorsed on the conveyance itself was unnecessary.

A question arises as to "how prior" can a consent be? Further, must a consent be given for a sale to a particular purchaser, or is a general consent to the sale of the family home to any purchaser sufficient? For example, can a wife in a deed of separation give a general consent to the selling of the family home, so as to enable her husband validly convey it to a third party at any time in the future, if he so wishes? Having regard to the wording of the section it appears that a sale of the family home subsequent to the giving of such a consent is valid.[45] The validity of such a sale could, however, be called in question if, prior to the completion of the conveyance, a wife notified the parties that she was withdrawing a consent so given. Whether the court would hold her bound by her agreement and her change of mind to be of no effect or whether it would only recognise the sale as valid in such circumstances, if a successful application to dispense with consent was made by her husband,[45a] remains to be seen.

Conveyance: A conveyance under the Act is said to include

> "a mortgage, lease, assent, transfer, disclaimer, release and any other disposition of property otherwise than by a will or a *donatio mortis causa* and also includes an enforceable agreement (whether conditional or unconditional) to make any such conveyance".

"Convey" is to be construed accordingly.[46]

As has already been seen, section 3(2) excludes from the application of the Act any conveyance made by a spouse pursuant to an enforceable agreement entered into before marriage. In *Hamilton v. Hamilton*[47] the Supreme Court held that the Act also does not apply to any conveyances completed after the Act came into force on the 12th of July 1976, the contracts for sale in relation to which were entered into prior to that date. In this case contracts for the sale of a mansion house and 215 acres of land for £150,000 were entered into by the husband and D. in 1973.[47a] The husband delayed completing the sale and following upon successful court proceedings for specific performance brought by D. the husband executed the documents required to enable the conveyance

---

44. (July, 1980) unreported (H.C.).

45. In *Hamilton v. Hamilton, supra,* at p. 486, Henchy J. stated that "the primary purpose of s.3 would appear to be the prevention of the unilateral alienation (by one of the spouses) of any interest, legal or equitable, in a family home." A sale following upon the giving of a general consent to sell could not be regarded as a unilateral alienation of the family home by the selling spouse to a third party.

45a. For the circumstances in which a court may dispense with a spouse's consent see p. 554 *post et seq.*

46. Sect. 1(1). "An enforceable agreement . . . to make any such conveyance" must be taken to mean an agreement enforceable but for the provisions of the Act. For example, if prior consent is not obtained to a contract for sale of the family home, the contract is one that would be enforceable if the Act did not render it void because of the absence of consent.

47. [1982] I.R. 466 (S.C.); (February, 1980) unreported (H.C.).

47a. In neither the High Court nor the Supreme Court was any detailed consideration given to the issue as to whether the 215 acres of land in addition to the house could come within the definition of a family home, and in particular be properly regarded as a "portion of ground attached to and usually occupied with the dwelling or otherwise required for the amenity or convenience of the dwelling" in accordance with section 2 of the Act.

to be completed in July 1979. Prior to completion, however, the wife instituted proceedings claiming that any conveyance of the property without her prior written consent was void. The wife's claim was successful in the High Court but was dismissed on appeal by a majority in the Supreme Court. Referring to all cases in which an enforceable contract to sell a family home had been entered into before the coming into operation of the Act of 1976 where the conveyance had not been completed until after its passing, Henchy J. stated:

> "The prohibition in s. 3 must be held to be directed only against post-Act 'conveyances' so as to enable the unilateral disposition of both legal and equitable interests in the family home to be barred so as to achieve basic fairness by honouring lawful transactions and, in particular, so that ignorance of the law will justifiably not excuse transactions which are declared void because they do not observe the requirements of the Act[48] . . . the power to veto or annul the disposition of an interest in a family home, as given to the non-disposing spouse by the Act applies . . . only to agreements to sell or to instruments of conveyance entered into after the coming into operation of the Act."[49]

The Act did not expressly provide that it was to have a retrospective effect and the learned judge was clearly of the view that if it had done so, it may have been open to constitutional challenge.[50]

It is clear from the decided cases[51] that a wife's "prior consent" is required not only to close a sale but also to render valid and enforceable any contract for sale entered into as and from the 12th of July 1976.[52] Thus, in order to protect the interests of the purchaser, it is not sufficient to wait until the requisition stage to enquire whether the property being sold is a "family home" within the terms of the Act. If no such inquiry is made and a wife's consent is not obtained prior to the signing of a contract for sale, if the contract is for the sale of a family home and the vendor subsequently reneges on his commitment, the contract will be of little value to the purchaser.[53] If, however, a wife has given her written consent to the sale of a family home prior to the execution of contracts for sale, it has been held that no further consent is required for the valid completion of the conveyance.[54]

In *Kyne v. Tiernan & Anor.*[55] the husband and the wife decided to sell their

48. [1982] I.R. at p. 486.
49. *Ibid.*, at p. 487.
50. In addition to the judgement of Henchy J., see also judgement of O'Higgins C.J. Both Griffin J. and Hederman J. agreed with the judgements of their colleagues. Costello J. delivered a dissenting judgement.
   A contrary view to that of the Supreme Court was taken by McMahon J. in *M.D. v. L.D. & Ors.* (December, 1978) unreported (H.C.). In that case contracts were entered into on the 5th of March 1976 between the husband L.D. and N. for the sale of the D.'s family home to N. The transfer was executed by the purchaser and the vendor and the purchase money handed over on the 5th of May 1976. Subsequently, N. decided he wished the house to be held jointly in the names of his wife and himself and a fresh transfer was executed. The house was on registered land and neither transfer was registered prior to the 12th of July 1976. N. was aware throughout the transaction that the property he was purchasing was a family home and that D. was married. At no stage was the wife asked to consent to the sale of the home. In proceedings brought by the wife, M.D., the High Court held that the transaction had been caught by the Act and that the wife's consent was required as a transfer of registered land does not operate as a conveyance until it is registered (see Registration of Title Act, 1964, Sect. 51). This decision was delivered over three years prior to the Supreme Court decision in *Hamilton v. Hamilton* and was not appealed to that court.
51. See in particular, *Nestor v. Murphy, supra; Hamilton v. Hamilton, supra.*
52. See J.C.W. Wylie, *Irish Conveyancing Law, supra*, pp. 212–215.
53. See judgement of Griffin J. in *Somers v. Weir, supra.*
54. See *Kyne v. Tiernan and Anor.* (July, 1980) unreported (H.C.).
55. *Supra.*

family home, the legal title of which was held by the husband in his sole name, and both co-operated with an auctioneer in arranging a sale. The wife was reluctant to attend at the offices of the husband's solicitor to sign a written consent to the sale endorsed on the contract for sale but signed a letter drafted by the husband unequivocally consenting to the sale. Subsequently, the contract for sale was signed by the purchaser. Matrimonial difficulties arose between the husband and the wife and the wife refused to endorse her consent to the sale on the deed of transfer to the purchaser. In proceedings brought by the purchaser, seeking an order for specific performance of the contract for sale, the court held on the evidence that both the husband and the wife had agreed to sell the home and that the wife had given an unconditional consent to the sale in the letter signed by her. The court concluded that the consent contained in the letter was sufficient to comply with the provisions of section 3 of the Act. As for whether the section required a further written consent by the wife for the valid completion of the conveyance, McWilliam J. stated:

> "I suppose it could be said on a strict interpretation of section 3 of the Act, that there must be a consent in writing to each conveyance, that is to say, both to the contract and to the final conveyance to the purchaser, but I cannot imagine that it could have been the intention of the legislature to require two consents for the completion of one transaction, namely, the sale of one house, and thus leave a purchaser in the position of conducting all the work and incurring all the expense necessary for the completion of a purchase only to find that a spouse had changed his or her mind about giving consent and require the whole transaction to be abandoned. Accordingly, I am of opinion that the consent given by the wife . . . is sufficient for the completion of the entire transaction."

A conveyance of a home which is jointly owned by a married couple and to which both spouses are parties was held by the Supreme Court in *Nestor v. Murphy*[56] to be outside the scope of section 3(1). The two defendants, a married couple, each signed a contract to sell their family home in which they were joint tenants to the plaintiff. Subsequently, they refused to complete the sale, contending that the contract was void because the wife did not consent to the sale in writing before the contract was signed. Delivering the judgement of the court Henchy J. stated:

> "The basic purpose of the subsection is to protect the family home by giving a right of avoidance to the spouse who was not a party to the transaction. It ensures that protection by requiring, for the validity of the contract to dispose and of the actual disposition, that the non-disposing spouse should have given a prior consent in writing. The point and purpose of imposing the sanction of voidness is to enforce the right of the non-disposing spouse to veto the disposition by the other spouse of an interest in the family home . . . an extension of that right of avoidance to spouses who have entered into a joint 'conveyance' would not only be unnecessary for the attainment of that aim but also enable contracts to be unfairly or dishonestly repudiated by parties who entered into them freely, willingly and with full knowledge . . . the spouse whose 'conveyance' is avoided (under) s.3(1) is a spouse who has unilaterally (i.e. without the other spouse

---

56. [1979] I.R. 326 (S.C.).

joining) purported to 'convey' an interest in the family home without having obtained the prior consent in writing of the other spouse."[57]

The defendants' appeal was dismissed and the order for specific performance made in the High Court was affirmed.

Two months later in *Mulhall & Anor. v. Haran & Anor.*[58] the High Court held that if a family home is in the joint names of a husband and wife and they both authorise an estate agent to enter into a contract for the sale of their home, the validity of the contract is not affected by the failure of the wife to give her prior consent in writing to it. Following the Supreme Court decision in *Nestor v. Murphy* and holding that section 3(1) had no application, Keane J. stated:

> "I do not regard it as material that . . . the wife in the present case did not sign the contract, although she was a party to it. The judgement of the Supreme Court is plainly based on the principle that a transaction to which both spouses are parties is not captured at all by the Act of 1976. In this context it is manifestly immaterial whether the spouse on whose behalf protection is claimed signs the contract herself or authorises someone to sign it on her behalf. If, for example, the evidence in *Nestor v. Murphy* had established that the wife's solicitor had signed the contract as agent on her behalf with her full authority because she was away at the time, I do not believe that the decision would have been any different."[59]

The Act's application to mortgages is of particular importance. The term "mortgage" is said to include "an equitable mortgage, a charge on registered land and a chattel mortgage".[60] Thus, if a husband wishes to raise a mortgage on the family home, he has to obtain the consent of his wife. This requirement is particularly important for the wife living in the family home. If such a wife's husband attempted to sell the home, it is unlikely that she would be unaware of his actions, as undoubtedly people would come to view it. If, however, he sought by means of a mortgage to raise money to put into a failing business, to secure his overdraft or for gambling or drinking purposes, a wife could know nothing about it until a bank or building society sought to enforce its security. Under the provisions of the Act for such a mortgage to be valid and the rights of the mortgagee to be enforceable the prior consent of the wife to the mortgage must be obtained. As has been seen, however, a spouse's prior consent is not required to enable a judgement creditor register a judgement mortgage against a family home.[61] Thus, if a husband incurs business or other debts for which he is personally liable, while he cannot raise money to discharge such debts by mortgaging the family home without his wife's prior written consent, if the debts are not discharged and a judgement is obtained against him for the money due, a judgement creditor may force a sale of the home having registered a judgement against it[62] so as to enforce payment of the monies due to him out of the husband's share of the proceeds realised from any such sale.[63] The limited nature of the

---

57. *Ibid.*, at pp. 328, 329.

58. [1981] I.R. 364 (H.C.).

59. *Ibid.*, at p. 373.

60. Sect. 1(1). See *C.P. v. D.P.* [1983] 3 I.L.R.M. 380, in particular p. 384 and the reference to equitable mortgages therein.

61. *Containercare (Ireland) Ltd. v. Wycherley, supra; Murray v. Diamond, supra.* See p. 543 *ante.*

62. See, however, p. 561 *post* where the powers of the court to protect the family home under section 5 of the Act and the limitations on the court's power to do so are discussed.

63. A judgement creditor is only entitled to receive payment out of that portion of the monies to which the judgement debtor is entitled upon a sale of the home taking place. See

protection afforded by section 3 of the Act in such circumstances was vividly illustrated by Finlay P. in *C.P. v. D.P.*[64] Referring to the plaintiff wife's allegation that her husband had deposited the title deeds to the family home with a bank as security for overdrafts totalling £11,000 he stated that:

> "Since there is clear evidence that the wife did not consent in writing to the deposit of the title deeds by way of equitable mortgage against the bank indebtedness ... that equitable mortgage was a void conveyance ... and accordingly, the bank could not immediately lawfully realise their interest as mortgagee. Having regard to the judgement of Carroll J. in *Containercare (Ireland) Limited v. Wycherley*[65] ... however, this is a distinctly academic point as the bank can with expedition, if it so wished, sue for the recovery of the entire of the monies due to it and register such judgement as a judgement mortgage against the defendant (husband's) interest in the premises."[66]

The Act does not require the consent of a non-owning spouse if property that is mortgaged is not a family home at the time the mortgage is taken out. Thus, where a mortgage is raised when a house is purchased, the consent of the spouse without title is not required to validate the mortgage, if the parties will not acquire possession of the house until the transaction has been completed. Only after the house has been purchased and the parties have taken up residence will it become a family home as defined by the Act. In practice, however, since the coming into force of the Act, mortgagees have required the consent of the non-owning spouse to the creation of a mortgage on a newly purchased house.

Section 3(1) of the Act does not apply retrospectively to conveyances completed prior to its coming into force. Thus, a mortgage of a family home entered into by a husband without the consent of his wife prior to the 12th July 1976, is unaffected by the section. Nevertheless, such a mortgage may be defeated in whole[67] or in part[68] if the wife did not agree to it being obtained or if she was not a party to it, if at the time of its execution she had a beneficial interest in the home.[69] Thus, in *Northern Bank Ltd. v. Henry & Ors.*[70] a second mortgage on the family home granted to the bank by the husband in 1974 was held not to have priority over the wife's beneficial interest in the home which arose in 1964 and which was proved in subsequent High Court proceedings between the spouses determined under section 12 of the Married Women's Status Act, 1957. Prior to completing the mortgage the bank had not made any enquiries or furnished any requisitions to ascertain whether any litigation was pending or threatened in relation to the home or as to whether the wife had any beneficial interest in it. The bank was held not to have "made such enquiries ... as ought reasonably to have been made"[71] and was held to have constructive notice of the wife's

Containercare (Ireland) Ltd. v. Wycherley, supra. See also *Curran v. A.C. Bamlett (Ireland) Ltd.* (March, 1981) unreported (H.C.). See further, *Tubman v. Johnston, supra*, discussed in footnote 34a above.

64. *Supra.*
65. Now reported as *Containercare (Ireland) Ltd. v. Wycherley* [1982] I.R. 143 (H.C.).
66. *Ibid.*, at p. 384. See, however, *E.D. v. F.D.* (December, 1981) unreported (H.C.) and *G.P. v. I.P.* (October, 1984) unreported (H.C.) and p. 561 *et seq.* If it can be proved that a husband has deliberately embarked on a course of conduct to render a wife homeless, she may be able to secure protection for the family home in section 5 proceedings.
67. *Northern Bank v. Henry, supra.*
68. See *G.N.R. v. K.A.R.* (March, 1981) unreported (H.C.).
69. If the wife only acquired a beneficial interest in the family home subsequent to the obtaining of the mortgage, the mortgagee's interest would have priority. See *K. v. K.* (October, 1980) unreported (H.C.).
70. *Supra.*
71. See the Conveyancing Act, 1882, Sect. 3(1).

interest.[71a]

Delivering judgement in the Supreme Court, Henchy J. stated:

"Notwithstanding that this purchase took place before the passing of the Family Home Protection Act, 1976, (which makes a transaction of this kind void for want of the prior written consent of the wife), the (bank) as purchasers, ought reasonably to have adverted to the fact that there were decisions showing that a wife who had made payments towards the acquisition of the home or towards the payment of the mortgage instalments on it acquired a corresponding share in the beneficial ownership. As a matter of ordinary care, therefore, an inquiry as to threatened or pending claims was called for."[72]

Parke J., in the course of his judgement, stated:

"I have no doubt that by the beginning of the year 1974 any person who was offered a title to a matrimonial home by one spouse should have been alerted to the possibility that the other spouse might have a claim which would be upheld by the Courts to at least a share in the beneficial interest in the property. In the present case a proper investigation would have revealed that the wife was not merely entitled to an unquantified share in the house, but to the entire beneficial ownership to the exclusion of the proposed mortgagee."[73]

71a. For a detailed discussion as to the doctrine of notice, both actual and constructive in conveyancing transactions generally see J.C.W. Wylie, *Irish Conveyancing Law, supra,* p. 203, para. 6.38 *et seq.*

72. [1981] I.R. at p. 10. See further, *Ulster Bank v. Shanks & Ors.* [1982] N.I. 143 (Ch.D.) in which it was held that although the wife had a prior equitable interest in a one third share in the home, a second mortgage obtained by the bank was valid as against the entire property as the wife was present when a discussion took place between the bank manager and her husband and knew that the husband was arranging a second mortgage with the bank to stave off action by the bank on his overdraft but gave no indication that she had any beneficial interest in the home or that her consent was necessary to give the bank the security it sought. Murray J. held that in the circumstances it could not be said that the bank ought reasonably to have made enquiries of the wife as to whether she had an interest in the house and that accordingly the bank did not have constructive notice of her interest. During the course of his judgement, the learned judge stated "if a person in the wife's position were deliberately to stay silent about her own equitable interest with a view to asserting it later if the mortgagee attempted to realise his security, it would in my view amount to conduct of which a court administering equity could not possibly approve and, indeed, would be conduct which would leave the owner of the equitable interest open to the charge of coming to court with hands that were not clean." *Supra*, at p. 150.

73. *Ibid.*, at p. 21. *Northern Bank v. Henry, supra* was concerned with unregistered land. See also the English case of *Williams & Glyn's Bank Ltd. v. Boland* [1981] A.C. 487 (H.L.) in which it was held that a legal mortgage of registered land granted to the plaintiffs by a husband alone and registered in the Land Registry was overridden by the beneficial interest in the matrimonial home of the wife "in actual occupation of the land" (home) within Sect. 70(1)(g) of the Land Registration Act, 1925. The equivalent provision in Irish legislation is to be found in the Registration of Title Act, 1964, Sect. 72(1)(j). In the subsequent English case of *Kingsworth Trust Ltd. v. Bell* [1986] 1 All E.R. 423 (C.A.) it was held that a wife in occupation of a matrimonial home in which she had a beneficial interest and who was fraudulently induced by her husband into consenting to his obtaining a second mortgage was not bound by the mortgage deed and that her beneficial interest and right of occupation in the home had priority to all rights vested in the mortgagees. See further, *K. v. K.* (October, 1980) unreported (H.C.) in which both the judgements of the Supreme Court and of the House of Lords in the above cases are discussed. In this case, the High Court had determined in proceedings brought under section 12 of the Married Women's Status Act, 1957, that the wife had a 50% beneficial interest in the lease of a hardware shop held by the husband in his sole name. The husband, in October 1975, had deposited the deeds relating to the shop with the Bank of Ireland by way of an equitable mortgage to secure all his future liabilities. Five days later a company was formed in which the wife had a 50% interest to manage the hardware shop. The High Court held that as no monies were initially paid for the lease, the proprietary interest in the shop was jointly owned by the parties as the rental payments had been made with the profits earned from the shop in

In *Northern Bank v. Henry*, the mortgage was wholly defeated as the entire beneficial interest in the home in the proceedings instituted under the Act of 1957 was held to have vested in the wife 10 years prior to the husband purporting to create a mortgage on the property. In *G.N.R. v. K.A.R.*,[74] in proceedings brought by the wife under the Act of 1957, the mortgagee's interest was diminished as a result of the High Court holding the wife to possess a 51% beneficial interest in the family home. The family home, the legal title of which was held by the husband in his sole name, had been built in 1973 and was partially financed by a mortgage for £12,000 obtained by the husband. As the wife was not a party to the obtaining of the mortgage, it was held that the mortgage was only secured by the husband's 49% beneficial share of the property.[75]

Registration: Section 12 of the Act empowers a spouse to register a notice in the Registry of Deeds pursuant to the Registration of Deeds Act, 1707, (in the case of unregistered land) or under the Registration of Title Act, 1964, (in the case of registered land) stating she is married to a person having an interest in particular property or land. By registering the fact of her marriage, a wife can ensure that the defence of *bona fide* purchaser cannot be successfully used so as

which both parties worked and which was run by the company jointly owned by them. Barrington J. held that at the time the deeds were deposited with the bank the wife had no beneficial interest in the shop and that the interest of the bank was "prior" in time to the interest of the wife. If, however, the bank's interest had not been prior in time, Barrington J. indicated he may still not have found in her favour on this issue emphasising that both *Williams & Glyn's Bank* and the *Northern Bank* cases turned "on the fact that the property in question was the matrimonial home" (see p. 9 of judgement) stating that "when the wife enters the market place trading with property which is not the matrimonial home . . . the social considerations stressed in the cases cited (above) have no application. On the contrary, it appears to me to be in the interest of traders in general and also . . . of the wife herself that she should be treated like any other trader in the market." See p. 10 of judgement. See also *Allied Irish Banks v. McWilliams* (1982) Northern Ireland Law Reports, Bulletin of Judgements (No. 7) (Ch.D.) in which it was held that the bank could not validly lodge a judgement mortgage against the family home as the entire beneficial interest in it was vested in the wife, although the property had been acquired in the joint names of the husband and wife.

The most recent judgement on this issue is *Kingsnorth Finance Co. Ltd. v. Tizard* [1986] 1 W.L.R. 783 (Ch.D.) in which it was held that the wife's 50% beneficial interest in the matrimonial home was not subject to the plaintiffs' legal mortgage as the wife was not a party to the obtaining of the mortgage and the plaintiffs had failed to make such inquiries "as ought reasonably to have been made". For a different approach, however, see *Bristol and West Building Society v. Henning* [1985] 2 All E.R. 606 (C.A.) and M.P. Thompson, "Relief for First Mortgagees?" (1986) 49 M.L.R. 245 in which the latter case is discussed. See also J. Martin, "Co-ownership and the Mortgagee: A Tangled Web" (1986) 16 Fam. Law 315.

See further, R.A. Pearce, "Joint Occupation and the Doctrine of Notice" (1980) I.J. (n.s.) 211; J.M.G. Sweeney, "Occupiers Rights: A New Hazard for Irish Conveyancers" (1981) 75 *Gazette of the Incorporated Law Society of Ireland* 103; J. Conlon, "Beneficial Interests, Conveyancers & the Occupational Hazard" (1985) 79 *Gazette of the Incorporated Law Society of Ireland* 59.

74. (March, 1981) unreported (H.C.).

75. In *Northern Bank v. Henry, supra*, the plaintiffs had instituted proceedings subsequent to the wife succeeding in her claim to the entire beneficial interest in the family home in proceedings instituted by her under the Married Women's Status Act, 1957. In *G.N.R. v. K.A.R., supra*, the husband and wife had reached an agreement settling the proceedings brought by the wife under the 1957 Act, agreeing on an equal division of the property. The mortgagees, Canada Life, were on notice of the proceedings but chose not to appear. Nevertheless, Carroll J. "felt it proper to hear evidence so that the mortgagees' interests were protected" (see p. 1 of judgement) and in the result the mortgagees ended up with 1% less interest in the property than they would have had under the terms of settlement. Whether the parties having settled their proceedings should have been put to the expense of a full oral hearing on the issue in order to "protect the interests" of a third party who was a notice party in the proceedings and who chose not to appear, must be questionable. See, however, *Ulster Bank v. Shanks, supra* — it is arguable that although the wife was not a party to the mortgage that as she must have known it was obtained her beneficial interest should have been held to be subject to the bank's mortgage.

to uphold the validity of a conveyance of the family home made by her husband without her prior consent. It is a necessary part of the investigation of title carried out by a purchaser's solicitor prior to the completion of a conveyance to conduct a registry of deeds search, in the case of unregistered land, and a land registry search, in the case of registered land and either search would reveal the existence of a notice registered by a wife in the appropriate registry. However, even if a wife fails to register a notice she will not be prejudiced as the section provides that the fact that a notice of marriage has not been registered "shall not give rise to any inference as to the non-existence of a marriage."[76]

Section 13 of the Act states that Section 59(2) of the Registration of Title Act, 1964, (which refers to noting upon the register provisions of any enactment restricting dealings in land) shall not apply to the provisions of the 1976 Act. Section 59 imposes a duty on the Registrar to note upon the Register the "prohibitive or restrictive provisions . . . of an enactment by which the alienation, assignment, subdivision or subletting of any land is prohibited or in any way restricted". Moreover, under the section such provisions even if not registered are held to be burdens on the land concerned under section 72 of the 1964 Act.

In *Guckian & Anor. v. Brennan & Anor.*[77] Gannon J. stated:

"The Act of 1976 does not create, nor invest a married person with any right affecting land or property in the nature of an interest in land which could fall within any of the classifications of burdens within section 72(1) of the Act of 1964. Such right as is conferred is a right which affects the instrument of transfer and its validity. If that instrument is invalid the transfer is ineffective; but the spouse for whose benefit the transfer is rendered ineffective obtains no estate or interest which can affect the ownership or title to the property described in the transfer."[78]

In the view of the learned judge section 13 took the provisions of the 1976 Act "out of the scope" of sections 59 and 72 of the 1964 Act. He held that the effect of section 13, taken together with section 31(1) of the 1964 Act, is that a purchaser of registered land when investigating title need only enquire into matters arising under the Family Home Protection Act in relation to "the particular intended contract of sale and the intended instrument of transfer"[79] to that purchaser. There is no obligation on the purchaser of such land to make enquiries as to the validity under the 1976 Act of prior transactions as the Register, in the absence of fraud or mistake, is conclusive as to the validity of any such transaction.[80]

---

76. Sect. 12(2). Sect. 12(3) provides that "no stamp duty, Registry of Deeds fee or land registration fee shall be payable in respect of any such notice."
77. [1981] I.R. 478 (H.C.). See further (1981) D.U.L.J. 86.
78. *Ibid.*, at p. 485. See also *Containercare (Ireland) Ltd. v. Wycherley, supra; Murray v. Diamond, supra.*
79. *Ibid.*, at p. 488.
80. Section 31(1) of the Registration of Title Act, 1964, provides that "The register shall be conclusive evidence of the title of the owner to the land as appearing on the register and of any right, privilege, appurtenance or burden as appearing thereon; and such title shall not, in the absence of actual fraud, be in any way affected in consequence of such owner having notice of any deed, document, or matter relating to the land; but nothing in this Act shall interfere with the jurisdiction of any court of competent jurisdiction based on the ground of actual fraud or mistake, and the court may upon such ground make an order directing the register to be rectified in such manner and on such terms as it thinks just".

Offences: Section 15 provides

"Where any person having an interest in any premises, on being required in writing by or on behalf of any other person proposing to acquire that interest to give any information necessary to establish if the conveyance of that interest requires a consent under section 3(1), knowingly gives information which is false or misleading in any material particular, he shall be guilty of an offence and shall be liable —

  (a) on summary conviction, to a fine not exceeding £200 or imprisonment for a term not exceeding twelve months or to both, or

  (b) on conviction on indictment, to imprisonment for a term not exceeding five years,

without prejudice to any other liability, civil or criminal."

Thus, if a husband in answer to a purchaser's written inquiry falsely states that he is single and that the house he intends to sell is not a family home within the meaning of the Act, he is liable to a conviction under the above section. The section does not, however, make it an offence for another to masquerade as a party's spouse. For example, A has forced his wife to leave the family home and is living with B. A wishes to sell the family home and B signs the consent pretending to be his wife. Whilst A may be liable to prosecution under this section, B is not.[81]

Dispensing with consent: Section 4 provides that if a spouse whose consent is required under section 3(1) "omits or refuses to consent", such consent may be dispensed with by the court subject to the following provisions.[82]

(i) The court cannot dispense with the consent of a spouse, unless it considers it is

"unreasonable for the spouse to withhold consent, taking into account all the circumstances including —

  (a) the respective needs and resources of the spouses and of the dependent children[83] (if any) of the family, and

  (b) in a case where the spouse whose consent is required is offered alternative accommodation, the suitability of that accommodation having regard to the respective degrees of security of tenure in the family home and in the alternative accommodation".[84]

---

81. If B has made a statutory declaration she may be guilty of an offence under the Statutory Declarations Act, 1938, Sect. 6.

82. Sect. 4(1).

83. Sect. 1(1) of the Act of 1976 as amended by the Adoption Act, 1976, and by Sect. 2(3) of the Age of Majority Act, 1985 defines a "dependent child of the family" in relation to a spouse or spouses as any child:

(a) of both spouses or adopted by both spouses under the Adoption Act, 1952-1976 or in relation to whom both spouses are *in loco parentis*, or

(b) of either spouse, or adopted by either spouse under the Adoption Acts, 1952-76 or in relation to whom either spouse is *in loco parentis*, where the other spouse, being aware that he is not the parent of the child, has treated the child as a member of the family who is under the age of 16 years, or, if he has attained that age:

  (i) is receiving full time education or instruction at any university, college, school, or other educational establishment and is under the age of 18 years, or

  (ii) is suffering from mental or physical disability to such extent that it is not reasonably possible for him to maintain himself fully.

84. Sect. 4(2).

As is indicated by the use of the word "including", (a) and (b) are not all embracing, the court being able to take into account other relevant circumstances.

In *Somers v. Weir* it was stated that the onus of proving that the withholding of consent is unreasonable rests "fairly and squarely" on the spouse seeking an order dispensing with consent.[85]

In *O'M. v. O'M.*[86] the parties' marriage had broken down and the wife and her children were living in a county council flat, whilst the husband still resided in the family home which was in his sole name. The husband wished to sell the home and sought an order to dispense with the wife's consent. Finlay P. was satisfied that it was not possible for the wife and children to reside in the home "having regard to the attitude and conduct of the husband" who had deliberately not worked for two years and who had placed the home in "relatively immediate peril of being sold by the mortgagees" by deliberately failing to make mortgage repayments. He ordered that the consent of the wife to a sale of the home should only be dispensed with upon terms that, following the sale of the premises, one half of the nett proceeds of sale be lodged in court to be made available to the wife towards the purchase by her of accommodation for herself and the children. The wife had no right to any beneficial interest in the proceeds of sale and Finlay P. concluded, stating that upon the purchase of a house he would "direct that the appropriate share by way of interest in that house, be registered in the name of the husband and that the balance be registered in the name of the wife" and emphasised that it would "be the house in which the wife and children shall be entitled to live . . . to the exclusion of the husband."[87]

In *S.O'B. v. M.O'B.*[88] the husband was residing in Hong Kong with another woman and the child of their relationship. The wife resided in the family home in Ireland with the two children of their marriage and part of her income was derived from renting out a portion of the family home. She also had a separate income of her own and received maintenance from her husband. The parties' marriage had been annulled by the Roman Catholic Church in proceedings originally initiated by the wife but which were ultimately processed with the concurrence of both parties. Following the grant of the Church nullity decree the husband had married the woman he was residing with in a church in Hong Kong.[89] As no civil decree of annulment had been sought or obtained by him or no recognisable foreign decree of divorce granted, the parties were still validly married to each other.

The husband sought to dispense with the wife's consent to a sale of the family home as he wished to return to reside in Ireland and to raise some money to enable him purchase a home for himself and his second "wife". He proposed that the nett proceeds of sale of the family home would be divided in such shares as would enable the wife to obtain reasonable alternative accommodation which would be suitable for her own needs and those of their two children. O'Hanlon J. concluded that both spouses were at fault for the break up of their marriage and that they both had "to live with the situation where two separate households have to be maintained out of whatever resources are available to all the parties in the new situation that has arisen".[90] The legal title to the family home was

---

85. See judgement of Griffin J.
86. (December, 1981) unreported (H.C.).
87. See p. 6 of judgement. In making the above order, Finlay P. clearly relied not only on Sect. 4 but also on the powers conferred on the court by Sect. 5 of the Act. See p. 5 of judgement. See further p. 561 *post et seq.*
88. (December, 1980) unreported (H.C.).
89. The second marriage was invalid under Irish law and arguably criminally bigamous.
90. See p. 8 of judgement.

held by the husband in his sole name and the wife was held to be entitled to no more than 25% beneficial interest in the property pursuant to a claim made by her in the same proceedings to a proprietary interest in it. Referring to this, O'Hanlon J. noted that the husband was willing to make available as much as half the nett proceeds of sale to the wife and that "she would be better off if she had a house she could call her own, even though it might be less commodious than the present family home, and even though it may not be as convenient to the school attended by the children."[91] In the learned judge's view "the financial problems stemming from the breakdown of the marriage (could) only be resolved by a sale of the family home"[92] and an order was made by him dispensing with the wife's consent. Although the judgement is ambiguous, it appears that it was intended by O'Hanlon J. that any property purchased for the wife and children to reside in was to be purchased in the wife's sole name.[93]

As has already been seen, in *Hamilton v. Hamilton*,[94] the Supreme Court held the Act of 1976 had no application as the husband had contracted to sell the family home and the land attached to it in 1973. At first instance, Gannon J. in the High Court had taken the contrary view and had held that the Act did apply to the intended conveyance. He then went on to consider in detail whether the wife's withholding of her consent was reasonable.[95] He held that in the circumstances of the case the matters included by the Act as being specific matters to which the court should have reference when determining such an application had no relevance (those contained in (a) and (b) on page 554) as the spouses in this case were still living together and that these matters referred to "a situation in which a family, so far as the two spouses are concerned, has ceased to be a family."

Further on in his judgement the learned judge stated:

> "The purchaser . . . asks the Court to declare that it is unreasonable for the plaintiff to withhold her consent solely on the grounds that she does so because of sentimental attachment . . . I believe it to be the law that the determination of whether the withholding of consent is unreasonable or not is not resolved by considering whether the reasons are commendable or acceptable . . . I must take account of the circumstances of the family as a unit and consider the interests of the family to the extent that it remains a unit. There is no evidence of division in this family or between the spouses who have, at all times, supported each other and complemented each other each in his and her proper functional area of ability. To me it is natural, proper and reasonable that the wife and mother in a family would be motivated by emotional and sentimental responses and for her these would

---

91. See p. 9 of judgement.
92. See p. 11 of judgement.
93. No final determination was made as to the exact share of the nett proceeds of sale that were to be released to the wife. It was ordered that the nett proceeds were to be held on deposit by the parties' solicitors to await the further order of the court and "in particular, with liberty to apply should any property suitable for the needs of the wife and the two children of the marriage become available for purchase in the name of the wife." Although the judgement contains a number of references to the husband's willingness to make available to the wife one half of the nett proceeds of sale, no indication is given in the judgement as to the basis upon which the court would determine any such subsequent application and the Act of 1976 does not expressly contain any statutory powers or lay down any criteria applicable to determine such application. The decision in this case was appealed to the Supreme Court but the appeal was subsequently withdrawn.
94. *Supra.* See p. 546 *ante.*
95. The High Court judgement which was delivered in February 1980 remains unreported.

have much higher priority than financial and commercial considerations. In a united family the spouses will disclose and balance their differing priorities in the ordinary course of family life and daily decisions. For many family and domestic decisions the wife's priorities will prevail and in many others the husband's will prevail, particularly in matters pertaining to the security and maintenance and advancement of the family. It may be unusual for the wife to persist in pressing her priorities in an area of decision in which the husband's judgement would normally prevail, but I could not say that it would be unreasonable."[96]

As for D.'s reliance on the circumstances as they existed at the time when the contract for sale was entered into, the learned judge stated that in determining whether to dispense with a consent he must consider the circumstances as they are at the time of the court proceedings. He continued:

"The evidence is that the plaintiff and her husband are both of the one mind, namely that they do not want to move . . . nor to live separately, nor to leave the family home. The value of the property is now estimated at over £640,000 and it would be impossible for the plaintiff and the first defendant (the husband) to acquire an alternative farm of land of reasonable equivalent quality of any more than 50 acres if they were to complete this sale. Without determining whether her attitude is commendable or acceptable I take the view that it is not unreasonable for the plaintiff to withhold her consent in all the circumstances to the proposed 'conveyance' and accordingly I may not dispense with her consent."[97]

As the Supreme Court was of the view that the Act of 1976 had no application to the particular transaction it did not have to pronounce on this issue.

In *R. v. R.*[98] McMahon J. refused to dispense with the wife's consent holding that her refusal to consent to her husband raising an additional mortgage on the family home was not unreasonable. The parties' marriage had broken down, the husband had formed a relationship with another woman and intended to move out of the home leaving his wife and children to reside in it. He wished to raise a mortgage to discharge various debts he had incurred and the wife refused to consent to his doing so. On the evidence it was held that if the husband was permitted to obtain the proposed mortgage, he would not have available sufficient income to maintain his family, support himself and make the mortgage repayments that would become due.

In two cases in which written judgements have been delivered, the High Court has considered the interaction between the jurisdiction conferred on it by the Act of 1976 to dispense with the consent of a spouse deemed to be "unreasonable" and that conferred by the Partition Acts, 1868—76 in so far as the latter empower the courts to order the sale of a family home or other property in which both

---

96. See pp. 25—26 of judgement.
97. See p. 27 of judgement.
98. (December, 1978) unreported (H.C.).

spouses hold a beneficial interest unless "good reason" to refuse an order for sale is proved.[99]

In *A.L. v. J.L.*[100] the wife who, the High Court ruled, held a 50% beneficial interest in the family home,[101] sought an order under the Partition Acts for the sale of it approximately four years after leaving her husband and going to reside with another man. There were no children of the marriage but at the date of the court proceedings two children had been born to the wife, fathered by the person with whom she was residing. The husband was living alone in the family home and it was a condition of his employment that he continue to reside in the same area in which it was situated. The wife sought to sell the house on the grounds that she was responsible for her two children and wished to have a capital asset to leave them in the event of anything happening to her. Delivering judgement Finlay P. stated:

> "Having regard to the provisions of the Family Home Protection Act, 1976, in the absence of an agreement between the parties, an order for sale cannot ... be made under the Partition Acts, unless the court is also satisfied that it should dispense with the consent of the non-agreeing spouse under section 4 of the 1976 Act."[102]

Having regard to the evidence given, the learned President concluded that he was "not satisfied that at present there are grounds on which it would be appropriate for the court to dispense with the consent of the husband" and he refused to make the order sought by the wife.

In the earlier case of *O'D. v. O'D.*[103] the family home was held by the husband and wife in their joint names. The husband, having moved out of the family home after the wife unsuccessfully tried to have him barred from it, sought an order for the sale of the home. He proposed that the monies realised from the sale be used to discharge the building society mortgage and that the balance be invested in a less expensive home "for the benefit of the wife during her life" and their dependent child. The property was valued at approximately £43,000 and Murphy J. accepted that at the date of the hearing the income of the husband was "inadequate to meet a reasonable claim for maintenance", the mortgage repayments and repayment of a loan to his father, as well as keeping the wife and himself "in the basic necessities of life". Declining to make the order for sale sought by the husband, and referring to the Partition Acts, he stated:

---

99. The right of a joint tenant or tenants in common at common law to compel a partition or physical division of the property so held on the other joint tenant or tenants in common was first conferred by a statute enacted in 1542 (33 Hen. 8, c.32 Ir.). This statute was amended in 1697 (9 Will. 3, c.12). These statutes have been repealed by the Statute Law Revision (Ireland) Act, 1878, and the Statute Law Revision (Pre-Union Irish Statutes) Act, 1962. The Partition Acts, 1868 and 1876 gave the court power to order a sale of the property as an alternative to partition and to order a division of the proceeds of sale in accordance with the proportionate interest in the property vested in the parties. The court is not bound by the Acts to order a sale as when one is sought, section 4 of the 1868 Act provides that it may refuse to order a sale if there is "good reason" not to do so. The onus to establish such "good reason" is placed on the person or persons resisting the sale. See, for example, *In the Matter of the Estate of Agnes B. Whitnell & Ors.* (1887) 19 L.R.I.r. 5 Eq. 572 (Ch.D.). See further footnote 106 *post* and J.C.W. Wylie, *Irish Land Law, supra*, p. 369.
100. (February, 1984) unreported (H.C.).
101. Although the wife had a 50% beneficial interest, the court held the husband was entitled to some credit for mortgage repayments made by him after the wife's departure from the home to which the wife had made no contribution.
102. See p. 6 of judgement.
103. (November, 1983) unreported (H.C.).

"An order (for sale) will not be made where the court sees good reason to the contrary[104] ... what constitutes good reason at the present time will properly have regard to the rights of the parties under the Family Home Protection Act, 1976."[105]

Referring to the contention that in determining whether an order for sale should be made in relation to a home in which both spouses have a beneficial interest, the court need not have regard to the provisions of the Act of 1976 and was bound to determine the issues solely by having regard to the provisions of the Partition Acts, he continued:

"It seems to me unthinkable that the court would direct a conveyance to be made under the 1868 Act without having regard to the right of a spouse to withhold his or her consent and indeed the express duty imposed on the court not to dispense with a consent without taking into account all the relevant circumstances ... in my view a court would be justified in concluding on the circumstances of present times, under our Constitution and of the rights conferred by the Family Home Protection Act that the loss of the statutory veto represented a good reason within the meaning of section 4 of the Partition Act, 1868."[106]

A further issue that arises under this section relates to what approach the courts will take to deal with the problem that would arise if a wife has concluded a deed of separation containing a statement whereby she renounces or waives all

---

104. See p. 9 of judgement.
105. See p. 10 of judgement.
106. See p. 11 of judgement. This case came to the High Court on appeal. The President of the Circuit Court had declined to order a sale of the family home but had ordered its partition. Dealing with the issue of partition in his judgement Murphy J. pointed out that the Act of 1542 had been repealed by the Act of 1962 (see footnote 99 *supra*) and queried whether the courts still retained a power to order partition. It was contended that while the Act of 1962 removed the court's statutory power to order partition, the jurisdiction to decree partition remained as part of the court's "inherent equitable jurisdiction". Murphy J. stated he had "some hesitation" in accepting this argument and for the purpose of the specific case he "assumed" rather than "accepted" that this contention was correct but ruled that "an order of partition on the basis of the evidence available would be wholly inappropriate." As the Acts of 1868 and 1876 effectively amended the earlier and now repealed legislation empowering the courts to order sale in lieu of partition, some doubt must now exist as a consequence of the above judgement as to the continued applicability of these statutes. Although decided after *O'D. v. O'D.*, this issue is not referred to by Finlay P. in his judgement in *A.L. v. J.L., supra*, which contains no reference to the former case. See also *N.D. v. A.D.* (December, 1982) unreported (H.C.) in which O'Hanlon J. made an order pursuant to the Partition Acts for the sale of a public house which was also used as a family home but the learned judge at no stage adverted to the issue raised by Murphy J. in *O'D. v. O'D.* In *F.F. v. C.F.* (December, 1985) unreported (H.C.) in an appeal from the Circuit Court to the High Court in proceedings instituted by the husband pursuant to the Partition Acts seeking the sale of a family home in which it was acknowledged both husband and wife had a joint interest, the issue was raised as to whether the court possessed jurisdiction to make an order for sale pursuant to the Partition Acts having regard to the fact that the statute of 1542 had been repealed by the Act of 1962. Giving judgement on this issue, Barr J. referred to Sect. 2(1) of the Act of 1962 which states that "This Act shall not affect any existing principle or rule of law or equity or any established jurisdiction, form or course of pleading, practice or procedure, notwithstanding that it may have been in any manner derived from, affirmed or recognised by an enactment hereby repealed" and stated that it was evident that this provision was intended by the Oireachtas as a "safety-net" and that he had no doubt that the right to seek an order for sale pursuant to Sect. 3 and 4 of the 1868 Act "is preserved by section 2(1) in that" the right in question is within the meaning and intent of the phrase "any existing principle or rule of law or equity". The learned judge also stated that "there is no doubt that the 1542 Act has been lawfully repealed" (see p. 4 of judgement). The law in this area will continue to remain uncertain until the issue is resolved by the Supreme Court or until such time as appropriate legislation to resolve the difficulty is enacted by the Oireachtas.

proprietary and possessory interest in the family home and subsequently refuses to consent to its sale, such deed containing no express provision whereby she unconditionally or irrevocably agrees to give any such consent pursuant to the provisions of the Act of 1976 in the event of it being sought. Whereas such a provision in a deed would undoubtedly be a circumstance to take into account in determining whether to dispense with a consent, it is submitted that such a provision would not lead to an automatic dispensing of consent. The court would still be bound to have regard to other circumstances including those listed in (a) and (b) referred to on page 554 *ante*.

Another question arises as to the manner in which the court would deal with a case in which a separation agreement contains a clause by which a wife promises to give her consent to the sale of the family home if required to do so at some future time, but subsequently refuses such consent. Would an order of specific performance to enforce such a clause be made? It is submitted that such a clause would again simply be one of the circumstances to be taken into account by the court upon an application being made to it, to dispense with consent.

(ii) If the spouse whose consent is required is in desertion of the other spouse, the court must dispense with the former's consent. Desertion is said to include

"conduct on the part of the former spouse that results in the other spouse, with just cause, leaving and living separately and apart from him".[107]

Thus, under the latter provision, if with just cause a wife leaves her husband, and the husband who owns the family home wishes to sell it, the husband and not the wife will be held to be in desertion, and the wife's consent to the sale will still be required. If, however, the wife leaves without just cause she will be held to be in desertion and the husband will be able to obtain a court order dispensing with her consent.

In *S.O'B. v. M.O'B.*[108] the husband alleged that his wife had forced him by her behaviour to move out of the family home and that she consequently was in constructive desertion of him. O'Hanlon J. rejected the husband's contention that he should dispense with the wife's consent to a sale of the family home by holding her to be in desertion, saying that he was "not willing to lay the blame (for the breakup of the marriage) fairly and squarely at the door of the husband or the wife."[109] He concluded, stating that:

"He was not prepared to hold that this (was) a case of constructive desertion of the husband by the wife, by conduct on her part making it impossible for him to continue living with her."[110]

and refused to dispense with the wife's consent on this ground. He did, however, as we have already seen, hold her to be unreasonable in withholding consent.[112]

(iii) If a spouse is incapable of consenting by

"reason of unsoundness of mind or other mental disability or has not after reasonable inquiries been found, the court may give the consent on behalf of that spouse if it appears to be reasonable to do so".[113]

---

107. Sect. 4(3).
108. *Supra.*
109. See p. 7 of judgement.
110. See p. 8 of judgement.
112. See p. 555 *ante.*
113. Sect. 4(4).

The President of the High Court has stated in a practice direction that where there is an application to dispense with a consent in circumstances **(ii)** and **(iii)** and the spouse whose consent is required cannot be served as a party, the fact of desertion, of unsoundness of mind or other mental disability or of inability to trace should be corroborated by an affidavit of some responsible disinterested person confirming the material facts contained in the affidavit of the applicant spouse.[114] An order to dispense with consent may in such circumstances be granted upon an *ex parte* application being made.

In *Somers v. Weir,*[115] the Supreme Court emphasised that an application under section 4 must be made before a conveyance takes place. The court has no jurisdiction to dispense with consent under the section after a conveyance has been completed. At that stage the court may determine, upon an application being made to it under section 3 of the Act, whether a conveyance is valid without consent or void *ab initio*, but it cannot make an order under section 4 dispensing with a consent.

Section 5 Proceedings: Section 5 of the Act confers on the court a general discretionary power to make orders to protect the right of a spouse to reside in the family home. Sub-section (1) provides,

"Where it appears to the court, on the application of a spouse, that the other spouse is engaging in such conduct as may lead to the loss of any interest in the family home *or* may render it unsuitable for habitation as a family home with the intention of depriving the applicant spouse or a dependent child[116] of the family of his residence in the family home, the court may make such order as it considers proper, directed to the other spouse or to any other person, for the protection of the family home in the interest of the applicant spouse or such child".

Judicial intervention can take place under the section in a wide variety of circumstances. The jurisdiction conferred by this section on the court may be invoked by a wife, for example, if a husband

(i)   attempts to demolish part of the family home or remove slates from the roof, *or*

(ii) cuts off or has cut off the electricity, gas, water or any other essential supplies, *or*

(iii) suffers a judgement in collusive proceedings brought by a friend with the intention of ultimately being "forced" to sell the home to meet the award made in the judgement following upon the friend registering a judgement mortgage against the home,[117] *or*

(iv) refuses or fails[118] to pay any further mortgage instalments due or rent payable in respect of the home and can afford to make such payments[119] or deliberately renders himself unable to afford to make such payments, for example, by giving up his employment,[120] *or*

---

114. See (1977) 111 I.L.T. & S.J. 176.
115. *Supra.* See also *H. & L. v. S., supra.*
116. For the definition of a dependent child under the Act see footnote 83 *supra.*
117. See *Murray v. Diamond* [1982] 2 I.L.R.M. at p. 115.
118. See *D.C. v. A.C.* [1981] 1 I.L.R.M. 357 (H.C.) in particular at p. 359.
119. See *A.D. v. D.D. & Anor* (June, 1983) unreported (H.C.) in particular at p. 11 of judgement.
120. See *O'M. v. O'M., supra*; see *C.B. v. S.B.* (May, 1983) unreported (H.C.).

    (v) breaches covenants in the lease of the home which could result in forfeiture, *or*

    (vi) advertises that the family home is for sale, or puts it onto an estate agent's books.

Behaviour such as that outlined in (i) and (ii) could be such as to render a house "unsuitable for habitation as a family home", whilst (iii)–(vi) could be regarded as conduct likely to lead to the loss of an interest in the family home. Such conduct by itself will, however, be insufficient for a successful invocation of the court's jurisdiction. For the court to intervene in such circumstances, the section requires proof that a husband acted in such a fashion "with the *intention* of depriving" his wife or a dependent child of the family of his or her residence in the family home.

In *C.P. v. D.P.*[121] Finlay P. rejected the contention that the necessary intention may be imputed to a spouse from the natural and probable consequences of his conduct, stating that he was satisfied he could not

> "construe the word 'intention' in s.5 sub-l. of the Act of 1976 as being equivalent to the implied or imputed intention which can arise from the natural and probable consequences of an act or omission. There must be . . . an element of deliberate conduct."[122]

He concluded that he was not entitled to make an order pursuant to section 5 transferring a family home[123] into the sole name of the plaintiff wife, although he was satisfied that the husband was substantially in debt and there was no doubt that the state of the husband's finances "lead to a significant danger of the loss of the family home".[124] He found that the debts had arisen as a result of the recession in the building industry affecting the husband's business as an architect; the breakup in his business partnership and from the separation of the spouses rendering it necessary to maintain two households rather than one. The husband, in the learned President's view, had "been struggling, though possibly unsuccessfully, with a difficult professional situation and with mounting debts"[125] and the most desirable thing for the future financial interests of the family would be for an earliest possible sale of the family home (which was estimated as being worth between £60,000 to £70,000) with the proceeds being applied in an agreed manner to discharge a "substantial portion of the debts of the husband" and to provide a stable and secure family home for the wife and children and proper accommodation separately for the husband.[126]

In the later case of *S. v. S.*[127] the wife also sought an order that the family home, which was in the joint names of herself and her husband, be transferred into her sole name but the husband was held to have lacked the necessary "intention". Approximately seven months prior to the court proceedings, the husband had disappeared having removed all his belongings and his passport from the family home. Shortly before his departure a representative of Allied Irish Banks had called to the family home and stated that because of the husband's severe financial difficulties the home would have to be sold. Subsequently,

121. [1983] 3 I.L.R.M. 380 (H.C.).
122. *Ibid.*, at p. 384.
123. Which was in the sole ownership of the husband.
124. *Supra*, at p. 384.
125. *Ibid.*, at p. 385.
126. *Ibid.*
127. [1983] 3 I.L.R.M. 387 (H.C.).

the wife learned that there were large sums of money being claimed from her husband by various creditors and that an investigation was under way with regard to possible criminal offences. McWilliam J. refusing to make an order transferring the family home into the sole name of the wife stated:

"The defendant appears to have looked after his wife and children to the best of his ability, possibly to a large extent with borrowed money. Although he may have acted improvidently and, possibly, dishonestly, and the natural and probable consequences of his actions may have been that the family home would be a target for his various creditors, it appears to me that it is unlikely that he formed any intention of depriving his wife and children of his residence in the family home and that it is much more likely that he left the country to escape the attentions of his creditors and other more distressing pursuers."[128]

The deliberate conduct required under the section does not necessarily require that a spouse must actually do something. In *D.C. v. A.C.*[129] Carroll J. stated that she was satisfied

"that the phrase 'engaging' in such conduct covers inactivity as well as activity"[130]

and held that the husband's failure to pay the mortgage instalments "could be described as engaging in such conduct as may lead to the loss of an interest in the family home."[131] The learned judge declined, however, to order that the home be transferred into the wife's sole name in the circumstances of the particular case as to do so

"would have the effect of divesting the husband of a valuable asset (i.e. his joint interest in the surplus monies that would be realised on a sale) at a time when both he and the wife have considerable debts incurred in the course of their marriage for their living expenses."

The learned judge indicated that following upon the sale of the home she would make elaborate orders under section 5(2) of the Act to provide for the discharge of these debts.[132]

If the requisite "intention" has been proved it is judicially accepted that section 5(1) confers a wide discretion on the court to determine what type of order it should make[133] and that this discretion may extend to ordering a spouse to transfer the family home or his interest in it to the other spouse. In *E.D. v. F.D.*[134] the husband had deserted the wife who resided with her three children in the family home. It was established that the husband, who lived in London, owed a "considerable amount of money" to creditors; had been sued in the past and that the sheriff had come to his home to enforce judgement; had allowed ejectment proceedings to be instituted for possession by the mortgagees of his family home and was living beyond his means. In the initial proceedings brought,

---

128. *Ibid.*, at p. 390.
129. [1981] 1 I.L.R.M. 357 (H.C.).
130. *Ibid.*, at p. 359.
131. *Ibid.*
132. See p. 565 *post.*
133. See the comments of McCarthy J. in *Weir v. Somers* [1983] I.R. 122; [1983] 3 I.L.R.M. 343 (S.C.); See also *O'M. v. O'M.* (December, 1981) unreported (H.C.) Finlay P. and *E.D. v. F.D.* (October, 1980) unreported (H.C.) Costello J.
134. *Supra.*

Costello J. accepted that the husband had "for some time acted in an improvident way" but stated that he did not "think that he (had) acted with the intention referred to in the section."[135] He ordered that the husband enter into discussions and negotiations with his various creditors, including the revenue authorities in both Ireland and the United Kingdom to ascertain the exact nature of his various liabilities and that he make arrangements to discharge them. He also ordered that the husband advise the wife's solicitors, on request, of the progress made and gave the wife "liberty to review the application under section 5 if thought fit."[136] Fourteen months later, upon the wife renewing her application, Costello J., delivering his second judgement in the case,[137] noted that the husband had failed "to take any steps in relation to his creditors and he has not given particulars to the (wife or her solicitors) when required to do so", and concluded that the husband's behaviour "is deliberate". Having stated that proceedings were about to be issued by creditors in some cases and that others were threatened, the trial judge stated that in his view the husband "is engaged in conduct with the intent required . . . with the result that the family home is on risk and very serious risk" as if a judgement was obtained by a creditor and registered against the family home as a judgement mortgage, the family home may be lost."[138] He ordered that the husband convey the family home to the wife but that the conveyance was to be "without prejudice to any equitable rights" which the (husband) may have in the family home.[139]

In *C.B. v. S.B.*[140] Barron J. concluded that not only was the husband unable to properly manage his own affairs but that he had "put his obligation to his wife and children at the bottom of his list of priorities, so much so that he has actually indulged in conduct which could only have been calculated to achieve the end of paying her nothing and ultimately of losing his interest in the family home."[141] He held that section 5(1) of the Act of 1976 "has been shown to apply"[142] and made an order that the wife and the couple's children had "a right of residence" in the home and that "the husband's interest" in the home "be held subject to that right of residence". The trial judge in the same case held the parties to have a joint beneficial interest in the property and to be each liable for one half of the mortgage repayments. No explanation is given by the trial judge for making the particular order referred to under section 5(1) and it is not clear what assistance this order gave to the wife in the circumstances of the case.

In *G.P. v. I.P.*[143] O'Hanlon J. held that the husband was "engaged on a course of conduct designed to deprive the plaintiff (wife) of the family home and to extract the maximum financial benefit from the premises for himself, without any regard for the needs of his wife and children."[144] In earlier proceedings, the

---

135. See p. 8 of judgement.
136. See p. 9 of judgement.
137. (December, 1981) unreported (H.C.).
138. See p. 2 of judgement.
139. See p. 3 of judgement. It is not certain what was meant by the order being made "without prejudice to any equitable rights" of the husband in the family home as if the husband retained an equitable or beneficial interest in the home after it was conveyed to the wife, a judgement mortgage still could have subsequently been registered against it. See J.C.W. Wylie, *Irish Land Law, supra*, p. 648 *et seq*, in particular para. 13.166.
140. (May, 1983) unreported (H.C.).
141. See p. 6 of judgement. Prior to determining the application brought under the Act of 1976, the court held the husband and wife each had a 50% beneficial interest in the family home.
142. See p. 10 of judgement.
143. (October, 1984) unreported (H.C.).
144. See p. 3 of judgement.

High Court had made an order dispensing with the wife's consent to the raising of a loan by the husband, the home to be used as security for the loan. The husband had stated that he required the loan for the setting up of a new business and the court had made an order authorising him to raise a sum not exceeding £20,000 subject to the condition that he was to use a portion of the money raised to discharge a bank debt of approximately £5,000 and had to advise his wife's solicitors of the exact amount of the mortgage liability incurred. The husband subsequently raised a sum of £7,000, did not use it for the purpose for which it was allegedly raised and failed to comply with the conditions imposed. Expressing the view that the husband was "an untruthful and untrustworthy person",[145] O'Hanlon J. ordered that he "forthwith" transfer the family home into the sole name of the wife; that he raise no further monies on the security of the home and that as and from the date of his judgement, that the wife

> "shall be deemed entitled to the entire beneficial estate and interest hither-to held by the (husband) in the house ... to the intent that no further arrangement entered into by the (husband) with a view to encumbering the ... property and no judgement registered against the (husband) which is sought to be converted into a judgement mortgage ... and which has not been so registered ... prior to the date of this judgement, shall take effect as a valid encumbrance against the property."[146]

Whilst sub-section 1 of section 5 seeks to protect the wife's right of residence in the family home, sub-section (2) empowers the court to award compensation to a wife deprived of a right to reside in the family home and also confers on the court a general discretionary power in respect of such a wife to make such other orders as are "just and equitable". It provides:

> "Where it appears to the court, on the application of a spouse that the other spouse has deprived the applicant spouse or a dependent child of the family of his residence in the family home by conduct that resulted in the loss of any interest therein or rendered it unsuitable for habitation as a family home, the court may order the other spouse or any other person to pay to the applicant spouse such amount as the court considers proper to compen-sate the applicant spouse and any such child for their loss or make such other order directed to the other spouse or to any other person as may appear to the court to be just and equitable."

If a husband fails or refuses to pay mortgage instalments on the family home resulting in a bank or building society obtaining court orders whereby it takes possession of and sells the home, a wife may apply for a compensation or "other order" under section 5(2). However, if the mortgage arrears accumulated due to a husband being genuinely financially unable to make the payments, no such order will be made.[147]

145. *Ibid.*
146. See pp. 3 and 4 of judgement.
147. If a husband deliberately leaves his employment to render himself financially unable to make mortgage repayments, the court will not regard him as "genuine" and may make an order under this section – see *O'M. v. O'M., supra,* discussed on p. 555 *ante.* See in particular p. 5 of judgement where Finlay P. stated, concluding that he should exercise the power conferred on the court by section 5 that "the defendant's (husband's) failure to make any income and his consequent failure which has gone on now for a number of years to make any mortgage repayments on the (family home) ... is a conscious and deliberate act intended to deprive his wife and children of the use of that house or of any alternative house which might result from selling it and purchasing another." In making an order that one half of the nett proceeds of sale should be paid into court and go towards the acquisition of a new home for the wife and children with "an appropriate share by way of interest" in the home being registered in the husband's name, the learned President did not clarify whether the order made was pursuant to sub-section (1) or sub-section (2) of section 5.

In *A.D. v. D.D. & Anor.*[148] dealing with such an application, McWilliam J. stated that:

> "Although there is no reference in sub-sect. (2) of Sect. 5 to 'an intention' to deprive a spouse of her residence in the family home as there is in sub-sect. (1), I am of the opinion that a failure to pay instalments due on a mortgage would not be conduct resulting in the loss of an interest in the family home sufficient to entitle a spouse to compensation under the sub-section unless it were established that the other spouse was financially able to pay the instalments."[149]

One of the reasons for McWilliam J. declining to make the compensation order sought by the wife was that on the evidence, in the learned judge's view "the husband did not have an income sufficient to meet the instalments."

A wife may also seek an order for compensation if a judgement creditor sells the family home to obtain payment of monies due arising out of a judgement obtained against her husband if the husband could otherwise have dishcarged the monies due pursuant to the judgement.[150] It is also arguable that a compensation order can be sought under this section by a battered wife against her husband if she is forced by his violence to move out of the family home, as such violence could be classified as "conduct" rendering the "family home unsuitable for habitation". It is, however, unlikely that the courts will regard section 5(2) as applicable to conduct directed by one spouse against the other that does not affect the physical amenity of the family home itself.

Not only an offending husband but also a third party can be the subject of directions or orders made under section 5. Thus, if the mortgage payments on a family home are in arrears, the court can not only order a husband under sub-section (1) to discharge the mortgage arrears but may also make an order restraining the bank or building society who provided the loan on the mortgaged family home from taking any steps to realise their security, to afford the husband time to discharge the arrears due in accordance with the court order made. An order can also be made under sub-section (1) to require a purchaser of a family home who has taken up residence in it to vacate the home, if the sale of it to him is void, being in contravention of section 3(1) of the Act.[151] A third party who has assisted a husband in carrying out works on the home so as to render it uninhabitable can be required by an order made under sub-section (1) to put the home back into proper condition, or under sub-section (2) to pay compensation to the wife deprived of her residence in it.

Sub-section (2) confers a wide discretionary power on the court to determine the type of order it should make. Thus, instead of ordering compensation, the

---

148. *Supra*.
149. See p. 11 of judgement.
150. See *Containercare (Ireland) Ltd. v. Wycherley* [1982] I.R. at p. 150.
151. See *Weir v. Somers* [1983] I.R. 122 (S.C.). It appears that subsequent to the Supreme Court holding that the sale of the family home was void pursuant to Sect. 3(1) of the 1976 Act (see *Somers v. Weir* [1979] I.R. 94 (S.C.) discussed on p. 541 *ante*) the wife sought and obtained a Circuit Court injunction requiring the "purchasers" to vacate the family home. Delivering the Supreme Court judgement in the case stated from the Circuit Court to the Supreme Court in the injunction proceedings issued by the wife, McCarthy J. explicitly referred to the "wide range of powers granted to the courts by Sect. 5" and emphasised the court's power to make orders under sub-section (1) against "any other person." It is submitted that the wife could have utilised the powers conferred by that sub-section to have the unfortunate purchasers evicted from the home without the necessity of bringing Circuit Court injunction proceedings.

court may order a husband to put a home rendered uninhabitable back into habitable condition, or to provide his wife and children with an alternative place of residence, or may order that monies realised from the sale be used to discharge debts incurred by the wife, or the husband and wife jointly, for family household purposes.[152] Whether the court may order a spouse who can afford to do so, to purchase an alternative home and to vest the beneficial interest in it in the spouse for whom it is purchased, has not yet been decided. It is submitted that as the courts have interpreted section 5(1) as conferring a power to order the transfer of a family home or an interest in it from one spouse to the other, there is no reason why section 5(2) should not also be held to confer power on the courts in an appropriate case, to make such an order.[153] In this context, it should be noted, however, that to date no case has been decided by the Supreme Court finally determining whether and in what circumstances an order may be made pursuant to section 5(1) transferring ownership of the family home from one spouse to the other.

Although the Family Home Protection Act has been in force for over ten years, the courts have not as yet fully explored the nature of the jurisdiction conferred by section 5 of the Act. In the context of section 5(2) a major defect in the Act relates to the absence of any legislative guidance as to the basis upon which the amount of compensation to be paid is to be calculated by the courts upon a finding being made that a spouse's conduct has deprived the other spouse of her residence in the family home and that the latter is entitled to be compensated. There is also no statutory guidance as to when orders other than "compensation orders" should be made and as to the nature of any such orders, other than a statement that such "other orders" should be "just and equitable". In the context of sub-section (1) the courts' refusal to infer or impute the existence of the necessary intention on the part of a spouse to deprive the other spouse of a right of residence in the family home by an objective, rather than a subjective, assessment of the former's conduct, has diluted the protection that could be afforded to dependent spouses and could inhibit the courts from intervening to ensure the continued availability of a family home for a dependent spouse and children in circumstances in which such intervention may be desirable.

The differences between sub-sections (1) and (2) have given rise to the curious anomaly that although a court may be unable to act under sub-section (1) to prevent the loss of a family home or to prevent a husband from rendering it uninhabitable, due to it not being possible to establish that the husband's conduct is done with the "intention of depriving" his wife of her residence in it, upon the husband's conduct having such a result, as the need to prove intention no longer arises, it may make a compensation order against the husband to require him to compensate the wife for conduct the court was powerless to prevent.[154]

---

152. See *D.C. v. A.C., supra*.
153. See *H.D. v. J.D.* (July, 1981) unreported (H.C.) in which Finlay P. raised the issue as to whether "the provisions of the Family Home Protection Act, 1976, give to the court a discretion which it should exercise to force the defendant (husband) out of the proceeds of any sale of (a family home) to provide a family home for his wife and children." Making an order restraining the husband from disposing of the home without the liberty of the court, he gave the parties "liberty to apply with regard to this question" since it involved "difficult points of law" and the value of the property concerned was "substantial" (see pp. 7–8 of judgement).
154. See further (1983) 8 I.L.T. 132.

Payment in arrears: Section 6(1) of the Act provides that

> "Any payment or tender made or any other thing done by one spouse in
> or towards satisfaction of any liability of the other spouse in respect of
> rent, rates, mortgage payments or other outgoings affecting the family home
> shall be as good as if made or done by the other spouse, and shall be treated
> by the person to whom such payment is made or such thing is done as
> though it were made or done by the other spouse."

Thus, in the event of a husband defaulting on mortgage repayments the
mortgagee is bound by this section to accept payments made by his wife and to
treat them as if they were made by the husband. Similarly, so long as a wife pays
the rent, a landlord will be unable to evict her for her husband's default. Moreover,
payment by her of rent in such circumstances will protect any rights accruing to
either spouse by virtue of their tenancy under the Housing (Private Rented
Dwellings) Act, the Landlord and Tenant Acts, etc. Such treatment, however,
does not affect any claim the wife making the payment may have to an interest
in the family home.[155]

The Act further provides that in proceedings for the sale or possession of the
family home by the mortgagee or landlord, if a wife is able to pay off the arrears
or repayments within a reasonable time and is able to make future periodical
payments falling due, the court may adjourn the proceedings "for such period
and on such terms as appear . . . to be just and equitable."[156] If the wife succeeds
in making the required payments and it appears to the court that payments
subsequently falling due will continue to be paid, it may make an appropriate
declaration to that effect.[157] Upon such a declaration being made, any term
in a mortgage or lease whereby the default in payment, that gave rise to the
initial proceedings, has at any time before, or after the initial hearing of such
proceedings, resulted or would have resulted, in the capital sum advanced there-
under, or any sum other than the periodical payments, becoming due, is of no
effect for the purpose of such proceedings or any subsequent proceedings in
respect of the sum so becoming due.[158]

A defect in the above provisions is that a mortgagee or lessor is not bound to
give a wife any notice of her husband's default. Thus, if proceedings are brought
and she only discovers the amount due shortly before, or at the date of the
hearing, so much arrears may have accrued as to make it impossible for her to pay
it all within "a reasonable time". However, in determining for what length of time
proceedings should be adjourned to enable arrears to be paid off, the court must

> "have regard in particular to whether the spouse of the mortgagor or lessee
> has been informed (by or on behalf of the mortgagee or lessor or otherwise)
> of the non-payment of the sums in question or of any of them".

A further defect in the above protection is that in order to enforce his security
a mortgagee need not always obtain a court order. The Conveyancing Act, 1881,
Sect. 19(1), confers a power of sale on all mortgagees, provided the mortgage
was made by deed. Thus, if a husband defaults on a legal mortgage, a sale may
take place without the wife's knowledge and without her being given an opportunity to make good her husband's default. In practice, however, if the husband

155. Sect. 6(2).
156. Sect. 7(1).
157. Sect. 8(1).
158. Sect. 8(2).

and wife are still living in the home the mortgagee will have great difficulty in finding a purchaser willing to buy the property.

Finally, if a wife discovers that the mortgage or rent payable in respect of the family home is in arrears, it is open to her to make an application under section 5 of the Act to seek a court order requiring her husband to discharge the arrears. Moreover, even if a landlord or mortgagee has obtained an order for possession of the family home, a wife may ask the court under section 5 to restrain the former from enforcing the order for possession and seek an order against her husband requiring him to discharge the arrears within a stipulated time. In practice, a number of orders of this nature have been made by the High Court in recent years.

Joint tenancies: The Act seeks to encourage spouses where the family home is owned by one of them to place the home in joint ownership. Section 14 provides that

> "No stamp duty, land registration fee, Registry of Deeds fee or court fee shall be payable on any transaction creating a joint tenancy between spouses in respect of a family home where the home was immediately prior to such transaction owned by either spouse or by both spouses otherwise than as joint tenants."

Household goods: Section 9 of the Act prevents a spouse from disposing of "household chattels" in certain circumstances. Household chattels for the purpose of this section are said to mean

> "furniture, bedding, linen, china, earthenware, glass, books and other chattels of ordinary household use or ornament and also consumable stores, garden effects and domestic animals, but does not include any chattels used by either spouse for business or proefessional purposes or money or security for money".[159]

(1) If matrimonial proceedings[160] have been instituted by either spouse, neither spouse "can sell, lease, pledge, charge or otherwise dispose or remove any of the household chattels" in the family home until the proceedings have been finally determined. A spouse however may so act

(a) with the consent of the other spouse, *or*

(b) with the permission of the court before which the proceedings have been instituted.[161]

A spouse who contravenes this provision is guilty of an offence and liable on summary conviction to a fine not exceeding £100 or to imprisonment for up to six months.[162]

---

159. Sect. 9(7).
160. Sect. 9(3) defines matrimonial proceedings as including "proceedings under Sect. 12 of the Married Women's Status Act, 1957, under the Guardianship of Infants Act, 1964, or under Sect. 21 or 22 of the Family Law (Maintenance of Spouses and Children) Act, 1976". Curiously, section 5 of the latter Act is not included. The reference to Sect. 22 of the Act of 1976 can now be read as a reference to proceedings under the Family Law (Protection of Spouses and Children Act, 1981.) See Sect. 9 of 1981 Act.
161. Sect. 9(2).
162. Sect. 9(4).

(2) Section 9(1) provides that

> "Where it appears to the court, on the application of a spouse, that there are reasonable grounds for believing that the other spouse intends to sell, lease, pledge, charge or otherwise dispose of or to remove such a number or proportion of the household chattels in a family home as would be likely to make it difficult for the applicant spouse or a dependent child of the family to reside in the family home without undue hardship, the court may by order prohibit, on such terms as it may see fit, the other spouse from making such intended disposition or removal."

This section may assist a wife in various circumstances. For example, the court may make an order preventing a husband who is a compulsive gambler from selling or pledging the furniture so as to obtain money for gambling or it may prevent a husband from removing all the furniture from the family home so as to force his wife to vacate it.

If a spouse contravenes an order made under (1) or (2) above or if he

> "has sold, leased, pledged, charged or otherwise disposed of or removed such a number or proportion of the household chattels in the family home as has made or is likely to make it difficult for the applicant spouse or a dependent child of the family to reside in the family home without undue hardship"

the court may order that spouse

> "to provide household chattels for the applicant spouse, or a sum of money in lieu thereof, so as to place the applicant spouse or the dependent child of the family as nearly as possible in the position that prevailed before such contravention, disposition or removal".[163]

Finally, if a third person, prior to any disposition of a household chattel to him by a spouse, is informed in writing by the other spouse that he intends to

> "take proceedings in respect of such disposition or intended disposition, the court in such proceedings may make such order, directed to the former spouse or the third person, in respect of such chattel as appears to it to be proper in the circumstances."[164]

Court jurisdiction: The District Court is conferred with jurisdiction only to hear proceedings under section 9 of the Act and only if the value of the household chattels which are the subject matter of the proceedings does not exceed £2,500. The High Court and Circuit Court are conferred with concurrent jurisdiction to hear all matters arising under the Act. Where the rateable value of the land to which proceedings relate exceeds £200 and the proceedings are brought in the Circuit Court, that court must, at the request of a defendant, transfer the proceedings to the High Court. However, any act done or order made prior to such transfer is valid until discharged or varied by order of the High Court.[165]

---

163. Sect. 9(5).
164. Sect. 9(6).
165. Sect. 10 as amended by the Courts Act, 1981, Sect. 13.

CRITICISMS AND SUGGESTED REFORMS

In Chapter 15 reference is made to the government's proposal to introduce legislation to provide for a presumption of co-ownership of the family home. No indication has been given by the government as to whether it intends in the context of such legislation to amend in any way the Family Home Protection Act, 1976. Even if a presumption of co-ownership of the family home is prescribed by statute, the Act of 1976 will still have an important role to play in protecting the family home and the right of a non-owning or co-owning spouse to reside in it. Some reference has already been made to a number of the difficulties that arise under the Family Home Protection Act that could be resolved by amending legislation. It is merely intended here to refer to four specific reforms that are necessary to render the protection afforded by the Act both more effective and more equitable.

1. Section 5 of the Act should be amended so as to enable court orders to be made to protect the family home where a spouse's conduct may lead to the loss of the home or to it being rendered uninhabitable without an applicant spouse having to prove that the spouse so behaving specifically intends that his or her conduct deprive the applicant spouse and/or dependent children of the family of their right to reside in the home. The Joint Oireachtas Committee on Marriage Breakdown specifically point out that "in cases where a spouse is simply a spendthrift by nature or where he or she has an alcohol, drug or gambling problem"[166] it may be impossible to prove the necessary intention. Nevertheless, where a spouse has such a problem it will be apparent in many cases that without judicial or other effective intervention the family home may ultimately be sacrificed by such a spouse's conduct and there should be no doubt about the court's right to intervene and make orders where necessary under section 5 of the Act of 1976 to preserve and protect the home.

2. The tenuous nature of the protection afforded by the Act to the family home upon a judgement being obtained against a spouse in whom is vested all or part ownership of the home, has been clearly exposed in those cases in which it has been held that the prior written consent of the other spouse is not required before a judgement mortgage can be registered against the home. If, however, the other spouse is aware that either proceedings have been issued or a judgement obtained against the home owning spouse and if she can prove that the latter has engaged in a course of conduct with the intention of depriving her and/or children of the family of their right to reside in the home, an application may be made to the court pursuant to section 5 of the Act to obtain an order so as to prevent a judgement being registered against the home and to have any proprietary interest in the family home of the debtor spouse transferred to the applicant spouse. Consequently, the extent to which the home is protected at present may largely depend on how quickly a spouse discovers the existence of court proceedings brought against a debtor spouse and how rapidly proceedings are instituted and determined under section 5 of the Act of 1976. The current law, it is submitted, is totally unsatisfactory in that it neither affords adequate protection to the right of a spouse and dependent children to reside in the family home nor to creditors to recover monies due.

---

166. See p. 65 of the Committee's Report.

It is unsatisfactory to spouses because a judgement may be registered against the home for a debt for which the debtor spouse is liable without the other spouse's prior consent being required and without the latter having to be informed, even where

(a) the debtor spouse has other assets out of which the judgement could be discharged, or

(b) the creditor was pre-warned by the other spouse that the debtor spouse's conduct could result in his incurring a debt or debts which he would be unable to discharge, or

(c) the other spouse had originally expressly refused to consent to the home being used as security for the debt for which judgement was obtained, prior to the debt being incurred.

It is unsatisfactory to creditors because at the time of the institution of proceedings against a debtor spouse a creditor may believe that monies due can be recovered following the registration of a judgement mortgage against the family home, only to discover upon the obtaining of a judgement, that a court order has been made in proceedings brought under section 5 of the Act of 1976 transferring the family home to the other spouse. It is possible at present for such proceedings to be determined without the creditor being informed of their being instituted, or appearing as a party in such proceedings or even being called as a witness. As a consequence, a court order made pursuant to section 5 may deprive a creditor of the only property against which he could recover payment of a debt properly incurred without any opportunity being afforded to him to appear in the section 5 court proceedings to seek to have the debt due to him discharged.

Comprehensive amending legislation is required to resolve the above difficulties. It is submitted that it should require a judgement creditor to notify the non-liable spouse of an intention to register a judgement mortgage against the family home and registration should require either the prior written consent of the non-liable spouse or, if such consent is not forthcoming within a specified time following such request, in the alternative, the consent of the court. Prior to permitting registration, the court should be empowered to require the judgement debtor to make a full disclosure of all capital assets with a view to ascetaining whether there is other appropriate property against which a judgement mortgage can be lodged and, if such property exists, the court should be empowered to direct that the judgement mortgage be lodged against it and not the family home. Where there is no other appropriate property, the court should have a discretionary power to determine whether a judgement creditor should be permitted to register a judgement mortgage against the family home having regard to the general circumstances in which the debt was incurred, the amount due in respect of the debt and the value of the family home. Whereas registration of a judgement mortgage should generally be permitted for debts incurred in a number of circumstances, such as damages awarded in actions for tort, it is submitted that as a general rule having regard to the spirit and intent of the Family Home Protection Act, in the absence of the necessary spousal consent, sums due in respect of business debts or loans obtained from financial institutions should not, in principle, be registerable as judgement mortgages against the family home. So as to afford some additional protection to creditors, however, there should be a duty imposed on a spouse who issues proceedings under section 5 of the Act seeking to have the family home transferred into her sole name so as to protect her right of residence in it, to notify any person who is known by her to have instituted proceedings against the house owning spouse for payment or recovery of monies, of the existence of the section 5 proceedings so that any such person may apply to appear in the proceedings as a notice party so as to ensure that the court is fully informed of the position in relation to any debt due and is in a position to determine what order should properly be made under section 5. At present, in the absence of such a requirement, it is open to spouses by collusion to effect a transfer by way of court order of an interest in the family home from one spouse to another that could otherwise be regarded as invalid and as defrauding creditors pursuant to existing bankruptcy legislation.[167]

3. Whilst a spouse may make mortgage repayments upon the default of the other spouse, which under section 6 of the Act the mortgagee must accept and which under section 7 of the Act, after the institution of proceedings for possession or sale of the home, the mortgagee can be required by a court to accept, neither section confers any specific power on the court to transfer part of the beneficial interest in the home to a spouse making such payments.[168] Thus, if the defaulting spouse, in whose sole name the property is held, wishes subsequently to sell the home, the other spouse may have to bring proceedings under section 12 of the 1957 Act in order to ascertain whether her payments gave rise to the acquisition by her of a beneficial interest in it, and if they did, the extent of that interest.[169] Alternatively, she may have to bring proceedings claiming compensation from the defaulter for the payments made by her on his behalf. Whether a claim to either a beneficial interest or compensation in such circumstances would be successful is uncertain. It is submitted that the Act should be amended so as to specifically provide that a spouse who makes mortgage repayments in default of the other spouse, acquires a beneficial interest in the family home, proportionate to the payments made.

4. If one spouse deserts the other, the court must dispense with the former's consent, if the latter applies to it to do so upon his wishing to sell the family home. On the other hand, if a spouse, guilty of adultery or cruelty, refuses consent, upon an application to dispense with consent, the court must consider all the circumstances including the needs and financial resources of the spouse and those of any dependent children, and the suitability of any alternative

---

167. See the Report of the Inter-departmental Working Party: *Irish Women — Agenda for Practical Action* (Dublin, February 1985) pp. 295–297 where it is stated that an amendment to the Family Home Protection Act providing that "a judgement should not be capable of being registered against a family home, unless, at some prior stage the other spouse consented to the debt" would go well beyond the purpose and the spirit of the Act. The working party stated that it was unable to support such a proposal. See, however, the *Report of the Joint Oireachtas Committee on Marriage Breakdown* at p. 66 where it states that "the Committee is of the view that legislative action should be taken immediately in order to prevent the spirit of the (1976) Act being defeated whereby judgement mortgages can be used to enforce the sale of the family home without the consent of either or both spouses."

168. An application for a transfer of the home into the sole name of the spouse paying the mortgage can in appropriate circumstances be made under section 5 of the Act. See p. 561 *ante.*

169. A beneficial interest may arise upon the payment of mortgage instalments by virtue of a resulting trust. Mortgage payments by the spouse in whom no legal title is vested are taken as evidence that it was the intention of the parties at the time of the acquisition of the property that the spouse in whom legal title was vested would hold all or part of the property on trust for the other spouse. However, if such payments are made under Sects. 6 or 7 of the 1976 Act, it is questionable whether such an intention would be inferred, and if it was it would be easily rebuttable. A spouse making such payments may, however, be held to be entitled to a beneficial interest by way of a constructive trust. See further *N.A.D. v. T.D.* [1985] 5 I.L.R.M. 153 (H.C.).

accommodation that has been offered, before it can make such an order. The Act has thus retained the concept of the matrimonial offence and as in the case of the recent legislation on maintenance, desertion is regarded as a more reliable indicator of 'guilt', than any other type of marital misbehaviour. It is submitted that desertion should merely be regarded as one of the circumstances to be taken into account by the court in determining whether the requirement of a spouse's consent should be dispensed with. Proof of desertion by itself should not conclude the matter.

CHAPTER 17

PROTECTION AGAINST SPOUSAL MISCONDUCT

This chapter examines the legal remedies available to ensure that spousal misconduct does not prevent the spouse against whom such misconduct is directed from exercising his or her right to reside in the family home and the circumstances in which a spouse may be excluded from the family home for misbehaviour towards his or her spouse and/or children of the family. While the remedies discussed can be invoked by either a husband or a wife, allegations of misconduct rendering it difficult, if not impossible, to continue to reside in the family home are most frequently made in court proceedings by wives against husbands. Accordingly, it will be assumed in the pages that follow, unless otherwise stated, that the wife is the person on whose behalf proceedings are initiated and that either she or the children of the family are the ones who require protection against a husband's misbehaviour.

This area of the law is most often invoked to seek protection for the "battered" wife. Prior to 1976 the injunction was the only civil law remedy available to a wife who required speedy and permanent protection from ill-treatment by her husband and who wished to have him excluded from the family home. While the injunction was and still can be effective in providing such protection, it also has certain limitations. For example, injunctions cannot be obtained in the District Court and the breach of an injunction, by itself, does not render a spouse liable to arrest or criminal prosecution. Moreover, prior to 1976 although injunctions could be granted by the Circuit Court, in practice most matrimonial injunctions were sought and granted in proceedings initiated in the High Court and the cost of initiating such proceedings put them outside the reach of the majority of battered wives in need of protection. As a result, many sought to circumvent the inadequacies of the civil law and utilised the criminal law to bring private assault summonses against violent husbands. The use of criminal law in this context is discussed in Chapter 6. Suffice it to note here that the criminal law cannot and does not extend to battered wives the necessary permanent protection that many require and is of no assistance at all to wives ill-treated by their husbands but never physically assaulted by them. In recognition of the need for an efficient and effective remedy to provide protection against spousal misconduct that would also protect the right of a spouse to reside in the family home, section 22 of the Family Law (Maintenance of Spouses & Children) Act, 1976, for the first time conferred jurisdiction on the courts to grant barring orders. This jurisdiction is now exercised pursuant to the provisions of the Family Law (Protection of Spouses & Children) Act, 1981, and it is the jurisdiction conferred on the courts by this Act to grant, enforce and discharge barring orders that is discussed in the first part of this chapter. In the second part we shall consider the remedy of the injunction.

BARRING ORDERS

The Family Law (Protection of Spouses & Children) Act, 1981, expressly confers jurisdiction on the District and Circuit Courts[1] to make an order barring a spouse from entering the home in which the other spouse is residing. This Act repealed and replaced section 22 of the Family Law . . . Act, 1976, which first introduced barring orders and which also expressly conferred jurisdiction to make them on the High Court. No such express jurisdiction is conferred on the High Court by the Act of 1981, save in the context of certain transitional provisions which are discussed later on.

The main purpose of the Act of 1981 is described in its long title as being to make "provision for the protection of a spouse and any children whose safety or welfare requires it because of the conduct of the other spouse." While the courts may make an order barring either a husband or a wife, this statute was enacted primarily to provide protection for the battered wife. Thus, in the discussion that follows, it will be assumed unless otherwise stated, that the wife is the person on whose behalf a barring order is sought.

Criteria applicable for the making of barring orders: Pursuant to section 2 of the Act, upon application being made to a court by a wife, if the court is of the opinion that there are reasonable grounds for believing that the safety or welfare of the wife or of any child[2] of the family so requires, it may

(a) order a husband, if he is residing at a place where the wife or child resides, to leave that place, and

(b) prohibit a husband from entering such place.[3]

An order prohibiting entry as in (b) can be made against a husband who is living apart from his wife or child, as well as against a husband who was residing in the same place as either of them, until ordered to leave by the court. Moreover, if the court thinks fit, a barring order may also prohibit a husband "from using or threatening to use violence against, molesting or putting in fear" his wife or any child of the family.[4]

If by his behaviour a husband forces his wife out of the family home, she is not prevented from seeking to obtain an order barring him from the home, if at the time of the application she is not residing in it. The Act expressly provides that a wife who, but for the conduct of her husband, would be residing at a place "shall be treated as residing at that place" when seeking to have her husband barred from it.[5]

The court is not confined in its jurisdiction to make barring orders only in respect of the family home as it is defined in the Family Home Protection Act, 1976. An order can be made under the Act of 1981 in relation to any property in which the wife is residing. Thus, for example, if a wife goes to reside in the home of a relation and wishes to remain there, in appropriate circumstances a husband

---

1. In *R. v. R.* [1984] I.R. 296 (H.C.) it was held that the High Court also possesses jurisdiction to make such order. See, however, p. 586 *post* and p. 43 *ante*.
2. "Child" means any child of either the applicant spouse or the respondent spouse or both of them or adopted by either or both of them under the Adoption Acts, 1952/1976 or in relation to whom either or both of them is or are *in loco parentis*, provided that he is under the age of 18 years or, if over that age, is suffering from mental or physical disability.
3. Sect. 2(1).
4. Sect. 2(2).
5. Sect. 2(6).

can be barred from entering the relation's home. The Act cannot be relied upon, however, to bar a husband from entering premises in which a wife is not resident and which are used by her solely for business purposes.

A barring order may be made "subject to such exceptions and conditions as the court may specify"[6] and can be varied by the court that made it upon a variation application being brought by either spouse.[7] Thus a husband, barred from the family home, may under this provision be permitted to enter the home once or twice a week for the purpose of having access to his children in the home or may be permitted to enter the home for access purposes when children are sick. If such an exception or condition attached to a barring order creates difficulties for either party, it is open to them to apply to the court by way of a variation application to have it amended or terminated.

Barring orders and the need for spousal misconduct: A barring order cannot be made by the courts simply because a marriage has irretrievably broken down or because spouses are incompatible[8] or because there is a personality clash between them.[9] It has been emphasized that having regard to "the very drastic and far reaching nature of the remedy"[10] and "the fundamental nature of the marriage contract as constitutionally recognised[11] and as . . . expressed in the words of the marriage service 'in sickness and in health'[12] something more than 'the ordinary wear and tear of married life' is required."[13]

In *C. v. C.*[14] O'Hanlon J. emphasized the necessity to prove spousal misconduct and expressed the view that a barring order:

> "should not be granted unless it can be shown that the spouse against whom the order is sought has been guilty of serious violence or other cruelty, whether mental or physical, or other serious misconduct which has jeopardized the safety or welfare of the other spouse and has earned the penalty and stigma of exclusion from the family home by such misconduct."[15]

In *O'B. v. O'B.*[16] O'Higgins C.J. adopted a similar approach. Referring first to the terms "safety" and "welfare" contained in the Act, he stated:

> "The use of the word 'safety' probably postulated a necessity to protect from actual or threatened physical violence emanating from the other spouse. The word 'welfare' . . . was intended to provide for cases of neglect or fear or nervous injury brought about by the other spouse."[17]

---

6. Sect. 2(2).

7. Sect. 2(3).

8. See *O'B. v. O'B.* [1984] I.R. 182; [1984] 4 I.L.R.M. 1 (S.C.). See in particular [1984] I.R. O'Higgins C.J. at pp. 189 and 190, Griffin J. at p. 194 and McCarthy J. at pp. 198 and 199. See also *C. v. C.* (December, 1982) unreported (H.C.), O'Hanlon J.

9. See *O'B. v. O'B.*, in particular McCarthy J. [1984] I.R. at p. 196. See also *C. v. C., supra.*

10. *C. v. C., supra, per* O'Hanlon J. at p. 1 of judgement.

11. *O'B. v. O'B., per* McCarthy J. [1984] I.R. at p. 199.

12. *Ibid.*

13. See *O'B. v. O'B.*, Griffin J., [1984] I.R. at p. 194.

14. *Supra.*

15. *Supra* at p. 2 of judgement.

16. *Supra.*

17. [1984] I.R. p. 188. He also stated that what endangers the "welfare" being considered must "be attributed to the conduct of the other spouse, whether that conduct consists of positive action or atttude or mere neglect." [1984] I.R. at p. 188.

In both instances, he said, it is the conduct of the accused spouse and its effect upon the other spouse or the children which the court has to consider.[18] Expressing the need for "serious misconduct" on the part of the offending spouse before a barring order could be made, he continued stating:

> "Something wilful and avoidable which causes or is likely to cause, hurt or harm, not as a single occurrence but as something which is continuing or repetitive in its nature"

was required.[19]

McCarthy J., in his judgement acknowledged that:

> "ordinarily ... the statute clearly contemplates positive action or conduct on the part of the guilty spouse, be it by way of physical or mental violence or the like"[20]

but also envisaged circumstances in which a barring order could be made, even though the spouse against whom the barring order was sought was not guilty of any serious misconduct, stating:

> "There may be circumstances, for example, mental disturbance of an aggravated kind, or even, infection with some highly contagious disorder in which a spouse, innocent of any serious misconduct towards the other spouse or any member of the family, may be subjected to a barring order."[21]

In neither *C. v. C.* nor *O'B. v. O'B.* did the wife who instituted proceedings ultimately succeed in having her husband barred. In *C. v. C.* O'Hanlon J. acknowledged that there had been "fairly constant friction" in the home and accepted that the husband "had caused the wife considerable distress and upset throughout (their) married life by insensitive behaviour and language and by failure or inability to demonstrate his affection for her in the manner she needed." He stated, however, that he did "not ... regard the wife as a person of a timid or submissive character who would be easily overborne by a stronger personality" and that many of the couple's difficulties had been caused by a "constant clash of personalities and ... incompatibility of temperament which neither party strove hard enough to eliminate."[22] In refusing to grant the order sought he noted that, in the two years immediately preceding the court hearing, the couple had "settled down to a state of co-existence under the one roof with few outbreaks of raised voices and open discord but without the atmosphere of a home where parents and children are living in a state of mutual harmony and affection."[23]

In *O'B. v. O'B.* the Supreme Court by a 2−1 majority allowed the husband's appeal and discharged a barring order made by the High Court.[24] O'Higgins C.J. summarising the evidence given in the proceedings noted that the parties had

---

18. See also *O'B. v. O'B.* [1984] I.R. at p. 193 where Griffin J. stated that "a barring order ought not be made unless the safety or welfare of such spouse or child is at risk by reason of the conduct of the other spouse."
19. [1984] I.R. at p. 189.
20. [1984] I.R. at p. 198.
21. *Ibid.*
22. *Supra* at p. 2 of judgement.
23. *Supra* at p. 3 of judgement.
24. O'Higgins C.J. and McCarthy J. were the majority. Griffin J., although in agreement with the general principles enunciated by his colleagues, on the facts of the case favoured dismissing the husband's appeal.

separated in April 1979, when the husband left the family home and that he had not returned to reside in it until September 1980.[25] His return revived the stresses and strains which formerly existed and the wife, in February 1981, obtained a District Court barring order which was set aside by the Circuit Court in June 1981. Upon the husband again returning to the family home "tensions, strains and difficulties were apparent" and the evidence indicated that "various incidents occurred — rudeness by the husband in front of the children, a lack of sensitivity in his manner to her and efforts by him at dominance in running the home."[26] This behaviour, in the Chief Justice's view, did not amount to serious misconduct. Allowing the appeal, he stated that while it was clear that the wife suffered severe nervous strain as a result of the husband residing in the same home it was "equally clear that this did not stem from any particular conduct on his part, but rather because he was there."[27]

McCarthy J. adopted a similar approach stating the main cause of the breakdown to be "a total personality clash between the parties" who were incompatible and that the provisions of the 1981 Act "were not intended to and do not cover the circumstances" of such cases.[28] Griffin J. in the minority, although agreeing with the general legal principles enunciated by his colleagues, in a vigorous dissenting judgement disagreed with their conclusions. Stating that he could "not agree that the conduct of the husband was no more than what might be expected in the ordinary wear and tear of married life as I understand it"[29] and that the husband had "constantly indulged in . . . conduct which . . . no woman should be required to put up with" he held the husband's appeal should be dismissed.[30]

It is clear as a result of the *O'B. v. O'B.* decision that in order to obtain a barring order a wife will ordinarily[31] have to establish serious misconduct on the part of the husband. The mere fact that she is under stress or strain because her marriage has broken down and the husband refuses to move out of the family home is no cause for the court granting a barring order. The mere existence of tension or disharmony in the home, by itself, is not sufficient justification. It is, however, not necessary to prove that a husband has been violent before such an order can be made. O'Higgins C.J. clearly stated that "threats of violence" are sufficient to invoke the court's jurisdiction.[32] Moreover, it is submitted that despite the Chief Justice's reference to the necessity for misconduct "which is continuing or repetitive"[33] the court may bar a husband who indulges in a single act of physical violence towards his wife in circumstances in which it is clearly established that such behaviour poses a danger to the wife's safety or welfare. To suggest otherwise could produce the absurd result that a court could not bar a husband who on a single occasion attempted to murder or seriously maim his wife and would have to wait until he made at least a second attempt. It is submitted that the Chief Justice's remarks were merely intent on emphasizing that a spouse should not be barred if guilty of a single minor transgression.[34]

---

25. During the period in which he resided outside the home, the husband had visited his children each week.
26. [1984] I.R. at p. 190.
27. *Ibid.*
28. [1984] I.R., pp. 196 and 199.
29. [1984] I.R. at p. 194.
30. [1984] I.R. at p. 195.
31. See judgement of McCarthy J., [1984] I.R. at p. 198.
32. [1984] I.R. at p. 189.
33. *Ibid.*
34. See further O'Connor, "Barring Orders" (1983) 1 I.L.T. (n.s.) 96.

It is more difficult to establish exactly what conduct or behaviour other than violence or threats of violence will result in the making of a barring order. Clearly conduct amounting to mental cruelty will justify the making of an order, as such conduct may clearly endanger a wife's welfare. In this context, the Chief Justice stated that the reference in the Act to "welfare" intended "to provide for cases of neglect or fear or nervous injury brought about by the other spouse."[35] In the view of Griffin J. welfare ordinarily referred "to health and wellbeing and included both physical and emotional welfare."[36] To determine whether a husband's behaviour is jeopardising his wife's welfare to the degree that would warrant the making of a barring order is a particularly subjective judicial exercise and, as a consequence, the result of each case that arises depends not only on its particular facts but also on the individual judicial perspective of the marital relationship and the type of conduct that should be tolerated by a couple who have married "for better or for worse".[37] The difficulty in determining whether conduct will be regarded as unacceptable or as merely indicative of incompatibility is well illustrated by the divergence in the views expressed by the majority and minority opinions delivered in the O'B. case.

In practice, many barring orders have been made by the courts in cases where a husband has been regarded as placing in jeopardy the safety or welfare of his wife and where allegations of violence have either played no part or only a minor part. The only such case in which a written judgement has been delivered to date is that of *McA. v. McA.*[37a] in which Costello J. held that the husband's continued refusal to communicate with his wife had adversely affected the wife's health and seriously affected her welfare. As a result, she had to attend regularly with a consultant psychiatrist and was on anti-depressant drugs for over two and a half years. The husband's conduct which also resulted in the granting of a decree of divorce *a mensa et thoro* on the grounds of mental cruelty, was held by the trial judge to justify the making of a barring order.

The Making of Barring Orders for the Protection of Children: Whilst an application to make a barring order must be made by a spouse, it is not necessary that the safety or welfare of the spouse be threatened before the other spouse can be barred. Such order may be made if required to protect the safety or welfare of a child of the family.[38] Thus, if a husband is violent towards his child or otherwise seriously mistreats his child he may be barred, even if his behaviour does not pose a threat to his wife. Such a case would in practice be unusual in that a husband who so behaved would usually also mistreat his wife and a barring order would normally be sought to afford protection not only to the child but also to the wife. Consequently, there have been a number of cases in which barring orders have been granted to protect spouses in which the courts have held that such an order was also required to protect the welfare of children.

In *D.C. v. A.C.*[39] when barring the husband who had been violent towards

---

35. [1984] I.R. at p. 188.
36. [1984] I.R. at p. 194. In the case of a child he stated "it would, in addition, include moral and religious welfare."
37. In *O'B. v. O'B.*, [1984] I.R. at p. 193 Griffin J. stated that for a barring order to be granted "there must be something in the nature of conduct on the part of the spouse against whom the barring order is sought which is over and above that which every spouse bargains for in accepting the other for 'better or worse'."
37a. [1981] 1 I.L.R.M. 357 (H.C.).
38. For the definition of a child under the Act see footnote 2 *ante*.
39. [1981] 1 I.L.R.M. 357 (H.C.).

the wife on a number of occasions, Carroll J. emphasized that "quite apart from the question of safety" the court is "entitled to make a barring order if the welfare of the spouse or children requires it".[40] Having noted that since the husband's departure from the family home "the children have improved" and that "the elder child, from being quite a disturbed boy, has settled down to a remarkable degree"[41] she concluded that she was satisfied on the evidence that "the welfare of the wife and children require his (the husband's) absence at least for a certain period."[42]

In *McA. v. McA.*[43] Costello J. concluded that the effect of the husband's conduct on his three year old daughter also justified making a barring order, stating that he was satisfied "from the evidence of the (wife) and from medical evidence that the barring order is necessary for the welfare of the infant" and that she was "affected by the very serious strain which presently exists in the family home and that her welfare requires that the order be made."[44]

Although the welfare and development of children may be affected by the nature of the relationship that exists between their parents and the interaction between them in the family home, it appears from the decision of the majority in *O'B. v. O'B.* that the fact that children are exposed to tension and a disagreeable atmosphere in the home due to the collapse of their parents' marriage will not, of itself, justify the court barring either spouse, if the behaviour of one spouse towards the other does not warrant the making of such an order.[45] *C. v. C.*[46] is the only case in which this issue has been considered in any detail in a written judgement. Referring to the contention that it is better for the welfare of children to reside in a peaceful home with one parent than with both parents in a home lacking "mutual harmony and affection", O'Hanlon J. refusing to bar the husband in the interests of the children's welfare, stated:

"I am not convinced that it would be better for the children that this less than desirable homelife should be exchanged for another arrangement under which they would live apart from their father and be subjected to the deplorable regime of rights of access exercised at particular times each week, interspersed with periodical visits to court to deal with holidays or changed arrangements for weekly contact with their parent. I think children are very sensitive indeed about having to reveal to their school friends and others that their father or mother are separated, and that there is something abnormal about their home and family life and I think it very probable that the children, if given the choice, would opt for the continuance of life

---

40. *Ibid.*, at p. 359.
41. *Ibid.*, at p. 358.
42. *Ibid.*, at p. 359.
43. *Supra.*
44. *Supra* at p. 362.
45. In *O'B. v. O'B.* O'Higgins C.J. ([1984] I.R. at p. 190) noted that "the children were exposed to tension and a disagreeable atmosphere in their home . . ." due to the situation which existed between their parents but this, in itself, was not a reason in the learned Chief Justice's view for barring the husband. Griffin J., in the minority, in the same case considered that not only the wife's but also the children's welfare justified the making of a barring order. He stated that the husband's conduct was "bound to have an adverse effect on the physical and emotional health of the plaintiff wife and of the children (and) the medical reports received in evidence at the hearing bore this out." He concluded that the original trial judge, Costello J. had been justified in holding that the welfare of the wife "and of the children was affected by the behaviour of the defendant" husband ([1984] I.R. at p. 195).
46. *Supra.*

at home with both parents even though the parents were not getting on well together and found each other's company difficult to tolerate."[47]

The principal difficulty with the learned judge's reasoning is that the family arrangements that a child might opt for are not necessarily the arrangements that would accord with the child's welfare.[47a] On the other hand, where marital disharmony was affecting a child's welfare, it would be particularly unjust to bar one spouse, if both spouses were equally contributing to the unhappy state of affairs in the home. It is clear that for a barring order to be made solely to protect the welfare of children, it must at least be proved that the threat to their welfare primarily stems from the conduct of the spouse against whom the barring order is sought.[48]

Emergency Relief: Particularly when violence is alleged, a wife may require immediate protection and may fear the likely consequences of court proceedings being served on her husband. Section 3 of the Act confers jurisdiction on the court to make a "protection order" to afford protection to a wife and children between the period when barring proceedings are initiated and finally determined by the court. If "there are reasonable grounds for believing that the safety or welfare of the wife or any child so requires" such an order may be

---

47. See p. 4 of judgement. See further *F.M. v. J.M.* (November, 1983) unreported (H.C.). When delivering judgement in this case and awarding custody of four children to the husband of the marriage, O'Hanlon J. refers to the fact that in an earlier application he declined to grant an order sought by the wife to have the husband restrained from entering the family home. It does not appear from the proceedings as if the husband sought to have the wife barred from the family home but, if he had done so, it appears that O'Hanlon J. may have considered granting such a barring order. Delivering judgement in this case O'Hanlon J. states "the atmosphere of mutual antipathy and of tension between the husband and the wife must be unbearable, and inevitably has affected deeply the four children of the marriage who have to live their lives in a household where their parents regard each other with distrust and dislike . . . I have come to the conclusion that the wife is, and has been for some years past, a rather irresponsible person; that she drinks too much and too often; that her behaviour particularly when under the influence of drink has often been highly objectionable; that she has failed to look after the moral and physical welfare of her children in the way she ought to have done, and that she, much more than the husband, has contributed to the total and irretrievable breakdown in the marriage which now appears to have taken place . . . I think it would not be in the best interests of any of the children to take them away from their father and to entrust their upbringing to the wife, subject only to such control and restraint as the husband could exercise while living apart from them." (See pp. 4 and 5 of judgement.) Later on in his judgement the learned judge expresses the opinion that "it would be in the best interest of the children, and of the husband and wife, if the wife were to move out of the family home and to live elsewhere" (see p. 7 of judgement) and concludes stating that "now that the wife has failed in her claim for custody of the children I would hope that she will come to realise that it is in the best interests of the entire family that she should live apart from her husband, leaving him to manage as best he can without uprooting the children from the family home." (See pp. 7 and 9 of judgement.)

47a. In this context, see *F.M. v. J.M., supra,* in which having urged the wife to vacate the family home in the interests of the children O'Hanlon J. declined to interview the children to ascertain their wishes stating "the fact that the wife may be more popular (than the husband) with some or all of the children – if such be the case – may well stem, in my opinion from the fact that the wife has courted such popularity by avoiding her responsibilities when it came to asserting any degree of parental control over the conduct and activities of the children in the past. In fact, she has gone further and has undermined the husband's authority over them and has encouraged them to disregard the husband's wishes and to show no respect for him as a father . . . I am also of the opinion that the wife has sought to vindicate herself in her own eyes and in the eyes of others by doing her utmost to antagonise the children against their father." (See pp. 8 and 9 of judgement.)

48. See further P. Charleton, "The Scope of the Remedy of the Barring Order" (1983) I.L.T. (n.s.) 79. See further the similar approach adopted by a majority in the House of Lords in *Richards v. Richards* [1984] A.C. 174 and P. McNally, "Barring Orders and Ouster Orders – Judicial Change of Attitude" (1983) 77 *Gazette of the Incorporated Law Society of Ireland* 279.

made prohibiting a husband from using or threatening "to use violence against, molest or put in fear" his wife or child. A protection order, unlike a barring order, does not require a husband to vacate the home or restrict his right to reside in it. It is merely an interim measure to prevent the husband from misconducting himself towards the wife or children pending the determination of barring proceedings by the court.

Both the District and Circuit courts may make a protection order upon an *ex parte* application being made[49] and, in practice, many such orders are granted to afford immediate protection to wives before barring proceedings are served on husbands who are alleged to have been violent. A protection order may also be sought in the Circuit Court by way of notice of motion.[50]

The Act does not confer any express power on any court to grant a barring order upon the making of an *ex parte* application but does expressly authorise the making of rules of court for the expeditious hearing of barring applications when such is required.[51] In practice, in appropriate cases of an emergency nature, barring orders have been granted upon the making of an *ex parte* application by both the Circuit Court, and by the High Court in proceedings originally initiated under the Act of 1976.[52] Finlay C.J., when President of the High Court, emphasized that the instances in which the courts would be justified in granting an *ex parte* barring order are rare.[53] Where a barring order is urgently required the more usual approach would be to issue Circuit Court barring proceedings and to apply to the relevant Circuit Court for short service of the proceedings and for an early hearing date, so as to enable the matter to be dealt with speedily (within 2 to 4 days) and also afford to the other spouse an opportunity to be heard.

Operation of Order: A barring or protection order takes effect upon notification of its being made being given to the husband.[54] If a husband is present in court when the order is made he is regarded as having been notified of its making. If he is not present,[55] oral communication of its making together with the production of a copy of the order is sufficient notification.[56] The court may also make an order providing for alternative forms of notification where appropriate, such as the sending of a telegram or of a solicitor's letter.

There is an obligation imposed on the court to supply a wife, a husband and the garda station "for the area in which is situate the place in relation to which the application for the barring order was made" with a copy of any barring or protection order made "as soon as practicable". Failure to comply with this requirement does not affect the validity of the barring order. Upon the variation or discharge of any such order a similar obligation arises.[57]

49. See the District Court [Family Law (Protection of Spouses & Children) Act, 1981] Rules, 1981 (S.I. No. 246 of 1981) Rule 7 and the Circuit Court Rules (No. 3), 1981 (S.I. No. 152 of 1982) Rule 4.

50. In practice, protection orders are also made following an initial court hearing of an application for a barring order if the court decides to adjourn the proceedings and postpone making a final determination until a later date, either for the purpose of hearing further evidence at a future hearing or so as to afford time to a spouse to improve his or her conduct whilst extending some protection to the other spouse.

51. Sect. 13. See the Circuit Court Rules, *supra*, Rule 6.

52. As for the High Court's jurisdiction see p. 585 *post*.

53. See Finlay P., "An Approach to Family Cases" (1977) 71 *Gazette of the Incorporated Law Society of Ireland* 175 at p. 177.

54. Sect. 4(1).

55. As most protection orders are granted upon the making of an *ex-parte* application a husband will rarely be present when such an order is made.

56. Sect. 4(2).

57. Sect. 5(1). A failure on the part of a court to comply with this provision does not affect the validity of any order made – see Sect. 5(2).

Effect of Order: A barring order does not affect any proprietary rights or interest in any property of any spouse barred from it, other than to suspend any right vested in the barred spouse to reside in or occupy the property during the currency of the barring order. Moreover, if as a consequence of a barring order being made against him, a spouse does not reside at a place for any period, he is deemed to be still residing there for the purposes of any rights he may have under the Landlord & Tenant Acts, 1967–1980, the Statute of Limitations, 1957 or the Housing (Private Rented Dwellings) Act, 1982.[58]

Appeals: Unless the court that made the original barring order or the court to which an appeal is brought agrees, the bringing of an appeal does not stay the operation of the order.[59] If a stay is granted, it may be subject to conditions. No stay can be granted in respect of the operation of a protection order.[60]

Breach of Order: A spouse who contravenes a protection order or a barring order is guilty of an offence and liable on summary conviction to a fine not exceeding £200 and/or to a term of imprisonment not exceeding six months.[61] Moreover, any such spouse can be arrested by a member of the gardai without warrant where the garda "has reasonable cause for believing" that the spouse is committing or has committed such an offence.[62] In the context of protection or barring orders made by any court other than the District Court, an application may also be made to the appropriate court to have a spouse in breach of either type of order attached and committed to prison for contempt of court.[63]

Termination of Protection and Barring Orders:

(1) Either spouse may apply at any time to the court that made it[63a] for the discharge of a protection or barring order. The court must grant such an application if it is satisfied that the safety or welfare of the spouse or child for whose protection the order was made does not require that the order should continue in force.[64] A protection order, if not previously discharged, ceases to have effect upon the barring proceedings in which it was granted being determined.[65]

(2) If a barring order is made by the District Court, it expires twelve months after the date of its making.[66] A further District Court barring order may be made with effect from the date of expiration, if an application for such order is made.[67] There is, however, in practice, a lack of uniformity in the approach

---

58. See Sect. 16.
59. Sect. 10(1).
60. Sect. 10(2).
61. Sect. 6(1). A person released on bail upon being charged with an offence under the Act who again commits such an offence, renders himself liable to consecutive terms of imprisonment – see Sect. 8.
62. Sect. 7.
63. See Sect. 6(2).
63a. See Sect. 17(5) by which orders made by the High Court in proceedings initiated under Sect. 22 of the Family Law ... Act, 1976, are to be treated "as if made by the Circuit Court". It would thus seem that any application to discharge such High Court order should be made to the Circuit Court.
64. Sect. 11(1).
65. Sect. 3(3).
66. Sect. 2(4).
67. Sect. 2(5).

of District Justices to such applications and some are very reluctant to renew a barring order previously made if a husband has not misbehaved during the period during which he was barred. Others will grant such application even if the husband has behaved properly during such period, if his behaviour prior to the granting of the original order gives reasonable cause for still believing that the safety or welfare of the wife or his children still require that he be barred.

Barring orders may be unlimited in time if made by the Circuit Court exercising its original jurisdiction, or by the High Court in proceedings originally initiated under section 22 of the Family Law ... Act, 1976, or in proceedings originally initiated under the Act of 1981, in so far as the High Court possesses jurisdiction under the latter Act.[67a] In practice, it is not unusual for a wife who has obtained a District Court barring order to subsequently apply to the Circuit Court for a further order so as to avoid remaining in a position whereby she may have to annually make barring applications to the District Court. Upon such application being made in such circumstances the Circuit Court has granted barring orders unlimited in time and there is no provision contained in the Act which restricts the Circuit Court's jurisdiction from doing so.

(3) A Circuit Court barring order or one made in the High Court need not be unlimited in time but may be made for a specific period of time. Thus, in *D.C. v. A.C.*[68] Carroll J. concluded that the husband's misconduct arose from his lack of maturity and barred the husband for a period of two years stating that it was possible that "in that time he might achieve some degree of maturity." Where such orders are stated to be for a specific period of time, as in the case of District Court orders, an application can be made by the spouse who obtained the original order for a further one to be made to take effect on the expiration of the initial order.[69]

(4) A court determining any matrimonial cause or matter between spouses or any proceedings between them under the Guardianship of Infants Act, 1964, may "if it thinks fit" discharge any protection order or barring order made against either spouse.[70] The Act nowhere defines what is a matrimonial cause or matter for the purpose of this provision. Thus, it is uncertain whether it merely applies to those matters traditionally so called that were formerly within the jurisdiction of the ecclesiastical courts, or whether it also applies to the determination of other matrimonial conflicts, for example, disputes as to maintenance determined under the provisions of the Family Law ... Act, 1976, or disputes determined under the Married Women's Status Act, 1957, section 12.

Court Jurisdiction

Under section 22 of the Family Law ... Act, 1976, jurisdiction to make barring orders was expressly conferred on the District, Circuit and High Courts. The Act of 1981 confines the jurisdiction to make such orders to the District and Circuit Courts.[71] By way of transitional provision it provides that any proceedings issued under section 22 of the Act of 1976 but not fully determined until after the Act of 1981 came into force on the 23rd of July 1981,[72] are to

---

67a. See below, section entitled "Court Jurisdiction".
68. *Supra.*
69. Sect. 2(5).
70. Sect. 11(2).
71. Sect. 1(1).
72. Sect. 18.

be dealt with by the High Court as proceedings issued under the latter Act.[73] Moreover, any barring orders made by the High Court prior to the commencement of the Act of 1981 or after it, in reliance on the transitional provisions, are to be treated as if made by the Circuit Court[74] and, as a consequence, it appears that any application to discharge any High Court barring order should be made to the Circuit Court.

Despite the express provisions of the Act, as we have already seen, it was held in *R. v. R.*[75] that the High Court still retains an original jurisdiction to grant barring orders, but the authority of that decision must now be open to question having regard to the decision of the Supreme Court in *Tormey v. Ireland.*[76]

Pursuant to the Circuit and District Court Rules made under the Act of 1981, applications for barring orders and, where required, protection orders to either court must be brought in either the District Court district or Circuit Court area in which the applicant spouse resides or where the home is situate from which it is sought to bar the other spouse.[77] Thus, if the family home is in Dublin and the wife is temporarily residing in Wicklow due to her husband's misbehaviour, the wife may bring barring proceedings against the husband before either the Eastern Circuit Court sitting in Wicklow Town or the Dublin Circuit Court. Finally, where a speedy Circuit Court hearing is required to obtain a barring order, the proceedings can be listed for hearing not only at the relevant local Circuit Court sitting but at any sitting of the court within the particular Circuit Court area.[78]

There is no difference in the criteria applicable by the District or Circuit Courts in determining whether to grant a barring order, the only difference between them being the length of time for which an order made by each may remain in force. As has already been seen, a District Court barring order must expire no later than twelve months after its making but a Circuit Court barring order may be unlimited in time or for a specific period of time. Appeals from the District Court are determined by the Circuit Court and, when exercising its appellate jurisdiction, the Circuit Court is also confined to making a barring order for a maximum period of twelve months.[79] Appeals from proceedings initiated in the Circuit Court are determined by the High Court.

An issue that has not been finally determined is whether a wife who fails to obtain a barring order in District Court proceedings can initiate new proceedings in the Circuit Court, as opposed to appeal proceedings, and seek a Circuit Court barring order on the same evidence as that given in the District Court proceedings. In *O'B. v. O'B.*[80] it was argued that the wife was not entitled to

---

73. Sect. 17(3).

74. Sect. 17(5).

75. *Supra*.

76. [1985] 5 I.L.R.M. 375 (S.C.). Confirmation that the High Court no longer retains an original jurisdiction under the Act of 1981 is implicit in the remarks of O'Higgins C.J. in *O'B. v. O'B.*, where he stated that the appeal brought to the Supreme Court against the High Court decision made in that case "probably constitutes the last occasion upon which this court can consider the proper application of the statutory provisions to the making of (barring) orders" [1984] I.R. at p. 187. See also the comments of McCarthy J. in *O'B. v. O'B.* [1984] I.R. at p. 197.

77. See District Court [Family Law (Protection of Spouses & Children) Act, 1981] Rules, 1981, *supra*, Rules 6 and 7; Circuit Court Rules (No. 3) 1982, *supra*, Rules 2 and 4. An urgent *ex-parte* application to the Circuit Court for a protection order may be made also to a judge of the relevant circuit "at any time or place approved by him by arrangement with the County Registrar".

78. Circuit Court Rule (No. 3), 1982, *ibid*, Rule 6.

79. Sect. 2(4).

80. *Supra*.

initiate High Court barring proceedings under the Act of 1976 as she had not succeeded in District Court barring proceedings previously brought[81] and it was contended that the matter was *res judicata*. This contention was rejected, however, on the basis that the High Court proceedings had not dealt with the same circumstances as those which had arisen for consideration in the District Court,[82] as part of the wife's evidence in the High Court as to the husband's conduct related to events that had taken place after the District Court proceedings had concluded. It is submitted, however, that if a wife brings barring proceedings and seeks a barring order in the Circuit Court under that court's original jurisdiction and presents evidence identical to that originally presented in District Court proceedings in which a barring order was refused, the Circuit Court may refuse to grant an order on the basis that the matter is *res judicata*.

---

81. A barring order had been made by the District Court but upon the husband appealing the wife's application had been dismissed by the Circuit Court.
82. By McCarthy J. and Griffin J. This issue was not dealt with by O'Higgins C.J.

THE INJUNCTION

An injunction may be mandatory or prohibitory. It is essentially an order of the court directing a party to do or refrain from doing a particular act. For example, if a husband has by violence forced his wife out of the family home, the court may grant a mandatory injunction ordering the husband to leave and a prohibitory injunction restraining him from re-entering the home or assaulting his wife.

An injunction can be perpetual or interlocutory. The former type of injunction is granted upon the final determination of a dispute before the court. It is made after both sides have been given an opportunity to be heard in court and to present their case in the normal way. If it appears to the court to be just and convenient to do so it will grant an interlocutory injunction before the final determination of an action.[1] In order to obtain such an injunction, a plaintiff must first serve notice on the defendant that on the next motion day he will apply to the court for an injunction, thus giving the defendant an opportunity to oppose the application. If the plaintiff's affidavit makes out a sufficient case, an interlocutory injunction will be granted which is effective until the trial of the action. If, however, a person requires immediate protection against the unlawful behaviour of another, an injunction may be granted upon an *ex parte* application being made to a judge of the Circuit or High Court if "the exigencies of the case require it."[2] Thus, while there is some doubt as to the jurisdiction of the courts to grant a barring order upon an *ex parte* application, there is no doubt as to the jurisdiction of both the Circuit and High Court to grant an injunction to exclude a spouse from the family home upon such an application being made in appropriate circumstances, for example, by a wife who has been seriously assaulted in the home by her husband and who requires the immediate protection of the court.

At the turn of the century, there was a reluctance on the part of the Irish courts to grant injunctions to exclude a spouse from the family home, even in cases in which allegations of serious misconduct made against a spouse were proved, the courts being of the view that it was more appropriate in such cases that a decree of divorce *a mensa et thoro* be sought. Thus, in *Gaynor v. Gaynor*[3] the court refused to grant an injunction restraining a violent husband from entering premises which comprised both the family residence and business, although it was willing to restrain him "from interfering with the property and the business" which was owned and run by the wife. Porter M.R. referred in his judgement to the right of "a husband to enjoy the society of his wife" and stated that he had a "great objection to do indirectly what could be done directly by proper proceedings, viz to grant a judicial separation."

During the 1960's and the first half of the 1970's the High Court, in practice, became more willing to grant injunctions in appropriate cases in which they were required to extend necessary protection to wives and, although there is a paucity of written judgements, a considerable number of such injunctions were granted. Due to the fact that neither the High Court nor the Supreme Court at any time during that period delivered a detailed written judgement stating the legal principles applicable to the granting of what can be described as matri-

---

1. See Supreme Court of Judicature (Ireland) Act, 1877, Sect. 28(8); The Rules of the Superior Courts (S.I. No. 72 of 1962) Order 50, Rule 6(1).
2. *Ibid.*, Order No. 50 Rule 6(7).
3. [1901] 1 I.R. 217 (M.R.).

monial injunctions, it is not possible to give a detailed exposition as to the law that was applicable in determining such applications. For example, the importance that the courts attached to the proprietary interest in the family home being vested in the spouse it was asked to exclude from it is uncertain. The fact of title in a family home being vested in a husband's sole name did not, in practice, prevent the High Court by injunction excluding a husband from it.

In *K. v. K.*[4] the husband was the sole tenant of a Dublin Corporation house. His wife was forced to leave the house following a number of serious assaults on her by the husband. Kenny J. upon an interlocutory application made by notice of motion, granted injunctions ordering the husband to vacate the matrimonial home, restraining him from entering it and from molesting or assaulting his wife or children.

In *C. v. C.*[5] the wife was forced to leave the matrimonial home because of her husband's violent conduct. The home was held in the husband's name. While he was away the wife returned to the home and changed the locks. Having moved back into the house, she successfully made an *ex parte* application to the High Court and was granted injunctions restraining her husband from entering the home and restraining him from assaulting or molesting her.

In *Conway v. Conway*[6] in proceedings brought under the Married Women's Status Act, 1957, section 12, the court held the matrimonial home to be owned jointly by a wife and her husband, although it was purchased solely in the latter's name. At the date of the proceedings the husband was living elsewhere. Prior to that date, he had turned off the electricity supply to the house and had disconnected the phone and had on many occasions returned home late at night in a drunken state and assaulted his wife. Although he was entitled to a half share in the family home, Kenny J. granted an injunction restraining the husband from entering it because of his "outrageous" conduct.

Following the enactment of section 22 of the Family Law ... Act, 1976, the importance of the injunction as a remedy to afford protection to the battered wife against spousal misconduct diminished and in the overwhelming majority of cases in which a wife sought protection from a violent husband and protection for her right to reside in the home, barring orders were sought. As a result of the enactment of the Family Law (Protection of Spouses & Children) Act, 1981, the uncertainty created about the High Court's present jurisdiction to grant barring orders and the doubt as to whether such orders can be granted upon *ex parte* application, the injunction has again assumed an importance in this area of family law. There is, however, only one recent family law case in which a written judgement has been delivered, since the power to make barring orders has been legislatively conferred on the courts, which contains any detailed reference to the legal principles applicable in determining a wife's application for an injunction to exclude a husband from the family home.[7]

---

4. 1975 No. 212 Sp. (H.C.). There was no written judgement in this case.

5. 1975 No. 148 Sp. (H.C.). There was no written judgement in this case.

6. [1976] I.R. 254; (1973) 111 I.L.T.R. 133 (H.C.). In this case Kenny J. expressed approval of *Gurasz v. Gurasz* [1970] P. 11 (C.A.).

7. In *O'Malley v. O'Malley* (1951) 85 I.L.T.R. 43 (S.C.) the court made it clear that the fact that title is vested only in the spouse seeking the injunction does not mean an application to grant an injunction excluding the other spouse will automatically be granted. In that case, the court refused to grant to a wife living in the United States an interlocutory injunction requiring her husband to vacate the matrimonial home which she wished to sell. In refusing the application the court noted that the wife was not in danger of any violence or cruelty and that there was no evidence that she would suffer irreparable damage if her application was refused. Today, an application of this nature by a wife seeking to sell a family home owned by her against the wishes of her husband would have to be brought initially to have his consent dispensed with under Sect. 4 of the Family Home Protection Act, 1976.

In *F. v. F.*[8] the wife alleged that the husband had been violent towards her on a number of occasions; that he rarely took her out and was frequently absent from the home; that he had a relationship with another woman; that he had threatened to take her life and that his behaviour was having a detrimental effect on her health. The husband denied the various allegations made against him and alleged that the wife had engaged in relationships with other men, an allegation which the wife denied. At the date of the proceedings the couple still resided and slept together in the family home and it was agreed that the husband had a good relationship with the children of the family. Murphy J. delivering judgement stated that it was

> "clear that (the) domestic situation has been far from satisfactory and that a way of life has evolved for which the husband is largely responsible as a result of which little or no affection now exists between the parties."[9]

The learned judge expressed the view that in determining whether an injunction should or should not be granted to prevent a husband from residing in the family home, the court should apply the same legal test as is applied to determining whether a husband should be barred,[10] that is, it

> "should be satisfied that there are reasonable grounds for believing that the safety or welfare of (the applicant) spouse or any dependent child of the family requires it."[11]

He concluded that he was not so satisfied "at the present time"[12] but adjourned the proceedings stating that if the husband failed "in future to make a more determined effort to co-operate in building a tolerable domestic relationship"[13] the court might well be justified in granting the injunction sought by the wife on a subsequent occasion.

It thus appears from this decision that the general criteria for the making of barring orders prescribed by the Act of 1981 and the principles enunciated by the courts in determining barring order applications may be applied in future applications to the courts for matrimonial injunctions to exclude a spouse from the family home.[14]

Making the Application: In practice the following injunctions are most usually sought in the family law context:

> 1. An injunction to restrain the defendant (in the majority of cases the husband) from attending at or near or entering upon or attempting to enter upon the family home, or restraining the defendant from approaching the family home without the express invitation of the plaintiff.

---

8. (May, 1982) unreported (H.C.).
9. See p. 6 of judgement.
10. In the judgement he states "an injunction should be granted or withheld on the same grounds as those specified in Sect. 22 of the Family Law (Maintenance of Spouses & Children) Act, 1976." By the date of the hearing of these proceedings this section had been repealed and replaced by the Act of 1981 and it is that Act to which Murphy J. should have referred.
11. See p. 6 of judgement.
12. *Ibid.*
13. *Ibid.*
14. Murphy J. expressly noted that the proceedings were "not a claim for a divorce *a mensa et thoro*" (see p. 5 of judgement) but does not seem to have made any further point as to the relevance of such proceedings in relation to matrimonial injunctions. There is certainly no suggestion of an approach similar to that adopted in *Gaynor v. Gaynor, supra.*

2. An injunction to restrain the defendant from molesting, assaulting, putting in fear or otherwise interfering with the plaintiff and the children of the family.

3. A mandatory injunction compelling the defendant to vacate the family home or any other property in which the plaintiff is resident.

4. An injunction to restrain the defendant from taking a child or children out of the custody of the plaintiff and/or out of the jurisdiction of the court (i.e. out of the country).

Application for an injunction on ground 4 above may, of course be made, when there is no dispute as to occupation of the family home or no question of a spouse being attacked. This type of injunction is the injunction most usually sought by a spouse fearing that a child or children of the family will be kidnapped by the other spouse.[15]

Breach of Injunction: The court may commit to prison for contempt of court a person who acts in breach of an injunction. Breach of an injunction does not, by itself, render a spouse liable to arrest or criminal prosecution and committal proceedings must be initiated by the spouse in whose favour the injunction was originally granted.

Court Jurisdiction: Proceedings claiming an injunction may be brought in either the High Court or the Circuit Court. The High Court has unlimited jurisdiction but the Circuit Court can only hear a claim for an injunction, otherwise than as ancillary to other relief, where the property concerned consists of land, the ratable valuation of which does not exceed £200.[16] In practice, the majority of applications for matrimonial injunctions are still made in the High Court. The Courts (Supplemental Provisions) Act, 1961, section 45(1) permits "applications of an urgent nature for relief by way of injunction" to be heard "otherwise than in public".[17]

CRITICISMS AND SUGGESTED REFORMS

The statutory provisions for the making of barring orders have significantly improved the legal protection available to the battered wife. There are, however, certain difficulties still to be overcome in this area.

1. Whereas a court may make a protection order prior to deciding an application for a barring order, there is no jurisdiction conferred by the Act of 1981 on the courts to make a protection order at the conclusion of barring proceedings, upon a determination being made that a barring order should not be granted. In practice, cases frequently arise in which allegations are made by a wife and are denied by a husband and in which a court may refuse to grant a barring order

---

15. Such injunctions are normally sought in conjunction with custody proceedings and are of particular relevance where a child has been kidnapped or where there is a fear that a child might be kidnapped and possibly taken out of the jurisdiction. See further p. 369 *ante*.

16. Courts (Supplemental Provisions) Act, 1961, Sect. 22(1) and Third Schedule, Ref. No. 27, as amended by the Courts Act, 1971, Sect. 2(1). See further Sect. 2 of the Courts Act, 1981.

17. In England there have been a great many reported cases relating to the area of matrimonial injunctions. Statute law development there is also a good deal more complex and confused than is the position in Irish law. For a recent account of English law, see S.M. Cretney, *Principles of Family Law*, 4th ed. (1984) Chapter 9.

due to the absence of any corroborative evidence. Judges have an understandable reluctance to bar a spouse from the home due to the drastic nature of the remedy. It is submitted, that upon a court refusing to make a barring order, it should possess the necessary jurisdiction to make a protection order in cases where there is a concern as to whether the behaviour of a husband may pose a danger or threat to the safety or welfare of a wife or dependent children but in which there is insufficient evidence presented upon which a barring order could be made.

2. There is a need to clarify by statutory provision the nature of the evidence upon which the District Court should base a determination as to whether to grant a further barring order, upon an application being made by a spouse to continue such order for a further twelve month period following upon the expiration of an order previously made. In particular, legislation should clarify whether spousal or parental misconduct by the barred spouse subsequent to the making of the expiring order is an essential pre-requisite before another barring order can be made.

3. The Joint Oireachtas Committee on Marriage Breakdown referred to "judicial inconsistency"[18] in the application of the criteria applicable to determine whether barring orders should be made, in particular in cases in which no allegations were made of physical violence. Undoubtedly, there is some disparity of approach on the part of individual members of the judiciary in determining barring order applications but this is inevitable having regard to the subjective nature of the determination that has to be made. It is submitted, however, that the courts have not yet sufficiently teased out the legal principles applicable to determine when conduct falling short of violence should result in the barring of a spouse on the grounds that such conduct poses a threat to the safety or welfare of the other spouse or dependent children. The Oireachtas Committee referred to the need for "a clear restatement of the law relating to barring orders".[19] What is required, it is submitted, is a more detailed judicial exposition of the general principles applicable by way of written judgements with reference to the specific areas referred to. It is curious that despite the fact that a great many barring orders have been granted by the courts since 1976 there have been relatively few written judgements delivered setting out the principles applicable to determine barring applications.

4. The Joint Oireachtas Committee noted that:

"A most unsatisfactory aspect of the present structure in relation to the making of barring orders is that in practically all cases no help is available to a person whose conduct has lead to him or her being barred"

and continued:

"That person is simply removed from the family home for a period of months or years during which time they are given no professional help to form an insight as to why their conduct was unacceptable or to ensure that similar conduct will not recur. This is yet another example of the complete

---

18. See *Report of the Joint Oireachtas Committee on Marriage Breakdown* (1985) at p. 69.
    19. *Ibid.*

lack of any adequate welfare or counselling service being available to those whose family difficulties are dealt with through the courts."[20]

It is submitted that upon the making of a court barring order the spouse barred should be automatically referred by the court to a court welfare officer for counselling and assistance in adjusting to the new family arrangements and that welfare officers should be appointed to the court specifically to fulfil such a function.

---

20. *Ibid.*, at p. 70. See also McNally, *supra*.

CHAPTER 18

THE FAMILY OUTSIDE MARRIAGE

The natural family or the family outside wedlock does not in Irish law possess the same legal rights and obligations as the family based on marriage. In this chapter it is intended to examine the present legal position of natural parents *vis-à-vis* each other and their children and to refer to the impact that the Status of Children Bill, 1986, as initiated, will have on this area of the law if it is enacted by the Oireachtas.

THE CONSTITUTION

We have already seen in chapter one that the courts have held that the mother and father of an illegitimate child and the child are not a family for the purposes of Articles 41 and 42 of the Constitution.[1]

In the leading case of *The State (Nicolaou) v. An Bord Uchtála*,[2] the Supreme Court stated that the words "family" and "parents" in Articles 41 and 42 referred only to a family and parenthood based on marriage and that the guarantees in these articles do not extend to a natural mother or a natural father. A mother's natural right to the custody and care of her illegitimate child was said to be protected by Article 40.3. Twelve years later in *G. v. An Bord Uchtála*,[3] a majority of the Supreme Court endorsed the approach in *Nicolaou* and confirmed that the rights of the mother of an illegitimate child were protected not by the family provisions of the Constitution but by the latter Article. O'Higgins C.J. stated that the plaintiff, who was the mother of an illegitimate child

> "as such . . . has rights which derive from the fact of motherhood and from nature itself. These rights are among her personal rights as a human being which the State is bound under Article 40.3.1. of the Constitution to respect and to defend and vindicate. As a mother she has the right to protect and care for and to have the custody of her infant child . . . This right is clearly based on the natural relationship which exists between a mother and child."[4]

---

1. See *State (Nicolaou) v. An Bord Uchtála* [1966] I.R. 567 (S.C.); *G. v. An Bord Uchtála* (1978) 113 I.L.T.R. 25 (S.C.); *In re M., an Infant* [1946] I.R. 334; (1946) 80 I.L.T.R. 130 (H.C.); *McNally v. Lee* (January, 1970) unreported (H.C.); *State (K.M. and R.D.) v. The Minister for Foreign Affairs and Ors.* [1979] I.R. 73 (H.C.).

2. *Supra.*

3. *Supra.* See also *E.M. v. E.M. & M.M.* (December, 1982) unreported (H.C.).

4. *Supra* at p. 35. See also judgements of Parke J. and Walsh J; Kenny J. and Henchy J. both held that the mother of an illegitimate child merely has a statutory or legal right and not a constitutional right to its custody. Henchy J. did however later in his judgement state "the mother's rights in regard to the child, although deriving from the ties of nature, are given a constitutional footing only to the extent that they are found on the constitutionally guaranteed rights of the child." (*Supra* at p. 52).

No such rights have been extended to the father of an illegitimate child. Walsh J., giving judgement for the Supreme Court in *Nicolaou*, stated:

"It has not been shown to the satisfaction of this court that the father of an illegitimate child has any natural right as distinct from legal rights, to either the custody or society of that child and the court has not been satisfied that any such right has ever been recognised as part of natural law."[5]

The court, thus, withheld constitutional recognition from the natural father not only under Articles 41 and 42 but also under Article 40.3.

In 1984 in *O'B. v. S.*[6] the Supreme Court unanimously re-affirmed that:

"the family recognised by the Constitution, particularly in Article 41, is the family based upon marriage — that is to say a marriage which was a valid subsisting marriage under the law of the State."[7]

As we have already seen, the courts have held that the position of the illegitimate child is not constitutionally inferior to that of the legitimate child. Thus, in *G. v. An Bord Uchtála*,[8] Henchy J. stated:

"All children, whether legitimate or illegitimate, share the common characteristic that they enter life without any responsibility for their status and with an equal claim to what the Constitution expressly or impliedly postulates as the fundamental rights of children."[9]

Moreover, in *O'B. v. S.*[10] Walsh J. delivering the judgement of the Supreme Court stated that:

"It cannot be contested that a person born outside marriage is, as a human person, equal to one born within marriage."[11]

The courts have emphasised that the innocent child of an extra-marital union possesses the same "natural and imprescriptible rights (under Article 42) as a child born in wedlock to religious and moral, intellectual, physical and a social education"[12] and "that the illegitimate child has an equal right with legitimate children to the constitutional protection of its personal rights of life, to be fed, to be protected, to be reared and educated."[13]

It has been stated, however, that this constitutional equality does not mean that in all instances legitimate and illegitimate children must be treated identically. Although Article 40.1 of the Constitution provides that "all citizens shall as human persons be held equal before the law", it permits the State in its enactments to "have due regard to differences of capacity, physical and moral and of social function".

---

5. [1966] I.R. at p. 643. See also *The State (K.M. & R.D.) v. The Minister for Foreign Affairs, supra.*
6. [1984] I.R. 316: sub nom *In the Goods of William Walker, Dcsd.* [1985] 5 I.L.R.M. 86 (S.C.).
7. [1984] I.R. at p. 333.
8. *Supra.*
9. *Ibid.,* at p. 51.
10. *Supra.*
11. [1984] I.R. at p. 332.
12. *Per* Gavan Duffy P. in *In re M., an Infant, supra* at p. 344. See also *State (Nicolaou) v. An Bord Uchtála, supra* at p. 642 — "These 'natural and imprescriptible rights' cannot be said to be acknowledged by the Constitution as residing only in legitimate children" *per* Walsh J.; *G. v. An Bord Uchtála, supra,* in particular judgements of Walsh J. at p. 41 and Henchy J. at pp. 51–52.
13. *Per* Murphy J. in *E.M. v. E.M. & M.M., supra,* at p. 6 of judgement.

A difference in "moral capacity and social function" between legitimate and illegitimate children was held in *The State (K.M. & R.D.) v. The Minister for Foreign Affairs & Ors.* [14] to justify a difference in treatment between legitimate and illegitimate children in a legislative provision concerning the removal of children under seven years of age from the State. The difference in treatment was, in that case, regarded as a desirable protection for the welfare of illegitimate children. [15]

In *O'B. v. S.* [16] the Supreme Court rejected the contention that a difference in treatment between legitimate and illegitimate children in the law of succession could arise from any difference of "physical or moral capacity" or "social function", Walsh J. acknowledging that "it could not be claimed that illegitimacy can, in itself, attribute any particular social function to the illegitimate person." [17] The court, however, accepted the argument that the difference in treatment between legitimate and illegitimate children could be constitutionally justified by the provisions of Article 41.1.2 under which the State has a duty to protect the family based on marriage. Accordingly, it was held to be constitutionally permissible for the State "to place members of the family based upon marriage in a more favourable position than other persons in relation to succession to property whether by testamentary disposition or intestate succession." [18] The court's acceptance of the proposition, that a succession law which treats illegitimate children less equally to legitimate children affords protection to the family

---

14. *Supra*. The constitutional challenge in this case was however successful on another ground. See p. 188 *ante*.

15. See also *State (Nicolaou) v. An Bord Uchtála, supra*, at p. 642 – "An illegitimate child has the same natural rights as a legitimate child though not necessarily the same legal rights" – *per* Walsh J. for the Succession Rights of illegitimate children see p. 623 *post*.

16. *Supra*.

17. [1984] I.R. at p. 333.

18. *Ibid.*, at p. 335. See also *In The Matter of the Estate of Norman Robert Wilson, Deceased, Eric John Wilson v. The Attorney-General and John Coughlan* (May, 1979) unreported (H.C.) In this case the claim of maternal cousins to be entitled to succeed to the estate of the deceased, who died intestate and was illegitimate was unsuccessful in the High Court. However, McWilliam J. in his judgement stated "There is a great deal to be said for the point of view that it is invidious to make a distinction for the purpose of inheritance between legitimate and illegitimate persons although it does not necessarily follow the depriving an illegitimate person of a right to inherit as next of kin offends against the provisions of the Constitution. In this case, however, it cannot be suggested that there is or was any discrimination against the illegitimate person. He is not deprived of any benefit or of any rights. He had full power of disposal over his property but did not choose to exercise it. The claim that must be made is that, because he was illegitimate, there was discrimination against his first cousins. Whatever claim might be made by him if he were deprived of rights to succeed to property of next of kin of his natural relations, I do not see how the converse can possibly give rise to the claim which can succeed on a constitutional ground."

For an analysis of the Supreme Court decision in *O'B. v. S.*, see P. O'Connor, "The Succession Rights of Illegitimate Children" (1984) I.L.T. (n.s.) 63. See also the following publications written prior to this judgement: W. Binchy, "The American Revolution in Family Law" (1976) 27 N.I.L.Q. 371; M. Staines, "The Concept of the Family under the Irish Constitution" (1976) 11 I.J. (n.s.) 223; T. O'Connor, "Illegitimate Children and Succession" (1979) 73 *The Gazette of the Incorporated Law Society of Ireland* 53 and "Illegitimacy and the European Convention on Human Rights" (1978) 112 I.L.T. & S.J. at p. 167 *et seq*; S. Maidment, "The Marckx Case" (1979) Fam. Law 228; The Law Reform Commission: *Report on Illegitimacy* (1982) at pp. 69–80 in which a number of decisions delivered by the United States Supreme Court are discussed. The relevance of the various United States cases cited and discussed in the preceding articles and publications was dismissed by Walsh J. in *O'B. v. S.* on the grounds that "no provision comparable to Article 41 exists in the United States Constitution and there is no part of the reasoning of the United States cases which is sufficiently pursuasive to negative the compelling provisions of Article 41, which provisions the court is obliged to take into its consideration of the issue raised in the present case". (see [1984] I.R. at p. 336). The learned judge, nevertheless, went on to examine and discuss many of the United States' Supreme Court decisions.

In Marckx the European Court of Human Rights held that provisions of the Belgium Civil Code relating to illegitimate children violated Articles 8 and 14 of the European Convention

based on marriage and maintains "the primacy of the family as the fundamental unit group of society",[19] raises a question as to the constitutional validity of any legislation that the Oireachtas might enact to provide equal treatment in the area of succession for both legitimate and illegitimate children. In this context, Walsh J. noted:

"It is not claimed in the present case that there are any particular limitations placed upon the ability of the Oireachtas by legislation to allow intestate succession by children to their parents when they are born outside marriage nor is this court called upon to express any opinion at this time on what limitations may exist in respect of any such legislative ability."[20]

As a result of the limitation of the application of Articles 41 and 42 to married couples, it has been held that a natural father has no right to appear before the Adoption Board upon an application by a third party for the adoption of his child.[21] It also seems that whereas married persons have a constitutional right to have access to contraceptives, a denial of such access being an invasion of marital privacy, a single person has no such right.[22] Further as these articles do not apply to the relationship between natural parents and their illegitimate child, there can be no constitutional objection to the welfare of such child being given paramount consideration in determining disputes between a parent and a third party as to its custody.[23] Finally, as we have seen in the chapter on adoption, the unmarried mother of an illegitimate child, by adopting her child may place it in the same legal position as a child born to her in marriage. Whether such an adoption renders the mother and child "a family" within the meaning of Articles 41 and 42 has never been judicially decided.[24]

---

for the Protection of Human Rights and Fundamental Freedoms. The Court in its judgement found certain limitations and discriminations in the area of succession to be in breach of the convention. In *O'B. v. S.* Walsh J. briefly referring to the Marckx case sought to distinguish it from the case being dealt with by the Supreme Court and dismissed its relevance as it could "have no bearing on the question of whether any provision of the (Succession) Act of 1965 is invalid having regard to the provisions of the Constitution." In so far as the Marckx case may be in conflict with the provisions of the Succession Act he noted "that this court is obliged to follow the provisions of the Act of 1965" (*supra* at p. 338). See Article 29.6 of the Constitution which states that "no international agreement shall be part of the domestic law of the State save as may be determined by the Oireachtas." It is this author's view that in the event of the appropriate proceedings being brought against this State, Irish succession laws will be held to be in breach of the Convention. At the time of writing judgement is awaited from the European Court in the case of *Johnston v. Ireland* (Application No. 9697/1982) in which such an allegation is raised.

19. [1984] I.R. at p. 334.
20. *Ibid.* See now Part V of the Status of Children Bill, 1986, discussed on p. 625 *post.*
21. *The State (Nicolaou) v. An Bord Uchtála, supra.* In contrast to the decision in *Nicolaou,* see *Stanley v. Illinois,* 405 U.S. 645 in which the United States Supreme Court held, contrary to the equal protection clause of the U.S. Constitution, a statutory provision which enabled the State of Illinois deprive a father of the custody of his illegitimate child without affording him a hearing. The U.S. Supreme Court has in later cases developed a distinction between the constitutional rights of the father where the parent-child relationship has developed as opposed to the position of the father where no such relationship has developed. See *Lehr v. Robertson* 463 US 248; *Caban v. Mohammed* 441 U.S. 380; *Quillon v. Walcott* 434 U.S. 246.
22. See *McGee v. A.G.* [1974] I.R. 284; 109 I.L.T.R. 29 (S.C.). See the contrasting approach of the United States Supreme Court in *Eisenstadt v. Baird* 405 U.S. 438. It should be noted that there is no express statutory prohibition on the supply to single people of contraceptives nor on their importation or use by them.
23. See p. 383 *ante et seq.*
24. Under the Status of Children Bill, 1986, as initiated, a child so adopted is, for the purposes of the Bill, defined as a "marital child".

GUARDIANSHIP AND CUSTODY

At common law a child born outside wedlock was said to be illegitimate or a bastard. He was a *filius nullius* (the child of no one) with no parents and no relations. None of the legal rights and duties which flowed from the relationship of parent and legitimate child were accorded to him or his parents. Natural parents were neither the guardians of their child nor did they have any right to its custody.[1]

In the 19th century the notion that the mother had some rights to her child slowly emerged. Initially her rights arose as a corollary to the duty imposed on her by the Poor Law legislation to provide maintenance. Although she was not regarded as the guardian of her child,[2] and her rights in relation to it were said not to be the same as the rights of the father of a legitimate child,[3] it became established that the "natural" relationship gave the mother a right to her child's custody.[4] Her wishes were to be primarily considered and observed unless contrary to its welfare.[5] However, the mother's wishes in relation to such a child could only prevail during her lifetime and if she was survived by the putative or natural father, he was entitled to custody of the child as against any guardian appointed by the mother.[6]

Section 6 of the Guardianship of Infants, 1964, clarified the legal position of a mother *vis-à-vis* her illegitimate child by providing that the mother of such child shall be its guardian and, pursuant to that section, she can appoint a testamentary guardian to act as guardian of her child after her death. Moreover, the mother can apply to the District, Circuit or High Court under section 11 of the Act for a direction on any question affecting the welfare of her child[7] and can enforce her right to custody by *habeas corpus* proceedings in the High Court. Section 11(4) of the Act of 1964, affords recognition to the natural father by providing that he can make an application to the court for an order seeking the custody of his child and a right of access to it. However, in the absence of a prior court order awarding him custody or a legal agreement signed by the mother granting custody to him, the father cannot institute *habeas corpus* proceedings to obtain custody, as he is not a guardian of his illegitimate child and has no right to custody. The Act of 1964 was passed while the *Nicolaou* case was under litigation. Today, if the natural father of a child was refused a hearing by the Adoption Board, or the board was going to make an order con-

---

1. See article entitled "The right to the Custody of Children" (1883) 17 I.L.T. & S.J. 417–8, 431–2, 445–6, 459–60, 473–4, 483–4. See also *Children in English Society*, by I. Pinchbeck and M. Hewitt, ch. XIX.
2. See *R. v. Nash* (1883), 10 Q.B.D. 454 (C.A.); *In re Ullee, Infants* (1885) 1 T.L.R. 667 (Ch. Div.); contra the dicta in *In re Darcys* (1860) 11 I.C.L.R. 298 (Ct. of C.P.).
3. *Barnado v. McHugh* [1891] A.C. 388 (H.L.); *In re Connor* [1919] 1 I.R. 361, 367 (M.R., C.A.).
4. *R. v. Nash, supra.*
5. *Barnado v. McHugh, supra. In re Connor, supra*; *In re Tamburrini* [1944] I.R. 508 (H.C.); *In re Cullinane, an Infant* [1954] I.R. 270 (H.C.).
6. *In re Kerr, an Infant* (1889) 24 L.R. Ir. 59 (Appeal); *In re Connor, supra*; *In re Crowe* (1883) 17 I.L.T.R. 72 (Q.B.D.). If the mother of an illegitimate child married there arose out of the husband's statutory duty to support her child, a right to the custody of the child – see *In re Gavagan, an Infant* [1922] 1 I.R. 148; (1922) 57 I.L.T.R. 33 (Ch. Div.).
7. The difficulties previously discussed relating to the jurisdiction of the High Court as a result of the Courts Act, 1981, the High Court decision in *R. v. R.* [1984] I.R. 296 and the Supreme Court decision in *Tormey v. Ireland* [1985] 5 I.L.R.M. 375 also apply to applications made to the High Court by either the mother or father or any other guardian of an illegitimate child pursuant to the provisions of the Guardianship of Infants Act, 1964. See further p. 47 *ante*.

trary to his wishes, he could at least delay the adoption process by applying for a custody order under the Act.[8]

The Act of 1964, does not extend any additional maintenance rights to an illegitimate child and a mother seeking to require a father to contribute towards the support of such child must rely on the provisions of the Illegitimate Children (Affiliation Orders) Act, 1930, under which she can obtain an affiliation order. In the context of any disputes relating to the guardianship, custody or upbringing of an illegitimate child, section 3 of the Act of 1964 applies so as to require the court to regard the welfare of the child as the first and paramount consideration.

We have already seen in the previous section that the natural mother's right to the custody of her child is now recognised as a constitutional right. As this right has been held to derive from Article 40.3 of the Constitution and not Articles 41 and 42 it is not an "inalienable or imprescriptible" right as are the rights possessed by the family under the latter Articles. It has been said that the mother's right to custody creates "corresponding obligations or duties"[9] to the child which are reflected in rights vested in the illegitimate child. Walsh J. in *G. v. An Bord Uchtála*[10] referring to this, stated:

> "The mother and her illegitimate child are human beings and each has the fundamental rights which spring from their relationship. These are natural rights ... the fact that a child is born out of lawful wedlock is a natural fact. Such a child is just as entitled to be supported and reared by its parents or parent who are the ones responsible for its birth, as a child born in lawful wedlock ... these obligations of the parent or parents amount to natural rights of the child and exist for the benefit of the child. The child's natural rights in these matters are primarily to be satisfied by the parent or parents."[11]

As Articles 41 and 42 do not apply to the relationship between natural parents and their illegitimate children and, more particularly, to the relationship between a mother and her illegitimate child, the constitutional difficulty in regarding a legitimate child's welfare as the first and paramount consideration in custody disputes between parents and third parties cannot arise in disputes as to the custody of an illegitimate child. The Supreme Court decision in *G. v. An Bord Uchtála* has, however, been held to give rise to a presumption of law that the constitutional rights of an illegitimate child to welfare "are ordinarily best served by entrusting the custody of the child to its natural mother",[12] and, clearly, the courts will normally award custody to a mother unless satisfied that the welfare of the child requires that the mother's claim to custody be overruled.

In *McNally v. Lee*[13] the High Court refused to make an order of custody in favour of the mother of an illegitimate child. In this case the mother M. having given birth to her child in 1959 "freely and fully" consented to its being adopted in 1960. The child was given to the L's but as Mrs. L. was under 30 an adoption order could not be made until she reached that age.[14] In 1964 the statutory form

---

8. See Adoption Act, 1952, Sect. 16(4). See p. 320 *ante*.
9. *Per* Walsh J. in *G. v. An Bord Uchtála* [1980] I.R. at p. 67.
10. *Supra*.
11. [1980] I.R. at pp. 67–68. Henchy J., in the minority, on the issue of the mother's rights stated that in his view a mother of an illegitimate child has a legal right, as opposed to a constitutional right, to custody but continued "the custody has a constitutional footing in so far as it satisfies a constitutional right of the child" (1980 I.R. at p. 87).
12. *E.M. v. E.M. & M.M.* (December, 1982) unreported (H.C.). See judgement of Murphy J. at p. 25. See also pp. 3 and 6 of judgement.
13. *Supra*.
14. See section 11(3) of the Adoption Act, 1952, which was subsequently amended by the Adoption Act, 1964.

of consent was sent to the mother and she refused to sign it. That same year the mother married a man who was not the father of the child. In 1969 an application by the mother for custody of the child was made to the High Court. Evidence was given that if the child was taken away from Mr. L.[15] the child would become emotionally disturbed. Kenny J. held that

> "the welfare of the child requires that he should remain with Mr. L. and that giving him to the custody of M. would be foolish and would probably destroy any prospect he has of a stable, settled life".

He also held that M. had abandoned the child and that under section 14 of the 1964 Act he would refuse to grant her custody.

In *J.L. (A Minor)*[16] an 8½ year old girl was placed in the custody of a third party (M) who was regarded by the girl as her mother and the court refused to make a custody order in favour of the girl's real mother, (K). J.L. was born in August 1969. Her mother, who had married a man who was not J.L.'s father in July 1969, was deserted within a few weeks of the child's birth. In November 1970, J.L. came with her mother to reside in F.'s household. F. was a widower with four children. For a period K. did the housework in F.'s home and reared her child there. In August 1972, M., a spinster, moved into the house and assisted F. in both running the household and in his business. Shortly after M.'s arrival J.L. went to sleep in M.'s bedroom and started to refer to her as "mammy".

In September 1974, K. left F.'s household, leaving J.L. behind her, returning only for short visits between then and January 1975. She stayed again for about five weeks in February, 1975, but never again returned to stay. J.L. remained part of F.'s household being brought up by F. and M.

In March 1978, Finlay P., holding that this was a case that came within sections 14 and 16 of the 1964 Act, ruled that it was in the interests of J.L.'s welfare that she remain in F.'s household. He concluded that on the evidence the child "had no overt awareness" of her relationship with K. Whilst making a custody order in favour of M., he also made elaborate access arrangements to enable a "gradual re-familiarisation" between K. and J.L. to take place.

In *E.M. v. E.M. & M.M.*[17] the High Court ordered that a girl just over three years of age be returned by grandparents to the custody of the mother. The child having been born in September 1980, had resided in her grandparents' home since December 1980. The mother, who was not married, remained living with the child in the grandparents' home until January 1982, when she again became pregnant and went to Northampton in England where she gave birth to a second daughter in March 1982. The evidence established that throughout the time the child resided with the grandparents it was the grandparents who took the immediate responsibility for her day to day needs and they were referred to by the child as "mammy and daddy". During her stay in Northampton, the mother was in communication with the grandparents by letter and by telephone. Upon the mother returning to Ireland to visit in August 1982, she informed the grandparents that she wished to have custody of her daughter and to take her back to Northampton in October 1982. The grandparents were opposed to the mother's plans and doubted her capacity to properly care for her child. At the date of the court hearing the mother had been allocated a house by Northampton County Council. There was evidence that she had considerably matured, was

---

15. Mrs. L. had by this time died.
16. (March, 1978) unreported (H.C.), Finlay P.
17. *Supra.*

very good with the baby and that there was good interaction between the mother and her daughter. Murphy J. held that the mother was capable and competent to look after her daughter and that it was in the child's "overall best interests, and in particular her long term interests, that she be in her mother's custody."[18]

As we have already seen, in both *G. v. An Bord Uchtála*[19] and in *R.C. & P.C. v. An Bord Uchtála*[20] the mothers succeeded in obtaining orders requiring the return to their custody of their one-year-old illegitimate children and the prospective adopters with whom the children in each case had been placed, failed in both cases to obtain an order dispensing with the consent of the mother to the making of an adoption order.[21]

Finally, Part III of the Status of Children Bill, 1986, as initiated on the 9th of May, 1986, proposes to amend the provisions of the Guardianship of Infants Act, 1964, so as to enable the father of an illegitimate child to be a guardian of his child or children jointly with the mother. Under the Bill, a father will have the same guardianship rights to his "marital children" as currently vest in the father of legitimate children. As a consequence, a father will automatically act with the mother as joint guardian to some children who are "illegitimate" and to whom a father under existing law has no guardianship rights.[22] For example, at present upon a voidable marriage being annulled, children of the parties to the marriage are rendered illegitimate and their father's rights as guardian terminate. Under this proposal, a father will, upon the granting of a nullity decree, remain the guardian of any such children. The Bill also contains provisions to enable the father of a "non-marital" child to become guardian jointly with the mother on application to the court. The Bill does not automatically confer guardianship rights on fathers of non-marital children but provides that a "special procedure" is to be provided for making guardianship orders where

"(a) the mother consents in writing to the appointment of the natural father as guardian, and

(b) the natural father is registered as the father in a register maintained under the Births & Deaths Registration Act, 1863–1986."[23]

Where the application of a father to become a guardian is opposed, the court in determining such application, will be bound to determine the issue on the basis of the welfare of the child being regarded as the "first and paramount consideration" pursuant to section 3 of the Act of 1964. No further guidance is given by the Bill to the courts as to the criteria to be applied in determining such applications.

Upon a dispute arising as to whether a person seeking a guardianship order is in fact the father of the child in respect of whom such order is sought, no

---

18. See p. 26 of judgement. Murphy J. in awarding custody to the mother made elaborate provision to ensure the future welfare of the child would be protected – see pp. 27–28 of judgement.
19. *Supra*.
20. (February, 1985) unreported (H.C.).
21. See further chapter 12, p. 299 *et seq* in which is discussed all the cases involving mothers of illegitimate children seeking to regain custody of their children from prospective adopters with whom such children had been placed for adoption in the context of proceedings initiated by adopters pursuant to section 3 of the Adoption Act, 1974, and cross proceedings for custody instituted by the mothers of the children concerned.
22. See chap. 11 at p. 288 *ante* where the categorisation of children as marital and non-marital is discussed.
23. See Sect. 11 of the 1986 Bill.

guardianship order can be made unless "it is proved on the balance of pro-babilities that he is the father of the child."[24] The provisions contained in Part VII of the Bill relating to blood tests can be invoked in the determination of a dispute as to paternity in guardianship proceedings.[25]

---

24. See Sect. 9, *ibid*.
25. See chap. 11 at p. 290 *ante*.

FINANCIAL SUPPORT

Introduction

Under Poor Law legislation a mother was under a duty to maintain her illegitimate child until it reached the age of 15 and any relief given to her child by a Poor Law Union was recoverable from her.[1] Upon her marrying, her husband came under the same duty.[2] The Public Assistance Act, 1939,[3] re-enacted these provisions, liability to maintain continuing until the child became 16 years of age. The Social Welfare (Supplementary Welfare Allowances) Act, 1975, repealed and replaced by the Social Welfare (Consolidation) Act, 1981, both retained this liability,[4] and a health board may recover from a mother or her husband, if the child was born prior to their marriage, a contribution towards any allowance granted by it for the child's support.[5]

The Courts Act, 1971,[6] enabled a deserted wife to seek maintenance from her husband for any illegitimate child under 16 who immediately prior to the husband's desertion was wholly or partly supported or maintained by the spouses. Under The Family Law . . . Act, 1976, either spouse may seek maintenance from the other for a dependent child of the family. Among the children within this category is a child of one spouse which the other spouse has treated as a member of the family, although aware that he is not the parent of the child.[7] A third party may also obtain an order requiring either spouse to maintain such a child in certain circumstances under this Act.[8] The Bastardy Law (Ireland) Act, 1863[9] enabled the Guardians of a Poor Law Union to recover the cost of relief given to an illegitimate child from the putative father of the child. In order to recover such costs it was necessary for the mother to identify the father upon oath and for her allegation of paternity to be supported by corroborative evidence.[10] It was not until the passing of the Illegitimate Children (Affiliation Orders) Act, 1930, that the mother of an illegitimate child was given power to directly force the father of her child to make a financial contribution towards its maintenance. The Act of 1930 repealed the one of 1863 in toto. Since the coming into force of the Family Law . . . Act, 1976, a third party may also seek a court order to require natural parents to maintain their

---

1. See the Poor Relief (Ireland) Act, 1838, Sects. 53–55.
2. See *In re Gavagan, an Infant* [1922] 1 I.R. 148; (1922) 57 I.L.T.R. 33 (Ch. Div.), where it was held that by virtue of his observance of his obligation to maintain his wife's illegitimate child under the 1838 Act the husband acquired a right to the custody of such child. The husband in this case was the father of the child but the same right to custody would have arisen even if he was not.
3. Sect. 27. See also Sect. 28 which enabled a public assistance authority to recover from those under an obligation to support an illegitimate child, the sum paid out by it to maintain such child.
4. See Sect. 16 of the 1975 Act, and section 214 of the 1981 Act.
5. See Sect. 17 of the 1975 Act and Sect. 215 of the 1981 Act.
6. Sect. 18(6).
7. Sect. 3 of the 1976 Act. An order may be made to maintain such a child until he reaches the age of sixteen "or if he has attained that age –
   (i) Is or will be or, if an order were made under this Act providing for periodical payments for his support, would be receiving full-time education or instruction at any university, college, school or other educational establishment and is under the age of twenty-one years, or
   (ii) is suffering from mental or physical disability to such extent that it is not reasonably possible for him to maintain himself fully."
This provision is not affected by the Age of Majority Act, 1985. See section 2(4) of the 1985 Act.
8. Sect. 5(1)(b), see p. 452 *ante*.
9. Replacing Sect. 18 of the Poor Relief (Ireland) Act, 1862.
10. See Sect. 2 and Sect. 3 of the Act of 1863.

child. Finally, whilst the mother of an illegitimate child is unable to claim maintenance for her own benefit from the father of her child, she has since 1973
been entitled to receive Unmarried Mother's Allowance.

It is now intended to engage in a detailed examination of the present law.

Affiliation Orders

The Illegitimate Children (Affiliation Orders) Act, 1930,[11] makes provision
for the mother of an illegitimate child to bring proceedings against the person
she alleges to be the father of her child, to oblige him to contribute towards the
maintenance of such child.[12] Formerly such proceedings could only be commenced in the District Court but the Courts Act, 1971,[13] expressly conferred
jurisdiction on the High Court concurrent to that of the District Court. The
Courts Act, 1981,[14] amended the 1971 Act by conferring jurisdiction on the
Circuit Court to hear such proceedings. Although the 1981 Act also deleted
from the 1971 Act explicit reference to the High Court's concurrent jurisdiction,
it appears that having regard to the judgement delivered in *R. v. R.*[15] the High
Court may still retain an original jurisdiction to hear proceedings initiated before
it under the 1930 Act.[16]

An order adjudging that a person alleged to be, is, the father of an illegitimate
child is called an affiliation order.[17]

Who may apply for an order: The mother of a child[18] or a local body administering relief to the poor[19] and actually giving relief to the mother or to her
illegitimate child. In practice no body that comes within the latter definition has
ever applied under the Act. An application for an affiliation order is always
made by the mother. The mother may only apply if a single woman, a widow,
a married woman living separate from her husband[20] or a married woman living
with her husband who gave birth to an illegitimate child before her marriage.[21]

---

11. See also the District Court Rules (No. 2) 1962, (S.I. No. 8 of 1962), and the Circuit
Court Rules (No. 6) 1982 (S.I. No. 158 of 1982).
12. Illegitimate Children (Affiliation Orders) Act, 1930, sect. 2.
13. Sect. 19(2)(a). See further *O. v. M.* [1977] I.R. 33 (S.C.).
14. Sect. 14.
15. [1984] I.R. 296 (H.C.).
16. See, however, *Tormey v. Ireland* [1985] 5 I.L.R.M. 375 (S.C.). See further p. 43
ante.
17. Sect. 3 of the 1930 Act.
18. A " 'child' means any child who is under the age of sixteen years, or, if he has
attained that age –
   (i) is or will be or, if an order was made under this Act providing for periodical pay-
      ments for his support, would be receiving full-time education or instruction at any
      university, college, school or other educational establishment and is under the age
      of twenty-one years, or
   (ii) is suffering from mental or physical disability to such extent that it is not reasonably
      possible for him to maintain himself fully". – Sect. 1 of the 1930 Act as amended
by the Family Law ... Act, 1976, Sect. 28(1)(a). This provision is not affected by the Age
of Majority Act, 1985. See section 2(4) of the 1985 Act.
19. Whilst in theory such a body could bring affiliation proceedings there is no reported
case of such a body doing so since the Act's inception.
20. A married woman seeking an affiliation order in respect of a child born to her
during marriage formerly had the difficulty of having to rebut the presumption of legitimacy and establish paternity without being able to give direct evidence herself of not
engaging in intercourse with her husband at any time during which conception could have
taken place. See p. 585 *et seq*. See, however, *O'Connell v. Broderick* (February, 1977)
unreported (H.C.) where this difficulty does not appear to have been considered.
21. See Sects. 1 and 2 of the 1930 Act.

Thus, if a woman becomes pregnant by a man other than the one that she subsequently marries, and her child is not born until after the marriage, she may only bring affiliation proceedings if she separates from her husband, or if he dies, or if their marriage is otherwise validly terminated.

There seems little valid reason for limiting in the above manner the circumstances in which an application may be made. It is illogical to deprive a family of extra support where a husband marries knowing his wife to be pregnant by another, and yet permit it to seek such support if the parties marry a week after the birth. This limitation on the making of an application for an order to require the father of an illegitimate child to contribute towards the support of his child will be removed from the law if the Status of Children Bill, 1986, is enacted and comes into force.

The issuing of Summons: In order for a summons to be issued the mother must first upon oath in writing identify the father of the child.[22] There are specific time limits laid down in the Act, within which a mother can apply for a summons to be issued. By section 2(2) as amended by the Family Law . . . Act, 1976,[23] an application can be made only:

(a) Before the birth of the child;[24]

(b) Within three years after the child's birth;

(c) At any time, if the alleged father has contributed towards the maintenance of the child within three years of its birth;[25]

(d) Within three years after the alleged father first takes up residence in the State,[26] if he was not resident in the State at the date of the child's birth, or if he ceased to be so resident within three years of its birth.

For time to run against the mother it is not necessary for her to know the place of residence of the father. Thus, if the father disappears before proceedings are commenced, without contributing to the child's maintenance and unknown to the mother takes up residence in Cork, if the mother living in Dublin does not discover his whereabouts until three years after the child's birth she will be unable to succeed in an application for an affiliation order. Similarly knowledge by the mother, of the father having taken up residence in the State is not required for time to run under (d) above.

---

22. *Ibid.*, Sect. 2(1); see *The State (O'Neill) v. Shannon* [1931] I.R. 691. A District Court affiliation summons is issued by a District Justice. A special summons to commence High Court affiliation proceedings may only be issued with the "prior leave" of a judge of that Court. The issuing of either is dependent on the making of a sworn information (District Ct.) or sworn affidavit (High Court) by the mother identifying the father of her child. An *ex parte* application is made to a judge of the relevant court grounded on the information or affidavit for leave to issue a summons. See *O. v. M., supra*. The service of a Circuit Court affiliation application must be preceded "by the filing of an affidavit made by the applicant verifying the facts of which the applicant has personal knowledge and deposing as to the belief in the truth of the other facts alleged in the application." It must also state that "no collusion or connivance exists between the applicant and any other party to the application." See Circuit Court Rules (No. 6) 1982, *supra*, Rule 9.

23. Sect. 28(1)(b).

24. By Sect. 2(3) where a summons is issued before the birth of a child the date for which the father is summoned to the court "shall not be earlier than 14 days after the day on which such child is expected to be born".

25. See *O'Connell v. Broderick, supra*. A contribution is not limited to a financial contribution, it can be a contribution in kind.

26. Prior to the coming into force of the Act of 1976 all the time limits were of six months. Further time under (d) started to run six months after the alleged father first "entered the State". On this see *The State (O'Callaghan) v. Buckley* [1960] I.R. 429 (H.C.).

Part IV of the Status of Children Bill, 1986, as initiated, proposes to repeal the Act of 1930 in its entirety, subject to the continuation of orders already made under the Act. Under the Bill, the mother of a non-marital child will be able to apply for a maintenance order to be made for the support of her child against the child's father, at any time during the child's dependency and the father of such child will similarly be able to apply for a maintenance order to be made for the child's support against the mother.[27] In conferring on the courts a new jurisdiction to make maintenance orders for the support of non-marital children, the Bill requires the court, when determining such application to apply provisions similar to those currently applicable in determining whether a maintenance order should be made against a parent for the support of a legitimate child under the Family Law . . . Act, 1976. In doing so, it repeals the statutory requirement in the 1930 Act that the mother must identify the father on oath prior to the issuing of proceedings and the provisions requiring proceedings to be instituted against an alleged father within specified time limits. In any case in which there is a dispute as to paternity or parentage, the Bill provides for such issue to be determined on the balance of probabilities prior to any maintenance order being made. The enactment and coming into force of Part IV of the Bill will not only simplify an unnecessarily complicated area of the law but will also render it more difficult for fathers of illegitimate or "non-marital" children to evade their responsibilities.

Effect of criminal charge: In relation to the bringing of affiliation proceedings, it has been held by the High Court in *O'Donnell v. Hegarty*[28] that an acquittal of a person on a charge of unlawful carnal knowledge of a girl aged between 15 and 17 is no bar to a subsequent application for an affiliation order by the same girl against that person in respect of an illegitimate child born to her as a result of the intercourse which grounded the criminal charge. The affiliation proceedings are not as a result of the acquittal *res judicata*; the acquittal does not work any estoppel in favour of the father and the plea of *autrefois acquit* by him in answer to the affiliation proceedings is bad. The reason for this is that different matters are in issue in the two types of proceedings. Similarly, if a person is acquitted on a charge of rape, the girl who it was alleged he raped is not estopped from bringing affiliation proceedings alleging that the person acquitted of the charge is the father of her child.

Procedure: The hearing takes place in the District, Circuit or High Court[29] and if the District Justice or the Circuit or High Court judge is satisfied that the alleged father is the father of the child an order can be made adjudging him to be the "putative" father.

By section 3(2) of the Act —

"No justice of the District Court[30] shall be satisfied that a person is the putative father of an illegitimate child without hearing the evidence of the

27. A non-marital child for the purpose of this Part is said in the Bill to include a child "deemed to be legitimate" and therefore a marital child under Sect. 6 of the Bill. See further p. 289 *ante*.
28. [1941] I.R. 538; (1941) 76 I.L.T.R. 12 (H.C.).
29. As to the High Court's jurisdiction see p. 49 *ante*.
30. Despite the Courts Acts, 1971, and 1981, expressly conferring this jurisdiction on other courts, this section has never been expressly amended to make specific reference for example to a "Judge of the Circuit Court" or to a "Judge of the High Court".

mother of such child and also evidence corroborative in some material particular or particulars of the evidence of such mother."

This involves two factors: (1) The giving of evidence by the mother; (2) The requirement of evidence corroborative of the mother's in some material particular.

1. As was seen earlier, no summons can be issued unless the mother upon oath in writing identifies the father of the child, and by section 3(2) she must give evidence in court. Thus, if she dies at the birth of the child or afterwards, but before the application is finally heard, or cannot give evidence for any other reason, no order can be made and the father cannot be legally obliged to support the child.[31] This can result in considerable injustice in that if the mother dies, a relation may wish to bring up the child. Such a third person should in such circumstances be able to get an order to force the father to meet his obligation to provide maintenance for the child. Obviously it would be more difficult for such a person to provide the necessary proofs for the court to make an order, but he or she should be given an opportunity to do so. There seems little point in not permitting the bringing of such proceedings. If they were successful it can be only for the benefit of the child.

2. A difficult factor and one that has been discussed in a large number of cases is that of finding evidence corroborative of the mother's evidence in some material particular. The burden of proving paternity is upon the applicant, and her evidence by itself is not sufficient for an order to be made. There must be corroborative evidence of some fact that implicates the alleged father.[32] The best evidence is a corroborated admission of paternity by the father but evidence of such will rarely be forthcoming.[33] Mere evidence of opportunity for intercourse is not sufficient,[34] nor is evidence that the defendant sought and obtained an interview with the applicant on hearing that she accused him of being the father.[35]

The leading case is *Morrissey v. Boyle.*[36] The applicant, Morrissey, brought affiliation proceedings against the defendant, Boyle. She stated in evidence that on two occasions B. who was introduced to her as Mr. Manning, took her with another girl and a civic guard for a motor drive; that they stopped at a public house and that they then went off walking in pairs through the fields near Stepaside, that B. had intercourse with her on one of these occasions, and on subsequent occasions, and that as a result of this intercourse a child was born. Some weeks after the birth of the child she met B. and told him that she had been in trouble and that "the baby is in a nursing home"; that he had asked her in what home and she told him; she also told him that she had been in trouble with her parents and that her father wanted to see him, and that B. then said he would arrange to meet her father but that it was too late that night; that her father then came up and B. arranged to meet him on the following night.

Her father gave evidence that he met B. on the same occasion and asked him

31. See further on section entitled "Third Party Maintenance Orders". Where a person has been adjudged the putative father or is the admitted father, a third person in charge of the child may bring maintenance proceedings against him.
32. *The State (Reilly) v. District Justice for Clones* [1935] I.R. 908 (H.C.).
33. *O'Neill v. Kelly* [1957] Ir. Jr. Rep. 81 (Cir. Ct.).
34. See *Seaver v. O'Toole* [1937] Ir. Jur Rep. 8 (Cir. Ct.); *The State (Smyth) v. Fawsitt* [1950] Ir. Jur. Rep. 25 (H.C.).
35. *McCarthy v. Hourihane* [1935] Ir. Jur. Rep. 37 (H.C.).
36. [1942] I.R. 514; (1941) 75 I.L.T.R. 228 (S.C.).

was he Mr. B. and when he said "Yes" he brought B. to the applicant and said "Now Mr. Manning this is my daughter and she will tell you her tale". The father then left them for 10 or 12 minutes and on his return the applicant said to her father "Mr. Boyle wants to make an appointment to see you" and they arranged to meet on the following night. Boyle did not keep the appointment.

On the following evening the applicant's father wrote to B. saying that he was surprised that he did not keep the appointment; that he was willing to meet him any evening and that he did not intend to allow the matter to remain any longer in abeyance, and should he wish to come to an amicable agreement he would expect an early reply to his letter. B.'s solicitor replied to the father's letter stating that if he wished to discuss any matter he should first communicate with him and not directly to B.

The guard also gave evidence which was at variance with that of the applicant as to the material dates and as to the parties separating when they left the motor car.

The District Justice dismissed the summons. On Appeal to the Circuit Court at the conclusion of the applicant's case, B. applied for a direction on the ground that there was no evidence "corroborative in some material particular" of the evidence of the applicant but the Circuit Court judge refused the application holding that there was such evidence. He, however, stated a case for the opinion of the Supreme Court.

There it was held that the Circuit Court was correct in holding that there was evidence corroborative in some material particular of the evidence of the applicant and that the application for a direction was rightly refused.

Because of its importance Sullivan C.J.'s judgement is quoted *in extenso*. Sullivan C.J., referring to section 3(2) stated[37]

"A similar provision in Sect. 4 of the Bastardy Laws (Amendment) Act, 1872, was considered by the Court of Appeal in England in *Thomas v. Jones*.[38] In his judgement in that case Scrutton L.J. there said:— 'What is meant by "Corroboration in some material particular" — that is in a material fact? The vital fact to be proved in a bastardy case is that a child has been born to the applicant as a result of sexual connection with the man. From the nature of the case it is almost inevitable that there never will be any direct corroboration of sexual connection. The evidence in corroboration must always be circumstantial evidence of the main fact, that is to say, evidence from which it may be inferred that the main fact happened. For instance, the fact that the man has had connection with the woman and a child has resulted is sometimes inferred from evidence of previous affection, that they had been seen together showing affection to each other. Sometimes it is inferred from the fact of subsequent affection — that the man and woman are seen together showing signs of affection. Sometimes it is inferred from the fact that the man has done acts which may be treated as recognising responsibility for the child as his child, statements that he will provide for the child, payments for the child, all facts from which as a matter of inference and probability it is more probable that the intercourse did take place than not . . . If the fact is such that the probabilities are equal one way or the other, an inference cannot legitimately be drawn from it one way or the

---

37. *Supra* at pp. 520, 521.
38. *Thomas v. Jones* [1921] K.B. 22 (C.A.).

other. It must show, even only slightly, more probability that intercourse took place than not, and if there is that balance of probability it is not for the Court to say that it is so slight that it would not have acted upon it'."

Sullivan C.J. continued[39]

"In my opinion the only reasonable interpretation of the appellant's evidence is that in the interview in question she charged the respondent with the paternity of her child. That such a charge was made is, I think, the reasonable inference from the fact that the respondent without asking for any explanation of the letter . . . instructed his solicitors to reply to it in the terms 'stated'. If such a charge was made, then the fact that the respondent did not repudiate it in the presence of the appellant's father, but made an appointment to meet him on the following night obviously with the object of discussing the matter is to my mind a most material circumstance from which the more probable inference is that the charge was well founded.

The appellant's evidence as to that material circumstance was corroborated by the evidence of her father."

In the same case Meredith J. stated:

"corroboration has not to go the length of being an unambiguous admission, for that would be conclusive: it is enough if there be something which tends to make you believe the story of the applicant to be the truth".[40]

Following *Morrissey's* case, in *Kiely v. Mulvihill*,[41] evidence was given that the appellant had shown affection towards the applicant over a long period of time and that, on one occasion the appellant entered a field with the applicant at about 3 a.m. and remained there for about two hours.

The court held that the entering of the field at that time of night was more than evidence of mere opportunity and that "[it] must show even only slightly more probably that intercourse took place than not".[42] Taking this fact together with evidence of affection it was held that there was sufficient corroboration of the applicant's evidence to satisfy the statute.

Alternatively, in *Cahill v. Reilly*,[43] evidence was given that the applicant and the defendant who were engaged to be married were sitting in the kitchen of the applicant's home at 2.30 a.m. in the morning. The applicant's sister corroborated the fact that they were in the kitchen at that time as she had shortly before left the room.

Judge Deale reached the conclusion that it was unlikely that the couple would have engaged in intercourse so soon after the interruption of their privacy. At best "the probabilities of intercourse and no intercourse are equal". Thus, the fact that the sister corroborated the presence of the parties in the kitchen did "not corroborate the material fact that they had sexual intercourse in her absence".

There seems on the face of it to be little difference between the facts of the two above cases. In both cases they were young people who had previously exhibited affection towards each other, in the latter instance, the parties being engaged. The difference between the cases was that it was regarded as more

39. *Supra* at p. 523.
40. *Supra* at p. 526.
41. (1947) 82 I.L.T.R. 1 (Cir. Ct.).
42. *Supra* at p. 2 *per* Judge B. O'Briain.
43. [1957] Ir. Jur. Rep. 77 (Cir. Ct.).

likely that parties would engage in sexual intercourse in a field at 3 a.m. in the morning than they would do so in a kitchen at 2.30 a.m. in the morning.

These two cases illustrate the difficulty in predicting the outcome of affiliation proceedings, an unknown factor in each case and one that may be crucial, being what sexual behaviour the court will regard as more probable than not in particular circumstances.[44] Finally, an order that is obtained as a result of perjured evidence by the corroborating witness will be quashed whether or not the party obtaining the order was privy to the perjury.[45]

The Law Reform Commission in its *Report on Illegitimacy* stated that it did not favour the retention of the requirement that a mother's evidence as to paternity be corroborated because it "could work injustice and hardship in certain instances" where a court "might be perfectly satisfied on the evidence (heard) that a person is the parent of a child" but can be obliged not to make an order in the absence of corroboration.[45a] The Status of Children Bill, 1986, in making provision for the maintenance of non-marital children takes cognisance of the Law Reform Commission's view by requiring proof of paternity on the balance of probabilities and omitting the corroboration requirement contained in the Act of 1930. It also drops the explicit statutory requirement that the mother's evidence as to paternity be heard before a maintenance order can be made against the father. This change will render it possible for a maintenance order to be sought against the father of a non-marital child where the mother dies at childbirth or prior to the determination of proceedings. At present no affiliation order can be sought in such circumstances.

Blood and Genetic Testing

As has already been seen, blood testing and genetic testing of both a mother, child and the alleged father can provide considerable assistance to a court in determining the question of paternity.[46] Genetic testing in particular can now establish to a high degree of certainty whether a person alleged to be, in fact is the father of a child. However, the 1931 Act does not empower the courts to require the parties to an affiliation action to undergo blood or genetic testing. In practice it is now usual for parties to such proceedings to voluntarily undergo such testing and if the genetic tests establish paternity the issue of paternity is not usually contested. Similarly, if the tests establish that an alleged father could not be the father of a particular child, it is usual that the plaintiff discontinues her proceedings against him.

A question that has yet to be determined by the Irish courts is whether an alleged father's refusal, without a reasonable excuse, to undergo genetic and blood testing at the request of the mother of an illegitimate child constitutes "evidence corroborative in some material particular" within the meaning of Sect. 3(2) of the 1931 Act so as to enable the mother in affiliation proceedings to obtain an affiliation order. If an alleged father contests paternity in affiliation proceedings after the results of such testing have proved consistent with the allegation of paternity, there is little doubt that the results of the tests carried

---

44. See also *Norwood v. Scott* (1939) 73 I.L.T.R. 200 (N.I. Recorders Ct.); *Edgar v. Wallace* [1957] N.I. 64 (C.A.).

45. *R. (Burns) v. Tyrone County Court Judge* [1961] N.I. 167 (Q.B.D.).

45a. See L.R.C. Report No. 4 at pp. 111 and 116.

46. See p. 287 *ante*.

out could constitute the necessary corroborative evidence.[47] As we have already seen, the Status of Children Bill, 1986, makes provision for blood testing for the purpose of establishing parentage. The provisions of the Bill as initiated, however, do not appear to adequately provide for genetic testing.[47a]

Orders that may be made:[48] If the court adjudges the defendant to be the putative father of the child, it may order him to make various payments. He may be ordered to pay the expenses incidental to its birth,[49] and if the child has died before the making of the order, also the funeral expenses to a sum not exceeding £200. In addition he may be ordered to pay a weekly sum for the maintenance and education of the child and the court may attach such conditions as it thinks proper to the payment or receipt of the money. The weekly sum that can be ordered in the Circuit or High Court is unlimited[50] and left to the judge's discretion, but no more than £30 can be ordered in the District Court.[51] A weekly sum may not commence earlier than the date on which the order is made.[52] As an alternative to a weekly sum, where the court deems it appropriate and the putative father consents, the latter can pay a lump sum fixed by the court in commutation of a weekly sum.[53]

Until recently no written judgement had been delivered by either the Circuit or High Court describing the manner in which the sums, that the court can order to be paid pursuant to the 1931 Act, should be calculated. In *N. McV. v. J. McG.,*[53a] Barron J. in the High Court in March, 1986, determining an affiliation case on appeal from the Circuit Court, noted that the Act does not specify the test to be applied by the court in determining the amount payable for the support of an illegitimate child and stated that "the appropriate test in any case is what is fair and reasonable as between the parties." He continued:

> "The ability of the defendant to pay must be the first consideration of the court . . . the court must also have regard to the financial circumstances of the mother."

In the learned judge's view, in this context,

> "Regard can be had to the attitude of the parents of both parties, both before and after the birth of the child and to whether or not assistance has been willingly given. If assistance has been given then it is in reality part of the financial circumstances of the party in receipt of it. Such assistance may have been given prior to the circumstances of the birth of the child or may have been given by reason of the existence of the birth of the child. If it is deliberately cut off, to require a defendant to pay more or less maintenance, it may be proper for a court to make a decision on the basis that such assis-

---

47. See (1932) 66 I.L.T. & S.J. 64 "Bernstein Blood Test as Evidence" in which is recounted the first occasion in which the results of blood testing was successfully used in affiliation proceedings in this country. On the result of a blood test constituting the necessary corroboration, see the recent English case of *Turner v. Blunden* [1986] 2 All E.R. 75; [1986] 2 F.L.R. 69 (Fam. Div.).

47a. See p. 290 *ante*.

48. See Sect. 3 of 1930 as amended by the Family Law . . . Act, 1976, Sect. 28.

49. By the Social Welfare (Consolidation) Act, 1981, sect. 28(2) in deciding whether or not to make an order for payment of expenses incidental to the birth of a child the court cannot take into consideration the fact that the mother of the child is entitled to maternity allowance. No statutory limit is imposed on the amount that can be ordered to be paid under this provision.

50. The Courts Act, 1971, section 19(2) as amended by the Courts Act, 1981, section 14. See also *R. v. R., supra; Tormey v. Ireland, supra;* and p. 47 *ante*.

51. The Courts Act, 1971, Sect. 19(3)(a) as amended by the Courts Act, 1981, Sect. 14.

52. Sect. 4(1) of 1930 as amended by the Family Law . . . Act, 1976, Sect. 28(1)(h).

53. Sect. 3(1)(c) of the 1930 Act.

53a. (March, 1986) unreported (H.C.).

tance is still available. This would not be a direction for assistance to be continued, but a recognition that the party no longer in receipt of such assistance has made a voluntary decision to manage on a smaller income."

On the facts of the case, Barron J. held the mother to have a marginally smaller income available to her than had the putative father and made an affiliation order in the sum of £30 per week.

In the same case Barron J. considered the plaintiff's claim for expenses totalling £2,132 incidental to the birth of her child. Of the sum sought, £780 was claimed for loss of wages during a period both before and after the child's birth and £400 for maternity clothes. The balance of £952 related to items of expenditure incurred for or on behalf of the child. In determining this claim, Barron J. stated that:

> "Having regard to the scheme of the Act, expenses incidental to the birth relate to those arising at or about the time of the birth and incurred on behalf of the child."

He held that the mother's loss of earnings was "not an expense nor is it referrable to the birth. It is a loss . . . referrable only in part to the fact of the birth and in the main to the period of pregnancy." He also held the cost of maternity clothing not to be such an expense as the cost of such clothing "is referrable to the period of pregnancy." The sum of £952 sought relating to the child was, however, held to come within the scheme of the Act and an order was made requiring the father to pay this sum in full to the mother, Barron J. ruling that it was "reasonable" that he should do so, having regard to the amount of the mother's loss of earnings and her expenditure on maternity clothing.

The court may also order the putative father to pay a sum not exceeding £200 for the purpose of apprenticing a child to a trade. An application for such an order cannot be made until the child is 14, and must be made not later than six months after such child has attained the age of 16.[54] If a child in respect of whom a weekly sum is payable dies, upon an application being made within two months of the death of such child, the court can order the putative father to pay the funeral expenses to an amount not exceeding £200.[55]

Normally money due under an affiliation order is payable to the mother. If the mother dies or for any reason the child is not in her custody the order is made payable to the person in whose custody the child is. It can also be made payable to a local body if the child or mother is in receipt of poor relief from them.[56]

If a putative father, liable to pay a weekly sum dies, liability for such sum attaches to his estate as a civil debt and is recoverable by the person to whom the weekly sum is payable.[57] Similarly, in such circumstances his personal representative can be ordered to pay the funeral expenses of such child or the sum fixed to enable the child to become apprenticed.[58]

The Status of Children Bill, 1986, as initiated, proposes to abolish the provision relating to the making of a payment to enable a child to be apprenticed and proposes that the courts' current jurisdiction to make payments of up to £200 individually in respect of expenses incurred incidental to the birth of a

---

54. *Ibid.*, Sect. 6 as amended by the Family Law . . . Act, 1976, Sect. 28(1)(j).
55. *Ibid.*, Sect. 7 as amended by the Family Law . . . Act, 1976, Sect. 28(1)(j).
56. *Ibid.*, Sect. 9(3).
57. *Ibid.*, Sect. 4(5) as amended by the Family Law . . . Act, 1976, Sect. 28(1)(h).
58. *Ibid.*, Sects. 6(1) and 7.

child or relating to the funeral of a child, in each case, be increased to a juris-diction to make a maximum order of up to £500.[58a] The Bill deletes from the law the provision whereby a father's liability to maintain his illegitimate child can be commuted by the making of a lump-sum order.

Appeals: Either party may appeal from a court's decision. Formerly, any party who wished to do so, had to enter into a recognizance. This, however, is no longer necessary.[59] An appeal to the Circuit or High Court is virtually a rehearing of the case and the mother again has to give evidence which must be corroborated. Consequently if she were to die before the appeal was heard the court would be bound to find for the defendant. The Circuit Court when exer-cising its appellate jurisdiction cannot make an order for the payment of a peri-odical sum exceeding £30 per week (the District Court maximum) for the maintenance and education of a child.

Variation Orders and Concurrent Jurisdiction: Upon the application of either the person by whom or to whom a weekly sum is payable, the court has full powers to vary the amount payable, change the person to whom it is payable, or vary all or any of the conditions relating to the payment or receipt of the money.[60] Upon the application by a person liable to pay a weekly sum, or upon the death of such person, upon the application of the person to whom such weekly sum is payable, the court can authorise the commutation of the weekly sum by payment of a lump sum.[61] Every lump sum fixed as a result of such an application has to be fixed with a view to securing for the illegitimate child benefits at least equal to those he would derive from a continuation of the weekly sum.

Section 14 of the Courts Act, 1981, confers jurisdiction on the District Court and Circuit Court to vary or revoke an order made by the High Court, under the 1930 Act, before the 12th of May 1982 (the date of commencement of the 1981 Act) if the circumstances to which the order related have changed[62] and in the case of the District Court, provided the provisions of the order would have been within the jurisdiction of that court if the 1981 Act had been in operation at the time when it was made. For instance, if a High Court order was made in 1980 to require a putative father to pay less than £30 per week towards the maintenance of his child, an application to vary the order can be made to an appropriate District Court.[63] If, however, the mother is seeking a sum in excess of £30 per week as the District Court cannot make an order greater than such sum under the 1981 Act, it would be of no assistance to the mother to bring such an application before the District Court and, in such circumstances, the application can be made under section 14 of the 1981 Act in the appropriate Circuit Court[64] or having regard to the judgement in *R. v. R.*[65] in the High Court. An order made by the High Court under the 1930 Act after the 12th

---

58a. The Bill proposes a general jurisdiction to make such order in relation to both marital and non-marital children — see Sect. 20.

59. See Illegitimate Children (Affiliation Orders) Act, 1930, Rules 1931, para. 7. See also *Lonergan v. Morrissey* [1947] 81 I.L.T.R. 130 (Cir. Ct.). The 1931 Rules were repealed by the District Court Rules (No. 2), 1962, *supra.*

60. Sect. 5(1) of the 1930 Act.

61. *Ibid.*, Sect. 8.

62. Other than by reason of the Act's commencement.

63. See Sect. 16(2) of 1981 Act.

64. See Sect. 16(1) of the 1981 Act.

65. *Supra.* Whether the High Court still exercises an original jurisdiction is doubtful — see *Tormey v. Ireland, supra* and p. 47 *ante.*

of May 1982 cannot be varied or revoked by the District Court or Circuit Court, and the District Court cannot vary or revoke any such order made by the Circuit Court exercising the original jurisdiction conferred on it by the 1981 Act.[66]

Section 14 is silent as to the power of the Circuit Court (otherwise than on appeal) to make an order in relation to a matter previously dealt with by the District Court. It is submitted, however, that the mother of an illegitimate child may initiate affiliation proceedings in the Circuit Court, seeking an affiliation order even if one has already been made in the District Court. If she could not do so she would be locked into the jurisdictional financial limits imposed on the lower court even if she required a larger weekly sum for the support of her child which the putative father could clearly afford to pay. The Courts Act, 1971, in expressly conferring jurisdiction on the High Court to determine affiliation proceedings was also silent as to the power of that court to make an order under the 1930 Act in relation to a matter previously dealt with by the District Court.[67] In *M.R. v. R. O'F.*[68] Kenny J. rejected the contention that the mother was estopped from seeking a High Court affiliation order as she had previously obtained a District Court affiliation order. He stated that the sum of maintenance payable for the support of an illegitimate child should depend in part, at least, on the putative father's means and held that the High Court had power to modify and amend the affiliation order made by the District Court. An order was made in that case increasing the amount to be paid by the father from the then District Court maximum of £5 to £10.

Termination of Affiliation Orders:[69] An order providing for periodical payments continues to be payable for the length of time specified in the order. All such payments cease to be payable upon

(a) the death of the child

(b) their commutation by payment of a lump sum

(c) an order of the court terminating the payments

(d) the child becoming 16 years of age, unless at the time of the making of the order, or at any time thereafter, before his attaining 16, the court on account of his educational needs or a physical or mental disability orders otherwise.

(e) the attainment by the child of the age of 21 where the court on account of his educational needs has ordered that payment be made after he has attained 16

(f) the adoption of the child by a person other than the natural mother.[70] Where a mother adopts her own child, the affiliation order remains in force.

The court may at any time on the application of the person making weekly payments under an affiliation order terminate the payments if satisfied

---

66. See Sect. 14 of 1981 Act.
67. See Sect. 19 of the Courts Act, 1971.
68. (1974) 109 I.L.T. & S.J. 25 (H.C.).
69. See Sect. 4 of the 1930 Act as amended by Sect. 28(1)(h) of the 1976 Act. See also Sect. 2(4) of the Age of Majority Act, 1985.
70. Adoption Act, 1952, Sect. 31.

(i)   that liability has ceased under the Act, *or*

(ii)   that justice requires that liability should cease.[71]

(a), (b), (d), (e) and (f) list the circumstances in which liability terminates under the Act. Despite none of these circumstances existing it is still possible for the court under (ii) above to terminate the order upon application by the party subject to it. An example of a situation in which the court may terminate an order in the interests of justice would perhaps be where the mother had become financially very well off, while the putative father was impecunious. The fact that the mother of the child marries subsequent to the making of an order does not automatically terminate liability under the order. If, however, she adopts the child together with her husband, liability ceases upon the adoption order being made.

The Family Law ... Act, 1976,[72] empowers the court to require a putative father to make further payments although the original affiliation order is discharged or payments have ceased. The amount payable and the period of time for which it is to be paid is left to the court's discretion. The court may only require the father to make such payments while the person for whose benefit they are made is still a child within the meaning of the Act. This provision introduces considerable flexibility to the law. Thus, if a father pays a lump sum in commutation of weekly payments, it is possible that the court will at some time in the future order him to make further payments. Similarly, if payments cease upon a child reaching 16 because the child is no longer attending school, and the child subsequently, when still under 21, resumes full-time education, the court may require further payments to be made.

Voluntary Agreement for the Maintenance of an Illegitimate Child:[73] A voluntary agreement can be made between the mother and the father of an illegitimate child whereby the father agrees to provide for the child. Such an agreement can be made either before or after the making of an affiliation order. It can be submitted to the court by either party and provided the benefits are substantially as beneficial as those which would be obtained under the 1930 Act, although they differ wholly or partly from such benefits, the court can record its approval. The recording of such approval acts as a complete bar to any proceedings or further proceedings (where an order has previously been made) being brought under the Act for an affiliation order.[74] Before a mother of an illegitimate child in respect of whom an order has not previously been made

---

71. Sect. 5(2) of the 1930 Act.
72. Sect. 4(4) of the 1930 Act as amended by Sect. 28(1)(h) of the 1976 Act.
73. See Sect. 10 of the 1930 Act.
74. *Ibid.*, Sect. 10(4). There is some doubt as to the accuracy of this statement. By virtue of Sect. 10(4) of the 1930 Act it is accurate. However, the Act of 1930, as amended by the Family Law ... Act, 1976, Sect. 28, now states in Sect. 4(4)(a) that "Where an affiliation order ... has been discharged ... or where payments under an affiliation order have ceased to be payable by virtue of this Act, the ... court may at any time thereafter, notwithstanding anything in this Act, by order direct the making by the putative father of further payments". An order to make further payments is regarded as an affiliation order. Thus it seems from this section that if prior to concluding an agreement a father has been subject to an affiliation order, despite the obtaining of the court's approval for the agreement, it will not bar the mother from bringing proceedings for further payments. However, if such an agreement is approved, without an affiliation order ever having been made as the father is never adjudged a "putative father" it seems that future affiliation proceedings cannot be brought.

can apply for the approval of the court for such an agreement, she must upon oath make an information in writing identifying the father of the child.[75] The father who signs such an agreement is known as the "admitted father".

In the case of an agreement made which is not submitted to the court for its approval, the question arises as to whether it is a bar to an affiliation action being brought in the future. Obviously, if such an agreement is concluded outside the statutory time limit for bringing proceedings, no problem arises as no proceedings could be brought in any case. However, if the father has contributed to the maintenance of such child within the statutory time limit, either by virtue of such an agreement or prior to its being concluded, an agreement not submitted to the court should not be a bar to the mother bringing affiliation proceedings. The Act provides that those agreements concluded and expressly approved by the court bar future proceedings. The purpose of the court seeing and approving an agreement is to protect the interests of the child by ensuring that an agreement is equally as beneficial to the child as any order that could be made by the court.

It is submitted that if an agreement was concluded containing a provision whereby the mother promised not to take affiliation proceedings, and if the circumstances were such that in the absence of such a provision the court would have jurisdiction to make an order, if such an agreement did not receive the approval of the court, such a provision would be unenforceable as contrary to the policy of the Act.[76] As has already been noted, the Status of Children Bill, 1986, makes no provision whereby the father of a non-marital child can be relieved of his obligation to pay continuing maintenance by the payment of a once-off lump sum either by agreement or court order. The government Memorandum entitled *The Status of Children*, published as a discussion document one year prior to publication of the 1986 Bill, stated that "it is regarded as inappropriate to enable a parent to terminate his maintenance obligations to his children by payment of a capital sum".[76a]

Procedure for Payment: The law as to the payment of an affiliation order is the same as that applying to payment of a maintenance order under the Act of 1976.[77] The court when making an order must direct that payment be made to the District Court clerk. The court is bound to make such a direction unless, at the request of the person on whose application the order was made, the court considers that it would be proper not to do so. If a direction of payment to the clerk is not made the court may at any time in the future make such a direction.

---

75. Sect. 10(5) of the 1930 Act. As we shall see further on whether or not the father was previously subject to an affiliation order, as the "admitted father" under the agreement, he may be subject to maintenance proceedings brought by a third party.

76. See *Follit v. Koetzow* (1860) 2 EI & EI. 730, 121 E.R. 274 (Ct. of Q.B.) where it was held that a mother could apply under Sect. 3 of the Poor Law Amendment Act, 1844, for an affiliation order, despite the existence of a legally enforceable agreement between her and the father, whereby she promised in effect not to bring affiliation proceedings in return for his paying her a sum for the support of the child. The agreement was held not to bar such proceedings. Payments ordered under the Act "not being made solely for the mother's benefit, she cannot renounce the right to it". *Per* Blackburn J. at p. 741. For the enforcement of agreements to contribute towards the support of one's illegitimate child see *Jennings v. Brown* (1842) 9 M. & W. 496; 152 E.R. 210 (Ct. of Exch.); *Ward v. Byham* [1956] I.W.L.R. 496 [1956] 2 All E.R. 318 (C.A.).

76a. See *The Status of Children*, a memorandum published by the Dept. of Justice (Dublin, May 1985, Stationery Office) at p. 10.

77. See Sect. 28(1)(g) of the 1976 Act.

The clerk is under a duty to transmit payments made to him to the person entitled to receive them. Where payments to the clerk are in arrears, upon a request in writing by the latter, the clerk may proceed in his own name for enforcement of the arrears. This does not prevent a person from taking enforcement proceedings in her own name if she wishes. Where the court has directed payment to the court clerk, it may discharge the direction on the application of the putative father if satisfied that having regard to his record of payments and other circumstances it would be proper to do so. The court must first give the person in receipt of the payments an opportunity to oppose the application.

Normally, the mother is the person entitled to receive the payments ordered by the court. If she dies or if for any reason the child is not in her custody, the money will be paid to the person that has custody of the child. It may also be paid to a local body if the child or mother receives poor relief from it.[78]

Enforcement of Orders: Every weekly or other sum ordered to be paid under the Act of 1930 may be recovered as a civil debt.[79] Other means of enforcing payment of affiliation orders are discussed in Chapter 14, commencing at page 456.

Third Party Maintenance Orders

Under section 4A of the Act of 1930, as appended by the Family Law ... Act, 1976, Sect. 28(1)(h) it is possible for a third party to seek a maintenance order for the benefit of an illegitimate child. If it appears to the court that a parent of an illegitimate child has failed to provide such maintenance for the child as is proper in the circumstances, the court may order the parent to make periodical payments for the support of the child to the person applying for maintenance. These payments are to be made for such period during the lifetime of the applicant, as the court determines. The court also has a general discretion to determine the amount of the payments and the times at which they are to be made. A parent under this provision means the mother, putative father or an admitted father of the child.

An order may not be made in relation to a parent, if that parent is already obliged by virtue of one of the other provisions of the 1930 Act to make payments for the child's benefit unless (a) he is not complying with his obligation and (b) the court having regard to all the circumstances thinks it proper to make an order. If the court does make such an order, any sums that would fall due for payment by virtue of other provisions of the Act, cease to be payable.

Under this provision not only the father but also the mother of an illegitimate child may be ordered to pay maintenance. Thus, the father, a relative of the mother, a social worker, or an institution looking after the child, could bring maintenance proceedings against her, to require her to make some financial contribution towards its upbringing. In so far as is appropriate, the provisions of the Act of 1976 relating to maintenance orders also apply to orders made under this section.

Unmarried Mother's Allowance

Family Law only provides for the maintenance of the child. Social Welfare

---

78. See Sect. 9(3) and (4) of the 1930 Act.
79. Sect. 11 of the 1930 Act.

legislation seeks to provide for unmarried mothers. Under section 197 of the Social Welfare (Consolidation) Act, 1981, an unmarried mother whose child or children are residing with her may qualify for Unmarried Mother's Allowance.[80] For the purposes of the section a woman is regarded as being an unmarried mother "if, not being or having been a married woman she is the mother of a child who has not been adopted".[81] Thus, if an unmarried mother adopts her own child it appears that by so doing she disqualifies herself from receipt of the allowance. Moreover, the Ministerial regulations made relating to payment of the allowance provide that "a woman shall be disqualified from receiving an allowance if and so long as she and any person are cohabiting as man and wife".[82]

To obtain the allowance a mother must satisfy a means test and the means test and the amount of allowance payable is the same as that applicable to a deserted wife with one child under the deserted wife's allowance scheme. If an unmarried mother has more than one child outside wedlock, she may claim for each additional child. There is no benefit payable to an unmarried mother equivalent to the deserted wife's benefit. Appendix H lists the total annual recipients of unmarried mother's allowance since 1973.

Other Social Welfare Schemes

Since the coming into force of the Social Welfare (Supplementary Welfare Allowances) Act, 1975, an unmarried mother, whose means are insufficient to meet her needs and those of her dependants may apply for supplementary welfare allowance. Child Benefit is also payable to an unmarried mother subject to the same conditions under which payment is made to a married parent.[83]

---

80. This provision replaced the Social Welfare Act, 1973, Sect. 8, which originally established unmarried mother's allowance.
81. See S.I. No. 190 of 1973, Article 4.
82. *Ibid*, Article 7.
83. See further p. 472 *ante*.

PROPERTY RIGHTS

The provisions of Section 12 of the Married Women's Status Act, 1957, do not apply to and cannot be used for the determination of proprietary disputes between an unmarried couple who are or have been cohabiting, unless such couple were engaged and the dispute relates to property in which either or both cohabitees had a beneficial interest during the course of their engagement.[1] Moreover, a cohabitee cannot invoke the provisions of the Family Law (Protection of Spouses & Children) Act, 1981, to obtain a barring order if her safety or welfare or the safety or welfare of any of her children are threatened by the person with whom she is residing. In appropriate circumstances, however, an injunction may be sought or criminal proceedings for assault instituted to obtain the necessary protection or relief. The Family Home Protection Act, 1976 also provides no protection for the cohabitee. Thus, if a woman is residing with a man in a home which is in the man's sole name and in which she has no proprietary or beneficial interest, her consent is not required prior to the home being validly conveyed to another. If a cohabitee refuses to vacate a home owned solely by the person with whom she is residing, the latter may successfully bring ejectment proceedings against her. A cohabitee who claims to have a proprietary or beneficial interest in property the legal title of which is vested in the sole name of the person with whom she is residing may, of course, in ejectment proceedings or in separate proceedings instituted by her, seek a court order to declare the extent of her interest in the property.

There have, to date, been two cases involving a proprietary dispute between cohabitees in which the Irish courts have delivered written judgements.

In *McGill v. S.*[2] the plaintiff and the defendant, who were not married to each other, lived together for a number of years in the defendant's flat in Germany. They spent holidays together in Ireland and on one of these, in 1967, the plaintiff purchased a house which was to be used by both of them as a holiday home. The plaintiff paid the entire purchase price of £1,775 and spent the sum of £9,750 on renovating and redecorating the house. The defendant believed the house was purchased for both of them but at no stage did any discussions take place between the parties concerning the defendant acquiring a beneficial interest in the house and the house was purchased in the plaintiff's sole name. The parties spent several holidays in Ireland working on the house and a considerable amount of work, mostly in the nature of cleaning, decoration and supervising tradesmen, was done by the defendant. She also spent £1,000 of her own money in repairing out-buildings as a present for the plaintiff. Early in 1973, following discussions with the plaintiff, the defendant came to reside permanently in the house with his permission. Towards the end of that year the plaintiff went to the United States of America on business and the parties' relationship ended. The defendant continued to reside in the house and subsequently the plaintiff, in Circuit Court ejectment proceedings, sought possession of the house from the defendant and the defendant, who contested the proceedings, counter-claimed that she was entitled to an equitable or proprietary interest in the house. The Circuit Court, rejecting the counter-claim, granted possession of the house to the plaintiff and this decision was affirmed by the High Court, dismissing the appeal by the defendant.

---

1. See the Family Law Act, 1981, Sect. 5. See further p. 72 *ante*.
2. [1979] I.R. 283 (H.C.).

It is clear from the judgement delivered by Gannon J. in the High Court that whilst the procedure provided by the Married Women's Status Act, 1957, section 12, cannot be invoked by cohabitees, the legal principles enunciated in the cases determined under that section may be applied in determining proprietary disputes between cohabitees. Rejecting the defendant's claim to a beneficial interest in the house, Gannon J. stated:

> "In the case of two persons who are not spouses evidence of a consensus derived from words or conduct and intended to have legal consequences would support a trust expressed or implied or constructive. But whether the party having the legal estate and the party claiming an equitable interest be spouses or not, the Court will not impute a relationship of trustee and cestui que trust from the facts of a couple living together in (or seemingly in) the married state and sharing expenses without any more cogent evidence . . .[3]

> As the counter-claiming defendant is not a spouse but claims to be a cestui que trust by virtue of indirect contributions in circumstances of a close domestic relationship corresponding to that between spouses, I think it is necessary to point out that indirect contributions which are unrelated to the acquisition of the property cannot found an equitable interest in it . . . the evidence of the defendant in support of her claim falls far short of what is required to enable the court to hold, by the implication of a trust for her benefit, that she has acquired any beneficial interest in the property which is the subject of the claim. In spite of having the means and the opportunity, she took no part in the negotiations and contributed no amount of the purchase price for the acquisition of the property of which the plaintiff is sole owner. Such as were her indirect contributions all came after the acquisition of the property had been completed (without continuing instalment payments) and did not bear any significant relationship whatever to either the capital sum of £1,775 or to the sum of £9,750 spent by the plaintiff."[4]

In these proceedings, the defendant also claimed that she had an irrevocable licence to continue to reside in the house. Rejecting this contention, Gannon J. stated:

> "On the facts of this case I am satisfied that the defendant was lawfully in occupation of the property which is the subject of the claim with the licence or permission of the plaintiff, but only as a licensee at will. For so long as the domestic and personal relations between the parties remained stable it was unlikely that the licence would be terminated, but the evidence does not support a licence by implied contract which could continue against the will of the plaintiff or even beyond the period of their mutual association. I am satisfied that the defendant's licence to occupy and have possession of the property was validly and effectively terminated by the institution of these proceedings at the latest."[5]

The learned judge also concluded that the defendant had no grounds for a claim to compensation for the termination of her licence to reside in the house.

---

3. *Ibid.*, at p. 289.
4. *Ibid.*, at pp. 291—292.
5. *Ibid.*, at p. 293.

Whilst the actual decision of Gannon J. in relation to the claim made to a beneficial interest in the property cannot be faulted, in discussing the legal principles applicable in determining when an indirect contribution by a cohabitee will result in the acquisition of a beneficial interest in property, it is clear that he adopted the more restrictive approach subsequently articulated in proceedings instituted under section 12 of the Married Women's Status Act, 1957, by Keane J. in *M.G. v. R.D.*[6] and approved of and followed by Murphy J. in *S.D. v. B.D.*[7] By comparison, McWilliam J. in the subsequent case of *Power v. Conroy*[8] appears to have adopted the more liberal approach subsequently articulated in the judgement of Finlay P. in *W. v. W.*[9] and reiterated by the Supreme Court in *D.McC. v. M.McC.*[10] It should be noted, however, that in *Power v. Conroy*, the claim made to a proprietary interest was based on both direct and indirect contributions made towards the purchase of property.

The home in which the defendant resided with the plaintiff and their child was purchased by him in his sole name. The plaintiff contributed £1,000 towards the deposit and paid a further £1,000 towards the building of the house. The defendant obtained a building society loan for the rest of the money and he had made mortgage repayments totalling approximately £1,700 at the date of the proceedings. Both contributed to the upkeep of the household. McWilliam J. held that there had been no agreement or even discussion between the parties as to how the house was to be owned and stated that:

> "The correct approach is to try to ascertain what sums have been paid by the parties towards the acquisition of the house and that, in doing this, I must take into account such contributions towards the household living expenses made by either party as enabled the other party to make such payments as were made by him or her. Having done this, I should treat the house as being held by the defendant, on trust for the parties in the shares which they contributed either directly or indirectly towards its purchase."[11]

The learned judge estimated the contribution of the plaintiff at 55% and that of the defendant at 45% and concluded that the defendant held the house "as to 11/20 on trust for the plaintiff", i.e. that the plaintiff held a 55% beneficial interest in the nett value of the house.[12]

Both of the above cases concerned claims by a female cohabitee to a beneficial interest in a home, the legal title of which was held by a male cohabitee in his sole name. It is clear that, generally speaking, the same legal principles are applicable to determine proprietary disputes between cohabitees as apply to determine such disputes between spouses. Moreover, in the resolution of both types of disputes there has now emerged the same divergence of judicial view as to when an indirect contribution will, of itself, give rise to the acquisition of a beneficial

6. (April, 1981) unreported (H.C.). See p. 502 *ante.*

7. (March, 1982) unreported (H.C.). See p. 504 *ante.* Gannon J. referred in his judgement to *Heavey v. Heavey* (1974) 111 I.L.T.R. 1 (H.C.); *Conway v. Conway* [1976] I.R. 254 (H.C.); *McFarlane v. McFarlane* [1972] N.I. 59 (C.A.); *Pettitt v. Pettitt* [1970] A.C. 777 (H.L.) and *Gissing v. Gissing* [1971] A.C. 886 (H.L.).

8. (February, 1980) unreported (H.C.).

9. (March, 1981) unreported (H.C.). See further p. 496 *ante.*

10. [1986] 6 I.L.R.M. 1 (S.C.). See further p. 501 *ante.*

11. See p. 4 of judgement. McWilliam J. referred to *Conway v. Conway, supra; L. v. L.* (December, 1979) unreported (H.C.) but did not refer to *McGill v. S., supra.*

12. See further M. Cooney, "Wives, Mistresses and Beneficial Ownership" (1979) 14 I.J. (n.s.) 1 for a critique of the approach adopted by Gannon J. in *McGill v. S., supra.*

interest in property. There is one particular aspect of the law applicable to spouses, however, that does not apply to cohabitees unless they are parties to a broken engagement and the dispute relates to property acquired during the course of their engagement — that is, that no presumption of advancement arises in favour of a female cohabitee upon a male cohabitee purchasing a property with his own money and placing it either in joint names or in the sole name of the female co-habitee.[13] As a consequence, future cases may arise in which a female cohabitee unsuccessfully claims a beneficial interest in property paid for by a male co-habitee and placed by him in her name, in circumstances in which if the parties were married to each other or had been previously engaged such a claim would have been successful.[14]

---

13. If the dispute relates to property in which either spouse had a beneficial interest during the course of their engagement the presumption of advancement may apply. See p. 73 *ante*.

14. For a discussion of the relevant English cases concerning proprietary disputes between cohabitees see S.M. Cretney, *Principles of Family Law*, 4th ed. (1984) pp. 660 *et seq*. See also *Ridgeway v. Murray* (1981) Northern Ireland Law Bulletin of Judgements No. 7 and *Grant v. Edwards* [1986] 2 All E.R. 426 (C.A.). See further R. Johnson, "Cohabitation Without Formal Marriage in England and Wales" (1986) 16 Fam. Law 47.

SUCCESSION RIGHTS

No matter for how long a man and woman cohabit, if not married to each other, upon the death of one the surviving cohabitee has no legal right to a share in the deceased's estate in the absence of a specific disposition contained in the deceased cohabitee's will. If the deceased dies intestate, the surviving cohabitee has no entitlement to claim a portion of the estate on intestacy. Cohabitees for this purpose include not only a couple residing together who have never celebrated a ceremony of marriage but also couples residing together who are parties to a void marriage. Thus, if a person unknowingly enters into a void marriage with a person, now deceased, and the latter makes no provision for the former in his will or dies intestate, then no claim can be made on the deceased's estate. Moreover, even if specific provision is made by will for the surviving party to a void marriage, the latter's share of the estate may be considerably reduced if a successful claim is made under the Succession Act, 1965, to a share in the deceased's estate by the deceased's lawful spouse, where at the date of death the deceased was validly married to another. The surviving cohabitee's share in the estate may be further reduced if a successful claim is also made by children of a valid marriage to a share in the estate under section 117 of the 1965 Act.[1] It has been recognised, however, that in determining claims made pursuant to section 117, the courts must take into account the moral duty of a deceased to provide for a person with whom he was cohabiting and any children of their relationship.[2]

An illegitimate child, being a *filius nullius* at common law, had no succession rights to either of his parents or to any of his relations and if he died intestate and unmarried there was no one to whom his property could pass. The Legitimacy Act, 1931, enacted a minor reform by giving an illegitimate child and his mother limited reciprocal rights of succession on the other's intestacy. By section 9(1) of the Act if the mother of an illegitimate child "dies intestate as respects all or any of her real or personal property" and she is not survived by any legitimate children, "the illegitimate child, or if he is dead, his issue" are entitled to take any interest "to which he or such issue would have been entitled if he had been born legitimate." Thus, such child has no right of succession on intestacy to his mother's estate under the Act if she later marries and has children. The Act confers on him no right of succession whatever to the estate of his natural father.

By Section 9(2) of the Act of 1931 if an illegitimate child "dies intestate in respect of all or any of his real or personal property", his mother, if still alive, possesses the same rights of succession as a last surviving parent to his legitimate child. Section 9 does not apply to or affect the right of any person to take by purchase or descent an estate in tail in real property.[3]

The Succession Act, 1965, did not affect the limited succession rights on intestacy conferred on illegitimate children by the Legitimacy Act, 1931. In *O'B. v. S.*[4] the Supreme Court held that the provisions in sections 67 and 69 of the Act of 1965 relating to intestate succession, which extend to the issue of an

---

1. See p. 520 *ante*.

2. See *L. v. L.* [1978] I.R. 288 (H.C.); *M.P.D. & Ors. v. M.D. & Ors.* [1981] 1 I.L.R.M. 179 (H.C.).

3. Legitimacy Act, 1931, Sect. 9(3). If an illegitimate child dies intestate and unmarried with no children of his own and is not survived by his mother, it appears that the State will take his property "as ultimate intestate successor". See the Succession Act, 1965, Sects. ö7–73 and *In the Matter of the Estate of Norman Robert Wilson, Decsd, Eric John Wilson v. The Attorney General & John Coughlan* (1979) unreported (H.C.).

4. [1984] 5 I.R. 316 (S.C.).

intestate an entitlement to a specific share in a deceased parent's estate, do not apply to illegitimate children and that "the only reasonable construction which can be put upon the word 'issue' in ss. 67 and 69 of the Act of 1965 is that it refers solely to issue born within marriage."[5]

In *O'B. v. S.* the deceased had died a bachelor. The respondent who was his illegitimate daughter and only child, claimed an entitlement to his estate on his intestacy. The court acknowledged that if she were legitimate, as the deceased's only child, she would have inherited the entire estate. In rejecting her claim to a share in her deceased father's estate, the Supreme Court also dismissed her challenge to the constitutional validity of sections 67 and 69.[6] Asserting that the different legislative treatment afforded to legitimate as compared with illegitimate children was constitutionally justifiable, the court stated that the essential difference between the defendant, the deceased's daughter, and the other persons claiming as next of kin, i.e. the deceased's four surviving sisters and one brother, was "the fact that the defendant is not the child of a family based upon marriage and the other next-of-kin are the issue of a family based on marriage."[7]

The above case was concerned with intestate succession but a parent may, if he or she wishes, specifically dispose of property to an illegitimate child by will. It is essential when doing so, however, that the illegitimate child is clearly identified, as it is an established rule of construction that in the absence of evidence clearly showing a contrary intention, words in a will or other disposition denoting family relationships are construed as referring to legitimate relations only. Thus, a disposition to "my children" would be presumed to apply to legitimate children only.[8]

If no specific disposition is made for the benefit of a legitimate, legitimated or adopted child by a parent who dies testate, such child may apply to the court under section 117 of the Succession Act, 1965, asking it to make such provision for him as is just, out of the estate of the deceased parent, alleging that such parent failed "in his moral duty to make proper provision" for him. The Act does not expressly define a child who can make such claim as including an illegitimate child and although no specific claim brought under this section by or on behalf of an illegitimate child has yet arisen for determination, it is clear from the judgement of Walsh J. in *O'B. v. S.* that the Supreme Court is of the view that section 117 of the 1965 Act cannot be availed of by an illegitimate child.[9] In that case, for the purpose of intestate succession, the Supreme Court refused to construe the word "issue" as including illegitimate children in the

---

5. *Ibid.*, at p. 330.
6. See p. 15 *ante*.
7. *Supra* at p. 333.
8. See, however, *O'Loughlin v. Bellew* [1906] 1 I.R. 487 (L.C.) — Whereas "children" is usually taken as referring to legitimate children, in this case, having regard to the surrounding circumstances, the court held that there was sufficient indication of intention to show that the testatrix used the word to include illegitimate children. See also *B. Deceased O. v. D.* [1916] 1 I.R. 364 (K.B.D.); *Andrews v. Andrews* (1885) 15 L.R. Ir. 199 (App.).
9. See, in particular, where Walsh J. makes reference to the Act of 1965 making "special provision to enable the children of the marriage of a testator to apply to the court under section 117 to have just provision made for them out of the estate" (*supra* at p. 335). See also the reference made to a child born outside marriage suffering "severe disappointment" if a parent dies testate leaving him no property (*supra* at p. 336). The learned judge clearly did not envisage that in such circumstances a child born outside marriage could bring a claim under section 117. See, however, *Report on Illegitimacy*: The Law Reform Commission (Report No. 4, September 1982) pp. 45–46 where it is suggested that an illegitimate child can make a claim under section 117 against the estate of his mother if she dies testate leaving no legitimate issue. It is respectfully submitted that this is not a correct view of the current law.

absence of the Succession Act, 1965, containing a specific definition of that term as being inclusive of such children. It is submitted that as the Act of 1965 does not specifically define a "child" for the purposes of section 117 as including an illegitimate child, the courts would similarly refuse to construe that section as conferring any right on such a child to apply for provision to be made for him out of a deceased parent's estate. It also appears that such an interpretation of the Act would not be open to constitutional challenge having regard to the judgement of the Supreme Court in the above case.

The fact that an illegitimate child cannot make a claim under section 117 of the 1965 Act does not mean that in the event of such claim being made by the legitimate children of a testator, the illegitimate child will automatically be deprived of property specifically left to him by a deceased parent. In two recent cases the courts have recognised that a testator has a moral duty towards his illegitimate child or children and that this duty must be taken into consideration by the court when making provision for legitimate children in proceedings brought under section 117.

In *L. v. L.*[10] a claim under section 117 was made by the two children of the deceased's first marriage. The deceased having been divorced by his first wife had remarried and a further two children had been born as a result of this marriage. Under the deceased's will, all his property had been left in trust for the benefit of his second wife.

Costello J. on a preliminary issue, held that in deciding a claim under section 117, the court must have regard to all a testator's moral duties. The deceased had a moral duty towards his second wife and the children of the second marriage, the nature and extent of which, he stated, could not be affected by the court failing to recognise the validity of the second marriage. It was thus not necessary to determine whether the second marriage was valid or not in determining what provision, if any, out of the deceased's estate should be made by the court for his two legitimate children.

In *M.P.D. & Othrs. v. M.D.*[11] a claim was made by the four legitimate children of the deceased to a share in his estate. Although the court held it had no jurisdiction to make an order under section 117 because the claim had not been initiated within the time provided by the 1965 Act Carroll J., nevertheless, held that if it had been brought within time, she would have made an order under section 117, but in doing so, would have taken into account the moral obligations of the deceased to make provision for the woman he was living with at the date of death and the two children of their relationship.

Part V of the Status of Children Bill, 1986, as initiated, proposes major reforms to the succession laws in so far as they apply to illegitimate children and their parents. Under the Bill, those children defined as "marital children" will possess the same rights in relation to both testate and intestate succession as currently vest in legitimate children. As we have already seen in chapter 11, marital children as defined in the Bill include some children who are under existing law regarded as illegitimate children. The Bill also extends to non-marital children the same rights on intestacy to the estate of a parent or relation as currently vest in legitimate children subject to the following:

---

10. *Supra.*
11. *Supra.*

(a) the extension of intestate rights of succession to non-marital children under section 67 of the Succession Act, 1965, only applies to an intestacy that occurs after the enactment of the Bill by the Oireachtas and the commencement of Part V.

(b) Where an intestate dies "leaving one or more children who are non-marital children" the court is to be empowered upon an application being made by the intestate's spouse or any surviving child, whether marital or non-marital, to vary the rules of distribution on intestacy provided for in the Succession Act, 1965, as amended by the Status of Children Bill, if it is "of opinion" that the applicant "has made a contribution of a substantial nature to the accumulation of the intestate's estate and that injustice would be caused" by applying the normal rules.[12] Prior to making an order under this provision, the court will have to have regard to any other provision made by the intestate for the applicant and no order made is to affect the legal right of a surviving spouse. As no application can be made under this provision unless an intestate parent is survived by a non-marital child, circumstances could arise where a marital child benefits to a greater extent from a deceased's estate because a non-marital child is entitled to claim a share in it by way of intestacy, than where no non-marital child exists to make such claim. For example, if a widowed father dies intestate owning a farm of 300 acres and is survived by his three marital children each is entitled under the law at present to a one third share of the farm, even if two of the children never showed any interest in the farm whilst the other child devoted 20 years of his life to working the farm with his father. However, if a non-marital child were to claim a share in the farm, under this proposed provision in the Bill, the child who devoted his life to working on the farm could in court proceedings succeed in obtaining a judgement that the major portion of the farm be vested in him.

The Bill also proposes to reverse the existing rules of construction whereby use of words such as "child" or "issue" in wills, deeds and other instruments is interpreted as referring only to legitimate and legitimated persons and those tracing their relationship through them, unless the contrary intention appears. Section 26 of the Bill provides that in "deducing any relationship" for the purpose of any disposition made after the commencement of Part V, the relationship between "a person and his father and mother shall unless the contrary intention appears be determined irrespective of whether the father or mother are or have been married to each other." The section is not to operate retrospectively to affect dispositions made before its commencement and, for the purposes of section 26, the Bill provides that a will made before its commencement shall not be treated as having been made later merely because it was confirmed by a codicil made after that date. Thus, following the coming into force of this provision, a devise to "my children" contained in a parents will made in 1985, unless the contrary intention appears, will not extend an entitlement to a share in the deceased's estate under the will to any illegitimate child of the testator.

In any case where a parent dies testate after the commencement of Part V of the Bill, a non-marital child of the testator will have a right to apply under

---

12. In many cases a non-marital child may not make a contribution to the accumulation of the intestate's estate because he was not permitted or given an opportunity to make a contribution. See further L.R.C. Report No. 4, *supra*, at p. 127.

section 117 of the Act of 1965 for proper provision out of his deceased parent's estate, irrespective of whether the will was made before or after the commencement date. This provision to some extent will ameliorate the effect of the construction provision discussed above. The right to make a section 117 application will, however, only subsist for a period of 12 months from the first taking out of representation of the deceased's estate.[13]

On the death of a non-marital child intestate, the Bill provides for the same rights of succession as currently pertain between a legitimate child and his parents and other family relations but establishes a rebuttable presumption that a non-marital child is not survived by his father or any person related to him through his father. Moreover, section 35 of the Bill provides that upon a non-marital child dying intestate, an application may be made to the court to declare that the father is "unworthy to share in the estate to which that child died intestate". The Bill contains no similar provision to have a mother declared unworthy to share in the estate of any non-marital child born to her.

---

13. See the Succession Act, 1965, Sect. 117(6).

CRITICISMS AND PROPOSALS FOR REFORM

The Illegitimate Child

It is not possible nor is it intended here to critically analyse all the provisions contained in the Status of Children Bill, 1986, as initiated. Undoubtedly the Bill, if enacted, will considerably improve the legal position of children born outside marriage and extend to them most of the statutory rights that currently vest in legitimate children. For this it is a most welcome measure, although there is little doubt that some of its provisions require amendment during the course of its passage through the Oireachtas either to ensure that the legislation will be fully effective[1] or to remove some legal anomalies that could arise from its implementation.[2]

Although the reforms that will derive from the enactment of the Bill are welcome, it is unfortunate that it does not implement the central recommendation of the Law Reform Commission and entirely remove from the law, distinctions made between children based on the marital status of their parents,[3] or more correctly in the context of the Bill as initiated, distinctions based on whether their parents have at any time celebrated together a ceremony of marriage, whether or not such ceremony results in a valid marriage under Irish law.[4]

The Bill does not abolish the status of illegitimacy as such and remove the concept entirely from the law. It merely re-defines and maintains a distinction between two groups of children, labelling most children who are currently held to be illegitimate as "non-marital". The government's decision not to accept the Law Reform Commission's recommendation that the father of a child should in all circumstances be a joint guardian of his child with the mother, whether the child was born inside or outside wedlock, resulted in it concluding, wrongly, that a conceptual distinction as between children had to remain part of the law.[5] It is

---

1. For example, in the context of requiring parties to co-operate in genetic testing in the determination of parentage or paternity disputes. See p. 290 *ante*.

2. For example, if all the surviving children of a deceased parent who dies intestate are marital children, why should the Succession Act, 1965, not be amended under Sect. 32 of the Bill so as to permit any child who has made a "contribution of a substantial nature to the intestate's estate" seek additional provision out of the estate upon proof that "injustice" would be caused if he was not permitted to do so? Similarly, why should it not be possible under Sect. 35 of the Bill to seek a court order that not only a father but that either a father or a mother "is unworthy to share in the estate" of a deceased non-marital child? On the basis of the Bill, as drafted, the mother of a non-marital child could automatically acquire a share in the estate of her deceased child even in circumstances in which she abandoned the child at birth and left it throughout its minority in the care of the father and had no contact of any nature with her child.

3. See Law Reform Commission, *Report on Illegitimacy* (L.R.C. Report No. 4, Dublin, 1982) at pp. 85–87.

4. A child may, of course, under the Bill be a "marital child" even when the parent has never celebrated a marriage i.e. where a child is adopted under the Adoption Acts, 1952–76 by its unmarried mother or unmarried father.

5. See *The Status of Children* (Department of Justice, Dublin, 1985), a Memorandum laid by the Minister for Justice before each House of the Oireachtas in May, 1985, in particular at pp. 5–7. See also speech delivered by the Minister of State at the Dept. of Justice, N. Fennell T.D., in the second stage debate in the Senate on the 9th day of July, 1986, 113 Seanad Debates 2198 in which she states that the Law Reform Commission's recommendation that the father of an illegitimate child should in all cases be a guardian, "took insufficient account of the interests of the child in each case: while the parents of a child born within marriage owe a duty of fidelity to each other and in consequence can be expected to provide a suitable family environment in which the child's interests will be given a high priority, the same bonds of fidelity do not necessarily apply to the parents of a child born outside marriage." It could be similarly argued that upon a married parent committing adultery he or she should be deprived of guardianship rights to his children born in marriage.

clearly possible to allocate legal rights between parents in accordance with the circumstances of a child's birth whilst in law regarding all children as possessing an equal status.[6] New Zealand legislation provides a valuable example of such an approach.[7]

The New Zealand Status of Children Act, 1969, section 3(1) provides that

> "For all purposes of the law of New Zealand the relationship between every person and his father and mother shall be determined irrespective of whether the father and mother are or have been married to each other and all other relationships shall be determined accordingly."

A year prior to its abolishing the status of illegitimacy, the New Zealand Parliament enacted the Guardianship of Infants Act, 1968, section 6 of which is concerned with the automatic acquisition of parental rights of guardianship. The section provides that generally "the father and the mother of a child shall each be a guardian of the child." However, the mother is a sole guardian if she has never been married to her child's father or if their marriage was validly dissolved prior to the child's conception and "she and the father of the child were not living together as husband and wife at the time the child was born." Thus, if the parents of a child born outside marriage are living together when their child is born, both are automatically joint guardians. If they are not so living together, the legislation provides a mechanism whereby the father can seek guardianship rights by court order.

The use of the above formula has the merit that it removes the necessity to retain a conceptual difference between children, whilst providing a formula to exclude an unworthy father, such as a rapist, from automatically acquiring guardianship rights. The adoption of such a formula in the Status of Children Bill, 1986, would not only have resulted in the Bill completely abolishing the status of illegitimacy but would also have removed the necessity for including in the Bill some of the more tortuous and legally convoluted provisions drafted to define the meaning of the terms "marital child" and "non-marital child". It is to be hoped that this central issue will be reconsidered during the course of the Bill's passage through the Oireachtas.

In this context it should be noted that one of the objectives of many of those who have sought reform in this area of the law in recent years has been to remove from innocent children the social stigma that attaches to the status of illegitimacy.[8] Thus, the Irish Roman Catholic Bishops in their pastoral *Love is for Life*,[9] published in 1985, stated

> "Children do not choose to be born out of wedlock. Children so born should not be stigmatised because of the circumstances of their birth."[10]

---

6. The approach adopted by the Status of Children Bill, 1986, as initiated is similar to that proposed by the English Law Commission in its final *Report on Illegitimacy* (Law Com. No. 118, London, 1982). See W. Duncan, "Abolishing Illegitimacy — A Discussion of the Law Reform Commission's Proposals" (1983) 5 D.U.L.J. 29; J. Eekelaar, "Second Thoughts on Illegitimacy Reform" (1985) 15 Fam. Law 261. In its original Working Paper (see Working Paper No. 74 of 1979) the approach of the English Law Commission was similar to that of the Irish Law Reform Commission.

7. See Sim & Inglis, *Family Court Code* (Butterworths, Wellington, New Zealand, 1983) at pp. 209–212 and p. 254 *et seq*. See also L.R.C. Report No. 4, *supra*, pp. 80–83.

8. See, for example, the Cherish Booklet, *Conference on the Unmarried Parent and Child in Irish Society* (Dublin 1974); The Irish Council for Civil Liberties, *Children's Rights and the Constitution* (Dublin, 1977).

9. (Veritas Publications, Dublin, 1985).

10. See p. 72. See also *Statement on Family Law Reform*, by the Episcopal Council for Social Welfare: A Committee of the Catholic Bishops Conference (Dublin, 1974) pp. 16–18.

Whilst abolition of the concept of illegitimacy would not have any immediate effect on social attitudes to children born outside marriage, the influence of such legislation would, in the long term, contribute to a reformulation of public opinion and the removal of much of the social stigma that currently attaches to such children. It is unlikely that changing the description of children born outside marriage from illegitimate to "non-marital" will have such influence.[11]

The Unmarried Couple

1. Jurisdiction should be conferred on the courts to make maintenance and lump sum financial orders and property transfer orders in appropriate circumstances for the support of a dependent person and children following the granting of a High Court nullity decree.[12]

2. Where an unmarried couple are cohabiting or have cohabited "as if husband and wife" and a child has been born of their relationship, consideration should be given to conferring jurisdiction on the courts to order that maintenance or a lump sum payment be provided, in appropriate circumstances, for the support of a dependent cohabitee during the minority of such child by the other party, unless the child is not in the former's custody. Consideration should also be given to amending the Family Law (Protection of Spouses & Children) Act, 1981, so as to empower the courts to make both protection and barring orders where the serious misconduct of a cohabitee places in danger the safety or welfare of the party with whom he is or was cohabiting or any child of his relationship with such person.

3. A person, who in good faith, entered into a void marriage with another, now deceased, should be able to make a court application for reasonable provision out of the deceased's estate whether the deceased person died testate or intestate.[13]

---

11. See further L.R.C. Report No. 4, *supra*, at p. 86.
12. See p. 156 *ante*.
13. See p. 157 *ante*.

APPENDIX A

1: TOTAL MARRIAGES REGISTERED IN THE YEARS 1961 TO 1985 INCLUSIVE AND THE MODE OF CELEBRATION

Year	Church of Ireland	Presby-terian	Methodist	Jewish	Other religious denomina-tions	Civil marriages	Total	Catholic marri-ages registered	Total marriages registered
	Marriages registered other than Catholic								
1961	375	92	29	17	5	39	557	14,772	15,329
1962	438	120	28	14	3	47	650	14,977	15,627
1963	430	112	30	12	6	78	668	14,888	15,556
1964	412	103	31	7	3	66	622	15,506	16,128
1965	429	83	33	9	7	56	617	16,329	16,946
1966	444	117	33	8	4	79	685	16,164	16,849
1967	475	103	30	3	6	74	691	17,097	17,788
1968	465	120	31	8	13	96	733	18,260	18,993
1969	567	116	36	15	5	124	863	19,441	20,304
1970	518	104	29	7	10	121	789	19,989	20,778
1971	566	111	30	6	13	170	896	21,118	22,014
1972	528	130	43	7	13	168	889	21,413	22,302
1973	491	113	25	12	3	179	823	21,993	22,816
1974	441	103	30	7	8	239	828	22,005	22,833
1975	426	82	24	5	2	224	763	20,517	21,280
1976	490	93	35	7	8	282	915	19,665	20,580
1977	342	88	27	8	5	266	736	19,280	20,016
1978	394	65	17	2	3	322	803	20,381	21,184
1979	325	60	15	6	8	351	764	20,042	20,806
1980	332	51	23	11	13	388	818	20,974	21,792
1981	392	63	25	4	27	454	965	19,647	20,612
1982	376	119	41	1	20	540	1,097	19,127	20,224
1983	404	71	23	2	19	902	1,421	18,046	19,467
1984*							1,133	17,222	18,355
1985*							860	17,692	18,552

Source: Annual Report on Vital Statistics, 1972 & 198. 1983 to 1985 the Yearly Summary of Births, Deaths and Marriages compiled by the Central Statistics Office.
*Figures relating to 1984 and 1985 are provisional.

2: TOTAL BIRTHS, ILLEGITIMATE BIRTHS AND ADOPTIONS IN IRELAND
1953–1981 (absolute figures and percentages)

Year	Total births	Illegitimate births	Per cent illegitimate births of total	Adoptions	Per cent adopted of illegitimate births
1953	62,558	1,340	2.14	381	28.43
1954	62,534	1,310	2.09	888	67.78
1955	61,622	1,234	2.00	786	63.69
1956	60,740	1,173	1.93	565	48.16
1957	61,242	1,032	1.69	752	72.86
1958	59.510	976	1.64	592	60.65
1959	60.188	959	1.59	501	52.24
1960	60,735	968	1.59	505	52.16
1961	59,825	975	1.63	547	56.10
1962	61,782	1,111	1.80	699	62.91
1963	63,246	1,157	1.83	840	72.60
1964	64,072	1,292	2.92	1,003	77.63
1965	63,525	1.403	2.21	1,049	74.76
1966	62,215	1,436	2.31	1,178	82.03
1967	61,307	1,540	2.51	1,493	96.94
1968	61,004	1,558	2.55	1,343	86,20
1969	62,912	1,642	2.61	1,225	74.60
1970	64,382	1,708	2.66	1,414	82.78
1971	67,551	1,842	2.73	1,305	70.84
1972	68,527	2,005	2.93	1,291	64.43
1973	68,713	2,167	3.15	1,402	64.69
1974	68,907	2,309	3.35	1,415	61.28
1975	67,178	2,515	3.74	1,443	57.37
1976	67,718	2,545	3.76	1,104	43,37
1977	68,892	2,879	4.18	1,127	39.14
1978	70,299	3,003	4.27	1,223	40.72
1979	72,539	3,337	4.60	988	29.60
1980	74,046	3,723	5.03	1,115	29.94
1981	72,158	3,914	5.44	1,191	30.42
1982	70,843	4,358	6.15	1,191	27.32
1983*	66,815	4,517	6.80	1,184	26.21
1984*	64,237	5,030	7.80	1,195	23.75
1985*	62,250	5,268	8.50	882	16.74

Sources:　For births, Annual Reports on Vital Statistics 1960, 1970 and 1982. The 1983–
1985 yearly summary – published by the Central Statistics Office. For adoptions,
Annual Report of An Bord Uchtála (Adoption Board), 1953–1985.

It should be noted that there is not an exact co-relation between the number of births and
the number of adoption orders made in any one year as the adoption process in respect of
a child is in many cases not completed until the new calendar year after the birth of the
child and in some cases in relation to some children may not be completed until they are
two or three years of age or older. It should also be noted that it is assumed that all adoption
orders made in each year specified were made in respect of illegitimate children. Orphaned
legitimate children and legitimated children may also be adopted but, in practice, very few
adoption orders are made in respect of such children. Thus, the above table is just a crude
measure of association which clearly illustrates the changing trend from the majority of
children born illegitimate being placed for adoption to the majority of such children being
retained in the care of their natural mothers. It should also be noted that the making of an
adoption order does not in all cases indicate that a mother has given up the care of her child
to others or another. In the period 1983–1985, 500 adoption orders were made in which
the natural mother adopted her own child, 16 being made in favour of the natural mother
alone and 484 in favour of a natural mother and her husband, the latter not being the father
of her child. (See further Appendix D).

*The births figures for the years 1983–1985 are provisional.

APPENDIX B

GOVERNMENT LAW CENTRES

45 Lr. Gardiner Street, Dublin 1. Tel: (01) 787295
Aston House, Aston's Place, Dublin 2. Tel: (01) 712177
9 Lr. Ormond Quay, Dublin 1. Tel: (01) 741711/748241
24 North Mall, Cork. Tel: (021) 275998
84 O'Connell Street, Limerick. Tel: (061) 314599
5 Catherine Street, Waterford. Tel: (051) 55814
5 Mary Street, Galway. Tel: (091) 61650
1 Teeling Street, Sligo. Tel: (071) 61647

PART-TIME LAW CENTRES

St. Catherines Social Services Centre, St. Joseph's Road, Carlow. Tel: (0503) 31063/31354
Social Services Centre, O'Connell Street, Ennis, Co Clare. Tel: (065) 28178
Health Centre, O'Brien Street, Mallow, Co. Cork. Tel: (022) 21484
Community Centre, Letterkenny, Co. Donegal. Tel: (074) 22761
Finglas Health Centre, Ballygall Road West, Finglas, Dublin 11. Tel: (01) 341215
6 High Street, Tralee, Co. Kerry. Tel: (066) 26900
Social Services Centre, Waterford Road, Kilkenny. Tel: (056) 21685/21409
Health Centre, Leitrim Road, Carrick-on-Shannon, Co. Leitrim. Tel: (078) 20308
Community Services Centre, Fair Street, Drogheda, Co. Louth. Tel: (041) 32908/ 36084
Social Services Centre, 15 Clanbrassil Street, Dundalk. Tel: (094) 37352
County Clinic, Castlebar, Co. Mayo. Tel: (094) 22333
Community Information Centre, 14 Wellington Street, Clonmel, Co. Tipperary. Tel: (052) 22267
Social Services Centre, Rossa Street, Thurles, Co. Tipperary. Tel: (0504) 22169
North Gate Street, Athlone, Co. Westmeath. Tel: (0902) 72174/74798
Wexford Community Services Council, St. Bridget's Centre, Roches Road, Wexford. Tel: (053) 23819.

APPENDIX C

SOME STATISTICS OF MARITAL BREAKDOWN AND NULLITY APPLICATIONS

Applications to the High Court for Civil Decrees of Annulment

Year	1976	77	78	79	80	81	82	83	84	85	Total
No. of Petitions Issued	3	11	11	10	16	21	21	33	20	29	175
No. of Decrees Granted	3	1	5	3	10	8	12	18	12	16	88

Source: Figures supplied by the Department of Justice.
During the above period 3 decrees of civil annulment of marriage were granted by the Supreme Court in circumstances where the High Court had refused to grant a decree of nullity. Thus, during a ten year period 91 civil decrees of annulment were granted.

Applications to the Regional Marriage Tribunals of the Roman Catholic Church for Ecclesiastical Annulments

Year	1976	77	78	79	80	81	82	83	84	85	Total
No. of Applications	732	813	698	567	954	584	580	631	740	829	7,128
No. of Decrees Granted	79	104	91	75	76	73	83	94	118	198	991

Source: Figures supplied by the Dublin Regional Marriage Tribunal.

High Court Matrimonial Proceedings (other than Nullity Proceedings) Initiated

Divorce a Mensa et Thoro Proceedings

Year	1976	77	78	79	80	81	82	83	84	85
Petitions Initiated	37	29	39	34	27	25	20	8	5	15

Guardianship of Infants Act, 1964*

Year	1976	77	78	79	80	81	82	83	84	85
Proceedings Initiated	86	182	211	285	379	478	335	1	22	31

Applications for Maintenance Orders under the Family Law (Maintenance of Spouses & Children) Act, 1976*

Year	1976	77	78	79	80	81	82	83	84	85
Proceedings Initiated	50	148	196	263	379	428	165	0	11	13

Married Women's Status Act, 1957

Year	1976	77	78	79	80	81	82	83	84	85
Proceedings Initiated	NA	NA	114	151	238	269	148	11	13	15

Family Home Protection Act, 1976

Year	1976	77	78	79	80	81	82	83	84	85
Proceedings Initiated	NA	NA	83	121	242	341	139	17	18	NA

Applications for Barring Orders under section 22 of the Family Law (Maintenance of Spouses & Children) Act, 1976 and under the Family Law (Protection of Spouses & Children) Act, 1981**

Year	1976	77	78	79	80	81	82	83	84	85
Proceedings Initiated	NA	NA	NA	NA	NA	21	27	0	7	4

Source: Report of Joint Oireachtas Committee on Marriage Breakdown (Dublin, Stationery Office, 1985) at p. 133 and 134 and figures supplied by the Department of Justice.
*A question mark hangs over the jurisdictional competence of the High Court to determine proceedings initiated under these Acts in the High Court on or after the 12th May, 1982, the date when the Courts Act, 1981 came into force – see pp. 47–50 *ante*.
**A question mark hangs over the jurisdictional competence of the High Court to determine proceedings initiated under this Act – see pp. 47–50 *ante*.

Circuit Court Divorce a Mensa et Thoro Proceedings

Year	1982	1983	1984	1985
No. of Applications Made	5	53	115	197

Circuit Court Family Law Proceedings (other than Mensa et Thoro Proceedings) Initated

Guardianship of Infants Act, 1964

Year ending 31st July,	1981	1982	1983	1984	1985
No. of Applications Made	8	54	370	276	294

Applications for Maintenance Orders under the Family Law (Maintenance of Spouses & Children) Act, 1976

Year ending 31st July,	1982	1983	1984	1985
No. of Applications Made	34	297	247	263

Married Women's Status Act, 1957

Year ending 31st July,	1982	1983	1984	1985
No. of Applications Made	7	112	151	177

Family Home Protection Act, 1976

Year ending 31st July,	1982	1983	1984	1985
No. of Applications Made	17	85	123	158

Family Law (Protection of Spouses & Children) Act, 1981

Year ending 31st July,	1982	1983	1984	1985
No. of Applications Made	41	251	140	180

Source: Report of Joint Oireachtas Committee on Marriage Breakdown, *supra*, at p. 133

and 134 and figures supplied by the Department of Justice. It should be noted that subsequent to the publication of the Joint Oireachtas Committee's Report the Department of Justice discovered that the statistics as to the Circuit Court Barring Order applications had been wrongly collated. The corrected statistics are published in this Appendix.

District Court Family Law Proceedings Initiated

Guardianship of Infants Act, 1964*

Year ending 31st July,	1979	1980	1981	1982	1983	1984	1985
No. of Applications Made	–	–	–	0	110	605	447

Family Law (Maintenance of Spouses & Children) Act, 1976

Year ending 31st July,	1979	1980	1981	1982	1983**	1984	1985
No. of Applications Made	1,706	1,842	2,095	1,812	872	2,160	1,974

Applications for Barring Orders under section 22 of the Family Law (Maintenance of Spouses & Children) Act, 1976 and under the Family Law (Protection of Spouses & Children) Act, 1981

Year ending 31st July,	1979	1980	1981	1982	1983**	1984	1985
No. of Applications Made	1,493	1,917	2,225	2,428	1,697	3,478	3,269

Source: Report of Joint Oireachtas Committee on Marriage Breakdown and Department of Justice. The District Court has only maintained annual statistics in relation to maintenance and barring proceedings since 1978.
*The District Court did not acquire a jurisdiction under the Guardianship of Infants Act, 1964 until the 12th of May, 1982.
**The 1982–83 figures are reduced due to the District Court Clerks going on strike following the coming into force of the Courts Act, 1981, on the 12th of May, 1982.

Number of Receipients of Deserted Wife's Allowance/Benefit

Date	Deserted Wife's Benefit	Deserted Wife's Allowance	Total
1976	1,675	3,110	4,785
1977	1,992	3,176	5,168
1978	2,215	3,022	5,237
1979	2,525	2,856	5,381
1980	2,873	2,920	5,793
1981	3,124	3,063	6,187
1982	3,416	3,282	6,698
1983	3,825	3,478	7,303
1984	4,403	3,653	8,056
1985	5,165	3,965	9,130

Source: Department of Social Welfare, Statistical Information on Social Welfare Services, 1985 (Stationery Office, Dublin, 1986), at p. 14.

APPENDIX D

DIVORCE AND THE ROMAN CATHOLIC HIERARCHY

EXTRACT FROM THE IRISH BISHOPS SUBMISSION TO THE TAOISEACH, 7TH APRIL, 1986

I. ENFORCEMENT OF THE LAW PROSCRIBING BIGAMY

1. The Catholic Church regards marriage as a sacrament and as a matter of profound religious and social importance. For this reason the Church cannot but specify the conditions under which its members can contract a valid marriage. If a particular country's laws differ from those of the Catholic Church on the question of what constitutes a valid marriage, it is not possible for the Church to change the conditions of validity in order to adjust in every respect to the provisions contained in the civil law.

Where the Catholic Church recognises as invalid a marriage which initially had the appearance of validity, it is obliged to take account of the status of the partners concerned as persons who were not in Church law united as husband and wife in virtue of that ceremony. In any conceivable arrangement the potential for difference in this area between the law of the Church and that of the State would continue to exist.

2. It is worth recalling the historical background to our present law. Catholic marriages were left outside the Marriages (Ireland) Act 1844 which set out formal requirements for marriages between persons of certain other denominations and for registry office marriages. To be formally valid, Catholic marriages must comply with the common law, that is, the body of non-statutory law built up over the years through judicial decisions. Although the precise scope of the common law rules relating to formal validity of marriage may be a matter of some uncertainty (cf. especially the discussions aroused by the decisions in *Reg v. Millis*, 1843), nevertheless there are good grounds for believing that the range of harmony between canon law and the common law on this matter is considerably greater than has been appreciated formerly. We believe that this is an area in which both Church and State should examine existing procedures with a view to maximising this range of harmony. Our remarks below concerning recent developments in the civil courts in regard to nullity point to one relevant factor in this context.

3. We wish to stress that divorce legislation is entirely inappropriate in relation to this matter. One of the policy justifications for any law of bigamy is that a person should not make a binding valid commitment to one person during the lifetime of another person to whom one has already made this commitment, whereas this is precisely the result which remarriage after divorce brings about. The essence of the bigamy legislation is frustrated by divorce.

II. NULLITY OF MARRIAGE

4. Since 1980 there have been several decisions of the High Court the effect of which has been to develop the civil law of nullity of marriage to a considerable extent. There is now no difference in substance between the law of nullity administered in the civil courts and the law administered in the religious Tribunals. The perceived 'gulf' between the two systems is at variance with the real situation. It is still of course possible that in a small number of individual cases the outcome of nullity proceedings in the civil court may be different from that in the ecclesiastical Tribunal.

5. In view of the above development we would be quite satisfied if the courts were to continue to rule on nullity proceedings in the absence of new and more specific legislative criteria. We are equally satisfied, however, with the recommendations as to *grounds* for nullity of remarriage contained in the Law Reform Commission's *Report on Nullity of Marriage*.

6. We are of the view that the present law as to maintenance and property entitlements after the nullity decree (at civil law) is harsh and unjust and that the Law Reform Commission's proposals as to reform on *these matters* contained in its *Report on Nullity of Marriage*, published two years ago, should be implemented without delay (pp. 190f.).

7. We wish to reiterate our conviction that the law of nullity of marriage should never be transformed so as to deal with cases involving *valid* marriages, where the effect could be to grant divorces under another name.

8. We would like to point out that the civil law of nullity of marriage applies to all members of our society without distinction so far as the essential grounds of validity are concerned. Members of several different denominations have sought to have their status determined in these proceedings.

9. We wish to observe that nullity proceedings are a normal feature of State law systems throughout the world and are found in countries of the most diverse legal traditions.

10. We endorse the recommendations of the Committee on Marriage Breakdown on the cost of nullity as outlined in 9.18-20 of its *Report*. Adequate civil legal aid in such matters ought to be available. The hearings should take place in the Family Court.

STATEMENT ISSUED BY THE HIERARCHY, 26 APRIL, 1986

Marital breakdown in our society is a distressing and growing problem. Through its pastoral ministry, the Catholic Church seeks in many ways to give practical expression to its compassion for those who suffer in this situation.

The proposals relating to marital breakdown published by the Government in recent days include a number of useful initiatives, for instance, those concerned with the introduction of a Family Court, mediation and conciliation, the age of marriage and the requirement of a minimum period of notice.

While these proposals are welcome, it is regrettable that in the Government statement of Wednesday, 24th April they are linked with the introduction of a divorce law. We wish to make a number of comments on this aspect of the Government's proposals:

1. The fundamental law of the State is a matter for the people and it is right that the people should have an opportunity to speak on a matter of this importance.

2. We recognise that many tragic problems arise in the context of marital breakdown. To alleviate these problems much improved legal provision is needed for mediation and conciliation, maintenance, custody of and access to children, the status of children, succession and legal separation. All this should be provided, and could be provided without the introduction of divorce.

3. It will be suggested that the proposal envisages a very restricted form of divorce. It is true that the granting of a divorce decree will be delayed, but the *grounds* suggested could scarcely be broader. 'Failure' of a marriage is in fact the basis for the most advanced and most unrestrictive form of divorce in the world today.

4. Nowadays, in situations of failure in life it tends to be taken for granted that people should be given a 'second chance'. It is understandable that people are tempted to apply the same kind of considerations to a 'failed' marriage. But in the case of marriage it must be asked what the giving of a second chance would imply. It would mean bringing about the situation where, as far as the civil law was concerned, the phrase 'till death do us part' or 'as long as we both shall live' would always be deemed to include the added clause 'or until one of us decides that the marriage has failed'. Civil law would cease to recognise any marriage as indissoluble.

5. A national debate of fundamental importance for the future of our society is now opened. We emphasise that in this debate opposing views should be fairly stated and honestly listened to and appraised.

6. In the meantime, we ask all our people to pray earnestly that God may direct them in their thinking and in their ultimate choice.

Source: Appendices in Marriage, the Family and Divorce, A Statement by the Irish Bishops (June, 1986).

APPENDIX E

ADOPTION SOCIETIES

Telephone No.

ST. ANNE'S ADOPTION SOCIETY
Cork and Ross Family Centre, 34 Paul Street, Cork . . . .   021—273213

ST. ATTRACTA'S ADOPTION SOCIETY
St. Mary's, Sligo . . . .   071—3058

ST. BRIGID'S ADOPTION SOCIETY
Holy Faith Convent, 16 The Coombe, Dublin 8 . . . .   01—754794

ST. CATHERINE'S ADOPTION SOCIETY
O'Connell Street, Ennis, Co. Clare . . . .   065—28178

CATHOLIC PROTECTION AND RESCUE SOCIETY OF
IRELAND
30 South Anne Street, Dublin 2 . . . .   01—779664

CHALLENGE ADOPTION SOCIETY
c/o Sion House, Kilkenny . . . .   056—21653

ST. CLARE'S ADOPTION SOCIETY
St. Michael's Presbytery, Castlepollard, Co. Westmeath . . . . .   044—412583

ST. JOHN'S ADOPTION SOCIETY
Cathedral Presbytery, 3 George's Street, Waterford . . . .   051—73759
                                                                       051—55819

ST. KEVIN'S ADOPTION SOCIETY
St. Joseph's Hospital, Dungarvan, Co. Waterford . . . .   058—42199

LIMERICK CATHOLIC ADOPTION SOCIETY
39 Catherine Street, Limerick . . . .   061—316655

ST. LOUISE ADOPTION SOCIETY
1 James's Street, Dublin 8 . . . .   01—537951

ST. MARY'S ADOPTION SOCIETY
20 Denny Street, Tralee, Co. Kerry . . . .   066—22524

ST. MURA'S ADOPTION SOCIETY
Nazareth House, Fahan, Lifford, Co. Donegal . . . . 080504—268592
                                                                      080504—262475

ST. NICHOLAS ADOPTION SOCIETY
Community Care Services, Newcastle Road, Galway . . . .   091—23112

P.A.C.T. SUPPORT & COUNSELLING SERVICE FOR
SINGLE PARENTS
71 Brighton Road, Rathgar, Dublin 6   01–972670
                                                                       01–972659

ST. PATRICK'S GUILD
82 Haddington Road, Dublin 4   01–681765
                                                                       01–681908

ROTUNDA GIRLS AID SOCIETY
82 Marlborough Street, Dublin 1 01–744262

SACRED HEART ADOPTION SOCIETY
Sacred Heart Convent, Blackrock, Cork   021–357730
                                                                       021–357841

ST. THERESE ADOPTION SOCIETY
Carmelite Priory, 56 Aungier Street, Dublin 2   01–758821

PLEASE NOTE that Health Boards may also place children for adoption.

APPENDIX F

ADOPTION STATISTICS

Analysis of Adoption Placements 1975–1985

	1975	1976	1977	1978	1979	1980	1981	1982	1983	1984	1985
No. of applications received	1426	1277	1296	1228	1234	1354	1189	1254	1115	956	883
No. of adoption orders made	1443	1104	1127	1223	988	1115	1191	1191	1184	1195	882
No. of orders made in respect of children placed by:											
– adoption societies	1164	905	938	1064	845	928	951	879	921	793	588
%	80.7	82.0	83.2	87.0	85.5	83.2	79.9	73.8	77.8	66.3	66.7
– health boards	123	91	79	52	42	77	80	80	75	85	54
%	8.5	8.2	7.1	4.2	4.3	6.9	6.7	6.7	6.3	7.1	6.1
– the natural mother with non-relatives	30	9	6	12	7	5	13	11	15	20	28
%	2.1	0.8	0.5	1.0	0.7	0.5	1.1	0.9	1.3	1.7	3.2
No. of orders made in respect of family adoptions*	126	99	104	95	94	105	147	221	173	297	212
%	8.7	9.0	9.2	7.8	9.5	9.4	12.3	18.6	14.6	24.9	24.0

Source: Reports of An Bord Uchtála (The Adoption Board) 1984 and 1985.
*Family adoptions relate to adoption orders made in favour of the natural mother alone or with her husband, the natural father alone or with his wife or in favour of other relations, such as grandparents, aunts and uncles.

ANALYSIS OF ADOPTION ORDERS MADE IN RESPECT OF FAMILY
MEMBERS 1982-1985

	1982	1983	1984	1985
No. of orders made in favour of:				
Natural mother	2	6	4	6
Natural mother and her husband	128	103	225	156
Natural father alone*	—	—	—	1
Natural father and his wife	4	1	4	1
Grandparents** or other relatives	87	63	64	48
Total	221	173	297	212

Source: Reports of An Bord Uchtála for the years 1982–1985. No such detailed breakdown of family placements is contained in the earlier reports.
*This category only appears in the 1985 report. It was previously subsumed under "Grandparents or other relatives".
**In 1985, out of the 48 orders made in this category, 29 were made in favour of grandparents. The exact number of orders made in favour of grandparents alone is not disclosed in the earlier reports.

Analysis of Adoption Orders made and Religion of Adopters 1953–1985

Year	Roman Catholic	Protestant, Jewish and others	Mixed Religion*	Total
1953	312	69		381
1954	811	77		888
1955	709	77		786
1956	512	53		565
1957	698	54		752
1958	550	42		592
1959	470	31		501
1960	478	27		505
1961	520	27		547
1962	660	39		699
1963	811	29		840
1964	972	31		1,003
1965	995	54		1,049
1966	1,127	51		1,178
1967	1,451	42		1,493
1968	1,303	40		1,343
1969	1,187	38		1,225
1970	1,368	46		1,414
1971	1,259	46		1,305
1972	1,265	26		1,291
1973	1,354	48		1,402
1974	1,387	28		1,415
1975	1,396	31	16	1,443
1976	1,075	16	13	1,104
1977	1,082	22	23	1,127
1978	1,173	31	19	1,223
1979	962	13	13	988
1980	1,074	23	18	1,115
1981	1,144	19	28	1,191
1982	1,138	22	31	1,191
1983	1,140	18	26	1,184
1984	1,148	25	22	1,195
1985	832	39	11	882
Total	32,363	1,234	220 =	33,817

Source: Reports of An Bord Uchtála, 1953–1977 and Reply to Dáil Question (20th March, 1986) 357 Dáil Reports Cols. 13–14. Information as to the religion of Adopters was not provided in the annual reports of the Board after 1977.

*Couples of mixed religion were unable to adopt until 1974 (see p. 296 *ante*). H.J. Abramson "Issues in Adoption in Ireland" (E.S.R.I. Broadsheet No. 23, July, 1984) notes that the proportion of non-Catholic adopters is lower than their percentages in the total Irish population (see Abramson at p. 31).

APPENDIX G

SOME STATISTICS RELATING TO CHILDREN AT RISK, IN CARE AND SUBJECT TO CRIMINAL PROSECUTION

The Planning Unit of the Department of Health has undertaken a detailed analysis of the total number of children in care in 1981 and 1982 and the reasons for their admission to care and in doing so collated the following information.

Number of Children in Care Analysed by Type of Care on 30 September, 1981 and 31 December, 1982

Type of Care	1981*	1982
Fostered children (through Health Boards)	1,241	1,272
Children maintained in residential homes	1,086	1,072
Privately fostered children	159	93
Supervisor at home**	—	9
Total	2,486	2,446

*Revised figures for 1981
**New category introduced in 1982

Children in Care during 1981 and 1982: Reason for Admission into Care

Reason for Admission	1981*	%	1982	%
Physical abuse of child	108	2.9	131	3.6
Sexual abuse of child	33	0.9	32	0.9
Emotional abuse of child	62	1.7	147	4.0
Neglect of child	489	13.3	509	13.9
One parent family unable to cope	1,788	48.7	1,377	37.5
Marital disharmony	297	8.1	331	9.0
Child out of control	117	3.2	159	4.3
Child abandoned	268	7.3	220	6.0
Both parents dead	61	1.7	58	1.6
Short-term crisis	451	12.3	479	13.0
Child awaiting adoption**	—	—	232	6.3
Total	3,674	100	3,675	100

*Revised figures for 1981
**New category introduced in 1982

As can be seen from the above statistics, while there are approximately 2,450 children in care at any one time, there are in the region of 3,650 who annually spend some time in care.

As can be seen from the table below, approximately 1,100 children who are in care for some portion of the year are re-united with family or relatives or adopted.

Children in Care:
Reason for Children Leaving Care during 1981 and 1982

Reason for Leaving Care	1981*	%	1982	%
Reached legal age limit	62	4.9	108	8.8
Reunited with family/relatives	786	61.6	781	63.5
In After Care/Self sufficient	23	1.8	22	1.8
Adopted	362	28.4	287	23.4
Absconded	18	1.4	8	0.7
Admitted to specialist unit**	—	—	10	0.8
Death of child**	—	—	1	0.1
Other	25	2.0	12	1.0
Total	1,276	100	1,229	100

*Revised figures for 1981.
**New category introduced in 1982.
Source: See Department of Health, Statistical Information Relevant to the Health Services, 1985 (Stationery Office, Dublin, 1986) in particular at pp. 35–36. See further "Children in Care, 1980/81" (Department of Health Publication).

Number of Children Taken into Care by Each of the Health Boards
in the Years 1982–85

Health Board	1982	1983	1984	1985	Total
Eastern	59	122	113	212	506
Midland	32	33	18	59	142
Mid-Western	27	36	9	20	92
North-Eastern	9	14	11	20	54
North-Western	5	5	17	19	46
South-Eastern	42	22	15	15	94
Southern	23	47	21	26	117
Western	10	18	13	23	64
Total	207	297	217	394	1,115

Number of Children Suspected of being Victims of Non-Accidental Injury on Lists Maintained by Directors of Community Care in each Health Board Area as at the 31st of December, 1985

Health Board	No. of Children Listed
Eastern	113
Midland	28
Mid-Western	28
North-Eastern	18
North-Western	18
South-Eastern	63
Southern	28
Western	27
Total	323

Source: Department of Health.

Dublin Metropolitan Children's Court — Care Proceedings 1983–85

	Year ended 31st July,		
	1983	1984	1985
(a) Number of Applications for Fit Person Orders	85	75	52
Number granted	53	60	36
Number refused	2	9	16
(b) Number of Applications for Committal to Industrial Schools	33	25	30
Number granted	25	15	13
Number refused	8	10	17
(c) Number of Applications for Place of Safety Orders	51	26	14
Number granted	51	26	13
Number refused	Nil	Nil	1

Provincial District Court – Care Proceedings 1984–1985

		1984	1985
(a)	Number of Applications for Fit Person Orders	133	109
	Number granted	114	94
(b)	Number of children committed to Industrial Schools	41	50
(c)	Number of Applications for Place of Safety Orders	76	46
	Number granted	76	37

Source: The Department of Justice.
In relation to Provincial District Courts, statistics of the number of applications refused under (a), (b) and (c) and of the number of applications under (b), are not available. Neither are statistics for the years prior to 1984.

In practice, a separate application is normally made in respect of each child that it is sought be taken into care. The number of children in respect of which applications were made, therefore, corresponds to the figures shown.

Dublin Metropolitan Children's Court – Criminal Proceedings
Number of Criminal Offences Involving Children and Young Persons in the
Dublin Metropolitan Area, 31st July, 1978–31st July, 1985

	No. of Criminal Cases Dealt With
Year ending 31st July, 1978	21,031
,, ,, ,, ,, 1979	19,566
,, ,, ,, ,, 1980	19,748
,, ,, ,, ,, 1981	16,332
,, ,, ,, ,, 1982	15,497
,, ,, ,, ,, 1983	14,269
,, ,, ,, ,, 1984	12,852
,, ,, ,, ,, 1985	12,602

Source: See (1983) 341 Dáil Reports Col. 1201 and (1986) 365 Dáil Reports Cols. 1221-1222.
The above figures do not represent the number of persons who appeared before the court but rather the number of alleged offences dealt with by the court. No statistics are compiled by the Dept. of Justice as to the number of criminal cases involving children and young persons dealt with by the District Courts sitting outside the Dublin Metropolitan area. Neither are any statistics compiled as to the exact number of children and young persons who are annually prosecuted for criminal offences in the District Court or in any other court or the numbers annually convicted. The former Minister for Justice, Mr. M. Noonan T.D., in reply to a Dáil Question on the 19th of April, 1983 stated that "experience shows that those appearing before the court are, on average, each charged with three or four offences." It is not known whether this statement can be applied to the figures for the years ending 31st July 1983, 31st July 1984 and 31st July 1985.

APPENDIX H

UNMARRIED MOTHER'S ALLOWANCE
RECIPIENTS AND ANALYSIS OF BENEFICIARIES

Date	No. of Recipients
31st December, 1976	3,334
" " 1977	3,799
" " 1978	4,041
" " 1979	4,574
" " 1980	5,267
" " 1981	6,222
" " 1982	7,592
" " 1983	8,534
" " 1984	10,309
" " 1985	11,530

Analysis of Beneficiaries

	1984 31st December, 1984	1985 31st December, 1985
No. of mothers	10, 309	11,530
No. of child dependants	12,685	14,324
Total Beneficiaries	22,994	25,854

Source: Department of Social Welfare, Statistical Information on Social Welfare Services, 1985 (Stationery Office, Dublin, 1986) see pp. 16 & 17.

APPENDIX I

FORM OF CONTRACT FOR CHILD BOARDED OUT OR PLACED IN FOSTERAGE BY HEALTH BOARD

THIS AGREEMENT made this   day of
19   , BETWEEN the   (hereinafter
called the health board) of the first part, and
of the second part, WITNESSETH that the said
(hereinafter called the foster parent), hereby accepts the charge of
born   (and hereinafter called the child); and in consideration
of the sum of   per month or such larger sum as may from
time to time be determined by the health board in respect of maintenance,
clothing and education of the child to be paid to the foster parent by the health
board as hereinafter mentioned, hereby covenants and agrees to bring up the
child as he (she) would a child of his (or her) own, to promote the proper
development of the child, and to observe and keep, in respect of the child, the
following conditions:

(1) The child shall be properly and sufficiently nourished and shall be
suitably accommodated in the same home as the foster parent.

(2) The child shall be brought up in the   religion and the foster parent shall cause the child when of sufficient age regularly to attend religious services at a place of worship of that religion.

(3) If the child shall at any time be suffering from illness or injury, medical aid shall be obtained for the child and if a registered medical practitioner shall advise admission to hospital, the foster parent shall cause the child to be so admitted.

(4) The foster parent shall inform the health board immediately of any serious occurrence affecting the child.

(5) The child shall be produced at all reasonable times to any authorised officer of the Minister for Health or of the health board when so required by any such officer; the foster parent shall furnish forthwith all such relevant information as may be required by any such officer and shall facilitate any such officer in inspecting the home in which the child lives.

(6) The child shall be returned to the health board at any time where the health board, with the consent of the Minister for Health, decides to remove the child from the foster parent or where the Minister for Health requires the health board so to remove the child.

(7) The foster parent shall cause the child to attend regularly a school in which such child will be instructed in the religion, or such other school as the health board, with the agreement of the nearest appropriate minister of that religion, may approve.

(8) If the foster parent intends to change his (or her) place of residence, the foster parent shall, at least fourteen days before doing so, notify the health board of his (or her) proposed new address.

(9) The foster parent shall not insure, or attempt to insure, directly or indirectly, the life of the child, and shall not have, or attempt to obtain, any interest in any insurance policy on the life of the child.

And the health board hereby covenants and agrees with the foster parent that so long as the child shall continue to be boarded out in his (or her) charge the health board will pay or cause to be paid to the foster parent the sum of   or such larger sum as may from time to time be determined by the health board, on the   day of each calendar month in respect of maintenance, clothing and education of the child, and a proportionate part of such monthly payment where the child is in the charge of the foster parent for portion of a calendar month.

Signed by
in the presence

Present when the Seal of
            was affixed
hereto

Source: Boarding Out of Children Regulations, 1983 (S.I. No. 67 of 1983).

INDEX

(The contents of the appendices are not included in this index.)

651

452, 453
Guardianship of Infant's Act, 1964, under, 453, 454
parental right to apply, 451, **454**
third party's right to apply, 452, 453
mother, rights of –
historical, 344 et seq.
present day, 352, 598
nullity of marriage, effect of in relation to, 144
reform of law, 166, 167, 288, 289, 290, 426, 427, 428, 428
rights to services of, 163 et seq.
school attendance, 409
third parties' right to apply to court, 376, 399, 401
wardship jurisdiction, 399, 400, 401
welfare, meaning of, 354
wishes of, as affecting court orders, 368, 369

CHILD BENEFIT, 472

CHURCH OF IRELAND
disestablishment of, 47
formalities of marriage, 85, 86, 87

CLERK, DISTRICT COURT
role of, in enforcing maintenance obligations, 449

COERCION
by husband of wife, ending of presumption of in criminal proceedings, 38, 181

COHABITATION
duty of, 159, 537
enforcement of duty, 159, 160, 161
divorce a mensa et thoro, effect of, 217
see also CONSORTIUM

COHABITEE
injunction for protection of, 619
property rights of, 619, 620, 621, 622
reform of the law applicable to, 630
succession rights of, 623

COLLUSION
divorce a mensa et thoro proceedings, bar to, 226, 227
nullity proceedings, relevance of, 142, 143

CONDONATION
divorce a mensa et thoro, relevance of, 223, 224, 225
maintenance proceedings, relevance of, 445, 446, 447
meaning of, 224

CONFLICT OF LAWS
adoption, in relation to, 328
divorce a vinculo, in relation to, 19, 20, 255 et seq.
marriage, in relation to, 78, 79

CONNIVANCE
divorce a mensa et thoro, bar to, 225, 226
maintenance proceedings, relevance of, 445, 446

CONSENT
adoption – see ADOPTION

marriage to – see NULLITY OF MARRIAGE
parental, to marriage – see FORMALITIES FOR MARRIAGE

CONSORTIUM, 159
action for interference with spouses right to, 162, 163, 165, 166
by husband, 162, 163
by wife, 163
loss of, by death, 168
damages, basis of assessment, 168, 169, 170

CONSPIRACY
unity of husband and wife, effect, of, 181

CONSTITUTION
access to the courts, right of, 43, 44
adoption, relevance to, 7, 8, 16, 24, 28, 36, 40, 292, 301, 302, 303, 304, 305, 306, 307, 308, 319, 320, 323, 597
beget children, right to, 33, 34
children, rights of, 6, 15, 21, 22, 23, 24, 26, 27, 28
contraceptives, right to, 29, 30, 171, 175, 597
dissolution of marriage, 18, 237 et seq.
family, constitutional meaning of, 4, 5, 6, 7, 8, 594, 595
foreign maintenance orders, enforcement of, and, 462, 463, 464, 465, 466
homosexuality, and, 14, 15, 31, 32, 33, 39
illegitimate children, position of, 6, 15, 26, 27, 28, 29, 371, 574, 575, 597
income tax, relevance to, 12, 13, 14
legal aid, right to, 44
legitimated children, position of, 7, 283
marriage, protection of, 10, 11, 12, 14, 15, 19
matrimonial property and the, 511n
non-citizens, application to, 9, 16, 17, 18
nullity, relevance to, 18, 19, 103, 104
parental rights, 20, 21, 343, 350, 351, 352, 594, 595
children's education over, 20, 21, 350, 351, 352, 383 et seq.
welfare of child, as opposed to, 21, 22, 23, 383 et seq.
personal rights,
access to contraceptives, 29, 30, 171, 175, 597
bodily integrity, to, 25
citizenship, to Irish, 37
equality, 36, 37, 38, 39, 40, 41
freedom of movement, to, 25
marital privacy, to, 29, 30, 31
marry, to, 25
mothers, to custody of illegitimate child, 26, 28, 29, 594
passport, to, 188, 189, 190
privacy, right to, 29, 30, 31, 32, 33, 51
set up home, to, 18n
spousal residence in the State, right to, 16, 17, 18
travel, to, 25n
recognition of foreign decrees of dis-